THE
ANNUAL REGISTER
Vol. 240

ANNUAL REGISTER ADVISORY BOARD

CHAIRMAN

H. V. HODSON

EDITOR

ALAN J. DAY

ASSISTANT EDITOR

VERENA HOFFMAN

JOHN BEETLESTONE
Emeritus Director of Techniquest, Emeritus Professor, University of Wales
NOMINATED BY
THE BRITISH ASSOCIATION FOR THE ADVANCEMENT OF SCIENCE

JAMES BISHOP
Editor-in-Chief, The Illustrated London News

M. R. D. FOOT
Formerly Professor of Modern History, University of Manchester
NOMINATED BY
THE ROYAL HISTORICAL SOCIETY

MICHAEL KASER
*Emeritus Fellow of St Antony's College, Oxford,
and Honorary Professor, University of Birmingham*
NOMINATED BY
THE ROYAL INSTITUTE OF INTERNATIONAL AFFAIRS

ALASTAIR NIVEN
Director of Literature, British Council
NOMINATED BY
THE BRITISH COUNCIL

RICHARD O'BRIEN
Principal, Global Business Network
NOMINATED BY
THE ROYAL ECONOMIC SOCIETY

Popperfoto/Reuter

[*Top*] The most published image of the year, discovered on a TV videotape in January 1998: President Clinton hugging Monica Lewinsky on the White House lawn in November 1996, when their sexual affair was still in progress. [*Bottom*] End of an era in Germany: installed as Chancellor on 27 October 1998, Gerhard Schröder (right) shakes hands with predecessor Helmut Kohl.

Popperfoto/Reuter
Where angels feared to tread: Pope John Paul II and President Fidel Castro listening to the Cuban national anthem on the Pope's arrival in Havana on 21 January 1998 for the first-ever papal visit to the Communist-ruled island.

THE
ANNUAL REGISTER

A Record of World Events
1998

Edited by
ALAN J. DAY

assisted by
VERENA HOFFMAN

FIRST EDITED IN 1758
BY EDMUND BURKE

Keesing's Worldwide, LLC

THE ANNUAL REGISTER 1998
Published by Keesing's Worldwide, LLC, 51 Monroe Street, 17th Floor, Suite M,
Rockville, MD 20850, United States of America

ISBN 1-886994-21-8

© Keesing's Worldwide, LLC 1999
All rights reserved; no part of this publication may be reproduced,
stored in a retrieval system, or transmitted in any form or by any
means, electronic, mechanical, photocopying, recording or otherwise
without either the prior written permission of the Publishers or a licence
permitting restricted copying issued by the Copyright Licensing Agency,
90 Tottenham Court Road, London, W1P 9HE

British Library Cataloguing in Publication Data
The Annual Register—1998
  1. History—Periodicals
  909.82'8'05   D410

ISBN 1-886994-21-8

Library of Congress Catalog Card Number: 4-17979

Set in Times Roman by
THE MIDLANDS BOOK TYPESETTING COMPANY, LOUGHBOROUGH

Printed in Great Britain by
MPG BOOK DIVISION, BODMIN

CONTENTS

	CONTRIBUTORS	viii
	IGO ABBREVIATIONS	xiv
	PREFACE TO 240th VOLUME	xv
	EXTRACTS FROM 1798, 1848, 1898 AND 1948 VOLUMES	xvi

I		OVERVIEWS OF THE YEAR	
1		Global Issues and Regional Realities	1
2		The International Economy	8

II		WESTERN AND SOUTHERN EUROPE	
1		i United Kingdom 16 ii Scotland 40 iii Wales 42 iv Northern Ireland 44	16
2		i Germany 51 ii France 56 iii Italy 61 iv Belgium 65 v The Netherlands 67 vi Luxembourg 69 vii Ireland 70	51
3		i Denmark 73 ii Iceland 75 iii Norway 76 iv Sweden 78 v Finland 80 vi Austria 81 vii Switzerland 84 viii European Mini-States 87	73
4		i Spain 91 ii Gibraltar 94 iii Portugal 96 iv Malta 99 v Greece 101 vi Cyprus 105 vii Turkey 108	91

III		CENTRAL AND EASTERN EUROPE	
1		i Poland 111 ii Baltic Republics 114 iii Czech Republic 118 iv Slovakia 120 v Hungary 122 vi Romania 124 vii Bulgaria 127	111
2		i Albania 130 ii Bosnia & Hercegovina 134 iii Croatia 137 iv Macedonia 139 v Slovenia 141 vi Yugoslavia 142	130
3		i Russia 147 ii Belarus, Ukraine, Moldova 153 iii Armenia, Georgia, Azerbaijan 156	147

IV		AMERICAS AND THE CARIBBEAN	
1		United States of America	158
2		Canada	178
3		Latin America: i Argentina 183 ii Bolivia 185 iii Brazil 186 iv Chile 187 v Colombia 188 vi Ecuador 190 vii Paraguay 191 viii Peru 192 ix Uruguay 194 x Venezuela 194 xi Cuba 195 xii Dominican Republic and Haiti 197 xiii Central America and Panama 198 xiv Mexico 201	183
4		Caribbean: i Jamaica 203 ii Guyana 205 iii Trinidad & Tobago 206 iv Barbados 206 v Belize 207 vi Grenada 208 vii The Bahamas 208 viii Windward & Leeward Islands 209 ix UK Dependencies 212 x Suriname 214 xi Netherlands Antilles and Aruba 214 xii US Dependencies 215	203

CONTENTS

V	MIDDLE EAST AND NORTH AFRICA	
1	Israel	217
2	i Arab World and Palestinians 221 ii Egypt 224 iii Jordan 226 iv Syria 228 v Lebanon 230 vi Iraq 232	221
3	i Saudi Arabia 235 ii Yemen 238 iii Arab States of the Gulf 240	235
4	i Sudan 245 ii Libya 247 iii Tunisia 249 iv Algeria 251 v Morocco 253 vi Western Sahara 255	245

VI	EQUATORIAL AFRICA	
1	i Horn of Africa 257 ii Kenya 261 iii Tanzania 264 iv Uganda 265	257
2	i Ghana 267 ii Nigeria 269 iii Sierra Leone 272 iv The Gambia 273 v Liberia 274	267
3	i West African Francophone States 275 ii Central African Franc Zone States 283	275

VII	CENTRAL AND SOUTHERN AFRICA	
1	i Democratic Republic of Congo 288 ii Burundi and Rwanda 291 iii Guinea-Bissau and Cape Verde 294 iv São Tomé & Príncipe 295 v Mozambique 296 vi Angola 297	288
2	i Zambia 299 ii Malawi 300 iii Zimbabwe 301 iv Botswana, Lesotho, Namibia and Swaziland 303	299
3	South Africa	308

VIII	SOUTH ASIA AND INDIAN OCEAN	
1	i Iran 313 ii Afghanistan 316 iii Central Asian Republics 319	313
2	i India 326 ii Pakistan 331 iii Bangladesh 334 iv Nepal 338 v Bhutan 339 vi Sri Lanka 341	326
3	i Mauritius 343 ii Seychelles, Comoros and Maldives 345 iii Madagascar 348	343

IX	SOUTH-EAST AND EAST ASIA	
1	i Myanmar (Burma) 349 ii Thailand 351 iii Malaysia 352 iv Brunei 354 v Singapore 354 vi Indonesia 355 vii Philippines 357 viii Vietnam 359 ix Cambodia 360 x Laos 363	349
2	i China 364 ii Hong Kong SAR 371 iii Taiwan 374 iv Japan 376 v South Korea 380 vi North Korea 382 vii Mongolia 384	364

X	AUSTRALASIA AND THE PACIFIC	
1	i Australia 387 ii Papua New Guinea 391	387
2	i New Zealand 393 ii Pacific Island States 395	393

XI	INTERNATIONAL ORGANIZATIONS	
1	United Nations	400
2	i Defence Organizations 413 ii Economic Organizations 417	413
3	i The Commonwealth 421 ii Francophonie and CPLP 423 iii Non Aligned Movement and Developing Countries 426 iv Oranization of the Islamic Conference 429	421
4	European Union	430
5	i Council of Europe 438 ii Organization for Security and Cooperation in Europe 440 iii European Bank for Reconstruction and Development 444 iv Nordic, Baltic and Arctic Organizations 445 v Other European Organizations 447	438

6	i Arab Organizations 450 ii African Organizations and Conferences 453 iii Asia-Pacific Organizations 457 iv American and Caribbean Organizations 462	450
XII	RELIGION	466
XIII	THE SCIENCES	
1	Scientific, Medical and Industrial Research	473
2	Information Technology	479
3	The Environment	484
XIV	THE LAW	
1	i International Law 492 ii European Community Law 497	492
2	Law in the United Kingdom	500
3	United States Law	506
XV	THE ARTS	
1	i Opera 509 ii Music 511 iii Ballet & Dance 514 iv Theatre 518 v Cinema 523 vi Television & Radio 526	509
2	i Visual Arts 531 ii Architecture 534	531
3	Literature	538
XVI	SPORT	546
XVII	DOCUMENTS AND REFERENCE	
1	Northern Ireland: Good Friday Agreement	556
2	Statute of International Criminal Court	567
3	Scotland and Wales: Devolution Acts	571
4	The Starr Report	577
5	UK Labour Cabinet	582
6	US Democratic Administration	583
7	International Comparisons: Population and GDP	584
8	Maastricht Convergence Criteria Performance	585
XVIII	OBITUARY	586
XIX	CHRONICLE OF PRINCIPAL EVENTS IN 1998	602
	INDEX	612
	MAPS AND TABLES	
	East Asia's Faltering Economies	11
	The Troubled Province of Kosovo	143
	US Mid-Term Election Results	169
	The Disputed Eritrean-Ethiopian Border	259
	United Nations Peace-keeping Missions	408

CONTRIBUTORS

EXTRACTS FROM PAST VOLUMES	**M.R.D. Foot,** Former Professor of Modern History, University of Manchester

PART I

GLOBAL ISSUES AND REGIONAL REALITIES	**John Roberts,** Formerly Vice-Chancellor of the University of Southampton and Warden of Merton College, Oxford
THE INTERNATIONAL ECONOMY	**Victor Keegan,** Assistant Editor, *The Guardian*

PART II

UNITED KINGDOM	**Alan J. Day,** MA, Editor, *The Annual Register*
UK ECONOMY	**Robert Fraser,** MA, Consulting Editor, *Keesing's Record of World Events*
SCOTLAND	**Charlotte Lythe,** MA, Senior Lecturer in Economic Studies, University of Dundee
WALES	**Gwyn Jenkins,** MA, Keeper of Manuscripts and Records, National Library of Wales, Aberystwyth
NORTHERN IRELAND	**Sydney Elliott,** BA, PhD, Senior Lecturer in Politics, The Queen's University, Belfast
GERMANY	**Charlie Jeffery,** PhD, Deputy Director, Institute for German Studies, University of Birmingham
FRANCE	**Martin Harrison,** Professor of Politics, University of Keele
ITALY	**Stephen Gundle,** Senior Lecturer in Italian, Royal Holloway, University of London
BELGIUM, NETHERLANDS LUXEMBOURG	**Peter Dixon,** Historian at the European Commission
REPUBLIC OF IRELAND	**Louis McRedmond,** MA, BL, Journalist, historian and broadcaster
NORDIC COUNTRIES	**David Smith,** PhD, Lecturer in Contemporary History and International Relations; member of Baltic Research Unit, Department of European Studies, University of Bradford
AUSTRIA	**Angela Gillon,** Researcher in West European affairs
SWITZERLAND	**Hans Hirter,** PhD, Editor, *Année Politique Suisse*. University of Berne
EUROPEAN MINI-STATES	**Stefan Kossoff,** Free-lance writer on European affairs
SPAIN, GIBRALTAR	**Richard Gillespie,** BA, PhD, Professor of Iberian and Latin American Studies, University of Portsmouth
PORTUGAL	**Antonio de Figueiredo,** Knight Commander of Portugal's Order of Freedom; Portuguese author, freelance journalist and broadcaster
MALTA	**D.G. Austin,** Emeritus Professor of Government, University of Manchester
GREECE	**Richard Clogg,** MA, St Antony's College, Oxford

CONTRIBUTORS

CYPRUS	**Robert McDonald,** Freelance writer and broadcaster; author on Greece, Cyprus and Turkey
TURKEY	**A.J.A. Mango,** BA, PhD, Orientalist and writer on current affairs in Turkey and the Near East

PART III

POLAND	**A. Kemp-Welch,** BSc(Econ), PhD, Dean, School of Economic and Social Studies, University of East Anglia
BALTIC REPUBLICS	**John Hiden,** Professor of Modern European History and Director, Baltic Research Unit, University of Bradford
CZECH REPUBLIC, SLOVAKIA	**Sharon Fisher,** MA, Analyst specializing in East European political and economic affairs
HUNGARY	**George Schöpflin,** Jean Monnet Professor of Politics and Director, Centre for the Study of Nationalism, School of Slavonic and East European Studies, University of London
ROMANIA	**Gabriel Partos,** Eastern Europe Analyst, BBC World Service
BULGARIA	**Stephen Ashley,** MA, DPhil, BBC News Programmes
ALBANIA	**Richard Crampton,** PhD, Professor of East European History, and Fellow of St Edmund Hall, University of Oxford,
EX-YUGOSLAV REPUBLICS	**John B. Allcock,** MA, PhD, Head of Research Unit in South-East European Studies, University of Bradford
RUSSIA, BELARUS, UKRAINE, MOLDOVA AND CAUCASUS	**Stephen White,** PhD, DPhil, Professor of Politics, University of Glasgow

PART IV

USA	**Neil A. Wynn,** MA, PhD, Reader in History and American Studies, University of Glamorgan
CANADA	**David M.L. Farr,** Professor Emeritus of History, Carleton University, Ottawa
LATIN AMERICA, CARRIBBEAN	**Peter Calvert,** AM, MA, PhD, Professor of Comparative and International Politics, University of Southampton

PART V

ISRAEL	**Joel Peters,** BSc, DPhil, Lecturer in International Relations, University of Reading
ARAB WORLD, EGYPT, JORDAN, SYRIA, LEBANON, IRAQ	**Christopher Gandy,** Formerly UK Diplomatic Service; writer on Middle Eastern affairs
SAUDI ARABIA, YEMEN, ARAB STATES OF THE GULF	**George Joffé,** Director of Studies, Royal Institute of International Affairs
SUDAN	**Ahmed al-Shahi,** DPhil, Social anthropologist and independent researcher
LIBYA, TUNISIA, ALGERIA, MOROCCO, WESTERN SAHARA	**R. I. Lawless,** PhD, Emeritus Reader in Modern Middle Eastern Studies, University of Durham

CONTRIBUTORS

PART VI
HORN OF AFRICA — **Patrick Gilkes,** Writer and broadcaster on the Horn of Africa

KENYA, TANZANIA, UGANDA — **William Tordoff,** MA, PhD, Emeritus Professor of Government, University of Manchester

GHANA — **D.G. Austin** (see Pt. III, Malta)

NIGERIA — **Guy Arnold,** Freelance writer specializing in Africa and North-South affairs

SIERRA LEONE, THE GAMBIA, LIBERIA — **Arnold Hughes,** Professor of African Politics, Centre of West African Studies, The University of Birmingham

CHAPTER 3 (SENEGAL to EQUATORIAL GUINEA) — **Kaye Whiteman,** Publisher, *West Africa*

PART VII
CHAPTER 1 (ZAÏRE TO ANGOLA) — **Robin Hallett,** MA, Writer and lecturer on African affairs

ZAMBIA, MALAWI — **Robin Hallett** (see above)

ZIMBABWE — **R. W. Baldock,** BA, PhD, Senior Editor, Yale University Press; writer on African affairs

NAMIBIA, BOTSWANA, LESOTHO, SWAZILAND, SOUTH AFRICA — **Greg Mills,** MA, PhD, National Director, South African Institute of International Affairs

PART VIII
IRAN — **Keith McLachlan,** BA, PhD, Emeritus Professor, School of Oriental and African Studies, University of London

AFGHANISTAN — **D.S. Lewis,** PhD, Editor, *Keesing's Record of World Events*

CENTRAL ASIAN REPUBLICS — **Shirin Akiner,** PhD, Lecturer in Central Asian Studies, School of Oriental and African Studies, University of London

INDIA, BANGLADESH, NEPAL, BHUTAN — **Peter Lyon,** BSc(Econ), PhD, Reader in International Relations and Academic Secretary, Institute of Commonwealth Studies, University of London; Editor, *The Round Table*, the Commonwealth journal of international affairs

PAKISTAN — **David Taylor,** Senior Lecturer in Politics with reference to South Asia, School of Oriental and African Studies, University of London

SRI LANKA — **Charles Gunawardena,** former Director of Information, Commonwealth Secretariat, London

SEYCHELLES, MAURITIUS, MALDIVES — **Harry Drost,** Writer on European and Third World affairs; editor, *The World's News Media*

MADAGASCAR AND COMOROS — **Kaye Whiteman** (see Pt. VI, Ch. 3)

PART IX
MYANMAR (BURMA), THAILAND, VIETNAM, CAMBODIA, LAOS MALAYSIA, BRUNEI, SINGAPORE — **Jonathan Rigg,** PhD, Reader in South-East Asian Geography, University of Durham

Michael Leifer, BA, PhD, Professor of International Relations, London School of Economics and Political Science

CONTRIBUTORS

INDONESIA, PHILIPPINES	**Norman MacQueen,** Head of Department of Politics University of Dundee
CHINA, TAIWAN, HONG KONG	**Robert F. Ash,** MSc(Econ), PhD, Director, EU-China Academic Network and Chiang Ching-Kuo Professor of Taiwan Studies, School of Oriental and African Studies, University of London
JAPAN	**Ian Nish,** Emeritus Professor of International History, London School of Economics and Political Science
KOREA, MONGOLIA	**Alan Sanders,** FIL, Former lecturer in Mongolian Studies, School of Oriental and African Studies, University of London

PART X

AUSTRALIA	**James Jupp,** MSc (Econ), PhD, FASSA, Director, Centre for Immigration and Multicultural Studies, Australian National University, Canberra
PAPUA NEW GUINEA	**Norman MacQueen** (see Pt.IX, Indonesia & Philippines)
NEW ZEALAND, PACIFIC ISLAND STATES	**Stephen Levine,** PhD, Associate Professor and Head of School, School of Political Science and International Relations, Victoria University of Wellington

PART XI

UNITED NATIONS	**David Travers,** BA(Wales), Lecturer in Politics and International Relations, Lancaster University; Specialist Adviser on UN to House of Commons' Foreign Affairs Committee
DEFENCE ORGANIZATIONS	**Donald Kerr,** Military information specialist; former Information Officer, International Institute for Strategic Studies (IISS), London
ECONOMIC ORGANIZATIONS	**Robert Fraser,** (see Pt. II, UK Economy)
COMMONWEALTH	**Derek Ingram,** Consultant Editor of *Gemini News Service*; author and writer on the Commonwealth
NON-ALIGNED MOVEMENT AND GROUP OF 77	**Peter Willetts,** PhD, Professor of Global Politics, Department of Sociology, The City University, London
ORGANIZATION OF THE ISLAMIC CONFERENCE	**Darren Sagar,** MA, Deputy Editor, *Keesing's Record of World Events*
EUROPEAN UNION	**Michael Berendt,** Expert on affairs of the European Union
COUNCIL OF EUROPE	**Christopher Shaw,** MA, Secretary to UK delegation to Parliamentary Assembly of the Council of Europe
ORGANIZATION FOR SECURITY AND COOPERATION IN EUROPE	**Adrian G.V. Hyde-Price,** BSc(Econ), PhD, Lecturer, Department of Politics, University of Southampton
EUROPEAN BANK FOR RECONSTRUCTION AND DEVELOPMENT	**Michael Kaser,** MA, DLitt, DSocSc, Emeritus Fellow of St Antony's College, Oxford, and Honorary Professor, University of Birmingham
NORDIC/BALTIC/ARCTIC ORGANIZATIONS	**David Smith** (see Pt. II, Nordic Countries)

xii CONTRIBUTORS

OTHER EUROPEAN ORGANIZATIONS	Stefan Kossoff (see Pt. II, European Mini-States)
ARAB ORGANIZATIONS	George Joffé (see Pt. V, Saudi Arabia, etc.)
AFRICAN ORGANIZATIONS AND CONFERENCES	Kaye Whiteman (see Pt. VI, Ch. 3)
ASIA-PACIFIC ORGANIZATIONS	Darren Sagar, MA (see above)
AMERICAN AND CARIBBEAN ORGANIZATIONS	Peter Calvert (see Pt. IV, Latin America etc.)

PART XII

RELIGION	Geoffrey Parrinder, MA, PhD, DD, Emeritus Professor of the Comparative Study of Religions, University of London

PART XIII

MEDICAL, SCIENTIFIC AND INDUSTRIAL RESEARCH	Martin Redfern, Deputy Science Editor, BBC World Service
INFORMATION TECHNOLOGY	David Powell, A director of Electronic Publishing Services Ltd and Interactive Media Publications Ltd
ENVIRONMENT	Richard Black, Journalist and broadcaster specializing in scientific and environmental affairs

PART XIV

INTERNATIONAL LAW	Christine Gray, MA, PhD, Fellow in Law, St John's College, Cambridge
EUROPEAN COMMUNITY LAW	N. March Hunnings, LLM, PhD, Editor, *Encyclopedia of European Union Law: Constitutional Texts*
LAW IN THE UK	David Ibbetson, MA, PhD, Fellow and Tutor in Law, Magdalen College, Oxford
LAW IN THE USA	Robert J. Spjut, ID, LLM, Member of the State Bars of California and Florida

PART XV

OPERA	Charles Osborne, Author; opera critic, *The Jewish Chronicle*
MUSIC	Francis Routh, Composer and author; founder director of the Redcliffe Concerts
BALLET/DANCE	Jane Pritchard, Archivist, Rambert Dance Company and English National Ballet
THEATRE	Jeremy Kingston, Theatre critic, *The Times*
CINEMA	Derek Malcolm, Film critic, *The Guardian*
TV & RADIO	Raymond Snoddy, Media Editor, *The Times*
VISUAL ARTS	David Cohen, MA, Independent art critic and lecturer
ARCHITECTURE	Paul Finch, Editor, *The Architects' Journal*
LITERATURE	Alastair Niven, Director of Literature, British Council; formerly Literature Director of the Arts Council of England

CONTRIBUTORS xiii

PART XVI
SPORT   Tony Pawson, OBE, Sports writer, *The Observer*;
                             cricket, football and fly-fishing international

PART XVIII
OBITUARY   H. V. Hodson, former Editor of *The Annual Register*;
                             Editor, *The Sunday Times*, 1950–61; Provost of the
                             Ditchley Foundation, 1961–71

PART XIX
CHRONICLE OF 1998   Verena Hoffman, Assistant Editor, *The Annual
                             Register*
MAPS   Michael Lear, MJL Graphics, N. Yorks, YO14 9BE

ACKNOWLEDGEMENTS

THE editor again gratefully acknowledges his debt to a number of institutions for their help with sources, references and documents, notably the UK Departments for Northern Ireland, Scotland and Wales, the UN Secretariat and the US Congress. Acknowledgement is also due to the principal sources for the national and IGO data sections (showing the situation as at end-1998 unless otherwise stated), namely *Keesing's Record of World Events* (Keesing's Worldwide), *Worldwide Government Directory* (Keesing's Worldwide), *World Development Report* (Oxford University Press for the World Bank) and the *Financial Times* (London). The AR advisory board and the bodies which nominate its members disclaim responsibility for any opinions expressed or the accuracy of facts recorded in this volume.

ABBREVIATIONS OF NON-UN INTERNATIONAL ORGANIZATIONS

AC	Arctic Council
ACP	African, Caribbean and Pacific states associated with EU
ACS	Association of Caribbean States
AL	Arab League
ALADI	Latin American Integration Association
AMU	Arab Maghreb Union
ANZUS	Australia-New Zealand-US Security Treaty
AP	Amazon Pact
APEC	Asia-Pacific Economic Cooperation
ASEAN	Association of South-East Asian Nations
Benelux	Belgium-Netherlands-Luxembourg Economic Union
BSEC	Black Sea Economic Cooperation
CA	Andean Community
Caricom	Caribbean Community and Common Market
CBSS	Council of the Baltic Sea States
CE	Council of Europe
CEEAC	Economic Community of Central African States
CEFTA	Central European Free Trade Agreement
CEI	Central European Initiative
CIS	Commonwealth of Independent States
COMESA	Common Market of Eastern and Southern Africa
CP	Colombo Plan
CPLP	Community of Portuguese-Speaking Countries
CWTH	The Commonwealth
EBRD	European Bank for Reconstruction and Development
ECO	Economic Cooperation Organization
ECOWAS	Economic Community of West African States
EEA	European Economic Area
EFTA	European Free Trade Association
EU	European Union
G–8	Group of Eight
GCC	Gulf Cooperation Council
IOC	Indian Ocean Commission
Mercosur	Southern Common Market
NAFTA	North American Free Trade Agreement
NAM	Non-Aligned Movement
NATO	North Atlantic Treaty Organization
NC	Nordic Council
OAPEC	Organization of Arab Petroleum Exporting Countries
OAS	Organization of American States
OAU	Oganization of African Unity
OECD	Organization for Economic Cooperation and Development
OECS	Organization of Eastern Caribbean States
OIC	Organization of the Islamic Conference
OPEC	Organization of the Petroleum Exporting Countries
OSCE	Organization for Security and Cooperation in Europe
PFP	Partnership for Peace
SAARC	South Asian Association for Regional Cooperation
SADC	Southern African Development Community
SELA	Latin American Economic System
SPC	Secretariat of the Pacific Community
SPF	South Pacific Forum
UEMOA	West African Economic and Monetary Union
WEU	Western European Union

PREFACE

THE publisher, editor and advisory board of *The Annual Register* mourn the passing of H.V. (Harry) Hodson, who died on 27 March 1999 at the age of 92. He was editor of the *Register* from 1973 to 1988 and chairman of the advisory board and contributor until his death. In accordance with the AR's strict rule of calendar year coverage, a full obituary will appear in the 1999 volume. Harry will be greatly missed by all in the AR circle.

Also mourned is John McLachlan, who died in the summer of 1998, having been the AR's contributor on the Benelux countries for almost 40 years.

The 1998 volume of the AR marks a significant departure in terms of content and arrangement, the aim being to consolidate the book's authority as an international reference work. Instead of an editorial, this volume begins with two global 'overviews' of the year, one focusing on strategic and political trends and the other on economic developments including the Asian economic crisis. After that, the former separate section on the United Kingdom is now included within Part II, covering Western and Southern Europe. In light of the new 'overview' chapters, the former sections on defence, disarmament and security and on economic and social affairs have been discontinued, while chapters on defence and economic organizations have been added to Part XI (International Organizations).

EXTRACTS FROM PAST VOLUMES

200 years ago

1798. *Letter from Admiral Nelson.* [London, 3 October] This day the court of common council was attended by two hundred members. The business was opened by the lord mayor reading the following letter, which he had received from Admiral Nelson, viz.

Vanguard, Mouth of the Nile, August 8, 1798
My lord,
Having the honour of being a freeman of the city of London, I take the liberty of sending to your lordship the sword of the commanding French admiral, Monsieur Blanquet, who survived after the battle of the 1st, off the Nile, and request that the city of London will honour me by the acceptance of it, as a remembrance, that Britannia still rules the waves; which that she may for ever do is the fervent prayer of
Your lordship's
Most obedient servant
Horatio Nelson.

150 years ago

1848. *Revolution in Paris.* [Paris, Tuileries, 24 February] Here were the wildest confusion and disorder. The throne was early pulled down and carried away: the curtains were torn to the ground—the lustres and candelabra smashed—the busts broken—the pictures riddled with balls; everywhere thronging, yelling, half-intoxicated crowds. In the theatre all was torn and broken; the people appeared to resent the past pleasures of the Royal Family. In the chapel the altar was respected, by the intervention of a young *élève* of the Polytechnic School, and the cross borne away by men, thus animated a sense of religious deference, to the church of St. Roch; but all else was, if possible, more disorderly still. There everything was recklessly destroyed: papers were hurled about in showers, like a snow storm.

100 years ago

1898. *Balfour on the death of Gladstone.* [London, House of Commons, 20 May] Mr Balfour felt himself unequal to dealing even with Mr Gladstone as a politician, as a minister, as a leader of public thought, as an eminent servant of the Queen. He would, therefore, rather speak of him as the greatest member of the greatest deliberative assembly that the world had yet seen. There was no gift which would enable one to move, to influence, and to adorn an assembly like that which Mr Gladstone did not possess in a super-eminent degree . . . . Every weapon of parliamentary warfare was wielded by him with the sureness and ease of a perfect, absolute and complete mastery.

50 years ago

1948. *The Marshall Plan.* Although the electoral contest cast its long shadow across the year, from the first speculation of January to the last post-mortem of December, it none the less, in all but its peak moments, ran a poor second to the serious concerns of the nation; this was equally and commendably true both of the principal contestants and of the electorate. In particular, the issues of foreign policy were accorded a place above, and often outside, the partisan politics of the election, and one such issue, the development and execution of the Marshall Plan, dominated all others in the public mind of the United States throughout 1948; its enactment and financing were a major concern of Congress, while upon its European implementation America's hopes for a stable world order came increasingly to depend.

THE ANNUAL REGISTER

FOR THE YEAR 1998

I OVERVIEWS OF THE YEAR

1. GLOBAL ISSUES AND REGIONAL REALITIES

NOTHING on the world stage appeared to change very much in 1998. The actors—people and institutions alike—were the same at the end of the year as at its beginning, the scenery had hardly altered. Much the same issues were preoccupying people. In Korea and Cuba the Cold War itself lingered on, even if a few straws in the wind suggested that ancient quarrels were (at least in the latter case) beginning to look less insurmountable. To discern what that signified, though, raises questions about criteria of historical importance and relevance and about the meaning of apparently simple facts. To Cubans, at least, a faint possibility that American economic sanctions might begin to crumble probably mattered less than the Pope's visit to the island and a Christmas celebrated, for the first time since 1969, as a public holiday.

Such things have symbolism as well as their own seemingly light weight. We have not only to overcome local or shallow perspectives. There are issues harder to resolve. No doubt the year's Indian and Pakistani tests of nuclear weapons registered long-term failure in the machinery for the international control of such weapons. Notable as they were, though, were those tests more or less important than the report in March that tuberculosis was now killing more people worldwide than any other infectious disease? After all, scientists were sure that three million people who would contract it in 1998 would die of it, yet any attempt to assess the implications of the nuclear tests for mortality was bound to be merely conjectural.

It was perhaps enormously important, too, that 1998 closed a phase in the history of a small country, Cambodia, with the death of a mass murderer of global scale and the elimination of the last Khmer Rouge strongholds; but what should that mean outside Cambodia? Should the world have cared more that in June the World Metereological Organization and the UN Environmental Programme reported that there was at least a little evidence that decisions taken ten years earlier in Montreal about chlorofluorocarbons (CFCs) were at last beginning to show that they had slowed down the rate of damage being done to the ozone layer? Acts of violence may symptomize worldwide stirring, but we still find it hard to assess them: outside Afghanistan's borders, should we take much account of the Taleban, who during the year won control of something like nine-tenths of the country's territory?

With no great international fact so evidently decisive to mark 1998 as the disappearance of the Soviet Union had marked 1991, it seems safest to start with the obvious: it remained true, as it had since the beginning of the decade, that world expectations, for good and ill, still focused above all on the behaviour of the United States. Most people, probably, would agree that it was the only superpower. Yet American actions did nothing to change the world in 1998. True, Americans witnessed astonishing drama in their domestic politics, and finished the year with the unprecedented spectacle of an elected President facing impeachment before the Senate. He did so, moreover, while enjoying a popularity in the opinion polls which surpassed that registered as the year began, when he had presented a buoyant State of the Union message. Even a few weeks later, as the first coils of the Lewinsky affair were already winding around his ankles, he sent to Congress the first balanced budget that the country had enjoyed for 30 years. In the troubled months that followed, too, Mr Clinton's seemingly categorical assertion of the integrity of his behaviour ('I did not have sexual relations with that woman') crumbled away, while other issues in the background (Whitewater, campaign contributions, earlier lies about sexual activity) continued to fester. Yet the President kept the sympathy of many Americans and the votes which had been so important in winning his second term, and carried his party to success in the mid-term congressional and gubernatorial elections.

Along the way a little history was made in the working of the US constitution. The Supreme Court decided that a sitting President had no immunity from civil proceedings; there was a notable circumscription of the defence of 'executive privilege' as a protection for witnesses and special privilege was denied to the US Secret Service. The President had to respond to a subpoena to appear before a grand jury. But none of this changed the big picture. At the end of the year the best indicators of political realities were that senators of both parties were looking for a way of avoiding prolonged impeachment proceedings. For all the bitterness of the party polemics, the Lewinsky affair (to stick to that simplifying label) cannot be said to have mattered much in world history. No doubt its failure to damage the President in popular esteem owed much to the continuing prosperity which had for years sustained him without major legislative or foreign policy success. In October Mr Clinton had been able to announce that the budget surplus for 1998 would be $70,000 million dollars, thus achieving four years ahead of its due date a target set in 1997.

Nor did the absence of success abroad seem to dent President Clinton's popularity. Yet it was a bad year for the major goals of American foreign policy. When bombs exploded at the US embassies in Nairobi and Dar es

Salaam, the promptness and violence of the American response (bombardment by cruise missiles of two sites in the Sudan and Afghanistan alleged to be connected with the presumed instigator of the atrocities) attracted less international awe than it did hostile criticism. The replacement of gunboat diplomacy by that of the guided missile had a notably negative moral effect (partly because of the questionable nature of the targets) and no convincing material success. Predictably, strong criticism came from Iraq, Iran and Libya, but so did a condemnation from the Arab League, while the allies of the United States in the Gulf remained silent. Pakistan and Russia also condemned the missile strikes; only Israel, the United Kingdom and Germany declared their support for them.

A similar disarray, and at best qualified success, accompanied four nights of US/UK bombardment of Iraq by missiles and aircraft in December. This was an escalation of the policy of preventing that country from equipping itself with biological, chemical and nuclear weapons. Inspections authorized by the United Nations had dragged on for six years, with the aim of uncovering Iraq's progress (or lack of it) towards equipping itself with the so-called 'weapons of mass destruction'. After a breakdown in late 1997 the inspections had been resumed with renewed assurance of cooperation by the Iraqi government. In May the announcement of a partial withdrawal of US forces from the Gulf seemed briefly promising. Yet in August the UN Security Council again condemned a new Iraqi refusal to cooperate with the inspection team. In November American military action was only countermanded at the last moment. In December, when renewed frustration was reported, the United States and Britain without more ado carried out their announced threat to bomb Iraq.

American policy had now entered a revolutionary mode; it became one of its acknowledged aims to overthrow Saddam Husain. Congress had already voted to give military aid to Iraqi opposition groups. In his State of the Union message the President had delivered an outright warning to Saddam Husain that he could not 'defy the will of the world' by obstructing the inspections authorized by the United Nations (and to which he had agreed), but he seemed likely to be able to continue to do so as 1998 ended. Though the military operation was proclaimed a technical triumph (no American or British casualties were reported), it was a public relations failure and hardly a convincing material success. Whatever damage it may have done to Iraq's capacity to produce weapons of mass destruction, it seemed likely that it could at best only have delayed their acquisition. In a larger context, the operation troubled other Arab states, and did nothing to ensure the continuing security of Israel. Britain, the sole ally of the United States to participate in the bombing campaign, shared in its discredit in the eyes of other members of the Security Council. The UN inspection teams had left Iraq before the attack began, and it was not easy to see on what fruitful basis they could return. The economic sanctions about which Iraq so bitterly complained (and of which it made good propaganda use) were still in place, but had proved a very blunt instrument and now had even less support. The 'degrading' of Iraq's military capacity had achieved only uncertain success. Over the whole operation, finally, there hung a cloud of suspicion, worthy or not, that its timing and nature had been directly linked to the American President's wish to win further support inside and outside Congress as a crucial vote on impeachment drew near.

Iraq was only part of a bad year in the Middle East. Palestinian-Israeli quarrels continued to show a disproportionate power to trouble the international scene. As 1998 opened, hopes engendered by the Oslo accords had long been blighted; as it unrolled, it became clearer than ever that Washington could exert no effective control over its ally, Israel. Although assiduous American effort succeeded in bringing together the Israeli Prime Minister and the Palestinian leader for a meeting in the United States, and in engineering an agreement to re-energize the Oslo process, Mr Netanyahu was confronted on his return to Israel with such criticism by supporters of his coalition government that it became evident that execution of the steps agreed (notably by withdrawing Israeli troops from areas of occupied Palestine) was unlikely, whether because of his own views or because he felt constrained by the need to hold his government together. By the end of the year it was clear that no further progress could be expected until new Israeli elections had been held, if then. These would be the first consultation of Israeli public opinion since Mr Netanyahu had come to power on a wave of disillusion with the Oslo agreements. Until then the frustration of the United States would continue.

The problems of the Middle East indeed looked as intractable as ever, and perhaps even more so than 12 months earlier. The consequences of the creation of the Zionist programme at the end of the nineteenth century and of the Balfour Declaration of 1917 were evidently as unmanageable as ever. The central issues of the stabilization of Palestine and the containment of what looked like an increasingly dangerous regime in Iraq were also tangled with, and cut across by, a variety of local inter-state problems, growing regional economic and social pressures (it was a year of depressed oil prices) and even a few lingering consequences of the Cold War. It was striking, nonetheless, that in spite of the persistence of the Gulf and Palestinian problems, the obvious link between them, pan-Islamic sympathy, did not itself seem to present more cause for worry at the end of the year than at the beginning. Again, this was hardly a change. The many long-term obstacles to cooperation within the Islamic world were as strong as ever. The ideological and institutional excesses (as the Western world often saw them) of the Taleban in Afghanistan, and the barbaric aspects of political struggle in Algeria and the Sudan, were alarming and often revolting, but hardly seemed surprising or of great consequence outside the countries concerned. The Prime Minister of Malaysia might endeavour to rally Islamic opinion in the aftermath of financial disaster by allegations of Jewish plots, but his wild protestations had an air of artificiality. Even in the Gulf there was still plenty of evidence of the impracticality and difficulty attending joint action by Islamic states.

In part, the Islamic factor in world politics had sometimes been confused with what some saw as a problem of 'rogue regimes'—some of them, notably North Korea, not Islamic—which threatened to disturb international peace, appeared to have unpredictable futures, and dabbled in the murky waters of international terrorism in default of more effective means of action. Syria had been one such country, but its position had seemed more predictable in recent years. Iraq, Iran and Libya, though, all still seemed to exemplify attitudes and qualities which tempted commentators to lump them together as problems of a new kind. All pursued (and advertised) fundamentally anti-American policies when they could, and loudly advocated them from time to time. They appeared, too, to be broadly anti-capitalist and therefore anti-Western. But they had lost much potential leverage with the collapse of the Cold War polarities. The USSR was no longer available as an ally of last resort against the United States; the position of China remained much more reserved than that of the old communist superpower. Some thought it significant, too, that an Islamic nation, Pakistan, had tested its own nuclear weapons. But this was in response to Indian tests in May. It was clear that the threats which Pakistan's rulers had in mind came from their neighbour, rather than from any more generalized anti-Islamic forces, far less from Western powers. As for the Indian explosions, their purpose may well have been to impress China (the victor of the fighting of the early 1960s, Indians remembered) rather than Pakistan. Meanwhile, these tests also indisputably revealed a spread of nuclear weaponry which made it more urgent than ever to secure wider adhesion to non-proliferation and control arrangements. But little could be said to have strengthened confidence in such arrangements during 1998, in spite of British and French ratification of the 1996 Nuclear Test-Ban Treaty in April.

There was tension between aspiration and achievement, too, even in the formal improvement in American relations with China. In July Mr Clinton paid that country a presidential visit to which both governments clearly attached great importance; it was the first since the Tiananmen Square killing nearly ten years before. Pressures had mounted on American policy to make more positive assertions of the need to protect and promote human rights in China and hopes of greater success in this area were occasioned by the presence of a new Chinese Prime Minister who as mayor of Shanghai had managed in 1989 to avoid violent confrontation and bloodshed with students in the aftermath of Tiananmen. President Jiang Zemin also gave a reassuring impression of unprecedented frankness and relaxation in a televised press conference which he shared with Mr Clinton; they discussed not only human rights in their more general aspects, but even the specific topic of Tiananmen Square. Yet Chinese actions towards political dissidents remained implacable. To human-rights watchers, the regime's language looked like little more than a polite response to the gesture made by the US government before the visit in announcing that it would in future not be giving its usual annual support to a resolution in the United Nations deploring the poor protection of human rights in China.

For a potential superpower, China's 1998 did not seem one of significant change either. Its government continued to promote its austerity campaign to combat recent inflationary tendencies. There were reforms in the banking system which, it was hoped, would enable it to avoid some of the economic and financial disasters which had already occurred in other Asian countries. Politically, though, the regime was firmly against overt liberalization. Trials followed by imprisonment or exile for those seeking to form new political parties accompanied benevolent phraseology and the signature of the International Convention on Civil and Political Rights. As for China's international role, Mr Clinton indicated that Taiwan's government had nothing to hope for from the United States; it looked as if China had only to wait for that fruit to fall from the tree. A first 'summit' with the European Union had been held in April, inaugurating what was intended to be a series of annual meetings. This could be interpreted as another step towards greater freedom of manoeuvre for China in international affairs, as could a small beginning in the definition of its frontiers with Russia. Relations with Japan remained cool after a visit by the Chinese President to that country which still failed to elicit what the Chinese regarded as due Japanese acknowledgment of crimes perpetrated 60 years earlier. For all the hopes which had surrounded the Clinton visit, too, Chinese irritation with American policy at the end of the year was made clear in references to the dangers of American 'hegemony' in the columns of the *People's Daily* of Beijing, and in the UN Security Council's discussion of Iraq.

Against this background, Africa's problems looked as insoluble as ever and perhaps also as much disregarded. In one state after another there was kaleidoscopic change, but only in governmental personnel, through coups, disorder, mutinies and rebellions—a story of persisting strife and, all too often, of genocidal massacre. There was little sign of that dawn of an African renaissance which had been heralded a few years before. Civilized government in the continent seemed as fragile a growth as ever. The only solid gain was the continued waning of the intense political interference by outsiders which had marked the Cold War era. But there were other threats. Studies suggested that, rather than the continent's endemic political and economic problems (which shadowed the future even of South Africa), the effects of AIDS might well come to transcend those of Africa's other ills.

In Europe, one troubled province, Kosovo, hovered again on the edge of open conflict as the Yugoslavian government sought to assert its authority over the Albanians who still lived there. Evidently all European nationalisms were not yet assured of non-violent solution, notwithstanding the slow edging forward of a negotiated settlement in Ireland. An agreement between the rival Irish nationalists and the responsible governments in April was followed by a referendum which put it to an immediate test; popular approval both sides of the border was probably the most important sign so far that Irish sentiment was beginning to overcome division and the bitterness it evoked. Elections in June to a new representative assembly were the next step. Tension between two nations was also eased when the Cyprus government decided, after all, not to install better anti-aircraft missiles on the island to counter the presumed Turkish threat. Meanwhile, the integration of Europe edged forward, even if the enlargement of the European Union seemed to face greater difficulty than ever. The most important event in its history since the reunification of Germany in any case had to wait until the first day of 1999: the introduction of a single European currency in 11 states. The United Kingdom, meanwhile, remained awkwardly aloof, distracted by the trivia of its own politics, and showing little awareness of the impending disaggregation latent in devolution for Scotland and Wales, or of the prospect that new institutions in Ireland must radically change old assumptions about the sovereignty exercised by Westminster.

For the potential giant of the European scene, Russia, it was an unhappy year, largely because of continuing economic difficulties. The devaluation of the rouble in August produced widespread discontent and it was evident for the rest of the year that President Yeltsin, more and more hampered by ill-health, was rapidly running out of room for political manoeuvre in finding a government to deal with his key problem, the economy. Here, too, was little change. In the actual onset of its greatest difficulties, Russia was nonetheless in part the victim of external forces. The financial crisis which it faced in the summer was detonated by a wave of difficulties rolling in from Asian countries.

The Asian economic epidemic continued to show characteristics familiar for years in Japan: the instability of over-committed banks, the erosion of currency value and the flight of foreign capital. The most radical effects in 1998 came in Indonesia, where economic discontent led eventually to the overthrow of a government which had successfully clung to power for a quarter of a century. From the collapse of the Indonesian currency, too, flowed reciprocal effects in other South-East Asian countries, notably Malaysia, whose Prime Minister vociferously denounced what he depicted as the efforts of speculators to undermine national policies. Elsewhere, by the end of the year some degree of containment of the damage appeared to have been achieved, though it remained an open question whether there might not be worse to come.

Whatever precise form it took, everywhere the same fundamental question hung over the year's end: could stability still be taken for granted?

Evidently, instability had not triumphed in the international political and economic system since the seismic change of the collapse of the Cold War system. Yet it remained to be seen whether it could still be contained. In a time of uncertainty, perhaps only a very long perspective provided some unambiguous encouragement: 1998 was, after all, the 50th anniversary of the signing of the UN Declaration of Human Rights. A Human Rights Watch organization was able to report favourably on the achievements of half a century, and the year brought at least two signs that, for all the sordid realities of government, progress continued. In July 120 nations signed a statute to set up a permanent international court with jurisdiction over war crimes and crimes against humanity. True, 60 would have to ratify the agreement before the court could actually come into existence. Nevertheless, it was, like the UN Declaration 50 years earlier, a significant tribute of vice to virtue and marked how far the tide had run since then. The second step was a decision in the highest of British courts—the House of Lords—that the extradition under a warrant from another country (Spain) of a former head of state, Senator Pinochet of Chile, to face trial for crimes committed against human rights under his rule, was legal. Almost at once, the ruling was overtaken by a decision to re-hear the case because of a possible technical disqualification of one of the judges; but this could not erase the significance of the decision in principle. It was an application of a universal jurisdiction over human rights violations in peacetime even when a former head of state was concerned—a setting-aside of a centuries-old view of sovereignty.

Coupled with such facts as the obvious concern the Chinese government was beginning to show over the use of the Internet by possible opponents of the regime—at the end of the year a person said to have 'incited the overthrow of state power' by giving a list of electronic addresses to the publisher of an electronic newsletter was put on trial—or with the continuing effectiveness of American constitutional procedures in exposing presidential inadequacies, it was possible for some to think 1998 not too bad a year. Of course, revelation of presidential misconduct did not mean that he would have to pay the price which some thought was due. Mr Clinton remained more popular than ever with those who talked to the pollsters, and especially with the black Americans and women who had voted for him. Democracy, after all, is not about getting what is good for you, but what you want.

2. THE INTERNATIONAL ECONOMY

THE world economy was thrown off course in 1998 by the predicted consequences of the Asian crisis and by some unexpected side-effects. It expanded by only 2.2 per cent, according to the International Monetary

Fund (IMF). This was a sharp shortfall compared with earlier estimates of 4.4 per cent made in October 1997 and contrasted with growth of 4.2 per cent in 1997. Growth was also unevenly distributed. The International Labour Office warned in September that up to one-third of the world's 3,000 million-strong workforce would be unemployed or under-employed by the start of 1999 as a result of the global recession. The UN Human Development Report reported that the poorest 20 per cent of the world's people had been left out of the consumption explosion. Globally the richest 20 per cent of people consumed 86 per cent of total private expenditures and the average African household in 1998 consumed 20 per cent less than it did 25 years ago.

By the late spring it had become obvious that the Asian crisis, which had begun in July 1997 with the devaluation of the Thai baht, was much deeper than expected for the main countries concerned but less serious than expected for the mainstream Western economies. This was particularly true of the United States, whose 3.7 per cent growth in 1998 was actually 0.8 percentage points higher than the OECD had predicted a year earlier. The European Union also managed slightly higher growth than the OECD had forecast (2.8 per cent against 2.7 per cent). Total growth in the OECD countries over the same period, at 2.2 per cent, was only 0.2 percentage points down on OECD estimates a year earlier. This was entirely due to a very sharp change of fortunes for Japan, whose economy shrank by an unprecedented 2.6 per cent in 1998 compared with previous expectations of a standstill. The recent deflationary trend in the OECD area continued, with the rate of price increases dropping to 3.3 per cent compared with 3.7 per cent in 1997. One of the chief ingredients of deflation was falling commodity prices. *The Economist* sterling index of commodity prices fell 20.5 per cent during the year, with oil (as reflected in the benchmark price North Sea Brent) dropping by 43 per cent, a phenomenon which hardly anyone had predicted.

The economic crisis that swept across the world during the year hit poorer and aspiring economies much harder than mature ones. Developing countries suffered a drop of more than 50 per cent in their rate of growth (from 5.7 to 2.8 per cent) mainly because of the meltdown in Asia. Unlike the West, Third World inflation started rising again—from 9.2 to 10.2 per cent. The worst hit countries were the so-called ASEAN-4 (Indonesia, Malaysia, Philippines and Thailand), which suffered an average fall in gross domestic product (GDP) of 10.6 per cent. Africa managed to increase its rate of growth slightly, to 3.6 per cent, but this was way below the near the 6 per cent achieved in 1996.

The IMF's handling of the Asian crisis produced an unusual clash with its sister organization, the World Bank, whose chief economist, Joseph Stiglitz argued that the high interest rates advocated by the IMF were counterproductive because they undermined economies that were already weak. The IMF countered this by stating that monetary policy had to be tightened in order to stop and reverse the excessive depreciation of exchange rates that had occurred. The IMF admitted, however, that 'like most observers' it misread the depth of the recession that had been provoked in Asia. (see map/diagram on facing page).

The most disappointing economy (apart from Japan's) was Russia's. After six years of extreme deprivation and economic contraction, it had appeared to have turned a corner in 1997 when it recorded its first positive growth rate (albeit only 0.7 per cent) since the collapse of communism in 1991. But in 1998 the economy imploded again—by 5.7 per cent—with no obvious recovery in sight (see below).

If Russia was once again the world's economic 'basket case' in 1998, then the prize for the most impressive performance would be fought for between three very different countries. First, the United States, despite the arithmetical handicap of being the largest economy in the world (accounting for almost a third of total OECD output), continued to expand strongly, while still keeping inflation at bay. Second, Ireland, the so-called 'emerald tiger', shrugged off the Asian crisis and its own adjustment difficulties in joining Europe's single currency to grow by more than any other country in the world and by over 9 per cent for the second year running. The third contender for the prize was China. Whether one believed its own growth figure of 7.8 per cent or the IMF's of 7.2 per cent did not really matter. The fact that it grew at all, by over 7 per cent, when nearly all of the countries around it in East Asia suffered sharp recessions, was a sort of miracle in its own right.

Economists conducted a lively debate about why the financial hurricane that swept the world in 1997–98 was so selective in its victims. It was agreed that the slump in Asia was made worse by the failure of the Japanese economy—by far the biggest in the region—to adopt successful recuperative policies and that Russia's unexpected defaulting on its debts in mid-August was seminal in transmitting the virus to industrialized countries hitherto immune. In theory, Russia was such a tiny economy that its problems should not have had much effect. But just as, in chaos theory, the flapping of a butterfly's wings can cause a storm on the other side of the world, so the Russian government's default on domestic debts and associated devaluation of the rouble brought a disproportionate response. It led people to realize that other governments could default on their debts and triggered a 'flight to quality' among investors. There was a rush to liquidate positions. This had knock-on effects all over the world, partly because of the involvement of hedge funds (unlike the situation in Asia, where most of the problem concerned non-tradeable inter-bank loans). These had very large exposures backed by limited capital because of the leveraged positions involved. The pressure was soon transferred to Brazil, the most important economy in South America, whose currency came under fierce speculative attack in the third quarter of the year.

Meanwhile, share markets in the United States and Europe continued

I.2. THE INTERNATIONAL ECONOMY

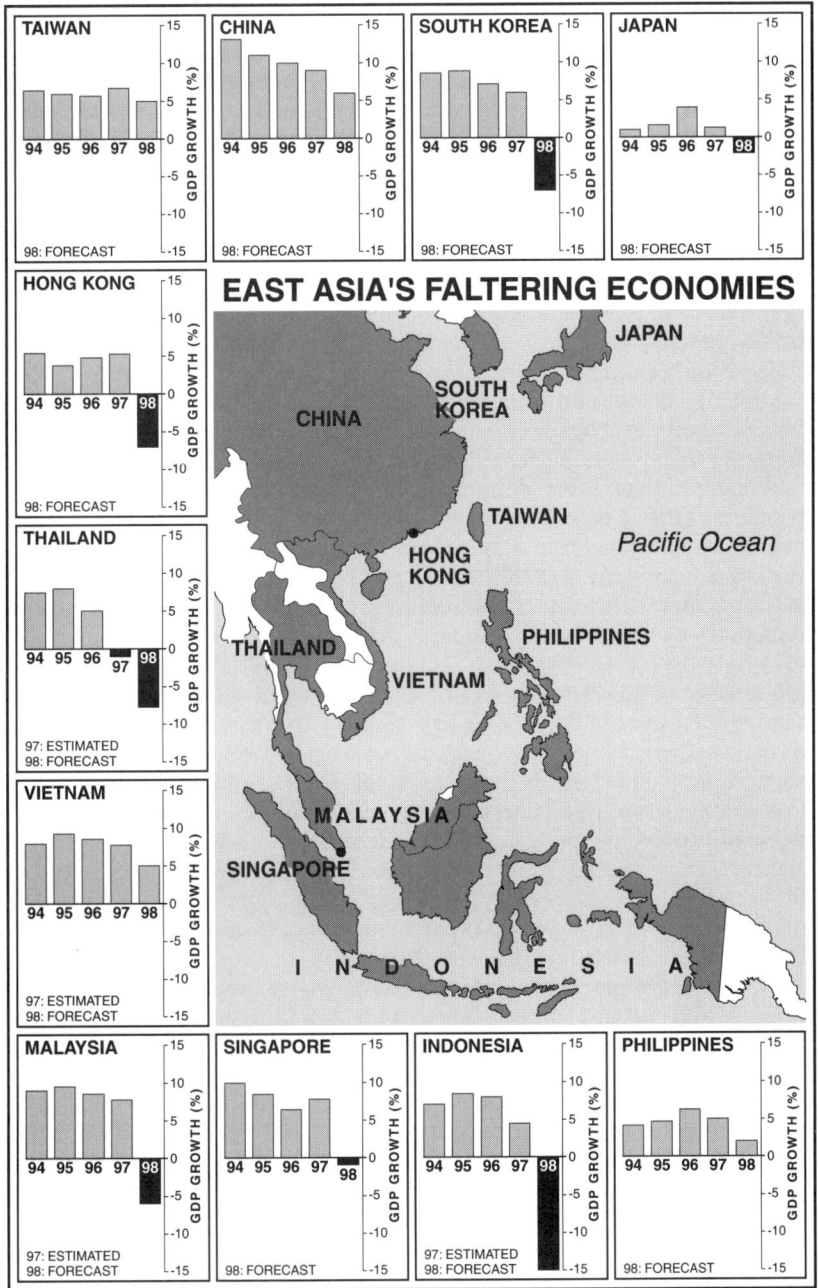

to rise, directly benefiting from the 'flight to quality' out of Asia, Russia and South America. However, towards the end of July investors began to worry that equity prices were simply unrealistically high by any standards. This worry coincided with concerns that the Asian crisis was starting to take its toll, a fear aggravated by the Russian situation. Suddenly, it seemed, everyone wanted to be out of shares—with the result that by October US equity markets had fallen by 20 per cent and those in Europe by as much as 35 per cent. The situation was aggravated by the near-collapse of the US hedge fund Long-Term Capital Management (LTCM), which had highly leveraged positions around the world and had to be bailed out with the help of the New York Federal Reserve Bank.

In response to these events the US Federal Reserve led a global reduction of interest rates with two cuts of 0.25 per cent in September. More than anything else, this action reversed the deteriorating trend in market sentiment—at least until the end of the year. Such was the thrust of the flow of money that by the end of 1998 Western share markets had recovered from the mid-year collapse and ended the year at high levels.

Asia's problems were dominated by the economic situation in Japan, which the OECD described as 'grave'. Japanese GDP growth of 5 per cent in 1996 had dropped to 1.4 per cent in 1997, followed by an actual contraction of 2.8 per cent in 1998, the biggest in recent memory. The economy suffered from a credit crunch, falling exports and investment, and a reluctance of consumers to spend. Nevertheless, Japan still had a number of very positive achievements. Its savings ratio (the proportion of net income not spent) was over 15 per cent (compared with almost nothing in the United States in the second half of the year), short-term interest rates were less than 0.5 per cent and the country sported a current-account surplus equivalent to 3.2 per cent of GDP. The government tried everything, from exhortation to the distribution of free vouchers, to persuade people to spend more of their savings, but without any obvious success. On 16 November the government announced the biggest-to-date of a series of reflationary packages—this one worth US$200,000 million—but hardly anyone was expecting Japan to bounce back into positive growth in 1999.

Japan's problems—particularly the lack of consumer spending—cast a shadow over the rest of East Asia, where a number of countries suffered from severe contractions in their economies, notably Indonesia (minus 17.4 per cent), Thailand (minus 11 per cent), South Korea (minus 7 per cent) and Malaysia (minus 8.6 per cent). The Hong Kong economy contracted by 7 per cent, but Taiwan expanded by almost 5 per cent and mainland China by between 7 and 8 per cent. China was helped by a strong public spending programme (equivalent to a 2.5 per cent fiscal stimulus), a lowering of interest rates and the fact that its currency, being only partly convertible, was insulated to a great extent from the troubles going on all around it. Even so, the Chinese economy was beginning to look more vulnerable by the end of the year. Elsewhere in Asia, India, Pakistan and Bangladesh all managed to grow by over 4 per cent. The Middle East experienced mixed fortunes. Egypt grew by an estimated 5.3 per cent, whereas Saudi Arabia, hit by the sharp fall in oil prices, managed only a modest 0.4 per cent. Iran's growth rate dropped from 2.6 per cent to 1.7 per cent and Jordan's from 2.2 to 0.5 per cent.

Russia's decision on 17 August to devalue the rouble and, in effect, to default on domestic government debt was a defining moment in the economic year. It caused a reaction out of all proportion to the size of the loans involved (only a third of which were held outside Russia anyway). It punctured the assumption that government-backed debt in emerging countries was safe and led to a global reappraisal of credit risks. No longer was any one emerging country 'too big to fail', even when there were strong political reasons to continue support. Investors around the world started unloading their securities in emerging markets and stopped making new investments. The effect was exaggerated by the unwinding of leveraged positions taken out by hedge funds. In the third quarter alone, shares in Latin America dropped in value by 27 per cent, while Asian shares lost a further 7.6 per cent.

For the first time since the end of communism in 1991, the Russian economy had actually expanded in 1997, by 0.7 per cent. In 1998, however, it lapsed into another contraction of over 5.5 per cent. The country's problems were aggravated by weak governance, collapsing oil prices and an inability to collect taxes. This led to a yawning budget deficit which could not be funded either by overseas borrowing or domestic tax collecting—so the government resorted to the printing presses, thereby expanding the money supply and undermining the real progress that had been made in reducing inflation to near-Western levels. According to *Russian Economic Trends*, real average wages fell by over 35 per cent between the end of July and the end of October. It was estimated that 29 per cent of Russia's population was living in poverty by the end of the year compared with 22 per cent before the crisis.

It was no surprise that the Russian crisis adversely affected neighbouring countries in transition. Ukraine, hit by reduced trade with Russia and persistent budget deficits, shrunk by another 1.7 per cent, while inflation nearly doubled to 26 per cent. Ukraine's economy retained the dubious distinction of having contracted every year since the break with communism—with no obvious light at the end of the tunnel. On the brighter side, there were signs that others were managing the post-communist transition more effectively. The IMF reported that the median growth rate for countries in transition was 4.2 per cent in 1998, up from 3.4 per cent a year earlier. Albania, Belarus and Azerbaijan all grew by 7–8 per cent, and a string of other East European economies expanded by 5 per cent or more, including Bulgaria, Poland, Estonia, Hungary, Latvia, Lithuania, Macedonia, Croatia and Armenia.

The US economy seemed to be defying gravity as it experienced its seventh successive year of sustained economic growth. Real GDP expanded in 1998 by 3.7 per cent, with inflation actually falling still further, from 2.4 per cent in 1997 to only 1.6 per cent in 1998. Share markets reflected this optimism, and the Dow Jones industrial average rose by 17.3 per cent. However, by the end of the year concern was being expressed at what was seen as excessive increases in the shares of companies engaged in developing the Internet, which were rising to exceptional heights even when the companies concerned were making losses. Unemployment dropped once more—from 4.9 to 4.6 per cent—though by the end of the year there was a general feeling that a slowdown in the economy would soon temper the surprising buoyancy of the labour market. Expansion was fuelled by a boom in household consumption. Spending was running well ahead of income, and in the third quarter the savings ratio actually turned negative for the first time in recent memory. Consumer confidence was kept high by the buoyancy of the share markets and the wealth thus generated gave people the confidence to keep on spending (though it also made economic growth vulnerable to a future shakeout in shares). The Federal Reserve continued to keep a deft hand on the tiller. It raised interest rates twice in September (by 0.25 percentage points each time) in order to restore liquidity to the markets after the sharp fall in share prices in mid-year. On the second occasion the decision was taken, unusually, between meetings of the Open Markets Committee. By giving an extra-strong signal to the markets, the US lead in reducing interest rates was soon followed by other key countries, including EU member states.

The economy of the European Union expanded by 2.8 per cent in 1998, according to the OECD, compared with 2.7 per cent the previous year. Within this total, the 11 economies which joined together in monetary union at the end of 1998 did rather better, with growth of 2.9 per cent against 2.5 per cent in 1997. Even so, growth was modest compared with the strong rates recorded in the second half of the 1980s. More recently they had been required to sweat down their economies by shedding surplus debt in order to meet the criterion laid down in the Maastricht Treaty that budget deficits must not be more then 3 per cent of GDP. France achieved GDP growth of 3.1 per cent (its best for a decade). Germany was not far behind with 2.7 per cent, though Italy managed only 1.5 per cent. But the sustained expansion that Europe had hoped for still looked elusive at the end of the year as the rate of growth slackened under the twin effects of the Asian crisis and high interest rates. Aware of the situation, the embryonic European Central Bank actually engineered an EU-wide reduction in interest rates shortly before it formally took over the reins at the beginning of 1999. The size of the challenge facing the 11 countries of 'Euroland' was underlined by the fact that unemployment was still almost 11 per cent at the end of 1998.

The United Kingdom, whose new Labour government had decided not to join the single European currency until the time was ripe, experienced growth of 2.7 per cent (the sixth successive year of respectable expansion) and low inflation (down to 2.6 per cent by the end of the year). Once again, however, Ireland was the star EU performer, and arguably in the whole world. The country recorded economic growth of 9 per cent, as if the Asian crisis had not existed. During the five years to the end of 1998, the Irish economy expanded by an average of 9 per cent a year, an achievement without parallel for Ireland or any other country. It managed to do this while maintaining a budget surplus and a healthy surplus on the current account of the balance of payments—and low inflation as well. No-one would be watching Ireland's future performance more closely than the United Kingdom, because Ireland had joined the single currency despite having same economic problem as Britain, namely, being out of step with the business cycle of the rest of Europe. In order to qualify for membership Ireland had to halve the country's short-term interest rates to 3 per cent in the last months of 1998. If Ireland could do this and succeed within the single currency area, then it was bound to have repercussions on Britain.

The 1998 Group of Eight (G-8 summit), held in Birmingham, England, in May, was overshadowed by the events in Asia, instability in Indonesia and the controversy surrounding India's nuclear tests. Tony Blair, the British Prime Minister, who was host, failed to persuade his G-8 colleagues, particularly Germany and Japan, to extend debt relief to developing countries. But members did pledge themselves to take urgent steps to strengthen the 'global financial architecture' in order to reduce the risks of crises recurring in future.

II WESTERN AND SOUTHERN EUROPE

1. UNITED KINGDOM—SCOTLAND—WALES—NORTHERN IRELAND

i. UNITED KINGDOM

CAPITAL: London   AREA: 244,100 sq km   POPULATION: 59,000,000 ('97)
OFFICIAL LANGUAGES: English; Welsh in Wales
POLITICAL SYSTEM: parliamentary democracy
HEAD OF STATE: Queen Elizabeth II (since Feb '52)
RULING PARTY: Labour Party (since May '97)
HEAD OF GOVERNMENT: Tony Blair, Prime Minister (since May '97); *for cabinet list see* XVII.5
MAIN IGO MEMBERSHIPS (non-UN): NATO, CWTH, EU, WEU, OSCE, CE, OECD, G-8
CURRENCY: pound sterling (end-'98 £1=US$1.66)
GNP PER CAPITA: US$20,710 by exchange-rate calculation, US$20,520 by PPP calculation ('97)

THE political year was inevitably dominated by Tony Blair, elected Prime Minister in May 1997 at the head of a 'New Labour' administration commanding the largest parliamentary majority since 1945 (see AR 1997, pp. 19–20). In addition to securing a potentially historic peace agreement in Northern Ireland (see II.1.iv), the government gave priority to constitutional reform in Britain, enacting devolution legislation for Scotland and Wales as well as setting in train the eventual abolition of the hereditary component of the House of Lords. It also used its new windfall tax on the privatized utilities to launch a New Deal 'welfare-to-work' programme designed to get the long-term unemployed into the labour market. However, little progress was made on the government's much-vaunted promise to initiate fundamental reform of the country's costly welfare system, not least because of divisions within ministerial ranks that were starkly exposed when Mr Blair carried out his first cabinet reshuffle in late July. The government became increasingly prone to scandals and political crises as the year progressed, culminating in the last quarter in the enforced resignations of two cabinet ministers, one of them, Peter Mandelson, a principal architect of the 'New Labour' project. By then, evidence of an economic downturn had obliged the government to halve its growth forecast for 1999, although it insisted that plans for large increases in social spending remained in place.

In the external policy sphere, Britain hosted a summit meeting of the G-8 group of industrialized countries in Birmingham on 15–17 May (see I.2). It also held the presidency of the European Union (EU) in the first half 1998; but the government's aspiration to be 'at the heart of Europe' was not assisted by Britain's non-participation in the new single European currency prepared for launch on 1 January 1999. At the end of the year, moreover, UK participation with the United States in renewed bombing of Iraq further highlighted the continuing supremacy of the US-UK alliance over Britain's continental relationships.

THE POLITICAL YEAR. The Government of Wales Act and the Scotland Act received the royal assent on 31 July and 19 November respectively, whereupon campaigning began in earnest in each country for the elections to their new devolved legislatures scheduled for May 1999 (see II.1.ii; II.1.iii; XVII.3). Apart from its declared belief in the principle of devolution, the government's strategy was to take the wind out of the sails of the pro-independence nationalists by granting different degrees of home rule to Scotland and Wales, thus ensuring the preservation of the United Kingdom. However, particularly in Scotland, devolution proved to be something of a Pandora's Box for Labour. The Scottish National Party (SNP) embraced the plan enthusiastically, as a step towards full independence, and benefited hugely in opinion polls of Scottish voting intentions, moving ahead of Labour by mid-year.

The government also faced difficulties at Westminster over the so-called 'West Lothian question'—the prospect that after devolution Scottish MPs at Westminster would continue to vote on legislation affecting England, whereas members representing English constituencies would have no corresponding power to influence Scottish legislation. A Conservative amendment to the Scotland Bill, tabled on 6 May, demanded an independent inquiry into these aspects of devolution. The government defeated the amendment, but revealed in mid-May that the House of Commons' regional affairs committee, which had not met for two decades, would be revived to give English MPs an opportunity to question ministers and to scrutinize legislation affecting England, without input from Scottish and Welsh members. There appeared to be little governmental appetite for embarking upon the devolution of power to regional assemblies in England, as also envisaged in the 1997 Labour election manifesto.

Even more problematical for the government was opposition in the House of Lords to the manner in which Labour intended to abolish the hereditary peers, numbering some 750 out of a total upper house complement of about 1,200 and overwhelmingly Conservative in allegiance. Astutely, most of their lordships did not oppose abolition as such, because it had featured in Labour's 1997 election manifesto, but rather the intention to create an interim second chamber as a stepping-stone to definitive reform. The battle-lines were drawn on 5 May when the then Conservative leader in the Lords, Viscount Cranborne, threatened to use his party's in-built majority to block government legislation if an attempt were made to eject the hereditary peers before proposals for comprehensive reform were tabled. Calling for a 'big bang' reform rather than piecemeal changes, Viscount Cranborne asserted that it would be 'perfectly possible' to block government bills without breaching the unwritten Salisbury Convention that the Lords should not defeat measures that had appeared in a ruling party's election manifesto.

The Tory peers' ultimatum was encouraged by Conservative Party leader William Hague, amid opposition claims that the Labour Party was bent on filling the upper chamber with 'Tony's cronies', i.e. friends of Prime Minister Blair. Pending disclosure of the government's precise intentions, opposition peers flexed their muscles by seeking major amendment of the European Parliamentary Elections Bill, which was intended by ministers to be in force for the European Parliament elections due in June 1999. The bill provided in particular for the replacement of 'first-past-the-post' contests in single-member constituencies by a proportional system based on multi-member electoral districts and voting for party lists. Opposition in the Lords focused on the envisaged presentation of candidates on 'closed' lists drawn up by party committees, on which an amendment was tabled seeking to give voters the option of expressing a preference for individual candidates. Whilst the bulk of the opposition came from Conservative ranks, some Labour peers also supported the amendment, amid disquiet in Labour circles at the recent 'de-selection' of several left-wing sitting members of the European Parliament. Passage of the amendment on two occasions before the summer recess, and the government's refusal to accept it, produced a deadlock that was not to be resolved until the broader confrontation on Lords reform was defused late in the year (see below).

The government encountered much less opposition to its plan for a directly-elected mayor and 25-member assembly for London, to provide the sort of city-wide strategic authority which had not existed since the abolition of the Greater London Council (GLC) by the Thatcher government. A referendum in London on 7 May, in which the voting turnout was 34 per cent, produced a 72 per cent majority in favour of the proposals. However, the Labour Party then had to grapple with the problem of who would be its mayoral candidate. The clear favourite among party members and the London electorate was Ken Livingstone, the former GLC leader who was now a left-wing Labour MP and member of the party's national executive committee (NEC). As a distinctly 'old Labour' politician, Mr Livingstone did not endear himself to the Blair leadership. The trouble was that no other putative Labour candidate came near to matching the popularity of 'Red Ken' in the capital. Pending the setting of a date for the London elections, therefore, the Labour candidacy issue remained unresolved at year's end, as did that of the Conservative Party. In the latter case, a determined bid for the mantle by former Conservative MP Lord (Jeffrey) Archer encountered resistance within the Tory hierarchy, which feared that various personal and financial allegations made against the millionaire novelist in recent years would get a new lease of life if he became the party's official candidate.

Local elections for over 4,000 council seats in England (including the 32

London boroughs), also held on 7 May, were notable mainly for attracting the lowest voter turnout (27 per cent) since records began in 1947. They produced modest net gains for the Conservatives, while Labour and the Liberal Democrats both lost ground compared with the previous contests in 1994. Labour nevertheless remained substantially the strongest party in local government, and the Conservatives failed to dislodge the Liberal Democrats as the second largest. The Conservatives recorded a net gain of 258 seats, regaining control of Tunbridge Wells and Runnymede but losing Bromley to the Liberal Democrats and failing to make inroads in other target areas. Councils lost by Labour included Liverpool to the Liberal Democrats, who also picked up seats in other high-spending 'old Labour' strongholds in the north and parts of inner London. However, the Liberal Democrats lost control in the Isle of Wight and in six other councils in the south and east, including their flagship London borough of Kingston-upon-Thames.

Plans for local government reform featured prominently in the government's output of policy papers in the first half of the year. A draft code of conduct published on 7 April aimed at rooting out corruption and malpractice among a 'small minority' of the UK's 20,000 local councillors and two million local government staff. The proposals included the establishment of an independent Standards Board, which would investigate corruption allegations and would be empowered to punish councillors found guilty by disqualification from office for up to five years. Such corruption, it was noted by commentators, tended to be found in 'one party' city councils long controlled by Labour. Deputy Prime Minister John Prescott followed this up on 30 July with a White Paper which he described as 'the most radical and comprehensive package of local government reform for generations'. It contained proposals for directly-elected mayors with executive powers (subject to local referendums to determine whether electors wanted them), annual council elections, an end to the 'capping' of council budgets by the central government, the replacement of compulsory competitive tendering by a 'best value' regime overseen by the Audit Commission and the establishment of regional standards boards to combat corruption.

The centre-piece of the government's domestic programme was the New Deal 'welfare-to-work' scheme, announced with great fanfare on 5 January by the Chancellor of the Exchequer, Gordon Brown, who promised a 'national crusade' against unemployment. Set to cost £3,500 million in total, the scheme aimed in its first phase, which began in April, to guarantee work or training for those aged 18 to 24 who had been unemployed for at least six months. Such young people would lose their unemployment benefit (the so-called 'job-seeker's allowance') if they refused to take a job, a place in full-time training or further education, or a place on an environmental task force. Employers participating in the programme would receive £60 a week per person employed for up to 26 weeks, which was to be funded out of the windfall tax. At the end of June the scheme was extended to over-24s who had been unemployed for two years or more.

Assessments of the efficacy of the New Deal differed widely. Conservative spokesmen claimed in late November that it had proved to be 'a chaotic flop', after the government had admitted that it had no idea how many of the 35,000 participating firms had taken on anyone under the scheme. Employment Minister Andrew Smith blamed this gap in knowledge on 'the woeful management information systems we inherited from the Tories'. By the end of the year the government had sufficient information to announce 'the good news that in total the New Deal has helped over 90,000 young people into jobs, training or work experience'. Of the 52,800 who had found employment, over three-quarters had gone into unsubsidized jobs. In the 25-plus age group some 3,500 people had been helped into work.

As the year progressed, efforts by Labour 'spin doctors' to keep the public focus on the government's achievements were undermined by increasingly serious scandals and other cases of alleged ministerial culpability. The police caution handed out to the son of Home Secretary Jack Straw on 12 January, after an undercover journalist had entrapped him into selling her cannabis in a London public house, was an embarrassment for Mr Straw as the minister responsible for the fight against drugs; but he was thought to have handled the affair responsibly. The press also had great fun in February and March with disclosures about the startling cost of the refurbishment of the Lord Chancellor's official apartments in the Palace of Westminster, and with Lord Irvine of Lairg's unwise comparison of himself to Cardinal Wolsey, his powerful 16th-century predecessor. Including £60,000 for wallpaper alone, the refurbishment eventually cost some £650,000, double the original estimate, but was justified by Lord Irvine on the grounds that his residence deserved to be maintained 'in an historically authentic manner'.

More ominous for the government were a series of investigations into the business affairs and personal finances of millionaire businessman and Labour MP Geoffrey Robinson, who had been appointed Paymaster-General in May 1997. Criticized by the parliamentary commissioner for standards on 20 January for failing to register an offshore trust of which he was a discretionary beneficiary, Mr Robinson was rebuked by the Commons' standards and privileges committee on 15 July for not declaring two paid directorships in the 1980s. Meanwhile, Foreign Secretary Robin Cook had come under intense pressure in May over the 'arms for Africa' affair (see External Relations and Defence, below), whilst an exposé in *The Observer* newspaper of 5 July had suggested that professional lobbyists close to the Labour government were using their contacts to secure preferential access to ministers and advisers and to obtain confidential information of commercial value.

The so-called 'cash for access' affair centred on the relationship between

Roger Liddle, a former political lobbyist and currently an adviser in the Prime Minister's policy unit, and Derek Draper, a lobbyist who had previously been research assistant to Peter Mandelson, then Minister without Portfolio in the Cabinet Office. According to *The Observer*, two freelance reporters posing as representatives of US companies had been introduced to Mr Liddle by Mr Draper at a recent Whitehall reception given by the GPC lobbying firm. Mr Liddle was said to have assured the two undercover reporters that Mr Draper was a member of 'the circle' and to have added: 'Whenever you are ready, just tell me what you want, who you want to meet, and Derek and I will make the call for you.' Mr Draper himself was quoted as having, in telephone conversations with the supposed US businessmen, made expansive claims about his access to government personnel and decision-making. He was also quoted as saying that his weekly column for *The Express* newspaper was regularly vetted by Mr Mandelson, whom he named as one of '17 people who count' in government circles (most of them not ministers), with all of whom he claimed to be intimate.

The response of the Prime Minister's Office was to insist that no firm evidence had been presented showing impropriety by ministers or their current advisers, whilst stressing that any such evidence would result in instant dismissals. For his part, Mr Liddle could only recall talking 'quite properly' to persons at the reception he had believed to be acting for companies interested in investing in Britain. He also insisted that he had no direct financial interest in GPC, having placed his substantial shareholding in a blind trust on joining the Prime Minister's policy unit. Mr Liddle kept his job, but Mr Draper was less fortunate, being dismissed by GPC and losing his *Express* column. In media interviews the ex-lobbyist admitted being 'an occasional big-mouth', but denied having been involved in any improper activity. In the Commons on 8 July Mr Hague gave what was widely regarded as his most effective performance to date as opposition leader, castigating Mr Blair for having surrounded himself with 'feather-bedding, pocket-lining, money-grabbing cronies'. The Prime Minister's rejoinder that 'not a single allegation in that *Observer* article is true' was later qualified by a spokesman as having been meant to apply only to government personnel. At the end of the month a new code of conduct on government contact with lobbyists was issued by the Cabinet Office, laying down rigorous rules as to what was acceptable and what was not.

The 'cash for access' affair cast something of a shadow over Mr Blair's first government reshuffle on 27–28 July, in which he dismissed four members of the cabinet and made various changes at junior ministerial level. Those leaving the cabinet were Harriet Harman (social security), Gavin Strang (transport), David Clark (Chancellor of the Duchy of Lancaster) and Lord Richard (Lord Privy Seal and Leader of the Lords). The incoming members were Mr Mandelson as Secretary of State for Trade and Industry; Stephen Byers as Chief Secretary to the Treasury; Nick Brown as Minister of Agriculture, Fisheries and Food; and Baroness Jay of Paddington as Lord Privy Seal, Leader of the House of Lords and Minister for Women. In changes of cabinet responsibility, Alistair Darling became Secretary of State for Social Security; Margaret Beckett succeeded Ann Taylor as President of the Council and Leader of the House of Commons; Mrs Taylor replaced Nick Brown as Government Chief Whip, while remaining in the Cabinet; and Jack Cunningham, hitherto Agriculture Minister, became Chancellor of the Duchy of Lancaster and Minister for the Cabinet Office, his new responsibilities including the role of what the press dubbed 'enforcer' of government policy across the various departments.

The most controversial aspect of the reshuffle proved to be the exit from the government of Frank Field, who as Minister of State for Social Security had been charged with 'thinking the unthinkable' of fundamental reform of the welfare state. It emerged that Mr Field had resigned after the Prime Minister had declined to appoint him to succeed Ms Harman as Secretary of State. In his resignation statement on 29 July, Mr Field told the Commons that the slow progress of welfare reform stemmed from the Prime Minister's refusal to give him executive responsibility and from the failure of Gordon Brown and other ministers to support the 'common endeavour'. Opposition spokesmen seized on this statement, and the fact that both Ms Harman and Mr Field had left the government, to claim that the government's much-publicized espousal of welfare reform was in disarray. Mr Field's later contributions included a claim that Ms Harman had blocked his welfare reform proposals, and a description of the activities of Labour 'spin doctors' as a 'cancer' in the government.

A report on the first year of the Labour government was presented by Mr Blair on 30 July, in partial emulation of the State of the Union address delivered annually by US Presidents. The 115-page document claimed that, of the 177 specific pledges given in Labour's 1997 election manifesto, 50 had been carried out, 119 were in hand and only eight remained to be tackled. This assessment was disputed by the opposition parties, whilst several political commentators also challenged the report's tally of pledges honoured. From this perspective, the document was seen as a classic example of the 'spin doctoring' of information, of which the Labour government was a dedicated and skilled practitioner in its ceaseless quest for a favourable public image.

Indeed, 'spin doctors' and 'spin doctoring' could lay claim to have been the most prominent feature of politics in 1998, certainly the most discussed. Critics of the burgeoning importance of this American import in the UK political process included the Speaker of the Commons, Betty Boothroyd, who more than once complained that important government policy statements were being leaked to the media before they were made in parliament. There was also concern among some MPs over the activities of the

Prime Minister's press secretary and 'spin doctor-in-chief', Alastair Campbell, especially after the revelation in early April that, unlike previous holders of the post, he attended meetings of the cabinet. An investigation of Mr Campbell's role by the Commons' public administration committee resulted in the publication on 6 August of majority and minority reports, the first such division in the present parliament. The Labour-backed majority report broadly exonerated Mr Campbell from charges of playing an overtly party political role in contravention of his status as a civil servant. The minority report published by Conservative and Liberal Democrat members demanded that political appointees should not be paid from the public purse where they were involved in the promotion of their party, finding that Mr Campbell and others were often so involved.

In any event, Labour 'spin doctors' continued to spin at the party's annual conference held in Blackpool on 27 September–2 October, when much was made of New Labour's discovery of a 'third way' between outdated socialism and unrestrained market capitalism. On the conference fringes, the concept's principal academic theorist, Professor Anthony Giddens of the London School of Economics, was in attendance to sign copies of his new book, entitled *The Third Way*. Also much on delegates' lips was the government's so-called 'Cool Britannia' initiative, seeking to 're-brand' Britain for the 21st century and to emphasize its prowess in the arts, design and new technology. But rumblings could be distinctly heard from 'old Labour' ranks that the government was getting its priorities wrong. A particular target for opprobrium was the expenditure of £758 million on construction of a 'Millennium Dome' at Greenwich in London to house a great exhibition marking the advent of the year 2000 (see AR 1997, pp. 512–13).

In his main address to delegates on 29 September, Mr Blair sought to develop the philosophical basis of New Labour, rejecting 'this nonsense that we are just more moderate Tories'. Under new procedural rules intended to curtail the expression of rank-and-file opposition to the leadership, traditional conference haggling over complex composite resolutions was superseded by discussion of policy documents prepared earlier in the party's new national policy forum. The four documents presented at Blackpool—on health, welfare reform, crime and European policy—were all approved by acclamation. Nevertheless, the party leadership did not get everything its own way. In elections to the restructured Labour NEC, four of the six successful candidates in the constituencies section belonged to the left-wing Grassroots Alliance. The failure of left-winger Dennis Skinner to secure re-election in the MPs' and MEPs' section, after 20 years of almost continuous NEC membership, was attributed by his supporters to the fear of many voters that their numbered ballot papers could be individually identified.

The Conservative Party's annual conference in Bournemouth on 6–9 October featured an abortive attempt by Mr Hague to heal the internal party rift on Europe. It had not been a good year for the Conservative leader so far. He had succeeded in pushing through more democratic leadership election rules and other party reforms early in the year, including the replacement of the Young Conservatives by a new organization called 'Conservative Future'. But his reshuffle of the shadow cabinet on 1 June, when the formidable Ann Widdecombe returned to the front bench as shadow health spokesman, had brought no improvement in the party's and his lowly opinion poll ratings. And pro-EU Conservatives had continued to infuriate the 'Euro-sceptic' majority by doubting the wisdom of opposition to UK participation in the single European currency. Mr Hague's recourse was to hold a pre-conference referendum of party members on the proposition that the next Conservative election manifesto should include a pledge to oppose membership of the single currency through the next parliament. As announced on 5 October, the result was an 84.4 per cent vote in favour, which Mr Hague described as showing 'the settled will of the party' that pro-European Conservatives would oppose only at the risk of becoming outcasts. However, former Deputy Prime Minister Michael Heseltine dismissed the referendum as 'an irrelevance' and warned that the party was making itself unelectable. Former Chancellor of the Exchequer Kenneth Clarke and other senior pro-European Conservatives also continued to argue that the party should not rule out early UK participation in the single currency.

The Liberal Democrats had assembled for their annual conference in Brighton on 20–24 September, making familiar calls for tax increases, proportional representation (PR) and UK participation in the single European currency. The extent to which the party should cooperate with the Labour government provided the main focus of debate, in light of the party's participation since July 1997 in a special cabinet committee dealing with constitutional reform (see AR 1997, p. 27). In his keynote speech on 24 September, party leader Paddy Ashdown gave qualified praise to the Blair government, whilst urging it to move speedily to the introduction of PR and a freedom of information bill and to curb its 'control freak' tendencies. Other prominent Liberal Democrats warned that Mr Ashdown would be opposed if he sought closer involvement with Labour before PR had been agreed for general elections. Undeterred, Mr Ashdown later entered into an extended Lib-Lab pact with Mr Blair. As announced on 11 November, it envisaged that the special cabinet committee's agenda would be extended to cover areas such as welfare reform, education, health policy and preparation for the single European currency.

The chances of the Liberal Democrats achieving PR for general elections in the foreseeable future appeared to recede as the year progressed. Opposition to any change to 'first-past-the-post' (FPTP) contests came not only from the Conservatives but also from growing numbers of Labour MPs and government ministers. The seminal event was the publication on 29 October of the report of the independent commission on electoral reform established in December 1997 under the chairmanship of Lord Jenkins of Hillhead (Liberal Democrat). It recommended that, with effect from the general election after next, the existing FPTP system should be replaced by a combination of alternative vote (AV) in 530 to 560 single-member constituencies and up to 150 'top-up' seats filled from 80 electoral districts to ensure greater proportionality between votes cast and representation gained in the constituency contests. Under the AV system, voters would be able to indicate an order of preference for candidates, the least-favoured being progressively eliminated and their votes redistributed until one candidate had 50 per cent plus one.

Although AV was not their favoured electoral system, the Liberal Democrats immediately endorsed the Jenkins proposals. Conservative spokesmen, in contrast, contended that their complexity demonstrated the folly of abandoning the simplicity of FPTP, also pointing out that most post-war elections would have produced coalition governments under the system proposed. The government gave a cautious welcome to the report's publication, but made no commitment to holding a referendum on electoral reform before the next general election, as urged by the Liberal Democrats. The crucial factor was likely to be the attitude of Mr Blair himself; but the Prime Minister, conscious of the strength of pro-FPTP sentiment in his own party, carefully avoided taking sides at the present stage of the debate.

There was much more political agreement on proposals for a far-reaching reform of the rules governing the funding of political parties and campaigns published on 13 October by the Committee on Standards in Public Life chaired by Lord Neill of Bladen. Drawn up in light of recent 'sleaze' cases involving both major parties, the Neill recommendations included a ban on all donations to parties from foreign sources; speedy disclosure by parties of national-level donations of over £5,000 and of local donations of over £1,000; a ban on 'blind trusts' by which individual politicians were financed by anonymous donors; a limit of £20 million per party on all campaign-related expenditure in general elections; a limit of £1 million on election campaign spending by 'third parties' (e.g. trade unions); a tripling of state funding for parliamentary opposition parties (from £1.6 million to £5 million a year); equal public funding for both sides in referendum campaigns; a ban on government (and European Commission) literature taking one side in a referendum; and creation of an independent electoral commission to monitor and enforce the new rules. Whilst entering reservations on the requirement for official neutrality in referendum campaigns, the government promised to publish a bill implementing most of the recommendations by mid-1999, for enactment before the next general election.

The next episode to shake the government was, however, not about financial corruption. On 27 October the Secretary of State for Wales, Ron

Davies, announced his resignation because of 'a serious lapse of judgment' the previous evening which had resulted in his being robbed at knifepoint in south London. He was replaced as Welsh Secretary by Alun Michael, hitherto Minister of State for Home Affairs, who also declared his aim to succeed Mr Davies as Labour candidate to lead the new Welsh administration due to be elected in May 1999 (see II.1.iii). In his resignation letter, Mr Davies gave only the following sparse account of his 'lapse of judgment': 'After driving back from Wales last night, I parked my car near to my home in south London. I went for a walk on Clapham Common. Whilst walking I was approached by a man I had never met before who engaged me in conversation. After talking for some minutes he asked me to accompany him and two of his friends to his flat for a meal. We drove, in my car, to collect his friends, one male, one female. Shortly afterwards the man produced a knife and together with his male companion robbed me and stole my car, leaving me standing at the roadside. I reported this matter immediately to the police.' According to police descriptions, the first man encountered by Mr Davies was a Rastafarian, and his two friends were also black.

In the absence of fuller details, press speculation centred on the fact that Clapham Common was a well-known meeting-place for homosexuals and that the robbery had occurred on a Brixton council estate notorious as a haunt of prostitutes and drug-dealers. Mr Davies repeatedly denied that either sex or drugs had been involved, asserting that he had a 'loving relationship' with his second wife. However, the press obtained and published detailed evidence that he had a history of casual homosexual encounters. It emerged that the Prime Minister's Office had been alerted to the episode, and of police concern about inconsistencies in Mr Davies's account, in advance of the latter's arrival for his resignation interview with Mr Blair. Media hopes that court proceedings would shed more light on the affair were disappointed when the Crown Prosecution Service (CPS) decided in late November not to prosecute a Rastafarian who had been arrested and charged with the theft of Mr Davies's car. The CPS had apparently concluded that there was little chance of obtaining a conviction because the only material witness was Mr Davies, who had changed his story when being interviewed by the Brixton police.

In a bizarre associated development, the management of the British Broadcasting Corporation (BBC) came under fierce criticism for attempted censorship when on 30 October it issued an instruction to its editors banning any reference in BBC programmes to the private life of Trade and Industry Secretary Mandelson (see also XV.1.vi). The move followed a BBC television interview about the Davies affair in which former Conservative MP Matthew Parris, a self-declared homosexual now writing for *The Times*, had named Mr Mandelson as one of the homosexual members of the cabinet. At that stage, the only self-acknowledged homosexual cabinet minister was Chris Smith, the Culture, Media and

Sport Secretary. Mr Parris later expressed regret for having referred to something that he thought was already in the public domain.

More on the same theme was to follow. In a statement issued late on 7 November, Agriculture Minister Nick Brown acknowledged that he was a homosexual, a few hours in advance of publication of a Sunday tabloid story featuring a claim by a former partner that Mr Brown had paid him for sex. There had been gifts, acknowledged Mr Brown, because he earned more than his former partner; but he had 'never' paid him or anyone else for sex. In light of this and other recent disclosures, *The Sun* newspaper on 9 November carried the front-page headline 'Tell us the truth, Tony: Are we being run by a gay mafia?' The Prime Minister's Office responded that Mr Brown enjoyed the full support of Mr Blair and that ministers' sexuality was a private matter provided that it did not impinge upon their public role.

Political attention then focused on the Queen's Speech outlining the government's legislative programme for the 1998–99 parliamentary session. It was delivered on 24 November at a state opening of parliament in which ancient ceremonial was somewhat reduced, in line with Labour's modernizing impulse. Measures announced in the speech included a bill to remove the right of hereditary peers to sit and vote in the House of Lords; two local government bills, one replacing compulsory competitive tendering for council contracts with 'best value' rules and the other establishing a Greater London Authority to be headed by an elected mayor; four bills on welfare reform, including one to make it compulsory for benefit claimants to attend job and training interviews; two bills on the National Health Service (NHS), including one to end the NHS internal market created by the previous government; and a bill creating a Financial Services Agency (FSA) as the single regulatory authority for the City of London.

Other legislation was promised on a range of issues, including a bill to create 'faster and fairer' procedures for dealing with political asylum applications (which spiralled to a record level of 46,015 in 1998) and a backlog of some 80,000 outstanding applications. Implementing the main provisions of a White Paper published by Mr Straw on 27 July, the bill would require political asylum seekers to reside in designated accommodation and to receive welfare benefits in the form of vouchers rather than cash. It would also institute greater regulation of immigration 'advisers' to combat what Mr Straw had described as 'abusive claimants and racketeers'. Also announced was a bill to reduce the age of homosexual sexual consent from 18 to 16 years, and thus to equalize it with the prevailing heterosexual age of consent. The government had already made an attempt to equalize the age of consent at 16, by means of a late amendment to its Crime and Disorder Bill during the 1997–98 parliamentary session. However, the amendment had been heavily defeated by the Lords on 22 July (by 290 votes to 122), despite a 336–129 vote in favour by the Commons the previous month.

In exchanges on the Queen's Speech in the Commons, the government was taunted by opposition spokesmen for omissions from the list of forthcoming bills, about which some Labour MPs also expressed disquiet. It was noted that no immediate action was intended on a freedom of information bill, direct election of mayors (outside London), creation of a food standards agency, greater regulation of former public utilities and the 'integrated transport policy' proposals set out in a White Paper in July (see 'The Economy in 1998', below). Ministers responded that draft bills and/or consultative documents would be published on most of these matters in due course.

The forthcoming bill to abolish the hereditary component of the Lords had been outlined in the upper chamber on 14 October by Baroness Jay, who had also announced that a Royal Commission would be appointed to consider options for definitive reform, pending which there would be a transitional chamber. Her announcement served to intensify Conservative anger that the government was bent on abolishing the hereditary peers without having a viable blueprint for a reconstituted second chamber. Tory peers were therefore emboldened to continue their opposition to the European Parliamentary Elections Bill, which was effectively rejected on three more occasions in November, making five in all and ensuring that it lapsed in the 1997–98 parliamentary session. The government immediately gave notice that it would invoke the 1911 and 1949 Parliament Acts to enforce passage of the reintroduced bill in the 1998–99 session. Its difficulty, however, was that the Lords could still have delayed the bill for a further year, thus preventing its implementation in time for the June 1999 Euro-elections.

The government's solution was to enter into a compromise agreement under which 91 hereditary peers would retain their seats in a transitional second chamber and the Euro-elections bill would be passed by the Lords early in the 1998-99 session. Of the 91 surviving hereditary peers, 75 would be elected by party group to reflect current party strengths and 14 would be elected by the whole house to serve in various official capacities. The Lord Great Chamberlain and the Earl Marshal would remain as hereditary offices. Including current life peers, the resultant breakdown of the interim chamber was likely to be Conservatives 214, Labour 161, Liberal Democrats 48, cross-benchers 148. The Prime Minister would then appoint enough new life peers to bring Labour up to parity with the Conservatives.

At Prime Minister's Questions on 2 December, shortly before the agreement was announced, Mr Hague sought to embarrass Mr Blair by referring to the government's 'huge climb-down' in proposing the continuation of some hereditary peers, making it clear that he did not support the compromise. The Prime Minister was able to retort that the Conservative leader in the Lords had agreed to the plan. It quickly emerged that Viscount Cranborne had negotiated the agreement with Labour leaders without the authorization of the shadow cabinet. Although a meeting of Conservative peers later in the day gave overwhelming backing to the agreement, Mr Hague in the early evening announced the dismissal of Viscount Cranborne, informing him by letter that 'it can never be acceptable for a member of the front bench to seek to bring about a change in the policy of the party without the knowledge or agreement of the party leader or the shadow cabinet'.

Viscount Cranborne, son and heir of the 6th Marquess of Salisbury and therefore an hereditary Tory grandee *par excellence*, admitted to journalists that he had behaved 'quite outrageously' but insisted that he stood by the agreement and would do the same again. He was replaced as Conservative leader in the Lords by Lord Strathclyde, hitherto opposition Chief Whip. The following day four Conservative front-bench spokesmen in the Lords resigned in protest against Mr Hague's action. In a rapid change of policy tack, the Conservative leader indicated that he was not opposed to the substance of the Cranborne agreement, only to the way that it had been reached.

The reintroduced Euro-elections bill was rejected for a sixth time by the Lords on 15 December, but this was essentially a procedural device enabling the government to override the upper chamber immediately and to secure enactment of the bill in time for the June 1999 Euro-elections. Invoked only three times since World War II, the Parliament Acts had last been used in 1991 under the previous Conservative government to secure passage of the War Crimes Bill.

As ministers began to relax at the start of the Christmas recess, the year proved to have one more political bombshell for the government—the most damaging so far in terms of adverse press coverage. The leading *dramatis personae* were Trade and Industry Secretary Mandelson and Paymaster-General Robinson, the former one of Mr Blair's closest associates in the New Labour project, credited with having master-minded Labour's 1997 election victory. On 22 December *The Guardian* disclosed that in 1996, when both were opposition backbenchers, Mr Mandelson had received a preferential loan of £373,000 from Mr Robinson to enable him to buy a luxury house in London's fashionable Notting Hill, at a reported cost of £475,000. The report noted tellingly that the latest of several official inquiries into the beleaguered Mr Robinson's business affairs was being conducted by the Department of Trade and Industry (DTI), of which Mr Mandelson had taken charge in July. As recently as 18 November, the Paymaster-General had been obliged to apologize to the Commons for non-disclosure of business interests, following an investigation by the standards and privileges committee.

Alerted to the imminent *Guardian* story, Mr Mandelson issued a statement late on 21 December confirming the existence of the loan but maintaining that it was 'always intended to be a short-term arrangement' and that he was in the process repaying the £332,375 balance outstanding 'with the help of my mother'. The statement continued: 'In September

1998 the permanent secretary of the DTI advised me that the department was considering allegations concerning Geoffrey Robinson's business affairs. We agreed that I should not be involved in this process. Since that conversation I have played no part whatsoever in the department's consideration of the matter. Because I was satisfied that any conflict of interest had been properly dealt with, I did not disclose the existence of the loan to the permanent secretary, as I had agreed with Geoffrey Robinson that it would be a private matter. However, when it became clear that the loan was in the public domain, I immediately told the permanent secretary and informed Number 10.' The statement concluded: 'I do not believe that accepting a loan from a friend and fellow MP was wrong. There is no conflict of interest in this.'

Resisting Conservative opposition demands for Mr Mandelson's (and Mr Robinson's) immediate dismissal, the Prime Minister's Office insisted during 22 December that Mr Blair retained full confidence in the Trade and Industry Secretary. In an attempt to defuse the controversy, late on 22 December Mr Mandelson wrote to the parliamentary commissioner for standards giving details of the loan and asking for a ruling on whether it should have been declared in the official register of MPs' interests. Nevertheless, media coverage of the affair intensified, focusing in particular on whether Mr Mandelson had deceived his building society by not declaring the loan when he applied for a mortgage for the balance of the house purchase price. On the morning of 23 December the Prime Minister and Mr Mandelson reportedly agreed by telephone that the affair was seriously damaging the government, with the result that the resignations of both Mr Mandelson and Mr Robinson were announced later that day. In his reply to Mr Mandelson's resignation letter, Mr Blair referred to 'a misjudgment' on his part but expressed confidence that 'in the future you will achieve much, much more with us'.

Mr Mandelson was immediately replaced as Trade and Industry Secretary by Stephen Byers, who had entered the cabinet in July as Chief Secretary of the Treasury. Mr Byers was succeeded in the latter position by Alan Milburn, hitherto Minister of State for Health, who at 40 became the youngest cabinet minister. The non-cabinet post of Paymaster-General was later allocated to Dawn Primarolo, hitherto Financial Secretary to the Treasury. Within Labour circles, the fall of Mr Mandelson was greeted with undisguised satisfaction by several left-wing and 'old Labour' figures, who said that the episode should serve as a warning to Mr Blair not to abandon Labour's true roots. In the media, attention subsequently centred on the source of the disclosure of the Mandelson loan, the main suspect being Charlie Whelan, press secretary to Chancellor of the Exchequer Brown. It was noted, in this context, that there had been no political love lost between Mr Mandelson and Mr Brown since the former switched his support from Mr Brown to Mr Blair prior to the 1994 Labour leadership contest.

The Prime Minister therefore had much to reflect upon at the end of the year, as he left London for a winter holiday in the Seychelles with his family. Labour remained far ahead in the prestigious MORI opinion poll ratings, ending 1998 on a record 56 per cent, two points higher than at the start of the year, whereas the Tories languished on only 24 per cent and the Liberal Democrats on 14 per cent. But the unpredictability of political 'events' had been brought home to him in no uncertain fashion.

THE ECONOMY IN 1998. Key features of the government's economic strategy during 1998 had been set out by the Chancellor of the Exchequer, Mr Brown, in his special budget in July 1997 and in other measures announced soon after the Labour administration was formed in May of that year (see AR 1997, pp. 21, 25–6). In 1998, however, other major factors affecting policy included Britain's relationship with the EU (notably the issue of when it might participate in the single European currency, the 'euro') and the effects on world economic and monetary stability caused by the severe financial disturbances in eastern Asia. Moreover, Britain's particular stance was further conditioned by its chairmanship in the first half of 1998 both of the EU Council of Ministers and of the G-8 grouping of leading industrialized countries (now embracing also Russia).

The complex interaction of the various forces operating worldwide, combined with individual national aims and circumstances, gave cause for considerable unease within the Labour movement, some sections of which felt that the government's determination firstly not to allow expenditure to escalate and secondly to hold back on taxation increases—i.e. not to follow a course of 'tax and spend' for which Labour was traditionally criticized by the opposition—was betraying those to whom the party was inherently linked. However, Mr Brown and his colleagues stressed the need to pursue a path of economic prudence, and later in the year there was some relaxation of this stringency with major plans for investment in key policy areas.

Five major indicators which became interwoven during 1998 were the external strength of sterling; interest rates; the level of unemployment; inflation; and stock market performance.

Sterling started the year at around 2.95 Deutsche Mark (DM), showing an appreciation of some 6 per cent since the May 1997 general election. By early April the pound was up to about DM3.09, but in the next month it lost this strength. At the end of the year the rate against the German currency was at approximately DM2.80 (around the mid-1997 level). The uncertainties of the international financial markets were reflected in the differing timing of fluctuations of sterling against the US dollar, against which the pound rose from US$1.64 at the beginning of the year to $1.70 by late September, closing at the end of the year at around $1.66.

Shortly after the Labour government was formed, Mr Brown had taken a key step relating to interest rates by transferring to the Bank of England responsibility for fixing the key base rate. The Bank of

England—whose governor, Eddie George, on 18 February had his term of office extended for a further five years—had already in 1997 raised the base rate in stages from 6.25 to 7.25 per cent, and on 4 June it went higher still to 7.5 per cent (a level not reached since late 1992). The monthly meetings of the Bank of England's monetary policy committee were torn between those determined to maintain a high rate and those who considered that the only way to improve the country's competitive edge was in fact to make reductions. Eventually, on 8 October, 5 November and 10 December, three successive cuts were made to bring the year-end base rate to 6.25 per cent—the level set by the Chancellor in May 1997.

However, the combination of the strong pound and high interest rates began to have a detrimental effect upon business confidence. Although the seasonally adjusted unemployment percentage continued its steady downwards trend, the fall slowed down during the year, from 4.9 per cent on the basis of claimant count at the end of 1997 to 4.6 per cent at the end of 1998. The situation was experienced unevenly across the country, especially hit being parts of the north-east, where a number of major foreign companies decided either not to proceed with large-scale investment or even to close down prestige plants (notably Siemens in July and Fujitsu in September).

The government's attitude towards the work force met some opposition from sections of the trade union movement, which were further enraged by the failure of the government to meet in full minimum wage proposals made by the Low Pay Commission. On 18 June the then Trade and Industry Secretary, Margaret Beckett, announced that legislation would be introduced for the establishment, effective April 1999, of a full adult flat-rate hourly minimum wage of £3.60 as recommended by the commission in its report of 27 May. However, a lower £3.00 rate would apply for workers aged under 22, and there would be no basic minimum for workers aged under 17. The Trades Union Congress subsequently, in September, demanded a minimum flat rate of £4.61 an hour.

Earlier in the year, the government had announced on 29 January that, while major sectors of the public service should have wage increases averaging 3.9 per cent, generally only around half was to be paid from April and the balance not until December—a type of phasing persistently attacked by Labour in opposition. This two-part wage award was made against a rate of inflation which, on the all-items (headline) basis, rose from 3.6 per cent on a year-on-year basis in December 1997 to 4.2 per cent by May, although it then declined to 2.8 per cent in December (when the 'underlying' rate was 2.6 per cent).

A separate part of the government's employment policy was unveiled on 21 May with the publication of the *Fairness at Work* White Paper, which set out basic conditions for compulsory recognition by employers of trade unions at their places of employment, although the threshold for such recognition and certain other aspects were criticized by many trade unionists. Further details of the *Fairness at Work* package were made public on 17 December.

The world financial uncertainties in the middle of the year also affected the London stock exchange. While the key FTSE 100 index had climbed steadily to an all-time peak of 6179.0 by 20 July, over the next ten weeks it fell to its lowest for the year, at 4648.7 on 5 October. After further fluctuations in the latter of the year, it was back by end-December at around 5900, showing a net improvement during 1998 of some 15 per cent.

The Chancellor of the Exchequer, Mr Brown, presented his 1998–99 budget on 17 March. With the aim of encouraging work and enterprise, he introduced a Working Families Tax Credit designed to guarantee that a family with at least one parent in full-time work would receive an income of at least £180 a week, while no income tax would be payable where earnings were below £220 a week. Tax credits would be introduced to meet up to 70 per cent of the costs of accredited child care, while child benefit for a first child would be increased by an additional £2.50 a week. From April 1999 the starting level above which employees' national insurance contributions would be payable would be raised from £66 to £81 a week, while the employer's contribution would effectively be adjusted from lower-paid jobs to higher-paid ones. Corporation tax would, effective April 1999, be cut from 31 to 30 per cent for large companies and from 21 to 20 per cent for smaller firms. The Chancellor further reported that the state's financial situation had improved and that additional allocations would be made, in particular to health, education and the public transport system.

On 11 June Mr Brown announced plans for privatizations and sales of assets amounting to £4,000 million a year over the next four years. The programme would include the partial sale of the Royal Mint, the air traffic control service (NATS), the Horserace Totalisator Board (the Tote) and holdings of the Commonwealth Development Corporation, although no definite steps towards these disposals had taken place by the end of 1998. At the same time, Mr Brown said that other unused government assets would be sold; that net investment in social and economic infrastructure projects would double to £14,000 million a year by 2002; that public spending would rise by 2.75 per cent a year over the remainder of the current parliament; and that a three-year rolling programme of departmental spending would be introduced.

In a further step towards increasing investment and other spending by some £57,000 million over three years, Mr Brown on 14 July announced his comprehensive spending review, including large boosts to allocations for health, education and transport, and on 3 November he gave further details in his pre-budget statement. In this latter statement Mr Brown noted that economic growth in 1999 was now expected to be in the range of 1–1.5 per cent against the previous budget forecast of 1.75–2.25 per cent, although in the following two years growth was expected to be in the ranges of 2.25–2.75 per cent and 2.75–3.25 per cent respectively.

Major plans for the energy sector were announced by the government on 25 June, including a policy designed to improve the competitiveness of coal as against gas in the electricity generation industry. Under this strategy, the construction of additional gas-fuelled stations was to be examined more closely on a case-by-case basis. The policy was strengthened on 8 October when the then Trade and Industry Secretary, Mr Mandelson, stated that new stringent constraints would be placed on the construction of such gas-fuelled stations, partly in view of the prospect that early in the next century Britain would become a net importer of gas. In September it was announced that a new energy regulator, Callum McCarthy, had been appointed to succeed both the present electricity regulator (OFFER), Professor Stephen Littlechild, and the gas regulator (OFGAS), Clare Spottiswoode.

A much-anticipated transport White Paper was eventually published on 20 July, aimed at reducing the use of the motor car in order to seek to avoid gridlock on the country's roads early in the 21st century. In due course legislation would be introduced to provide, among other things, for new toll charges in cities and towns and for charges for workplace parking, and for the establishment of a new strategic rail authority. Other measures included five-year local transport plans, approved by the central government; partnerships between local authorities and bus companies to improve services; and the establishment of a national public transport information system. Further details of plans for reducing traffic congestion in towns (including new parking charge arrangements and charges for keeping vehicles within designated areas of certain towns) were announced in a consultation paper on 8 December by Mr Prescott, the Environment, Transport and Regions Secretary and Deputy Prime Minister.

EXTERNAL RELATIONS AND DEFENCE. Britain's external policy endeavours were dominated in the first half of the year by its occupancy of the rotating chairmanship of European Union (EU) ministerial bodies. The Labour government sought to use its six-month term to demonstrate that Britain now wanted full cooperation and involvement with its European partners, after what it depicted as nearly two decades of Tory obstructionism. However, the government's declared 'wait and see' policy on the single European currency—that Britain would join 'when and if' the national interest so dictated, and certainly not at its launching on 1 January 1999— meant that Britain effectively excluded itself from the most important EU deliberations in 1998.

At a special EU summit held in Brussels on 1–3 May, Mr Blair nominally presided over familiar wrangling about which member state's nominee should be appointed to a top EU post, in this case the presidency of the new European Central Bank; but he played little real part in the messy compromise with the French under which Wim Duisenberg of the

Netherlands got the job, for at least part of the official eight-year term (see XI.4). On 15–16 June a regular EU summit was hosted by Mr Blair in Cardiff, intended to highlight the forthcoming devolution of power to Wales; but most important decisions were deferred because of the impending elections in Germany and the prospect of a change of government in the EU's most powerful member state (see II.2.i). The British Prime Minister's close friendship with the new German Chancellor elected in September, Gerhard Schröder, made no noticeable dent in the rock of the Franco-German alliance at the core of EU decision-making. Nor did it prevent the new German Finance Minister, Oskar Lafontaine, wrong-footing Mr Blair by calling for the 'harmonization' of EU members' taxation policies—an objective categorically rejected by a UK government sensitive to domestic fears of loss of more sovereignty to Brussels.

A proposal by Mr Blair at a special EU summit at Pörtschach, Austria, on 24–25 October that attention should be given to creating a 'European defence identity' capable of responding to international crises was received politely. In December plans for enhanced defence cooperation were agreed between Britain and France. But the minds of most other EU leaders were by then focused on the imminent birth of the euro. Of particular concern to London was the creation by the 11 euro participants of the 'Euro-11 Committee', seen as an inner EU decision-making forum in which the four non-participants would play no part. At a regular EU summit held in Vienna on 11–12 December, moreover, Mr Blair was again on the defensive, over Germany's stated intention to use its forthcoming EU presidency to achieve a fairer scale of national contributions to the EU budget—in particular a reduction in the disproportionately large German share. Although Mr Blair's insisted publicly that there was no question of Britain's giving up its budget rebate (won by Mrs Thatcher in 1984 and currently worth over £2,000 million a year), other EU leaders made it clear that all aspects of the budget arrangements were up for renegotiation. Hoping to divert attention from this difficult prospect at home, Mr Blair laid stress on his return on having helped to secure a reprieve for the sale of duty-free goods to air and sea travellers between EU countries. This popular concession was earmarked for abolition in mid-1999 under a Brussels directive which, the Prime Minister pointed out, had been approved by the previous Conservative government.

The only real EU success for the government in 1998 was in persuading its partners to end the ban on British beef exports, imposed in March 1996 in light of the discovery of a possible link between bovine spongiform encephalopathy (BSE, or 'mad cow disease') in British herds and the fatal new variant Creutzfeldt-Jakob disease (nvCJD) in humans (see AR 1996, pp. 17, 392–3). An important step in this direction came on 1 June with the lifting of the export ban in respect of Northern Ireland, where 97 per cent of beef herds had never been infected with BSE. Finally, on 23 November, the EU Agriculture Ministers voted to lift the ban for the rest of the UK, subject to Britain completing a cull of calves born of BSE-infected cattle and obtaining EU approval for its exporting facilities. Even when exports could be resumed, however, British beef producers were expected to find it extremely difficult to recapture former markets in continental Europe and elsewhere.

The power of the Internet was tangentially demonstrated in the 'arms for Africa' affair which broke over the Foreign and Commonwealth Office (FCO) in May. According to press disclosures, the FCO had known that a British firm of 'security consultants', Sandline International, had sent arms to Sierra Leone early in 1998 for use in the restoration to power of President Ahmed Tejan Kabbah, in apparent contravention of a UN arms embargo (see also VI.2.iii). It emerged that a Liberal Democrat peer, Lord Avebury, had alerted FCO officials to Sandline's dubious role on 5 February, after finding details on a Sierra Leonean website on the Internet. Amid much confusion about when FCO ministers had first been informed of the company's activities, Mr Cook repeatedly insisted that the arms supplies had received no ministerial sanction. In announcing on 6 May that an inquiry would be held into the FCO's conduct, the Foreign Secretary expressed 'deep concern' that ministers had not been informed earlier of the suspicions about Sandline, describing the omission as 'unfair to parliament'. The response of the colourful head of Sandline, Lieut.-Colonel (retd) Tim Spicer of the Scots Guards, was to claim on 8 May that the company's activities in Sierra Leone had been carried out 'with the full prior knowledge and approval of Her Majesty's government'.

Mr Blair took charge of the government response on 11 May, dismissing the furore over arms supplies to Sierra Leone as 'hoo-ha' and asserting that FCO officials had been 'quite right' to work for the restoration of President Kabbah. Whatever technical breach of UN sanctions there might have been, he was interpreted as saying, an outcome that was in accord with UK, Commonwealth and UN policy should be welcomed. Nevertheless, FCO ministers and officials were subsequently grilled, and sometimes forced to squirm and retract, by the Commons' foreign affairs select committee, which also came into conflict with Mr Cook over its insistence, eventually successful, on having sight of relevant FCO telegrams. Relief was provided for the government by the FCO inquiry report, by former civil servant Sir Thomas Legg, published on 27 July. Although he criticized FCO ministers and officials for 'repeated and partly systemic failures of communication', Sir Thomas found no evidence of ministerial collusion in the arms supplies, so that Mr Cook was able to portray the report as a full exoneration of ministers. The select committee continued to probe, however, hearing evidence on 3 November from Peter Penfold, the UK high commissioner to Sierra Leone who had played a key role in the restoration of President Kabbah and had been criticized in the Legg report for exceeding his authority. Mr Penfold told the committee that he had 'no doubt at all that everything I did was being done properly in fulfilment of legal requirements and in fulfilment of British government policy'.

Important official visits to Britain in 1998 included those of the heads of state of two former enemy countries. During his visit on 25–29 May, Emperor Akihito of Japan was invested with the Order of the Garter by Queen Elizabeth but encountered protests by former British prisoners-of-war held by the Japanese during World War II. They were demanding financial compensation for their suffering, as well as a fuller apology than anything offered by Japan so far. Five months later, on 27 October, President Carlos Saúl Menem of Argentina arrived for a visit intended to heal the wounds of the 1982 war over the Falklands/Malvinas (see also IV.3.i). The President laid a wreath in St Paul's Cathedral for victims of the 1982 conflict and signed three cooperation agreements with the British government. He also restated Argentina's claim to sovereignty over the Falklands, eliciting the familiar British response that sovereignty was not negotiable. On 17 December Britain announced a partial lifting of its embargo on arms sales to Argentina, which would henceforth be considered on a case-by-case basis and judged as to whether they would jeopardize the security of the Falklands.

Much less planned were the strains in Britain's relations with traditional ally Chile which developed as a result of the arrest in London on 16 October of former Chilean dictator General (retd) Augusto Pinochet Ugarte on a warrant for his extradition to Spain to face charges that his 1973–90 regime had committed 'crimes of genocide and terrorism', some of them against Spanish nationals (see also IV.3.iv). The 82-year-old General, now a life senator in Chile, was paying one of his regular visits to his 'favourite' country, both to obtain medical treatment for a back condition and to discuss possible arms sales to Chile with British companies. His many supporters in London included Baroness Thatcher, who recalled that he had been an invaluable friend to Britain during the 1982 Falklands conflict with Argentina. The democratic government in Santiago, anxious to preserve the post-Pinochet political accommodation between left and right, also called for his release, claiming that General Pinochet enjoyed diplomatic immunity.

Chile and Spain then watched closely as a unanimous Court of Appeal ruling of 28 October that General Pinochet, as a former head of state, enjoyed 'sovereign immunity' from arrest and extradition was overturned by a 3 to 2 decision by five law lords of the House of Lords on 25 November (the ex-dictator's 83rd birthday). When Home Secretary Straw on 9 December authorized the opening of formal extradition proceedings, the Chilean ambassador was withdrawn from London 'for consultations'. However, in an unprecedented decision on 17 December, another panel of law lords unanimously quashed the previous ruling because one of the five judges, Lord Hoffmann, had been found to have undeclared links with Amnesty International, which was a party to the attempt to extradite General Pinochet to Spain. As the legal establishment in London contemplated the damage done to the reputation of the country's legal system in the eyes of the world (see also XIV.2), the Chilean government formally requested Mr Straw to rescind his decision of 9 December. The British response was that the outcome of a further hearing of the Pinochet appeal, by a new panel of law lords, should be awaited. Meanwhile, General Pinochet remained under arrest but on bail, residing in a rented house in Surrey under police supervision.

As Christmas (and the Muslim holy month of Ramadan) approached, the United States and Britain on 16 December launched a series of massive air and missile strikes against Iraq with the aim of 'degrading' the Iraqi regime's military capability. The first such action against Iraq since January 1993 (when the French had also participated—see AR 1993, pp. 31, 221), the five-day assault, code-named Operation Desert Fox, was ordered by President Clinton and Mr Blair following the final breakdown of efforts by UN inspectors to eliminate Iraq's weapons of mass destruction, as required by UN resolutions governing the end of the 1991 Gulf War (see also V.2.vi). No explicit UN authorization was given for the US-UK action, with the result that France, China and Russia, the other three permanent members of the Security Council, all declared their opposition. However, the US and UK governments maintained that no further authorization was necessary since the Security Council had in March threatened Iraq with the 'severest consequences' if it reneged on its latest commitment to cooperate with the UN weapons' inspectors.

In a statement issued late on 16 December, Mr Blair described Saddam Husain as 'a serial breaker of promises' who harboured a desire to develop weapons of mass destruction; if he was not stopped, 'the consequences to our peace are real and fundamental'. Stressing that the targets had been selected to 'degrade' Iraq's military capability and that 'every possible care' was being taken to avoid civilian casualties, the Prime Minister insisted that there was 'no realistic alternative to military force' and that 'we act because we must'. The reaction in the country, according to opinion polls, was a somewhat lukewarm acceptance that the strikes were necessary. At Westminster, the unity of the government and opposition front benches in support of the action was challenged by a vociferous small band of Labour MPs led by left-winger Tony Benn, but to no avail.

British spokesmen echoed US military claims that the strikes had achieved most of their objectives and that no casualties had been suffered by US-UK forces. The Iraqi regime insisted, predictably, that little real damage had been done to its military capability and that civilian casualties had been high. By the end of the year it was clear that Saddam Husain was bent on continued confrontation in the UN-imposed 'no-fly zones' over northern and southern Iraq, declaring them to be illegal. London and Washington therefore faced the prospect of open-ended tensions and regular clashes with Iraq, amid a serious breach with the other three

Security Council members over the most effective, or least ineffective, method of dealing with the Baghdad regime.

The dangers facing Western visitors to Muslim lands had been illustrated before Operation Desert Fox when the severed heads of three Britons and one New Zealander taken hostage in October were found in the breakaway Russian republic of Chechenya on 8 December (see III.3.i). Following the assault on Iraq, three British tourists and one Australian were killed in southern Yemen on 29 December in what appeared to be a bungled attempt by Yemeni forces to rescue a group of 16 tourists who had been taken hostage the day before (see V.3.ii). Yemeni members of the Islamic Jihad fundamentalist group were widely rumoured to have been responsible for the kidnapping, motivated in part by a desire to respond to the US-UK attack on Iraq. The UK government called upon the Yemeni authorities to undertake a full investigation into the episode.

The logistical requirements of Operation Desert Fox and its aftermath demonstrated the rationale of the main thrust of the government's *Strategic Defence Review* published on 8 July, which was that Britain's expeditionary capability should be enhanced by the creation of a 15,000-strong rapid reaction force. The plans envisaged a £915 million reduction in defence expenditure in real terms over three years (to £23,000 million in 2001–02, or 2.4 per cent of GDP), but also provided for an increase of 3,300 personnel in the regular armed forces. Two new large aircraft carriers would be constructed with a capacity of 50 warplanes each (to replace the Royal Navy's existing three carriers); a helicopter-equipped 'air cavalry', including the Parachute Regiment, would be created; and Royal Air Force and Royal Navy warplanes would be combined in a 'Joint Force 2000'. The fleet of destroyers and frigates would be reduced from 35 to 32, and attack submarines from 12 to 10, while the number of minesweepers would be increased from 22 to 25. Britain's fleet of Trident nuclear-armed submarines would be four in number as previously planned, but with only one always on patrol, with its missile capacity reduced from 96 to 48 warheads. The fourth Trident submarine, HMS *Vengeance*, was subsequently launched at Barrow-in-Furness on 19 September, having cost some £500 million to build.

As foreshadowed in the July review, Defence Secretary George Robertson on 17 November confirmed that a controversial plan to reduce the size of the auxiliary Territorial Army (TA) by about 25 per cent would go ahead. Those dubious about the reduction, to a complement of 41,200, apparently included the Scottish Secretary, Donald Dewar, who was revealed in correspondence leaked to the press to have warned that cuts in the TA might leave the authorities unable to cope with civil unrest. Of particular concern to Mr Dewar, it appeared, was the possibility that at the end of 1999 there might be serious dislocation of public services, and resultant popular protest, as a result of the 'millennium bug' problem, whereby computers would crash because they could not recognize the advent of the new century (see XIII.2).

ii. SCOTLAND

PLANNING for the Scottish parliament to be elected in May 1999 dominated the political scene. The bill to establish the parliament received its second reading on 12 January, the legislation eventually receiving the royal assent in November (see XVII.3). The Conservative Party moved from opposition to devolution to attempting to influence the form it took and the powers to be devolved to the Scottish parliament, but the Conservatives' weakness in the UK parliament and in Scotland meant that debate in Scotland was primarily about Scottish National Party (SNP) proposals to strengthen devolution.

Thanks partly to the creation in January of an all-party steering group on the constitution, the eventual form of the legislation was very close to the original government proposals, giving the Scottish parliament control mainly over matters currently administered by the Secretary of State for Scotland. But there was elbow-room for expansion of its activities, principally because the legislation specified which functions were not to be devolved, rather than those which were. The elections to the parliament would be in two stages, 73 candidates being elected by a first-past-the-post procedure, and 56 selected from regional party lists so as to achieve some proportionality of representation. Electors would have two votes, one for a candidate and the other for a party.

Controversy was aroused by the physical arrangements for the parliament—where it should be located, who should be the architect, and where the interim location should be until the new building was ready. Despite some vigorous pressure from Scottish Office civil servants based in Leith, the location chosen was at Holyrood, in the historic heart of Edinburgh. The successful Enric Miralles design, announced on 4 July, made few compromises with the architecture of its setting. Glasgow had had strong hopes of being the successful bidder to provide a temporary home for the parliament, but on 20 March the government announced that Edinburgh's General Assembly Hall (normally the venue of Church of Scotland assemblies) would be used instead.

A big issue, especially within the Labour Party, was how to select candidates to stand for the Scottish parliament, either in the first-past-the-post contests or on the party lists. The Labour leadership was anxious to weaken the hold on Scottish politics of some of its entrenched members, particularly west of Scotland councillors. It therefore circumvented local democracy in the selection of candidates. This meant that two sitting 'old Labour' Westminster MPs were not selected as candidates for the Scottish parliament, much to their chagrin.

Labour's difficulties with some of its local representatives continued. The party dropped its attempts to remove Pat Lally, the Lord Provost of Glasgow, and to discipline Tommy Graham, MP for West Renfrewhire, both accused of bringing the party into disrepute; but on 23 July Donald Dewar, the Secretary of State for Scotland, ordered East Ayrshire and North Lanarkshire councils to wind up their loss-making 'direct labour' organizations, and on 17 August Harry McGuigan resigned as Labour leader in North Lanarkshire. Mohammed Sarwar, elected to Westminster for Glasgow Govan in 1997 and Britain's first Muslim MP, remained suspended from the privileges of party membership. In September he was formally charged with criminal offences in connection with his election campaign and was due to stand trial early in 1999.

It was a good year for the SNP, which at times was given public opinion poll ratings ahead of the Labour Party. There were no parliamentary by-elections in the year, but 21 local government seats fell vacant. Of these, ten changed hands, Labour recording a net loss of eight seats and the SNP and Conservatives net gains of six and two seats respectively. Perhaps the more significant indicator, albeit on a very low turnout of 20.5 per cent, was the European Parliament by-election caused by the death on 25 August of Allan Macartney, MEP for Scotland North-East. Dr Macartney had won the seat for the SNP in 1994, taking it from Labour. The by-election on 26 November returned local man Ian Hudghton for the SNP, with 48 per cent of the vote. Labour's main embarrassment was that, having proclaimed the election to be a two-horse race, its candidate was beaten into third place with only 18.5 per cent. The Conservative candidate, an Ayrshire farmer and the only avowed 'Euro-sceptic' in the field, came second with just under 20 per cent. The outcome marked a further recovery for the Conservatives, who had on 6 September appointed David McLetchie as their new leader.

In higher education, debate about the implications for Scottish universities of the charging of tuition fees continued well into the summer. A government bill provided that Scottish and non-UK European Union students would have to pay fees for only three of the four years of an honours degree, but that students from England, Wales and Northern Ireland must pay for all four years. After sustained attack in the House of Lords, the government agreed to commission an inquiry to examine the effects of the measure on the Scottish universities. More positively, the new University of the Highlands and Islands (UHI) moved nearer to reality, as the first students on what were planned to become UHI degree programmes were enrolled in the autumn. UHI courses were to be provided face-to-face in the participating colleges and also by 'distance learning'.

On 24 August the UK and US governments agreed that the two Libyans suspected of bombing the airliner which exploded over Lockerbie in 1988 could be tried at The Hague under Scottish law (see also V.4.ii). On 22 September the government named the Scottish lawyers who would make up the prosecution team, but at year's end it remained uncertain whether the Libyan authorities would agree to send the suspects to the Netherlands.

The Scottish economy suffered from the world glut of computer components. On 26 June Hyundai confirmed the indefinite suspension of its proposed factory at Dunfermline, and on 29 September Viasystems closed plants in Galashiels and Selkirk (which had been a valuable source of jobs in an area hit by the loss of textile employment). At the beginning of December official estimates suggested that farming income in 1998 had fallen by about 42 per cent from the previous year (as against the average UK decline of 33 per cent). The Scottish economy, however, displayed modest growth overall. Most of the new employment opportunities created by inward investment were in telephone-call services.

iii. WALES

IT was another eventful year in Welsh politics. It began with the continued argument over the most suitable location for the National Assembly due to be elected in May 1999, the two rival cities of Swansea and Cardiff being seen as the most credible options. Swansea's proposal was both imaginative and forward-looking. However, according to Ron Davies, when he was still Secretary of State for Wales, the case for locating the National Assembly in the capital city was 'too compelling to resist'. Mr Davies decided in favour of a new £17 million building to be located in Cardiff Bay, adjacent to the impressive Victorian Pierhead building and attached to the less attractive 1980s office block, Crickhowell House. In October, following an architectural competition, it was announced that the building would be based on a modernistic design submitted by the London architects Richard Rogers Partnership (see XV.2.ii).

The Government of Wales Bill finally received the royal assent on 31 July (see XVII.3). The new 60-strong National Assembly, scheduled to meet for the first time during the summer of 1999, was to assume virtually all the executive functions currently held by the Secretary of State for Wales. It would only be able to pass subordinate legislation and would have no tax-raising powers, but it would take control of the Welsh Office's £7,000 million budget. The Secretary of State received advice on the new political structure from an all-party advisory group which reported in August. However, there were fears that Welsh Office civil servants were seeking to ensure that their own powers would be preserved.

Mr Davies spent much of the summer campaigning to win the leadership of the Labour Party in Wales. Victory would almost certainly ensure that he would become the Welsh Assembly's first secretary in 1999. His opponent, Rhodri Morgan, MP for Cardiff South, received strong support from the constituency parties, but the electoral college system employed by the party meant that the overwhelming support for Mr Davies from the trade union block vote gave him a comfortable victory in a specially convened conference at Newport on 19 September.

It therefore appeared that Mr Davies's ambition to continue to be the leading figure in Welsh politics was to be realized. However, on 27 October, in a dramatic statement, he announced his resignation as Secretary of State and, soon after, as leader of the Labour Party in Wales. He claimed that he had been attacked at knifepoint following a walk on Clapham Common, in an area notorious for casual homosexual contact; despite being a victim of a crime, he felt he had committed 'a serious lapse of judgement' and was therefore obliged to resign (see also II.1.i). Subsequently, in an emotional speech to the House of Commons, he stated cryptically: 'We are what we are. We are all different, the product both of our genes and experiences.' Although the public remained mystified by the events surrounding the resignation, there was far greater sympathy for Mr Davies in Wales than elsewhere, and he was encouraged to consider seeking nomination as a candidate for the new Assembly.

The personal tragedy for Mr Davies was also a major blow to the devolution process as he had shown a rare ability to unite the Labour Party as well as gaining a wide measure of confidence among those outside the party who were committed to building a new inclusive political structure in Wales.

Mr Davies's successor, Alun Michael, the MP for Cardiff South and Penarth and Minister of State in the Home Office, was considered able and fair-minded, but fears were expressed as to his apparently lukewarm attitude to devolution. He was challenged for the leadership of the Labour Party in Wales by Mr Morgan, who refused to stand down for the sake of party unity. By the end of the year, following weeks of acrimony, it was by no means clear who would win the leadership election, which was to be held in February 1999. It appeared that Mr Morgan had substantial support from constituency parties who were unhappy with the perceived interference in Welsh politics by the Prime Minister's Office and Labour Party headquarters at Millbank.

A European Union (EU) summit was held in Cardiff on 15-16 June, with 15 heads of government and over 1,500 officials visiting the capital city. Another eminent visitor was the President of South Africa, Nelson Mandela, who was granted the freedom of Cardiff. The warm welcome given to Mr Mandela contrasted with the protests by ex-servicemen which greeted Emperor Akihito of Japan when he had also visited the capital city a few weeks earlier. Akihito's staff distributed leaflets detailing the £1,500 million of Japanese investment in Wales, which had created nearly 20,000 jobs over a 25-year period.

This was a timely reminder, as the Welsh economy was not immune to the effects of the economic crisis in the Far East. There had been a high concentration of inward investment from Japan and South Korea, and there were particular concerns about the future of the major development by the South Korean company LG in Newport. Not all parts of Wales had benefited from inward investment. In April the Welsh Development Agency reported that of the £6,400 million foreign investment obtained during the past five years only £700 million, barely 10 per cent, had been in the poorer parts of west Wales.

The agricultural sector remained in crisis. Welsh Office figures showed that farm incomes had fallen by up to 90 per cent; because of low milk prices and a strong pound, it was predicted that up to a thousand Welsh dairy farmers faced bankruptcy within two years. In September farmers blocked the Second Severn Crossing bridge, causing a massive traffic jam on the M4 motorway, while later in the month livestock farmers refused to sell stock in markets throughout Wales because prices for lambs were too low. There were also protests at supermarkets because, it was claimed, the gap between market prices and prices paid by consumers was too great. Farmers received some encouragement in November with a winter aid package and the lifting of the worldwide EU ban on the export of beef.

In early November it was announced that the National Trust had succeeded in raising the £4 million required to purchase a large tract of land on the southern flank of Yr Wyddfa (Mount Snowdon), the highest peak in Wales and one of symbolic significance. There had been concern in the summer that the land might be sold privately, but a major appeal led by the actor Sir Anthony Hopkins, who contributed £1 million himself, received generous support. However, doubts were raised by the Countryside Council for Wales and others that, as the land was not open to development because of environmental restrictions, the price paid was substantially over-inflated.

It was a particularly successful year for Welsh pop music, with groups such as The Manic Street Preachers, The Stereophonics and Catatonia receiving a worldwide recognition unprecedented in the history of Welsh entertainers in this field.

iv. NORTHERN IRELAND

It was a year in which political accommodation, in the shape of the Good Friday Agreement signed on 10 April, came out ahead of increased violence and won the journalistic accolade of historic. Six months later the award of the 1998 Nobel Peace Prize jointly to the two party leaders most responsible, David Trimble of the Ulster Unionist Party (UUP) and John Hume of the nationalist Social Democratic and Labour Party (SDLP), symbolized international acclaim for the achievement. By then the work of implementing the agreement was beset by some familiar and some new difficulties, although confidence remained high that the peace process had been given unstoppable momentum.

The shooting dead of Billy Wright, leader of the Loyalist Volunteer Force (LVF), by two Irish National Liberation Army (INLA) prisoners in the Maze prison on 27 December 1997 (see AR 1997, p. 48) produced a spate of sectarian killings in January and February which sucked in the Ulster Freedom Fighters (UFF) and the Irish Republican Army (IRA). In addition, the LVF, the INLA and the Continuity IRA remained active and outside the talks. The Continuity IRA exploded car bombs in Enniskillen, Moira and Portadown in the first three months of the year, many others being intercepted and defused.

The failure of the political talks to agree an agenda before the 1997 Christmas recess, and the threat by loyalist prisoners to review their support for talks, produced an exceptional political response. On 8 January the Secretary of State for Northern Ireland, Dr Marjorie (Mo) Mowlam, visited the Maze to reassure loyalist and republican inmates. Four days later the British and Irish governments presented the parties with a heads of agreement document. It proposed balanced constitutional change north and south of the border, a Northern Ireland assembly, a new British-Irish agreement, an inter-governmental council representing assemblies and parliaments throughout the British Isles, a North/South ministerial council accountable to the Northern Ireland assembly and to the Dáil (the Irish parliament), and suitable implementation bodies.

The talks moved to Lancaster House, London, on 26 January in the hope of speeding progress. However, the admission by the UFF of its involvement in 'a measured military response' resulted in the Ulster Democratic Party (UDP), the UFF's political 'advisers', withdrawing ahead of formal expulsion at Lancaster House. The Chief Constable of the Royal Ulster Constabulary (RUC) also informed the Secretary of State that the IRA had been involved in two murders, with the result that Sinn Féin, the IRA's political wing, was suspended from the talks under protest on 20 February. Although invited to return on 9 March, Sinn Féin refused until after party leaders had had a meeting with Prime Minister Tony Blair and then delayed a further 11 days until 23 March. Intensive meetings between Mr Blair and the Irish Prime Minister, Bertie Ahern, at the beginning of April enabled the talks chairman, former US senator George Mitchell, to present a paper on 7 April. The parties went into a final round of negotiations with a deadline of 9 April. Although the UUP initially described the document as 'a Sinn Féin wish list', agreement was eventually reached some 20 hours after the deadline, at around 6pm on Good Friday, 10 April.

The text of what was christened the Good Friday Agreement was widely circulated in the succeeding days (see XVII.1). It set out new devolved democratic institutions for Northern Ireland, proposed a North/South ministerial council in a new British-Irish agreement, a British-Irish Council involving the new assemblies for Northern Ireland, Scotland and Wales as well as the legislatures of the Isle of Man and the Channel Islands and the British and Irish parliaments. It also made extensive provision for the protection of human rights. Since the agreement envisaged a peaceful as well as a democratic society, there were arrangements for the decommissioning of weapons under the supervision of an international body, proposals for reduced security and a commission on policing, as well as proposals for the accelerated release of prisoners. These proposals were to be implemented in a related way over a period of two years. The resultant system of government was far removed from the Westminster model. It was best described as 'consociational' in its internal arrangements but with federal aspects in its UK dimensions and confederal in some aspects of its Irish dimensions. It required consensus between the main unionist party, the UUP, and the main nationalist party, the SDLP; otherwise the extensive checks and balances could result in deadlock.

The next stage in the process required endorsement of the agreement in referendums in Northern Ireland and the Republic of Ireland. The five-week campaign served to exacerbate the divisions in the unionist community. The Democratic Unionist Party (DUP) and the UK Unionist Party (UKUP) had left the talks two months before Sinn Féin entered them in September 1997 (see AR 1997, p. 46) and firmly opposed the agreement. The UUP council backed Mr Trimble in supporting the agreement, but six out of 10 UUP MPs opposed it and the Orange Order would not endorse it, even after a meeting with the Mr Blair, who visited Northern Ireland three times during the campaign, on 6, 14 and 20 May. On the first occasion he was accompanied by former Prime Minister John Major in a joint appeal for a 'yes' vote and announced a fund for victims of violence. On 12 May the Chancellor of the Exchequer, Gordon Brown, announced a 'peace through prosperity' economic investment package of £350 million. Opinion moved towards 'yes' in the last seven days of the campaign, during which the image of Mr Hume and Mr Trimble at a concert by the pop group U2 on 19 May seemed to signal the new politics. On 20 May Mr Blair issued five hand-written pledges to reassure unionist voters, after his speech and visit on 14 May had been regarded by many as insufficient. President Clinton, at the G-8 summit in Birmingham on 15–17 May, said that the agreement safeguarded the principle of consent and that everyone would gain from its endorsement, also predicting that it would facilitate investment.

There was no uncertainty in the nationalist community about the agreement, which was regarded by the SDLP as very close to its own prescription. A Sinn Féin special *ardfheis* (conference) on 10 May in Dublin, attended by leading IRA prisoners from the Maze and Portlaoise prisons, called for a 'yes' vote north and south, and 331 out of 350 delegates voted in favour of the party taking up seats in the new Northern Ireland assembly, reversing a boycott policy of 77 years. During the campaign, dissident republicans attacked the RUC stations at Belleek and Armagh, while on 15 May the LVF declared a ceasefire and called for a 'no' vote in the referendum.

On polling day, 22 May, the question on the ballot paper was very straightforward: 'Do you support the agreement reached at the multi-party talks on Northern Ireland and set out in Command Paper 3883?' The result, announced during the afternoon of 23 May, was as follows: Yes 676,966 (71.1 per cent), No 274,879 (28.9 per cent), invalid votes 1,738, turnout 81.1 per cent. The turnout was the second highest of any election in Northern Ireland, exceeded only by the 89 per cent recorded in the 1921 elections to the first parliament of Northern Ireland. In the simultaneous referendum in the Irish Republic on new and revised articles in the constitution, the changes proposed were passed overwhelmingly, although on a much lower turnout (see II.2.vii).

The referendum result acted as a starting flag for the assembly elections on 25 June. The campaign, especially among the unionist parties, was essentially a re-run of the referendum. Among the nationalist parties, the SDLP and Sinn Féin competed for dominance, after the former had rejected an electoral pact. The electorate of 1,177,969 had a choice of 277 candidates from some 17 parties and three groups of independents for the 108 seats. The results showed that pro-agreement candidates had polled 75 per cent of the vote and won 80 seats, while anti-agreement candidates took 25 per cent and won 28 seats. With the unionist vote shredded between six parties, the UUP (21.3 per cent) was knocked off top position in terms of first-preference votes by the SDLP (22 per cent), while Sinn Féin experienced its fifth increase in support since 1993, winning 17.6 per cent.

However, in the allocation of seats the UUP came out as the largest party with 28, followed by the SDLP with 24. Of the other 28 seats won by pro-agreement parties, Sinn Féin took 18, the Alliance Party (AP) 6, the Northern Ireland Women's Coalition (NIWC) 2 and the Progressive Unionist Party (PUP) 2. In the anti-agreement camp, the DUP won 20 seats, the UKUP 5 and independent Unionists 3 (see table on p. 48).

The new assembly, meeting in shadow form when required by the Secretary of State, had its first meeting on 1 July. The session elected Mr Trimble (UUP) as first minister and Seamus Mallon (SDLP) as deputy first minister, set up two business committees and agreed to meet next on 14 September. The temporary presiding officer, appointed by the Secretary of State, was Lord Alderdice (AP). The opening was remarkably smooth despite the history of hostile relations between many of the parties and members.

The Orange Order church parade at Dumcree near Portadown on 5 July, re-routed by the Parades Commission on 29 June, produced an enormous build-up of security forces, including two extra army battalions and the construction of a steel wall across the Garvaghy Road, amid communal

Party	1st preference	%	Seats
SDLP	177,963	22.0	24
UUP	172,225	21.3	28
DUP	146,989	18.1	20
Sinn Féin	142,858	17.6	18
AP	56,636	6.5	6
UKUP	36,541	4.5	5
Ind U	24,399	3.0	3
PUP	20,634	2.5	2
NIWC	13,019	1.6	2
Others	23,098	2.9	0
Total	810,317	100.0	108

Electorate 1,178,556
Total poll 824,391
Invalid votes 14,074
Valid votes 810,317
Turnout 68.76% (of valid vote)

tension marked by attacks on church property. When the march was prevented from returning to Portadown via the Catholic-populated Garvaghy Road, the Orangemen refused to disperse, vowing to stay as long as it took to complete the march. Nightly confrontations developed, but neither an Orange meeting with the Prime Minister on 9 July nor indirect talks with Garvaghy Road residents on 11 July produced a solution, as 'sympathetic' actions broke out in Protestant working-class areas. By 8 July the police had experienced 400 attacks; there had been 12 shooting incidents and 25 bombings; and many officers were being intimidated at their homes. The death of three young brothers, Richard, Mark and Jason Quinn, in a fire-bomb attack on their Ballymoney home on 11 July was immediately labelled a sectarian attack by the RUC. It divided Orange opinion between those in favour of the principle of walking traditional routes and the view of Rev William Bingham that the protest should end because 'no road is worth a life'. Celebrations for 12 July were muted and one of the additional battalions was withdrawn on 16 July. The protest by Portadown Orangemen was still continuing at the end of the year.

On 28 July Dr Mowlam declared the Ulster Defence Association (UDA), the Ulster Volunteer Force (UVF) and the IRA to be officially 'inactive', to enable their prisoners to benefit from early release schemes under the Northern Ireland (Sentences) Act. The beginning of the schemes brought a statement from the LVF on 8 August saying 'our war is over' and making their May ceasefire permanent. The revelation that £1.4 million was to be spent rehabilitating the 400 paramilitary prisoners from the Maze prison was criticized by victims' organizations.

Dissident republican violence continued during the summer. A 200-pound bomb severely damaged Newtownhamilton the day before the assembly elections and was, surprisingly, claimed by the INLA. There was a failed mortar attack on Newry RUC station on 21 July and a Real IRA car bomb destroyed the centre of Banbridge on 1 August. However, it was the Real IRA bomb in the market town of Omagh on Saturday 15 August which became the most infamous, as the worst single incident of the troubles. The bomb killed 29 men, women and children (one of the victims dying some days later) and injured 310, when it exploded during a civic festival week. There was worldwide condemnation of the bombing. After some equivocation, the Real IRA suspended all military operations from 18 August, announcing a complete cessation from 8 September. On 22 August the INLA also announced a 'complete ceasefire', and accompanied it with an apology for the deaths of innocent civilians in their campaign. Accordingly, only the Continuity IRA remained active to face new anti-terrorist measures introduced simultaneously by the British and Irish governments.

The Omagh outrage also brought movement in Sinn Féin and the IRA. The latter encouraged the Real IRA to disband, while Sinn Féin condemned the bombing. On the eve of a visit by President Clinton on 3 September, Sinn Féin leader Gerry Adams went close to meeting the widespread demand for a statement that the war was over when he spoke of violence as 'a thing of the past, over, done with and gone'. His deputy, Martin McGuinness, was appointed to liaise with the international decommissioning body. President Clinton urged an audience in Belfast's Waterfront Hall to grasp the opportunity for peace. He also visited Stormont, along with Mr Blair, and met assembly members before going on to Omagh and Armagh.

A week after the US President's visit, Mr Trimble had a one-to-one meeting with Mr Adams, the first between a Unionist and a Sinn Féin leader for 76 years. The next day the first seven prisoners gained early release, and a week later the first prisoner with a murder conviction was freed. On 12 September patrols by the army in the Belfast area were ended, and ten days later the RUC Chief Constable said that another 300 to 400 troops could leave Northern Ireland.

After the summer recess the assembly resumed on 14 September, in refurbished premises at Stormont, to hear interim reports from its two committees and from the first and deputy first ministers. The main problems in the autumn were decommissioning and the formation of the new Northern Ireland executive. No date had been specified in the Good Friday Agreement for the beginning of decommissioning, and Sinn Féin was determined to stick to the letter of the deal, whereas the UUP refused to form an executive before the IRA began decommissioning. At the same time, the opposition Conservatives at Westminster called for the end of prisoner releases and a bar on executive appointments for Sinn Féin if the IRA did not decommission. By the end of September it was clear that there were serious differences between Mr Trimble and Mr Mallon, a statement by one invariably being contradicted by the other. The formation of the Union First movement within the UUP on 9 October left Mr Trimble with even less room for manoeuvre at his party's conference on 24 October. Mr Adams made it clear that he would not help him out by securing a gesture towards decommissioning from the IRA. The result was that the 31 October date mentioned in the agreement for the creation of a North-South Council was missed.

Despite this setback, UK-Irish relations remained as good as they had ever been, represented by a visit by Prince Philip to Ireland on 10 November and by the joint opening the next day by Queen Elizabeth and President Mary McAleese of a memorial to Irish World War I dead at Messines Ridge, Belgium. The Northern Ireland Act, setting the Good Friday Agreement in legislative form, became UK law on 19 November. On the same day Mr Trimble told the Irish Association in Dublin that the gaps were narrowing on North-South implementation bodies, but continued to resist Sinn Féin being given executive positions in the absence of any arms decommissioning. Two days later Mr Ahern told RTE of the 'irresistible dynamic towards a united Ireland within 20 years', thereby presenting ammunition to unionist opponents of the agreement.

Mr Blair had talks with assembly parties in Belfast on 25 November, en route to Dublin, where on 26 November he became the first British Prime Minister to address the two houses of the Irish parliament. He returned to Northern Ireland on 2 December and met each of the parties in an effort to resolve the deadlock. When he left early the next day the SDLP claimed that a deal had been reached, whereas the UUP said that it had not. On 10 December Mr Hume and Mr Trimble received the Nobel Peace Prize at a ceremony in Oslo, amid general pessimism about any further progress being made before Christmas. However, at 3am on 18 December agreement was reached on a ten-department executive and six North-South implementation bodies. A full report was promised to the assembly on 18 January. The good news did not end there, for the LVF handed in nine guns, 350 bullets, two pipe-bombs and six detonators as a token of decommissioning, calling on others to follow suit.

In her Christmas message Dr Mowlam said that Northern Ireland was enjoying a 'new season of hope' and pointed to the Good Friday Agreement as 'a powerful model for divided societies everywhere'. There were still hurdles ahead. The first minister and his party were determined that Sinn Féin could not take their two executive seats without a start to IRA decommissioning; the Democratic Unionists and the UKUP began to plan in anticipation of what they saw as Mr Trimble's submission to the two governments. Further, an IRA convention early in December firmly rejected decommissioning—the IRA's third such rejection in 1998.

The New Year Honours' list included awards for many associated with the Good Friday Agreement, notably an honorary knighthood for Mr Mitchell and the Companionship of Honour for Mr Major.

In a year which ostensibly brought the peace process to fruition, there was a marked increase in the level of violence. There were 55 terrorist-related deaths, of which 53 were civilians, one RUC and one army. Republican terrorists were responsible for 38 deaths and loyalists for 16. According to figures issued by FAIT (Families Against Intimidation and Terror (FAIT), it was one of the worst years for 'punishment' attacks. Loyalist paramilitaries were responsible for 119 and republicans for 118 such attacks, which were mainly the work of groups with representatives in the talks process. The ceasefires were therefore tenuous. Among republicans, the Continuity IRA remained active as a focus for dissidents. Among loyalists, the LVF ceasefire in August, soon produced the Red Hand Defenders and the Orange Volunteers as active groups.

Unemployment continued to fall—by some 11,000 over the year, to about 8 per cent of the labour force. Despite a new government programme to deal with the long-term unemployed aged 25 and over, there was a fall of only 1.9 per cent in this group, which made up 45 per cent of the total. The biannual census of employment showed 600,676 persons employed as at September, the highest-ever total and an increase of 27,795 jobs or 5 per cent over the two years. The largest increases were in services with 3,000 new jobs, followed by 530 in manufacturing, while construction gained 250 and 'others' 700. The main growth was in information technology, sales, engineering and construction.

2. GERMANY—FRANCE—ITALY—BELGIUM—THE NETHERLANDS—LUXEMBOURG—IRELAND

i. GERMANY

CAPITAL: Berlin   AREA: 357,000 sq km   POPULATION: 82,100,000 ('97)
OFFICIAL LANGUAGE: German
POLITICAL SYSTEM: federal parliamentary democracy
HEAD OF STATE: President Roman Herzog (since July '94)
RULING PARTIES: Social Democratic Party (SPD) & Alliance 90/Greens
HEAD OF GOVERNMENT: Gerhard Schröder (SPD), Federal Chancellor (since Oct '98)
MAIN IGO MEMBERSHIPS (non-UN): NATO, EU, WEU, OSCE, CE, CBSS, AC, OECD, G-8
CURRENCY: Deutsche Mark (end-'98 £1=DM2.76, US$1=DM1.1.67)
GNP PER CAPITA: US$28,260 by exchange-rate calculation, US$21,300 by PPP calculation ('97)

GERMAN politics in 1998 were marked by a milestone event: the establishment of a new 'red-green' federal government following the general election of 27 September. This was the first time in the post-war era that a sitting government had been voted out of office. Previous changes of government (in 1966, 1969 and 1982) had resulted from parties switching coalition allegiance. This time, Chancellor Helmut Kohl and his centre-right coalition of the Christian Democratic Union (CDU), the Christian Social Union (CSU) of Bavaria and the Free Democrats (FDP), in office since 1982, were decisively rejected in the polling booths to be replaced by a 'red-green' coalition of Social Democrats (SPD) and Greens.

It was an election of many other milestones. The former CDU/CSU-FDP coalition fared unusually badly at the polls, the FDP scoring its worst result since 1969 and the CDU/CSU its worst since the first post-war election in 1949. The SPD did unusually well, achieving its best result since 1980. And, replicating a model now well-established in the German *Länder* (states), the first-ever SPD-Green coalition was established at the federal level, led by the former Minister-President of Lower Saxony, Gerhard Schröder. The election outcome was as follows (1994 results in parentheses):

	seats	% of vote
Social Democratic Party	298 (252)	40.9 (36.4)
Alliance 90/Greens	47 (49)	6.7 (7.3)
Christian Democratic Union	198 (244)	28.4 (34.2)
Christian Social Union	47 (50)	6.7 (7.3)
Free Democratic Party	44 (47)	6.2 (6.9)
Party of Democratic Socialism	35 (30)	5.1 (4.4)
Others	0 (0)	6.0 (3.5)

The election results reflected at least as much on the unpopularity of Herr Kohl's government as on the popularity of its challengers. Put simply, German public opinion was gripped by a strong mood for change throughout 1998. In power for 16 years, the Kohl team—and in particular the 68-year-old Chancellor himself—found it difficult to generate an impression of vigour and renewal to maintain the electorate's enthusiasm.

More than this, though, there was overt dissatisfaction with a government which had failed to address key problems effectively. Foremost among these was unemployment, which had stagnated at a post-war high of over four million (11 per cent of the labour force). Unemployment was an especially potent issue in eastern Germany, where amid ongoing problems of post-unification economic reconstruction the unemployment rate had persistently remained around the 18 per cent mark through 1998. An 11.2 per cent fall in the CDU vote in eastern Germany (compared with a more modest 4.5 per cent fall in the west) was eloquent testimony to the ebbing patience of the east German electorate in waiting for the 'flourishing landscapes' promised by Herr Kohl at the time of unification in 1990.

At the same time, opinion polls showed that the electorate's view of the SPD as the main alternative was ambivalent; at best it was seen as less bad than the existing Kohl government. What the SPD did have, and skilfully played upon, was a younger and more dynamic leadership figure. In a highly professionalized campaign, Herr Schröder, carefully avoiding specific commitments, projected the theme of renewal for those tired of Chancellor Kohl, alongside reassurances of continuity to appeal to the middle ground of a notoriously cautious electorate.

The challenge of transforming this vision of a 'new middle ground' (*'neue Mitte'*) in German politics from electoral strategy into clear policy direction proved difficult to meet once Herr Schröder formally took office on 27 October. Contrary to many expectations, this had little to do with difficulties in cooperating with the Greens. By common consent, the Greens' contribution to establishing the new government and its programme was constructive, in that they balanced their radical environmentalist heritage effectively against the practicalities of government. Among the results were a commitment to raising 'green' energy taxes incrementally over the coalition's period of office; a long-term programme to phase out nuclear power; and, in line with the Greens' commitment to multiculturalism and equality of opportunity, a planned reform of Germany's antiquated citizenship law (still based on the concept of bloodline rather than birthplace), so as to offer fuller prospects for equal rights and social integration for Germany's seven million non-German inhabitants.

The failure to establish a clear direction for the government lay within the SPD. Herr Schröder was nominated as the SPD's candidate for the chancellorship only in March 1998. The decision was taken immediately after his third election victory in a row as minister-president of Lower Saxony on 1 March, when he unexpectedly increased his vote and successfully defended the SPD's absolute majority in the regional parliament. His victory—in a high-profile campaign styled in the media as a dry-run for the September general election—amply confirmed his vote-winning capacities to a party eager to return to power after 17 years of opposition. However, the lateness of the nomination did not allow him much time to stamp his authority on the SPD, of which he did not even become leader. This distinction continued to fall to Oskar Lafontaine, the new Finance Minister, on whom Herr Schröder was reliant for 'delivering' the party behind the government.

Problems quickly arose from the fact that these two key figures in the administration hailed from different wings of the party. Herr Lafontaine was seen as an old-style Social Democrat, with a broadly Keynesian vision of economic management based on redistributive taxation, public investment and demand management. He also succeeded in creating a robust power-base by strengthening the remit of the Finance Ministry at the expense of the traditionally powerful Economics Ministry during negotiations on the formation of the government. Herr Schröder by contrast had an image—and a policy track-record in government in Lower Saxony— rather more like that of Tony Blair in Britain: remote from the traditions of the 'workers' party', focused on pragmatic supply-side reforms and on working closely with business to promote employment through labour market flexibility. How these two backgrounds, and these two dominant personalities, would be combined remained unclear. The result was a blurring of the government's message on core policies such as tax reform and employment policy.

The rather lacklustre start by the new government was accompanied by a difficult period of adaptation for the main opposition parties. In recognition of their responsibility for electoral defeat, the leaders of the CDU (Herr Kohl) and the CSU (former Finance Minister Theo Waigel) both announced their resignations immediately after the election. Herr Kohl was replaced by his anointed successor, former CDU party chairman Wolfgang Schäuble. Herr Waigel was set to be replaced in early 1999 by Edmund Stoiber, minister-president of Bavaria.

Herr Stoiber's profile and influence were raised by his success in leading the CSU to another absolute majority of votes and seats in the Bavarian regional election held just two weeks before the general election in September. This resounding success (which fleetingly raised hopes of a CDU/CSU recovery in the general election) followed a hard-hitting campaign focused on 'Euro-scepticism' and law and order concerns, the latter linked to immigration flows into Germany. It was instructive that by year's end the issue on which the CDU/CSU had most clearly chosen to profile its opposition to the new federal government was immigration, directed against the government's plans to reform the German citizenship law. This suggested that Herr Stoiber and the CSU had ratcheted up their influence in the Christian Democratic camp, exploiting the leeway opened up as Herr Schäuble attended to the urgent process of policy and personnel renewal in a CDU dominated for well over 20 years by Herr Kohl. Accordingly, a harder, more conservative brand of CDU/CSU politics was perhaps in prospect in the coming years.

The FDP, under the leadership of Wolfgang Gerhardt, greeted opposition as an opportunity for renewal—in particular a sharpening of its deregulationist and tax-cutting agenda—away from the constraints of the coalition with the CDU/CSU since 1982 (and before that with the SPD since 1969). However, the party's electoral base outside the federal parliament remained extremely fragile. It failed to win the 5 per cent of the vote necessary to qualify for seats in any of the regional elections held during 1998 (in Lower Saxony, Saxony-Anhalt, Bavaria and Mecklenburg-West Pomerania). Failure to improve on this record in the raft of regional and European elections due in 1999 would revive doubts about its viability—not least because the Greens had usurped the FDP's traditional role as majority-maker in federal coalition-building.

The Party of Democratic Socialism (PDS) continued to confound expectations of its demise. From an unpromising start as the discredited successor to the Socialist Unity Party of the former German Democratic

Republic, it had shed most of the more unappealing ideological remnants of its Soviet-bloc heritage to become a highly successful articulator of east German interests. It maintained its run of successes in east German regional elections in Saxony-Anhalt in April (19.9 per cent) and Mecklenburg-West Pomerania in September (24.4 per cent). Its steady progress towards political respectability was marked by an extension of the 'toleration' arrangement in Saxony-Anhalt, maintaining a minority SPD government in office, and, even more significantly, by the first-ever formal 'red-red' (SPD-PDS) coalition in Mecklenburg-West Pomerania. Its success in clearing the 5 per cent hurdle for parliamentary representation in the September general election despite its enduring weakness in western Germany (where it won just 1.1 per cent of the vote) confirmed its status as a regional party for the east (where it won 19.5 per cent).

German foreign policy in 1998 broadly adhered to the continuity of direction one had come to expect under Herr Kohl—even under the direction of the new Foreign Minister (and Vice-Chancellor), the leading Green Joschka Fischer. Given that the Greens were once committed to withdrawal from NATO and until recently deeply suspicious of the European Union (EU), this continuity provided clear confirmation of the Greens' newfound pragmatism. Thus, the long process of 'normalizing' Germany's role in the international community continued via the reaffirmation of political and military commitments to peace-keeping operations in the former Yugoslavia (amid only mild murmurings of discontent from the Green Party's rank and file).

In the field of European integration, moreover, Herr Fischer presented messages of closer European integration and, ultimately, political union which were reminiscent of Herr Kohl himself *circa* 1991. Perversely, the then Chancellor had been moved to take a half-heartedly 'Euro-sceptical' stance in the general election campaign in the attempt, under pressure from Herr Stoiber and the CSU, to recover electoral support. His defeat saw EU policy normality duly restored.

Neither Herr Kohl's dabbling in scepticism nor the change of government hampered progress on the key issue of European economic and monetary union, which culminated in the launch of the euro at the turn of the year. At the same time, the advent of a new government provoked an intense debate on the economic management of 'euroland'. In particular, Finance Minister Lafontaine (who had added international economic relations to his ministry's remit) revived the question of creating a 'political' counterweight to the European Central Bank, while also questioning the rigour with which the EU Stability Pact negotiated by his predecessor, Herr Waigel, needed to be observed if member states preferred strategies of fiscal expansion. In November Herr Lafontaine joined ten other Finance Ministers from centre-left EU governments in launching *The New European Way* as the manifesto of the EU Socialists for the European Parliament elections due in June 1999. It called for economic policies to be more coordinated in pursuit of growth and jobs, public spending to be higher and taxes to be more harmonized.

Given that these issues had long stood on the agenda of the Socialist Jospin government in France, they provided a sound basis for injecting new life into the Franco-German axis in the EU. The result was a burst of Franco-German agenda-setting for the German EU presidency in the first six months of 1999 which flagged up budgetary issues (i.e. reducing the German contribution) and movement towards tax harmonization across the EU as priorities. On both counts there was opposition in Britain, because of the obvious implications for the budget rebate negotiated by Prime Minister Thatcher in the 1980s and for the UK's status as a low-tax location for inward investment. The result was a distancing of the new German government from its UK counterpart despite the close personal relationship which had built up prior to the German election between Herr Schröder and Prime Minister Blair.

ii. FRANCE

CAPITAL: Paris   AREA: 544,000 sq km   POPULATION: 59,000,000 ('97)
OFFICIAL LANGUAGE: French
POLITICAL SYSTEM: presidential parliamentary democracy
RULING PARTIES: Rally for the Republic (RPR) holds presidency; Socialist Party (PS), French Communist Party (PCF), Greens and other groups form government
HEAD OF STATE & GOVERNMENT: President Jacques Chirac (RPR), since May '95
PRIME MINISTER: Lionel Jospin (PS), since June '97
MAIN IGO MEMBERSHIPS (non-UN): NATO, EU, WEU, OSCE, COE, OECD, G-8, Francophonie
CURRENCY: franc (end-'98 £1=F9.29, US$1=F5.59)
GNP PER CAPITA: US$26,0500 by exchange-rate calculation, US$21,860 by PPP calculation ('97)

PRESIDENT Jacques Chirac sombrely reflected on 'difficult and uncertain times' in his New Year message, mentioning 'too much violence, too much insecurity in the schools, on public transport and on the streets'. With unemployment, this was 'the number one concern'. Certainly both problems challenged the Jospin government. The year opened with a national rail strike, street protests turning to vandalism and sit-ins at benefit offices by unemployed workers. Over a third of the 3.1 million unemployed had been out of work for over a year and were now on minimum benefits. More than one household in ten was below the poverty line. Lionel Jospin won praise for his handling of the rail strike. However, the sit-ins commanded widespread sympathy, not least from several ministers. The job-seekers wanted minimum benefits of F5,000 per month and a F3,000 end-of-year bonus. Faced with the F70,000 million bill and with economic and monetary union (EMU) imminent in the European Union (EU), the government was unreceptive. However, Martine Aubry, the Minister of Labour, promised F500 million to finance training programmes, while M. Jospin pledged an extra F1,000 million for emergency unemployment benefits. And in the run-up to local elections Mme Aubry unveiled a F50,000 million three-year plan to reduce dependence on benefits, help the jobless find work and provide health care for the uninsured. Benefits for the long-term unemployed were raised by 8 per cent.The government's main hopes of reducing unemployment lay in the introduction of the 35-hour working week. By the year 2000 firms with 20 or more employees would have to pay overtime if they worked more than 35 hours; smaller firms would have a longer period of grace. Companies taking on additional staff would receive a state subsidy of F120,000 a year for five years for each one. The government hoped to create over 100,000 extra jobs; employers insisted labour costs would rise by 11 per cent and many thousands of jobs would go. The bill's slow passage through parliament was marked by hundreds of opposition amendments, while many government supporters felt that it was nowhere near enough.

In January the Prime Minister announced an increase of 35,000 in the security forces, a review of the law on juvenile delinquency and a scheme to counter violence in schools—the third such in three years. The most serious law and order situation remained Corsica. In February gunmen assassinated the prefect, Claude Erignac. He had apparently been unduly zealous in tackling the murders and racketeering endemic in the island. President Chirac vowed that 'crime and disregard for the law' would not be allowed to take root in the island. But the killers were not brought to justice. Also in February, 36 Islamic militants were sentenced to up to ten years imprisonment for involvement in bomb attacks in 1995 (see AR 1995, p. 51).

The government also wrestled with the intractable issue of some 70,000 immigrants living illegally in France. A case-by-case review regularized the position of many thousands, while others were deported. But thousands still remained illegally in the margins of society, a source of grievance to the racist right.

In the regional elections in March left-wing parties gained considerable ground. On a lowish turnout, the Socialists won 396 seats compared with 318 in 1992 and the Communists 147 (115), though the divided Greens dropped from 106 to 68. The neo-Gaullist Rally for the Republic (RPR) fell from 318 seats to 285 and the centrist Union for French Democracy (UDF) from 305 to 262. The governmental majority had done well—but not well enough to win as many regions outright as it had hoped, while the doubling of support for Trotskyist parties to 4.4 per cent sounded a warning note on its left. The far-right National Front (FN), with 15 per cent of the vote and 275 seats (239 in 1992), now held the balance in a number of regions. Several right-wing provincial leaders, defying appeals from their national parties and President Chirac, clung to their regional chairmanships by doing deals with the Front, though some pulled back when the left won over 400 seats and took 11 councils from the right in subsequent departmental elections. The mainstream centre-right parties were plunged into disarray. One regional chairman, Charles Millon (a former Defence Minister), who retained his position thanks to a deal with the Front, founded a new party, La Droite (The Right), based on a closer relationship with the far right. And the former Prime Minister, Edouard Balladur, stirred a hornet's nest by calling for an examination of 'national preference'—political code for the Front's policy of discriminating against foreigners. In May, however, the Front lost its only parliamentary seat in a by-election at Toulon, when conservative voters swung behind the Socialist candidate in the run-off ballot.

All was not well within the National Front. Longstanding tension between its leader, Jean-Marie Le Pen, and his deputy, Bruno Mégret, burst into open warfare. In April M. Le Pen was convicted of assaulting a Socialist candidate during the 1997 elections and sentenced to a three-year suspended sentence, a F20,000 fine and disqualification from public office for two years. He proposed that his wife—no politician—should head the Front's list in the 1999 European elections in his stead. The ensuing row led to M. Mégret's expulsion in December and a damaging split.

The right was also divided over Europe. In April RPR deputies refused to follow President Chirac's call to back the euro, following which challenges to his authority at the party's congress came close to success. The FN and the Communists were also hostile to closer European integration. The Communist leader, Robert Hue, called unsuccessfully for a referendum on the Treaty of Amsterdam—ratification of which required constitutional amendments, according to a Constitutional Council ruling in January, in view of the transfers of sovereignty over immigration, asylum and border controls. Here again, the RPR was divided. Ratification had still to be completed as the year ended. With 57 per cent of the French reportedly thinking their politicians corrupt, such sentiments were bolstered by evidence of kickbacks, illicit party funding and phantom jobs in Paris city government. These revelations brought the whiff of scandal close to the President himself, since he was for many years mayor of the city. An attempt by centre-right councillors to oust the current mayor, Jean Tiberi, who, with his wife, was caught up in these allegations, was unsuccessful. His purge of 12 'disloyal' assistant mayors added to the RPR's internal disarray. Some 50 people were now facing charges relating to the illegal funding of the party. The (Socialist) president of the Constitutional Council and former Foreign Minister, Roland Dumas, was embroiled in allegations that his mistress was paid by the Elf oil company to lobby him. François Léotard, a UDF former minister, was also under criminal investigation over party funding.

In another long-running scandal—though with no element of corruption—former Prime Minister Laurent Fabius was sent for trial for manslaughter, with two former ministers, over contaminated blood in 1985 that resulted in the deaths of nearly 300 people from AIDS. Even the Tour de France, the premier event of the French sporting year, was tainted almost to the point of collapse by the revelation of endemic doping (see also Pt XVI). This punctured the euphoria following France's unexpected victory in the football World Cup—though not before the contrast between the ethnic diversity of the winning team and the National Front's view of who was worthy of being considered 'French' was widely noted.

Meanwhile, the economy boomed and public finances swelled with record receipts from partial privatizations of state industry, a policy rejected by the Socialists before taking office. Introducing the budget in July the Finance Minister, Dominique Strauss-Kahn, projected growth of 3.0 per cent in 1998, 400,000 new jobs and a public-sector deficit of only 2.3 per cent of GDP. He refused to spend more on social welfare but cut taxation, mostly on companies, by F28,000 million—partly to allay business concerns over the 35-hour week. He reduced value-added tax (VAT) on household gas and oil but increased tax on diesel and on personal fortunes exceeding F100 million. The unions were unhappy that the minimum wage rose only 2 per cent, while a fresh round of measures to contain remorselessly rising health expenditure antagonized the doctors. However, the biggest threat to M. Strauss-Kahn's policy lay in the threat of recession. By the end of the year his optimistic growth projections had to be trimmed back. But whatever 1999 might bring, in 1998 retail prices rose only 0.3 per cent, the lowest figure for 40 years, and GDP was up almost 3 per cent. Even unemployment, though still much too high, edged down from 12.5 to 11.5 per cent.

Nevertheless, the government had a difficult autumn. October brought nationwide demonstrations by 500,000 secondary school children demanding more teachers and funds for building improvements and equipment and a loosening of centralized control. As so often, sporadic violence followed in the wake, stirring uneasy memories of 1968 (see AR 1968, pp. 236–8). Extra funding and reforms were promised. A rash of deaths among the homeless during November's cold snap momentarily gave consciences their annual jolt over those whom prosperity and welfare provision failed to benefit. Earlier, the government had to withdraw proposals to reform the method of electing French MEPs in the face of opposition by the Senate. And a proposed 'civil solidarity pact' for couples who 'cannot or do not wish to marry' drew the wrath of churchmen and conservatives for undermining marriage and legitimizing homosexual unions; for a time, the proposal paralysed the parliamentary agenda. Another bill, ostensibly increasing the independence of state broadcasting and improving its quality by reducing its dependence on advertising, was 'deferred' after a savage reception. There was persistent antagonism between the Labour and Finance Ministers, while the outspoken Environment Minister, Dominique Voynet, broke ranks on several issues. Nevertheless, M. Jospin's personal popularity remained unfailingly buoyant.

With the expanding importance of the EU, the old distinction between 'home' and 'foreign' affairs was increasingly blurred. And 'Europe' was a major preoccupation. The central aim of monetary and economic policy was a healthy entry into EMU and the euro currency. France wanted the new European Central Bank (ECB) to be sensitive to wider considerations than inflation, and looked to it as a way of achieving greater influence on monetary policy than in the years when the franc had simply shadowed the Deutsche Mark. Hence President Chirac's highly controversial attempt to impose a French president of the ECB (see XI.4), and hence a readiness to endorse the new German government's attempts to influence the ECB's approach. France moved rapidly to cement the Franco-German relationship after Gerhard Schröder's election as Chancellor (see II.2.i), while also agreeing closer defence cooperation with Britain in December (see II.1.i).

In February M. Jospin announced a consolidation of the Ministries of Foreign Affairs and Cooperation, with the aim of targeting bilateral aid more effectively and coherently. A parliamentary commission undertook an investigation of the French role in arming the Hutu troops and militias who massacred hundreds of thousands of Tutsis in Rwanda in 1994 (see AR 1994, pp. 292–4). Two former Prime Ministers, Edouard Balladur and Alain Juppé, rejected all criticism of France's role during the genocide when they appeared before the commission. The inquiry raised little public interest. Nor was there much official or public discussion of the continued brutal bloodletting in Algeria. France did seek a role in promoting peace in the Democratic Republic of the Congo, though without immediate success. Its continuing interest in Africa found happiest expression in the Franco-African summit held in Paris in late November, attended by 49 African countries, with 34 heads of state present. However, critics pointed to the number of dictators and human rights abusers attending, at least one of whom sought assurance that he would not meet General Pinochet's fate (see II.1.i; IV.3.iv).

France remained hostile to military action against Iraq and distanced itself from the Anglo-American action in December, also signalling sympathy for the easing of UN sanctions (see V.2.vi). Meanwhile, the ending of conscription after two centuries was forcing the transformation of the armed forces onto a wholly professional basis. As the last cadres of conscripts were serving their time, the impact not only on the military but on other public services that had depended on conscripts and on the economies of the garrison towns was becoming clear, sometimes painfully so.

iii. ITALY

CAPITAL: Rome   AREA: 301,000 sq km   POPULATION: 57,250,000 ('97)
OFFICIAL LANGUAGE: Italian
POLITICAL SYSTEM: parliamentary democracy
HEAD OF STATE: President Oscar Luigi Scalfaro (since May '92)
RULING PARTIES: Left Democrats (DS) head six-party centre-left coalition
HEAD OF GOVERNMENT: Massimo D'Alema (DS), Prime Minister (since Oct '98)
MAIN IGO MEMBERSHIPS (non-UN): NATO, EU, WEU, OSCE, CE, CEI, OECD, G-8
CURRENCY: lira (end-'98 £1=Lit2,743.43, US$1=Lit1,648.94)
GNP PER CAPITA: US$20,120 by exchange-rate calculation, US$20,060 by PPP calculation ('97)

AT the start of the year it was still not clear whether Italy would be admitted to the group of countries joining the single European currency. Although the budget deficit at the end of 1997 was, at 2.7 per cent of gross domestic product (GDP), within the criteria set down at Maastricht, Dutch and German ministers voiced fears that the country's very large public debt would pose a threat to the stability of the euro. In fact, Italy was included in the list approved in the spring and participated enthusiastically in the launch of the new currency at the end of the year.

In an interview in *La Repubblica* of 30 December, Romano Prodi (who had vacated the premiership in October) said that entry had been achieved despite a certain scepticism both abroad and at home. He added that France had been Italy's strongest sponsor and that data had been transmitted on a daily basis to European treasury departments to assure them of the country's improving situation. The internal sceptics referred to by Professor Prodi included the governor of the Bank of Italy and the former managing director of Fiat, Cesare Romiti. They took the view that the struggle to meet the main Maastricht criteria for monetary union had meant that major issues such as the pension system, which remained generous despite reform, and the problems of development and unemployment had not been sufficiently addressed. The hard-line Communist Refoundation (RC), whose votes had kept the Prodi government in office, also called for a significant change of economic policy, although in a somewhat different direction. RC's power was shown when, much to the dismay of the employers' organization Confindustria, a law was passed reducing the working week to 35 hours by 2001.

The coalition remained broadly stable for the first half of the year, although the general political situation continued to be fluid. The lack of any shared view on political reform was demonstrated when none of the points proposed by the bicameral commission on institutional reform were adopted. In its report, presented in January, the commission proposed several far-reaching changes. These included the adoption of federalism, direct election of a non-executive president, reinforcement of the position of prime minister, and reduction of the size of both houses of parliament. By May, however, it was clear that, despite the best efforts of the commission president, Democratic Party of the Left (PDS) leader Massimo D'Alema, the project would not command wide support. Sensing that there was political mileage to be gained by championing the cause of presidentialism, the right-wing Liberty Pole (PL) alliance denounced the commission's work as a shabby compromise. Its attitude was also determined by the failure of the leader of Forza Italia (FI), Silvio Berlusconi, to secure majority support for his bid to trade backing for reform for curbs on the investigative activities of the judiciary.

Signor Berlusconi continued to accuse Milan magistrates of waging a political campaign against him. His speeches on this theme became more numerous and intemperate as his own legal circumstances worsened. In July he was found guilty in two separate trials of bribing officials of the Finance Police who were inspecting the accounts of his Fininvest company and of illegally financing the Italian Socialist Party in the 1980s. He was also summoned to appear before magistrates in Spain to explain alleged irregularities in Fininvest's foreign operations. When the FI leader denounced the Milan magistrates as 'terrorists', he received a prompt and vociferous response from the magistrate-turned-politician Antonio Di Pietro, who emerged as his principal antagonist. Signor Di Pietro enhanced his status as a populist leader by campaigning against plans to reintroduce public financing of political parties and for the abolition of the proportional quota which, it was said, distorted the tendentially bipolar nature of the party system.

Despite his personal troubles, Signor Berlusconi was active in seeking to relaunch his party as the successor to the former ruling Christian Democrats (DC). In April the first congress of Forza Italia was held and in June the party was granted membership of the European Popular Party (the European Christian Democrats), in spite of the opposition of Professor Prodi and the Italian Popular Party (itself a successor to the DC). There were a number of other innovations in the party system, one of the most significant being the transformation of the PDS into the Left Democrats (DS) in February. For Signor D'Alema, the change of name was part of the process whereby the former Communist Party (which became the PDS in 1991) completed its transformation into the sole party of socialist inspiration in Italy. The 'new' formation absorbed several small political groups, including the Republican Left, the Unitary Communists, the Social Christians and the Labourists. The rose symbol of the Party of European Socialists replaced the hammer and sickle, which had still occupied a place in the PDS symbol. The changes were criticized both by those who felt that any refounding of a left party should involve citizens rather than minor groupings and by those who wanted to strengthen the then ruling Olive Tree coalition. A step towards the latter objective occurred in May when an Olive Tree committee was established which comprised the leaders of all the member parties, five mayors and two regional presidents.

One new political party appeared on the scene, namely the Democratic Union for the Republic (UDR). Founded by former President Francesco

Cossiga in February, the UDR drew in moderates and former Christian Democrats hostile both to Signor Berlusconi and to the Olive Tree. Its parliamentary group was made up of refugees from both right and centre-left blocs. The UDR's aim was to regroup the centre and, in the medium if not the short term, to replace the PL as the main alternative to the left.

Comparatively few electoral tests occurred during the year. But the outcome of those which did was not very comforting for the government. In local elections in May and June the PL made gains in the north-east, Sicily and Sardinia, while the centre-left lost control of Parma, Piacenza and other cities. In December, on a low poll, it lost the presidency of the province of Rome. Only Friuli saw the DS gain, although no centre-left majority resulted. Commentators took these results as a sign of the failure of the Olive Tree to develop a programme of action which went beyond the struggle for admission to the new euro. In education, health, employment and other areas, no major initiative had been undertaken.

The government endeavoured to answer some of these points in its economic and financial planning document, which was also seen as an opportunity to bind the RC into pledging strategic support for the ruling coalition. In April a draft was published which presented a three-year plan for continuing rigour, restitution of the 'euro-tax' and no tax increases, further privatization and measures to promote employment. Eventually the RC gave its approval to the document when a plan was included to create 600,000 jobs in two years.

It proved much more difficult to win RC backing for the Finance Bill. The RC leader, Fausto Bertinotti, demanded a radical policy turn to tackle injustice through increased public investments. Despite the promise of an extra Lit.1,200,000 million on social spending, he still withheld support. When Professor Prodi refused further concessions, and it became clear that Italy's first left-oriented administration since 1945 could fall, 22 RC deputies broke away and supported the government. Nevertheless, the government was defeated on a confidence motion on 9 October by 313 votes to 312. Thus, after 875 days, the curtain fell on the Olive Tree administration, the 55th and second-longest government of the post-war period.

When it became clear that the UDR would support a new administration that was not headed by Professor Prodi (who symbolized the Olive Tree), the task of forming it fell to Signor D'Alema. The first former Communist to become Prime Minister, and the first professional politician since 1992 to hold the office, Signor D'Alema headed a centre-left government that included both the 'Italian Communists' (the name adopted by those who had split from RC) and the centrist UDR, as well as the Italian Popular Party, the Italian Renewal Party and other component of the Olive Tree coalition. The new administration possessed certain advantages compared with its predecessor. In the first place, it could rely on a parliamentary majority and was not subject to the blackmail of the RC;

second, it was headed by a highly astute politician well used to mediating between different forces; third, it was no longer obliged to subordinate all to the exigencies of EU monetary union; and fourth, it was broadly in line politically with the social democratic orientation of other major European governments.

Signor D'Alema retained the key ministers of the Prodi administration, but there were a few significant modifications. Giuliano Amato, Prime Minister in 1992–93, became Minister for Reforms—an indication that, following the failure of the bicameral commission, the new government intended to tackle constitutional reform. In addition, the popular mayor of Naples, Antonio Bassolino, became Labour Minister and was given responsibility for dealing with the issue of unemployment in southern Italy.

At the end of the year the government achieved a notable success when it succeeded in winning the approval of the unions and employers for a 'social pact' to encourage investment and promote equitable growth. In essence, the pact was a continuation of the similar accord reached in July 1993. Under the terms of the new agreement, industrial behaviour was regulated with the aim of lowering inflation and maximizing investment. The government provided incentives to establish youth training schemes and promised new public works. It also pledged to reduce the red tape involved in setting up new businesses and to increase social spending in line with growth in the economy. The new government succeeded in winning back the confidence of industry after the clash over the 35-hour week, but it was not able to deliver abolition of the split level of negotiation for workers' contracts (national and company). The unions also refused to countenance any discussion of labour market 'flexibility'. Interpretations of the pact differed, but most of the parties involved saw it as an essential condition for the relaunch of the economy.

Three foreign policy issues arose during the year. First, the problem of illegal immigration came to a head. As the main source, Albania presented a major concern. In August Italy intervened heavily in that country's turbulent internal situation to prevent it from degenerating into civil war (see III.2.i). In November an agreement was reached with the Albanian Prime Minister to combat the organized crime syndicates that were responsible for the flux of immigrants. In August an accord was also reached with Tunisia under which development aid was to be paid in return for cooperation in preventing clandestine migration. In spite of these moves, the sheer numbers of immigrants seeking to regularize their position in Italy escalated beyond the quotas set earlier in the year. As a result, Italy earned disapproval in Europe for what appeared to be a soft line on immigration.

Relations with Turkey became badly strained when the exiled Kurdish leader, Abdullah Öcalan, arrived in Rome in November, requested political asylum and was arrested on a German warrant (see II.4.vii). When

Chancellor Schröder declined to apply for his extradition, Italy was pressured to send him to Turkey, where he was wanted on terrorism charges. The government refused, on human rights grounds, and found itself at the centre of a controversy which remained unresolved at year's end.

The US-UK bombing of Iraq in December led to the government voicing cautious criticism of the United States. Throughout the year Italy had sought to promote a peaceful solution and had shown reluctance to allow the use of NATO airbases in Italy for air-strikes on Iraq. The RC and the Greens had dissented from then Prime Minister Prodi's cautious approval of the US raids on terrorist bases in Sudan and Afghanistan in August, threatening to vote against the government if it cooperated with the United States over Iraq. When the US-UK assault occurred in December, however, the government adopted a view of respectful dissent that stopped short of condemnation. While the right-wing opposition expressed support for the bombing, the government requested that the United Nations be restored to a central role.

iv. BELGIUM

CAPITAL: Brussels   AREA: 30,500 sq km   POPULATION: 10,154,000 ('97)
OFFICIAL LANGUAGES: French, Flemish & German
POLITICAL SYSTEM: federal parliamentary democracy based on language communities
HEAD OF STATE: King Albert II (since Aug '93)
RULING PARTIES: Christian People's Party (CVP/Flemish), Christian Social Party (PSC/Walloon), Socialist Party (SP/Flemish) & Socialist Party (PS/Walloon)
HEAD OF GOVERNMENT: Jean-Luc Dehaene (CVP), Prime Minister (since March '92)
MAIN IGO MEMBERSHIPS (non-UN): NATO, EU, WEU, Benelux, OSCE, CE, OECD, Francophonie
CURRENCY: Belgian franc (end-'98 £1=BF57.16, US$1=BF34.35)
GNP PER CAPITA: US$26,420 by exchange-rate calculation, US$22,370 by PPP calculation ('97)

THE coalition of Christian Democrats and Socialists, both French- and Flemish-speaking, continued in office, although in 1999 it faced not only an election for the Chamber of Deputies but also elections for the Senate, the regions and the European Parliament. Tension between the fairly advanced and high-tech economy of Flanders and the more depressed French-speaking Wallonia, and the linguistic divide between them, remained a running sore within the country. However, the real shock to the political system in 1998 came from the Dutroux paedophile scandal, which combined with other issues to throw into doubt the integrity of the Belgian state and its political class as a whole.

The grisly discovery in August 1996 of the bodies of victims of suspected paedophile Marc Dutroux (see AR 1996, p. 55) had caused a frenzy of speculation in the Belgian press about a much wider and perhaps highly-placed ring (see AR 1997, pp. 61–2). The authorities investigating the case were accused by a committee of the Chamber of Deputies of 'amateurism and incompetence'. What made matters worse was the brief escape in April of Dutroux himself. The Justice and Interior Ministers were obliged to resign, although the government of Jean-Luc Dehaene survived a vote of confidence in the Chamber by 81 votes to 64.

Following the vote of confidence, the government announced the speeding-up of plans to restructure the police and judiciary. The ruling coalition and four opposition parties agreed to work together in the so-called 'octopus agreement', thus ensuring the necessary two-thirds majority to amend the constitution (eventually achieved on 22 October). The reforms included the creation of a federal prosecutor's office to carry out nationwide investigations of serious offences. There would also be a new Supreme Council of Justice to supervise the work of the judiciary, including nominations to posts, which had long been bedevilled by the issue of political affiliation. The restructuring of the police was intended to remedy the existing situation where different branches (judicial police, gendarmerie, local police) worked alongside each other while being responsible to different ministers.

There were other law and order issues. The mysterious murder in 1991 of former Socialist Deputy Prime Minister André Cools came back into the news on 3 June when two Tunisian nationals were found guilty by a Belgian Court of the assassination and sentenced to 25 years in prison. However, it was apparent that they were hired killers, and it remained unclear who gave the orders and why. The arrest in April of members of the Armed Islamic Group (GIA) was welcomed by the Algerian government, which had accused Belgium of providing a base for terrorists. Even the Catholic Church was not immune from the general crisis of confidence, being ordered in April to pay damages in respect of a priest convicted of paedophile acts.

On 19 June there was a further government change, when Philip Maystadt became head of the Walloon Christian Social Party (PSC) and was replaced as Finance Minister by Jean-Jacques Viseur. Jean-Pol Poncelet (PSC) stayed on as Minister of Defence but took over M. Maystadt's role as a Deputy Prime Minister, whilst another Deputy Prime Minister, Elio de Rupo, took over M. Maystadt's foreign trade portfolio.

At the end of April the government introduced an employment action plan entitled 'Invest in Work' and setting out a range of innovative measures aimed especially at youth unemployment (running at over 20 per cent among under-25s). The plan was also designed to tackle the problem of Belgium's high labour costs and their adverse impact on job creation. The Employment Minister, Miet Smet, said that over six years the social security contributions paid by employers would be reduced by BF108,000 million, bringing Belgium into line with neighbouring countries.

A UK-Belgium gas pipeline became operational between Bacton in Norfolk and Zeebrugge in Belgium. It was designed to transmit up to

20,000 million cubic metres of natural gas a year into the continental gas grid and 9 million in the reverse direction. The Belgian company Distrigas, the second largest international transit gas carrier in the European Union, aimed to enhance the role of Zeebrugge as a gas transit hub. Work was in progress on a 300-kilometre pipeline from Zeebrugge to the German border, with a branch to the Netherlands.

On 9 July the European Court of Justice condemned Belgium for failing to change its constitution to allow residents of other EU countries to vote in local elections. The failure was an obvious result of fears that foreigners might upset the political balance between Flemish and French speakers in certain areas.

Along with Italy, Belgium was ostensibly furthest of the 11 EU countries countries participating in the euro from meeting the criteria laid down by the Maastricht Treaty concerning public debt, which was estimated at 118.1 per cent of GDP in 1998 as against the 60 per cent permissible, though it was scheduled to fall to 114.2 per cent in 1999. Nevertheless, to fairly general public approval, Belgium became part of the single currency at the end of 1998, with one euro fixed at 40.34 Belgian francs (see XI.4).

v. THE NETHERLANDS

CAPITAL: Amsterdam   AREA: 37,000 sq km   POPULATION: 16,000,000 ('97)
OFFICIAL LANGUAGE: Dutch
POLITICAL SYSTEM: parliamentary democracy
HEAD OF STATE: Queen Beatrix (since April '80)
RULING PARTIES: Labour Party (PvdA), People's Party for Freedom and Democracy (VVD) & Democrats 66 (D66)
HEAD OF GOVERNMENT: Wim Kok (PvdA), Prime Minister (since Aug '94)
MAIN IGO MEMBERSHIPS (non-UN): NATO, EU, WEU, Benelux, OSCE, CE, OECD
CURRENCY: guilder (end-'98 £1=f3.12, US$1=f1.88)
GNP PER CAPITA: US$25,820 by exchange-rate calculation, US$21,340 by PPP calculation ('97)

THE three-party coalition formed in August 1994 came successfully through the parliamentary elections held on 6 May. Local elections held on 4 March had shown little change in the position of two of the coalition partners, the Labour Party (PvdA) and the right-wing liberal People's Party for Freedom and Democracy (VVD), but had produced big losses for the third partner, the centre-left Democrats 66 (D66). In the general election, however, the PvdA strongly improved its position, winning 45 of the 150 seats (a gain of eight) and 5 per cent more of the vote. The VVD also gained eight seats to win 38, but the fall in support for D66 was confirmed, reducing the party from 24 to 14 seats and 9.0 per cent of the vote.

The opposition Christian Democratic Appeal (CDA), which had held firm in the local elections, continued its decline at the national level by falling from 34 to 29 seats. In contrast, the smaller left-wing parties managed to increase their aggregate representation, including the ably-led and 'Euro-sceptic' Green Left, which rose from five to 11 seats.

Led again by Wim Kok (PvdA), the new cabinet included six PvdA, six VVD and three D66 members, plus two ministers plenipotentiary for Aruba and the Netherlands Antilles. Four of the appointments were women. Jozias van Aartsen remained at the Foreign Ministry, with added responsibilities. The special concerns of the government were reflected in the new appointment of a Minister for Urban Policy and Integration of Ethnic Minorities.

In the government programme presented in August, European integration was given first spot, followed by a long section on public safety, crime and the rule of law. Other elements included health, the environment and social cohesion (especially as affecting the young), and there was strong stress on urban regeneration.

The main issue facing the Netherlands was European economic and monetary union (EMU). A poll early in the year showed a 51 per cent majority against participation in the single currency, but its eventual introduction at the turn of the year was welcomed by 68 per cent. By then Dutchman Wim Duisenberg had been confirmed as president of the new European Central Bank, albeit on the basis of a messy compromise with the French over the time he would serve (see XI.4). On the more general EMU issue, there had been CDA criticism of Finance Minister Gerrit Zalm (VVD) for taking too relaxed an attitude to the reduction of budget deficits. The government had responded that planned additional social expenditure would leave the budget deficit well within the limits specified at Maastricht.

A focus of increasing attention in the Netherlands was the country's large net contribution to the EU budget. This was especially important because of the government's support for eastward enlargement of the EU and its call for firm control of EU expenditure, together with a mechanism to correct budgetary imbalances. At the same time, the Finance Minister had adopted a more active policy in seeking EU funds for the Netherlands, especially for the inner cities and the pig industry, which had been ravaged by a serious outbreak of swine fever accompanied by a massive slaughter programme.

Among the political surprises of the year was the appointment of H.H.F. Wijffels, a Christian Democrat and former banker, to the presidency of the Social and Economic Council. There was a small stir in October when the National Court of Audit rebuked Prime Minister Kok, Finance Minister Zalm and Central Bank president Nout Wellink for their unauthorized spending of $50 million of the bank's 1998 profits on acquiring an abstract painting by Piet Mondrian and other works. The paintings were donated to a Dutch museum.

The reduction in public debt from 72.1 per cent in 1997 to a projected 67.7 per cent in 1999 was regarded as acceptable in terms of the 60 per cent criterion laid down in the Maastrich Treaty for joining the single currency. Thus the Netherlands became part of the 'Euro-11' zone at the end of 1998, with the rate against the guilder being fixed at 2.20. Unemployment appeared to be on a downward trend, from 5.2 per cent in 1997, to 3.7 per cent in the last quarter of 1998, although it remained much higher for the under-25s. Although higher than in the other Benelux countries, inflation remained modest at an estimated 2.3 per cent for 1998. In the index of purchasing power per head, the Netherlands stood at 105 against an EU average of 100.

vi. LUXEMBOURG

CAPITAL: Luxembourg   AREA: 3,000 sq km   POPULATION: 422,000 ('97)
OFFICIAL LANGUAGE: Letzeburgish
POLITICAL SYSTEM: parliamentary democracy
HEAD OF STATE: Grand Duke Jean (since Nov '64)
RULING PARTIES: Christian Social People's Party (PCS) & Luxembourg Socialist Workers' Party (LSAP)
HEAD OF GOVERNMENT: Jean-Claude Juncker (PCS), Prime Minister (since Jan '95)
MAIN IGO MEMBERSHIPS (non-UN): NATO, EU, WEU, Benelux, OSCE, CE, OECD, Francophonie
CURRENCY: Luxembourg franc (end-'98 £1=LF57.16, US$1=LF34.35)
GNP PER CAPITA: US$45,330 by exchange-rate calculation, US$34,460 by PPP calculation ('97)

THE beginning of 1998 was marked by a scandal concerning false invoices at the Ministry of Health. Johnny Lahure, the minister, was forced to resign on 22 January and was replaced by fellow Socialist Georges Wolfahrt, whose role as State Secretary for Foreign Affairs was surprisingly taken by Lydie Err, a lawyer. At the same time, Marc Fischbach (Christian Social) resigned as Minister of Justice to become a judge at the European Court of Justice and was replaced by Luc Frieden.

Following the European Union (EU) 'employment summit' in Luxembourg in November 1997 (see AR 1997, pp. 407–8), in April the government presented proposals for combating unemployment focusing on the long-term and young unemployed. The programme would cost LF1,600-2,000 million, of which LF750 million would be financed by a one franc per litre increase in the price of petrol. The measures would be implemented over 18 months rather than the five years envisaged by the EU summit.

The achievement of the single European currency was of tremendous importance to Luxembourg, being given symbolic form when European Commission president Jacques Santer presented another former Luxembourg Prime Minister, Pierre Werner, with the first copy of the EU's *Official Journal* of 31 December 1998 listing the fixed euro exchange rates. It was nearly 25 years since Mr Werner's own report had called for economic and monetary union by 1980, a project thwarted partly by the oil shock of 1973.

Of the 11 countries joining the euro zone, Luxembourg met the necessary economic indicators far better than any other participant. Luxembourg enjoyed the lowest accumulated public debt of all EU countries, estimated at 7.1 per cent of GDP in 1998, compared with the Maastricht Treaty qualification of 60 per cent. Unemployment in 1998 averaged 2.8 per cent of the labour force, but was three times higher among the under-25s. Price inflation in 1998 was put at 1.6 per cent and forecast at 1.7 per cent for 1999. A survey by Eurostat showed that among EU countries the gap between the highest and lowest paid workers was highest in Italy and Luxembourg.

In April Grand Duke Jean bestowed considerable constitutional powers on his son and heir, Prince Henri, 42, in what was seen as a preparation for the latter's accession to the throne. He was empowered to deputize for his father in all official capacities, including receiving foreign ambassadors and signing legislation.

vii. REPUBLIC OF IRELAND

CAPITAL: Dublin   AREA: 70,280 sq km   POPULATION: 3,700,000 ('98)
OFFICIAL LANGUAGES: Irish & English
POLITICAL SYSTEM: parliamentary democracy
HEAD OF STATE: President Mary McAleese (since Nov '97)
RULING PARTIES: coalition of Fianna Fáil (FF) & Progressive Democrats (PD)
HEAD OF GOVERNMENT: Bertie Ahern (FF), Prime Minister/Taoiseach (since June '97)
MAIN IGO MEMBERSHIPS (non-UN): EU, OSCE, CE, OECD
CURRENCY: punt (end-'98 £1=IR£1.16, US$1=IR£0.67)
GNP PER CAPITA: US$18,280 by exchange-rate calculation, US$16,740 by PPP calculation ('97)

RECONCILIATION and prosperity were the dominant themes of the year. The intensive joint involvement of the Taoiseach (Prime Minister), Bertie Ahern, and his British counterpart, Tony Blair, in the negotiations preceding the Good Friday Agreement on Northern Ireland (see II.1.iv; XVII.1), and in the subsequent repeated efforts to surmount the difficulties of implementation, marked the highest point reached in sustained collaboration between the Dublin and London governments since the establishment of the independent Irish state in 1922.

The endorsement of the agreement by a massive majority in the Republic as well as Northern Ireland at referendums held on 22 May confirmed the consensus long felt to exist, but until then unproven, between the people in both parts of Ireland on the need for a settlement incorporating a compromise between nationalist and unionist views on the Northern question. The vote in the Republic in favour of the Agreement was 94.5 per cent but there was some disappointment in the fact that only 55.6 per cent of the electorate chose to vote by comparison with 81.1 per cent in Northern Ireland. The major concession made by the Republic was dropping the claim in its constitution to jurisdiction over Northern Ireland.

The constitution was amended to acknowledge *inter alia* that, while it was the 'firm will of the Irish nation... to unite all the people who share... the island', it was recognized 'that a united Ireland shall be brought about only by peaceful means with the consent of a majority of the people, democratically expressed, in both jurisdictions'. The *quid pro quo* for this effective recognition of Northern Ireland as part of the United Kingdom and substitution of an aspirational statement for the previous assertive claim was the British (and unionist) acceptance of the right of Northern people to Irish citizenship if they should choose it and the Republic's right to participate in the affairs of Northern Ireland through the establishment of institutions 'with executive powers and functions' shared between the two jurisdictions. The number and scope of these institutions, together with the problems of paramilitary decommissioning and the formation of a Northern executive, were to occupy much of the later months of the year, but across the entire agenda the two Prime Ministers continued to cooperate with every appearance of harmony in endeavouring to persuade the Northern parties to find common ground.

Other events reflecting newly harmonious relations included reaction to the Omagh bombing on 15 August. The Irish President, Mary McAleese, went immediately to the stricken town to express solidarity with the victims' families, and the Northern Ireland first minister, David Trimble attended a Roman Catholic funeral service in the Republic for those killed who had been visiting Omagh from across the border. A remarkable sign of reconciliation between the Republic and Great Britain was the attendance of the Irish President at the Armistice Day commemorations in Belgium together with Queen Elizabeth II and King Albert II of the Belgians. The three heads of state, as well as units from the armies of each country, joined in the dedication of a memorial to the thousands of soldiers from Ireland, South and North, who had died as British servicemen in the battle of Messines Ridge in 1917. It was the first occasion ever, in the 76 years of Irish independence, that the nationalist state specifically acknowledged the considerable Irish involvement in World War I. The memorial, in the form of a Celtic 'round tower', had been built by volunteer workers from both parts of Ireland on the initiative of two former politicians, Paddy Harte who had been a junior minister in the Irish government, and Glenn Barr who had once been an influential spokesman for loyalist paramilitaries in the North. A further happening, equally inconceivable in past, was the address by the British Prime Minister on 26 November to a joint session of the houses of the Irish parliament. In a country as susceptible to symbolism as Ireland, these gestures carried much greater social and political significance than might have been apparent elsewhere, even in Britain. They signalled the retirement of long-hardened traditional attitudes.

Notwithstanding the international apprehension arising from the collapse of Asian economies, the economic improvement of recent years in the Republic continued at a near hectic rate. The Commission of the European Union (EU) towards the end of October predicted growth in Ireland of 11.4 per cent for the year (by comparison with a 3 per cent average for the EU as a whole), and it foresaw further growth of 8.4 per cent in 1999 and of 9 per cent in 2000. The long-feared inflation seemed to be showing itself in the form of a 3 per cent rate at mid-summer, up from 1.5 per cent 12 months earlier, but had begun to slip back at year's end despite record spending in the Christmas season. Among the signs of prosperity were a fall in unemployment to 7.8 per cent (against an EU average of 10.2 per cent), while immigration by Irish people returning to take up employment at home helped to boost the population to 3.7 million, the highest figure for the 26 counties now constituting the Republic since 1881. The leading growth sectors providing new jobs were the construction and computer industries: in 1998 the Republic was the second largest exporter of software after the United States.

Interestingly, the government went to some lengths to cast doubts on what it considered to be overly optimistic assessments of the Irish situation. The EU, according to Finance Minister Charlie McCreevey, had failed to allow for the likely effect in Ireland of deteriorating economic conditions abroad. Two factors combined to influence government caution. Constant talk of prosperity was stimulating wage demands in the public service, and the EU Commission was beginning to look on Ireland as a wealthy country which would no longer qualify for regional aid on the scale it had so far enjoyed. In his December budget, however, Mr McCreevey was able to allow significant concessions to the lower paid, removing the liability for income tax from substantial numbers of them entirely, which with other reforms promised greatly to facilitate the achievement of a moderate national wage agreement in 1999—thus continuing an important element in the strategy underlying the current prosperity (see AR 1997, p. 66).

A referendum to approve ratification of the Amsterdam Treaty (see XI.4) took place on the same day as the poll on Northern Ireland and caused momentary alarm when only 62 per cent voted in favour. This was much the lowest support recorded for a major EU proposal since the Republic became a member in 1973. However, most commentators agreed that the outcome represented less a decline in popular backing for the EU than a rebuke to the government and opposition alike, who had failed adequately to explain the implications of the complex treaty, acceptance of which they had recommended. The people were seen, not for the first time, to have served a sharp reminder on the political establishment that their opinions were not to be presumed upon. A survey sponsored by the *Irish Times* later found substantial satisfaction with the EU and its institutions.

As if in confirmation, the approach of economic and monetary union (EMU) with ten other EU member states at the end of the year was awaited with remarkable equanimity despite the decision of the United Kingdom, still the Republic's biggest trading partner, to remain outside the system for the time being. Criticism of the long-heralded development, which would mean loss of Irish control over much of Irish economic policy, remained confined to some academic economists, journalists and a small lobby group which had won little public support for its anti-EU stance down the years. In conformity with all but one of its EMU partners, the Republic adopted interest rates of 3 per cent at the beginning of December. At midnight on 31 December the exchange rate of the punt against the euro became irrevocably fixed at 0.787564, pending final elimination of the Irish and other national currencies in mid-2002.

The tribunals set up to investigate financial matters relating to certain politicians (see AR 1997, p. 68) were slowed down by applications to the courts but remained sufficiently in the news to keep alive public suspicion over links between politics and business. Concern spread wider when allegations of tax evasion, supposedly involving the operation of 'non-resident' accounts in fictitious names by the country's largest bank (Allied Irish Banks) seven years earlier, led to contradictory statements by the bank and the revenue authorities at hearings before the parliamentary committee of public accounts.

Anxiety was also expressed at what some believed to be incipient racism in demands for government action to curb an influx into Ireland of refugees from Africa and the former Soviet bloc. Human rights activists, meanwhile, charged the government with providing insufficient care for the refugees, especially those seeking political asylum. Complaints continued that the benefits of economic buoyancy were not being passed on to the chronically poor—the homeless, the long-term unemployed. Elements of cynicism and idealism thus combined to modify any excess of euphoria generated by Ireland's new-found prosperity.

3. DENMARK—ICELAND—NORWAY—SWEDEN—FINLAND—AUSTRIA—
SWITZERLAND—EUROPEAN MINI-STATES

i. DENMARK

CAPITAL: Copenhagen   AREA: 43,000 sq km   POPULATION: 5,250,000 ('97)
OFFICIAL LANGUAGE: Danish
POLITICAL SYSTEM: parliamentary democracy
HEAD OF STATE: Queen Margrethe II (since Jan '72)
RULING PARTIES: coalition of Social Democrats (SD) & Radical Liberals (RV)
HEAD OF GOVERNMENT: Poul Nyrup Rasmussen (SD), Prime Minister (since Jan '93)
MAIN IGO MEMBERSHIPS (non-UN): NATO, EU, NC, CBSS, AC, OSCE, CE, OECD
CURRENCY: krone (end-'98 £1=DKr10.59, US$1=DKr6.36)
GNP PER CAPITA: US$32,500 by exchange-rate calculation, US$22,740 by PPP calculation
   ('95)

THE gamble of Prime Minister Poul Nyrup Rasmussen in bringing forward parliamentary elections to 11 March paid off, as the ruling coalition secured re-election and a one-seat majority in the 179-member Folketing. Opinion polls had suggested a narrow victory for the six-party centre-right opposition led by Uffe Ellemann-Jensen. Whilst the Liberals narrowly increased their representation, the election was a disaster for the Conservatives, who lost 10 seats. Mr Ellemann-Jensen subsequently resigned as chairman of the Liberal Party (*Venstre*), to be replaced by Anders Fogh Rasmussen.

In announcing the election, Mr Nyrup Rasmussen stressed the need to avoid undue political speculation in the run-up to the 28 May referendum on the European Union's Amsterdam Treaty (see AR 1997, p. 69). In reality, the pro-Amsterdam stance of the mainstream parties ensured that the campaign was fought mainly on economic issues. Here the government pointed to its impressive record of growth and falling unemployment, whilst promising improvements in welfare provision. The opposition made tax cuts the centre-piece of its programme.

Ultimately, the election hinged upon results in the Faroe Islands, where a candidate allied to the opposition lost his seat by a margin of 100 votes. The outcome was made uncomfortable by Faroese demands for compensation from the Danish government and Den Danske Bank (DDB) for their part in the sale of Faroya Bank to the islands' government in 1993. The Faroes were later obliged to bale out the bank, which, it transpired, had many bad loans on its books. Whilst Mr Nyrup Rasmussen was quick to pin the blame on DDB, the Faroese Social Democrat elected to the Folketing indicated that his support for the ruling coalition would depend upon a 'fair and just' solution to the bank affair. Meanwhile, the new Faroese government, elected in April, declared itself in favour of full independence from Denmark.

As the May referendum loomed, the government was boosted by the decision of the Supreme Court to reject the legal challenge to the Maastricht Treaty brought by anti-EU activists (see AR 1997, p. 70). A month later the Amsterdam Treaty was approved by a margin of 57 to 43 per cent, despite the strong 'no' campaign mounted by extreme left and right alike. Tensions over the poll were heightened by a two-week national strike which began when union members rejected a wage deal in late April. In the worst bout of industrial action since the mid-1980's, over half a million workers walked out, bringing transport to a halt and seriously disrupting the export sector. The final government-imposed settlement—providing for an average 4 per cent wage increase—merely fuelled fears of an overheating economy. The government responded by increasing taxes on fuel and energy, whilst simultaneously cutting mortgage relief and corporation tax. These unpopular measures were compounded by welfare cuts in a 1999 budget dedicated to further reducing the national debt. The trade unions were particularly incensed by proposals to restrict entitlement to early retirement, and polls taken in November showed that support for the Social Democrats had fallen by nearly 10 per cent since the election. The government faced further discomfiture over the opt-out from EU economic and monetary union (EMU) approved in the May referendum. The official policy of 'shadowing' the ecu/euro within a narrow band was thrown into question by financial market speculation against the krone during the autumn. A poll conducted in October showed a narrow majority in favour of joining EMU. Whilst the Prime Minister stuck to his 'wait and see' policy of holding a referendum in 2002, his Liberal namesake insisted that the poll should be brought forward by a year.

In February, Denmark became the first NATO member to ratify the admission of the Czech Republic, Poland and Hungary, highlighting its continued strong support for expansion of the alliance to Central and Eastern Europe. Another notable international event during the year was the June opening of the suspension bridge between the Jutland peninsula and Zealand—Europe's longest—carrying road and rail traffic across the Great Belt straits.

ii. ICELAND

CAPITAL: Reykjavík   AREA: 103,000 sq km   POPULATION: 272,000 ('97)
OFFICIAL LANGUAGE: Icelandic
POLITICAL SYSTEM: parliamentary democracy
HEAD OF STATE: President Ólafur Ragnar Grímsson (since Aug '96)
RULING PARTIES: Independence (IP) & Progressive (PP) parties
HEAD OF GOVERNMENT: David Oddsson (IP), Prime Minister (since April '91)
MAIN IGO MEMBERSHIPS (non-UN): NATO, EFTA/EEA, NC, OSCE, CE, OECD
CURRENCY: króna (end-'98 £1=ISkr115.33, US1=Isk69.32)
GNP PER CAPITA: US$27,580 by exchange-rate calculation, US$22,500 by PPP calculation
   ('97)

WITH parliamentary elections scheduled for spring 1999, the fortunes of Davíd Oddsson's centre-right government remained buoyant at the end of the year. Opinion polls showed support for the ruling parties running at nearly 70 per cent, as opposed to 20 per cent for the United Left opposition. Cooperation between the Social Democrats, the Women's Alliance and the far-left People's Alliance (PA) got off to a difficult start in October, as several members of the PA rejected the joint platform and departed to form their own 'left-green' party.

The government's popularity rested on continued economic growth and low unemployment and inflation. A predicted trade deficit of $750 million did little to dispel fears of overheating (see AR 1997, p. 70), yet the government continued its quest to diversify the economy and attract inward investment. The inauguration of Iceland Herring Ltd during July was an important step towards ending state involvement in the export trade, but plans to transform Iceland into a major offshore banking centre were set back after the government decided to postpone the sale of two state-run banks until after the elections.

Intense discussion surrounded the activities of the biotechnology firm deCode Genetics and the proposal to create a centralized database of health records for use by the company. The genetic homogeneity of Iceland's population, it was argued, offered unparalleled opportunities for research into common cardiovascular, psychiatric and metabolic diseases. To this end, deCode concluded a five-year deal with the Swiss pharmaceutical company Roche at the start of the year. The database proposal was not without its critics, who regarded the scheme as a dangerous breach of individual rights. Yet surveys revealed majority support for the research, described by President Ólafur Ragnar Grímsson as the most important task undertaken by Icelanders since settlement of the island.

Plans to generate further hydroelectric power—also integral to the quest for overseas investment—proved no less controversial, attracting powerful opposition from local authorities and environmental groups anxious to protect the country's central highlands.

The government expressed its satisfaction with the new Schengen Accord arrangements giving Iceland and Norway joint representation with the participating European Union (EU) states in all decision-making short of the ministerial level (see II.3.iii). Holding the chairmanship of EFTA from January to June, Iceland continued to exert pressure for reform of the EU common fisheries policy—still the most potent barrier to full Icelandic EU membership—whilst beginning negotiations on a free trade agreement with Canada. Negotiations with Greenland and Norway on a new capelin treaty finally bore fruit during May. The year was also notable for the accent placed upon relations between the 'West Nordic' troika of Iceland, Greenland and the Faroe Islands, whose leaders met in Reykjavík during October. The Prime Minister promised to emphasize this connection during Iceland's 1999 presidency of the Nordic Council.

iii. NORWAY

CAPITAL: Oslo   AREA: 324,000 sq km   POPULATION: 4,500,000 ('97)
OFFICIAL LANGUAGE: Norwegian
POLITICAL SYSTEM: parliamentary democracy
HEAD OF STATE: King Harald V (since Jan '91)
RULING PARTIES: Christian People's Party (KrF) heads minority coalition with Centre and Liberal parties
HEAD OF GOVERNMENT: Kjell Magne Bondevik (KrF), Prime Minister (since Sept '97)
MAIN IGO MEMBERSHIPS (non-UN): NATO, EFTA/EEA, NC, CBSS, AC, OSCE, CE, OECD
CURRENCY: krone (end-'98 £1=NKr12.68, US$1=NKr7.62)
GNP PER CAPITA: US$36,090 by exchange-rate calculation, US$23,940 by PPP calculation ('97)

THE strain of running the weakest minority government in Norway's history began to tell on Kjell Magne Bondevik during August, as the Prime Minister was forced to take two weeks' sick leave. The 'depressive reaction' which he suffered coincided with the nadir of the centrist government's fortunes during a year which had begun promisingly. Eschewing traditional political divisions of left and right, the coalition of Christian Democrats, Centrists and Liberals had signalled its readiness to cooperate with all parties in the Storting, apparently safe in the knowledge that anyone who attempted to unseat it would immediately have to seek the support of the centrist parties to establish an alternative government. However, Mr Bondevik's initially high approval ratings quickly evaporated amidst real fears of economic overheating.

In producing a fiscally expansive budget for 1998, the government had banked on continued moderation during the annual wage negotiations in April-May. In fact, state-sector unions were able to obtain sizeable increases for members who had long lagged behind wage-earners in the private sector. Pay rises averaging 6 per cent brought predictions of inflation, declining competitiveness and renewed unemployment. The value of the stock market and the krone were also hit by declining oil prices and financial turmoil in Russia and the Far East. Interest rates rose by 3.5 per cent during March-August as the government struggled to obtain Storting approval for its planned austerity measures. Amendments to the 1998 budget proposal were only passed after the issue was made a vote of confidence in the government.

In return for cooperation on the 1999 budget, the Labour party demanded that the government abandon its flagship reform of child benefit passed with the support of the right-wing parties the previous autumn (see AR 1997, p. 73). The right-wing parties for their part were reluctant to sanction any further increases in taxation. In a significant about-turn, Labour then signalled its willingness to form a new coalition government with the Conservatives. This move provoked the Centre Party—the most radical of the ruling formations—to such an extent that the government eventually bowed to right-wing demands over the budget. Short-term survival was thus ensured, but the future of the Bondevik coalition remained uncertain at the end of the year.

A satisfactory renegotiation of the Schengen Accord (see AR 1997, p. 73) appeared close after the European Union (EU) agreed on Norwegian and Icelandic participation in a new 'mixed committee' to discuss political issues connected with the agreement. The government's cause was helped by the decision of Anne Enger Lahnstein's 'Euro-sceptic' Centre Party to abandon its previous opposition to the agreement. Ms Lahnstein, often regarded as the architect of Norway's 'no' to the EU in 1994, later resigned as Centre Party leader during December. In January, Foreign Minister Knut Vollebæk called for renewed debate on the EU in the light of the new challenges posed by current European developments. His sentiments were later echoed by Labour, which suggested a new referendum on membership following the EU's projected admission of new members from Central-East Europe. Opinion polls, however, suggested that public support remained lukewarm towards the proposal.

In March the government expelled two diplomats from the Russian embassy, whilst declaring three other officials based in Russia to be *personae non gratae*. The five had allegedly attempted to recruit Norwegians to spy for Russian intelligence. Their activities were exposed by Svein Lamark, an employee in the Ministry of Local Government, who for years had worked as a Norwegian Police Security Service (POT) double agent. Mr Lamark subsequently embarrassed his bosses by revealing his identity through a national newspaper. Among other things, he claimed that the spy affair was timed to coincide with the conclusion of a government investigation into POT's operations. The Danielsen Committee had been established by the previous government following revelations in 1996 that POT had illegally registered Norwegian citizens on political grounds. Its final report in April called for greater scrutiny and political control over POT's activities.

The spying scandal—which foreshadowed a similar case in Finland later in the year (see II.3.v)—led to the tit-for-tat expulsion of two Norwegian diplomats resident in Moscow. Ultimately, however, the affair proved to be little more than a temporary glitch in Norwegian-Russian relations. A visit by King Harald and Queen Sonja to Moscow during May was used by officials to advance proposals for new, groundbreaking cooperation on nuclear safety.

iv. SWEDEN

CAPITAL: Stockholm   AREA: 450,000 sq km   POPULATION: 9,000,000 ('97)
OFFICIAL LANGUAGE: Swedish
POLITICAL SYSTEM: parliamentary democracy
HEAD OF STATE: King Carl XVI Gustav (since Sept '73)
RULING PARTY: Social Democratic Labour Party
HEAD OF GOVERNMENT: Göran Persson, Prime Minister (since March '96)
MAIN IGO MEMBERSHIPS (non-UN): EU, NC, CBSS, AC, PFP, OSCE, CE, OECD
CURRENCY: krona (end-'98 £1=SKr13.49, US$1=SKr8.12)
GNP PER CAPITA: US$26,220 by exchange-rate calculation, US$19,030 by PPP calculation ('97)

LIKE its Norwegian counterpart a year before, the ruling Social Democratic Labour Party (SAP) registered its worst performance for 70 years in September's Riksdag elections. Whilst the SAP remained the largest party by a comfortable margin, its share of the vote declined by 8 per cent compared with the last elections in 1994. The result reflected widespread discontent at fiscal austerity and the perceived failure by the government to get to grips with unemployment. In official terms, the number out of work (6.4 per cent) was almost 2 per cent down on the previous year. Yet this decline was attributed mainly to new government-funded retraining programmes (*kunskapslyftet*), whose participants were excluded from unemployment statistics. Critics of the scheme continued to maintain that unemployment would be better tackled through deregulation of the labour market.

In the wake of the elections, Prime Minister Göran Persson was left to negotiate a pact with the former communist Left Party—the main beneficiary of the drift from the Social Democrats—and the Greens in order to remain in office. The centre-right parties, meanwhile, fell 16 seats short of an overall majority. Prospects for a viable non-socialist coalition, already slim given the longstanding disagreements between the opposition parties (see AR 1997, pp. 74–5), were dashed after Moderates' leader Carl Bildt failed to capitalize on the initially high popularity ratings which accompanied his return from Bosnia the previous year. His party lost out to the Christian Democrats, who virtually trebled their representation. After Lennart Daleus replaced Olof Johansson as leader of the Centre Party in June, the party finally abandoned its support of the government and threw in its lot with the Christian Democrats and Liberals. This move, however, did not bring about the hoped-for revival of the Centrists' fortunes in the elections. The expected shut-down of the Barsebäck nuclear reactor (a key Centre Party aim—see AR 1997, p. 75), moreover, did not materialize. After considering an appeal by power company Sydkraft, the Supreme Administrative Court ordered a judicial review of the closure plans during May.

In return for supporting the Persson government, Left leader Gudrun Schyman called for the creation of 100,000 new public-sector jobs and increased subsidies to local authorities. However, although the Prime Minister reiterated his aim of 4 per cent unemployment by 2000, Finance Minister Erik Åsbrink ruled out any significant changes to the 1999 budget, since public expenditure ceilings had already been agreed by parliament. In spite of an initial fall in share values, financial markets reacted calmly to the election result.

More serious was persistent downward pressure on the krona throughout the year, which intensified pressure on the government to set a firm timetable for a referendum on economic and monetary union (EMU) in the European Union. Opinion polls during the autumn suggested a narrowing of the majority opposed to the single currency, yet the agreement with the fiercely 'Euro-sceptic' Left would make it harder for the government to commit itself more wholeheartedly to European integration. In October Mr Persson also reaffirmed his commitment to Swedish neutrality, despite polls indicating rising support for NATO membership. The security debate had intensified after cabinet secretary Leif Leifland published a work entitled *Farewell to Neutrality* in August.

Uncomfortable reminders of Sweden's wartime role emerged in July, when it was concluded that the Riksbank and government had been aware that shipments received from Nazi Germany might have contained gold looted from Holocaust victims (see AR 1997, p. 75). Earlier, in May, the Supreme Court rejected an application for a re-trial of Christer Pettersson—the man once convicted of shooting Olof Palme in

1986—on the grounds that assembled new evidence lacked credibility so long after the event (see AR 1997, p. 75).
Tragedy struck in October, when 60 died and 190 were injured in a fire at a discotheque in Gothenburg. The mainly teenage victims, many of Macedonian and Somali origin, were attending a Halloween dance at the building of the local Macedonian immigrant association. The scale of the disaster was attributed to inadequate security arrangements: 400 people were crammed into a venue licensed to hold only 150 and one of the two fire exits was blocked.

v. FINLAND

CAPITAL: Helsinki   AREA: 338,000 sq km   POPULATION: 5,150,000 ('97)
OFFICIAL LANGUAGES: Finnish & Swedish
POLITICAL SYSTEM: presidential democracy
HEAD OF STATE: President Martti Ahtisaari (since Feb '94)
RULING PARTIES: Social Democratic Party (SSDP), National Coalition (KOK), Left-Wing Alliance (VAS), Swedish People's Party (SFP) & Green Union (VL)
HEAD OF GOVERNMENT: Paavo Lipponen (SSDP), Prime Minister (since April '95)
MAIN IGO MEMBERSHIPS (non-UN): EU, NC, CBSS, AC, PFP, OSCE, CE, OECD
CURRENCY: markka (end-'98 £1=Fmk8.42, US$1=Fmk5.06)
GNP PER CAPITA: US$24,080 by exchange-rate calculation, US$18,980 by PPP calculation ('97)

THE government's enthusiastic pursuit of deeper integration in the European Union (EU) continued to mark Finland out from its Nordic neighbours during the year. Entry to economic and monetary union (EMU) was confirmed in April, when parliament voted by 135–61 to adopt the euro from 1 January 1999. Public opinion, evenly divided at the time of the vote, had become more favourable by September, when 53 per cent expressed support for the single currency against 31 per cent who remained opposed. This rising support undermined claims by the opposition Centre Party that EMU would fatally divide the nation. Indeed, Centre Party leader Esko Aho—whose government took Finland into the EU in 1995— began to moderate his 'Euro-scepticism' ahead of the parliamentary elections scheduled for March 1999. Year-end polls indicated that the three main parties—Social Democrats (SSDP), Conservatives (KOK) and Centre—were neck and neck, each commanding 22–24 per cent of the vote.

The ruling parties clashed in June, when KOK, with the support of the Centre, overruled the SSDP to secure the appointment of Matti Vanhala as central bank governor. Extension of the SSDP-KOK axis was also placed in doubt by disagreements over fiscal policy. The global economic downturn led many analysts to question forecasts of 5 per cent growth; however, with the notable exception of the rural north, the government's economic policy continued to enjoy wide support. Privatization revenues ensured that the net borrowing requirement was reduced from Fmk15,000 million to Fmk5,000 million, while 1999 was expected to see the first budget surplus for over a decade. The sale of state holdings, however, was not without its critics, particularly after revelations in December that the director of telecom firm Sonera had benefited excessively from the company's share flotation.

The Sundqvist affair (see AR 1997, p. 77) resurfaced during the autumn, when it was alleged that the Prime Minister himself had ordered the reduction of the damages awarded against the former politician and banker. The government, which survived a vote of no confidence over the issue, was forced to reconsider the validity of the Sundqvist deal.

In the light of Finland's upcoming presidency of the EU in the second half of 1999, Prime Minister Paavo Lipponen called for reform of European institutions, casting his country as a champion of small states' interests and a valuable intermediary between Europe and Russia. The expulsion of a Russian diplomat and suspension of a Finnish Foreign Ministry official on grounds of suspected espionage thus proved embarrassing for the government during September. Official policy towards NATO remained unchanged, despite indications that a narrow majority of the public now favoured membership of the alliance. However, intra-governmental tensions became apparent during December, when Mr Lipponen criticized KOK and the Swedish People's Party (SFP) for their alleged 'flirtation' with NATO. These comments were seen as being specifically directed against Elizabeth Rehn (SFP), who had emerged as front-runner for the 2000 presidential elections, well ahead of incumbent Martti Ahtisaari (SSDP).

vi. AUSTRIA

CAPITAL: Vienna   AREA: 84,000 sq km   POPULATION: 8,050,000 ('97)
OFFICIAL LANGUAGE: German
POLITICAL SYSTEM: federal parliamentary democracy
HEAD OF STATE: Federal President Thomas Klestil (since Aug '92)
RULING PARTIES: Social Democratic (SPÖ) & People's (ÖVP) parties
HEAD OF GOVERNMENT: Viktor Klima (SPÖ), Federal Chancellor (since Jan '97)
MAIN IGO MEMBERSHIPS (non-UN): EU, OSCE, CE, PFP, CEI, OECD
CURRENCY: schilling (end-'98 £1=Sch19.49, US$1=Sch11.72)
GNP PER CAPITA: US$27,980 by exchange-rate calculation, US$21,980 by PPP calculation ('97)

THE big event of 1998 was Austria's first European Union (EU) presidency in the second half of the year. Coming less than four years after its entry to the EU, this was a real baptism of fire which severely tested bureaucratic skills and organizational capacity. Federal Chancellor Viktor Klima declared in July that he wanted a 'workmanlike' presidency. Nonetheless, imperial Austria's magnificent legacy of historic buildings duly provided memorable settings for big presidency events, and enlivened the dull round of Euro-meetings.

At year's end the Austrians were confident that they had acquitted themselves creditably and that Austria had been confirmed as a useful and effective EU member. They had chalked up some modest successes, and nothing had gone disastrously wrong. Formal negotiations on enlargement were successfully begun; progress was made on the transport and research dossiers; and agreement was reached with Switzerland on some longstanding problems. No progress was made on the difficult Agenda 2000 issues at the Vienna European Council in December (see XI.4), but this surprised no-one, and the Austrians were pleased with the smooth run-up to the launch of the euro on 1 January 1999. The Austrian public grumbled at the very considerable expense, and the leader of the opposition Freedom Party (FPÖ), Jörg Haider, commented disobligingly on the little there was to show for it all. On the whole, however, people seemed pleased to see Austria back at the centre of European affairs.

Of Austria's own particular EU concerns, the most important was probably the question of enlargement, about which there continued to be public unease, particularly over its possible impact on employment. This was fuelled by Dr Haider and the FPÖ with claims that enlargement would result in more crime, fewer jobs and hundreds of thousands of immigrants arriving in Austria. The government argued that overall prosperity and security would increase, but was clearly on the defensive in view of the general election scheduled to take place by autumn 1999.

Another touchy subject was the question of future security policy, on which the coalition partners differed, with the Social Democrats (SPÖ) reluctant to abandon traditional neutrality and the People's Party (ÖVP) strongly in favour of NATO membership. The ÖVP reacted angrily when Chancellor Klima announced in March that the SPÖ was ruling out NATO membership for the foreseeable future, but would push for close cooperation with the Western defence alliance and for a strengthening of a European security policy within the European Union. A joint report on future security policy, intended for parliamentary debate and promised for March, could not in the end be agreed, but the issue was largely set aside in the interests of EU presidency cohesion.

Internally the political situation remained calm throughout the year, which was also the 80th anniversary of the foundation of the Austrian Republic (on 12 November 1918). The major event was the presidential election held on 19 April, won outright by the incumbent, Thomas Klestil, who was re-elected with 63.5 per cent of the vote after a dull campaign. In a *Land* election held in Lower Austria on 22 March, the ÖVP won 27 seats, the SPÖ 19, the FPÖ 9 and the Green Party 2. This represented a gain of one seat for the ÖVP and two for the FPÖ, at the expense of the SPÖ and the Liberal Forum Party.

For the FPÖ and Dr Haider, 1998 brought major problems, In April the FPÖ transport spokesman, MP Peter Rosenstingl, absconded with large sums of private and party investors' funds, several of his associates being arrested. In August there were splits in the party in Vienna and Salzburg, when many FPÖ members resigned or were sacked by Dr Haider for refusing to sign his 'Democracy Pact' making all elected FPÖ officials legally accountable to the party for their policies in the wake of the Rosenstingl affair. On 4 November the FPÖ's economic spokesman also resigned. By December, with the FPÖ down to 19 per cent in the polls, its prospects for the 1999 general election suddenly looked less promising, as did Dr Haider's alternative strategy of seeking election as governor of Carinthia in the *Land* election due there in March 1999.

By contrast, the coalition partners continued to work together in reasonable harmony, and were rewarded at the end of the year by opinion poll support of 42 per cent for the SPÖ and 25 per cent for the ÖVP. Public perception of a successful EU presidency contributed to this, as did continued strong economic performance. The government announced in February that it had formally fulfilled the Maastricht Treaty criteria, producing a financial deficit of 2.5 per cent of GDP and a ratio of national debt to GDP of 66.1 per cent in 1997 (down from 69.5 per cent in 1996). Real growth in GDP for 1998 was strong at 3.3 per cent, while retail prices increased by only 0.9 per cent over the previous year. The unemployment rate remained at 4.5 per cent.

EU presidency responsibilities made this an exceptionally busy year for foreign visits and visitors, particularly from Central Europe, the Balkans and countries engaged with the Middle East peace process. Apart from a mid-year row with Slovakia over its activation of a nuclear reactor at Mochovce judged unsafe by outside experts (see III.1.iv), external relations were generally cordial. The Pope paid a third visit to Austria in June, though there was disappointment that he did not attempt to address religious scandals and controversies of concern to the Austrian faithful. Also in June, the 50th anniversary of the Universal Declaration of Human Rights was marked by a major international conference organized jointly with the UN in Vienna.

The government continued to work for a more open and honest appraisal of the Nazi past. On 5 May Austria celebrated for the first time a national day against violence and racism, honouring the memory of the victims of Nazism with commemorative ceremonies in both houses of parliament. In September the government decided to appoint an independent commission of historians, to shed new light on confiscations and forced sales of property in Austria during the Nazi era, and on subsequent restitution and compensation practice. In November parliament enacted a law providing for the return of Jewish-owned works of art which had been plundered by the Nazis or unwillingly 'donated' to the state after World War II.

vii. SWITZERLAND

CAPITAL: Berne AREA: 41,300 sq km POPULATION: 7,096,800 ('97)
OFFICIAL LANGUAGES: German, French, Italian & Rhaeto-Romanic
POLITICAL SYSTEM: federal canton-based democracy
RULING PARTIES: Christian Democratic People's (CVP), Radical Democratic (FDP), Social Democratic (SPS) & Swiss People's (SVP) parties
HEAD OF GOVERNMENT: Flavio Cotti (CVP), 1998 President of Federal Council and Foreign Minister
MAIN IGO MEMBERSHIPS: OECD, OSCE, CE, EFTA, PFP
CURRENCY: Swiss franc (end-'98 £1=SwF2.28, US$1=SwF1.37)
GNP PER CAPITA: US$44,320 by exchange-rate calculation, US$26,320 by PPP calculation ('97)

THE behaviour of Switzerland and its banks during and after World War II ceased to be the top political issue that it had been in 1996–97 (see AR 1996, p. 76; 1997, pp. 80–1). New reports published by the US administration refrained from singling out Switzerland for special blame, while Jewish organizations started to make claims against other European and US banks and industrial firms which had done business with Germany or employed Jewish and other slave workers in their factories in Nazi-occupied countries.

In the United States, the class action by a group of Holocaust survivors against the major Swiss banks, demanding compensation of US$20,000 million, was settled by a New York court on 12 August. After long deliberations, the banks agreed to pay a total of US$1,250 million to the claimants and to Jewish organizations. The banks remained silent on their reasons for the settlement. For analysts, however, it was evident that a long dispute before the US courts, and the effects of continuing negative reports in the US media, would have been a greater encumbrance for the banks. In the wake of the settlement, officials of several US states confirmed their intention to boycott Swiss banks, also threatening to include other Swiss firms in the action if the banks were not accommodating.

Switzerland's bilateral negotiations with the European Union (EU)—which had lasted for more than four years—were finally brought to an end with the signature of a trade and cooperation agreement on 1 December. Representatives of both sides declared that all differences had been settled; but the agreement still had to be ratified by Switzerland, the European Parliament and the EU member states. In Switzerland, a referendum was seen as likely, because several small right-wing parties announced their opposition to ratification and their intent to collect the required 50,000 signatures for a popular consultation.

The trade agreement covered seven areas, namely transport by land, integration of Switzerland into a liberalized aviation market, unrestricted reciprocal access to labour markets, Swiss participation in EU research programmes, mutual recognition of technical regulations and standards, reciprocal free access to public contracts and reciprocal partial liberalization of agricultural markets. The Federal Council decided to present the agreement as a whole package, to prevent opponents picking out critical issues—immigration by the right-wingers or long-distance road transport by the environmentalists—and to allow citizens to make their judgement on the totality of the advantages and risks. The main employers' association (Vorort), which favoured the full integration of Switzerland into the liberalized markets of the EU, quickly launched a publicity campaign in support of the agreement.

The EU negotiations had occupied front stage in the Swiss political debate throughout the year, even though, from the seven issues mentioned above, only the regulation of transport by land across the Swiss Alps remained to be settled. In January EU transport commissioner Neil Kinnock and Swiss Transport Minister Moritz Leuenberger reached a compromise. Having already agreed to abandon its 28-tonne limit on trucks, Switzerland was allowed to tax lorries transiting the country by up to SwF325 per passage to cover the resultant costs and, as a side-effect, to induce them to use railway facilities. When this compromise was presented to the EU Council of Transport Ministers, the German representative declared his absolute opposition on the grounds that the tax was still too high. The Swiss authorities considered his opposition to be very much related to the ongoing campaign for the German elections in September (see II.2.i) and therefore refrained from making a new offer. After the German elections, this assumption proved to be correct. The new Social Democratic-Green government had no objections to the tax as proposed, so that the last obstacle to a conclusion of the bilateral agreement between the EU and Switzerland was removed.

Swiss voters supported the government's transport policy in two referendums, despite the combined opposition of the road transport organizations and the electorally advancing Swiss People's Party (SVP). The citizens thereby gave a sign to Brussels that they were determined to reduce the transport of goods by road by both Swiss and foreign lorries and that they were ready to spend considerable amounts of money to protect the Alps from the nuisance of long-distance road transport. On 27 September they voted by a 57 per cent majority in favour of a tax on all road freight transports (not only transits). As a European novelty, this tax would not be a flat rate, but depend on the weight of the load and the distance travelled, the main argument for this differentiation being that heavy users of the roads caused more damage to them and to the environment and should in consequence pay more. With this measure, long-distance transportation of goods by road would become appreciably more expensive and so, the Swiss hoped, be switched to the less polluting railway system. The government estimated the total annual yield of the new tax at almost SwF1,500 million, of which about a third would be paid by foreign lorries using Swiss roads.

In the second vote, on 29 November, the citizens decided on how the

SwF30,000 million bill (SwF1.5 million a year over 20 years) for the construction of the two new railway tunnels through the Alps (Gotthard and Lötschberg) and some additional railway projects (e.g. the connection with the French TGV system) would be covered. According to this decision, roughly one half of the money would come from the allocation of two-thirds of new tax on road transport (the remaining third to be used for road works). The other half would be financed by using part of an existing special tax on fuel (until now strictly reserved for road construction) and by a slight increase in the rate of value-added tax (VAT).

The economy was in a much better shape than in the previous year, the rate of growth being provisionally estimated at 2 per cent. The number of unemployed was reduced by almost a third, falling from 180,549 at end-1997 to 124,309 in December 1998 (3.4 per cent of the workforce). The inflation rate for the year was exactly zero, the lowest level since 1959. To the relief of Swiss business, the citizens rejected by a majority of 67 per cent an initiative for a complete ban on research into, and use of, genetically-transformed material. Considering the widespread fear of those new technologies, and the fact that this initiative was supported by the Social Democrats, the Green Party and all environmentalist organizations, the result of the vote was unexpectedly clear. According to analysts, this was mainly due to the fact that many prominent scientists (among them several Nobel Prize winners) had actively campaigned against the proposed restriction on research.

The deficit in the public finances remained one of the most important topics of Swiss politics. At the invitation of Finance Minister Kaspar Villiger, representatives of the four governmental parties, the cantons, the trade unions and the employers' associations gathered at 'round-table' discussions on 7 April, agreeing cuts in federal expenditure of SwF2,000 million. The agreement had no legal implications, but was fully respected by the parliament when it decided on the budget for 1999. In addition, the citizens demonstrated their wish for the budget to be balanced in the future. Against the opposition of the Social Democrats and the unions, on 6 June they voted by a 70 per cent majority to approve a governmental scheme to reduce the deficit to zero by 2001.

Federal Councillor and Minister of Economy Jean-Pascal Delamuraz, who had been in bad health for several years, resigned in March (subsequently dying in October at the age of 62). It was clear from the beginning that his successor had also to come not only from the Radical Democratic Party (FDP) but also from the French-speaking part of Switzerland, while some pressure was exerted by the media and public opinion that a second woman should be elected to the seven-member federal government. This latter requirement was not easy for the FDP to comply with, because well-known female politicians were rather scarce in the French-speaking part of Switzerland (in contrast with the German-speaking part). Eventually, two candidates were nominated, namely Pascal Couchpin and Christiane Langenberger. M. Couchepin had the advantage of a long political career, whereas his female opponent had only been a member of parliament since December 1995. It was therefore no surprise that M. Couchepin was elected to the Federal Council, where he took over the Department of Economy.

In the past the choice of candidates for the Federal Council had often been handicapped by the constitutional provision that no canton should provide more than one member of the government. Parliament now decided to replace this rule by a less restrictive provision, requiring only 'fair representation' of the different regions and language groups.

On 9 December the federal Vice-President and Minister of Interior, Ruth Dreifuss (Social Democrat), was elected to the annually-rotating post of President of the Federal Council for 1999. She would be the first woman to head the Swiss government.

viii. EUROPEAN MINI-STATES

Andorra
CAPITAL: Andorra la Vella   AREA: 460 sq km   POPULATION: 71,000 ('97)
OFFICIAL LANGUAGE: Catalan
POLITICAL SYSTEM: parliamentary democracy
HEADS OF STATE: President Jacques Chirac of France & Bishop Joan Martí Alanis of Urgel (co-princes)
HEAD OF GOVERNMENT: Marc Forné Molne, President of Executive Council (since Dec '94)
MAIN IGO MEMBERSHIPS (non-UN) CE
CURRENCY: French franc & Spanish peseta

Holy See (Vatican City State)
CAPITAL: Vatican City   AREA: 0.44 sq km   POPULATION: 870 ('97)
OFFICIAL LANGUAGES: Italian & Latin
POLITICAL SYSTEM: theocracy
HEAD OF STATE: Pope John Paul II (since '78)
HEAD OF GOVERNMENT: Cardinal Angelo Sodano, Secretary of State (since Dec '90)
MAIN IGO MEMBERSHIPS: OSCE
CURRENCY: Vatican lira (at par to Italian lira)

Liechtenstein
CAPITAL: Vaduz   AREA: 160 sq km   POPULATION: 32,000 ('97)
OFFICIAL LANGUAGE: German
POLITICAL SYSTEM: parliamentary democracy
HEAD OF STATE: Prince Hans Adam II (since Nov '89)
RULING PARTY: Patriotic Union (VU)
HEAD OF GOVERNMENT: Mario Frick, Prime Minister (since Dec '93)
MAIN IGO MEMBERSHIPS (non-UN): EFTA/EEA, OSCE, CE
CURRENCY: Swiss franc
GNP PER CAPITA: US$44,000 ('97 est.)

Monaco

CAPITAL: Monaco-Ville   AREA: 1.95 sq km   POPULATION: 32,000 ('97)
OFFICIAL LANGUAGE: French
POLITICAL SYSTEM: constitutional monarchy
HEAD OF STATE: Prince Rainier III (since '49)
HEAD OF GOVERNMENT: Michel Lévêque, Minister of State (since Feb '97)
MAIN IGO MEMBERSHIPS (non-UN): OSCE
CURRENCY: French franc

San Marino

CAPITAL: San Marino   AREA: 60.5 sq km   POPULATION: 25,500 ('97)
OFFICIAL LANGUAGE: Italian
POLITICAL SYSTEM: parliamentary democracy
HEADS OF STATE & GOVERNMENT: Captains-Regent Pietro Berti & Paolo Bollini (Oct '98–March '99)
RULING PARTIES: Christian Democratic & Socialist parties
MAIN IGO MEMBERSHIPS (non-UN): OSCE, CE
CURRENCY: Italian lira

IN MONACO, the ruling National and Democratic Union (UND) won all 18 seats in elections for the National Council, the unicameral legislature, held in early February. Both the Union for the Future of Monaco (UNA), which fielded 13 candidates, and the Rally for the Monegasque Family (six) failed to win a seat. On 19 February Michel Lévêque was reappointed as Minister of State, the head of the four-member Council of Government which exercised executive power under the authority of Prince Rainier III, the head of state. Towards the end of the year speculation grew in the press that Prince Rainier's daughter, Princess Caroline, who had already been once divorced and once widowed, intended to marry her long-term boyfriend, Prince Ernst August of Hanover.

In ANDORRA, the centre-right Liberal Union (UL) led by Marc Forné, the President of the Executive Council (Cabinet), remained in office during 1998 following its overwhelming victory in the previous year's general election (see AR 1997, p. 84).

In elections held in SAN MARINO on 31 May, the ruling Christian Democratic Party (PDCS) retained its grip on power after winning 41 per cent of the vote and 25 seats in the principality's 60-member Grand and General Council (the unicameral legislature). The PDCS's coalition partner, the Socialist Party (PSS), won 23 per cent of the vote and 14 seats. The main opposition parties, the Progressive Democratic Party (PPDS) and the Popular Democratic Alliance (APDS), took 11 and six seats respectively.

In LIECHTENSTEIN, the ruling Patriotic Union (VU) led by Prime Minister Mario Frick stayed in office during 1998 despite the break-up of its coalition with the Progressive Citizen's Party (FBP) following elections the previous year (see AR 1997, pp. 84–5).

In the HOLY SEE (Vatican), an air of mystery surrounded the killing on 4 May of the newly-appointed commander of the Swiss Guards (the Vatican's army), Colonel Alois Estermann, and his Venezuelan-born wife

Gladys. The couple were reportedly shot dead in their apartment by Cedric Tornay, a lance-corporal in the Swiss Guards, whose body was found nearby after he had apparently committed suicide. In a statement issued following the deaths, the Vatican claimed that Lance-Corporal Tornay had shot the couple in a 'fit of madness' after Colonel Estermann had excluded him from an earlier medal ceremony.

The official version of events was treated with scepticism by the Italian press, however, which searched for other motives for the murders. There was speculation that Lance-Corporal Tornay had been systematically bullied by Colonel Estermann, who was also rumoured to have been murdered by other persons out of resentment of his humble origins. By tradition, commanders of the Guards had always been chosen from the Swiss nobility, and Colonel Estermann had only been confirmed as commander after a seven-month search for an aristocratic candidate had proved fruitless. Further doubts over the official account also emerged when Lance-Corporal Tornay's mother publicly claimed that her son had been killed and subsequently 'framed' in a Vatican 'cover-up'. In particular, Muguette Borday-Tornay cast doubt on the authenticity of her son's alleged suicide note, which she claimed contained several factual inaccuracies and was addressed to her in her married name, whereas her son had always used her maiden name. Reports in the press at the end of the year suggested, however, that an investigation into the deaths would soon endorse the Vatican's version of events and recommend that the case be shelved. On 2 June Pope John Paul II appointed Colonel Pius Segmüller, a 46-year-old Swiss army officer, as the new commander of the Swiss Guards.

The Vatican published on 16 March its definitive assessment, prepared over ten years, of the role of the Roman Catholic Church during the Holocaust. The report, entitled *We Remember, a Reflection on the Shoah*, expressed deep regret that many individual Catholics had failed to defend the Jews. However, it levelled no serious criticism of church policy and defended the then Pope, Pius XII, against those who had condemned his public silence on the Nazi exterminations. The report met with a mixed response from Jewish scholars and organizations. Many criticized it as a wholly inadequate apology, especially in its abdication of institutional responsibility, and its side-stepping of the Church's centuries-old demonization of the Jews. Amongst the more specific omissions cited were the Church's support for the pro-Nazi regime established in Croatia during World War II, and the Vatican's alleged role in helping SS officers escape from Europe in 1945.

The Vatican faced further condemnation from Jewish groups for the beatification on 3 October of Cardinal Aloysius Stepinac, the controversial cardinal who had been sentenced to 16 years in prison by the former Communist regime in Yugoslavia on charges of collaborating with the pro-Nazi Croatian regime.

Despite his continuing frailty, the Pope made a number of important overseas visits during the year, beginning with a much-heralded visit to Cuba on 21-25 January, when he became the first pontiff to ever visit the island (see IV.3.xi). Although both sides insisted that it was a pastoral visit, the Pope used the last of his four open-air masses in the country to deliver a strong political message. As well as calling for greater freedom and openness inside Cuba, he vigorously denounced the USA's longstanding economic embargo of the island. The visit also helped to loosen many of the restrictions which had long been imposed by the ruling Communist regime on Roman Catholicism. For example, the Church was allowed airtime on state television as part of the preparations for the papal visit, and in both 1997 and 1998 Christmas Day was declared a public holiday for the first time since the late 1960s.

In March the Pope paid a high-profile visit to Nigeria during which he met with the country's military ruler, General Sani Abacha (who subsequently died in June—see Pt XVIII: Obituary). Throughout the visit the Pope repeatedly and publicly urged the ruling regime to improve the human rights situation in the country. The Pope also paid a three-day visit in late April to Austria at a time of great divisions in the country's Roman Catholic Church. In recent years the Austrian Church had been buffeted by sexual abuse charges levelled at the former Archbishop of Vienna, Cardinal Hans Hermann Groer, and by a 500,000-strong petition calling for the liberalization of church policy. Whilst the Pope criticized the Church for the public discussion of its divisions, he made no direct reference to the Groer case or other controversial areas of church policy.

With the health of the Pope visibly declining, concerns were raised over his ability to lead the Roman Catholic Church during 1999, when he would be required to take on a hectic schedule of official duties to commemorate the 2,000th anniversary of Christ's birth. As well as preparing for the arrival of an estimated 25 million pilgrims in Rome, he was also expected to pay a number of high-profile visits abroad, including a visit to the Middle East, where he was due to make a journey retracing the life of Abraham.

4. SPAIN—GIBRALTAR—PORTUGAL—MALTA—GREECE—CYPRUS—TURKEY

i. SPAIN

CAPITAL: Madrid   AREA: 505,000 sq km   POPULATION: 40,100,000 ('97)
OFFICIAL LANGUAGE: Spanish
POLITICAL SYSTEM: parliamentary democracy
HEAD OF STATE: King Juan Carlos (since Nov '75)
RULING PARTY: Popular Party (PP)
HEAD OF GOVERNMENT: José María Aznar López, Prime Minister (since May '96))
MAIN IGO MEMBERSHIPS (non-UN): NATO, EU, WEU, OSCE, CE, OECD
CURRENCY: peseta (end-'98 £1=Ptas235.75, US$1=Ptas141.70)
GNP PER CAPITA: US$14,510 by exchange-rate calculation, US$15,720 by PPP calculation ('97)

INITIATIVES aimed at ending the conflict in the Basque Country raised hopes during 1998 of an eventual settlement, while at the same time stirring fundamental controversies about the structure of the Spanish state.

Against a background of successive reverses for the paramilitary Basque Homeland and Liberty (ETA) organization and its growing isolation, the mainstream Basque Nationalist Party (PNV) made efforts to negotiate an end to 30 years of political violence. In February-March a plan announced by the then Basque regional president, José Antonio Ardanza, envisaged the eventual admission of the pro-ETA Herri Batasuna (HB) into multi-party talks, following an ETA ceasefire. However, both the ruling People's Party (PP) and the opposition Socialist Party (PSOE) remained sceptical, fearing that the plan implied Basque self-determination. Disagreements with the PP on occasion led to a withdrawal of PNV support for José María Aznar's PP government but political stability was unaffected, thanks to backing from the Catalan Nationalists (CiU) and Canary Islands Coalition (CC) in the Congress of Deputies.

An anti-terrorist united front of all the democratic political parties, as maintained since 1988, proved impossible to sustain. ETA's main target had become the PP and its government, condemned by the Basque nationalist parties for keeping over 500 ETA members in prisons a long way from the Basque Country. On 25 June Manuel Zamarreño became the sixth PP councillor to be assassinated by ETA in a year, but was also the organization's last victim in 1998.

PNV contacts with HB eventually led to a meeting in Estella (known to Basques as Lizarra) on 12 September, attended by 22 Basque nationalist groups and parties and the United Left (IU). The assembly called on ETA to declare an indefinite ceasefire to facilitate an inclusive political dialogue. It demanded too that any solution to the Basque conflict should be based on self-determination, to be exercised in Euskal Herria (the existing Spanish region of Euskadi, plus neighbouring Navarra and the French Pays Basque). ETA then called a ceasefire on 16 September, starting officially two days later.

The Basque radicals were encouraged by signs of PNV flexibility and by joint efforts by the mainstream Basque, Catalan and Galician nationalist parties to press for constitutional reform. The nationalist parties demanded recognition of the national status of their homelands and proposed a confederal reconfiguration of the Spanish state. Their ideas were opposed by the PP and the PSOE.

ETA's ceasefire averted a predicted loss of support for Herri Batasuna in elections to the Basque parliament held on 25 October, which the HB radicals entered as part of a new coalition, the Basque Citizens (EH). The principal gains in the election were made by EH and the PP, while the pluralism of Euskadi was underlined by the victory of different parties in its three provinces. The balance between nationalist and non-nationalist parties in the regional parliament remained unchanged, at 41 and 34 seats respectively. However, following the failure of coalition negotiations between the PNV and the Socialists, the outcome was the first exclusively nationalist Basque government supported by a majority in parliament. EH promised to uphold the new government, without entering the coalition.

The Spanish government reacted cautiously to these developments, with measures designed to encourage pacification while avoiding political concessions to the radicals. Indirect contacts with ETA were established and Sr Aznar declared his readiness to include EH among the government's interlocutors. However, attempts to develop a peace process were hampered from November by a resumption of attacks on property by the HB youth organization Jarrai, which the government described as 'low-intensity terrorism'.

In apparent preparation for an eventual amnesty gesture towards ETA, the government introduced measures to compensate the victims of terrorism and to pardon figures associated with counter-terrorism under the previous PSOE administration. In July former Interior Minister José Barrionuevo and former head of state security Rafael Vera had been sentenced to ten years imprisonment for kidnapping (an ETA suspect) and embezzlement, in a trial arising from the activities of the Anti-Terrorist Liberation Groups (GAL), responsible for killing some 27 ETA suspects during the 1980s. Sr Aznar's government sought to avoid political responsibility for the fate of the former Interior Ministry officials by awaiting the advice of the Supreme Court. In December the latter recommended a two-thirds reduction in the prison sentences, after which partial pardons were granted just before Christmas, provoking protests from Basque nationalists.

The government also followed a judicial lead when it acted upon a request from Judge Baltasar Garzón for former Chilean dictator Augusto Pinochet to be extradited from London on charges of genocide, terrorism and torture, following a High Court ruling on 30 October that the Spanish courts were competent to judge crimes allegedly committed by the former military regimes of Chile and Argentina (see also II.1.i; IV.3.iv). General

Pinochet's arrest on 16 October had caused acute embarrassment to Sr Aznar, for it came during the eighth Ibero-American summit, held in Oporto (Portugal), at which the Latin American and Iberian political leaders were assembled (see XI.6.iv). On 6 November, following the Spanish government's processing of the extradition request, Chilean ambassador Sergio Pizarro was recalled to Santiago. On 25 November the commander-in-chief of the Chilean army, General Ricardo Izurieta, called for a break in diplomatic relations with Spain and Britain in the event of the Frei government failing to secure the release of General Pinochet. Seeking to minimize the political and commercial effects of the crisis, on 1 December Sr Aznar told the Chilean Foreign Minister, José Miguel Insulza, that if the British Home Secretary decided to let General Pinochet return to Chile, Spain would not stand in the way.

In contrast, the Oporto summit was used by Spain as an opportunity for rapprochement with Cuba, following the naming of a new Spanish ambassador in April, after 16 months without one. A subsequent visit to Havana by Foreign Minister Abel Matutes in November brought an agreement to go ahead with a visit by King Juan Carlos and Queen Sofía in spring 1999 (see IV.3.xi).

Important issues for Spain were raised meanwhile by the European Commission's proposed financial reforms known as Agenda 2000, which focused on the European Union (EU) budget for 2000–2006. While the Commission recommended the retention of the cohesion fund, from which Spain was the prime beneficiary, Madrid was faced with the prospect of a much reduced volume of aid, not only from this source but also from other structural funds and agricultural subsidies. These proposals overshadowed another Commission recommendation, made on 25 March, that Spain should be among 11 countries to enter the new EU economic and monetary union from the start (see also XI.4).

At the EU summit in Cardiff on 15–16 June, Spain led southern European countries in pushing for a formula to base future budget contributions on the per capita wealth of each member state. The Spaniards clashed with the Germans over the relative contributions and benefits that would be determined by the new EU budget. Spain allied with France over the proposed changes to the common agricultural policy and received British support in resisting German and Scandinavian threats to the cohesion fund. At the EU summit in Vienna in December, a compromise formula was reached, with the final declaration echoing certain German cost-cutting proposals but retaining Agenda 2000 as the basis for future negotiations. This seemed to ensure the survival of the cohesion fund, but threatened to deprive Spain of half its income from it.

Spanish concern about the financial impact of the EU's future eastern enlargement did not prevent Sr Aznar from expressing support for the entry of Poland and the Czech Republic during visits in January and December respectively. Among the European leaders, the Spanish Prime

Minister meanwhile showed a readiness to go against majority positions by indicating support for Israeli Prime Minister Binyamin Netanyahu, during his first visit to the Middle East on 29 June, and by supporting US and British policy on Iraq. Spain did not participate in the attack on Iraq in December, but described the bombing as 'necessary'.

The important American dimension to Sr Aznar's foreign policy was reflected also in other events: official visits to Peru and Colombia; Spain's offer of $5,000 million to an emergency aid fund for Latin America in September, as the effects of the Asian financial crisis threatened Spanish investments in that region; and a $189 million aid package for Central America in response to Hurricane Mitch (see IV.3.xiii; XIII.3), including a moratorium on regional debt until 2001.

On the domestic front, the year saw significant changes within the parties of the left. On 24 April former minister José Borrell defeated general secretary Joaquín Almunia to become the PSOE's candidate for Prime Minister in the next general election (the first time internal party primaries had been used for this purpose in Spain). The PSOE went on to overtake the PP in opinion polls in May, although by July the 'Borrell effect' had been nullified and the PP went on to lead by 3.7 points in September. Finally, on 5 December, at the 15th congress of the Spanish Communist Party (PCE), Julio Anguita retired as general secretary and was replaced by Francisco Frutos.

In a major disaster at home on 25 April, toxic waste from a mine at Aznalcóllar flooded 40 kilometres of the bed of the River Guadimar in the Doñana national park, causing great damage to wildlife and the natural habitat.

ii. GIBRALTAR

CAPITAL: Gibraltar AREA: 6.5 sq km POPULATION: 33,000 ('97)
OFFICIAL LANGUAGE: English
POLITICAL STATUS: Crown Colony, parliamentary democracy
HEAD OF STATE: Queen Elizabeth II
GOVERNOR: Sir Richard Luce
RULING PARTY: Gibraltar Social Democrats (GSD)
HEAD OF GOVERNMENT: Peter Caruana, Chief Minister (since May '96)
CURRENCY: Gibraltar pound (at par with UK pound)

PROGRESS towards resolving the Gibraltar dispute between Britain and Spain seemed possible during the first seven months of the year. In April there was an unprecedented invitation from Spain for Gibraltar's Chief Minister, Peter Caruana, to attend bilateral talks in Madrid, and indications from the Rock that it was welcome. In July Britain and Spain reached an agreement that prevented the Gibraltar issue from disrupting plans to modernize NATO. Madrid agreed that Gibraltar could be used as a communications centre during NATO exercises, but maintained its ban on military aircraft using Spanish airspace en route to or from the colony. Days later, the Gibraltar authorities offered to share the use of the local airport with Spain, a formula which they had blocked in 1987, following agreement between London and Madrid, because it was feared that it might imply recognition of Spanish sovereignty over the isthmus upon which the airport was built.

The stage seemed set for direct dialogue between Spain and Gibraltar, an idea acceptable to 54 per cent of Gibraltarians, according to an opinion poll published in the *Gibraltar Chronicle* in April. However, only 2 per cent of the respondents welcomed Spain's proposal of a lengthy period of co-sovereignty followed by Gibraltar's reintegration into Spain (with considerable autonomy). In contrast, 35 per cent favoured integration with Britain and 22 per cent wanted Gibraltar to acquire a status similar to that of Jersey (as proposed by Mr Caruana). Moreover, Madrid now showed less commercial interest in Gibraltar's airport than ten years earlier, owing to the development of airports in southern Spain.

From August a fishing dispute underlined the fact that the Gibraltar problem had not really evolved. On 21 August Gibraltan patrol boats prevented trawlers from the nearby Spanish port of Algeciras from fishing in Rosia Bay, in waters protected by local environmental legislation since 1991. Nevertheless, Spanish fishermen continued to fish there, while Madrid continued to reject the notion of British territorial waters around the Rock. Foreign Ministers Robin Cook and Abel Matutes discussed the problem on 5 October, but later differed over what had been agreed. Spanish displeasure brought a tightening of border controls, leading to long traffic queues for the rest of the year.

There were also Spanish complaints about the opaqueness of Gibraltar's economy, the registration of some 53,000 phantom companies having enabled Gibraltar to become the third largest property investor in Andalucía. Towards the end of the year, the situation prompted Spanish threats to denounce the Rock's non-fulfilment of European financial legislation to the European Court of Justice.

Spain welcomed one event during this dispute: the arrest on 13 August of 13 people, including a prestigious Gibraltar lawyer, on charges relating to drug-trafficking. However, although Britain and Spain were cooperating increasingly over other issues, notably within the European Union, the year ended on a note of confrontation

iii. PORTUGAL

CAPITAL: Lisbon   AREA: 92,000 sq km   POPULATION: 10,000,000 ('97)
OFFICIAL LANGUAGE: Portuguese
POLITICAL SYSTEM: presidential/parliamentary democracy
HEAD OF STATE: President Jorge Sampaio (since March '96)
RULING PARTY: Socialist Party (PS)
HEAD OF GOVERNMENT: António Guterres, Prime Minister (since Oct '95)
MAIN IGO MEMBERSHIPS (non-UN): NATO, OECD, EU, WEU, OSCE, CE, CPLP
CURRENCY: escudo (end-'98 £1=Esc284.05, US$1=Esc170.73)
GNP PER CAPITA: US$10,450 by exchange-rate calculation, US$13,840 by PPP calculation ('97)

THE dominant event in Portugal for most of the year was Lisbon's grandiose Expo'98, a state-of-the-art $2,000 million world trade fair of 150 pavilions, stands and exhibits, which ran from May to September. It was preceded by the inauguration of other major infrastructure projects, notably the opening in March of the majestic six-lane Vasco da Gama bridge stretching 18 kilometres across the Tagus estuary.

Dedicated to the theme 'the oceans and oceanography', Expo'98 had a deeper national significance than met the eye. Designed to turn the derelict site of the centuries-old Lisbon docklands into a futuristic urban zone and leisure/cultural centre, the fair was seen by the Portuguese as the catalyst of a renaissance that most of them had not expected to happen only a quarter of a century after the end of Portugal's 500-year-old overseas empire. The older generation had been conditioned by decades of autocratic nationalist/colonialist rule to the belief that Portugal, comparatively poor as it was, would become economically unviable if it lost its remaining overseas possessions. In fact, the democratic coup of 1974 and speedy decolonization ushered in an accelerated process of development and growing prosperity which rapidly restored national confidence and facilitated Portugal's admission to the European Union (EU) in 1986. Symbolizing the transformation, Expo'98 was, in the words of the man mainly responsible for it, Mega Ferreira, 'a celebration of the success of Portuguese democracy'. The coincidental award of the 1998 Nobel Prize for literature to José Saramago—the first to a Portuguese writer—was hailed as another confirmation of Portugal's renaissance (see XV.3).

Accelerated socio-economic and changing national perspectives had some curious consequences, including the emergence of what observers described as a duality in the balance of Portugal's incoming and outgoing investment. On the one hand, Portugal as a state was a major beneficiary of the EU Cohesion Fund and an enthusiastic recipient of EU investment; on the other, in 1998 it confirmed its position as one of the seven biggest international investor countries. Portuguese investment was directed at countries as near as Spain and Morocco or as far away as Brazil (in telecommunications), Mozambique (in banking) and even Poland, where a Portuguese supermarket chain was expanding. Underlining

Portugal's presence in the global market economy, the sharp worldwide collapse in share prices in April was particularly felt on the Lisbon stock exchange, which on 27 April registered the biggest fall in Europe, amounting to Esc740,000 million and widely described as a 'mini-crash'. In the year's later financial crises, however, a recognition of Portugal's close trading and financial relations within the EU meant that it was not so directly exposed to Asian and other market turmoil, with the result that investors gradually recovered their confidence.

Internally, the process of democratization was mostly—some would say only—noticeable in rampant consumerism. It was reported during the year that the Portuguese had one of Europe's highest rates of mobile phones per thousand of the population. And one of Lisbon's newest shopping centres, the Centro Colombo, became so overcrowded that admissions had to be controlled to ease customer and traffic congestion. The trend away from an interest in ideology and party politics was perhaps best encapsulated by the use of the popular tune *Grandola, Vila Morena*—previously identified with the advent of democracy in 1974—in a television advertisement for a brand of olive oil.

The lack of public interest in politics extended to social issues, including a referendum on abortion held on 28 June. Only a generation ago the issue would have been beyond discussion in a country with a 98 per cent baptism rate and with over 70 per cent of the population being practising Catholics. In the event, the referendum produced an extremely narrow 'no' majority of 50.9 per cent against any relaxation of current abortion restrictions. But the vote had no legal effect, because the turnout was only 32 per cent. Under Portuguese law, participation of at least 50 per cent was required for a referendum decision to be binding.

Other social indicators were more conclusive, notably statistics showing that for every 100 male university students registered in 1998 there were 170 female students. No immediate explanation was offered for this reversal of the old male-dominated social order or of the factors that had led young men to fall so far behind. In line with the trend in other European countries, the ruling Socialist Party (PS) laid plans to establish quotas for women candidates in parliamentary elections, starting with the election due in 1999.

The narrowing of the GNP per capita gap between Portugal and the EU average, from 50 per cent in 1985 to less than 30 per cent in the late 1990s, was sustained in 1998 by means of growth of over 4 per cent, well above the EU average. Another encouraging indicator was that, despite the stronger escudo, exports to the rest of the EU continued to grow faster than the average EU rate, thus increasing the share of Portuguese products in the European market.

There were few major events or commotions in party politics, apart from a leadership dispute within the Popular Party (PP), the second formation in the centre-right opposition after the Social Democratic Party (PSD). At the PP national congress in Braga on 22 March, former journalist Paulo Portas replaced rival Manuel Monteiro as party leader, reportedly attracting overtures from PSD leader Marcelo Rebelo de Sousa to discuss a PSD-PP electoral alliance to oppose the ruling PS. While PS Prime Minister António Gutteres was in some respects a political precursor of the Blairite brand of socialism in Britain, the programme of Sr Portas, which he described as 'pro-European but non-federalist', resembled that of the British Conservatives. In articles and press interviews, Sr Portas denounced the PS for being 'elected by the workers but governing as capitalists'.

Sr Portas gained additional prominence as one of the leading campaigners against the decriminalization of abortion in the June referendum. He also opposed the government in the year's other referendum, held on 8 November on regionalization plans envisaging the decentralization of mainland administration into eight autonomous regions. Such a reform might have been rational, and certainly enjoyed some support among those who resented the traditional political and economic dominance of Lisbon. But emotional emphasis on the 'natural cohesion' of a small country resulted in a 63.6 per cent vote against the proposals, in a turnout of 51.7 per cent. Accordingly, apart from the autonomous Atlantic archipelagos of Madeira and the Azores, Portugal remained one of Europe's most centralized nations, with a regional structure unchanged from the pre-democratic era. The fact that only 9 per cent of the national budget was allocated to local authorities (compared with 25 per cent in most EU countries) and the persistence of great economic disparities between different mainland regions ensured that the 'regionalization' question remained a contentious issue.

Portugal had its share of corruption and sleaze cases in 1998. The most sensational involved the treasurer and publicity director of Expo'98, who were jointly charged with embezzling Esc1,000 million. Another case, albeit on a minor scale, involved the production of counterfeit money on Expo'98 photocopying machines. Also in evidence was a novel confidence trick whereby old-age pensioners were persuaded to exchange their savings in escudos in return for fake credits in euros at supposedly preferential rates.

Finance Minister António Sousa Franco had some success in implementing much-needed efficiency in tax collection, in a situation where until recently the majority of self-employed professionals tended to show no profits in their tax returns, or even losses. According to an OECD report, government measures to curb tax evasion and reduce arrears were expected to add Esc400,000 million to tax receipts for the period 1996-2009.

On 28 October the European Commission recommended an EU embargo on Portuguese exports of beef and cattle pending the successful implementation of measures to eradicate 'mad cow disease' (BSE), which had been found in a small number of animals. The previous month the Portuguese government had banned the use of meat and bone meal in cattle feed with the aim of preventing any spread of BSE. There were no reported cases of human victims.

The impact of EU membership was also reflected in increasingly close economic relations with Spain, featuring growing investment and trade in both directions as well as new links in gas, electricity, telecommunications and other industries. An eventual merger between the TAP Portuguese national airline and Iberia of Spain was also contemplated. Nevertheless, while most people regarded the process of 'Iberianization' as welcome or inevitable, others preferred 'Europeanization' rather than domination by Spain.

The city of Oporto on 18 October hosted the eighth Ibero-American summit (see XI.6.iv), which was notable for the coincidental diplomatic embarrassment to Spain and Chile arising from the Spanish request for the extradition of General Augusto Pinochet from London (see II.1.i; IV.3.iv). The summit also heard an eloquent 'state of the world' speech by President Fidel Castro of Cuba, who was scheduled to host the ninth summit in Havana in 1999 in a further demonstration of Ibero-American solidarity in defiance of the US boycott of Cuba.

As regards bilateral issues such as the dispute with crisis-ridden Indonesia over East Timor (see IX.1.vi) or the concluding arrangements for the scheduled transfer of Macao to Chinese sovereignty in December 1999, it was clear that EU membership conferred a degree of confidence on Portugal. The same applied to relations with the Community of Portuguese-Speaking Countries (see XI.3.ii). Membership of the EU had strengthened the value of the Portuguese passport and given clout to the country's diplomacy. As the year ended, Portugal's participation in the launch of the euro from 1 January 1999 highlighted its status as one of the best national study cases of the advantages of meeting EU goals.

iv. MALTA

CAPITAL: Valletta   AREA: 316 sq km   POPULATION: 376,000 ('97)
OFFICIAL LANGUAGES: Maltese & English
POLITICAL SYSTEM: parliamentary democracy
HEAD OF STATE: President Ugo Mifsud Bonnici (since April '94)
RULING PARTY: Nationalist Party (NP)
HEAD OF GOVERNMENT: Edward Fenech Adami, Prime Minister (since Sep '98)
MAIN IGO MEMBERSHIPS (non-UN): NAM, CWTH, OSCE, CE
CURRENCY: lira (end-'98 £1=Lm0.63, $US1=Lm0.38)
GNP PER CAPITA: US$8,630 ('97)

MALTA went to the polls on 5 September, less than two years after the Labour Party had turned out the Nationalists in October 1996 (see AR 1996, pp. 88–9). The see-saw of public opinion moved back to the Nationalist end: Dr Alfred Sant and the Labour Party lost office, Dr Eddie Fenech Adami was sworn in again as Prime Minister. The Nationalists won 51 per cent of the vote, and a majority of five in the parliament of 65 seats. The Labour government was the first in Malta's democratic record not to last its full term.

The explanation was simple. Economics and politics joined forces. The cost of living and the rate of unemployment had risen as the worldwide recession took hold; the Labour Party was divided and unable to sustain its narrow position in parliament. The crisis was long in the making. On 19 March Dom Mintoff, the fiery octogenarian of Maltese politics, withheld his support from the government on what had become a vote of confidence; Dr Sant, with a majority of one, was obliged to rely on the casting vote of the Speaker. In July Mr Mintoff voted against the government, effectively bringing down the party of which he had once been the leader.

The debate came after a bitter six-week battle over the Cottonera quayside development scheme in Victoriosa in Mr Mintoff's own constituency. When the government lost the vote on the bill to approve the waterfront project, Dr Sant asked President Ugo Mifsud Bonnici to dissolve parliament. The President was reported as saying (3 August) that 'he felt he should not exercise his discretion to refuse to dissolve parliament. . . as he did not feel it is in Malta's interests for the government to continue when it does not have a consistent parliamentary majority to sustain it'.

Mr Mintoff did not contest his seat at the election, thus closing a political life which went back to the 1930s. In his own constituency he had successfully contested 14 elections since 1945, and had been four times Prime Minister until standing down in 1984. Politics in Malta were traditionally democratic and boisterous, and both elements were evident in the long career of Dom Mintoff.

The return to power of the Nationalist Party reopened the question of Malta's relationship with the European Union (EU). On 5–6 February a representative of the European Commission visited Malta to discuss relations with the island. The full text of an agreement was published in Valletta, its principal argument being that 'complete free trade' between Malta and the EU should be in place within three years, and that Malta should take steps to bring its Customs and Excise Tax Act into line with EU requirements. The change of government in September left the agreement untouched, but Dr Fenech Adami repeated his government's determination to renew the island's lapsed bid for full EU membership.

A three-year economic plan, drawn up by civil servants and codenamed 'Operation Value 2000', was published on 2 February. The plan focused on the six main pillars of the economy—tourism, manufacturing, information technology, financial services, agriculture and 'hub services' (stressing Malta's Mediterranean position as major free port). A plan for Gozo followed on 26 March. Tourism suffered a little in July when holiday-makers from Britain sued a London-based holiday firm on the grounds that their hotel was dirty and unhygienic—legal history being made in Britain when the judge decided that the only solution was to fly to Malta for a 'site inspection'. His judgment was that the hotel gave 'fair value for rock-bottom prices', and he awarded only minimal damages to the complainants.

The public were more worried about rising crime and drug-related offences. In July an international gang was gaoled in Manchester following one of Britain's largest smuggling operations, in which seven tonnes of cannabis from Cambodia were found in a container in Malta. The first recorded Maltese death from the drug ecstasy was reported on 17 August, and at the end of the month a quarry owner was charged with assault and drug offences uncovered in investigations by the assistant commissioner of police, Michael Cassar, into sales of heroin and cocaine.

A singular event took place towards the close of the year. In September the Knights of Malta opened their Rome headquarters to the public in the Grand Priory high on the Aventine Hill above the Tiber. Subsequently, in December, 200 years after the Order had been expelled by Napoleon, the Knights returned to Valletta. In a grand ceremony (4–6 December) attended by 1,000 members, Count Carlo Marullo, the Order's Grand Chancellor, signed an agreement with Dr Fenech Adami which granted a 99-year lease on Fort St Angelo, the scene of the Order's victory over the Turks in the great military siege of 1565.

v. GREECE

CAPITAL: Athens   AREA: 132,000 sq km   POPULATION: 11,000,000 ('97)
OFFICIAL LANGUAGE: Greek
POLITICAL SYSTEM: parliamentary democracy
HEAD OF STATE: President Kostas Stephanopoulos (since March '95)
RULING PARTY: Pan-Hellenic Socialist Movement (PASOK)
HEAD OF GOVERNMENT: Kostas Simitis, Prime Minister (since Jan '96)
MAIN IGO MEMBERSHIPS (non-UN): NATO, EU, WEU, OSCE, CE, BSEC, OECD
CURRENCY: drachma (end-'98 £1=Dr485.93, US$1=Dr280.06)
GNP PER CAPITA: US$12,010 by exchange-rate calculation, US$13,080 by PPP calculation ('97)

DOMESTIC politics were dominated by the consequences of the determination of the PASOK government headed by Kostas Simitis to prepare Greece for membership of the European Union's economic and monetary union in 2001. Part of these preparations included a 14 per cent devaluation on 14 March to enable the drachma to join the EU's exchange rate mechanism, at a rate of 357 drachmas to the European currency unit (ECU). The Athens stock market reacted enthusiastically, as did the IMF and the EU. The EU Commission did note, however, that Greece had yet to meet the Maastricht Treaty criteria with respect to inflation, interest rates and the budget deficit. At the same time, the Commission was mildly encouraging about Greece's recent economic progress.

Concomitant measures to privatize parts of the large state-controlled sector and tough wage restraint measures enshrined in the 11 November budget prompted a series of strikes. These included a 24-hour strike on 9 April called by the General Confederation of Greek Workers. This was followed by another general strike on 27 May. These stoppages brought much of the public sector, including banks, to a halt. There was also a prolonged strike by employees of the Ionian and Popular Bank of Greece, which had been targeted by the government for privatization. At one stage striking bank employees physically attacked the governor of the bank, Haris Stamatopoulos. The strike was called off when the government, while refusing to abandon its privatization plans, made concessions over job security. The first attempt to sell the bank in August failed. Another target for restructuring prior to privatization was Olympic Airways, whose employees were the highest paid in the public sector. The airline was subject to minor industrial action throughout much of the year.

As many as half of the country's schools came under occupation by pupils in December. The occupations were in protest against curriculum changes and, in particular, proposals to replace the highly competitive university entrance examinations by a system of continuous assessment.

In municipal elections held in October, the opposition New Democracy party made a strong showing, the mayorships of Athens and Thessaloniki remaining in conservative hands. Mr Simitis responded to PASOK's poor performance in the local elections by engaging in a minor government reshuffle on 29 October. Georgios Romaios was replaced as Minister of Public Order by Phillipos Petsalnikos, formerly Minister for Macedonia and Thrace. Mr Romaios had been severely criticized in the wake of a bungled attempt in September to end a hostage-taking incident which resulted in deaths and injuries. This episode had already brought about the resignation of the chief of the Athens police, Lieut.-General Athanasios Vassilopoulos. Stephanos Tzoumakas was replaced as Minister of Agriculture by Georgios Anomeritis. Costas Geitonas, as Minister to the Prime Minister, was charged with parliamentary liaison, and in particular with dealing with dissent among backbench PASOK deputies opposed to the government's austerity measures.

At the same time, Mr Simitis challenged the 11 dissenting deputies by calling on 3 November for a vote of confidence and threatening to expel them if they refused to back him. He comfortably survived the vote, securing 163 votes to 136. Ten PASOK deputies had voted against legislation enacted in February aimed at reducing the deficits of public sector enterprises by reducing benefits, overtime and collective bargaining rights. New Democracy also had internal disciplinary problems. In July a deputy, whose house had recently been burgled, was expelled from the party for nine months for brandishing a pistol at the Minister of Public Order.

Greece's foreign relations were once again dominated by friction with Turkey. Despite pressure from President Clinton, Mr Simitis blocked moves at the Cardiff summit in June to release EU aid to Turkey in an effort to soothe Turkish anger at being excluded from the EU enlargement process. Shortly afterwards serious tension arose when Greece dispatched four F-16 fighters and two C-130 transports to the Andreas Papandreou airbase near Paphos on Cyprus (see also II.4.v). Turkey retaliated by sending six F-16s to the Gecitkale airbase near Famagusta. The crisis prompted the US government to dispatch the aircraft-carrier USS *Eisenhower* to the vicinity of the island. In January the Greek Defence Minister, Akis Tsokhatzopoulos, had declared that the recently completed Paphos base had the status of a mainland airbase and that any attack on it would provoke immediate retaliation.

Much of the tension between Greece and Turkey arose from the declared intention of the Cyprus government to deploy Russian-made S-300 missiles on the island. This prompted the Turkish government to declare that it would remove these by force if necessary. The Greek government was in constant contact with Nicosia over the issue and proposed the demilitarization of the island as a solution to the problem of the missiles. These negotiations culminated in a stormy meeting in Athens in November between Mr Simitis and the Cypriot President, Glafkos Clerides, at which the latter rejected Greek proposals that the missiles be sited on the island of Crete, where they would be well out of range of the Turkish mainland. At the year's end, however, the Cyprus government announced its decision that, instead of being based in Cyprus, the missiles should be redeployed to Crete. This proposal provoked an angry reaction from Turkey.

Greek-American relations were disturbed in July when the Foreign Minister, Theodoros Pangalos, accused President Clinton of lying over his pre-election promises to give Cyprus a high priority in US foreign policy.

In November the Prince of Wales paid a rare official visit to Greece by a member of the British royal family, which had close family ties with the deposed Greek royal family. On a visit by Prince Charles to the Acropolis, Culture Minister Evangelos Venizelos expressed the hope that it would be a symbolic first step towards the return of the Elgin Marbles, removed from the Parthenon by Lord Elgin in the early nineteenth century. Likewise, the mayor of Athens, Dimitris Avramopoulos, in making Prince Charles an honorary citizen of the Greek capital, suggested that he should resolve the question on the day that he became king. Earlier in the year controversy over the Elgin Marbles was revived with the publication of further evidence of their aggressive cleaning in the 1930s by the British Museum authorities. This prompted a demand by the Greek government for an independent inquiry into the matter.

At the end of May King Juan Carlos of Spain paid an official visit to Greece accompanied by Queen Sofia, the sister of former King Constantine of Greece. There were minor demonstrations by royalists but overall the visit passed off without incident.

In July a Thessalonika court ordered the deletion of one of the meanings of 'Bulgarian' from a newly-published dictionary of the Greek language. Athenian football fans were apparently in the habit of taunting players and supporters of Thessaloniki teams with the epithet 'Bulgarians'. Professor George Babiniotis, the author of the dictionary, listed this as one of the subsidiary, insulting meanings of the word. When this became known, however, uproar ensued, and a Thessalonika municipal councillor filed a petition with the courts calling for the removal of the offending definition. The judge duly decreed its removal, failing which Professor Babiniotis faced a two million drachma fine or one month's imprisonment.

During the summer months forest fires wreaked their now routine devastation. In July some 180 fires resulted in widespread destruction of forest land and caused six deaths, including those of three firemen and a civilian volunteer. Seven deaths from forest fires were recorded in August, when the government was forced to declare a state of emergency in Attica and in the prefecture of Ilia in the Peloponnese. Some 400,000 acres of forest were said to have been destroyed. There were allegations that some of the fires had been started deliberately by property developers.

Seemingly the last of the 'dinosaurs'—as the grand old men of Greek politics were known, not always affectionately—died on 23 April at the age of 91. This was Konstantinos Karamanlis, the conservative politician and uncle of the present leader of New Democracy, Kostas Karamanlis. With the late Andreas Papandreou, he had dominated the political life of Greece in the second half of the twentieth century (see Pt XVIII: Obituary).

Archbishop Serapheim of Athens, the head of the Orthodox Church in Greece, died on 10 April at the age of 85 (see Pt XVIII: Obituary). A wartime resistance fighter, he had been appointed as archbishop during the closing stages of the military regime that ruled Greece between 1967 and 1974. His successor as Archbishop of Athens and All Greece was the 59-year-old Christodoulos, who soon gave indications of an activist tenure of the office.

vi. CYPRUS

CAPITAL: Nicosia   AREA: 9,250 sq km   POPULATION: 852,657 ('97): 651,800 Greek Cypriots in the south (Planning Bureau est.); 200,857 Turkish Cypriots and Turks in the north ('97 revision of '96 census).
POLITICAL SYSTEM: separate presidential/parliamentary democracies in Greek Cypriot area and in Turkish Republic of Northern Cyprus (recognized only by Turkey)
HEAD OF STATE & GOVERNMENT: President Glafkos Clerides (since Feb '93); Rauf Denktash has been President of Turkish Cypriot area since Feb '75
RULING PARTIES: Democratic Rally (DISY) holds presidency and heads coalition government in Greek Cyprus; Democratic Party (DP) holds presidency in TRNC, National Unity Party (UBP) and Communal Liberation Party (TKP) form coalition government
MAIN IGO MEMBERSHIPS (non-UN): (Greek Cyprus) NAM, OSCE, CE, CWTH
CURRENCY: Cyprus pound (end-'98 C£1=£0.83, US$1=£0.50); in TRNC Turkish lira
GNP PER CAPITA: Greek Cyprus US$14,930 ('97); TRNC n.a.

THERE were elections both in the Republic and in the Turkish Republic of Northern Cyprus (TRNC). In February the incumbent President of the Republic, Glafkos Clerides (78), was narrowly re-elected for a second term with 50.8 per cent of the vote. In a second round run-off, he defeated former Foreign Minister George Iakovou, who with the backing of the Communists (AKEL) and the centrist Democratic Party (DIKO) had headed the first round. In the effort to secure victory, both candidates undertook to form coalition governments. After his victory, Mr Clerides formed a cabinet consisting of representatives of the conservative Democratic Rally (DISY), which he had led before becoming President; the United Democrats (KED) headed by former President George Vassiliou; the Socialist Party (EDEK), which had been the decisive force in swinging the election; and the Liberals, who made such a poor showing in the election that they dissolved and joined forces with DISY.

In the TRNC the fractious coalition government of the National Unity Party (UBP) led by Dervis Eroglu and the Democratic Party (DP) headed by Rauf Denktash's son, Serdar Denktash, staved off repeated threats of collapse until elections were held early in December, the last month of the outgoing parliament's term. The UBP took 40.3 per cent of the votes and 24 of the seats in the 50-seat assembly. The DP claimed only 22.6 per cent and 13 seats. The centrist Communal Liberation Party (TKP), with relatively moderate views on the national issue, took 15.4 per cent and seven seats and the former chief opposition party, the left-of-centre Republican Turkish Party (CTP), trailed last with just 13.4 per cent of the votes and six seats. On 29 December the UBP and the TKP formed an uneasy coalition government under Mr Eroglu.

International efforts to find a solution to the division of the island were thwarted by the determination of Turkey and the Turkish Cypriot community to secure recognition of the sovereignty of the TRNC, which had been declared an independent state in 1983 but was recognized only by Turkey. Elaborately prepared UN-sponsored inter-communal talks in 1997 had foundered after the European Union (EU) decided that the Republic of Cyprus could proceed with negotiations for accession in the next round of enlargement, whereas Turkey was deemed not to qualify as a 'fast-track' candidate (see AR 1997, pp. 98, 102–3, 408–10). The Turkish Cypriot leader, Rauf Denktash, had claimed that the EU decision denied the TRNC's putative sovereignty, which he claimed constituted the cornerstone of his negotiating position. Thereafter, the TRNC and Turkey adopted a policy that every step of harmonization of the legislation and the economy of the Republic with that of the EU was to be matched by corresponding measures to 'integrate' the TRNC with Turkey.

In January a high-level Partnership Council signed a 'functional and structural cooperation protocol' to initiate the creation of a TRNC-Turkish 'integrated economic area'. There were further meetings of the Partnership Council late in March and in July. Until the July meeting the Turkish authorities had been careful to distinguish between integration and annexation. The TRNC, it was argued, would continue as a politically autonomous state for which Turkey would provide an international presence in terms of defence and external affairs, a relationship analogous to that between the UK and the Channel Islands or the USA and Puerto Rico. However, during a visit to the island on 25 July, the Turkish President, Süleyman Demirel, referred to the TRNC as an economic 'province' of Turkey where 'the Turkish state and army are in control'.

On 10 March the Turkish Cypriot parliamentary assembly had passed a resolution asserting that 'the reality of the existence of two states in Cyprus should be taken as a basis in the subsequent stages of the negotiating process'. During a visit to the island at mid-month by the UN Secretary-General's special representative, Diego Córdovez, Dr Denktash demanded that the UN abandon any efforts to convene further inter-communal talks and insisted that in future the TRNC would only attend state-to-state negotiations. The Turkish Cypriot leader then flew to Geneva to urge Secretary-General Kofi Annan to persuade the UN Security Council to 'modify its position to fit the new realities'.

On 26 June the UN Security Council adopted two resolutions (1178 and 1179) renewing the Secretary-General's mission of good offices in the pursuit of the resumption of negotiations and extending the mandate of UNFICYP. Dr Denktash met with Sr Córdovez in July and said that the resolutions were invalid because they referred to the government of the Republic as the government of Cyprus. He also rejected draft constitutional proposals presented by the special representative as the basis for negotiation. In September the UN named Dame Ann Hercus (New Zealand) as the Secretary-General's deputy special representative stationed on the island. In October she began a process of shuttle diplomacy, seeking to find common ground in three areas: matters of substance, steps to reduce tension and measures to restore confidence.

Turkey and the Turkish Cypriots on 31 August advanced a joint proposal for a confederated Cyprus consisting of two states each with special relationships with their respective motherlands. The proposal envisaged that the guaranteed rights of Greece and Turkey established in the 1960 constitution should continue. It also said that the proposed confederation could pursue accession to the EU, but coupled this with an ambiguous comment to the effect that, pending Turkey's admission to the EU, it would have 'full rights and obligations of an EU member state with regard to the Cyprus confederation'. The Turkish camp said that this was its final offer on reunification of the island. The proposal was rejected by President Clerides on the grounds that it would create a legal framework for the dissolution of the confederation and its replacement by two separate states.

The EU Luxembourg summit in December 1997 had confirmed that the negotiations for the accession of the Republic could proceed provided that the benefits that would accrue would be for the whole population of the island and provided that the Greek Cypriots sought to incorporate Turkish Cypriots into their negotiating team. Accordingly, the government of the Republic offered two places to Turkish Cypriots, including the post of deputy chief negotiator, on condition that their participation should in no way signify direct or indirect recognition of the TRNC. The Turkish Cypriots declined the offer. On 31 March the EU commenced the process of review for compatibility with the Community *acquis* of the national legislation of Cyprus and the other five states included in the first round of enlargement (Poland, Hungary, the Czech Republic, Slovenia and Estonia). The French government questioned the wisdom of allowing the Cypriot entry negotiations to proceed prior to a settlement, arguing that the EU did not want to import a dispute with the potential for hostilities. The Greek government threatened to block negotiations with the other five candidates. The then UK presidency of the EU said that the negotiations should be allowed to proceed to term, at which time there should be a review of the situation.

In January the Greek Cypriots completed construction of a military base at the civilian airfield of Paphos designed to allow forward deployment of up to 12 Greek fighter aircraft on an 'as needs' basis. The government of the Republic insisted that it would take delivery of Russian-made S-300 missiles to protect the airbase (see AR 1997, p. 98). Turkey, which had some 150 warplanes stationed on the mainland within seven minutes' flying time of the island, saw the deployment as a challenge to its traditional domination of the skies over Cyprus. It threatened to destroy the missiles if they were deployed. After Greek aircraft conducted manoeuvres at the Paphos base in June, Turkey landed warplanes at the mothballed Lefkoniko (Geçitkale) airport and said that it would be upgraded to active status. Mainland troops from both countries participated with local conscript forces in live-fire exercises in their respective sectors in the autumn. As the year-end deadline for delivery of the S-300 missiles approached, the Turks stepped up their threats to destroy them.

At the end of the year the Greek government, committed to support Cyprus in the event of any hostilities involving Turkey and concerned lest it be drawn into a conflict not of its own making, persuaded President

Clerides not to take delivery of the missiles and to allow them instead to be deployed on the Greek island of Crete. The decision taken on 29 December defused the military confrontation but caused Mr Clerides serious loss of face. The two EDEK Socialist members of the coalition government resigned, as did a presidential adviser. The Greek Cypriots cited, as grounds for their decision, two UN Security Council resolutions passed on 22 December (1217 and 1218), which called for the parties to refrain from the threat or use of force, for staged reduction of forces and armaments on the island and for the resumption of negotiations on the 'core aspects of a comprehensive Cyprus settlement'. Couched in stronger than usual terms, the resolutions urged 'compliance' by both sides. The Greek Cypriots argued that they had complied and that it was now up to the Turkish Cypriots to do likewise.

vii. TURKEY

CAPITAL: Ankara   AREA: 779,000 sq km   POPULATION: 64,000,000 ('97)
OFFICIAL LANGUAGE: Turkish
POLITICAL SYSTEM: parliamentary democracy
HEAD OF STATE: President Süleyman Demirel (since May '93)
RULING PARTIES: Caretaker administration in office at end-'98
HEAD OF GOVERNMENT: Mesut Yilmaz (Motherland Party), caretaker Prime Minister
   (originally appointed July '97)
MAIN IGO MEMBERSHIPS (non-UN): NATO, OSCE, OECD, CE, OIC, ECO, BSEC
CURRENCY: lira (end-'98 £1=LT524746.8, US$1=LT315,400.0)
GNP PER CAPITA: US$3,130 by exchange-rate calculation, US$6,430 by PPP calculation ('97)

IN spite of political instability and of social tension between secularists and Islamists and between dominant Turkish nationalists and minority Kurdish nationalists, self-confidence and an awareness of national strength marked the celebration of the 75th anniversary of the proclamation of the republic on 29 October.

The minority secularist coalition government, formed by Mesut Yilmaz, leader of the centre-right Motherland Party (ANAP), led a precarious existence, as Deniz Baykal's centre-left Republican People's Party (CHP), on whose support it relied, threatened repeatedly to bring it down. On 21 July Mr Yilmaz announced that he had agreed with Mr Baykal to step down at the end of the year and allow a caretaker administration to conduct early elections. On 31 July the Grand National Assembly (Turkey's unicameral parliament) voted to hold local and parliamentary elections simultaneously on 18 April 1999. The government did not last the year. On 24 September it was shaken when a Minister of State, Eyüp Asik, resigned following the publication of a tape recording of his conversations with a fugitive from justice, arrested in France. On 25 November Mr Yilmaz resigned when the CHP voted with the opposition and parliament endorsed a motion censuring the Prime Minister for alleged improper interference in the sale (later cancelled) of a state bank to a businessmen accused of contacts with criminals. However, the government remained in office in a caretaker capacity until after the end of the year, as no alternative administration could be formed.

One reason for the lengthy crisis was the determination of the secularist establishment, spearheaded by the armed forces, to exclude Islamist politicians from office. On 16 January the Constitutional Court closed down the Islamist Welfare Party (RP), confiscated its assets and banned leader Necmettin Erbakan and six of his lieutenants from politics for five years. The court found that RP had become the focus of activity against the secular nature of the state. Most of the party's MPs then transferred to the recently-formed Virtue Party (FP). On 14 May Recai Kutan, an elderly former minister in the Erbakan government, which had been brought down the previous year (see AR 1997, pp. 101-2), was elected to the leadership of the new party. His attempts to conciliate secularists found no favour with the armed forces. On 23 September the court of appeal confirmed the sentence of ten months' imprisonment, with loss of political rights, passed by the mixed civil-miltary state security court on the Islamist mayor of Istanbul, Recep Tayyip Erdogan. On 14 September a hijacker diverted a Turkish Airways flight in protest at the ban on the wearing of headscarves by women students. The ban, which had been confirmed by the Constitutional Court, led to demonstrations outside university premises throughout the year and to the dismissal of university teachers sympathetic to the protesters.

Domestic weakness did not affect the firm conduct of foreign policy by the Yilmaz government. The statement at the end of the Cardiff European Union (EU) summit on 16 June, that the membership application of Turkey and of other candidate countries were subject to the same criteria, and the reiteration of this assurance at the Vienna summit in December, did not lead to a resumption of the political dialogue between Turkey and the EU (see also XI.4). On 20 July the Prime Minister went to northern Cyprus to mark the 24th anniversary of the landing of Turkish troops on the island and repeated that Turkey would respond to the threat posed to the Turkish Republic of Northern Cyprus (TRNC, recognized only by Turkey) by the planned installation of Russian-built S-300 missiles in southern Cyprus (see II.4.vi). On 25 July President Süleyman Demirel paid a first official visit to northern Cyprus to inaugurate the shipment of fresh water by balloons towed from Turkey. On 31 August the Turkish Foreign Minister, Ismail Cem, went to the TRNC to unveil proposals for the establishment in Cyprus of a confederation of two sovereign states, one Greek, the other Turkish. The proposal was turned down by the Greeks.

Turkish security forces continued their efforts to put an end to the armed campaign waged since 1984 by the Kurdistan Workers' Party (PKK), a radical Kurdish nationalist movement. The Turkish army repeatedly entered northern Iraq in pursuit of the PKK, enlisting the help of the Iraqi Kurdistan Democratic Party (KDP) of Mesud Barzani. Turkey complained that it had been kept out of the US-sponsored negotiations which resulted on 17 September in an agreement between Mr Barzani and Jalal Talabani, leader of the rival Patriotic Union of Kurdistan (PUK). On 1 October President Demirel threatened retaliation if Syria continued to afford facilities to the PKK and shelter its leader, Abdullah Öcalan. The Egyptian President, Husni Mubarak, visited Ankara on 6 October to discuss the crisis, and on 20 October Syria signed a protocol promising to desist from any action against public order in Turkey.

Syria promptly expelled Mr Öcalan, who had a brief stay in Moscow and then turned up in Rome on 12 November in the company of a hardline Italian Communist MP. This caused a crisis in relations with Italy, which had already been strained when the PKK-influenced Kurdish parliament-in-exile had been allowed to meet on the premises of the Italian parliament (see II.2.iii). The Turkish authorities retaliated officially by excluding Italian firms from arms procurement tenders, while encouraging unofficially a boycott of Italian goods and services. The decision of an Italian court that Mr Öcalan could not be extradited to Turkey so long as that country retained the death penalty on its statute book (even although it had not been applied for many years), and the subsequent decision to free the PKK leader from detention stoked Turkish indignation. However, Turkey's extradition request continued to be processed. As the year ended, Mr Öcalan was still in Rome and the problem posed by his presence remained unresolved, although a visit by an Italian minister to Turkey in December suggested that tempers had begun to cool.

The Turkish economy was affected by the financial crisis in the Far East and then, more seriously, by the one in Russia, Turkey's second most important trading partner. An estimated US$8,000 million of foreign capital left the country, and by 31 December the Istanbul stock exchange had lost half its capitalization, dropping by 50 per cent in dollar terms year-on-year. The economy's growth also halved from (an admittedly unsustainable) annual rate of 8 per cent in 1997 to an estimated 4 per cent. The slowdown helped the government to reduce inflation, and by the end of the year the rise in retail prices had dropped from 99 per cent in 1997 to 70 per cent, and in wholesale prices from 91 to 54 per cent. The budget primary surplus rose in line with the government programme monitored by IMF staff under an agreement made early in the year. This success was due largely to a wide-ranging tax-reform law passed by the Yilmaz government on 20 July, but then eased on 2 September in response to the rapid downturn in the economy.

As the year ended, the Istanbul stock exchange was rising again. But while the external balance of payments and, with it, the convertibility of the Turkish lira were safeguarded by revenue from tourism and other services, the burden of servicing the domestic debt (at exorbitant rates which neared 150 per cent at one time, and dropped to 'only' 135 per cent by the end of the year) was the main economic problem which the Yilmaz government bequeathed to its successor.

III CENTRAL AND EASTERN EUROPE

1. POLAND—BALTIC REPUBLICS—CZECH
REPUBLIC—SLOVAKIA—HUNGARY—
ROMANIA—BULGARIA

i. POLAND

CAPITAL: Warsaw   AREA: 313,000 sq km   POPULATION: 39,000,000 ('97)
OFFICIAL LANGUAGE: Polish
POLITICAL SYSTEM: presidential democracy
HEAD OF STATE: President Aleksander Kwasniewski (since Dec '95)
RULING PARTIES: Solidarity Electoral Alliance (AWS) & Freedom Union (UW)
HEAD OF GOVERNMENT: Jerzy Buzek (AWS), Prime Minister (since Oct '97)
MAIN IGO MEMBERSHIPS (non-UN): OSCE, CE, PFP, CEI, CEFTA, CBSS
CURRENCY: new zloty (end-'98 £1=Zl.5.84, US$1=Zl.3.51)
GNP PER CAPITA: US$3,590 by exchange-rate calculation, US$6,380 by PPP calculation ('97)

THE centre-right coalition, brought to power by the 1997 elections (see AR 1997, p. 105), consolidated its policies of free-market reform through rapid privatization and sought to place Poland at the front of the queue for the next round of European Union (EU) enlargement. This led to conflict with organized labour unions, including Solidarity, whose founder, ex-President Lech Walesa, declared that they should more clearly separate their trade union and political roles. The former communist establishment, now in opposition, was threatened with investigation into its period of rule

An optimistic budget for 1998 forecast 5.6 per cent growth, and reduction of the annual deficit to 1.5 per cent of GDP. Central to budgetary constraints was an accelerated programme for restructuring heavy industry. The government announced that state subsidies for the coal industry were to end in the year 2000. Almost half the country's collieries were to be closed by 2002, with the loss of 110,000 jobs. Some 50 mines stopped work in early December when the government insisted that miners should continue to work until 65. The strikes ended when the right to retire after 25 years' service was restored.

The government also announced that the steel industry was to be privatized in 2001, as part of a modernization plan to be completed in 2005. It was to shed 50,000 workers, while productivity was planned to remain the same. Similar plans for the copper industry were put on hold after ten days of strikes in Rudna. They ended on 10 April when management rescinded plans for job transfers.

A dispute over rail privatization led to the resignation of the Transport Minister, Eugeniusz Morawski, on 23 November on the grounds that rail unions were blocking a restructuring programme. This aimed to reduce the workforce by 60,000 (from 218,000) ahead of privatization due to be completed by 2002. In the meantime, the railways continued to be run at a loss. The state monopoly of telecommunications was to be ended with issues of 25 to 35 per cent of shares to a 'strategic investor' and a further 25 per cent to the general public. Further privatizations (announced on 14 July) included the largest insurance company (PZU), the national airline (LOT) and the Ursus tractor plant outside Warsaw.

Rural protests against government policies culminated on 10 July in a mass rally of 10,000 farmers in Warsaw, which called for a state grain procurement programme for 1998, higher state subsidies for farming and higher tariffs on food imports. They also demanded intensive investment by the state to modernize Polish farming prior to EU entry. The strike was suspended when Deputy Premier Leszek Balcerowicz, who had been the architect of 'shock therapy' in 1989, agreed to talks. Three days later the government announced delays to the introduction of value-added tax on farm products and also of a tax on farm incomes. These would be phased in gradually during 1999 to avoid an inflationary rush of food price increases. Despite these concessions, protests continued. On 4 December some 6,000 farmers again demonstrated in Warsaw for increased state subsidies and government grants.

EU entry negotiations remained difficult. Poland requested exemptions from various EU regulations concerning the free movement of labour and capital and sought to restrict the penetration of foreign capital into certain service sectors, including insurance. Relations were further strained by a cut of 34 million ecus in Poland's allocation under the PHARE programme for Central and East European reconstruction. Poor presentation of projects for EU funding was blamed, and the Under-Secretary of State responsible for preparing them, Slawomir Zawadzki, was dismissed.

The transition into NATO, which Poland had been formally invited to join in July 1997 (see AR 1997, pp. 106, 437-8), was much smoother. Progress was facilitated by urgent modernization and joint manœuvres between Polish and Western armed forces. The scheduled date of entry itself—NATO's 50th anniversary in April 1999—was reconfirmed by President Chirac of France and Chancellor Kohl of Germany when they met Poland's President, Aleksander Kwasniewski, under the auspices of the 'Weimar Triangle' in Poznan on 21 February.

Disputes flared up on Poland's eastern border. Russia and Belarus made diplomatic protests as the government introduced new visa regulations designed to accord with EU pressures to limit illegal immigration and imports from the east. There were also angry demonstrations by Polish traders against restrictions on their lucrative cross-border commerce, including the blockade of border crossings in the Bialystok region on 9 February. Despite concessions by the Polish government, relations with Belarus remained strained. The Polish ambassador to Minsk, Ewa Spychalska, resigned on 14 February.

One long-running international issue approached resolution. The Auschwitz synagogue, destroyed by the Nazis, was rededicated at a ceremony attended by Polish, Israeli and US officials on 10 November. The government put in motion a programme to restore seized property or to compensate Poland's Jewish community for losses suffered in the period. Moreover, crimes committed in the post-war period were also condemned. These included expulsions or enforced flight from Poland during an antisemitic and anti-intellectual pogrom in 1968. President Kwasniewski publicly condemned this shameful episode from the communist past, announcing the restoration of citizenship to those affected and an invitation to return home.

Two changes of law aimed to streamline domestic politics. Firstly, the government repealed earlier legislation under which as few as 15 electors could register a political party—producing a massive proliferation, with some 360 parties registered at the 1997 general election. From the beginning of 1998 a minimum of 1,000 signatures were required. A mere 65 parties had been registered by 13 April. Secondly, parliament reduced the number of provinces (voivodships) from 49 to 16, earlier reductions to 12 and 15 having been vetoed by the President. In the first elections under the new structures on 11 October, the opposition Democratic Left Alliance (SLD) gained control of half the new provinces, while the ruling Solidarity Electoral Alliance (AWS), which won the most seats, took six provinces. The Freedom Union (UW) gained control of one. Overall turnout improved to 45 per cent, but in some provinces, such as Szczecin, remained below 20 per cent.

The ruling coalition took a more robust approach than its predecessors to the communist past. In a reversal of earlier policies, parliament on 18 June passed a resolution condemning the 'communist dictatorship imposed on Poland by force and against the nation's will by the Soviet Union and Joseph Stalin'. The former Polish communist party (PZPR) was held to have been responsible for the 'crimes and offences' of the communist period. On 3 December the military court issued an arrest warrant for an elderly woman, now a naturalized British citizen, who had been a military prosecutor in the Stalinist period, and extradition proceedings were begun.

There was also much greater candour towards the treatment of ordinary citizens. Parliament established an Institute of National Remembrance (IPN) to house secret service files compiled between 1944 and 1989. From the end of 1999 the public was to have access to personal files, enabling victims to be traced and revealing the names of agents and informers. It was to be overseen by a nine-member council, elected by parliament, with powers to decide which documents to declassify.

The settlement of ancient political scores, taken together with the speeding-up of privatization, marked a clear defeat for the old Polish left, as well as showing that the political right was regrouping for a significant comeback. A newly-formed Christian Democratic Party of the Third

Republic held its inaugural congress in Wroclaw on 24 January, electing Mr Walesa as titular head. It was widely thought that this might offer the former President a suitable platform for contesting the next presidential election in 2000.

ii. ESTONIA—LATVIA—LITHUANIA

Estonia
CAPITAL: Tallinn   AREA: 45,000 sq km   POPULATION: 1,500,000 ('97)
OFFICIAL LANGUAGE: Estonian
POLITICAL SYSTEM: democratic republic
HEAD OF STATE: President Lennart Meri (since Oct '92)
RULING PARTIES: Estonian Coalition Party (EK) heads coalition
HEAD OF GOVERNMENT: Mart Siiman (EK), Prime Minister (since March '97)
MAIN IGO MEMBERSHIPS (non-UN): OSCE, CE, PFP, CBSS
CURRENCY: kroon (end-'98 £1=K22.19, US$1=K13.34)
GNP PER CAPITA: US$3,330 by exchange-rate calculation, US$5,010 by PPP calculation ('97)

Latvia
CAPITAL: Riga   AREA: 64,000 sq km   POPULATION: 2,600,000 ('97)
OFFICIAL LANGUAGE: Latvian
POLITICAL SYSTEM: democratic republic
HEAD OF STATE: President Guntis Ulmanis (since July '93)
RULING PARTIES: Latvia's Way (LC) heads minority coalition
HEAD OF GOVERNMENT: Vilis Kristopans (LC), Prime Minister (since Nov '98)
MAIN IGO MEMBERSHIPS (non-UN): OSCE, CE, PFP, CBSS
CURRENCY: lats (end-'98 £1=L0.94, US$1=L0.57)
GNP PER CAPITA: US$2,430 by exchange-rate calculation, US$3,650 by PPP calculation ('97)

Lithuania
CAPITAL: Vilnius   AREA: 65,000 sq km   POPULATION: 4,000,000 ('97)
OFFICIAL LANGUAGE: Lithuanian
POLITICALSYSTEM: democratic republic
HEAD OF STATE: President Valdas Adamkus (since Feb '98)
RULING PARTIES: Homeland Union (TS) heads coalition
HEAD OF GOVERNMENT: Gediminas Vagnorius (TS), Prime Minister (since Dec '96)
MAIN IGO MEMBERSHIPS (non-UN): OSCE, CE, PFP, CBSS
CURRENCY: litas (end-'98 £1=L6.66, US$1=L4.00)
GNP PER CAPITA: US$2,230 by exchange-rate calculation, US$4,510 by PPP calculation ('97)

THE durable President of ESTONIA, Lennart Meri, who had the satisfaction of being named 'European of the Year' by the French weekly *La Vie* at a selection meeting chaired by Jacques Delors, appeared less than impressed by the lacklustre government of his own country. In his end-of-year political review he urged Estonians to examine the politicians critically when voting in the 1999 elections. His call for a less splintered parliament and the need to end stagnation was interpreted as a charge of indecisiveness against Prime Minister Mart Siimann, whose Coalition Party-led minority government controlled only 37 of the 100 seats in the Riigikogu (parliament). One reason for Mr Siimann's failure to broaden his government's base was the reluctance of his coalition partners to join forces with the opposition Reform Party under Siim Kallas.

There were coalition strains in LATVIA too. Ministers of the Saimnieks

Democratic Party successfully challenged Prime Minister Guntars Krasts on budgetary issues in cabinet and criticized him and his Fatherland and Freedom/LNNK party over the handling of relations with Russia, before dropping out of the government in April. Mr Krasts managed to obtain a confidence vote from parliament on 30 April, but his public image was tarnished by earlier reports of the equivalent of US$3 million going missing from the accounts of the state power utility, Latvenergo, at a time when he had been Economics Minister in the ill-fated government of Andris Skele. The latter had meanwhile become head of a new People's Party, formed on 2 May, and promptly attracted two defectors from Mr Krasts' other coalition partner, Latvia's Way.

Mr Skele's party went on to top the poll at the parliamentary elections on 3 October, with Latvia's Way and Fatherland and Freedom/LNNK coming second and third respectively. However, President Guntis Ulmanis chose to invite former Transport Minister and one-time basketball star Vilis Kristopans, of Latvia's Way, to form the government. Hopes that he might build a majority government by getting agreement with the People's Party were disappointed. There was too much distrust of Mr Skele and his personality clashed with that of Mr Kristopans. The latter had to be content instead with only 46 out of the 100 seats in the Saeima (parliament), gaining the backing of the right-wing Fatherland and Freedom/LNNK and the centrist New Party. His minority government then secured unexpectedly large parliamentary approval in a vote on 26 November. That did not prevent President Ulmanis from voicing his disappointment over the lack of a stable government majority for the tasks ahead.

In LITHUANIA, the political year began with the installation of the Lithuanian-American Valdas Adamkus as President on 25 February. The incumbent conservative government under Gediminas Vagnorius presented itself for consideration by President Adamkus, who duly confirmed the cabinet on 25 March. As expected, few changes were made, although Laima Andrikiene, hitherto European Affairs Minister, was not reappointed following an incident earlier in the month when her car had apparently been involved in the death of a demonstrator in Kaunas. It was eventually decided, to the pleasure of the Christian Democrat coalition partners, that her post should be abolished.

Rumours of clashes within the Conservative Party, and specifically between parliamentary Speaker Vytautas Landsbergis and Prime Minister Vagnorius, were confounded momentarily by the unity shown at the party conference in May, but resurfaced throughout the summer. Mr Landsbergis was also accused by the opposition Lithuanian Democratic Labour Party (LDDP)—wrongly according to Mr Vagnorius—of ordering surveillance tactics on officials and their families. In December the irrepressible Speaker proposed a bill banning ex-communists from serving in high level positions in government, to be in effect for five years.

Political manœuvring within the Baltic governments did little to deflect them from the continuing drive to become full European Union (EU) members. In June the Latvian parliament voted 57 to 16 for a series of amendments making citizenship legislation more responsive to European criticism. The naturalization 'window', which had previously limited numbers eligible to apply for citizenship in any given year, was abolished and children born in Latvia after the restoration of its independence could automatically become Latvian citizens. Critics in parliament, prominent among them Juris Dobelis of Fatherland and Freedom/LNNK, then collected enough signatures to force a referendum in an attempt to reverse the amendments. However, the referendum, held on the same date as the general election, upheld the changes by a vote of 52.5 per cent. Mr Dobelis was more successful in pushing the adoption of a language law in October, intended to make Latvian the sole language of instruction in public schools over the next decade. In December the Estonian parliament also voted to allow children born after February 1992 to apply for citizenship without passing a language test.

Latvia's more enlightened stance on citizenship removed one of the last remaining obstacles to the country sooner rather than later taking its place alongside Estonia—already selected as a candidate for earlier EU entry. Baltic association agreements signed with the EU in 1995 came into force on 1 February 1998. Although the financial crisis in Russia, as well as the generally tight international markets, prompted the IMF to revise Baltic growth rates downwards, they were still regarded as healthy. Nevertheless, when leaders of the 15 EU states had their Vienna summit in December they took the decision not to invite any new members for the moment. Latvian and Lithuanian opinion was greatly disappointed, but the governments of both countries rightly recognized that the decision did not reflect on their capacity, but was rather evidence of a growing concern, following the installation of Gerhard Schröder as Germany's new Chancellor, to reform the EU budget before real expansion took place.

The snail's pace of the march of Estonia, Latvia and Lithuania towards European integration was matched by their lack of any real progress in joining NATO. Supreme patience was again demanded of the Baltic states, but both President Meri and Mr Landsbergis succumbed to frustration, publicly voicing irritation at the manifest slowing-down of NATO enlargement (see XI.2.i). There remained a lack of clarity about the specific criteria to be met by new applicants, although the signature of the US-Baltic Charter at the beginning of the year underlined the commitment of the United States to supporting the NATO aspirations of Estonia, Latvia and Lithuania.

In May the US Secretary of State, Madeleine Albright, delivered a particularly forthright defence of the Baltic republics' entitlement to join NATO. By contrast, European leaders continued to show less resolve, in spite of their mantra about NATO being primarily a defence organization, the door to which would continue to remain open to applicants. Confusingly, NATO Secretary-General Javier Solana insisted in March that the alliance was not currently considering the admission of new members.

Hesitancy among the European governments undoubtedly reflected a fundamental unwillingness to upset Russian sensitivities. President Yeltsin told the Russian parliament in February that Baltic membership of NATO would threaten Russian security. In June the then Russian Foreign Minister, Yevgenii Primakov, insisted that 'we do not want the NATO expansion process again'. In December the strength of the anti-NATO group within the Russian Duma was revealed when it began formulating a non-binding resolution linking the ratification of the START-II treaty limiting nuclear weapons to an agreement by Western military leaders not to extend NATO to the area of the former Soviet Union. The Baltic states were expressly mentioned in this context.

Undoubtedly, Russian displeasure with Latvia in particular was intensified following a clash in Riga in March, when force used by police against mainly elderly Russian protesters prompted Moscow to protest about human rights abuses. The temperature rose again when, later in the same month, veterans from the former Latvian Waffen SS held an anniversary parade in the Latvian capital. Astonishingly, the armed forces commander, Colonel Juris Dalbins, took part in the commemoration, together with a few members of parliament. Colonel Dalbins was dismissed in June.

There were occasional placatory noises from Moscow during the year, but Latvia and Estonia did not receive the expressions of good will reserved by Moscow for Lithuania. It proved impossible for the two Baltic states to finalize either their border agreements with Russia or to stop Moscow from inflicting double tariffs on Estonian and Latvian exports to Russia. At a December meeting with Estonian Prime Minister Siimann, Deputy Russian Prime Minister Valentina Matviyenko again tied Russian cooperation over tariffs to improved treatment of Russian minorities. Other demands included better treatment for pensioners and the return of the Alexander Nevsky cathedral to the Moscow-based Russian Orthodox Church. In the same month, Russian Foreign Minister Igor Ivanov stressed his country's concern for its minorities abroad to Latvian Foreign Minister Valdis Birkavs, notwithstanding the positive outcome of the referendum on citizenship law amendments.

iii. CZECH REPUBLIC

CAPITAL: Prague   AREA: 30,450 sq km   POPULATION: 10,400,000 ('97)
OFFICIAL LANGUAGE: Czech
POLITICAL SYSTEM: parliamentary democracy
HEAD OF STATE: President Václav Havel (since Jan '93)
RULING PARTY: Czech Social Democratic Party (CSSD)
HEAD OF GOVERNMENT: Milos Zeman (CSSD), Prime Minister (since July '98)
MAIN IGO MEMBERSHIPS (non-UN): OSCE, CE, PFP, CEI, CEFTA, OECD
CURRENCY: koruna (end-'98 £1=K49.96, US$1=K30.03)
GNP PER CAPITA: US$5,200 by exchange-rate calculation, US$11,380 by PPP calculation ('97)

THE year in the Czech Republic was characterized by political change and economic recession. In January, following the collapse of Vaclav Klaus's centre-right cabinet in November 1997 (see AR 1997, p. 111), a caretaker government headed by Czech National Bank governor Josef Tosovsky took office. Elections to the Chamber of Deputies were held two years ahead of schedule on 19-20 June, bringing a left-inclined government to power for the first time since the fall of communism in 1989. In the pre-election period, political uncertainty was prevalent because of President Vaclav Havel's poor health and funding scandals that discredited several major parties. Mr Havel was narrowly re-elected on 20 January for a second five-year term, but he faced several serious operations and was bedridden much of the year.

The elections resulted in a major advance for the centre-left Czech Social Democratic Party (CSSD), which won 32.3 per cent of the vote and 74 of 200 lower house seats, followed by the right-wing Civic Democratic Party (ODS), with 27.7 per cent and 63 seats. To form a majority government, both the CSSD and the ODS needed the cooperation of at least two of the three smaller parliamentary parties—the Christian Democratic Union (KDU-CSL), the Freedom Union (US) and the Communists—although the last were not regarded as a real option. Following the collapse of both parties' talks with the KDU-CSL and the US, CSSD Chairman Milos Zeman and his long-term rival, ODS chairman Vaclav Klaus, forged a controversial 'opposition agreement', according to which the ODS agreed to tolerate a CSSD minority government. In return, Mr Klaus became chairman of the Chamber of Deputies and the two parties agreed to discuss changing the proportional electoral system to a majority one with a view to reducing the influence of small parties.

The new CSSD cabinet's programme statement centred on fighting economic crime and corruption, improving capital market transparency and speeding up economic growth. In an effort to achieve the third goal, there was discussion of limiting the Czech National Bank's independence. The ODS labelled the CSSD programme 'populist', but ODS deputies ensured its approval by leaving the chamber during the vote. In September the ODS formed a shadow cabinet to differentiate itself from the CSSD government and to prepare for future elections. In the same month, KDU-CSL chairman Josef Lux, who had been diagnosed as suffering from chronic leukæmia, announced that he would leave politics.

By the end of the year Czechs seemed disenchanted with politics, and turnout was low in the local and Senate elections held on 13–14 November, with the latter continuing in a second round a week later. The ODS was the winner in the local polling, followed by the CSSD. A new coalition uniting the KDU-CSL and US with two non-parliamentary parties won more seats than expected in the Senate elections, but the CSSD and ODS in aggregate retained their constitutional majority in both houses. In accordance with the 'opposition agreement', ODS representative Libuse Benesova was elected as Senate chairwoman in December.

Regarding the economy, the Tosovsky government implemented a series of unpopular reforms in the first half of the year, including the deregulation of rents and energy prices. Attempts were also made to restructure firms and complete the privatization process, most notably through the sale in March of a 36 per cent stake in the troubled Investicni a Postovni Banka to the Japanese corporation Nomura. Once the CSSD cabinet took over, there was limited room to manœuvre, since the country was facing budgetary problems, a widening foreign trade deficit, declining GDP and growing unemployment. The state budget deficit surpassed K26,000 million in 1998, while the foreign trade deficit was expected to reach K85–100,000 million. In the third quarter of 1998 GDP fell by 2.9 per cent from the same period the previous year, and was expected to decrease 1.9 per cent for the year as a whole. Unemployment rose steadily throughout the year, reaching 7.5 per cent in December, while the annual inflation rate was 10.7 per cent.

Meanwhile, the CSSD government was also restrained by its dependence on right-wing opposition parties to approve economic legislation. The CSSD's initial draft of the 1999 state budget was quickly rejected by the parliament, and discussions on the second version, which planned for a deficit of K31,000 million, continued into 1999.

In the foreign affairs sphere, the new government worked towards strengthening the country's European integration efforts and improving relations with neighbouring countries. Upon taking office, Mr Zeman undertook his first foreign visit to neighbouring Austria, which at the time held the European Union chairmanship. During the summer the Prime Minister sparked a new argument with German representatives about the Sudetenland issue when he compared Sudeten Germans to Czech political extremists. However, bilateral ties improved after Germany's September parliamentary elections brought the Social Democrats to power (see II.2.i). Czech-Slovak relations improved markedly following the formation of a new Slovak cabinet in late October (see III.1.iii).

iv. SLOVAKIA

CAPITAL: Bratislava   AREA: 18,930 sq km   POPULATION: 5,500,000 ('97)
OFFICIAL LANGUAGE: Slovak
POLITICAL SYSTEM: parliamentary democracy
HEAD OF STATE: Co-Presidents (acting) Mikulas Dzurinda & Jozef Migas (since Oct '98)
RULING PARTIES: coalition of Slovak Democratic Coalition (SDK), Party of the Democratic Left (SDL), Party of the Hungarian Coalition (SMK) & Party of Civic Understanding (SOP)
HEAD OF GOVERNMENT: Mikulas Dzurinda (SDK)), Prime Minister (since Oct '98)
MAIN IGO MEMBERSHIPS (non-UN): OSCE, CE, PFP, CEI, CEFTA
CURRENCY: koruna (end-'98 £1=K61.27, US$1=K36.83)
GNP PER CAPITA: US$3,700 by exchange-rate calculation, US$7,850 by PPP calculation ('97)

SLOVAKIA's parliamentary elections on 25–26 September were the dominant event of 1998, marking a major turning-point in domestic politics and signalling an end to the rule of Prime Minister Vladimir Meciar and his Movement for a Democratic Slovakia (HZDS). Citizens demonstrated their desire for change by giving four opposition parties a constitutional majority of 93 out of 150 seats in the unicameral legislature.

Throughout the pre-election months the atmosphere was extremely tense, much energy being focused on the parliament's approval in May of government-sponsored amendments to the electoral law. The amendments created one electoral district covering the entire country, prohibited campaigning through the private electronic media, and specified that each party needed to win at least 5 per cent of the vote to enter parliament, even if competing in a coalition. After two opposition coalitions—the Slovak Democratic Coalition (SDK) and the Hungarians (SMK)—had dealt with these changes by transforming themselves into single parties, attention was devoted mainly to the media provisions. During the campaign state-run Slovak Television showed clear loyalty towards the HZDS, while an ownership struggle at the private TV Markiza sparked fears that the station was being taken over by HZDS allies, leading to several days of protests throughout Slovakia just days before the elections.

Despite pre-election anxiety, the voting process went smoothly and turnout reached 84.24 per cent. The HZDS's highly visible and costly campaign ensured that the party came out on top, with 27 per cent of the vote and 43 of the 150 seats. However, the SDK was close behind with 26.3 per cent and 42 seats. The four other parties to gain representation were the Party of the Democratic Left with 14.7 and 23 seats, the SMK (9.1 per cent and 15 seats), the Slovak National Party (9.1 per cent and 14 seats) and the Party of Civic Understanding (8.0 per cent and 13 seats). An HZDS-instigated referendum on the non-privatization of strategic energy and gas firms, held simultaneously with the elections, was declared invalid, since only 44.05 per cent of eligible voters had participated. After the elections, only the Slovak National Party supported HZDS efforts to form a new government, which therefore failed. A disappointed Mr Meciar gave up his parliamentary seat and announced that he would withdraw from politics. After the other four parliamentary parties had signed a coalition agreement, a new government was appointed on 30 October, with SDK chairman Mikulas Dzurinda as Prime Minister.

The Slovak presidency was vacant for most of the year. After Michal Kovác's term expired on 2 March, no candidate managed to win the necessary three-fifths majority in a series of parliamentary votes. Most powers of the head of state were transferred to the Prime Minister, and a constitutional amendment approved in July allowed the parliamentary chairman to take those that remained. After the September elections, the new government decided to delay presidential elections until early 1999 and to amend the constitution to allow citizens to choose the head of state by direct election.

Slovakia's GDP growth in 1998 was approximately 5 per cent, while inflation was recorded at only 5.6 per cent. Nevertheless, numerous imbalances indicated that the country was heading for an economic crisis. In November the trade deficit reached a cumulative total of K72,500 million, while the state budget deficit had grown to K65,200 million by year's end. Despite several years of steady economic growth, unemployment remained high, at 13.76 per cent in September. On 1 October the central bank was forced to float the crown and to abolish the 7 per cent fluctuation band within which the currency was fixed against a mark/dollar basket.

Slovakia's ties with the West and with some of its neighbours continued to be rocky in the first part of the year. Controversy over the Mochovce nuclear plant and the Gabcikovo-Nagymaros dam complicated bilateral relations with Austria and Hungary respectively. Meanwhile, ties with London were troubled by an exodus of Slovak Roma (Gypsies) applying for refugee status in Britain. The situation of Roma in Slovakia was particularly difficult in 1998, when summer floods hit two villages and killed some 50 people. Following the appointment of the Dzurinda government, however, Slovakia's relations with the West and with its neighbours showed a marked improvement, most noticeably with the Czech Republic. The new cabinet also promised to pay closer attention to the problems of ethnic minorities. At the December summit of the European Union (EU) in Vienna, Slovak officials were disappointed that Slovakia continued to be excluded from the list of 'fast-track' applicants for EU membership. They vowed to keep trying.

v. HUNGARY

CAPITAL: Budapest   AREA: 93,000 sq km   POPULATION: 10,250,000 ('97)
OFFICIAL LANGUAGE: Hungarian
POLITICAL SYSTEM: parliamentary democracy
HEAD OF STATE: President Arpád Göncz (since Aug '90)
RULING PARTIES: Young Democrats (Fidesz) head coalition with Independent Smallholders' Party (FKGP) & Hungarian Democratic Forum (MDF)
HEAD OF GOVERNMENT: Viktor Orban (Fidesz-MPP), Prime Minister (since July '98)
MAIN IGO MEMBERSHIPS (non-UN): OSCE, CE, PFP, CEI, CEFTA
CURRENCY: forint (end-'98 £1=Ft358.20, US$1=Ft215.29)
GNP PER CAPITA: US$4,430 by exchange-rate calculation, US$7,000 by PPP calculation ('97)

THE defining event of the year for Hungary was the change of government following the May elections. The Hungarian Socialist Party (MSP)-Free Democrats coalition, which had won a solid majority in the 1994 elections, lost fairly badly in 1998 and was replaced by a centre-right coalition of the Young Democrats (Fidesz), the Independent Smallholders (FKGP) and the Hungarian Democratic Forum (MDF). The pattern of alternating governments between right and left established in 1994 was set to continue.

There were various explanations for the failure of the centre-left at the polls. Although at the start of the year it looked as if the then ruling parties would hold on to their vote, support for the government melted away during the spring. Weakened by a lacklustre election campaign, the MSP was seen by voters as too confident, too assured of its power, while Fidesz impressed opinion by its dynamism. At the same time, the Free Democrats were widely seen as having failed to attain what they had set out to do four years earlier—to act as a curb on the MSP. As the communist successor party, the MSP was certainly held back from any serious lurch to the left, but the Free Democrats were quite unsuccessful in reining in the Socialists' propensity for corruption. Crucially, there was no sense that the MSP had any serious concept of accountability to the electors or that it was prepared to listen to its junior partner on this issue. Hence both the centre-left parties lost heavily, the one for its corruption and the other for its inadequate control over that corruption.

The swing to the right was convincing, though not overwhelming. Given Hungary's extraordinarily intricate electoral system, the swing was hard to calculate, but the centre-right now had 213 deputies in the unicameral National Assembly to the centre-left's 158. Considerable concern was aroused, however, by the success of the extreme-right Hungarian Justice and Life Party led by the demagogue Istvan Csurka, which returned 14 deputies. However, the new Prime Minister, Viktor Orban, the leader of Fidesz, firmly insisted that the coalition would not do a deal with Mr Csurka's party.

The composition of the new government, which took office on 8 July after extensive negotiations, was striking for its heavy reliance on non-party technocrats. Several key ministries, including foreign affairs and finance, went to people who were not formally active politicians. None of the Independent Smallholders' four portfolios (including agriculture) were of central significance, while the MDF took the justice portfolio. Furthermore, the style of governing was reformed by the creation of a strong prime ministerial office with supervisory tasks. There was a clear impression that the new government would concentrate on technical efficiency in order to make its mark.

With respect to policies, however, the centre-right found itself in the standard dilemma of post-communist conservatism—what should it actually conserve? Reference to the past was problematical, because it was a communist past and thus a part of the left's heritage, while any attempt to move in a radical direction would undermine the right's moderate credentials. As the rest of the year passed, the impression that the new government created was that it had not really resolved this dilemma. It tended to concentrate on issues of power and style rather than seek to develop a new philosophy.

The new government made it fairly evident that it regarded its predecessor's approach to the ethnic Hungarians in the neighbouring states of Romania and Slovakia with disfavour. It indicated that it wanted to adopt a higher-profile position on this issue, duly making a number of declarations that pointed in that direction. In relations with Romania, the major issue was that of the projected Hungarian-language university to serve the Hungarian community in that country. This was a highly sensitive problem, given the depth of the opposition to the project in some Romanian circles, which were fearful that such a university was no more than a prelude to ethnic Hungarian separatism (see III.1.vi). Intervention from Budapest was regarded as evidence to fuel these fears, even although the Romanian government coalition, of which the ethnic Hungarian party in Romania was a member, had more or less committed itself to permitting the university to be set up. As regards Slovakia, it was clear that no movement towards an easing of the pressures on the ethnic Hungarian minority there could be expected as long as the Meciar government was in power. However, after a new Slovak government had taken office in July (see III.1.iv), Budapest moved to reassure its northern neighbour of its goodwill. Generally, Hungarian-Slovak relations were much improved thereafter.

The most significant foreign policy issue, however, continued to be Hungary's relationship with the European Union (EU). Again, the new government's style changed somewhat. Whereas the centre-left coalition had seemed to be almost passive in acquiescing in whatever Brussels requested, the new government made a point of stressing that there were a number of questions that it wished to dispute with the EU. The two most significant of these were the automatic acceptance of the Schengen Accord regime on visas and the freedom for foreigners to buy land in Hungary. These were both potentially emotive issues. Hungary had one of the most open visa-free regimes in Europe, and it was seen as particularly important that Romanian, Yugoslav and Ukrainian citizens (including ethnic Hungarians) could travel freely to Hungary. Any suggestion that Hungary's eastern and southern borders should come under Schengen restrictions was therefore most unwelcome. There were indications that Brussels was ready to listen on this point. On the other hand, restrictions on the sale of land to non-citizens seemed quite out of the question if Hungary wanted to join the EU.

As far as the economy was concerned, the improvement registered in the previous couple of years continued, though Hungary suffered briefly from the flight of 'hot money' after the Russian collapse in August. Inflation remained uncomfortably high at not far short of 20 per cent, while unemployment dwindled only rather slowly. However, the overall mood was more cautiously optimistic than it had been for some years.

vi. ROMANIA

CAPITAL: Bucharest   AREA: 237,500 sq km   POPULATION: 23,000,000 ('97)
OFFICIAL LANGUAGE: Romanian
POLITICAL SYSTEM: presidential democracy
HEAD OF STATE: President Emil Constantinescu (since Nov '96)
RULING PARTIES: Christian Democratic National Peasants' Party (PNTCD) heads coalition including Hungarian Democratic Union of Romania (UDMR), Democratic Party (PD) & National Liberal Party (PNL)
HEAD OF GOVERNMENT: Radu Vasile (PNTCD), Prime Minister (since April '98)
MAIN IGO MEMBERSHIPS (non-UN): OSCE, CE, CEI, PFP, BSEC
CURRENCY: leu (end-'98 £1=L18,301.30, US$1=11,000.00)
GNP PER CAPITA: US$1,420 by exchange-rate calculation, US$4,290 by PPP calculation ('97)

ROMANIA's year began with a prolonged government crisis; continued with the appointment of a new Prime Minister, Radu Vasile; and ended with a major restructuring of the administration in which six ministerial portfolios were abolished or merged. In between these milestones of the political year, several ministers resigned or were dismissed. Yet these constant changes at the top were less a demonstration of the centrist coalition's determination to guide Romania firmly onto the path of economic reform than a symptom of the general confusion and disagreement over what course the country should follow. As a result, the economy performed much worse than expected, disappointing not only large sections of the population but also Romania's foreign creditors.

The longstanding discord within the coalition came to a head in late January when the Democratic Union (PD), the second largest party in the administration, announced that it was withdrawing its ministers from the government while continuing to support the coalition in parliament. The PD's move followed sustained criticism of Prime Minister Victor Ciorbea for incompetence, inefficiency and doctrinaire conservatism—and had been prompted, in part, by his failure to appoint a PD candidate to one of the key economic posts in the government.

Mr Ciorbea's new government proved short-lived. By the end of March he had lost the support of other coalition partners as well as that of substantial groups within his own Christian Democratic National Peasants' Party (PNTCD), the leading force in the government. He resigned and was replaced by Mr Vasile, the secretary-general of the PNCTD. An economics professor known for his pragmatic views and business-like approach, Mr Vasile quickly assembled a new government in which the PD regained several key portfolios and finally got a long-sought economic portfolio with the appointment of Radu Berceanu as Minister of Industry.

The new Prime Minister promised to speed up privatization and the restructuring of the still considerable state-owned sector of the economy by closing down loss-making companies, particularly in mining and the public utilities. To show that he meant business, Mr Vasile even issued a timetable for legislation and privatization deals. But these promises were to backfire later on as the schedule repeatedly got blown off course by disputes within the coalition and by personality conflicts which claimed several ministerial careers.

The first to depart, though for an entirely different reason, was Francisc (Ferenc) Baranyi, the ethnic Hungarian Minister of Health, after it was revealed that as a family doctor in the 1960s he had signed an agreement with the Securitate (the communist-era secret police) to work as an informer. Mr Baranyi was forced to resign in June even though he claimed that he had acted under duress in signing up and that he had never actually worked as an informer.

Mr Baranyi's departure was little more than a distraction. Much more serious was the disagreement over economic policies between Mr Vasile and Daniel Daianu, the highly-respected and politically independent Minister of Finance. Their dispute centred on the Prime Minister's determination to press ahead with a controversial scheme involving the purchase of 96 military helicopters, at a cost of $1,500 million, from Bell-Textron of the United States in exchange for the American partner's investment in a joint venture in Brasov. Mr Vasile had the enthusiastic backing of President Emil Constantinescu for the deal, which they both regarded as tying Romania closer to the United States and improving Bucharest's chances of being included in a future further enlargement of NATO.

Mr Daianu, who opposed the deal on grounds of cost and the resulting big increase in the defence budget, was dismissed in September and was replaced by Traian Decebal Remes, chairman of the budget and finance committee of the Chamber of Deputies. Within weeks another senior figure, Sorin Dimitriu resigned as Minister of Privatization after being blamed by Mr Vasile for the slow pace of disposals of state property. The Prime Minister announced that he was adding the privatization portfolio to his other duties on a temporary basis.

The last of the many ministerial changes—a process that was widely regarded as highly disruptive—came with the restructuring of the government in December. The Ministries of Tourism and Communications were abolished and a number of other portfolios were merged. The restructuring came shortly after Mr Vasile's government had comfortably survived (by 283 votes against 163) a vote of no-confidence in the two chambers of parliament.

Although the opposition remained weak in parliament and ex-President Ion Iliescu's Party of Social Democracy in Romania showed no signs of recovery from its 1996 electoral defeat, opinion polls were showing a huge surge in support for the ultra-nationalist Greater Romania Party (PRM) led by the populist Senator Corneliu Vadim Tudor. The PRM's newly-recruited members included Miron Cosma, the charismatic leader of the miners' violent marches on Bucharest in 1990–91, who was released from gaol after serving 18 months for the illegal possession of firearms. Following extensive mine closures and planned further cuts under the Ciorbea and Vasilu governments, miners were once again becoming militant. They were not alone: during December alone labour unrest erupted on the railways, in steel-making and car plants and among rubbish collectors in Bucharest. An opinion poll released just a few weeks earlier showed that a majority (51 per cent) of those asked believed that life had been better under communist rule.

The growing militancy among the workforce and disenchantment across society had been brought about by the poor state of the economy. According to preliminary figures, GDP declined by over 4 per cent in 1998 as against a planned zero-growth target; unemployment went up from 7 to 9 per cent; and inflation, though reduced by nearly two-thirds from the 1997 level, was still well above the planned annual figure of 40 per cent. As a result of the rapid devaluation of the leu, average monthly incomes fell to just over $100 during the year.

Although some of these economic ills were the negative by-products of otherwise essential reforms—the mine closures had contributed to unemployment—much of the failure to revive the economy was due to divisions within the coalition. The privatization programme, in particular, continued to lag behind schedule. The partial sale of RomTelecom, the state telephone company, which was originally planned for April, was repeatedly delayed until the deal was finally clinched in November. Overall figures showed that the government had sold off only one-fifth of its portfolio of assets due for privatization.

The slow pace of restructuring in industry and in the financial sector led to strains in relations with the International Monetary Fund and the World Bank. The IMF's latest loan package lapsed in May with much of the credits on offer remaining unused. The Fund made subsequent assistance conditional on Romania demonstrating a tight budget policy and consistently implementing its oft-promised restructuring plans. Substantive talks on fresh aid were postponed until 1999.

The slow progress of economic reform and widespread social discontent also had a negative impact on Romania's twin foreign policy objectives—joining NATO and the European Union (EU). Hopes that Bucharest might be included in a second wave of NATO expansion, soon after the enlargement due in 1999, were beginning to fade. But Romania continued to forge closer links with the EU and the United States through frequent high-level visits.

Romania's relations with its neighbours remained largely uneventful, though Bucharest showed its concern over the outbreak of fighting in Kosovo and its likely impact on stability in the region. Relations with Budapest were not affected adversely by the election of a more nationalist government in Hungary, partly because the new Hungarian coalition was led by the kind of pragmatic conservatives who were also in office in Romania (see III.1.v).

Within Romania, relations between the majority community and the ethnic Hungarian minority continued to improve steadily but were by no means free of problems. Attention continued to focus on education, and at one stage the ethnic Hungarians' party, the Hungarian Democratic Union of Romania, threatened to leave the coalition government by the end of September unless its long-standing demand for the opening of a separate Hungarian university was met. The threat was averted following a compromise deal which left a government committee in charge of exploring the possibility of establishing a Hungarian-German bilingual university.

vii. BULGARIA

CAPITAL: Sofia   AREA: 110,000 sq km   POPULATION: 8,500,000 ('97)
OFFICIAL LANGUAGE: Bulgarian
POLITICAL SYSTEM: parliamentary democracy
HEAD OF STATE: President Petar Stoyanov (since Jan '97)
RULING PARTIES: Union of Democratic Forces (UDF) & People's Union (PU), allied as United Democratic Parties
HEAD OF GOVERNMENT: Ivan Kostov (UDF), Prime Minister (since May '97)
MAIN IGO MEMBERSHIPS (non-UN): OSCE, CE, PFP, CEI, CEFTA, BSEC, Francophonie
CURRENCY: lev (end-'98 £1=L2,771.64, US$1=L1,665.90)
GNP PER CAPITA: US$1,140 by exchange-rate calculation, US$3,860 by PPP calculation ('97)

SINCE the end of communism, Bulgaria had been plagued by economic turmoil and constant changes of government. This year, however, saw a welcome return to stability. Ivan Kostov's cabinet survived, without a single major change of personnel, while his party, the Union of Democratic Forces (UDF), built on the political ascendancy it won in the April 1997 election (see AR 1997, p. 120). It was assisted by recriminations and infighting within the defeated Bulgarian Socialist Party (BSP) and a formal split in the ethnic Turkish party, the Movement for Rights and Freedoms.

Mr Kostov also profited from a more favourable international climate, which saw the European Union (EU), NATO and the IMF expand their relations with Bulgaria.

On the anniversary of his taking office on 15 May, Mr Kostov claimed the restoration of national consensus and the start of economic recovery as his government's achievements. The key was last year's agreement with the IMF, creating a currency board that linked the lev to the Deutsche Mark and cut inflation to some 11 per cent by mid-summer. In August the government introduced a three-year draft budget as a framework for its eventual overhaul of the Bulgarian economy. It forecast movement towards an annual inflation rate of 5.4 per cent and a growth-rate of almost 5 per cent by 2002. On 24 September the IMF approved a new credit worth around $800 million for debt-servicing and to underpin the reforms. At the start of the new parliamentary year in September, Mr Kostov outlined a more long-term strategy. Its priorities were to complete the structural reform under IMF guidance, to step up the campaigns for EU and NATO membership and to defeat organized crime.

On 22 September the government reinstated the national holiday of Independence Day, marking the 90th anniversary of cutting the final ties to Ottoman Turkey. The eight-year schism in the Orthodox Church was healed on 2 October, when a convention upheld the authority of the much-criticized communist-era head, Patriarch Maksim. Such events should have helped engender national confidence, but public morale remained strangely low. Surveys found Bulgarians to be the most pessimistic nation in Europe and the most eager to emigrate. Approval ratings of the government also declined. By the end of the year, much of the country's press had turned against Mr Kostov, accusing him of placing party interests first, of failing to halt corruption and of achieving little more than predecessors, who had failed to attract significant foreign investment, privatize major enterprises or complete the redistribution of arable land.

President Petar Stoyanov, despite his UDF allegiances, criticized the slow pace of reform and the lack of transparency in government. Like his predecessor, Dr Zhelyu Zhelev, he used his veto to return several laws, including ones on the media and the judiciary. Together with the Foreign Minister, Nadezhda Mihaylova, he sought to promote Bulgaria internationally, helped by the fact that, for the first time in a decade, his office and the government were not pursuing conflicting foreign policies. Mr Stoyanov visited the United States in February and Russia in August to promote trade and seek approval for the European ambitions of the UDF. In Russia he side-stepped conflict over Bulgarian obligations to NATO to discuss a lowering of trade tariffs and fix a deal whereby Moscow partly repaid its $48 million debt to Sofia with military supplies. His talks were facilitated by the conclusion on 27 April of a 12-year agreement, ending disputes over the terms of trade in Russian natural gas. The deal also provided for Bulgaria to transport gas to Turkey, Greece, Macedonia and Yugoslavia and to pay one-fifth of its bill by barter.

Mrs Mihaylova was a frequent traveller to EU capitals. The government's drive to end what it saw as an unhelpful international isolation was helped by visits from the NATO secretary-general, Javier Solana, in April and the EU enlargement commissioner, Hans van den Broek, in September. On 23 March the government adopted a strategy for EU accession, focusing on the adoption of EU legislation in Bulgaria. The country accepted its exclusion from the six candidates fast-tracked for entry in July, acknowledging that the delay of key reforms had undermined its case. Bulgaria joined the Visegrad Group (the Central European Free Trade Agreement) on 17 July.

Another theatre of diplomacy was the Balkans, where the UDF sought to promote regional cooperation and limit the repercussions of the Kosovo conflict. Steps towards better relations with Turkey included agreements on 1 June demarcating the marine border in the Black Sea and on 5 November regularizing pensions for ethnic Turks who emigrated during the assimilation campaign of the 1980s. On 12 November the Deputy Prime Minister, Veselin Metodiev, made a public apology for the repression of Muslims under communism, speaking in the presence of his Turkish counterpart, Bülent Ecevit, in the southern city of Kurdzhali. Bulgaria was instrumental in drafting a joint Balkan declaration on 25 March calling for the peaceful restoration of autonomy in Kosovo. Sofia renewed its ban on arms sales to Yugoslavia in May, quarrelled with Belgrade over its treatment of its ethnic Bulgarian minority and offered the city of Plovdiv as the base for a joint Balkan rapid-reaction force under the aegis of NATO. On 11 October the newly-created National Security Council offered NATO east-west passage through Bulgarian air-space in the event of military operations against Serbia.

Bulgarian troops participated in their largest military exercise for 12 years in north-eastern Bulgaria in June, when the concept of the rapid-reaction force was tested. Other preparations for NATO entry included appointing new heads of the navy and the artillery and a new deputy commander of the air force. In July the government announced plans to privatize a large part of the military industrial sector. The Commander of the General Staff, Colonel-General Miho Mihov, outlined a major army reform in August. It involved approximately halving the size of the armed forces, offering more professional soldiering contracts and fully legalizing conscientious objection to military service.

The government claimed to be winning its fight against the Mafia but the public and media were more sceptical. New laws strengthened measures against tax evasion, money-laundering, compact disc piracy, car theft, drug-trafficking and the operation of protection rackets. A purge of the police involved sacking more than 100 police officers just in the city of Varna. Nevertheless, the underworld remained active, fighting for territory across the country. On 20 December the head of one unlicensed security company, Ivo Karamanski, was shot dead at a private party. Some 112 bomb incidents were reported, the most serious being an attack on the newspaper *Trud* on 17 January. Bulgaria abolished the death penalty on 10 December to bring its penal code into line with EU standards.

Two former heads of state were in the news. On 4 June the Constitutional Court ruled that most of ex-King Simeon's properties, including two palaces and five villas, should be returned. On 23 December the Court was asked to judge whether the 1946 referendum that abolished the monarchy should be declared invalid. Todor Zhivkov, who ruled Bulgaria for 35 years until 1989, died on 5 August, aged 86 (see Pt XVIII: Obituary). He was refused a state funeral. President Stoyanov said that Mr Zhivkov's death marked the final end of the communist era. UDF leaders called the BSP's thinly-attended public rally in honour of Mr Zhivkov 'a ridiculous political event'.

2. ALBANIA—BOSNIA & HERCEGOVINA—CROATIA—
MACEDONIA—SLOVENIA—FEDERAL YUGOSLAVIA

i. ALBANIA

CAPITAL: Tirana AREA: 29,000 sq km POPULATION: 3,500,000 ('97)
OFFICIAL LANGUAGE: Albanian
POLITICAL SYSTEM: parliamentary democracy
HEAD OF STATE: President Rexhep Mejdani (since July '97)
RULING PARTY: Socialist Party of Albania (PPS) holds presidency and heads government coalition
HEAD OF GOVERNMENT: Pandeli Majko (PS), Prime Minister (since Oct '98)
MAIN IGO MEMBERSHIPS (non-UN): OSCE, PFP, CE, CEI, BSEC, OIC
CURRENCY: lek (end-'98 £1=AL232.84, US$1=AL139.95)
GNP PER CAPITA: US$750, by exchange-rate calculation ('97)

THE disorders which had wracked Albania in 1997 (see AR 1997, pp. 122–5) did not disappear entirely in 1998 when, even according to official figures, there were 5,562 reported violent crimes. These included 548 murders, 19 of them of policemen, and 62 kidnappings. The UEFA European football association was moved to postpone a qualifying match in the Euro-2000 competition scheduled to be played in Tirana on 17 October. Towards the end of the year there was also a rash of attacks on high-voltage power lines and water pipelines.

Many of the nation's political developments were related to acts of violence, past or present, alleged or real. The northern city of Shkodër saw a number of violent incidents in January and February. The leader of the opposition Democratic Party of Albania (PDS), Sali Berisha, used these incidents to urge Prime Minister Fatos Nano, of the Socialist Party of Albania (PPS), to call early elections. Mr Nano declined, and Albania seemed to be returning to a more regular and regularized public life on 12

March when Mr Berisha agreed to end the PDS boycott of parliament instituted in September 1997 after the murder of a PDS deputy. Mr Berisha said that he did this to achieve the national unity which the Kosovo emergency demanded.

Political divisions soon re-emerged. On 14 March a closed session of the People's Assembly voted to remove from office the chairman of the Constitutional Court, who was accused of cooperating with the communist-era secret police. He had since changed allegiance and joined the PDS. On 17 March the general secretary and 27 other prominent members of that party were arrested for defying a police order not to organize a demonstration in Tirana on 25 February.

Much more serious tensions broke surface in the summer. On 6 July the Assembly adopted a report from the commission it had established to inquire into the disorders of 1997. The report had been published on 11 February. It held Mr Berisha, who was President at the time, responsible for the collapse of the pyramid investment schemes and also declared that the disorders would not have spread beyond Tirana had he not had recourse to the illegal deployment of armed police and specialized military units. In retaliation, Mr Berisha reinstituted the PDS boycott of parliament, and most local government officials of the PDS severed their links with the authorities in Tirana, thus further weakening Albania's already exiguous centralized administration. On 22 August six *prominenti* in the PDS were arrested for 'crimes against humanity' committed during the disorders of 1997. They were held in custody with no date set for their trial. This time Mr Berisha's retaliation was to organize a demonstration against the government on 27 August; about 3,000 people joined the demonstration in Tirana.

The most dramatic turn of events came on 11 September with the assassination of Azem Hajdari, a close associate of Mr Berisha and a popular leading figure in the PDS. The murder occasioned two days of intense violence in which the Prime Minister's office was ransacked and seven people were killed and 80 injured. The disorders did not spread beyond the capital and, compared with the previous year, order was restored relatively easily, this being a reflection of the government's strength. Mr Nano nevertheless declared that the PDS had been trying to bring about a violent coup. On 18 September the Assembly deprived Mr Berisha of his parliamentary immunity.

Though it had contained the September riots, the Nano government had lost some of its credibility. It was further weakened by persistent accusations, not least from Mr Berisha, of rampant corruption and of not doing enough to support the Albanian cause in Kosovo. On 29 September it was announced that Mr Nano would step down as Prime Minister as soon as an alternative administration could be formed. This took place on 2 October when Pandeli Majko, also of the PPS, was sworn in.

Mr Majko's government differed little from that of its predecessor. It too was a five-party coalition—the PPS, the Party of Democracy in Albania, the Social Democratic Party of Albania, the Agrarian Party and the Union for Human Rights. The most striking difference was that its leader had barely entered his 30s and therefore had no connections with the communist past, having in fact been a leader of the students who brought down the totalitarian system in the early 1990s. His objectives now, he declared, were to restore peace and stability, to draft a new constitution, to establish a dialogue with the PDS and to combat crime.

The question of the constitution was critical. Albania had not had a new constitution since the fall of communism, the one major effort having failed when a referendum in 1994 had rejected one introduced by Mr Berisha's administration. A commission established to prepare a new document completed its work in August. Its draft was approved by parliament on 21 October; the most significant feature of the proposed system was that it reduced the presidency to little more than a ceremonial role. A national referendum was held on 22 November. The PDS, however, refused to participate, objecting to clauses which allowed Albanians to change their nationality and to the fact that the referendum would be valid regardless of the voter turnout. When voting was held, the official returns gave a turnout of 50.57 per cent, though the PDS insisted that the real figure was only 39.6 per cent. Of those who did vote, 93.5 per cent were in favour of the new constitution. International observers were satisfied that the poll had been properly conducted.

After the referendum, Mr Berisha and the Majko government clashed again over the issue of the alleged September putsch. In December the PDS leader was ordered to appear before prosecutors to testify in an investigation into the alleged coup attempt in September. Mr Berisha refused, and questioned the partiality of the leading prosecutor; but his position was weak. He and his party had been criticized by the OSCE and the US State Department for their boycott of parliament and for their unwillingness to end the polarization which had paralysed much of Albanian public life.

Towards the end of the year Mr Berisha made a number of significant conciliatory moves. On 21 December he met Mr Majko for the first time, ostensibly to discuss a student hunger strike then in its 12th day. The two leaders agreed a common stance on Kosovo, and also that a new prosecutor should be appointed in the inquiry into the murder of Mr Hajdari and the subsequent riots. A threat from the prosecutor-general to arrest Mr Berisha was dropped and the students ended their hunger strike.

The Kosovo problem dominated external affairs, although Albania's palpable weakness meant that it could not be an effective actor in seeking a solution to the problem (see also III.2.vi). In party terms, Mr Berisha's PDS tended to be more strident in its calls for action to help the Albanians of the area, issuing calls for Kosovo to be granted independence and for arms to be sent to the Kosovo Liberation Army (UKC). The Socialist government took a more realistic view and confined itself to backing any possible use of force by NATO, preferring air strikes but supporting the use of ground forces should it be necessary. Inevitably, given the weakness of the Albanian central authorities and the nature of the terrain, some weapons found their way to the UKC via Albania.

Another aspect of external affairs was Albania's relationship to Islamic fundamentalism. In July Albania deported to America an Egyptian subject who had been accused of a number of acts of terrorism in the United States and was suspected of involvement in the murder of the Speaker of the Egyptian parliament in 1990. In June the Tirana regime had begun a crackdown on Muslim extremists in the country. Some of these had come en route for Kosovo, but there were also indications of more sinister forces. In October a Muslim was brought to trial accused of murder. The accused did not deny the charge and was sentenced to 20 years in gaol; but the case hinted at links with Osama Bin Laden, who had been in Albania in 1994 and who came to international prominence in 1998 as the alleged instigator of terrorist attacks on US targets (see V.4.i; VI.1.ii; VII.1.ii). In November the Albanian police declared that they had uncovered a network of Bin Laden's supporters in Albania.

In accordance with its declared aim of combating crime, the Majko government in November set up a special body to deal with the Albanian Mafia. In the same month it concluded an agreement with Italy to coordinate activity against organized criminals. Many of the latter were involved in smuggling people into Western Europe, and in an effort to interdict this activity Italian speedboats were deployed along Albania's southern coast (see II.2.iii).

Despite its problems, Albania continued to benefit from foreign loans and credits, albeit limited ones. The European Union granted $34 million to help modernize agriculture and Denmark offered $17 million to finance improvements in the judicial system. In May the IMF agreed that Albania should receive $35 million under the enhanced structural adjustment facility scheme.

ii. BOSNIA & HERCEGOVINA

CONSTITUENT ENTITIES: Federation of Bosnia & Hercegovina & Republika Srpska (Serb Republic) CAPITAL: Sarajevo   AREA: 51,129 sq km
POPULATION: 4,500,000 ('97 est)
OFFICIAL LANGUAGE: Serbo-Croat
POLITICAL SYSTEM: federal republic
MAIN RULING PARTIES: Coalition for a Single and Democratic Bosnia & Hercegovina (KCD), Sloga Coalition & Croatian Democratic Union (HDZ)
HEADS OF STATE AND GOVERNMENT: Živko Radišić (President of Republic of Bosnia & Hercegovina); Ejup Ganić (President of Muslim-Croat Federation); Nikola Poplašen (President of Republika Srpska)
PRIME MINISTERS: Haris Silajdzic & Boro Bosić (Republic of Bosnia & Hercegovina); Edhem Bicakćić (Muslim-Croat Federation); Milorad Dodik (Republika Srpska)
MAIN IGO MEMBERSHIPS (non-UN): OSCE, CEI
CURRENCY: marka (at par with Deutsche Mark)
GNP PER CAPITA: US$3,590 ('90 est)

FOLLOWING the November 1997 elections in the Serb entity, the Republika Srpska (RS) (see AR 1997, p. 127), the Social Democrat Milorad Dodik was elected on 18 January as its Prime Minister. Mr Dodik had been fostered as a moderate and modernizing alternative to the strident nationalism of Radovan Karadžić and the Serbian Democratic Party (SDS). His 'government of experts' steered a careful line: no representatives from the more hardline formations were given ministerial positions, and no representatives of Muslim parties were included either. Ministerial appointees from the Serb National Alliance (SNS) of RS President Biljana Plavšić agreed to suspend their party memberships during their terms of office.

Among Mr Dodik's first acts, on 31 January, was to table a motion to move the capital of the RS from the small ski resort of Pale to Banja Luka—signalling his determination to move away from the obdurate secessionism formerly pursued by the SDS. The replacement of Major-General Pero Zolić as commander-in-chief of the Bosnian Serb army by General Momir Talić, on 16 February, was also taken as indicating a further marginalization of the nationalists.

Responding supportively to these signs of change, the Foreign Ministers of the European Union (EU) on 26 January voted for aid amounting to 6 million ecus for the RS. A USAID package of $75 million was also made partly available to the RS.

Within both Bosnian entities there was evidence of sustained struggle between parties and factions committed to the defence of ethnic interest, and between those and others which sought to built inter-ethnic cooperation. In the Muslim-Croat Federation hopes were raised of a move away from the domination of ethnic parties by the formation in March of a Liberal Social Party of Bosnia & Hercegovina, led by representatives of the three main ethnic communities. The Croatian Democratic Union (HDZ) split in June, with former collective presidency member Krešimir Zubak founding his own party, the New Croatian Initiative (NHI). In the

RS, the Speaker of the Assembly was ousted in June after a power struggle within the SDS.

On 12–13 September elections were held to the collective presidency of the union, the union legislature and the assemblies of both entities. A contradictory picture emerged, in which some leaders clearly identified with particular ethnic groups did well. The Muslim Alija Izetbegović and the Croat Ante Jelavić were returned to the collective presidency of the union, while the moderate Serb Živko Radišić was newly elected (and on 13 October became the first Serb to hold the chairmanship of the presidency). In the RS, Nikola Poplašen (SDS) comfortably defeated Mrs Plavšić for the presidency as the SDS remained narrowly the largest assembly party, while Vojislav Šešelj's hardline Radicals also polled strongly. Nevertheless, parties without ethnic designations, and those pursuing more moderately nationalist platforms, made significant gains in the various contests. At all levels governments could only be formed and sustained by means of coalition and compromise. On 13 November Mr Šešelj was expelled from Bosnia by the NATO-led Stabilization Force (SFOR), accused of endangering the peace.

Within the union government, cooperation between the three members of the collective presidency remained difficult to achieve. The design of a new flag was imposed on 4 February by UN high representative Carlos Westendorp after the parties in the union Assembly had failed to reach agreement. It was also necessary in July for Sr Westendorp to impose privatization legislation, delayed because of disagreements over the prerogatives of federal and entity governments. More positively, an agreement was signed between the Ministries of the Interior of the two entities on 3 June concerning cooperation between their police forces.

The United States suspended parts of its military aid programme on 5 June because of the difficulty of securing cooperation between the predominantly Bosniak (Muslim) army of Bosnia & Hercegovina and Croat military units. The persuasive efforts of Sr Westendorp were also required to secure the ratification on 22 November of three agreements between Bosnia & Hercegovina and Croatia. Although these included urgently-required transit agreements between the two states, there was widespread concern that the mention of a 'special relationship' between the two states would further alienate the RS.

The return of refugees continued slowly in many regions. A limited stimulus was given by new legislation in the Muslim-Croat Federation facilitating the recovery of formerly-confiscated properties. Attention was drawn to the difficulties associated with the return process when on 5 March Sr Westendorp dismissed the nationalist Croat mayor of Stolac for resisting the return of Muslim refugees to the municipality. On 17 April two Serb refugees were killed by Croat extremists while attempting to return to the majority-Croat region of Drvar. Action by international agencies in April secured the dismissal of the council of the Serb-dominated

Srebrenica municipality, because of its obstruction of the return process. In November UN High Commissioner for Refugees reported that an estimated 110,000 refugees would have returned to their homes by year's end (about half the projected total), leaving some 865,000 still dispersed across the region and 148,000 in other countries.

On 15 March an international arbitration commission announced that a decision on the fate of the disputed north-western Bosnian town of Brčko (unresolved by the Dayton agreements of 1995—see AR 1995, pp. 126–8, 561) would be delayed until after the September elections to the federal Assembly. The move was widely interpreted as a lever to impel the RS into closer cooperation with the Muslim-Croat entity. A final decision was still pending by the year's end.

Recognition by the international community of the need for a long-term commitment to a military presence in Bosnia was marked by the proposal of the NATO Council on 18 February to reconstitute the SFOR Stabilization Force of 34,000 troops as a 'Dissuasion Force' (DFOR). Accordingly, the UN Security Council voted on 15 June to extend the mandate for operations in Bosnia & Hercegovina for a further year—in stark contrast to the optimistic one-year mandate of the original Intervention Force in 1995 (see AR 1995, p. 560).

The election of a new *Reis-ul-Ulema* (head of the Islamic community) took place on 20 November. The new *Reis*, Dr Mustafa Zerić, was the first to be elected in the post-communist era. A graduate of Chicago, with experience in Kuala Lumpur, he was believed to be of moderate and liberal opinion. As religious leader of all Muslims in the region, he would exercise influence extending beyond Bosnia & Hercegovina, notably in the neighbouring Sandžak (Serbia).

A conference of international aid donors, meeting in Brussels on 7 May, voted an additional $1,200 million for reconstruction in Bosnia & Hercegovina. Economic rehabilitation was taken a significant step forward with the launch on 22 June of a new currency, the 'convertible mark' (KM), pegged one-for-one to the German currency. On 28 October a meeting of the Paris Club of creditors agreed to debt-relief measures amounting to around $1,000 million.

The operation of the International War Crimes Tribunal (IWCT) at The Hague continued to test the sensitivity of Bosnian politics, especially since the two most prominent indicted persons, Dr Karadžić and Ratko Mladić, remained at large (see also XIV.1.i). A number of arrests of indicted suspects were made, beginning in February with Goran Vasić, a Bosnian Serb accused of the murder of Bosnian Deputy Premier Hakija Turaljić in January 1993 (see AR 1993, p. 130). Arrests of indicted suspects (and occasional self-surrenders) continued throughout the year. In April a UN forensic mission began examination of mass grave sites in the Srebrenica area in eastern Bosnia (see AR 1995, pp. 125–6). Public interest in the IWCT, both internationally and in Bosnia, was stimulated by intermittent speculation about plans to arrest Dr Karadžić (who was believed to have been granted asylum in Belarus) or that he might be negotiating voluntary surrender. In August the trial began at The Hague of six Bosnian Croats accused of a massacre at Ahmići in April 1993.

The decision in May to drop charges against a number of those indicted, because the IWCT had insufficient resources, drew attention to the problems faced by the International Police Task Force (IPTF). The potentially embarrassing nature of this development was underlined by the almost simultaneous discovery in eastern Bosnia of mass graves containing around 7,500 bodies. Responding to this situation, the UN Security Council resolved on 21 May to increase the strength of the IPTF to 2,057. A further discovery of a mass grave near Zvornik on 8 October revealed the bodies of 274 Muslims.

iii. CROATIA

CAPITAL: Zagreb   AREA: 56,538 sq km   POPULATION: 4,777,000 ('94 est)
OFFICIAL LANGUAGE: Croatian
POLITICAL SYSTEM: presidential republic
RULING PARTY: Croatian Democratic Union (HDZ)
HEAD OF STATE & GOVERNMENT: President Franjo Tudjman (since May '90)
PRIME MINISTER: Zlatko Matesa (since Nov '95)
MAIN IGO MEMBERSHIPS (non-UN): OSCE, CE, CEI
CURRENCY: kuna (end-'98 £1=K10.38, US$1=K6.24)
GNP PER CAPITA: US$4,610 by exchange-rate calculation ('97)

CROATIA on 15 January resumed control of the last of the Serb-controlled enclaves in its territory of Eastern Slavonia (see AR 1991, p. 172). The handover brought to a close the UN Transitional Administration (UNTAES), in place since January 1996 (see AR 1996, p. 118). A number of incidents were reported from the area, related to inter-ethnic tension. Serb political rallies were banned in Eastern Slavonia in March, although opposition critics and some international observers attributed this to the government's efforts to control the expression of dissent in general. The most serious incident, on 15 June, left two policemen dead after a shoot-out with a group attempting to cross illegally from Serbia into Croatia. Following substantial international pressure, new government guidelines were introduced in May regulating the return of Serb refugees to their former homes in Croatia, and easing the process by which they could obtain Croatian citizenship.

Although suffering from cancer, President Franjo Tudjman was re-elected as president of the ruling Croatian Democratic Union (HDZ) at the party's convention on 21 February, papering over the infighting between aspiring successors. His address to the congress on 23 February, in which he referred to the restoration of the mediæval kingdom of Tomislav, caused international and domestic outrage, since it was interpreted as indicating that Croatia had designs on the territory of Bosnia & Hercegovina. A European Union (EU) statement described the President's remarks as 'inconsistent with Croatia's international understandings'. Internal HDZ divisions became more serious after the death of his close ally Gojko Sušak on 3 May (from cancer). Mr Sušak, formerly a businessman in the United States, had made a substantial contribution to the early electoral success of the HDZ and had been a vigorous advocate of the union of Croatia and the majority Croat areas of Bosnia & Hercegovina.

A series of large industrial actions and demonstrations took place throughout the year, notably strikes of teachers in June and December The determination of the government to minimize effective opposition by all available means was repeatedly made clear. Charges of libel, brought in April by members of the cabinet against the editor-in-chief of the opposition daily *Globus*, however, were not upheld in court.

A crisis was precipitated in the banking system when it was announced on 2 April that Dubrovačka Banka had made 'doubtful' loans in excess of US$230 million. Following an unsuccessful government rescue attempt, it became clear that this was only one component of more extensive problems in the banking system. Foreign debt had also become a serious problem by the year's end, rising to per capita levels in excess of those which had precipitated the collapse of Yugoslavia after 1989. Unemployment remained relatively high (officially over 18 per cent) and the signs had begun to emerge by the end of the year of the return of serious inflation.

The steadily deteriorating state of the Croatian economy was underlined by rioting in the capital, Zagreb, on 20 February. Dissatisfaction with the intolerant attitude of the ruling HDZ resulted, on 12 November, in the withdrawal by all opposition and independent Assembly members of cooperation with government committees. They were particularly unhappy about the government's refusal to institute an independent inquiry into the operation of the intelligence services. Miroslav Tudjman, the son of the President, resigned his position as head of Croatia's intelligence services on 20 April, for reasons which remained unclear. Equally mysterious was the resignation on 4 May of Hrvoje Šarinić, as President Tudjman's *chef de cabinet*, although it was widely believed that his departure was in protest against the involvement of senior HDZ figures in the collapsed Dubrovačka Banka.

Significant moves were made towards the stabilization of Croatia's relations with its neighbours. The mandate of the UN Observer Mission in Prevlaka, supervising the sensitive border between Croatia and Montenegro (see AR 1996, p. 118), was extended for a further six months on 13 January. A draft proposal for the regularization of the border, agreed by Montenegrin and Croat representatives, was laid before the United Nations on 23 June. It drew an angry response from the Yugoslav federal government, which had been marginalized in the negotiations. The UN Prevlaka mandate was given a further six-month renewal on 15 July. Government measures to aid the return of Croat refugees to Eastern Slavonia—involving the eviction of large numbers of Serbs displaced by the war—led to controversy in the latter part of the year.

On 10 September Croatia signed an agreement with the Bosnian government which allowed Bosnia access to the Adriatic Sea through the Neretva port of Ploče, in return for which Croatia was permitted free transit across the isthmus of Bosnian territory at Neum. The dispute with Bosnia & Hercegovina over Croatian military occupation of the small border town of Martin Brod remained unresolved.

The shadow of World War II touched Croatia when on 30 April Dinko Sakić was arrested in Buenos Aires in connection with crimes allegedly committed under the Pavelić dictatorship (1941–44). An order for his extradition to Croatia was signed on 15 May.

iv. MACEDONIA

CAPITAL: Skopje   AREA: 25,713 sq km   POPULATION: 2,000,000 ('97)
OFFICIAL LANGUAGE: Macedonian
POLITICAL SYSTEM: presidential republic
HEAD OF STATE & GOVERNMENT: President Kiro Gligorov (since Dec '90)
RULING PARTIES: Social Democratic Alliance of Macedonia (SDSM) holds presidency;
    Internal Macedonian Revolutionary Organization–Democratic Party for Macedonian
    National Unity (VMRO-DPMNE), Democratic Alliance (DA) & National Democratic
    Party (NDP) form government
PRIME MINISTER: Ljubčo Georgievski (VMRO-DPMNE), since Nov '98
MAIN IGO MEMBERSHIPS (non-UN): OSCE, PFP, CE, CEI
CURRENCY: denar (end-'98 £1=D85.77, US$1=D51.55)
GNP PER CAPITA: US$1,090 by exchange-rate calculation ('97)

THE deteriorating situation in Kosovo (see III.2.vi) overshadowed Macedonia throughout the year. In January bombs exploded in the mainly ethnic-Albanian cities of Tetovo and Gostivar, widely attributed to the Kosovo Liberation Army (UCK). Large demonstrations took place on 10 June in Skopje, in which local Albanians voiced support for the UCK. Controversy erupted during January and February over the proposal to establish a safe corridor for the transit of refugees from Kosovo to Albania. Tension remained high along Macedonia's borders with Albania and Kosovo.

The seriousness with which the international community took the vulnerability of Macedonia to destabilization was recognized in the further extension in January of the mandate of the UN Preventative Deployment Force (UNPREDEP) originally deployed in 1993 (see AR 1993, p. 128).

The strategic significance of Macedonia was underlined by the prominent part played by the republic in NATO's planning to deal with the Kosovo crisis. A base was established outside Kumanovo as the headquarters for an emergency 'extraction force' for the international monitoring mission in Kosovo—the scene of international exercises in June and September.

Relations between the majority Macedonian Slav population and the Albanian minority remained difficult. Although sentences imposed on three ethnic Albanian municipal officials in 1997, for flying the Albanian flag on occasions not sanctioned by law (see AR 1997, pp. 131–2), were reduced by the Court of Appeal on 19 February, the fact that they were not quashed provoked Albanian resentment. On 13 April the Democratic Party of Albanians announced that, partly as a consequence, it was to withdraw from the governing coalition and from all state bodies. The incident was also the occasion for opposition demonstrations in Skopje on 5 May. The death of an ethnic Albanian politician, Beqir Limani, in a clash with security forces in Kičevo on 20 September led to escalating inter-ethnic tension in the run-up to parliamentary elections in October.

Held on 18 October and 1 November, the elections resulted in a change of government. The former communists of the Social Democratic Alliance of Macedonia (SDSM) were defeated by an alliance of the right-of-centre Internal Macedonian Revolutionary Organization–Democratic Party for Macedonian National Unity (VMRO-DPMNE) and the Democratic Alternative (DA), a new pro-business party. With the VMRO-DPMNE/DA alliance commanding 62 of the 125 Assembly seats, VMRO-DPMNE leader Ljupčo Georgievski eventually finalized a new cabinet in early December which included representatives of the ethnic-Albanian National Democratic Party (NDP). Although formerly regarded as ultra-nationalist, the VMRO-DPMNE offered major concessions to ethnic Albanians, including greater autonomy for local government and recognition of the Albanian-language university at Tetovo (see AR 1995, p. 122). The participation of Albanian representatives in government was generally recognized as necessary to minimize ethnic conflict. The success of the DA, led by former communist youth leader and collective presidency member Vasil Tupurkovski, reflected widespread dissatisfaction with the slowness of economic modernization.

International economic support for Macedonia was expressed on 17 February in the granting of a World Bank loan of US$35 million for the modernization of power generation capacity. Substantial additional loans were made available by the German Development Bank, the Dutch Development Corporation and the EBRD.

The privatization of former 'social property' made relatively rapid progress in Macedonia in comparison with other ex-Yugoslav republics (with the exception of Slovenia). Legislation approved on 22 April made provision for the extensive return to private ownership of land and other property expropriated under communist nationalization measures between

1945 and 1948. A scheme was also introduced to modernize agriculture through the leasing of individual holdings to large agrarian enterprises. However, the difficulties of economic transition continued to haunt Macedonia, as was evident in June in trials arising from the failed TAT pyramid investment scheme (see AR 1997, p. 131).

The longstanding dispute between Skopje and Greece over the use the name 'Macedonia' continued, with the Macedonian authorities tightening visa regulations for Greeks, in response to a similar action by the Greeks the previous November. On the other hand, preliminary negotiations between representatives of the Macedonian Orthodox Church and the Serbian and Greek Churches, designed to end the non-recognition of the autonomous Macedonian church, made significant progress and were scheduled to continue.

v. SLOVENIA

CAPITAL: Ljubljana   AREA: 20,251 sq km   POPULATION: 2,000,000 ('97)
OFFICIAL LANGUAGE: Slovene
POLITICAL SYSTEM: presidential republic
HEAD OF STATE & GOVERNMENT: President Milan Kučan (since April '90)
RULING PARTIES: Liberal Democracy of Slovenia (LDS), Slovene People's Party (SLS) &
   Democratic Party of Pensioners (DeSUS)
PRIME MINISTER: Janez Drnovšek (LDS), since April '92
MAIN IGO MEMBERSHIPS (non-UN): OSCE, CE, PFP, CEI
CURRENCY: tolar (end-'98 £1=T269.24, US$1=T161.82)
GNP PER CAPITA: US$9,680 by exchange-rate calculation, US$12,520 by PPP calculation ('97)

SLOVENIA's determination to emphasize the distance between its democratic aspirations and its communist past were shaken in January by the arrest on Croatian territory of two members of its intelligence forces, who were found to be in possession of electronic surveillance equipment. Defence Minister Tit Turnšek resigned on 25 February as a consequence of the affair, which strained relationships between the Slovene People's Party (SLS), which he represented, and the dominant Liberal Democracy of Slovenia (LDS). The episode was followed by a major restructuring of the Slovene security services in October. Relations with Croatia were further tested by the Slovene decision in August to cut off electricity from the Krško nuclear power station until the Croat authorities paid an outstanding debt equivalent to US$14.4 million.

Progress towards Slovenia's accession to the European Union (EU) encountered a setback in January when its stock market law was criticized by EU negotiators for its rigidity. However, this principal foreign policy plank of successive post-independence governments was aided by agreement on 4 February with Italy over the issue of compensation to ethnic

Italians who had been forced to flee Slovenia at the end of World War II. Italy had threatened not only to block Slovene accession to the EU but even to abrogate the Osimo and Rome agreements of 1975 and 1983 (see AR 1994, p. 135; 1995, p. 123). The seriousness with which Slovenia took the goal of EU accession was highlighted in March when Assembly members voted to cut their salaries by 5 per cent as part of a package to reduce public expenditure to meet EU targets. The costs of this single-minded endeavour were reflected in unemployment rates of 14–15 per cent and a struggle to keep inflation below 10 per cent.

vi. FEDERAL REPUBLIC OF YUGOSLAVIA

CONSTITUENTS: Montenegro (13,812 sq km), Serbia (88,316 sq km)   CAPITAL: Belgrade
AREA: 102,128 sq km POPULATION: 10,600,000 ('97 est)   OFFICIAL LANGUAGE: Serbo-Croat
POLITICAL SYSTEM: federal republic
RULING PARTIES: Socialist Party of Serbia heads coalition in Serbia; For a Better Life alliance heads coalition in Montenegro
HEAD OF STATE & GOVERNMENT: President Slobodan Milošević (since July '97)
PRESIDENTS OF REPUBLICS: Milan Milutinović (Serbia) & Milo Djukanović (Montenegro)
PRIME MINISTERS: Momir Bulatović (Yugoslavia); Mirko Marjanović (Serbia); Filip Vujanović (Montenegro)
MAIN IGO MEMBERSHIP (non-UN): OSCE
CURRENCY: new dinar (end-'98 £1=ND16.59, US$1=9.98)
GNP PER CAPITA: n.a.

DOMESTIC and international perception of Yugoslavia was dominated throughout the year by the escalation of tension into civil war, between the Serbian authorities and the insurgent Kosovo Liberation Army (UCK).
   The deterioration in the security situation, particularly the deaths of four police officers on 28 February, led to an emphatic attempt to dislodge the UCK during March. Serious fighting, especially in the vicinity of Drenica, led to more than 80 deaths, and Albanian accusations of Serb atrocities. The United States and the European Union (EU) reacted strongly, the Clinton administration threatening the imposition of additional economic sanctions against Yugoslavia. Attempts to mobilize UN intervention in early March were blocked by Russia and China, which opposed interference in Yugoslavia's internal affairs. Visits by US State Department envoy Robert Gelbard and British Foreign Secretary Robin Cook in the first week of March put pressure on the Serbs to moderate their action in Kosovo. Nevertheless, fighting intensified. Following a meeting on 9 March of Foreign Ministers of the international Contact Group for Kosovo (the United States, Germany, France, Italy and the UK), together with a Russian observer, a package of economic sanctions was reimposed on Serbia, despite Russian dissent. Meetings of representatives of five Balkan states (on 10 March) and of the EU Foreign Ministers in

III.2.vi. YUGOSLAVIA

THE TROUBLED PROVINCE OF KOSOVO

Edinburgh (13 March) also called for restraint. Following a visit to Belgrade by the Foreign Ministers of France and Germany on 19–20 March, informal talks took place between Serb and Kosovar representatives.

On 22 March elections were held to a legislature and the presidency of the 'Republic of Kosovo', returning overwhelming support for Ibrahim Rugova and his Democratic Alliance of Kosovo (LDK), which advocated passive resistance to Serbian rule. As in the previous such poll in 1992, the Serbian authorities declared the latest election illegal and refused to recognize its results. A new Serbian government coalition was established on 24 March, following the defeat in the assembly of the administration of Mirko Marjanović. The new coalition involved Slobodan Milošević's Socialist Party of Serbia (SPS), the Yugoslav United Left (JUL) and Vojislav Šešelj's Serbian Radical Party (SRS). The intransigent nationalism of Mr Šešelj, whose party held 15 of the 36 ministerial portfolios, undermined any possibility of compromise with the Albanians.

A UN Security Council resolution of 31 March imposed an arms embargo on the Federal Republic, further measures also being taken to freeze Yugoslav assets abroad. Nevertheless, the Serb leadership continued to refuse to negotiate with 'terrorist' representatives of an armed insurrection, the Albanians would not begin negotiations without the withdrawal of Serbian special forces. Bowing to mounting pressure from international bodies, however, the Serbian government held a referendum on 23 April on whether to accept foreign intervention in the settlement of the Kosovo problem. Boycotted by the ethnic Albanians, it produced a vote of 95 per cent against intervention (although the result was challenged by non-governmental observers).

The UCK extended its reach steadily, claiming by mid-May to control between a third and a half of Kosovo, with only the larger cities and main roads being dominated by the Serbian forces. On 15 May both sides bowed to growing international pressure, especially the mediating efforts of US envoys Richard Holbrooke, Robert Gelbard and Christopher Hill, and the first of a series of meetings between President Milošević and Dr Rugova took place in Belgrade. Although progress was reported, with significant concessions coming from the Kosovars, on 25 May the Serbs launched a large-scale counter-offensive, bringing in armoured units. NATO Foreign Ministers responded by announcing on 28 May that contingency plans were being drawn up for the deployment of troops along the province's borders, to prevent the spread of the conflict, and to cut the flow of arms into Kosovo from Albania.

By mid-June UCK strength was estimated at around 12,000 troops and their units were threatening the large mining and power generation resources in the north of the province. By the end of June, however, Serbian security forces had begun to reverse the UCK gains, taking several UCK strongholds in heavy fighting. Calls in the UN Security Council on 24

August for a ceasefire were ignored by both sides. On 6 July diplomatic observers from nine countries, including principally members of the Contact Group, began patrols in Kosovo designed to monitor the activities of the Serbian security forces. On 14 July a team from the Organization for Security and Cooperation in Europe (OSCE) arrived in Belgrade in an attempt to persuade the Serbs to permit international monitoring of the conflict, although their task was made difficult by the fact that the OSCE had suspended Yugoslav membership in 1992.

International concern over Kosovo was stimulated by revelations about atrocities committed against civilians, particularly the discovery of mass graves at Gornje Obrinje, Golubovac and Vraniq. Although the Serbs were criticized repeatedly for the indiscriminate use of force in their attempts to defeat the UCK, the latter was held responsible for the murder of nine Serb workers captured in the assault on the Belaševac mine in late June. The UCK was also accused of the widespread terrorization of ethnic Albanians believed to have cooperated with the Serb authorities. A team of investigators from the International War Crimes Tribunal at The Hague was refused permission to operate in Kosovo on 5 November.

A meeting of NATO Defence Ministers in Brussels on 11 June drafted plans for military intervention in Kosovo. By the end of the month NATO was in a position to issue an ultimatum to the Serbian government. US envoy Holbrooke saw President Milošević again on 23 June, also meeting representatives of the UCK, but after four days of negotiation reported little progress. The Contact Group continued its efforts throughout July, and on 9 August tabled at the UN proposals suggesting that Kosovo be given a large degree of autonomy while retaining its constitutional link with Serbia. Local powers would include control over the police as well as tax-raising powers, the use of national emblems and external representation. The initial response from both sides was cool, since the plan fell short of the independence sought by the Albanians but exceeded the degree of autonomy acceptable to the Serbs.

The Serb offensive of September was generally interpreted as an attempt to weaken the UCK before the government bowed, inevitably, to international pressure for mediation. Kosovar proposals for the future of the province were finally put forward on 20 September. UN Security Council resolution 1199 of 23 September demanded an immediate ceasefire, and the following day NATO issued an 'activation warning' asking member states to make available the forces necessary to mount military intervention in Kosovo. On 28 September Serbian Prime Minister Marjanović announced that security operations in Kosovo had been brought to a successful conclusion. A temporary ceasefire was secured, permitting the deployment during November of a force of 1,800 unarmed OSCE 'verifiers'. Intense diplomatic activity during October enabled Ambassador Hill to hand a US peace plan to President Milutinović on 14

November. Intermittent fighting continued between the two sides throughout the rest of the year.

The attempts of outside bodies to enforce mediation in Kosovo were complicated during the year by the emergence of serious political and tactical differences between the Kosovar Albanian factions. In mid-April a splinter group of the LDK under Rexhep Qosia emerged as the 'New Democratic League of Kosovo', openly abandoning 'President' Rugova's policy of non-violent resistance. Following the Serbian offensive of May, the Albanian population of Kosovo polarized rapidly, with the Rugova line steadily losing support to more militant groups. Divisions within the Kosovar side led to repeated delays in the composition of a negotiating team. A good deal of the efforts of both Mr Holbrooke and Mr Hill were devoted to mediating between different Kosovar factions.

By mid-summer international aid agencies estimated that 250,000 people had been displaced from their homes by the fighting, resulting in the flight of waves of refugees into Montenegro, Macedonia and Serbia as well as into Albania. Many were believed to be living in makeshift encampments in the hills away from the roads along which fighting was concentrated.

The continuing political difficulties of the Serbian leadership following the restructuring of the ruling coalition in March became apparent also on the economic front. New banking rules were introduced in February, although several economists suggested that these could compel the banks to operate when technically insolvent, underlining the inability of the government to address seriously the imperative need for economic structural reform. Deputy Serbian Premier Danko Djunić resigned on 9 April, protesting at the 'bureaucratic blockade' against economic reform, including privatization, and government toleration of increasingly high rates of inflation, signalled by a 45 per cent devaluation of the dinar against the Deutsche Mark.

The atmosphere of semi-legality and scandal surrounding federal government was enhanced by the arrest on 19 February of Nenad Djordjević, a close associate of President Milošević's wife Mirjana Marković, on charges of embezzlement. Government intolerance of dissent was illustrated by the fine of the equivalent of $244,000 imposed on the weekly *Evropljanin* on 24 October, for publishing an item critical of the President. During November Ljubiša Stanišić (head of the security services) and Chief of Staff General Momčilo Perišić were removed from office because of growing differences with President Milošević. Loyalty oaths were demanded of academics at Belgrade University.

The inauguration of Milo Djukanović as President of Montenegro in January 1997 (see AR 1997, p. 135), attended by demonstrations and riots by the supporters of the ousted Momir Bulatović, had signalled the beginning of a long process of struggle between Podgorica and Belgrade. The Montenegrins withdrew from a succession of cooperative arrangements between the two constituent republics of the federation, perhaps presaging their eventual separation. Growing distance between the Serbian and Montenegrin leaderships was emphasized by President Djukanović's criticism of the April referendum on Kosovo as 'collective suicide', and by proposals for major reforms of the federal system critical of the policy and practice of the Serbian leadership. Relations between the two republics deteriorated further when on 18 May federal Prime Minister Radoje Kontić (of Montenegrin birth) was dismissed, after he had been increasingly critical of President Milošević's policies. He was replaced by Momir Bulatović. In August it emerged that the Montenegrins had refused Serbian requests that they should send forces to participate in operations in Kosovo.

Assembly elections were held in Montenegro on 31 May, under a new electoral law providing for a 78-seat Assembly to replace the former 125-seat legislature. The 'For a Better Life' coalition, led by President Djukanović's Democratic Party of Socialists of Montenegro, took 42 seats and 49.5 per cent of the vote. The new Assembly promptly revoked the mandates of the 20 Montenegrin representatives in the upper house of the Federal Assembly, replacing them with Djukanović supporters. This move ensured that President Milošević could no longer command the two-thirds majority needed to introduce further constitutional change.

3. RUSSIA, EASTERN EUROPE AND THE CAUCASUS

i. RUSSIA

CAPITAL: Moscow   AREA: 17,075,000 sq km   POPULATION: 146,000,000 ('98)
OFFICIAL LANGUAGE: Russian
POLITICAL SYSTEM: federal republic
HEAD OF STATE & GOVERNMENT: President Boris Yeltsin (since June '91)
RULING PARTIES: Our Home is Russia (NDR) heads fluid coalition
PRIME MINISTER: Yevgenii Primakov, since Sept '98
MAIN IGO MEMBERSHIPS (non-UN): CIS, OSCE, G-8, CE, PFP, CBSS, BSEC, AC, APEC
CURRENCY: rouble (end-'98 £1=R35.85, US$1=R21.55)
GNP PER CAPITA: US$2,740 by exchange-rate calculation, US$4,190 by PPP calculation ('97)

COMMUNIST rule had ended later in Russia than in Eastern Europe, and it had lasted longer. For these reasons its 'transition' was slower and more erratic. Its economy, already contracting in the last years of Soviet rule, shrank by about half in the years that followed. Its political system, which had been dominated by a Communist Party in the Soviet period, remained highly centralized, even if the central agency of decision-making was now a powerful presidency. There was a very slow development of 'civil society', or of the associations among ordinary people that might have sustained a more open and participatory politics, and little sign of a new middle class on which the post-communist system might have depended. The defeat of the Communist challenger at the 1996 presidential election (see AR 1996, pp. 128–9) appeared to demonstrate that most Russians had no wish to return to a version of the Soviet past. But there was little commitment to the post-communist order. And as the financial and political convulsions of 1998 made clear, its stability could not be taken for granted.

President Yeltsin, ill at the beginning of the year, had recovered sufficiently to give his annual 'state of the union' address to the Russian parliament in February. He called for 'strict order' in public finance and a 'realistic budget' for 1998, and warned that if these 'strategic tasks' were not accomplished they would 'have a different government'. How different became apparent in March, when in a series of decrees Mr Yeltsin dismissed Prime Minister Viktor Chernomyrdin and his entire cabinet and named the 35-year-old Energy Minister, Sergei Kirienko, as the new Prime Minister. Explaining his actions in a television address, the Russian President said that he wished to 'give the economic reforms more energy and efficiency'. His nomination, however, required the approval of the Duma (parliament), which would itself be dissolved if it failed three times to confirm the President's choice. The Duma rejected Mr Kirienko in a first vote on 10 April, and still more decisively in a second vote a week later. In the third vote, on 25 April, Mr Kirienko won by a decisive margin, with 251 votes in favour and only 25 against, although many deputies refused to vote at all. In spite of their party's firm opposition to the nomination, it was clear that many Communist deputies had used the opportunity provided by a secret ballot to accept it.

Many politicians, clearly, already had their eyes on the parliamentary elections due in December 1999, and still more so on the presidential elections scheduled for July 2000. Mr Chernomyrdin, who had been Prime Minister from 1992 up to his sudden dismissal, was the first to announce his candidature. Another expected candidate, the former Secretary of the Security Council, Alexander Lebed, strengthened his position enormously when he was elected governor of the vast Krasnoyarsk region of Siberia. Having led in the first round, ex-General Lebed defeated the incumbent governor with 57 per cent of the vote in the second round on 17 May. Speaking on television, the new governor indicated that he saw 'no reason to aspire' to the presidency 'for the time being'; but he began to champion the cause of the regions that were rich in natural resources against the central government, and it was likely that this would form the substance of his presidential challenge. Other candidates declaring their hand later in the year included the Moscow mayor, Yuri Luzhkov, who announced in October that he would stand if there were 'no more worthy candidates', and the Speaker of the Duma, Gennadii Seleznev.

The year had begun with relatively good news on the economic front, when the State Statistics Committee reported 0.4 per cent growth in GDP in 1997, the first annual rise since the demise of the USSR in 1991. Industrial output grew by 1.9 per cent, and the annual inflation rate fell to 11.3 per cent as compared with 21.8 per cent in 1996. Government forecasts for the year assumed growth of 2 per cent, and a further fall in inflation to between 5 and 8 per cent. A further instalment of IMF support was paid over in January, and a redenomination (by which 1,000 old roubles became one new rouble) went smoothly. But a nationwide day of protest against unpaid wages was held in numerous Russian cities in April, organized by the Federation of Independent Trade Unions (who claimed that 4.5 million people had taken part). And in late May there was a worrying sign of instability on the financial markets, with a sharp fall in the value of the rouble; the Central Bank was obliged to treble interest rates to restore a measure of stability, although it was regarded as no more than an interim measure. A package of measures, announced on 29 May, indicated that attempts would be made to improve tax collection and that further state assets would be sold as part of a longer-term solution.

Coal-miners began their own protest against unpaid wages in May, blocking railway lines and cutting off eastern Siberia from the rest of the country. Other sectors of the labour force, including scientists and teachers, began to press similar demands. The government responded by attempting to revive its privatization programme, and seeking assistance from international financial institutions (among which the IMF, after discussions with the Russian government, announced further support in July). In early June President Yeltsin met a group of the wealthy 'oligarchs', who issued a public statement in favour of the 'tough but necessary measures' being undertaken by the government in response to what they described as the 'biggest financial crisis in recent years'. A more comprehensive 'anti-crisis programme' was published at the end of June, and adopted with some amendments by the Duma in July. Unpaid wages, nonetheless, remained the leading public concern throughout the year, fuelling another day of action on 7 October. According to the Interior Ministry, 600,000 people took part, but this figure excluded strikers. The trade unions themselves claimed that 17 million had been involved. The demonstrators' demands included the resignation of the President as well as action on back pay.

Meanwhile, a much deeper crisis had erupted in August, the most serious since the bloodshed of October 1993. The markets were already nervous as a result of the financial crisis that had begun in Asia the previous year. Tension was heightened on 13 August when the financier George Soros published a letter in the London *Financial Times* suggesting a devaluation of the rouble of up to 20 per cent. President Yeltsin ruled out devaluation in a public appearance the following day, but on 17 August, in an abrupt about-turn, the government was obliged to announce a widening of the exchange-rate 'corridor' (in effect, a devaluation of 34 per cent) and a freeze on the repayment of foreign loans (in effect, a default). In a joint statement, the government and the Central Bank explained their action by referring to the Asian crisis and a further fall in the world price of oil. In a speech to the Duma, Prime Minister Kirienko conceded that these were 'emergency decisions', asserting that they were unavoidable as long as the state was spending more to service its debt than it was raising in revenue. The Duma adopted a resolution describing the government and the Central Bank's performance as 'unsatisfactory', and the Communist leader, Gennadii Zyuganov, called for the resignation of the President himself. The rouble, meanwhile, continued to lose value and the banking system moved into still deeper difficulties.

The economic crisis became a combined political and economic crisis on 23 August when President Yeltsin, who had been on holiday for much of the month, dismissed the Kirienko government and reappointed Viktor Chernomyrdin as Prime Minister. The most prominent reformers left the government at the same time, including Deputy Premier Boris Nemtsov and the presidential envoy to international financial institutions, Anatolii Chubais. In a difficult economic situation, the President explained in a television address on 24 August, they needed 'heavyweights' like Mr Chernomyrdin, and the 'experience and authority' that he commanded. Mr Yeltsin made it clear, in another broadcast, that he would not be resigning his own office but would remain until the end of his term in 2000. Mr Chernomyrdin, however, was widely blamed for Russia's economic crisis, his appointment appearing to owe much to the pressure of the 'oligarchs', who had become nervous about Mr Kirienko's attempted reform of the banking system. On 31 August the nomination was voted down by the Duma more decisively than when it had first rejected Mr Kirienko. The nomination was rejected a second time on 7 September.

On this occasion it was President Yeltsin who yielded, rather than nominate Mr Chernomyrdin a third time and risk a further rejection that would have forced a dissolution of the Duma and early elections. In discussions among the parties, a number of alternative candidatures were discussed, including the chairman of the upper house of parliament, Yegor Stroyev, and the Moscow mayor, Yuri Luzhkov. In the end, the choice fell on Foreign Minister Yevgenii Primakov, who was nominated on 10 September and approved by the Duma the following day. Born in Kiev (Kyiv) in 1929 and a former journalist and academic, Mr Primakov had specialized in Arab affairs and was regarded as hostile to Western governments, particularly the United States; he was also a longstanding friend of Iraqi leader Saddam Husain. He was certainly a rather more 'Soviet' figure than his predecessor, as a former member of the Communist Party (CPSU) politburo and later (after 1991) the head of foreign intelligence.

Mr Primakov's appointment appeared to reflect a shift back to a greater measure of state regulation than had been practised by previous postcommunist governments. Among the first to be confirmed in his position was Yuri Maslyukov, another former member of the CPSU politburo and head of the state planning agency in the Soviet period; already Minister of Industry and Trade, he became a First Deputy Premier with overall responsibility for economic policy. The new Finance Minister, Mikhail Zadornov, who was also confirmed in his position, had a more liberal reputation. The economic programme of the new government, reflecting these different views, took some time to emerge, and was believed to include the printing of substantial quantities of currency, raising inflationary fears. Other elements in the programme included a restoration of state control over alcohol production and sale, and an attempt to protect domestic producers. A further contribution, it was hoped, would be made by international financial institutions, although an IMF delegation left at the end of October without reaching agreement—a consequence, Mr Primakov explained, of the government's declared intention of restoring a measure of state control.

President Yeltsin's health remained erratic. In mid-October he had to cut short a visit to Uzbekistan and Kazakhstan after stumbling at a reception ceremony in the Uzbek capital, subsequently leaving for a period of convalescence by the Black Sea. The new Prime Minister naturally assumed a number of Mr Yeltsin's responsibilities in these circumstances, including foreign trips: he visited Austria for discussions with European Union representatives in late October, and India in December. Some had come to speak of him as the 'virtual President' by the end of the year, and there were indications that he would be a widely supported presidential candidate in due course, although he disclaimed any such ambitions. The Constitutional Court ruled in November that Mr Yeltsin would not be allowed to stand for office himself when the elections took place, even if he wished to do so. In light of the Russian constitution's stipulation that a President could not serve more than two consecutive terms, the Court ruled that Mr Yeltsin's election to the presidency of the Russian republic in 1991, while it was still a part of the USSR, was to be regarded as the first such election.

The President took part in an unusual ceremony in July, when the bodies of Russia's last Tsar, Nicholas II, his wife Alexandra, three of their four daughters, their doctor and three servants were buried in a vault at the Peter and Paul fortress in St Petersburg on the anniversary of their execution by Bolshevik forces in Yekaterinburg during the civil war. After some indecision, Mr Yeltsin attended the funeral and spoke movingly of his wish for forgiveness and reconciliation. It was recalled that he had been responsible, when Communist Party first secretary in the region, for the destruction of the house in which the shootings had taken place. Numerous Romanov descendants and members of foreign ruling houses attended the ceremony, but not the senior hierarchy and Patriarch of the Orthodox Church, who continued to entertain doubts about the authenticity of the 'Yekaterinburg remains'.

A public occasion of a rather different kind took place in November, namely the funeral of the prominent liberal politician Galina Starovoitova, who had been shot dead in St Petersburg in what appeared to be a political killing. Figures published in 1998 showed that the Russian murder rate had become the highest in the world after South Africa.

Mr Yeltsin had been well enough in February to visit Italy, where he met the Pope as well as the Italian Prime Minister. In March he played host in Moscow to the French President and the German Chancellor, hailing it as the 'starting-point of a multi-polar world', although Chancellor Kohl of Germany made a point of emphasizing that their gathering had 'not been directed against anyone'. The domestic crisis rather overshadowed a two-day summit in Moscow in early September with President Clinton (who had his own difficulties—see IV.1). The US President met opposition as well as government figures, including the Communist leader, Mr Zyuganov, and Mr Lebed, and promised to support a greater measure of financial assistance from the West provided the reform process was carried forward. The two Presidents also agreed to reduce their countries' stocks of weapons-grade plutonium by 50 tonnes each, and to share early warnings of the launch of ballistic missiles and space rockets worldwide.

Relations with Russia's longstanding ally India were advanced during Mr Primakov's visit in December; a ten-year weapons agreement was signed, and the Russian Premier called for a closer association between their two countries and China as part of a move towards the 'multi-polar world' that his own country favoured. Relations with the United States and Britain, however, worsened sharply the same month when the Russian government took sharp exception to the US-UK bombing raids on Iraq (see II.1.i; IV.1; V.2.vi). The two countries, Mr Yeltsin declared, had 'crudely violated' the UN Charter by their 'unprovoked' attack on Iraq. A meeting with NATO representatives was abruptly cancelled; the Duma became even less inclined to ratify the START-II Treaty of 1993; and the Russian ambassadors in Washington and London were recalled for the first time since the worst years of the Cold War. Similar tensions developed in October in relation to Kosovo, where Russian representatives insisted on diplomatic rather than military methods to resolve a deteriorating situation (see III.2.vi).

ii. BELARUS—UKRAINE—MOLDOVA

Belarus
CAPITAL: Minsk   AREA: 208,000 sq km   POPULATION: 10,500,000 ('97)
OFFICIAL LANGUAGES: Belarusan & Russian
POLITICAL SYSTEM: presidential
HEAD OF STATE & GOVERNMENT: President Alyaksandr Lukashenka (since July '94)
RULING PARTY: Belarusan Patriotic Movement (BPR)
PRIME MINISTER: Syargey Ling, Prime Minister since July '94
MAIN IGO MEMBERSHIPS (non-UN): CIS, OSCE, PFP, CEI, NAM
CURRENCY: Belarusan rouble (end-'98 £1=BR364,361.20, US$1=BR219,000.00)
GNP PER CAPITA: US$2,150 by exchange-rate calculation, US$4,840 by PPP calculation ('97)

Ukraine
CAPITAL: Kyiv   AREA: 604,000 sq km   POPULATION: 50,090,000 ('98)
OFFICIAL LANGUAGE: Ukrainian
POLITICAL SYSTEM: democratic republic
HEAD OF STATE & GOVERNMENT: President Leonid Kuchma (since July '94)
RULING PARTY: Inter-Regional Reform Bloc (MBR) links ruling circle
PRIME MINISTER: Valery Pustovoytenko (since July '97)
MAIN IGO MEMBERSHIPS (non-UN): CIS, OSCE, CE, PFP, BSEC, CEI
CURRENCY: hryvna (end-'98 £1=K6.70, US$1=K4.03)
GNP PER CAPITA: US$1,040 by exchange-rate calculation, US$2,170 by PPP calculation ('97)

Moldova
CAPITAL: Chisinau (Kishinev)   AREA: 34,000 sq km   POPULATION: 4,400,000 ('97)
OFFICIAL LANGUAGE: Moldovan
POLITICAL SYSTEM: democratic republic
HEAD OF STATE & GOVERNMENT: President Petru Lucinschi (since Jan '97)
RULING PARTY: Agrarian Democratic Party of Moldova (PDAM)
PRIME MINISTER: Ion Ciubuc (since Jan '97)
MAIN IGO MEMBERSHIPS (non-UN): CIS, OSCE, CE, CEI, PFP, BSEC
CURRENCY: Moldovan leu (end-'98 £1=ML14.03, US$1=ML8.43)
GNP PER CAPITA: US$540 by exchange-rate calculation ('97)

IN BELARUS, Russia's nearest neighbour, the economy was beset by economic difficulties that affected the whole region. The government had to take emergency measures in March to sustain the currency, and the governor of the national bank was dismissed. There was also harsh government action in relation to domestic opposition. Official sources announced in January that a 'strategic plan' to overthrow the President and his government had been uncovered; and the leader of the youth wing of the Belarusan Popular Front was taken into custody in early April on charges of 'malicious hooliganism' following an unauthorized demonstration against the Russian-Belarus treaty of union that had been concluded the previous year (see AR 1997, p. 141).

Relations with Russia were, as this suggested, a central concern, and there were domestic as well as foreign policy implications in a declaration that the two Presidents agreed in December. Under the terms of their agreement, a formal treaty of union was to be drawn up by the summer of 1999; by that time both countries promised to have worked out a mechanism for joint defence, security and foreign policy, and undertook to unify their civil and tax legislation and to create a single budget and a single currency. The two countries, President Yeltsin declared, would be 'entering the 21st century in a new capacity, moving together towards a union state'. President Lukashenka of Belarus was even more enthusiastic.

Relations with the wider international community, however, deteriorated sharply in June when the ambassadors of most of the Western nations left Belarus following attempt to evict them from their official residences in Minsk to enable 'urgent plumbing repairs' to be carried out. The real reason, it was thought, was that the Belarusan President wanted to extend his own residence in the same vicinity—an impression that was confirmed when in October the ambassadors were allowed to return except for the US, French and German representatives, whose residences had been 'absorbed' by Mr Lukashenka.

Political life in UKRAINE was dominated in 1998 by the parliamentary elections that took place on 29 March, under a new electoral law which (as in Russia) allocated half the seats to single-member constituencies and half to a national contest among party lists, with seats allocated proportionally among all the parties that secured at least 4 per cent of the vote. Thirty parties and blocs contested the elections, but only eight exceeded the threshold; the turnout was put at 69.9 per cent. The Communist Party of Ukraine (KPU) was by some margin the most successful of the party-list contenders, winning 24.7 per cent of the vote, followed by the People's Movement of Ukraine (Rukh) with 9.4 per cent. These were also the two parties that won the largest numbers of single-member seats, although about half went to independents. With 430 of the 450 seats declared, the KPU had a total of 119 seats, which left it a long way short of an overall majority, although it was the best represented of the parties. There were protracted difficulties in electing a new parliamentary Speaker in these circumstances: not until 7 July, after 19 ballots, was Peasant Party leader Oleksandr Tkachenko approved for the post.

Ukraine's economic difficulties during the year paralleled those of the Russian Federation (see III.3.i), and were affected by them. As in Russia, coal-miners went on strike over unpaid wages, marching to government offices to press their case. A promised IMF loan was placed in jeopardy in August because of the turmoil on the Russian currency markets, and at the end of the month the Ukrainian currency reached the upper limit of its currency 'corridor' against the US dollar. A new limit was announced in early September, but the economic situation continued to worsen. In late September it was announced that Ukraine, like Russia, had in effect defaulted on its domestic debt. Agreement had, however, been reached with the IMF on a stabilization and structural reform programme for the period up to 2001. A first instalment of an agreed three-year credit was made available at the end of October, after the IMF had declared itself satisfied by Ukraine's successful restructuring of its debt and by the stabilization of its currency.

In February President Kuchma paid an official visit to Moscow, where he and President Yeltsin signed a treaty of economic cooperation for the period 1998–2007, within which the volume of trade between the two countries was expected to double. This continued an improvement in relations that had begun with the signature of a friendship treaty the previous year (see AR 1997, p. 142). There remained some uncertainty about Ukraine's international allegiances. It was the most reluctant member of the Commonwealth of Independent States (CIS), and government ministers did not necessarily rule out membership of NATO at some future point. An agreement with the United States was concluded in May allowing Ukraine to import the technology that was needed to modernize its nuclear power industry; it followed Ukraine's agreement that it would not supply turbines for a planned nuclear plant in Iran. The European Bank for Reconstruction and Development agreed in the same month to grants worth $160 million to help to reinforce the crumbling sarcophagus around the fourth reactor at Chernobyl, where the world's worst nuclear accident had taken place in 1986 (see AR 1986, pp. 100–1).

Parliamentary elections also took place in MOLDOVA, on 22 March. They were contested by 15 parties and electoral blocs, none of which was able to secure an overall majority. The largest share of the vote (30 per cent) and 40 of the 104 seats went to the Moldovan Party of Communists (PCM), which had only been permitted to re-register in late 1994 and had not been able to contest the parliamentary elections at the end of that year. The Agrarian Democratic Party, which had been the largest party after the 1994 election, won no seats at all; a right-wing alliance, the Democratic Convention of Moldova, came second with 26 seats and 19.2 per cent of the vote. In discussions that took place in Moscow the same month at prime ministerial level, a ten-year economic cooperation agreement was agreed that would come into effect in 1999.

156   III CENTRAL AND EASTERN EUROPE

iii. ARMENIA—GEORGIA—AZERBAIJAN

Armenia
CAPITAL: Yerevan   AREA: 30,000 sq km   POPULATION: 4,000,000 ('97)
OFFICIAL LANGUAGE: Armenian
POLITICAL SYSTEM: democratic republic
HEAD OF STATE & GOVERNMENT: President Robert Kocharyan (since Feb '98)
RULING PARTIES: Pan-Armenian National Movement heads ruling coalition
PRIME MINISTER: Armen Darbinyan (since April '98)
MAIN IGO MEMBERSHIPS (non-UN): CIS, OSCE, PFP, BSEC
CURRENCY: dram (end-'98 £1=D847.48, US$1=D509.38)
GNP PER CAPITA: US$530 by exchange-rate calculation, US$2,280 by PPP calculation ('97)

Georgia
CAPITAL: Tbilisi   AREA: 70,000 sq km   POPULATION: 5,500,000 ('97)
OFFICIAL LANGUAGE: Georgian
POLITICAL SYSTEM: democratic republic
HEAD OF STATE & GOVERNMENT: President Eduard Shevardnadze (since Oct '92)
RULING PARTIES: Citizens' Union coordinates fluid coalition
MAIN IGO MEMBERSHIPS (non-UN): CIS, OSCE, PFP, BSEC
CURRENCY: lari
GNP PER CAPITA: US$840 by exchange-rate calculation, US$1,980 by PPP calculation ('97)

Azerbaijan
CAPITAL: Baku   AREA: 87,000 sq km   POPULATION: 7,600,000 ('97)
OFFICIAL LANGUAGE: Azeri
POLITICAL SYSTEM: democratic republic
HEAD OF STATE & GOVERNMENT: President Geidar Aliyev (since June '93)
RULING PARTY: New Azerbaijan Party (YAP)
PRIME MINISTER: Artur Rasizade (since July '96)
MAIN IGO MEMBERSHIPS (non-UN): CIS, OSCE, PFP, BSEC, OIC, ECO
CURRENCY: manat (end-'98 £1=M6,571.81, US$1=M3,950.00)
GNP PER CAPITA: US$510 by exchange-rate calculation, US$1,520 by PPP calculation ('97)

IN ARMENIA, Levon Ter-Petrosyan resigned as President in February following a collapse of support in the National Assembly for his attempt to reach a gradual resolution of the long-running conflict with Azerbaijan over Nagorno-Karabakh. Mr Ter-Petrosyan had originally been elected in 1991 shortly after Armenia had declared its independence from the Soviet Union, and was re-elected in September 1996 in controversial circumstances (see AR 1996, p. 133). In the first round of presidential elections on 16 March, Prime Minister Robert Kocharyan won 38.8 per cent of the vote, with the former Communist Party first secretary Karen Demirchyan in second place with 30.7 per cent; in the second round of voting on 30 March, Mr Kocharyan took 59.5 per cent of the vote and Mr Demirchyan 40.5 per cent.

Mr Kocharyan, a former president of Nagorno-Karabakh, was inaugurated as President of Armenia on 9 April. He identified as his main priorities the consolidation of Armenia as an independent state and international acceptance of the right to self-determination of the people of the disputed enclave. He appointed Armen Darbinyan, who had been Minister of Finance and the Economy, as Prime Minister on 10 April. The new Prime Minister was regarded as a strong supporter of radical economic reform and privatization. However, two ministers of the new administration were from the Armenian Revolutionary Party (Dashnak), a strongly nationalist grouping that had been banned by President Ter-Petrosyan on grounds of alleged terrorism and drug-trafficking.

In neighbouring GEORGIA, President Shevardnadze survived another assassination attempt in February, when unidentified gunmen attacked him while he was being driven on official business through Tbilisi. Two of the President's bodyguards were killed, but the President himself remained unscathed. There was further turbulence in October when an armed insurrection broke out in the west of the republic, apparently instigated by supporters of former President Zviad Gamsakhurdia. Relations with the breakaway republic of Abkhazia continued to be difficult throughout the year; hostilities broke out in May, although a ceasefire was quickly negotiated and a more formal agreement followed in late June.

Presidential elections were held in AZERBAIJAN on 11 October, in spite of requests from several opposition parties for their cancellation. In the first ballot, incumbent President Geidar Aliyev, in office since October 1993, secured the two-thirds of the vote necessary for his outright re-election, being credited with 76.1 per cent against just 11.6 per cent for his nearest rival. The entire government resigned, as the constitution required, but on 23 October Mr Aliyev reappointed Artur Rasizade as Prime Minister. By the end of the month he had reappointed the Ministers of Defence, National Security, Internal Affairs and Foreign Affairs.

President Aliev visited Britain in July, when he signed new oil exploration contracts worth $5,000 million with three UK companies providing for the further development of oilfields in the Caspian Sea. He also welcomed the increasing economic cooperation between Azerbaijan and Britain.

IV THE AMERICAS AND THE CARIBBEAN

1. UNITED STATES OF AMERICA

CAPITAL: Washington, DC   AREA: 9,372,614 sq km   POPULATION: 272,000,000 ('97)
OFFICIAL LANGUAGE: English
POLITICAL SYSTEM: democratic federal republic
HEAD OF STATE & GOVERNMENT: President Bill Clinton, Democrat, since Jan '93 (*for full cabinet list see* XVII.6)
RULING PARTIES: President is a Democrat; Congress is controlled by the Republicans
MAIN IGO MEMBERSHIPS (non-UN): NATO, OSCE, OECD, G-8, OAS, NAFTA, APEC, AC, CP, SPC, ANZUS
CURRENCY: dollar (end-'98 £1=US$1.66)
GNP PER CAPITA: US$28,740 ('97)

IN an eventful year which included mid-term elections and foreign military engagements, one name alone dominated the American news—that of the 24-year-old former White House intern, Monica Lewinsky. Ms Lewinsky's name emerged in January when lawyers acting for Paula Jones in her sexual harassment suit against President Clinton (see AR 1994, p. 162; 1997, p. 146) tried to establish a 'pattern of behaviour' on his part which would strengthen their client's claims. They alleged that he had an 18-month affair with Ms Lewinsky between 1995 and 1997. President Clinton's denials of a sexual relationship, in his testimony of 17 January and in a subsequent television broadcast, then became part of the investigation led by the special prosecutor, Kenneth Starr. Although he had originally been appointed to investigate the Whitewater affair (see AR 1994, p. 164), Mr Starr's brief had been extended to include other suggestions of presidential wrongdoing such as the 'Travelgate' scandal and possible misuse of FBI files. Now he attempted to determine whether the President had committed perjury by lying to Ms Jones's lawyers and had suborned a witness in getting Ms Lewinsky to lie too. After protracted hearings and debates, and revelations of an often shocking private nature about the President's relationship with Ms Lewinsky, the investigation resulted in Mr Clinton becoming the first President to be impeached since Andrew Johnson in 1868.

Despite the constant revelations in the so-called 'Zippergate' affair, the President lived up to his nickname of 'The Comeback Kid', as favourable opinion polls and a good result in the mid-term elections indicated that the American people wanted neither his impeachment nor his resignation. The public seemed more preoccupied with the healthy state of the economy or the duel between baseball players Mark McGwire of the St Louis Cardinals and Sammy Sosa of the Chicago Cubs to break the record of most home runs in a single season. McGwire won with a total of 70, nine more than the record set in 1961 by Roger Maris (see Pt XVI).

Extremes of weather also dominated the news at different at times. Severe storms and tornadoes hit parts of the country in spring. It was believed that 60 people died on 9 April alone, after storms swept through Alabama, Georgia and Mississippi. This brought the total number of tornado deaths in the South to 112 since January. Further storms between 30 May and 3 June caused widespread destruction in the mid-west and north-east, and the deaths of at least ten people. Six people were killed and more than 150 injured when a tornado virtually destroyed the town of Spencer, South Dakota. More than 20 people died in storms and flooding between 30 June and 2 July in Wisconsin, Minnesota, Indiana, Ohio, West Virginia and Vermont. Meanwhile, fierce fires which raged from late May into mid-June destroyed hundreds of homes and thousands of acres of woodland across parts of Florida. A heatwave in late July was thought to be responsible for 129 deaths in south-western states, and on 25 July Texas and Georgia were declared agricultural disaster areas. On 27 September 1.5 million people in the New Orleans area experienced a mandatory evacuation when Hurricane Georges hit the Gulf states. At least 15 people were killed in central and east Texas during torrential rain storms on 17 and 18 October.

SCANDAL AND POLITICS. In January the sexual harassment case against President Clinton brought by Paula Jones in Arkansas entered its discovery phase in advance of the full trial scheduled for May. On 17 January Mr Clinton became the first sitting President to testify as a defendant in a court case when he gave evidence under oath before videotape cameras in closed session. Unconfirmed reports suggested that in the course of his evidence the President had denied the sexual harassment charge, but had admitted that he might have met Ms Jones alone in the hotel in Arkansas in 1991. The President apparently denied asking Ms Jones for oral sex, but did admit to a sexual relationship with Gennifer Flowers, an allegation he had rejected during the 1992 presidential election campaign (see AR 1992, p. 154).

It was in the course of this session that allegations relating to the President's relationship with Monica Lewinsky emerged. On 21 January Mr Clinton publicly denied that he had had a sexual relationship with Ms Lewinsky or that he asked her to deny any such affair in her deposition in the Jones case at the start of the month. However, it became apparent that the independent prosecutor investigating the Whitewater affair, Kenneth Starr, had extended his investigation to include the possibility that the President had committed perjury and suborned a witness. It also emerged that Linda Tripp, a former White House aide, had provided Mr Starr with tape-recordings of telephone conversations in which Ms Lewinsky gave details of an 18-month relationship with the President. The tapes apparently referred to presents given and received, and to the fact that Ms Lewinsky performed oral sex on the President because he believed that this did not constitute adultery. Subsequent reports concerned a dress owned by Ms Lewinsky which she claimed was stained with the President's semen.

Faced with mounting accusations and suggestions that he might resign or be impeached, President Clinton appeared in a public broadcast on 26 January and stated categorically: 'I did not have sexual relations with that woman, Miss Lewinsky. I never told anybody to lie, not a single time, never. These allegations are false.' This denial was further strengthened by First Lady Hillary Clinton in an interview on breakfast television on 27 January in which she said that 'Bill and I have been accused of almost everything, including murder, by some of the same people who are behind these allegations'. Her suggestion that a right-wing conspiracy was responsible for the attacks on her husband was taken up by other Clinton supporters, who also accused Mr Starr, a known Republican, of acting out of partisan motives.

Amid continuing reports that the Starr investigators had seized papers, records and items of personal clothing from Ms Lewinsky's home, doubts were expressed about her credibility. On 28 January investigators interviewed Andy Bleiler, Ms Lewinsky's former lover. He suggested that she was obsessed with sex and was not always truthful. On 29 January Judge Susan Webber Wright of the US district court in Little Rock, Arkansas, announced that she would not admit any evidence from Ms Lewinsky in the Jones case. It also seemed unlikely that a deal would be reached between Mr Starr and Ms Lewinsky which would give her immunity from prosecution for perjury if she retracted her earlier statement denying an affair with Mr Clinton.

President Clinton made no reference to these matters in his State of the Union address to Congress on 27 January. Rather, he concentrated on domestic issues. Insisting that 'these are good times for America', he outlined a record of achievement in economic affairs, in welfare, health provision and child care. In addition to the lowest unemployment in 24 years, Mr Clinton pointed to an anticipated federal budget deficit of $10,000 million in the current fiscal year (compared with a projection of $357,000 million when he took office) and suggested that the deficit would soon be zero. Looking ahead to a future surplus in the budget, he proposed a simple slogan for its use: 'Save Social Security First'. The President indicated that a series of discussions culminating in a White House conference on social security in December would take place throughout the year. Reaffirming his administration's commitment to education, he assured every family listening that 'your children can go to college', also announcing funding for the hiring of new teachers and for the building of new schools.

The President emphasized the importance of trade and of manufacturing, and the need to train or re-train workers. He proposed 'one single GI bill for workers' that would fund individuals with a 'simple skills grant' and replace the tangle of existing training programmes. Referring to the economic crisis in South-East Asia, Mr Clinton said

America should help countries which 'undertake serious economic reform' and continue to support the International Monetary Fund (IMF).

Mr Clinton reiterated his support for the expansion of NATO to include former Iron Curtain countries and for the continued presence of US troops in Bosnia. He called upon the Senate to approve the 1996 Comprehensive Nuclear Test-Ban Treaty and reaffirmed America's opposition to Iraq's development of weapons of mass destruction. He further called for an improved inspection system to enforce the Biological Weapons Convention.

Finally, Mr Clinton spoke of the nation's commitment to equality and urged all Americans to help 'build one America'. Looking to the new millennium, he proposed a public-private partnership to advance the arts and humanities and to celebrate the millennium by saving America's treasures and preserving the past. He proposed a 21st Century Research Fund 'for path-breaking scientific inquiry', and urged support for medical and other research.

Investigations into the Lewinsky affair continued through February, as Mr Starr subpoenaed members of the White House staff, including the President's personal secretary, Betty Currie. In her testimony, which was leaked to the press on 7 February, Ms Currie apparently contradicted the President's claims that he had not spent time alone with Ms Lewinsky. There was also some suggestion that the President might have tried to influence Ms Currie's testimony. Secret Service logs showed that Ms Lewinsky did appear to have had unprecedented access to the White House. Considerable publicity was given to the issue of whether Mr Starr would grant Ms Lewinsky immunity from prosecution in return for her evidence if it contradicted previous sworn testimony. Questions about her reliability continued to be raised, as further details of her telephone conversations with Ms Tripp emerged, including her confession that she had been 'a liar all my life'.

Further leaked details of the President's January deposition appeared in March. They included an admission that he 'may have been alone' with Ms Lewinsky and details of gifts exchanged between the two, including clothing, jewellery and a book of poetry from the President. The President acknowledged that Ms Currie had on more than one occasion provided assistance for Ms Lewinsky in her quest for employment and that he had spoken to Ms Lewinsky 'at some point' about the possibility that she would be called as a witness in the Jones suit. These details appeared to contradict other evidence provided by Secret Service personnel and cast further doubt on the President's veracity. White House spokesmen angrily accused Mr Starr of deliberately leaking information to the press.

The pressure on the President increased following an interview on 15 March on CBS television in which a former White House volunteer worker, Kathleen Willey, claimed that Mr Clinton had lied under oath to Ms Jones's lawyers when he denied that he had made physical sexual advances to her in a private meeting on 29 November 1993. According to Ms Willey, the President had embraced and kissed her and fondled her breasts—advances that she had found shocking and unwelcome. Mr Clinton denied the accusations, and the White House released letters from Ms Willey to the President after the alleged incident. Their friendly tone appeared to cast doubt on her version of events.

Businessman Vernon Jordan, the President's close friend, gave evidence before the grand jury reviewing the evidence of the Starr inquiry over two days early in March. His testimony largely related to his help in finding employment for Ms Lewinsky. The President invoked executive privilege on 20 March to prevent Bruce Lindsey (a White House counsel) and Sidney Blumenthal (a communications adviser) from giving evidence.

Meanwhile, lawyers acting for Paula Jones in Little Rock, Arkansas, claimed on 27 March that Mr Clinton had not submitted all letters and notes relating to the Willey incident. As further evidence against the President, the lawyers cited an accusation of rape made by an Arkansas woman who claimed that she had been assaulted by Mr Clinton in a hotel room in 1978. The White House immediately denounced the allegation as 'outrageous and false' and claimed that the alleged victim had provided Jones's lawyers with a sworn deposition that the incident had never occurred.

The Senate committee investigating alleged campaign finance irregularities in the 1996 elections (see AR 1997, pp. 148–9) presented its final report on 10 March. The committee had failed to find any conclusive evidence that the Chinese government had made covert donations to either congressional or presidential campaigns, or that the President or Vice-President had committed any illegal acts. However, in a separate but related case, Democratic Party fund-raiser Johnny Chung pleaded guilty in a Los Angeles US district court on 16 March to four counts of fraud, tax evasion and conspiracy to break the law on campaign donations.

On 1 April Judge Susan Webber Wright in Little Rock dismissed the suit brought by Ms Jones against the President. The judge ruled that, even if the events had happened as Ms Jones described them, this would not constitute sexual harassment as defined in law, but rather 'a mere sexual proposition or encounter, albeit an odious one'. She also said that the lawyers had not demonstrated that Ms Jones had suffered emotionally or in career terms as a result of the incident. At a press conference on 16 April in Dallas, Ms Jones indicated that she would appeal against the decision in order to obtain 'justice and my day in court'. The conservative Rutherford Institute, which had paid Ms Jones's legal fees, guaranteed that it would continue to do so.

Public opinion surveys showed that the President's 'job approval' rating remained at 67 per cent; a similar proportion of those asked thought that investigations into his sexual relations should stop. The public mood was no doubt encouraged by an official report which indicated that the

Whitewater investigation had cost $30 million in the three years up to October 1997. Adverse publicity notwithstanding, Mrs Clinton faced questioning by Mr Starr and his team for almost five hours in the White House on 25 April. The interview, videotaped for the Arkansas grand jury, concerned Mrs Clinton's work at the Rose Law Firm on behalf of Madison Guaranty Saving and Loan, a company involved in the Whitewater deals. There was some suggestion that Mr Starr hoped to bring an indictment against Mrs Clinton before the expiry of the grand jury's term in May. In the event, the grand jury stood down on 5 May without producing any indictments against either the President or Mrs Clinton in relation to Whitewater, despite four years of investigation.

In a related development on 30 April, Mr Starr secured indictments against Webster Hubbell, a former Associate Attorney-General and a former law partner of Mrs Clinton's in Arkansas, with his wife, lawyer and accountant, for tax evasion and conspiracy to defraud the Internal Revenue Service. The indictment related to payments of $500,000 which Mr Hubbell had received in 1994 and 1995 after resigning his position in the Justice Department, and which Mr Starr believed had been made to secure his silence in the Whitewater-related investigations.

In May the judge supervising the grand jury investigation in Washington, DC, into the Lewinsky affair ruled that White House claims of executive privilege to prevent testimony by senior presidential aides were outweighed by the need to secure evidence in a criminal investigation. In a separate ruling, the judge later ruled that there was no 'unique privilege' or function preventing Secret Service personnel from giving testimony.

One of the people linked with the Clintons in the Whitewater affair, Susan McDougal, was indicted on charges of criminal contempt and obstruction of the Whitewater investigation by the grand jury in Arkansas on 4 May, following her refusal to testify about a note on a cheque dated 1983 which read 'pay off Clinton'. Mrs McDougal had already refused to testify in 1996 and had spent 18 months in prison, and had only just begun a two-year sentence for fraud following a conviction in 1996 (see AR 1996, p. 144). Mrs McDougal's husband, James (Jim) McDougal, had died on 8 March while serving a three-year sentence for fraud in the Fort Worth prison in Texas. Mrs McDougal was unexpectedly released on 25 June on medical grounds, but still faced the possibility of further imprisonment arising from the later charges.

Meanwhile, in the course of the campaign finance investigations it was reported on 16 May that Johnny Chung had told Justice Department officials with whom he was cooperating that he had channelled tens of thousands of dollars from China into Democratic campaigns and that he had submitted evidence to support his claim. Reports on 18 May suggested that the Justice Department had begun an investigation into whether there was any link between such donations and the Clinton administration's decision to allow the export of commercial satellites to China in 1996 and 1998.

At the beginning of June the White House announced that it would not appeal against court decisions relating to claims for executive privilege in the Lewinsky affair, but indicated that attorney-client privilege would be cited to prevent senior presidential aides from giving evidence. On 2 June it was reported that President Clinton himself had repeatedly turned down requests to appear before the grand jury in person. Lawyers acting for Mr Starr in the Whitewater investigation on 8 June asked the Supreme Court for a ruling as to whether attorney-client privilege continued after the death of the client in question. This matter was raised in connection with papers belonging to the former deputy White House counsel, Vincent Foster, who had committed suicide in 1993 (see AR 1993, p. 156).

On 28 July Ms Lewinsky's lawyers reached an agreement with Mr Starr granting their client full immunity in return for 'a full and truthful testimony' about her relationship with the President. The following day President Clinton agreed to submit to videotaped questioning at the White House in return for a withdrawal of the subpoena compelling him to testify in front of the grand jury. Appeal Court decisions in July ruled that government lawyers could not invoke attorney-client privilege and that Secret Service personnel could not appeal to 'protective function privilege' to avoid testifying before the grand jury. In the latter case, the Chief Justice of the Supreme Court, William Rehnquist, ruled that the secret service officers could give evidence before the court gave a final ruling, with the result that Mr Starr immediately began taking testimony from officers. However, the special prosecutor then suffered two setbacks. On 25 June the Supreme Court ruled that attorney-client privilege did survive the death of the client, while on 1 July a federal district court dismissed tax evasion charges against Webster Hubbell and his wife and two associates on the grounds that the Mr Starr had exceeded his brief in pursuing such charges.

After months of negotiation, Monica Lewinsky finally testified before the grand jury for almost six hours on 6 August. Leaked reports suggested that she had admitted to an affair with the President in which she had engaged in acts, including performing oral sex on him, which might be deemed 'sexual relations' as defined in the Paula Jones case, i.e. 'contact with the genitalia, anus, groin, breast, inner thigh, or buttocks. . .with an intent to arouse or gratify sexual desire'. She reportedly claimed that Mr Clinton had suggested ways to cover up the affair, including returning presents, and that both had agreed to deny the affair to lawyers acting for Ms Jones. She did not appear to have suggested that she had been offered help in finding employment in return for her cooperation.

Mr Clinton became the first sitting President to give evidence before a grand jury when he testified from the White House via closed-circuit television to a Washington federal court house on 17 August. Although this evidence was also supposedly secret, reports indicated that the President had admitted to 'inappropriate physical contact' with Ms Lewinsky but claimed that this had not constituted sexual relations as defined in the Jones case. In a television broadcast to the nation later that night, President Clinton admitted that, while his answers to the lawyers in the Jones case in January were 'legally accurate', he did 'not volunteer information' and that he 'did have a relationship with Ms Lewinsky that was not appropriate' and was in fact 'wrong'. While Mr Clinton expressed regret at misleading people, particularly his wife, he said that his actions had stemmed from a desire to avoid personal embarrassment and to protect his family. He also cited his concerns about the intrusive nature of the Starr investigation which he said had 'gone on too long, cost too much, and hurt too many innocent people'.

The political response to the President's speech was mixed. Some Republicans, such as House Speaker Newt Gingrich, said that they would reserve judgment until they had received the Starr report. However, a number of leading Democrats, including Senator Daniel Patrick Moynihan and Richard Gephardt, clearly felt that they had been misled by the President and that his statement was 'inadequate'. Nonetheless, public opinion polls still indicated a high job approval rating for the President, even though 70 per cent of those asked believed that Mr Clinton and Ms Lewinsky had had a sexual relationship and 66 per cent thought that the President had lied in his deposition in January. Only about 45 per cent of respondents thought the President should be impeached even if he was shown to have committed perjury.

Despite the public mood, there was mounting criticism of President Clinton for his failure to give an explicit apology in his 17 August address. In a speech in the Senate on 3 September, Senator Joseph Lieberman, a long-time Clinton supporter, criticized the President's behaviour as 'immoral' and 'disgraceful'. Mr Clinton responded with a series of public apologies and a show of contrition. During his visit to Dublin on 4 September he said: 'I made a bad mistake. It's indefensible and I'm sorry about it.' He continued to express his remorse throughout early September, and in a speech before a group of clergymen at the White House on 11 September he admitted that he had sinned and expressed his sorrow to family, friends, staff, and to Ms Lewinsky and her family, as well as to the American people.

Mr Starr submitted his report and 18 boxes of evidence to Congress on 9 September. Despite attempts by the President's aides and Democratic representatives to delay publication in order that the White House might prepare a rebuttal, the 445-page report was made public on 11 September and placed on Internet sites (see XVII.4 for summary). It did not find grounds for impeachment in the original areas of investigation, namely Whitewater, the 'Travelgate' affair or the possible misuse of FBI files. However, Mr Starr listed 11 possible impeachable offences committed by the President, including five cases of perjury and five of obstruction of justice. The report gave sexually explicit details of ten occasions between November 1995 and March 1997 when the President and Ms Lewinsky had engaged in sexual activity. The detail recorded the use of sex aids which included on one occasion a cigar.

The White House issued an immediate denial of the charges and suggested that the report contained little more than 'the details of a private sexual relationship told in graphic detail with intent to embarrass'. Nothing, it was claimed, could be deemed to have fallen into the category of 'treason, bribery of other high crimes and misdemeanours' punishable by impeachment. In a second response released on 12 September, the President's lawyers described the report as 'pornographic' and as a 'hit-and-run smear campaign'.

While public opinion still seemed to favour the President, and to be looking for some form of censure rather than impeachment or resignation, on 18 September the House judiciary committee voted to release a four-hour videotape of the President's grand jury testimony of 17 August. Following the endorsement of this decision by the House, the tape was immediately screened by several television stations on 21 September. Contrary to expectations, the tape did not appear particularly damaging to the President. While he sometimes appeared uncomfortable—and his definition of 'sexual relations' as excluding an act of oral sex strained credibility—he generally seemed calm, restrained and remarkably dignified in trying circumstances. Remarkably, public opinion polls indicated a rise in his approval ratings after the broadcast.

Despite suggestions, notably from former President Gerald Ford, that the President should be given some form of official rebuke rather than face impeachment, on 5 October the House judiciary committee voted on party lines by 21 to 16 in favour of seeking authority from the full House to initiate a formal impeachment inquiry. In doing so the committee began only the third presidential impeachment in history and the first since 1974 (when President Nixon had resigned rather than face such proceedings). The House voted by 258 votes to 176 on 8 October to authorize the judiciary committee's inquiry. Of those in favour, 31 were Democratic representatives, while only one Republican voted against.

The mid-term elections in November provided an unexpected boost for President Clinton and the Democratic Party. Many commentators had anticipated that in the light of the Lewinsky affair the voters would give overwhelming support to Republican candidates. In the event, there appeared to be a reaction the other way, as Mr Clinton became only the third President this century to see his party gain in mid-term elections. In the Senate elections the Republicans won 16 of the 34 contested seats. Among their victories was that in Illinois of Peter Fitzgerald over Carol Moseley-Braun, who had become the first African-American woman to win a Senate seat in 1992. Democratic senators were also defeated in Ohio and Kentucky. Some Republican candidates also lost, however, most notably the abrasive Alfonse D'Amato of New York, to Charles Schumer. Mr D'Amato had chaired the Senate Whitewater hearings and had been particularly critical of President Clinton. Sitting Republican senators were also defeated in Indiana and North Carolina. The overall balance remained unchanged, at 45 Democrats to 55 Republicans. Although the Republicans also retained control of the House of Representatives, they lost five seats to Democrats. As a result, the overall distribution was 223 Republicans to 211 Democrats, with one independent (see results map on p. 169).

A similar pattern emerged in the 36 state gubernatorial elections, in which the Democrats won 11 contests and maintained their total of 17 states, while the Republicans won 23 contests and, with a net loss of one, saw their governorships fall from 32 to 31. The most significant victory for the Democrats was in California, which was an 'open' contest, where the incumbent was not seeking re-election. In defeating Republican state attorney-general Dan Lungren, Gray Davis became the first Democratic governor in 16 years and only the fourth this century. Significant victories were also scored by the Democrats in Alabama and South Carolina, suggesting that they were recovering ground lost to the Republicans in the Reagan era. However, the Republican victories in Texas, where George W. Bush secured re-election, and in Florida, where his brother Jeb Bush also won, pointed to the fact that the party could attract the vote of women and Latinos. Both men, sons of former President George Bush, were identified as likely future presidential candidates. One upset for the Republicans was the loss of Minnesota to Ross Perot's Reform Party candidate, James George Janos, a former wrestler also known as Jess 'the body' Ventura. His campaign had benefited from state laws which limited campaign spending and provided a public subsidy for those who had attracted more than 5 per cent of the vote in earlier primaries.

A number of state ballots also included referendums. In Washington state 58 per cent voted in favour of the prohibition of affirmative action programmes in employment, education and public procurement, while voters in Alaska, Arizona, Nevada and Washington state approved the medical use of marijuana. In Washington and Colorado a proposal to restrict late-term abortions ('partial birth abortion') was rejected, while voters in Michigan said 'no' to a proposition that would have allowed medically-assisted suicides in certain circumstances. Only Oregon currently allowed such a practice.

President Clinton described the election results as 'astonishing', amid suggestions by many commentators that the results did not provide an obvious mandate for impeachment. Within the Republican Party, there was considerable criticism of the leadership of House Speaker Gingrich, both for his support of bi-partisan approaches to the budget and taxation issues and for his handling of the Starr report and the Lewinsky affair. On

6 November Bob Livingston (Louisiana), chair of the House appropriations committee, announced that he would challenge Mr Gingrich in the party elections scheduled for 18 November. Steve Largert (Oklahoma) and Jennifer Dunn (Washington) both indicated that they would stand against the Republican majority leader, Dick Armey. The conflict abated to some extent when Mr Gingrich announced his resignation as Speaker late on 6 November, also indicating that he would vacate his Georgia seat in the House at a later date. Mr Armey retained his position in the internal Republican elections on 18 November, when Mr Livingston's candidacy to succeed Mr Gingrich was unopposed.

On 5 November Henry Hyde, the chair of the House judiciary committee, announced an expedited schedule for the impeachment inquiry indicating an intention to complete the hearings before the end of the year. Testimony would be heard only from Kenneth Starr. Mr Hyde indicated that this timetable was dependent upon the cooperation of the White House, and on 5 November he sent President Clinton a letter asking him to affirm or deny 81 findings from the Starr report.

Mr Starr submitted two boxes of evidence to the House judiciary committee on 13 November, relating to allegations made during the Lewinsky investigations that the President had physically harassed White House volunteer Kathleen Willey in 1993. In a separate and unexpected development on the same day, it was announced that President Clinton had agreed to pay Paula Jones $850,000 in settlement of the sexual harassment suit. The settlement did not include any form of apology or admission that the events she described had occurred. In October it had been reported that negotiations had broken down when the President had refused to offer more than $700,000. At that point Abe Hirschfeld, a New York property developer, had offered to pay Ms Jones $1 million in addition to any settlement from Mr Clinton, to settle the case and to enable her to pay her previous team of lawyers.

Also on 13 November, Mr Starr secured an indictment against former Associate Attorney-General Hubbell on charges of fraud and misleading federal regulators in matters arising from the Whitewater affair. He submitted four boxes of material on this case to the House judiciary committee on 17 November. The special prosecutor appeared before the House judiciary committee himself on 19 November. In the course of a two-hour presentation, Mr Starr conceded that he could find no evidence of wrong-doing in the three original areas of his investigation —Whitewater, the dismissal of White House office staff or the related alleged improper use of FBI files. However, with regard to the Lewinsky affair, he said: 'On at least six different occasions from 17 December 1997 through to 17 August 1998 the President had to make a decision. He could choose truth or he could choose deception. On all six occasions, the President chose deception, a pattern of calculated behaviour over a span of months.' He therefore believed that the President

IV.1. UNITED STATES OF AMERICA 169

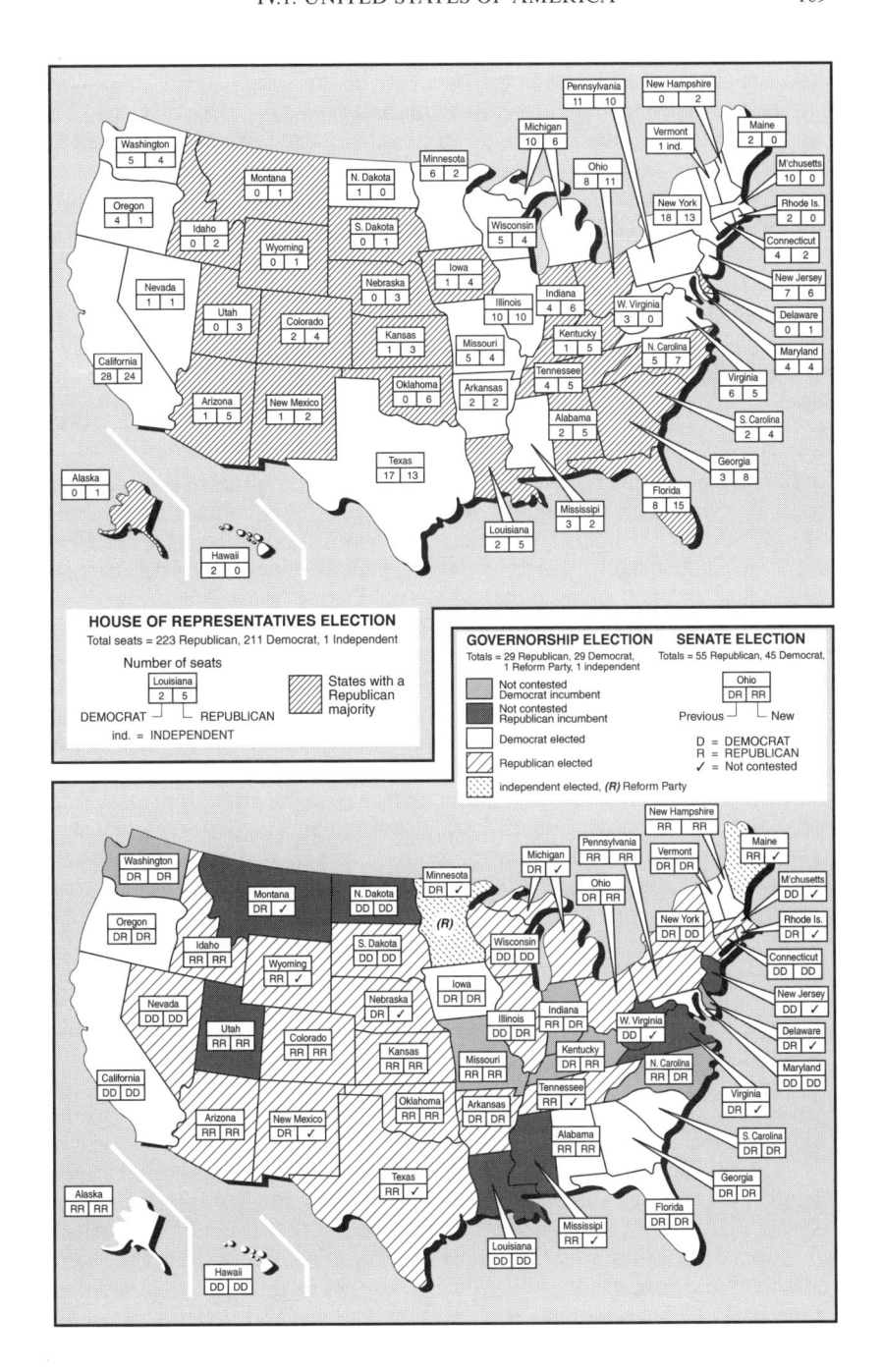

was guilty of obstruction of justice, perjury, subornation of witnesses and the abuse of executive privilege.

Attorney-General Janet Reno announced on 24 November that she would not recommend the appointment of an independent counsel to investigate alleged improper fund-raising activities by Vice-President Al Gore during the 1996 campaigns (see AR 1997, p. 149). Ms Reno said that evidence that Mr Gore had lied to FBI agents was 'insubstantial'. It was reported that both Mr Gore and Mr Clinton had been interviewed earlier by Justice Department investigators concerning the use of party funds to pay for advertising in support of the President's re-election. Also on 24 November a Washington district judge dismissed eight charges against Mike Espy, the former Secretary of Agriculture, but accepted 30 counts that he had received gifts and favours from poultry companies while serving in the Clinton administration (see AR 1994, p. 163).

In representations before the House judiciary committee in the impeachment hearings on 8 December, White House special counsel Greg Craig argued that the President's behaviour was 'sinful' and immoral rather than illegal, and that his evidence in the Paula Jones sexual harassment case had been 'evasive, incomplete, misleading, even maddening', but 'not perjury.' The President's actions, he contended, did not merit impeachment. He added: 'The President wants everyone to know that he is genuinely sorry for the pain and the damage he has caused and for the wrongs he has committed.' Given the composition of the committee, it was clear that these remarks were intended to gain public support in opposition to impeachment.

Despite such appeals, the House judiciary committee approved four articles of impeachment on 12 December, namely that the President had given perjurious answers to the grand jury, had perjured himself in answer to questions, had obstructed justice and had committed perjury in sworn statements in answer to written questions. The articles of impeachment alleged that the President had 'undermined the integrity of his office' and had 'acted in a manner subversive of the rule of law and justice, to the manifest injury of the people of the United States'.

Mrs Clinton, who sometimes seemed strained in her relations with her husband in this period, broke her silence on 18 December by calling for 'reflection and reconciliation' in the nation. She continued to urge Democratic representatives to support the President in the run-up to the vote on impeachment.

The impeachment debate in the House of Representatives was temporarily delayed during the military action against Iraq which began on 16 December (see below). Indeed, some of the President's critics questioned the timing of the attacks on Iraq, suggesting that they were launched to divert attention from the debates or to influence the outcome. Following an impassioned and at times rancorous debate, in which

Republicans refused to limit their reprimand of the President to a vote of censure, on 19 December the House voted on the four articles of impeachment. The first article was passed by 228 votes to 206; the second was rejected by 229 votes to 205; the third was dismissed by 286 votes to 148; the fourth was approved by 221 to 212. The matter was then referred to the Senate, where Mr Clinton would face trial in 1999. In the course of the debates, the newly-elected Speaker of the House, Republican Bob Livingston, announced that he would resign following revelations of his marital infidelity published in *Hustler*, a pornographic magazine. Mr Livingston called upon the President to follow his example.

There were other calls for the President's resignation, including some from among his own party. However, the congressional action seemed at odds with the public mood. Two days after the vote, Mr Clinton's popularity ratings shot up. A Gallup poll showed that over 70 per cent of those asked approved of the President, his highest rating ever. Former Presidents Ford and Jimmy Carter also indicated their opposition to impeachment in favour of some form of censure.

As the year ended, it was still not clear what form the trial of President Clinton would take. On 29 December Senate leader Trent Lott ruled out any deal to avoid a trial, but offered the possibility of a fast-track procedure if the President did not dispute any of the facts presented. Ironically, Mr Clinton was on that day laying a wreath in memory of Andrew Johnson, the only other President to have faced a Senate impeachment trial (in 1868), in the traditional commemoration of a former President's birthday.

SOCIAL AND LEGAL AFFAIRS. It was announced on 15 January that, following settlements in Mississippi and Florida in 1997 (see AR 1997, p. 157), five cigarette manufacturers had agreed to pay the state of Texas $7,250 million over 25 years in respect of the costs of treating tobacco-related illness. This was the largest out-of-court settlement agreed by the tobacco industry. In June legislation to settle the national liability of tobacco companies was set aside when it became apparent that it could not secure sufficient congressional support to overcome procedural obstacles. Opponents felt that the $368,500 million to be paid over 25 years was excessive, while others believed that the restrictions placed on the companies were still insufficient. In November a proposed $206,000 million settlement between the four largest companies and 46 states was revealed as an alternative to the legislation. The companies also agreed to fund anti-smoking campaigns and to spend $250 million over ten years to reduce teenage smoking.

In January the jury in a federal court in Denver failed to agree on imposing the death penalty on the second Oklahoma bomber, Terry Nichols. He had been convicted of conspiracy and involuntary manslaughter on 23 December 1997 for the bombing of the federal court house in Oklahoma city in 1995 (see AR 1997, p. 154). Having described

Nichols as 'an enemy of the United States constitution,' Judge Richard Matsch on 4 June sentenced him to life imprisonment without the possibility of parole. A third individual, Michael Fortier, was sentenced to 12 years in prison on 27 May for failing to warn the authorities of the bomb plot.

Also in January, Theodore Kaczynski, the so-called 'Unabomber' (see AR 1997, p. 155), agreed to plead guilty in his trial in Sacramento, California, in the face of overwhelming evidence linking him to ten bombings which had killed two people and injured 29 others. The plea bargain, which had previously been rejected, was accepted by the Justice Department following reports that Kaczynski had attempted suicide on 8 January and that he was suffering from paranoid schizophrenia. On 4 May he was sentenced to four consecutive life terms, plus 30 years, with no possibility of parole.

On 8 January Ramzi Ahmed Yousef was sentenced to 240 years' imprisonment without the possibility of parole following his conviction for the bombing of the World Trade Center in 1993 (see AR 1997, p. 154). Judge Kevin Duffy also imposed fines of $4.5 million and damages of $250 million to be paid to victims in order to ensure that Yousef could not benefit financially from any media exploitation of his life story. The judge further recommended that Yousef should serve his sentence in solitary confinement. Eyad Ismoil, the driver of the van used in the bombing, was also sentenced to 240 years imprisonment without parole on 3 April.

The Microsoft Corporation agreed in January to meet Justice Department concerns that it had not complied with an injunction to stop requiring personal computer manufacturers to install its Internet Explorer browser as a condition for licensing its Windows 95 system (see also XIII.2). In June the corporation won a victory in the anti-trust litigation when the District of Columbia court of appeals ruled that it should be allowed to sell Internet Explorer as part of the Windows 95 system. However, the company still had to face litigation with regard to Windows 98. Following a breakdown of negotiations, the Justice Department and several states initiated anti-trust suits against the company on 18 May, and the case opened in October.

On 29 January an off-duty police officer working as a security guard was killed, and a nurse was seriously injured, when a bomb exploded outside an abortion clinic in Birmingham, Alabama. In February a group called 'The Army of God', which had previously claimed responsibility for the bombing of another clinic and a gay night-club in Atlanta in 1997, admitted responsibility. It was reported on 28 February that federal investigators had forensic evidence linking all these bombings with that of the 1996 Olympic Games in Atlanta (see AR 1996, p. 139; 1997, p. 156). Police announced that they were searching for Eric Robert Rudolph, a North Carolina man seen near the Birmingham clinic before the bomb exploded. Federal authorities announced on 14 October that Rudolph had been charged *in absentia* with the bombings, a reward of $1 million being placed on his head. Anti-abortion attacks continued, and on 5 October it was reported that bombs had been found outside two abortion clinics in Fayetteville, North Carolina. On 23 October Dr Barnett Slepian, an obstetrician who performed abortions, was shot dead by a sniper in Buffalo, New York state.

FBI agents arrested two men in Henderson, Nevada, on 18 February after an informant had warned that they planned to put anthrax into the New York underground system. Larry Wayne Harris and William Leavitt were charged in Las Vegas on 19 February with conspiracy to possess and possession of anthrax. Reports associated the men with white supremacist organizations, but Leavitt was released on 21 February after tests had revealed the chemicals to be non-lethal anthrax. Harris was kept in prison, having violated a probation order relating to the purchase of bubonic plague cultures in 1995.

On 26 February five New York City policemen were indicted on federal charges of denying Abner Louima, a Haitian immigrant, his constitutional rights by assaulting him while in police custody. The case had attracted particular attention because of the brutality of the assault and its racial aspects (see AR 1997, p. 159).

Opponents of capital punishment were outraged when Karla Faye Tucker became the first woman to be executed in Texas since the Civil War despite her conversion to Christianity whilst in prison and a number of late appeals. Convicted for her part in a double murder in 1984, Tucker died on 4 February as a result of lethal injection after Governor Bush approved the execution.

There were a number of significant Supreme Court rulings during the year. On 4 March the Court unanimously ruled that a federal law against sexual harassment in the workplace applied even where the individuals involved were of the same sex. The Court also, on 23 March, upheld a ruling which had declared a 1995 Ohio state law banning 'partial birth' abortions as unconstitutional. On 25 June the Court struck down the 'line-item veto' which allowed the President to remove individual taxes or items of expenditure from within broad legislation. Mr Clinton had used the measure on 82 occasions since August 1997, but the court ruled that the President only had the power to sign legislation or veto it in its entirety.

A court martial on 13 March found army instructor Sgt.-Major Gene McKinney not guilty of 19 charges of sexual misconduct arising out of allegations of indecent assault and sexual harassment (see AR 1997, p. 156). He was found guilty of one charge of conspiracy to obstruct justice and was sentenced to a demotion and an official reprimand. Sgt.-Major McKinney, an African-American, had always denied the charges, which he claimed were racially motivated.

Concern about children's access to guns was raised again following the killing of four pupils and a teacher in a school in Jonesboro, Arkansas, on 24 March by two boys, aged 11 and 13, armed with rifles and handguns. Eleven other people were wounded. As an indication of the government's determination to control guns, on 6 April President Clinton issued an executive order imposing a permanent ban on the import of foreign-made semi-automatic assault weapons. Further concerns were expressed when on 21 May a 15-year-old student, Kipland Kinkel, shot dead his parents at home and then killed two fellow pupils and wounded 22 others at a school in Springfield, Oregon, after he had previously been expelled.

The supreme court of Massachusetts on 16 June upheld Judge Hiller Zobel's decision in November 1997 to reduce the sentence of British au pair Louise Woodward, for the second-degree murder of the baby in her charge, from 15 years to time served (see AR 1997, p. 154–5). The ruling, by a 4–3 majority, meant that Ms Woodward was free to return to Britain.

There was widespread public revulsion following two separate brutal murders, one racially motivated and the second sexual. On 6 June, outside Jasper, near Houston, Texas, a 49-year-old African American, James Byrd, was chained to the back of a vehicle, which was then driven at such speed that Mr Byrd was decapitated and an arm severed from his body. Three white men were charged with the murder, the apparent racial motivation of which meant that they could also face federal charges. The murder of gay student Matthew Shephard in Laramie, Wyoming, led to calls for the extension of the federal 'hate crime' laws, which imposed severe penalties for attacks on individuals due to their race, religion or ethnic origin, to include violence against gays and lesbians. Mr Shephard died on 12 October, five days after being found severely beaten and tied to a fence. Two men, both aged 21, were charged with kidnapping, murder and robbery. In December the prosecutors announced that they would be seeking the death penalty.

Two police officers were shot dead in the US Capitol by a lone gunman, Russell Eugene Weston, on 24 July. Weston was himself critically injured by one of the officers and a tourist was also wounded in the exchange. It was believed that Weston, who had a history of mental illness, bore a grudge against the government.

A federal court in New York City on 27 August charged Mohammed Saddiq Odeh and Mohammed Rashed Daoud Owhali with 12 counts of murder in connection with bomb attacks on the US embassies in Kenya and Tanzania on 7 August in which 12 US citizens were killed (see VI.1.ii; VI.1.iii). Both men had been flown from Kenya that day. On 4 November the Saudi Arabian Islamic militant, Osama bin Laden, and his associate, Mohammed Atef, were indicted *in absentia* by a Manhattan federal grand jury on 238 charges relating to the attacks. Indictments were also issued against the two men for earlier attacks on US forces in Somalia, Saudi

Arabia and Yemen, and for attacks in the United States, including the bombing of the World Trade Center in 1993.

On 1 September the Senate veterans' affairs committee issued a report which concluded that there was insufficient evidence to conclude that the illnesses known as 'Gulf War syndrome' were the result of exposure to Iraqi nerve gas. The report also criticized federal agencies for their failure to investigate the issue sufficiently.

THE ECONOMY. If sexual scandal threatened to destroy the Clinton presidency, the strength of the US economy seemed likely to save it. Unemployment rates continued to fall, down to 4.3 per cent by the end of the year, the lowest level since 1969. The rate of inflation was 0.9 per cent, again the lowest since the 1960s, despite a continued consumer boom.

On 2 February President Clinton presented his budget proposal for fiscal year 1999 to Congress. The first balanced budget to appear before Congress since 1969 (three years ahead of the target date set in 1997), the budget initiated the bargaining process between the administration and Congress to agree a final budget and tax plan. The proposals, based on a conservative estimate of 2 per cent economic growth in 1999, included $21,000 million for child care and $7,300 million in new education spending, including provision for 100,000 new teachers at infant and primary level over seven years. Tax reductions for low-income parents for child care were also included, while benefits for 730,000 legal immigrants, cut off by welfare reform measures in 1996, would be restored. An increase in social spending of $65,000 million was to be offset by monies raised over ten years by a national tobacco settlement. Extra spending to allow people aged between 55 and 64 to buy into Medicare was also to be made. Additional funding was also to be provided to improve law and order, with more money for the FBI and for drug control. Revenue raised by broadcasting licences would be used to offset the costs of assisting public broadcasters to switch to digital technology.

Mr Clinton underlined the administration's successful economic policy when he announced the first US budget surplus since 1969 on 30 September. The surplus, of $70,000 million for 1998, was achieved four years early as a result of the strong economy.

The omnibus budget bill for 1999 was signed by President Clinton on 21 October following its approval by Congress. The budget, which included $18 million in funding for the IMF and $1,100 million in additional education spending, was seen as a victory for Mr Clinton. However, Republicans took some pleasure from the inclusion of $9,000 million in additional military spending and also from the exclusion of funds to pay $1,600 million in US arrears to the United Nations.

On 21 December the US Trade Department announced a new list of imports from the European Union (EU) which would face 100 per cent duties in February in response to the alleged favourable treatment given to banana imports from former Caribbean colonies (see XI.4). Denmark and the Netherlands were to be excluded from the duties because they had voted against the EU's policy on banana imports.

EXTERNAL RELATIONS. President Clinton made an unprecedented week-long visit to six African countries beginning on 23 March. Speaking in Uganda on 24 March, he expressed regret for US support of oppressive regimes during the Cold War and US participation in the slave trade. He suggested that Africa had been subject to American 'neglect and ignorance' and proposed $180 million in future aid. On 26 March Mr Clinton became the first US President to visit South Africa.

Despite some opposition at home because of China's record on human rights, the Clinton administration continued a policy of 'constructive engagement' with Beijing. Secretary of State Madeleine Albright visted China in May, and Mr Clinton announced his intention to approve most-favoured-nation (MFN) trade status for another year on 3 June, although this subsequently was changed to 'normal trade' relations. Mr Clinton paid a nine-day visit to China at the end of June, the first by a US President since the Tiananmen Square massacre in 1989. In the course of his stay the President spoke several times on human rights, and he stated publicly that 'the use of force and the tragic loss of life was wrong'. He also urged the Chinese to open negotiations with Tibet's spiritual leader, the Dalai Lama, and reaffirmed US policy of no change with regard to the status of Taiwan. In his final press conference he praised President Jiang Zemin as a man of 'vision' and expressed the hope that communism would disappear in China in his life-time. His visit was generally deemed to have been very successful.

Following the attacks on US embassies in Africa on 7 August, the United States launched cruise missile attacks on 20 August against alleged terrorist bases in Afghanistan and Sudan. Breaking his vacation in Martha's Vineyard to give a televised address to the nation, President Clinton claimed that there was 'convincing information' linking the Islamic militant Osama bin Laden to the recent attacks and a number of earlier ones, and 'compelling information' that further attacks were planned against US citizens. Some critics suggested that the US response was intended to divert attention away from the Lewinsky investigation, parallels being drawn with a fictional President in the film *Wag the Dog* who began a war when faced with a sex scandal. Such charges were vehemently denied by administration spokesmen.

President Clinton visited Russia on 1–2 September (see also III.3.i). Following meetings with President Yeltsin and opposition leaders, he pledged continued financial support provided that 'the reform process can be completed'. Mr Clinton then travelled to Ireland, where he expressed continued support for the peace process in the course of his three-day visit (see II.1.iv; II.2.vii).

On 15 October Mr Clinton formally opened talks between Israeli Prime Minister Binyamin Netanyahu and Palestinian leader Yassir Arafat at the

Wye River Plantation in Maryland in an attempt to revive the Israeli-Palestinian peace accords (see V.1; V.2.i). After nine days of negotiation, in which the President was personally involved, an agreement was finally reached on 23 October. The talks had been threatened by disagreements between the Americans and the Israelis over the fate of Jonathan Pollard, a US naval officer gaoled in 1986 for spying for Israel; however, a discussion on that issue was postponed until after the Wye agreement had been reached.

The Lewinsky affair even followed President Clinton on a two-day visit to Japan in November. In the course of a public meeting on 19 November, asked how he had said sorry to his family, he replied that he had done so 'in a direct and straightforward manner' and that he believed that they forgave him.

Following up the Wye agreement, Mr Clinton visited the Middle East in December. After meeting with the Israeli government on 13 December, the following day he became the first incumbent President to visit Palestine. Addressing the Palestine National Council, he thanked the members for 'standing tall' in their 'commitment to peace and negotiations' and in abandoning their commitment to the overthrow of the state of Israel. Although he failed to achieve further agreement between the respective parties before his visit ended on 15 December, Mr Clinton insisted that he had achieved what he had intended. Even on this trip, however, he was dogged by questions about impeachment. He indicated that he had no intention of resigning, and in response to questions on 14 December said that he did not think impeachment and a trial were in the 'interest of the United States and the American people'.

Having called off air strikes against Iraq at the last minute in November, on 16 December, following receipt of the Butler report of the UN arms inspection team and consultations with members of Congress, the US forces, supported by British units, launched 'Operation Desert Fox' against positions in Iraq (see V.2.vi). In a televised address to the American people, President Clinton claimed that President Saddam Husain's policies posed 'a clear and present danger' to people in the Gulf and elsewhere. He also said that 'so long as Saddam remains in power, he threatens the well-being of his people, the peace of his region, the security of the world'. He reiterated these points in a Ramadan message to the Arab world on 19 December prior to the cessation of hostilities. Following an attack by US aircraft on an Iraqi missile battery on 28 December, President Clinton insisted that the US would continue to police the no-fly zones in northern and southern Iraq.

2. CANADA

CAPITAL: Ottawa   AREA: 9,9970,610 sq km   POPULATION: 30,700,000 ('97)
OFFICIAL LANGUAGES: English & French
POLITICAL SYSTEM: federal parliamentary democracy
HEAD OF STATE: Queen Elizabeth II (since Feb '52)
GOVERNOR-GENERAL: Roméo Leblanc (since Feb '95)
RULING PARTY: Liberal Party (since Oct '93)
HEAD OF GOVERNMENT: Jean Chrétien, Prime Minister (since Oct '93)
MAIN IGO MEMBERSHIPS (non-UN): NATO, OECD, OSCE, G-7, OAS, NAFTA, APEC, CP, CWTH, Francophonie
CURRENCY: Canadian dollar (end-'98 £1=Can$2.56, US$1=Can$1.54)
GNP PER CAPITA: US$19,290 by exchange-rate calculation, US$21,860 by PPP calculation ('97)

QUEBEC'S future as a part of Canada—the central question of recent Canadian history—continued to hang over the country in 1998. A Supreme Court ruling in August stated plainly that a unilateral declaration of independence by the French-speaking province would be illegal; a provincial election in Quebec in November returned to office a government committed to secession. Polls throughout the year revealed that most Quebeckers wished to remain part of Canada. At the end of 1998 the issue remained in much the same state as it had in the beginning.

One change had occurred, however. A new figure emerged to lead the federalist forces in Quebec. He was Jean Charest, chosen unopposed to take over the leadership of the Quebec Liberal Party on 30 April. M. Charest succeeded Daniel Johnson, leader for the past four years, who dramatically announced his resignation on 2 March. Colourless in manner, M. Johnson had failed to give momentum to the federalist cause in Quebec. In addition, he did not possess the full confidence of Prime Minister Jean Chrétien and the governing Liberal Party in Ottawa. M. Chrétien blamed M. Johnson for the poor showing of the federalist side in the 1995 sovereignty referendum, a vote which the federalists won by the narrowest of margins (see AR 1995, pp. 162–4).

M. Charest had been a forceful protagonist in the referendum campaign, participating at the time as the leader of the national Progressive Conservative Party (PCP). When M. Johnson resigned, M. Charest came under intense pressure to leave his party and assume command of the Liberals in Quebec. His qualifications seemed clear to all. A committed federalist yet a loyal Quebecker, a charismatic figure immensely popular across the province, relatively young (40), energetic and superbly bilingual, he had gained federal experience as a minister over the years 1986–93 in the PCP administration of Brian Mulroney. A wave of enthusiasm greeted M. Charest's decision to enter Quebec politics. Polls showed separatist sentiment at a low ebb and predicted that M. Charest as Liberal leader could defeat the Parti Québécois (PQ) government, led by another charismatic figure, Lucien Bouchard.

M. Bouchard (60), who had also served in Mr Mulroney's cabinet before defecting to the separatist cause, had devoted his government's attention to policies designed to restore Quebec's economic and financial position, weakened by the years of uncertainty over the prospect of secession. An overhanging deficit in the public finances of the province had been gradually reduced and was scheduled to be eliminated by the year 2000. An overgrown public service had been cut back and grants for health, social services and education curtailed. As a result of these actions the PQ government appeared to have suffered a loss in popularity—a factor that was expected to play into the hands of M. Charest and the Liberals at the next election. As well, there were tensions within the separatist camp. M. Bouchard, who had always maintained that his goal was to forge a partnership between a sovereign Quebec and the rest of Canada, was not entirely trusted by the hard core of militant separatists. This distrust was enhanced when the premier refused to commit himself on the timing of another referendum on independence. (Quebec had already held two referendums on the concept of 'sovereignty-association', in 1980 and 1995, both of which the separatists had lost.) At a party convention on 19-20 September, M. Bouchard forced through a resolution giving him authority to hold a vote on separation only when 'winning conditions' occurred. The passage of this resolution gave the PQ leader more flexibility in dealing with attitudes in his own party and with broad changes in the public mood.

Worried that support for M. Charest was building, M. Bouchard decided to call an early election in Quebec. He announced that polling would take place on 30 November, four years after the PQ had come to power under M. Bouchard's predecessor, Jacques Parizeau. His appeal was straightforward: the record of his government in bringing the province's finances under control. Separation was still his long-term goal, but in the meantime Quebec would be prepared to work within the federal system to gain additional desired powers. The message was reassuring to those committed to the separatist cause but did not alarm the moderate 'soft nationalists' who were nervous of major change. M. Charest countered with a platform that emphasized lower taxes and measures to stimulate the economy. Unwisely, he attacked the interventionist role that the Quebec government had always played in the economy. Most residents of the province were comfortable with this role, symbolized by the powerful publicly-owned electric utility company, Hydro-Québec, which had been a major force in the growth of the Quebec economy. M. Charest was obliged to tone down his public statements on this point, but it was an aspect of his message that was not well received. On the constitutional front, he made it plain that if he formed a government after the election he would not move for another referendum on the province's future. A vote on this question would be an unnecessary distraction from the real tasks of government, which should focus on economic renewal.

As the campaign proceeded, polls showed residents of the province turning away from the Liberals. M. Bouchard seemed to many voters a more authentic son of Quebec, fully understanding of its aspirations and trustworthy in implementing them. A powerful, emotional orator, the PQ leader skilfully made the most of the expressions of confidence which he seemed to inspire. By the end of the campaign, polls suggested a possible landslide victory for the separatists. It appeared that M. Bouchard's 'winning conditions' for a successful referendum were at hand.

In the event, the results of the election closely resembled those of the previous contest in 1994. The PQ took 76 seats in the 125-member Quebec national assembly and the Liberals 48, while the leader of a small nationalist third party was also elected. Liberal strength, as expected, was concentrated in ridings on the island of Montreal, in the Eastern Townships south of Montreal towards the US border, and in the Ottawa valley. Here there were substantial proportions of English-speaking residents and others whose mother tongue was neither English nor French. Separation possessed no appeal to these groups. Over the 70 electoral districts with a majority of French-speaking voters, however, the PQ took seat after seat. Yet the popular vote gave the Liberals a slight overall majority of 43.7 per cent compared with the PQ's 42.7 per cent. The third party, the Action Démocratique du Quebec, took 11.8 per cent even though only its leader, 28-year-old Mario Dumont, was elected.

M. Bouchard was disappointed by the electoral results. The contest revealed how evenly the parties were divided in popular support. The PQ would continue in office for a second term, but without the sweeping majority which the premier had expected to provide 'winning conditions' for a successful referendum. But M. Charest had also not fulfilled the expectations raised by his move into Quebec politics. Indeed, the electoral results which he had obtained were almost identical to those gained by Daniel Johnson in 1994. Thus M. Charest would be a forceful spokesman for federalism in Quebec but not its saviour. A referendum had been put off indefinitely. The ambiguity of Quebec's position in Canada remained. Was the foremost loyalty of its inhabitants to Canada or to a new sovereign state?

The federal government, which had at first been cautious on the challenge of Quebec nationalism, had taken a stronger stand in recent years. A central feature of its new approach was the decision announced in September 1996 to refer the question of whether Quebec could secede unilaterally to the highest court in the land, the Supreme Court of Canada. Hearings before the court were spread over four days beginning on 16 February. The nine members of the Supreme Court, four of whom were French-speaking, issued a unanimous ruling on 20 August. The 78-page decision was written in a clear fashion, intelligible to the average citizen.

To the first question referred to it—'Does Quebec have the right to secede unilaterally?'—the court was blunt. The Canadian constitution had no provision for secession; therefore, such a step would 'violate the Canadian legal order'. But Canadians in the rest of Canada, the court added, could not be indifferent to a clear expression by the majority of Quebeckers if they decided that they wished to leave Canada.

A second question—'Does international law give any sanction for Quebec to secede?'—was also dealt with in the negative. Precedents for such action could only be found in colonial situations or where individuals and groups suffered under intolerable oppression. Quebec was hardly in these categories. It was not a colony but an original and equal member of a democratic federation. Its citizens, enjoying the same rights as other Canadians, were in no sense 'oppressed'. Moreover, there was no conflict between domestic and international law over Quebec's secession (the third question). Neither form of law permitted separation. A referendum on secession could therefore have no legal effect. Secession could only be achieved by negotiations in good faith with the federal government and the other nine provinces of Canada.

The court did not deal with the difficult questions surrounding the process of negotiation. How should the constitution be amended to permit secession? What would constitute a sufficient majority to support the decision for secession? Would Quebec's borders remain unchanged if partition occurred? How would the rights of aborigines—who were under federal jurisdiction and had made it plain that they did not want to be part of an independent Quebec—be protected if Quebec desired to leave Canada? All these questions, the court stated, would have to be dealt with by the 'political actors' (governments) involved in the process. All in all, the court remarked with disarming understatement, it would not be 'an easy set of negotiations'.

Each side took what comfort it could from the court's ruling. The Quebec government, which had refused to participate in the hearings, claimed that the decision had legitimized independence as a democratically-endorsed option for Quebec. The Canadian government and the provinces, it argued, were duty-bound to negotiate separation if Quebec raised it. For its part, the Chrétien government took the view that the court had validated its constitutional position but it did not gloat over the result. It would continue, it stated, to revise the federal system to meet the legitimate concerns of Quebec and the other nine provinces.

Prime Minister Chrétien made only two minor changes in his cabinet in 1998, during which his Liberal Party maintained a comfortable majority in the House of Commons. Party standings in the 301-seat Commons at year's end were: Liberals 156, Reform Party (official opposition) 59, Bloc Québécois (separatist) 45, New Democratic Party 21, Progressive Conservatives 19, independent 1. Needing a new leader after M. Charest left the party, the Progressive Conservatives turned to a former head, Joe Clark (59), an Albertan who had been Prime Minister in the short-lived PCP administration of 1979–80.

The Canadian economy, especially in the Pacific province of British Columbia, suffered from the Asian financial collapse. The Canadian dollar fell steadily against its US counterpart, the Bank of Canada being forced to intervene in August to raise its trend-setting interest rate. Any earlier increase had been resisted for fear of curbing economic growth. By the end of the year the Canadian dollar was trading at approximately 66 US cents. The fall in commodity prices, especially in such Canadian staples as oil, metals, forest products and wheat, was a principal reason for the currency's depreciation. Inflation was kept to around 1 per cent, while unemployment remained higher than in the United States, at 8 per cent at the end of the year.

Finance Minister Paul Martin presented his fifth budget on 24 February. For the first time since 1969–70, the federal budget would be balanced in the fiscal year ending 31 March 1998. A later statement, on 14 October, reported that an actual surplus of Can$3,500 million had been recorded in the year just passed. Canada thus became the first of the major industrialized countries to eliminate its public deficit. Tax cuts of Can$7,200 million over the next three years were promised, as well as a Millennium Scholarship Fund to aid 100,000 post-secondary students in the ten years after 2000.

Canada suffered the worst natural disaster in its recorded history when successive storms dumped as much as 100 millimetres of freezing rain across eastern Ontario and Quebec on 4–10 January. The load of ice brought down about 1,000 power transmission towers and some 30,000 wooden utility poles. Around 3 million people lost electricity and heat at a time of extreme winter conditions. At least 25 people died as a result of the storm and about 700,000 insurance claims were filed for resultant property damage.

In a vote on 8 October, Canada won election to one of the ten non-permanent seats on the UN Security Council, to serve a two-year term from 1 January 1999. Along with the Netherlands, Canada was chosen to represent a miscellaneous group of countries designated 'Western Europe and Others', having been so elected once every decade since the foundation of the UN. Foreign Affairs Minister Lloyd Axworthy stated that Canada would use its place on the Council to support its policies on global humanitarian issues such as the eradication of anti-personnel land mines and a check on the illicit trade in 'light weapons'. On the difficult question of reforming the Security Council, Canada opposed naming any new permanent members but believed that five more states should be elected to represent the five existing groupings on the Council.

Ratifications of the 1997 treaty banning anti-personnel land mines (see AR 1997, pp. 165, 442–3, 566–8) continued to arrive in Ottawa. By November 52 states had approved the treaty, allowing it to come into force, earlier than expected, in March 1999. Significant non-ratifiers were the United States, Russia and China.

Canada took an active role at a meeting of 120 countries in Rome in July at which a treaty setting up the world's first permanent War Crimes

Tribunal was adopted (see XIV.1.i; XVII.2). Canada also participated in a conference in Oslo, also in July, which discussed means to restrain the trade in 'light weapons' such as assault rifles, hand grenades and small mortars. These arms, rather than large weapons systems, were known to have caused the greatest bloodshed in international and internal conflicts.

3. LATIN AMERICA

ARGENTINA—BOLIVIA—BRAZIL—CHILE—COLOMBIA—ECUADOR—PARAGUAY—PERU—URUGUAY—VENEZUELA—CUBA—DOMINICAN REPUBLIC AND HAITI—CENTRAL AMERICA AND PANAMA—MEXICO

i. ARGENTINA

CAPITAL: Buenos Aires   AREA: 2,766,890 sq km   POPULATION: 36,000,000 ('97)
OFFICIAL LANGUAGE: Spanish
POLITICAL SYSTEM: federal presidential democracy
HEAD OF STATE & GOVERNMENT: President Carlos Saúl Menem (since July '89)
RULING PARTY: Justicialist (Peronist) Party (since Dec '89)
MAIN IGO MEMBERSHIPS: OAS, SELA, ALADI, Mercosur
CURRENCY: peso (end-'98 £1=AP1.66, US$1=AP1.00)
GNP PER CAPITA: US$8,570 by exchange-rate calculation, US$9,950 by PPP calculation ('97)

IN late January a presidential decree stripped retired Navy Captain Alfredo Ignacio Astiz of his rank and pension after he had boasted in a newspaper interview of his role in the 'dirty war' of the 1970s; the deaths of two French nuns, however, were apparently ordered not by him, as hitherto believed, but by Captain Jorge Acosta. President Carlos Saúl Menem had just announced plans to demolish the notorious Naval Mechanical School (ESMA) and the interview provoked moves by the opposition Front for a Country in Solidarity (Frepaso) to repeal both the 'Full Stop' Law of 1986 and the Law of Due Obedience of 1987. The initial debate in the Chamber of Deputies broke up amid much wrangling. The decision of the administration to pay substantial sums in compensation to seven Brazilian families who had lost relatives during the war angered relatives of Argentine victims. On 24 and 25 March the Frepaso bill passed both houses by large majorities, soon after the Senate (on 18 March) had approved a bill for the reorganization of the armed forces. On 9 June a federal judge ordered the arrest of the former de facto President Jorge Rafael Videla for illegal placing for adoption of children born to detainees during the 'dirty war'. This charge not apparently being covered by either the 1986 'Full Stop' Law or President Menem's amnesty in 1990, on 24 November former

Admiral Eduardo Emilio Massera was also arrested and charged. In December a Swiss judge issued an international arrest warrant for General Videla.

In January the Supreme Court upheld the validity of the presidential decree of September 1997 privatizing the country's 33 airports, but the move was opposed in Congress and suspended in April after a court found irregularities. On 3 September Congress finally passed the long-delayed labour reform bill, submitted to them by Labour Minister Antonio Ermán González in February, which cut redundancy payments as well as ending the three-month so-called 'rubbish contracts'. However, the IMF criticized the labour reform package as inadequate and falling short of the country's obligations under the US$2,800 million extended fund facility loan approved in February.

After the federal electoral appeals court had ruled on 1 June that President Menem could not be a candidate to succeed himself in 1999, on 21 July he formally announced that he would not seek a third term. Ramón 'Palito' Ortega, former governor of Tucumán, had already emerged in March as the front-runner for the Peronist presidential nomination and in April was appointed Secretary of Social Development. On 17 October Governor Eduardo Duhalde launched his candidature, while former Economy Minister Domingo Cavallo decided to run as an independent.

Accusations of governmental corruption were reawakened by the suicide on 20 May of Alfredo Yabrán after a warrant had been issued for his arrest in connection with the murder of press photographer José Luis Cabezas in 1997 (see AR 1997, p. 166). In October, however, Eduardo César Angeloz, former UCR presidential candidate, was acquitted of charges of 'illicit enrichment' and returned to his seat in the Senate. In open primaries on 29 November, former senator Fernando de la Rua, currently mayor of Buenos Aires, who had been chosen by the opposition Radical Civic Union (UCR) on 3 April, was endorsed as joint presidential candidate of an opposition alliance between the UCR and Frepaso.

Externally, relations with Iran soured in May when an Iranian national was arrested, and five days later four Iranian diplomats were expelled, for alleged complicity in the bombing of the Argentine-Israeli Mutual Association (AMIA) in 1994. President Menem and President Eduardo Frei Ruiz-Tagle of Chile signed an new agreement on the Southern Glaciers question in Buenos Aires on 15 December. Argentinian-UK relations improved in the months leading up to the official visit of President Menem to Britain in October (see I.1.i), although on 22 April the Senate approved a bill imposing sanctions on companies drilling in the waters around the Falkland Islands without Argentine permission. In November, in a so-called 'charm offensive', President Menem wrote a conciliatory letter to the islands' inhabitants. News on 17 December that Britain was to lift its embargo on most arms sales to Argentina was greeted as an important step in improved relations.

ii. BOLIVIA

CAPITAL: La Paz and Sucre   AREA: 1,099,000 sq km   POPULATION: 8,000,000 ('97)
OFFICIAL LANGUAGES: Spanish, Quechua, Aymará
POLITICAL SYSTEM: presidential democracy
HEAD OF STATE & GOVERNMENT: President Hugo Banzer Suárez (since Aug '97)
RULING PARTIES: Democratic Nationalist Action (AND) heads coalition with Civic Solidarity Union (UCS), New Republican Force (NFR) & Movement of the Revolutionary Left (MIR)
MAIN IGO MEMBERSHIPS (non-UN): NAM, OAS, ALADI, SELA, AG, CA
CURRENCY: boliviano (end-'98 £1=Bs9.40, US$1=Bs5.65)
GNP PER CAPITA: US$950 by exchange-rate calculation ('97)

BOLIVIA's economic position remained difficult throughout the year, the tone being set when the Bolivian Workers' Central (COB) held a second strike on 12 January in protest at the government's November 1997 reform package (see AR 1997, p. 168). The country was the first in Latin America to be designated by the IMF as eligible for debt service relief under the heavily-indebted poor countries (HIPC) initiative. In September it was granted a three-year loan equivalent to US$137 million under the enhanced structural adjustment facility. During an official visit on 15–16 March by Prime Minister José Maria Aznar, Spain agreed two concessionary loans totalling some $130 million to combat drugs and relieve poverty.

Unemployment remained high and coca growers became increasingly active in stirring up resistance to the government's plans to stamp out all illegal production by 2002. In clashes between demonstrators and police in Cochabamba and Chaparé in April, at least ten people died and 40 were injured. Fresh violence erupted in September after compensation payments to farmers were sharply cut.

At the beginning of August President Hugo Banzer Suárez reshuffled his cabinet, appointing Herbert Muller Costas of the Movement of the Revolutionary Left (MIR) as Finance Minister, following the involuntary departure of the Conscience of the Fatherland (Condepa) members. On 13 November he appointed Admiral Jorge Zabala Ossio as commander-in-chief of the armed forces in place of General Carlos Béjar Molina.

At least 100 people died when a series of earthquakes measuring up to 6.8 on the Richter scale hit central Bolivia on 22 May.

iii. BRAZIL

CAPITAL: Brasília   AREA: 8,512,000 sq km   POPULATION: 164,000,000 ('97)
OFFICIAL LANGUAGE: Portuguese
POLITICAL SYSTEM: federal presidential democracy
HEAD OF STATE & GOVERNMENT: President Fernando Henrique Cardoso (since Jan '95)
RULING PARTIES: Brazilian Social Democratic Party (PSDB) heads coalition with Brazilian Labour Party (PTB), Liberal Front Party (PFL), Brazilian Progressive Party (PPB), Popular Socialist Party (PPS) & Brazilian Democratic Movement Party (PMDB)
MAIN IGO MEMBERSHIPS (non-UN): OAS, ALADI, SELA, Mercosur, AP, CPLP
CURRENCY: real (end-'98 £1=R2.01, US$1=R1.21)
GNP PER CAPITA: US$4,720 by exchange-rate calculation, US$6,240 by PPP calculation ('97)

It was announced in January that former President Fernando Collor de Mello had been acquitted on eight counts of illegal enrichment. On 12 February President Fernando Henrique Cardoso was able finally to sign a bill first introduced in 1991 making serious environmental crimes punishable by up to five years' imprisonment. In March the Senate finally approved the civil service bill, the main purpose of which was to reduce public expenditure by the dismissal of some 33,000 civil servants.

Meanwhile, demonstrations and looting of shops and supermarkets spread throughout the north-east as endemic drought problems intensified by El Niño weather distortion affected some 10 million people in eight states. The Landless Workers' Movement (MST) offered support to destitute peasants on 5 May, and both the Conference of Brazilian Bishops (CNBB) and the left-wing Workers' Party (PT) supported their demands. Government officials admitted that some US$45 million budgeted for famine relief had been used to pay off the national debt. Francisco de Assis Araujo, coordinator of the Organization of Indigenous Peoples, was shot dead on 10 May, probably by farmers who had occupied tribal lands. On 29 June MST national coordinator José Rainha Júnior and his wife, who had been arrested in 1995 following a land occupation in São Paulo, were sentenced to two years' imprisonment for illegal association.

On 29 July the sale went ahead, amid street protests, of a controlling interest in Telebrás, the 12 companies making up the federal telecommunications network. Most were purchased at auction by European telephone companies, for a total of US19,100 million. News that on 3 September the New York ratings agency Moody's had downgraded Brazil's debt rating to B2 precipitated a crisis on the stock market, followed by a series of interest-rate rises to staunch capital flight and maintain the parity of the real. With the IMF and other lending agencies pledging their support, President Cardoso announced on 23 September a substantial package of austerity measures.

Despite these difficulties, Sr Cardoso on 4 October became the first Brazilian President to be re-elected for a further term in a free election, winning 53.1 per cent of the votes cast against 31.7 per cent for his nearest rival, Luiz Inácio ('Lula') da Silva (PT). Results of elections for the Chamber of Deputies gave the ruling coalition more than the three-fifths majority needed to amend the constitution. The President's Brazilian Social Democratic Party (PSDB) won 99 seats, the Liberal Front Party (PFL) 105, the Brazilian Democratic Movement Party (PMDB) 82, the Brazilian Progressive Party (PPB) 60 and the Brazilian Labour Party (PTB) 31. For the opposition, the PT won 58 seats and the Democratic Labour Party (PDT) 26. A variety of smaller parties shared the remaining 52 seats.

A new fiscal stability programme sent to Congress on 28 October proposed far-reaching changes in tax and pension provisions, following a joint understanding with the IMF which led to a bailout package worth some $40,000 million. On 2 December, however, Congress rejected pensions reform—a key part of the package—by 205 votes to 187, and so reawakened fears of a fiscal collapse and devaluation of the real.

During a visit by UN Secretary-General Kofi Annan on 13 June, President Cardoso signed Brazil's accession to the Nuclear Non-Proliferation Treaty (NPT) and also ratified the Comprehensive Nuclear Test-Ban Treaty (CTBT).

iv. CHILE

CAPITAL: Santiago   AREA: 756,000 sq km   POPULATION: 15,000,000 ('97)
OFFICIAL LANGUAGE: Spanish   POLITICAL SYSTEM: presidential democracy
HEAD OF STATE & GOVERNMENT: President Eduardo Frei-Tagle (since March '94)
RULING PARTIES: Christian Democratic Party (PDC) heads Coalition for Democracy (CPD)
MAIN IGO MEMBERSHIPS (non-UN): OAS, ALADI, SELA, NAM, APEC
CURRENCY: peso (end–'98 £1=Ch$787.37, US$1=Ch$473.25)
GNP PER CAPITA: US$5,020 by exchange-rate calculation, US$12,080 by PPP calculation ('97)

ON 10 March the former dictator General Augusto Pinochet Ugarte retired as army commander-in-chief and took up the seat as senator-for-life provided for in the 1980 constitution (which he had imposed). He was succeeded by Major-General Ricardo Izurieta. General Pinochet's decision to retain his army post till the last possible moment, which triggered the resignation of Defence Minister Eduardo Pérez Yoma, was strengthened by a resolution of the Chamber on 7 January repudiating his appointment as senator. Several further efforts were made to challenge the appointment, but the Constitutional Tribunal refused to rule on the matter. An attempt to impeach General Pinochet failed when on 9 April, after 12 hours of debate, 11 of the 35 deputies of the Christian Democratic Party (PDC) failed to vote for the motion, which was defeated by 52 votes to 62 with one abstention. In early May investigations into the disappearance of some 1,120 people under General Pinochet's rule disclosed three pits in the vicinity of the Pisagua (First Region) detention camp, containing the remains of more than 150 prisoners summarily shot in 1973.

A number of legal cases had already been brought in Chile against General Pinochet, though without success. However, on 16 October the former dictator was arrested while in hospital in London, under an extradition warrant issued in Spain (see II.1.i). Despite a series of high-level efforts to secure his release and return to Chile, on 25 November (the General's 83rd birthday) the British House of Lords ruled that he could be extradited. This ruling, and the decision of UK Home Secretary Jack Straw on 9 December to authorize formal extradition proceedings, produced intense anger among the General's supporters. Under pressure from the armed forces, the government of President Eduardo Frei Ruiz-Tagle renewed its efforts and dispatched Foreign Minister José Maria Insulza to London to request his return to Chile, promising to place him on trial there. When the Lords' ruling was quashed on 17 December and re-hearing ordered, because of possible bias in one of the judges, Sr Insulza formally requested Mr Straw to rescind his decision authorizing extradition proceedings.

When the Lords' original ruling was announced, British reporters in Chile were attacked and beaten by Pinochet supporters, though Chilean exiles and the relatives of the 'disappeared' were moved to tears of joy. Violent clashes had earlier occurred between demonstrators and the police (*carabineros*), despite heavy security surrounding the marches held on 11 September to commemorate the 25th anniversary of the 1973 coup and the death of President Salvador Allende. Two died and at least 60 were arrested. At the request of President Frei, Congress had voted to abolish the annual celebration of the coup date but to observe a new day of national unity at the beginning of September.

Abroad, free trade agreements were concluded with Mexico on 16 March, to come into effect on 1 October, and with Peru in May, to come into effect on 1 July.

v. COLOMBIA

CAPITAL: Santa Fe de Bogotá   AREA: 1,141,750 sq km   POPULATION: 38,000,000 ('97)
OFFICIAL LANGUAGE: Spanish   POLITICAL SYSTEM: presidential democracy
HEAD OF STATE & GOVERNMENT: President Andrés Pastrana Arango (since Aug '98)
RULING PARTIES: Social Conservative Party (PSC) heads Great Alliance for Change
MAIN IGO MEMBERSHIPS (non-UN): OAS, ALADI, SELA, AG, CA, ACS, NAM
CURRENCY: peso (end-'98 £1=Col$2,574.65, US$1=Col$1,547.50)
GNP PER CAPITA: US$2,280 by exchange-rate calculation, US$6,720 by PPP calculation ('97)

IN February five prosecutors from the Fiscalia General de la Nación were suspended facing charges of having fabricated evidence against aides of President Ernesto Samper Pizano. Soon afterwards former Defence Minister Fernando Botrero Zea, who had been imprisoned for illicit enrichment following charges that he had channelled money from the Cali drugs cartel into President Samper's campaign, was released. A week later police captured the leader of the Valle del Norte cartel, José Nelson Urrego Cárdenas, who was thought to be the last of the major drug barons still at large.

In legislative elections in March the ruling Liberal Party (PL) retained a narrow majority in both houses, after a series of attacks on security forces by both the Revolutionary Armed Forces of Colombia (FARC) and the National Liberation Army (ELN) which constituted one of the most concerted offensives in 30 years of civil war. Although the FARC declared US drug advisers and technicians legitimate targets, the US government, while failing to certify Colombian cooperation as satisfactory, decided to lift sanctions, which had cost Colombia some US$800 million in aid and investment in 1996 and 1997. Roger Eliezer Pombo ('El Flaco'), arrested in Barranqilla on 5 March and believed to be the second-in-command of the Coast cartel, became the first Colombian to be extradited to the United States under the November 1997 extradition law. The cartel's head, Alberto Orlandes Gamboa ('El Caracol'), was captured on 6 June.

To general surprise, in the first round of the presidential elections on 31 May the PL candidate, Horacio Serpa Uribe, a former Interior Minister who had only recently been cleared of criminal charges resulting from his role in the 1994 election, narrowly led Andrés Pastrana Arango of the Social Conservative Party (PSC), who was the son of former President Misael Pastrana Borrero and a former mayor of Bogotá. Numerous violent incidents had taken place in the days leading up to the election, including the murder on 12 May of General (retd.) Fernándo Landazábal Reyes, who had been forced to resign as Defence Minister in 1994 because of his tough stand against Colombia's guerrillas. In the second round on 21 June, however, Sr Pastrana won a decisive victory over his Liberal rival and was sworn in on 7 August, appointing Guillermo Fernández de Soto as Foreign Minister. On 2 September, in response to international financial pressure, the new government devalued the peso by 9 per cent, as part of a package of stabilization measures welcomed by the IMF.

Negotiations between the government and the FARC continued fitfully throughout the year, and most of the hostages taken in March were freed or managed to escape. In talks in Spain in March the government reached a preliminary agreement with the ELN, whose leader, the Spanish-born former priest Gregorio Manuel Pérez Martínez, had died of hepatitis B on 14 February. A collective ELN leadership had then been formed, with José Nicolás Rodríguez Bautista as political leader and Antonio García as military commander. On 24 May some 350 convicts escaped after an FARC attack on San Isidro prison, where one of their leaders was detained. In May paramilitaries killed 11 suspected guerrillas at Barrancabermeja, a stronghold both of the ELN and the Popular Liberation Army (EPL). A further 25 taken hostage were also later killed.

In an unprecedented move, President-elect Pastrana met personally with FARC leader Manuel Marulanda Vélez ('Tirofijo') on 9 July and agreed a timetable and conditions for negotiations on peace with the FARC. However, a show of strength at the beginning of August to greet the new President left some 200 dead in a string of attacks across the country. In

October President Pastrana secured congressional support before reaching an agreement in turn with the ELN and the FARC on a timetable for talks, as finally confirmed on 15 December. Despite an ELN attack on 18 October on the Ocensa oil pipeline, which destroyed two villages in Antioquia and killed at least 66 people, and a costly FARC offensive at the beginning of November, the government went ahead with plans to evacuate a large area in which to hold talks.

vi. ECUADOR

CAPITAL: Quito   AREA: 270,500 sq km   POPULATION: 12,000,000 ('97)
OFFICIAL LANGUAGE: Spanish   POLITICAL SYSTEM: presidential democracy
HEAD OF STATE & GOVERNMENT: President Jamil Mahuad Witt (since July '98)
RULING PARTIES: Popular Democracy (DP) heads coalition
MAIN IGO MEMBERSHIPS (non-UN): OAS, ALADI, SELA, AG, CA, NAM
CURRENCY: sucre (end-'98 £1=S/.11,363.40, US$1=S/6,830.00)
GNP PER CAPITA: US$1,590 by exchange-rate calculation, US$4,820 by PPP calculation ('97)

THE Constituent Assembly elected in November 1997 (see AR 1997, p. 174) met in the early part of the year, but proposed only limited changes to the existing electoral procedure and none to the length of the presidential term. Its president, Osvaldo Hurtado Larrea, resigned on 20 April in protest against the Assembly's decision not to reform the country's social security system. In March the National Congress voted to decriminalize the consumption of drugs.

In January a convention of the Ecuadorian Roldosista Party (PRE) nominated former President Abdalá Bucaram Ortiz as candidate for the presidency, despite his conviction by the Supreme Court two days earlier for criminal libel against two politicians. One, Jaime Nebot Saadi, the unsuccessful candidate for the Social Christian Party (PSC) in 1992 and 1996, decided subsequently not to run for election to succeed interim President Fabián Alarcón Rivera, with the result that Sr Bucaram was replaced by Alvaro Noboa Pontón as the PRE candidate.

The first round of the presidential election on 31 May was inconclusive, though in the concurrent legislative elections the centre-right Popular Democracy (DP) did well. In the second round on 12 July, the mayor of Quito, Jamil Mahuad Witt (DP), was elected President with 51.16 per cent of the votes cast, to 48.83 per cent for Sr Noboa. Retaining José Ayala Lasso as Minister of Foreign Affairs, he appointed a cabinet otherwise consisting largely of political independents and was sworn in on 10 August.

Severe economic measures imposed by the new government on 14 September led to a general strike, protests and riots, but it was soon forced by the regional economic crisis and the impact of low oil prices to devalue the sucre by some 15 per cent. In November, however, Congress passed a law replacing income tax with a 1 per cent tax on the circulation of capital, a move criticized by the banks as likely to lead to a reduction in liquidity.

Talks held in Brasília on 27–28 September between the new President and President Alberto Keinya Fujimori of Peru led to agreement on a trade and navigation treaty and the clearance of minefields in the disputed frontier zone of the Corderilla del Cóndor, though not on the delimitation of the frontier itself. An earlier agreement on 13 August had committed both parties to pull back their troops 'temporarily' from the disputed territory, under the supervision of the Ecuador-Peru Military Observer Mission (MOMEP) set up by the four guarantor states of the 1942 Protocol of Rio. Following congressional agreement in each case, the two Presidents then signed a formal agreement in Brasília on 26 October accepting the arbitration of the four guarantor states on the disputed frontier zone and its future administration, thus bringing this long-running dispute to a satisfactory conclusion. The border integration treaty was ratified by Congress on 20 November.

vii. PARAGUAY

CAPITAL: Asunción   AREA: 406,752 sq km   POPULATION: 5,000,000 ('97)
OFFICIAL LANGUAGE: Spanish   POLITICAL SYSTEM: presidential democracy
HEAD OF STATE & GOVERNMENT: President Raúl Cubas Grau (since Aug '98)
RULING PARTY: Colorado Party (ANR-PC)
MAIN IGO MEMBERSHIPS (non-UN): OAS, ALADI, SELA, Mercosur
CURRENCY: guarani (end-'98 £1=G4,724.22, US$1=G2,839.50)
GNP PER CAPITA: US$2,010 by exchange-rate calculation, US$3,870 by PPP calculation ('97)

ON 9 March the Special Military Court found General (retd.) Lino César Oviedo Silva guilty of rebellion (see AR 1997, pp. 174–5) and sentenced him to ten years imprisonment and a dishonourable discharge. A specially constituted military tribunal attempted to reverse the verdict on 1 September but its decision was ruled 'absolutely lacking in validity' by the Supreme Court, which had already confirmed the original decision on 17 April. The following day his candidature had been voided by the Supreme Electoral Tribunal and he had been replaced by Raúl Cubas Grau as presidential candidate of the ruling Colorado Party (ANR-PC).

Despite protests, the elections went ahead as planned on 10 May. Sr Cubas obtained some 54 per cent of the votes cast to 42 per cent for Domingo Laino of the Democratic Alliance on an 85 per cent turnout. Results of elections for the Senate were: ANR-PC 24, Democratic Alliance 20, Blanco Party 1; and for the Chamber of Deputies: ANR-PC 45, Democratic Alliance 35.

Having taken office on 15 August, President Cubas, a wealthy engineer who was said to have made his money from contracts for the Itaipú Dam, appointed two Oviedista generals to his cabinet and commuted General Oviedo's sentence to time already served. The new Congress immediately voted to condemn the pardon and to institute impeachment proceedings against the new President. On 2 December, moreover, the Supreme Court ruled that the pardon was unconstitutional, though a presidential decree rejected that ruling. The new President's position had meanwhile been weakened by an agreement between his opponents and the faction of the Colorado Party led by his Vice-President, Luis María Argaña, under which supporters of the latter obtained the presidencies of both chambers. On 21 August the President's brother Carlos resigned as Minister of Industry and Commerce in protest against the pardon of General Oviedo, while former President Juan Wasmosy, who had spent the night of 19 August in the Argentine embassy to avoid arrest on charges relating to $58 million worth of state contracts granted to two of his companies, took his seat as senator-for-life as provided for in the constitution.

viii. PERU

CAPITAL: Lima   AREA: 1,285,000 sq km   POPULATION: 25,000,000 ('97)
OFFICIAL LANGUAGES: Spanish, Quechua, Aymará
POLITICAL SYSTEM: presidential democracy
HEAD OF STATE & GOVERNMENT: President Alberto Keinya Fujimori (since July '90)
RULING PARTIES: New Majority-Change 90 heads government coalition
PRIME MINISTER: Alberto Pandolfi Arbulu (since April '96)
MAIN IGO MEMBERSHIPS (non-UN): NAM, OAS, ALADI, SELA, CA, AP, APEC
CURRENCY: new sol (end-'98 £1=NS5.25, US$1=NS3.16)
GNP PER CAPITA: US$2,460 by exchange-rate calculation, US$4,390 by PPP calculation ('97)

IN January El Niño weather distortion brought heavy rains and the worst flooding for 50 years. Some 70 people died and 22,000 were rendered homeless. President Alberto Keinya Fujimori's bid for re-election in 2000 received support in February when the Supreme Court ruled that there was no constitutional impediment. Members of the Constitutional Tribunal, which had previously ruled it was unconstitutional, were dismissed by Congress. In July, however, 1.4 million people signed a petition to request a referendum on the third-term issue in a bid to stop it.

All seven members of the National Council of the Judiciary resigned on 13 March after Congress had voted to reduce their powers, an action widely seen as further evidence of the President's intention to undermine the judiciary and with it the rule of law. The World Bank responded by cancelling a loan of US$22.5 million for judicial reform. The 'people's rights' ombudsman, Jorge Santiestevan de Noriega, complained that 'the rule of law is being dismantled', while in early April the dean of the Bar Association, Delia Revoredo Marsana (one of those removed from the Constitutional Tribunal), condemned tax evasion charges that had subsequently been brought against her and her husband as false. Taking refuge in the Costa Rican embassy, Sra Revoredo blamed Captain Vladimiro Montesinos, the presumed real head of President Fujimori's secret Intelligence Service (SIN), for the systematic persecution of critics such as herself by various technical devices. On 4 December Congress voted to continue the so-called 'reorganization' of the judiciary for a further two-year period. Other reports of the routine use of torture and the murder of suspected guerrillas and the systematic surveillance of opposition politicians by the SIN confirmed allegations of abuses made by the Frecuencia Latina TV station (owned by Baruch Ivcher) and by the UN Committee Against Torture in a report in May. An international warrant for the arrest of Sr Ivcher was issued by the Peruvian authorities on 30 November on charges of falsifying legal documents. The government meanwhile was able to report on 20 April the capture of Pedro Domingo Quinteros Ayllón ('Comrade Luis'), alleged to be second-in-command of the militant and still-active Red Path faction of Sendero Luminoso led by Oscar Ramírez Durand ('Feliciano').

Following the shooting of mine owner Luis Hochschild Pflaud, Congress on 12 May granted President Fujimori exceptional powers to legislate by decree. In a draconian so-called 'law against aggravated terrorism' issued on 21 May, the President redefined all organized crime as a form of terrorism. Not only would it be subject to military law but would carry the same drastic penalties first imposed for terrorism in 1992 (AR 1992, pp. 181–2). On 2 November the President was able to report the capture of 'Yoel', the current leader of the Túpac Amaru Revolutionary Movement (MRTA).

Meanwhile, the Prime Minister, Alberto Pandolfi Arbulu, had resigned on 4 June following conflict with the Civil Defence Agency, which had been put in charge of reconstructing houses and roads damaged by the floods. He was replaced by a long-standing critic of the President's authoritarian tendencies, Javier Valle Riestra. Within days the President had rejected his advice to free Lori Berenson, a US citizen imprisoned on terrorism charges. Having initially refused to accept Sr Valle Riestra's offer of resignation, the President did so on 7 August after a series of further policy clashes, Sr Pandolfi being reappointed. On 20 August the President dismissed the commander of the armed forces, General Nicolás Hermoza Ríos, because of his opposition to an agreement with Ecuador on disputed border territory (see IV.3.vi). He was replaced by General César Saucedo Sánchez, whose post as Defence Minister went to General Julio Salazar Monroe, hitherto official chief of the SIN.

Dispute over the frontier question also precipitated the resignation (on 2 October) of the Foreign Minister, Eduardo Ferrero Costa, who was replaced by Fernando de Trazegnies. In local elections on 11 October the ruling party decided not to run candidates because of the President's declining popularity. News of the border settlement caused widespread demonstrations, especially at the cession of Tiwintza. Nevertheless, the border integration treaty was ratified by Congress on 13 November, the President announcing that the money saved on the purchase of armaments would be devoted instead to education.

ix. URUGUAY

CAPITAL: Montevideo AREA: 176,200 sq km POPULATION: 3,250,000 ('97)
OFFICIAL LANGUAGE: Spanish
POLITICAL SYSTEM: presidential democracy
HEAD OF STATE & GOVERNMENT: President Julio María Sanguinetti (since March '95)
RULING PARTIES: Colorado Party holds presidency and heads government including Blanco Party, People's Government Party & Civic Union
MAIN IGO MEMBERSHIPS (non-UN): OAS, ALADI, SELA, Mercosur, NAM
CURRENCY: new peso (end-'98 £1=NUr$17.93, US$1=Nur10.77)
GNP PER CAPITA: US$6,020 by exchange-rate calculation, US$8,460 by PPP calculation ('97)

IN a cabinet reshuffle in late-January President Julio María Sanguinetti appointed Didier Opertti as Foreign Minister in place of Alvaro Ramos. Sr Opertti was succeeded as Interior Minister by Senator Luís Hierro López. On 3 October Vice-President Hugo Batalla died; he was replaced by Senator Hugo Fernández Faingold. Bitterness over the events of the 1976–85 military dictatorship continued, but in November a court ruled that there was insufficient evidence to proceed with the case against those accused of the murder of the former Chilean secret agent Eugenio Berrios Sagredo.

In December the Senate finally approved the construction of a 4.5-kilometre bridge across the River Plate between Colonia and Buenos Aires, at a cost of more than US$1,000 million.

x. VENEZUELA

CAPITAL: Caracas AREA: 912,000 sq km POPULATION: 23,000,000 ('97)
OFFICIAL LANGUAGE: Spanish POLITICAL SYSTEM: presidential democracy
HEAD OF STATE & GOVERNMENT: President Rafael Caldera Rodríguez (since Feb '94)
PRESIDENT-ELECT: Hugo Chávez Frias
RULING PARTIES: 17–party National Convergence (CN) coalition
MAIN IGO MEMBERSHIPS (non-UN): OAS, ALADI, SELA, CA, ACS, OPEC, NAM
CURRENCY: bolívar (end-'98 £1=Bs939.19, US$1=Bs564.50)
GNP PER CAPITA: US$3,450 by exchange-rate calculation, US$8,530 by PPP calculation ('97)

THE ruling National Convergence (CN) coalition led by President Rafael Caldera Rodríguez found itself under attack from all sides as the country slid into financial chaos. In February the Planning Minister, Teodoro Petkoff Maleo, reached an agreement with employers and workers to raise the minimum wage by 33 per cent, ahead of the government's inflation target. Reforms of the social security system in March opened the way for a loan of US$350 million from the Inter-American Development Bank (IADB). On 14 April former President Carlos Andrés Perez, who had been imprisoned in May 1996 for misappropriation of public funds (see AR 1996, p. 173), was again charged with illegal enrichment during his period of office. Meanwhile, the news that the government faced serious financial problems as a result of a shortfall in oil revenues coincided with the resignation of Finance Minister Freddy Rojas Parr on 6 June.

On 16 June Sr Petkoff therefore announced a new economic adjustment package to close the fiscal gap and avert the threat of devaluation. Congress still refused to pass the necessary measures, with the result that on 19 August the President was authorized by the cabinet to seek special powers to introduce them by decree. The government reacted with anger to the decision on 3 September of the New York agency Moody's to downgrade its debt rating, Sr Petkoff condemning the action as 'irresponsible and lacking in seriousness'. In mid-October the government belatedly established a macroeconomic stabilization fund (FEM), the purpose of which was to stabilize oil revenues. At the end of November, at the inauguration of the Brazil-Venezuela trunk road, President Caldera stated that his country had not given up its claim to the Essequibo region of Guyana, the dispute over which was currently under UN arbitration.

For the first time in four decades neither of the two main parties fielded a candidate in the presidential elections on 6 December. The centre-right Social Christian Party (COPEI) decided on 7 May to give active support to the independent candidature of Irene Sáez, then front-runner in the polls. More surprisingly, the Movement Towards Socialism (MAS)—against the advice of Sr Petkoff, its co-founder, who resigned from the party—decided on 12 June to back the 44-year-old populist Colonel Hugo Chávez Frias, running as candidate of the Movement for a Fifth Republic (MVR). Colonel Chávez, who had led the unsuccessful coup of 1992 (AR 1992, pp. 183–4), promised to declare a moratorium on repayments of the $22,000 million foreign debt, to restrict oil production and to replace Congress by a new constituent assembly more representative of the people. On election day he achieved a record majority, obtaining 3,673,685 votes (56.20 per cent) to 2,613,161 (39.97 per cent) for the moderate independent former state governor, Henrique Salas Römer. Sra Sáez won only 2.82 per cent standing as the Integration, Renewal, New Hope (IRENE) candidate, and the other nine candidates got only 1.01 per cent between them.

xi. CUBA

CAPITAL: Havana   AREA: 115,000 sq km   POPULATION: 11,100,000 ('97)
OFFICIAL LANGUAGE: Spanish   POLITICAL SYSTEM: one-party republic
HEAD OF STATE & GOVERNMENT: President Fidel Castro Ruz (since Jan '59)
RULING PARTY: Cuban Communist Party (PCC)
MAIN IGO MEMBERSHIPS (non-UN): ACS, SELA, NAM
CURRENCY: peso (end-'98 £1=Cub$38.27, US$1=Cub$23.00)
GNP PER CAPITA: n.a.

THE second direct elections to the National Assembly of People's Power were held on 11 January, when 14 provincial assemblies were also elected. The first act of the new Assembly on 24 February was to confirm Dr Fidel Castro Ruz as President of the Council of State for a further five-year term and endorse the single list of members of the Council. The highlight of the year was the visit of Pope John Paul II on 21-25 January (see also II.3.vii; Pt XII). In the course of the visit, the pontiff officiated at four well-attended open-air masses carried live on state television, in the last of which, in Havana, he called for greater freedom in Cuba and also denounced the US embargo. Following the visit, the Foreign Ministry announced an amnesty for 299 prisoners, 75 of whom had been among the 302 recommended for clemency on the occasion of the Pope's visit. Later in the year Christmas was formally reinstated as a public holiday after more than 30 years.

On 3 February President Castro indignantly rejected a US proposal, originating with Senator Jesse Helms, that food and medical supplies should be donated to Cuba through charitable organizations. The US government, however, on 20 March unilaterally announced the easing of sanctions to permit such supplies and to restore direct flights between Cuba and the United States, which began on 15 July. The US government's annual resolution condemning Cuba before the UN Human Rights Commission was defeated for the first time since 1991, while on 26-28 March the Canadian Prime Minister, Jean Chrétien, condemned sanctions during an official visit to the island, as well as launching negotiations on a bilateral agreement to protect and encourage foreign investment in face of US pressure. Soon afterwards Spain normalized diplomatic relations with Cuba, and the Dominican Republic became the last of the Caribbean countries to restore full diplomatic ties on 21 April.

The admission by Luis Posada Carriles to the *New York Times* on 12-13 July that he had organized the 1997 wave of bombings in Havana (see AR 1997, p. 179) confirmed suspicions long held of the involvement of the militant exile Cuban American National Foundation (CANF). It was followed by orders from President Clinton to US coastguards to intercept illegal incursions into Cuban waters and confirmation by President Castro in a television interview on 21 October that his government had planted agents among Cuba-American exiles in the USA.

The former head of the DGI Intelligence Directorate, Manuel Pineiro Losada ('Barba Roja'), died as the result of a traffic accident on 12 March. On 29 August a Tupolev-154 aircraft of Cubana de Aviación burst into flames on take-off and crashed in a football field near Quito, Ecuador, killing 74 of the 90 on board and five children playing on the ground. Crops suffered serious damage from Hurricane Georges in late September.

xii. DOMINICAN REPUBLIC AND HAITI

Dominican Republic
CAPITAL: Santo Domingo AREA: 48,400 sq km POPULATION: 8,000,000 ('97)
OFFICIAL LANGUAGE: Spanish POLITICAL SYSTEM: presidential democracy
HEAD OF STATE & GOVERNMENT: President Leonel Fernández (since Aug '96)
RULING PARTY: Dominican Liberation Party (PLD)
MAIN IGO MEMBERSHIPS (non-UN): OAS, SELA, ACS, ACP
CURRENCY: peso (end-'98 £1=RD$26.29, US$1=RD$15.80)
GNP PER CAPITA: US$1,670 by exchange-rate calculation, US$4,540 by PPP calculation ('97)

Haiti
CAPITAL: Port-au-Prince AREA: 27,750 sq km POPULATION: 7,400,000 ('97)
OFFICIAL LANGUAGE: French POLITICAL SYSTEM: presidential democracy
HEAD OF STATE & GOVERNMENT: President René Préval (since Feb '96)
RULING PARTY: Lavalas Political Organization
PRIME MINISTER: vacant
MAIN IGO MEMBERSHIPS (non-UN): OAS, SELA, ACS, ACP, Francophonie
CURRENCY: gourde (end-'98 £1=G27.56, US$1=G16.57)
GNP PER CAPITA: US$330 by exchange-rate calculation, US$1,150 by PPP calculation ('97)

IN HAITI, Vasco Thernalan of the ruling Lavalas—later renamed the Organization of the Struggling People (OPL)—was in January elected president of the Chamber of Deputies to succeed Kely Bastien. Political crises continued, however, and planned economic reforms were delayed. Despite his rejection in late 1997 (see AR 1997, p. 180), Hervé Denis was again nominated as Prime Minister by President René Préval, proving to be acceptable to the Chamber of Deputies but failing to gain the approval of the Senate on 15 April. Following an agreement with the new leader of the OPL, therefore, on 15 July the President nominated Jacques Edouard Alexis, currently Education Minister, and this nomination was grudgingly ratified by Congress on 18 December.

In the DOMINICAN REPUBLIC, José Francisco Peña Gómez, leader of the centre-left Dominican Revolutionary Party (PRD) and three times an unsuccessful candidate for the presidency, died of cancer on 10 May. In legislative elections on 16 May, the PRD won a decisive majority and the conservative Christian Social Reform Party (PRSC) of former President Joaquín Balaguer lost heavily. The results for the Senate were: PRD 24, Dominican Liberation Party (PLD) 4, PRSC 2; for the Chamber of Deputies they were: PRD 83, PLD 49, PRSC 50. The PRD also took control of 90 per cent of the country's municipalities. On 9 July the newly-elected Congress approved an amnesty law absolving all public servants of responsibility for actions taken since September 1978.

Haiti and the Dominican Republic bore the brunt of Hurricane Georges in September, the majority of the 300 dead losing their lives in floods and landslides on the island. The IMF subsequently approved financial assistance packages to assist rehabilitation in both parts of the island.

xiii. CENTRAL AMERICA AND PANAMA

Guatemala
CAPITAL: Guatemala City   AREA: 109,000 sq km   POPULATION: 11,000,000 ('97)
OFFICIAL LANGUAGE: Spanish   POLITICAL SYSTEM: presidential democracy
HEAD OF STATE & GOVERNMENT: President Alvaro Arzú Irigoyen (since Jan '96)
RULING PARTIES: National Advancement Party (PAN) heads coalition
MAIN IGO MEMBERSHIPS (non-UN): OAS, SELA, CACM, ACS, NAM
CURRENCY: quetzal (end-'98 £1=Q11.16, US$1=Q6.71)
GNP PER CAPITA: US$1,500 by exchange-rate calculation, US$3,840 by PPP calculation ('97)

El Salvador
CAPITAL: San Salvador   AREA: 21,400 sq km   POPULATION: 6,000,000 ('97)
OFFICIAL LANGUAGE: Spanish   POLITICAL SYSTEM: presidential democracy
HEAD OF STATE & GOVERNMENT: President Armando Calderón Sol (since June '94)
RULING PARTY: National Republican Alliance (Arena)
MAIN IGO MEMBERSHIPS (non-UN): OAS, SELA, CACM, ACS
CURRENCY: colón (end-'98 £1=C14.54, US$1=C8.74)
GNP PER CAPITA: US$1,810 by exchange-rate calculation, US$2,810 by PPP calculation ('97)

Honduras
CAPITAL: Tegucigalpa   AREA: 112,000 sq km   POPULATION: 6,000,000 ('97)
OFFICIAL LANGUAGE: Spanish   POLITICAL SYSTEM: presidential democracy
HEAD OF STATE & GOVERNMENT: President Carlos Roberto Flores Facussé (since Jan '98)
RULING PARTY: Liberal Party of Honduras (PLH)
MAIN IGO MEMBERSHIPS (non-UN): OAS, SELA, CACM, ACS, NAM
CURRENCY: lempira (end-'98 £1=L22.92, US$1=L13.77)
GNP PER CAPITA: US$700 by exchange-rate calculation, US$2,200 by PPP calculation ('97)

Nicaragua
CAPITAL: Managua   AREA: 120,000 sq km   POPULATION: 5,000,000 ('97)
OFFICIAL LANGUAGE: Spanish   POLITICAL SYSTEM: presidential democracy
HEAD OF STATE & GOVERNMENT: President Arnaldo Alemán (since April '97)
RULING PARTY: Liberal Alliance (AL)
MAIN IGO MEMBERSHIPS (non-UN): OAS, SELA, CACM, ACS, NAM
CURRENCY: córdoba (end-'98 £1=C$18.51, US$1=C$11.12)
GNP PER CAPITA: US$410 by exchange-rate calculation, US$2,370 by PPP calculation ('97)

Costa Rica
CAPITAL: San José   AREA: 51,000 sq km   POPULATION: 3,600,000 ('97)
OFFICIAL LANGUAGE: Spanish   POLITICAL SYSTEM: presidential democracy
HEAD OF STATE & GOVERNMENT: President Miguel Angel Rodríguez (since May '98)
RULING PARTY: Social Christian Unity Party (PUSC)
MAIN IGO MEMBERSHIPS (non-UN): OAS, SELA, CACM, ACS
CURRENCY: colón (end-'98 £1=C451.57, US$1=C271.42)
GNP PER CAPITA: US$2,640 by exchange-rate calculation, US$6,410 by PPP calculation ('97)

Panama
CAPITAL: Panama City   AREA: 77,000 sq km   POPULATION: 2,600,000 ('97)
OFFICIAL LANGUAGE: Spanish   POLITICAL SYSTEM: presidential
HEAD OF STATE & GOVERNMENT: President Ernesto Pérez Balladares (since Sept '94)
RULING PARTIES: Democratic Revolutionary Party (PRD) heads coalition
MAIN IGO MEMBERSHIPS (non-UN): OAS, SELA, NAM
CURRENCY: balboa (end-'98 £1=B1.66, US£1=B1.00)
GNP PER CAPITA: US$3,080 by exchange-rate calculation, US$5,980 by PPP calculation ('97)

IN May huge tracts of wood and grassland throughout Central America were destroyed as fires flared out of control in the worst drought for 70 years. This was followed at the beginning of November by Hurricane

Mitch, the worst tropical storm to hit Central America in the twentieth century, which devastated Honduras and Nicaragua in particular, washing away roads and bridges, villages and crops, and setting back their development, it was said, by 30 years (see also XIII.3). In Honduras some 6,500 people died, 11,000 were reported missing and up to two million suffered loss; in Nicaragua, where on 30 October a landslip from the volcano Casitas buried five villages in a mudslide which claimed some 1,500 lives, another 1,000 died and 1,900 were missing. The storm, one of the strongest on record, with wind speeds approaching 190 mph (300 kph), also caused some loss of life and extensive damage in El Salvador and Guatemala.

In HONDURAS, following the vote by the Congress in September 1997 to abolish the position of commander-in-chief (see AR 1997, p. 182), in January the Committee for the Defence of Human Rights in Honduras brought charges against General Mario Raúl Hung Pacheco and two other generals of complicity in the 'disappearance' of student leader Roger Samuel González. However, with the country paralysed and the people starving after Hurricane Mitch, it was the army which had to coordinate the relief effort in September when international agencies confronted a devastated country from a capital that had itself been partially destroyed by floods.

Earlier in the year, on 19 January, President Carlos Roberto Reina Idiaquez and the President of El Salvador, Armando Calderón Sol, had signed an agreement in Tegucigalpa delimiting the common frontier and settling citizenship rights in the formerly disputed area delimited by the International Court of Justice in 1992 (see AR 1992, pp. 189, 465). In February the former chief of the secret police, Colonel Juan Blas Salazar, was acquitted of the abduction and torture of six university students in 1982 on the grounds that he was covered by the amnesty forming part of the Esquipulas II peace agreements of 1987.

In May a new economic programme was approved by Congress, substantially worsening the plight of the poor by increasing sales tax substantially while cutting corporation tax and the banana levy. After Hurricane Mitch, however, the government was forced to appeal to the international community both for aid and for a moratorium on debt repayments. On 7 December the IMF approved an emergency package amounting to $1,000 million in interest-free credits for both Honduras and Nicaragua, although two days later the Paris Club refused to allow a write-off of the countries' current international debt.

In NICARAGUA, the Sandinista (FSLN) newspaper *Barricada*, already in serious financial difficulties, was handed over to its workforce in February. Accusations of sexual abuse against former President Daniel Ortega Saavedra published on 2 March by his stepdaughter seemed intended to prevent his re-election as leader of the FSLN and were dismissed by the Managua criminal court on 29 May. Meanwhile, the National Assembly had voted to compensate those whose property had been expropriated under the provisional government, the cost of US$200 million to be raised through a bond issue. In April, however, the Supreme Court ordered a halt to the return of properties to their pre-1979 owners on the grounds that the government did not have the power to do this by administrative act. In March the IMF approved a three-year package under the enhanced structural adjustment facility (ESAF) to support the government's economic programme and on 21 April the Paris Club granted $200 million in debt relief over the next three years, with the prospect of relief on the principal in 2000 under the highly-indebted poor countries (HIPC) initiative.

The former Contra leader, Edén Pastora Gómez, began a hunger strike on 22 August, 20 years after his daring capture of the National Palace during the 1978 Sandinista Revolution. His action successfully forced the National Assembly to review its decision barring him from candidature at the presidential elections due in 2001, and in July a new centrist alliance was formed to oppose the ruling Liberal Alliance of President Arnaldo Alemán Lacayo. Internal criticism of President Alemán led the government on 12 August to rescind an agreement made on 30 July allowing Costa Rica free navigation on the San Juan River.

In EL SALVADOR, the president of the Central Bank, Roberto Orellana, resigned in May following allegations of prior knowledge of a savings fraud. On 24 June three of the five National Guardsmen convicted of the murder of three nuns in 1980 were conditionally released to reduce prison overcrowding. In September the opposition Farabundo Martí National Liberation Front (FMLN) chose Facundo Guardado as its candidate for the March 1999 presidential elections. At the year's end the Defence and Public Security Minister, General Jaime Guzmán Morales, unexpectedly resigned.

President Alvaro Arzú Irigoyen of GUATEMALA announced in January his government's intention to resume diplomatic relations with Cuba, which had been suspended in 1961. However, efforts to extradite former President Jorge Serrano Elias from Panama to face charges connected with his attempted 'self-coup' (*autogolpe*) of May 1993 (see AR 1993, p. 187) failed for the third time on 20 March. On 14 March the UN Human Rights Commission decided to remove Guatemala from the list of countries under observation; however, the work of the UN Mission overseeing the implementation of the 1996 agreement (see AR 1996, p. 177) would go on. After three years of work, the Catholic Church on 24 April released a report, *Guatemala: nunca más* ('never again') giving as much detail as was known of over 55,000 crimes committed during the 36 years of civil war, including 25,123 murders and 3,893 'disappearances'. Four-fifths of the crimes had been committed by the armed forces and 92 per cent of the victims were civilians. Two days later, the Auxiliary Bishop of Guatemala and head of the archbishopric's human rights office, Mgr Juan José Gerardi Conadera, was bludgeoned to death, his murder provoking a great popular outcry. The extreme-right death-squad organization, Jaguar Justice (JJ), claimed responsibility. Three suspects were subsequently arrested, and in December three members of paramilitary 'civil defence patrols' were sentenced to death for killing at least 269 people during the civil war.

The former leader of the Guatemalan National Revolutionary Unity (URNG), Ricardo Arnaldo Ramírez de León ('Comandante Rolando Morán'), died of a heart attack on 11 September. The movement was formally registered as a political party on 18 December.

In elections in COSTA RICA on 4 February, Miguel Angel Rodríguez Echeverría of the opposition Social Christian Party (PUSC) defeated the candidate of the ruling National Liberation Party (PLN), José Miguel Corrales, by 650,399 votes to 616,600. In elections to the 57-seat Legislative Assembly, the PUSC won 27 seats and the PLN 23. President Rodríguez, who took office on 8 May, appointed Roberto López Rojas as Foreign Minister and Leonel Baruch as Minister of Finance. Meanwhile, in April the outgoing Assembly had approved plans extending private competition in areas formerly under state control, but the Labour Minister, Farid Ayales, had been forced to resign, charged with illegal administration of ministry funds.

In a referendum on 30 August, the voters of PANAMA rejected by a large majority a package of constitutional measures that would have allowed President Ernesto Pérez Balladares to seek re-election. The result was seen as an implicit rejection of the free-market policies of the ruling Democratic Revolutionary Party (PRD), which on 25 October nominated as its candidate in the 1999 presidential election Martin Torrijos Espino, son of former President Omar Torrijos Herrera. Alberto Vallarino was chosen as candidate of the Christian Democratic Party (PDC) in a primary election on 29 November. In March the Legislative Assembly had substantially extended the scope of the privatization law.

Continuing drought affected the Panama Canal. For 109 days ships had to pass through it less than fully laden, until on 30 June a combination of early rainfall and strict water-conservation measures enabled the ban to be lifted.

xiv. MEXICO

CAPITAL: Mexico City   AREA: 1,958,000 sq km   POPULATION: 97,000,000 ('97)
OFFICIAL LANGUAGE: Spanish   POLITICAL SYSTEM: federal presidential democracy
HEAD OF STATE & GOVERNMENT: President Ernesto Zedillo Ponce de León (since Dec '94)
RULING PARTY: Party of the Institutionalized Revolution (PRI), since 1929
MAIN IGO MEMBERSHIPS (non-UN): OAS, SELA, ALADI, ACS, APEC, NAFTA, OECD
CURRENCY: peso (end-'98 £1=Mex$16.45, US$1=Mex$9.89)
GNP PER CAPITA: US$3,680 by exchange-rate calculation, US$8,120 by PPP calculation ('97)

FOLLOWING the massacre of 45 Tzotzil Indians in Acteal, Chiapas, on 22 December 1997 (see AR 1997, p. 185), both the Interior Secretary, Emilio

Chuayffet Chemor, and the governor of the state, Julio César Ruiz Ferro, were forced to resign. The former was replaced by Francisco Labastida Ochoa and the latter by Roberto Albores Guillén. In one of a series of massive demonstrations against the armed forces and paramilitary action in Chiapas, one woman was killed and others injured at Ocosingo on 12 January when police fired into the crowd; the leader of the pro-Zapatista Democratic State Assembly, Rubicel Ruiz Gamboa, was later assassinated. On 1 February the government reiterated its acceptance of the 1995 San Andrés Larráinazar accords, but its proposal to resume the peace talks broken off in September 1996 was immediately rejected by the Zapatistas (EZLN).

On 1 March Sr Labastida Ochoa unilaterally proposed action under the accords, following which an Indian rights and culture bill modified to take account of government objections was introduced in Congress on 15 March. Immediately it ran into a storm of criticism, notably from Bishop Samuel Ruiz, head of the national mediation commission (CONAI). On 8 June, however, the Bishop resigned and CONAI disbanded, accusing the government of militarizing the conflict and preparing a final attack on the EZLN. Soon afterwards fighting broke out for the first time since the January 1995 truce. A gun-battle in the village of Los Plátanos left two dead and four injured, and security forces then entered the municipality of San Juan de la Libertad. There was resistance and one police officer and eight EZLN sympathisers were killed. Meanwhile, on 7 June 11 members of the Popular Revolutionary Army (EPR) had been killed when troops mounted a surprise attack on a meeting in El Charco (Guerrero).

Although the ruling Party of the Institutionalized Revolution (PRI) won most of the legislative seats and control of most of the town councils in Chiapas in elections on 4 October, it did so on a minority vote on a very low turnout. More than 11,000 fires were reported over 3,800 square kilometres of the drought-stricken south between January and May, at least 61 people being killed. Between 4 and 11 September, however, torrential rains brought widespread flooding; about 400 people died and more than 100,000 were rendered homeless. In an ominous development for the government, on 18 November some 50 dissident soldiers staged a protest march in the capital.

The PRI proved able to continue its rule by negotiation. Rosario Green Macias became Secretary of External Affairs on 7 January, after José Angel Gurría Treviño had been appointed to the vacant finance portfolio two days before. In gubernatorial elections on 5 July the PRI recaptured Chihuahua from the National Action Party (PAN), held Durango, but lost Zacatecas to the Democratic Revolutionary Party (PRD), which was supporting a PRI defector. Five days before the elections, the director of the Federal Judicial Police, Adrián Carrera Fuentes, was sentenced to four years' imprisonment for obstruction of justice by the torture of witnesses to implicate Raúl Salinas de Gortari (brother of former President Carlos

Salinas de Gortari) in the 1994 murder of José Francisco Ruiz Massieu, former PRI secretary-general. Sr Salinas admitted having received large sums in bribes from the Juárez drug cartel, which he had given to Sr Ruiz Massieu's brother Mario. The procurator-general subsequently demanded that he serve the maximum penalty of 50 years' imprisonment for complicity in murder.

In state elections in August and October, the PRI held Veracruz, Oaxaca and Tamaulipas, but lost control of Aguascalientes to the PAN. On 9 November the PRI retained the governorships of Puebla and Sinaloa, but the PRD-led coalition candidate gained Tlaxcala. Meanwhile, the PRD had refused to accept a framework agreement for the rescue of Mexico's banking system reached in September by Finance Minister Gurría Treviño, although on 11 December the opposition PAN dropped its demand for the resignation of the Central Bank head, Guillermo Ortiz Martínez, and a modified agreement was ratified the next day. The government's austerity budget, presented to the Chamber of Deputies on 13 November, imposed severe spending cuts, but was passed with the aid of PAN deputies on 31 December, after a proposed 15 per cent telephone tax had been dropped.

4. THE CARIBBEAN

JAMAICA—GUYANA—TRINIDAD & TOBAGO—BARBADOS—
BELIZE—GRENADA—THE BAHAMAS—WINDWARD AND LEEWARD
ISLANDS—UK DEPENDENCIES—SURINAME—NETHERLANDS ANTILLES
AND ARUBA—US DEPENDENCIES

i. JAMAICA

CAPITAL: Kingston   AREA: 11,000 sq km   POPULATION: 3,000,000 ('97)
OFFICIAL LANGUAGE: English   POLITICAL SYSTEM: parliamentary democracy
HEAD OF STATE: Queen Elizabeth II
GOVERNOR-GENERAL: Sir Howard Cooke
RULING PARTY: People's National Party (PNP)
HEAD OF GOVERNMENT: Percival J. Patterson, Prime Minister (since March '92)
MAIN IGO MEMBERSHIPS (non-UN): OAS, SELA, ACS, Caricom, ACP, CWTH, NAM
CURRENCY: Jamaican dollar (end-'98 £1=J$61.64, US$1=J$37.05)
GNP PER CAPITA: US$1,560 by exchange-rate calculation, US$3,470 by PPP calculation ('97)

FOLLOWING the general election in December 1997 which had returned him to power (see AR 1997, p. 186), Prime Minister Percival J. Patterson announced his new cabinet on 2 January. Changes included Robert Pickersgill at mining and energy, Paul Robertson at industry and investment, Peter Philips at transportation and works, and Roger Clarke at agriculture.

The victory in December of the opposition Jamaica Labour Party (JLP) candidate for West Central St Andrew, Andrew Holness, was challenged on the grounds of irregularities at a cluster of polling stations and subsequently annulled. At a second re-election in the constituency on 30 June, however, his election was confirmed. Deficiencies in the count had earlier been blamed by the director of elections, Danville Walker, on the failure of the computer system supplied by a US-based company.

In the local government elections held on 10 September, 118 of the 475 candidates were women. In a low turnout, the ruling PNP won 84 divisions to 36 for the JLP in 11 parishes. The arrest of a JLP candidate, an attempt to steal ballot boxes and the accidental injury of a PNP outdoor agent by a shotgun pellet marred the proceedings only slightly.

Continuing financial crisis threatened the stability of the banking system. At the end of February the Workers' Savings and Loan Bank was taken into receivership and on 30 November the Minister of Finance and Planning, Dr Omar Davies, announced that it and three other banks also taken over by the Financial Sector Adjustment Company (FINSAC)—Citizens' Bank/ Horizon, Eagle Commercial Bank and Island Victoria Bank—were to merge under the management of a US-based bank and a US management and consultant firm. The new firm would trade as Union Bank Holding Company Ltd.

At a long-delayed annual general meeting of the general utility Jamaica Public Service Company (JPSCo), it was confirmed that the company had overcharged its customers by some J$2,000 million in 1996-97, but that the government in March had given approval for the company to keep the money it had 'over-recovered', since it had already been spent in paying for electrical capacity supplied by three independent power companies.

Welcoming President Fidel Castro Ruz of Cuba to the island on 29 July, the Prime Minister condemned the US embargo against Cuba and specifically the 1996 Helms-Burton Act (see AR 1996, p. 155). President Castro in return recalled the common history shared by Cuba and Jamaica and criticized moves by the World Trade Organization (WTO) to eliminate the Caribbean Community's preferential trade arrangements, singling out as 'inhumane' their likely impact on the islands' banana industries. Dr Castro was reported to have chatted animatedly about his boyhood days in Cuba during a courtesy call on Governor-General Sir Howard Cooke and Lady Cooke.

Acting on behalf of the government, the Prime Minister on 30 April signed the Declaration of Chapultepec promoted by the Inter-American Press Association in defence of press freedom. On 25 November, moreover, the government introduced a Freedom of Information Bill to repeal the (British) Official Secrets Act of 1911. At the same time, the slowness of appeals against the death sentence for murder continued to irritate the government, which at the beginning of December threatened to withdraw from the Inter-American Commission on Human Rights if its appeal procedures were not speeded up. In the course of the year 13 policemen were killed in the course of duty, it being argued that the death penalty was a necessary sanction for such crimes.

ii. GUYANA

CAPITAL: Georgetown   AREA: 215,000 sq km   POPULATION: 848,000 ('97)
OFFICIAL LANGUAGE: English POLITICAL SYSTEM: cooperative presidential democracy
RULING PARTY: People's Progressive Party-Civic (PPP-C)
HEAD OF STATE & GOVERNMENT: President Janet Jagan (since Dec '97)
PRIME MINISTER: Sam Hinds (since Dec '97)
MAIN IGO MEMBERSHIPS (non-UN): OAS, SELA, AP, ACS, Caricom, ACP, CWTH, NAM
CURRENCY: Guyana dollar (end-'98 £1=G$252.56, US$1=G$151.80)
GNP PER CAPITA: US$800 by exchange-rate calculation, US$2,890 by PPP calculation ('95)

AN agreement brokered by a Caribbean Community (Caricom) commission on 17 January put a temporary end to the demonstrations and civil unrest that had troubled Georgetown, the capital, since the elections of 17 December 1997 (see AR 1997, pp. 187–8). The polling had resulted in victory for the People's Progressive Party–Civic (PPP-Civic) and the election of Janet Jagan, the US-born widow of the late Cheddi Jagan, as President. The opposition People's National Congress (PNC) led by former President Desmond Hoyte, on the other hand, continued to exploit racial feelings among the one-third of the country's population of Afro-Guyanese origin and to do everything it could to reverse the verdict of the electorate. Both sides initially agreed to an independent 'audit' of the election results by Caricom, the suspension of all demonstrations and the appointment of a commission on constitutional reform. However, tensions again rose before arrangements for the audit were approved by the National Assembly on 16 March.

The Caricom report on 2 June disclosed no evidence of fraud. Accordingly, at their summit which opened in St Lucia at the end of the month, Caricom leaders called upon President Jagan and Mr Hoyte to resume talks. The PNC had refused to accept the findings of the report, however, and organized violence had broken out again. Protesters attacked shops owned by Indo-Guyanese and the Finance Ministry was burnt down on 22 June. Firebombs were also found at the Ministry of Health and Inland Revenue buildings, but successfully defused. Eventually, in July, talks in St Lucia between government and opposition representatives resulted in an agreement to cut short President Jagan's five-year term by two years, while in December agreement was finally reached on how far opposition representation could be allowed on state boards and committees.

On 15 July the IMF approved a loan to the beleaguered government to support its structural adjustment programme over the next three years. On 22 October the World Bank agreed an emergency credit of US$9 million to improve flood protection in low-lying parts of Georgetown and to restore agricultural capacity in drought-stricken areas of the countryside.

iii. TRINIDAD & TOBAGO

CAPITAL: Port of Spain   AREA: 5,128 sq km   POPULATION: 1,300,000 ('97)
OFFICIAL LANGUAGE: English   POLITICAL SYSTEM: parliamentary republic
RULING PARTIES: United National Congress (UNC) & National Alliance for Reconstruction (NAR)
HEAD OF STATE: President Arthur N.R. Robinson (NAR), since March '97
HEAD OF GOVERNMENT: Basdeo Panday (UNC), Prime Minister (since Nov '95)
MAIN IGO MEMBERSHIPS (non-UN): OAS, SELA, ACS, Caricom, ACP, CWTH, NAM
CURRENCY: Trinidad & Tobago dollar (end-'98 £1=TT$10.43, US$1=TT$6.25)
GNP PER CAPITA: US$4,230 by exchange-rate calculation, US$6,410 by PPP calculation ('97)

DESPITE evidence of weaker economic performance in the third quarter, unemployment at 13.4 per cent was at its lowest since 1984. Crime remained a chief preoccupation of the government of Prime Minister Baseo Panday and there were calls for the government to agree a bi-partisan approach to the question with opposition leader Patrick Manning. The financial year having been changed to start on 1 October, the annual budget statement was presented to parliament at its opening on 5 October by the Minister of Finance, Senator Brian Kwei Tung. In it he claimed that the government had already done more for youth and the aged than any previous Trinidad government. There was also a strong emphasis on the rule of law and the need for an investor-friendly environment.

William Demas, the first secretary-general of the Caribbean Community (1973–74), died of renal failure aged 69 in hospital in Port-of-Spain on 27 November.

iv. BARBADOS

CAPITAL: Bridgetown   AREA: 430 sq km   POPULATION: 270,000 ('97)
OFFICIAL LANGUAGE: English   POLITICAL SYSTEM: parliamentary democracy
HEAD OF STATE: Queen Elizabeth II
GOVERNOR-GENERAL: Sir Clifford Husbands
RULING PARTY: Barbados Labour Party (BLP)
HEAD OF GOVERNMENT: Owen Arthur, Prime Minister (since Sept '94)
MAIN IGO MEMBERSHIPS (non-UN): OAS, SELA, ACS, Caricom, ACP, CWTH, NAM
CURRENCY: Barbados dollar (end-'98 £1=B$3.35, US$1=B$2.01)
GNP PER CAPITA: US$6,590 by exchange-rate calculation ('97)

FOLLOWING the introduction of value-added-tax (VAT) in 1997 (see AR 1997, pp. 190–1), there was concern both about the increased level of government spending and its likely effect on inflation. However, government support remained strong and one MP, Rev. Joseph Atherley, switched to the government of Prime Minister Owen Arthur from the opposition Democratic Labour Party (DLP) only four months before the general election due in January 1999.

The Commission for Pan-African Affairs, established in July to forge new links between Barbados, Africa and the African diaspora, commenced operation in November. A new Penal System Reform Bill introduced by Attorney-General David Simmons in December proposed a range of alternatives to imprisonment for minor offences.

v. BELIZE

CAPITAL: Belmopan   AREA: 23,000 sq km   POPULATION: 228,000 ('97)
OFFICIAL LANGUAGE: English   POLITICAL SYSTEM: parliamentary democracy
HEAD OF STATE: Queen Elizabeth II
GOVERNOR-GENERAL: Sir Colville Young
RULING PARTY: People's United Party (PUP)
HEAD OF GOVERNMENT: Said Musa, Prime Minister (since Aug '98)
MAIN IGO MEMBERSHIPS (non-UN): OAS, SELA, ACS, Caricom, ACP, CWTH, NAM
CURRENCY: Belize dollar (end-'98 £1=BZ$3.33, US$1=BZ$2.00)
GNP PER CAPITA: US$2,740 by exchange-rate calculation, US$4,110 by PPP calculation ('97)

IN a general election held on 27 August the opposition People's United Party (PUP) won a landslide victory, taking 59.4 per cent of the votes cast and 23 of the 29 seats in the House of Representatives. The ruling United Democratic Party (UDP) won 39.1 per cent and only three seats, on a turnout of 78.1 per cent. The outgoing Prime Minister, Manuel Esquivel, who lost his own seat by more than 400 votes, subsequently resigned as leader of the UDP. He was succeeded by his former deputy, Dean Oliver Barrow, who, together with his two colleagues, boycotted the official opening of the new House in Belmopan on 12 September, after the new government had claimed that its predecessor had effectively bankrupted the treasury.

The new Prime Minister, Said Musa, who was sworn in on 28 August, assumed the portfolios of finance and foreign affairs himself and appointed John Briceño as Deputy Prime Minister with responsibility for natural resources and environment. A task force formed by the new Minister for the Sugar Industry, Florencio Marin, to advise on ways of increasing production held its first meeting on 23 November.

In an unprecedented move, the new government on 1 December banned reproduction in Belize of an article from the British newspaper *The Independent*. The article had been critical of the Chief Justice, Sir George Brown, who had, despite his judicial rank, openly advocated the speedy execution of eight prisoners held on capital charges in Hattieville prison.

Relations with neighbouring Guatemala continued to improve. In talks held in Miami, Florida, on 20 November, representatives of Belize and Guatemala agreed to set up a new mixed commission to deal with technical problems of immigration, transit and the rights of citizens.

vi. GRENADA

CAPITAL: St George's   AREA: 344 sq km   POPULATION: 99,000 ('97)
OFFICIAL LANGUAGE: English   POLITICAL SYSTEM: parliamentary democracy
HEAD OF STATE: Queen Elizabeth II
GOVERNOR-GENERAL: Sir Daniel Williams
RULING PARTY: New National Party (NNP)
HEAD OF GOVERNMENT: Keith Mitchell, Prime Minister (since June '95)
MAIN IGO MEMBERSHIPS (non-UN): OAS, SELA, ACS, Caricom, OECS, ACP, CWTH, NAM
CURRENCY: East Caribbean dollar (end-'98 £1=EC$4.49, US$1=EC$2.70)
GNP PER CAPITA: US$3,000 by exchange-rate calculation, US$4,450 by PPP calculation ('97)

FOLLOWING the death of Sir Eric Gairy in August 1997 (see AR 1997, pp. 193, 578), a convention of his right-wing Grenada United Labour Party (GULP) on 24 May elected former Deputy Prime Minister Herbert Preudhomme as its leader. At the beginning of August, during a state visit to the island, President Fidel Castro Ruz of Cuba unveiled a plaque at Pointe Salines international airport in memory of the Cuban construction workers killed during the US intervention in 1983 which resulted in the overthrow of the short-lived Revolutionary Military Council (RMC) government. The Prime Minister, Dr Keith Mitchell, had previously visited Cuba and praised its role in helping the development of Grenada between 1979 and 1983.

On 29 November Dr Raphael Fletcher resigned as Foreign Minister because of concern at integrity in government, leaving the government without a majority. At the same time, he resigned as chairman of the ruling New National Party (NNP), stating his intention to join the GULP. A general election was therefore called for 18 January 1999. Mark Isaac took Dr Fletcher's place at foreign affairs, while Senator Claris Modest succeeded Mr Isaac at health. Elvin Nimrod, Minister of Carriacou and Petit Martinique Affairs, became Minister of Legal Affairs.

On 8 December the GULP executive agreed that in view of Mr Preudhomme's poor state of health, Dr Fletcher should lead the party into the election. A week later the party agreed with the other main opposition party, the National Democratic Congress (NDC), a strategy of 'limited cooperation' within a United Front with The National Party (TNP) and the Democratic Labour Party (DLP).

vii. THE BAHAMAS

CAPITAL: Nassau   AREA: 14,000 sq km   POPULATION: 289,000 ('97)
OFFICIAL LANGUAGE: English   POLITICAL SYSTEM: parliamentary democracy
HEAD OF STATE: Queen Elizabeth II
GOVERNOR-GENERAL: Sir Orville Turnquest
RULING PARTY: Free National Movement (FNM)
HEAD OF GOVERNMENT: Hubert Ingraham, Prime Minister (since Aug '92)
MAIN IGO MEMBERSHIPS (non-UN): OAS, ACS, Caricom, ACP, CWTH, NAM
CURRENCY: Bahamas dollar (end-'98 £1=B$1.66, US$1=B$1.00)
GNP PER CAPITA: US$11,830 by exchange-rate calculation ('97)

FINANCE Minister William Allen announced in February that he would bring forward regulations for the creation of a stock exchange by the end of the year. In May the government returned some 200 Cuban refugees to Cuba despite the fact that the government of Nicaragua had been prepared to offer them temporary asylum. On 19 June the Foreign Minister, Janet Bostwick, concluded an agreement with Cuba providing for the 'more expeditious' repatriation of Cuban refugees in future. In line with practice in Britain and the United States, the new agreement would not allow the UN Human Rights Commission to interview refugees to decide whether or not their reasons were political.

Public demand for the return of the death sentence rose following the murder of two tourists early in the year. Despite an appeal to the Inter-American Commission on Human Rights and international calls for clemency, two convicted murderers were executed by hanging on 15 October.

viii. WINDWARD AND LEEWARD ISLANDS

Antigua & Barbuda
CAPITAL: St John's   AREA: 440 sq km   POPULATION: 66,000 ('97)
OFFICIAL LANGUAGE: English   POLITICAL SYSTEM: parliamentary democracy
HEAD OF STATE: Queen Elizabeth II
GOVERNOR-GENERAL: Sir James B. Carlisle
RULING PARTY: Antigua Labour Party (ALP)
HEAD OF GOVERNMENT: Lester Bird, Prime Minister (since March '94)
MAIN IGO MEMBERSHIPS (non-UN): OAS, ACS, OECS, Caricom, ACP, CWTH
CURRENCY: East Caribbean dollar (end-'98 £1=EC$4.49, US$1=EC$2.70)
GNP PER CAPITA: US$7,380 by exchange-rate calculation, US$8,720 by PPP calculation ('97)

Dominica
CAPITAL: Roseau   AREA: 750 sq km   POPULATION: 74,000 ('97)
OFFICIAL LANGUAGE: English   POLITICAL SYSTEM: parliamentary republic
HEAD OF STATE: President Vernon Shaw (since Oct '98)
RULING PARTY: United Workers' Party (UWP)
HEAD OF GOVERNMENT: Edison James, Prime Minister (since June '95)
MAIN IGO MEMBERSHIPS (non-UN): OAS, ACS, OECS, Caricom, ACP, CWTH, Francophonie
CURRENCY: East Caribbean dollar (see above)
GNP PER CAPITA: US$3,120 by exchange-rate calculation, US$4,470 by PPP calculation ('97)

St Christopher (Kitts) & Nevis
CAPITAL: Basseterre   AREA: 260 sq km   POPULATION: 41,500 ('97)
OFFICIAL LANGUAGE: English   POLITICAL SYSTEM: parliamentary democracy
HEAD OF STATE: Queen Elizabeth II
GOVERNOR-GENERAL: Sir Cuthbert Sebastian
RULING PARTY: St Kitts-Nevis Labour Party (SKNLP)
HEAD OF GOVERNMENT: Denzil Douglas, Prime Minister (since July '95)
MAIN IGO MEMBERSHIPS (non-UN): OAS, ACS, Caricom, OECS, ACP, CWTH
CURRENCY: East Caribbean dollar (see above)
GNP PER CAPITA: US$6,100 by exchange-rate calculation, US$7,730 by PPP calculation ('97)

St Lucia

CAPITAL: Castries   AREA: 616 sq km   POPULATION: 160,000 ('97)
OFFICIAL LANGUAGE: English   POLITICAL SYSTEM: parliamentary democracy
HEAD OF STATE: Queen Elizabeth II
GOVERNOR-GENERAL: Perlette Louisy
RULING PARTY: St Lucia Labour Party (SLP)
HEAD OF GOVERNMENT: Kenny D. Anthony, Prime Minister (since May '97)
MAIN IGO MEMBERSHIPS (non-UN): OAS, ACS, OECS, Caricom, ACP, CWTH, NAM
CURRENCY: East Caribbean dollar (see above)
GNP PER CAPITA: US$3,620 by exchange-rate calculation, US$5,030 by PPP calculation ('97)

St Vincent & the Grenadines

CAPITAL: Kingstown   AREA: 390 sq km   POPULATION: 112,000 ('97)
OFFICIAL LANGUAGE: English   POLITICAL SYSTEM: parliamentary democracy
HEAD OF STATE: Queen Elizabeth II
GOVERNOR-GENERAL: Charles James Antrobus
RULING PARTY: New Democratic Party (NDP)
HEAD OF GOVERNMENT: Sir James F. Mitchell, Prime Minister (since July '84)
MAIN IGO MEMBERSHIPS (non-UN): OAS, ACS, OECS, Caricom, ACP, CWTH
CURRENCY: East Caribbean dollar (see above)
GNP PER CAPITA: US$2,500 by exchange-rate calculation, US$4,320 by PPP calculation ('97)

THE Commonwealth of Dominica, St Kitts & Nevis and St Lucia all suffered substantial damage from Hurricane Georges in September. On 10 December the World Bank approved credits and loans totalling US$19.08 million for the three countries in support of the first phase of an emergency recovery and disaster management programme proposed by the Organization of Eastern Caribbean States (OECS). On 17 December the IMF also approved an emergency SDR1.625 million credit for St Kitts & Nevis for relief and rehabilitation over a period of up to five years.

In ANTIGUA & BARBUDA, substantial new consignments of arms were reported to have been delivered in November for the use of the police and defence forces.

In DOMINICA, the House of Assembly chose Vernon Shaw as the new President on 2 October, to succeed Crispin Sorhaindo, whose bid for re-election was unsuccessful. Mr Shaw, who had served as cabinet secretary under former Prime Minister Eugenia Charles, was sworn in on 6 October. Washington's threat of sanctions against the European Union (EU) if the banana regime were not changed (see XI.4) aroused particular concern when Prime Minister Edison James reported to parliament on the negotiations on 14 December. As with other smaller island territories in the region, Dominica faced financial ruin if the protection hitherto afforded by the EU's Lomé Convention was removed. However, the Clinton administration in the United States, responding to an appeal from the head of the US transnational corporation Chiquita, continued to escalate the trade dispute by threatening to impose punitive retaliatory tariffs on a select list of EU products.

On 20 July ST KITTS & NEVIS became the first Commonwealth Caribbean state for 17 years to carry out an execution. David Wilson was hanged for the murder of a security guard in 1994. The execution came at a sensitive time, when a number of other Caribbean states, notably Barbados and

Trinidad & Tobago, were challenging the continued reluctance of the judicial committee of the UK Privy Council to sanction capital punishment. In a referendum held on 10 August at the request of the Nevis secessionist movement, 61.8 per cent of voters approved secession. However, since this margin was short of the two-thirds majority required under the constitution, the Prime Minister, Denzil Douglas, agreed to negotiate an arrangement that would allow Nevis greater autonomy within the federation.

In ST LUCIA, plans announced in June to introduce a US$10 per night hotel tax were quickly suspended, and eventually dropped, following strong protests from all-inclusive hotel resorts. In a press conference at the annual Caribbean Community (Caricom) summit, held in Castries on 30 June-4 July (see XI.6.iv)), Prime Minister Kenny Anthony urged the heads of government to advance the implementation of a Caribbean Court of Justice, saying: 'I think this is a very, very important development because it seems that at long last we will be completing the process of repatriating our constitutions to the Caribbean.' At the same gathering, Foreign Minister George Odlum called for a joint Caricom battle against rising crime levels. Later, at the beginning of December, Dr Anthony announced arrangements for the privatization of the National Commercial Bank. Shares were to be offered to the public in February 1999 with incentives for wide share ownership, the disposal being expected to raise some US$14.4 million.

In ST VINCENT & THE GRENADINES, the Prime Minister, Sir James Mitchell, reshuffled cabinet responsibilities in early January. Among those receiving altered duties were John Horne at trade and consumer affairs, Bernard Wyllie at agriculture, industry and labour, and Allan Cruickshank at foreign affairs, tourism and information. In May the Prime Minister used his prerogative to call a general election on 15 June, several months before the expiry of the current parliament. After a brief campaign, the ruling National Democratic Party (NDP) won 54.2 per cent of the votes cast and eight of the 15 seats in the House of Assembly and therefore formed the government for the fourth successive time. The opposition Unity Labour Party (ULP) won the remaining seven seats. In the new cabinet sworn in on 18 June, Arnhim Eustace was appointed Minister of Finance. The leader of the ULP, Vincent Beache, resigned at the end of November, following complaints from opposition members that the government was repeatedly delaying the convening of parliament. In December the Regional Security System and US Marines mounted a ten-day operation to eradicate marijuana on mountain farms.

ix. UK DEPENDENCIES

Anguilla
CAPITAL: The Valley   AREA: 96 sq km   POPULATION: 8,300 ('97)
OFFICIAL LANGUAGE: English   POLITICAL SYSTEM: representative democracy
GOVERNOR: Alan Poole
RULING PARTIES: Anguilla United (AUP) & Anguilla Democratic (ADP) parties
HEAD OF GOVERNMENT: Hubert Hughes (AUP), Chief Minister (since March '94)
MAIN IGO MEMBERSHIPS: OECS, Caricom (obs.)
CURRENCY: East Caribbean dollar (end-'98 £1=EC$4.49, US$1=EC$2.70)

Bermuda
CAPITAL: Hamilton   AREA: 53 sq km   POPULATION: 64,000 ('97)
OFFICIAL LANGUAGE: English   POLITICAL SYSTEM: representative democracy
GOVERNOR: Thorold Masefield
RULING PARTY: Progressive Labour Party (PLP)
HEAD OF GOVERNMENT: Jennifer Smith, Prime Minister (since Nov '98)
MAIN IGO MEMBERSHIPS: Caricom (obs.)
CURRENCY: East Caribbean dollar (see above)

British Virgin Islands
CAPITAL: Road Town   AREA: 153 sq km   POPULATION: 18,000 ('97)
OFFICIAL LANGUAGE: English   POLITICAL SYSTEM: representative democracy
GOVERNOR: David MacKilligin
RULING PARTY: Virgin Islands Party (VIP)
HEAD OF GOVERNMENT: Ralph O'Neal, Chief Minister (since May '95)
MAIN IGO MEMBERSHIPS: OECS (assoc.), Caricom (assoc.)
CURRENCY: East Caribbean dollar (see above)

Cayman Islands
CAPITAL: George Town, Grand Cayman   AREA: 259 sq km POPULATION: 35,000 ('97)
OFFICIAL LANGUAGE: English   POLITICAL SYSTEM: representative democracy
GOVERNOR: John Owen
MAIN IGO MEMBERSHIPS: Caricom (obs.)
CURRENCY: East Caribbean dollar (see above)

Montserrat
CAPITAL: Plymouth   AREA: 102 sq km   POPULATION: 3,000 ('98)
OFFICIAL LANGUAGE: English   POLITICAL SYSTEM: representative democracy
GOVERNOR: Frank J. Savage
HEAD OF GOVERNMENT: David Brandt, Chief Minister (since Aug '97)
MAIN IGO MEMBERSHIPS: OECS, Caricom, ACS
CURRENCY: East Caribbean dollar (see above)

Turks & Caicos Islands
CAPITAL: Cockburn Town   AREA: 430 sq km   POPULATION: 14,500 ('97)
OFFICIAL LANGUAGE: English   POLITICAL SYSTEM: representative democracy
GOVERNOR: John Kelly
RULING PARTY: People's Democratic Movement (PDM)
HEAD OF GOVERNMENT: Derek H. Taylor, Chief Minister (since Jan '95)
MAIN IGO MEMBERSHIPS: Caricom (assoc.)
CURRENCY: East Caribbean dollar (see above)

IN BERMUDA, Prime Minister Pamela F. Gordon of the United Bermuda Party (UBP), who had held the post since March 1997 (see AR 1997, p. 197), announced a major reshuffle of her cabinet on 6 May. Two new ministries were created: one for development and opportunity, under Jerome Dill (previously Education Minister) and the other for government and community services, under Senator Yvette Swan. At the general election on 9 November, however, the UBP, which had won every election since the introduction of party politics in the 1960s, was heavily defeated. The UBP obtained only 44.1 per cent of the votes cast and 14 seats, against 54.2 per cent and 26 seats for the opposition Progressive Labour Party (PLP), whose leader, Jennifer Smith, formed the new government. In its own view, the UBP suffered electorally from its association with past white dominance. A sluggish economy and dissension about immigration policy were also factors. In the new cabinet, the Prime Minister also assumed responsibility for the education portfolio, Eugene Cox became Deputy Prime Minister and Minister of Finance, and Paula Cox Minister for Home Affairs and Public Safety.

The 1999 budget for the BRITISH VIRGIN ISLANDS, presented in December, recorded that the economy was generally healthy. A three-year datagathering project was launched by the BVI National Parks Trust with support from the Darwin Initiative funding agency, to collate data on biodiversity within the islands and to allow for the better planning of tourism and other uses. There was some concern, however, that European proposals to launch space exploration rockets from Sombrero Island (Anguilla) might give rise to problems with falling debris.

The government of the CAYMAN ISLANDS took over the chairmanship of the Caribbean Financial Action Task Force (CFATF) at a full meeting of the Council in the islands in December, announcing plans for the group to address issues of harmful tax competition.

In retrospect, the volcanic eruption in the Soufrière hills that had rendered two-thirds of MONTSERRAT uninhabitable (see AR 1997, p. 198) reached a peak of intensity with the collapse of the lava dome on Boxing Day 1997 following two days of intense seismic activity. The collapse of the southerly lobe had built up in the preceding months to a height of some 1,020 metres and sent a pyroclastic flow of lava down the White River valley towards the sea, where it caused a small tsunami. The explosion was accompanied by intense surge activity generating a convective ash cloud which reached an altitude of some 1.3 kilometres (47,000 feet) and mantled much of the south-west of the island. Fortunately, both effects were well away from the remaining 3,000 inhabitants on their foothold in the far north of the island. Dome growth resumed almost immediately afterwards, but was accompanied by a comparatively low level of seismicity. By the year's end it was clear that the new growth had come to an end in March. The consensus of experts was that the eruption might be expected to last for some two or three more years. Although the danger of new pyroclastic flows could not be discounted, they were likely to be relatively local events and activity generally could be expected to subside.

Meanwhile, Chief Minister David Brandt (appointed in August 1997) continued to express his bitterness at what he saw as the slow and inadequate response of the UK government. In January he again accused the UK government of delaying relief funds to force islanders to leave. After a formal visit to the island by Foreign Secretary Robin Cook on 14 February, however, the British government, which had already spent more than £60 million on emergency relief over the previous three years, pledged to allocate £75 million for the next three. In June, moreover, the UK Home Office ruled that all present and departed islanders would be allowed to settle in Britain (some 3,500 having already done so).

In the TURKS & CAICOS ISLANDS, the government of Chief Minister Derek H. Taylor of the People's Democratic Movement (PDM) remained in office all year.

x. SURINAME

CAPITAL: Paramaribo   AREA: 163,000 sq km   POPULATION: 437,000 ('97)
OFFICIAL LANGUAGE: Dutch   POLITICAL SYSTEM: republic
HEAD OF STATE: President Jules Wijdenbosch (since Sept '96)
RULING PARTIES: National Democratic Party (NDP) heads coalition
HEAD OF GOVERNMENT: Vice-President Pretaapnarain Radhakishum (since Sept '96)
MAIN IGO MEMBERSHIPS (non-UN): OAS, SELA, AP, ACS, Caricom, ACP, NAM
CURRENCY: Suriname guilder (end-'98 £1=Sf667.16, US$1=Sf401.00)
GNP PER CAPITA: US$1,240 by exchange-rate calculation, US$2,740 by PPP calculation ('97)

THE President of Guyana, Janet Jagan, paid a state visit to Suriname in December. In the course of discussions she and President Jules Wijdenbosch agreed that after two years of inactivity the joint border commission established to settle the boundary dispute between the two countries, arising out of Suriname's claim to a triangle of land between the New and Corentyne rivers in south-east Guyana, should resume operation.

xi. NETHERLANDS ANTILLES AND ARUBA

Netherlands Antilles
CAPITAL: Willemstad (Curaçao)   AREA: 800 sq km   POPULATION: 204,000 ('97)
OFFICIAL LANGUAGES: Dutch, Papiamento, English
POLITICAL SYSTEM: parliamentary, under Dutch Crown
GOVERNOR: Jaime M. Saleh
RULING PARTIES: National People's Party (PNP) heads coalition
HEAD OF GOVERNMENT: Susanne Camelia-Romer (PNP), Prime Minister (since May '98)
CURRENCY: Neth. Antilles guilder (end-'98 £1=Naf2.98, US$1=NAf1.79)
GNP PER CAPITA: n/a

Aruba

CAPITAL: Oranjestad   AREA: 193 sq km   POPULATION: 80,000 ('97)
OFFICIAL LANGUAGE: Dutch
POLITICAL SYSTEM: parliamentary, under Dutch Crown
GOVERNOR: Olindo Koolman
RULING PARTIES: Aruban People's Party (AVP) & Aruban Liberal Organization (OLA)
HEAD OF GOVERNMENT: Jan Hendrick (Henny) Eman (AVP), Prime Minister (since July '94)
CURRENCY: Aruba guilder (end-'98 £1=Af2.98, US$1=Af1.79)
GNP PER CAPITA: US$16,640 by exchange-rate calculation ('97)

IN a general election in the NETHERLANDS ANTILLES on 31 January the Antillean Reconstruction Party (PAR), which had led the coalition government since 1994, lost more than half its support and retained only four seats in the new States-General, the remaining 18 seats being shared by 10 parties. A new six-party coalition government was eventually formed under the premiership of Susanne Camelia-Romer of the National People's Party (PNP).

A total eclipse of the sun was visible for over three minutes on ARUBA on 26 February.

xii. US DEPENDENCIES

Puerto Rico

CAPITAL: San Juan   AREA: 9,103 sq km   POPULATION: 3,800,000 ('97)
OFFICIAL LANGUAGES: Spanish & English   POLITICAL SYSTEM: democratic commonwealth
GOVERNOR: Pedro Rosselló
RULING PARTY: New Progressive Party (PNP)
CURRENCY: US dollar (end-'98 £1=EC$1.66)

US Virgin Islands

CAPITAL: Charlotte Amalie   AREA: 342 sq km   POPULATION: 100,000 ('97)
OFFICIAL LANGUAGE: English   POLITICAL SYSTEM: democratic dependency
GOVERNOR: Roy Schneider (independent)
CURRENCY: US dollar (see above)

THE island of PUERTO RICO suffered considerable damage to roads, bridges and housing from Hurricane Georges on 21 September. Earlier, protests had failed to halt a proposal to privatize the government-owned telephone company. On 24 June the bill to sell the company to a consortium led by the US telecommunications company GTE was signed into law by Governor Pedro J. Rosselló. The following day a series of bomb threats received by the Commonwealth's largest bank, Banco Popular (a member of the consortium), was followed by a bomb explosion which injured a policeman. The 6,500 workers of the company stopped work in protest and were supported by a general strike which paralysed half the island on 6–7 July. On 9 December US Customs seized 400 pounds of Colombian heroin and arrested 25 suspected traffickers.

The Governor, who favoured US statehood for the island, failed to obtain from the US Congress legislation for a binding referendum. On 25 July he called instead for a non-binding plebiscite to be held on the future political status of the island before the end of the year. Of the four options on offer in the referendum, which was held on 13 December, continuation of the island's existing Commonwealth status was effectively favoured by 50.17 per cent of the electors, while 46.49 per cent supported statehood, only 2.53 per cent independence and only 0.3 per cent self-government in free association with the United States. The Governor stated his intention of continuing to pursue the statehood option, despite the fact that it was exceedingly unlikely that the US Congress would be prepared to accept it.

In the US VIRGIN ISLANDS, on the 150th anniversary of emancipation on 25 June, Governor Roy C. Schneider formally inaugurated a new bus service to alleviate congestion at Cruz Bay, St John. Earlier, on 11 May, the Virgin Islands National Park was forced to drop plans to charge visitors a US$4 fee to fund conservation work after Carnival Cruise Lines, the largest operator of tours to the islands, cancelled future visits to St John. The scheme to charge fees to the nearly 200,000 visitors a year had received strong public support at a March public meeting. The US Secretary of the Interior, Bruce Babbitt, paid his first visit to the islands on 10 August.

V MIDDLE EAST AND NORTH AFRICA

1. ISRAEL

CAPITAL: Jerusalem   AREA: 22,000 sq km   POPULATION: 6,000,000 ('97)
OFFICIAL LANGUAGE: Hebrew   POLITICAL SYSTEM: parliamentary democracy
HEAD OF STATE: President Ezer Weizman (since March '93)
RULING PARTIES: Likud-Gesher-Tsomet alliance heads coalition with Shas, National Religious Party, Yisrael Ba-Aliya, Third Way & United Torah Judaism
HEAD OF GOVERNMENT: Binyamin Netanyahu (Likud), Prime Minister (since June '96)
CURRENCY: new shekel (end-'98 £1=NSh6.92, US$1=NSh4.18)
GNP PER CAPITA: US$15,810 by exchange-rate calculation, US$16,960 by PPP calculation ('97)

THE year witnessed Israel's 50th anniversary celebrations, albeit somewhat subdued. Many people in the country found it difficult to rejoice as the Jewish state reached this landmark. Israel in its 50th year, fraught with uncertainty about its future direction, was a country deeply divided over issues concerning the peace process with the Palestinians, its socio-economic fabric and secular-religious relations. Political uncertainty characterized the year, as Binyamin Netanyahu's shaky coalition went from crisis to crisis and ultimately collapsed in December.

After a year of political uncertainty and two-and-a-half years into Mr Netanyahu's term in office, the Knesset (parliament) voted on the 21 December to dissolve itself and call for early elections in the spring of 1999. There was little surprise that the coalition had failed to survive its full four-year term. At the beginning of the year David Levy, the charismatic Sephardi leader of the Gesher party, resigned as Foreign Minister, announcing that he had lost confidence in Mr Netanyahu's leadership and that the government was 'going nowhere'. Mr Levy's resignation and the departure of Gesher from the coalition left Mr Netanyahu with a wafer-thin majority of one in the Knesset. Mr Levy's resignation prompted widespread speculation that the government would quickly collapse. Whilst this did not immediately occur, it left him considerably weakened and at the beck and call of various members of his coalition.

Criticism of Mr Netanyahu came not only from the opposition parties, but from within Likud itself. Benny Begin, who had resigned as Science Minister in protest against the Hebron accord signed in January 1997 (see AR 1997, p. 203), and Dan Meridor, the former Finance Minister, both leading members of the Likud party, frequently absented themselves in voting on motions of no confidence in the government. In May the mayor of Tel Aviv, Roni Milo, announced that he was leaving the Likud to set up a new centre movement called 'Atid' and would run for the position of Prime Minister in the next elections. Mr Netanyahu's prospects of survival, already doubtful, became increasingly slim when, in mid-December,

Finance Minister Ya'acov Ne'eman, one of the Prime Minister's most loyal erstwhile supporters, faxed him his resignation whilst on a skiing holiday in Switzerland.

Mr Netanyahu ultimately fell on account of the inherent contradictions within his coalition concerning the peace process with the Palestinians and over the agreement and implementation of the Wye River accords signed with the Palestinians on 23 October (see also V.2.i). Those on the moderate wing of his coalition, notably the Third Way, consistently threatened to leave the coalition should he not advance the peace process, whilst those on the right, namely the National Religious Party and several members of the Likud, threatened to bring down the government should he withdraw from the West Bank. The delicate balancing-act achieved by the Prime Minister between these two opposing positions was no longer sustainable with the implementation of the Wye accords.

Throughout the year intensive US mediation sought to revive the dormant peace process between Israel and the Palestinians. The Americans were keen to bring about a further redeployment of Israeli troops from the West Bank as called for by the Oslo accords and the endorsed in the Hebron deal signed the previous year. This mediation consisted of getting the two sides to agree to an American proposal that the next phase of troop redeployment should consist of a withdrawal from a further 13 per cent of the West Bank territory. The British Prime Minister, Tony Blair, lent his support to the US efforts during his April visit to Israel. In May Mr Netanyahu and the Palestinian leader, Yassir Arafat, flew to London for talks; however, despite continued US-UK efforts to push forward the peace process, little progress was made in rebuilding confidence and trust between the two sides.

In the middle of October, despite his domestic difficulties surrounding the publication of the Starr Report and the Monica Lewinsky affair (see IV.1), President Clinton put his prestige on the line and called on Mr Netanyahu and Mr Arafat to meet at the Wye River Plantation outside Washington for intensive negotiations to put the peace process back on track. After nine days of talks, which at various times seemed to be on the brink of collapse, and with the direct involvement of President Clinton and King Husain of Jordan (who left his sick-bed in Minneapolis to attend the talks—see V.2.iii), the Israeli and Palestinian leaders finally put their signatures to the Wye River agreement on 23 October.

Israel agreed to a further redeployment of 13 per cent from the West Bank, despite the fact that only days before the departure of the Israeli delegation, Ariel Sharon, who was appointed Foreign Minister on 9 October, had declared that a such redeployment would constitute a grave threat to the national security of Israel. Originally Israel had insisted that it could not accept a 'double digit' withdrawal. As a way of overcoming Israeli concerns relating to the original American proposal of 13 per cent, which the Palestinians had accepted at during the year, 3 per cent of the territory to be returned to the Palestinians was to be designated a nature reserve. The Wye River accords also called for a renewal and intensification of cooperation between Israeli and Palestinian security forces in the fight against terrorism, a commitment by the Palestinians to confiscate illegal weapons in the West Bank and to work against incitement to violence and terror against Israel, and for a reduction of the Palestinian police force to 30,000 as stipulated in the Oslo peace accords. In order to ensure the effective implementation of the security cooperation clauses, the US Central Intelligence Agency (CIA) would be brought in to assess whether the Palestinians were keeping to their side of the agreement.

Of particular significance was the demand by Israel that a full meeting of the Palestinian National Council (PNC) be convened to annul the clauses in the Palestinian Charter calling for the destruction of Israel. Palestinian claims that these clauses had already been anulled did not hold water with the Israeli government. As a compromise, the Palestinians acceded to the demand and President Clinton agreed to attend a meeting of the PNC in Gaza to witness the nullification of the offending articles. The Wye River memorandum also agreed to the release of 750 Palestinian prisoners held in Israeli gaols, to the opening of an international airport in Gaza and to the creation of two safe passages between the West Bank and Gaza and to the start of final-status negotiations between the two sides.

The signing ceremony of the Wye River memorandum nearly failed to materialize at the 11th hour over Israel's request for the release of Jonathan Pollard, the Israeli spy serving a life sentence in an American gaol. Mr Netanyahu believed that he had received an assurance from President Clinton that Pollard would be released in return for Israel's willingness to sign the deal. When it later transpired that Pollard would not in fact be released, Mr Netanyahu threatened to return to Israel without an agreement. In his speech at the signing ceremony, Mr Clinton announced that he would review the Pollard case but gave no assurances that he would be granted an early release.

Enjoying the support of the overwhelming majority of the Israeli public, the Wye accords were approved by the Knesset on 17 November by a vote of 75 to 19, with nine abstentions. Few expected that within a month the government would fall. Ten days later Israel began the first phase of its redeployment from the West Bank. However, the spirit and hopes of Wye quickly evaporated over the vexed issue of the release of Palestinian prisoners, especially when, contrary to Palestinian expectations, Israel announced that no prisoners who had 'blood on their hands' would be released. It soon became apparent that the agreement had done little to rebuild confidence and trust between the two sides. On 12 December Mr Clinton arrived in the Middle East on a three-day visit to Israel and the Palestinian Authority to witness the annulling of the clauses of the Palestinian National Charter and to get the parties back together for the continued implementation of Wye. This time, despite his best efforts, the President returned to the USA empty-handed.

More significantly, the right-wing opposition within the government to any further withdrawal from the West Bank created an increasingly untenable situation for the Prime Minister, especially since these groups threatened to support a bill in the Knesset providing for early elections. In order to buy back their support, Mr Netanyahu assured his coalition partners on the right that, since the Palestinians were not keeping to their side of the agreement, no further withdrawal would take place, whilst simultaneously telling the more moderate members of his coalition that he was fully committed to implementing the agreement. The Prime Minister's foot-dragging led the Labour opposition—which had originally announced that it would nullify the threats of the right to vote against the government by offering parliamentary support to Mr Netanyahu so long as he was implementing the Wye accords—to reverse its position and work actively for the new elections. With the writing on the wall, Mr Netanyahu announced that his government had reached the end of the road and that he too would be voting for early elections.

Meanwhile, Lebanon continued to take its toll on the lives of Israeli soldiers (see also V.2.v). A total of 22 Israeli soldiers were killed during the year, leading to increasing calls from within Israel for a unilateral withdrawal from Lebanon.

Municipal elections were held in November. In Jerusalem Ehud Olmert (Likud) was re-elected mayor; in Tel Aviv and Be'er Sheva the Labour Party regained the mayorship. However, the most significant element of the results was the collapse in the vote and support for both major parties—Likud and Labour—and the rise in the number of small interest groups, such as the Green Party, Dor Shalem and new Russian parties. This voting pattern, particularly the collapse in support for main parties, occasioned great fear about the continuing fragmentation of the Israeli political system and the consequences for the elections of 1999.

It was not a good year for the Israeli economy. Growth was only 2 per cent, whilst the inflation rate reached an overall level of 8.5 per cent and unemployment entered double figures at 10 per cent. At the end of April the government approved the complete liberalization of the exchange rate and money markets. This made the shekel a fully convertible currency and allowed Israelis to take money out of the country in any quantity, to hold bank accounts abroad and to purchase property overseas. With the growing uncertainty in the global money markets and the financial crisis in the Far East, the shekel came under increasing attack and speculation from abroad. At the beginning of the year the shekel's exchange rate to the dollar stood at 3.53. In the space of one-and-a-half months from late September its value against the dollar depreciated by nearly 25 per cent, reaching an all-time high of 4.30 by the end of October. Although the government refused to intervene to stabilize the currency, it was forced to raise domestic interest rates—a move which led to widespread opposition from the industrial and manufacturing sectors.

President Ezer Weizman was re-elected for a second term of office on 4 April. However, for the first time in Israeli history an incumbent President running for a second term was challenged by an opponent, Knesset member Shaul Amor, who was supported by Mr Netanyahu. Mr Weizman was voted in by the narrowest of majorities, receiving 63 Knesset votes out of 120.

General Amnon Lipkin-Shahak retired as Chief of Staff of the Israeli Defence Forces on 9 July and was succeeded by General Shaul Mofaz.

2. ARAB WORLD AND PALESTINIANS—
EGYPT—JORDAN—SYRIA—LEBANON—IRAQ

i. THE ARAB WORLD AND THE PALESTINIANS

ALTHOUGH the United States was now displaying more understanding of the Palestinians, the Israeli government showed little flexibility towards them or firmness in controlling its own extremists. Even after the signing of the historic Wye agreement of 23 October extending Palestinian control in the occupied territories (OT), Jewish settlement there continued to expand. The Palestinian administration remained under the autocratic leadership of Yassir Arafat and its failings strengthened the Palestinian extremists.

The Israelis extended Jewish settlements in Arab territory, especially at Har Homa on the fringes of Arab Jerusalem. They were planning 30,000 new homes for Jews in the OT. Israel, said Prime Minister Binyamin Netanyahu, had never viewed such extension as inconsistent with the Oslo agreements. The Palestinians had long hesitated to abandon the by now antique Palestinian commitment to the destruction of Israel, but in January Mr Arafat had confirmed to President Clinton in writing that this commitment was no longer valid. Mr Netanyahu went on raising it.

The Israeli Prime Minister was also demanding from the Palestinians more zeal in preventing attacks on Israeli civilians, but this would never have been easy. The Israeli authorities were regularly closing the border, thus reducing the livelihood of thousands of Palestinians. There was sporadic violence towards the often provocative Jewish settlers in the OT. Mr Netanyahu regularly used this as an excuse to halt withdrawals from the OT.

The Israelis had never found it easy to show a friendly face to Mr Arafat; but any amicable gesture by him towards them raised hackles among his own people. They resented the extension of Jewish settlement, particularly in the overcrowded Gaza Strip. Violence, often indiscriminate and pointless on the Arab side, was answered with calculated and ruthless efficiency by the Israelis. Their insistence, because of Hebron's biblical past, on maintaining and protecting the tiny Jewish enclave there was a particular irritant—as was the clamorous pleasure which Palestinians displayed at the antics of Iraqi leader Saddam Husain.

On 13 January the Israelis halted the withdrawals at Hebron promised in January 1997 (see AR 1997, p. 206), alleging that the Palestinian authorities had not met their corresponding undertaking to counter violence. Next day the Israeli cabinet decided to retain existing settlements, protecting them with buffer zones and safety perimeters, particularly in the Jordan valley and around Jerusalem.

The US government now sought movement from the Israelis. Mr Netanyahu suggested a meeting with Mr Arafat, who refused until Israel had further redeployed its troops. In late March the UN Secretary-General urged Israel to exchange territory for peace. There was little progress, the Israelis refusing to evacuate even the reduced territory which Mr Arafat had been persuaded by the Americans to accept. An Israeli newspaper published American proposals that the Palestinians should eventually fully control 17.7 per cent of the West Bank and partially control another 21 per cent; that the Israelis should build no new settlements nor significantly expand existing ones; and that the Palestine National Council (PNC) should endorse Mr Arafat's ending of the Palestinian commitment to the destruction of Israel.

These proposals omitted the issue of Jerusalem, on which various steps, often contradictory, were taken and many declarations made. The Israeli government squashed efforts by a Jewish millionaire from Chicago to establish a new Jewish quarter in Arab Jerusalem but planned to extend the city to six times its present size. This was condemned by the Palestinians, the Arab world, the European Union (EU), the US government and the UN Security Council.

Mr Arafat went on promising an independent Palestine, though many thought that such controversial topics should await the solution of more immediate matters. After one of Mr Arafat's statements, Mr Netanyahu threatened that any declaration of independence would end the peace process.

In late September President Clinton called Mr Arafat and Mr Netanyahu to Washington to arrange a peace summit. He persuaded the Palestinian leader not to declare independence meanwhile, and on 15 October brought the two together at the Wye plantation. The so-called Wye agreement was signed on 23 October. By it Israel finally agreed to more Palestinian control in the OT and to release 750 Palestinian prisoners in return for the Palestinian side's undertakings to reinforce its anti-terrorism measures, to reduce its police force and to cancel, once again, the anti-Israel clauses of Palestinian National Charter: Mr Netanyahu was still using this pretext to delay ratification of the agreement. Gaza airport was to open and the Gaza Strip to have a corridor joining it to the West Bank.

President Clinton visited Gaza on 14 December to witness the formal abandonment of the Palestinians' anti-Israel commitment. On this occasion, and during his subsequent visit to Bethlehem, the President was loudly cheered by Palestinians, while many others in Syria, Lebanon and Jordan were burning effigies of Mr Arafat and the US leader.

There were still many clouds in the Israeli-Palestinian sky. Mr Arafat again promised independence in May 1999 and the recovery of Jerusalem, but withdrew when Mr Netanyahu again suspended the implementation of the accord. Terrorist attacks by dissidents in the OT and protests against the Israeli failure to release political prisoners continued. The peace process stopped in December when Mr Netanyahu called early elections (see V.1).

Longstanding intra-Palestinian divisions deepened. The openly intransigent groups, Hamas and Islamic Jihad, opposed the Palestinian administration from outside; even inside it, mutually hostile factions fought each other. There was high-handed or brutal behaviour by policemen and several deaths in police custody. On 29 March a prominent dissident from an extremist group was murdered. The affair was implausibly patched up by blaming the Israelis.

Accusations of corruption inside the Palestinian National Authority (see AR 1997, p. 208) became more serious. On 24 June, to forestall a vote of no confidence by the legislature, Mr Arafat accepted the resignation of his cabinet. But the new one he formed on 5 August still included three ministers accused of corruption, and a substantial minority voted against it. Next day one of its best-known members, Hannan Ashrawi, joined a colleague in resigning.

Britain's presidency of the EU in the first half of 1998 brought its government into temporary prominence in the OT. In March the UK Foreign Secretary, Robin Cook, visited Israel and delighted the Palestinians but enraged the Israeli government. Less heat was engendered by Prime Minister Blair's visit to the OT next month, when he met Mr Arafat and agreed to establish a joint EU-Palestinian security committee The Europeans also followed Palestinian affairs closely and were generous donors to the almost penniless Palestinians

The economy of the OT was precarious. The administration managed its finances and invested donors' funds effectively: but income per head was down by 25 per cent since 1993 and unemployment had risen to 30 per cent. Gross national product was hardly rising and living standards were falling. Thus the general population was badly off, 20 per cent being below the poverty line. The workforce depended partly on jobs in Israel, which lapsed whenever the Israelis closed the frontier. Some Palestinian businessmen were doing well, but many of them lived in Jordan and needed their money there.

The Palestinian authorities had prepared a budget of $3,800 million, most of which had to come from abroad. Help from the oil-rich Gulf did not appear significant. The biggest external aid was coming from Europe, slightly larger than that of the Americans. The World Bank had approved a loan of $10 million to start an industrial zone in Gaza and the European Investment Board was lending $39 million to improve power in the OT. The British government was finding smaller sums, both directly and through the UN Relief and Works Agency (UNRWA). Other plans for aid followed: the USA pledged $3,000 million over the next 5 years.

There was some dishonesty in the Palestinian administration. In December the EU reported that $20 million had already been spent on luxury quarters for Mr Arafat's supporters. An internal Palestinian audit found that more than 50 per cent of the Palestinian authority's budget had been lost in corruption or mismanagement.

ii. EGYPT

CAPITAL: Cairo   AREA: 1,000,000 sq km   POPULATION: 61,500,000 ('97)
OFFICIAL LANGUAGE: Arabic   POLITICAL SYSTEM: presidential democracy
HEAD OF STATE & GOVERNMENT: President Mohammed Husni Mubarak (since '81)
RULING PARTY: National Democratic Party (NDP)
PRIME MINISTER: Kamal Ahmad Ganzuri (since Jan '96)
MAIN IGO MEMBERSHIPS (non-UN): AL, OAPEC, OAU, OIC, NAM
CURRENCY: Egyptian pound (end-'98 £1=E£5.67, US$1=E£3.41)
GNP PER CAPITA: US$1,180 by exchange-rate calculation, US$2,940 by PPP calculation ('97)

THE continuing tension between the Arabs and the West over the future of the Palestinians, and now over Iraq, left Egypt in the middle, often treated coolly by the Arabs, contemptuously by the Israelis and not fully supported by the United States. President Husni Mubarak was still much concerned with the peace process (see V.2.i) and the Iraq crisis (see V.2.vi). Fresh outrages by extremist Muslims provoked violent police reactions. The government continued to restrict press freedom, but human rights activists and judges did something to defend it. Sales of state assets continued, but an IMF mission found the private sector still responsible for only 12 per cent of gross domestic product. The rate of inflation fell slightly.

In June the Israeli Prime Minister, Binyamin Netanyahu, criticized President Mubarak for rejecting a new Madrid-style conference and again in September accused the Egyptian media of anti-semitism. The Egyptian leader replied that Egypt was sticking by the Oslo agreement and that Mr Netanyahu could not reasonably object to press freedom abroad while allowing it at home. Egypt followed other Arab states by not supporting the Anglo-American attack on Iraq in December. Cairo accused Britain of over-tolerance to exiled Egyptian fundamentalists in Britain. London rejoined that it had denied visas to some and would cooperate with Egypt in fighting terrorism; it had to seek judicial authority to discipline asylum seekers.

There was still no genuine multi-party system or tolerance of groups believed to be allied with the fundamentalists. The courts forbade Muslim

Brotherhood supporters to register their party under another name. But the worst horrors of 1997 were not repeated: by November 'only' 40 people were reported killed; and 3,000 fundamentalist prisoners had been released after promising better behaviour. With its large Christian community and dependence on foreign tourism, Egypt had strong economic reasons for concern about fundamentalists. The latter were increasingly divided, those in prison seeming now less intransigent, while some exiled fundamentalists advocated a less violent strategy.

There were still, however, many thousands of political prisoners and the police were underpaid, poorly trained and sometimes heavy-handed. In January they clashed with a crowd at Luxor, killing four people. Then in July, after two murders of Copts in upper Egypt, the police reacted by arresting and maltreating hundreds of the Coptic population. The local Coptic bishop reported the episode to the Egyptian Organization for Human Rights (EOHR) and it was highlighted by the foreign press, while government publicity played it down.

The disclosure irritated President Mubarak, who was obsessed with the press and its periodic non-conformity. In February, while scolding businessmen for other things, he also accused them of publicizing their disputes in the press. In March he ordered the dismissal of the editor of *Rose al Yusuf* and accused the press of 'spoiling Egypt's image', i.e. they were revealing things which the regime wanted hidden. Another paper lost its licence by reporting a threat by the Jama'at al Islamiyya to kill some Christian businessmen. In April the parliament's press council purged independent-minded editors from state-owned papers. Several journalists went to prison or were dismissed. In November two were found guilty of libelling a pro-government politician and some important newspapers were forcibly closed. The EOHR was accused of being the agent of a foreign government because it accepted a modest cheque from a British sister organization: its head was briefly imprisoned. But the most influential newspaper, *Al Ahram*, wrote that the government should have tried to benefit from the report and in July a judge ordered a retrial for pro-Islamic journalists who had criticized the son of a former minister.

The government reinstated the ban on female circumcision (not anyhow part of Islamic doctrine) and the President himself was reportedly opposed to it, although the powerful reactionary, Yusuf al Badri, a television star, spoke in its favour. The Shaykh of Al Azhar (the Muslim university) was reported to be modernizing its syllabus, and a book on Muhammad by French scholar Maxime Rodinson was being used there.

Egypt's economy was still badly affected by the fall in tourism after the massacre at Luxor (see AR 1997, p. 209) but the government tried to follow the IMF's advice by cutting public spending and pursuing privatization, which by July had realized $2,500 million since 1993. Enabling legislation was introduced to shift part of the postal and power services into the public sector and to introduce other limited privatizations, for example shipping, commercial banking, insurance and chemicals. Even so, the private sector was producing only 12 per cent of gross domestic product, less than in other developing countries.

In January parliament approved a plan to increase taxation for the rich and lower it for the poor. The IMF, meanwhile, was urging a reduction in tariffs and other barriers to trade. Most modernization projects concerned the towns, leaving the countryside untouched; mainly because of emigration from country to town, children now formed, reportedly, 70 per cent of the rural labour force. The huge project to extend cultivation to the west of the Nile (see AR 1997, p. 210) had attracted help from three Arab development funds, but also Ethiopian complaints that Egypt would be taking more than its fair share of Nile water.

One technical triumph was the April launch by a French company of a television satellite, 'Nilesat', receivable throughout the Middle East. A quite different modernization was celebrated by the President when he gave a party on the occasion of repairs to climatic damage caused to the Sphinx.

Shaykh al Sha'rawi died on 17 June, having made a fortune, much of it in Saudi Arabia, out of religion and television combined. He had been the late President Sadat's Minister of Awqaf but had been less welcome to the present regime.

iii. JORDAN

CAPITAL: Amman   AREA: 97,000 sq km   POPULATION: 5,200,000 ('97)
OFFICIAL LANGUAGE: Arabic   POLITICAL SYSTEM: monarchy
HEAD OF STATE & GOVERNMENT: King Husain ibn Talal (since Aug '52)
PRIME MINISTER: Fayez Tarawneh (since Aug '98)
MAIN IGO MEMBERSHIPS (non-UN): AL, OIC, NAM
CURRENCY: dinar (end-'98 £1=JD1.18, US$1=JD0.71)
GNP PER CAPITA: US$1,570 by exchange-rate calculation, US$3,430 by PPP calculation ('97)

KING Husain, was diagnosed as having cancer. For some weeks in the spring, and again from mid-July onwards, he was in hospital in the United States, whence his guiding hand was still felt: only internal affairs were delegated to his brother, Prince Hasan. Jordan was still straddled uncomfortably between the governments of Israel and those of neighbouring Arab states. Many Jordanians, especially Palestinians, were reluctant to accept the King's policy of coexistence with Israel. Relations with the deeply Arab nationalist government of Syria were uncomfortable. Jordan had essential and indissoluble economic links with Iraq, which, despite its repugnant regime, was embarrassingly popular with Husain's own subjects. In August maladministration brought down the government under Abdul Salam Majali, which was replaced by one under Fayez Tarawneh.

In foreign affairs, relations with Israel and the latter's treatment of the Palestinians were, as usual, the biggest worry. The year began badly when, in early January, Jordan sent an observer to joint US-Israeli naval manœuvres and was criticized for it by Arabs abroad and at home. The King was angry when Ariel Sharon said in February on television that Israel's 1998 attack on a Palestinian activist in Amman (see AR 1997, pp. 203-4, 212) might be repeated (Sharon had thought it enough to promise not to do so on Jordanian soil) and disappointed to find the Americans not pressing Israel harder to accept their proposals. In April the King, after meeting Israeli Prime Minister Binyamin Netanyahu at Eilat, wrote to him that without progress towards peace the whole region might plunge into destructive darkness.

To Jordan, relations were also important with Iraq, whence it was getting cheap oil in settlement of debts. Some Jordanians in Iraq had been executed for smuggling (see AR 1997, pp. 211, 213); but to placate Jordanian opinion the Iraqis unexpectedly released 92 Jordanians from prison. They had refused to do so when asked by the Jordanian government but now complied with a request from its leading opponent, Leith Shubailat. On 17 January several people, including diplomats, were killed in the Iraqi embassy in Amman. This later proved unconnected with politics, being the work of Jordanian gangsters. At about the same time it was reported that President Clinton had rejected the King's advice to hold direct US-Iraqi talks. Meanwhile, Jordan ruled that its airspace must not be used for Anglo-American attacks on Iraq and the police tried vainly to ban pro-Iraqi demonstrations which broke out again in February in Ma'an after a pro-Iraqi sermon.

Much of the opposition to the government stemmed from its most prominent long-term critic, Mr Shubailat, head of the Engineers' Federation. In February he gave a pro-Iraqi sermon in a mosque and was arrested. King Husain then visited the town, following which those arrested, including Mr Shubailat, were released and the opposition called off further demonstrations. But Mr Shubailat, who enjoyed support from professional associations, was in active opposition throughout the year. Arrested in May for holding illegal meetings, he was released on bail but refused a pardon because he wanted a general amnesty for political offenders. He was then rearrested while others connected with the unrest in Ma'an were released.

Domestic politics included one perennial and embarrassing issue—Jordan's division between the Transjordanians who, by and large, ran the government, and the Palestinians who ran business. When a Transjordanian appeared on Qatari television to maintain that the Palestinians should just 'go home', the official reaction—understandable but inadequate—was that such talk undermined national unity. On 17 February the cabinet was reshuffled to introduce one of the less intransigent of the King's opponents, Bassam al Ammush, once deputy head of the opposition Islamic Action Front (IAF).

Much of internal political importance before King Husain left for America concerned the press and his efforts to control it without muzzling it altogether. In April he asked for a new law to restrict criticism of the Palestinian Authority, while the Prime Minister promised legal sanctions on papers which threatened national unity and impaired relations with Arab and Palestinian authorities. Another empowered the government to demand financial guarantees from papers before publication could be allowed, to sue papers, and to shut them down if necessary.

Then in August, after the King's departure, came a big scandal and a major change of government. In the second week of July Amman's water turned cloudy and malodorous. At first the authorities pretended that this was not dangerous. When they were proved wrong, first of all the minister responsible, and then the whole government, including the Prime Minister, resigned and a very largely new cabinet took office under Fayez Tarawneh, a Palestinian who had been head of the Royal Diwan.

The economy was still dependent on foreign aid for its foreign exchange. In January the Foreign Minister visited the United States to seek more aid above the $225 million which Congress had allotted (besides $75 million for military aid). Later, the German government agreed to reschedule $51 million of debt and to help finance the care of refugees (mostly from the Gulf) and remedy poverty in outlying districts. In June the World Bank expressed concern over the economic slowdown, growth being only 2.5 per cent as against a forecast of 5.2 per cent. There was a standing tendency for the government, under pressure from foreign lenders, to cut government expenditure while parliament was asking for increases. One no doubt inevitable increase was a rise in pay for the armed services costing $37 million. Despite protests, partial or complete privatization of industries and services continued, covering in particular the national airline, the cement industry and the state telecommunications company.

iv. SYRIA

CAPITAL: Damascus   AREA: 185,000 sq km   POPULATION: 15,000,000 ('97)
OFFICIAL LANGUAGE: Arabic   POLITICAL SYSTEM: presidential
HEAD OF STATE & GOVERNMENT: President Hafiz al-Asad (since March '71)
RULING PARTY: Baath Arab Socialist Party
PRIME MINISTER: Mahmud Zuabi, Prime Minister (since Nov '87)
MAIN IGO MEMBERSHIPS (non-UN): AL, OAPEC, OIC, NAM
CURRENCY: Syrian pound (end-'98 £1=S£74.87, US$1=S£45.00)
GNP PER CAPITA: US$1,150 by exchange-rate calculation, US$2,990 by PPP calculation ('97)

TENSION with Israel and the West increased as Israeli policy hardened under the Netanyahu government, while relations with the US government cooled further. Syria still dominated the Lebanon, but less obtrusively. Relations with Iraq strengthened; Turkey, coming closer to Israel, forced Syria to stop supporting the Turkish Kurds. The climate with Jordan grew frostier. President Hafiz al-Asad's health and degree of control seemed unaltered and he paid a grand visit to Paris.

Syria retained its primacy in Lebanon. Together they resisted Israel's attempts to separate its occupation of the security zone in southern Lebanon (SZ) from its presence on the Golan Heights, which Israel had captured in 1967. When the President met the UN Secretary-General in June, he was adamant that Israel must evacuate both. Syria's presence in Lebanon had also led to arrests of Syrian exiles or refugees there. Under what was believed to be French pressure, the Syrians released many but not all of these. The new Lebanese regime seemed likely to be less close to Syria than its predecessor (see V.2.v).

Rapprochement with Iraq continued. Both resented American policy in the Middle East, were at odds with Turkey and had complementary rather than conflicting economic interests. The two countries signed an agreement to reopen the Kirkuk-Banyas pipeline, increase its capacity and establish a new refinery on the Syrian coast. Dues at Syria's Mediterranean ports were reduced to encourage their use for trade from Iraq. A Syrian minister visited Baghdad, the first to do so for many years. There was a corresponding cooling with Jordan, not only because of the latter's relations with Israel and the United States, but also because each government accused the other of encouraging and arming its own dissidents. Amman protested that Syrians had attacked Jordan on a commercial television programme from Qatar. President Asad offered no public expression of sympathy for King Husain in his serious illness.

There was more friction with Turkey, partly for historical reasons, such as Turkey's continued occupation of Hatay (Alexandretta). Other factors were Turkey's increasingly friendly relations with Israel, its building of dams on the Euphrates which menaced Syria's water supply (another point where Syria had common interests with Iraq) and, above all, Syria's assistance to the Kurdish liberation movement, the PKK, including sheltering the Kurdish leader, Abdullah Öcalan. In October the Turks talked of attacking Syria if this support did not cease. Egypt and Iran intervened and in late October Syria and Turkey made an agreement whereby Syria undertook to expel 3,000 of the PKK fighters, including Mr Öcalan himself, and promised not to support the PKK materially or allow it to use Syria as a basis for propaganda (see II.3.vii).

On 8 February the President's brother, Rifa'at Asad, was stripped of his nominal vice-presidency. From Geneva, his habitual base, he had reportedly been advocating a move away from dictatorship to pluralism and even a settlement with Israel. His son, Sawmar Asad, was running a satellite television station from London which had recently softened its tone towards his grandfather's regime and now appeared to be funded by the Saudi royal family. Another former pillar of the regime, General Hikmat Shihabi, was retired with comparative honour, while the head of military intelligence, Bashir Najjar, was simply dismissed.

Syria's most pressing economic problem was foreign debt. When a new trade agreement with Russia was signed in January there was also discussion of the estimated $10,000 to $12,000 million debt accumulated during years when Moscow regularly sold arms in exchange for influence. Russia now wanted its money back and was reported to be supplying Syria with short-range anti-tank rockets. Large sums were also owed to the World Bank, which said that Syria was faithfully keeping to the agreement of 1997 to repay loans, and to Germany, to which Syria owed $900 million, mostly incurred with the former East Germany.

An eminent Syrian poet, Nizar Qabbani, died in London on 21 March.

v. LEBANON

CAPITAL: Beirut   AREA: 10,000 sq km   POPULATION: 4,000,000 ('97)
OFFICIAL LANGUAGE: Arabic   POLITICAL SYSTEM: presidential, power-sharing
HEAD OF STATE & GOVERNMENT: President Émile Lahoud (since Nov '98)
RULING PARTIES: government of national unity
PRIME MINISTER: Salim al Hoss, Prime Minister (since Dec '98)
MAIN IGO MEMBERSHIPS (non-UN): AL, OIC, NAM, Francophonie
CURRENCY: Lebanese pound (end-'98 £1=L£2,516.42, US$1=L£1,512.50)
GNP PER CAPITA: US$3,350 by exchange-rate calculation, US$5,990 by PPP calculation ('97)

PRESIDENT Elias Hrawi had been in office for nine years, but the multi-millionaire Rafiq Hariri, Prime Minister since 1992, had been the dominant figure. Both were replaced in the autumn. The new President, General Émile Lahoud, was a respected soldier unlikely to follow his predecessor by accepting second place in the government, while the new Prime Minister, Salim al Hoss, had a reputation for integrity. Israel was still occupying Lebanese territory, with resulting frontier violence, and Syria still supervising Lebanese politics. Public finances still appeared sound but over-dependent on foreign borrowing, because of reluctance to impose adequate taxes.

In January the Israelis offered to return the large (850 square kilometres) part of south Lebanon—the so-called security zone (SZ)—which they had been occupying since 1982, still refusing, however, to return the Golan Heights to Syria. But neither Lebanese nor Syrians would negotiate only on the SZ or undertake to prevent Shia guerrillas from attacking Israeli territory. Meanwhile, Shia guerrillas continued to harry the Israeli occupation forces. The latter suffered smaller casualties than did their Lebanese opponents from Israeli air attacks, but the Israelis felt them more.

From January onwards there were Israeli suggestions for a unilateral Israeli withdrawal from Lebanon, but on condition that the Lebanese army manned the frontier, prevented guerrilla attacks across it, provided employment for the (Christian and pro-Israeli) South Lebanese Army (SLA), disarmed the Hizbullah and so on. The Syrian and Lebanese governments called repeatedly for simultaneous and unconditional withdrawal from the SZ and the Golan.

These demands were supported in April by the French, who offered to give asylum to the SLA leader, General Antoine Lahad. A minor proposal that the SLA should evacuate one largely Christian enclave was rejected on 26 September by Mr Hariri, who refused to agree that the government should act as border policeman while Israel and Lebanon were, technically, still at war. When faced with more violence during the autumn, Israeli Prime Minister Binyamin Netanyahu responded that it would not force an Israeli withdrawal. Some Israelis called for reprisals on Beirut. In December the US government urged restraint by Lebanon, Syria and Israel.

Despite the continued presence of the UN Interim Force in Lebanon (UNIFIL), whose mandate was twice renewed in 1998, violence in the south, around the SZ, continued and many lives were lost. More of these were Lebanese than Israeli. Reprisals from both sides followed: Israel's were more lethal. But casualties were taken more seriously by the Israeli public—the Israelis and their Lebanese allies were ready to exchange 60 prisoners for the body of one dead Israeli—and led to increasing pressure to give up the SZ. The year ended with the death of a mother and six children in an Israeli air raid on southern Lebanon, followed by retaliatory rocketing by Hizbullah. The leader of the Israeli Labour opposition now demanded withdrawal from the SZ.

President Hrawi had long wanted to resign. Local elections in May-June had shown unexpected support for the anti-government Hizbullah and reduced backing for the Prime Minister. General Émile Lahoud, the army chief of staff, was unopposed in the presidential election held in the Lebanese parliament on 15 October. Even before declaring his candidature, he was the favourite, being widely respected and enjoying Syrian support. His election was welcomed by the Maronites but criticized by the Druze leader, Walid Jumblatt, and by some pro-democracy organizations, who maintained that the constitution barred the election of serving officers.

General Lahoud was sworn in on 24 November. He promised to fight corruption, called for national unity to deal with economic problems and praised those fighting Israel in the south. His references to corruption and sectarian wheeler-dealing seemed to be criticism of the Hariri style. He nevertheless, on 27 November, asked the incumbent Prime Minister to form a new government; but Mr Hariri, nettled not to be unanimously supported by the deputies, effectively resigned on 30 November—a decision which the President at once accepted.

Two days later Salim al Hoss was overwhelmingly elected Prime Minister. His years in political life had not blemished his reputation for honesty. He said that priority must go to reducing public expenditure and indebtedness, which now exceeded Lebanon's gross domestic product, and promised to attend to the problems of those displaced by Israeli action and to liberate the occupied south. Keeping only two of the former ministers, he formed a cabinet combining technocrats with parliamentarians.

Accusations followed of corruption in the Hariri/Hrawi regime. Documents revealing embezzlement of public funds had vanished as Mr Hariri left office. Others dealt with the alleged illegal transfer of property to the giant development company Solidère. Legal provision had been made to discourage accusations of peculation.

There was continued preoccupation with the government's debts. Parliament approved in January a budget where revenue was only half of expenditure, the balance to be met by borrowing abroad. Kuwait, Saudi Arabia and the United Arab Emirates lent the central bank large sums at below market rates to help stabilize the Lebanese pound. American economic advisers warned of a financial crisis unless the budget deficit and public debt (now up to $12,900 million) were reduced. It was, as usual, politically difficult to impose—or practically to collect—income tax; but to replace it with a turnover tax would raise prices, warned the Finance Ministry. Meanwhile, official statistics showed average monthly income at only $132. There was another confrontation between government and trade unions over the salaries of civil servants.

The government's irritation with news broadcasts by private television stations (see AR 1997, p. 217) led in January to a complete ban. There was more, and more serious, trouble in the Beqa'a Valley (see AR 1997, p. 216) with a former Hizbullah leader, Shaikh Tufayli. Clashes between his supporters and government forces caused several deaths; Shaikh Tufayli himself disappeared. In the following month Muslim and Maronite clergy protested at the government's proposal to introduce civil marriage. So heated was the argument that the President publicly slapped the face of a journalist who had criticized this reform.

vi. IRAQ

CAPITAL: Baghdad   AREA: 438,000 sq km   POPULATION: 22,000,000 ('97)
OFFICIAL LANGUAGE: Arabic   POLITICAL SYSTEM: presidential
HEAD OF STATE & GOVERNMENT: President Saddam Husain (since July '79), also Prime
    Minister & Chairman of Revolutionary Command Council
RULING PARTY: Baath Arab Socialist Party
MAIN IGO MEMBERSHIPS (non-UN): AL, OPEC, OAPEC, OIC, NAM
CURRENCY: Dinar (end-'98 £1=ID0.52, US$1=ID0.31)
GNP PER CAPITA: n/a

THE history of Iraq in 1998 repeated that of 1997, being dominated by the conflict between President Saddam Husain and the British and American governments. Other governments in Europe and the Middle East were increasingly reluctant to follow the Anglo-Saxons, who now contemplated his forcible removal.

In December the US and UK governments finally acted, to disapproval or lack of support from many other states, including their allies in Europe and even from Arab governments in the Gulf. Anglo-Saxon bombing did not weaken Saddam's control over his own country, his subjects seeming even to rally to support him against this attack. It also raised his popularity with ordinary Arab people and sharpened their long-standing resentment against the Americans.

The first crisis came in January when Iraq prevented the US-dominated UN Special Committee on Iraq (UNSCOM) from carrying out inspections, alleging, not unfoundedly, that one of its American members was an Israeli spy. This member, Scott Ritter, admitted later that he had been cooperating with Israel to investigate Iraq. In February Iraq sent envoys round some of the Arab states and agreed to free all non-Iraqi Arab prisoners. The Vice-President, Tariq Aziz, said he had agreed with France, Russia and the Arab League to allow UN inspection of some extra sites under certain conditions.

Kofi Annan, the UN Secretary-General, visited Baghdad in February and Iraq and promised UNSCOM unrestricted access to presidential sites. Those inspecting the palaces would be accompanied by international worthies and the UN undertook to respect Iraq's legitimate concern for its dignity and security. On 25 March UN Security Council resolution 1154 endorsed Mr Annan's agreement but emphasized that Iraq must meet its obligations and threatened serious consequences if it did not (see also XI.1).

The Americans continued their military preparations and their contacts with the numerous but divergent groups of anti-Saddam exiles, who agreed that military action against Saddam should be avoided. Little help was to be expected from the Kurds (see below).

The UNSCOM chairman, Richard Butler, returned to Iraq in early August but left immediately when the Iraqis rejected his proposal for accelerated inspections. Tariq Aziz now accused the inspectors of serving US policy and denied again that Iraq retained any weapons of mass destruction. At the end of October the government announced that it would not cooperate with UNSCOM until the Security Council recognized Iraq's right to demand an end to sanctions, removed Mr Butler and reorganized UNSCOM.

On 5 November the UN Security Council condemned the Iraqi decision and demanded that Iraq resumed cooperation with the inspectors. Iraq refused and the inspectors left. The Americans sent another aircraft carrier to the Gulf and announced that there would be no ultimatum before they launched air strikes, a policy supported by Britain, which warned its nationals to leave Iraq. These Anglo-American moves received little support. Other permanent members of the Security Council—and other Arab states—called on Iraq to resume working with the inspectors but opposed the use of force. Arab public opinion broadly sympathized with the Iraqi people.

Iraq itself promised to respond to any diplomatic initiative but condemned the United States for killing Iraqis with sanctions and again described UNSCOM as a subsidiary of Israeli intelligence. However, on 15 November they suddenly readmitted the inspectors. President Clinton therefore countermanded air strikes but promised to intensify efforts to remove Saddam Husain and support the Iraqi opposition.

The Iraqi President was soon once more refusing to produce documents for the inspectors and blocking their access to Ba'ath party headquarters. Accordingly, Mr Butler declared that Iraq had not fulfilled its pledges of cooperation. By 16 December all the inspectors had left and US/UK aircraft began bombing Iraqi targets, continuing for four nights. Military targets in Baghdad and other places were bombed but the Anglo-Americans claimed that they had spared civilian targets. On 28 December US aircraft attacked an Iraqi military base which had fired on an American patrol.

Another sanction against Iraq was to limit its permitted oil exports to a certain level, the proceeds being divided between minimum necessary humanitarian supplies for Iraq itself and compensation to victims of Iraqi aggression; but the arrangement did not run smoothly. The Iraqis saw it as an encroachment on their liberty which became more burdensome as world oil prices suddenly fell: Iraq could not now, with its run-down oil industry, produce enough oil to earn the same number of dollars. When in early February the UN Secretary-General recommended a doubling of permitted exports, Iraq declared the proposal to be impracticable. In September the UN official running the 'oil-for-food' programme was forced to cut humanitarian supplies because the Iraqis lacked money to pay for them and resigned in frustration. In November the oil export quota was raised to $5,200 million, not enough to meet the costs involved.

Continental Europe was unenthusiastic about the Anglo-American line. The Arabs, even Saudi Arabia and Kuwait, which had suffered Iraqi aggression, were more critical. Their peoples were against action to overthrow the Iraqi government, most markedly in Jordan and the Israeli-occupied Palestinian territories, where there were noisy pro-Iraqi demonstrations.

Relations with Jordan were affected by the murder of Iraqi diplomats (see V.2.iii). The Kuwaitis had reason to detest Saddam, who had invaded them and still detained many Kuwaitis, but their government was uncomfortable with the presence of so many US and UK servicemen. Even Egypt, with its special links to the United States, was ill-at-ease. The Syrians were steadily becoming closer to Iraq. In July the two governments agreed to reopen the Banias pipeline to the Mediterranean and to build another, larger, one. The two governments were also brought together by their joint opposition to Turkey's distraining Euphrates water.

Relations with Iran improved, despite the murders in April of Iranian divines near the Shia Holy Cities in southern Iraq. The Foreign Minister visited Tehran in January to discuss the reciprocal return of prisoners-of-war, while in August a group of Iranian pilgrims came to Iraq, the first since 1980.

In Iraq itself, Saddam's grip on power seemed undiminished, even after the Anglo-American attack in December. He exercised it with his habitual brutality, though lurid stories from Iraqi exiles—for example, that 4,000 political prisoners had been gaoled below ground and that Iraq's prisons now held five times their capacity—could not be confirmed.

In Kurdistan, the two factions were too busy quarrelling with each other to trouble Baghdad much. The latter had indeed reached an understanding with one of them, Mustafa Barzani's Kurdish Democratic Party (KDP). The two rival Kurdish groups met in Washington in September but apparently failed to end the conflict between them.

3. SAUDI ARABIA—YEMEN—ARAB STATES OF THE GULF

i. SAUDI ARABIA

CAPITAL: Riyadh   AREA: c.2,000,000 sq km   POPULATION: 20,000,000 ('97)
OFFICIAL LANGUAGE: Arabic   POLITICAL SYSTEM: monarchy
HEAD OF STATE & GOVERNMENT: King Fahd ibn Abdul Aziz (since June '82), also Prime Minister
HEIR APPARENT: Crown Prince Abdullah ibn Abdul Aziz (since June '82), also First Deputy Prime Minister
MAIN IGO MEMBERSHIPS (non-UN): AL, OPEC, OAPEC, GCC, OIC, NAM
CURRENCY: riyal (end-'98 £1=SRls6.24, US$1=SRls3.75)
GNP PER CAPITA: US$6,790 by exchange-rate calculation ('97)

THE year opened for Saudi Arabia with the depressing realization that the collapse in oil prices was not going to improve in the short term and that the compromise reached in Jakarta in November 1997 by the Organization of the Petroleum Exporting Countries (OPEC), designed to control members' output (see AR 1997, p. 221), would not solve the crisis. Oil revenues in 1998 were expected to be 18 per cent lower than in 1997—an optimistic estimate as matters turned out. The Saudi draft budget seemed increasingly unrealistic, based as it was on average oil prices during the year of $14–$15 per barrel. The draft forecast a deficit of SR18,000 million despite revenue increases of 8 per cent to SR196,000 million and expenditure rises of 8.5 per cent to SR178,000 million, with GDP growth cut to 2 per cent, compared with 7.1 per cent in 1997.

In response to weakening oil prices, Saudi oil production rose in February towards the country's 8.4 million barrels per day (b/d) quota. At the same time, Oil Minister Ali al-Naimi indicated that the kingdom would be prepared to consider cutting back on output to improve the price situation. In March, in a surprise initiative to support oil prices, Saudi Arabia joined with Venezuela and Mexico in a move intended to remove 2 million b/d from world oil markets. Under the so-called 'Riyadh pact', Saudi

Arabia was to cut back production by 300,000 b/d, Venezuela by 100,000 b/d and Mexico by 1 million b/d. Iran later accepted the Saudi proposals over cuts at an OPEC meeting in Jakarta.

Despite these moves, however, the full force of the recession hit the kingdom in mid-year. By then crude prices were 32 per cent lower than a year earlier and oil and gas liquids income was 25 per cent below budget estimates. The budget deficit was expected to hit $10,000 million and the current account deficit $11,000 million with GDP growth virtually stagnant at 0.3 per cent. In a desperate move to contain the damage, the Kingdom, along with Iran, persuaded its OPEC partners in June to make production cuts of 2.6 million b/d which would last until June 1999 in the hope of removing the market production overhang with non-OPEC cooperation. The Oil Minister also suggested that the time had come to create an informal group of the seven-to-nine major world oil producers who would seek to respond quickly to market over-supply in future.

Saudi Arabia had little room for manœuvre over the crisis. There was little freedom for budget cuts, since 85 per cent of current budgetary expenditure was directed towards maintenance costs, while significant tax increases or subsidy cuts were considered to politically risky. Nor could the capital budget be easily cut, because it was the motor of the economy. It was decided to privatize the telecommunications sector and the Saudia national airline, a single telecommunications company being created in April as a first step. The Saudi Telecommunications Company, in which the state would eventually have only a 20 per cent holding, was expected to have annual revenues of $16,000 million and was to be upgraded by IT&T prior to privatization at a cost of $4,300 million. At the same time, the Saudi Basic Industries Corporation (SABIC) pushed ahead with planned expansions, despite a 25 per cent profits fall in the first quarter of the year, in order to catch the expected Asian rebound.

Although the private sector could offer little hope of salvation in the short term, in a speech to the Jiddah chamber of commerce in April King Fahd called for it to become the prime mover in economic regeneration, with a growth rate of 4 per cent per year (compared with an overall annual rate of 1 per cent). He highlighted the need to increase the number of Saudis employed in the private sector, and legislation soon followed to force firms to accept a 5 per cent Saudi participation level in their workforces, rising to 10 per cent in 1999. Illegal migrants—an estimated 250,000 out of 3 million in the Eastern Provinces alone—were arrested. The King had also called for diversification away from oil dependence, but the major private-sector activities, such as petrochemicals and basic industrial goods, were severely hit by the economic crisis in Asia.

In the meantime, it was clear that the Saudi banking system would have to cover government revenue shortfalls with additional lending. By mid-1998 25 per cent of the sector's asset base of $99,000 million had been lent to government and, given the fact that bank profits continued to rise, there were also hopes that the $470,000 million in Saudi funds invested abroad might soon be attracted home. In an additional move to ease the crisis—by now the government was paying contractors late and issuing bonds to raise funds—a 10 per cent across-the-board cut on contracts in force was decreed, together with a freeze on new contracts, increases in the domestic prices of petrol, water and electricity, and a minor tax move on foreign travel which was expected to raise $85 million annually. Government debt had risen to 100 per cent of GDP, compared with 79 per cent in 1997; the budget deficit had reached SR50,000 million ($13,200 million) and was now equivalent to 10 per cent of GDP.

Despite these moves, the crisis continued, and at the end of August international currency speculators moved against the riyal, hoping to force a Saudi devaluation for the first time since 1986. They had noted the worsening revenue position and the fact that imports had continued to rise—by 12 per cent in the first half of 1998 compared with the same period in 1997. Anxieties over King Fahd's health made the situation worse, and the Saudi government had to spend $1,000 million in fighting off the speculators. Although this eased the short-term crisis, anxieties persisted that government action was inadequate to contain the crisis, as Moody's credit rating agency downgraded Saudi external debt holdings, together with those of three banks. Nonetheless, by the end of the year plans for privatization were in full swing, with the electricity sector to be added to telecommunications, despite the likely job losses.

Problems also existed in the field of foreign affairs, with Saudi Arabia being unwilling to support planned UK-US bombing actions against Iraq in February or the actual operation carried out in December (see V.2.vi), although facilities for aircraft operating the no-fly zone in southern Iraq were maintained. Relations with the United States worsened further in May when the Saudi Interior Minister, Prince Nayef, made it clear that the Kingdom did not accept American theses that the al-Khobar bombing in 1996 was the work of Iranian agents or sympathizers, arguing instead that Saudi nationals had been responsible. Claiming that they had been denied cooperation by the Saudi authorities, FBI agents in the Kingdom were withdrawn in consequence.

In a further move that irritated Washington, the former Iranian President, Ali Akbar Rafsanjani, visited the Kingdom at the start of March to cement the improved relations symbolized by Crown Prince Abdullah's visit to Tehran in November 1997 (see AR 1997, pp. 220, 400). He brought a large delegation, including the Iranian Oil Minister, and extended his stay in order to visit the Shia-dominated Eastern Provinces. Caution remained over the new relationship and Iran's ambitions of regional hegemony, however, and the Saudi government responded to Iranian suggestions of a non-aggression pact by arguing that the Iranian-UAE dispute would have to be resolved first. The former Iranian President's visit was followed by one from the pro-Khatami Iranian Interior Minister, Abdullah

Nouri, and in late May by a visit by the Saudi Foreign Minister to Tehran, where he signed a cooperation agreement and sought expanded economic contacts.

Relations with Yemen worsened during the year, as Saudi Arabia laid claim to islands in the Red Sea, and there were also incidents along the land border between the two countries in July (see V.3.ii).

In domestic terms, Crown Prince Abdullah was able to reassert his position, particularly after King Fahd had two minor operations in July. However, given the Crown Prince's age and tensions among the king's full brothers—the so-called 'Sudairi Seven'—his succession could only introduce a transitional regime. In November the Crown Prince made a month-long world tour which took him to Britain, France and the United States. His visit was accompanied by rumours that the Saudi government was now ready to allow American oil companies to invest in the Saudi upstream oil sector. In the event, this turned out to be incorrect and only downstream opportunities were made available—to considerable disappointment.

In May the two British nurses convicted in September 1997 of murdering a colleague in Dhahran in 1996 (see AR 1997, pp. 220–1) were released from prison and allowed to fly home, after their sentences had been commuted by King Fahd. In December one of them, Lucille McLauchlan, was found guilty by a Scottish court of theft from a patient and forgery committed before she went to work in Saudi Arabia.

The annual *haj* month was marred by an accident in which 118 pilgrims were crushed to death in a stampede in Mina (near Mecca) on 9 April. Unofficial sources put the death toll at 180. The incident recalled a similar disaster in 1994, when 270 persons died (see AR 1994, p. 237). During the past 23 years, some 3,000 persons had died during the *haj*, from which Saudi Arabia earned around $1,600 million a year. In 1998 the habitual Iranian political demonstrations which had marred past pilgrimages were completely absent, thus suggesting that a sea-change has occurred in the Kingdom's relations with its largest regional partner—or rival.

ii. YEMEN

CAPITAL: Sana'a   AREA: 540,000 sq km   POPULATION: 16,000,000 ('97)
OFFICIAL LANGUAGE: Arabic   POLITICAL SYSTEM: presidential
HEAD OF STATE & GOVERNMENT: President (Gen.) Ali Abdullah Saleh (since May '90)
RULING PARTY: General People's Congress (GPC)
PRIME MINISTER: Abdulkarim al-Iryani (since April '98)
MAIN IGO MEMBERSHIPS (non-UN): AL, OIC, NAM
CURRENCY: Yemeni rial (end-'98 £1=YRls227.39, US$1=YRls136.68)
GNP PER CAPITA: US$270 by exchange-rate calculation, US$720 by PPP calculation ('97)

FOR Yemen, the year was dominated by continuing tensions with Saudi Arabia over their common border and by a worsening economic situation compounded by a government crisis. On 24 April the Yemeni Premier, Faraj Said bin Ghanem, resigned and was replaced on a temporary basis by the Deputy Premier and Foreign Minister, Abdulkarim al-Iryani. There had been tensions between the former Premier and President Ali Abdullah Saleh over proposed government changes and the economic reform programme. In the event, the new Premier, who was soon confirmed in his post, introduced a new cabinet which was substantially the same as its predecessor and the reform programme continued on track. All cabinet members except for the holders of the health and religious affairs portfolios were members of the President's ruling party, the General People's Congress (GPC). The government crisis came in the wake of a rift between the two former coalition parties, the GPC and the Islah Party, over the IMF-sponsored budget and the proposed privatization programme.

The domestic scene continued to be difficult, with five leaders of the South Yemen secessionist movement in the 1994 civil war being sentenced to death *in absentia* by a Sana'a court in late March. At the start of the following month, either in reaction to the sentences or because of more local grievances, bombs exploded in the diplomatic quarter of the capital. More bombs exploded in late May and early June in the south of the country, causing several deaths. It was not clear whether these were politically motivated or part of widespread protests at 40 per cent price rises caused by the IMF-proposed removal of subsidies on food and petrol prices in June, which caused demonstrations in Sana'a, Taiz, Ibb and Marib. There were other bombs in Aden in September and, in November, a bomb exploded outside the German embassy in Sana'a, although it was not clear that the embassy was the intended target.

In what was certainly a local issue, a British family on their way to Sana'a airport were held ransom by local tribesmen, being released only on 3 May after mediation. The Yemeni Consultative Council met at the start of May to discuss what should be done about the rash of kidnappings—there had been 21 in 1997 and 16 to date in 1998. It decided on much tougher action, culminating in July in a new law imposing the death penalty for kidnapping. Three British journalists in Yemen were arrested for illegal filming and were only released after diplomatic intervention in June. More tragically, a group of nuns were killed in July by what the government claimed were 'deranged extremists'.

Right at the end of the year four tourists (including three Britons) died when Yemeni security forces tried to rescue a group of 16 Western tourists who had been kidnapped by tribesmen in the southern Abyan province the day before. Amid uncertainty as to the motives of the kidnappers, the UK government strongly condemned the premature use of force and called for a full investigation into the exact circumstances of the deaths.

Relations with Saudi Arabia, which began well with the renewal of migration visas for Yemenis in May (for the first time since the end of the Gulf War in 1991), soon deteriorated over the longstanding border dispute between the two countries. Although two-thirds of the border had been agreed, attention shifted to the Red Sea, where Saudi Arabia occupied islands claimed by Yemen and forced out the resident population. In part, this was motivated by a Saudi desire to prevent Yemen supporting Ethiopia in its border dispute with Eritrea (see VI.1.i). In July Saudi forces shelled the islands in dispute, killing three Yemenis, one week after Saudi forces had crossed the land border—at a time when the Yemeni government was already engaged in pacification operations against local tribes enjoying Saudi backing in their struggle against the central government. Despite protests from the Yemeni President, the two sides eventually agreed in August to seek a peaceful solution to their differences.

On a happier note, on 1 November Yemen took over control of the majority of the Hanish archipelago islands which had been claimed and occupied by Eritrea in 1995 (see AR 1995, pp. 221, 241; 1996, p. 239), as a result of an award made on 9 October by an arbitration tribunal of the International Court of Justice. The procedure adopted by the two parties to this dispute was a pointer to the way in which Yemen's dispute with Saudi Arabia might eventually be solved.

iii. ARAB STATES OF THE GULF

United Arab Emirates
CONSTITUENTS: Abu Dhabi, Dubai, Sharjah, Rasal-Khaimah, Fujairah, Umm al-Qaiwin, Ajman
FEDERAL CAPITAL: Abu Dhabi   AREA: 77,000 sq km   POPULATION: 3,000,000 ('97)
OFFICIAL LANGUAGE: Arabic   POLITICAL SYSTEM: federation of monarchies
HEAD OF STATE: Shaikh Zayad bin Sultan al-Nahayyan (Ruler of Abu Dhabi), President of UAE (since Dec '71)
HEAD OF GOVERNMENT: Shaikh Maktoum bin Rashid al-Maktoum (Ruler of Dubai), Vice-President and Prime Minister of UAE (since Nov '90)
MAIN IGO MEMBERSHIPS (non-UN): AL, OPEC, OAPEC, GCC, OIC, NAM
CURRENCY: dirham (end-'98 £1=Dh6.11, US$1=Dh3.67)
GNP PER CAPITA: US$17,360 by exchange-rate calculation ('97)

Kuwait
CAPITAL: Kuwait   AREA: 18,000 sq km   POPULATION: 1,640,000 ('97)
OFFICIAL LANGUAGE: Arabic   POLITICAL SYSTEM: monarchy
HEAD OF STATE: Shaikh Jabir al-Ahmad al-Jabir al-Sabah (since Dec '77)
HEAD OF GOVERNMENT: Crown Prince Shaikh Saad al-Abdullah as-Salim as-Sabah, Prime Minister (since Feb '78)
MAIN IGO MEMBERSHIPS (non-UN): AL, OPEC, OAPEC, GCC, OIC, NAM
CURRENCY: dinar (end-'98 £1=KD0.50, US$1=KD0.30)
GNP PER CAPITA: US$22,110 by exchange-rate calculation, US$24,270 by PPP calculation ('97)

Oman

CAPITAL: Muscat   AREA: 300,000 sq km   POPULATION: 2,200,000 ('97)
OFFICIAL LANGUAGE: Arabic   POLITICAL SYSTEM: monarchy
HEAD OF STATE & GOVERNMENT: Shaikh Qaboos bin Said (since July '70)
MAIN IGO MEMBERSHIPS (NON-UN): AL, GCC, OIC, NAM
CURRENCY: rial (end-'98 £1=OR0.64, US$1=OR0.39)
GNP PER CAPITA: US$4,950 by exchange-rate calculation, US$8,690 by PPP calculation ('97)

Qatar

CAPITAL: Doha   AREA: 11,400 sq km   POPULATION: 675,000 ('97)
OFFICIAL LANGUAGE: Arabic   POLITICAL SYSTEM: monarchy
HEAD OF STATE & GOVERNMENT: Shaikh Hamad bin Khalifa al-Thani (since June '95)
MAIN IGO MEMBERSHIPS (non-UN): AL, OPEC, OAPEC, GCC, OIC, NAM
CURRENCY: riyal (end-'98 £1=QR6.06, US$1=QR3.64)
GNP PER CAPITA: US$11,570 by exchange-rate calculation ('97)

Bahrain

CAPITAL: Manama   AREA: 685 sq km   POPULATION: 619,000 ('97)
OFFICIAL LANGUAGE: Arabic   POLITICAL SYSTEM: monarchy
HEAD OF STATE: Shaikh Isa bin Sulman al-Khalifah (since Dec '61)
HEAD OF GOVERNMENT: Shaikh Khalifa bin Sulman al-Khalifa, Prime Minister (since Jan '70)
MAIN IGO MEMBERSHIPS (non-UN): AL, OAPEC, GCC, OIC, NAM
CURRENCY: dinar (end-'98 £1=BD0.63, US$1=BD0.38)
GNP PER CAPITA: US$7,820 by exchange-rate calculation ('97)

FOR the Arab states of the Gulf, the year was marked by the chronic and worsening state of world oil prices. The result was to be widening budget deficits and stagnation in economic growth. In Oman, the January draft budget forecast a deficit of OR295 million ($766 million)—an increase of OR32 million over the previous year—even though the current five-year plan had predicted the disappearance of the budget deficit by 2001. The Kuwaiti budget draft was placed before the National Assembly in April and approved in August despite a deficit of KD1,733 million ($5,700 million) compared with KD1,273 million in 1997. When the 10 per cent of revenues committed annually to the Kuwaiti Fund for Future Generations was included, the gross deficit rose to KD2,163 million. Qatar's budget, in the same month, anticipated a budget deficit of QR3,310 million ($910 million), an increase of 10 per cent over the previous year.

The UAE's February budget draft, which was approved in July, was out-of-date by the time it was approved and optimistically set the anticipated deficit at only AD1,750 million ($479 million). Oil revenues represented 80 per cent of UAE budget revenues, even though the oil sector provided only 31 per cent of GDP; the projected budget deficit of BD80 million ($210.5 million) for 1998 was equivalent to 3 per cent of GDP. Bahrain, the Gulf state least affected by oil price declines, nevertheless depended on oil income for 55 per cent of its budgetary revenues.

These worsening budget figures were paralleled throughout the year by declines in economic activity and growing cutbacks in public expenditure, as general budgetary assumptions based on oil price averages of $15 per barrel proved too optimistic. Kuwait's economic downturn was typified by the decline in its stock exchange activity, as was the situation in Oman, where the stock exchange lost 37 per cent of its value in the first six months of the year, compared with a rise of 141 per cent in 1997. Foreign concern over the situation was typified by an IMF report on the Omani economy. Although the report praised Oman's economic management and response to the oil price crisis, it expressed anxieties over medium-to-long-term strategy. It called for accelerated privatization, liberalization of foreign investment restrictions and diversification away from oil dependence, which had increased from 75 per cent in 1992 to 77 per cent in 1997. Nonetheless, Oman pressed ahead with its application for World Trade Organization membership.

Moody's rating agency added to the gloom at the end of the year by predicting a bleak 1999 for Bahrain despite the fact that the country was not oil dependent and was a key financial centre for the region, with 45 offshore banks, 32 investment banks, 40 representative foreign bank offices and 19 commercial banks. Those financial institutions dealing with Asia, however, experienced difficult times throughout 1998.

The decline in oil prices brought cuts in capital expenditures throughout the region. For example, Qatar made a 35 per cent cut, although projects connected with the North Field gas exploitation, on which Qatar's future success depended, were left untouched—indeed, manufacturing investment had risen by 4 per cent in 1997. Since Qatar's foreign debt reached $10,070 million in 1998, or 100.6 per cent of GDP, it sought unsuccessfully to raise a $500 million bond issue in mid-year and anticipated raising $1,000 million over the year to cover the costs of these developments. In Abu Dhabi, 35 per cent of planned investment for the 1998-2000 period was postponed.

The effects of the oil price crisis were also seen in GDP declines—from 8 per cent to 1.2 per cent between 1996 and 1997 in the UAE, for example, with growth anticipated to be even lower in 1998 as re-export trade to Iran and the gold trade to India declined. In Oman, the forecast GDP growth of 4.5 per cent for 1998 was over-optimistic despite 20 per cent reductions in government expenditure; its public sector contributed only 38 per cent of overall GDP, the lowest level in the Gulf. Public sector spending in Kuwait was cut by 25 per cent.

Attempts were made during the year to start major privatization programmes, but only Qatar was able to privatize 45 per cent of its telecommunications industry, Q-Tel. In Kuwait a similar move was stalled in the National Assembly. In the UAE, after a collapse of 12 per cent in unofficial share trading at the start of the year, a law to regulate an official stock exchange was promulgated towards the end of the year, making the Emirates the last Gulf state to open an official exchange. Despite this difficulty, the UAE maintained its reputation as the second-largest regional arms purchaser, after Saudi Arabia, with 25 per cent of total expenditure up to 2001 being committed to this purpose.

The UAE hosted three arms shows during the year and, despite its traditional closeness to France, in May purchased 80 US F-16 fighters from Lockheed-Martin at a cost of $8,000 million, despite furious Iranian protests. The country was able to cover the costs from earnings of $10,000 million annually on its foreign investments of $150,000 million. The purchase was also designed to balance the 30 Mirage fighter-bombers purchased from France in December 1997 at a cost of $3,200 million. In Qatar, a visit by French Defence Minister Alain Richard in late 1998 to renew a 1994 defence agreement was accompanied by joint exercises between Qatari and French forces, as well as a gift of ten AMX tanks from France. Qatar rejected a US attempt to persuade it to purchase an American missile defence system, preferring, instead, to consider the purchase of France's Leclerc main battle tank, 36 of which had already been sold to the UAE. The French Premier was expected to visit Qatar in 1999.

In the political sphere, Bahrain experienced the retirement in February of its veteran head of security, Ian Henderson, and his replacement by Shaikh Khalid bin Mohamed al-Khalifah, a member of the ruling family. In December six persons accused of sabotage, arms smuggling and the possession of explosives were arrested amidst fears of renewed political instability. The alleged leader, Suhail Mahdi Shehadi, was a Shia Lebanese who had organized the training of his five colleagues in southern Lebanon, apparently in the wake of the murder of a Bahraini security official in Lebanon in July 1998. Although violence continued sporadically during the year, with attacks on shops predominating, most of the victims were not Bahraini citizens, suggesting that violence was now stimulated by economic competition rather than because of continuing Shia-Sunni tensions, as in past years.

Elsewhere in the Gulf, political circumstances improved. Although in February three nationals were convicted of involvement in the 1996 coup attempt against the Emir in Qatar (see AR 1996, p. 223), following the trial of 100 persons which had opened in November 1997 (see AR 1997, p. 225), greater political freedoms were also authorized. In July a law enabling municipal elections under universal suffrage was passed, and in mid-November a committee was appointed to draw up a new permanent constitution involving a parliament also elected by universal franchise. Meanwhile, the life of the Consultative Council was extended in June until 2002.

Tensions developed in Kuwait in January when the Prime Minister refused to accept the resignation of the Deputy Premier and Oil Minister, Abdullah al-Roudhan, who had been questioned by the National Assembly in November 1997 over state corruption. (He was eventually allowed to resign in November.) In mid-April the situation worsened when the entire cabinet resigned to avoid a National Assembly no-confidence vote called by the Islamist faction and directed against the Information Minister, who was accused of having allowed 'un-Islamic' books to appear at the Kuwait book fair the previous year. The Prime Minister was immediately reinstated by the Emir, and the former Interior Minister was given the oil portfolio in the new cabinet. More trouble occurred in June when the Islamists in the Assembly tried to cross-examine the Interior Minister, who was alleged to be implicated in drugs and human rights abuses. The interior portfolio was traditionally in the Emir's sovereign gift, as were the premiership and the defence and foreign affairs portfolios. He rejected the Assembly's initiative and called on the Assembly Speaker to ensure that government and Assembly should 'work together'.

In foreign affairs, the year was dominated by American initiatives to maintain the policy of 'dual containment'. In February, the Anglo-American threat to bomb Iraq for hindering UN weapons inspections failed to find any support amongst Gulf states, although Kuwait agreed to pay the costs of the associated military preparations. Qatar, indeed, even sent a representative to Baghdad to discuss the matter, in a deliberate snub to American sensibilities. The Gulf states, nevertheless, repeatedly called on Iraq to avoid unnecessary tension by complying with UN demands, in the wake of the compromise negotiated in February by the UN Secretary-General, Kofi Annan. The Iraqi failure to comply meant that the Anglo-American attacks on Iraq in December (see V.2.vi) were not condemned by Gulf states, even though none of them, except for Kuwait, participated in or facilitated the Anglo-American action.

In relations with Iran, the Gulf states increasingly ignored American preferences. In early March the former Iranian President, Ali Akbar Rafsanjani, visited Bahrain as part of the ongoing Iranian attempt to improve relations with the Gulf states, before going on to Saudi Arabia (see V.3.i). Although further tensions were avoided by a visit to the UAE in late May by the Iranian Foreign Minister, Kamal Kharrazi, no progress towards resolving the Abu Musa and Tunbs islands disputes between the UAE and Iran was made during the year.

The Qatar-Bahrain maritime boundary dispute, now being considered by the International Court of Justice at The Hague, was envenomed in April when Qatar was accused of submitting forged documents to the Court. At the end of the year Qatar withdrew the documents in question. Qatar's relations with Egypt also worsened early in the year after Egyptians employed in the public sector in Qatar were suddenly forced to leave their jobs. In March, however, relations improved after 700 of those dismissed were offered compensation.

4. SUDAN—LIBYA—TUNISIA—ALGERIA—MOROCCO—WESTERN SAHARA

i. SUDAN

CAPITAL: Khartoum   AREA: 2,500,000 sq km   POPULATION: 29,000,000 ('97)
OFFICIAL LANGUAGE: Arabic   POLITICAL SYSTEM: Islamist/military regime
HEAD OF STATE & GOVERNMENT: President (Gen.) Omar Hasan Ahmed al-Bashir (since Oct '93), previously Chairman of Revolutionary Command Council (since June '89)
RULING PARTY: National Islamic Front (NIF)
MAIN IGO MEMBERSHIPS (non-UN): AL, OAU, COMESA, OIC, ACP, NAM
CURRENCY: dinar (end '98 £1=D326.01, US$1=D196.00)
GNP PER CAPITA: US$280 by exchange-rate calculation ('97)

THE major event of the year was the missile attack on 20 August on the Al-Shifa pharmaceutical factory in Khartoum by the United States on the grounds that it produced nerve gas. This came as a retaliation to the suspected involvement of Sudan's National Islamic Front (NIF) regime in the bombing of the American embassies in Nairobi (Kenya) and Dar es Salam (Tanzania), where a number of Sudanese were arrested (see VI.1.ii; VI.1.iii). The Al-Shifa plant was assumed to have been built with financial assistance from Osama bin Laden, who was implicated in the bombing of the two embassies, but doubts were raised as whether the US strike had destroyed the right factory.

In February the US government had claimed that Iraq had been helping Sudan in the development of chemical weapons since 1991. Sudan insisted that the Al-Shifa factory was producing half of Sudan's medicine needs and that it possessed no chemical weapons, though opposition groups claimed otherwise. Sudan sought the help of the international community to condemn the United States, but the United Nations rejected a Sudanese request for an investigation into the US attack. In light of the UK government's strong support for the strike, the British embassy in Khartoum was stoned and all staff were withdrawn, while Sudan withdrew its ambassador in London. The United States renewed the economic sanctions imposed on Sudan in 1997 (see AR 1997, p. 230) and urged the Khartoum regime to cut its links with Osama bin Laden and renounce terrorism.

In August President Mubarak of Egypt met leaders of the opposition National Democratic Alliance (NDA), who were attending a meeting in Cairo, and urged them to end the civil war in the south. The leaders rejected an offer by the government to return to Sudan, since they suspected the intentions of the regime in introducing a multi-party democracy. Eritrea continued to be the base from which the NDA and its armed-wing, the Sudan Alliance Force (SAF), operated. The SAF engaged government forces near the towns of Kassala and Gadarif in eastern Sudan. The spate of bombing in Khartoum in August was attributed to the NDA, though it denied involvement.

The rapprochement between Egypt and Sudan continued when their Foreign Ministers met on 12–13 January to normalize relations. Sudan agreed to return seized Egyptian properties and to resume shipping services in Lake Nasser. The inclusion of Egypt in November as a member of the Inter-Governmental Authority for Development (IGAD) was not welcomed by the Sudan People's Liberation Army (SPLA) because of Egypt's opposition to self-determination for people in the south.

Sudan's relations with neighbouring African countries were strained. Eritrea and Sudan accused each other of shelling border areas, efforts by Qatar and Libya to mediate producing no settlement of differences. Sudan accused Ethiopia of exerting pressure when the latter demanded in February a review of its treaty with Sudan and Egypt on the use of Nile waters. In April Uganda put its forces on alert on the border with Sudan to prevent the Sudan-based Ugandan opposition group, the Lord's Resistance Army (LRA), from crossing into the country (see also VI.1.iv). It was reported that the LRA was fighting against the SPLA, alongside Sudanese government troops. Reports in November suggested that Sudanese troops were to be found in the Democratic Republic of the Congo in support of President Laurent Kabila. This intervention was apparently aimed at Ethiopia, Uganda, Eritrea and the SPLA, which all supported the forces opposed to President Kabila. As a result of the Congo conflict, southern Sudanese refugees living there started to flow back to Sudan.

A number of towns and military garrisons in southern Sudan changed hands between central government troops and the SPLA. In December guards at the home of the SPLA leader, Colonel John Garang, and the offices of the Sudan Relief and Rehabilitation Association in Nairobi foiled attacks by armed men thought to be loyal to dissident SPLA commander Kerubino Kuanyin Bol. Representatives of the SPLA and the government met in May to discuss self-determination in the south, but further talks held in August collapsed without agreement on important issues such as boundaries and religion. In July Derek Fatchett, the British Foreign Office Minister of State, succeeded in securing a three-month truce between the government and the SPLA in order to allow vital aid supplies into areas affected by the civil war. The government in September closed universities in order to send students to fight in the south. Compulsory conscription into the army continued to be resented, and in April over 200 young people were either drowned or gunned down in an attempt to escape from their military training camp south of Khartoum.

In November the government and the SPLA separately renewed the ceasefire and agreed to facilitate the work of convoys. Care International, Oxfam UK, Médecins Sans Frontières, the Save the Children Fund, the NDA and the government all urged the UN Security Council to take an effective role in ending the civil war. The severity of the famine in Bahr el Ghazal prompted the UN World Food Programme's 'Operation Lifeline Sudan' to start airdrops of necessary supplies to affected areas, while the Red Cross resumed aid operation in the south. Public appeals in Britain to help the victims of the famine raised $3.2 million and the British government allocated $6.8 million. The civil war had always posed a threat to aid workers, and the year saw the killing of three Sudanese nationals attached to the Norwegian People's Aid Agency.

As a gesture of support for the regime, but to the disgust of non-Muslim people, Louis Farrakhan, leader of the US black separatist Nation of Islam, visited Sudan in January and urged non-Muslims to embrace Islam. A request by the UN Human Rights Commissioner to open an office in Sudan was turned down by the government.

The death in a plane crash on 12 February of the First Vice-President, Major-General Al-Zubair Muhammed Saleh, deprived the government of one of the leaders who played a key role in the 1989 military coup which brought the present regime to power. Ali Uthman Muhammed Taha, a powerful figure in the NIF, was appointed First Vice-President instead. The approval by referendum of a new constitution in March and the decision in November to reintroduce a multi-party system, banned since 1989, were viewed with caution by opposition groups.

The latest IMF review of Sudan's economic performance was encouraging, though it criticized the government's high level of military expenditure. Inflation had declined to 32 per cent by the beginning of the year, and Sudan continued to link its economic recovery with impending oil export. Contracts were signed with Chinese, Argentinian, British and German companies to construct the 1,600-kilometre petroleum pipeline from the south-west of the country to Basha'ir harbour on the Red Sea. Work was scheduled for completion in 1999. In October Canada's Talisman Energy completed the acquisition of Arakis Energy Corporation, which was involved in oil exploration and production in Sudan. The Inter-Church Coalition on Africa appealed to the Canadian Foreign Minister to bring in legislation making Sudanese oil operations difficult for Talisman.

In September a Nile flood, thought to be worse than that of 1988, devastated Northern State. It left many of the rural population homeless, destroying most of the farms by the banks of the river.

ii. LIBYA

CAPITAL: Tripoli   AREA: 1,760,000 sq km   POPULATION: 5,292,000 ('97)
OFFICIAL LANGUAGE: Arabic   POLITICAL SYSTEM: socialist 'state of the masses'
HEAD OF STATE: Col. Muammar Qadafi, 'Leader of the Revolution' (since '69)
HEAD OF GOVERNMENT: Mohammed Ahmed al-Manqoush, Secretary-General of General People's Committee (since Dec '97)
MAIN IGO MEMBERSHIPS (non-UN): AL, OPEC, OAPEC, AMU, OAU, OIC, NAM
CURRENCY: dinar (end-'98 £1=LD0.75, US$1=LD0.45)
GNP PER CAPITA: n/a

A resolution of the Lockerbie affair and the lifting of UN sanctions against Libya, in place since 1992, appeared to move a step closer by year's end. In

March the International Court of Justice ruled that it would hear Libya's complaints that the US and UK governments were acting unlawfully by insisting that the two Libyan suspects in the 1988 Lockerbie bombing should stand trial in Scotland or the USA. Libya claimed an important victory and won support from a growing number of countries in Africa and the Arab world but also in Europe for its proposal that the two suspects stand trial in a third country.

The USA and Britain continued to oppose Libya's proposal, and at its review session in March and again in July the UN Security Council decided to keep sanctions against Libya in place. In June, however, the Organization of African Unity resolved that from September its members would cease to comply with UN sanctions unless the USA and Britain agreed to a trial being held in a neutral third country, and authorized flights to Libya on humanitarian, religious or diplomatic missions with immediate effect. In the following months several African heads of state openly flouted the air embargo and flew directly to Libya for talks with Colonel Qadafi.

In late August the USA and Britain, faced with mounting diplomatic pressure, sought to regain the initiative and agreed to a trial of the two Libyan suspects in the Netherlands before a panel of Scottish judges and in accordance with Scottish law. Soon after the offer was made, the UN Security Council unanimously approved a resolution allowing the lifting of UN sanctions against Libya as soon as the two suspects were handed over for trial. The US however threatened to tighten sanctions to include a multilateral oil embargo should Libya reject the new offer.

Colonel Qadafi gave a cautious welcome to the proposal, but the Libyan authorities later asked for negotiations about the terms of a trial in the Netherlands. The USA and Britain made it clear that their offer was non-negotiable but agreed to clarify any technical or legal points through the office of the UN Secretary-General. The Libyan government also appointed a new high-level legal team to represent the two suspects, headed by a former Foreign Minister, suggesting to some observers that the interests of the Libyan regime rather than those of the accused would now be given priority. By the time Kofi Annan, the UN Secretary-General, visited Libya in early December, Colonel Qadafi had agreed to a trial in the Netherlands under Scottish law but a problem remained over US and British insistence that if convicted the two men must serve their sentences in a Scottish prison. The Libyan leader assured Mr Annan that he wished to see a final solution to the Lockerbie issue, and in mid-December, just before the tenth anniversary of the bombing, the General People's Congress, the country's highest legislative body, gave its approval to a trial in the Netherlands, a move which appeared to clear the way for the two men to be handed over. A Scottish legal expert and adviser to the families of UK victims of the bombing expressed serious doubts that the evidence against the two Libyan suspects was strong enough to secure a conviction.

After years of promoting the virtues of Arab unity, in September the official news agency announced that the General People's Committee for Unity had been abolished and emphasized that Libya belonged to the African continent. The change, which was possibly only a tactical move, reflected Colonel Qadafi's growing frustration with Arab countries for not giving Libya stronger support on the Lockerbie issue in marked contrast to the states of sub-Saharan Africa. Libya continued to promote closer relations with countries south of the Sahara, and in February initiated the Community of Sahel and Saharan States (Comessa) to promote economic, social and cultural exchanges. In his capacity as president of Comessa, Colonel Qadafi attempted to mediate in a number of African disputes but these initiatives had more symbolic value than substance.

More significant were improvements in relations with European countries, notably Italy, Libya's major trading partner. A wide-ranging accord was signed in Rome in July providing for joint infrastructure projects especially in the energy sector, and in which Italy expressed regrets for its colonial past. France and Libya agreed that the six Libyans implicated in the 1989 bombing of a French airliner over Niger could be tried *in absentia*.

On the domestic front the Islamist opposition remained active especially in the mountains east of Benghazi, and a number of successful arms raids led to speculation that the militant Islamist groups had infiltrated the security forces. Reports of an assassination attempt on the Libyan leader by Islamist extremists near Benghazi in late May were denied by the authorities but in the weeks that followed the security forces mounted a major offensive against Islamist strongholds in the north-eastern part of the country. A serious hip injury which Colonel Qadafi sustained in July could have resulted from another assassination attempt, although officially he suffered an accident while exercising. A decline in oil production and the dramatic fall in oil prices during the year aggravated the country's economic problems although projected state spending remained virtually unchanged.

iii. TUNISIA

CAPITAL: Tunis   AREA: 164,000 sq km   POPULATION: 9,200,000 ('97)
OFFICIAL LANGUAGE: Arabic   POLITICAL SYSTEM: presidential
HEAD OF STATE & GOVERNMENT: President (Gen.) Zayn al-Abdin Ben Ali (since Nov '87)
RULING PARTY: Constitutional Democratic Rally (RCD)
PRIME MINISTER: Hamid Qarwi (since Sept '89)
MAIN IGO MEMBERSHIPS (non-UN): AL, AMU, ICO, OAU, OIC, NAM, Francophonie
CURRENCY: dinar (end-'98 £1=D1.82, US$1=D1.09)
GNP PER CAPITA: US$2,090 by exchange-rate calculation, US$4,980 by PPP calculation ('97)

AT its congress in July the ruling party, the Rassemblement Constitutionnel Démocratique (RCD), endorsed Zayn al-Abdin Ben Ali's candidature for a third term in presidential elections due to take place in March 1999. In his speech to delegates the President emphasized his commitment to pursuing gradual change and to balancing economic liberalization with social justice and integrating Tunisia into the world economy without destroying its identity. Congress approved the government's decision to increase the proportion of seats in parliament allocated to opposition parties to 20 per cent at the next legislative elections, urged the party to develop stronger relations with non-governmental organizations and associations throughout the country, and agreed that it was necessary to press ahead with the programme of industrial modernization, reform of the country's financial system and efforts to increase both domestic and foreign investment.

Responding to the President's call for Tunisians to *'dépasser la mentalité d'assisté'*, congress recommended reforms to the welfare system which would require more affluent families to pay for their own health-care and for higher education. There was also support for the government's plan to reduce the cost of food subsidies and ensure that subsidies benefited those in greatest need. The RCD's central committee was enlarged from 200 to 236 members and the Foreign Minister, Said Ben Mustapha, was appointed to the party's political bureau.

Earlier in the year President Ben Ali had again rejected international criticism of the country's human rights record and insisted that there were no political prisoners in Tunisia. Criticism of Tunisia by human rights organizations continued. Activists in France demanded the release of Khemais Ksila, vice-president of the Ligue Tunisienne des Droits de l'Homme, sentenced to three years' imprisonment in February for issuing a statement accusing the government of using fear to eliminate dissent. Ignoring constitutional guarantees of freedom of speech, the sentence was later upheld by the appeal court.

A report by Article 19, the London-based anti-censorship organization, condemned press restrictions imposed by the Ben Ali regime and urged the European Union (EU) to put pressure on the Tunisian authorities to respect press freedoms. Tunisia's association agreement with the EU was formally implemented in March and at the first meeting of the EU-Tunisia Association Council in July, Wolfgang Schüssel, the Austrian Foreign Minister, indicated that as part of the political dimension of the agreement, the EU would wish to discuss its concerns over civil liberties in Tunisia.

In September the Brussels-based pressure group, Human Rights Watch, called on the European Parliament to send a clear message that the human rights performance of the Tunisian government fell far short of what was expected under the association agreement. In an open letter to MEPs the group stated that overall the human rights situation in Tunisia remained unchanged, that there were hundreds of political prisoners and that detainees were frequently tortured during interrogation.

Problems over fishing zones and illegal immigration again caused friction with Italy, Tunisia's main trading partner after France and an important source of foreign aid. After meeting President Ben Ali in Tunis in June, the Italian Prime Minister, Romano Prodi, insisted that these minor problems could easily be resolved, but the following month a sharp increase in illegal immigrants from Tunisia provoked an angry rebuke from the Italian Foreign Minister, Lamberto Dini, who accused the Tunisian authorities of not doing enough to stem the flow. The row quickly subsided and in August the two countries signed an accord under which Tunisia agreed to do more to prevent Tunisians entering Italy illegally and to take back those illegal immigrants apprehended by the Italian authorities in exchange for a substantial development aid package.

Reports in the early part of the year that Tunisia's close relations with Libya and Iraq and President Ben Ali's refusal to host the next economic conference on the Middle East and North Africa (MENA) had caused a rift in relations with the USA appeared to have been exaggerated. In June during a visit to Tunis the US Under-Secretary of State, Stuart Eizenstat, praised Tunisia as a 'model for the developing world' and proposed a new economic partnership with the United States to encourage structural change and to promote greater US investment. Although a Tunisian request for US military aid was not granted, the meeting of the Tunisian-US military committee, postponed in May, took place in September in Washington attended by the Defence Minister, Habib Ben Yahia, while the Minister for International Cooperation and Foreign Investment, Mohamed Ghannouchi, reported continued progress in economic cooperation with the USA, notably in the energy sector. The last diplomat at Tunisia's interests office in Tel Aviv was withdrawn and relations with Israel remained suspended.

iv. ALGERIA

CAPITAL: Algiers   AREA: 2,382,000 sq km   POPULATION: 29,000,000 ('97)
OFFICIAL LANGUAGE: Arabic   POLITICAL SYSTEM: quasi-military regime
HEAD OF STATE & GOVERNMENT: President (Brig.-Gen.) Liamine Zéroual (since Jan '94)
RULING PARTIES: National Democratic Rally (RND) heads coalition
PRIME MINISTER: Ismael Hamdani (since Dec '98)
MAIN IGO MEMBERSHIPS (non-UN): AL, OPEC, OAPEC, AMU, OAU, OIC, NAM
CURRENCY: dinar (end-'98 £1=DA101.07, US$1=DA60.75)
GNP PER CAPITA: US$1,490 by exchange-rate calculation, US$4,580 by PPP calculation ('97)

As the year opened, the horrific massacres of civilians continued with more than 1,300 men, women and children slaughtered during the holy month of Ramadan alone. International concern at the increasing scale of the violence led to the dispatch of a European Union (EU) delegation to Algiers in late January. Although the Algerian authorities reluctantly agreed to receive the mission, it achieved little of substance. The Algerian government continued to reject all offers of outside mediation or assistance for the victims of the violence and firmly to oppose any form of independent inquiry into the massacres. During meetings with the EU delegation, Algerian officials repeated their complaints that European governments were not doing enough to crack down on radical Islamist networks operating in EU member-states.

In the following months the security forces mounted a wave of offensives against Islamist strongholds and the authorities claimed that the Groupes Islamiques Armés (GIA) had sustained significant losses. Officials also pointed out that the ceasefire of the Armée Islamique du Salut (AIS) continued to hold and that the AIS had persuaded several smaller armed groups to declare a truce and seek a political solution to the conflict. The Islamist opposition remained deeply divided, however, and later in the year there were reports that the AIS was cooperating with the security forces against its GIA rivals. A number of European countries moved to arrest Algerians suspected of providing support for the GIA. In spite of claims by the Algerian authorities that the conflict was nearly over, massacres, ambushes and bomb attacks continued, although not on the scale experienced at the beginning of the year.

In April over 100 people—including policemen, leaders of self-defence groups armed by the government, and local government officials, among them two mayors and a member of the ruling Rassemblement Nationale Démocratique (RND)—were arrested in Relizane for alleged involvement in the massacre of civilians, providing confirmation that the regime and its supporters had been responsible for some of the recent atrocities. Those arrested were said to have been involved not only in eliminating suspected Islamists but in killings linked to criminal activities and tribal rivalries. While officials admitted that some abuses were committed by the security forces and their allies, they insisted that such incidents were rare. In July Algeria's ambassador to the UN told a meeting of the UN Human Rights Committee that his government rejected claims of state-sponsored killings.

Human rights groups continued to insist that the security forces were responsible for numerous extra-judicial executions of both individuals and groups of people, while the fate of the many *'disparus'* attracted growing international attention. A high-level UN fact-finding mission, led by Mario Soares, a former President of Portugal, visited Algeria in late July-early August with the stated objective of determining the severity of the crisis and ascertaining the country's human rights and economic situations. The six-member panel met with government officials, the military, opposition leaders (but not with the banned Front Islamique du Salut, FIS)) and women's groups, visited Algiers Serkadji prison, and sites of several massacres. Their report, released in September, avoided any condemnation of human rights abuses or proposals for dealing with the Islamist underground and was criticized by human rights groups for giving too much credence to the views of the Algerian government.

In early July the highly controversial Arabization law came into effect fuelling unrest in Berber-speaking Kabylia, a region already in turmoil after the assassination of the popular Berber singer and leading anti-Islamist, Lounes Matoub, at the end of June. While Kabyle-based political parties organized large peaceful demonstrations in Algiers to denounce '*la loi scélérate sur l'arabisation totalitaire*', rumours circulated about the emergence of Kabyle extremist groups committed to violent protest and separatism.

In a dramatic television address on 11 September, President Zéroual announced that he would stand down as head of state after new presidential elections to be held in early 1999, nearly two years before the end of his five-year term of office. It was generally agreed that General Zéroual, although also suffering from poor health, was being forced out following a particularly vicious round of infighting within the army high command. His announcement followed a series of vitriolic articles in sections of the press attacking General Mohamed Betchine, the President's closest political ally, and clearly aimed at the President himself. General Betchine resigned as presidential adviser in October along with the Justice Minister, Mohamed Adami, another of President Zéroual's allies. The episode was seen as a victory for the 'clan' led by the chief of staff, Lieut.-General Mohammed Lamari.

Ahmed Ouyahia, regarded by some as a possible presidential candidate, resigned as Prime Minister in mid-December and was succeeded by Ismail Hamdani, a career diplomat. In October Mr Ouyahia had stated that rising oil and gas production and steady foreign reserves would shield the economy from the sharp decline in world oil prices, at least until the end of the century; but this was little comfort to an embattled population facing rising levels of unemployment and falling living standards. Powerful commercial mafias linked to senior figures in the military continued to enrich themselves at the expense of the country's declining manufacturing sector.

v. MOROCCO

CAPITAL: Rabat   AREA: 460,000 sq km   POPULATION: 28,000,000 ('97)
OFFICIAL LANGUAGE: Arabic   POLITICAL SYSTEM: monarchy
HEAD OF STATE & GOVERNMENT: King Hassan II (since '61)
RULING PARTIES: Socialist Union of Popular Forces (USFP) heads broad coaliton
PRIME MINISTER: Abderrahmane Youssoufi (USFP), Prime Minister (since May '94)
MAIN IGO MEMBERSHIPS (non-UN): AL, AMU, OIC, NAM
CURRENCY: dirham (end-'98 £1=DH15.39, US$1=DH9.25)
GNP PER CAPITA: US$1,250 by exchange-rate calculation, US$3,130 by PPP calculation ('97)

ON 4 February King Hassan named Abderrahmane Youssoufi, the veteran leader of the Union Socialiste des Forces Populaires (USFP), the largest single party in the new wholly elected Chamber of Representatives (see AR 1997, p. 238), as Prime Minister. This was the first time that the King had chosen an opposition politician as Premier since he came to the throne in 1961. On 14 March, after weeks of difficult negotiations, Mr Youssoufi formed a coalition government in which 23 of its 41 members were from the opposition Al-Koutlah al-Democratiyya alliance (14 from the USFP, six from Istiqlal and three from the Parti du Renouveau et du Progrès (PRP)), three from two small opposition splinter parties (the Front des Forces Démocratiques and the Parti Socialiste Démocrate) and nine from two centre-right parties, the Rassemblement National des Indépendants (RNI) and the Mouvement National Populaire (MNP), which took six and three posts respectively.

Although hailed as the country's first *'gouvernement d'alternance'*, with opposition parties taking charge of the key areas of economic and social policy, six cabinet posts—interior, foreign affairs, justice, religious endowments and Islamic affairs, together with the Secretary-General of the Government and the Minister-Delegate for National Defence—were appointed directly by the King. Driss Basri, the long-serving and powerful Interior Minister remained in post and former Prime Minister Abdellatif Filali retained the foreign affairs and cooperation portfolio. Some opposition activists were quick to point out that not only the security services but also important networks of economic influence were outside the new Prime Minister's control, restricting his room to manœuvre.

The new government's programme, presented to parliament in mid-April, was adopted by a comfortable majority. Mr Youssoufi and his senior ministers outlined ambitious plans but stressed that they did not underestimate the gravity of the problems or the constraints confronting them. The Prime Minister stated that his mission was to promote the democratization of the country's social and political life, and pledged to raise standards of morality in public life, to promote transparency and openness in government, respect for the rule of law and for human rights, and to seek solutions through negotiation and consensus. He outlined a range of measures to tackle urgent social problems, in particular unemployment, illiteracy, acute deficiencies in basic health-care, schooling and housing provision, and to combat social inequalities and exclusion. Reform of public administration and the justice system would also be undertaken.

On the economy, the Prime Minister stated that it was vital to achieve strong and sustainable growth that would create new jobs. Improving the competitiveness of the productive sector, particularly industry, would be one of the government's priorities. A special effort was made to reassure the private sector and to establish a 'climate of confidence' between government and the business community, while calling for dialogue with the trade unions and promoting measures to reinforce the rights of employees. The privatization programme would be completed 'in transparency and speed' to raise funds for investment in infrastructure.

Mr Youssoufi immediately ordered all civil servants, cabinet ministers and MPs to disclose their wealth and private interests. The Justice Minister began the enormous task of reforming the justice system, bringing disciplinary charges against 50 magistrates, mainly on corruption charges. Budget allocations to the departments of solidarity and employment, health, housing, youth and sport, and culture were increased substantially. But several months after taking office, little progress had been made on human rights issues, including the case of exiled dissident Abraham Serfaty, whose dossier remained with the Interior Ministry.

In foreign affairs the new government paid customary lip-service to strengthening relations with other Maghreb countries, Arab-Islamic cooperation and support for the Middle East peace process, but its attention was focused primarily on the European Union. During Prime Minister Youssoufi's visit to France in early October the French government announced an extra aid package of $765 million and plans for a second debt-swap agreement between the two countries. Bilateral relations with Spain, Portugal and Italy were strengthened, and tough measures were introduced to curb illegal immigration to Europe.

vi. WESTERN SAHARA

CAPITAL: Al Aaiún   AREA: 252,000 sq km   POPULATION: 164,000 ('82)
STATUS: regarded by Morocco as under its sovereignty, whereas independent Sahrawi Arab Democratic Republic (SADR) was declared by Polisario Front in 1976

MOROCCO's new opposition-led government which took office in March (see V.4.v) declared that its overriding priority was closing the dossier on 'the Moroccan Sahara' by ensuring unambiguous international recognition of the kingdom's sovereignty over this part of its territory. Responsibility for the Western Sahara, however, remained firmly with the palace. In spite of the Houston agreement brokered in 1997 by UN Special Envoy James Baker (see AR 1997, p. 239), voter registration continued to be plagued by disputes and the process had not been completed by 31 May, the date set by Kofi Annan, the UN Secretary-General, for finalizing electoral lists.

In October it was reported that some 147,000 voters had been identified as eligible for the UN referendum on self-determination and accepted by both Morocco and the separatist movement, Polisario. But Morocco also insisted on the registration of another 65,000 members of three contested tribes on the basis that they were Sahrawis who had migrated to southern Morocco in the late 1950s to escape Spanish colonial rule. Although Polisario agreed to accept 4,000 members of the contested tribes as eligible to vote and was prepared to allow others to present themselves at UN voter registration centres on an individual basis, it accused Morocco of an attempt at mass registration and electoral fraud. There was growing impatience within the international community at Moroccan obstructionism. As attempts to resolve the latest dispute continued, the referendum rescheduled for December suffered yet another delay and was postponed until the second quarter of 1999. The Western Sahara issue remained a major source of tension between Morocco and Algeria because of the latter's support for Polisario.

VI EQUATORIAL AFRICA

1. HORN OF AFRICA—KENYA—TANZANIA—UGANDA

i. ETHIOPIA—ERITREA—SOMALIA—DJIBOUTI

Ethiopia
CAPITAL: Addis Ababa   AREA: 1,128,000 sq km   POPULATION: 60,000,000 ('97)
OFFICIAL LANGUAGE: Amharic   POLITICAL SYSTEM: presidential
HEAD OF STATE: President Negaso Gidada (since Aug '95)
RULING PARTIES: Ethiopian Peoples' Revolutionary Democratic Front (EPRDF) coalition
HEAD OF GOVERNMENT: Meles Zenawi, Prime Minister (since Aug '95)
MAIN IGO MEMBERSHIPS (non-UN): OAU, COMESA, ACP, NAM
CURRENCY: birr (end-'98 £1=Br11.63, US$1=Br6.99)
GNP PER CAPITA: US$110 by exchange-rate calculation, US$510 by PPP calculation ('97)

Eritrea
CAPITAL: Asmara   AREA: 94,000 sq km   POPULATION: 3,827,000 ('97)
OFFICIAL LANGUAGES: Arabic & Tigrinya   POLITICAL SYSTEM: presidential
HEAD OF STATE & GOVERNMENT: President Issaias Afewerki (since May '93)
SINGLE RULING PARTY: People's Front for Democracy and Justice (PFDJ)
MAIN IGO MEMBERSHIPS (non-UN): OAU, COMESA, ACP, NAM
CURRENCY: nakfa, at par with Ethiopian birr (see above)
GNP PER CAPITA: US$210 by exchange-rate calculation ('97)

Somalia
CAPITAL: Mogadishu   AREA: 638,000 sq km   POPULATION: 10,130,000 ('97)
OFFICIAL LANGUAGES: Somali & Arabic   POLITICAL SYSTEM: transitional
HEAD OF STATE & GOVERNMENT: Disputed
MAIN IGO MEMBERSHIPS (non-UN): AL, OAU, ACP, OIC, NAM
CURRENCY: shilling (end-'98 £1=SSh4,359.02, US$1=SSh2,620.00)
GNP PER CAPITA: n/a

Djibouti
CAPITAL: Djibouti   AREA: 23,000 sq km   POPULATION: 636,000 ('97)
OFFICIAL LANGUAGES: Arabic & French   POLITICAL SYSTEM: presidential
HEAD OF STATE & GOVERNMENT: President Hassan Gouled Aptidon (since June '77)
RULING PARTY: Popular Rally for Progress (RPP)
PRIME MINISTER: Barkat Gourad Hamadou (since Sept '78)
MAIN IGO MEMBERSHIPS (non-UN): AL, OAU, ACP, OIC, NAM, Francophonie
CURRENCY: Djibouti franc (end-'98 £1=DF295.68, US$1=DF177.72)
GNP PER CAPITA: US$780 ('93)

ETHIOPIA. In May, despite apparently close relations, a border dispute with Eritrea flared into violence. Following the death of several Eritrean soldiers near Badme, in the north-west of Ethiopia's Tigray region on 6 May, Eritrean forces seized an area previously administered by Ethiopia, but claimed by Eritrea. Over the next month clashes at several disputed border points left hundreds of casualties; in early June Ethiopian aircraft attacked Asmara airport, and Eritrean planes bombed Makelle and Adigrat. Serious fighting stopped in mid-June, but spasmodic artillery exchanges continued for the rest of the year. Both sides built up their forces, buying significant quantities of arms, mostly from Eastern Europe and China, and carried out an extensive barrage of propaganda.

In June Ethiopia began rounding up Eritreans with military training or members of Eritrea's ruling People's Front for Democracy and Justice (PFDJ). A process of expulsion rapidly expanded; by December Eritrea claimed that over 40,000 Eritreans, or Ethiopians of Eritrean origin, had been deported; Ethiopia claimed that as many Ethiopians had been driven out of Eritrea. Each alleged that their nationals had been seriously mistreated. Hundreds of thousands more were displaced on both sides of the border.

Ethiopia diverted its import/export trade to Djibouti, and cross-border trade with Eritrea came to a standstill. The conflict highlighted longstanding problems, including Ethiopian resentment over the cost of access to the port of Assab, and Eritrean anger over Ethiopia's insistence on using dollars for trade transactions after the introduction of the Eritrean nakfa in 1997.

Mediation efforts made little progress. Both sides claimed a serious commitment to peace, but of the 11 proposals produced by the OAU in November Eritrea rejected those calling for an Eritrean withdrawal from the territory occupied after 6 May, and the return of the previous (Ethiopian) administration to the Badme area. Without this, Ethiopia refused to discuss other issues, though both apparently accepted the principles of deployment of an international force and UN demarcation of the disputed border. An earlier US/Rwandan mediation similarly failed, with Eritrea claiming it had deployed troops only inside Eritrea.

The conflict threatened the collapse of the US strategy for containing Sudan (see also V.4.i). The former US National Security Council Adviser, Anthony Lake, made several trips to the region in the latter part of the year. Although he found enough encouragement to continue his visits, he made no visible progress towards a solution.

Hard-liners appeared to be in control on both sides for much of the year, but the conflict improved the standing of Prime Minister Meles, previously criticized for a too-close relationship with President Issaias of Eritrea. Some opposition movements prepared to back the government, but failed to extract any concessions. Others stood aside. There were indications that the Eritrean government was prepared to back the new hardline leadership of the externally-based opposition Oromo Liberation Front, elected in May. An ethnic conflict in the Oromo region in July between Gudji and Gedeo peoples left, according to government sources, 140 dead and 100,000 displaced.

The dispute with Eritrea affected economic progress in 1998, already hit by a significant fall in agricultural production, after erratic rains and reduced fertilizer usage following the removal of subsidies in 1997-98. In February an FAO/WFP report noted that annual per capita GDP remained less than $100; in April three-quarters of a million people needed urgent food aid. In September the Central Statistical Authority announced that Ethiopia had a population growth rate of 2.9 per cent a year and that its population of nearly 60 million would be over 80 million by 2010. Agricultural prospects for 1998–99 were excellent, but greatly increased military expenditure and extra transport costs via Djibouti were expected to affect any possible surplus. In October the IMF agreed to resume a structural adjustment facility suspended a year earlier.

Human rights abuses continued to cause international concern. The government was strongly criticized over the Eritrean expulsions, and human rights organizations continued to report extensive harassment of suspected opponents, journalists remaining a prime target. Statistics showed that Ethiopia detained more people than any other country in Africa. A conference in May discussed the establishment of a national human rights commission and an ombudsman, but neither proposal made speedy progress. Amnesty International and Human Rights Watch/Africa, with critical reports in April and January respectively, were not invited. Torture allegations were made in several trials, including that of Professor Asrat Woldeyes, imprisoned chairman of the opposition All-Amhara People's Organization. He was allowed abroad for seriously overdue medical treatment in December.

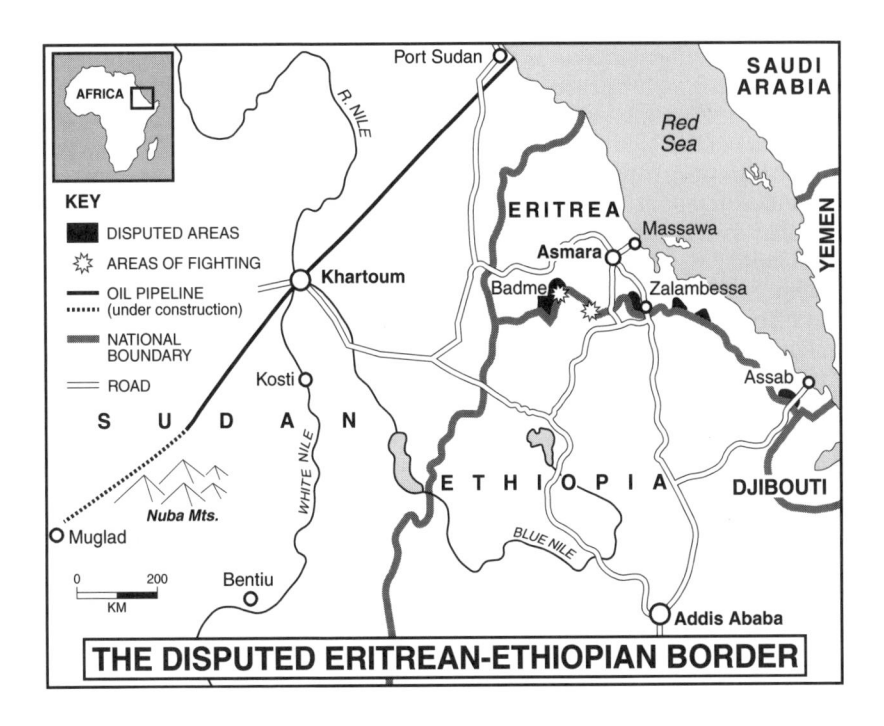

THE DISPUTED ERITREAN-ETHIOPIAN BORDER

ERITREA. The economy was seriously affected by the conflict with Ethiopia. By mid year Assab was at a virtual stand-still and an already substantial trade gap rising sharply due to the increased military spending. The government encouraged Eritreans overseas to contribute; remittances remained the government's largest source of revenue. In December it announced the sale of government bonds to help raise funds.

During the year Eritrea made a sustained effort to improve relations with the Arab world, particularly with Libya, agreeing to exchange ambassadors in February. In July one of President Issaias's advisers said that Eritrea would apply for membership of the Arab League. In October Eritrea accepted an International Court of Justice decision awarding the Hanish Islands to Yemen; Yemen was granted the main islands, while Eritrea was given two groups of tiny islets, and fishing rights in Yemen waters (see also V.3.ii). Relations with Sudan remained poor. Eritrea continued to allow the Sudanese National Democratic Alliance rebels to operate from Eritrea; in March President Issaias predicted that the Sudanese government was on the verge of collapse. The Eritrean and Sudanese Foreign Ministers met in Qatar in November, but a month later Eritrea-accused Sudan of giving logistic support to Ethiopia.

Externally-based opposition continued to criticize the lack of political activity and the government's record on human rights. Ruth Simon, an Agence France-Presse (AFP) correspondent detained in April 1997 after quoting President Issaias as saying that Eritrean troops were fighting in Sudan, was finally released in December, after 20 months without charge.

SOMALIA. The National Reconciliation Conference follow-up to the 1997 Cairo meetings was postponed all year, being replaced by attempts to organize regional and clan-based alternatives. In July 'Puntland' was created as a separate administrative entity by the Darod clans in northeast Somalia, with a president, government and assembly; however, its claim to represent Darod clans in neighbouring Somaliland was sharply rebuffed. A month later Hawiye clan leaders in Mogadishu announced the creation of a 'Benadir' regional administration, with a police force of demobilized clan militia, which was provided with pay and uniforms by Egypt and Libya in November; however, disputes among faction leaders prevented Mogadishu's port or airport reopening. Plans for another Darod administration, in Jubaland in the south-west, came to nothing, with Kismayo remaining a centre of conflict.

The 1998 grain harvest was the worst for five years, with flooding in the Juba and Webi Shebelli valleys, and serious pest infestations. Humanitarian programmes were affected by insecurity; World Food Programme planes were attacked in March, and the Red Cross suspended activities after ten of its staff were taken hostage in Mogadishu in April.

The trend towards de facto recognition of the self-proclaimed Republic of Somaliland continued. President Mohammed Ibrahim Egal visited

Ethiopia, France and Italy, and Eritrea agreed to an informal exchange of representatives. In July the UN representative for Somalia was declared *persona non grata* in Hargeisa (the Somaliland capital). Nevertheless, during the year UNICEF agreed to complete the restoration of Hargeisa's water supply, while UNCTAD carried out training and improved services at Berbera. The economy was affected by a Saudi Arabian ban on livestock exports in February, worth at least $150 million a year, but Berbera benefited from the closure of Assab to Ethiopian shipping after May, helping to ease pressure on the port by importing food aid for Ethiopia. The government continued to integrate clan-based militias into its 12,000-man national army; six more assistant ministers were appointed in September.

DJIBOUTI. With French aid declining, and under IMF pressure, austerity measures in March included civil service salary cuts and increased taxes on petrol and on the narcotic khat (the source of 14 per cent of government revenue). The diversion of Ethiopian trade after May boosted the economy but stretched port facilities. Modernization and expansion plans were speeded up and extended. In August President Hassan Gouled Aptidon visited China, Japan and Malaysia, to press Djibouti's case as a trans-shipment hub port for the Red Sea and Gulf.

In June Ismail Omar Guellah, *chef de cabinet* and probable successor to the President, spoke of possible union with Ethiopia. This would be acceptable to France, seen as a significant element in regional stability by Ethiopia, but not to Eritrea or Somaliland. In November Djibouti broke off relations with Eritrea after accusations that it was helping Ethiopia against Eritrea.

Ethiopian troops were deployed to help in internal security operations after an attack on Ethiopian trucks in October, one of several small-scale operations carried out by Ahmed Dini's anti-government Front for the Restoration of Unity and Democracy (FRUD). The government suspected that FRUD was backed by Eritrea. In September two former ministers and several military officers were given suspended sentences and fined for alleged involvement in an attempted uprising.

ii. KENYA

CAPITAL: Nairobi   AREA: 580,000 sq km   POPULATION: 30,000,000 ('97)
OFFICIAL LANGUAGES: Kiswahili & English   POLITICAL SYSTEM: presidential
HEAD OF STATE & GOVERNMENT: President Daniel Arap Moi (since Aug '78)
RULING PARTY: Kenya African National Union (KANU)
MAIN IGO MEMBERSHIPS (non-UN): OAU, COMESA, ACP, CWTH, NAM
CURRENCY: shilling (end-'98 £1=Ksh102.78, US$1=Ksh61.77)
GNP PER CAPITA: US$330 by exchange-rate calculation, US$1,110 by PPP calculation ('97)

A terrorist attack on the United States embassy in Nairobi on 7 August caused the death of over 250 people, of whom 12 were Americans, and injured over 5,000 others. The bombing was attributed by the US government to groups linked to the Saudi-born Islamic militant Osama bin Laden (see IV.1) and resulted in US missile strikes on 'terrorist targets' in Sudan and Afghanistan (see V.4.i; VIII.1.i). The Kenyan government expressed outrage at the Nairobi bombing, while distancing itself from the subsequent US retaliatory action.

This tragic event had a temporary unifying effect on life in the capital, which had been absorbed in political infighting since the elections of December 1997 (see AR 1997, p. 244). In January Mwai Kibaki, leader of the Democratic Party (DP), and Raila Odinga, leader of the National Development Party (NDP), called for a re-run of the presidential elections which had returned Daniel Arap Moi to power for a fifth and final five-year term. However, the other opposition parties accepted the results, being convinced that without prior political and constitutional reforms any new elections would again be marred by widespread irregularities.

The ruling Kenya African National Union (KANU) emerged weakened from the parliamentary elections, in which 12 out of 25 cabinet ministers lost their seats. With a final tally of 113 MPs, KANU had an overall majority of only four in the 222-member House. With the opposition parties divided, mainly on ethnic lines, the President was able to exploit the situation to his own and his party's advantage: a partnership was forged between KANU and three opposition parties with roots in Western Kenya—the Luo-based NDP (22 MPs), Ford-Kenya (18 MPs) and the Kenya Social Congress (1 MP). This coalition emerged at the expense of the DP (41 MPs), whose leader, former national Vice-President Kibaki, had swept the Kikuyu vote in the Central Province, Nairobi and Nakuru and won strong support among the neighbouring Meru and Embu.

The post-election cabinet had a new look. George Saitoti was demoted from Vice-President to Development Planning Minister; Musalia Mudavadi moved to agriculture and was replaced at finance by Simeon Nyachae, a wealthy businessman and political heavyweight; and Nicholas Biwott left the President's Office to become Minister for East African and Regional Cooperation. Dr Amukowa Amangwe, a University of Nairobi lecturer, was made responsible for cooperative development; he was one of a small, new breed of minister appointed on grounds of ability rather than party allegiance. The post of Vice-President—widely seen as the gateway to the presidency in 2002—was left vacant. Manœuvring for the presidential succession added to the factional divisions within KANU.

A grim economic situation was made worse by extensive flooding, severely damaging crops and infrastructure; corruption and mismanagement in the coffee and several other sectors; and rampant crime, which sapped business confidence and discouraged investment and tourism. At a rally in Nairobi on 14 March the large crowd protested against taxes, rising food prices and corruption, and chanted 'Moi-butu must go'. The economic problems were addressed in April at a World Bank and donor-sponsored economic forum which brought together political leaders and donor representatives. The forum agreed to set up a 19-member committee chaired by the Minister of Finance, who made a frank assessment of the situation. An angry President Moi denounced the forum and reprimanded the large number of KANU MPs who had attended it and openly supported its critical findings.

In his June budget speech Mr Nyachae stated that the slow economic growth rate of 1997—it fell to 2.3 per cent—would continue for most of 1998, but must be increased to at least 7 per cent if the problems of poverty and unemployment were to be tackled realistically. His intention was to pursue a strategy of debt-reduction through expenditure cuts, encourage the purchase of long-term bonds, and achieve much higher levels of investment and public-sector productivity. The completion rate of a scaled-down number of existing investment projects would be improved; staffing levels in the public sector would be reduced; privatization would be carried further and local government reforms undertaken. The budget was widely welcomed, though its success was jeopardized by the strike for increased pay of 260,000 teachers on 5 October. Fortunately, the strike was called off after 15 days.

In April President Moi used a legal pretext to revoke the licences acquired by the media Nation Group, allegedly out of fear that independent radio broadcasts would undermine KANU's grip on power and patronage. With Amnesty International stating that human rights violations were on the increase, the government had to tread warily if it was to persuade the IMF to release the desperately-needed $205 million aid package which had been suspended in July 1997 on the grounds of official corruption and poor governance. It sought to win favour by at last bringing to trial some of those charged with the Goldenberg financial scandal of 1991–93 (see AR 1993, p. 250); however, no action was taken against George Saitoti, former Minister of Finance, or Eric Kotut, the former Central Bank governor. The dire legacy of the early 1990s remained: many of the sizeable, unsecured loans then made were still unpaid; debtors, who included a number of ministers and former ministers, were called upon to repay them. To keep the troubled National Bank of Kenya liquid, Mr Nyachae injected KSh2,000 million of public money into the bank by issuing more of the 90-day treasury bills which he was committed to phase out.

It needed more than Andrew Morton's flattering biography *Moi: The Making of an African Statesman*, published in November, to restore the damaged reputation of the President and his government.

iii. TANZANIA

CAPITAL: Dar es Salaam/Dodoma   AREA: 945,000 sq km   POPULATION: 31,000,000 ('97)
OFFICIAL LANGUAGES: Kiswahili & English   POLITICAL SYSTEM: presidential
HEAD OF STATE & GOVERNMENT: President Benjamin Mkapa (since Nov '95)
PRESIDENT OF ZANZIBAR: Salmin Amour (since Oct '90)
RULING PARTY: Chama cha Mapinduzi (CCM)
PRIME MINISTER: Frederick Sumaye (since Nov '95)
MAIN IGO MEMBERSHIPS (non-UN): OAU, COMESA, SADC, ACP, CWTH, NAM
CURRENCY: shilling (end-'98 £1=Tsh1,124.82, US$1=Tsh676.08)
GNP PER CAPITA: US$210 by exchange-rate calculation ('97)

THE budget presented in June by Daniel Yona, the Minister of Finance, sought to tackle the grim financial situation largely caused by drought and heavy rains. The agricultural sector, which accounted for approximately 50 per cent of GDP, performed badly and was responsible for a sharp decline in export earnings.

The budget aimed to strengthen revenue collection: the introduction of value-added tax (VAT) at 20 per cent (though not on exports, which were zero-rated) would broaden the tax base and reduce scope for tax evasion. Mr Yona predicted a modest GDP growth of 3.5 per cent in 1998–99 and an annual inflation rate of 7.5 per cent by June 1999. Taxes on vehicles were reduced and fuel was exempted from VAT. In future, housing benefit was to be assessed at 15 per cent of an employee's emoluments, a change adversely affecting employees with company accommodation. Local manufacturers were worried about the impending revival of the East African Community, wound up in 1977; under the treaty, originally scheduled to be signed in July, all internal tariffs were to be eliminated by the year 2000. Manufacturers were convinced that the treaty would benefit Kenya more than Tanzania, which needed to reduce tariffs more slowly than its neighbour.

The weak financial position of Zanzibar, caused mainly by the collapse of the price of cloves on the world market, forced its government to seek IMF assistance in improving revenue collection; the IMF recommended that VAT should be introduced, as on the mainland. The freezing of development aid to Zanzibar by the donor community forced the government to abandon nearly half of its donor-supported development projects.

Tanzania remained a very poor country but, having broken the terms of its structural adjustment agreement with the IMF in 1995, the six-year rule of continuous involvement with the Fund meant that it could not qualify for relief under the HIPC initiative until the year 2000. In the meantime, the country carried a US$7,400 million debt and this entailed spending some 35 per cent of export earnings on debt-servicing. President Benjamin Mkapa asked the World Bank and IMF for relief. He undertook to tackle vigorously the mounting problem of corruption; some progress had been made over the past two years: 122 government officers had been dismissed for corruption and a further 840 were under investigation.

In August the United States embassy in Dar es Salaam, at the same time as the mission in Nairobi (see VI.1.ii), was bombed by terrorists, 11 Africans being killed. The following month the President appointed four new ministers and reshuffled others after the High Court had nullified the election to parliament of two ministers and a third had resigned. The Ministry of Regional Administration and Local Government was re-established and, in the light of a report prepared by the NORDIG Consulting Group, a major reorganization of local government was begun. The government also set about reforming the civil service and encouraged investment by offering attractive incentives under a new Investment Act. The Ashanti Goldfields Corporation of Ghana pushed ahead with the development of an ambitious gold-mining project at Geita. But overall the results of the investment drive were disappointing and the government had difficulty selling off parastatals scheduled for privatization.

In Zanzibar, the 1995 presidential elections continued to be the cause of bitter internal division between the ruling Chama cha Mapinduzi (CCM) and the Civic United Front (CUF) coalition. An agreement brokered by a Commonwealth mission failed to satisfy hardliners on either side. There were reports of a deteriorating human rights situation in the islands: Dr Salmin Amour's government was accused of persecuting the people of Pemba and discriminating in employment and education against the CUF opposition. President Mkapa refused to intervene in Zanzibar's internal politics.

iv. UGANDA

CAPITAL: Kampala   AREA: 240,000 sq km   POPULATION: 21,500,000 ('97)
OFFICIAL LANGUAGE: English   POLITICAL SYSTEM: presidential
HEAD OF STATE & GOVERNMENT: President Yoweri Museveni (since Jan '86)
RULING PARTY: National Resistance Movement (NRM) heads broad-based coalition
PRIME MINISTER: Kintu Musoke (since Nov '94)
MAIN IGO MEMBERSHIPS (non-UN): OAU, COMESA, ACP, CWTH, OIC, NAM
CURRENCY: new shilling (end-'98 £1=Ush2,264.37, US$1=Ush1,361.00)
GNP PER CAPITA: US$320 by exchange-rate calculation, US$1,050 by PPP calculation ('97)

IN his June budget Gerald Sendawula, the Minister of Finance, said that coffee exports had fallen because of bad weather and that GDP had grown at 5.5 per cent rather than at the predicted 7 per cent. Annual inflation was below 3 per cent. Traders claimed that the budget favoured importers and would not eradicate poverty despite the poverty action plan which the Minister announced. This plan stipulated that savings made available by debt relief to Uganda under the IMF's 'heavily-indebted poor countries' (HIPC) initiative—estimated at some US $37 million in 1998–99—would be channelled mainly through district councils, with primary education receiving preferential treatment.

Early in December the report of a parliamentary inquiry revealed that privatization had been 'derailed by corruption'; three senior ministers were implicated. The banking sector was shown to be in crisis. Major-General Salim Saleh, President Yoweri Museveni's younger brother, resigned as presidential adviser on defence after confessing to 'improper conduct' in the takeover of the Uganda Commercial Bank (UCB); the bank had lent millions of dollars in unsecured loans, of which at least US$2 million had gone to firms in which General Saleh had an interest. The government responded to the report, and the criticism of the outspoken Kampala press, by issuing an anti-corruption plan and pledging to reduce political interference in privatization. These assurances, coupled with the government's socio-economic achievements, proved enough to satisfy Uganda's aid donors who announced aid to Uganda of $2,200 million (£1,300 million) over the next three years.

Though at present manageable, defence spending was likely to increase to counter the attacks launched by rebel groups across the country's northern, north-western and western borders. The main groups were the Sudan-based Lord's Resistance Army (LRA), which rendered meaningful development in northern Uganda impossible; the West Nile Bank Front (WNBF), which made the West Nile a virtual no-go area; and the Allied Democratic Forces (ADF), which was now based in the Ruwenzori mountains. Of these, the ADF was said to have Islamic tendencies and was held responsible for terrorist attacks in Kampala, resulting in the adoption of tight security measures.

President Museveni justified his decision to send troops to the eastern region of the Democratic Republic of the Congo to fight alongside the Rwandan army against the forces supporting President Laurent Kabila (see VII.1.i), as calculated both to prevent Ugandan rebels attacking Uganda and the genocide of ethnic Tutsis. But the deployment overstretched the resources of an army badly in need of modernization—the remedy proposed being to replace many of the serving officers with university graduates.

The President continued to insist that his brand of no-party democracy was the best way forward if the country was to avoid crippling regional and ethnic divisions. The opposition parties accused him in December of having already launched his campaign for a 'no' vote to multi-partyism, though it was over two years before a referendum on this issue was due. A section of the ruling National Resistance Movement was said to be secretly worried about the personalization of power and the lack of any mechanism to choose a presidential successor.

2. GHANA—NIGERIA—SIERRA LEONE—THE GAMBIA—LIBERIA

i. GHANA

CAPITAL: Accra   AREA: 240,000 sq km   POPULATION: 18,000,000 ('97)
OFFICIAL LANGUAGE: English
POLITICAL SYSTEM: presidential
HEAD OF STATE & GOVERNMENT: President Jerry Rawlings (since Nov '92), previously Chairman of Provisional National Defence Council (since '81)
RULING PARTIES: National Democratic Congress (NDC) heads coalition
MAIN IGO MEMBERSHIPS (non-UN): OAU, ECOWAS, ACP, CWTH, NAM
CURRENCY: cedi (end-'98 £1=C3,893.18, US$1=C2,340.00)
GNP PER CAPITA: US$370 by exchange-rate calculation, US$1,790 by PPP calculation ('97)

ON 15 January President Rawlings delivered his seasonal address to parliament. He warned of difficult times to come, including food shortages in the north. Poor rains and the insufficient flow of the River Volta through its Akosombo dam resulted in water shortage and an erratic electricity supply—for which, however, higher prices would be needed. El Niño weather distortion was apparently to blame. The President also declared renewed war on corruption and promised to take his message to the country. Grassroots radicalism and harsh economic measures were back on the national agenda.

Other worries lay at the heart of the ruling party's problems. The National Democratic Congress (NDC) wanted a candidate for the presidential election in 2000. President Rawlings was debarred from standing under the constitution, having been elected in 1992 and 1996. Much of the political argument during the year was concerned with the dilemma. Could the constitution be changed to allow a third term? Should Nana Konadu Agyeman (the President's wife) be encouraged to stand? Was it possible for John Atta-Mills, the Vice-President, to campaign with Flight-Lieut. Rawlings as his vice-presidential candidate? Ambition should be made of sterner stuff, but at party conferences on 9 July and 17 December the decision was taken to defer the choice.

That there was discontent with the NDC was seen in September when a Reform Group came out into the open to broadcast its criticism, first on Joy Radio in Accra and later on cassette during visits by the President to the United States and Cuba. The group was led by Sam Garba and Augustus Tanoh. Its members were harassed by the Bureau of National Investigation (BNI) under Security Minister Kofi Totobi-Quakyi and Local Government Minister Kwamena Ahwoi; however, as always in Ghana, opposition was hydra-headed, shaped by ethnic, ideological and personal ambition.

The opposition New Patriotic Party (NPP) was also concerned about choosing a leader. The party met in Sunyani (Ashanti) on 24 October to decide between six candidates. The winner, with 64.6 per cent of the vote, was John Agyekum Kufuor, NPP presidential candidate in 1996. Nana Akufo Addo, son of the former President (1969–72), won 31 per cent, while J.H. Mensah, NPP parliamentary leader, was given only three votes by the 1,984 delegates. Accusations of bribery were quick to be made, the lure of money being a perennial factor in Ghanaian politics.

The economy itself was in difficulties. Compared with the rest of tropical Africa, Ghana was a success. An *Economist* report (3 October) showed the country well ahead in terms of GDP, with an average annual growth since the mid-1980s of nearly 5 per cent. But success came at a price. Aid from the World Bank amounted to 11 per cent of GDP, or four times the value of the country's exports. Debt service cost $150 million annually, or more than three years' worth of capital spending. In September the government braved public outcry and imposed a 10 per cent value-added tax and higher electricity prices. The World Bank noted that 'current growth cannot be sustained without commensurate growth in both agricultural and non-agricultural production', the key element being rising costs and low prices for cocoa and palm oil to the point where many families were now engaged only in subsistence farming.

The public was concerned less with party arguments than with crime and the behaviour of the police. There was widespread criticism of the brutality of law enforcement. When rioting broke out in the diamond town of Akwatia and in the Nima area of Accra, the police used armoured cars, full riot gear and live ammunition. Inevitably there were deaths which the police dismissed as accidental. That was not what President Rawlings had promised in his campaign to revitalize Ghanaian democracy.

When President Clinton visited Accra in March, he addressed a huge crowd in Independence Square, saying (on 23 March): 'Let us find a future here in Africa, the cradle of humanity.' However, words needed to be translated into deeds. Later in the year the Fokker-28 presidential jet taking President Rawlings across the Atlantic developed a fault and had to be grounded in Miami. His supporters welcomed him back in October with placards urging him to 'change the flying coffin'; but there were no available funds even for that.

Two leading politicians died, Hilla Limann from Tumu in Upper Ghana on 23 January (see Pt XVIII: Obituary), and K.A. Gbedemah from the Volta region on 11 July. Komla Gbedemah's place in Ghanaian history was assured from his role as principal lieutenant to independence leader Kwame Nkrumah, and he probably did more than any other leader to win the critical first election in 1951. A decade later he fell out with Nkrumah, but returned from exile to contest (unsuccessfully) the 1969 election.

ii. NIGERIA

CAPITAL: Abuja   AREA: 924,000 sq km   POPULATION: 120,000,000 ('97)
OFFICIAL LANGUAGE: English   POLITICAL SYSTEM: military rule
HEAD OF STATE & GOVERNMENT: General Abdulsalam Abubakar, Chairman of and of Federal Executive Council (since June '98)
MAIN IGO MEMBERSHIPS (non-UN): OAU, ECOWAS, OPEC, ACP, OIC, NAM
CURRENCY: naira (end-'98 £1=N148.07, US$1=N75.67)
GNP PER CAPITA: US$260 by exchange-rate calculation, US$880 by PPP calculation ('97)

THE death of General Sani Abacha on 8 June, followed a month later by the similar death of Chief Moshood M.K.O. Abiola (the winner of annulled 1993 presidential elections), profoundly altered the political prospects of Nigeria. General Abdulsalam Abubakar, Chief of the General Staff, succeeded as head of state and promised that he would return the country to civilian rule. (For obituaries of Abacha and Abiola, see Pt XVIII.)

The Minister of Finance, Chief Anthony Ani, presented the budget in mid-January. He abolished excise duties and capital gains tax—a move that was welcomed by investors and manufacturers—but left the dual exchange rate intact. One result was that the IMF was unable to give an accurate estimate of the true state of Nigeria's international debt. According to the budget presentation the government's leading priorities were job creation, sustainable growth, expanded production, sustained fiscal discipline, improved social services and infrastructure.

A bank crisis erupted on 20 January when riot police occupied 26 commercial banks after the government had ordered their liquidation. They had accumulated huge debts, so that substantial losses for savers were expected to follow. A total of N16,330 million was effectively wiped out when the Central Bank withdrew the operating licences of the banks. It was expected that N5,990 million, slightly more than a third of the losses, would be paid out by the Nigerian Deposit Insurance Corporation (NDIC). The government also at this time announced plans for a massive retrenchment of the civil service that could affect up to 800,000 jobs; 30 per cent of civil service employees were likely to be made redundant, while the remainder would have salary increases in the hope of boosting productivity.

On 14 February 26 people accused of participation in the 'coup plot' of December 1997 (see AR 1997, p. 253) were brought to trial before a military tribunal at Jos; they included 16 military officers and ten civilians. One of the leading accused, Lieut.-General Oladipo Diya (then Chief of the General Staff), accused the government of framing the evidence against him. The trial was suspended in March when the judges disputed the reliability of prosecution evidence although it was resumed in April and on 28 April sentences of death were passed on six of the accused, while three more were given life imprisonment and 12 were released. Appeals for clemency were made by Britain, the Commonwealth and South Africa. In July

1998, after General Abacha's death, the sentences were reduced and the six death sentences commuted to 20 years' imprisonment.

Results of the state and National Assembly elections which had been held in December 1997 for a total of 989 seats were released on 22 January, as follows: United Nigeria Congress Party (UNCP) 637, Democratic Party of Nigeria (DPN) 199, Committee for National Consensus (CNC) 61, Grassroots Democratic Movement (GDM) 50, National Centre Party of Nigeria (NCPN) 23. A further 19 seats awaited by-elections. Meanwhile, the Abacha Solidarity Movement (ASOMO) was launched by Alhaji Abayomi in Abuja, and during February a number of rallies were held to persuade General Abacha to run for the presidency. On 1 May the police in Ibadan opened fire on demonstrators demanding that the General should quit office; seven people were killed and 40 arrested.

General Abacha was 55 when he died on 8 June, apparently of a heart attack. He had ruled Nigeria since November 1993 and had been widely condemned for his dictatorial methods and ruthless treatment of opponents, as well as for the incompetence and corruption of his government. General Abubakar was sworn in as his successor on 9 June with the agreement of the 23-man Provisional Ruling Council, promising to return the country to civilian rule in October. Aged 56, he was a close associate of former ruler General Ibrahim Babangida and had neither held office nor enjoyed patronage. On 15 June nine leading political prisoners, including former head of state General Olusegun Obasanjo, were released, followed by a further 17 on 21 June.

Chief Abiola, who had been imprisoned since 1994, died in detention on 7 July, also apparently of a heart attack; his death led to widespread disturbances in Yorubaland in which 60 people died, and the government imposed curfews in Lagos, Ibadan and Abeokuta (Chief Abiola's birthplace). In response to accusations that Chief Abiola had been poisoned or had died of maltreatment in prison, the Abubakar government agreed to allow international pathologists to examine the body; they found that he had died of natural causes.

On 20 July General Abubakar announced a new electoral timetable to replace the one envisaging elections on 1 October, which by then was seen as unrealistic. He promised to create a new independent electoral body, to remove restrictions on political activity and the formation of political parties, to release all political detainees and to respect human rights. On 22 August he appointed a new Federal Executive Council of 23 members, eight of whom were military officers; an effort was made to achieve a regional balance. Two of his appointments were especially well received by Western diplomats: Ismaila Usman (deputy governor of the central bank) as Finance Minister; and Ignatius Olisemeka (a former ambassador to the United States) as Foreign Minister.

A new electoral timetable was issued on 25 August by the new Independent National Electoral Commission (INEC): local elections on 5

December 1998; state legislative elections on 9 January 1999; National Assembly elections on 20 February 1999; and presidential elections on 27 February 1999. The President and Assembly would be inaugurated on 29 May 1999.

In September General Abubakar released the draft of a civilian constitution which had been drawn up in 1995 (and then suppressed) and invited the public for comments prior to promulgation of a final version. At the same time he proposed to reorganize the Ministry of Petroleum Resources and the Nigeria National Petroleum Corporation (NNPC) and to establish an independent commission to monitor the crucial petroleum sector. He also appealed for Nigerian exiles to return to the country, though many were wary of doing so while legislation remained in place under which they could be prosecuted. However, the writer Wole Soyinka returned to the country for a six-day visit on 14 October.

By 10 September 25 of 32 political parties which had collected registration forms had returned these to the INEC, which extended the time allowed for registration until 10 October. On 5 October the INEC launched a two-week campaign to encourage people to register for voting, hoping that the estimated 60 million eligible voters would respond. At the end of the month General Obasanjo joined the People's Democratic Party (PDP); then in early November he announced his intention of seeking the PDP nomination as its presidential candidate. He said the PDP, the most broad-based of the current parties, aimed to overcome ethnic divisions and keep Nigeria united.

Revelations about the 'lootocracy' of General Abacha and his family surfaced during November, when the government recovered $750 million of an estimated $1,300 million seized by him. One of General Abacha's sons was caught with $100 million and the late ruler's wife attempted to leave the country with 38 suitcases found to be stuffed with foreign currency. General Abacha's former security adviser, Ishmael Gwarzo, returned $250 million, which he had withdrawn a few days before the General died. This was to have been taken to the annual conference of the Organization of African Unity (OAU), to be distributed to leaders whom the Nigerian regime wanted to influence. These and other revelations put General Abacha on a par in public estimation with the late Mobutu Sese Seko of Zaïre.

In November Ijaw youths boarded an oil rig off the coast of Bayelsa state in protest against oil pollution and ordered the oil companies to pull out by 30 December. When the deadline was reached, however, clashes with the military led to at least 19 deaths. The oil confrontations here and elsewhere in Nigeria were the result of years of neglect of the people living in the oil-producing region in south-western Nigeria. An example of the deteriorating condition of oil installations was a fuel pipeline explosion on 17 October near the city of Warri, which produced a fireball that killed at least 700 people.

The first move in the return to democracy came with the local elections during December. If the time-schedule for the various stages of the return to civilian rule was adhered to, the military were expected to return to barracks at the end of May 1999, when a new President and Assembly would be inaugurated.

iii. SIERRA LEONE

CAPITAL: Freetown   AREA: 72,000 sq km   POPULATION: 5,000,000 ('97)
OFFICIAL LANGUAGE: English   POLITICAL SYSTEM: presidential
HEAD OF STATE & GOVERNMENT: President Alhaji Ahmed Tejan Kabbah (since March '96)
MAIN IGO MEMBERSHIPS (non-UN): OAU, ECOWAS, OIC, ACP, CWTH, NAM
CURRENCY: leone (end-'98 £1=Le2,495.62, US$1=Le1,500.00)
GNP PER CAPITA: US$200 by exchange-rate calculation, US$510 by PPP calculation ('97)

A return to political normality continued to elude Sierra Leone. This was despite a promising beginning when, in February, forces composed largely of Nigerians, operating under the command of the regional ECOMOG (Economic Community of West African States Monitoring Group) organization, succeeded in dislodging the military regime which had itself seized power in May 1997 (see AR 1997, pp. 253–4), not only from the capital, Freetown, but also from much of the countryside. The operation created a political furore in Britain, referred to in the news media as the 'Arms for Africa' scandal, over whether the Foreign Office knew that Sandline International, a private British security company, was providing arms and military assistance to the exiled Sierra Leone government, in apparent breach of a UN embargo on selling weapons to any party in the conflict (see II.1.i).

The deposed head of state, Ahmed Tejan Kabbah, who had been forced to take up residence in Conakry, the Guinean capital, was able to return to Freetown on 10 March, to begin the daunting process of political reconstruction and economic and social rehabilitation. Over 1,300 persons were detained on suspicion of supporting the ousted military regime, the Armed Forces Ruling Council (AFRC). Of these, some 30 were executed and others given prison sentences. Among those gaoled was the former head of state and army chief, Joseph Momoh, who received a ten-year sentence. Lieut.-Colonel Johnny Paul Koroma, the AFRC leader, managed to escape, but a younger brother of his was among the rebel soldiers executed.

Other rebel soldiers fled into the interior to seek escape across the border to Liberia, or to join the guerrilla forces of the Revolutionary United Front (RUF), against whom they had previously been fighting. The brutal war against government and ECOMOG forces therefore continued, characterized by appalling atrocities against civilians. Foday Sankoh, the RUF leader previously detained in Nigeria, was returned to Sierra Leone and sentenced to death, although the sentence had not been carried out by the end of the year.

By October ECOMOG forces, supported by local village militias, known as kamajors, were claiming major successes against rebel forces, now pushed back to the eastern and southern borders of the country. President Kabbah and his Sierra Leone People's Party, with international financial backing, were also beginning the process of re-establishing the administration and tackling the enormous damage to the infrastructure and economy resulting from the seven-year civil war and junta rule, during which an estimated 1,500,000 people had been displaced.

However, the survival of the government was once more in question at the close of the year. Rebel forces, bolstered by foreign mercenaries (reportedly including several hundred Ukrainians fighting on the side of the RUF) and unidentified financial backers, renewed their onslaught on Freetown in the last days of December. The rebels were widely believed to have the support of the Liberian government, although the latter denied any involvement.

iv. THE GAMBIA

CAPITAL: Banjul AREA: 11,300 sq km POPULATION: 1,200,000 ('97)
OFFICIAL LANGUAGE: English POLITICAL SYSTEM: presidential
HEAD OF STATE & GOVERNMENT: President (Col.) Yahya Jammeh (since Sept '96), previously Chairman of Armed Forces Provisional Revolutionary Council (from July '94)
RULING PARTY: Alliance for Patriotic Reorientation and Construction (APRC)
MAIN IGO MEMBERSHIPS (non-UN): OAU, ECOWAS, ACP, CWTH, OIC, NAM
CURRENCY: dalasi (end-'98 £1=D929.40,US$1=D558.62)
GNP PER CAPITA: US$350 by exchange-rate calculation, US$1,340 by PPP calculation ('97)

ALTHOUGH politically unassailable following their election successes in 1996–97 (see AR 1996, pp. 251–2; 1997, p. 254), President Yahya Jammeh and the Alliance for Patriotic Reorientation and Construction continued to face opposition and accusations of political intimidation, particularly on the part of supporters of the main opposition United Democratic Party. These charges, backed by an Amnesty International report in December 1997 condemning human rights violations in The Gambia, did not prevent the government from improving its relations with donor countries and international aid agencies or from seeking to play a constructive part in resolving conflict in the immediate sub-region. Both the long-drawn-out ethnic separatist insurrection in the Casamance region of Senegal and the military deadlock in Guinea-Bissau, between rebel forces and troops loyal to President Vieira, impinged upon The Gambia, owing to its ethnic and economic links with the two countries.

President Jammeh made several changes to his cabinet during the year; there was a major reshuffle in March and other ministerial departures took place later in the year. No explanations were given for the changes.

v. LIBERIA

CAPITAL: Monrovia AREA: 97,750 sq km POPULATION: 2,894,000 ('97)
OFFICIAL LANGUAGE: English POLITICAL SYSTEM: republic
HEAD OF STATE & GOVERNMENT: President Charles Taylor (since July '97)
RULING PARTY: National Patriotic Party of Liberia (NPPL)
MAIN IGO MEMBERSHIPS (non-UN): OAU, ECOWAS, ACP, NAM
CURRENCY: Liberian dollar (end-'98 £1=L$1.66, US$1=L$1.00)
GNP PER CAPITA: n/a

ALTHOUGH spared the large-scale violence that continued to ravage neighbouring Sierra Leone (see VI.2.iii), the normalization of political life in Liberia remained uncertain. While the 1997 peace settlement had resulted in a return to elected government (see AR 1997, pp. 255–6), there was growing evidence of a breakdown in the political consensus that accompanied the end of protracted civil war.

President Charles Taylor, contrary to the peace agreement worked out by the warring factions and to his earlier willingness to give opposition leaders appointments in his government, was accused of seeking to pack the administration and the reconstituted security forces with his own followers in the National Patriotic Party of Liberia. He was also accused of seeking to crush opposition groups by force and legal intimidation. His main target was the United Liberation Movement of Liberia (ULIMO), one of the leading military factions during the civil war and a political rival of the government. Roosevelt Johnson, leader of the Krahn faction of ULIMO, despite having earlier served in the Taylor administration, was forced to flee (after several attempts on his life) to the US embassy in Monrovia, from where he was flown to safety, initially to Sierra Leone and then to Nigeria. Mr Johnson, Alhaji G.V. Koroma (leader of the Mandingo wing of ULIMO) and over 30 other prominent opposition leaders were formally charged in September with plotting to overthrow the government. Guinea was also accused of involvement in the plot.

Relations between President Taylor and the remaining ECOMOG forces in Liberia, led by and principally made up of Nigerians, were also strained. The President's well-known antipathy towards Nigeria and ECOMOG, and his sympathy both for the deposed military junta and the rebel forces in Sierra Leone (see VI.2.iii), led to a number of confrontations between government forces and ECOMOG units. Consequently, growing internal political discord and continuing difficulties with neighbouring countries cast doubts about the success of the democratization process in Liberia.

3. WEST AFRICAN FRANCOPHONE STATES—CENTRAL AFRICAN FRANC ZONE

i. SENEGAL—MAURITANIA—MALI—GUINEA—
CÔTE D'IVOIRE—BURKINA FASO—TOGO—BENIN—NIGER

Senegal
CAPITAL: Dakar   AREA: 196,000 sq km   POPULATION: 9,000,000 ('97)
OFFICIAL LANGUAGE: French   POLITICAL SYSTEM: presidential democracy
HEAD OF STATE & GOVERNMENT: President Abdou Diouf, since Jan '81
RULING PARTIES: Socialist Party (PS) heads coalition
PRIME MINISTER: Mamadou Lamine Loum (PS), since July '98
MAIN IGO MEMBERSHIPS (non-UN): OAU, ECOWAS, UEMOA, ACP, OIC, NAM, Francophonie
CURRENCY: CFA franc (end-'98 £1=CFAF929.40, US$1=CFAF558.62)
GNP PER CAPITA: US$550 by exchange-rate calculation, US$1,670 by PPP calculation ('97)

Mauritania
CAPITAL: Nouakchott   AREA: 1,000,000 sq km   POPULATION: 2,400,000 ('97)
OFFICIAL LANGUAGES: French & Arabic   POLITICAL SYSTEM: presidential
HEAD OF STATE & GOVERNMENT: President (Col.) Maaouyia Ould Sidi Mohammed Taya (since Jan '92); previously Chairman of Military Council of National Salvation (from Dec '84)
RULING PARTY: Democratic and Social Republican Party (PRDS)
PRIME MINISTER: Cheikh El-Avia Ould Mohammed Khouna (since Nov '98)
MAIN IGO MEMBERSHIPS (non-UN): OAU, ECOWAS, AMU, AL, OIC, ACP, NAM, Francophonie
CURRENCY: ouguiya (end-'98 £1=OM338.98, US$1=OM203.75)
GNP PER CAPITA: US$450 by exchange-rate calculation, US$1,870 by PPP calculation ('97)

Mali
CAPITAL: Bamako   AREA: 1,240,000 sq km POPULATION: 10,750,000 ('97)
OFFICIAL LANGUAGE: French   POLITICAL SYSTEM: presidential
HEAD OF STATE & GOVERNMENT: President Alpha Oumar Konaré (since April '92)
RULING PARTY: Alliance for Democracy in Mali (ADEMA)
PRIME MINISTER: Ibrahim Boubakar Keita (since April '92)
MAIN IGO MEMBERSHIPS (non-UN): OAU, ECOWAS, UEMOA, AL, OIC, ACP, NAM, Francophonie   CURRENCY: CFA franc (see above)
GNP PER CAPITA: US$260 by exchange-rate calculation, US$740 by PPP calculation ('97)

Guinea
CAPITAL: Conakry   AREA: 246,000 sq km   POPULATION: 7,000,000 ('97)
OFFICIAL LANGUAGE: French   POLITICAL SYSTEM: presidential
HEAD OF STATE & GOVERNMENT: President (Gen.)Lansana Conté (since Dec '93); previously Chairman of Military Committee for National Recovery (from April '84)
RULING PARTY: Party of Unity and Progress (PUP)
PRIME MINISTER: Sidya Touré (since July '96)
MAIN IGO MEMBERSHIPS (non-UN): OAU, ECOWAS, OIC, ACP, ACP, NAM, Francophonie
CURRENCY: Guinean franc (end-'98 £1=GF1,863.84, US$1=GF1,136.00)
GNP PER CAPITA: US$570 by exchange-rate calculation, US$1,850 by PPP calculation ('97)

Côte d'Ivoire

CAPITAL: Abidjan   AREA: 322,000 sq km   POPULATION: 15,000,000 ('97)
OFFICIAL LANGUAGE: French   POLITICAL SYSTEM: presidential
HEAD OF STATE & GOVERNMENT: President Henri Konan Bédié (since Dec '93)
RULING PARTY: Democratic Party of Côte d'Ivoire (PDCI)
PRIME MINISTER: Daniel Kablan Duncan (since Dec '93)
MAIN IGO MEMBERSHIPS (non-UN): OAU, ECOWAS, UEMOA, ACP, NAM, Francophonie
CURRENCY: CFA franc (see above)
GNP PER CAPITA: US$690 by exchange-rate calculation, US$1,640 by PPP calculation ('97)

Burkina Faso

CAPITAL: Ouagadougou   AREA: 275,000 sq km   POPULATION: 11,000,000 ('97)
OFFICIAL LANGUAGE: French   POLITICAL SYSTEM: presidential
HEAD OF STATE & GOVERNMENT: President (Capt.) Blaise Compaoré (since Dec '91); previously Chairman of Popular Front (from Oct '87)
RULING PARTY: Congress for Democracy and Progress (CDP))
PRIME MINISTER: Kadre Desiré Ouedraogo (since Feb '96)
MAIN IGO MEMBERSHIPS (non-UN): OAU, ECOWAS, UEMOA, OIC, ACP, NAM, Francophonie
CURRENCY: CFA franc (see above)
GNP PER CAPITA: US$240 by exchange-rate calculation, US$990 by PPP calculation ('97)

Togo

CAPITAL: Lomé   AREA: 57,000 sq km   POPULATION: 4,000,000 ('97)
OFFICIAL LANGUAGES: French, Kabiye & Ewe   POLITICAL SYSTEM: presidential
HEAD OF STATE: President (Gen.) Gnassingbé Eyadéma (since '67)
RULING PARTY: Rally of the Togolese People (RPT)
PRIME MINISTER: Kouassi Klutse (since Aug '96)
MAIN IGO MEMBERSHIPS (non-UN): OAU, ECOWAS, UEMOA, ACP, NAM, Francophonie
CURRENCY: CFA franc (see above)
GNP PER CAPITA: US$330 by exchange-rate calculation, US$1,790 by PPP calculation ('97)

Benin

CAPITAL: Porto Novo   AREA: 113,000 sq km   POPULATION: 6,000,000 ('97)
OFFICIAL LANGUAGE: French   POLITICAL SYSTEM: presidential
HEAD OF STATE & GOVERNMENT: President Mathieu Kérékou (since March '96)
MAIN IGO MEMBERSHIPS (non-UN): OAU, ECOWAS, UEMOA, ACP, NAM, Francophonie
CURRENCY: CFA franc (see above)
GNP PER CAPITA: US$380 by exchange-rate calculation, US$1,260 by PPP calculation ('97)

Niger

CAPITAL: Niamey   AREA: 1,267,000 sq km   POPULATION: 10,000,000 ('97)
OFFICIAL LANGUAGE: French   POLITICAL SYSTEM: republic
HEAD OF STATE & GOVERNMENT: President (Brig.-Gen.) Ibrahim Barre Mainassara (since Jan '96)
RULING PARTY: National Union of Independents for Democratic Renewal
PRIME MINISTER: Ibrahim Assane Maiyaki (since Dec '97)
MAIN IGO MEMBERSHIPS (non-UN): OAU, ECOWAS, UEMOA, ACP, OIC, NAM, Francophonie
CURRENCY: CFA franc (see above)
GNP PER CAPITA: US$200 by exchange-rate calculation, US$920 by PPP calculation ('97)

SENEGAL. Parliamentary elections held in two rounds on 24 May and 6 June were the key event of Senegal's political year. They led to a majority of 93 seats in the parliament of 140 for the ruling Socialist Party (PS). Second place with 23 went to the Senegalese Democratic Party (PDS) of Maître Abdoulaye Wade. This result was generally seen as a setback for the main opposition party, since in the previous Assembly they had held 27 out of 120 seats. It was probably due to the emergence of a new force in the ranks of the opposition—the Union for Democratic Renewal (URD), which obtained 11 seats. The URD was led by former Interior Minister Djibo Kâ, who had tried to create a reformist tendency within the PS in 1997 but had been obliged to leave to set up his own party, taking some important PS leaders with him. The remainder of the 47 opposition seats were won by eight smaller parties.

A notable development in the post-election situation was the virtual absence of any of the opposition parties from the new government formed on 4 July under a new Prime Minister, the technocrat Mamadou Lamine Loum. He replaced Habib Thiam, who had been in the post for 15 years and had always been perceived as being very close to President Abdou Diouf. The only non-PS minister was Serigne Diop, from a small faction allied to the PDS, who was promoted from communications to the justice portfolio.

Otherwise, the idea of an enlarged presidential majority—encouraged between recent elections, notably by the appointment of Me Wade for two terms as Minister of State—came to an end, perhaps in preparation for the next great contest, the presidential elections due in 2000. To prepare for this, Me Wade resigned his seat in the National Assembly, while Moustapha Niasse, who apparently at his own request had not been reappointed Foreign Minister, was also seen as a possible presidential candidate. However, although reputed to be both wealthy and popular, M. Niasse had never shown any sign of establishing a party structure of his own.

For the opposition parties, whose combined strength after the elections was actually higher than after the 1993 contest, a number of issues arose for them to get their teeth into. These included increased tension on the social front, with the arrest of electricity union leader Mademba Sock, and the involvement of Senegalese troops in Guinea-Bissau following the outbreak of hostilities there on 8 June (see VII.1.iii). This involvement was occasioned by the connection of the secessionist movement in Senegal's southernmost province of Casamance with the Bissau rebels. The latter had been charged with selling arms in Casamance, and official Senegalese pressure had been one of the main factors causing the rift in President Vieira's government.

The lack of a clear statement by the Diouf administration either on the objectives of the Guinea-Bissau intervention—which had been based on faulty intelligence about the strength of the support for President Vieira—or on troop losses (believed to be heavy) was a gift to the opposition parties. However, a patriotic unwillingness to be seen attacking their own troops (the neutral and technocratic army enjoying high standing in Senegalese political society) muted the criticisms. There was relief at the Abuja peace agreement of 2 November, which provided for Senegalese withdrawal with honour from a costly and damaging involvement.

The opposition staged a small coup in October when the seven principal parties organized a protest demonstration in Paris on the same day as President Diouf addressed the French National Assembly, thereby attracting much of the publicity. Their main demand was for a change in the constitution to limit the number of seven-year terms a President could serve to two. President Diouf had in fact served two five-year terms before embarking on his current seven-year term. He had already been adopted as the PS candidate for another beginning in 2000.

MAURITANIA. It was a year without elections, but the political atmosphere remained sour. Ministers were dismissed on several occasions, allegedly for mismanaging their departments, and in November the Prime Minister, Mohammed Lemine Ould Guig, was removed, after a little under a year in office (see AR 1997, p. 259). He was replaced by his predecessor, Cheikh El-Avia Ould Mohammed Khouna, in charge of a slightly reshuffled government. No reason was given for the change, although observers commented that M. Guig was not a popular political figure.

In March five human rights campaigners were gaoled for 13 months each for taking part in a French television film on slavery in Mauritania, but were later pardoned by presidential decree. When the five were arrested in March there had been demonstrations in their favour in the capital, Nouakchott.

MALI. The status of Alpha Oumar Konaré as one of Africa's new-style democratic leaders continued to be belied by the disappointing state of democracy in Mali, despite the President's best intentions—seen, for instance, in his reaffirmation at the end of the year that he had no intention of seeking a third term in 2001. Political life continued to be plagued by the opposition's uncooperative attitude towards the government and the ruling Alliance for Democracy in Mali (ADEMA). This arose, ironically, from the dominance of the ruling party, the counterpart of which was the weakness of the opposition, which had been boycotting elections since the affair of the bungled parliamentary elections of the previous year (see AR 1997, pp. 259-60).

The impasse was seen again in June in the first phase of municipal elections, which had already been postponed three times in the hope of persuading the opposition coalition to participate. Because the opposition continued its boycott, ADEMA swept the board. The second phase, due to have been held in November, was postponed to enable another session of a 'national forum' to discuss political reconciliation to be held. However, the promised session had not taken place by the end of the year.

Meanwhile, as a kind of ominous reminder of Mali's recent undemocratic past, the trial of former dictator Moussa Traoré and his wife on charges of 'economic crimes' continued sporadically during the year. In October it was suspended for two months when their lawyers walked out because of the continued refusal to have direct radio broadcasting of the trial. The two defendants had already been sentenced to death for 'blood crimes', but the sentences had been commuted to life imprisonment.

GUINEA. It was a difficult year, in which the problems of neighbouring countries interleaved uneasily with domestic politics. Mounting in importance through the year was the milestone of Guinea's second multi-party presidential elections since independence, held on 14 December. These were conducted in an atmosphere of violence and were followed by charges of rigging by the ruling Party of Unity and Progress (PUP), whose candidate, incumbent President Lansana Conté, was announced the winner with 56.12 per cent of the vote. In a 70 per cent turnout, the other main candidates polled as follows: Mamadou Ba, of the Union for a New Republic (UNR), 24.63 per cent; Alpha Condé, of the Guinea People's Rally (RPG), 16.58 per cent. The remaining 2.67 per cent went to two minor candidates. Although he had been out of the country for much of the campaign, the turnout for M. Condé was considered surprisingly low in view of the known support for the party in Guinea's largest ethnic group, the Malinké. M. Ba's candidacy benefited from being endorsed by other Peulh leaders, such as Siradiou Diallo, who had been a candidate in the 1993 presidential elections.

Following the opposition's charges of electoral fraud, there was a large military and police deployment in the capital, Conakry, and a closure of all land borders. Then M. Condé was arrested in the far east of the country, allegedly trying to flee across the border. A former minister and supporter of M. Condé, Marcel Cros, was also arrested, following the discovery of five guns in his house, and charged with preparing a 'coup with the aid of mercenaries based abroad'. M. Ba was placed under house arrest and there were demonstrations against the regime in several cities. Ten people were killed when troops fired on a crowd in the town of Siguiri.

Through the year Guinea was called on to deploy its troops in both its northern and southern neighbours. For some time it had had several hundred men in the ECOMOG force in Sierra Leone (see VI.2.iii), the only francophone country to support the Nigerians and Ghanaians in that operation. Guinea was also called upon, in June, to send 500 troops in support of the Senegalese intervention to prop up President Vieira in Guinea-Bissau (see VII.1.iii). The troubles to both north and south not only meant an increasingly costly military commitment, but also resulted in a large refugee influx from both countries. This inevitably caused added burdens for the Guinean budget, in spite of support from the international community.

Despite being mineral-rich, Guinea had still not achieved the kind of economic take-off some might have expected. Although it registered a good growth rate of 5 per cent in 1998 and continued to have the blessing of the International Monetary Fund, it continued to suffer from the dislocations of its first 25 years of independence and remained aloof from its francophone neighbours' cooperation within the framework of the franc zone.

CÔTE D'IVOIRE. Although the next round of presidential and parliamentary elections were still two years away in the year 2000, manœuvres were already taking place in preparation. On the one hand, it seemed as though the constitutional disqualification, for reasons of nationality and residence, of former Prime Minister Alassane Ouattara might no longer apply. On the other, an alliance within a limited framework between the ruling Democratic Party (PDCI) and the opposition Ivoirian Popular Front (FPI) of Laurent Gbagbo appeared to be in preparation. The party that M. Ouattara would lead on his return in 1999 (from a four-year term as deputy managing director of the IMF in Washington) was the Republican Democratic Rally (RDR). It was still waiting for him patiently, the more so since its leader in parliament, where it had several seats, Djény Kobena, died suddenly in October.

The performance of the Ivoirian economy continued to give satisfaction, not just to the local business class (which remained strongly interlocked with the political class) but to international donors, who had a strong interest in the country's economic success. Annual growth in GDP per capita remained at over 6 per cent (albeit down on growth of over 7 per cent in 1995) and plans were predicated on further increases. However, debt servicing still amounted to 50 per cent of administrative expenditure, and there was some tailing-off of external aid as well as other revenue, in part because of the uncertain state of world commodity prices for cocoa, coffee and cotton in the wake of the Asian economic collapse. Battles continued with the IMF and World Bank over economic deregulation, notably the dismantling of Caistab (the state-run commodity price stabilizing structure). However, the removal of Caistab was nearly complete by the end of the year. Because it had been used in the past as a patronage vehicle by the ruling party, its removal was expected to affect the coming political contest.

BURKINA FASO. The holding of the annual summit of the Organization of African Unity in Ouagadougou at the beginning of June and the presidential elections of November were the main events of the year. The summit was somewhat distracted by the outbreak of two wars during the meeting (see XI.6.ii) and a third two months later; but this meant that in his new role as OAU chairman President Blaise Compaoré was keen to be perceived as a dynamic African leader. He was particularly involved in a series of unsuccessful mediations between Eritrea and Ethiopia (see VI.1.i) and in some meetings in southern Africa on the conflict in the Democratic Republic of the Congo (see VII.1.i).

The presidential elections in November saw President Compaoré sweep back to power with 87.52 per cent of votes, against 6.61 per cent for Ram Ouedraogo and 5.87 per cent for Frederic Guirma, neither of whom presented any threat. The two main opposition leaders, Joseph Ki-Zerbo and Herman Ouedraogo, boycotted the election, so the result could not be seen as an accurate reflection of the actual state of the parties, although it was noted that voter participation was more than double the 25 per cent shown in the last presidential poll in 1991.

The investiture of President Compaoré on 21 December was marred by major demonstrations in the capital and other towns in protest at the alleged murder in a car fire of a prominent journalist, Norbert Zongo. The protests were seen as an indication of the continued strength of the opposition, in spite of the election outcome.

TOGO. The central political event of the year was the presidential election of June. The crisis which followed it, both domestically and internationally, had not been defused by the end of the year.

The crisis was rendered the more acute by the peculiarly close involvement of the European Union (EU) in the election. This followed a deal in 1997 between President Gnassingbé Eyadéma and European Commissioner João de Deus Pinheiro, which permitted the EU-ACP Joint Assembly (involving the European Parliament) to be held in Togo, as well as providing for 1.2 million ecus to assist the conduct of the polling and for a high-powered team of EU observers. The condition was that the election would be fully transparent. This condition was more or less observed during the campaign, which was supervised by an independent electoral commission and featured shared radio and television time. Also important was the participation of the Union of the Forces of Change (UFC), the party of the self-exiled Gilchrist Olympio, President Eyadéma's arch-enemy, who was still obliged for reasons of his own personal security to remain in neighbouring Ghana for most of the election campaign.

When it came to election day, however, government members of the electoral commission were pressured into resigning, and the Minister of the Interior, General Seyi Memené, took over the counting of votes, as well as the announcement of the results. Although these were later confirmed by the Constitutional Court, the opposition claimed that there had been blatant interference in the process, because the first returns in the capital, Lomé, had shown large majorities for the UFC. Whereas the figures put out by the government showed President Eyadéma as having obtained 52.13 per cent of the vote, with Mr Olympio second with 34.06 per cent, the opposition said that according to their counts at polling stations the UFC candidate had won a clear majority. The important aspect was that the EU team also expressed its unhappiness at the events, although its actual report had not been published by year's end.

Some dubiously pro-Eyadéma observer groups were found to authenticate the result, and General Eyadéma procceded to be sworn in as President on 22 July. However, the European Commission made it clear that it rejected the result, with support from key member-states, notably Germany and France, and continued its suspension of aid, while invoking a consultation process under the Lomé Convention. This involved two missions to Brussels by Prime Minister Kouassi Klutse, but by the end of the year the explanations offered were not satisfactory. Attempts at domestic consultation with opposition groups, prior to the holding of parliamentary elections scheduled for February 1999, also proved inconclusive.

Meanwhile, President Eyadéma sought continued diplomatic backing from Togo's West African neighbours, who obliged by making him chairman of ECOWAS at the organization's summit at the end of October (see XI.6.ii).

BENIN. It was a quiet election-free year, with nonetheless a measure of political manœuvring. Most conspicuously, in May, Adrien Houngbedji, loser in the 1996 presidential election, was ousted from the position of Prime Minister which he had held since the election. He had apparently sought from President Mathieu Kérékou a definition of the role of Prime Minister, a job not provided for in the constitution. The President responded by doing without a Prime Minister in the new government, although this was seen as taking a risk, since without support from M. Houngbedji, his coalition government was in danger of being put in a minority in parliament.

NIGER. There were signs in December that the opposition parties were preparing to create conditions for an end to the crisis which had prevailed since the coup and presidential elections of 1996 (see AR 1996, pp. 258–9), and which had rumbled on during the year. Mediation from the new Abubakar regime in Nigeria was said to have played a part in the new detente.

The year had begun with considerable tension surrounding an assassination plot alleged to have been fomented by one of the opposition leaders, former Premier Amadou Hama. Despite the charges, M. Hama was not arrested, and the affair died down. In July there was a purported agreement to end the crisis, which did not stick, so that the municipal elections due in November were postponed. In October some minor opposition parties crossed to support the government.

ii. CHAD—CAMEROON—GABON—CONGO-BRAZZAVILLE— CENTRAL AFRICAN REPUBLIC—EQUATORIAL GUINEA

Chad
CAPITAL: Ndjaména   AREA: 1,284,000 sq km   POPULATION: 7,000,000 ('97)
OFFICIAL LANGUAGES: French & Arabic   POLITICAL SYSTEM: presidential
HEAD OF STATE & GOVERNMENT: President (Col.) Idriss Déby (since Dec '90)
RULING PARTIES: Patriotic Salvation Movement (MPS) & Union for Democracy and the Republic (UDR) head fluid coalition
PRIME MINISTER: Nassour Owaido Guelendouksia (since May '97)
MAIN IGO MEMBERSHIPS (non-UN): OAU, CEEAC, OIC, ACP, Francophonie, NAM
CURRENCY: CFA franc (end-'98 £1=CFAF929.40, US$1=CFAF558.62)
GNP PER CAPITA: US$240 by exchange-rate calculation, US$1,070 by PPP calculation ('97)

Cameroon
CAPITAL: Yaoundé   AREA: 475,000 sq km   POPULATION: 14,000,000 ('97)
OFFICIAL LANGUAGES: French & English   POLITICAL SYSTEM: presidential
HEAD OF STATE & GOVERNMENT: President Paul Biya (since Nov '82)
RULING PARTY: Democratic Rally of the Cameroon People (RDPC)
PRIME MINISTER: Peter Mafany Musonge (since Sept '96)
MAIN IGO MEMBERSHIPS (non-UN): OAU, CEEAC, OIC, ACP, Francophonie, NAM
CURRENCY: CFA franc (see above)
GNP PER CAPITA: US$650 by exchange-rate calculation, US$1,980 by PPP calculation ('97)

Gabon
CAPITAL: Libreville   AREA: 268,000 sq km   POPULATION: 1,350,000 ('97)
OFFICIAL LANGUAGE: French   POLITICAL SYSTEM: presidential
HEAD OF STATE & GOVERNMENT: President Omar Bongo (since March '67)
RULING PARTY: Gabonese Democratic Party (PDG)
PRIME MINISTER: Paulin Obame-Nguema (since Oct '94)
MAIN IGO MEMBERSHIPS (non-UN): OAU, CEEAC, OPEC, OIC, ACP, Francophonie, NAM
CURRENCY: CFA franc (see above)
GNP PER CAPITA: US$4,230 by exchange-rate calculation, US$6,540 by PPP calculation ('97)

Congo-Brazzaville
CAPITAL: Brazzaville   AREA: 342,000 sq km   POPULATION: 3,000,000 ('97)
OFFICIAL LANGUAGE: French   POLITICAL SYSTEM: presidential
HEAD OF STATE & GOVERNMENT: President Denis Sassou-Nguesso (since Oct '97)
RULING PARTIES: Congolese Movement for Democracy and Integral Development (MCDDI) is included in ruling coalition
MAIN IGO MEMBERSHIPS (non-UN): OAU, CEEAC, ACP, Francophonie, NAM
CURRENCY: CFA franc (see above)
GNP PER CAPITA: US$660 by exchange-rate calculation, US$1,380 by PPP calculation ('97)

Central African Republic
CAPITAL: Bangui   AREA: 623,000 sq km   POPULATION: 3,500,000 ('97)
OFFICIAL LANGUAGE: French   POLITICAL SYSTEM: presidential
HEAD OF STATE & GOVERNMENT: President Ange-Félix Patassé (since Sept '92)
RULING PARTY: Central African People's Liberation Party (MPLC)
PRIME MINISTER: Michel Gbezera-Bria (since Jan '97)
MAIN IGO MEMBERSHIPS (non-UN): OAU, CEEAC, OPEC, OIC, ACP, Francophonie, NAM
CURRENCY: CFA franc (see above)
GNP PER CAPITA: US$320 by exchange-rate calculation, US$1,530 by PPP calculation ('97)

Equatorial Guinea
CAPITAL: Malabo   AREA: 28,000 sq km   POPULATION: 421,000 ('97)
OFFICIAL LANGUAGES: Spanish & French POLITICAL SYSTEM: presidential
HEAD OF STATE & GOVERNMENT: President (Brig.-Gen.) Teodoro Obiang Nguema Mbasogo (since Aug '79)
RULING PARTY: Democratic Party of Equatorial Guinea (PDGE)
PRIME MINISTER: Angel Serafin Seriche Dugan (since March '96)
MAIN IGO MEMBERSHIPS (non-UN): OAU, CEEAC, ACP, Francophonie, NAM
CURRENCY: CFA FRANC (see above)
GNP PER CAPITA: US$1,050 by exchange-rate calculation, US$3,600 by PPP calculation ('97)

CHAD. If President Idris Déby appeared increasingly to dominate the political scene within Chad, there was still unease about his authoritarian methods. Although most of the former zones of dissidence were quiescent, the situation in the south appeared to deteriorate sharply early in the year, as the Republican Guard composed of Déby loyalists carried out a number of punishment raids on areas believed to be supporting the Forces d'Action pour une République Fédérale (FARF) of Laokein 'Frisson' Bardé, which had broken the 1997 truce. However, in April a new peace agreement was reached, following, it later emerged, the death of M. Bardé, who was variously reported to have been killed in a government ambush or by his own FARF colleagues. Later in the year turbulence in the south died down, although the outspoken southern parliamentarian, Yorongar Ngarlejy, was gaoled for three years in June for criminal libel in claiming that Abdelkader Kamougué, Speaker of the National Assembly, had been bribed by oil companies.

Oil was an increasingly important theme in both domestic politics and international relations. The proposed 1,050-kilometre pipeline from Doba in southern Chad to Kribi on the Cameroon Atlantic coast ran into opposition from environmental lobbies in Europe and the United States. This delayed the World Bank financing decision on which the major raising of funds for the whole project, totalling $3,000 million, would depend. The oil companies involved—Exxon, Shell and ELF—were not overly concerned by the delay, in light of the fall in world oil prices resulting from the Asian recession. But the project was still expected to go ahead and come on stream by 2002. The importance of a stable and relatively moderate regime in Chad was still important in the West, because of its close proximity to the 'loose cannon' states of Libya and Sudan.

CAMEROON. After the tensions of election year in 1997 (see AR 1997, p. 264), Cameroon settled down to concentrate on putting its economy in order, with the political situation in semi-cold storage. The one remaining party of significance still in opposition, the Social Democratic Front (SDF), was more preoccupied with its own divisions, while still holding out on any temptation to take office. Observers noted that threats of opposition frustrations converting into violence failed to materialize. Relations with Nigeria remained tense because of the continuing dispute over the oil-bearing Bakassi peninsula (still under consideration by the International Court of Justice), but verbal threats did not deteriorate into combat.

Signs of economic recovery continued to be seen, although relations with the Washington institutions remained difficult. The privatization of Cameroon's numerous top-heavy and sclerotic state enterprises, one of the main bones of contention, was said to have made important strides in the sugar, railways and cement sectors. Arrangements for the Cameroon Development Corporation in the anglophone south-west were complete by the end of the year. The problem of selling off Cameroon Airlines remained to be faced.

GABON. The presidential elections of 6 December confirmed predictions that the winner would be President Omar Bongo, who had held the supreme office since December 1967, making him Africa's third longest-serving head of state (after the King of Morocco and the President of Togo). According to the Constitutional Court, he obtained a further seven-year term with 66.55 per cent of the vote. His erstwhile main rival, Father Paul Mba Abessole, managed only third place, with 13.41 per cent, compared with the 16.54 per cent obtained by maverick politician Pierre Mamboundou. This led M. Mba, and his Lumberjacks' Party to denounce 'fraud on a massive scale'. The French press noted that there was 'suspicion' around some of the apparently neutral observers, who had been recruited by a close adviser of President Bongo.

Relations with France were passing through one of the periodic periods of coolness, in part because of perceived criticism from the socialists now in parliamentary power in Paris. President Bongo refused to attend the Franco-African summit in Paris in November, because he objected to the large number of non-francophone countries attending.

CONGO-BRAZZAVILLE. Having been imposed by force in October 1997 (see AR 1997, pp. 265–6), the government of President Denis Sassou-Nguesso spent much of the year in a quest for legitimacy in the face of an increasingly troubling security situation. At the same time, he embarked upon the uphill struggle of persuading the international community to sink funds into the shattered country, especially the capital Brazzaville, ruined by the four months of intensive fighting between militias from June to October 1997.

While a Forum for Transition drew up a programme for the restoration of a democratic system by the year 2001, and supporters of the former President Pascal Lissouba seemed to have melted away, the same could not be said of the 'Ninja' militia of former Prime Minister Bernard Kolélas. His support came especially from the Lari areas in the vicinity of Brazzaville. Operating in certain suburbs of the capital, his supporters also received general sympathy from the southern part of the country, especially in all the areas of the Bakongo (the broader grouping of the Lari). Whereas the situation was reported as 'calm' in mid-year, by December there was a sharp deterioration, featuring fighting between 'Ninjas' and the pro-Sassou-Nguesso 'Cobras'.

In view of his domestic problems, President Sassou-Nguesso was careful not to become involved in the new ructions in neighbouring Congo-Kinshasa (see VII.1.i), especially since he was still dependent on an admittedly low-key Angolan military presence.

CENTRAL AFRICAN REPUBLIC. Although the delicate political/military situation continued to dictate that foreign troops were needed to maintain order and retrain the national army, there was an important evolution early in the year. On 15 April the Mission to Monitor the Bangui Accords (MISAB) was replaced by the United Nations Mission to the Central African Republic (MINURCA). The MISAB had been set up following the Franco-African summit in Ouagadougou in December 1996, to take charge of security in the country following the three army mutinies of that year (see AR 1997, pp. 266–7). The successor UN force continued to be composed of troops from several francophone African countries (Senegal, Chad, Togo, Gabon and Burkina Faso, expanded to include Côte d'Ivoire), with logistics, funds and a handful of personnel from France. Canada also decided to come under the UN umbrella in a force totalling over 1,000 personnel, whereas Ghana, which was to have offered a token anglophone presence, withdrew at the last minute, officially for budgetary reasons.

The mandate of the UN mission as approved by the Security Council was to reinforce security, to continue to collect weapons and to maintain order in the capital, as well as to retrain the police force to lighten the load of the army. The continuation of MINURCA was, even so, to depend on the political evolution of the country and on the implementation of economic reforms. Above all, its presence hinged upon the successful holding of parliamentary elections intended to reinforce the democratic process. After some delays, these were eventually held in November. The first round proved inconclusive, with the ruling Central African People's Liberation Movement (MPLC) of President Ange-Félix Patassé obtaining 26 seats in the 109-seat Assembly and the combined opposition 17, three seats going to independents. The second round, still supervised by MINURCA, was held on 13 December, but the results had not been announced by the end of the year.

EQUATORIAL GUINEA. The year opened explosively, with an armed attack on three localities on Bioko island (formerly Fernando Po). Announcing the attack on 23 January, President Obiang Nguema Mbasogo said that the Movement for Self-Determination for Bioko (MAIB)—composed mainly of the Bubi ethnic group, the original inhabitants of the island—had orchestrated the attack. The MAIB denied this charge, but claimed that the Bubi were undergoing a 'veritable genocide' at the hands of 'the army of the Fang' (the majority tribe of the mainland territory of Rio Muni). The attack was followed by a wave of arrests on the island, especially in the capital, Malabo, and reported attacks and looting against the 10,000-strong Nigerian community on the island. Nigerian media reported widespread killings, but these were denied by the Malabo authorities.

Arrests of Bubi militants in April were followed by an growing campaign in Spain, the former colonial power, against the Obiang dictatorship, in both media and parliament. The ensuing trial resulted in death sentences being passed on 15 of the alleged ringleaders by a military court (using colonial laws reportedly unchanged since the Franco dictatorship), but President Obiang commuted the sentences. An announced reconciliation with Nigeria following the January incidents was put on ice with the death of Nigerian leader Sani Abacha on 8 June (see VI.2.ii), remaining cool for the rest of the year. Relations with Spain remained difficult, with the Malabo government requesting the extradition of opposition leader Severin Moto, in self-exile in Madrid for more than a year. More arrests of Bubis, especially relatives of those condemned in June, were reported in December.

VII CENTRAL AND SOUTHERN AFRICA

1. CONGO-KINSHASA—BURUNDI AND RWANDA—GUINEA-BISSAU AND CAPE VERDE—SÃO TOMÉ & PRÍNCIPE—MOZAMBIQUE—ANGOLA

i. DEMOCRATIC REPUBLIC OF THE CONGO (EX-ZAÏRE)

CAPITAL: Kinshasa   AREA: 2,345,000 sq km   POPULATION: 47,000,000 ('97)
OFFICIAL LANGUAGE: French   POLITICAL SYSTEM: presidential
HEAD OF STATE & GOVERNMENT: President Laurent Kabila (since May '97)
RULING PARTIES: Alliance of Democratic Forces for the Liberation of the Congo (AFDL) heads coalition with Union for Democracy and Social Progress (UDPS) & Patriotic Front (FP)
MAIN IGO MEMBERSHIPS (non-UN): OAU, CEEAC, ACP, Francophonie, NAM
CURRENCY: zaïre (end-'98 £1=Z228,765.60, US$1=Z137,500.00)
GNP PER CAPITA: US$110 by exchange-rate calculation, US$790 by PPP calculation ('97)

SERIOUS doubts were being expressed by early 1998 as to whether the government of President Laurent Kabila, who had taken power in May 1997 (see AR 1997, pp. 268–71), had the capacity to hold the country together. By the end of the year the worst fears had been confirmed: the country was again rent by civil war with the main line of division lying between east and west but with serious internal divisions within both those larger areas. It seemed highly doubtful whether the Congo would ever again resume the shape imposed on it by King Leopold of the Belgians more than a hundred years earlier.

The new government faced a formidable range of problems. There were many uncontrolled armed groups still active in different parts of the country. Hutu militants, some of them well-equipped ex-soldiers, were still using bases in North Kivu for launching attacks into Rwanda. In other parts of North and South Kivu small but distinct ethnic groups had taken to arms in defence of their own autonomy against all comers. Former soldiers of ex-President Mobutu's Zaïrean Armed Forces (FAZ) were still at large, some of them having acquired safe havens in neighbouring Congo-Brazzaville and the Central African Republic. And there was a high degree of insecurity along the Angolan frontier.

President Kabila himself lacked a really solid land base. Even in Katanga, from which he drew most of his support, there was a significant secessionist movement. His victory in 1997 had been largely due to the support offered by the Bamyamulenge (ethnic Tutsi of South Kivu) and by the armies of Rwanda and Uganda. This alliance was coming under increasing strain with the growth of widespread resentment in Kinshasa at the role of 'the Tutsi'. M. Kabila spurned the support he might have received from Etienne Tshisekedi, the leader of the Union for Democracy and Social Progress (UDPS), the country's largest political party, with a firm base in Eastern Kasai. M. Tshisekedi was subjected to four months' 'internal exile'. Other dissidents, several of whom had been among the President's most prominent supporters, found themselves in prison. Falling back on the methods adopted by ex-President Mobutu, M. Kabila started filling key posts with members of his own family or with 'ethnic kinsmen' from Katanga.

Taking a fiercely nationalist line, the new government found that it could count on little practical support from the country's traditional aid donors. The government strongly resented the work of the UN team appointed to investigate allegations of human rights abuses and in particular massacres of thousands of Hutu refugees by M. Kabila's forces in 1997. In the face of increasing obstruction, the UN team withdrew in April. Its report, published on 30 June, confirmed the allegations of massacres and recommended that an international tribunal be established to prosecute those responsible.

Potential aid donors were involved in drawing up plans for a reconstruction programme that would need US$1,500 million, of which close on half would have to come from aid donors. By mid-year no more than $100 million had been offered. The government was confident that the country's massive mineral resources would attract substantial private investment, but the initial enthusiasm of foreign businessmen cooled as soon as they came face to face with the many practical difficulties of investing in so unstable a country. Nevertheless, the government could claim some successes. Hyperinflation, put at over 600 per cent in 1997, disappeared; the inflation rate was no more than 14 per cent in 1998. A new currency was introduced in June, intended to replace the four or five different currencies circulating in the last years of the Mobutu regime. On 25 May President Kabila issued a decree establishing a 300-member constituent legislative assembly but the government reserved the right to control the selection of members.

Signs of really serious strain emerged in July when the government, fearing a possible coup, started removing Tutsi, both Rwandans and Banyanulenge, from key positions in the military establishment. With the growth of anti-Tutsi sentiment, other Banyamulenge began moving back to their homeland in South Kivu. The Rwandan authorities were also deeply worried by evidence that President Kabila was now providing training camps for Hutu extremists.

On 2 August military units in Goma and Bukavu mutinied and so took the first steps in a major rebellion. Two weeks later the rebels announced the formation of the Congolese Democratic Rally (RCD). Banyamulenge Tutsi with strong Rwandan and Ugandan backing formed the core of the new movement, but both military and civilian leaders from other regions joined the rebels, and a history professor of Bakongo origin, Ernest Wamba dia Wamba, became president of the RCD.

On 4 August the rebels carried out a spectacularly daring strike: using civilian planes captured at Goma airport, they transported several thousand of their best troops to the military base at Kitoma, not far from the Atlantic port of Matadi. Most of the soldiers at Kitoma were former members of Mobutu's army undergoing 're-education'. Many of them joined the rebels, who set out to march on Kinshasa. They occupied the dam and hydroelectric works at Inga and reached Kinshasa's airport. In this desperate situation, unable to rely on his own forces, President Kabila appealed for help to Angola and Zimbabwe, both countries with well-trained armies and air forces. Their intervention proved decisive. Angolan troops moved south from Cabinda to take the rebels in the rear. Under attack from Angolan and Zimbabwean planes, the rebels retreated into northern Angola and took up guerrilla tactics. Over the next few weeks Namibia, Congo-Brazzaville, the Central African Republic, Sudan, Chad and Gabon pledged support to President Kabila and provided small military contingents or financial aid.

The rebels had failed in their attempt to win the war by a 'lightning strike', but by the end of August they had driven government forces from a large triangle of territory with a base running from the border with Sudan to northern Katanga and an apex at Kisangani, the country's third largest town. But many local groups remained fiercely opposed to what they saw as 'Tutsi domination'.

One of the most significant features of this new civil war was that it represented an exclusively African conflict, with the Western powers (the United States, France and Belgium) which had hitherto been deeply involved in the Congo standing impotently on the side-lines. African military intervention was accompanied by vigorous diplomatic initiatives aimed at bringing about a ceasefire. The first peace conference attended by all the intervening states, with neutral Zambia in the chair, was held at Victoria Falls (Zimbabwe) on 7 September. Subsequent meetings involved members of the Southern African Development Community and the Organization of African Unity. The Congo crisis was a major item at the 20th Franco-African conference held in Paris at the end of November (see XI.3.ii). Senior US officials also attempted to bring the two sides together. But it proved impossible to overcome the intransigence shown both by President Kabila and by the rebels.

In September and early October the rebel advance continued. Particular significance was attached to the capture of Kindu, upstream from Kisangani, an important garrison town and air base well sited for an assault on Katanga and Eastern Kasai. To counter further rebel advances, more Angolan and Zimbabwean troops were brought in. In the north-east rebel groups independent of the RCD but supported by the Ugandan army made substantial progress. But by the end of the year the war seemed to have reached stalemate.

In the meantime, the Congo's neighbours sought ways of compensating themselves for the expense of their intervention. The Angolans struck a deal over oil; the Zimbabweans acquired valuable stakes in the copper and cobalt industries; the Namibians obtained access to diamonds; and the Ugandans to gold. 'The main players in Congo are seen by many', wrote *The Economist* (London) on 24 October, 'as greedy warlords with readymade armies at their disposal and a clear interest in enriching themselves. Continued war could be their best way of doing this.'

ii. BURUNDI AND RWANDA

Burundi
CAPITAL: Bujumbura   AREA: 28,000 sq km   POPULATION: 7,000,000 ('97)
OFFICIAL LANGUAGE: French & Kirundi   POLITICAL SYSTEM: transitional
HEAD OF STATE & GOVERNMENT: President (Maj.) Pierre Buyoya (since July '96)
MAIN IGO MEMBERSHIPS (non-UN) OAU, CEEAC, ACP, Francophonie, NAM
CURRENCY: Burundi franc (end-'98 £1=Fbu840.40, US$1=Fbu505.12)
GNP PER CAPITA: US$180 by exchange-rate calculation, US$590 by PPP calculation ('97)

Rwanda
CAPITAL: Kigali   AREA: 26,300 sq km   POPULATION: 8,000,000 ('97)
OFFICIAL LANGUAGES: French, Kinyarwanda & English
POLITICAL SYSTEM: presidential
HEAD OF STATE & GOVERNMENT: President Pasteur Bizimungu (since July '94)
RULING PARTIES: Rwandan Patriotic Front (FPR) & Republican Democratic Movement (MDR) head coalition
PRIME MINISTER: Pierre-Célestin Rwigyema (MDR), since Aug '95
MAIN IGO MEMBERSHIPS (non-UN): OAU, CEEAC, ACP, Francophonie, NAM
CURRENCY: Rwanda franc (end-'98 £1=RF533.45, US$1=RF320.63)
GNP PER CAPITA: US$210 by exchange-rate calculation, US$630 by PPP calculation ('97)

BURUNDI. 'The opposing sides in the four-year-old civil war in Burundi raped, tortured and killed thousands of civilians and looted and destroyed civilian property.' This was the conclusion of the New York-based Human Rights Watch in its World Report 1998, summing up the situation in 1997 (see AR 1997, pp. 271–2). Particular brutality was shown by the army in enforcing its '*regroupmemt*' policy, 'going systematically through the countryside, looting and burning homes, and hunting down anyone who resisted being "regrouped" [killing] thousands of unarmed civilians, many of them women, children and elderly'. The report continued: 'The military also carried out numerous attacks, targeting specific individuals who were summarily executed or "disappeared". Most of those killed were community leaders whom the armed forces feared might organize resistance or young men who might some day join the rebel groups ... The most widespread human rights abuse by rebel groups was looting from the civilian population, but the rebels also killed a number of unarmed civilians, both Hutu and Tutsi, in indiscriminate attacks.'

One particularly well-publicized attack was that made on January 1 on a military camp and village close to Bujumbura by rebels belonging to the military wing of the National Council for the Defence of Democracy (CNDD). In this attack, the first made on a target near the capital for two years, at least 284 people, most of them Hutu civilians, were reported killed. Rebel attacks in the same area continued for the next four months, but gradually violence died down and by the end of the year life in the capital was reported as being back to normal.

The draconian methods used by the army were undoubtedly one cause for the pacification of the country. Another development—in the long run far more significant—was the remarkable progress made towards a political accommodation between Tutsi and Hutu. Pressure on the government to work out a peaceful settlement was intense. Delegations from the UN, foreign governments, religious groups and non-governmental organizations continued to visit Bujumbura to urge the cause of peace. The trade embargo imposed by regional powers after the military coup of 1996 was still in force. Above all, demographic necessity—the fact that the Tutsi were outnumbered five to one by Hutu—made a settlement the only alternative to an armed struggle in which the Tutsi could never hope to be completely victorious.

In 1996 Julius Nyerere, the former President of Tanzania and the region's foremost elder statesman, had been appointed regional mediator. A generous grant from the European Union was provided to meet the cost of mediation. In May a wide range of political groups from Burundi came together in Dar es Salaam. Further meetings were held in Arusha in June and July. On 6 June Colonel Buyoya, the head of the military government, promulgated a Transitional Constitutional Act which partially restored the civilian constitution of 1992. The settlement established a power-sharing government with the 22 ministerial posts being equally divided between Tutsi and Hutu. The post of Prime Minister was replaced by two Vice-Presidents, one Hutu, the other Tutsi. The National Assembly was enlarged from 81 to 121 members.

Colonel Buyoya was formally sworn in as President on 11 June. The new settlement did not pass unopposed. Charles Mukasi, a Hutu but chairman of Uprona (Union for National Progress), the main Tutsi party, denounced members of the Front for Democracy in Burundi (Frodepu), the main Hutu party, as '*genocidaires*' and refused to participate. Nevertheless, most Uprona members backed the agreement, and M. Mukasi was later forced to resign as Uprona chairman and replaced by another prominent Hutu. Frodebu was also divided, but with a majority favouring settlement. The militant Hutu CNDD denounced the settlement as 'an act of treason', but the party was riven by factional differences, with some factions sending representatives to the Arusha conference in June. The power-sharing agreement was seen as only the first step towards an enduring settlement. An effective ceasefire still needed to be established.

Serious incidents of violence continued in some areas. In November, for example, at least 100 Hutu civilians were killed by the army in retaliation for an attack on a camp sheltering Tutsis, launched by the military wing of Party for the Liberation of the Hutu People (Palipehutu). With the army completely dominated by Tutsi, effective reform would involve opening up government service, both military and civilian, to Hutu nominees; however, given the intensity of fear and hatred on both sides, such a reform presented formidable difficulties.

At the end of the year the trade embargo was still formally in place, but by now it was riddled with loopholes: Kenya, Rwanda and Zambia had for some time been disregarding the restrictions on trade with Burundi, while on 7 November the UN Security Council called for sanctions to be at least suspended. With ex-President Nyerere, hitherto the foremost advocate of sanctions, also turning against them, President Buyoya could hope to see them removed early in 1999. Such a move was likely to bring about an economic upturn, a development which could only strengthen his position.

RWANDA. A total of 1,575 civilians had been killed by the army or by rebels in Rwanda in 1996, according to a UN report. According to a Human Rights Watch (HRW) report, in the first nine months of 1997 the death toll rose to 6,000. No figures were yet available for 1998, but judging from the number of incidents reported the incidence of violent death seemed unlikely to be much reduced. The north-west remained the most troubled region: the state of civil war prevailing in 1997 (see AR 1997, p. 273) continued in 1998. Serious incidents also occurred in central Rwanda.

The rebels, mostly drawn from the pre-1994 Interahamwe militia, seemed as yet to have no clear political organization. But in June a group calling itself the Rwandan Liberation Army (RLA) claimed responsibility for an attack on a camp for Tutsi refugees from Kivu (Democratic Republic of the Congo). The RLA described itself as the armed wing of People in Arms for the Liberation of Rwanda (Palir). Although most of the attacks launched by Hutu extremists were seen as the work of groups which had established bases in the less accessible forested areas of Rwanda, some groups were still operating from bases across the border in Kivu. The government was also deeply concerned by reports that President Kabila was now offering training facilities to Interahamwe still living in Congo-Kinshasa.

On 24 April the first public executions of those found guilty of participating in the 1994 genocide took place: 22 people faced the firing squad in Kigali and other towns. On 2 September the UN International Criminal Tribunal for Rwanda passed its first 'guilty' verdict, convicting Jean-Paul Akayesu, mayor of Taba, of genocide and crimes against humanity. The verdict was reported to be the first by any international court for the specific crime of genocide. On 2 October M. Akayesu was sentenced to three life terms in prison.

Kofi Annan, the UN Secretary-General, visited Rwanda on 7 May, addressing the National Assembly. Three days before his visit a report in the US press asserted that in January 1994 the commander of the UN force in Rwanda had sent a warning of plans by Hutu for the systematic massacre of Tutsi. Rwandan Foreign Minister Anastace Gasana, who spoke after Mr Annan, accused the UN of 'lack of political will' in failing to prevent the genocide. A further indication of strained relations with the UN came with the publication of the UN report on human rights abuses in Congo-Kishasa, in which Rwandan troops were accused of participating in the killing of Hutu refugees. In July the UN Human Rights Field Office withdrew from Rwanda after it became clear that its staff would not be free to visit all parts of the country.

Both Amnesty International and the HRW produced reports critical of the government in 1998. 'The government responded to attacks [by insurgents] with an excessive and indiscriminate use of force', HRW asserted in its *World Report 1998*. 'Soldiers and government officials also killed hundreds of civilians in circumstances other than military operations.' In spite of these and other criticisms relating to the judicial process, the Rwandan government continued to receive a substantial amount of foreign aid, the United States being the main supporter.

iii. GUINEA-BISSAU AND CAPE VERDE

Guinea-Bissau
CAPITAL: Bissau AREA: 36,000 sq km POPULATION: 1,100,000 ('97)
OFFICIAL LANGUAGE: Portuguese POLITICAL SYSTEM: presidential
HEAD OF STATE & GOVERNMENT: President (Brig.-Gen.) João Bernardo Vieira (since Nov '80)
RULING PARTY: African Party for the Independence of Guinea and Cape Verde (PAIGC)
PRIME MINISTER: Francisco Fadul (since Dec '98)
MAIN IGO MEMBERSHIPS (non-UN): OAU, ECOWAS, ACP, OIC, NAM, CPLP
CURRENCY: CFA franc (end-'98 £1=PG929.40, US$1=PG558.62)
GNP PER CAPITA: US$240 by exchange-rate calculation, US$1,070 ('95) by PPP calculation ('97)

Cape Verde
CAPITAL: Praia AREA: 4,000 sq km POPULATION: 400,000 ('97)
OFFICIAL LANGUAGE: Portuguese POLITICAL SYSTEM: presidential
HEAD OF STATE & GOVERNMENT: President Antonio Mascarenhas Monteiro (since March '91)
RULING PARTY: Movement for Democracy (MPD)
PRIME MINISTER: Carlos Veiga (since Jan '91)
MAIN IGO MEMBERSHIPS (non-UN): OAU, ECOWAS, ACP, NAM, CPLP
CURRENCY: Cape Verde escudo (end-'98 £1=CVEsc157.25, US$1=CVEsc94.52)
GNP PER CAPITA: US$1,090 by exchange-rate calculation, US$2,980 by PPP calculation ('97)

GUINEA-BISSAU was plunged into violence by an army mutiny on 7 June. Most of the country's 9,000 soldiers joined the mutineers, who seized the international airport and the main barracks. They were under the leadership of General Ansumane Mane, who had been sacked from his post as chief of staff in January after being accused of smuggling arms to the rebel movement in the Senegalese province of Casamance (see also VI.3.i). With Diola people living on both sides of Guinea-Bissau's northern border with Senegal, close ethnic ties existed between many soldiers and the people of Casamance. The soldiers complained of low pay and the threat of redundancy. They were also affected by the unpopularity of President Vieira, who had been in power for 18 years and had recently shifted the country's foreign policy away from its natural allies, the Lusophone states, coming closer to the Francophone states, especially Senegal.

Left with little more than the presidential guard to protect him, President Vieira appealed to Senegal and Guinea, which sent in more than 3,000 troops. Panic gripped the people of the capital, Bissau, most of whose 250,000 inhabitants were reported to have fled. Heavy fighting continued until the end of July, when the first ceasefire was arranged.

CAPE VERDE played a prominent part in the peace negotiations. The Community of Portuguese-Speaking Countries (CPLP) held a summit meeting (only the second in its history) in Cape Verde in mid-July and set up a contact group which brokered the ceasefire and went on to cement it. Suspecting the Lusophone states of sympathy for the rebels, President Vieira looked towards the Economic Community of West African States (ECOWAS) for support, hoping that under Nigerian leadership the organization would send in, as it had already done in Liberia and Sierra Leone, a large peace-keeping force. At a meeting held in Lomé (Togo) on 14 December the ECOWAS states persuaded President Vieira and General Mane to accept a transitional power-sharing government with an ECOWAS force brought in to keep the peace.

iv. SÃO TOMÉ & PRÍNCIPE

CAPITAL: São Tomé   AREA: 965 sq km   POPULATION: 138,000 ('97)
OFFICIAL LANGUAGE: Portuguese   POLITICAL SYSTEM: presidential
HEAD OF STATE & GOVERNMENT: President Miguel Trovoada (since March '91)
RULING PARTY: Movement for the Liberation of São Tomé and Príncipe-Social Democratic Party (MLSTP-PSD)
PRIME MINISTER: Guiherme Posser da Costa (since Dec '98)
MAIN IGO MEMBERSHIPS (non-UN): OAU, CEEAC, ACP, NAM, CPLP
CURRENCY: dobra (end-'98 £1=Db3,976.36, US$1=Db2,390.00)
GNP PER CAPITA: US$270 by exchange-rate calculation ('97)

A series of articles in *The Courier* (the journal of the European Union and the ACP states) in March–April provided a rare insight into the islands' problems. 'There is a widespread feeling', it said, 'that the economic stagnation which is taking root is due, at least partly, to inertia within the political class.' There existed a long-running conflict between President Miguel Trovoada and Manuel Pinto da Costa—the former elected unopposed as an independent candidate in 1991 but later linked to the opposition Independent Democratic Action (ADI), the latter a former President and leader of the majority party, the São Tomé and Príncipe Liberation Movement—Social Democratic Party (MLSTP-PSD). The tension between them, reported *The Courier*, had produced 'an ill-tempered, reluctant power-sharing arrangement'.

Cocoa, the basis of the economy, continued to provide 80 per cent of export earnings, but production fell from 11,000 tonnes before independence in 1975 to 3,500 tonnes in 1997. 'All observers', reported *The Courier*, 'agreed that the country was on the verge of catastrophic bankruptcy', unless the IMF, using its highly-indebted poor country (HIPC) facility, cancelled 80 per cent of the $300 million external debt. Plans to establish a 'free zone' on Príncipe to attract investment and to encourage oil exploration in offshore waters were seen as palliatives: effective agricultural reform was vital but difficult to achieve with a population that was becoming steadily poorer. Society showed a lack of strong communal ties but some positive changes were being introduced with the help of foreign non-governmental organizations.

In a parliamentary election held on 8 November, the MLSTP-PSD increased its number of seats in the 55-seat National Assembly from 27 to 31 in a turnout of 65 per cent. Its coalition partner, the Democratic Convergence Party (PCD), fell from 14 to 8, while the opposition ADI increased from 15 to 16. Having also come into conflict with Prime Minister Raul Bragança Neto, President Trovoada on 23 December appointed the MLSTP-PSD vice-chairman, Guiherme Posser da Costa (a former Foreign Minister), to head the new government. However, the President promptly vetoed several of Sr da Costa's proposed ministerial appointments, so that no new government was in place at year's end.

v. MOZAMBIQUE

CAPITAL: Maputo   AREA: 800,000 sq km   POPULATION: 19,000,000 ('97)
OFFICIAL LANGUAGE: Portuguese   POLITICAL SYSTEM: presidential
HEAD OF STATE & GOVERNMENT: President Joaquim Alberto Chissano (since Nov '86)
RULING PARTY: Front for the Liberation of Mozambique (Frelimo)
PRIME MINISTER: Pascoal Mocumbi (since Dec '94)
MAIN IGO MEMBERSHIPS (non-UN): OAU, COMESA, SADC, ACP, CWTH, OIC, NAM, CPLP
CURRENCY: metical (end-'98 £1=Mt20,492.50, US$1=Mt12,317.10)
GNP PER CAPITA: US$90 by exchange-rate calculation, US$520 by PPP calculation ('97)

MOZAMBIQUE continued to maintain its reputation in the international community as a model case of transition from a long civil war to peaceful national reconciliation. The country also succeeded in maintaining a growth rate of 8 per cent, one of the highest in Africa. Impressed by the government's commitment to reform, the World Bank held out the promise that more than half the country's $5,500 million of external debt would be cancelled by 1999.

In Maputo the evidence of foreign investment was clearly visible—for instance in the many new Portuguese– and South African-owned supermarkets. In rural areas most of the schools destroyed in the war had been rebuilt and three-quarters of the 1,250 state farms had been privatized. But the existence of an estimated 500,000 land-mines continued to present a cruel obstruction to the development of peasant agriculture. President Chissano was committed to keeping strict restraints on public spending: he promptly vetoed an attempt by members of the National Assembly to vote themselves fat pensions. The President also took decisive action in dealing with cases of corruption.

Nevertheless, the hope that the country might make steady progress towards a genuine democratic order was not fulfilled. Municipal elections for 33 urban centres were due to be held in April. In the face of complaints by the National Resistance Movement (Renamo) and other opposition parties, polling was postponed till June; but the opposition parties carried out their threat to boycott the election and only 14.5 per cent of the urban electorate actually voted. Given the absence of genuine grievances, the opposition parties' boycott was seen as a means of covering up their own lack of effective organization. But there was no hint of the opposition contemplating violence, in striking contrast to the situation in Angola (see VII.1.vi).

vi. ANGOLA

CAPITAL: Luanda   AREA: 1,247,000 sq km   POPULATION: 12,000,000 ('97)
OFFICIAL LANGUAGE: Portuguese   POLITICAL SYSTEM: presidential
HEAD OF STATE & GOVERNMENT: President José Eduardo dos Santos (since Sept '79)
RULING PARTY: Popular Movement for the Liberation of Angola-Workers' Party
   (MPLA-PT) heads nominal coalition
PRIME MINISTER: Fernando José da França Dias van Dunem (since June '96)
MAIN IGO MEMBERSHIPS (non-UN): OAU, COMESA, SADC, ACP, NAM, CPLP
CURRENCY: kwanza (end-'98 £1=Kw427,796.60, US$1=Kw257,128.00)
GNP PER CAPITA: US$340 by exchange-rate calculation, US$940 by PPP calculation ('97)

IT was a dreadful year featuring a steady escalation of violence between Unita and government forces, leading to an outbreak of fighting on a scale which some described as Angola's 'fourth war'. (The three earlier wars were the anti-colonial struggle of 1961–74, the civil war and foreign intervention of 1975–91 and the renewed civil war 1992–94). Yet in the first three months of 1998 there were not unhopeful signs that an enduring peace might still be achieved.

Most senior Unita officials moved to Luanda, the capital, as the government appointed Unita governors to three provinces. Unita withdrew from the important diamond-mining area in the Cuango valley, and it was announced that Unita's demobilization had finally been completed. But the Unita leader, Dr Jonas Savimbi, still refused to come to Luanda, arguing that even with a large bodyguard his safety could not be guaranteed. Unita also refused to hand over its key areas, especially that round its headquarters at Bailundo in the Central Highlands. Acts of violence continued to be reported from many parts of the country, some the work of armed gangs without political associations. On 30 March the government sent an open letter to the UN special envoy, asserting that Unita was preparing for war with 8,000 well-equipped troops at its disposal. Later estimates put Unita's forces at 25,000. The government blamed the UN Observer Mission in Angola (UNOMA) for failing to prevent Unita's build-up of arms.

Alioune Blondin Beye, the UN special envoy in Angola since 1993, was killed in an aircraft crash in Côte d'Ivoire on 26 June. Sr Beye had built up close contacts with both sides, so that his death was a serious blow to the UN's already weakened position in Angola. A West African diplomat, Issa Diallo, was appointed as the new UN special envoy on 6 August.

In June President dos Santos embarked on a series of visits to build up international support. In Moscow he negotiated a large arms deal with the Russian government. He later strengthened ties with Portugal and the Lusophone states at their summit in Cape Verde in July (see XI.3.ii), also receiving vigorous professions of support from members of the Southern African Development Community (SADC). In July the UN Security Council imposed further sanctions on Unita. In August Angolan troops crossed into Congo-Kinshasa to help the hard-pressed government of President Kabila (see VII.1.i)). As the situation worsened, SADC members meeting in Luanda on 1 October called for 'a swift and rapid campaign to rid the region of Unita'.

The discovery of 'enormous' new oil reserves in Angola's offshore waters attracted a wide range of international oil companies and helped to boost the government's position. It was left to a few independent observers to point out the MPLA government's serious shortcomings. 'The government', wrote *The Economist* on 25 July, 'has squandered the four years of relative peace in which it could have been fostering national reconciliation.' Instead of building up desperately-needed social services in areas taken over from Unita, said the report, the government sent in heavily-armed police to search out, arrest, torture and even execute Unita suspects. What were described as government 'press-gangs' roamed the country looking for new recruits for the army, 'going from school to school rounding up boys as young as 15'. Meanwhile, Unita's tactics were becoming more apparent. 'Insiders from Unita', *Africa Confidential* reported on 7 August, 'insist that Savimbi is still determined to be Angola's President', his troops having been ordered into 'a series of carefully-orchestrated hit-and-run attacks against government positions'. Eventually, in Dr Savimbi's opinion, all-out war would result in the tearing-up of the 1994 Lusaka protocol (see AR 1994, p. 298) and make possible a settlement favourable to his own ambitions.

On 1 September the government suspended all Unita minsters and Assembly deputies in Luanda. Clearly with the government's foreknowledge, a group of Unita minsters led by Jorge Valentim immediately rejected Dr Savimbi's leadership and announced the establishment of 'Unita Renewed'. The new party attracted little support from Unita deputies, even though many of them were highly critical of Dr Savimbi's bellicose tactics.

In the first week of December the Angolan army launched an all-out attack on Unita's main base at Bailundo. There had been much fighting earlier, but this assault was seen as a de facto declaration of war, especially as it was accompanied by the replacement of 'doves' by 'hawks' at the ruling MPLA-PT's annual party conference taking place in Luanda at the same time. The government forces encountered tough resistance, and Unita launched a vigorous counter-attack, while lacking the resources needed for a convincing victory. On 26 December a plane carrying UN observers crashed near Huambo; both sides accused each other of shooting it down but denied UN officials access to the site. It was a brutal indication of the ultimate impotence of the international community. Meanwhile, the number of internal refugees from the war zone rose to over half-a-million.

2. ZAMBIA—MALAWI—ZIMBABWE—BLNS STATES

i. ZAMBIA

CAPITAL: Lusaka   AREA: 750,000 sq km   POPULATION: 9,300,000 ('97)
OFFICIAL LANGUAGE: English   POLITICAL SYSTEM: presidential
HEAD OF STATE & GOVERNMENT: President Frederick Chiluba (since Nov '91)
RULING PARTY: Movement for Multi-Party Democracy (MMD)
MAIN IGO MEMBERSHIPS (non-UN): OAU, COMESA, SADC, ACP, CWTH, NAM
CURRENCY: kwacha (end-'98 £1=K4,109.48, US$1=K2,470.00)
GNP PER CAPITA: US$380 by exchange-rate calculation, US$890 by PPP calculation ('97)

IN 1998 Zambia was dependent on Western aid donors to meet one-third of the government's budgeted expenditure. This gave donors a powerful leverage, which they attempted to use to correct the government's alleged human rights abuses. The government was urged to end the state of emergency imposed after the abortive coup of October 1997 (see AR 1997, pp. 278–9), to release detainees and to investigate allegations of torture which had been documented in Human Rights Watch's most recent report on Zambia published in May under the title 'No Model for Democracy'. The government gave only partial satisfaction to these demands. Former President Kenneth Kaunda, the most prominent of the detainees, was released on 1 June; shortly afterwards he retired from his post as president of the opposition United National Independence Party (UNIP) and announced that he was withdrawing from domestic politics. Other detainees were put on trial, however, and further arrests were made in June.

In search of more congenial aid donors, the government approached China and received an encouraging response. Expressing an interest in taking over some of the copper mines and in providing training for the army, the Beijing government appeared to be viewing Zambia as a possible bridgehead into Africa. Western aid donors were particularly anxious to see the process of privatization completed by the selling-off of the largest of the state-owned industries, Zambia Consolidated Copper Mines, which was reported to be running at a loss of $2 million a day. An international consortium, of which the South African Anglo-American Corporation was the largest member, made a bid, but its offer price was turned down. The government hoped to get a better deal from Asian investors, Indian as well as Chinese.

The Zambian government prudently avoided becoming involved in the civil war in Congo-Kinshasa (see VII.1.i), thus allowing President Chiluba to gain a measure of international status as a mediator in the conferences held to try to resolve the conflict. With UNIP deeply divided after Mr Kaunda's resignation, and the smaller opposition parties in a state of disarray and further weakened by a government announcement on 18 October that 14 parties had been de-registered for failing to meet 'required standards', President Chiluba's position seemed secure, even if he enjoyed little popularity.

ii. MALAWI

CAPITAL: Lilongwe AREA: 118,500 sq km POPULATION: 10,300,000 ('97)
OFFICIAL LANGUAGE: English POLITICAL SYSTEM: presidential
HEAD OF STATE & GOVERNMENT: President Bakili Muluzi (since May '94)
RULING PARTIES: United Democratic Front (UDF) heads coalition with Malawi National Democratic Party (MNDP) & United Front for Multi-Party Democracy (UFMD)
MAIN IGO MEMBERSHIPS (non-UN): OAU, COMESA, SADC, ACP, CWTH, NAM
CURRENCY: kwacha (end-'98 £1=MK35.45, US$1=MK21.60)
GNP PER CAPITA: US$220 by exchange-rate calculation, US$700 by PPP calculation ('97)

IN an uneventful year the government of President Bakili Muluzi and the United Democratic Front came under criticism especially from donor countries for corruption which led to the sacking of at least one minister and for its failure to make significant improvements in the state of the economy. The government's shortcomings helped the opposition Malawi Congress Party to regain some of the support it had enjoyed during the 30 years in which it had been the dominant party under the late President Hastings Banda. Presidential and Assembly elections were due in 1999.

iii. ZIMBABWE

CAPITAL: Harare   AREA: 390,000 sq km   POPULATION: 12,000,000 ('97)
OFFICIAL LANGUAGE: English POLITICAL SYSTEM: presidential
HEAD OF STATE & GOVERNMENT: President Robert Mugabe (since Dec '87); previously Prime Minister (from April '80)
RULING PARTY: Zimbabwe African National Union-Patriotic Front (ZANU-PF)
MAIN IGO MEMBERSHIPS (non-UN): OAU, COMESA, SADC, ACP, CWTH, NAM
CURRENCY: Zimbabwe dollar (end-'98 £1=Z$61.92, US$1=Z$37.22)
GNP PER CAPITA: US$750 by exchange-rate calculation, US$2,280 by PPP calculation ('97)

THE year began, as 1997 had ended, with President Robert Mugabe and his ZANU-PF government at the depths of unpopularity and the country's economy in acute crisis. On 19 January riots and looting in the centre of the capital, Harare, and surrounding townships followed a sudden hike in the cost of basic foodstuffs, a consequence of the collapse of the country's currency the previous November (see AR 1997, p. 281). In February a two-day strike organized by the Zimbabwe Congress of Trade Unions (ZCTU) was supported by more than 75 per cent of the urban workforce.

While street protests were ruthlessly contained by the police and security forces, increasingly widespread calls for Mr Mugabe to retire in advance of the expiry of his current presidential term in 2001 led to recriminations within the ruling party itself, and a clamping down on the state-owned and independent media. In February Margaret Dondo, the country's only independent MP and an articulate opponent of the government, claimed she had escaped an attempt upon her life.

The start of the year also brought a highly symbolic commercial defeat for the government which, for five years, had campaigned to deny the franchise for NetTwo, the country's second cellular telephone service, to the talented Harare entrepreneur Strive Masiyiwa and his company Econet. On 15 January the government accepted a High Court judgement in favour of Econet's bid over that of the officially-backed Telecel. Mr Masiyiwa, a political outsider and long-standing critic of the ZANU-PF government, welcomed the government's change of mind, observing that 'a revolution ends when it begins to eat its own children'.

Economic uncertainty delayed resolution of the often-postponed issue of the redistribution and resettlement of the country's prime agricultural land (see AR 1997, p. 281). In September a conference of aid donor states in Harare approved the principle of land redistribution, but only on the basis that it would be financially sustainable, transparently fair and geared towards the reduction of poverty. Sceptical of the policy framework document tabled by the government, the donor countries declined to provide the financial assistance necessary to administer the scheme beyond the £40 million already allocated.

Two months later, however, and in open defiance of international opinion, Mr Mugabe encouraged squatters to occupy white-owned land in the Enterprise Valley, east of Harare. And on 19 November he wrote to the owners of 841 white-owned farms declaring that their properties were immediately forfeit, without compensation. The move, seen as a tactic to win internal popularity, backfired. A spokesman for the International Monetary Fund (IMF) declared that discussions on current loans to Zimbabwe had ended 'as of now', and the Catholic Commission on Justice and Peace described the President's action as 'not only a misjudgment but a criminal misjudgment'. In the absence of external funding, the land redistribution exercise was unenforceable. At the end of the year the targeted farmers were still in possession of their land, and under instruction to plant the new season's crops, though summary dispossession remained a real threat.

As a distasteful diversion, the country was preoccupied with the long-running prosecution of the former President, the Rev. Canaan Banana, for sodomy and indecent assault. When Rev. Banana was convicted on 26 November, the ruling party's reactionary stance on sexual minorities (see AR 1995, p. 278) appeared to have found its most conspicuous victim. By then, however, the former President had fled, first to Botswana and then to South Africa, where he had a private meeting with President Mandela on 3 December. South Africa ignored Zimbabwe's extradition request.

Further major disruption to Zimbabwe's economic stability followed the government's surprise decision, in August, to send 6,000 troops, fighter aircraft and attack helicopters to the Democratic Republic of the Congo to support the regime of Laurent Kabila against rebel forces (see VII.1.i). By November the military intervention was costing the country an estimated Z$60 million a day, and the budget that month provided for a 46 per cent increase in defence spending. Reasons advanced for the intervention, which pitted Zimbabwe, Angola and Namibia against Rwanda and Uganda, included the security of commercial contracts and mining concessions negotiated by Zimbabwean companies since President Kabila's ascendancy, some involving businesses controlled by relatives and close associates of Mr Mugabe. Others referred to the growing personal antipathy between Mr Mugabe and South Africa's President, Nelson Mandela, the latter being strongly committed to a negotiated peace through the agency of the Southern African Development Community (SADC).

Hostility to what seemed an extraneous and unwinnable war helped to ignite further public protest in October. Demonstrations in Harare against a 67 per cent increase in the price of fuel were followed on 11 and 18 November by successful national strikes organized by the increasingly powerful Zimbabwe Congress of Trade Union (ZCTU). When the government called on business, labour and civic representatives to join talks to resolve the country's economic stalemate, the ZCTU agreed to suspend further action. But the *Financial Gazette*, a newspaper critical of the government, declared that it was too late for talks: 'What is needed is the sheer willpower and the courage to take painful but so glaringly obvious measures.'

The combination of military involvement in Congo-Kinshasa, a scandal involving the War Victims' Compensation Fund (see AR 1997, p. 280), the collapse of the United Merchant Bank and a decline in confidence in the government's overall financial competence had a severe impact on the Zimbabwe Stock Exchange, which lost 60 per cent of its value during the year. In December the IMF, which had been committed to a US$176 million standby facility, announced that it had taken Zimbabwe off its agenda pending reassurance on the financial impact of the war on land acquisition reforms, and on financial targets.

By the close of the year, the 18th of ZANU-PF rule, the Zimbabwean dollar had declined to a rate of 62 to the pound sterling, inflation stood at 47 per cent and interest rates were close to 50 per cent. Unemployment rose to a new record high and the country's foreign currency reserves reached their lowest-ever level. The independent *Sunday Standard* newspaper reported that a number of senior army officers were arrested on 17 December on grounds of inciting colleagues to join a military coup; the government immediately detained the editor and journalists responsible for the story. When President Mugabe and his wife left for a much-publicized pre-Christmas shopping trip to London, the British press greeted him with pointed references to the fate of the former Chilean dictator, General Augusto Pinochet (see II.1.i; IV.3.iv).

iv. BOTSWANA—LESOTHO—NAMIBIA—SWAZILAND

Botswana
CAPITAL: Gaborone   AREA: 580,000 sq km   POPULATION: 1,510,000 ('97)
OFFICIAL LANGUAGE: English   POLITICAL SYSTEM: presidential democracy
HEAD OF STATE & GOVERNMENT: President Festus Mogae (since March '98)
RULING PARTY: Botswana Democratic Party (BDP)
MAIN IGO MEMBERSHIPS (non-UN): OAU, SADC, SACU, ACP, CWTH, NAM
CURRENCY: pula (end-'98 £1=P7.41, US$1=P4.45)
GNP PER CAPITA: US$3,260 by exchange-rate calculation, US$8,220 by PPP calculation ('97)

Lesotho
CAPITAL: Maseru   AREA: 30,000 sq km   POPULATION: 2,300,000 ('97)
OFFICIAL LANGUAGES: English & Sesotho   POLITICAL SYSTEM: monarchy
HEAD OF STATE: King Letsie III (since Jan '96)
RULING PARTY: Lesotho Congress for Democracy (LCD)
HEAD OF GOVERNMENT: Bethuel Pakalitha Mosisili, Prime Minister (since June '98)
MAIN IGO MEMBERSHIPS (non-UN): OAU, COMESA, SADC, SACU, ACP, CWTH, NAM
CURRENCY: loti/maloti (end-'98 £1=M9.79, US$1=M5.88)
GNP PER CAPITA: US$670 by exchange-rate calculation, US$2,480 by PPP calculation ('97)

Namibia

CAPITAL: Windhoek   AREA: 824,000 sq km   POPULATION: 2,000,000 ('97)
OFFICIAL LANGUAGES: Afrikaans & English   POLITICAL SYSTEM: presidential democracy
HEAD OF STATE: President Sam Nujoma (since March '90)
RULING PARTY: South West Africa People's Organization (SWAPO)
HEAD OF GOVERNMENT: Hage Geingob, Prime Minister (since March '90)
MAIN IGO MEMBERSHIPS (non-UN): OAU, SADC, SACU, ACP, CWTH, NAM
CURRENCY: Namibian dollar/SA rand (end-'98 £1=N$9.79, US$1=N$5.88)
GNP PER CAPITA: US$2,220 by exchange-rate calculation, US$5,440 by PPP calculation ('97)

Swaziland

CAPITAL: Mbabane   AREA: 17,350 sq km   POPULATION: 952,000 ('97)
OFFICIAL LANGUAGES: English & Siswati   POLITICAL SYSTEM: monarchy
HEAD OF STATE: King Mswati III (since '86)
HEAD OF GOVERNMENT Sibusiso Barnabas Dlamini, Prime Minister (since July '96)
MAIN IGO MEMBERSHIPS (non-UN): OAU, COMESA, SADC, SACU, ACP, CWTH, NAM
CURRENCY: lilangeni/emalangeni (end-'98 £1=E9.79, US$1=E5.88)
GNP PER CAPITA: US$1,440 by exchange-rate calculation, US$3,560 by PPP calculation ('97)

SOME progress was made during the year towards revising the revenue-sharing formula of the Southern African Customs Union (SACU), involving South Africa, Botswana, Lesotho, Swaziland and Namibia (see AR 1997, p. 284). SACU members met in Gaborone, Botswana, in November to work out a new agreement, the details of which had to be in place by April 1999. A new agreement excluding excise duties from the pool was reached during the year, reflecting an anticipated ongoing fall in tariff levels. These were expected to drop sharply as a result of the mooted free trade and development agreement between South Africa and the European Union (EU). Smaller states within SACU, such as Swaziland and Lesotho, which were dependent on the formula for about half of government revenue, started to look for ways to diversify income sources.

Given the problems involved in attempting to institute a free trade regime in the 14 member states of the Southern African Development Community (SADC), it was increasingly felt that the SACU might prove a less-unwieldy kernel for a regional integration process. The tariff liberalization offer presented by SACU states to the SADC in September was seen by officials as a kick-start to the process of establishing a regional free trade zone.

Tax evasion through fictitious exports and smuggling inspired moves by Pretoria to charge value-added tax (VAT) on imports from other SACU states. Implementation of this plan was delayed until January 1999, however.

BOTSWANA. President Sir Ketumile Masire stepped down after 18 years at the helm in March and was succeeded by the Vice-President and Finance Minister, Festus Mogae. Pending presidential elections in 1999, however, Mr Mogae was expected to face tough opposition to his leadership from various factions within the ruling Botswana Democratic Party (BDP), coming to a head at the party congress scheduled for July 1999. Mr Mogae took the presidency without an election through party structures, his path being smoothed by his predecessor and mentor, Sir Ketumile. Faced with in-fighting within the BDP, President Mogae chose a Vice-President not identified with any single BDP faction, namely Lieut.-General Ian Khama, the 45-year-old son of former President Sir Seretse Khama and the commander of the Botswana Defence Force (BDF). The challenge to Mr Mogae in the 1999 elections was expected to come from either Lieut.-General Khama or Ponatshego Kedikilwe, the current Minister of Finance and Development Planning and chairman of the BDP.

Sir Ketumile stepped down amidst controversy over his pension plans. Under the recently-enacted President Pensions and Retirement Bill, the former President was entitled to a tax-free monthly stipend equivalent to his old salary or 80 per cent of the incumbent's salary. It also stipulated that the former President would be provided with staff, including security officers, two drivers, one private secretary, one secretary and one attendant, plus a fully-equipped office, a furnished residential house, two maids and a gardener. As was to be expected, this act came under attack from the opposition.

In October President Mogae announced a government programme aimed at providing long-term economic growth and the improvement of social conditions. Known as 'Vision 2016', the plan set various targets to be achieved by 2016, including a threefold increase in per capita income to US$8,500 per annum, 9 per cent annual economic growth and 12 years of free schooling for every child. It also sought to boost manufacturing from the current level of 5 per cent to 30 per cent of GDP. The IMF projected Botswana's GDP growth at 3.5 per cent in 1998, down from 4.2 per cent in 1997 and 6.8 per cent in 1996.

President Mogae also announced plans to give AIDS patients a monthly allowance of 90 pula. Botswana expected 18 per cent of its 1.5 million people to be infected with HIV by the year 2000. A study released in July estimated that the cost of AIDS and HIV would climb sevenfold by 2004 and account for 5 per cent of the country's wage bill.

Relations with Namibia remained tense after alleged Caprivi Strip secessionists fled to Botswana to escape prosecution. This episode complicated already tense diplomatic relations over disputed islands in the Chobe River in the Caprivi Strip. BDF soldiers shot dead two alleged Namibian poachers in the Kwando area in July. Botswanan fears over water security in the Okavango Delta apparently lay behind these tensions, given Namibian plans to pump water from the Kavango river to Windhoek. Tensions with Namibia were suggested as the main reason for the relatively large-scale arms purchases made by Botswana over the past two years, including 20 tanks from Austria and 13 F-5 fighter-aircraft from Canada.

Botswana continued to play an active role in regional politics. In September a BDF contingent supported the South African National Defence Force peace-enforcement mission in the troubled mountain Kingdom of Lesotho (see below).

LESOTHO. Events in Lesotho were dominated by the outcome of the general election held on 23 May in which the ruling Lesotho Congress for Democracy (LCD) won 79 of the 80 seats in the enlarged National Assembly. Following the release of the findings of a commission of inquiry on the election outcome led by Judge Pius Langa of South Africa, a military revolt was put down by a joint South African-Botswana military intervention on 22 September. The intervention, under the mantle of the SADC, resulted in widespread destruction to buildings in the capital, Maseru, at an estimated cost of over R1,000 million, and in the deaths of nine South African National Defence Force (SANDF) and over 20 Lesotho Defence Force (LDF) soldiers.

Soon after the election, the opposition parties (which had taken nearly 40 per cent of the vote under the first-past-the-post electoral system) began a campaign of civil disobedience and demonstrations, apparently enjoying the full support of King Letsie III. By 10 August South African Deputy President Thabo Mbeki had established a troika comprising South Africa, Botswana and Zimbabwe to mediate in the growing political crisis. Although opposition leaders had demanded the dissolution of parliament, new elections and the amendment of the constitution to allow for the restoration of traditional authority, the Langa Commission found that no large-scale electoral fraud could be identified.

Following various shootings outside the palace, and a mutiny within the army resulting in the resignation of the LDF commander, Prime Minister Pakalitha Mosisili sent an urgent letters to the Presidents of South Africa, Botswana, Mozambique and Zimbabwe requesting SADC military assistance to avert a possible coup. Mr Mosisili had taken over as Premier from the veteran politician, Ntsu Mokhehle, after the May election. Some speculation existed about the legality of the resultant SADC action, given the absence of a UN mandate, although the South African government justified the action on the grounds of an agreement struck with Lesotho. There was no doubt in most minds, however, that the military operation was hastily conceived and poorly executed, resulting in an unexpectedly high loss of life and damage to property.

In November the conflicting parties agreed on the establishment of a 'Lesotho Interim Political Authority'. This multi-party structure would prepare the country for fresh elections in 18 months. The agreement was the result of ongoing dialogue led by the South African Minister of Safety and Security, Sydney Mufamadi.

NAMIBIA. Namibia's political landscape was dominated by three issues during 1998: first, the decision by President Sam Nujoma to amend the 1990 constitution to enable an incumbent President to seek a third term of office; second, the deployment of an estimated 600 troops in support of Zimbabwean and Angolan forces assisting Laurent Kabila's government in the Democratic Republic of the Congo (DRC); and third, the problems of instability in the Caprivi Strip bordering Angola, Zambia and Botswana.

In October Prime Minister Hage Geingob introduced the Namibian Constitution Amendment Bill to change the country's constitution to allow President Nujoma to serve a third term. Mr Geingob said that Mr Nujoma sought a third term for reasons of higher national interest rather than for personal gain or power. The ruling South West African People's Organization (SWAPO) had the necessary two-thirds majority to ensure safe passage of the bill, though there was some opposition within SWAPO ranks. In August the Namibian high commissioner to the United Kingdom, Ben Ulenga, resigned over the President's plans. Nevertheless, the bill was approved in November, paving the way for Mr Nujoma to stand in the presidential elections scheduled for November 1999.

President Nujoma went on national television in September to justify Namibia's decision to deploy troops in the DRC (see VII.1.i), describing President Kabila's opponents as puppets. Critics of the intervention argued that it violated the Namibian constitution's restriction of the use of Namibian armed forces to the defence of the country's security.

Also in October, Namibian troops swooped on secret training camps in the Caprivi Strip which were allegedly being used as bases by elements seeking the secession of Caprivi from the rest of Namibia. More than 100 secessionists fled to Botswana, where they sought asylum. Windhoek demanded that Botswana extradite the suspects to stand trial in Namibia. This followed several flare-ups between the two countries over two disputed islands—Kasikili and Situngu—in the Chobe River. The secessionists were predominantly San (Bushman) people from the Kxoe community in the western Caprivi, though they were believed to have links with a group seeking the breakaway of the Western Barotse province of Zambia. Those who fled to Botswana included the former Namibian Democratic Turnhalle Alliance (DTA) opposition leader Meshake Muyongo, DTA parliamentarian Francis Sizimbo and Caprivi governor Johnnie Mabuku. Mr Muyongo had been replaced as leader of the DTA in September by Katuutire Kaura as a result of controversial remarks made on the secession of the north-eastern province.

Namibia's growth expectations for 1998 failed to materialize. The linking of the Namibian dollar to the South African rand meant that the currency was dragged down by the 21 per cent depreciation of the rand in May and June (see VII.3). In the first quarter growth was 6.4 per cent, but the rate declined to only 1 per cent in the second quarter. Poor rainfall and the resultant expected increase in cereal imports contributed to the relative downturn, though the fishing sector's production rose by 30 per cent in the second quarter. Despite South Africa's decision in 1997 to write off Namibia's R700 million 'colonial' debt, the level of state debt continued to rise. A major contributory factor was a downturn in mining revenues due to the Asian financial crisis.

On a positive note, the Trans-Kalahari highway, linking the Namibian port of Walvis Bay to South Africa via Windhoek and Gaborone, opened early in the year.

SWAZILAND. The run-up to the Swazi general elections on 16 and 24 October was marked by strikes and other actions in protest at the monarchy's failure to reform the traditionalist *tikhundla* system of government, under which candidates for the House of Assembly were chosen by primary elections in each of the country's chiefdoms. In October there were 350 candidates for the 55 elective seats, the 55 elected members being joined by ten members nominated by the King. The new Assembly proceeded to elect ten members to the 30-member Senate (the upper chamber), the other 20 members being named by the King.

The opposition Swaziland Federation of Trade Unions (SFTU) called for a boycott of the elections, which were held under a 1973 decree banning political parties and granting the King absolute governing powers. SFTU leader Jan Sithole was arrested shortly after polling in connection with a bomb blast, although he was subsequently released. The government attempted to ensure a better turnout than the 17 per cent level recorded in 1993 by postponing the deadline for voter registration three times. In the event, blustery weather resulted in polling on 16 October being adjourned to 24 October, although the turnout was still sparse.

The central bank reported moderate economic growth of 3.5 per cent for 1997/98, just above the population growth rate of 2.7 per cent. High levels of government consumption and a regional economic slowdown made the task of debt-reduction more difficult. Tourism receipts increased by 50 per cent over the previous year, though most areas of agricultural production were down. The notable exception was sugar, Swaziland's chief export, production of which increased by 1 per cent, with exports rising by 5.6 per cent.

3. SOUTH AFRICA

CAPITAL: Pretoria   AREA: 1,220,000 sq km   POPULATION: 40,000,000 ('97)
OFFICIAL LANGUAGES: Afrikaans, English & nine African languages
POLITICAL SYSTEM: transitional multi-racial democracy
HEAD OF STATE & GOVERNMENT: President Nelson Mandela (since May '94)
RULING PARTIES: African National Congress (ANC) & Inkatha Freedom Party (IFP)
MAIN IGO MEMBERSHIPS (non-UN): OAU, SADC, SACU, CWTH, NAM
CURRENCY: rand (end-'98 £1=R9.79, US$1=R6.88)
GNP PER CAPITA: US$3,400 by exchange-rate calculation, US$7,490 by PPP calculation ('97)

FOR South Africa it was a year of political stability, economic uncertainty and greater regional assertiveness. The central political event was the submission on 29 October of the much-anticipated report of the Truth and Reconciliation Commission (TRC), although its elucidation of some of the truth of the apartheid era did not bring much reconciliation, at least among the political parties.

Submission of the report to President Mandela by the TRC chairman, Archbishop Desmond Tutu, was the culmination of 30 months of hearings involving testimony by some 21,000 witnesses. Its main finding was that 'apartheid as a form of systematic racial discrimination constituted a crime against humanity', notably in that its application in the period 1960–90 'sought to protect the power and privilege of a racial minority'. However, while the report found that the state under successive National Party (NP) governments had been the 'primary perpetrator' of human rights abuses, it also recognized that the African National Congress (ANC), the Inkatha Freedom Party (IFP) and the Pan-Africanist Congress (PAC) were accountable 'both politically and morally' for comparable violations. Prominent individuals censured in the report included former President P.W. Botha, who was found to have overseen numerous human rights violations; the former chief of the South African Defence Force (SADF), General Constand Viljoen; IFP leader Chief Mangosuthu Buthelezi (now Home Affairs Minister); and Winnie Madikizela-Mandela, the President's ex-wife, who was found to have been implicated in at least 12 cases of assault, abduction and murder, including the killing of Stompie Moeketsi Seipei in 1988 (see AR 1997, p. 290).

In a deluge of criticism by the parties whose past actions it had censured, the TRC report's findings were condemned by the ANC as 'misdirected, arbitrary and capricious' and tantamount to the 'criminalization of the liberation struggle'. The PAC described the TRC as a 'circus' and the IFP dismissed its report as 'preposterous and comical', while the NP and General Viljoen's Freedom Front (FF) claimed that the TRC was the 'political tool of the ANC'. All of these parties, including the ANC, boycotted the report's handover ceremony. On 6 December President Mandela ruled out any general amnesty for crimes committed in the apartheid era, maintaining the existing position whereby individual amnesty applications had to be made to the TRC. Of over 7,000 applications made to date, less than 200 had been granted.

Notwithstanding the fault-lines displayed by publication of the TRC report, South Africa continued to be blessed with a strong legal and financial system, a durable, democratic and effective government, tolerable levels of inflation and international trade exposure, low external debt and fiscal austerity. The key was an ongoing government commitment to its conservative Growth, Employment and Redistribution (GEAR) macroeconomic reform strategy. The downside was reflected in the relatively high level of population expansion, low GDP growth, high unemployment, high interest rates and low external liquidity, along with a volatile (and falling) currency value.

South Africa had some success in managing the three deficits critical to developing countries, those of the fiscal deficit (down as a percentage of GDP from 10.1 per cent in 1993/94 to 4.2 per cent in 1997/8 and a projected 3.9 per cent in 1998/99); current account deficit (which doubled to 1.5 per cent over the year, demanding high interest rates to attract inward capital flows and maintain monetary stability), and the social deficit. Though there was progress in terms of service delivery (between 1994–98, some 650,000 houses of the government's promised total of one million had been constructed), the latter area remained the most troubling.

South Africa suffered from unemployment figures as high as three million, or over 30 per cent of the working population. A 'presidential job summit' staged in October had less to do with job-creation than the need to maintain the tripartite government-business-labour working relationship and commitment to the GEAR strategy. An estimated 560,000 new jobs were needed each year to redress the high jobless figure and provide for those entering the labour market. A failure to do so, combined with a high rate of AIDS infection, created a cocktail for social dislocation and, possibly, populist politics.

The Actuarial Society of South Africa released a report in December which estimated that 10.4 per cent of South Africa's population was HIV-positive. This figure would rise to 12.5 per cent by 2006 and stabilize in that year, when 11.4 per cent of men and 13.6 per cent of women were likely to have contracted the disease. As a result, the population growth rate would drop from its current 1.9 per cent a year to 0.7 per cent in 2006.

The political landscape remained stable throughout the year. In the run up to the 1999 general election—the first since the ground-breaking 1994 poll (see AR 1994, pp. 311–5)—the opposition political parties focused their campaign around the need to prevent the ruling African National Congress (ANC) from obtaining a two-thirds parliamentary majority, which would enable it to change the constitution unchallenged. Opinion polls in 1998 indicated that the ANC was on course to attract 57 per cent of the vote, with the NP next on 11 per cent (down from 20 per cent in 1994), followed by the Democratic Party on 10 per cent (up from 1.7 per cent in 1994), the IFP (8.4 per cent), and the United Democratic Movement (6.5 per cent). Controversy erupted over the need for voters to have barcoded identity books to register to vote in the 1999 elections, which was seen as unfairly favouring the ANC-led alliance.

Most of the opposition to ANC policies continued to come from its major allies within the government, notably the South African Communist Party (SACP) and the Congress of South African Trade Unions (COSATU), rather than the major opposition parties. At the SACP's 10th congress held in July in Johannesburg, South African Deputy President Thabo Mbeki accused the Communists of siding with right-wing reactionaries and called on them not to target the wrong enemy. SACP secretary-general Blade Nzimande responded by describing the party's alliance with the ANC as sacrosanct and the only body that could take the country forward.

While Mr Mbeki's criticism was interpreted as proof of the government's commitment to the GEAR, even in the face of populist pressures, and may have provided solace to foreign investors, South Africa still found it difficult to obtain the levels of foreign investment initially hope for in 1994. The slow pace of privatization, the Asian financial crisis and the end of the post-isolation investment wave were all cited as additional reasons for the investment slowdown. Nevertheless, according to the UN Conference on Trade and Development (UNCTAD), foreign direct investment into South Africa more than doubled between 1996 and 1997, from US$760 million to $17,000 million, making it the largest recipient of foreign capital in Africa. Reflecting increasing openness, South African firms increased their investments from $57 million in 1996 to $2,300 million in 1997. Over the same period investment into the southern African region by South African companies increased from less than $50 million to over US$4,000 million.

Foreign investors appeared to remain sceptical of the government's relationship with its left-wing allies, which had led to the passage of contentious legislation such as the Labour Relations Act and the Employment Equity Act, regulating the labour market and seeking, *inter alia*, to give affirmative action a legal basis. Investors' concerns were heightened by a combination of the fall-out from the Asian financial crisis for emerging markets generally and specific concerns over high rates of crime in South Africa. Low rates of productivity and high economic transaction costs also continued to deter foreign and local investors. The real GDP growth rate was just 0.2 per cent in 1998, far below the 3.0 per cent level originally projected. Polls showed that South Africans remained equally divided on whether the country was going in the right direction, though those who felt that it was not had increased substantially since 1994.

The impact of violent crime on society remained a deterrent to foreign investors. South Africa's past of racial oppression, violence and dehumanization, along with increasing inaccessibility to the material targets of crime and decreasing fear on the part of criminals of punishment, combined to increase the violence of criminal acts in South Africa. Murders on farms in the Gauteng (Johannesburg-Pretoria) area increased by over 500 per cent in 1997–98. Among Interpol reporting countries, South Africa also remained the worst country for rape; had the second-highest rate of robbery with aggravating circumstances; and the third-highest incidence of murder. The murder of police officers was also among the highest in the world, 120 being killed in the first six months of 1998 alone.

Increasing numbers of attacks on farmers resulted in a high-level 'rural crime summit' in October. This was followed by a two-day public service anti-corruption conference in parliament in November. The government also sought to put words into deeds: in November the Prevention of Organized Crime Bill was passed, placing South Africa in the forefront of international efforts to fight trans-national crime.

Against this backdrop, the announcement in October that one of South Africa's major conglomerates, the Anglo American Corporation, was to list its share price 'offshore' in London, was greeted by many as a vote of no confidence in the South African economy. Anglo's action was followed by similar moves by South African Pulp and Paper Industries (SAPPI) and the beer giant, South African Breweries. Yet these moves were accepted stoically by the government as an inevitable consequence of globalization and the opening-up of South African markets and institutions to the global economy.

Indeed, in the four years since the 1994 election, South Africa had actively sought to participate in global politics. During 1998, for many observers, Pretoria's foreign policy finally came of age in accepting both regional and global responsibilities. Numerous visits by heads of state, including one in March by Bill Clinton, who became the first serving US President to visit South Africa since Jimmy Carter, and by South African leaders abroad were complemented by the key role played by the Republic in trying to mediate peaceful solutions to conflicts in the Democratic Republic of the Congo (DRC), Angola and Lesotho (see VII.1.i; VII.1.vi; VII.2.iv). This role in conflict mediation was seen as part of Deputy President Mbeki's 'African renaissance' vision, whereby African states had to accept greater responsibility for the continent's problems and solutions.

In the case of Lesotho, the new approach led in September to the first-ever deployment of South African National Defence Force (SANDF) troops in a peace-enforcement mission. Although subject to questions about its legality and *modus operandi*, this mission was widely seen to have set a precedent for similar South African-led peace-support operations elsewhere on the African continent, particularly in the light of increasing reluctance by Western nations to commit their own resources. The year ended with an undertaking by the South African Department of Foreign Affairs to send peace-keeping forces to the DRC.

South Africa's hosting of the 12th summit of the Non-Aligned Movement (NAM) in Durban on 31 August–3 September (see XI.3.iii) was seen as a great success. South Africa took over the chairmanship of the organization for three years, promising a greater relevance for the NAM in focusing on economic issues affecting developing nations. Less certain, however, was the prospect of the much-debated South Africa-European Union (EU) free trade and development agreement. Under negotiation since the start of 1996, the agreement appeared in October to have stalled over South Africa's reluctance in the face of EU insistence to give up use of the terms 'port' and 'sherry' (regarded under EU law as uniquely the property of Portugal and Spain respectively). Compromise was reached on this issue by year's end, however, and the conclusion of the agreement was expected to be achieved by March 1999.

Problems with the EU paralleled difficulties in making progress in implementing the free trade protocol of the 14-member South African Development Community (SADC). By the end of 1998 only four countries had ratified the protocol originally signed in 1996 (see AR 1996, pp. 278, 285, 413) and designed to create a free trade region by 2004. South Africa's relations with Robert Mugabe's Zimbabwe and José Eduardo dos Santos' Angola remained tense, primarily because of their role in sending troops to prop up the regime of Laurent Kabila in the DRC.

VIII SOUTH ASIA AND INDIAN OCEAN

1. IRAN—AFGHANISTAN—CENTRAL ASIAN REPUBLICS

i. IRAN

CAPITAL: Tehran   AREA: 1,650,000 sq km   POPULATION: 63,500,000 ('97)
NATIONAL LANGUAGE: Farsi (Persian)   POLITICAL SYSTEM: Islamic republic
SPIRITUAL GUIDE: Ayatollah Seyed Ali Khamenei (since June '89)
HEAD OF STATE & GOVERNMENT: President Mohammed Khatami (since Aug '97)
MAIN IGO MEMBERSHIPS (non-UN): OPEC, ECO, CP, OIC, NAM
CURRENCY: rial (end-'98 £1=Rls4,991.25, US$1=Rls3,000.00)
GNP PER CAPITA: US$1,780 by exchange-rate calculation, US$5,530 by PPP calculation ('97)

DOMESTIC politics was dominated by a confrontation between factions within the ruling regime. Every attempt at modernization by President Mohammed Khatami and his allies was blocked by the conservatives through legal and parliamentary means. Lay political and human rights groups attempted to reinforce the trend towards secularism or modernization but violence was used against them by the conservative Islamists to delay their progress.

The centre-piece of the conflict was the arrest by the hard-line judiciary on 4 April of Gholamhossein Karbaschi, the mayor of Tehran and close political ally of President Khatami. He was found guilty of corruption on 23 July and sentenced to a 1 million rials fine, a 20-year ban from public office and 60 lashes. The trial polarized factions within the regime and led to unrest on the streets of the capital. A new Minister of the Interior, Moussavi Lari, was appointed on 27 July following the impeachment of his reformist predecessor, Abdollah Nouri, by the Majlis (parliament).

There was a particular attack by the hard-liners against the freedom of the press, including suspension of newspapers such as *Tous*, *Tavana* and *Rah-e Now* in September and *Asr-e Ma* in October. Several prominent journalists were arrested in connection with the banning orders against their newspapers. In November the hard-line campaign against liberalization culminated in the murder in Tehran of the head of the Iran National Party, Dariush Foruhar, and his wife, together with the killing of four other important intellectual figures.

President Khatami, whilst speaking out in support of the rights of the intellectuals and the press, seemed powerless to halt the violent activities of his opponents. There were also assassinations of hard-line personalities. Assadollah Lajevardi, former manager of Iran's notorious Evin prison during the period of revolutionary activity against secular opponents, was killed in August, and on 13 September an unsuccessful attempt was made on the life of the head of the Foundation for the Oppressed, Mohsen Rafiqdust. The Mujaheddine Khalq organiation, based in Iraq, was blamed for these attacks.

Elections for the influential Assembly of Experts on 23 October reinforced the strength of the conservative factions within the Islamic Republic. Out of the 86 new members elected, 49 were affiliated to the conservative wing of the regime—which was not surprising in view of the careful pre-election screening of the official list of candidates by the hardline factions.

Iran's internal political divisions were reflected in the nation's foreign policy. Relations with the USA, on which the lifting of trade sanctions against Iran depended, at one level improved. Sports diplomacy, which included Iranian and US joint participation in international events such as the football World Cup in France (where the Iranian team beat the USA 2–1—see Pt XVI) and wrestling in the USA, indicated that a new, more cordial normality was emerging between the two sides. At the political level, however, there were deep contradictions. The Iranian spiritual leader, Ali Khamenei, was adamant in rejecting any contacts with the USA in his speech on 19 January; with the hard-line conservatives in support, he maintained this stance throughout the year.

Meanwhile, President Khatami continued to promise that Iran would open itself to the world at large, not least to the USA, and Foreign Minister Kamal Kharrazi made it clear that he was working towards an ultimate rapprochement with the administration in Washington. However, the adoption by the USA of further sanctions legislation against Iran on 23 May and the inception of 'Free Radio' broadcasts to Iran in October were taken in Iran as setbacks for the liberal faction in its efforts at rapprochement with the USA.

Development of Iranian relations with the European Union (EU) states made good progress following the announcement by President Khatami on 24 September that the 1988 death decree against British author Salman Rushdie would not be implemented. Although other lesser frictions remained to blight EU-Iranian links, and Britain did not immediately resume full diplomatic representation in Iran, the groundwork was laid in 1998 for increased future commercial and industrial exchanges between Iran and the EU.

In the Persian Gulf, Iran reiterated on 5 February its claim to ownership of the islands of Abu Musa and the Tunbs and called for new talks with the United Arab Emirates (UAE) to settle the matter. Ex-President Rafsanjani visited Saudi Arabia on 23 February, but no real progress was made on the issue of the Persian Gulf islands (see V.3.i; V.3.iii). The Arab side in the dispute demanded that the question be referred to the International Court of Justice, while Arab League Foreign Ministers in March demanded that Iran should cease to occupy the three islands. Iran held naval manoeuvres in the Persian Gulf on 4 December which did little to reassure its Arab neighbours on the nature of its determination to underwrite its possession of the islands by military means.

Conflict arose with Afghanistan over Iran's alleged support for the Shia opponents of the Taleban authorities in Kabul (see VIII.1.ii). In March a number of Iranians were detained by Taleban forces in northern Afghanistan. Despite a joint Iran-Pakistan peace mission to end factional fighting in Afghanistan in early July, in August nine Iranian diplomats and newsmen were killed by the Taleban when Mazar-i-Sharif in northern Afghanistan was captured. This incident led to Iranian military mobilization on the Afghan frontier in September, with the result that at one stage as many as 200,000 Iranian regular army troops were assembled in a show of force in the frontier region. Iran demanded a return of all Iranians held in Afghanistan and the punishment of the killers of the eight diplomats in Mazar-i-Sharif.

The recurrent crises between Iraq and the UN (see V.2.vi; XI.1) inevitably affected Iran. On 28 April Iraq offered again to renew the 1975 Algiers Accord on border arrangements provided that Iran withdrew its financial claims for compensation for the 1980–88 war. Travel for Iranian pilgrims to the Shia shrines in Iraq was eased and some further exchanges of prisoners took place. Despite these moves, problems remained. Iran demanded that Iraq should cease to give refuge to the Mujaheddine Khalq and be less repressive to its Shia population, while Iraq resented the apparent Iranian financial and moral support given to Iraqi dissident groups such as the Iraqi National Congress. During the US-UK air strikes on Iraq in December, Iran officially took a stance of disapproval but did nothing to hinder allied operations against Iraq.

The Iranian economy stagnated in 1998 as a result of poor world oil prices. Oil revenues were estimated to have run at approximately $10,000 million for the year as a whole, more than 40 per cent down on 1997. Great efforts were made to attract foreign investment into oil exploration and development, with some successes, notably in the offshore zone of the Persian Gulf; but depressed prices for crude on the international market adversely affected current oil revenue flows. The Iranian rial weakened abroad and the economy at home suffered an inflation rate of 20 per cent. Foreign debt was officially claimed to be $11,300 million in mid-1998, but in reality, including trade-related items and other unpaid claims, was rather higher at some $22,000 million.

A new economic recovery plan was published on 2 August, calling for greater social justice, an end to officially-sponsored monopolies and better control of inflation, but also a continuation of state subsidies. By the end of the year there were few signs that President Khatami was making the plan work effectively, confronted as he was by resistance to change from vested interests within the regime and an acute lack of financial resources, the latter exacerbated by continuing high levels of expenditure on defence and security.

ii. AFGHANISTAN

CAPITAL: Kabul   AREA: 650,000 sq km   POPULATION: 19,000,000 ('97)
OFFICIAL LANGUAGES: Pushtu, Dari (Persian)
POLITICAL SYSTEM: transitional
LEADERSHIP: Mohammad Omar, Leader of the Taleban (in power since Sept '96),
   Mohammad Rabbani, Chairman of Interim Council (since Sept '96)
MAIN IGO MEMBERSHIPS (non-UN): ECO, CP, OIC, NAM
CURRENCY: afghani (end-'98 £1=Af7,902.81, US$1=Af4,750.00)
GNP PER CAPITA: n/a

THE civil war in Afghanistan continued during 1998 with the Taleban regime making significant military progress against the opposition United Islamic Front for Salvation of Afghanistan (UIFSA). The Taleban also maintained its control of Kabul (the capital) and continued to impose strict Islamic fundamentalist rule over those within their jurisdiction.

The inconclusive fighting of the early part of the year was punctuated by increased US diplomatic pressure for peace negotiations. Bill Richardson, the US permanent representative to the UN, on 17 April became the highest-ranking US official to visit Afghanistan in almost 20 years when he held talks with Mullah Mohammed Rabbani, Deputy President of the Taleban regime, and a number of UIFSA representatives, including ethnic Uzbek leader General Abdul Rashid Dostam. Although the two sides agreed to hold face-to-face negotiations in Islamabad (Pakistan), the talks collapsed without progress on 3 May.

The breakdown signalled the resumption of fighting throughout the country. Some of the heaviest clashes occurred close to Kabul in May and June, and a number of civilians were killed in the city by UIFSA rocket attacks. The Taleban launched a major offensive on 11 July, rapidly overrunning Fariab province and continuing to drive north. On 3 August they captured Sheberghan—the site of General Dostam's headquarters— some 120 kilometres west of Mazar-i-Sharif (the last significant city to remain outside Taleban control). Its fall was strategically significant since, with General Dostam fleeing to neighbouring Uzbekistan, the road to Mazar-i-Sharif lay open to the Taleban.

A massed assault on 8 August quickly overcame the city's defences. Claims that the victorious Taleban troops perpetrated a series of massacres were upheld by a UN report (published in November) into the circumstances of the city's capture. It concluded that more than 6,000 civilians had been systematically slaughtered, with the minority (Shia) Hazaras being singled out for particular attention. The atrocities were in part motivated by a thirst to avenge the alleged summary execution of as many as 3,000 Taleban prisoners in Mazar-i-Sharif in May 1997 after the city had been recaptured by UIFSA forces following a brief period of Taleban control (see AR 1997, p. 296).

In an effort to exploit the strategic victory in Mazar-i-Sharif, on 10 August Taleban forces defending Kabul advanced north towards the Panjsher valley and engaged UIFSA forces under the command of former Defence Minister Ahmed Shah Masud. The manoeuvre meant that by mid-August the Taleban had effectively severed all communication between General Masud's forces and the remaining UIFSA troops in the northern province of Bamian. On 12–13 September the Taleban captured Bamian, the last major town outside their control. Its fall meant that significant military opposition to the Taleban regime was restricted to General Masud's stronghold in the Panjsher valley. Although General Masud's forces launched a series of rocket attacks against Kabul, causing significant civilian casualties, the Taleban's victories meant that by the end of the September they controlled about 90 per cent of Afghanistan.

The rapid Taleban advance prompted consternation amongst the country's northern neighbours, particularly Tajikistan, where Russian border troops were reinforced. Other countries, including Uzbekistan and Turkmenistan, also announced the strengthening of their border defences.

There was particular tension with Iran, as news of the massacres of Shia civilians during the capture of Mazar-i-Sharif by the (Sunni) Taleban fuelled anti-Taleban sentiment in predominantly Shia Iran. Relations were also damaged by the seizure by Taleban forces of nine Iranian diplomats from Iran's diplomatic mission in Mazar-i-Sharif during the city's capture. On 28 August the UN Security Council adopted resolution 1193 (1998), which demanded the release of the Iranians and called upon all foreign states to end the supply of arms and military assistance to any of the warring factions within Afghanistan. The Taleban initially denied any knowledge of the disappearance of the diplomats, a move which prompted Iran to stage three days of military manoeuvres on its eastern border during the first week of September.

On 10 September the Taleban announced that the bodies of the Iranians had been recovered but stressed that the killings had been carried out by renegade Taleban units. The funerals of six of the diplomats took place in Tehran on 18 September and were accompanied by mass demonstrations and emotional calls for the invasion of Afghanistan. The situation appeared to be escalating dangerously as Iran announced that its armed forces had been placed on high alert and that further deployments meant that there were 200,000 troops on the border, supported by heavy artillery, tanks and aircraft (see also VIII.1.i).

The new Iranian deployments led to increased diplomatic efforts to defuse the crisis, and on 21 September an informal group (dubbed 'two plus six') comprising of representatives from the USA, Russia, China, Iran, Pakistan, Tajikistan, Uzbekistan and Turkmenistan met in New York to discuss the situation.

In early October the Iranian authorities reported that a Taleban incursion across the border at Saleh-Abad, in the Iranian province of Khorassan, had been repulsed with casualties. The Taleban denied that any fighting had taken place, however, claiming instead that their forces in the region had shown great restraint, despite coming under several days of artillery fire from Iran.

In October the UN special envoy to Afghanistan, Lakhdar Brahimi, held a series of talks with officials from the Taleban, Iran and Pakistan in an attempt to defuse the tension. As a result, on 11 October the Taleban returned to Iran the last of the bodies of the murdered diplomats and, on 13 October, released 10 Iranian prisoners. They also promised to punish the renegade militia which they alleged had been responsible for the deaths of the diplomats. Mr Brahimi also negotiated a new security agreement with the Taleban which cleared the way for UN staff to return to Afghanistan. (UN agencies had left Afghanistan in August following the death of an official in a revenge attack for the US air strikes against training camps commanded by Saudi-born Islamic militant Osama bin Laden—see IV.1; V.4.i.)

In late October the Taleban suffered a military setback when General Masud's troops captured the strategically important town of Taloqan, on Afghanistan's north-eastern border with Tajikistan. The town was an important link in General Masud's supply route to his Panjsher valley stronghold. In November General Masud's forces made territorial gains in Kapisa province, some 60 kilometres north of Kabul. Although these were of little strategic significance, they served to emphasize that the Taleban military victory was not yet complete. The year ended with General Masud's forces continuing to conduct anti-Taleban military operations of limited scope, and subjecting Kabul to artillery and rocket attack.

Throughout the year there was no relaxation in the Taleban's imposition of strict Islamic codes in all areas of public and private life. In June the authorities closed more than 100 private schools. Many of these had been run by women teachers from their own homes, and had been educating as many as 6,000 girls in defiance of the Taleban's ban on female education. On 8 July Mohammed Qalamuddin, deputy head of the Taleban's Religious Ministry, announced a ban on the ownership or operation of televisions, video cassette recorders, satellite dishes and video cassettes. Owners of the proscribed items were told to dispose of them within 15 days or face punishment under Islamic law. For men, the wearing of beards remained compulsory, and in December, as the holy month of Ramadan began, police were reported to have arrested dozens of those whose beards were deemed to be insufficiently full.

Despite the Taleban's military success and its firm grip on the population, international recognition remained limited. In October Taleban leader Mullah Mohammad Omar made a public offer to halt the production of opium poppies—Afghanistan was estimated to be the world's second largest producer of opium—in exchange for international recognition of his regime. The offer coincided with the decision of Saudi Arabia to downgrade diplomatic relations with Afghanistan and recall its chargé d'affaires from Kabul. This move was significant since Saudi Arabia, Pakistan and the United Arab Emirates were the only countries to have recognized the Taleban regime. The decision followed a request from Saudi Arabia, acting under pressure from the USA, to extradite Osama bin Laden on terrorist charges which included the US embassy bombings in East Africa in August (see VI.1.ii). The Taleban prevaricated, however, offering to try bin Laden if sufficient evidence was produced against him. When this was not furnished, the Taleban Supreme Court, after an inquiry into the case, announced on 21 November that bin Laden had been totally exonerated.

The remote north-eastern provinces of Takhar and Badakhshan, some 280 kilometres north of Kabul, were struck by two severe earthquakes during 1998. The first, on 4 February, measured 6.1 on the Richter scale and had an epicentre near the town of Rostaq. Communication difficulties resulting from the war and the inaccessibility of the region meant that news of the disaster did not emerge until 6 February, thereby causing a significant delay in relief operations. The earthquake and its strong aftershocks killed more than 4,000 people, destroyed as many as 30 villages, and left some 15,000 homeless. The second earthquake, measuring 7.1 on the Richter scale, with its epicentre near the town of Shari Basurkh, struck on 30 May. It killed at least 3,000 people, destroyed some 60 villages and left 30,000 homeless.

iii. KAZAKHSTAN—TURKMENISTAN—UZBEKISTAN— KYRGYZSTAN—TAJIKISTAN

Kazakhstan
CAPITAL: Astana   AREA: 2,717,300 sq km   POPULATION: 17,000,000 ('97)
OFFICIAL LANGUAGES: Kazakh & Russian   POLITICAL SYSTEM: presidential
HEAD OF STATE & GOVERNMENT: President Nursultan Nazarbayev (since Feb '90)
RULING PARTY: Party of People's Unity of Kazakhstan (PNEK)
PRIME MINISTER: Nurlan Balgimbayev (since Oct '97)
MAIN IGO MEMBERSHIPS (non-UN): CIS, PFP, OSCE, OIC, ECO
CURRENCY: tenge (end-'98 £1=T139.64, US$1=T83.93)
GNP PER CAPITA: US$1,340 by exchange-rate calculation, US$3,290 by PPP calculation ('97)

Kyrgyzstan
CAPITAL: Bishkek   AREA: 198,500 sq km   POPULATION: 5,000,000 ('97)
OFFICIAL LANGUAGES: Kyrgyz & Russian   POLITICAL SYSTEM: presidential
HEAD OF STATE & GOVERNMENT: President Askar Akayev (since Oct '90)
RULING PARTIES: Democratic Movement of Kyrgyzstan heads loose ruling coalition
PRIME MINISTER: Jumabek Ibrahimov (since Dec '98)
MAIN IGO MEMBERSHIPS (non-UN): CIS, PFP, OSCE, ECO, OIC
CURRENCY: som
GNP PER CAPITA: US$440 by exchange-rate calculation, US$2,040 by PPP calculation ('97)

Tajikistan

CAPITAL: Dushanbe   AREA: 143,100 sq km   POPULATION: 6,000,000 ('97)
OFFICIAL LANGUAGE: Tajik   POLITICAL SYSTEM: presidential
HEAD OF STATE & GOVERNMENT: President Imamali Rakhmanov (since Nov '92)
RULING PARTIES: People's Democratic Party of Tajikistan & United Tajik Opposition head loose coalition
PRIME MINISTER: Yahya Azimov (since Feb '96)
MAIN IGO MEMBERSHIPS (non-UN): CIS, PFP, OSCE, ECO, OIC
CURRENCY: Tajik rouble
GNP PER CAPITA: US$330 by exchange-rate calculation, US$930 by PPP calculation ('97)

Turkmenistan

CAPITAL: Ashgabat   AREA: 448,100 sq km   POPULATION: 5,000,000 ('97)
OFFICIAL LANGUAGE: Turkmen   POLITICAL SYSTEM: presidential
HEAD OF STATE & GOVERNMENT: President (Gen.) Saparmurad Niyazov (since Jan '90)
RULING PARTY: Democratic Party of Turkmenistan (DPT)
MAIN IGO MEMBERSHIPS (non-UN): CIS, PFP, OSCE, ECO, OIC, NAM
CURRENCY: manat
GNP PER CAPITA: US$630 by exchange-rate calculation, US$1,410 by PPP calculation ('97)

Uzbekistan

CAPITAL: Tashkent   AREA: 447,400 sq km   POPULATION: 24,000,000 ('97)
OFFICIAL LANGUAGE: Uzbek   POLITICAL SYSTEM: presidential
HEAD OF STATE & GOVERNMENT: President Islam Karimov (since March '90)
RULING PARTY: People's Democratic Party (PDP)
PRIME MINISTER: Otkir Sultonov (since Dec '95)
MAIN IGO MEMBERSHIPS (non-UN): CIS, PFP, OSCE, ECO, OIC, NAM
CURRENCY: sum (end-'98 £1=S773.64, US$1=S465.00)
GNP PER CAPITA: US$1,010 by exchange-rate calculation, US$2,450 by PPP calculation ('97)

THERE were several changes of senior government personnel in the Central Asian states in 1998. The first reshuffle occurred in Kazakhstan in February. Changes included the appointment of Uraz Jandosov, previously National Bank chairman, to the post of First Deputy Prime Minister and head of the State Investment Committee, while Kadyrjan Damitov, a former presidential adviser, became chairman of the National Bank. There were further attempts to restructure the government apparatus in the summer, when a number of ministries and state agencies were merged on the grounds of improving efficiency.

In Kyrgyzstan, there were also radical government shake-ups. In March the Prime Minister, Apas Jumagulov, resigned; his place was taken by the 41-year-old Kuvachbek Jumaliyev. In April two out of three deputy prime ministers, six out of 15 ministers and ten heads of state agencies were replaced. Among the most significant new appointments were those of Feliks Kulov, previously National Security Minister, to the post of acting mayor of the capital, Bishkek, while the former mayor of the city, Boris Silayev, was made First Deputy Prime Minister. The changes were officially ascribed to the need to bring younger people into the government in order to carry through the reform programme. Six months later there was a further reshuffle when a number of ministers and chairmen of state committees were dismissed for 'grave breaches of the state's financial discipline'. On 23 December, moreover, the President dismissed the entire government for its 'unsatisfactory performance in dealing with the economic crisis'. A new Prime Minister, Jumabek Ibrahimov, was appointed with 'special and additional powers'. A new government was formed on 30 December; some 12 ministers retained their former posts.

In Uzbekistan, Rustam Azimov, the long-standing chairman of the National Bank, was made Minister of Finance in October. A more dramatic change was the dismissal of Ismoil Jorabekov, the powerful First Deputy Prime Minister. A number of other senior government officials were also removed from office at this time as part of a drive against corruption. According to President Karimov, 'negative phenomena such as regionalism, arrogant behaviour, favouritism and tribalism' were creating 'an intolerable situation'. In Turkmenistan, too, several ministers were dismissed on charges of corruption. These included Deputy Defence Minister Bayramberdi Garayev and Deputy Economics Minister Avez Agayev. The chairman of the State Oil and Gas Construction Concern, Orazmurad Niyazbiyev, was replaced by his former deputy, Rejepturdy Atayev.

With presidential elections looming in Kyrgyzstan and Kazakhstan, preparatory measures to strengthen the chances of re-election for the incumbent leaders were initiated. In July the Kyrgyz Constitutional Court ruled that President Akayev was eligible to run for re-election in 2000; although this would amount to a third term of office (not permitted under the constitution), his first term was deemed not to count because it was during the pre-independence Soviet period. Opposition deputies strongly attacked this decision, following which President Akayev himself suggested that he might not stand for re-election. In Kazakhstan, presidential elections were also not due to be held until 2000, but in October a decree was suddenly passed bringing them forward to January 1999. At the same time, Akezhan Kazhegeldin, the former Prime Minister and only real rival to President Nazarbayev, was barred from entering the presidential race on a legal technicality. Three other presidential candidates were allowed to register, but they were hampered by a lack of adequate time for preparation of their campaigns; also, although there were no actual violations of the law on media coverage, the press was heavily biased in favour of President Nazarbayev. Thus, even before the elections had taken place, there was a general feeling that the outcome of the poll was a foregone conclusion.

In Turkmenistan, polling was held on 5 April for the 50 directly-elective seats in the People's Council, the supreme representative and supervisory chamber also including the 50 members of the unicameral Majlis (legislature) and a varying number of appointed and ex-officio members. According to the Central Electoral Commission, 99.5 per cent of the electorate turned out to vote. Unlike the parliamentary elections in 1994, there were alternative candidates this time. However, their political platforms were almost identical, so the choice was between individuals rather than policies.

The Decree on the Privatization of Land, for long a contentious issue in Kyrgyzstan, was finally signed by President Akayev on 14 October, three days before a national referendum on both constitutional reform and proposals for land reform. The decree laid down that the land would become real estate, to be traded in keeping with the Civil Land Code. Kyrgyz citizens who already cultivated plots of land would assume ownership of them free of charge, without having to renew the existing documents entitling them to use the land. To date, almost 2.5 million citizens had received plots of land and over 700,000 leases of up to 99 years had been issued. The decree banned foreigners, non-citizens and joint ventures with foreign participation from owning land.

In May the Kyrgyz-Canadian gold-mining enterprise Kumtor, the largest joint venture with foreign partners in Kyrgyzstan, was involved in an environmental accident that rapidly escalated into a political crisis. A vehicle carrying sodium cyanide for the enterprise overturned and discharged its contents into a nearby river. Two people died as a result and more than 800 were admitted to hospital. The opposition used the incident to criticize both the government and the joint venture, being accused by the Kumtor managing director of 'trying in every way to use the accident for its mercenary purposes' and of 'exaggerating and juggling with the facts'. A forum of 140 non-governmental organizations, set up in the wake of the spill, demanded that the Kyrgyz government should terminate its contract with Kumtor. Reports from Russian and US doctors suggested that the majority of the symptoms presented were of psychogenic origin. Nevertheless, the incident fuelled a wave of xenophobia and Kumtor's image was seriously undermined. By the end of the year the incident was still the cause of dispute and bitterness.

Astana (formerly Akmola, and during Soviet times Tselinograd) was inaugurated as the capital of Kazakhstan on 10 June. The ceremony was attended by high-level delegations from all Commonwealth of Independent States (CIS) countries, as well as by President Demirel of Turkey and a delegation from China. There were celebrations throughout the country and the National Bank issued a new 20-tenge coin to mark the occasion. However, the leader of the Communists, Serikbolsyn Abdildin, stated that the party was against the hasty removal of the capital and was pressing parliament to forbid the use of money from the state budget for the construction of new government buildings in Astana. A Japanese architect, Kise Kurokawa, won the international competition to design the principal buildings for the new capital.

The Tajik peace process gradually moved forward. The leader of the Islamic-led United Tajik Opposition (UTO), Sayed Abdullo Nuri, and first deputy leader Haji Akbar Turajonzoda, finally returned from exile in Afghanistan in February. Haji Turajonzoda at once proposed a referendum on replacing the words 'secular state' in the constitution with 'people's state' to ensure that the Islamic Rebirth Party could compete with other parties on equal terms in future parliamentary elections. The presidential spokesman insisted that there could be no such revision of the constitution, since 'faith must remain outside politics'. A ban was passed by parliament on religion-linked political parties; however, this decision was subsequently reversed when President Rakhmonov vetoed the law.

The situation in Tajikistan remained unstable. Negotiations on the government posts that, according to the 1997 peace agreement, were to be allocated to the UTO (30 per cent of the total) progressed slowly. The registration and demobilization of opposition troops also continued. Meanwhile, there were numerous instances of shootings, assault and abduction, perpetrated by both sides. In July a UN observer team and their Tajik interpreter and driver were killed while they were driving through central Tajikistan, some 170 kilometres east of the capital. The head of UN operations in Tajikistan immediately recalled all other UN observers to Dushanbe, and all but essential personnel were evacuated from the country.

In November there was an armed anti-government uprising in northern Tajikistan. The insurgents, according to the Tajik government, had been trained in northern Afghanistan and in Uzbekistan. Tajik radio also claimed that the UN observers had had prior information about the plot and that that was the reason for their withdrawal from the area. The UN mission denied this charge. The Uzbeks also rejected the allegations, as 'groundless and unsubstantiated'. The uprising was soon suppressed, but it caused a severe deterioration in relations between Uzbekistan and Tajikistan.

During the year moves were undertaken to strengthen the Central Asian Union, comprising Kazakhstan, Kyrgyzstan, Tajikistan and Uzbekistan. In July it was renamed the Central Asian Economic Community. An accord was signed on preventing and dealing with environmental disasters, natural and man-made. The agenda had originally included the drawing-up of a statement on measures to increase security, but this was deferred as the Kazakh President felt that the document needed to be reconsidered. A second meeting of the grouping was held in the Kazakh capital in December.

The power of drug-traffickers appeared to be growing throughout Central Asia. Analysis of statistical information, where available, showed a noticeable increase over the past couple of years in the scale of such operations throughout the CIS. The international aspect of the drugs trade had also grown and there was evidence of the involvement of corrupt government officials and police. In Uzbekistan, over the past five years the National Security Services had confiscated over 23 tonnes of drugs and some 500 people had been convicted of drug dealing. The Tajik President urged that particular attention be paid to Afghanistan as a source of drugs smuggling. He was concerned that drug barons might play a destabilizing role in the fragile peace process in Tajikistan. Elsewhere in the region, the Kzyl Orda province in southern Kazakhstan was shown to be a crucial transit area for dealers smuggling drugs from Afghanistan and Pakistan to the European part of the CIS and thence to Western Europe. One of the largest-ever seizures of a heroin cargo, totalling 1,000 kilograms, was made in Kushka, a town near the Turkmen-Afghan border. However, attempts to prevent the spread of drug-dealing in the CIS were complicated by the disintegration of security services dealing with organized crime, as well as of the prosecution system.

Kazakhstan's relations with Russia received a boost in 1998 as a result of President Nazarbayev's official visit to Moscow in July. The leaders of the two countries signed 'a treaty of eternal friendship and alliance' which envisaged, amongst other provisions, military assistance in the event of aggression from a third party. They also concluded an agreement 'on the delimitation of the Caspian Sea in compliance with sovereign rights for using mineral resources'—although this did not empower the signatories to claim sovereignty over the resources of the sea. The long-standing dispute over the Baikonur space facility (located in Kazakhstan but under Russian control) was also finally settled. Under the terms of the deal, Kazakhstan's debts to Russia were written off and Kazakhstan dropped its claims for rent from Baikonur for the period 1992–98, and also for compensation for the environmental damage caused by the facility since its inception. From 1999 Russia would pay rent for the use of Baikonur totalling US$65 million a year in hard currency.

The financial turmoil in Russia (see I.2; III.3.i) inevitably had an effect on the Central Asian economies. However, the leaders of the republics were careful to stress that they were no longer as dependent on Russia as they had once been. The Uzbek President stressed that his country did not buy foodstuffs from Russia: trade with Russia accounted for only 15–17 per cent of Uzbekistan's total turnover. Moreover, Uzbekistan's currency reserves were more that US$1,000 million. The Turkmen President likewise claimed that his country would not be affected. However, by the end of the year restrictions on the conversion of currency had been introduced in Turkmenistan. Trips abroad were only permitted in exceptional cases (for health reasons, education and government business). In Tajikistan, the main concern was that currency dealers might try to take advantage of the situation by importing large quantities of Russian roubles, then exchanging them for dollars that could be taken out of the country. The Tajik National Bank called on the public to refrain temporarily from conducting business transactions in roubles.

Similarly, in Kyrgyzstan and Kazakhstan there was an attempt to minimize the consequences of the Russian economic crisis. However, it gradually became clear that both countries would be seriously affected. In Kazakhstan it was announced in September that the budget might be cut by 60,000 million tenge (US$750 million), rather than the 45,000 million tenge cut announced the previous month. Shortly afterwards new curbs on official spending were announced: foreign trips, courses and seminars were cancelled, and the use of cellular telephones banned. Special government permission was now required for any officials to go abroad and strict limits were set on the amount of hard currency available. In Kyrgyzstan the draft budget for 1999 was amended to take account of an anticipated massive shortfall in revenue. The situation was exacerbated by a fall in gold sales (which accounted for over 40 per cent of the country's export earnings). Moreover, increasing sums of money were being required to service debts and to pay the large backlog of wages and pensions. Speculation in the dollar market resulted in panic buying of dollars by the general public.

The legal status of the Caspian Sea remained unresolved. In September the Kazakh Foreign Minister addressed the UN General Assembly and called for a decision on the issue. The Iranians continued to favour a joint approach to the sea, in part because of their concern over pollution, a major threat to the spawning beds of the caviar-producing sturgeon. In early September it was announced that the five littoral states had approved what was described as a 'comprehensive plan' to reduce pollution levels and work out a balanced and sustainable plan for the use of the biological resources of the sea.

A number of new Caspian Sea oil deals were concluded. The Kazakh state oil company Kazakh Oil signed agreements with the US-based Phillips Petroleum Company for exploration and extraction of oil from the Caspian shelf, and to refine and transport gas. The 40-year contract was to cover ten blocks of the northern Caspian section of the shelf, from which it was estimated that hydrocarbons worth some US$7,000 million would be extracted. Under another agreement, the Japanese companies Marubeni, Mitsui and Mitsubishi undertook, amongst other commitments, the upgrading of the Atyrau oil refinery. In Turkmenistan, the National Iranian Drilling Company concluded an agreement to drill four oil wells in the Turkmenbashi region, in the vicinity of the Caspian Sea; a team of technical experts, as well as three oil platforms, were to be supplied by the Iranian side. The Turkmen government undertook to cover the cost of drilling.

Pipeline projects continued to attract attention. The Caspian Pipeline Consortium (CPC) project to build a 1,580-kilometre pipeline from western Kazakhstan to the Black Sea, under consideration for several years, began to make some progress. By November the CPC had secured all the necessary approvals from Russian and Kazakh government experts. The feasibility study was given final approval at a CPC shareholders' meeting on 23–24 November. It was anticipated that construction would begin in January 1999, with a budget of US$854 million; the estimated completion date of the first stage of construction was set at October 2001. Stakeholders in the CPC included Russia (24 per cent), Kazakhstan (19 per cent) and Oman (7 per cent), with the remaining 50 per cent shared by a number of foreign companies, headed by Chevron (15 per cent). According to the Kazakh Foreign Minister, Kasymzhomart Tokayev, the CPC project remained the 'most practical option'. However, Kazakhstan also concluded an agreement with three Western companies (Royal Dutch/Shell Group, Mobil and Chevron) for a feasibility study on parallel oil and gas pipelines under the Caspian Sea to Azerbaijan. Moreover, a memorandum was signed between Shell International Gas and Romania's ROMGAZ public gas company and the National Agency for Mineral Resources for a feasibility study for transporting Turkmen gas through Romania to European and Turkish markets.

Notable foreign visitors to the Central Asian states during the year included King Juan Carlos of Spain to Kazakhstan and President Herzog of Germany to Kyrgyzstan in February; Mongolian President Bagabandi and Brazilian President Cardoso to Kazakstan in March; and Turkish President Demirel to Turkmenistan in November. Central Asian presidential visits abroad included those of President Niyazov of Turkmenistan to Brussels and Munich in February, to the USA in April and to China in September; President Karimov of Uzbekistan to Israel in September; and President Akayev of Kyrgyzstan to Hungary in November.

2. INDIA—PAKISTAN—BANGLADESH—NEPAL—BHUTAN—SRI LANKA

i. INDIA

CAPITAL: New Delhi   AREA: 3,287,000 sq km   POPULATION: 980,000,000 ('97)
OFFICIAL LANGUAGES: Hindi & English   POLITICAL SYSTEM: parliamentary democracy
HEAD OF STATE: President Kocheril Raman Narayanan (since July '97)
RULING PARTIES: Bharatiya Janata Party (BJP) heads 11-party coalition
HEAD OF GOVERNMENT: Atal Bihari Vajpayee (BJP), Prime Minister (since March '98)
MAIN IGO MEMBERSHIPS (non-UN): SAARC, CP, CWTH, NAM
CURRENCY: rupee (end-'98 £1=Rs70.70, US$1=Rs42.50)
GNP PER CAPITA: US$390 by exchange-rate calculation, US$1,650 by PPP calculation ('97)

THIS was a year which, from mid-March onwards, saw a coalition government in office in New Delhi headed by the Hindu-nationalist Bharatiya Janata Party (BJP), after the BJP had made advances in a general election. The new government soon startled the world by setting off nuclear tests in May, a move which initially elicited much approval within India and adverse comment and some sanctions from foreign powers. The BJP suffered electoral setbacks in state elections late in the year.

India's general election was staggered over four days between 16 February and 7 March. It produced, as expected, an inconclusive result. The BJP and its allies won 252 of the 545 seats in the Lok Sabha (lower house), while the Congress Party, with its allies, obtained 165. After two weeks of intense horse-trading, BJP leader Atal Bihari Vajpayee was sworn in as Prime Minister on 19 March, heading a coalition of many parties and factions. Aged 71, Mr Vajpayee had been Foreign Minister in the late 1970s and Prime Minister for a mere 13 days in 1996 (see AR 1996, p. 299).

The election, carried out at 900,000 polling stations manned by 4.5 million election officials, was marred by nearly 100 deaths. The worst incidents were in the region of Coimbatore, in India's deep south-western state of Kerala.

As Mr Vajpayee took office, veteran Congress leader Sitaram Kesri resigned, under pressure from Italian-born Sonia Gandhi (widow of former Prime Minister Rajiv Gandhi), who refused to let him share a campaign platform with her. On 7 March she was elected president of Congress and then, a few days later, chairman of the parliamentary party, even though she was not an MP. The post of parliamentary chairman had been created for her mother-in-law, Indira Gandhi, in 1977 and had been vacant since her assassination in 1984.

The new government won a 274–261 vote of confidence in the Lok Sabha on 18 March. The next day Mr Vajpayee was sworn in as Prime Minister and head of a 22-member cabinet; 21 ministers of state were also appointed. Mr Vajpayee himself took six portfolios, including that of external affairs. Former bureaucrat Yashwant Sinha became Finance Minister; the BJP president, L.K. Advani, was appointed Minister of Home Affairs; and George Fernandes became Defence Minister. Mr Sinha was quick to try to reassure investors: 'We are not out of another planet. We are ready to welcome foreign investors in sectors in which we feel foreign investment has a major role to play'. However, this assertion was not convincingly driven home either in his interim budget issued on 25 March or in his main budget presented on 1 June.

During the election campaign there was some international concern and criticism because the BJP manifesto said that a BJP government would build, test and deploy nuclear weapons. On 11 May, despite earlier Western warnings of international sanctions, India conducted three underground nuclear tests at Pokharan in the Thar desert, under 100 miles from the Pakistan border. Two days later it carried out two further tests, completing the series. The timing of the tests appeared to have taken foreign governments by surprise, and US intelligence agencies apparently had not detected the preparations.

The tests inspired an immediate surge of national pride unmatched since the military victory over Pakistan in 1971 or the end of the British Raj in 1947—though there were a few articulate critical voices from within India. For about a fortnight BJP leaders and their supporters triumphantly proclaimed India's new power status, to widespread domestic approval across the country's diverse political spectrum. They dismissed international criticism and opprobrium as the price of earning

India's 'rightful place' in the world. Soon, however, the party which had promised India 'stable government and an able Prime Minister', was thrown on the defensive. Lambasted by domestic businessmen and foreign critics for lack of coherence and purposive direction, the government's policies were rebuffed by the markets. Moreover, the BJP soon became ensnared in feuds with some of its coalition members that threatened its continuance as the core of the central government. This raised the bigger and more searching question: what could the government achieve, even if it did survive? A political turning-point was the June budget, which was laden with tax and spending measures and heralded a return to greater protectionism. Dismissively, the colourful weekly magazine *India Today* summarized a prevailing view with the headline that the BJP-led government had enjoyed a first '100 days of just being there'.

World reaction to India's tests was mostly hostile. Pakistan immediately followed suit (see VIII.2.ii), having accused India of threats and of damaging the security situation in South Asia. On 13 May President Clinton, on the eve of a visit to Britain for a meeting of the G-8 leaders, signed an order for economic sanctions against India. For a variety of reasons the US leader did not fulfil an earlier plan to visit India in 1998. Japan suspended aid. UK Prime Minister Tony Blair said that the tests gravely weakened the security of the entire world, but he did not threaten British sanctions. Officials said that European leaders believed that sanctions might be counter-productive. Russia also opposed sanctions. The World Bank cancelled the annual donors' meeting. Many Commonwealth countries deplored India's tests, notably Australia, Canada, New Zealand and South Africa (a country which had destroyed its own nuclear arsenal). Initial Chinese reaction was cautious and then more openly critical after India's new Defence Minister, Mr Fernandes, had repeated his earlier claim that China was India's main security worry. A Chinese statement said that India had shown 'outrageous contempt for the common will of the international community'.

Later in the year India worked hard to repair and improve its international relationships, with some apparent success. Jaswant Singh, one of the Prime Minister's closest aides (who was made Foreign Minister in December), and Brijesh Mishra, his principal secretary and a former diplomat, made many journeys across the globe—notably to Washington, New York, London, Paris and Moscow—to explain India's views and policies. New Russian Premier Yevgenii Primakov's visit to India in early December (as a substitute for the ailing President Yeltsin) produced a number of indications of continuing Indian-Russian cordialities and cooperation.

India and Pakistan exchanged artillery fire across Kashmir's disputed borders, accompanied by sporadic, localized violence inside the state throughout the year. There was much mutual vituperation after the nuclear testings in May; however, by the end of the year they had resumed bilateral talks at official level. The discussions were about their territorial disputes and other contentious issues such as terrorism, drug-trafficking and economic plans. No major agreements resulted, but both sides agreed to continue their dialogue in 1999.

Perhaps more indicative of the dominant note in Indo-Pakistan relations in 1998 was the fact that about 60,000 troops were involved in India's largest military exercise for a decade, conducted in early December close to the border with Pakistan, and included training in nuclear and chemical weapons warfare. Pakistan moved 20,000 troops close to the border in response, although both countries kept their forces about 80 miles apart in line with international norms.

There were many reports of communal clashes during the year, of Hindus attacking Christians, or, as in early December, when paramilitary forces were put on alert to protect a Sufi shrine in southern India as militant Hindus threatened to storm it in a mass rally.

A slow-down of reforms and sluggish industrial growth plagued the Indian economy for the second consecutive year. Investor confidence touched its lowest ebb since economic reforms were initiated in 1991. Few shared the government's much-repeated claim that there would soon be an industrial and economic upsurge. Few seemed to believe the government's forecast that the economy would return to the growth rates of up to 7 per cent achieved between 1994 and 1997, although many economists expected India to do better in financial year 1998/99 than in the previous year, with good monsoon rains boosting agricultural output. It was notable that India achieved growth of 5.1 per cent for the year ended 31 March 1998, in a region where most economies plunged deeper into crisis.

Nevertheless, foreign and domestic investors who had been optimistic that the BJP-led government would accelerate the dawdling pace of reforms soon learned that it was not conspicuously better than its predecessors in this respect. Reforms in the areas of insurance and infrastructure remained sluggish or inoperative, much to the disappointment of foreign investors. In October a cabinet committee recommended that foreign insurance companies be permitted to hold stakes of up to 26 per cent in Indian-owned insurance companies, with an additional 14 per cent allowed for non-resident Indian investors and financial institutions. Controversial legislation to facilitate the liberalization of what hitherto had been a state-monopoly industry was tabled in parliament in December.

The rupee came under heavy pressure in the first quarter of financial year 1998/99 (April to June) and was allowed to slide by 7.5 per cent to settle at about 43 rupees to the US dollar, compared with 38 rupees a year before. The pressure on the exchange rate reflected the international situation and a fall in investor confidence after India's nuclear tests in May, followed by sanctions from the USA, Japan and some other G-8 countries. Foreign institutional investors withdrew more than $400 million from the stock markets in May and June, and rating agencies such as Moody's downgraded India's sovereign rating. Foreign institutional investment fell to $1,000 million for 1997/98, from $1,900 million in 1996/97. In contrast, foreign direct investment increased to $3,200 million in 1997/98, from $2,700 million the preceding year.

The World Bank, in its annual India report released in June, warned that recent developments pointed to deteriorating prospects for the economy. The slow-down in growth had raised serious doubts about the country's prospects in the longer term to attain and sustain the level of growth required to reduce poverty. The World Bank said that the budget deficit—one of the world's largest at about 6 per cent of GDP—should be reduced. It also said that deregulation of external and internal markets should be speeded up to encourage efficiency improvements and higher private investment.

Implemenation of the Women's Reservation Bill, guaranteeing one-third of the seats in the national and state legislatures to women, was delayed until consensus could be reached. On 13 July, when MPs debated the issue, some opposition MPs snatched a copy of the draft bill from the Law Minister and tore it to shreds. The Prime Minister said that this behaviour was disgraceful and that he had not seen anything like it in his 40 years in parliament.

Draft legislation creating the three new states of Uttaranchal, Vananchal and Chattisgarh—to be carved out of Uttar Pradesh, Bihar and Madhya Pradesh respectuvely—was approved by the cabinet on 3 August.

The foundation stone was laid on 5 November of the Centre of India Tower, planned to become the tallest building in the world, at 2,222 feet. Situated in the village of Karoda, Madhya Pradesh, it would be 700 feet taller than the Petronas Towers in Kuala Lumpur. Designed by the firm that produced the World Trade Center in New York, the building was the brainchild of the Maharishi Mahesh Yogi and was intended to be the home for 100,000 Hindu sages rather than office space.

One of the regional coalition partners in the BJP-led government, the Madras-based AIADMK, which controlled 27 seats, threatened to pull out of the Union government because of a dispute over a water-sharing scheme in southern India. The plan aimed to create a River Valley Authority and to end a long-running dispute over the distribution of water between Tamil Nadu and Karnataka. After intense and protracted talks, the AIADMK decided on 13 August to stay within the coalition.

In late November the BJP coalition government suffered a series of setbacks in regional elections. Congress did remarkably well in three elections to state legislatures. It took two-thirds of the seats in Delhi, dislodged the BJP from office in Rajasthan and kept control of Madhya Pradesh, although it lost Mizoram to a regional party. The results were regarded by a number of analysts as a first striking success for Sonia

Gandhi as newly-installed leader of Congress, following her vigorous campaigning in the general election earlier in the year.

On 22 September President Narayanan sent back to the cabinet a request that the Bihar state government should be dismissed because of a breakdown in constitutional procedures. The BJP-led government had complained of Bihar's 'bad governance, social anarchy, rank casteism and criminalization of politics'. When the President effectively rejected the request, the Union government dropped its demand. All the opposition parties in the Lok Sabha, and even some of the coalition parties, opposed the imposition of presidential rule in Bihar, although the state governor had called for it. Chief Minister Lalu Prasad Yadav claimed that the presidential intervention was a 'victory for democracy over communal force'. In 1997 Mr Yadav had been sent to gaol and had appointed his wife, Rabri, in his place (see AR 1997, p. 306). He had been released on bail, but was imprisoned again on 28 October for involvement in a financial scandal.

India gained some vicarious kudos in October when the 1998 Nobel Prize for Economics was awarded to Professor Amartya Kumar Sen, the Indian-born master of Trinity College, Cambridge (UK), for his work on welfare economics which had 'helped explain the economic mechanisms underlying famine and poverty'. By studying catastrophes in India, Bangladesh, Ethiopia and Saharan Africa, he had found that a shortage of food was not always the main explanation for famine; other factors, such as flooding, were often responsible as well. The award to Professor Kumar Sen, who was formerly a professor of philosophy and economics at Harvard University (USA), marked a further move away from awarding Nobel prizes to economic theorists in favour of those, like Professor Sen, who dealt with practical problems.

ii. PAKISTAN

CAPITAL: Islamabad   AREA: 804,000 sq km   POPULATION: 130,600,000 ('98)
OFFICIAL LANGUAGE: Urdu   POLITICAL SYSTEM: parliamentary democracy
HEAD OF STATE: President Mohammed Rafiq Tarar (since Dec '97)
RULING PARTY: Pakistan Muslim League (PML)
HEAD OF GOVERNMENT: Mohammed Nawaz Sharif, Prime Minister (since Feb '97)
MAIN IGO MEMBERSHIPS (non-UN): OIC, SAARC, ECO, CP, CWTH, NAM
CURRENCY: Pakistan rupee (end-'98 £1=PRs81.58, US$1=PRs49.02)
GNP PER CAPITA: US$490 by exchange-rate calculation, US$1,590 by PPP calculation ('97)

PAKISTAN'S political stability remained fairly fragile during 1998, despite or because of Prime Minister Nawaz Sharif's assertion of power, but the focus of events was more the economic crisis and defence issues. The country teetered throughout the year on the edge of financial default, while in May it decided that it had no choice but to match India's decision to test a series of nuclear devices (see also VIII.2.i).

Nawaz Sharif, who had won a major battle against the judiciary at the end of 1997 (see AR 1997, pp. 310–11) and who continued to enjoy a substantial parliamentary majority, moved to consolidate his position within the state apparatus. He successfully took on the army by forcing the resignation in October of General Jehangir Karamat, Chief of the Army Staff, who had made a public statement calling for the government to sort out the country's problems. His successor, General Parvez Musharaf, was promoted over the heads of two more senior officers, who resigned in protest.

At the end of August Mr Sharif announced an amendment to the constitution to introduce Islamic law in all areas of the country's life, the measure being passed by the National Assembly on 9 October. If implemented, it would have given the Prime Minister much greater discretionary power. However, the absence of a sufficient majority in the Senate prevented its final adoption.

In September the Prime Minister broke with the Muttahida Qaumi Movement (MQM), with which he had been in alliance both nationally and locally in Sindh province. The issue at stake was control of Karachi, home to most of the MQM's Urdu-speaking supporters, where Mr Sharif claimed the MQM had orchestrated violence and the latter that the national government was seeking to diminish the MQM's political power base. In November he used his constitutional powers to dismiss the Sindh ministry, suspend the legislature and impose federal control. As in the past, the dismissal was followed by army action in Karachi. The death toll in the city during the year was in the region of 1,000. Mr Sharif's authoritarian approach also led to his losing the support of local allies in the provinces of Balochistan and the North-West Frontier. The opposition Pakistan People's Party (PPP) made little progress during the year. Its leader, Benazir Bhutto, was tied down by charges of corruption and spent much of the year abroad, although she was able to address some well-attended public meetings.

Sectarian violence remained a major problem, as demonstrated by a massacre of over 20 Shia Muslims by militant Sunnis in Lahore in January. In May the Roman Catholic bishop of Faisalabad committed suicide as a protest against the use of Pakistan's controversial blasphemy law.

The economy faced major difficulties throughout the year as a result of internal and foreign deficits. In February the governor of the State Bank of Pakistan resigned in protest at the government's unwillingness to curb spending and thus reduce the fiscal deficit. In terms of the balance-of-payments gap, the government had to look both to foreign banks for short-term financing as well as to overseas Pakistanis, who were encouraged to make foreign exchange deposits with Pakistani banks. The sanctions that followed the nuclear tests in May were almost the last straw. The IMF suspended disbursements of previously agreed loans, and Pakistan was forced to delay payments on several loans from commercial banks, although a total default was averted. A state of emergency was declared under which foreign exchange accounts totalling $11,000 million held by Pakistani citizens were frozen, although this inevitably had negative consequences in the longer term.

The budget was introduced as usual in June, but chose to ignore the crisis rather than introduce drastic measures. In October the Moody's ratings agency downgraded the country's credit rating to almost the bottom of the scale, and at the end of that month foreign exchange reserves fell to $425 million. With the partial lifting of sanctions, however, negotiations resumed with the IMF, and in November there was provisional agreement on a new $5,600 million package, although final IMF approval was outstanding at the end of the year.

In the middle of the year the government turned on foreign investors in the power sector, accusing them of having secured their contracts to construct private sector power plants through kickbacks to the previous PPP government. At the end of June one such contract was cancelled and others were put on notice.

A much-delayed population census was held during the year and recorded a population of 130.6 million. This was lower than had been expected, and indicated that the population growth rate had declined to 2.6 per cent in the 1988–97 decade.

In May the newly-elected government of the Hindu nationalist Bharatiya Janata Party (BJP) in India detonated a series of nuclear devices, in a clear challenge to the existing nuclear regime. Although India attempted to portray the tests in terms of India's global role, it was inevitably seen in Pakistan as an attempt to assert Indian hegemony in the region. Despite some domestic voices urging caution and strong pressure from the US government, Pakistan responded at the end of May with its own series of tests. It thus rendered itself liable to the same sanctions as were imposed on India. In practice, however, although the sanctions had a major impact on an already-fragile economy, Pakistan was in no position to make any unilateral concessions, given the strength of domestic public opinion. In the event, the US government in effect decided after a few months that sanctions would not work so far as India was concerned. Congress passed a resolution in October allowing the President to waive some of the sanctions, and this was implemented for both countries the following month. At the end of the year the USA announced its willingness to settle Pakistan's compensation claims for F-16 aircraft paid for in 1991 but never delivered because of earlier sanctions.

The USA's carrot-and-stick policy was supplemented by intensive talks between US representatives—mainly Strobe Talbott, the Deputy Secretary of State—and the two South Asian protagonists. Mr Sharif visited Washington in early December. No formal agreements had been reached by the end of the year, although both India and Pakistan had clearly signalled that they were willing to consider signing the 1996 Comprehensive Nuclear Test-Ban Treaty or making comparable commitments. Even before the nuclear tests, Indo-Pakistan relations were distinctly cool, not least because of the speed with which each side was evidently developing its missile capability. In April Pakistan tested its longest-range missile so far. Named Ghauri, it had a range of 1,500 kilometres and was intended to counter India's development of its Prithvi range of missiles. Unconfirmed reports suggested that Pakistan had acquired some of the technology for its missile from North Korea. Immediately after the tests Indo-Pakistan bilateral relations reached a low point, but prime ministerial contacts at multilateral events led eventually to Foreign Secretary-level talks in October and November, first in Islamabad and then in New Delhi, although little substantive progress was reported.

Relations with the USA were further complicated when the latter's missile attack in August on Osama bin Laden's headquarters in Afghanistan crossed Pakistan airspace (see IV.1; VIII.1.ii). Although the US government had earlier given tacit support to the Taleban regime in Kabul, by 1998 it had decided to change its stance. Pakistan meanwhile continued to support the Taleban as the best bet for political stability in Afghanistan, although this policy led to worsening relations with Iran (see VIII.1.i).

iii. BANGLADESH

CAPITAL: Dhaka   AREA: 144,000 sq km   POPULATION: 124,000,000 ('97)
OFFICIAL LANGUAGE: Bengali   POLITICAL SYSTEM: parliamentary democracy
HEAD OF STATE: President Shahabuddin Ahmed (since July '96)
RULING PARTIES: Awami League heads coalition
HEAD OF GOVERNMENT: Sheikh Hasina Wajed, Prime Minister (since June '96)
MAIN IGO MEMBERSHIPS (non-UN): SAARC, CP, OIC, CWTH, NAM
CURRENCY: taka (end-'98 £1=Tk80.69, US$1=Tk48.50)
GNP PER CAPITA: US$270 or US$1,050 by PPP calculation ('97)

CONTINUING intense and bitter political competition, together with flooding unprecedented in its severity even in a country recurrently afflicted by the adverse buffets of nature: these were the two main motifs of 1998 for Bangladesh. The Awami League, led by Sheikh Hasina Wajed as Prime Minister, continued as the head and core of the ruling coalition government throughout the year, opposed principally by the Bangladesh National Party (BNP) led by former Prime Minister Begum Khaleda Zia.

In a document published early in the year, the World Bank pronounced a telling judgment on the prevailing character of Bangladesh's politics, in the following terms: 'Confrontation between the Awami League and the BNP became the norm, initially in parliament, but then also on the streets .... Though the two parties' development policies are similar, the BNP has not shied away from attacking policies it had initiated, such as privatization. This is having something of a chilling effect on reforms.'

The BNP ended its long-running boycott of parliament in early March, following a provisional agreement made with the ruling party. The appointment of two BNP MPs as junior ministers by the Prime Minister, in defiance of a constitutional provision against floor-crossing, was seen as provocative by the BNP. It was also characterized as a 'great blunder' by some of the ruling party's own back-benchers.

In an unprecedented joint statement in May, the presidents of six of the country's major trade bodies issued a declaration which said: 'The country's trade and industry is deeply worried over the breakdown of law and order and increasing criminalization of society. The first threat to the rule of law is the dependence of major political parties on armed criminals to ensure support for their political programmes. This has brought about a near-collapse of the rule of law .... The business community cannot remain silent as the abduction of businessmen, rapes and attacks on children continue unabated.'

Rising corruption and deteriorating law and order not only made normal life difficult but also affected the investment climate. As well as the activities of criminals, and much evidence of political violence, the local press reported many instances of brutality and corruption in the police. The World Bank's country director, Pierre Landell-Mills, described corruption as 'outrageous' and said that it 'threatens to retard growth .... Toll collection, bribing public officials ... are hurting the investment of the country.'

Millions of people were forced from their villages between July and September as two-thirds of the country spent more than two months under water. The flooding left food supplies at dangerously low levels and turned vast swathes of farmland into water-logged wastelands. The opposition accused the government of putting politics above need as it distributed relief aid and organized food-for-work programmes. As the political battle intensified, some observers feared that relief efforts could grind to a halt, with malnutrition spreading. In mid-November the seven-party opposition alliance led by Begum Khaleda organized strikes that paralysed 60 cities and towns around the country in protest against the government's handling of relief efforts. The opposition repeatedly accused Sheikh Hasina of misusing funds meant for flood victims.

Although Bangladesh was often exposed to devastating floods, those of 1998 were the worst for decades. The flooding, which lasted an unprecedented 11 weeks, was caused by the simultaneous rise of the Ganges, Brahmaputra and Meghna rivers, which usually crested at different times. The disaster claimed at least 1,500 lives and the World Bank estimated that 30 million people—almost a quarter of the entire population—lost their source of income. More than 500,000 homes and 14,000 schools were severely damaged. Some 1,500 kilometres of roads, including the highway between Dhaka and the main port of Chittagong, were washed out, making the distribution of assistance difficult. The devastation was expected to have a lasting adverse impact on the economy. The World Bank predicted GDP growth would slow to 3–4 per cent in the fiscal year which began in July. In the previous year growth had been almost 6 per cent.

The country generally, and Dhaka especially, was obstructed and intermittently brought to standstills by politically-motivated strikes, much to the distress of local and foreign businessmen and investors. In late November Sheikh Hasina said that general elections would be held in the year 2000, one year ahead of schedule. She also announced that the Awami League would never again call a general strike. By the end of the year the BNP, the Jatiya Party and the Jamaat-e-Islami Party were trying to forge a tactical alliance with the aim of forcing the government to call an early election. The Jatiya Party was led by former military ruler General Mohammed Hossain Ershad, of whom Begum Khaleda had once been a bitter opponent.

As in recent years, Bangladesh was active at the United Nations as well as in a number of international agencies during 1998. The Prime Minister's official visits were cut down when compared with the previous 18 months, because of her preoccupations at home. However, having attended the Tehran summit of Islamic states in December 1997 (see AR 1997, pp. 400–2), in July she was also present at the summit of the South Asian Association for Regional Cooperation (SAARC) in Colombo (see XI.6.iii).

At the beginning of the year the first-ever one-day meeting of the Prime Ministers of India, Pakistan and Bangladesh was held in Dhaka. Leading businessmen were included in the three delegations, and the meeting was billed as an economic summit. In fact, it was as much a political as an economic meeting, as the three then incumbent Prime Ministers—I.K. Gujral of India, Nawaz Sharif of Pakistan and Sheikh Hasina—renewed personal contacts and began discussing outstanding issues. Dhaka-based sources said that Sheikh Hasina would host a second India-Pakistan-Bangladesh economic summit some time early in 1999 depending on political developments.

Further evidence of Bangladesh's desire to raise its international profile was provided in the announcement that it would host the next summit of the Non-Aligned Movement (NAM) in Dhaka in August-September 2001, thereby succeeding South Africa for a three-year term in the NAM chair (see XI.3.iii). Several top-class hotels and a new convention centre were to be built in the capital before this event; and Bangladesh, with South Africa, would immediately play a prominent part in NAM consultative processes.

Extensive and protracted negotiations between government officials and the Shanti Bahini tribal rebels in the south-eastern Chittagong Hill Tracts (CHT), under the terms of the December 1997 peace treaty (see AR 1997, p. 315), continued into 1998—although the agreement seemed to have brought anything but peace either to the trouble-torn CHT or to party political differences on this issue. On 6 February the government declared a general amnesty for all armed rebels in the CHT. By its terms no charges were to be made against individuals who had previously been active in the Shanti Bahini or its political wing, the Parbatya Chattagram Janasanghati Samiti (PCJSS). Shanti Bahini rebels, who had been fighting for 23 years for autonomy in the CHT, formally surrendered their arms on 10 February. However, some of the Chakma people of the CHT opposed the accord from the beginning, claiming that it betrayed the tribal populations. The government's refusal to debate the four 'peace' bills in parliament, and the haste with which they were pushed through without the opposition being allowed to speak, highlighted the persisting divisions and differences on the CHT.

The peace accord was made possible principally because the Indian government had pressed for it. The Indian authorities repeatedly accused Bangladesh of providing sanctuary and training facilities to Indian tribal rebels from some of the eastern Indian states—a charge that Bangladeshi spokesmen always denied. After the Awami League, with its marked pro-Indian elements, returned to office in mid-1996, New Delhi's attitude changed and the December 1997 agreement was signed. A similar story could be told of the 30-year Ganges Water Treaty which had been signed between India and Bangladesh in December 1996. These agreements signalled Sheikh Hasina's determination to maintain good relations with India, even though the accords did not bring an end to all Indian press criticism of Bangladesh.

A 171-page judgment was delivered by a Dhaka court in November whereby 15 former army officers were sentenced to public execution for their alleged involvement in the killing of Sheikh Mujibur Rahman, independent Bangladesh's first Prime Minister, and most of his family in the August 1975 military coup. Only two of the 15 accused were in the country; the others were hiding overseas (and four other accused were acquitted). The case had been reopened when Sheikh Mujib's daughter, Sheikh Hasina, became Prime Minister in 1996. When the family home was stormed on 15 August 1975, she had been out of the country, but 21 members of the family were massacred. A constitutional amendment amnestying the murderers and their accomplices had allowed them to go free. However, on taking office, Sheikh Hasina had restored the power of the courts to try her father's killers. After the court verdict, the opposition BNP renewed its campaign to oust the government and called a 48-hour strike. Demonstrations followed.

Charges relating to three more corruption cases were filed against Begum Khaleda in July and August, relating to her period as Prime Minister (1991–96). Earlier in the year 69 cases had been filed against her, members of her family and former ministers.

iv. NEPAL

CAPITAL: Kathmandu   AREA: 147,000 sq km   POPULATION: 23,000,000 ('97)
OFFICIAL LANGUAGE: Nepali   POLITICAL SYSTEM: parliamentary democracy
HEAD OF STATE: King Birendra Bir Bikram Shah Deva (since '72)
RULING PARTIES: Nepali Congress Party (NCP) heads coalition
HEAD OF GOVERNMENT: Girija Prasad Koirala (NCP), Prime Minister (since April '98)
MAIN IGO MEMBERSHIPS (non-UN): SAARC, CP, NAM
CURRENCY: Nepal rupee (end-'98 £1=NRs110.97, US$1=NRs66.70)
GNP PER CAPITA: US$210 by exchange-rate calculation, US$1,090 by PPP calculation ('97)

FAMILIAR but generally intensifying political in-fighting between and within Nepal's political parties continued throughout 1998.

On 8 January Prime Minister Surya Bahadur Thapa heightened political uncertainty when he asked King Birendra to dissolve the bicameral legislature and set a date for general elections. Mr Thapa's three-month old coalition government was the fourth since the general election of November 1994 had failed to provide any one party with a workable majority in the legislature (see AR 1997, pp. 316–7). The government was a coalition between Mr Thapa's right-wing National Democratic Party (NDP) and the Nepali Congress Party (NCP), based on an 'understanding' between the parties' presidents, respectively Mr Thapa and Girja Prasad Koirala, that they would take turns in the post of Prime Minister until November 1999, when the term of the present parliament ended. This understanding was soon shown to be inoperable, however.

In February the United Communist Party Party–Marxist-Leninist (UCPN-ML), which had 89 seats in the 205-member House of Representatives, split into two factions, a breakaway group forming the Communist Party of Nepal–Marxist-Leninist (CPN-ML), with 40 MPs. This left the NCP, with 87 seats, as the largest single party and enabled it to form a minority government in April under Mr Koirala, for the second time since the November 1994 polls. The NCP had been an element in each of the past three coalition governments, but also an ultimate defector from each of them.

The NCP then entered into lengthy negotiations with the CPN-ML on the formation of a new government coalition. Initially, many members inside both parties were opposed to an alliance on ideological and other grounds. Eventually, King Birendra acted on Mr Koirala's recommendation and in August reconstituted the government by appointing 13 CPN-ML ministers and removing 13 NCP ministers. Soon afterwards the Prime Minister and the CPN-ML leader, Sahana Pradhan, signed a 25-point programme which envisaged the rebuilding of the national economy; ending the three-year Maoist insurgency; evacuating Indian troops stationed in the Kalapani border area since the 1962 Sino-Indian border war; calling general elections in May 1999; and repatriating more than 100,000 Bhutanese refugees of Nepalese descent who had been sheltering in south-eastern Nepal since 1990.

On 16 October the Speaker of the House of Representatives survived an impeachment motion sponsored by the opposition UCPN-ML. The Speaker, who had been accused of breaking legislative rules in order to push through a bill on autonomy for local councils, was supported by 123 deputies, whilst 55 deputies voted for the motion. The Deputy Speaker, from the UCPN-ML, had resigned her seat on 10 October in order to avoid the humiliation of a forced resignation after the ruling NCP and CPN-ML had tabled a retaliatory impeachment motion against her.

King Birendra travelled to London in the second half of November for a medical check-up, following what a palace source described as a mild heart attack on 4 November. It was an awkward time for the King to be suffering from health problems, since Nepal was grappling with a Maoist insurgency in the countryside and difficult relations with Bhutan. In addition, Mr Koirala's government was exposed to considerable pressure from a raft of rival political parties and movements, including royalists. In late November the government offered an amnesty to Maoist rebels if they agreed to abandon the 'people's war' that had already left hundreds dead. The rebels had joined with the Nepal Communist Party–Maoist in demanding that the constitutional monarchy be replaced by a people's republic.

Nepal agreed to host the 11th South Asian Association for Regional Cooperation (SAARC) summit in October 1999. During 1998 Nepal maintained virtually trouble-free relations with all its neighbours (especially India and China) apart from Bhutan (see VIII.2.v), though some irritants remained evident in its relations with India over the Indian troops in the Kalapani border area.

Predictably, the coalition between the NCP and the CPN-ML did not survive the year, collapsing in mid-December then the CPN-ML ministers resigned in protest against Mr Koirala's alleged failure to honour parts of the government's agreed programme. Amidst much political confusion, Mr Koirala was reappointed Prime Minister on 24 December, this time at the head of a coalition between the NCP, the UCPN-ML and a smaller party. It was Nepal's sixth government since the 1994 election.

v. BHUTAN

CAPITAL: Thimphu   AREA: 46,500 sq km   POPULATION: 736,000 ('97)
OFFICIAL LANGUAGES: Dzongkha, Lhotsan, English   POLITICAL SYSTEM: monarchy
HEAD OF STATE & GOVERNMENT: Dragon King Jigme Singye Wangchuk (since '72)
MAIN IGO MEMBERSHIPS (non-UN): SAARC, CP, NAM
CURRENCY: ngultrum (end-'98 £1=N70.70, US$1=N42.50)
GNP PER CAPITA: US$400 by exchange-rate calculation ('97)

THE main political event of 1998 came in late June when King Jigme Singye Wangchuk dismissed his entire cabinet—becoming the first monarch to do so in the country's long history—and issued a royal decree authorizing the 15-member National Assembly to elect new ministers. By the new rules, ministers would serve fixed five-year terms, whereas previously there was no time-limit on cabinet posts.

Much controversy and some compromises ensued. The Assembly asked the King, and he agreed, to present a list of acceptable candidates with corresponding portfolios, so that it would not have to vote 'without guidance'. Candidates were duly nominated by the King and were elected with clear majorities. But the ballot was secret and not all Assembly members voted in their favour. Six new ministers were elected, all in their 40s and highly regarded by foreign observers in Bhutan. They replaced ministers from the country's traditional political elite who had served in their posts for years, some even for decades.

Various explanations were offered for these changes, ranging from generational conflict and resentments amongst the ruling elites and pressure from aid-giving donor countries. Bhutanese dissidents living abroad asserted that the reforms fell well short of their demands for 'genuine democracy', including the right to form political parties. Whatever the King had in mind when he surprised the Assembly with his reform programme, the outcome was seen none the less as a significant step towards a more representative system of government within one of the world's few remaining absolute monarchies.

The first year of Bhutan's eighth five-year plan came to an end in 1998 and recorded economic growth in most areas. During the year GDP grew by 6 per cent and inflation remained below 10 per cent, according to the government's review of the 1997/98 budget. There was no budgetary deficit and the balance of payments continued to register a surplus, leading to healthy growth of 26.7 per cent in external reserves. Bhutan thus now had $215 million in foreign exchange reserves, or enough to meet import requirements for at least two years. Hydroelectric power and controlled, up-market tourism were increasingly important factors in generating economic growth.

Bhutan, however, continued to be heavily dependent on foreign aid. India provided nearly 2,000 million ngultrums (US$54 million) in grants and aid during the year, while 1.5 million ngultrums came from other foreign donors and international agencies. Domestic revenue covered current expenditure, while the financing of capital expenditure remained donor-driven. The Bhutanese remained some of the least taxed people in the world, as the government laid emphasis on sustainable growth and self-reliance.

The Prince of Wales arrived in Bhutan on 9 February on the last leg of a three-country South Asian tour which included Nepal and Sri Lanka. Human rights activists seized the chance to publicize the plight of about 100,000 ethnic (Hindu) Nepalese who had been expelled from Bhutan in 1990 under King Jigme Singye Wangchuk's 'one nation, one people' policy. Nepal's Foreign Minister, Lyonpo Dawa Tshering, said that claims of repression of the Nepalese refugees were 'exaggerated'. The majority of the exiles were now in UN refugee camps on Nepalese soil. Those who stayed in Bhutan were required to embrace the Buddhist culture and language of the indigenous Drukpa population. Prince Charles met with King Wangchuk on 10 February in the capital, Thimphu, though palace sources said afterwards that the refugee issue was not discussed.

vi. SRI LANKA

CAPITAL: Colombo   AREA: 64,500 sq km   POPULATION: 18,500,000 ('97)
OFFICIAL LANGUAGES: Sinhala, Tamil, English   POLITICAL SYSTEM: presidential democracy
HEAD OF STATE & GOVERNMENT: President Chandrika Bandaranaike Kumaratunga (since Nov '94)
RULING PARTIES: Sri Lanka Freedom Party (SLFP) heads People's Alliance coalition
PRIME MINISTER: Sirimavo Bandaranaike (since Nov '94)
MAIN IGO MEMBERSHIPS (non-UN): SAARC, CP, CWTH, NAM
CURRENCY: rupee (end-'98 £1=SLRs113.85, US$1=SLRs68.43)
GNP PER CAPITA: US$800 by exchange-rate calculation, US$3,460 by PPP calculation ('97)

SRI Lanka ended 1998, its 50th year as an independent nation, with the government still battling the Liberation Tigers of Tamil Eelam (LTTE), whose violent campaign to carve a separate state out of the country's northern and eastern provinces had begun in 1983. There were increasing calls for agreement between the two main national political forces—the ruling People's Alliance and the opposition United National Party (UNP)—on a political settlement that could be offered to the island's Tamil minority (an eighth of the whole population). But the two groups remained wide apart. The UNP's refusal to support a government plan to devolve power to the country's nine provinces as a way of meeting Tamil demands for autonomy in the north and east blocked its legislative passage. Towards the year's end, both parties came under pressure from a coalition of business leaders to seek a common position on the ethnic issue. But there were few signs that even that effort would bring the two together.

The government, while maintaining that it was committed to power-sharing through devolution and to a political solution, continued its efforts to weaken the LTTE militarily, but with mixed results. Its bid to open a land route to the Jaffna peninsula in the north through territory under Tiger control made very slow progress. The army suffered a heavy blow in September when the LTTE overran its important base at Kilinochchi, a town south of Jaffna. With some 1,500 soldiers killed, many others wounded and a large stock of equipment seized, this setback for the army was not fully offset by its capture of nearby Mankulam. Tiger losses were also heavy. The government, producing a group of child Tigers who, it claimed, had surrendered, charged the LTTE with reneging on a promise not to deploy children, given to UN envoy Olara Otunnu earlier in the year.

Besides giving the army a hard time, the LTTE continued to attack civilian targets, including Tamil political figure who would not toe its line. It opened the score on 26 January by sending suicide bombers to strike at the Temple of the Tooth, the holiest shrine of Sri Lanka's Buddhist majority, in Kandy. The last seat of Sri Lanka's kings—it was captured by the British in 1815—Kandy was to have been the centre of celebrations to mark the 50th anniversary of the end of British rule in 1948. The attack, which enraged Buddhists and strengthened resistance to concessions to the LTTE, made the government shift the ceremonies to Colombo. But the heightened security fears did not deter Britain's Prince Charles from gracing them as chief guest, as the Tigers would have hoped. Besides the three bombers, a dozen pilgrims were killed.

Many more died when the Tigers brought down an aircraft flying from Jaffna to Colombo on 29 September. All 55 persons on board, most of them Tamils, were presumed dead, the plane having crashed into the sea. With the government thinking it prudent to ban all civilian flights to and from Jaffna, the LTTE action added to the tribulations of Tamils in Jaffna.

Insisting on being regarded as the sole authentic representative of the Tamil people, the LTTE continued its policy of silencing non-subservient Tamil voices by assassinating, on 18 May, Sarojini Yogeshwaran, who had been elected mayor of Jaffna in March. Her successor, Ponnuthurai Sivapalan, was killed in a bomb blast, along with several civic and security officials, on 11 September. Both mayors belonged to the moderate Tamil United Liberation Front. Mrs Yogeswaran's husband, an MP, had been an LTTE victim some years earlier. An MP who led another Tamil political group was nearly killed when suspected LTTE members whom he was visiting in a gaol set upon him.

There was a minor flurry of excitement in November when LTTE leader Velupillai Prabhakaran said he was ready to negotiate with the government. President Chandrika Bandaranaike Kumaratunga's government, which had felt let down soon after assuming office when the LTTE abruptly abandoned talks in 1995 (see AR 1995, pp. 312–3), was in no hurry to meet the LTTE. The offer was surrounded with qualifications. Crucially, the invitation was not so much to negotiations on the key political issues but to talks to create a climate for them. The LTTE had to contend with the wide belief that it was ready to talk only when under pressure and needing time to recoup its strength. It was also held that Mr Prabhakaran was trying to repair the Tigers' dented image by appearing to desire a negotiated settlement.

Internationally, the tide favoured the government. The UN had adopted a convention against terrorist bombings, and in several Western countries official attitudes hardened against groups engaging in terrorist violence. Britain, for instance, reacted to the Omagh bombing in Northern Ireland in August by introducing legislation that would ban organizations from promoting terrorist acts abroad (see II.1.iv). One sequel to these developments was a request by President Kumaratunga to President Nelson

Mandela to prevent the LTTE from shifting some of its external operations to South Africa, where it had some support among the many Tamils in the country's Indian population.

Sri Lanka played a prominent role in regional diplomacy in 1998, hosting the tenth summit of the South Asian Association for Regional Cooperation (SAARC) in July. President Kumaratunga, as SAARC's new chairman, took its message to the UN General Assembly in September. Relations with big neighbour India received special attention amid concern that the new Indian administration might be susceptible to pro-LTTE influence from supporters in the Indian state of Tamil Nadu. Colombo avoided any comment that would upset India, or Pakistan, after their competitive nuclear tests (see VIII.2.i; VIII.2.ii). President Kumaratunga returned from a state visit to New Delhi in December with a bilateral free trade agreement which did not, however, please everybody. Some feared it would favour the economically stronger partner much more than the weaker one.

The economy, having functioned robustly in 1997, faced difficulties in 1998. GDP growth was reckoned to have dipped below 5 per cent after touching 6.4 per cent in 1997, as the economic collapse in Russia, a big buyer of Sri Lankan tea, added to the repercussions of the East Asian downturn.

3. INDIAN OCEAN STATES

i. MAURITIUS

CAPITAL: Port Louis   AREA: 2,040 sq km   POPULATION: 1,150,000 ('97)
OFFICIAL LANGUAGE: English   POLITICAL SYSTEM: parliamentary democracy
HEAD OF STATE: President Cassam Uteem (since June '92)
RULING PARTY: Mauritius Labour Party (MLP)
HEAD OF GOVERNMENT: Navin Ramgoolam (MLP), Prime Minister (since Dec '95)
MAIN IGO MEMBERSHIPS (non-UN): OAU, COMESA, SADC, OIC, ACP, CWTH, Francophonie, NAM
CURRENCY: rupee (end-'98 £1=MRs41.14, US$1=MRs24.73)
GNP PER CAPITA: US$3,800 by exchange-rate calculation, US$9,360 by PPP calculation ('97)

THE economic boom in Mauritius—generating, since the mid-1980s, the highest growth rates in Africa—was sustained in 1998. But the steady depreciation of the rupee against the US dollar, widely seen as reflecting concern about the long-term outlook, became a serious problem in the second half year. Overall the rupee lost 11 per cent of its value in 1998, after losing 12 per cent the previous year (see AR 1997, p. 321).

Provisional figures showed that GDP grew by 5.6 per cent in 1998 (fractionally higher than the previous year), while unemployment remained relatively low around 5 per cent. Inflation was expected to rise from 5.4 per cent in the 1997/98 financial year to 8–9 per cent in 1998/99. The hike was triggered by the imposition of a 10 per cent value-added tax (replacing the 8 per cent sales tax) in September, by a large pay award to the country's 80,000 public-sector workers granted in the same month, and by the rupee's depreciation.

In an effort to strengthen confidence the 1998/99 budget unveiled on 8 June contained a number of measures aimed at further closing the budget deficit from 3.7 per cent of GDP in 1997/98 to 1.8 per cent in 1998/99. Another measure was the establishment of an investment board to streamline procedures to attract foreign direct investment. This move was a response to complaints by business leaders that such investment was hampered by excessive bureaucracy.

In an episode which underlined the country's delicate ethnic balance, the governor and managing director of the Bank of Mauritius, Dan Maraye and Bud Gujadhur, resigned on 21 November after widespread protests from the Tamil community forced the central bank to withdraw a group of new banknotes. Notes traditionally carried the denominations written in English, Tamil and Hindi scripts, in that order. The new set changed the order to English, Hindi and Tamil. Although Tamils constituted around 10 per cent of the population, their claim to precedence over the 40 per cent Hindi speakers was based on traditional practice and the argument that their ancestors had arrived earlier on the island. Rameshwurlall Basant Roi and Anil Gujadhur were appointed to the central bank's top posts as from 1 December.

On 7 October Prime Minister Navin Ramgoolam announced a series of measures aimed at restoring confidence in the police force. The measures included better training and equipment, as well as the creation of an emergency unit, a police authority to handle complaints and the introduction of a policing charter. The reforms followed the publication in July of a government-commissioned report (by retired British police officer David Shattock) which had criticized the police for failing to provide adequate services, combat drugs-trafficking and other crimes effectively and stamp out corruption.

On 26 October Mr Ramgoolam created four new full ministries (housing and lands, social security and national solidarity, fisheries and cooperatives, and youth and sports), thereby expanding the number of cabinet posts to 24.

ii. SEYCHELLES, COMOROS AND MALDIVES

Seychelles
CAPITAL: Victoria   AREA: 454 sq km   POPULATION: 78,000 ('97)
OFFICIAL LANGUAGES: Seychellois, English & French   POLITICAL SYSTEM: presidential
HEAD OF STATE & GOVERNMENT: President France-Albert René (since June '77)
RULING PARTY: Seychelles People's Progressive Front (SPPF)
MAIN IGO MEMBERSHIPS (non-UN): OAU, COMESA, IOC, ACP, CWTH, Francophonie, NAM
CURRENCY: rupee (end-'98 £1=SR9.07, US$1=SR5.45)
GNP PER CAPITA: US$6,880 by exchange-rate calculation ('97)

Comoros
CAPITAL: Moroni   AREA: 1,860 sq km   POPULATION: 650,000 ('97)
OFFICIAL LANGUAGES: Arabic & French   POLITICAL SYSTEM: presidential
HEAD OF STATE & GOVERNMENT: Interim President Tajiddine Ben Said Massounde (since Nov '98)
RULING PARTIES: Forum for National Recovery (FRN) & National Rally for Development (RND)
PRIME MINISTER: Abbas Djoussouf (FRN), since Nov '98)
MAIN IGO MEMBERSHIPS (non-UN): OAU, COMESA, OIC, ACP, CWTH, Francophonie, AL, OIC, NAM
CURRENCY: Comoros franc (end-'98 £1=FC694.16, US$=FC417.23)
GNP PER CAPITA: US$400 by exchange-rate calculation, US$1,590 by PPP calculation ('97)

Maldives
CAPITAL: Malé   AREA: 300 sq km   POPULATION: 262,000 ('97)
OFFICIAL LANGUAGE: Divehi   POLITICAL SYSTEM: presidential
HEAD OF STATE & GOVERNMENT: President Maumoun Abdul Gayoom (since Nov '78)
MAIN IGO MEMBERSHIPS (non-UN): SAARC, CP, CWTH, OIC, NAM, SADC
CURRENCY: ruffiya (end-'98 £1=R19.58, US$1=R11.77)
GNP PER CAPITA: US$1,150 by exchange-rate calculation, US$3,230 by PPP calculation ('97)

IN the SEYCHELLES, France-Albert René and the Seychelles People's Progressive Front (SPPF) were returned to office with increased majorities in presidential and legislative elections on 20–22 March. (For the previous elections, see AR 1993, p. 328.) M. René secured 66.7 per cent of the vote, against 19.5 per cent for Wavel Ramkalawan and 13.8 per cent for former President Sir James Mancham. The SPPF gained 61.7 per cent of the vote and 30 seats in the 34-member National Assembly, the United Opposition (UO) 26.1 per cent and three seats, and the Democratic Party (DP) 12.1 per cent and one seat. The SPPF captured all but one of the 25 directly-elected seats. A key feature of the election was the replacement of Sir James Mancham as opposition leader by Mr Ramkalawan, an Anglican priest and leader of the UO.

The 12-member cabinet, sworn in on 30 March, included three new members, one of whom was Ronny Jumeau, who took over as Agriculture and Fisheries Minister from his father, Esme Jumeau, who had retired at the election.

The Seychelles' main economic problem—a budget deficit that reached 13 per cent of GDP in mid-year—prompted the government to take a number of revenue-raising measures. On 15 July it announced plans to introduce a US$100 tax on all tourists and other foreign nationals arriving at Mahé airport and an increase in the departure tax on Seychelles nationals from 20 rupees to 100 rupees. The new departure tax rate was implemented in August; however, following pressure from local and European tour operators, the introduction of the arrival tax was postponed until November 1999.

In a confidential report leaked to the opposition weekly *Regar* on 21 August, the International Monetary Fund blamed the poor state of the public finances on an expanding welfare system, substantial transfers to parastatal enterprises, a large public-sector pay bill and substantial capital-spending programmes. The Seychelles welfare state had been created in the 1980s and was largely financed by the foreign-exchange earnings generated by tourism. The Seychellois continued to enjoy the highest standard of living by far in sub-Saharan Africa.

The National Youth Service (NYS), a programme set up in 1979 (when the SPPF was the sole legal party and pursuing a radical-left agenda), was abolished at the end of 1998. The NYS had long been criticized for its outmoded emphasis on military training and political education, for the enforced separation of 15- and 16-year-olds in camps and for its cost. The official reason given for its abolition was the need to bring education 'in line with developments in the modern world'.

On 26 November the Seychelles hosted the 'Miss World' beauty pageant for the second year running. The event was strongly promoted by the government as a means of boosting the country's image as a tourist destination. Following changes to the format and much greater interest by television companies, the event was broadcast in 130 countries and was thought to have reached a worldwide audience of 2,000 million. Miss Seychelles, Alvina Grandcourt, won the 'Miss Personality' title.

In the COMOROS, the crisis over the secessionist movement on the island of Anjouan (Nzwani), proclaimed on 3 August 1997 (see AR 1997, p. 323), rumbled on without a solution throughout 1998, with the year ending amid continued fighting. In March the separatists held a referendum on a new 'constitution' for independent Anjouan, which produced a heavy warning from France and the OAU, both of which were involved in trying to mediate a solution to the crisis. The OAU in particular held several reconciliation meetings, notable for their lack of progress. Meanwhile, in March, the leadership of Mohéli island, which had seceded after Anjouan in 1997, said that it was not seeking full independence, but only full autonomy.

In May discontent in Moroni, the capital of the Comoros, was apparent in protest strikes by unpaid civil servants. After appeasing the strikers, in June President Mohammed Taki tried to retake the initiative by reshuffling his government, introducing Mohammed Abou Madi, a former Premier who had rallied to the cause of the secessionists and then withdrawn. At the same time the President released from detention a prominent secessionist, Ahmed Charikane, who had been held in detention in Moroni. On 6 July, however, the President was booed at ceremonies for the island's 23rd independence anniversary. The next day the situation became bogged down further when fighting erupted between rival camps on secessionist Anjouan after the 'President', Abdallah Ibrahim, dismissed the 'prime minister', Chamassi Said Omar. At the end of the month a new government on the island was appointed under Abdou Mohammed, but Anjouan remained divided into two armed camps.

The situation took a surprising new twist in November with the sudden death of President Taki at the age of 62. He was replaced by the president of the High Council of the Republic, Tajiddine Ben Said Massounde, as provided in the constitution, pending the holding of a presidential election within 90 days. He appointed as interim Prime Minister the opposition leader, Abbas Djoussouf; but the chances of conciliation with the secessionists became further complicated by the intensification of the conflict on Anjouan. Chamassi Said Omar took control of much of the capital, Mutsamudi, allegedly with support from far-right groups in France who favoured an alliance between Anjouan with Mayotte as a French overseas department, although the Jospin government in Paris totally rejected such a move. The government on Anjouan was thought to be more favourable to reconciliation in view of the lack of international support for the secession, but Chamassi Said Omar represented a harder-line pro-independence tendency.

Where some thought that the death of President Taki in November might ease the situation, since he had been a main target of attack by the secessionists, it was too soon to see if the new President was going to make a difference. Certainly the outbreak of hostilities in December did not bode well, although the fact that there were between different factions on Anjouan bidding for control of the capital indicated a weakening of the 17-month-old secessionist movement.

In the MALDIVES, President Abdul Gayoom was re-elected for a fifth term on 16 October. The sole candidate, he secured 91 per cent of the vote on a turnout of 75 per cent. Under new election procedures, multiple nominations were allowed for the first time. The elections commissioner submitted five approved nominations to the Majlis (parliament), which decided a final candidate by secret ballot, and the choice was put to a national referendum. (Previously, the Majlis had selected a presidential candidate by open vote and without taking nominations.)

On 13 November President Gayoom appointed a new 23-member cabinet. A surprise appointment was that of his brother-in-law, Ilyas Ibrahim, as Transport Minister. He had stood against the President in the previous election (see AR 1993, p. 329) and had subsequently been convicted of bribery. President Gayoom retained the key portfolios of defence and finance, while Fathulla Jameel remained as Foreign Minister.

The new government's priorities were defined as (i) increasing the observance of Islamic values and ideals in society, and (ii) encouraging a more active role for the private sector in the economy.

In June plans were announced to nearly double the capacity of the tourism industry—the country's main foreign-exchange earner—from 12,000 beds to 22,500 by 2005. Development would not be at the expense of the environment, however.

In October the government described as 'baseless' allegations made by Amnesty International that political opponents were arrested without charge, held without trial and detained in inhuman conditions. 'There are no political prisoners or prisoners of conscience in the country', an official statement declared.

iii. MADAGASCAR

CAPITAL: Antananarivo　AREA: 587,000 sq km　POPULATION: 14,000,000 ('97)
OFFICIAL LANGUAGES: Malagasy & French　POLITICAL SYSTEM: presidential
HEAD OF STATE & GOVERNMENT: President (Adm.) Didier Ratsiraka (since Jan '97)
RULING PARTIES: Vanguard for Economic and Social Recovery (ARES) heads coalition
HEAD OF GOVERNMENT: Tantely Andrianavino (since July '98)
MAIN IGO MEMBERSHIPS (non-UN): OAU, COMESA, IOC, ACP, Francophonie, NAM
CURRENCY: Malagasy franc (end-'98 £1=FMG8,684.77, US$1=FMG5,220.00)
GNP PER CAPITA: US$250 by exchange-rate calculation, US$910 by PPP calculation ('97)

IT was an arduous political year for President Didier Ratsiraka, but one in which he appeared to have emerged strengthened. In February he survived an impeachment motion because the opposition failed to obtain the needed two-thirds majority. In March a referendum was held on an amended constitution. By a very narrow majority (50.96 per cent) the 'great red island' became a federal republic with six autonomous provinces and a strong presidential regime. What was known as the 'Third Republic Mark 3' was ushered in on 8 April, in spite of protests from the opposition Union of Democratic Living Forces (UVFD), which had boycotted the poll but not prevented a reported 70 per cent of the electorate from voting. Malagasy churches protested against the new constitution, especially the replacement of the word 'justice' with the word 'progress' in the national motto. Former President Albert Zafy said that the opposition, of which he was leader, would do everything to overthrow the regime through legal means, including civil disobedience.

National Assembly elections in May attracted a much lower turnout, in spite of the lack of a boycott, possibly because of the reduced power of the Assembly under the new constitution. President Ratsiraka's ARES party obtained only 63 of the 150 seats, but a new complex of alliances, and the defection of the party of former Premier Norbert Ratsirahonana from opposition to government, permitted the establishment of a new presidential majority. The new Prime Minister was Tantely Andrianarivo, a member of ARES and hitherto Deputy Prime Minister.

IX SOUTH-EAST AND EAST ASIA

1. MYANMAR (BURMA)—THAILAND—MALAYSIA—BRUNEI—
SINGAPORE—INDONESIA—PHILIPPINES—VIETNAM—
CAMBODIA—LAOS

i. MYANMAR (BURMA)

CAPITAL: Yangon (Rangoon) AREA: 676,500 sq km POPULATION: 50,000,000 ('97)
OFFICIAL LANGUAGE: Burmese POLITICAL SYSTEM: military regime
HEAD OF STATE & GOVERNMENT: Gen. Than Shwe, Chairman of State Peace and Development Council and Prime Minister (since April '92)
MAIN IGO MEMBERSHIPS (non-UN): ASEAN, CP, NAM
CURRENCY: kyat (end-'98 £1=K10.40, US$1=K6.25)
GNP PER CAPITA: n/a

ON 7 July National League for Democracy (NLD) leader Aung San Suu Kyi defied the orders of the State Peace and Development Council (SPDC) and left Yangon to visit supporters in Minhla. Her car was turned back 80 kilometres from the capital. On 24 July Ms Suu Kyi attempted to reach Bassein, again to visit NLD supporters, and again her route was blocked by security forces. After a six-day stand-off during which concerns grew for her health, she was forcibly driven back to Yangon. The NLD leader made a third attempt to break through on 12 August when she once more set out for Bassein—and once more the authorities barred her way. Ms Suu Kyi announced that she would give up if more than 40 NLD supporters detained in May were released. With her health deteriorating, she returned to Yangon in an ambulance on 24 August.

In August Ms Suu Kyi said that in the light of the SPDC's intransigence she would call a 'people's parliament'. On 9 September the NLD reported that 300 of its members had been detained. By the end of the month this had reportedly risen to 800. The NLD claimed that the government was trying to prevent the people's parliament from convening. A ten-member committee was created to represent the people's parliament until a full session could be called. During October and November around 300 of the 800 detained NLD members were released. On 27–30 October UN assistant secretary-general Alvaro de Soto visited Myanmar and met government ministers as well as Ms Suu Kyi. It was reported that Sr de Soto had offered a deal of UN/World Bank financial and humanitarian aid in exchange for political progress.

A cabinet reshuffle on 15 November appeared to strengthen the position of military intelligence chief and First Secretary Lieut.-General Khin Nyunt, a 'moderate' within the SPDC. Among the changes Win Ayung, a close supporter, was appointed Minister of Foreign Affairs. Earlier, on 25 September, Khin Nyunt had established a 16-member political affairs committee, naming himself its chairman.

On 1 March the SPDC announced the arrest of 40 people suspected of involvement in a plot to bomb government buildings and foreign embassies. The authorities accused the suspects of having links with the All Burma Student Democratic Front (ABSDF) and with the NLD. The ABSDF rejected the accusations. On 30 April the SPDC announced that six of the 40, four of whom were allegedly linked to the ABSDF, had been sentenced to death for carrying explosives.

The Japanese government on 11 March agreed partially to resume aid, which had been suspended following the 1988 demonstrations and crackdown. On 5 September the World Bank said that it had cut financial links with Burma because of Yangon's failure to make repayments on past loans.

On 27–28 May 400 NLD members held a congress to mark the eighth anniversary of the NLD's 1990 election victory. The NLD released a statement condemning the SPDC and calling on it to restore democratic principles. At the beginning of September thousands of Yangon-based students demonstrated against the SPDC.

In March the Democratic Karen Buddhist Army (DKBA), with support from government forces, attacked refugee camps on the Myanmar-Thai border loyal to the rival Karen National Union (KNU). At the end of the month KNU troops mounted a reprisal attack against DKBA bases in Myanmar. An Amnesty International report released in mid-April alleged that the army had tortured and killed hundreds of Shan associated with the Shan State National Army (SSNA). The SPDC repudiated the claim as a 'fabrication'. In early May the Burmese army reportedly crossed into Thai territory in pursuit of SSNA guerrillas.

Prominent pro-democracy activist and NLD member Daw San San was sentenced to 25 years in prison on 21 April, allegedly for contravening the conditions of her early release from a previously-imposed 25-year sentence for treason. In May it was reported by the opposition 'Democratic Voice of Burma' radio station that 80-year-old Thakin Ohn Minh, adviser to Aung San Suu Kyi, had been sentenced to a seven-year prison term for supplying documents to the ABSDF. On 14 August 18 foreign activists were given sentences of five years' hard labour—and were then immediately expelled from the country.

ii. THAILAND

CAPITAL: Bangkok AREA: 513,000 sq km POPULATION: 61,000,000 ('97)
OFFICIAL LANGUAGE: Thai POLITICAL SYSTEM: constitutional monarchy
HEAD OF STATE: King Bhumibol Adulyadej (Rama IX) (since June '46)
RULING PARTIES: Democrat Party (DP) heads seven-party coalition
HEAD OF GOVERNMENT: Chuan Leekpai, Prime Minister (since Nov '97)
MAIN IGO MEMBERSHIPS (non-UN): ASEAN, CP, APEC, NAM
CURRENCY: baht (end-'98 £1=B60.45, US$1=B36.34)
GNP PER CAPITA: US$2,800 by exchange-rate calculation, US$6,590 by PPP calculation ('97)

THE year was one of continued economic malaise and (relative) political stability. Just two days into 1998, Prime Minister Chuan Leekpai warned the Thai people to expect 'tougher times'. This theme was reiterated through to the final days of 1998, with expected economic 'growth' for the year being downgraded from minus 0.9 per cent in January to minus 7 per cent by August as the economic situation deteriorated.

In February the IMF agreed to ease the original terms of its US$17,200 million financial rescue package (see AR 1997, p. 328) and allow the Thai government to run a budget deficit of 2 per cent of GDP; in May the government raised this to 3 per cent but continued to stress the primacy of exchange rate stabilization. The IMF applauded the Thai authorities for their handling of the crisis. However, growing domestic pressures caused promised legislation to be delayed or diluted. Chuan Leekpai paid an official visit to the USA on 11–17 March and came away with an additional $1,700 million in aid.

On 20 January the cabinet approved the creation of a new bank to take on the performing assets of the 56 finance companies closed in December 1997. Three days later the central Bank of Thailand (BoT) took control of the Bangkok Metropolitan Bank, and a week after that the BoT announced it was lifting all foreign currency controls. In early May Chaiyawat Wibulswasdi resigned as governor of the BoT ahead of an independent report critical of his handling of the crisis. On 16 December the government held its long-awaited auction of $10,000 million worth of assets seized from the liquidated finance companies. Afterwards the Financial Sector Restructuring Agency announced that it had accepted bids for only $882 million worth of assets. Commentators suggested that the auction had been compromised by political pressures and nationalist sentiment.

The government on 14 August unveiled a $7,240 million bank restructuring programme. Enthusiastically endorsed by the IMF, it provided additional capital to ailing banks on the conditions that they restructured their bad debts and welcomed foreign partners. A new foreign investment law was introduced on 19 August, lifting many of the restrictions on foreign ownership.

Chuan Leekpai's coalition faced a no-confidence vote on 20 March— which was defeated. On 15 September Health Minister Rakkiat Sukthana resigned following allegations of corruption; he was joined on 1 October by Deputy Agriculture Minister Virat Rattanaset. Coinciding with the latter resignation, the Prime Minister announced that the 51-seat Chart Pattana Party was joining the government. At the end of May the Muan Chon Party, led by Chalerm Yubamrung merged with the main opposition party, the New Aspirations Party, led by Chaovalit Yongchaiyut.

Foreign Minister Surin Pitsuwan unveiled a new policy of 'flexible engagment' at the ASEAN Foreign Ministers' meeting in Manila in July. He also raised questions about the success of the Association's policies towards fellow ASEAN member Myanmar.

General Surayud Chulanot was appointed commander-in-chief of the army and promised to distance the army from politics. Former Prime Minister Chatichai Choonhavan died in London on 6 May, aged 78.

On 11 December a Thai Airways Airbus crashed near Surat Thani in the south; over 100 of the 146 passengers were killed.

iii. MALAYSIA

CAPITAL: Kuala Lumpur   AREA: 132,000 sq km   POPULATION: 21,000,000 ('97)
OFFICIAL LANGUAGE: Bahasa Malaysia   POLITICAL SYSTEM: federal democracy
HEAD OF STATE: Ja'afar ibni Abdul Rahman, Sultan of Selangor (since April '94)
RULING PARTY: National Front coalition
HEAD OF GOVERNMENT: Dr Mahathir Mohamad, Prime Minister (since July '81)
MAIN IGO MEMBERSHIPS (non-UN): ASEAN, APEC, CP, OIC, CWTH, NAM
CURRENCY: ringitt (end-'98 £1=M$6.32, US$1=M$3.80)
GNP PER CAPITA: US$4,680 by exchange-rate calculation, US$10,920 by PPP calculation ('97)

MALAYSIA experienced unprecedented political turbulence from the beginning of September when Prime Minister Dr Mahathir Mohamad dismissed his Deputy Prime Minister and Finance Minister, Anwar Ibrahim, who was subsequently arrested and put on trial on charges of corruption and sexual misconduct. Tensions between the Prime Minister and his acknowledged successor had mounted with the onset of Malaysia's economic adversity. With the overthrow of President Suharto of Indonesia in May, Anwar began to make speeches echoing the idiom of the political reform movement in Jakarta in which he stressed the need to cleanse society of corruption and nepotism. These speeches were interpreted as a direct challenge to Dr Mahathir, with whom he differed over economic policy.

In mid-June, at the annual general assembly of the politically-dominant United Malays National Organization (UMNO), Zahid Hamid, the head of UMNO Youth and a known supporter of Anwar, drew attention to the debilitating impact of corruption on the party. Dr Mahathir then turned the tables on Anwar's camp by producing a list of names of people who had benefited from government contracts, including those of Zahid and Anwar's father and brother. The Prime Minister bolstered his position a few days later by announcing the appointment of former Finance Minister and confidant, Daim Zanuddin, to a new cabinet post of Minister with

Special Functions in charge of economic development—in effect, as an alternative finance minister. On 1 September, in the wake of the announcement that GDP had contracted by 6.8 per cent during the second quarter, the government reversed economic policy and imposed capital account and currency controls in an attempt to insulate the country from financial crisis.

Anwar Ibrahim was dismissed on 2 September, after refusing to resign his offices. He was expelled from UMNO, of which he was deputy president, on the following day. Dr Mahathir, who assumed the office of Finance Minister on 7 September, justified the dismissal on the grounds of Anwar's 'low morals', which corresponded with allegations in a tract entitled *50 Reasons Why Anwar Cannot Become Prime Minister* which had circulated at UMNO's general assembly in June. In the wake of his dismissal, Anwar launched a public campaign calling for political reform and Dr Mahathir's resignation, which attracted mass backing and prompted violent confrontations between his supporters and the security forces. He was arrested on 20 September coincident with the arrival in Kuala Lumpur of Queen Elizabeth II to preside over the closing ceremony of the Commonwealth Games (see Pt XVI). When Anwar made his first appearance in court on 25 September, his neck and arms were badly bruised and he had a black eye, which indicated that he had been beaten in police custody. Anwar pleaded not guilty to the charges claiming that he was the victim of a political conspiracy, while his cause was take up outside prison by his wife, Azizah Ismail.

Anwar's treatment in detention provoked interventions from President Estrada of the Philippines and from President Habibie of Indonesia as well as from Western governments, including the United States, and Kofi Annan, the Secretary-General of the United Nations. The first phase of his trial on five charges of corruption (abuse of political power) before a single judge began on 2 November, with an adjournment between 14–23 November while the Asia-Pacific Economic Cooperation (APEC) conference in Kuala Lumpur was in session (see XI.6.iii). During the conference, Vice-President Al Gore of the USA made a public statement of indirect support for Anwar which provoked a very strong Malaysian government reaction. The initial course of the trial was marked by doubtful testimony by prosecution witnesses and evidence of sinister police practices. By the end of the year, however, public protest in support of Anwar and political reform had died down, while Dr Mahathir showed no intention of appointing a deputy prime minister in succession to Anwar Ibrahim.

In August tension revived with Singapore after its government announced the transfer of its customs, immigration and customs posts from the Tanjong Pagar railway station in the south of the island on land owned by the Malaysian government to Woodlands close to the causeway linking the two countries. Malaysia insisted on keeping its own posts at Tanjong Pagar, despite the lack of legal authority. Those tensions were aggravated by the publication in mid-September of controversial memoirs by Lee Kuan Yew, former Prime Minister and currently Senior Minister of Singapore. The same month Malaysia announced that it would not participate in that year's Five-Power Defence Arrangements exercises with Singapore, Australia, New Zealand and the United Kingdom, and also imposed restrictions on the use of its air space by Singapore's air force. At the end of November, however, Defence Minister Hamid Albar announced that Malaysia would resume participation in the military exercises in 1999.

iv. BRUNEI

CAPITAL: Bandar Seri Bagawan   AREA: 5,765 sq km   POPULATION: 300,000 ('97)
OFFICIAL LANGUAGES: Malay & English   POLITICAL SYSTEM: monarchy
HEAD OF STATE & GOVERNMENT: Sultan Sir Hassanal Bolkiah (since '67)
MAIN IGO MEMBERSHIPS (non-UN): ASEAN, APEC, OIC, CWTH, NAM
CURRENCY: Brunei dollar (end-'98 £1=B$2.75, US$1=B$1.65)
GNP PER CAPITA: US$25,090 by exchange-rate calculation ('97)

ON 10 August Prince Al-Muhtadee Billah Bolkiah, the eldest son of Sultan Sir Hassanal Bolkiah, was invested as Crown Prince of Brunei. The investiture took place against the background of the dismissal at the end of July of the Sultan's younger brother, Prince Jefri, as chairman of the Brunei Investment Agency, which controlled the overseas assets of the Sultanate and from which large sums had been misappropriated to finance non-governmental projects. In early August Prince Jefri had been removed also from control of Amedeo, a construction-based conglomerate which had collapsed with considerable debts. Prince Jefri refused to return from overseas to attend his nephew's investiture, while a firm of international accountants was appointed to handle Amedeo's interests and to investigate its collapse.

v. SINGAPORE

CAPITAL: Singapore   AREA: 620 sq km   POPULATION: 3,000,000 ('97)
OFFICIAL LANGUAGES: Malay, Chinese, Tamil, English
POLITICAL SYSTEM: parliamentary
HEAD OF STATE: President Ong Teng Cheong (since Aug '93)
RULING PARTY: People's Action Party (PAP)
HEAD OF GOVERNMENT: Goh Chok Tong, Prime Minister (since Nov '90)
MAIN IGO MEMBERSHIPS (non-UN): ASEAN, APEC, CP, CWTH, NAM
CURRENCY: Singapore dollar (end-'98 £1=S$2.78, US$1=S$1.70)
GNP PER CAPITA: US$32,940 by exchange-rate calculation, US$29,000 by PPP calculation ('97)

SINGAPORE moved into recession for the first time in 13 years with the announcement in November that the economy had contracted by 3.5 per cent of GDP in the third quarter. The government sanctioned cuts in wages and in employers' contributions to pension funds in an attempt to sustain business competitiveness within a regional context of acute economic adversity.

Relations with Malaysia deteriorated sharply from late July with Singapore's decision to relocate its customs, immigration and quarantine facilities from Tanjong Pagar railway station in the south of the city to Woodlands on the Strait of Johor. The deterioration followed the breakdown of talks on the status of the property of the railway (owned by Malaysia under an agreement reached during the colonial period) and on the supply of water to Singapore beyond the terms of an accord running until 2061. The launch in mid-September of the first volume of Lee Kuan Yew's memoirs dealing with Singapore's entry into, membership of, and separation from, Malaysia served to aggravate matters. The same month, Malaysia banned Singapore's military aircraft from its air space with the exception of case-by-case permission. Relations improved in October after a hastily-arranged visit to Kuala Lumpur by Prime Minister, Goh Chok Tong, but in mid-December, Malaysia's Prime Minister, Dr Mahathir Mohamad, rejected any offer of financial help from Singapore in return for a deal over water supply.

In February opposition Workers' Party member Tang Liang Hong—who owed more than S$4.4 million in libel damages to government ministers—was declared bankrupt. In July the Court of Appeal dismissed a plea by J.B. Jeyaratnam, secretary-general of the Workers' Party, against libel damages due to Prime Minister Goh Chok Tong and raised them five-fold to S$100,000. In October, however, Mr Jeyaratnam reached an agreement to pay the damages in five instalments, which would allow him to avoid bankruptcy and to continue as a member of parliament. At the end of November Chia Thye Poh, who had been arrested in October 1966 and held in detention until 1989, and then been subject to residence restrictions, had all restrictions lifted on his movements.

In November Singapore entered into a memorandum of understanding under which the United States was offered the use of the new Changi naval base which, on completion, would accommodate aircraft carriers.

vi. INDONESIA

CAPITAL: Jakarta   AREA: 1,905,000 sq km   POPULATION: 200,000,000 ('97)
OFFICIAL LANGUAGE: Bahasa Indonesia   POLITICAL SYSTEM: presidential
HEAD OF STATE & GOVERNMENT: President Bacharuddin J. Habibie (since May '98)
RULING PARTY: Joint Secretariat of Functional Groups (Golkar)
MAIN IGO MEMBERSHIPS (non-UN): ASEAN, APEC, CP, OIC, OPEC, NAM
CURRENCY: rupiah (end-'98 £1=Rp13,226.80, US$1=Rp7,950.00)
GNP PER CAPITA: US$1,110 by exchange-rate calculation, US$3,450 by PPP calculation ('97)

IN May a 32-year era of Indonesian history ended with the resignation of President Suharto. Appointed for a seventh five-year term only in March, he was swept from office by the political backwash from Indonesia's economic meltdown. The year began with continuing wrangles between the regime and the IMF over the terms of the latter's US$43,000 million rescue programme (see AR 1997, p. 334). The value of the rupiah had fallen by 80 per cent against the principal world currencies in the previous six months (sinking briefly at the end of January to Rp17,000 to the US dollar). With apparent insouciance, however, President Suharto appointed a new cabinet still dominated by the very 'crony capitalists' and economic nationalists singled out by the IMF and most foreign observers as a primary source of Indonesia's economic ills. Over the next two months the social and political consequences of the crisis continued to mount and by May anti-government demonstrations were spreading throughout Java and Sumatra.

The main mobilizing force in these protests were university students, products in many cases of the very middle class which owed its prosperity to the years of growth presided over by the Suharto regime. On 12 May the tense stand-off between the protesters and the security forces ended with the killing of six students at the private Trisakti University in Jakarta. Within days the capital and other large cities had collapsed into chaos. Rioting and looting by the urban poor (frequently aimed at the ethnic Chinese community) now replaced student protest as the main challenge to the government. The regime appeared surprisingly unprepared for the explosion, and speculation mounted over the position of the army, the key to Indonesian politics since independence. The army commander, General Wiranto, despite warning statements, was thought to have some sympathy with the protesters. However, the hard-line commander of the Strategic Reserve Command, General Prabowo Subianto, favoured a crackdown on the protests, a position perhaps unsurprising on the part of President Suharto's son-in-law.

This uncertainty accounted in part for a missing element in the crisis: a strong and unified opposition leadership. While the students had orchestrated the protests, recognized opposition politicians seemed reluctant to challenge the regime head-on. Both Megawati Sukarnoputri and the Muslim leader, Amien Rais, were initially tentative in their calls for change at the top, conscious no doubt of the bloodbath which had followed the collapse of the previous presidential regime—that of Megawati's father General Sukarno in 1965–66. A major protest planned for 20 May, Indonesia's 'Day of National Awakening', which would likely have forced the issue to a resolution, was called off by Rais amid fears of major violence (the riots having already led to around 1,200 deaths). In the event, a combination of parliamentary and international pressure forced President Suharto's departure. Threatened with impeachment at home and urged to consider his position by Washington, he finally recognized the extent of his isolation and resigned on 21 May.

The crisis did not appear to be resolved by General Suharto's exit, however. His nominated successor was Vice-President B.J. Habibie, whose initial nomination as 'number two' in January had caused some dismay abroad. He had a reputation as a somewhat eccentric technocrat, obsessed with unrealistic grand projects (most notoriously the development of an indigenous aircraft industry). He was not, in short, 'IMF-friendly'. At the same time, he was regarded with deep suspicion by the opposition as a Suharto crony who merely represented the continuation of the regime by other means. There were few at home or abroad who would have offered odds on his completing a full term in office.

The protest movement lost momentum after the departure of General Suharto, however, and despite continuing student demonstrations President Habibie survived his crucial first months in office. His position was buttressed by both continued caution on the part of opposition leaders and by some genuine, if rather random, reforming moves. General Prabowo was relieved of his command within days of his father-in-law's departure and then, in August, dismissed from the army. Greater autonomy was proposed for the troubled areas of north Sumatra, East Timor and Irian Jaya, though specific plans were not produced. A number of prominent political prisoners were released, and by July over 40 new political parties had been formed and officially 'approved'.

The economic upheaval which had precipitated the succession persisted, however. Food supplies declined and prices rose steadily. GDP fell by around 20 per cent over the year. The May riots themselves contributed to economic regression, and not only in terms of destruction and looting. One consequence was the flight of a considerable section of the Chinese community, whose crucial skills and capital the country could not afford to lose. Protests and public disorder continued spasmodically over a range of grievances throughout the year. Despite the momentous political events of 1998, there were few signs at the end of the year that underlying problems were much closer to solution than at the beginning.

vii. PHILIPPINES

CAPITAL: Manila AREA: 300,000 sq km POPULATION: 73,000,000 ('97)
OFFICIAL LANGUAGE: Filipino POLITICAL SYSTEM: presidential democracy
HEAD OF STATE & GOVERNMENT: President Joseph Ejercito Estrada (since June '98)
RULING PARTY: Struggle of the Nationalist Philippines Masses (LMMP)
MAIN IGO MEMBERSHIPS (non-UN): ASEAN, APEC, CP, NAM
CURRENCY: peso (end-'98 £1=P64.72, US$1=P38.90)
GNP PER CAPITA: US$1,220 by exchange-rate calculation, US$3,670 by PPP calculation ('97)

THE major event of 1998 in the Philippines was the presidential election held in May. As usual, the race began with an inflated field—over 80 candidates at the beginning of the year—which was eventually reduced to 11 and only two serious contenders. The 'anointed' candidate of retiring President Fidel Ramos was the Speaker of the House of Representatives, Jose de Venecia, who faced Vice-President and former film actor Joseph 'Erap' Estrada (see AR 1997, pp. 335–6). Mr Estrada, a charismatic populist in a political culture where this was a high qualification, soon took a commanding lead over the 'machine politician' Mr de Venecia in the campaign. This was translated into a convincing victory, with Mr Estrada taking 39.9 per cent of the vote against Mr de Venecia's 15.9 per cent.

Joseph Estrada's party, the 'Struggle of the Nationalist Philippines Masses' (LMMP), had conducted the campaign on an anti-establishment, anti-corruption manifesto which had caused apprehension within the business community. In particular, there were fears that the economic liberalization of the Ramos years might now be reversed. Despite a continued rhetorical commitment to redistributive policies, however, Mr Estrada made it known that he would not interfere with the new economic disposition. His credibility in this was strengthened, paradoxically, by the fact that his defeated rival's running-mate, Gloria Macapagal-Arroyo, won the separate vice-presidential election. A respected economist (and daughter of former President Diosdado Macapagal-Arroyo), Ms Macapagal-Arroyo was appointed by President Estrada to the Ministry of Social Welfare. The 1998–99 budget, introduced in August, indicated an increase of about 10 per cent in government spending on the previous year, but the worst fears of the business community were not realized. The year was not without its industrial problems, however, the now-privatized Philippines Airlines apparently being liquidated in September after union-management conflicts, although it resumed operations the following month.

The tragi-comedy of the Marcos family continued to entertain, infuriate and inspire the Filipinos in roughly equal measure in 1998. The 68-year-old Imelda Marcos began the year facing a lengthy prison sentence following her conviction in 1993 for corruption. Now a congresswoman—and at one stage a potential presidential candidate—she remained confident of her continued liberty. Sure enough, the government recommended the setting-aside of her gaol term at the beginning of June, and the Supreme Court acquiesced in October. With daughter Imee Marcos also in Congress and son Bong Bong Marcos elected a provincial governor in 1998, the family's penetration of the Philippines political class seemed secure. Its position appeared further enhanced when a number of Marcos cronies found favour with President Estrada's new administration after he assumed office at the end of June. The new President's populist instincts momentarily deserted him, however, when he acquiesced in Mrs Marcos' campaign to have the body of her late husband, Ferdinand Marcos, interred in Manila's 'Cemetery of Heroes'. The consequential outcry led to a retreat and Mrs Marcos' agreement to keep her husband's body in its frozen state for a little longer. The family suffered a more material reverse in June when the Swiss authorities finally authorized the return of some US$270 million from Marcos accounts to the Philippines state, despite protracted appeals by the family.

During the election campaign, Mr Estrada had undertaken, rather extravagantly, to bring peace to the country within six months. The main challenge to be overcome in pursuit of this objective was the continuing separatist struggle in the largely Muslim province on Mindanao. Despite earlier ceasefire agreements (see AR 1996, p. 326; AR 1997, p. 336), no final settlement had been reached by year's end and sporadic violence continued. The government was more successful in negotiations with the leftist New People's Army, with which a final agreement was signed in the Netherlands in March.

viii. VIETNAM

CAPITAL: Hanoi   AREA: 330,000 sq km   POPULATION: 77,000,000 ('97)
OFFICIAL LANGUAGE: Vietnamese
POLITICAL SYSTEM: socialist republic
RULING PARTY: Communist Party of Vietnam (CPV)
HEAD OF STATE: President Tran Duc Luong (since Sept '97)
PARTY LEADER: Gen. Le Kha Phieu, CPV general secretary (since Dec '97)
HEAD OF GOVERNMENT: Phan Van Khai, Prime Minister (since Sept '97)
MAIN IGO MEMBERSHIPS (non-UN): ASEAN, APEC, NAM, Francophonie
CURRENCY: dong (end-'98 £1=D23,114.50, US$1=D13,893.00)
GNP PER CAPITA: US$320 by exchange-rate calculation, US$1,670 by PPP calculation ('97)

THE politburo of the ruling Communist Party of Vietnam (CPV) on 6 January appointed five members to a new politburo standing board. The board was headed by CPV general secretary General Le Kha Phieu and included President Tran Duc Luong, Prime Minister Phan Van Khai, National Assembly chairman Nong Duc Manh and Pham The Duyet. The board was said to consist of the inner circle of the leadership and to have strengthened its 'conservative' faction.

On 16 January Phan Van Khai hinted at disagreements within the leadership. It emerged that in May a group of 11 veteran CPV members had sent a joint letter to the party accusing politburo standing board member Pham The Duyet of corruption, and calling for his resignation. In a surprise move, a December session of the National Assembly rejected a CPV decision that the 1993 land law be amended to allow larger land holdings and longer leases—all with a view to encouraging commercial agriculture.

Three businessmen convicted of corruption were executed outside Ho Chi Minh City on 7 January. Vietnamese radio reported on 23 January that 13 people accused of 'disruption of public order' during the Thai Binh disturbances in 1997 (see AR 1997, p. 337) had been sentenced to gaol terms of between six months and eight years. At the end of July 30 more were sentenced to terms of 18 months to over 11 years. At the beginning of September four prominent dissidents were released from prison as part of a National Day amnesty.

There were several periods of tension between Hanoi and Beijing. At the beginning of February the Vietnamese accused the Chinese of altering the course of a river in the north, and in April the Vietnamese Foreign Ministry issued warnings over planned Chinese tourist developments on the disputed Paracel Islands in the South China Sea. On 8 September a Chinese Foreign Ministry spokesman demanded that the Vietnam navy withdraw from two reefs it had 'unlawfully occupied' in the Spratly Islands group.

Asia's economic crisis significantly affected Vietnam during 1998. On 16 February the central State Bank of Vietnam announced a devaluation of the dong against the US dollar from 11,175 to 11,800, while retaining the 10 per cent trading band each side of the new rate. At the beginning of August there was a further 7 per cent devaluation. In January a new foreign investment decree was approved to boost foreign interest by easing licensing and export rules. On 11 March US President Bill Clinton signed a waiver exempting Vietnam from the trade-restricting Jackson-Vanik amendment, which was expected to increase US business interest in the country. On 8 December the World Bank announced that donors had pledged US$2,700 million to help Vietnam alleviate the effects of the regional economic crisis and to encourage economic reform.

Former Foreign Minister and reformist politburo member Nguyen Co Thach died on 10 April aged 75. On 27 April Nguyen Van Linh, former general secretary of the CPV and initiator of the '*doi moi*' economic renovation programme, died aged 82. On 25 May members of a high-level military delegation to Laos were killed in a plane accident in Xieng Khouang. Among the dead were the Chief of General Staff and Deputy Defence Minister, General Dao Trong Lich. In September it was reported that Vu Van Mau, South Vietnam's last Prime Minister, had died in Paris aged 84.

ix. CAMBODIA

CAPITAL: Phnom Penh   AREA: 181,000 sq km   POPULATION: 11,000,000 ('97)
OFFICIAL LANGUAGE: Khmer   POLITICAL SYSTEM: monarchy
HEAD OF STATE: King Norodom Sihanouk (elected Sept '93)
RULING PARTIES: Cambodian People's Party (CPP) & United National Front for an
   Independent, Neutral, Peaceful and Cooperative Cambodia (FUNCINPEC)
HEAD OF GOVERNMENT: Hun Sen, Prime Minister (since July '97)
MAIN IGO MEMBERSHIPS (non-UN): CP, Francophonie, NAM
CURRENCY: riel (end-'98 £1=R6,438.71, US$1=R3,870.00)
GNP PER CAPITA: US$300 by exchange-rate calculation ('97)

POLITICS in Cambodia was dominated by efforts to reconcile the country's competing factions, as well as by Pol Pot's death (see XVIII: Obituary) and the collapse of the Khmers Rouges (KR) as a military force. Reports that former KR leader Pol Pot had died in a remote jungle hideout in the north on 15 April were confirmed by journalists invited to view his body the following day. Stretched out on a simple wooden bed, Pol Pot was reported to have died from a heart attack. He was 73.

Unconfirmed reports that the KR might be disintegrating in mutinous conflict filtered out of northern Cambodia in March. A hard-line faction led by Ta Mok retreated further into the mountains, claiming that it would be willing to negotiate. Fighting between the remnants of the KR and government forces continued during April and into May, displacing thousands and bringing the total number of Cambodian refugees in Thailand to 87,000. The government reported 3,000 KR defections in early May. In December most of the remnants of the KR army surrendered to government forces, leaving just a handful of men under Ta Mok still at large.

Second Prime Minister Hun Sen agreed on 17 February to a Japanese-brokered peace plan allowing exiled former First Prime Minister Prince Norodom Ranariddh to return to Phnom Penh. Under the plan, Prince Ranariddh would be tried *in absentia* and then receive an amnesty from his father, King Norodom Sihanouk, permitting Prince Ranariddh to participate in the July elections. Prince Ranariddh accepted the plan, and on the 27 February government troops and forces loyal to him announced ceasefires. On 4 March Prince Ranariddh was tried on charges of smuggling and conspiring with the KR, found guilty on both counts, sentenced to five and 30 years in prison respectively, and then granted a full pardon by the King. Prince Ranariddh returned to Phnom Penh at the end of the month for a short visit, his first since the coup in July 1997 (see AR 1997, pp. 338–9). On 22 May the *Phnom Penh Post* published documents purporting to show that Prince Randarridh and the KR had forged a military alliance—something that the former First Prime Minister had always strenuously denied.

There was sporadic violence in the months leading up to the 26 July elections to the National Assembly. In May talks on the reintegration into the army of forces loyal to Prince Ranarridh broke down. Despite opposition threats of a boycott, all parties participated in the elections. While there were reports of irregularities, international observers considered the poll to have been generally peaceful and fair. The National Election Committee (NEC) reported a high turnout of around 90 per cent, and Hun Sen's Cambodian People's Party (CPP) claimed an overwhelming victory. But on 28 July Prince Ranarridh and leading opposition politician Sam Rangsi, in a joint statement, said they would not recognize the result without an independent investigation.

The official results were released by the NEC on 5 August. The CPP won 41.1 per cent of the 4.9 million votes, Prince Ranariddh's Funcinpec 31.7 per cent and the Sam Rangsi Party (SRP) 14.3 per cent, the remainder of the votes going to 36 other parties. The allocation of seats in the Assembly was expected to be 64, 43 and 15 respectively for the three main parties. Hun Sen's offer to bring Funcinpec and the SRP into a coalition was refused. A series of demonstrations and vigils outside the Assembly—which quickly became known as 'Democracy Square'—were organized by the opposition at the end of August, despite a government ban. Prince Ranarridh and Sam Rangsi said that they would end their resistance if the system for allocating seats was changed so that the CPP did not command a majority.

A grenade attack on Hun Sen's residence on 7 September led to a crackdown on the demonstrators outside the National Assembly. Clashes between government forces and demonstrators continued until 15 September, when Prince Ranarridh, Sam Rangsi and Hun Sen agreed to talks presided over by King Sihanouk. These were held in Siem Reap on 22 September, and following reported good progress the 122-seat National Assembly opened at Angkor Wat on 24 September. While a grenade attack on Hun Sen's convoy marred proceedings, commentators were hopeful that the talks might mark a return to some semblance of normality.

Talks between the CPP and Funcinpec on 14 November led to the formation of a coalition government. It was agreed that Hun Sen would become sole Prime Minister and Prince Ranarridh chairman of the National Assembly. Chea Sim, chairman of the CPP, would lead a newly-created upper house, the Senate, and act as head of state during King Sihanouk's frequent absences. The CPP and Funcinpec took control of 12 and 11 ministries respectively, with defence and interior shared. The other key portfolios were controlled by the CPP. At the beginning of December Cambodia was given permission to occupy its UN seat, and on 29 December KR leaders Khieu Samphan and Nuon Chea flew to Phnom Penh and pledged their allegiance to the new coalition government.

At a summit meeting in Hanoi on 15–16 December, leaders of the Association of South-East Asian Nations (ASEAN) announced that they had agreed on the admission of Cambodia to the grouping, but at an unspecified date (see XI.6.iii).

The UN High Commissioner for Human Rights, Mary Robinson, visited Cambodia on 22–25 January to press for an investigation into the deaths of more than 40 Ranariddh supporters during the July 1997 coup. Prime Minister Hun Sen accused the UN of unwarranted interference. In early April the UN special representative for human rights in Cambodia, Thomas Hammarberg, said that he and his colleagues had uncovered evidence of 50 political killings between August 1997 and March 1998. A spokesman for the Prime Minister dismissed the report as 'propaganda'.

x. LAOS

CAPITAL: Vientiane   AREA: 237,000 sq km   POPULATION: 5,000,000 ('97)
OFFICIAL LANGUAGE: Laotian   POLITICAL SYSTEM: people's republic
RULING PARTY: Lao People's Revolutionary Party (LPRP)
HEAD OF STATE: President (Gen.) Khamtay Siphandon (since Feb '98)
HEAD OF GOVERNMENT: Gen. Sisavath Keobounphanh, Prime Minister (since Feb '98)
MAIN IGO MEMBERSHIPS (non-UN): ASEAN, CP, Francophonie, NAM
CURRENCY: new kip (end-'98 £1=KN6,993.57, US$1=KN4,203.50)
GNP PER CAPITA: US$400 by exchange-rate calculation, US$1,290 by PPP calculation ('97)

THE fourth National Assembly met on 23–26 February and formally endorsed a major leadership reshuffle. Outgoing Prime Minister and chairman of the ruling Lao People's Revolutionary Party (LPRP), Khamtay Siphandon, replaced 84-year-old Nouhak Phoumsavan as President. Former Vice-President Sisavath Keobounphanh became the new Prime Minister, and Oudom Khattigna was appointed to the post of Vice-President. In addition, there were a number of changes to the cabinet, with eight new appointments and five members with altered responsibilities. Reformist Deputy Prime Minister Khamphoui Keoboualapha was given the critical finance portfolio. Commentators noted that the changes did not indicate any fundamental change in the political complexion of the leadership.

Laos was buffeted by the Asian economic crisis, and especially by Thailand's economic collapse (see IX.1.ii). The governor of the central bank blamed the dramatic depreciation of the domestic currency, the kip, on 'speculative attempts by opportunists' as it plummeted to 3,300 to the US dollar by mid-year. Inflation rose significantly and was expected to reach 100 per cent by year's end, while the trade deficit widened. Approved foreign investment was a paltry US$65 million in the first quarter (including $57 million from Thailand), and commentators expected little of this to materialize.

At the end of January 44 people, including three US, one French and one Thai citizen, were detained for causing 'social turmoil'. In April a South Korean-built hydro-power project came on stream in the south and was expected to boost GDP by 7 per cent through the sale of electricity to Thailand.

2. CHINA—HONG KONG—TAIWAN—JAPAN—SOUTH KOREA—
NORTH KOREA—MONGOLIA

i. PEOPLE'S REPUBLIC OF CHINA

CAPITAL: Beijing   AREA: 9,600,000 sq km   POPULATION: 1,226,260,000 ('97)
OFFICIAL LANGUAGE: Chinese   POLITICAL SYSTEM: people's republic
HEAD OF STATE: President Jiang Zemin (since March '93)
RULING PARTY: Chinese Communist Party (CCP)
PARTY LEADER: Jiang Zemin, CCP general secretary (since June '89)
CCP POLITBURO STANDING COMMITTEE: Jiang Zemin, Li Peng, Zhu Rongji, Li Ruihuan, Hu Jintao, Wei Jianxing, Li Lanqing
CCP CENTRAL COMMITTEE SECRETARIAT: Hu Jintao, Ding Guangen, Wei Jianxing, Wen Jiabao, Zhang Wannian, Luo Gan, Zeng Qinghong
CENTRAL MILITARY COMMISSION: Jiang Zemin, chairman (since Nov '89)
PRIME MINISTER: Zhu Rongji (since March '98)
MAIN IGO MEMBERSHIPS (non-UN): APEC
CURRENCY: renminbi (RMB) denominated in yuan (end-'98 £1=Y13.77, US$1=Y8.28)
GNP PER CAPITA: US$860 by exchange-rate calculation, US$3,570 by PPP calculation ('97)

IN the face of both new and familiar challenges, the Chinese government displayed a basic continuity of policies at home and abroad during 1998. The most important new factor facing the government was the regional financial crisis. Its economic impact, exacerbated by the effects of devastating flooding in central and north-eastern provinces, was serious and for the first time in the 1990s China's GDP growth target was not fulfilled. Preliminary official estimates indicated that the momentum of rapid development had nevertheless been broadly maintained, although the persistence of underlying economic difficulties suggested a much less buoyant economic situation.

In the first full meeting of the Ninth National People's Congress (NPC) on 5–18 March, delegates strongly endorsed the policies and principles inherited from the 15th national congress of the ruling Chinese Communist Party (CCP) held in September 1997 (see AR 1997, p. 343). They reaffirmed the enshrinement of Deng Xiaoping Theory ('building socialism with Chinese characteristics') as the party's core ideology. The State Council submitted a plan for the restructuring of government institutions, designed to facilitate political reform. This was duly adopted by NPC delegates, who also elected new senior state officials (including the State President, chairmen of the NPC standing committee and Central Military Commission, president of the Supreme People's Court and procurator-general of the Supreme People's Procuracy). The appointment of Zhu Rongji as the new Premier of the State Council in place of Li Peng was also confirmed.

A principal theme of the 15th party congress had been the government's determination to embrace difficult reforms in order to enhance efficiency and eliminate massive indebtedness within the state-owned enterprise (SOE) sector. Subsequent lay-offs resulted in employment in SOEs being cut by 2.73 million in the first half of 1998. But under the impact of slowing growth throughout the economy (including collectively-owned enterprises, where 1.62 million workers were laid off) employment pressures became increasingly severe. The government's response was to retreat from its SOE reform programme in favour of renewed investment in state-owned manufacturing industries, including loss-making units. As a short-term expedient, this response promised to stem rising unemployment. In the longer term, however, it was likely to be no substitute for reforms that were essential to reviving the state enterprise sector. Since the main source of SOEs' investment funding was state-owned banks, not government revenue, the government's action also had grave implications for reform of the financial sector and the creation of an accountable, commercial banking system.

It was not only in the urban sector that the government faced difficult choices, the third plenum of the 15th CCP central committee also focusing on conditions in the countryside. The outcome was the adoption of an important decision on agricultural and rural policy, designed to strengthen the agricultural base and raise peasant incomes through the more rapid development of the farm and rural sectors. The fulfilment of such goals was intended to facilitate the creation, during the next decade, of a 'socialist new countryside with Chinese characteristics', while giving support to China's modernization programme.

China's pursuit of a vigorous diplomatic offensive, designed to enhance its global status as a major political and economic actor, met with continued success. In particular, reciprocal exchanges took place between senior government officials in China, Russia and the United States. The single most important visit was that undertaken by the American President, when he travelled to China and Hong Kong in June. Jiang Zemin said that his talks with Mr Clinton had generated a 'new and extensive consensus' and revealed a shared determination to extend cooperation over a wide of variety of fields. Later in the year, President Jiang went to Moscow, where fruitful discussions with President Yeltsin underlined the positive momentum of bilateral relations.

Following several years of strained relations, there were signs of the beginnings of renewed rapprochement between mainland China and Taiwan (see IX.2.iii). Less auspicious was President Jiang's high-profile visit to Japan, where his discussions with Prime Minister Keizo Obuchi failed to resolve long-standing differences between the two countries in regard to the interpretation and handling of wartime events and issues.

In September the death was announced of Yang Shangkun, one of the last remaining members of China's gerontocracy. He was 92. After 1949, Yang had risen to high office, eventually becoming secretary-general of the CCP central committee. During the Cultural Revolution he was dismissed from his official posts and spent 12 years in prison. In 1979 he resumed his party and political career, the culmination of which was his appointment, in 1988, as State President.

THE ECONOMY. In 1997 China could reasonably claim that it had successfully achieved a 'soft landing' without sacrificing the momentum of economic growth. In 1998, however, domestic economic problems were exacerbated by the impact of the financial crisis in other parts of East and South-East Asia. The result was to inhibit growth and threaten fulfilment of macro-economic targets. However, despite pressure on the renminbi as a result of the falling value of the Japanese yen and other Asian currencies, the Chinese government earned the plaudits of many governments by resisting the temptation to devalue its own currency. Instead, it sought to stimulate domestic demand by directing more funds to infrastructural construction (especially in transport, water conservation, environmental protection and residential housing).

Slowing growth had characterized the Chinese economy since 1993, and the downward trend continued through 1997 and 1998. In 1997 the decline in GDP expansion from 9.7 to 8.8 per cent reflected government success in restraining former inflationary pressures and slowing an over-heated economy. A similar interpretation was less convincing in 1998, when GDP growth fell by almost a further percentage point to 7.8 per cent (marginally below the target of 8 per cent). Such official estimates doubtless exaggerated reality by including output that merely added to huge existing inventories. In any case, the intensification of the downward trend during 1998 mostly served to highlight underlying structural weaknesses in the Chinese economy and the negative consequences of the Asian financial crisis.

In 1997 all three major sectors contributed, albeit in differing degrees, to GDP expansion. Industrial growth (10.8 per cent) once more outstripped that of agriculture (3.5 per cent) and services (8.2 per cent), although the tertiary sector was unique in registering more rapid growth in 1997. The implied increase in average per capita GDP was 7.7 per cent, compared with 8.6 per cent in 1996. Mirroring the fall in aggregate GDP growth, industrial expansion in 1998 fell by two percentage points to 8.8 per cent. Within the industrial sector, the lagging performance of state-owned units was clearly evident despite its receipt of more investment funds. Thus, in contrast to growth rates of 8.8 and 13.5 per cent in collective and foreign-funded enterprises, the value-output of SOEs rose by only 4.8 per cent.

The plight of ailing SOEs was again to the forefront of Chinese leaders' economic concerns. SOE reform was not only essential to efforts to improve efficiency in the industrial sector. It also impinged directly on the government's ability to fulfil its goal of creating a modern, commercial banking system. From this perspective, the sharp rise in state investment in the second half of 1998—most of it financed through bank lending and much of it destined for loss-making state enterprises—marked a retreat from the earlier commitment to industrial and financial reforms. The outcome was a further deterioration in the quality of loan portfolios held by the major state-owned banks. With non-performing loans already accounting for 25 per cent of total loans extended by such banks—higher than in pre-crisis Thailand, Indonesia and South Korea—the implications of this worsening situation were all too apparent.

In July and August China suffered its worst flooding since 1954. The natural disasters followed unusually severe rainfall, but also reflected serious problems of environmental degradation associated with inappropriate growth-maximizing policies. Early reports indicated that 21 million hectares of land—almost 14 per cent of China's total sown area—had been damaged by the summer floods, of which 13 million hectares had suffered a total crop loss. Direct economic losses were said to total some 166,600 million yuan (equivalent to 2.2 per cent of GDP in 1997). Even so, early reports indicated a 1998 grain harvest of 490 million tonnes—a mere percentage point lower than in the previous year. Road and rail networks suffered extensive damage and operations were suspended in many industrial enterprises.

Almost 250 million people were affected by the floods, of whom 13.4 million had to be relocated. The official death toll was put at 3,004. More than 5.5 million houses were destroyed and a further 12 million damaged, giving rise to widespread homelessness. In the aftermath of the floods, Premier Zhu Rongji called for an immediate ban on logging of natural forests on the middle and upper reaches of the Yangtze and Yellow rivers. He also urged a package of measures, including silt removal, soil loss reduction, dike reinforcement and afforestation in order to improve ecological balance in threatened regions.

The recent erratic trend of China's merchandise trade performance was repeated in 1997 and 1998. From a low of 3.2 per cent in 1996, the combined value of exports and imports expanded by 12.1 per cent in 1997. In a reversal of the previous year's pattern, exports increased more rapidly than imports, facilitating a rise in China's trade surplus from US$12,300 million to US$40,300 million. Trade conducted by foreign-funded enterprises maintained its high growth momentum, as did the share of machinery and electronic products in total exports. There were also large rises in the value of China's trade with Latin American and African countries.

China's foreign trade growth was reversed in 1998, merchandise shipments falling by almost 2 per cent. In May negative export growth was experienced for the first time in almost two years, and in September exports fell by 6.7 per cent year on year. By the end of the year the value of exports was at about the same level as in the previous year, although with imports having fallen by 3.8 per cent, China's trade surplus rose by almost 12 per cent to reach US$45,000 million. No less serious than the downturn in merchandise trade was the threat to macroeconomic stability posed by capital flight under the guise of current-account transactions.

The sharp deceleration in export growth mainly reflected the impact of the regional financial crisis. The impact would have been greater if a sharp reduction in shipments to Japan, South Korea and South-East Asia had not been partly offset by closer ties with non-Asian countries. Slowing trade and declining competitiveness resulting from currency depreciations by China's major Asian partners led to speculation that China might devalue the renminbi. Despite some voices arguing to the contrary, the government was consistent in its refusal to do so. Instead, it argued that, given the high import content of finished Chinese exports, depreciation would bring few economic benefits and might be counter-productive if it led to a further round of competitive devaluations by other countries. In any case, with foreign exchange reserves of over US$140,000 million, China had sufficient resources to cover its existing foreign debt four times over and to fund a whole year's worth of capital imports.

Increasingly pessimistic external perceptions of China's economic prospects were reflected in a decline of almost 16 per cent in utilized foreign investment in 1998. The collapse, in October, of the Guangdong International Trust and Investment Corporation (GITIC) and Beijing's clearly-stated refusal to guarantee GITIC's unregistered debts, as well as the downgrading of China's foreign currency debt status, merely added to the loss of confidence among overseas investors.

POLITICS AND SOCIETY. Li Peng's government work report to the ninth NPC—his last as Chinese Premier—noted that the existing framework of government organization had become unwieldy and inadequate to meet the new needs of a socialist market economy. He announced a programme of organizational restructuring, designed to reduce from 40 to 29 the number of ministries and commissions under the State Council. More than 16,000 employees were expected to be transferred to other jobs. Meanwhile, all levels of government would be expected to simplify and streamline their organizational and staff structures.

At the ninth NPC various senior government appointments were announced. Jiang Zemin was simultaneously reconfirmed as State President and chairman of the Central Military Commission. Hu Jintao was appointed Vice-President, while Li Peng was elected as chairman of the NPC standing committee. On 17 March Jiang Zemin issued a presidential decree, formally appointing Zhu Rongji as Premier of the State Council in succession to Li Peng.

Authoritative reports again acknowledged the poor state of social order in China. One of these referred to increasing criminal activities and highlighted the role of young people and members of the 'floating population' in fuelling the deterioration in urban public order. An important political initiative was contained in a directive, issued jointly by the CCP central committee and State Council and designed to enhance democratic practice in the countryside.

On 27 July the information office of the State Council published a White Paper on China's national defence. The document reaffirmed China's adherence to a peaceful policy of national reunification, insisting that it would never resort to 'foreign aggression and expansion'. It reiterated the government's determination to subordinate national defence construction to the core task of economic development, and gave a renewed undertaking to cut troop numbers by a further 500,000 within the next three years. It noted that the Chinese government had already undertaken major reductions in defence spending, official expenditure of $9,800 million in 1997 being a mere 3.67 per cent of that of the United States.

Continuing unrest in the Muslim regions of north-west China was again a source of concern to the central government. The Xinjiang party secretary's admission that 'the situation in the struggle against the enemy is still very grim' highlighted the continuing threat from separatists.

EXTERNAL RELATIONS. In his government work report to the ninth NPC, Li Peng referred to his government's determination to pursue an independent and peaceful foreign policy. The then Chinese Premier spoke of the enhancement of China's relations with the United States and Russia, although his remarks on Sino-Japanese ties were more cautious and reserved. He reiterated his government's willingness to develop cooperation with European Union (EU) member states and other European countries, as well as its desire to participate more actively in the activities of members of ASEAN, APEC and the EU-sponsored Asia-Europe Meeting. As well as repeating China's intention to recover Macao on 20 December 1999, Li insisted that Taiwan meanwhile remained an 'inalienable part of the inviolable territory of China'.

The single most important event affecting relations between China and the USA in 1998 was the visit to China by President Clinton (25 June-3 July)—the fifth by an incumbent American President. President Clinton held talks with Jiang Zemin on bilateral relations as well as on major international and regional issues. Both leaders noted the favourable impact of recent positive trends in the two countries' relations, although President Jiang also highlighted the threats to future global development posed by regional conflicts, environmental degradation, international crime and financial disorder. The Presidents were in agreement on the need to extend their dialogue on economic and financial issues, as well as on such matters as human rights and global security. President Jiang later revealed that, as a demonstration of their new cooperative partnership, the two sides had decided to de-target their nuclear weapons from one another. In a reference to still-unresolved differences, President Clinton urged the Chinese government to engage in a closer dialogue with the authorities in Taiwan and with the Dalai Lama of Tibet, and he revealed that his talks with Jiang Zemin had embraced questions of China's human rights record (see also IV.1). Continuing sensitivities impinging on Sino-American relations were reflected in official Chinese condemnation of remarks contained in the US State Department's *Human Rights Report* (1997). China's decision to sign the Covenant on Civil and Political Rights was, however, instrumental in persuading the US government not to sponsor a UN resolution critical of China's human rights' record.

In the wake of the successful retrocession of British sovereignty over Hong Kong in mid-1997 (see AR 1997, pp. 350–3), relations between China and Britain displayed a new momentum. Evidence of a shared commitment to stronger bilateral ties was reflected in a series of visits to China by senior British officials throughout the year, culminating in that of the Prime Minister Tony Blair in October. The desire to strengthen political, economic and other ties between member states of the EU and China was endorsed during a visit to China in October by the president of the European Commission, Jacques Santer.

The summer floods having forced the postponement of Jiang Zemin's intended September visit to Russia, the Chinese President eventually travelled to Moscow on 22 November. The indisposition of the President Yeltsin forced the two leaders to hold an informal meeting in a Moscow hospital where they reviewed bilateral and other issues of common concern, the discussions reportedly generating positive results, including progress towards a settlement of outstanding border issues (see also III.3.i). President Yeltsin also accepted an invitation to visit China in 1999.

As in previous years, reciprocal high-level visits testified to China's wish to develop cooperative relations with Central Asian countries. In the course of talks in Beijing in May, Premier Zhu Rongji told his Kazakh counterpart of Beijing's wish to join Kazakhstan in developing a long-term bilateral relationship, based on comprehensive cooperation—but with the oil industry as the key focus of joint efforts. Later in the year, during talks in Almaty with President Nursultan Nazarbayev, Jiang Zemin noted that with the signing on 2 July of a second supplement to the bilateral border demarcation agreement, China and Kazakhstan had resolved all outstanding border issues.

Despite reciprocal visits by senior government officials, the further progress of Sino-Japanese relations in 1998 was frustrated by continuing mutual distrust. During a visit to Tokyo in March Chinese Defence Minister Chi Haotian took the opportunity to reiterate his government's opposition to the 1997 Japan-US Defence Agreement (see AR 1997, p. 348). In August the new Japanese Foreign Minister held talks in Beijing with his Chinese counterpart on the regional economic crisis, bilateral economic cooperation and global issues (including nuclear disarmament). It was revealed that Japan was already drawing up plans to extend a further round of yen loans to China.

By far the most important event affecting Sino-Japanese relations was Jiang Zemin's visit to Japan in November—the first such visit ever undertaken by a Chinese head of state (see also IX.2.iv). Chinese sources let it be known in advance that President Jiang intended to raise the question of Japan's wartime activities in China, although Japanese sources suggested that

Premier Keizo Obuchi would go no further than giving an oral apology for Japan's wartime conduct. The joint statement issued after the completion of the talks reaffirmed the importance of efforts to establish a 'friendly cooperative partnership' between the two countries. However, despite protestations of a shared determination to promote a 'long-term neighbourly relationship of friendly cooperation', many observers regarded the absence of an explicit Japanese apology for its wartime activities as the most significant omission, the statement merely referring to Japan's 'responsibility. . .and deep retrospection' for its aggression against China.

After a period in which relations between mainland China and Taiwan had remained at a low ebb, there were real signs of an easing of tension and a renewed rapprochement across the Taiwan Strait in 1998. The climax of this process were visits, in October, to Shanghai and Beijing made by Koo Chen-fu, chairman of Taiwan's Straits Exchange Foundation (see IX.2.iii).

Through official visits and tours, as well as active participation in major international organizations, China maintained its programme of diplomatic activity throughout the rest of the world. Chinese officials were also active in involvement in major trouble-spots, expressing condemnation of nuclear tests undertaken by Pakistan and (especially) India in May, showing concern at deteriorating public order in Indonesia, and calling for peaceful negotiations to resolve crises in Iraq and Kosovo (Yugoslavia).

ii. HONG KONG SPECIAL ADMINISTRATIVE REGION

CAPITAL: Victoria   AREA: 1,073 sq km   POPULATION: 6,502,100 ('97)
STATUS: Special Administrative Region of the People's Republic of China (from 1 July 1997
CHIEF EXECUTIVE: Tung Chee-hwa (from July '97)
ADMINISTRATIVE SECRETARY: Anson Chan (since July '97), previously Chief Secretary (since Sept '93)
MAIN IGO MEMBERSHIPS: APEC
CURRENCY: Hong Kong dollar (end-'98 £1=HK$12.89, US$1=HK$7.74)
GDP PER CAPITA: US$26,600 by exchange-rate calculation ('97)

FEARS that China's recovery of sovereignty over Hong Kong (see AR 1997, pp. 351–52) would have a serious negative impact on local political and socio-economic conditions proved unfounded and there was a consensus that the Chinese government had handled the post-handover period with tact and caution. Throughout 1998 the People's Liberation Army (PLA) garrison stationed in the Hong Kong Special Administrative Region (HKSAR) maintained a very low profile, while pro-democracy demonstrations took place without serious incident—most notably on 4 June, when up to 40,000 people came together on the ninth anniversary of the Tiananmen Square massacre in Beijing (see AR 1989, pp. 339–40). There was no doubting the increasingly severe economic and social problems that confronted Hong Kong in 1998; their origin was, however, not interference from Beijing, but the impact of the regional financial crisis.

The emerging economic recession was responsible for a scaling-down of the celebrations originally intended to mark the first anniversary of the handover of Hong Kong to Chinese rule. Even so, President Jiang Zemin's presence in Hong Kong for the anniversary afforded him the opportunity to reaffirm China's continued commitment to the principle of 'one country, two systems' and to cite the experience of the previous year as evidence of its ability to guarantee long-run prosperity and stability in the region. He praised the efforts of Chief Executive Tung Chee-hwa and his government in their handling of the internal and external challenges facing Hong Kong and promised to provide help in the face of its current economic difficulties.

In January Hong Kong's reputation as a safe and popular tourist destination was damaged by an outbreak of avian influenza, which caused the deaths of six people and necessitated the slaughter of its entire poultry stock. Shortly afterwards the appearance of toxic algae in local waters destroyed 1,500 tonnes of farmed fish—equivalent to half of total production in 1997.

In February Financial Secretary Donald Tsang unveiled the HKSAR's first budget. With accumulated fiscal reserves of almost HK$450,000 million and a record budget surplus (HK$77,000 million) in the 1997–98 fiscal year, he was able to announce a package of measures—including a four-year programme of tax cuts worth HK$100,000 million—designed to combat worsening economic conditions. Meanwhile, Mr Tsang's projections indicated that GDP growth would fall from 5.2 to 3.5 per cent during 1998. Subsequent events showed these projections to be wide of the mark. In his half-yearly economic report Mr Tsang revised his annual GDP growth forecast to a negative 4 per cent. At the end of May, in the wake of a 2.8 per cent fall in first-quarter GDP growth (the first such decline since 1985) and with unemployment at 3.9 per cent, he was forced to introduce further stimulatory financial measures in an attempt to stabilize the property market and improve banking liquidity.

The following month Tung Chee-hwa unveiled a HK$32,000 million package designed to combat what had clearly become a serious recession in Hong Kong. Following a 40 per cent fall in property prices in the previous six months, its central feature was the suspension, until April 1999, of sales of government-owned land. Through its impact on government revenue, this initiative was expected to push the 1998–99 government budget from a projected surplus of HK$11,000 million into a HK$21,400 million deficit. Other measures sought to lower import and export duties, improve small and medium-sized enterprises' access to loans, and freeze government salaries.

In August speculative activity by currency traders and others in the face of fears that declining competitiveness might cause the abandonment of the currency peg to the US dollar led to massive government intervention (of HK$118,000 million) in the local stock market. Mr Tsang referred to 'improper measures' having been used to undermine the Hong Kong dollar and provoke a stock market collapse, but reaffirmed the HKSAR government's commitment to the peg and insisted that recent government intervention in the financial market portended no change in its support of the traditional free-market approach to Hong Kong's economic affairs. In any case, falling interest rates and rising stock market values appeared to vindicate the government action, even though the severity of the underlying economic malaise was also apparent in a further rise in unemployment to over 5 per cent, implying 180,000 jobless, especially in retailing, construction, manufacturing and investment banking.

Elections to the first HKSAR Legislative Council (Legco) took place on 24 May. By law 2.8 million citizens were entitled to vote in direct elections for 20 of the 60 Legco seats, a further 30 members being elected through functional constituencies and the remaining 10 being returned by an 800-strong election committee. The Democratic Party emerged from the elections as the largest party, holding 13 Legco seats, nine of them through direct election. It was followed by the Liberal Party (10 seats, but none achieved in the direct elections), the Democratic Alliance for the Betterment of Hong Kong (9), the Progressive Alliance (5) and the Frontier Party (3). Despite inclement weather, the turnout in the direct elections was 53.29 per cent.

Following his visit to mainland China (see IX.2.i), President Clinton travelled to Hong Kong on 2–3 July. Underlining remarks in which he stressed the dynamism of economic relations between the USA and Asia, it was reported that the United States was Hong Kong's second-largest trading partner and second-largest export market. In 1997 the value of two-way trade was HK$442,000 million—6 per cent higher than in 1996. Hong Kong's exports to the USA were valued at HK$316,000 million.

Senior British officials, including Prime Minister Tony Blair, made separate visits to Hong Kong during 1998, testifying to the new warmth of relations between China and Britain following the successful handover of Hong Kong. Although China's recovery of sovereignty ended the formal role of the Sino-British Joint Liaison Group, its 43rd meeting was convened on 15–16 September in order to consider a number of outstanding issues. Against the background of a decision, taken in January, to end the 'port of first asylum' policy hitherto applied to Vietnamese 'boat people', one such issue was the handling of the remaining 1,100 Vietnamese refugees interned in Hong Kong.

On 2 July President Jiang Zemin officially opened the new Hong Kong airport at Chek Lap Kok (CLK). Four days later the old Kai Tak airport was closed, after 73 years, and CLK instituted commercial operations. However, in the face of serious computer problems (causing flight delays, baggage loss and disruption of cargo facilities), all cargo handling was suspended until 18 July.

iii. TAIWAN

CAPITAL: Taipei AREA: 35,981 sq km POPULATION: 21,500,000 ('97)
OFFICIAL LANGUAGE: Chinese POLITICAL SYSTEM: presidential
HEAD OF STATE & GOVERNMENT: President Lee Teng-hui (since Jan '88, popularly elected March '96)
RULING PARTY: Kuomintang (KMT)
PRIME MINISTER: Vincent Siew (since Sept '97)
MAIN IGO MEMBERSHIPS : APEC
CURRENCY: new Taiwan dollar (end-'98 £1=NT$53.60, US$1=NT$32.22)
GDP PER CAPITA: US$12,872 by exchange-rate calculation ('96 est.)

IN 1998 Taiwan's pursuit of domestic development and conduct of its foreign relations were again enacted under the shadow of mainland China. But for the first time in several years there was evidence of a thawing of relations between Taiwan and the People's Republic (PRC) and the beginnings of renewed rapprochement across the Taiwan Strait. Early in the year mainland Chinese leaders renewed calls for cross-Strait political talks to take place. Taiwan's cautious reaction was highlighted in its rejection of the 'one country, two systems' formula as a basis for China's peaceful reunification. But in February and March Taiwanese government sources responded positively to two letters sent by the PRC Association for Relations Across the Taiwan Strait (ARATS), setting out the possibility of visits to mainland China, at appropriate times, by Koo Chen-fu, chairman of the Straits Exchange Foundation (SEF)—the counterpart of ARATS in Taiwan—and business, cultural and academic representatives.

In the following months sensitivities surrounding the possibility of renewed contacts between ARATS and SEF were reflected in the caution with which the two sides approached the increasing likelihood of a resumption of talks between representatives of the two semi-official bodies in Beijing and Taipei; but on 15 September ARATS finally issued a formal proposal for the visit to take place in October. Koo Chen-fu duly arrived in Shanghai on 14 October. His subsequent talks with Wang Daohan was the first meeting ever to take place on the mainland between ARATS and SEF leaders, the previous encounter between the two having taken place in Singapore in 1993.

Reports indicated that the discussions in Shanghai had resulted in a frank exchange of views on political issues between the two sides. According to Taiwanese sources, Mr Koo stressed the significance of the resumption of talks between ARATS and SEF, drawing attention to the equal status of the two parties and expressing the hope that unresolved issues could in due course be reopened and discussed through the same channel of communication. PRC sources went further and suggested that cross-Strait relations had now entered the stage of 'political dialogue'. They also called for the swift establishment of the 'three links', namely, direct trade, transportation and communications between Taiwan and mainland China. The most concrete outcome of the talks was a four-point agreement, which allowed for further dialogue between SEF and ARATS on various issues, including political and economic questions. The two sides undertook to strengthen cooperation in order to protect the lives and property of citizens of the two countries. Wang Daohan accepted Mr Koo's invitation to visit Taiwan at an appropriate date in the future.

Following his talks in Shanghai, Mr Koo returned to Beijing for the first time for 55 years. In a courtesy meeting with President Jiang Zemin, the latter reviewed the major issues impinging on cross-Strait relations. He endorsed Mr Koo's efforts to promote closer ties and welcomed the four-point consensus that had emerged out of his discussions in Shanghai. Mr Koo himself was said to have urged Beijing to recognize the reality of the separate rule of mainland China and Taiwan during the previous half-century. He also repeated a suggestion made earlier in the year that the two sides should take joint action in an effort to resolve the Asian financial crisis.

Agreement was reached on 4 March for a PRC shipping company to operate a direct shipping link between Shanghai and the port of Chi-lung—the first direct link across the Taiwan Strait since the severance of sea links in 1949. Later the same month the Mainland Affairs Council also endorsed an agreement for joint oil exploration between the Chinese Petroleum Corporation (Taiwan) and the China National Overseas Offshore Oil Company (PRC).

Taipei's efforts to maintain a high diplomatic profile in the international community suffered a series of setbacks in 1998, with three countries (the Central African Republic, Guinea-Bissau and Tonga) breaking off ties with Taiwan in favour of the establishment of full diplomatic relations with the PRC. In September the Malagasy cabinet also decided to abolish the 'special agreement' which it had signed with Taiwan in 1990. The only political success enjoyed by Taiwan was the establishment, in November, of full diplomatic relations with the Marshall Islands. In an effort to prevent such transfers of diplomatic recognition, it was announced that Taiwan's foreign aid budget would be increased from US$57,000 million to US$183,000 million. Meanwhile, President Lee Teng-hui was explicit in his advocacy of 'pragmatic diplomacy', and in the course of the year Vice-President Lien Chan and Premier Vincent Siew separately undertook supposedly secret or private visits to countries of the Middle East and South-East Asia.

The ruling Kuomintang (KMT) made an impressive showing in the year's local and national-level elections. In January the KMT took 233 out of 319 contested seats in elections for township chiefs and city mayors, while in simultaneous county and city council elections the party won 524 out of 890 seats. But more significant was the outcome of elections held on 5 December, when 68.09 per cent of 14.9 million eligible voters elected 225 members of the Legislative Yuan. The results showed the KMT to have taken 123 of the 225 seats, with 46.43 per cent of the vote. By contrast, the Democratic Progressive Party (DPP) secured 70 seats, the New Party

11, the Democratic Alliance four, and the Taiwan Independence Party and New Nation Alliance (the latter newly-established in September) one seat each. Independent candidates won the 12 remaining seats, with 9.43 per cent of the vote.

Although less affected by the regional financial crisis than some other Asian countries, Taiwan was not immune from its impact. With unemployment rising to 3 per cent in August and with exports shrinking (down by 9 per cent during January-October), early forecasts of annual GDP growth of 6.2 per cent were revised downwards to 5.1 per cent. Meanwhile, in the face of continued exchange rate and stock market volatility, the government unveiled an expansionary package worth NT$652,000 million for the 1998–99 fiscal year. In October, against a background of emerging problems in the private sector, Premier Siew unveiled further growth-enhancing measures based on technological upgrading and stronger international cooperation.

A resolution passed by the US Congress in July sought to reaffirm the US commitment to continue arms sales to Taiwan. The next month the US Defence Department announced plans to sell US$350 million of arms to Taiwan, including 61 Stinger anti-aircraft missile launchers and 728 missiles. Meanwhile, in October Taiwan took delivery of the last of 60 Mirage 2000–5 jet fighters ordered from France in a deal struck in 1993.

iv. JAPAN

CAPITAL: Tokyo   AREA: 378,000 sq km   POPULATION: 126,000,000 ('97)
OFFICIAL LANGUAGE: Japanese   POLITICAL SYSTEM: parliamentary democracy
HEAD OF STATE: Emperor Tsugu no Miya Akihito (since Jan '89)
RULING PARTY: Liberal-Democratic Party (LDP)
HEAD OF GOVERNMENT: Keizo Obuchi, Prime Minister (since July '98)
MAIN IGO MEMBERSHIPS (non-UN): APEC, CP, OECD, G-8
CURRENCY: yen (end-'98 £1=Y187.67, US$1=Y112.80)
GNP PER CAPITA: US$37,850 by exchange-rate calculation, US$23,400 by PPP calculation ('97)

JAPAN suffered throughout 1998 from economic difficulties which continued from previous years: severe recession, fears of rising unemployment, official corruption and 'bad loans' held by major financial institutions. The government and the bureaucracy found it hard to revive the stagnant economy. This led to continuing criticism of the government and brought to light weaknesses in the bureaucracy, especially the Ministry of Finance, which had hitherto been respected for its leadership in times of economic crisis.

The Ministry of Finance came under investigation for the first time in 50 years for failing to recognize the heavy losses, which had led to the collapse of Yamaichi Securities in 1997 (see AR 1997, p. 359), and take appropriate action. More generally, its officials were blamed for receiving lavish expense-account entertainment, undue closeness to the banks and general lack of transparency. After investigation, various senior officials were arrested and the minister resigned in January, assuming responsibility for the scandal. The job of inspection was removed from the Ministry of Finance and a new Financial Supervision Agency set up. Similar criticisms were made of the Bank of Japan and resulted in the resignation of the governor.

In general, the Liberal-Democratic (LDP) government of Ryutaro Hashimoto faced three problems: how to find a way out of the slump which had gripped the country for most of the 1990s; how to assist in the stabilization of the weaker economies of Asia; and how to respond to international criticism of its dilatoriness, especially from the United States. The government, by a supplementary budget in February, again injected vast amounts of public money into the economy, involving public works expenditure in order to revive the economy and save the financial system. These remedies had been tried before without succeeding in stimulating consumer confidence and boosting domestic demand. Some of the other steps envisaged had run into political opposition within the LDP.

The depressing financial scene was relieved by the Winter Olympics, which took place in Nagano prefecture for 16 days in February (see Pt XVII). It was far and away the most elaborate and expensive Games ever held and was a great achievement of planning and organization, since it was held outside a metropolitan area. The performance of the Japanese athletes (whose tally of five gold medals was the best they had ever achieved) was widely covered on television and greatly boosted national morale.

Another promising development was in relations with Russia, with which Japan had a long-standing territorial dispute over the 'Northern Territories'. At the end of February the then Foreign Minister, Keizo Obuchi, signed a fisheries pact in Moscow which allowed Japanese boats to fish within the waters of these Russian-held islands in return for certain technical assistance. Japan further promised about $1,500 million in untied loans to Russia. These agreements were confirmed when President Yeltsin met Mr Hashimoto at Kawana on 18–19 April. It was additionally agreed that the joint committee already in existence should speed up its endeavours to conclude a peace treaty by the year 2000, which would formally end the state of war between the two countries.

The opening of the Akashi Kaikyo bridge on 5 April joined up the main island of Honshu with the east of Shikoku island. It was the world's largest suspension bridge (3.9 kilometres) and had the capacity to resist earthquakes registering up to 8.5 on the Richter scale.

Emperor Akihito and Empress Michiko conducted a series of state visits to Britain (see II.1.i), Portugal and Denmark. So far as Britain was concerned, the ground had been prepared by a visit to Tokyo in January by Prime Minister Tony Blair, when Mr Hashimoto took the occasion to express Japan's deep remorse and heartfelt apology for wartime atrocities towards prisoners-of-war. Though the protest by British PoWs and their demands for compensation caught the headlines, the imperial visit to Britain at the end of May was generally apolitical and was a popular success. Later in the year the issue surfaced again when the Tokyo district court on 26 November dismissed claims by former PoWs from four countries for compensation for wartime atrocities committed against them.

From the spring onwards, political parties were jockeying for position in view of the forthcoming Upper House elections due in July. The LDP, which had a small overall majority in the House of Representatives, found it difficult to get its legislation through, and internal party disputes imposed delays in implementing economic reforms. The survival of the LDP depended on the weakness and fragmented nature of the opposition. To overcome these divisions, the centrist opposition parties (many of them small) formed an anti-LDP bloc in the Diet called Minyuren. The Democratic Party became the main opposition party, while the Social Democratic and Sakigake parties announced their intention to pull out of the loose coalition which had existed with LDP for over a year. One of the outcomes of all this was that the opposition on 12 June felt strong enough to table a motion of no-confidence against Mr Hashimoto because of his deflationary economic policies; but it was defeated by 273 votes to 207.

The elections for half the 252 seats in the Upper House took place on 12 July. The poll was widely regarded as a popular test of confidence in the Hashimoto government's handling of the economy and brought out an unexpectedly large number of voters (58.8 per cent). The governing party did badly, its seats dropping from 60 to 45. The Democratic Party and the veteran Communist Party made significant gains of 27 and 15 respectively. The end-result was that the LDP, having become a minority party in the Upper House, was expected to have difficulty in getting its legislation through without allies. Mr Hashimoto therefore resigned; and three candidates offered themselves for election as president of the LDP. By the votes of existing Diet members, Keizo Obuchi, the outgoing Foreign Minister, came through comfortably with 225 of the total votes cast (376). In announcing his new minority LDP cabinet, Mr Obuchi controversially appointed former Prime Minister Kiichi Miyazawa (1991–93) to the finance portfolio.

The latter half of the year was taken up with efforts to form a coalition between the LDP and the small Liberal Party led by Ichiro Ozawa. In spite of exhaustive attempts at policy accommodation, agreement was not clinched by year's end. It was opposed by some in LDP ranks and by New Komeito, with which the LDP had a working arrangement for collaboration on selected policies.

At the end of August North Korea tested a rocket which overflew northern Japan and landed in the Pacific Ocean (see IX.2.vi). It was unclear what the rocket was carrying; but the Japanese naturally felt their vulnerability and protested strongly against their airspace being violated. They suspended talks to normalize diplomatic relations with Pyongyang and held up food aid.

With the autumn, the visiting season began. In September Mr Obuchi, as incoming Prime Minister, went to Washington to meet President Clinton. In a significant state visit on 7 October, President Kim Dae Jung of South Korea received an expression of remorse from Japan for 36 years of Japanese colonial rule in the peninsula (see XI.2.v). He responded favourably and proposed the signing of an agreement with Japan setting up a free-trade zone. The good atmosphere created suggested the emergence of new cordial relationship. On 12 November Mr Obuchi met President Yeltsin in Moscow in order to expedite the process for resolving the 'Northern Territories' issue by 2000. The two countries were understood to be toying with the idea that the Russian-held northern Kuriles would be designated a 'special area' where Japan would enjoy specific rights.

President Clinton flew to Japan on 20 November. His visit followed a prefectural governorship election in Okinawa, bringing to power the LDP nominee, Keiichi Inamine. The governor for six years, Masahide Ota, who stood on a platform of insisting on the removal of American bases from his territories, was voted out of office. The new governor declared his readiness to discuss building a new airfield to take over the functions of the existing US Marines' base at Futenma, thus removing one of the sources of US-Japanese friction. Another was that the USA and Japan had, following President Clinton's visit in 1997, agreed on guidelines for US-Japan defence cooperation; but the bills to bring these undertakings into force had been held up because of disagreements within the governing party over how to interpret the peace clauses in the Japanese constitution. While urging speedy action on this matter, the US President also appealed to Japan to take bolder economic measures.

The Chinese President, Jiang Zemin, took part in a large number of talks with Japanese ministers during a six-day visit from 25 November (see also XI.2.i). This first state visit to Japan by a Chinese head of state marked the 20th anniversary of the peace treaty between the two countries. China's priority was to obtain clarification from Japan of its position regarding past conflicts. Mr Obuchi offered a personal apology. Moreover, while declining Beijing's request for an official apology, Japan appeared to have raised no objection to China referring in the final communique to 'Japanese aggression'. On Taiwan, another thorny issue, Japan agreed to respect China's position that the island was an integral part of Chinese territory. By contrast, Japan wanted to concentrate discussion on the future in terms of trade expansion, the Asian financial crisis and security considerations on the Korean peninsula. The parties abstained from signing a joint statement after the formal sessions, suggesting that they were still some distance from a meeting of minds.

In South-East Asia, Prime Minister Obuchi attended the APEC summit in Kuala Lumpur in November and the ASEAN meeting in Hanoi in

December (see XI.6.iii)). At both, Japan stressed its Asia Aid programme, the so-called 'Miyazawa initiative' which the government had earlier published as an indication of its sense of responsibility for assistance to Indonesia, Malaysia, Thailand and South Korea.

These visits took place against the background of a renewed economic crisis in the autumn. On 23 October, after intense public debate about indebted banks, the Obuchi government announced the temporary nationalization of the Long-term Credit Bank, which was suffering from debts exceeding its assets by Y340,000 million. On 13 December it was the turn of the Nippon Credit Bank, with liabilities of Y94,400 million in excess of assets, which was placed under temporary state control.

The year ended on a note of self-doubt. The general public were sceptical about the Japanese government's ability to bring about economic and political improvements. The government announced yet another stimulus package, including massive spending on public works and personal and corporate tax cuts, while the LDP promised a tax reform plan. On the political front, reform of the party structure and the bureaucracy was still awaited, as the LDP appeared to be more inclined to forge coalitions to stay in power than to tackle longer-term factors.

v. SOUTH KOREA

CAPITAL: Seoul   AREA: 99,392 sq km   POPULATION: 46,000,000 ('97)
OFFICIAL LANGUAGE: Korean   POLITICAL SYSTEM: presidential democracy
HEAD OF STATE & GOVERNMENT: President Kim Dae Jung (since Feb '98)
RULING PARTIES: National Congress for New Politics (NCNP) & United Liberal Democrats (ULD)
PRIME MINISTER: Kim Jong Pil (ULD), since March '98
MAIN IGO MEMBERSHIPS (non-UN): APEC, CP, OECD
CURRENCY: won (end-'98 £1=SKW2,000.60, US$1=SKW1,202.50)
GNP PER CAPITA: US$10,550 by exchange-rate calculation, US$13,500 by PPP calculation ('97)

KIM Dae Jung, inaugurated President of the Republic of Korea in February amidst the country's worst-ever financial crisis (following his election in December 1997—see AR 1997, pp. 361-2), was plunged immediately into a political crisis as well. Underlining the difficulties that his minority National Congress for New Politics (NCNP) would face, the opposition in the National Assembly blocked his choice of Prime Minister, Kim Jong Pil, leader of the United Liberal Democrats (ULD). Installed in March, he was inaugurated only in August. The Foreign Affairs and Trade Minister, Park Chung Soo, was forced to resign in August after a dispute with Russia over mutual spying allegations. He was replaced by Hong Soon Yung, former ambassador in Moscow. The same month Yi Hoe Chang was elected president of the opposition Grand National Party (GNP) in place of Lee Hoi Chang, who faced corruption charges.

President Kim's IMF-mandated efforts to rein in the *chaebol* (industrial conglomerates) aimed to impose discipline on big business, but they resisted reform strongly. The government wanted the banks to be catalysts of corporate restructuring, but they were preoccupied with their own survival. Liquidation of commercial banks was ruled out, but 16 small merchant banks closed. Some SKW64,000,000 million had been set aside to buy back bad loans and recapitalize the banking system, but total non-performing loans were estimated at SKW160,000,000 million. In October the five biggest *chaebol* were ordered to limit their debts, and in December the President's office announced their restructuring through mergers and disposals. Analysts who considered closures and sackings to be the only way of curbing the *chaebol* saw Kim Dae Jung as weak and inept. His suggestion that foreign investment was as important as restructuring the *chaebol* met with suspicion.

In October President Kim paid an official visit to Japan. Emperor Akihito expressed 'deep sorrow' for Korea's suffering under Japanese colonial rule (1910–45) and Prime Minister Keizo Obuchi issued a statement about Japan's 'deep remorse and heartfelt apology'. A new fisheries agreement compromised over the disputed ownership of some border islands, and Japan offered South Korea $3,000 million in economic aid.

Just before Kim Dae Jung's inauguration, North Korea sent through Panmunjom dozens of letters addressed to the President-designate, political parties and civic groups seeking dialogue. A North Korean official was reported as saying: 'We are willing to have a dialogue and negotiate with anyone in South Korea, including political parties and organizations.'

Reflecting President Kim's 'sunshine' policy of improving relations with the North, Seoul pledged in March that the South would not force unification on the North, although the South's economic troubles made this problematical anyway. The first North-South meeting in four years, held in Beijing in April, collapsed after the South refused to supply fertilizer. During his official visit to Washington in June, President Kim told the US Congress of the need for a 'confident, coordinated and composed' approach to the North.

A North Korean midget submarine was seized in South Korean waters in July, and the bodies of nine crew found inside were returned to the North. Only a few days later, however, another North Korean submersible was discovered, together with the body of a diver. President Kim demanded an apology from the North and a promise to stop armed infiltration. In August the North rejected the President's proposal to send envoys to Pyongyang (the North Korean capital) and to set up vice-ministerial contacts.

Two rounds of four-party talks between the USA, China and the two Korean states were held in Geneva in March and October. It was agreed to set up two sub-committees, to discuss a Korean peace treaty and confidence-building measures, and to meet again in January 1999. During his official visit to Beijing in November, President Kim encouraged President Jiang Zemin to involve China more actively in the four-party talks, suggesting that Japan and Russia might also be included. However, the South Korean leader had to admit that the time for bilateral talks was 'not ripe'.

The range of contacts with North Korea not requiring government permission was expanded in March. The founder of the South Korean Hyundai Corporation, Chung Ju Yung, crossed into the North at Panmunjom in June with gifts of 50 lorries, 500 head of cattle and 10,000 tons of maize, and had talks with officials about plans to develop Mount Kumgang as a tourist resort. He returned at the end of October with another 500 cattle and 20 Hyundai cars, and was received by North Korean leader Kim Jong Il. In November 800 South Korean tourists set off aboard a cruise ship to visit Mount Kumgang. US President Bill Clinton, who was on an official visit to South Korea at the time, saw on television the South Korean tourists setting off for Mount Kumgang and remarked that 'nothing could ever be put in that hole in the ground [at Kumchangri—see IX.2.vi] that would give the North Koreans as much advantage, as much power, as much wealth, as much happiness as more of those ships going up there full of people from here'.

vi. NORTH KOREA

CAPITAL: Pyongyang   AREA: 123,370 sq km   POPULATION: 23,500,000 ('97)
OFFICIAL LANGUAGE: Korean   POLITICAL SYSTEM: people's republic
RULING PARTY: Korean Workers' Party (KWP)
PARTY LEADER: Kim Jong Il, KWP general secretary (since Oct '97)
PRIME MINISTER: Hong Song Nam (since Sept '98)
MAIN IGO MEMBERSHIPS (NON-UN): NAM
CURRENCY: won (end-'98 £1=NKW3.66, US$1=NKW2.20)
GNP PER CAPITA: US$741 ('97 South Korean est.)

THE first elections to the Supreme People's Assembly (SPA) since 1990 were held on 26 June. It was claimed that 99.85 per cent of the electorate had voted and that each of the 687 candidates (one per constituency), including Kim Jong Il, general secretary of the Korean Workers' Party (KWP), had received 100 per cent support.

The first session of the 10th SPA on 5 September re-elected Kim Jong Il to the post of chairman of the National Defence Commission (NDC), described in amendments to the 1972 constitution approved by the SPA as the 'highest office' in the country, overseeing political, economic and military affairs. The amended constitution made the late President Kim Il Song 'State President in perpetuity', but the state presidency and Central People's Committee were abolished and the routine duties of head of state fell to Kim Yong Nam, who was elected chairman of the SPA presidium.

Other revisions to the constitution introduced a small-scale market economy by permitting private income from subsistence farming and small business and allowing companies and cooperatives to own land, machinery and equipment.

Cabinet appointments approved by the SPA included those of Hong Song Nam (Prime Minister, previously acting), Paek Nam Sun (foreign affairs) and Kim Il Chol (people's armed forces). The SPA session focused attention on government structure at a time of military ascendancy. Over 100 members of the new SPA were thought to be soldiers, 60 of them generals. The army was estimated to absorb a quarter of the country's $22,000 million GDP. On the 50th anniversary of the Korean People's Democratic Republic on 9 September Kim Jong Il reviewed a massive military parade in central Pyongyang.

The launching on 31 August of a multi-stage rocket, *Taepodong-1*, into the Pacific raised a flurry, especially in Japan, whose territory was overflown. Whether or not the rocket launching was an attempt to orbit a satellite—Pyongyang and Moscow said that it had succeeded, Washington said that it had not—the military implications were clear. The North Korean government had declared in June its intention to continue developing, testing and exporting ballistic missiles unless the USA was prepared to offer compensation: $500 million was mentioned.

In April then Foreign Minister Kim Yong Nam stated that the sealing of the last 200 spent fuel rods from Yongbyon nuclear facility had been halted until the USA delivered the promised quantity of fuel oil and restarted work on the light-water reactor project at Kumho under the 1994 'framework agreement' between the USA, Japan and North and South Korea (see AR 1997, p. 363). In protest against US 'economic sanctions', the North Koreans halted the removal of spent fuel rods from Yongbyon in July. In September they agreed at New York talks to restart the sealing of spent fuel rods. The USA promised to resume shipments of fuel oil and announced 300,000 tons of emergency food aid.

At another New York meeting in August the USA protested about a suspected new underground nuclear weapons plant under construction at Kumchangri, about 15 kilometres from Yongbyon, spotted by satellite reconnaissance. The USA also demanded an end to the transfer of North Korean missile technology to Iraq, Iran, Pakistan and Syria. Talks about the Kumchangri facility and missile technology transfer continued in September and October. The US envoy in charge of the New York talks, Charles Kartman, visited Pyongyang in mid-November, but failed to gain access to the Kumchangri facility. Pyongyang said that US demands for inspection were interference in its internal affairs; if inspection failed to show a nuclear link, the USA must pay compensation: $300 million was mentioned.

The first meetings in seven years at Panmunjom between the UN Command and North Korean army in June and July were described as part of the 'crisis management mechanism' by the UN Command. In the event of attack from the North, the US and South Korean military had developed a new strategy not limited to containment but providing for the capture of Pyongyang and destruction of Kim Jong Il's regime. President Clinton emphasized during his November visit to South Korea (see IX.2.v.) that the North must dismantle its nuclear weapons programme and 'halt efforts to develop and proliferate chemical and biological weapons and ballistic missiles'. Former Defence Secretary William Perry, appointed the new US coordinator for North Korea policy, visited Seoul, Tokyo and Beijing in December in search of new ideas.

South Korean specialists who visited the North reported that better-quality seed and more fertilizer could treble maize production. Most of the one million tons of imported grain was set aside to feed children, but defectors claimed that some was going to the army. UN organizations criticized North Korean officials for slackness in disaster relief efforts. Thousands of North Koreans were fleeing into China, or seeking food supplies there to take home across the heavily-guarded border to their starving families.

vii. MONGOLIA

CAPITAL: Ulan Bator   AREA: 1,566,500 sq km   POPULATION: 2,387,100 ('97 est.)
PRINCIPAL LANGUAGE: Halh (Khalkha) Mongolian
POLITICAL SYSTEM: republic
HEAD OF STATE: President Natsagiyn Bagabandi (since June '97)
RULING PARTIES: Democratic Alliance (of Mongolian National Democratic & Social Democratic parties) has majority in parliament
PRIME MINISTER: Janlavyn Narantsatsralt (since Dec '98)
MAIN IGO MEMBERSHIPS (non-UN): NAM
CURRENCY: tögrög (end-'98 £1=T1,508.05, US$1=T902.00)
GNP PER CAPITA: US$390 by exchange-rate calculation ('97)

MONGOLIA'S ruling Democratic Alliance (DA), beset with problems arising from the opposition's use of unparliamentary tactics and complicated by the coalition's own internal squabbling, formed two new governments in 1998. Elected for a four-year term in 1996 (see AR 1996, p. 354), the DA coalition of the Mongolian National Democratic Party (MNDP) and Mongolian Social Democratic Party (MSDP) found itself in difficulties after the triumph of Natsagiyn Bagabandi of the opposition Mongolian People's Revolutionary Party (MPRP) in the 1997 presidential election, followed by the by-election victory of new MPRP leader Nyambaryn Enhbayar in Bagabandi's constituency (see AR 1997, p. 364). The MPRP's 25 members in the 76-seat Great Hural (National Assembly) were unable to outvote the DA's 50 members; however, with help from the one sitting member of the United Heritage (conservative) Party, they disrupted government business by boycotting sessions and preventing the formation of a quorum (51 members). The MPRP won another seat from the DA in a June by-election.

Under article 29/1 of the constitution, members of the Great Hural 'may not concurrently engage in other work or occupy another post not related to their duties as defined by law'. In the light of a Constitutional Court ruling reinforcing this article, Prime Minister Mendsayhany Enhsayhan and his cabinet appointed in 1996 were not members of the Great Hural. However, in early 1998 the DA leaders decided that Great Hural members could serve concurrently in the cabinet, after amendment of the Law on the Government and the Law on the Status of Great Hural Members. MNDP president Tsahiagiyn Elbegdorj was elected leader of the DA majority group in the Great Hural, whereupon the Enhsayhan government resigned and Mr Elbegdorj was appointed Prime Minister by the Great Hural on 23 April.

The new government inherited a confrontation with Russia over the joint copper-mining enterprise at Erdenet. Mr Enhsayhan's decision not to renew the contract of the Mongolian director-general, Shagdaryn Otgonbileg, was opposed by the MPRP, of which Mr Otgonbileg was a prominent member, by the Russian government, and by President Bagabandi, who wrote to President Boris Yeltsin supporting the Russians. Mr Otgonbileg was given a compromise extension to his contract, but when it ran out he refused to give up his post, suing in court for illegal 'dismissal'. The Elbegdorj government imposed a 'special regime' on Erdenet and installed a new director-general, Dambyn Dorligjav, Mr Enhsayhan's Defence Minister. An audit at Erdenet showed that Mr Otgonbileg had illegally privatized parts of the enterprise and withheld revenue from the national budget. Mr Dorligjav's appointment was approved by the Russians at a joint shareholders' meeting.

The pretext for the MPRP boycott of the Great Hural's spring session was the Elbegdorj government's decision to merge the bankrupt state-owned Reconstruction Bank with the private Golomt Bank. The MPRP combined its boycott with efforts to stall the merger in the courts. Encouraged by some DA members the government amended its decision, then cancelled it. The MPRP returned to the Great Hural and tabled a vote of confidence which, on 24 July, the government lost, 15 DA members voting with the opposition.

The DA decided to nominate Davaadorjiyn Ganbold, MNDP vice-president and chairman of the Great Hural's economic standing committee, as the next Prime Minister. However, President Bagabandi refused to back Mr Ganbold's nomination, on the grounds that he had failed to resolve the bank merger crisis. By the end of August Mr Ganbold's nomination had been forwarded to the President and rejected by him six times. Controversy raged over whether the President had the right to overrule the coalition's nominations. According to the constitution, his powers included 'proposing to the Great Hural the candidate for Prime Minister in consultation with the majority party'. In May 1993 Natsagiyn Bagabandi himself, then the chairman (speaker), during a debate on the Law on the President, had asked the Great Hural: 'Who has the final say, the party or the President? Let us vote for the proposition that in any situation the majority party has priority.'

President Bagabandi's own prime ministerial candidate, MNDP Great Hural member Dogsomyn Ganbold (not related to Davaadorjiyn Ganbold), proved unacceptable. The DA proposed Rinchinnyamyn Amarjargal, acting Minister of External Relations and a member of the MNDP general council. President Bagabandi raised no objections to Mr Amarjargal's nomination, but when put to the Great Hural in early September it was rejected by one vote. The President then turned down two other DA candidates.

On 2 October Sanjaasürengiyn Zorig, acting Minister of Infrastructure Development, was murdered during a robbery. It was said after Mr Zorig's death that the President had just agreed to his nomination as Prime Minister. Mr Zorig had been the founder of the Mongolian democratic movement in 1989, and political activity halted for his state funeral. Next, President Bagabandi issued a list of six nominees, including Dogsomyn Ganbold again as well as Janlavyn Narantsatsralt, the mayor of Ulan Bator. The DA ignored the list and with the written support of all DA members of the Great Hural nominated Davaadorjiyn Ganbold for the seventh time. The President rejected him yet again.

Formation of the government was then further complicated by a new Constitutional Court ruling saying specifically that Great Hural members could not serve concurrently in the government. Consultations on the way ahead took place in November between the MNDP, MSDP and MPRP leaders, but ended inconclusively. Dogsomyn Ganbold was elected deputy chairman of the Great Hural, which was boycotted again by the MPRP after the autumn session's 1999 budget debate.

Finally, the DA proposed President Bagabandi's candidate, Ulan Bator mayor Mr Narantsatsralt, and the Great Hural appointed him Prime Minister on 9 December. The focus of the MPRP's boycott then turned to contention over the vacant post of mayor of the capital, and by the year's end only two new ministers (external relations and the environment) had been approved. The cost of the damage done by these months of wrangling was indicated by the acting Minister of Finance, Bat-Erdeniyn Batbayar: $70 million of debts at Erdenet, a budget deficit of $110 million, and the withdrawal of IMF support for bank restructuring.

X AUSTRALASIA AND THE PACIFIC

i. AUSTRALIA

CAPITAL: Canberra   AREA: 7,687,000 sq km   POPULATION: 19,000,000 ('97)
OFFICIAL LANGUAGE: English   POLITICAL SYSTEM: federal parliamentary democracy
HEAD OF STATE: Queen Elizabeth II
GOVERNOR-GENERAL: Sir William Deane
RULING PARTIES: Liberal-National coalition
HEAD OF GOVERNMENT: John Howard, Prime Minister (since March '96)
MAIN IGO MEMBERSHIPS (non-UN): APEC, SPC, SPF, CP, ANZUS, OECD, CWTH
CURRENCY: Australian dollar (end-'98 £1=A$2.71, US$1=A$1.63)
GNP PER CAPITA: US$20,540 by exchange-rate calculation, US$20,170 by PPP calculation ('97)

AUSTRALIA weathered the expected storm from the crises in several Asian economies. While the Australian dollar continued to exchange at record low levels and unemployment remained at 8 per cent, there was no immediate sign that the economy was moving into recession. Share prices remained buoyant although the current account balance caused some concern, partly reflecting low international prices for primary commodities. Privatization continued, with the national government seeking to float the remainder of the telecommunications giant Telstra but meeting Senate resistance (see AR 1997, p. 367). The government also sought to shore up the declining private health funds with a large tax bonus to those taking out private insurance.

The ruling Liberal-National coalition retained power at the general election on 3 October. The Australian Labor Party (ALP) was narrowly elected in Queensland on 13 June and in Tasmania on 29 August. The newly-formed One Nation Party did very well in the Queensland election but not so well in October and was plagued, as in 1997, by very volatile support and internal dissension (see AR 1997, p. 367). Major political issues during the year included Aboriginal land rights, tax reform and industrial relations. International affairs were mainly dominated by the Asian crises and especially by the disorder in Indonesia. The republican issue was important at the start of the year but its resolution was relegated to 1999 and debate died down quickly after the holding of a constitutional convention.

The constitutional convention met in Canberra in the first week of February and attracted more attention than had seemed likely when it was elected by less than half the voters (see AR 1997, p. 369). It was fully televised and included many prominent and well-known Australians from a much wider social range than the national parliament. It soon emerged that republicans had a substantial majority but that they were divided on the issue of how a new head of state would be elected. The formal political parties took part only as representatives of the national and state parliaments, and the divisions which developed crossed conventional partisan lines. The model favoured by the Australian Republican Movement (ARM) eventually succeeded after amendment, requiring that the head of state should be endorsed by a parliamentary two-thirds majority on the basis of a single nomination made by the Prime Minister after consultations. The supporters of a popularly-elected President were often quite hostile to this proposal and to the ARM, while the monarchists simply argued that these divisions proved that no change was necessary. The various republican cases were cogently argued, and in the end Prime Minister John Howard, although a monarchist, promised that the amended ARM proposal would be put to a referendum late in 1999. Further debate centred around a proposed change to the constitutional preamble, which was drawn up in the reign of Queen Victoria and was regarded by many as inappropriate. Popular interest in the issue declined rapidly after the convention, but most participants agreed that it had been a useful exercise despite much initial scepticism.

The Liberal Party easily retained power in the Australian Capital Territory elections on 21 February. A new system of proportional representation caused large changes in the ALP and a completely new leadership was elected in response to the low Labor vote in what was normally the Labor stronghold of Canberra. In Queensland on 13 June the state elections shocked the major parties with the rapid increase in One Nation support, after they had slumped in the opinion polls earlier in the year. The final result was: ALP 44 seats (38.9 per cent of the vote), National 23 seats (15.2 per cent), One Nation 11 seats (22.7 per cent), Liberal 9 seats (16.1 per cent). Two independents were also elected who agreed to give general support to the Labor government formed by Peter Beattie.

The One Nation support in Queensland was far larger than most outside that party had expected. Its seats were largely gained on National and Liberal preferences, as those parties miscalculated the One Nation vote and tried to entice it back to themselves. However, Labor also lost seats to the new party. One Nation's support came mainly from coastal retirement areas, provincial and rural areas and in some peripheral areas around Brisbane, though not in the city itself. This was widely interpreted as showing disaffection with declining rural living standards and resentment at what were seen as privileges for Asian and Aboriginal Australians. Sections of the gun lobby also supported One Nation, although there were at least three other minor parties with similar programmes. One Nation was awarded election expenses of over A$2 million, enough to set up its organization for the future but also a bone of contention for many of its candidates expecting reimbursement of their expenses. One new parliamentarian resigned after a suicide attempt, and the consequent by-election saw a large drop in the One Nation vote.

The Liberal-National coalition went into the October general election determined to gain a mandate for its taxation proposals, despite its defeat on similar plans in 1993 (see AR 1993, p. 374). Despite its massive defeat in 1996 (see AR 1996, p. 358), the opposition ALP became increasingly confident of victory during the campaign. However, although gaining 18 seats and securing a higher vote than the government, it remained in opposition. The Senate remained hostile to the government by the narrowest majority, which consisted of two independents and the Australian Democrats. New senators would not take their seats until June 1999, but the election outcome did not improve the government's position. One Nation recorded nearly one million votes, to become the third largest party in terms of popular support, but it won only one Senate seat and its leader, Pauline Hanson, was defeated for the House of Representatives.

Voting for the major parties was: Labor 40 per cent, Liberal 34.1 per cent, National 5.6 per cent, One Nation 8.4 per cent, Democrats 5.1 per cent. The final strengths in the House of Representatives were: Liberal 64 (a loss of 11), National 16 (a loss of three), Labor 67 (a gain of 18). The five independents, who had emerged mainly through defections from the Liberal Party, were reduced to one. The government's comfortable majority was interpreted by the Prime Minister Howard as a mandate to introduce the goods and services tax (GST), which he had previously promised 'never' to introduce following the 1993 debacle. This was questioned not only by the ALP but also by the Democrats, who were opposed to the imposition of GST on food and books and began long negotiations with the government accordingly.

The other major outcome of the election was the defeat of Ms Hanson in Queensland and of Graeme Campbell in Western Australia, removing two of the most outspoken opponents of immigration and multiculturalism. The former leader of the Australian Democrats, Cheryl Kernot (see AR 1997, p. 370), was elected for the ALP by an extremely narrow margin. Post-election analysis was confused by the very large vote gained by One Nation for little return, but it was generally agreed that the main party to suffer from this was the National Party. Victory muted earlier criticisms of the leadership of Mr Howard and of National Party leader Tim Fischer. Labor leader Kim Beazley remained secure, but his deputy, Gareth Evans, resigned and was replaced by former trade union leader Simon Crean. Heather Hill was returned from Queensland as the only One Nation senator, but her status was being challenged at the end of the year on the grounds that she was ineligible under the constitution because she had not renounced her United Kingdom citizenship upon becoming an Australian.

The major issues from the national government's viewpoint were resolution of the native title question, industrial relations, taxation and privatization. On all of these the government could not guarantee a Senate majority and was forced to negotiate. The Native Title Amendment Bill, based on Mr Howard's ten-point plan (see AR 1997, p. 368), was eventually passed through all stages in July after threats that an election would be fought on the issue, which most wanted to avoid for fear of encouraging One Nation. Relations between the government and Aboriginal leaders continued to be cool, but there were signs of improvement after the October election victory. A minister was appointed to assist in the work of the Council for Reconciliation, though his work was not helped by the cancellation of Aboriginal scholarship schemes by one of his colleagues in December.

The government also tackled the issue of waterfront reform by attacking the Maritime Union of Australia in an attempt to break its control of the labour force, an issue recurring in Australian history for at least a century. Amid charges of collusion and conspiracy, the second-largest stevedoring company trained workers in Dubai and then introduced them to the wharves under the protection of security guards and dogs, provoking a national maritime dispute. The dogs and uniformed guards were withdrawn as they created a less than conciliatory image, but the dispute lingered on with the official support of the trade union movement, while the National Farmers' Federation actively supported the employers. After court proceedings against the dismissal of the entire workforce, an agreement was finally accepted on 15 June. The Minister for Workplace Relations, Peter Reith, damaged his reputation by his active endorsement of the employers. He also failed to secure Senate approval of a new workplace relations bill which would have withdrawn the wrongful dismissal protection for employees legislated for by the previous ALP government. Public opinion was divided, but the union case was well presented and many were anxious about the principle of sacking workers for belonging to a specific union. This was, however, the only major victory for the unions. Union membership continued to decline, a tendency assisted by legislation which favoured contracts between employees and employers without union participation.

Voters in the Northern Territory surprised the territory government and the national coalition by rejecting an offer of statehood in a referendum held jointly with the federal election. This, together with the promise of extending the railway from Alice Springs to Darwin, had been a perennial election inducement for Northern Territory voters, who compounded their decision by voting in an ALP member of parliament as well. Another perennial, the proposed high-speed Sydney-Canberra railway, moved forward in August when a tender favouring a French-type system was approved by the territory government over the Maglev system originating in Germany.

In Tasmania on 29 August the Liberal government was defeated by the ALP under Jim Bacon. The Tasmanian economy was the weakest in Australia and Labor later won all five lower house seats in the national election. The two major parties colluded to reduce the size of the House of Assembly in a successful bid to cut Green representation, on which they had both uncertainly relied in the past. The Green leader, Christine Milne, was consequently defeated and only one Green member remained.

Western Australia legislated on abortion in May to correct an anomaly which threatened prosecutions against two Perth doctors, the first such case in 30 years. This issue divided all the parties, activated right-to-life demonstrations and produced a defensive reaction from the medical profession anxious to ascertain its legal position. Ultimately, abortion was removed from the Criminal Code and regulated by specific amendments to the Health Act.

Two major crises were produced by a breakdown in water quality control in Sydney and an accident at a natural gas plant which stopped nearly all heating for Melbourne. Both were the subject of official inquiries revealing practices which needed improvement.

Among those who died during the year was the veteran Catholic activist Bob Santamaria, aged 82, who had campaigned influentially on social, political and moral issues since the 1930s. The annual Sydney-Hobart yacht race between Christmas and New Year was marred by very heavy seas which caused the deaths of six participants.

ii. PAPUA NEW GUINEA

CAPITAL: Port Moresby   AREA: 463,000 sq km   POPULATION: 5,000,000 ('97)
OFFICIAL LANGUAGES: Pidgin, Motu, English   POLITICAL SYSTEM: parliamentary democracy
HEAD OF STATE: Queen Elizabeth II
GOVERNOR-GENERAL: Sailas Atopare
RULING PARTIES: PNG First heads coalition
HEAD OF GOVERNMENT: Bill Skate (PNC), Prime Minister (since July '97)
MAIN IGO MEMBERSHIPS (non-UN): APEC, CP, SPC, SPF, ACP, CWTH, NAM
CURRENCY: kina (end-'98 £1=K3.41, US$1=K2.05)
GNP PER CAPITA: US$940 by exchange-rate calculation, US$2,390 by PPP calculation ('97)

IN 1998 Papua New Guinea's chaotic political party system touched new levels of instability. In April Prime Minister Bill Skate, in an attempt to consolidate his hold on office, announced the merger of his own People's National Congress and a number of smaller groupings into a new PNG First Party. Two months later, however, Mr Skate's key coalition partner, Pangu Pati leader Chris Haiveta, left the government after a bitter personal feud with the Prime Minister. Pangu Pati, the country's longest-established party, itself then split, with a number of ministers unwilling to follow their leader into opposition. In October, moroever, the People's Progress Party also left the coalition, and the following month its leader, Michael Nali, began to mobilize an opposition grouping to pursue a parliamentary no-confidence motion. During the year this limping administration was required to deal with major issues on a number of separate fronts.

In April a 'permanent' peace agreement was signed between the central government and the Bougainville Revolutionary Army (BRA). The ceremony took place in Arawa on Bougainville in the presence of the

Foreign Ministers of Australia, New Zealand and PNG's smaller Pacific neighbours. The accord built on the Christchurch (New Zealand) talks of the previous October (see AR 1997, p. 372) and was based on the creation of a new level of autonomous government for the province. Ominously (and characteristically), however, the elusive BRA military leader, Francis Ona, was absent from the Arawa ceremony and announced a few days later that his faction would fight on. But it was unclear whether he any longer commanded the men and resources to pursue his campaign for total independence.

Meanwhile, the Bougainville crisis continued to take its corrosive toll on the fabric of public life. In February a second 'Sandline inquiry' began into the government's use of that company's mercenaries against the BRA. This reported in September and recommended that former Defence Minister Benias Sabumei should be charged in relation to a $500,000 'consultancy fee' paid to him by Sandline. It also found that former Deputy Prime Minister Chris Haiveta had received a corrupt payment of $150,000 on the eve of the signing of the Sandline contract. Former Prime Minister Sir Julius Chan, who had been forced to resign over the mercenary issue, was exonerated by the inquiry. Meanwhile, Brigadier-General Jerry Singherok, the defence force commander dismissed by Sir Julius when he threatened to act against the government over the Sandline contract, was reinstated by Mr Skate in October—only to be charged the following month with sedition for his actions the previous year (see AR 1997, p. 371).

The sequence of natural disasters which had plagued PNG in recent years dealt its worst single blow on 17 July. A ten-metre-high tidal wave, generated by an off-shore earthquake, swept two kilometres inland in the Aitape district of the north coast, destroying all in its path and leaving at least 2,000 dead. Only a massive Pacific regional response prevented the disaster taking a much higher toll through subsequent famine and disease.

These political and natural misfortunes were accompanied by what Treasury Minister Iairo Lasaro described as 'the worst financial crisis since independence'. Although not in the front line of the disaster which overtook the economies of the 'Asian Tigers' to the west, PNG inevitably suffered from its contingent effects. Additionally, foreign investment continued to be deterred by political instability, frequent public disorder and the country's apparently permanent violent crime wave. Attempts to deal with the economic crisis through IMF– and World Bank-directed fiscal stringency were only partly successful. The government appeared to back down when threatened with industrial action over cuts in the swollen public sector in November.

2. NEW ZEALAND—PACIFIC ISLAND STATES

i. NEW ZEALAND

CAPITAL: Wellington   AREA: 270,000 sq km   POPULATION: 4,000,000 ('97)
OFFICIAL LANGUAGE: English   POLITICAL SYSTEM: parliamentary democracy
HEAD OF STATE: Queen Elizabeth II
GOVERNOR-GENERAL: Sir Michael Hardie Boys
RULING PARTY: National Party (NP)
HEAD OF GOVERNMENT: Jenny Shipley, Prime Minister (since Dec '97)
MAIN IGO MEMBERSHIPS (non-UN): ANZUS (suspended), APEC, SPC, SPF, CP, OECD, CWTH
CURRENCY: New Zealand dollar (end-'98 £1=NZ$3.15, US$1=NZ$1.89)
GNP PER CAPITA: US$16,480 by exchange-rate calculation, US$16,600 by PPP calculation ('97)

THE coalition government of Jenny Shipley, New Zealand's first woman Prime Minister (see AR 1997, p. 373), collapsed in August following a walk-out from a cabinet meeting by Deputy Prime Minister Winston Peters and the other New Zealand First (NZF) ministers. While it was unclear whether Mr Peters had been seeking to end the coalition with the National Party (NP), which had been formed following the 1996 election, Ms Shipley took the opportunity to end an arrangement which had been unpopular with the electorate since its formation.

The departure from parliament of Ms Shipley's predecessor, Jim Bolger, to become New Zealand's ambassador to the United States contributed to the coalition's demise. A by-election held in May saw Mr Bolger's majority of 10,223 votes fall to only 966, as the NP had difficulty retaining what had been one of its safest seats. The share of the vote won by its then coalition partner, NZF, dropped even more dramatically, its candidate being unable to win even 3 per cent of the votes. While the coalition government's loss of support had been a feature of nationwide opinion polls for some time, the effect of their partnership on the fortunes of both parties was highlighted in the by-election results.

The slump in the NP's standing among what were traditionally its most loyal supporters demonstrated that any improvement in its position following the change of leadership in December 1997 had ended. Pressures within the NP to distance itself from its coalition partner were paralleled by intra-party conflict within NZF, which began to disintegrate. Its deputy leader, Tau Henare, was removed from the position in mid-July. Two weeks later an NZF MP, Neil Kirton, who had been dismissed from his ministerial post by Winston Peters in August 1997, left the party, attacking Mr Peters for his 'deceits and betrayals'. On 9 August Mr Peters identified government plans to sell the public shareholding in Wellington's airport as a fundamental issue for the party, given NZF's history of opposition to state asset sales. Following the NZF walkout from the cabinet meeting three days later, during a discussion of options in connection with the sale proposal, the remaining NP ministers approved the airport sale. Two days later Ms Shipley sacked

Mr Peters as Deputy Prime Minister and as Treasurer, effectively ending the coalition with NZF. She invited the remaining NZF ministers to keep their positions in exchange for their support and most accepted the offer. Over the next few days the NZF party split, eight MPs (including Winston Peters) remaining with the party and the other eight choosing to leave. Subsequently five of the defecting MPs announced the formation of a new party, Mauri Pacific, while the others remained in parliament as independents.

While the NP-NZF relationship was fragmenting, relations between the opposition Labour and Alliance parties were improving. Labour leader Helen Clark was invited to address the Alliance's annual conference, and the two parties announced their readiness to form a coalition government after the next election. This was in marked contrast to the 1996 election, the first to be held under a new electoral system based on proportional representation, when the Alliance and Labour had been unable to enter into a pre-election agreement (see AR 1996, pp. 363–5).

While the shattering of the coalition was fascinating for the media, and appeared to be popular with the public, it had only a short-term effect on the government's standing. The decision by Ms Shipley to remain in office at the head of a minority NP government, dependent for support from a mix of ex-NZF MPs and other representatives on an issue-by-issue basis, placed her government in a weak position. Opinion polls showing the NP lagging behind Labour and the Alliance made the option of an early election unappealing, however. The government won a confidence vote in September by a narrow margin (62–58), but subsequently proved unable to proceed with several items of legislation. Suggestions of a 'grand coalition' between the NP and Labour were rejected by Ms Clark.

The economic and social environment also deteriorated during 1998. In October a demonstration converged on parliament, drawing attention to issues of jobs, housing, health services, education and poverty. At the same time, New Zealand began to suffer from the downturn in Asian economies, with revised forecasts predicting a renewed budget deficit after several years of surpluses and debt repayment. The New Zealand dollar fell to its lowest point in more than five years and a growing current-account deficit led to a downgrading of the country's credit rating.

There were some positive, and somewhat historic, developments as well. In February the new Museum of New Zealand was opened in Wellington, providing a new facility to house the nation's artefacts and treasures. Known also by its Maori name, Te Papa ('Our Place'), the museum was soon facing objections and protest (not all peaceful) over claims that some of the artwork being exhibited was obscene, blasphemous and offensive to Christian visitors. In September parliament enacted the Ngai Tahu Claims Settlement Act, bringing about what was expected to be a final resolution of land claims and grievances with the South Island's largest Maori tribe.

The government was also able to point towards some international successes, if the electorate was interested. In January New Zealand played an important role in mediating an end to the long-running civil war in the Papua New Guinea island of Bougainville (see X.1.ii). Subsequently, Foreign Affairs Minister Don McKinnon emerged as a leading candidate for the position of secretary-general of the Commonwealth. The government was also giving its support to the effort of Labour MP and former Prime Minister Mike Moore to become head of the World Trade Organization (WTO). New Zealand was selected to host the APEC summit meeting in 1999, while at the 1998 meeting in Malaysia Ms Shipley, referring to criticism of Malaysia's human rights record by US Vice-President Al Gore, distanced herself from what she called 'megaphone diplomacy' when she held her own talks with Prime Minister Mahathir Mohamad (see IX.1.ii; XI.6.iii).

The minority government's problems with the electorate were complicated by difficult decisions which it faced with respect to defence spending. At a time of economic slowdown, the government faced the need for a decision on the purchase of a third frigate from Australia, as well as requests for spending for the air force and the army. None of these items was popular with a public concerned about hospital waiting lists. Further signs of discontent were to be found in a petition calling for a reduction in the size of parliament, from the present 120 members down to 99. Problems of coalition coherence and stability contributed further to the loss of enthusiasm for the new electoral system. There were calls at the NP's own conference for a referendum to be held in 1999 on its replacement.

In December the government decided against purchasing a further frigate, but its decision to upgrade the capacity of the air force significantly by leasing 28 F-16s from the United States brought about the resignation from parliament of one of the independent MPs on whom it had been relying for support, reducing the government's advantage over the opposition to only a single vote.

ii. PACIFIC ISLAND STATES

Federated States of Micronesia
CAPITAL: Palikir (Pohnpei)   AREA: 701 sq km   POPULATION: 118,000 ('97)
OFFICIAL LANGUAGES: English
POLITICAL SYSTEM: republic
HEAD OF STATE & GOVERNMENT: President Jacob Nena (since May '97)
MAIN IGO MEMBERSHIPS (non-UN): SPC, SPF
CURRENCY: US dollar
GNP PER CAPITA: US$1,980 by exchange-rate calculation ('97)

Tuvalu

CAPITAL: Fongafle   AREA: 26 sq km   POPULATION: 9,750 ('97)
OFFICIAL LANGUAGE: English   POLITICAL SYSTEM: constitutional monarchy
HEAD OF STATE: Queen Elizabeth II
GOVERNOR-GENERAL: Tomasi Puapua
HEAD OF GOVERNMENT: Bikenibeu Paeniu, Prime Minister (since Dec '96)
MAIN IGO MEMBERSHIPS: SPC, SPF, ACP
CURRENCY: Australian dollar (end-'98 £1=A$2.71, US$1=A$1.63)
GNP PER CAPITA: n/a

Samoa

CAPITAL: Apia   AREA: 2,842 sq km   POPULATION: 173,000 ('97)
OFFICIAL LANGUAGES: English & Samoan   POLITICAL SYSTEM: constitutional monarchy
HEAD OF STATE: Susuga Malietoa Tanumafili II (since Jan '62)
RULING PARTY: Human Rights Protection Party
HEAD OF GOVERNMENT: Tuilaepa Sailele Malielegaoi, Prime Minister (since Nov '98)
MAIN IGO MEMBERSHIPS (non-UN): SPC, SPF, ACP, CWTH
CURRENCY: tala (end-'98 £1=T5.02, US$1=T3.02)
GNP PER CAPITA: US$1,150 by exchange-rate calculation ('97)

Fiji

CAPITAL: Suva   AREA: 18,375 sq km   POPULATION: 815,000 ('97)
OFFICIAL LANGUAGES: Fijian, Hindi & English
POLITICAL SYSTEM: republic
HEAD OF STATE: President Ratu Sir Kamisese Mara (since Nov '93)
RULING PARTY: Fijian Political Party (SVT)
HEAD OF GOVERNMENT: Maj.-Gen. Sitiveni Rabuka (SVT), Prime Minister (since May '92)
MAIN IGO MEMBERSHIPS (non-UN): SPC, SPF, CP, ACP, CWTH
CURRENCY: Fiji dollar (end-'98 £1=F$3.29, US$1=F$1.98)
GNP PER CAPITA: US$2,470 by exchange-rate calculation, US$4,040 by PPP calculation ('97)

Tonga

CAPITAL: Nuku'alofa   AREA: 750 sq km   POPULATION: 99,000 ('97)
OFFICIAL LANGUAGES: Tongan & English   POLITICAL SYSTEM: monarchy
HEAD OF STATE: King Taufa'ahua Tupou IV (since Dec '65)
HEAD OF GOVERNMENT: Baron Vaea, Prime Minister (since Aug '91)
MAIN IGO MEMBERSHIPS: SPC, SPF, ACP, CWTH
CURRENCY: pa'anga (end-'98 £1=T$2.71, US$1=T$1.63)
GNP PER CAPITA: US$1,830 by exchange-rate calculation ('97)

Kiribati

CAPITAL: Tarawa   AREA: 1,000 sq km   POPULATION: 83,000 ('97)
OFFICIAL LANGUAGES: English & Kiribati   POLITICAL SYSTEM: republic
HEAD OF STATE & GOVERNMENT: President Teburoro Tito (since Sept '94)
RULING PARTY: Christian Democratic Unity Party (CDUP)
MAIN IGO MEMBERSHIPS: SPC, SPF, ACP, CWTH
CURRENCY: Australian dollar (end-'98 £1=A$2.71, US$1=A$1.63)
GNP PER CAPITA: US$910 by exchange-rate calculation ('97)

Nauru

CAPITAL: Domaneab   AREA: 21.4 sq km   POPULATION: 11,000 ('97)
OFFICIAL LANGUAGES: Nauruan & English   POLITICAL SYSTEM: republic
HEAD OF STATE & GOVERNMENT: President Bernard Dowiyogo (since June '98)
MAIN IGO MEMBERSHIPS: PC, SPF
CURRENCY: Australian dollar (end-'98 £1=A$2.71, US$1=A$1.63)
GNP PER CAPITA: n/a

Vanuatu

CAPITAL: Port Vila   AREA: 12,000 sq km   POPULATION: 177,000 ('97)
OFFICIAL LANGUAGES: English, French & Bislama
POLITICAL SYSTEM: republic
HEAD OF STATE: President Jean-Marie Leye Lenelgau (since March '94)
RULING PARTIES: Vanuaaku Pati (VP) & Union of Moderate Parties (UMP)
HEAD OF GOVERNMENT: Donald Kalpokas (UMP), Prime Minister (since March '98)
MAIN IGO MEMBERSHIPS (non-UN): SPC, SPF, ACP, CWTH, Francophonie
CURRENCY: vatu (end-'98 £1=VT217.12, US$1=VT130.50)
GNP PER CAPITA: US$1,310 by exchange-rate calculation, US$3,020 by PPP calculation ('97)

Marshall Islands

CAPITAL: Dalap-Uliga-Darrit   AREA: 200 sq km   POPULATION: 58,000 ('97)
OFFICIAL LANGUAGES: English & Marshallese
POLITICAL SYSTEM: republic
HEAD OF STATE & GOVERNMENT: President Imata Kabua (since Jan '97)
MAIN IGO MEMBERSHIPS (non-UN): PC, SPF
CURRENCY: US dollar
GNP PER CAPITA: US$1,770 by exchange-rate calculation ('97)

Solomon Islands

CAPITAL: Honiara   AREA: 28,000 sq km   POPULATION: 401,000 ('97)
OFFICIAL LANGUAGE: English   POLITICAL SYSTEM: parliamentary democracy
HEAD OF STATE: Queen Elizabeth II
GOVERNOR-GENERAL: Sir Moses Puibangara Pitakaka
RULING PARTY: Liberal Party (LP) heads Alliance for Change coalition
HEAD OF GOVERNMENT: Bartholomew Ulufa'alu (LP), Prime Minister (since Aug '97)
MAIN IGO MEMBERSHIPS (non-UN): SPC, SPF, ACP, CWTH
CURRENCY: Solomon Islands dollar (end-'98 £1=SI$7.92, S$1=SI$4.76)
GNP PER CAPITA: US$900 by exchange-rate calculation, US$2,350 by PPP calculation ('97)

THE annual South Pacific Forum meeting was held in August in Pohnpei, capital of the FEDERATED STATES OF MICRONESIA. Issues considered by the 16-member Forum included nuclear testing by India and Pakistan, economic reform, trade, the Asian economic crisis, the peace process on Bougainville, climate change and the establishment of a South Pacific whale sanctuary (see also XI.6.iii). Environmental issues affecting the Pacific Islands were addressed in other ways as well. The International Atomic Energy Agency (IAEA) issued a report on French nuclear testing in the Pacific on 31 May, claiming that the tests (carried out from 1966–96) posed no health risk for the inhabitants of the atolls of Mururoa and Fangataufa in FRENCH POLYNESIA. The report also stated that there were no risks to the atolls' flora or fauna.

In TUVALU, Bikenibeu Paeniu won a third term as Prime Minister following elections in March. Mr Paeniu won 10 of the 12 votes cast in the country's parliament, to take office by the largest margin in the country's brief history.

Presidential elections were held in KIRIBATI on 27 November, following the election of a new parliament in October. President Teburoro Tito was re-elected with more than half of the popular vote.

The Prime Minister of SAMOA, Tofilau Eti Alesana, resigned in November because of ill-health. He had first been elected to the position in July 1988 and was co-founder of the country's first political party, the Human Rights Protection Party. He was succeeded by the Deputy Prime Minister and former Minister of Finance, Tuilaepa Sailele Malielegaoi.

An arson attack on FIJI's main power station (supplying 90 per cent of the country's power) occurred as a result of long-standing land grievances on the part of indigenous Fijian landowners seeking compensation for the loss of land taken for the hydroelectric project. The attack and resulting blockade of the access road brought Prime Minister Sitiveni Rabuka back from an overseas trip to deal with the issue. Fiji was also suffering from a severe drought, which at one stage led children to leave school to search for food. The drought affected more than 200,000 people, more than a quarter of the population, who were being assisted by government-distributed food rations. A new constitution went into effect on 27 July (see AR 1997, p. 379), 11 years to the day after the previous constitution had been promulgated by the military government which had taken power following the Pacific's first military coup in 1987.

In TONGA, the King's son, Crown Prince Tupuoto'a, resigned as Minister of Foreign Affairs and Defence, announcing his desire to withdraw from public life. The King appointed his youngest son, Prince Lavaka-Ata-'Ulukalala, as replacement in October, a week after his return to Tonga from Australia, where he had added a master's degree in international relations to another in strategic studies. Shortly afterwards Tonga switched diplomatic allegiances to Beijing, closing Taiwan's diplomatic mission and abrogating all agreements signed between Tonga and Taiwan (see also IX.2.iii).

Members of the royal family of TONGA were involved in other issues as well. In March Tonga's Supreme Court acquitted pro-democracy member of parliament 'Akilisi Pohiva of charges of criminal libel, arising out of a 1994 article in the *Wall Street Journal* in which he was quoted as attacking the King as 'dictatorial'. A dispute arose between Prince Tupuoto'a and his sister, Princess Pilolevu Tuita, over control of Tongasat, a company which received substantial royalties for use of Tonga's rights to equatorial satellite positions.

Tonga was also involved in an unusual competition with Kiribati, Fiji and New Zealand's Chatham Islands to establish where each new day began, in a bid to secure rights to the claim of being the first country to usher in the new millennium. Attempts to gain that privilege, and any accompanying economic and tourist advantages, led to attempted readjustments to the international dateline and the timing of daylight savings. Tonga awarded rights to organize its millennium celebrations to a Saudi businessman, Hussein Khashoggi. Samoa was also developing plans for a celebration at the village of Falealupo, at the western end of Samoa, where each day ended.

The Prime Minister of the New Zealand dependency of the COOK ISLANDS, Sir Geoffrey Henry, made his first official visit to China, following the establishment of diplomatic relations with the mainland government in 1997.

NAURU gained the right to host the world weightlifting championships in the year 2001, following approval of its bid by the International Weightlifting Federation. The Nauru government, which defeated applications from Germany and Poland, could have been helped by the success of Nauru's Marcus Stephen in winning three gold medals at the Commonwealth Games in Kuala Lumpur. President Kinza Clodumar announced that Nauru intended to apply for UN membership in an effort to increase its international influence, as well as full membership of the Commonwealth (in which it was an associate member).

Voters in the French dependency of NEW CALEDONIA took part in a referendum on 8 November on proposals for autonomy, leading to a further vote on independence in 15–20 years. The voter turnout was substantial (74 per cent) and the returns showed a solid majority (72 per cent) in favour. The referendum followed the Noumea accords, signed by both pro- and anti-independence parties in May 1997 and approved by the French parliament in July. The agreement was based on the 1988 Matignon agreement, which had ended violence in the territory.

In VANUATU, the coalition government led by Prime Minister Donald Kalpokas changed its composition in October, dropping the National United Party of founding Prime Minister Walter Lini from the government. The coalition was formed following elections on 6 March, following which Mr Kalpokas was elected Prime Minister on 30 March.

In the SOLOMON ISLANDS, a major cabinet reshuffle by Prime Minister Bartholomew Ulufa'alu in July and his abrupt dismissal of a minister in early August caused sufficient defections from the ruling coalition to endanger his parliamentary majority. On 18 September, however, the government survived a no-confidence vote, which was tied at 24–24 and therefore deemed to have been lost under parliamentary rules.

Similarly in the MARSHALL ISLANDS, the government of President Imata Kabua faced a no-confidence motion on 3 September, following the dropping of several ministers in a reshuffle the previous month. He survived by walking out of the legislature with his supporters, leaving the opposition without a quorum.

XI INTERNATIONAL ORGANIZATIONS
1. UNITED NATIONS AND ITS AGENCIES

DATE OF FOUNDATION: 1945   HEADQUARTERS: New York, USA
OBJECTIVES: To promote international peace, security and cooperation on the basis of the equality of member-states, the right of self-determination of peoples and respect for human rights
MEMBERSHIP (END-'98): 185 sovereign states; those not in membership of the UN itself at end-1997 were the Holy See (Vatican), Kiribati, Nauru, Switzerland, Taiwan (Republic of China), Tonga and Tuvalu, although all except Taiwan were members of one or more UN specialized agency
SECRETARY-GENERAL: Kofi Annan (Ghana)

THIS was an eventful year for the UN. The Security Council lifted three sanctions decisions, and imposed three new ones; created two new peace-keeping forces; and condemned terrorist attacks against US embassies in Kenya and Tanzania, as well as the killing of Iranian diplomats in Afghanistan. The General Assembly adopted a new opening format; the second committee held a number of expert seminars; and the third committee conducted dialogues with the High Commissioners for Refugees and Human Rights. The UN Secretary-General, Kofi Annan, played an important role in helping to avert two air-strikes against Iraq and bore with dignity a harrowing trip to Rwanda. The organization mourned staff lost in air crashes in Guatemala, in Angola (including the Secretary-General's special representative) and in Canada, as well as personnel killed in Afghanistan, Angola, Sudan and Tajikistan. A statute for an International Criminal Court was adopted. Finally, the UN web page on the Internet became available in all the official languages.

53RD GENERAL ASSEMBLY. In an attempt to rationalize the work of the Assembly and to allow organizational and logistical issues to be resolved more easily, the 53rd session was convened on Wednesday 9 September instead of the third Tuesday of the month. The general debate was reduced from three to two weeks, making it more compact and allowing for more time for consultations among the visiting statesmen. The committees were given firm adjournment dates and the first part of the Assembly was due to recess on 11 December (but had to be extended for one week to allow the fifth committee to finish its work). A special meeting of the Assembly was held on 17–18 September to discuss 'the social and economic impact of globalization and interdependence and their policy implications'.

On 9 September the General Assembly by acclamation elected Didier Opertti, Foreign Minister of Uruguay, as its president. On 8 October the Assembly elected Argentina, Malaysia, Namibia, Canada and the Netherlands as non-permanent members for a two-year period beginning on 1 January 1999. The other five non-permanent members, serving until 31 December 1999, were Bahrain, Brazil, Gabon, Gambia and Slovenia.

A total of 180 speakers addressed the Assembly, including 26 heads of state, one vice-president, one crown prince, 15 prime ministers, 14 deputy prime ministers and ministers for foreign affairs, 105 foreign ministers and six other ministers. A representative of Palestine, with it unique observer status granted by the resumed 52nd Assembly, spoke for the first time in the general debate.

UK Prime Minister Tony Blair emphasized in his speech to the Assembly that the founding values of the UN remained valid today but that new applications were required. The reform of the UN must not be allowed to falter. The authority of the Security Council needed to be strengthened with new permanent seats for the developing world as well as Germany and Japan. Clear principles were needed to demonstrate the collective will in keeping the peace: prevention was better than cure; peace-keepers should be given a clear and achievable task; the UN must be able to act and respond quickly and peace-keeping must be accompanied by peace building. Mr Blair announced that within six months Britain intended to sign an agreement with the UN so that it would have rapid use of British military resources when they were needed—the first such agreement by a permanent member of the Security Council.

50TH ANNIVERSARIES. The General Assembly on 6 October adopted a declaration at a special commemorative meeting marking the 50th anniversary of UN peace-keeping. On 2 December, in a resolution adopted on the 50th anniversary of the Convention on the Prevention and Punishment of the Crime of Genocide, the Assembly called upon all states to seek full implementation of the convention provisions. On 9–10 December it celebrated the 50th anniversary of the adoption of the Universal Declaration of Human Rights.

20TH SPECIAL SESSION ON DRUG PROBLEM. The 20th special session of the General Assembly, on 'countering the world drug problem together', met in New York on 8–10 June. The session concentrated on six crucial areas: demand reduction, elimination of illicit crops and alternative development, money-laundering, amphetamine-type stimulants, judicial cooperation and precursor chemicals. It adopted without vote a political declaration, a declaration on the guiding principles of drug demand reduction and a resolution on measures to enhance international cooperation to counter the world drug problem

10TH EMERGENCY SESSION. At its resumed 10th emergency session on 17 March the Assembly again condemned Israel's failure to comply with previous UN resolutions, including the call for an end to the settlement policy at Jabel Abu Ghneim (Har Homa), south of occupied East Jerusalem and of all other settlement activity in the occupied territories. The voting was 120 in favour, three against (Federated States of

Micronesia, Israel and the USA) and five abstentions (Australia, Bulgaria, Marshall Islands, Romania and Swaziland).

THE REFORM PROCESS. Mr Annan formally appointed Louise Fréchette of Canada to the newly-created post of Deputy Secretary-General at the end of February. The secretariat claimed that those reforms within the authority of the Secretary-General—managerial, structural, coordinational and operational—were already in place, particularly the changes to senior management. It said that they had profoundly altered the culture of the UN system, in that everybody had become part of the same team—although some problems of rivalry and duplication remained.

On the other hand, by year's end the General Assembly had acted on only one of the five important reforms that Mr Annan had addressed to member states (see AR 1997, pp. 381–2). It decided in December to designate its 55th session in 2000 as the 'Millennium Assembly of the UN' and that it should include as an intregal part a 'Millennium Summit'. It was not able to reach decisions on specific time-limits for new mandates, results-based budgeting, the 'revolving credit fund' and the development account.

Nor was there any visible movement from words to deeds in reform of the Security Council. After 65 meetings of the working group during the 52nd Assembly, it was unable to agree any resolution on any substantive issue. The 53rd Assembly, however, took a major decision when it decided that it would not adopt any resolution or decision without the affirmative votes of at least two-thirds of the 185 member countries. On the basis that 124 votes would therefore be needed for any change, negotiations would continue in 1999 in the open-ended working group.

FINANCE. Joseph Connor, under-secretary-general for management, informed the 5th committee that for the first time in four years the UN was borrowing less from peace-keeping funds to cover the regular budget activities and that cash balances were higher.

In 1998 assessments for the regular budget, peace-keeping and the two *ad hoc* criminal tribunals were $2,000 million. The financial review at the end of 1998, based on an analysis of cash, unpaid assessments and amounts owed to members for troops and contingent owned equipment, revealed that total combined cash in 1998 was $736 million compared with $669 million in 1997; that unpaid assessments were $2,031 million compared with $2,062 million in 1997; and that the amount owed to member states which had undertaken peace-keeping activities was $872 million in 1998 compared with $884 million in 1997.

If the organization's total cash was separated into peace-keeping and regular budget, several trends appeared. Peace-keeping cash was reduced from $923 million four years ago to $768 million at the end of 1998. This large decrease flowed from lower peace-keeping assessments: these had been over $3,000 million in 1994 and 1995, about $1,500 million in 1996 and in 1998 had declined to about $900 million. It was inevitable that a decrease in peace-keeping assessments would lead to a decrease in peacekeeping cash unless member states reduced their debts significantly.

The regular budget assessments provided for a fairly constant level of resources to fund mandated activities which allowed the secretariat to project regular budget cash deficits. The anticipated deficit for 1998 had been $50 million; the actual figure was $40 million. This was the lowest figure for three years. There were two main reasons for this. The largest contributor, the USA, had made payments that totalled 119 per cent of its regular budget assessment. And it had made a larger regular payment— $197 million—in the final quarter of 1998 than in earlier years because Congress had permitted quicker payment of appropriations. (This payment prevented the USA from losing its vote in the General Assembly from 1 January 1999, as stipulated in Article 19.) The second reason was that a record number of member states (117) had paid their regular budget assessments in full by the end of the year, compared with 100 in the previous year. This meant that the need to borrow substantial amounts from the peace-keeping cash to fund the shortfall in the regular budget had been sharply reduced.

Mr Connor observed that, while peace-keeping assessments were declining, and the regular budget assessments were stable, the assessment for the two war crimes tribunals was rising—from $27 million in 1995 to $99 million in 1998 and $155 million for 1999—partly because of increased activities and partly because they were being assessed in full for the first time; previously they had been subsumed under peace-keeping. He noted that there had been a substantial reduction in the regular budget debt but an increase in the peace-keeping and tribunal arrears. Regular budget debt had been $564 million in 1995 but had fallen to $417 million at the end of 1998. The US share had fallen by $98 million; the combined total for all other members was reduced by $49 million. The USA owed 76 per cent of the outstanding regular budget payments, Brazil 7 per cent and 65 states the remaining 17 per cent.

Unpaid peace-keeping assessments amounted to $1,594 million at the end of 1998, about $20 million more than the previous year. US debt had increased by $36 million and the Ukraine's by $2 million; but the Russian Federation had reduced its arrears by $10 million and the other members states had reduced theirs by $8 million. Unpaid assessments for the two tribunals were $20 million, compared with around $14 million in 1997.

Finally, Mr Connor pointed out that the organization owed member states $139 million for peace-keeping troops and $745 million for equipment at the beginning of 1998. New peace-keeping costs during 1998 were $204 million; in line with the Secretary-General's intention not to allow the total level of debt to rise, most new obligations had been met.

Additionally a revaluation had reduced equipment debt by $34 million. But the overall debt to member governments had only decreased by $12 million. The outstanding debt could not be met without large arrears payments.

The question of preferential payment to states which could least afford to have these debts owed to them had been discussed in the secretariat; but member states had not provided the authority to make such payment. Moreover, the organization had a highly structured method of payment. Before it could make payments for contributions to a particular mission it must have cash in that specific peace-keeping account. There was no cash in either the Somalia or the Former Yugoslavia account. The UN could not pay money that it did not have.

Mr Connor concluded that the UN's financial future was held hostage to a number of unstable conditions: a smaller amount of peace-keeping cash; the unknown level and timing of US payments; large arrears in assessment collection; and the debt to member states for troops and equipment. Thus, because the UN had no capital and no reserves, it would have to continue to borrow from some member states to make up for the income that it did not receive from other member states.

Reliable additional sources of funds for the UN were provided by philanthropists, however. CNN head Ted Turner had established the UN Foundation to administer his $1,000 million gift to the organization (see AR 1997, p. 384). In 1998 it granted $55 million to 39 projects selected by the UN and meeting the priorities and criteria of the foundation. On 22 April the UN Population Fund announced that it had received a grant of $1.7 million over three years from the William H. Gates Foundation for two population and development programmes. And on 2 December it was announced that Microsoft chief Bill Gates and his wife had pledged $100 million to help vaccinate children around the globe. The grant would be administered by UNICEF, the World Health Organization and the Seattle-based Program for Appropriate Health.

54TH SESSION OF HUMAN RIGHTS COMMISSION. The Commission met in Geneva from 16 March to 24 April. It adopted 83 resolutions and 13 decisions, mostly by consensus. Interestingly, on one occasion the chairman, Jacob Selebi (South Africa), locked several delegations in his office, urging them to reach agreement on a draft resolution on 'constructive dialogue' and 'enhancement of understanding' in the field of human rights. He later refused to have a text on 'enhancement of understanding' approved by anything but consensus. Noteworthy results of the session included the adoption of a draft declaration on human rights defenders, after 13 years of negotiation, which was subsequently approved by the General Assembly on 9 December; the termination of 19 years' monitoring of Guatamala's human rights record; and the defeat for the first time since 1991 of a draft resolution on the human rights situation in Cuba.

In April Secretary-General Annan was obliged to withdraw a team sent to the Democratic Republic of the Congo (DRC) in August 1997 to investigate allegations of massacres and other human rights violations since September 1996. The team had experienced persistent non-cooperation and harassment from the authorities. Its report was presented to the Security Council, which on 13 July called upon the governments of the DRC and Rwanda to investigate the allegations in the report.

The Secretary-General also asked a panel of eminent persons to visit Algeria between 11 July and 4 August and prepare a report on conditions there. This was presented to the Algerian government and then published. In August Mr Annan appointed a team to evaluate existing evidence on crimes committed by the Khmer Rouge leaders in Cambodia during the years 1975 to 1979.

PEACE ENFORCEMENT. The Security Council on 15 June, by resolution 1174, authorized member states acting through or in cooperation with the North Atlantic Treaty Organization (NATO) to continue for a further 12 months the multinational Stabilization Force (S-For) in Bosnia & Hercegovina (see III.2.ii).

SANCTIONS. On 16 March the Council, by resolution 1156, ended petroleum sanctions against Sierre Leone. On 5 June, by resolution 1171, it lifted the arms embargo on the government. It decided that the sale of arms and related material and petroleum products to parties other than the government and the ECOMOG forces of the Economic Community of West African States (ECOWAS) should be prevented, and it maintained travel restrictions on the leading members of the former military junta and the Revolutionary United Front.

By resolution 1160, on which China abstained, the Council on 31 March imposed an arms embargo on the Federal Republic of Yugoslavia, including the arming and training for terrorist activities in Kosovo (see below).

On 9 April, by resolution 1161, the Council reactivated for six months the international commission of inquiry which had been established in 1995 to investigate reports of the sale and the supply of arms and related material to former government forces and militias of Rwanda and to make recommendations relating to the illegal flow of arms in the Great Lakes region of Africa.

By resolution 1173, the Council on 12 June imposed diplomatic, financial, travel and trade restrictions, including a ban on the sale of diamonds, on the Unita movement in Angola (see VII.1.vi). On 15 October the Council, by resolution 1202, requested the sanctions monitoring committee to investigate reports that the Unita leader, Jonas Savimbi, had travelled outside Angola and that Unita forces had received foreign military training, assistance and arms in violation of the Council's decisions.

As regards UN sanctions on Libya, on 27 August the Council decided, by resolution 1192, that it would suspend sanctions against Libya once the Secretary-General had reported that the two Libyans suspected of involvement in the 1988 Lockerbie bombing had arrived for trial in the Netherlands under Scottish law and when the Libyan government had satisfied French judicial authorities investigating the 1989 bombing of a French airliner over West Africa.

PEACE-KEEPING. On 27 March the Security Council, by resolution 1159, created the UN Mission in the Central African Republic (MINURA) for an initial three-month period from 15 April with up to 1,350 military personnel. It had a law and order, disarmament and police training mandate. MINURA replaced the Inter-African Mission, which had been set up to monitor the implementation of the Bangui Agreements.

By resolution 1162 adopted on 17 April, the Council approved the deployment of up to ten UN military and security advisers to assist the special envoy of the Secretary-General in Sierre Leone. This was followed on 13 July by the establishment of the UN Observer Mission in Sierra Leone (UNOMSIL) by Council resolution 1181, initially until 13 January 1999. Consisting of up to 70 military observers, a small medical unit and civilian support staff, the mission was to monitor the military situation, the disarmament process and respect for international humanitarian law.

As of the end of 1998, there were a total of 17 UN peace-keeping missions deployed in various parts of the world (see table on pages 408–11).

IRAQ AND UNSCOM. The Security Council discussed Iraq ten times in 1998 and was often divided on how to respond to Iraqi non-compliance with its disarmament obligations, including its refusal to cooperate fully with the UN Special Commission (UNSCOM) weapons inspectors (see V.2.vi). While the Council deplored and then condemned Iraq's non-compliance in January, September and October, major attempts at securing Iraqi cooperation were undertaken by the Secretary-General. In February he negotiated a memorandum of understanding under which Iraq undertook to cooperate fully with UNSCOM and which outlined special procedures for the inspection of Iraqi presidential sites—to which UNSCOM had been denied access—by a newly-constituted group which included senior diplomats appointed by Mr Annan and members of UNSCOM and the International Atomic Energy Agency (IAEA). This understanding was endorsed by the Council on 2 March through resolution 1154. On 6 May the travel restrictions imposed on Iraqi officials in 1997 for noncooperation with UNSCOM were removed by the Council at the request of the chairman of UNSCOM, Richard Butler.

A further crisis developed on 31 October when Iraq announced an end to all cooperation with UNSCOM until the Security Council lifted UN sanctions on Iraq and dismissed Mr Butler. On 13 November the Secretary-General sent a letter to Iraq on future cooperation, and received a positive reply. Mr Annan then, at the request of some members of the Council, sought clarification about certain points in the letter and its appendix. On 15 November the Council's president announced that Iraq had decided to resume cooperation and to allow the inspectors to return, and that the Council would undertake a comprehensive sanctions review once the Secretary-General had confirmed Iraq's full cooperation. Although Mr Annan was again able, as in February, to defuse the crisis and to prevent Anglo-American air strikes against Iraq, he was unable to do so when on 15 December the UNSCOM chairman reported that Iraq had not cooperated fully and that his inspectors were unable to conduct their mandated tasks. In the ensuing Council debate on the use of force by the USA and the United Kingdom, the permanent members were even more divided, with Russia and China asserting that the UNSCOM chairman had acted dishonourably. The year ended with UNSCOM unable to return and with deadlock in the Council on a new policy towards Iraq.

'OIL FOR FOOD' PROGRAMME. The programme suffered a major blow when Dennis Halliday, the UN's humanitarian coordinator for Iraq, resigned on 30 September in protest against the impact of sanctions on innocent civilians. The Security Council met four times in 1998 to review and extend the programme. In February it decided that Iraq should be allowed to increase its oil exports from $2,000 milion to $5,256 million over six months and in June that oil industry spare parts could be imported. A further six-month extension of the arrangement was agreed by the Council on 24 November. However, because of the sharp decrease in world oil prices and Iraq's limited export capacity, it was thought unlikely that the new target could be met.

KOSOVO. The Council considered the violence in Kosovo in four meetings between March and the end of October. In resolutions and presidential statements, in addition to imposing an arms embargo on the Federal Republic of Yugoslavia (see above), the Council demanded an end to all forms of violence, the maintenance of a ceasefire, the creation of a political dialogue about the status of Kosovo, the establishment of conditions that would allow refugees and displaced to return to their homes, and access for humanitarian organizations. The Council also demanded that the Yugoslav government should cooperate fully with the OSCE and NATO verification missions to be established in and above Kosovo (see III.2.vi).

AFGHANISTAN. Between April and September the situation in Afghanistan (see VIII.1.ii) was examined by the Council in three presidential statements, two resolutions and a day-long open debate. The Council repeatedly called upon the parties to agree to a ceasefire and to enter into a political dialogue aimed at national reconciliation and the formation of a

UNITED NATIONS PEACE-KEEPING MISSIONS

	ESTABLISHED	PRESENT STRENGTH	RENEWAL DATE
1. UNTSO: United Nations Truce Supervision Organization	June 1948	168 military observers supported by international and local civilian staff	
2. UNMOGIP: United Nations Military Observer Group in India and Pakistan	January 1949	45 military observers, supported by international and local civilian personnel	
3. UNFICYP: United Nations Peace-keeping Force in Cyprus	March 1964	1,230 troops, 35 civilian police, supported by around 270 international and local civilian staff	Security Council resolution 1217 (1998) extended the mandate of the Force until 30 June 1999
4. UNDOF: United Nations Disengagement Observer Force (Golan Heights)	June 1974	1,046 troops assisted by approximately 80 military observers from UNTSO, supported by international and locally-recruited civilian staff	Security Council resolution 1211 (1998) extended the mandate until 31 May 1999
5. UNIFIL: United Nations Interim Force in Lebanon	March 1978	4,480 troops assisted by approximately 50 military observers from UNTSO, supported by international and local civilian staff	Security Council Resolution 1188 (1998) extended the mandate until 31 January 1999
6. UNIKOM: United Nations Iraq-Kuwait Observation Mission	April 1991	1,120 military personnel consisting of 922 troops and support personnel and 195 military observers, supported by some 200 international and local civilian staff	The mandate of UNIKOM is reviewed by the Security Council every six months
7. MINURSO: United Nations Mission for the Referendum in Western Sahara	April 1991, became operational in September 1991	202 military observers, 117 troops and 78 civilian police supported by a number of international and local civilian staff	Security Council Resolution 1214 (1998) extended the mandate until 31 January 1999
8. UNOMIG: United Nations Observer Mission in Georgia	August 1993	81 military observers, supported by international and local civilian staff	Security Council resolution 1187 (1998) extended the mandate until 31 January 1999

UNITED NATIONS PEACE-KEEPING MISSIONS continued

	ESTABLISHED	PRESENT STRENGTH	RENEWAL DATE
9. UNMOT: United Nations Mission of Observers in Tajikistan	December 1994	81 military observers and 2 civilian police officers, supported by international local civilian staff	Security Council resolution 1206 (1998) extended the mandate until 15 May 1999
10. UNPREDEP: United Nations Preventive Deployment Force (The former Yugoslav Republic of Macedonia)	March 1995	748 troops, 35 military observers and 26 civilian staff (July 1998)	Security Council resolution 1186 (1998) extended the mandate until 28 February 1999 and authorized an increase in troop strength up to 1050

Previous mission:
UNPROFOR: United Nations Protection Force February 1992 to March 1995 located in Bosnia & Hercegovina, Croatia, the Federal Republic of Yugoslavia and the former Yugoslav Republic of Macedonia. Authorized strength: 44,870 troops and police, almost 1,000 civilian staff, 1500 international contractual personnel and more than 3,000 local staff. Maximum 39,922 including 38,614 troops, 637 military observers and 671 civilian police (30/9/94)

| 11. UNMIBH: United Nations Mission in Bosnia and Herzegovina | December 1995 | 1,959 civilian police. 3 military support staff, assisted by international and local civilian staff | Security Council resolution 1174 (1998) extended the mandate until June 1999 |

Previous missions:
UNPROFOR: February 1992 to March 1995 (see above mission 10)
UNPROFOR: March 1995 to December 1995. Maximum strengths 30,574 troops, 278 military observers and 17 civilian police

| 12. UNMOP: United Nations Mission of Observers in Prevlaka | January 1996 | 28 military observers | Security Council resolution 1183 (1998) extended the mandate until 15 January 1999 |

Previous missions:
UNPROFOR: February 1992-March 1995
UNCRO: United Nations Confidence Restoration Operation March 1995-January 1996. Maximum strength 14,663 troops, 328 military observers, 531 civilian police, supported by international and local civilian staff.

UNITED NATIONS PEACE-KEEPING MISSIONS continued

	ESTABLISHED	PRESENT STRENGTH	RENEWAL DATE
13. MONUA: United Nations Observation Mission in Angola	July 1997	716 troops, 92 military observers and 405 civilian police monitors supported by international and local civilian staff	Security Council resolution 1213 (1998) extended the mandate until end of February 1999

Previous missions:
UNAVEM I: United Nations Angola Verification Mission I
January 1989-May 1991: 70 military observers (April to December 1989 supported by international and local civilian staff)
UNAVEM II: United Nations Angola Verification Mission II
May 1991-February 1995. Maximum authorized: 350 military observers and 126 civilian police; a civilian air unit and medical unit; 87 international civilian and 155 local staff; during the elections there were 400 electoral observers
UNAVEM III: United Nations Angola Verification Mission III
February 1995-June 1997: Authorized strength 350 military observers, 7,000 troops and military support personnel, 260 civilian police, 420 international civilian staff, 300 locally-recruited staff and 75 United Nations Volunteers.

	ESTABLISHED	PRESENT STRENGTH	RENEWAL DATE
14. MIPONUH: United Nations Civilian Police Mission in Haiti	December 1997	300 police monitors including 90-strong special police unit to provide protection for international personnel and property supported by international and local civilian staff	Security Council resolution 1212 (1998) extended the mandate until 30 November 1999

Previous missions:
UNMIH: United Nations Mission in Haiti
September 1993-June 1996. Maximum strength 6,065 troops and military support personnel; 887 civilian police, supported by international and locally-recruited staff.
UNSMIH: United Nations Support Mission in Haiti
July 1996-June 1997. Maximum 1,297 military, 291 civilian police supported by international and local civilian staff. 700 of its military personnel paid for by Canadian and United States governments.
UNTMIH: United Nations Transition Mission in Haiti
August to November 1997. 250 civilian police, 50 military personnel and additional military personnel paid for by voluntary funding.

UNITED NATIONS PEACE-KEEPING MISSIONS continued

	ESTABLISHED	PRESENT STRENGTH	RENEWAL DATE
15. United Nations Civilian Police Support Group (in Eastern Slavonia, Baranja and Western Sirmium)	January 1998 for a period of nine months by Security Council resolution 1145 (1997) 19 December 1997	179 civilian police personnel and 31 troops supported by international and police members supported by local civilian staff	This mission was replaced by OSCE

Previous missions:
UNPROFOR: February 1992-March 1995
UNCRO: March 1995-January 1996
UNTAES: United Nations Transitional Administration for Eastern Slavonia, Baranja and Western Sirmium January 1996-January 1998. Maximum strength 5,009 troops, 95 military, 457 civilian police, supported by international civilian and local staff.

| 16. MINURCA: United Nations Mission in Central African Republic | April 1998 | 1,362 troops, 17 civilian police, supported by civilian international and local staff | Security Council resolution 1201 (1998) extended the mandate until 28 February 1999 |

Previous mission:
MISAB: The Inter-African Mission to Monitor the Implementation of the Bangui Agreements. 8 February 1997-15 April 1998. 800 troops

| 17. UNOMSIL: United Nations Observer Mission in Sierra Leone | July 1998 | 70 military observers, 15 personnel medical unit, 5 civilian police advisers assisted by international civilian personnel and locally recruited staff | Security Council resolution 1181 (1998) provides an initial mandate of six months until 13 January 1999 |

Previous mission:
April 1998. Up to 10 United Nations military and security advisers for 90 days to assist the Special Envoy of the Secretary-General in Sierra Leone

broadly-based fully representative government. It also called upon states in the region to cease providing military support. It asked the Taleban regime to stop impeding the work of humanitarian organizations and condemned the killing of UN staff. It also deplored the killing of Iranian diplomats in August (see also VIII.1.i) and demanded that these should be investigated. In December the Council supported the Secretary-General's proposal to establish a civil affairs unit in the UN special mission to Afghanistan to promote respect for, and to deter systematic violations of, human rights and humanitarian law.

SPECIAL DEBATES. A report on 'the causes of conflict and the promotion of durable peace and sustainable development in Africa', requested by the Security Council from the Secretary-General in September 1997, was considered in a day-long debate on 24 April in which there were 52 speakers, including for the first time the representative of the Holy See. In May, by resolution 1170, the Council established an *ad hoc* working group which prepared proposals on regional cooperation, strengthening African peace-keeping capacity, increasing the effectiveness of Council-imposed arms sanctions, an international mechanism to assist host governments in maintaining the security and neutrality of refugee camps, illicit arms flows and enhancing the capacity of the Council to monitor activities authorized by it. These were subsequently adopted by the Council by resolution and presidential statements in September and November. In May the Council had also stated that it would convene at ministerial level on a biennial basis to assess progress in promoting peace and security in Africa. The first such meeting was held on 24 September.

The Council also held special debates on humanitarian assistance for refugees and others in conflict situations and on the impact of armed conflict on children and post-conflict peace building. In addition, it held open debates on the Lockerbie issue, the Arab occupied territories, Angola, Afghanistan and the nuclear tests conducted by India and Pakistan (see VIII.2.i; VIII.2.ii).

TRANSPARENCY. The Council made further attempts to improve its transparency, in response to a memorandum presented by the ten non-permanent members in December 1997 (see AR 1997, pp. 385–6). Steps taken included the enhancement of consultations with troop-contributing countries and establishment of a mechanism for alerting non-members of unscheduled or emergency meetings of the Council. In its annual report to the General Assembly, the Council included for the first time the 12 monthly assessments of the work of the Council presented by the Council presidents (serving one-month terms). The Council was briefed in open session by Sadako Ogata, the UN High Commissioner for Refugees, who then responded to questions from members; by the chairman of the Sierra Leone sanctions committee on the efficacy of sanctions and conditions in that state; and by the under-secretary-general for peace-keeping on Mr Annan's progress report on UNOMSIL.

INTERNATIONAL TRIBUNALS. A UN conference in Rome on 17 July adopted the statute of an International Criminal Court (ICC), by an unrecorded vote of 120–7 with 21 abstentions. The statute provided that states parties accepted the jurisdiction of the ICC with respect to genocide, crimes against humanity, war crimes and the crime of aggression (see XIV.1.i; XVII.2). It would enter in force when there were 60 ratifications. The Court would be complimentary to national criminal jurisdictions and its seat would be at The Hague in the Netherlands.

The Security Council established new third chambers for the International Tribunals for Rwanda and for the Former Yugoslavia to help them meet increased workloads and to prevent undue delay to trials. New judges were elected by the General Assembly from lists approved by the Security Council. In September the Rwanda Tribunal made the first-ever judgment by an international court on the crime of genocide. On 17 November, by resolution 1207, the Council condemned the failure of the government of the Federal Republic of Yugoslavia to execute arrest warrants issued by the Former Yugoslavia Tribunal and affirmed that a state could not invoke provisions of its domestic law as justification for its failure to perform binding obligations under international law.

2. DEFENCE AND ECONOMIC ORGANIZATIONS

i. DEFENCE ORGANIZATIONS

North Atlantic Treaty Organization (NATO)
DATE OF FOUNDATION: 1949   HEADQUARTERS: Brussels, Belgium
OBJECTIVES: To ensure the collective security of member states
MEMBERSHIP (END-'98): Belgium, Canada, Denmark, France, Germany, Greece, Iceland, Italy, Luxembourg, Netherlands, Norway, Portugal, Spain, Turkey, United Kingdom, United States (*total 16*)
PROSPECTIVE MEMBERS: Czech Republic, Hungary, Poland (to accede in April '99)
SECRETARY-GENERAL: Javier Solana (Spain)

Partnership for Peace (PFP)
DATE OF FOUNDATION: 1994   HEADQUARTERS: Brussels, Belgium
OBJECTIVES: To provide a framework for cooperation between NATO and the former communist and neutral states of Europe and ex-Soviet Central Asia
MEMBERSHIP (END-'98): Albania, Armenia, Austria, Azerbaijan, Belarus, Bulgaria, Czech Republic, Estonia, Finland, Georgia, Hungary, Kazakhstan, Kyrgyzstan, Latvia, Lithuania, Macedonia, Malta, Moldova, Poland, Romania, Russia, Slovakia, Slovenia, Sweden, Switzerland, Turkmenistan, Ukraine, Uzbekistan (*total 28*)

Western European Union (WEU)

DATE OF FOUNDATION: 1952   HEADQUARTERS: Brussels, Belgium
OBJECTIVES: To provide a framework for defence and security cooperation between European states
MEMBERSHIP (END-'98): Belgium, France, Germany, Greece, Italy, Luxembourg, Netherlands, Portugal, Spain, United Kingdom (*total 10*)
SECRETARY-GENERAL: José Cutileiro (Portugal)

THE Czech Republic, Hungary and Poland were invited, as an outcome of the Madrid summit in 1997, to accede to membership of the North Atlantic Treaty Organization (NATO) on its 50th anniversary in April 1999 (see AR 1997, pp. 437–9). The announcement of the enlargement sparked off debate as to the advisability of adding East European states to the alliance. That the invited states had recently been members of the Warsaw Pact, which had existed as a counter to NATO, and that they were located on the western frontiers of the former Soviet Union served to intensify the argument.

Questions in the USA as to whether the security of East European states might be ensured within other existing partnerships aimed at enhancing peace in Europe—NATO's Partnership for Peace, for instance—were disposed of, finally, by the US Senate's approval of the invitations to the Czech Republic, Hungary and Poland on 30 April. Three weeks later President Clinton formally ratified the invitation to the three new potential member states. By the end of 1998 all 16 existing NATO member states had deposited their documents ratifying the accession protocols in respect of all three prospective new members.

Russia's response to NATO enlargement had been hostile from the first. The NATO-Warsaw Pact confrontation, having lasted some 50 years, had created habits of thought on each side which made it difficult to see virtue in any act or proposal of the other. To the Russian government, NATO was an organization to be regarded with suspicion: it had been traditionally hostile; it was armed with nuclear weapons; and the proposed enlargement was potentially going to lead to the stationing of NATO forces—possibly with nuclear armaments—on the former Soviet borders. To make matters worse, the nuclear threat which might be emplaced in Czech, Hungarian or Polish territory would be made up of tactical weapons systems, capable of rapid deployment and use, in theory without warning. The possibility of surprise nuclear attack on Russian territory had always been a major concern in Moscow.

That the potential areas of deployment in the territories of the new invitees were not directly adjacent to present Russian lands was not a factor likely to reduce Russian concern. Belarus and Ukraine, the ex-Soviet republics sharing borders with Poland and Hungary and within range of tactical weapons, might be independent entities but that status was of short standing and either of the two might return to union with Russia in the future, especially if the Russian economy could be returned to a more healthy condition than had been the case since the collapse of the Soviet

Union. In that event, NATO deployment, particularly in Poland, would become a matter of direct concern to Russia.

The negotiations with the Russian government demanded delicate handling. The continuing downward slide of the Russian economy, emphasized by devaluation of the rouble and continuing evidence of degradation of the efficiency and capability of the armed forces, served to remind Russians of how far the country had fallen from its position as a great power. In such circumstances, the natural course for Russia would be to rely increasingly on the protection of the most reliable segments of its armed forces. The classification of 'reliable' best fitted the Strategic Rocket Forces; and in a time of threat, however misperceived, Russia would be impelled to abstain from any process tending to limit or reduce the capability of those forces. Hence it was no surprise that the State Duma, the Russian parliament, continued to delay ratification of the START-II agreement (the second Strategic Arms Reduction Treaty).

The most obvious drawback to the enlargement of the NATO alliance was the level of cost to be expected. To bring the armies and air forces of the new allies (and a navy in the case of Poland) to a level of equipment and training at which they could represent a significant enhancement to the security of NATO member states was an expensive undertaking. An additional factor was the need to upgrade infrastructure to make it realistic (or even possible) to base NATO forces in the new member states. Such liabilities were seen by some analysts as outweighing the obvious benefit of adding some 200,000 military personnel to NATO strength in Europe.

To the obvious sources of cost, such as standardization of equipment and munitions, had to be added the costs accompanying the increasing technical complexity of all types of modern military equipment. Increasingly, routine maintenance of equipment of many types required the use of sophisticated test-equipment, which sometimes required to be housed in controlled environments. Detailed evaluation was therefore required of facilities in the new member states to identify which required alteration or replacement.

Following the appearance in 1997 of various estimates of the probable costs of enlargement (see AR 1997, pp. 438–9), in February the US Department of Defence reported to Congress that the cost analysis produced by the NATO Senior Resource Board the previous year had been validated as militarily sound. The NATO assessment of 'common-funded costs' of enlargement of approximately US$1,500 million over ten years was therefore accepted as a planning figure, the US share being expected to be some $400 million. Agreement on a single estimate of costs would not only reduce uncertainty as to time-scale of expansion of the alliance, but would have significance for decisions on military procurement and upgrading of capabilities.

A breakdown of the assessed costs indicated that the major capital cost item ($694 million, from a total capital cost figure of $1,311 million) was expected to be incurred in providing reception facilities for reinforcement of the new member states. This item was largely concerned with the provision of airfields and airfield services essential for alliance pre-positioning, operations and re-supply. Next in size was a projected $560 million for air defence, this estimate reflecting the complex nature of modern air defence systems. To bring the three new partners into membership would require not only the introduction of common procedures unfamiliar to the newcomers, but also the extension of the existing NATO Command and Control communications network into the new territories. A consequence of this was that computer systems and software would have to be made compatible across the whole of the alliance.

A different aspect of NATO enlargement was an economic one. Although entry was bound to be costly for the new members, who would have to meet some of the costs of updating resources essential to enable NATO to operate within its standard criteria, there were potential economic benefits which might be indirect but were likely to be significant. Commercial investment was often sought from non-national financial sources, and a factor vital in a lender's decision to invest was assessment of political stability in a borrower country and the implications of this for the security of investment and the future servicing of debt. To be accepted as a member of an effective mutual security alliance would, in part, qualify a government and business within its country as a sound prospect for international investment. Another consideration was that work necessary for the improvement of transport infrastructure and other facilities to meet NATO specifications would provide the possibility for local companies to tender for projects which would not otherwise have existed, with attendant social benefit and greater commercial prosperity.

The Western European Union (WEU) continued to build on its central role as the link between NATO and the European Union (EU), functioning as agent of the central civil and military entities of European security. At a meeting in Rhodes in May, the WEU Ministerial Council announced the establishment of a new WEU military structure intended to strengthen relations with NATO and to facilitate the realization of a 'European security and defence identity' (ESDI). Terms of reference were agreed for the creation of a 'planning cell' at WEU headquarters in Brussels. Among the roles agreed for the WEU were development of military capability to assist in civil crisis situations and monitoring of European compliance with arms-control measures, with a focus on the present initiative to outlaw the use of land-mines.

The second 1998 meeting of the Ministerial Council, held in Rome in November, welcomed the fact that, following NATO's invitations to Poland, Hungary and the Czech Republic, these three states had made application for associate membership of the WEU.

The WEU was at an early point in its development, as proposed in the 1997 Amsterdam Treaty, into the operational arm of the EU. The course being followed placed the WEU in a unique central position within the emerging framework of a defence and security structure for Europe. The place of military commands in the provision of physical assistance to civil powers in emergency was recognized, as was the utility of military information resources in dealing with emergency situations. From its potential to provide those services, the WEU was continuing to develop an essential link function, not only between NATO and the EU, but between the EU and other organizations such as Organization for Security and Cooperation in Europe (OSCE), the Partnership for Peace and the Contact Group on former Yugoslavia.

An important asset in coping with its own responsibilities, and in providing assistance to other agencies, was the WEU Satellite Centre, situated at Torrejón de Ardoz near Madrid, an air base long used by NATO forces. Access to satellite data in general, and imagery in particular, was essential for prompt and informed decision and action in emergency situations, and for sound assessment in the control of long-term projects.

ii. ECONOMIC ORGANIZATIONS

International Monetary Fund (IMF)
DATE OF FOUNDATION: 1945   HEADQUARTERS: Washington DC, USA
OBJECTIVES: To promote international monetary cooperation and to assist member states in establishing sound budgetary and trading policies
MEMBERSHIP (END-'98): 179 UN members plus Kiribati, Switzerland & Tonga (*total 182*)
MANAGING DIRECTOR: Michel Camdessus (France)

International Bank for Reconstruction and Development (IBRD/World Bank)
DATE OF FOUNDATION: 1946   HEADQUARTERS: Washington DC, USA
OBJECTIVES: To make loans on reasonable terms to developing countries with the aim of increasing their productive capacity
MEMBERSHIP (END-'98): 178 UN members plus Kiribati, Switzerland & Tonga (*total 181*)
PRESIDENT: James D. Wolfensohn (United States)

World Trade Organization (WTO)
DATE OF INAUGURATION: 1995 (successor to General Agreement on Tariffs and Trade, GATT)   HEADQUARTERS: Geneva, Switzerland
OBJECTIVES: To eliminate tariff and other barriers to international trade and the facilitate international financial settlements
MEMBERSHIP (END-'98): 134 acceding parties
DIRECTOR-GENERAL: Renato Ruggiero (Italy)

Organization for Economic Cooperation and Development (OECD)
DATE OF FOUNDATION: 1960   HEADQUARTERS: Paris, France
OBJECTIVES: To promote economic growth in member states and the sound development of the world economy
MEMBERSHIP (END-'98): Australia, Austria, Belgium, Canada, Czech Republic, Denmark, Finland, France, Germany, Greece, Hungary, Iceland, Ireland, Italy, Japan, South Korea, Luxembourg, Mexico, Netherlands, New Zealand, Norway, Poland, Portugal, Spain, Sweden, Switzerland, Turkey, United Kingdom, United States (*total 29*)
SECRETARY-GENERAL: Donald Johnston (Canada)

Organization of the Petroleum Exporting Countries (OPEC)
DATE OF FOUNDATION: 1960   HEADQUARTERS: Vienna, Austria
OBJECTIVES: To unify and coordinate member states' oil policies and to safeguard their interests.
MEMBERSHIP (END-'98): Algeria, Indonesia, Iran, Iraq, Kuwait, Libya, Nigeria, Qatar, Saudi Arabia, United Arab Emirates, Venezuela (*total 11*)
SECRETARY-GENERAL: Rilwanu Lukman (Nigeria)

INTERNATIONAL MONETARY FUND. The IMF was concerned during 1998 with the plight of a number of key main countries whose deteriorating circumstances threatened to cause severe disruption of the world economic balance. These included countries which had already received major IMF and associated assistance in 1997, such as Russia, South Korea, Indonesia and Thailand. Major new assistance was also provided in 1998, notably for Argentina in February ($2,800 million), the Philippines in March ($1,400 million), Russia with an augmented arrangement in July (extra support of $11,200 million), Indonesia in July (a further $1,300 million), Ukraine in September ($2,200 million) and Brazil in December (a huge $18,000 million arrangement as part of an overall $41,500 million package). During 1998 the Fund continued to come under some external criticism over the stringent economic measures which it required to be fulfilled before passing over further tranches of its aid, while in the case of Russia the IMF was in September-December engaged in sharp confrontation over that country's fraught economic situation and continued to withhold further releases (see III.3.i).

The Brazil arrangement brought together for the first time two essential elements designed to improve the Fund's capacity to meet particularly large demands: the Supplemental Reserve Facility, established in December 1997, and the New Arrangements to Borrow (NAB), formally established in November 1998. The NAB effectively complemented the General Arrangements to Borrow (initially set up in 1962 and last used in July 1998 in connection with Russia's augmented arrangement), and comprised credit arrangements with 25 countries or institutions to provide supplementary resources to the Fund to forestall or cope with an impairment of the international monetary system or to deal with an exceptional situation which posed a threat to the stability of that system. Total resources under the NAB and GAB combined were some $48,000 million.

In December the IMF lowered its forecasts of world economic growth in 1999 from 2.5 to 2.2 per cent, and its prediction of the growth of world trade from 4.6 to 4.4 per cent. As a further means to increase the Fund's capacity to meet growing needs, it was agreed in February that member countries' quotas would be increased by on average 45 per cent to some $297,000 million. The final key US approval to this increase was given in October.

WORLD BANK/INTERNATIONAL DEVELOPMENT ASSOCIATION. The International Bank for Reconstruction and Development (IBRD—the World Bank) participated in a number of the IMF's rescue attempts during 1998, as in 1997 (see AR 1997, pp. 537–8). These joint and essentially relatively short-term emergency operations were seen by some as blurring the conceptual division between the two bodies. However, at the IMF/World Bank annual meetings session in Washington DC the World Bank president James Wolfensohn on 6 October stressed the social dimensions of the Bank's work, saying that if there were not 'greater equity and social justice' there would not be political stability, and that without the latter no rescue packages could create financial stability.

The 12th replenishment of the World Bank's soft-loan affiliate, the International Development Association (IDA), was agreed on 19 November, when 39 donor countries pledged a total of $11,600 million for the next three years. Taken together with other sources of funds, the replenishment meant that available resources for IDA lending during this period would total over $20,000 million.

WORLD TRADE ORGANIZATION. A vexed issue exercising the World Trade Organization (WTO) during 1998 was the dispute, essentially between the United States and the European Union (EU), over the latter's banana imports from countries within the African, Pacific and Caribbean (ACP) grouping, principally former colonies of EU member states (see also XI.4). The EU's draft regime, announced in January, abolished current import licensing arrangements and introduced a new system of quotas, but US dissatisfaction with the new regime and failure to reach agreement through the WTO led the US administration on 21 December to impose, in retaliation, heavy duties on a range of imports from most EU countries. While the USA did not itself export bananas to EU countries, many of the companies exporting from non-ACP Central American and northern South American countries were US-controlled multinationals, and certain of the governments concerned were joined with the United States in the appeal to the WTO.

In another dispute, a WTO appeal panel on 12 October upheld an earlier ruling that the United States had exercised 'arbitrary and unjustifiable discrimination' against India, Pakistan, Thailand and Malaysia when, in 1996, it had imposed a ban on the import into the USA of shrimps caught with nets which did not have turtle excluders. The panel ruled that, while the protection of an endangered species was a legitimate objective, the ban unilaterally imposed US law intended to protect turtles on other countries. Many environmentalists criticized the decision as confirming the principle that free trade took precedence over the need to protect the environment.

ORGANIZATION FOR ECONOMIC COOPERATION AND DEVELOPMENT. The OECD on 17 November published its half-yearly *Economic Outlook*, in which it noted that the possibility of a general recession throughout the world had now receded. However, it had reduced its forecast for growth in its 29 member countries for 1999 from 2.5 per cent to only 1.7 per cent (compared with the 2.2 per cent growth anticipated for 1998), and it warned that although a degree of stability had returned to financial markets over the past months there were still grave threats to economic well-being. Moreover, it criticized the failure of many OECD countries to reduce their interest rates quickly enough in the face of the continuing world economic difficulties.

Negotiations within the OECD on the proposed Multilateral Agreement on Investment (MAI) were suspended for four years on 4 December, following the withdrawal of France from the discussions on 14 October and of Australia on 2 November. The MAI talks had been launched in 1995 to construct a liberalized global framework for international investment, but opposition had grown both within some governments and within the public, which increasingly saw the MAI as over-sympathetic to big business and multinationals and as a possible threat to labour and environmental standards.

ORGANIZATION OF THE PETROLEUM EXPORTING COUNTRIES. The 11-member OPEC in 1998 sought to come to terms with the drastically falling world market for crude petroleum, affected as it was by the dramatic downturn in demand from countries caught up in the Asian meltdown, by the unusually warm winter in the northern hemisphere and by intensified energy conservation measures. (The internationally-recognized forward price for benchmark Brent crude fell from nearly $17 at the beginning of 1998 to about $10.50 at the end.) However, it was far from clear to what extent individual OPEC members actually conformed to agreed oil production cuts or to their theoretical quotas. Discussions also took place with certain non-OPEC countries on the demand and production outlooks.

On 30–31 March OPEC agreed to cut production (excluding Iraq) by 1,245,000 barrels a day (b/d) until the end of the year (compared with current quotas totalling around 26,500,000 b/d). On 24 June, moreover, it agreed on reductions of about another 1,355,000 b/d for the next 12 months, bringing the combined cut to around 10 per cent.

3. OTHER WORLD ORGANIZATIONS

i. THE COMMONWEALTH

DATE OF FOUNDATION: 1931   HEADQUARTERS: London, UK
OBJECTIVES: To maintain political, cultural and social links between (mainly English-speaking) countries of the former British Empire and others subscribing to Commonwealth democratic principles and aims
MEMBERSHIP (END-'98): Antigua & Barbuda, Australia, Bahamas, Bangladesh, Barbados, Belize, Botswana, Britain, Brunei, Cameroon, Canada, Cyprus, Dominica, Fiji, The Gambia, Ghana, Grenada, Guyana, India, Jamaica, Kenya, Kiribati, Lesotho, Malawi, Malaysia, Maldives, Malta, Mauritius, Mozambique, Namibia, Nauru, New Zealand, Nigeria (*suspended*), Pakistan, Papua New Guinea, St Kitts & Nevis, St Lucia, St Vincent & the Grenadines, Samoa, Seychelles, Sierra Leone, Singapore, Solomon Islands, South Africa, Sri Lanka, Swaziland, Tanzania, Tonga, Trinidad & Tobago, Tuvalu, Uganda, Vanuatu, Samoa, Zambia, Zimbabwe (*total 54*)
SECRETARY-GENERAL: Chief E. Chukwuemeka Anyaoku (Nigeria)

THE sudden death of General Sani Abacha in Nigeria on 8 June (see XVIII: Obituary) dramatically changed the Commonwealth political landscape. An apparently intractable situation opened up overnight when the new Nigerian head of state, General Abdulsalam Abubakar signalled an about-face in relations with the Commonwealth. For two years General Abacha had refused to talk to secretary-general Chief Emeka Anyaoku; now his successor was at once in touch and wanting Commonwealth help in the handover to civilian rule, rescheduled for 1999 (see VI.2.ii).

Chief Anyaoku visited Nigeria at the end of June, holding amicable talks with General Abubakar and seeing in detention the perceived winner of the 1993 presidential election, Chief Moshood Abiola, a week before he too died (see XVIII: Obituary). President Abubakar visited London on 22 September, talked with British Prime Minister Tony Blair and again with Chief Anyaoku. He urged that Nigeria be returned to full Commonwealth membership. He was told that this could not happen until elections had been held and civilian rule restored.

When the Commonwealth Ministerial Action Group (CMAG) held its tenth meeting in London (8–9 October), it received a Nigerian delegation led by the new Foreign Minister, Ignatius Olisemeka. Technical help was offered to the Independent National Election Commission (INEC) for the four-stage elections. The secretariat sent officials to advise on and observe stage one—local elections on 5 December.

In terms of democracy and good governance, the CMAG's other immediate concern was the situation in Sierra Leone (see VI.1.iii). The restoration of Ahmed Tejan Kabbah as President in February was followed by a Commonwealth mission to Freetown led by the Zimbabwean Foreign Minister and CMAG chairman, Dr Stan Mudenge. Commonwealth help was offered in rebuilding the judiciary and police, restoring the mining sector and developing projects for youth and employment. This work was seriously disrupted at year's end when rebels were on the verge of fighting their way back into Freetown, with attendant havoc and mayhem.

The CMAG meeting produced some disappointment when the ministers failed to endorse proposals allowing the group to widen its area of operation and look at human rights abuses in other parts of the Commonwealth, as provided for in the Millbrook Action Plan (see AR 1995, pp. 381–2). With several signs of deterioration in human rights during the year, notably in Zambia, Zimbabwe and Kenya, intentions to buttress good governance, expressed at the Auckland and Edinburgh CHOGMs, seemed to be postponed.

The Commonwealth tried for several months to help settle the long-standing dispute between government and opposition in the Tanzanian island of Zanzibar (see VI.1.iii). Chief Anyaoku visited the island himself as the year began, and his special envoy, Dr Moses Anafu, spent several weeks there. However, when a solution seemed near in October, hopes were dashed again and Chief Anyaoku adjourned the talks.

For the presidential and National Assembly elections in Seychelles on 20–22 March (see VIII.3.ii), the Commonwealth teamed up for the first time with the Francophone Community (Francophonie). A joint observer group was led by St Lucia's former Prime Minister, Sir John Compton. It included two Canadians—representing each grouping—and observers from Mauritius and Cameroon (see also XI.3.ii). The group expressed some concern about the conduct of polling. So too did an observer group headed by the former Prime Minister of the Bahamas, Sir Lynden Pindling, which was sent to Lesotho for the National Assembly elections on 23 May. It was disappointed that the voting had not produced a multi-party parliament and suggested adoption of a proportional representation system. Subsequently, a government crisis led to the intervention of South African and Botswanan troops and some bloodshed (see VII.2.iv).

The Commonwealth Games were boosted as an institution by the considerable success of the 16th Games, held in Kuala Lumpur on 11–24 September (see Pt XVI), despite the Asian economic downturn and the serious political crisis that erupted in Malaysia coincidentally (see IX.1.iii). For the first time, team sports were included, such as seven-a-side rugby, cricket, netball and hockey. Sports commentators compared the facilities and organization favourably with the 1996 Atlanta Olympics. A record number of some 6,000 athletes from 70 countries and territories took part.

The annual Finance Ministers' meeting in Ottawa (30 September-1 October), held against a backdrop of increasing world economic instability, renewed the pressure for debt relief on the international financial institutions. In the Ottawa Commonwealth statement on the global economic crisis, a global meeting to stabilize the economic and financial system was proposed. Immediately beforehand, the recently-established Commonwealth Business Council held a seminar in Ottawa, addressed by seven ministers and top businessmen, which urged an immediate review of the global financial architecture.

Two further regional funds to boost investment in the Commonwealth were set up by the secretariat during 1998. The Kula Fund for the Pacific (US$16.9 million) was launched in February. The Tiona Fund for the Caribbean (US$25 million) was announced during the Finance Ministers' meeting. Funds for Africa and South Asia were already in existence. All were being managed by the Commonwealth Development Corporation under the Commonwealth Private Investment Initiative (CPII) launched by Finance Ministers in 1995.

Commonwealth Environment Ministers, meeting in New York on 28 April, agreed to create a Commonwealth-wide information network to link water experts and institutions in all member countries. A Youth Ministers' meeting in Kuala Lumpur on 25–30 May approved a plan of action on youth empowerment designed to help countries harness better the potential of their youth for development and to give young people a bigger say in decisions affecting them. The 12th meeting of Health Ministers in Barbados on 15–19 November discussed the kind of health systems governments would manage and the care they could give their citizens in the next millennium.

Commonwealth determination to raise international interest in the problems of small states was pressed home in July when a team of five ministers, led by Prime Minister Owen Arthur of Barbados, met leaders of international financial institutions in Washington, Geneva and Brussels.

An annual Commonwealth lecture was inaugurated in May. The first, on human rights, was delivered in London by Indian-born Professor Amartya Kumar Sen, Master of Trinity College, Cambridge. Later Professor Sen won the 1998 Nobel Prize for Economics (see VIII.2.i). On the retirement of Sir Humphrey Maud, Dame Veronica Sutherland, formerly British ambassador to Ireland, was named Commonwealth deputy secretary-general (economic)—the first woman to hold such a post.

ii. FRANCOPHONE AND PORTUGUESE-SPEAKING COMMUNITIES

Francophone Community (Francophonie)
DATE OF FOUNDATION: 1997   HEADQUARTERS: Paris, France
OBJECTIVES: To promote cooperation and exchange between countries wholly or party French-speaking and to defend usage of the French language
PARTICIPATION (END-'98): Belgium (French-speaking community), Benin, Bulgaria, Burkina Faso, Burundi, Cambodia, Cameroon, Canada, Central African Republic, Chad, Comoros, Democratic Republic of Congo, Republic of Congo, Côte d'Ivoire, Djibouti, Dominica, Egypt, Equatorial Guinea, France, Gabon, Guinea, Guinea-Bissau, Haiti, Laos, Lebanon, Luxembourg, Madagascar, Mali, Mauritania, Mauritius, Moldova, Monaco, Morocco, New Brunswick (Canada), Niger, Quebec (Canada), Romania, Rwanda, St Lucia, São Tomé & Príncipe, Senegal, Seychelles, Togo, Tunisia, Vanuatu, Vietnam (*total 46*)
SECRETARY-GENERAL: Boutros Boutros-Ghali (Egypt)

Community of Portuguese-Speaking Countries (CPLP)
DATE OF FOUNDATION: 1996   HEADQUARTERS: Lisbon, Portugal
OBJECTIVES: To promote political, diplomatic, economic, social and cultural cooperation between member-states and to enhance the status of the Portuguese language
MEMBERSHIP (END-'98): Angola, Brazil, Cape Verde, Guinea-Bissau, Mozambique, Portugal, São Tomé & Príncipe (*total 7*)
EXECUTIVE SECRETARY: Marcolino Moco (Angola)

FRANCOPHONE COMMUNITY. After the excitements of the first summit of the reformed Francophonie in Hanoi in November 1997 (see AR 1997, pp. 393–5), which saw the establishment of a secretariat of the Francophone Community and the conversion of the ACCT cooperation agency into a more broad-ranging Francophone Agency, francophone organizations took a much lower profile in 1998. There was a ministerial meeting, as well as a session of Education Ministers, and gatherings of francophone universities and media as well as others on the level of technical and cultural cooperation.

On the personal/institutional level that had led to the new reinforced dispensation making a confused start at the Hanoi summit, relations between the new septuagenarian secretary-general of the Community, the Egyptian Dr Boutros Boutros-Ghali, and the head of the new Francophone Agency, Roger Dehaybe, settled into peaceful coexistence, with an understood demarcation of functions. Dr Boutros-Ghali spent part of his first year in office doing his best to prove that he was no enemy of 'Anglo-Saxons', undertaking an exchange of visits with the Commonwealth secretary-general for the purpose of stepping up cooperation between the two organizations. One example of this cooperation was the joint monitoring of elections in the Seychelles in March, where they even produced some modest criticism of the running of the elections, won yet again by President René (see VIII.3.ii; XI.3.i)).

More curious was the involvement of the Francophonie secretariat in the crisis over the fraudulent result of the Togolese elections (see VI.3.i). Here Dr Boutros-Ghali apparently felt that the grouping could mediate between the European Union and Togo (which had been able to rally a measure of African support, especially in francophone west Africa). This was felt to be rather thin ice, since in militant francophone circles Togo's opposition leader, the UK-educated Gilchrist Olympio, with his closeness to the Rawlings regime in Ghana, was perceived as the ultimate Trojan horse for 'Anglo-Saxonism'. His father, President Sylvanus Olympio, who had been assassinated by Gnassingbe Eyadema in 1963, had been perceived in the same way 35 years previously.

For Dr Boutros-Ghali it was a question of trying to keep the institution relevant, indeed to justify its existence, although it was bound to look marginal in the face of the extensive publicity given at the close of the year to the Franco-African summit held in Paris in November. This regular event, now known by the more downbeat title 'Conference of African States with

France', had begun in 1973 as a way of pinning France down to its commitment to francophone African states at a period when disengagement was feared. It had progressively widened its scope to include nearly all African countries (even though the francophone leaders still maintained a separate meeting and dinner on the eve of the main event). In 1998 the non-francophone presence was particularly marked, to the point that President Bongo of Gabon boycotted the event on the grounds that it had lost its identity. A surprising total of 32 Presidents took part, more than attended most OAU summits, as well as participants from 48 of the 54 independent African states, including Egypt, Nigeria, and South Africa.

The political focus of the Paris summit was on some of the main players in the crisis over the war in the eastern Democratic Republic of the Congo (see VII.1.i), including the Presidents of Congo, Uganda, Rwanda, Zimbabwe and Namibia, whose arguments dominated the meeting. Regrettably, the deliberations made little progress towards a ceasefire, in spite of the presence at the conference of UN Secretary-General Kofi Annan.

COMMUNITY OF PORTUGUESE-SPEAKING COUNTRIES. The second summit of heads of state and government from the seven CPLP countries was held in Praia, capital of Cape Verde, on 16–17 July. The highlight of the agenda was the signing of a 'general agreement of cooperation' aiming at the coordination of the various projects of inter-ministerial cooperation discussed at separate CPLP meetings during the year, as well as cooperation between educational and scientific institutions. A new protocol on the spelling of the Portuguese language was signed, to ensure basic uniformity of a language spoken by and taught to nearly 200 million people in countries geographically and economically far apart. Another highlight was the formal constitution of the International Institute of the Portuguese Language, to be permanently based in Cape Verde, geographically the most central of the CPLP countries and, with its miscenated Afro-European population, representative of the Community as a whole.

The Praia summit decided to extend CPLP observer status to East Timor, which was still recognized by the UN as a territory 'under Portuguese administration' and was the subject of a 22-year-old diplomatic dispute with Indonesia. The dispute remained unresolved in 1998, despite the process of democratization in Indonesia that followed the resignation of President Suharto in May and the succession of B.J. Habibie (see XI.1.vi).

The continuing armed confrontation in Angola between the MPLA government and Unita (see VII.1.vi) prompted the summit to adopt a statement deploring Unita's actions in contravention of the Lusaka peace agreement. However, the subsequent increase in hostilities in Angola later in the year showed that the CPLP's appeals for peace had gone unheeded. As regards the renewed insurgency in Guinea-Bissau (see VII.1.iii), the summit created a 'contact group', headed by Cape Verde, which achieved a temporary ceasefire. However, further negotiations between the warring parties were carried out in Abuja, the Nigerian capital, apparently also with only temporary success.

With Angola and Guinea-Bissau riven by armed antagonisms, and Brazil beset by growing financial and social problems (see IV.3.iii), the CPLP as an institution could achieve little more than organizational progress in 1998, rather than the hoped-for political and practical impact. However, various inter-ministerial meetings on culture, tourism and defence were held during the year. In January the Lisbon-based 'Radio/TV Africa' launched a new four-hour daily news and cultural service, and the CPLP pavilion at Expo'98 in Lisbon (see II.4.iii) was given pride of place to promote the ideals of joint cooperation.

The Praia summit elected Dr Marcolino Moco, a former Prime Minister of Angola, for a further two-year term as CPLP executive secretary. The third summit was scheduled to be held in Maputo, Mozambique, in 2000.

iii. NON-ALIGNED MOVEMENT AND DEVELOPING COUNTRIES

Non-Aligned Movement (NAM)
DATE OF FIRST SUMMIT: 1961   HEADQUARTERS: rotating with chair every three years
OBJECTIVES: Originally to promote decolonization and to avoid domination by the concerns of either the Western industrialized world or the Communist bloc; since the early 1970s to provide an authoritative forum to set the political and economic priorities of developing countries; in addition, since the end of the Cold War to resist domination of the UN system by the USA
MEMBERSHIP (END-'98): 114 countries (*those listed in AR 1995, p. 386, plus Belarus*)
CHAIRMAN: President Nelson Mandela of South Africa (since Sept '98)

Group of 77 (G-77)
DATE OF FOUNDATION: 1964   HEADQUARTERS: United Nations centres
OBJECTIVES: To act as an international lobbying group for the concerns of developing countries
MEMBERSHIP (END-'98): 133 developing countries (*those listed in AR 1996, p. 385, minus South Korea, plus China, Eritrea & Turkmenistan*)

THE Coordinating Bureau of the Non-Aligned Movement (NAM) met in Cartagena, Colombia, in May to prepare for the 12th NAM summit conference. This took place in Durban, South Africa, on 2–3 September, with 103 of the members attending. The 11 absentees included Yugoslavia, Uzbekistan and Turkmenistan, plus eight small countries. Despite the absence of the two members from the former Soviet Union, another— Belarus—joined in Durban, bringing the total to 114 countries. In addition, four other former Soviet republics (Armenia, Kazakhstan, Kyrgyzstan and Ukraine), Croatia, China and seven Latin American countries attended as 'observers', while the Russian Federation, Japan, ten members of NATO and 16 other countries, mainly from Europe, were 'guests'. This was the first time that the USA, Britain or Japan had been accorded guest status. In addition, there were even six NGO guests. At the start of the summit, President Nelson Mandela of South Africa took over the NAM chairmanship for the next three years, succeeding President Pastrana of Colombia.

The summit adopted a short *Declaration for the New Millennium*, which stated the general values of the Movement. After expressing satisfaction with the progress achieved in the previous four decades, it stressed that globalization was not just a promise of prosperity but also a threat, unless the South could gain 'dignified partnership, as full equals, with the North'. Eradicating poverty was both a possibility and an imperative. In addition, a final document endorsed detailed positions on all current global issues, with little change in the overall approach from the previous summit (see AR 1995, pp. 383–6).

Although the first Indian nuclear tests occurred immediately before the Cartagena meeting (see VIII.2.i), the Movement did not at this point produce any response beyond its regular condemnation of the nuclear policies of the 'great powers'. In July the South Africans circulated their first draft of the summit's final document. They broke with the standard practice of simply updating the Bureau's communique and introduced major amendments of their own. In particular, they expressed their 'deep concern at the re-emergence of the nuclear arms race'. At the summit, the Bureau's communique was reinstated as the basis for the debate. Nevertheless, a long addition was made putting pressure on India and Pakistan not to conduct any further tests, and in Durban for the first time the Movement called for universal adherence to the 1996 Comprehensive Test-Ban Treaty (see AR 1996, pp. 542–3). The Indians also found that the nuclear tests had damaged their case on the Kashmir question. President Mandela, in his opening speech, called for negotiations between India and Pakistan to resolve the dispute. Despite strong protests in the Indian press and by Prime Minister Vajpayee, the summit endorsed an oblique allusion to 'the need for bilateral dialogue'.

The South African draft had also proposed a strengthening of the NAM's commitment to the elimination of landmines. Despite this lead, and lobbying by the International Campaign to Ban Landmines (a guest NGO), the summit declaration dropped any reference to the Ottawa Convention (see AR 1997, pp. 442–3, 566–8). In practice, by the end of 1998 77 NAM members had committed themselves to abolishing landmines and 30 were among the 58 countries that had ratified the convention. The summit unequivocally condemned the US bombing of Sudan in August as an act of aggression against a pharmaceutical plant (see V.4.1), whereas no mention was made of the simultaneous US bombing of Afghanistan (see VIII.1.ii). Total rejection of unilateral action by the United States did not prevent the strongest possible condemnation being made of terrorism. As a new counter-initiative, the Movement called for a global summit to formulate a joint organized response to terrorism.

Strong support was given to the Palestinians by the Durban summit.

The new elements were a call for the Palestinians to move to full membership of the United Nations and for the Israeli credentials to be rejected with respect to the occupied territories and Jerusalem. In the various African civil wars—in Sierra Leone, Somalia, Liberia and Angola—the overriding concern was for an end to the violence. The Unita leader, Dr Jonas Savimbi, was condemned as being personally accountable for the resumption of hostilities in Angola (see VII.1.vi). The summit was not able to adopt any position on the war in the Democratic Republic of the Congo (see VII.1.i), despite the active diplomacy on the fringes of the conference.

In the debate on economic policy during the year, the Non-Aligned were divided between those who rejected globalization as threatening and those who thought it could provide opportunities for growth in developing countries. The Cartagena meeting mainly stressed the negative impact, while the South African summit draft was somewhat more positive. The Durban summit reinstated virtually all the text from Cartagena. Even so, the Movement fully endorsed the World Trade Organization (WTO) and its principles, not least because it was seen as offering some defence against unilateral economic coercion by the United States. The main concern was to integrate the WTO, plus the IMF and the World Bank, into the UN system and to achieve free trade in food and textiles to benefit developing countries. Concern about the economic crisis in East Asia shifted during the year from advocacy of dampening rapid movement of unpredictable, speculative financial flows to support for 'creating a model for a new international financial system capable of preventing financial crises'. The Durban summit revived a 1983 NAM proposal that an international conference should be held on money and finance, so that all countries, and not just the major industrialized states, could be involved in redefining the role of the IMF.

The summit tried yet again to stimulate greater cohesion in the Movement, with two new initiatives. A panel of economists led by former UNCTAD secretary-general Gamani Corea had produced a report, *Elements for an Agenda of the South*, on the need to formulate alternatives to the 'Washington consensus'. The South African government was mandated to carry out consultations to follow up the report in a practical manner. Similarly, a working group was to prepare 'a complete plan of action' for cooperation between the Movement's members. The old Action Programme of the NAM finally disappeared from sight. It was decided that Bangladesh would host the 13th NAM summit in Dhaka during 2001 (see VIII.2.iii).

The idea of a 'South summit' slowly moved forward (see AR 1997, p. 397), a Group of 77 (G-77) preparatory meeting being held in Jakarta in August. Finally, the 22nd annual meeting of the G-77 in New York on 25 September decided to hold the summit in Cuba at some point in 2000. This meeting also admitted Turkmenistan as a member of the Group, bringing the total to 132 plus China. The developing country representatives in Washington dealing with IMF and World Bank business, the Group of 24, decided to establish a permanent secretariat; but the decision taken in 1996 to create a secretariat for the G-77 in New York had still not been implemented. In February the Centre for South-South Technical Cooperation, funded by the Brunei and Indonesian governments on behalf of the NAM, was opened in Jakarta. A G-77 trade fair was held in New Delhi in November and a meeting of regional cooperation secretariats was held in Bali in December.

iv. ORGANIZATION OF THE ISLAMIC CONFERENCE (OIC)

DATE OF FOUNDATION: 1970   HEADQUARTERS: Jeddah, Saudi Arabia
OBJECTIVES: To further cooperation among Islamic countries in the political, economic, social, cultural and scientific spheres
MEMBERSHIP (END-'98): Afghanistan, Albania, Algeria, Azerbaijan, Bahrain, Bangladesh, Benin, Brunei, Burkina Faso, Cameroon, Chad, Comoros, Djibouti, Egypt, Gabon, The Gambia, Guinea, Guinea-Bissau, Indonesia, Iran, Iraq, Jordan, Kazakhstan, Kuwait, Kyrgyzstan, Lebanon, Libya, Malaysia, Maldives, Mali, Mauritania, Morocco, Mozambique, Niger, Nigeria, Oman, Pakistan, Palestine, Qatar, Saudi Arabia, Senegal, Sierra Leone, Somalia, Sudan, Suriname, Syria, Tajikistan, Togo, Tunisia, Turkey, Turkmenistan, Uganda, Uzbekistan, United Arab Emirates, Yemen, Zanzibar (total 56)
SECRETARY-GENERAL: Azeddine Laraki (Morocco)

FOLLOWING a 'two-summit year' in 1997 (see AR 1997, pp. 399–402), activity within the Organization of the Islamic Conference (OIC) was relatively low-key and routine during 1998.

OIC Foreign Ministers held their 25th meeting in Qatar in mid-March. The ministers had held their 24th meeting in Indonesia in December 1996. In a final communique issued at the close of the meeting, the Foreign Ministers called on those Islamic states which had taken steps towards establishing relations with Israel 'to reconsider such relations by closing missions and bureaus until Israel completes its withdrawal from all occupied Arab territories and fulfils the legitimate rights of the Palestinian people'. They further called on the international community to avoid any action that might recognise Jerusalem as Israel's capital. Expressing full solidarity with the Palestinian Liberation Organization, they urged the USA and Russia (the two co-sponsors of the Middle East peace process) to place pressure on Israel not to make any geographical or demographic transformation in Jerusalem during the course of any future Israeli-Palestinian 'final status' negotiations.

Calling for a peaceful settlement of the Kashmir issue, the ministers condemned 'the continuing massive violations of human rights of the Kashmiri people' and called for the respect of their basic human rights including the right to self-determination. They also called upon member states to take all necessary measures to persuade India to cease forthwith 'the gross and systematic violations of the rights of the Kashmiri people'.

The conference reaffirmed its condemnation of the 'military aggression' by the USA against Libya in 1986 and urged the UN Security Council immediately to suspend the sanctions imposed on Libya.

The conference reaffirmed its support for UN Security Council resolutions which called on Iraq not to use armed forces again in an aggressive manner to threaten neighbouring countries. It expressed sympathy with the Iraqi people and noted with great concern the constant deterioration in the food, health and humanitarian condition of the Iraqi people (see V.2.vi). It called on member states to redouble efforts to assist Iraq in halting human suffering.

The conference affirmed its total rejection of the arbitrary use of military forces against civilians in Kosovo and strongly condemned the large-scale repression of human rights of the Albanian people committed by the Federal Republic of Yugoslavia (see III.2.vi). The conference also reaffirmed the commitment of the OIC member states for the preservation of the unity, territorial integrity and sovereignty of Bosnia & Hercegovina.

The conference decided to hold the next Foreign Ministers meeting in Burkina Faso in April 1999.

4. EUROPEAN UNION

DATE OF FOUNDATION: 1952   HEADQUARTERS: Brussels, Belgium
OBJECTIVES: To seek ever-closer union of member states
MEMBERSHIP (END-'98): Austria, Belgium, Denmark, Finland, France, Germany, Greece, Ireland, Italy, Luxembourg, Netherlands, Portugal, Spain, Sweden, United Kingdom (*total 15*)
PRESIDENT OF EUROPEAN COMMISSION: Jacques Santer (Luxembourg)
EUROPEAN CURRENCY UNIT: £1=ECU1.42, US$1=ECU0.85 (end-'98)

ONE of the most significant developments in the European Union (EU) in 1998 was the shift in the political balance in the EU as a whole. The coming to power of a Red-Green coalition in Germany, just a few weeks before the launch of the euro, together with the installation of a coalition government in Italy led by a former communist, meant that by the end of the year 13 of the 15 EU member country governments were on the centre-left of the political spectrum. The sequence of socialist election successes which had begun the previous year in the UK and France flowered elsewhere in 1998.

Perhaps this shift represented a public reaction to years of lean budgets and public spending controls as required by the Maastricht conditions for EU economic and monetary union. It certainly brought a new tone to the discussions about economic and monetary policy, and a virtual *volte-face* in German policy towards public spending and interest rates. Not that these centre-left governments were all of one mind: the Blair government, for instance, continued to defend liberalized markets and reduction of labour costs, while the incoming German leaders tended to look to more traditional policies for stimulating economic growth and creating new jobs.

ECONOMIC AND MONETARY UNION. In the early months of the year the Commission and the European Monetary Institute (EMI) had to analyse the economic performance of the 15 EU countries in the light of the Maastricht convergence criteria and recommend which countries would be ready to introduce the euro from January 1999.

For the Commission the dramatic EU-wide improvement in public debt and deficit, inflation and interest rates marked the 'advent of a culture of stability in Europe' and opened the way for lower social security charges. The EMI took a darker view, saying that the reduction in budget deficits below 3 per cent of GDP had in part been achieved by *ad hoc* measures and expressed concern that public debt still averaged more than 70 per cent of GDP, against the Maastricht target of 60 per cent, with Belgium and Italy above 120 per cent. The EMI questioned whether overall debt had declined enough and warned of the need for structural reforms in the economy, especially in labour markets. Without such reforms, it said, sustainable improvement of public finances would be extremely arduous. The Germans and the Dutch were both cautious about the Belgian and Italian figures. Chancellor Kohl of Germany wanted a thorough examination of the reports (including a report from the Bundesbank) before a decision could be taken and Dutch Prime Minister Wim Kok said Italy still had major problems.

The weekend of 1–3 May was the moment of decision. European leaders meeting in Brussels under British presidency had to decide formally which countries would introduce the euro from 1 January 1999, the date laid down by the treaty for the launch of the European currency. The Brussels meeting determined that 11 European countries would subsume their national currencies into the euro at the end of the year, namely Belgium, Germany, Spain, France, Ireland, Italy, Luxembourg, the Netherlands, Austria, Portugal and Finland. A monetary union would be created accounting for about 20 per cent of world economic output—roughly equivalent to that of the United States. Of the other four EU member states, the UK and Denmark had no plans to join at that stage. The same applied to Sweden, which in any case did not meet the criteria of currency stability. Greece did not yet qualify because of its level of public spending and interest rates, although the Council welcomed its commitment to join on 1 January 2001.

As leader of a country which had already opted out of the first wave of euro membership, Prime Minister Tony Blair found himself in a difficult position. He had to underline the importance of the new currency while rejecting Britain's part in it. His position as Council president was made more uncomfortable by President Chirac's demand that Jean-Claude Trichet, governor of the Bank of France, should be nominated as the first president of the European Central Bank (ECB) rather than Dutchman Wim Duisenberg, who was supported by the other member states and who had been heading the EMI, precursor of the ECB.

The weekend's arguments made for an inauspicious start to an historic venture and were greeted with widespread cynicism by press and public. M. Trichet's appointment was opposed by 14 member countries, which supported Mr Duisenberg for the full eight-year term stipulated in the Maastricht Treaty. After negotiations described by Chancellor Kohl as among the most difficult he had ever experienced, there was a fudged understanding that Mr Duisenberg might voluntarily step down after four years, making way for the French candidate. That was just enough to pacify the French President.

In an oral statement included in the summit communique, Mr Duisenberg was quoted as saying that, in view of his age, he did not wish to serve the full term; that he wished to see through the transitional arrangements until the withdrawal of national notes and coins (June 2002); that this was 'my decision and my decision alone . . . not under pressure from anyone'; and that 'in future the decision to resign will be my decision alone'. This, he said, 'must be clearly understood'. The ECB was established in Frankfurt on 1 July. Its executive board consisted of six members with varying terms: Mr Duisenberg (the Netherlands), president, eight (possibly four) years; Christian Noyer (France), vice-president, four years; Otmar Issing (Germany), eight years; Tommaso Padoa Schioppa (Italy), seven years; Eugenio Domingo Solans (Spain), six years; Sirkka Hämäläinen (Finland), five years.

The Bank prepared for launch of the euro under challenging political circumstances. Despite coordinated interest rate cuts to 3 per cent in ten of the 11 euro-zone countries in early December—Italy retained slightly higher rates—the new German Finance Minister, Oskar Lafontaine, demanded further cuts to stimulate faltering economic activity and to boost employment. He also joined with his French opposite number to call for a more competitive rate for European currencies on world markets. The ECB stood firm. On 22 December it confirmed that it would set the main short-term interest rate at 3 per cent, Mr Duisenberg stating that the Bank 'was not seeking to signal a further rate cut in the near future'. To underline his independence, the ECB president told *Le Monde* just before Christmas that he had no plans to step down after four years.

There was a political price to pay for Britain's isolation from the prospective euro-zone. The formation of the 'Euro-11 Committee' was especially worrying to the government in London. It formed an inner group of those countries which would espouse the euro from the start. The Committee's first meeting was held immediately following the Brussels summit. The British concern was that this group might hammer out economic policy proposals among themselves and then present their conclusions to the full

Council of 15 member states as a done deal. In areas such as taxation and social security, this was a dangerous prospect.

The preparations for the launch of the euro went according to plan. The final step on the evening of 31 December was publication of the rates at which national currencies would be fixed against the euro as from midnight. The 11 national currencies would become units of a new currency, would no longer fluctuate against each other and would themselves disappear in 2002. The published rates against the euro were as follows: 13.7603 Austrian schillings; 40.3399 Belgian francs; 5,94573 Finnish marks; 6.55957 French francs; 1.95583 German marks; 0.787564 Irish pounds; 1,936.27 Italian lira; 40.3399 Luxembourg francs; 2.20371 Netherlands guilders; 200.482 Portuguese escudos; 166.386 Spanish pesetas.

TAXATION POLICY. Corporate and personal taxation were issues increasingly dominating the political agenda as the launch of the euro approached. One of the first public statements of the new German Finance Minister argued the need for harmonization of taxes and a clampdown on tax havens both inside the EU and further afield. In the view of the German government, the ability of companies and individuals to escape high German taxes by establishing their companies elsewhere or shifting their savings abroad had seriously damaging consequences for the German economy. Herr Lafontaine told his fellow Finance Ministers that he would make harmonization of corporate taxes and elimination of tax havens top priorities for the German EU presidency in the first half of 1999. He also made it clear that he believed that EU fiscal decisions should be taken by qualified majority vote rather than unanimity.

The new German Chancellor, Gerhard Schröder, also described the harmonization of corporate taxation as a priority and revived attacks on 'social dumping', with the implication that those member states with lower rates of taxation should increase them, so becoming less attractive for investors. It was significant that the heads of government meeting at Pörtschach in Austria in October no longer called for a reduction in the non-wage costs of labour, as had most such meetings for the last five years, and concentrated instead on setting minimum social standards and coordinating economic policies as ways of increasing employment

The German initiatives on taxation provoked an unusually outspoken reaction from a dismayed European commissioner, Mario Monti, who had been striving to build a consensus for voluntary tax reform and feared that the whole process would be destabilized, jeopardizing the progress already made. The German moves would be 'premature', he said. The Commission also believed that any moves to harmonize corporate tax levels upwards would damage job creation in Europe. Signor Monti said that it was better to implement the package on harmful tax competition and encourage tax structures which would create more jobs. To illustrate how difficult even this would be, a new Danish finance bill introduced a low tax regime for foreign holding companies—just the sort of measure which a code of conduct agreed 12 months earlier had been intended to phase out.

The tax question could not have come at a worse time for the British government, which was no doubt hoping that a smooth and uncontroversial launch for the euro would make it easier to prepare British public opinion for eventual UK acceptance of the new currency. The statements of German ministers seemed to bear out the fears of those who claimed that EMU would lead to harmonization of tax and social security systems across Europe. The British press gave the issue extended coverage, forcing the government onto the defensive.

The Commission made proposals in May for a withholding tax of 20 per cent on individual earnings from cash and bonds. This tax would apply to investments held in another member state by an EU citizen, with the alternative option of exchanging information on any earnings with the country of residence of the beneficiary. Luxembourg was strongly opposed to introduction of such a measure, while the British were concerned about its impact on the City of London market in eurobonds.

ENLARGEMENT. Formal accession talks with countries wishing to join the EU were launched on 30 March. Six countries were in 'fast track' negotiations, namely Cyprus, the Czech Republic, Estonia, Hungary, Poland and Slovenia; but the accession process was also begun with five second-phase countries, namely Bulgaria, Latvia, Lithuania, Romania and Slovakia. Ten 'accession partnerships' were agreed for the ten countries in Central/Eastern Europe. These outlined the principles, priorities, objectives and conditions for each of the applicants. Individual applicant countries would prepare a national programme for adoption of the body of EU law (the *acquis communautaire*).

A Commission report in November said that the negotiations were broadly on track but did not envisage moving any of the second-phase countries onto the priority list, although there had been substantial progress in Latvia and Lithuania. Malta once again asked to be considered for membership, making 12 candidate countries altogether, not including Turkey. The Turkish position raised serious problems. In an effort to assuage the Turks' intense resentment that they had not been included in either list of candidate countries, EU ministers planned a standing conference on 12 March for all the accession countries plus Turkey. The Turks would not play, though. They refused to participate in the conference, which was held in London, and raised the possibility of annexing the Turkish-controlled zone of Cyprus if the EU should begin negotiations with Nicosia (see II.4.vi).

Signs that the enlargement timetable was slipping became evident at the Pörtschach summit in Austria on 24–25 October. This brought together a new mix of European leaders with new priorities. Change was in the air. Chancellor Kohl, who had dominated European Councils for many years, was coming to the end of his long term in office, and Chancellor-designate Schröder was invited to attend part of the Council as a guest and to participate in the accompanying meeting of Socialist and Social Democratic leaders. A new Italian Prime Minister, former communist Massimo D'Alema, was also among the new faces.

The major victim of changing priorities at Pörtschach was enlargement to the east. Bringing in new member countries would imply far-reaching change, with increased spending, diversion of budget resources away from the traditional beneficiaries, low-cost imports of agricultural products in particular, the likelihood of increased immigration and generally difficult adjustment for the EU. Herr Kohl's enthusiasm for enlargement was replaced by a more cautious approach on the part of his successor, who warned that 'the process will be more difficult and complicated than first thought', adding: 'We must conduct accession negotiations in a measured fashion and not awaken false hopes among candidate countries'. It was important, said Herr Schröder, that too much should not be asked of the EU and its citizens.

AGENDA 2000. In March the European Commission set out detailed proposals elaborating its 'Agenda 2000' programme published in July 1997, covering the EU structural funds, the common agricultural policy (CAP), aid to candidate countries and the EU budget arrangements for 2000–2006. Under these proposals, 218,000 million ecu would be voted for the period 2000–2006 for structural funds (the Regional and Social Funds) to stimulate investment and training in the disadvantaged regions of the Union. The funds would be simplified and concentrated on areas of greatest need, covering 35–40 per cent of the population rather than the current 51 per cent, with strong emphasis on competitiveness and job-creation. No EU country would see an increase in the number of regions benefiting from the funds.

On agriculture, the proposals would extend the reforms launched in 1992, with further reductions in agricultural price support levels and increased direct payments to farmers. The Commission argued that this would improve the competitiveness of EU agriculture on domestic and world markets, reducing the risk of returning to expensive surpluses. The level of subsidy would be reduced for large farms and there would be more scope for individual governments to compensate farmers for more environmentally-friendly husbandry.

Aid to the countries applying to join the Union would total ECU 3,000 million ecu a year from 2000 to 2006. Ministers agreed to mobilize these sums by setting up two funds, the first (ISPA) to provide regional investment incentives and training and the second (SAPARD) to help modernize agriculture and promote rural development. Parallel assistance from the existing PHARE programme would be devoted to strengthening administration and the law. As for the EU budget, the Commission proposed that the ceiling on 'own resources' (which consisted of the Union's four sources of income) should be fixed at 1.27 per cent of GDP. The Council of Ministers had failed to come to grips with most of these issues by the end of the year. The series of interlocking issues making decisions more difficult included Germany's determination to cut the level of its net contribution (forcefully expressed by the new government), Britain's refusal to abandon the rebate limiting its payments to the budget, Spain's concern to maintain its level of income from the structural funds and the commitment of France to the maintenance of the CAP.

EU-US RELATIONS. Trade relations between the United States and the EU fluctuated violently during the year, beginning with idealistic plans for a new relationship and ending with a bitter dispute over bananas. In March the European Commission proposed the creation of a new 'trans-Atlantic market-place', which would have included the removal of tariff and non-tariff barriers to trade between the parties, complete elimination of industrial tariffs by 2010 (subject to international support), free trade in services and liberalization of investment, public procurement and intellectual property. The architect of the plan, Commission Vice-President Sir Leon Brittan, said that such an agreement would bring fresh political momentum to trans-Atlantic relations as well as economic benefits.

However, Sir Leon's formula was viewed with deep suspicion by the French government, for which the plan was a way of building a free trade area while calling it something else. It was left to the British presidency to construct an agreement at the EU-US summit held in London on 18 May which was accepted by the EU Council of Ministers and the US administration by the end of the year. The 18 May agreement had various interlocking elements. It covered sanctions on investments by European firms in Cuba, Iran and Libya, created a 'Trans-Atlantic Economic Partnership' to deal with economic issues, promised new initiatives for trade liberalization at the World Trade Organization (WTO) and established a stronger basis for political cooperation.

The sanctions issue had bedevilled EU-US relations for some time, since approval of the Helms-Burton and D'Amato Acts by the US Congress. At the London meeting President Clinton agreed that any sanctions against European companies should be waived. In return, the Europeans accepted certain definitions of expropriated property—of special importance to the Cuba lobby in the US. The EU also gave a range of commitments to work against arms proliferation in Iran—especially in the field of missiles—and to ratify 11 anti-terrorism conventions. The deal meant that projects such as Total's Iranian oil pipeline would not attract US sanctions and that future European projects in the region would not be targeted, although the US side refused a blanket EU exemption. The Europeans were able to underline that it was up to companies to decide on investments.

The Trans-Atlantic Economic Partnership (TEP), which had taken the place of the 'trans-Atlantic market-place', made no mention of a free trade area or tariff elimination, but did provide for extensive bilateral negotiations to remove non-tariff barriers in areas like services, investment, public procurement, intellectual property and regulatory barriers to trade. The details of the TEP were fleshed out during the year and finally endorsed at the Washington summit in December.

Despite this apparent progress on the political front, individual cases were causing serious damage. The most difficult issue concerned bananas. A WTO panel had ruled that the European import regime for bananas—which favoured Caribbean producers—must be changed to respect international trading rules. The EU revised the import arrangements, but American exporters of Latin American bananas complained to the US administration that there was still discrimination. Accordingly, the US government announced in October that it would impose 100 per cent import duties on a range of European products unless the EU changed its banana regime. In December, moreover, it announced its 'hit list' of European products. The European Commission condemned the US action, calling on the Americans to go back to the WTO for a new ruling. 'It is difficult to think of a more obvious breach of the multilateral trading system than to take the law into your own hands', said Sir Leon Brittan. Both the EU and Ecuador approached the WTO dispute settlement body in Geneva for new rulings, but Jamaica and the USA used their veto to delay this process.

Another issue which threatened trouble was the EU data-protection legislation, which came into force in October. This would oblige companies transferring personal data outside the EU to demonstrate that the other country involved had equivalent controls. The absence of such controls in the USA led to difficult negotiations between the two sides, which had not resolved the matter by the end of the year (see XIII.2).

FOREIGN AND SECURITY POLICY. The launch of the euro was the main internal preoccupation for the EU in 1998. The main external challenge came from instability in the international economic environment, with the Russian and Asian crises putting in jeopardy the growth forecasts so confidently made and relied upon to cut Europe's 10–11 per cent unemployment figures and boost economic activity. Against this background, the common foreign and security policy showed little sign of life. There was not much common ground between the EU partners concerning the two principal trouble-spots, Serbia/Kosovo and Iraq. The British government acted with the Americans in both regions, while little attempt was made to coordinate a European policy.

The UK did begin to ask questions about the future of European defence. At the Pörtschach meeting in Austria Mr Blair recognized the need for a 'European defence identity' as conceived in the Maastricht Treaty and launched a debate, but there were still differences as to how it might be achieved. One possibility was to establish a right of European action under NATO without American involvement; another was to merge the Western European Union (WEU) and the EU, which raised big questions about NATO's status; and a third was to disband the WEU and transfer its military capability to NATO. There was no consensus during the Pörtschach meeting.

THE PARLIAMENT'S CHALLENGE. The year ended badly for the Commission. The European Parliament flexed its muscles and refused to sign off the budget accounts for 1996, conscious that European elections would be held in June 1999. As an increasing catalogue was put together of alleged fraud, maladministration and bending of the budgetary rules, the parliamentarians saw an opportunity to strengthen their own position at the expense of the Commission. The Commission responded with plans to restructure its organization and to set up an independent fraud investigation office. Commission president Jacques Santer announced that a review of internal management was taking place, whose conclusions would be available in 1999. The new fraud investigation office would be independent of any EU institution with the remit of investigating suspected fraud or corruption both in these institutions and in the member states. The MEPs were dissatisfied by the tone and the content of the Commission's response, however, and by the end of the year were threatening a vote of censure on the whole college.

5. EUROPEAN ORGANIZATIONS

i. COUNCIL OF EUROPE

DATE OF FOUNDATION: 1949   HEADQUARTERS: Strasbourg, France
OBJECTIVES: To strengthen pluralist democracy, the rule of law and the maintenance of human rights in Europe and to further political, social and cultural cooperation between member-states
MEMBERSHIP (END-'98): Albania, Andorra, Austria, Belgium, Bulgaria, Croatia, Cyprus, Czech Republic, Denmark, Estonia, Finland, France, Germany, Greece, Hungary, Iceland, Ireland, Italy, Latvia, Liechtenstein, Lithuania, Luxembourg, Macedonia, Malta, Moldova, Netherlands, Norway, Poland, Portugal, Romania, Russia, San Marino, Slovakia, Slovenia, Spain, Sweden, Switzerland, Turkey, Ukraine, United Kingdom (*total 40*)
SECRETARY-GENERAL: Daniel Tarschys (Sweden)

THE action plan agreed at the Council of Europe's second summit in October 1997 (see AR 1997, pp. 412, 559–61) provided the backdrop and motivation behind much of the organization's activities throughout the year.

The 'committee of wise persons', set up subsequently to re-examine the Council of Europe's structure and decision-making processes in the light of its expanded membership, reported to the Council of Ministers towards the end of 1998. It called for a clearer affirmation of the organization's responsibility for democratic stability through the promotion of pluralist democracy, human rights and the rule of law. The committee recommended that the highest priority be given to the monitoring of commitments given by member states and to the provision of assistance necessary to help newer members fulfil their obligations. Consequently, it believed that an increase in resources was necessary. The committee called for improved practical cooperation with the European Union and the Organization for Security and Cooperation in Europe (OSCE), something which was already being pursued in high-level meetings during the year. Proposals to streamline the structure of the secretariat were to be complemented by the simplification of decision-making procedures in the Council of Ministers. These recommendations were set to be considered by the Committee of Ministers and the Assembly in the early part of 1999.

The new emphasis on the monitoring of commitments given by member states was reflected in the work of the Parliamentary Assembly's monitoring committee. It kept under review progress in Albania, Bulgaria, Croatia, Latvia, Moldova, Russia, Slovakia, 'the former Yugoslav Republic of Macedonia', Turkey and Ukraine. Following a debate over the ratification of the Ukrainian delegation in January, the committee later expressed deep concern over the failure of Ukraine to meet its obligations, particularly on the cessation of capital punishment. Assistance continued to be provided in the monitoring of elections in member states, often in conjunction with an OSCE monitoring team (see XI.5.ii). The elections in Macedonia in October (see III.2.iv) were viewed to have been conducted satisfactorily, as were those in Latvia (see III.1.ii). In respect of the presidential election in Azerbaijan, however, the Assembly delegation recognized the progress that had been made since the 1995 elections but drew attention to serious shortcomings and believed that 'a radical change of mentalities' was needed if a genuinely democratic climate were to be maintained (see III.3.iii).

Perhaps the most significant achievement of the Council of Europe during the year was the establishment of the single European Court of Human Rights, under the terms of the 11th Protocol of the Human Rights Convention. The judges were elected—one from each country—by the Parliamentary Assembly during the early part of the year, and the new Court was inaugurated at a ceremony in Strasbourg on 1 November. Only the Russian judge remained to be appointed by the end of the year. The Council of Ministers also developed proposals to establish a Human Rights Commissioner to promote awareness of and respect for human rights.

A formal application for membership of the Council of Europe was received from the Federal Republic of Yugoslavia, but the deteriorating situation there (see III.2.vi) led to the issue being shelved. Belgrade was told that a radical change of policy was required before the application would be seriously considered. The two-year-old membership application from Georgia received support from the relevant Assembly committees in December. In calling for the Council of Ministers to issue a formal invitation, the political affairs committee set out a long list of commitments which would need to be met, including the legal guarantee of broad autonomy for the existing three autonomous territories within Georgia. Aside from these applications, the Council of Europe maintained varied programmes of assistance and cooperation with Albania, Belarus, Bosnia & Hercegovina and Croatia.

The 'committee of wise persons' recommended the strengthening of the Social Development Fund (SDF) and its expansion to support projects in non-Fund member states. Already, a campaign to increase the membership of the SDF had encouraged the accession of over 30 member states. A new Convention on the Protection of the Environment through the Criminal Law was adopted and opened for signature.

The Committee of Ministers aimed to reach agreement on the restructuring of the Council of Europe to provide better support for its redefined role by the time of its 50th anniversary in May 1999. The celebrations surrounding this anniversary would provide an opportunity for the Council of Europe to enhance this role and raise its profile in Europe's institutional landscape.

ii. ORGANIZATION FOR SECURITY AND COOPERATION IN EUROPE (OSCE)

DATE OF FOUNDATION: 1975   HEADQUARTERS: Vienna, Austria
OBJECTIVES: To promote security and cooperation among member states, particularly in respect of the resolution of internal and external conflicts
MEMBERSHIP (END-'98): Albania, Andorra, Armenia, Austria, Azerbaijan, Belarus, Belgium, Bosnia & Hercegovina, Bulgaria, Canada, Croatia, Cyprus, Czech Republic, Denmark, Estonia, Finland, France, Georgia, Germany, Greece, Holy See (Vatican), Hungary, Iceland, Ireland, Italy, Kazakhstan, Kyrgyzstan, Latvia, Liechtenstein, Lithuania, Luxembourg, Macedonia, Malta, Moldova, Monaco, Netherlands, Norway, Poland, Portugal, Romania, Russian Federation, San Marino, Slovakia, Slovenia, Spain, Sweden, Switzerland, Tajikistan, Turkey, Turkmenistan, Ukraine, United Kingdom, United States, Uzbekistan, Yugoslavia (suspended) (*total 55*)
SECRETARY-GENERAL: Giancarlo Aragona (Italy)

IN 1998 the OSCE celebrated its 25th anniversary. On 3 July 1973 the then 35 participating states had met to open the Conference on Security and Cooperation in Europe (CSCE). The result was the 1975 Helsinki Final Act (see AR 1975, pp. 474–9), which marked the high tide of détente in Europe. From those inauspicious beginnings, the OSCE had developed into Europe's primary instrument for conflict prevention, crisis management and post-conflict rehabilitation, in a geographical area stretching eastwards from Vancouver to Vladivostock. The contemporary importance of the OSCE was underlined by US Secretary of State Madeleine Albright. In her address to the OSCE's permanent council on 3 September she described the organization as 'our instrument of choice for defending democracy' and as 'uniquely suited to occupy the middle ground between diplomacy and force'.

The year began with the handover of the chairmanship of the OSCE from Denmark to Poland. The new chairman-in-office (CIO) was Polish Foreign Minister Bronislaw Geremek, one of the generation of East European dissident intellectuals who had drawn sustenance from the CSCE's commitment to human rights during the 1970s and 1980s. Not surprisingly, in his first speech as chairman-in-office, Mr Bronislaw stressed that 'solidarity'—in the sense of a shared responsibility for common values and objectives—'should serve as a common denominator for developing in the OSCE a common strategy for implementing all commitments, eliminating injustice and protecting the weak'.

Mr Geremek's diplomatic rhetoric reflected the high expectations which often surrounded the OSCE. In reality, much of its work in 1998 was more prosaic. A major function of the OSCE was to provide an institutionalized forum for regular diplomatic discussions and negotiations on a comprehensive range of issues among its 55 member states. The main body for political consultation and decision-making was the permanent council, which met weekly in the Hofburg congress centre in Vienna. A senior council, composed of high-ranking officials, met occasionally, and once a year constituted an economic forum (on 1–5 June it met in Prague to discuss the security aspects of energy development). In December OSCE Foreign Ministers met in Oslo for a ministerial council. In addition, the OSCE parliamentary assembly held its seventh annual meeting in Copenhagen from 7–10 July, bringing together 300 parliamentarians from 54 participating states (the Federal Republic of Yugoslavia having been suspended from the OSCE since 1992).

With its many forums for regular diplomatic exchange, the OSCE functioned as a mini-UN—indeed, it formally constituted a regional arrangement under Chapter VIII of the UN Charter. If, however, the OSCE were only a means of diplomatic 'jaw-jaw', it would excite little interest. What made the organization of growing importance in contemporary Europe was its role as an instrument for preventive diplomacy, crisis management and post-conflict rehabilitation. It was these activities—particularly in the Balkans, Caucasus and Central Asia—which generated most public interest.

During 1998 the bulk of the OSCE's time, energy and resources were concentrated on former Yugoslavia. The OSCE's biggest mission to date was in Bosnia & Hercegovina, where the organization had primary responsibility for implementing the civilian tasks of the Dayton Accords (see AR 1995, pp. 559–62). This mission, headed by ambassador Robert

Barry (USA), was working to strengthen the fragile process of democratization and inter-ethnic reconciliation. In early 1998 a major preoccupation was ensuring the implementation of the September 1997 municipal election results (see AR 1997, pp. 126–7), resolving disputes through binding arbitration where necessary. The mission also organized a bus service from Banja Luka to Sarajevo to facilitate movement across the 'inter-entity boundary line', and ran a multi-media campaign on the theme of 'tolerance and non-discrimination'. Finally, ambassador Henry Jacolin (France) was appointed as the CIO's special representative with the task of negotiating further regional arms control measures in and around Bosnia.

In neighbouring Croatia the OSCE mission worked hard to bolster the Croatian authorities' half-hearted efforts at democratization and inter-ethnic reconciliation, focusing in particular on the safe return of Serbian refugees. With the handover of UNTAES peace-keeping responsibilities for Eastern Slavonia to Croatia on 15 January (see III.2.iii), the OSCE became the main international organization in Croatia. The OSCE also acquired a new responsibility on 15 October when it began deploying civilian police monitors. At the end of the year, however, the OSCE mission was forced to report that, despite the many promises of the Croatian government, discrimination and intimidation against the Serb minority persisted. Such behaviour, they warned, was harming Croatia's prospects of joining the European integration process.

Throughout 1998 increasing attention was paid by the OSCE to the deepening crisis in Kosovo (see III.2.vi), and it was here that the organization was to face its toughest and most high-profile challenge. During the year the OSCE monitored the deteriorating situtation from its missions in neighbouring Albania and Macedonia (FYROM). Following a major Serb offensive in August, and calls for NATO military intervention, it was announced on 13 October that the OSCE was to organize, deploy and run a 2,000-strong, unarmed mission to verify the fragile ceasefire. The Kosovo Verification Mission (KVM) was to be headed by ambassador William Walker (USA) and would be supported by NATO air surveillance. A NATO 'extraction force' was also deployed in Macedonia in the event that the ceasefire collapsed completely.

As Mr Geremek noted, the creation of the KVM provided the OSCE with both a 'tremendous challenge and a tremendous opportunity'. The KVM was ten times the size of any previous OSCE mission, so that organizing and deploying it presented major logistical problems. Although it was not expected to be fully operational until January 1999, by year's end 1,125 staff were already in the field. Unfortunately, their presence was not able to prevent further fighting and atrocities, and throughout December they reported an escalating number of ceasefire violations. One thing was clear: the Kosovo mission amounted to a major test for the OSCE. Its performance would greatly colour perceptions of the OSCE's utility and credibility, and would therefore have important consequences for the future of the European security system.

Outside the Balkans, the OSCE was involved in a series of other conflict prevention and crisis management activities, particularly around the fringes of the former Soviet Union. In Georgia, the OSCE mission continued to support UN efforts to end the conflicts in Abkhazia and South Ossetia, although with little success. In the conflict over Nagorno-Karabakh between Armenia and Azerbaijan (known in diplomatic parlance as 'the conflict dealt with by the OSCE Minsk conference'), the OSCE continued its mediation efforts, but to little avail. In mid-February OSCE monitoring of the 'line of contact' between the warring parties was suspended after the monitoring team were shot at. Monitoring resumed on 11 May, but no political settlement was in sight.

In Moldova, the OSCE mission continued to mediate between the Moldovan government and the authorities in Transdnestria, and to monitor the withdrawal of Russian troops. In war-torn Chechenya, the OSCE assistance group now constituted the only permanent presence by any international organization. Its role had expanded from mediation between Russians and Chechens to include the delivery of humanitarian aid, particularly after a series of severe spring landslides. Unfortunately, OSCE efforts could not prevent renewed fighting in July and a new wave of hostage-taking.

More positively, the OSCE welcomed the simplified naturalization procedures and new citizenship law in Latvia (see III.1.ii), which the organization had been advocating for some time. The OSCE also carried out the last inspection of the Skrunda radar station, which was shut down on schedule on 31 August as part of an OSCE-brokered deal between Russia and Latvia. In Ukraine, the OSCE mission played a part in facilitating the return of the Crimean Tatars from Uzbekistan to Ukraine. An OSCE advisory and monitoring group began work in Belarus, seeking to promote democracy, the rule of law and respect for human rights. The OSCE also strengthened its presence in Central Asia by opening three new centres. Finally, the newly-appointed OSCE representative on freedom of the media, Freimut Duve (Germany), began his work to strengthen 'the implementation of our common values and democratic convictions'.

The OSCE had many weaknesses and limitations: it lacked funds and resources; was short of trained personnel; had cumbersome decision-making procedures; and had to fight turf battles with the Council of Europe, the UN and the European Union. Nonetheless, its impact on European affairs had been overwhelmingly positive. Timothy Garton-Ash, the British writer who was awarded the OSCE prize for journalism and democracy by the parliamentary assembly in July, praised it for being 'one of the few organizations really to try to seize the chance that was opened in 1989, a chance . . . of building a liberal order for the whole of Europe, not just for a part of it'.

iii. EUROPEAN BANK FOR RECONSTRUCTION AND DEVELOPMENT (EBRD)

DATE OF FOUNDATION: 1991   HEADQUARTERS: London, UK
OBJECTIVES: To promote the economic reconstruction of former Communist-ruled countries on the basis of the free-market system and pluralism
MEMBERSHIP (END-'98): Albania, Armenia, Australia, Austria, Azerbaijan, Belarus, Belgium, Bosnia & Hercegovina, Bulgaria, Canada, Croatia, Cyprus, Czech Republic, Denmark, Egypt, Estonia, European Investment Bank, European Union, Finland, France, Georgia, Germany, Greece, Hungary, Iceland, Ireland, Israel, Italy, Japan, Kazakhstan, Kyrgyzstan, South Korea, Latvia, Liechtenstein, Lithuania, Luxembourg, Macedonia, Malta, Mexico, Moldova, Morocco, Netherlands, New Zealand, Norway, Poland, Portugal, Romania, Russia, Slovakia, Slovenia, Spain, Sweden, Switzerland, Tajikistan, Turkey, Turkmenistan, Ukraine, United Kingdom, United States, Uzbekistan (*total 60*)
PRESIDENT: Horst Köhler (Germany)

SHORTLY after the Russian financial crisis, precipitated by devaluation and a debt moratorium on 17 August (see III.3.i), the EBRD's board of directors reviewed the consequences of defaults in a country to which it had committed 2,700 million ecu (27 per cent of its total commitments) and already disbursed in loans or equity investments 1,400 million ecu (26 per cent). Although the Russian central bank explicitly assured the EBRD that these investments were exempted from the moratorium, the depreciation of the rouble, the collapse of share prices and the renewed downturn in national economic activity reduced the Bank's prospective earnings on them and posed the danger of default by private-sector borrowers, 34 per cent of disbursements to Russia having been to commercial banks and 18 per cent to oil and gas enterprises. The former were part of the August crisis and the latter had diminished profit prospects by reason of the sharp fall in the world market price of oil.

Having previously made provision against 171 million ecu of the funds disbursed in Russia, the Bank added a further 180 million ecu. The board announced that, unlike in previous years, its end-year accounts would show a loss. When the year's accounts were released, provisions of 553.1 million ecu were set against profit of 291.8 million ecu, producing a loss of 261.2 million ecu. Steven Kaempfer (Netherlands), the EBRD vice-president for finance, declared: 'The Bank is strongly capitalized and its financial viability is not affected.' It was later announced that projects worth 2,400 million ecu had been signed in 1998. On 1 October the new EBRD president, Horst Köhler (Germany), and the EU commissioner for economic, financial and monetary affairs, Yves-Thibaud de Silguy, agreed to establish a joint working group to monitor the situation in Russia and to coordinate their work in three key areas—restructuring the banking sector, supporting small and medium-size enterprises and strengthening the investment climate in Russia.

Herr Köhler had been appointed by the EBRD board of governors in July and took office for a four-year term on 1 September, following which he visited Moscow for discussions with the Russian Prime Minister, Yevgenii Primakov. His nomination for the post had been seen to be in the lead (over French, Italian and Spanish candidates) during the Bank's annual meeting in Kiev (Ukraine) on 16–20 April and was in part made politically possible by the appointment of a Dutchman as governor of the new European Central Bank (see XI.4). Herr Köhler had previously been president of the Deutscher Sparkassen- und Giroverband (DSG).

Among large projects supported by the EBRD during the year was a financing package of US$450 million—of which the Bank and the World Bank's International Finance Corporation provided $250 million—to supplement the owner's $350 million finance for Ispat Karmet in Kazakhstan, one of the world's biggest integrated steel plants. Another was the allocation of $190 million to help towards the $1,700 million needed by the Ukrainian government to close the Chernobyl nuclear power station (see AR 1986, pp. 100–1) and to complete two other reactors started in the Soviet period.

In accordance with the alternation of EBRD annual meetings between London headquarters and a member state, the 1999 session was to be held in the UK capital and the 2000 session in the Latvian capital, Riga.

iv. NORDIC, BALTIC AND ARCTIC ORGANIZATIONS

Nordic Council
DATE OF FOUNDATION: 1952   HEADQUARTERS: Stockholm, Sweden
OBJECTIVES: To facilitate legislative and governmental cooperation between member states, with particular reference to proposals of the Nordic Council of Ministers
MEMBERSHIP (END-'98): Denmark, Finland, Iceland, Norway, Sweden (*total 5*)
SECRETARY-GENERAL: Anders Wenström (Sweden)

Baltic Council
DATE OF FOUNDATION: 1992   HEADQUARTERS: rotating
OBJECTIVES: To promote political, economic and social cooperation between the three Baltic republics
MEMBERSHIP (END-'98): Estonia, Latvia, Lithuania (*total 3*)

Council of the Baltic Sea States (CBSS)
DATE OF FOUNDATION: 1992   HEADQUARTERS: Stockholm, Sweden
OBJECTIVES: To promote political, economic and other cooperation between Baltic littoral and adjacent states
MEMBERSHIP (END-'98): Denmark, Estonia, Finland, Germany, Latvia, Lithuania, Norway, Poland, Russia, Sweden (*total 10*)

Arctic Council (AC)
DATE OF FOUNDATION: 1996   HEADQUARTERS: Ottawa, Canada
OBJECTIVES: To promote cooperation between Arctic states (involving indigenous communities) on environmental issues and on the social and economic development of the region
MEMBERSHIP (END-'98): Canada, Denmark, Finland, Iceland, Norway, Russia, Sweden, United States (*total 8*)

LITHUANIA took over the chairmanship of the Council of the Baltic Sea States (CBSS) from Denmark in July. As expected, the organization created a permanent secretariat during the autumn. Based in Stockholm, the new body would be concerned with long-term planning, coordination and dissemination of information on regional initiatives. The location of the secretariat underlined Sweden's continued efforts to place itself at the centre of the emerging regional architecture.

In January the Latvian capital, Riga, provided the historically symbolic setting for the second summit of CBSS heads of government, which saw the first-ever meeting of German and Russian leaders on the territory of the Baltic states. The heads of government voiced their satisfaction with the work of the task force on organized crime established following their last meeting in 1996. They also expressed support for the creation of an integrated 'energy ring' which would open the region to Norwegian and North Sea oil and gas supplies. This initiative would serve to reduce the current dependence of the Baltic states on Russian gas whilst simultaneously opening a broader regional market for Russia's energy exports. The espousal of the proposals by then Prime Minister Viktor Chernomyrdin was regarded in some circles as a belated recognition by Russia of the commercial and strategic advantages to be gained from regional cooperation. However, forecasts of enhanced Russian involvement in Baltic affairs were likely to need some revision in the light of the crisis which hit the country later in the year (see III.3.i).

The Danish presidency of the CBSS concluded with the eighth ministerial council held in Nyborg on 22–23 June. Building on the earlier heads of government meeting, CBSS Foreign Ministers launched the implementation phase of 'Baltic 21', a common regional action programme for sustainable development which particularly emphasized environmental protection and infrastructure development.

The increased emphasis given by the CBSS to environmental issues dovetailed with the work of the Arctic Council, which met at Iqaluit, Canada, in September. Similarly, representatives of the Barents Euro-Arctic Region (BEAR) emphasized the need for greater coordination with the programmes of other northern European actors during the fifth BEAR council meeting at Lulea, Sweden in January. Sweden's chairmanship of the organization concluded with a proposed action plan for the management of energy resources and improvement of energy efficiency. The chair then passed to Norway, which would host the next meeting early in 1999.

European economic and monetary union again figured prominently on the agenda at the 50th session of the Nordic Council in November. Earlier, Council president Berit Brørby Larsen had warned that the organization would be reduced to a 'cultural club' if the constituent states did not adopt a more active role towards the European Union (EU). Nordic leaders were therefore urged to seize the opportunities offered by EU enlargement, which would increase the prominence of large regional units such as Norden and the Baltic. As such, the Council presidium welcomed the Finnish initiative on the 'Northern Dimension' (see AR 1997, p. 77). The importance attached to the 'adjacent areas' of Russia was also apparent in proposals for a parliamentary dimension to Barents Sea cooperation. In addition, the Council pledged to strengthen further joint Nordic efforts in the field of peace-keeping operations, which had yielded good results in the Balkans.

In a similar vein, the inter-parliamentary Baltic Assembly again sought to downplay tensions arising from the projected eastwards enlargement of the EU (see AR 1997, p. 419). Addressing the Assembly's 12th session at Ventspils, Latvia, in May, Estonian Prime Minister Mart Siimann argued that common foreign policy objectives should stimulate rather than impede cooperation between the Baltic states. To this end, the three countries undertook to harmonize regulations on intra-Baltic trade and transit shipments, with a view to creating a joint economic area. At its next meeting in Tallinn during November, the Assembly underlined the importance of ongoing military cooperation and the joint contribution to peace-keeping operations. A joint declaration called upon the forthcoming NATO summit to include Estonia, Latvia and Lithuania in a second round of expansion of the alliance.

v. OTHER EUROPEAN ORGANIZATIONS

European Free Trade Association (EFTA)
DATE OF FOUNDATION: 1960   HEADQUARTERS: Geneva, Switzerland
OBJECTIVES: To eliminate barriers to non-agricultural trade between members
MEMBERSHIP (END-'98): Iceland, Liechtenstein, Norway, Switzerland (*total 4*)
SECRETARY-GENERAL: Kjartan Jóhannsson (Iceland)

Central European Free Trade Association (CEFTA)
DATE OF FOUNDATION: 1992   HEADQUARTERS: rotating
OBJECTIVES: Reducing trade barriers between members with a view to their eventual membership of the European Union
MEMBERSHIP (END-'98): Czech Republic, Hungary, Poland, Romania, Slovakia, Slovenia (*total 6*)

Central European Initiative (CEI)
DATE OF FOUNDATION: 1992   HEADQUARTERS: rotating
OBJECTIVES: To promote the harmonization of economic and other policies of member states
MEMBERSHIP (END-'98): Albania, Austria, Belarus, Bosnia & Hercegovina, Bulgaria, Croatia, Czech Republic, Hungary, Italy, Macedonia, Moldova, Poland, Romania, Slovakia, Slovenia, Ukraine (*total 16*)

Black Sea Economic Cooperation Council (BSEC)
DATE OF FOUNDATION: 1992   HEADQUARTERS: Istanbul, Turkey
OBJECTIVES: To promote economic cooperation between member states
MEMBERSHIP (END-'98): Albania, Armenia, Azerbaijan, Bulgaria, Georgia, Greece, Moldova, Romania, Russia, Turkey, Ukraine (*total 11*)
DIRECTOR: Eugeny Kutuvoy (Turkey)

HAVING achieved a heightened profile in 1997 (see AR 1997, pp. 420-1), the European Free Trade Association (EFTA) continued to be visible during 1998. At a ministerial meeting in Loèche-les-Bains, Switzerland, on 30 November, the four member states signed an interim free trade agreement with the Palestine Liberation Organization (PLO), acting on behalf of the Palestinian Authority. EFTA had now concluded 14 free trade agreements with partners in Central/Eastern Europe and the Mediterranean, as well as declarations on cooperation with a further six. Free trade negotiations with Cyprus, Jordan and Egypt were also opened during 1998, whilst talks with Tunisia continued to progress. It was further anticipated that recent contact with the Gulf Cooperation Council (GCC) might lead to the signature of an EFTA-GCC declaration on cooperation in the near future. Ministers confirmed that the final aim was the creation of a comprehensive Euro-Mediterranean free trade zone by 2010. They also expressed satisfaction at the opening of negotiations with Canada, which were intended to prepare the way for the first-ever trans-Atlantic free trade agreement.

Since three of EFTA's four members (Iceland, Liechtenstein and Norway) participated in the European Economic Area (EEA) with the 15 European Union (EU) member states, relations with the EU remained of paramount importance for EFTA. These were considerably enhanced when Switzerland (the one EFTA member not included in the EEA) signed on 4 December its own free trade agreement with the EU after four years of negotiations (see also II.2.vii). The agreement, which was expected to add 0.5 per cent to Swiss GDP annually, covered road and air transport, research, procurement, agriculture and preferential access to markets, the free movement of people, and the mutual application of trade standards. A breakthrough in the bilateral negotiations had come when Swiss and EU Transport Ministers agreed on an accord for Alpine charges on lorries. This involved lifting a Swiss ban on vehicles over 28 tonnes in return for a toll based on environmental damage caused by such vehicles. It was estimated that access to shorter trade routes through the Alps would save the EU more than 50 million ecu per year in transport costs. However, the agreement had yet to be ratified by the Swiss Federal Assembly, commentators pointing out that in the past the Swiss had expressed reluctance to forge closer links with the EU. It was also noted that the agreement could still be challenged by a public referendum.

Bulgaria announced on 17 July that it would join the Central European Free Trade Association (CEFTA) on 1 January 1999, thereby becoming the organization's seventh member state. With CEFTA planning to phase out tariffs between member-states by 2002, membership of the organization was seen as a first step towards accession to the EU. At the annual CEFTA summit held in Prague on 11 September, the attending heads of government agreed to set up a sub-committee on agricultural trade to help solve trade disputes. Poland and Romania had both recently imposed taxes on agricultural imports from Hungary, and Slovakia announced at the summit that it would impose a 70 per cent levy on grain imports from

Hungary. Claiming that such actions violated CEFTA norms, Hungarian Prime Minister Viktor Orban pledged to lodge a complaint with the World Trade Organization (WTO). The hostile atmosphere was further reinforced when Mr Orban expressed support for a Czech initiative to give CEFTA a 'political dimension' in the face of stiff opposition from the Romanian and Slovak Prime Ministers.

Mr Orban and his Czech and Polish counterparts, Milos Zeman and Jerzy Buzek, agreed at a meeting in Budapest on 21 October to resume the Visegrad Group (the forerunner to CEFTA, formed in 1991) to coordinate the three countries' bid to join the EU and the North Atlantic Treaty Organization (NATO). The leaders resolved to meet at least twice a year and welcomed the possibility of Slovakia's return to the group following the defeat of the Meciar government in the country's September general election. It was also announced that cooperation between the member countries would be extended to the spheres of culture and telecommunications.

The loosely-organized Central European Initiative (CEI), with 16 member states, continued to be the biggest grouping in Central/Eastern Europe. In 1998 the CEI presidency was held by Croatia, its 'troika' for the year also including Bosnia & Hercegovina (which had held the presidency in 1997) and the next-in-line Czech Republic. Croatia's main priority goals for the year were to increase cooperation between member states across all fields and to promote increased dialogue with the EU. (Of the CEI members, the Czech Republic, Hungary, Poland and Slovenia had already opened bilateral accession negotiations with the EU, whilst several other states had expressed a desire to join.)

On 26–27 January the national coordinators of the 16 CEI member states met in Zagreb to draw up the organization's agenda for the year and to discuss several joint projects. A Foreign Ministers' meeting was subsequently held in the Brijuni Islands, Croatia, on 5–6 June. At the meeting a final document was adopted calling for the further enlargement of both the EU and NATO to incorporate those CEI countries which had applied to join the two organizations. The Foreign Ministers also issued a separate statement on the conflict in Kosovo, the disputed province of the Federal Republic of Yugoslavia, in which they called for 'an immediate halt to the escalating violence' and an end to all forms of terrorism and ethnic cleansing. They also stated their intention to send a fact-finding mission of the CEI troika to Albania to assess the current situation on its borders with Yugoslavia.

Alongside its annual heads of government summit, the CEI held its first Economic Forum in Zagreb on 19–21 November, attended by around 700 ministerial and other official participants, including business leaders from the 16 member states. During the summit, Trade and Economic Ministers issued a joint statement expressing their support for further trade liberalization between member states and an increase in foreign investment across the region. The summit also hosted an *ad-hoc* meeting between the then chairman of the EU, Austrian Foreign Minister Wolfgang Schüssel, and the Foreign Ministers of the three troika countries. The two sides agreed that regular annual meetings should take place between the CEI and the EU and that they should work on establishing permanent communication and cooperation in areas such as transport, communications and fighting organized crime.

Heads of state and government of the Black Sea Economic Cooperation (BSEC) group met for a summit in Ukrainian town of Yalta on 5 June. On the same day the participants signed a charter which formally upgraded the regional grouping to an official international organization. Heralding the agreement, Ukrainian President Leonid Kuchma claimed that the BSEC was now 'transforming itself into a major component of Europe's new security system' and called on member states to build on their achievement by establishing a free trade zone.

At the first conference under its new status, held in Sofia, Bulgaria, on 22 October, the 11 member states agreed to seek closer cooperation in the fields of transport, tourism and telecommunications in order to promote the development of the Black Sea region. It was also confirmed that the Black Sea Trade and Development Bank, whose opening in the Greek city of Thessaloniki had been delayed since May 1997, would finally begin operations in January 1999.

6. ARAB, AFRICAN, ASIA-PACIFIC AND AMERICAN ORGANIZATIONS

i. ARAB ORGANIZATIONS

League of Arab States
DATE OF FOUNDATION: 1945   HEADQUARTERS: Cairo, Egypt
OBJECTIVES: To coordinate political, economic, social and cultural cooperation between member-states and to mediate in disputes between them
MEMBERSHIP (END-'98): Algeria, Bahrain, Comoros, Djibouti, Egypt, Iraq, Jordan, Kuwait, Lebanon, Libya, Mauritania, Morocco, Oman, Palestine, Qatar, Saudi Arabia, Somalia, Sudan, Syria, Tunisia, United Arab Emirates, Yemen (*total 22*)
SECRETARY-GENERAL: Ahmad Esmat Abdel Meguid (Egypt)

Gulf Cooperation Council (GCC)
DATE OF FOUNDATION: 1981   HEADQUARTERS: Riyadh, Saudi Arabia
OBJECTIVES: To promote cooperation between member states in all fields with a view to achieving unity
MEMBERSHIP (END '98): Bahrain, Kuwait, Oman, Qatar, Saudi Arabia, United Arab Emirates (*total 6*)
SECRETARY-GENERAL: Jameel al-Hujilan (Saudi Arabia)

Arab Maghreb Union (AMU)
DATE OF FOUNDATION: 1989   HEADQUARTERS: Casablanca, Morocco
OBJECTIVES: To strengthen 'the bonds of brotherhood' between member-states, particularly in the area of economic development
MEMBERSHIP (END-'98): Algeria, Libya, Mauritania, Morocco, Tunisia (*total 5*)
SECRETARY-GENERAL: Mohammed Amamou (Tunisia)

THE Gulf Cooperation Council (GCC) presided over a dismal year, ending with Crown Prince Abdullah of Saudi Arabia warning delegates at the annual GCC meeting in December: 'The days of affluence are over and they will never come back!' He went on to argue that, given the continuing depression of world oil prices, the GCC would have to initiate basic reforms and give far greater control of the economies of individual members to the private sector. Furthermore, the region would need strong and unified Gulf economies and, therefore, the construction of a common Gulf market with unified customs tariffs and a strong private-sector-dominated industrial base to reduce reliance on imports was essential. The meeting agreed to support the rolling over the OPEC production cuts set in June from their end date of June 1999 for six months to the end of that year, as a measure designed to strengthen oil prices (see XI.2.ii).

The call for the creation of a Gulf common market echoed an oft-declared objective of the GCC over the past decade which had still not been achieved. The call had been repeated at the October ministerial meeting, which decided to put a similar call made in 1994 into effect. One possible stumbling-block was the requirement for the free movement of GCC nationals throughout the new market once it had been created—something which Saudi Arabia regarded with suspicion since it feared renewed labour migration would threaten its attempt to force the Saudi private sector to employ more Saudi nationals (see V.3.i). As a move towards encouraging greater economic integration, the Economic Ministers of the GCC decided in November to clarify the status of their proposed unified customs law with the World Trade Organization.

At an earlier GCC Foreign Ministers' meeting in March, Iran had been called upon to act on assurances of its desire for close cooperation with the Arab Gulf states. The call came in the wake of an improvement in Saudi relations with Iran and the visit by former Iranian President Rafsanjani to several Gulf states in the same month. Iran was specifically requested to abandon its claims on Abu Musa island—also claimed by Sharjah—and the Tunbs Islands, also claimed by Abu Dhabi. As usual, Iraq was called upon to comply with UN demands in the wake of the narrowly-averted Anglo-American attack on the country in February—in which the Gulf states had refused to join (see V.2.vi).

The GCC's demand that Iran should give up its territorial demands on the United Arab Emirates (UAE) was repeated in June at another GCC Foreign Ministers' meeting in Riyadh. It was repeated yet again at the December heads of state meeting in Doha, alongside the GCC's renewed desire for good relations with Iran and a suggestion that Iran should take seriously UN Secretary-General Kofi Annan's offer, made in a speech to the summit, to mediate in the dispute. The Doha meeting repeated its call for Iraqi compliance with UN weapons inspection requirements, just before the Anglo-American bombing raids on Iraq at the end of the year. The heads of state also, somewhat forlornly, called on Israel to sign the Nuclear Non-Proliferation Treaty in order to make the Middle East into a zone free of weapons of mass destruction. The meeting concluded by reappointing Jameel al-Hujilan (Saudi Arabia) as secretary-general for a further three-year term.

The only 1998 meeting held by the Damascus Declaration group of countries, consisting of the GCC states together with Egypt and Syria, occurred in mid-November, when they called on Iraq to observe UN resolutions on arms inspections. The Arab League was more active, however. Its members met in Cairo in mid-December, in response to a Yemeni request, to consider the Anglo-American attacks on Iraq, although the meeting had been postponed by one week at American insistence. The organization had also tried to intervene in the February crisis, proposing a deal to end the deadlock over UN inspection of Iraqi presidential sites (which was ignored by the United States) and then welcoming the agreement brokered by the UN Secretary-General.

Much of the League's time throughout the year was spent on the Lockerbie issue (see V.4.ii). The League's secretary-general, Ahmad Esmat Abdel Meguid, made several trips to Libya to ease the situation in favour of trial in a third country, as Arab League members repeatedly made clear their support for the Libyan position. They were not, however, prepared to ignore the UN sanctions against Libya, which were intended to force Libya to hand over the two named suspects in the incident to Scottish or US jurisdiction. Libya, on the other hand, began to insist that its position should be formally adopted by the League, particularly after the Organization of African Unity had made it clear that it would abandon the sanctions unilaterally in September unless Britain and the United States had accepted the principle of a trial in a third country. When a meeting of Arab Foreign Ministers in Cairo in mid-September decided that they would not comply with the Libyan demand, Libya abandoned its support for pan-Arab nationalism—the founding ideology of the League, which had also been at the root of Libya's own idiosyncratic political vision—and declared itself to be an African state instead.

As regards another of its perennial problems, the League condemned Israeli proposals for peace in Lebanon and the Israeli government's plans for Jerusalem (see V.1; V.2.ii). In another move in early January, Arab Interior Ministers meeting under League auspices in Tunis approved a draft of an inter-Arab anti-terrorism agreement which would strengthen border controls and facilitate extradition arrangements.

ii. AFRICAN ORGANIZATIONS AND CONFERENCES

Organization of African Unity (OAU)
DATE OF FOUNDATION: 1963   HEADQUARTERS: Addis Ababa, Ethiopia
OBJECTIVES: To promote the unity, solidarity and cooperation of African states, to defend their sovereignty and to eradicate remaining traces of colonialism
MEMBERSHIP (END-'98): Algeria, Angola, Benin, Botswana, Burkina Faso, Burundi, Cameroon, Cape Verde, Central African Republic, Chad, Comoros, Democratic Republic of the Congo, Republic of Congo, Côte d'Ivoire, Djibouti, Egypt, Equatorial Guinea, Eritrea, Ethiopia, Gabon, Gambia, Ghana, Guinea, Guinea-Bissau, Kenya, Lesotho, Liberia, Libya, Madagascar, Malawi, Mali, Mauritania, Mauritius, Mozambique, Namibia, Niger, Nigeria, Rwanda, Sahrawi Arab Democratic Republic, São Tomé & Príncipe, Senegal, Seychelles, Sierra Leone, Somalia, South Africa, Sudan, Swaziland, Tanzania, Togo, Tunisia, Uganda, Zambia, Zimbabwe (*total 53*)
SECRETARY-GENERAL: Salim Ahmed Salim (Tanzania)

Economic Community of West African States (ECOWAS)
DATE OF FOUNDATION: 1975   HEADQUARTERS: Abuja, Nigeria
OBJECTIVES: To seek the creation of an economic union of member states
MEMBERSHIP (END-'98): Benin, Burkina Faso, Cape Verde, Côte d'Ivoire, Gambia, Ghana, Guinea, Guinea-Bissau, Liberia, Mali, Mauritania, Niger, Nigeria, Senegal, Sierra Leone, Togo (*total 16*)
EXECUTIVE SECRETARY: Lamine Kouyate (Guinea)

West African Economic and Monetary Union (UEMOA)
DATE OF FOUNDATION: 1994   HEADQUARTERS: Ouagadougou, Burkina Faso
OBJECTIVES: To promote the economic and monetary union of member states
MEMBERSHIP (END-'98): Benin, Burkina Faso, Côte d'Ivoire, Guinea-Bissau, Mali, Mauritania, Niger, Senegal (*total 8*)

Southern African Development Community (SADC)
DATE OF FOUNDATION: 1992   HEADQUARTERS: Gaborone, Botswana
OBJECTIVES: To work towards the creation of a regional common market
MEMBERSHIP (END-'98): Angola, Botswana, Democratic Republic of the Congo, Lesotho, Malawi, Mauritius, Mozambique, Namibia, Seychelles, South Africa, Swaziland, Tanzania, Zambia, Zimbabwe (*total 14*)
EXECUTIVE SECRETARY: Kaire Mbuende (Namibia)

Common Market for Eastern and Southern Africa (COMESA)
DATE OF FOUNDATION: 1993 (succeeding Preferential Trade Area)
HEADQUARTERS: Lusaka, Zambia
OBJECTIVES: To establish a full free-trade area
MEMBERSHIP (END-'98): Angola, Burundi, Comoros, Democratic Republic of the Congo, Eritrea, Ethiopia, Kenya, Lesotho, Madagascar, Malawi, Mauritius, Namibia, Rwanda, Sudan, Swaziland, Tanzania, Uganda, Zambia, Zimbabwe (*total 19*)
SECRETARY-GENERAL: Bingo wa Mutharika (suspended)

Economic Community of Central African States (CEEAC)
DATE OF FOUNDATION: 1983   HEADQUARTERS: Libreville, Gabon
OBJECTIVES: To establish a full free-trade area
MEMBERSHIP (END-'98): Burundi, Cameroon, Central African Republic, Chad, Democratic Republic of the Congo, Republic of the Congo, Equatorial Guinea, Gabon, Rwanda, São Tomé & Príncipe (*total 10*)
SECRETARY-GENERAL: Kasasa Mutati Chinyata

East African Commission (EAC)
DATE OF FOUNDATION: 1996 (reviving former East African Community)
HEADQUARTERS: Nairobi, Kenya
OBJECTIVES: To promote economic integration between member states
MEMBERSHIP (END-'98): Kenya, Tanzania, Uganda (*total 3*)

THE Organization of African Unity (OAU), still recognized as pivotal in Africa's security problems, had a difficult year because of the increasing number of conflicts in Africa, and the clear impotence of the continental organization in providing the means to solve them. This was the more disheartening, since the year began with the message of 'African renaissance', with a new leadership and a more purposive way of doing things, coined by the Mandela-Mbeki duo in South Africa and taken up by President Bill Clinton on his African tour in March-April.

If the most dramatic setback was the outbreak of new hostilities at the end of July in the Great Lakes region of the eastern Democratic Republic of the Congo (see VII.1.i), the change of atmosphere had actually reached crisis level earlier, during the 34th annual OAU summit, held in Ouagadougou (Burkina Faso) on 8–10 June.

First, on 5 June, open conflict broke out between Eritrea and Ethiopia, featuring Eritrean bombing of Mekele and subsequent hostilities on a wide front (see VI.1.i). On 7 June, the day before the OAU summit was due to open, a military uprising took place in Guinea-Bissau, just as President Vieira was about to leave for the conference (see VII.1.iii). These two events threw the Ouagadougou meeting into confusion, compounded by the announcement on 8 June of the sudden death of General Sani Abacha, the Nigerian head of state (see VI.2.ii; XVIII: Obituary), which led to the sudden departure of the head of the Nigerian delegation from the Foreign Ministers' meeting held in the week prior to the summit. In the circumstances, the unexpected crises drew attention to the OAU's own difficulty in solving regional conflicts, although the summit did agree on a mediation mission for the Ethiopia-Eritrea quarrel. The sending of troops to Guinea-Bissau by Senegal and Guinea in the middle of the summit was a bilateral move for which the governments only subsequently sought wider endorsement, and even then from the regional Economic Community of West African States (ECOWAS) rather than from the OAU. The OAU was not included in any peace discussions, which were worked out in a complicated quadrille between ECOWAS, the Community of Portuguese-speaking Countries (CPLP) and the warring parties (see also XI.3.ii).

The OAU summit meeting perforce went ahead as planned, attended by 29 heads of state, with some remarkable set pieces, including the speech marking the last attendance at an OAU summit by President Nelson Mandela of South Africa. Quoting from Pablo Neruda's poem *The Century of Death,* he said that the new generation of African leaders should ensure that the 21st century would be different and that it should be an 'African century', as well as challenging some of the OAU's basic precepts and assumptions. He questioned whether the OAU's doctrine of non-intervention and respect for state sovereignty meant non-intervention against tyrannies, asking: 'Do not responsible governments have a duty to protect the rights of other countries' citizens?' In a similar challenging vein, he suggested that, if the OAU's 'mechanism for conflict prevention, management and resolution' was not working, the OAU should find another way to ensure that Africa 'truly and collectively' takes charge of its own security.

The summit was nevertheless presented as an achievement for President Blaise Compaoré of Burkina Faso, who had ambitiously, in his opening speech, called for a redefinition of the OAU to cope with the economic and political pressures of globalization. His call was underlined by the presence of the managing director of the IMF, Michel Camdessus, who again demonstrated his personal concern for Africa's economic problems—and indeed made an appeal for faster growth.

President Compaoré also pressed hard for a strengthening of the OAU's conflict resolution mechanism. In the event, the assembled leaders were too preoccupied with their immediate problems, although they did state in the final declaration that 'peace, security and political stability in Africa' were a preoccupation of the highest order. The declaration also took up the institutional question, saying that African leaders had decided to provide the OAU with structures capable of identifying the dynamics of change in different societies, to be done by coordinating sector-based policies and by implementing the decisions of specialized commissions. The leaders also noted the slow pace of new information and communication technology in Africa.

President Compaoré, as OAU chairman, took the Eritrea-Ethiopia mediation seriously by attending several meetings himself, although there was a plethora of other mediators, none of them achieving very much. But the outbreak of fighting in eastern Congo-Kinshasa proved a much more preoccupying peace-keeping exercise, especially as the fighting in the Horn of Africa died down, even without a formal ceasefire. The main initiative for peace in the Democratic Republic of the Congo (DRC), however, came from neighbours and from the Southern African Development Community (SADC) rather than the OAU. President Compaoré convened a peace meeting in Ouagadougou in mid-December, but this was unable to register any progress towards a ceasefire.

The Congo problem proved to be a major crisis for SADC, being the first time that it had been really tested politically. The problem arose because of the military engagement of three SADC members, Angola, Zimbabwe and Namibia, on the side of President Kabila of the DRC (which had joined the SADC in 1997). President Mugabe of Zimbabwe, as chairman of the SADC's security committee, claimed that the intervention was on behalf of the regional organization, but this view was disputed by other members, notably South Africa, which held the SADC chair. Various SADC states, notably Zambia, were also involved in mediation, still ongoing at the end of the year. Nonetheless, in its report to the annual summit in Mauritius in September, the SADC secretariat presented a favourable economic picture for the 12 members, even though the Asian economic crisis and the effects of El Niño-induced weather distortion had led to reduced growth.

The divisions of 1998 meant that the SADC countries were not in a favourable position to face the challenge of relations with the European Union (EU), which opened negotiations with the African, Caribbean and Pacific (ACP) states for the conclusion of a new Lomé Convention by February 2000. The SADC was one of the regional groupings with which the EU was hoping to form a free trade area, as part of a proposed new trade dispensation, even though the EU-South Africa negotiations had not been concluded at the end of 1998 (see VII.3).

The other main organizations cited by the EU for potential free trade links were the newly-revived East African Commission (EAC), grouping of Kenya, Tanzania and Uganda, and the West African Economic and Monetary Union (UEMOA), whose seven francophone members formed a powerful nucleus within the 16-nation Economic Community of West African States (ECOWAS). During the year the UEMOA further reinforced ties between members with the launch of a regional stock exchange in Abidjan. In addition, the EU agreed that the franc zone would be officially attached to the new euro-zone from 1 January 1999—the currency of the franc zone, the CFA franc, having been linked to the French franc since the colonial period.

Although still blocked in the key area of trade liberalization, ECOWAS held a successful summit in Abuja at the end of October, at which Nigeria profited from the changed political climate following the death of General Abacha. The main achievement of new Nigerian head of state General Abdulsalam Abubakar was to broker a peace deal for Guinea-Bissau, where there had already been a mostly successful ceasefire since July. The ECOWAS summit also approved the organization's own security mechanism for conflict resolution, as well as launching ECOWAS travellers' cheques, as a harbinger of an eventual, if distant, monetary union. ECOWAS remained more focused on its political problems, as witnessed by the presence of the President of Sierra Leone, Ahmed Tejan Kabbah, who had been restored to power by Nigerian troops acting in the name of ECOWAS in February (see VI.2.iii).

The francophone countries continued to wrestle with the problems of Air Afrique, their common airline, in which ten of them, with France, were shareholders. The airline had run up huge debts for unwise purchase of aircraft (two of which were impounded in July), and the servicing of the debts had created a grave financial crisis. However, the privatization solution, which might have helped the airline out of its problems, continued to be blocked.

Notwithstanding the presentation externally of various new plans for Africa, there was more concern in Africa itself about the role of what had been seen as the continent's own bank, namely the African Development Bank (AfDB). At the AfDB's annual meeting in May it was agreed that a 35 per cent capital increase of $7,650 million would be allowed, the fifth in the bank's 35-year history. Under the decision, the shareholding of non-Africans in the bank would increase from 33 to 40 per cent, a shift in the balance of power within the bank which was said to reflect 'financial reality'. The capital increase did not make much difference for the poorest countries, since credit rules effectively prevented 39 of its 53 members from borrowing. The 'non-regionals' also insisted that all bank decisions should be ratified by 66 per cent of shareholders, which appeared to shift power decisively into the hands of the external donors who provided much of the capital.

iii. ASIA-PACIFIC ORGANIZATIONS

Association of South-East Asian Nations (ASEAN)
DATE OF FOUNDATION: 1967   HEADQUARTERS: Jakarta, Indonesia
OBJECTIVES: To accelerate economic growth, social progress and cultural development in the region
MEMBERSHIP (END-'98): Brunei, Indonesia, Laos, Malaysia, Myanmar, Philippines, Singapore, Thailand, Vietnam (total 9)
SECRETARY-GENERAL: Rodolfo C. Severino (Philippines)

Asia-Pacific Economic Cooperation (APEC)
DATE OF FOUNDATION: 1989   HEADQUARTERS: Singapore
OBJECTIVES: To promote market-oriented economic development and cooperation in the Pacific Rim countries
MEMBERSHIP (END-'98): Australia, Brunei, Canada, Chile, China, Hong Kong, Indonesia, Japan, South Korea, Malaysia, Mexico, New Zealand, Papua New Guinea, Peru, Philippines, Russia, Singapore, Taiwan, Thailand, United States, Vietnam (total 21)
EXECUTIVE DIRECTOR: Jack A. Whittleton (Canada)

Pacific Community (SPC)
DATE OF FOUNDATION: 1947 (as South Pacific Commission)
HEADQUARTERS: Nouméa, New Caledonia
OBJECTIVES: To facilitate political and other cooperation between member states and territories
MEMBERSHIP (END-'98): American Samoa, Australia, Cook Islands, Fiji, France, French Polynesia, Guam, Kiribati, Marshall Islands, Federated States of Micronesia, Nauru, New Caledonia, New Zealand, Niue, Northern Mariana Islands, Palau, Papua New Guinea, Pitcairn Islands, Samoa, Solomon Islands, Tokelau, Tonga, Tuvalu, United Kingdom, United States, Vanuatu, Wallis & Futuna Islands (total 27)
DIRECTOR-GENERAL: Bob Dun (Australia)

South Pacific Forum (SPF)
DATE OF FOUNDATION: 1971   HEADQUARTERS: Suva, Fiji
OBJECTIVES: To enhance the economic and social well-being of the people of the South Pacific, in support of the efforts of the members' governments
MEMBERSHIP (END-'98): Australia, Palau, Cook Islands, Fiji, Kiribati, Marshall Islands, Federated States of Micronesia, Nauru, New Zealand, Niue, Papua New Guinea, Samoa, Solomon Islands, Tonga, Tuvalu, Vanuatu (total 16)
SECRETARY-GENERAL: Noel Levi (Papua New Guinea)

South Asian Association for Regional Cooperation (SAARC)
DATE OF FOUNDATION: 1985   HEADQUARTERS: Kathmandu, Nepal
OBJECTIVES: To promote collaboration and mutual assistance in the economic, social, cultural and technical fields
MEMBERSHIP (END-'98): Bangladesh, Bhutan, India, Maldives, Nepal, Pakistan, Sri Lanka (total 7)
SECRETARY-GENERAL: Nacem ul-Hasan (Pakistan)

Indian Ocean Rim Association for Regional Cooperation (IORARC)
DATE OF FOUNDATION: 1997
OBJECTIVES: To promote cooperation in trade, investment, infrastructure, tourism, science, technology and human-resource development in the Indian Ocean region
MEMBERSHIP (END-'98): Australia, India, Indonesia, Kenya, Madagascar, Malaysia, Mauritius, Mozambique, Oman, Singapore, South Africa, Sri Lanka, Tanzania, Yemen (*total 14*)

MEETINGS of the major regional organizations in the Asia-Pacific region were again largely dominated by the economic crisis that had engulfed the region in mid-1997. The crisis was the main topic on the agenda of the second Asia-Europe Meeting (ASEM) which took place in London in early April. (The first ASEM had been held in Thailand in March 1996.) The second ASEM was attended by heads of state and/or government from ten Asian countries and the 15 member states of the European Union (EU). The Asian countries represented included seven of the nine member states of the Association of South-East Asian Nations (ASEAN)—Brunei, Indonesia, Malaysia, Philippines, Singapore, Thailand and Vietnam—plus China, Japan and South Korea.

In the months prior to the meeting Asian leaders had expressed some discontent with the EU for having contributed little to the US- and IMF-instigated economic rescue packages for the region. In a speech delivered at the opening of the conference, however, UK Prime Minister Tony Blair insisted that European states were 'not fair-weather friends but partners for the long-term, ready to stick by Asia through thick and thin'. Mr Blair's proposal to create an ASEM trust fund to provide technical assistance to some Asian countries received unanimous support from the other ASEM leaders. The then Japanese Prime Minister, Ryutaro Hashimoto, also committed his country to making a major contribution to Asian recovery by announcing US$3,000 million in special assistance to support reforms in the Asian financial system.

In the 'chairman's statement' issued at the end of the summit, the meeting endorsed new environmental protection initiatives and increased cooperation in the fight against crime, illicit drugs and money-laundering. In addition, the meeting adopted a Trade Facilitation Action Plan (TFAP) and an Investment Promotion Action Plan (IPAP) intended to facilitate greater two-way trade and investment flows between Europe and Asia. The meeting discussed whether to extend ASEM membership to countries such as Australia, India, Pakistan and New Zealand, but it was left to the third ASEM meeting, scheduled for South Korea in 2000, to determine any possible expansion.

The heads of state and government of the nine member states of ASEAN held a summit meeting in Vietnam in mid-December. It was the first such gathering since an informal summit in Malaysia in December 1997 (see AR 1997, p. 429). At the meeting the leaders sought to devise a twin-track strategy to promote political and economic integration of the region in an effort to restore the credibility of ASEAN, which had been weakened by the Asian economic crisis and riven by internal divisions.

The conference was distracted by the continuing dispute over Cambodia's application to join ASEAN. Its scheduled entry in July 1997, alongside Myanmar and Laos, had been deferred pending a settlement of the ongoing internal conflict in Cambodia. Vietnam lobbied vigorously for Cambodia's immediate admission during the summit, with support from Indonesia and Malaysia, but Thailand, Singapore and the Philippines were adamant that entry should be delayed until a recently-formed Cambodian coalition government had proved its stability (see IX.1.ix). A face-saving formula allowed Vietnamese Prime Minister Phan Van Khai to announce, in his closing speech to the summit, agreement on the admission of Cambodia at an unspecified future date.

The meeting of ASEAN Foreign and Finance Ministers which preceded the summit had produced a range of agreed measures to accelerate trade and investment liberalization. The ASEAN Free Trade Area (AFTA) programme to liberalize trade in most goods and services, originally agreed at the 1992 summit, would be launched a year earlier than planned, in 2002. The more recent ASEAN members (Vietnam, Laos and Myanmar) would be allowed up to 2008 to implement the cuts. Divisions on economic policy remained evident, however, as Goh Chok Tong, Prime Minister of Singapore, advocated further economic liberalization to attract international capital, in contrast to Malaysian Prime Minister Mahathir Mohamad's defence of his own country's imposition of currency controls.

ASEAN Finance Ministers had met for a one-day meeting in Indonesia in late February. They agreed to implement proposals, suggested by Prime Minister Mahathir, to promote regional trade by using local currencies for payments instead of the US dollar. Singapore, the Philippines, Malaysia and Thailand agreed to establish bilateral payment arrangements as soon as possible in order to enable two trading partners to channel payments through central banks and pay only the difference in trade flows in US dollars. The ministers also endorsed the idea of a mechanism to monitor the region's economies—a suggestion put forward by Asian finance and central bank deputies in November 1997.

ASEAN Economic and Trade Ministers held a series of meetings in the Philippines in early October. The officials agreed to set up an ASEAN Investment Area to minimize barriers to direct investment flows. Under the accord, all ASEAN direct investment within member states would be treated on the same basis as for domestic investors by 2010, and this treatment would be extended to all investors by 2020. The ministers also announced the establishment of a joint surveillance system to provide early warning of future economic problems in the region. In a departure from past ASEAN policy of non-interference in each other's affairs, the system was to be based on 'peer review' and information exchange in areas such as interest rate levels, exchange rates and capital flows. The information would be submitted voluntarily to a monitoring committee based in Indonesia, and would then be discussed at meetings of ASEAN Finance Ministers at least twice a year.

ASEAN Foreign Ministers held their 31st annual meeting in late July in the Philippines. The meeting took place amidst unprecedented divisions among the nine member states over whether to abandon the organization's cardinal principle of non-intervention in the internal affairs of members. Thailand and the Philippines supported a new approach, characterized as 'flexible engagement', which would allow members to debate economic and political differences openly and, if necessary, criticize members whose policies were seen to be having a detrimental impact outside their own borders. Thailand in particular considered that ASEAN's traditional diplomacy had failed with regard to Myanmar's ruling military junta, whose continuing recalcitrance in the areas of political reform and human rights (see IX.1.i) had damaged ASEAN as a whole, most notably in its relations with the USA and the EU. Nevertheless, the notion of replacing the non-interference principle with one of 'flexible engagement' was not approved, because of strong opposition from almost all the other ASEAN countries. There was collective agreement, however, on a new term—'enhanced interaction'—which was intended to express a greater openness to the discussion of some regional issues, but which did not extend to interfering in the internal affairs of member states on issues such as human rights.

A joint communique issued at the end of the meeting called on Japan to implement economic measures in support of the economic recovery in ASEAN countries. The Foreign Ministers also urged international financial institutions and donor countries to consider the overall impact of structural adjustment measures, which were being implemented by a number of ASEAN countries, on the vulnerable sectors of their societies.

The fifth ASEAN Regional Forum (ARF) was held in the Philippines in late July. The meeting was attended by delegates from 21 participants, in addition to Mongolia, which was admitted as the ARF's newest member. The gathering was dominated by discussions concerning the financial crisis in the region and the nuclear tests carried out by India and Pakistan (see VIII.2.i; VIII.2.ii). In the official statement issued at the end of the meeting, the ARF maintained that it 'strongly deplored the recent nuclear tests in South Asia, which had exacerbated tension in the region and raised the spectre of the nuclear arms race'. The Indian delegation dissociated itself from the statement, however, claiming that the ARF should not engage in criticism of its own members.

Heads of state and government and Trade Ministers of the 21 member countries of the Asia-Pacific Economic Cooperation (APEC) forum held their sixth annual meeting in mid-November in Kuala Lumpur, the Malaysian capital. During the summit three countries—Russia, Peru and Vietnam—were formally admitted as APEC's newest members, thereby expanding the number of member states from 18 to 21.

The gathering was preceded by a meeting of APEC Trade Ministers, which was dominated by disagreements over proposals for a fast-track trade liberalization agreement. Under the Early Voluntary Sectoral Liberalization (EVSL) package launched by heads of state at the 1997 Vancouver summit (see AR 1997, pp. 429–30), member states had agreed to cut tariffs and liberalize trade across nine sectors. Whilst the plan was strongly endorsed by the USA and a number of other member countries, Japan resisted tariff reductions in two politically-sensitive sectors—forestry and fisheries. An earlier meeting of APEC Trade Ministers in Malaysia in June had also been dominated by disputes between Japan and the other APEC countries over the EVSL scheme.

During the course of negotiations over the tariff elimination proposals, the US and Japanese delegations became embroiled in a series of acrimonious exchanges. An uneasy compromise deal was eventually forged, however, as the Trade Ministers agreed to send the whole package to the World Trade Organization (WTO) for further negotiation.

Another controversy was triggered on the eve of the summit when US Vice-President Al Gore offended his Malaysian hosts with a pre-summit banquet speech in which he strongly backed the pro-reform movement led by the imprisoned former Deputy Prime Minister and Finance Minister Anwar Ibrahim (see IX.1.iii). Standing in because President Clinton was dealing with the latest crisis with Iraq, Mr Gore praised 'the brave people of Malaysia' for taking their pro-democracy campaign to the streets in protest against Prime Minister Mahathir. Not surprisingly, his remarks were vigorously attacked by the Malaysian delegation. Trade Minster Rafidah Aziz described them as 'the most disgusting speech' she had ever heard. Mr Gore's speech also distracted attention from one of the main positive developments at the APEC summit, when the USA and Japan unveiled a plan—in cooperation with the World Bank and the Asian Development Bank (ADB)—to provide US$10,000 million to help debt-ridden Asian economies.

The heads of state summit eventually opened in disarray on 17 November, as Malaysia issued a formal complaint over US interference in its domestic affairs and over what it described as Vice-President Gore's 'incitement to lawlessness'. The dispute between the two countries overshadowed discussions on other issues, and it also opened up a rift within APEC itself, as member states clashed over the wisdom of Mr Gore's intervention. A number of countries, including those normally sympathetic to the USA such as Australia and New Zealand, criticized the US Vice-President for indulging in what was described as 'megaphone diplomacy' and 'hectoring'.

Nonetheless, at the conclusion of the APEC summit on 18 November, the leaders issued a joint statement in which they pledged to pursue a 'cooperative growth strategy' to hasten economic recovery in Asia. The document called for better regulation of global financial markets and for restrictions to be imposed on the activities of hedge funds and other large institutional investors. The APEC leaders also stressed the need to push for the swift restructuring of banks and companies in recession-hit countries to help revive private sector activity. Some analysts criticized the final communique, however, for failing to include any detailed proposals or concrete financial pledges.

The heads of government of the 16-member South Pacific Forum (SPF) held their annual summit in the Federated States of Micronesia in late August. The summit was a relatively low-key event, due largely to the absence of a number of leaders because of domestic political considerations, notably the Prime Ministers of Australia, New Zealand and Papua New Guinea, respectively John Howard, Jenny Shipley and Bill Skate. The summit's final communique was dominated by economic and environmental issues, with the leaders calling on former nuclear-testing countries in the region—France, Britain and the USA—to accept liability for their actions and to pay compensation for any harmful consequences.

The communique urged all countries to ratify the 1997 Kyoto protocol on climate change (see AR 1997, pp. 466-7, 568-72), and it endorsed an Australian proposal for the establishment of a whale sanctuary in the South Pacific. An additional proposal for the establishment of a free trade zone in the region was referred for further research.

The South Pacific Commission formally changed its name to the Pacific Community in February. The decision had been approved at the commission's annual conference in Australia in October 1997 (see AR 1997, p. 431).

In July Mitsuo Sato (Japan) announced that in January 1999 he would resign as president of the Asian Development Bank, the region's leading multilateral lending institution.

iv. AMERICAN AND CARIBBEAN ORGANIZATIONS

Organization of American States (OAS)
DATE OF FOUNDATION: 1951   HEADQUARTERS: Washington DC, USA
OBJECTIVES: To facilitate political, economic and other cooperation between member states and to defend their territorial integrity and independence
MEMBERSHIP (END-'98): Antigua & Barbuda, Argentina, Bahamas, Barbados, Belize, Bolivia, Brazil, Canada, Chile, Colombia, Costa Rica, Cuba (*currently excluded*), Dominica, Dominican Republic, Ecuador, El Salvador, Grenada, Guatemala, Guyana, Haiti, Honduras, Jamaica, Mexico, Nicaragua, Panama, Paraguay, Peru, St Kitts & Nevis, St Lucia, St Vincent & the Grenadines, Suriname, Trinidad & Tobago, United States, Uruguay, Venezuela (*total 35*)
SECRETARY-GENERAL: César Gaviria Trujillo (Colombia)

Rio Group
DATE OF FOUNDATION: 1987   HEADQUARTERS: rotating
OBJECTIVES: To provide a regional mechanism for joint political action
MEMBERSHIP (END-'98): Argentina, Bolivia, Brazil, Chile, Colombia, Ecuador, Guatemala, Mexico, Panama, Paraguay, Peru, Trinidad & Tobago, Uruguay, Venezuela (*total 14*)

Southern Common Market (Mercosur)

DATE OF FOUNDATION: 1991 HEADQUARTERS: Montevideo, Uruguay
OBJECTIVES: To build a genuine common market between member states
MEMBERSHIP (END-'98): Argentina, Brazil, Paraguay, Uruguay (*total* 4)
ADMINISTRATIVE SECRETARY: Manuel Olarreaga (Uruguay)

Andean Community (CA)

DATE OF FOUNDATION: 1969 HEADQUARTERS: Lima, Peru
OBJECTIVES: To promote the economic development and integration of member states
MEMBERSHIP (END-'98): Bolivia, Colombia, Ecuador, Venezuela (*total* 4)
SECRETARY-GENERAL: José Antonio García Belaunde (Peru)

Latin American Integration Association (ALADI)

DATE OF FOUNDATION: 1980 (as successor to Latin American Free Trade Association founded in 1960) HEADQUARTERS: Montevideo, Uruguay
OBJECTIVES: To promote Latin American trade and development by economic preference
MEMBERSHIP (END-'98): Argentina, Bolivia, Brazil, Chile, Colombia, Cuba, Ecuador, Mexico, Paraguay, Peru, Uruguay, Venezuela (*total* 12)
SECRETARY-GENERAL: Antônio de Cerqueira Antúnes (Brazil)

Latin American Economic System (SELA)

DATE OF FOUNDATION: 1975 HEADQUARTERS: Caracas, Venezuela
OBJECTIVES: To accelerate economic and social development in member states
MEMBERSHIP (END-'98): Argentina, Barbados, Bolivia, Brazil, Chile, Colombia, Costa Rica, Cuba, Dominican Republic, Ecuador, El Salvador, Grenada, Guatemala, Guyana, Haiti, Honduras, Jamaica, Mexico, Nicaragua, Panama, Paraguay, Peru, Spain, Suriname, Trinidad & Tobago, Uruguay, Venezuela (*total* 27)
PERMANENT SECRETARY: Carlos Moneta (Argentina)

Caribbean Community and Common Market (Caricom)

DATE OF FOUNDATION: 1973 HEADQUARTERS: Georgetown, Guyana
OBJECTIVES: To facilitate economic, political and other cooperation between member states and to operate certain regional services
MEMBERSHIP (END-'98): Antigua & Barbuda, Bahamas, Barbados, Belize, Dominica, Grenada, Guyana, Haiti, Jamaica, Montserrat, St Kitts & Nevis, St Lucia, St Vincent & the Grenadines, Suriname, Trinidad & Tobago (*total* 15)
SECRETARY-GENERAL: Edward Carrington (Trinidad & Tobago)

Association of Caribbean States (ACS)

DATE OF FOUNDATION: 1994 HEADQUARTERS: Port of Spain, Trinidad
OBJECTIVES: To foster economic, social and political cooperation with a view to building a distinctive bloc of Caribbean littoral states
MEMBERSHIP (END-'98): Caricom members (*see above*) plus Colombia, Costa Rica, Cuba, Dominican Republic, El Salvador, Guatemala, Haiti, Honduras, Mexico, Nicaragua, Venezuela (*total* 25)
SECRETARY-GENERAL: Simón Molina Duarte (Venezuela)

Organization of Eastern Caribbean States (OECS)

DATE OF FOUNDATION: 1981 HEADQUARTERS: Castries, St Lucia
OBJECTIVES: To coordinate the external, defence, trade and monetary policies of member states
MEMBERSHIP (END-'98): Antigua & Barbuda, Dominica, Grenada, Montserrat, St Lucia, St Kitts & Nevis, St Vincent & the Grenadines (*total* 7)
DIRECTOR-GENERAL: Swinburne Lestrade (Dominica)

THE eighth Ibero-American summit was held in Porto, Portugal, on 18 October. The heads of state and government of Portugal, Spain and 23 Latin American countries were present. In the Declaration of Porto they called for common action to combat the current economic crisis in Latin America and appealed to the international financial institutions not to penalize states consistently pursuing structural adjustment programmes. Calling at the same time on other states to respect the principles of national sovereignty and non-intervention, they condemned the US Helms-Burton Act, extraterritorial enforcement of national laws and covert operations (such as the US 'Operation Casablanca') in friendly countries.

The 12th summit of the 14-member Rio Group was held in Panama on 4–5 September and attended by heads of state or government from all the countries in the region except Argentina, Brazil and Uruguay. The summit called for urgent action from international financial institutions and the major developed countries to mitigate the impact on the region of the financial crisis in Asia and Russia.

The eighth meeting of Foreign Ministers from the Rio Group with their counterparts from the European Union (EU), held in Panama City, concluded on 12 February with the issuing of a Declaration of Panama declaring both sides' opposition to the annual US procedure of 'certifying' as acceptable the efforts of other states to combat drug-smuggling.

On the recommendation of a meeting of Trade Ministers held in San José, Costa Rica, on 19 March, negotiations to create a Free Trade Area of the Americas (FTAA) were formally launched at the second 'Summit of the Americas' held in Santiago de Chile on 18 and 19 April (see AR 1994, p. 450). On the proposal of the Southern Common Market (Mercosur) countries, and against the wishes of the US administration, it was resolved that the negotiations would take place as a single process, though with a separate negotiating table for agriculture. Members called for Cuba to be included in future summit meetings and to be reinstated into membership of the OAS. They also called for an objective procedure to replace US certification of efforts against drug-trafficking, but endorsed a US proposal for the Inter-American Human Rights Commission (IAHRC) to appoint a special 'watchdog' for freedom of expression. In return, the US government announced a package of loans worth some $45,600 million over three years which, in conjunction with a further US$45,000 million in loans from the Inter-American Development Bank (IADB) and the World Bank, were intended to develop education, strengthen democracy, promote economic integration and combat poverty and discrimination in the Caribbean Basin area.

The five Central American states signed a free trade agreement with the Dominican Republic on 16 April. The intention was to link up with the Caribbean Community (Caricom) in a 22-nation regional trade bloc, to which end the Dominican Republic on 22 August signed a free trade agreement with Caricom, to take effect on 1 January 1999. At the 19th Caricom summit meeting, held in Castries, St Lucia, from 30 June to 4 July, its leaders called on President Janet Jagan of Guyana and opposition leader Desmond Hoyte to sign an agreement to resume talks aimed at concluding the months of violence fomented by Mr Hoyte and his followers, and subsequently welcomed the agreement arrived at (see IV.4.ii). The summit's other measures included a decision, in principle, to establish a Caribbean Court of Justice, with original jurisdiction in the interpretation of the organization's founding Treaty of Chaguaramas (1973) and the granting of associate membership of the organization to the UK dependency of Anguilla.

Also on 16 April the Andean Community (CA or Ancom) signed a framework agreement with Mercosur. Earlier, at a presidential summit of the Ancom countries held at Guayaquil, Ecuador, on 5 April, a similar agreement had been signed with Panama.

On 6 November Cuba, which had enjoyed observer status since 1986, was readmitted to full membership of the Latin American Integration Association (ALADI). This move was seen as an important one in Cuba's reintegration into the inter-American system. However, remarks made by President Fidel Castro Ruz at the closing session of the Latin American Economic System (SELA), held in Havana on 2 December, caused a major diplomatic incident and threatened Cuba's normally good relations with Mexico. President Castro had criticized Mexico for its membership of the North American Free Trade Agreement (NAFTA) and of the Organization for Economic Cooperation and Development (OECD) and had accused it of succumbing to US influence and turning its back on its poorer Latin American neighbours. In the end the Cuban leader felt it expedient to apologize for his remarks.

XII RELIGION

FAITH AND REASON. In October Pope John Paul II, marking the 20th anniversary of his papacy, published his 13th encyclical, *Fides et Ratio*, in which he described 'faith and reason' as the 'two wings on which the human spirit rises to the contemplation of truth'. Addressed primarily to bishops for the training of priests, the encyclical called on philosophers outside the Church not to be content with details but to confront the central questions of human existence. Uniquely in such a document, the Pope praised oriental philosophies in his opening paragraphs, the quest for meaning being found not only in the sacred writings of Israel and among the philosophers and dramatists of Greece, but also in the Indian Veda, Persian Avesta, Chinese Confucius and Lao Tze, and the preachings of Tirthankara and Buddha. 'In India it is the duty of Christians now to draw from this rich heritage the elements compatible with their faith, in order to enrich Christian thought.' This had been done by the Church in the past, Augustine in the fourth century drawing on Greek philosophy and Aquinas in the thirteenth studying Arab philosophers. Today, said the Pope, 'my thoughts turn immediately to the lands of the East', where 'a great spiritual impulse leads Indian thought'.

Yet engagement with oriental cultures recently had led to Vatican action against venturesome theologians, though the excommunication of Fr Tissa Balasuriya of Sri Lanka was lifted on 15 January (see AR 1997, pp. 448–9). The priest signed a 'statement of reconciliation', regretting the 'harm caused' by his writings, though he had hoped for more open dialogue, and accepting Pope Paul VI's *Credo of the People of God*, while the Vatican dropped its demand that Fr Balasuriya should sign a text stating that the Church did not have the authority to ordain women.

In August the Vatican Congregation for the Doctrine of the Faith criticized the writings of Indian Jesuit Fr Anthony de Mello, who had died in 1987, as 'incompatible with the Catholic faith' and capable of causing 'great harm', by stating that all religions, including Christianity, were obstacles to the discovery of truth. Nevertheless, religious leaders in the Philippines, in an open letter to the Congregation, praised the contribution of Fr de Mello to inter-religious dialogue showing 'how truly possible it is to integrate our Christianity with our local cultures'.

In November the Vatican Congregation opened an investigation into the theological views of an eminent Belgian Jesuit, Fr Jacques Dupuis, a professor at the Gregorian University in Rome and an expert on dialogue between religions. His 433-page book, *Towards a Christian Theology of Religious Pluralism*, had been presented at a public conference of the university in 1997 and criticized the old axiom that 'outside the Church there is no salvation', claiming instead that religious pluralism was 'part of God's plan'. The Roman Catholic Archbishop of Calcutta wrote that he 'could hardly believe the news' of the investigation. Fr Dupuis was noted for his orthodoxy and also for his affirmation of the presence of God 'in the teaching of other religions'.

In February the Vatican Congregation launched an inquiry into the work of a popular Australian Catholic priest, Fr Paul Collins. His book *Papal Power* contained 'certain doctrinal problems', appearing to reject papal primacy and infallibility as 'not in accord with tradition', and attacking the condemnation of modernism. But Fr Collins claimed that he had not been addressed directly by the Congregation, and that this body 'should be abolished' as having 'no place in the contemporary Church'.

In April another Australian priest, Fr Michael Morwood, was told by his archbishop that his book *Tomorrow's Catholic* contained 'serious errors' and was not to be displayed, sold or used by any Catholic church or school. Fr Morwood's book challenged 'the way Roman authority has played God' on issues such as female ordination.

In England a well-known Catholic priest, Fr John Wijngaards, a former vicar-general of the Mill Hill mission, announced in September that he was leaving the active ministry. He had been 'increasingly uncomfortable with the Church's official decrees concerning sexual doctrine and ethics', the ban on contraception for married couples, the 'arbitrary imposition' of celibacy on clergy in the West and, the 'last straw', the bar against women's ordination to the priesthood, 'in spite of there being no proven objections from scripture or tradition'. Fr Wijngaards believed that there had been 'great damage to the Body of the Church' by such official teaching, and he wanted to stand with those 'who are so casually and unjustly dismissed by the Vatican' in resigning from the priestly ministry, though he remained 'a conscientious and orthodox Catholic'. Also in September a national conference of priests in Birmingham warned that Vatican efforts to outlaw discussion of women's ordination hindered 'the credibility of the Church'.

In Northern Ireland a rebel priest, Fr Pat Buckley, who had been consecrated as bishop without papal authority in June, was held to have incurred automatic excommunication. Fr Buckley admittedly remained a priest and declared that his ministry included divorcees, homosexuals and married priests. In September he ordained a nun, Frances Meigh, as the first Irish woman priest. She said that she would continue to live as a hermit in St Andrew's Church, Omeath, act as the church's administrator and celebrate Mass every day.

In September British Roman Catholic bishops published a document, *One Bread One Body*, restricting the practice of open Communion between Churches. Whereas Catholics in Germany, South Africa and Australia allowed regular, even weekly, sharing in the Eucharist, the British bishops regarded this as only allowable exceptionally, a decision which the Catholic journal *The Tablet* said 'may be regretted later' since the laity were voting with their feet for greater latitude. In April President Clinton and his wife, who were Baptist and Methodist respectively, received Communion in a South African Roman Catholic Church, but this was regarded unfavourably by the Vatican.

PAPAL TRAVELS. In January Pope John Paul II paid a five-day visit to communist-ruled Cuba, meeting President Fidel Castro and saying Masses in the open air, which had not been allowed in Cuba for 35 years (see also II.3.viii; IV.3.xi). After the abortive Bay of Pigs invasion in 1961 (see AR 1961, pp. 192, 371), most foreign priests and teachers had left Cuba and Catholic schools had been nationalized. In 1967 the state had been declared officially atheist and believers were not allowed to join the Cuban Communist Party. However, in 1991 the ban on believers as party members had been removed and the following year all commitments to official atheism had been annulled, although the state remained secular. In the last 15 years there had been a religious revival in Cuba, with missionaries coming even from the right-wing Opus Dei movement (see AR 1992, p. 441). The Pope received a great welcome wherever he went, with a climax in the Plaza de la Revolución in Havana, where he appealed for ideals and commitment, religious and political liberty, freedom for dissidents, attacking the abuse of sex and drugs and stressing the contribution of Christians to society. As a result, some dissidents were freed, and Christmas was re-established as a public holiday, having been banned since 1970.

In March the Pope spent three days in Nigeria, meeting huge crowds in the southern provinces where there were Christian majorities. He announced the beatification of a Nigerian monk, Fr Cyprian Tansi, the first so blessed in West Africa. At the federal capital, Abuja, he met the then head of state, General Abacha, and asked for clemency for detainees. To Muslim leaders he stressed the teachings that Christianity and Islam had in common.

On 21 February Pope John Paul II created 20 new cardinals, bringing their number to a record 165, of whom 122 would be electors for the next Pope. The cardinals were from 55 countries and all continents, though with 56 cardinals Europe had the largest number. Latin America had 23 cardinals, North America 13, Asia 14, Africa 12 and Oceania four.

On 27 April Bishop Juan Conedera, aged 75, was beaten to death with a cement block at his home in Guatemala City, his murder giving rise to three days of national mourning. Two days earlier in the Catholic cathedral Bishop Conedera, a champion of human rights, had launched a report, *Guatemala Never Again*, listing 55,000 cases of human rights abuses, 80 per cent of them by the army during 36 years of civil conflict. The Catholic Institute for International Relations compared this murder to that of Archbishop Romero in El Salvador (see AR 1980, pp. 87, 378) and concluded that it was the work of a death squad.

LAMBETH CONFERENCE. The 13th Lambeth Conference of the worldwide Anglican Communion was held in Canterbury from 18 July to 9 August. The Anglican Church claimed 70 million members in 37 provinces, of which the largest was England with 26 million and the second largest Nigeria with 17.5 million. Some 850 bishops attended the conference, including for the first time 11 women bishops from the USA, Canada and New Zealand. The last conference, in 1988, had been criticized as too English, but this one opened with Latin American dancing, African drumming, gospel-reading in Portuguese and Arabic, and prayers in French and Swahili. It had been feared that debates on homosexuality and female ordination would dominate the programme, but Asian and African delegates brushed these aside and concentrated on regional problems of persecution in Muslim lands and world debt. The bishops did, however, vote by a large majority in favour of a resolution stating that homosexual relations were 'incompatible' with Christian scripture.

On 9 July ten modern Christian martyrs were uniquely commemorated by statues placed on the west front of Westminster Abbey in niches vacant since the Reformation. Unveiled by the Archbishop of Canterbury, in the presence of Queen Elizabeth II, Cardinal Hume and representatives of many countries and churches, these heroes of the faith were, from left to right: Fr Maximilian Kolbe (Poland), Manche Masemola (a South African girl), Archbishop Janani Luwum (Uganda), Grand Duchess Elizabeth (Russia), Pastor Martin Luther King (USA), Archbishop Oscar Romero (El Salvador), Pastor Dietrich Bonhöffer (Germany), Esther John (a Pakistani teacher), Lucian Tapiedi (a Papua New Guinea evangelist) and Pastor Wang Zhiming (China).

While many churches saw declining numbers, with fewer young people replacing the old, conservative fundamentalism showed some startling growth. In August a huge new church, Kingsway International Christian Centre near Hackney in east London, which had cost some £3 million, attracted 5,000 worshippers. Assisted by a 100-strong choir, guest bands, songs and prayers in different languages, the congregation was encouraged to 'jump for Jesus'. Headed by a Nigerian-born pastor, Matthew Ashimolowo, most of the church members were black and there were extensive social facilities and training centres.

The Anglican Holy Trinity, Brompton (see AR 1997, p. 448), had a regular congregation of 2,500 and annual income of £2.3 million. Its introductory course on Christianity, called 'Alpha', had spread to 7,500 other churches and denominations in five years and to 55 countries. The 'Alpha' programme began with a shared meal, followed by Bible-study of hard-line evangelicalism; an accompanying book asserted that homosexuality was 'an indirect result of sin' and that other religions were inadequate because Jesus was 'the only way to God'.

ORTHODOX TENSIONS. In February Patriarch Bartholomew of Constantinople spent a month visiting Orthodox congregations in the USA. The senior leader of Orthodoxy and Greek Orthodox Ecumenical Patriarch, but himself a Turkish citizen, Bartholomew had only a small community in Istanbul and frequently visited communities of the diaspora, especially in North America, Britain and Australia. The Patriarch's tour was extensive and was marked by his criticism of relations with Roman Catholicism, stating that 'the divergence between us continually increases'.

In Romania the anniversary of 'the Union of All Romanians' was celebrated by a national holiday on 1 December, marking 50 years since a governmental decree had suppressed the Romanian Greek Catholic Church (Uniate) and forbidden relations with any foreign body, cutting Catholics off from the Vatican. Even now Romanian Catholics had received back only 50 of the 2,008 churches confiscated at the suppression, though they had 300,000 adherents.

On 17 July the state burial of the remains of Russian Tsar Nicholas II and his family took place in the cathedral of St Peter and St Paul in St Petersburg and was shown on national television (see III.3.i). Noticeably absent from the ceremony was Patriarch Alexis of Moscow, though President Boris Yeltsin gave a powerful speech, referring to 'murdered innocents', and Orthodox priests sang dirges. The Moscow Patriarchate was said to be uncertain as to the genuineness of the remains. The Russian Church in Brussels had a set of rival relics, and there was also fear of demands for the canonization of Nicholas II. However, the chief reason for the Patriarch's absence seemed to have been fear of annoying the Communist Party, which might return to power. Although numbers of churches and monasteries had increased in Russia, and many children in the cities were baptized, at most only 6 per cent of the population claimed to go to church once a month. Bishops enjoyed public prominence but were generally conservative, and in May books by three modern Orthodox theologians were burnt on episcopal orders.

JEWISH RELATIONSHIPS. Disputes between branches of Anglo-Jewry followed the funeral of Rabbi Hugo Gryn (see AR 1997, p. 451), but in November a peace agreement was signed by lay leaders of the Orthodox United Synagogue and the three main non-Orthodox groups—Reform, Liberal and Masorti—and this was backed by Chief Rabbi Jonathan Sacks. Orthodox rabbis could not take part in or speak at non-Orthodox services, but their attendance was 'within their discretion'. Conservative members of the Orthodox Beth Din at once forbade Orthodox rabbis to attend such services.

In March a Vatican document, *We Remember: a Reflection on the Shoah* (the Holocaust of Jews), expressed 'deep sorrow' and 'repentance' for Christians who had failed to resist Nazi persecution. Jewish reactions were critical, especially of the document's support for the silence of Pope Pius

XII. The Chief Rabbi of Israel, Yisrael Lau, a survivor of Auschwitz, said it was 'too little, too late'.

Further disagreement arose on 11 October when Pope John Paul II declared the canonization of Jewish-born Edith Stein, who had been killed in Auschwitz. An atheist in early life, Edith Stein had been baptized a Catholic in 1922 and had become a Carmelite nun. She had been arrested in the Netherlands with other Dutch Catholics of Jewish origin during World War II, apparently in reprisal against Dutch bishops who had denounced persecution of Jews (it being claimed that this had caused Pius XII to prefer covert action to public denunciation). But making Edith Stein a saint angered many Jews, and a French rabbi said that 'she was murdered because she was Jewish, not because she was Christian'. Moves for the canonization of Pius XII himself provoked further criticism of the Vatican.

Continuing antisemitism in Poland was apparent in the stationing of crosses at Auschwitz concentration camp. A Carmelite convent located there had been moved at Pope John Paul II's personal direction (see AR 1989, p. 428), but a 27-foot-high cross installed by local residents remained and was justified by Cardinal Joseph Glemp of Warsaw. Jewish groups requested the relocation of this huge cross, but when the Polish authorities agreed to its transfer hundreds of small crosses appeared against the wall of the camp. Some local church leaders, and commentators in other countries, condemned this 'manipulation of patriotic and religious feeling'.

Certain Jewish and Christian fundamentalists believed that the Temple in Jerusalem, destroyed in 70 AD, should be rebuilt on what had later become the Dome of the Rock Muslim holy shrine. On 7 October a group of Jewish extremists was prevented by Israeli police from entering the mosque complex to start the temple reconstruction.

ISLAMIC CONCERNS. On 27 April a Pakistani Christian, Ayub Masih, was condemned to death in Punjab province for allegedly saying to a friend that if he read Salman Rushdie's novel *The Satanic Verses* he would know 'the true face of Islam' (see AR 1988, p. 440; 1989, p. 493). Ayub Masih denied the charge and there was widespread protest, led by Bishop John Joseph of Faisalabad, whose action stirred the country. The first Punjabi Roman Catholic bishop, Bishop Joseph had a long history of non-violent struggle on behalf of minorities. On 6 May he was taken at night to the court house, but then shot himself in the head. Thousands of people gathered for his funeral, and Bishop Joseph was declared 'man of the year for peace' in Faisalabad. The Vatican seemed uncertain how to present his action, however, since suicide was against the Church's teaching and even martyrdom should not be sought. The bishop's nephew wrote that it was not a suicide denying the grace of God, but the act of a shepherd giving his life for his sheep. Following his death, Muslim and Christian leaders in Pakistan met several times to ease tensions between the communities. Christians in Pakistan numbered three million in a population of 130 million.

In the Indonesian capital, Jakarta, Christians were attacked by Muslims in November, and several churches were damaged or destroyed, following reports that mosques had been stoned. In East Timor 22 churches were sacked, and in revenge mobs burnt or wrecked six mosques. The Archbishop of Jakarta apologized and asked Catholics to help rebuild the mosques.

In August two Catholic priests were arrested in Khartoum, and 19 others in the days following, on suspicion of involvement in bomb explosions in the Sudanese capital. The 21 defendants were formally charged in October, but lawyers for the defence questioned the independence of the military court. Almost all the Christians were refugees from the civil war in the south, and Amnesty International launched an appeal for their help. Baroness Cox, travelling in the Sudan with a group from Christian Solidarity Worldwide, told how she had bought slaves to save them from enforced Arabization and Islamization.

In other places inter-religious cooperation was manifest in reciprocal visits to mosques and churches. Young people from a Methodist Church at Orpington, Kent, went to prayers at a mosque of the Naqshbandi Sufi Order in London. In return Sheikh Nazim, leader of the Order, attended worship at the Methodist Church in February, with 40 Muslims, including a Malaysian prince.

BOOKS OF THE YEAR. Twelve books of the Bible were published in separate volumes with modern introductions by various writers, the book of Job being described as 'insidiously subversive', and Revelation as 'psychotic nightmare'. *Concise Encyclopedias* of Christianity, Judaism and Hinduism were packed with information on people and movements. *Man of the Century* by Jonathan Kwitny presented Pope John Paul II as the most influential 'political' figure of the past 20 years. In *Speak of the Devil*, J.S. La Fontaine examined allegations of Satanic cults in the 1980s, concluding that there was no hard evidence for them, 'no bodies, no bones, no bloodstains, nothing'. In *The Smoke of Satan*, M.W. Cuneo provided a sociological analysis of extreme groups in American Catholicism. D.J. Davies, in *Death, Ritual and Belief*, gave valuable material on a neglected subject, with many forms of 'words against death'. *The Bible and Colonialism*, by Michael Prior, described ways in which Bible stories of the conquest of the Promised Land had been used to justify the oppression of indigenous populations in America, South Africa and Palestine. Stephen Turnbull's *The Kakure Kirishitan of Japan* told of the 'hidden Christians' who kept the faith during two-and-a-half centuries of persecution. In *Beyond Belief: Islamic Excursions among the Converted*, V.S. Naipaul returned to the fundamentalism which he described in *Among the Believers* (see AR 1981, p. 381). In *Qur'an, Liberation and Pluralism*, Farid Esack, a Muslim theologian, showed how pluralism, working with people of other religions, helped in the struggle against apartheid in South Africa. In *Christianity in the Arab World*, Hasan bin Talal, Crown Prince of Jordan, acknowledged the Church's role in opening up Islam to the Greek heritage and to modern ways.

XIII THE SCIENCES

1. SCIENTIFIC, MEDICAL AND INDUSTRIAL RESEARCH

SPACE, ASTRONOMY AND PHYSICAL SCIENCES. 1998 was the year in which the first modules of the International Space Station (ISS) finally got off the ground. First to leave was the Russian manufactured *Zarya* module, which left the Baikonur cosmodrome in Kazakhstan on 20 November, several months behind schedule. That was followed in December by the first connecting node, called *Unity*, which was linked up by US astronauts on board the space shuttle *Endeavour*. When complete, the ISS was expected to be bigger than a football stadium and to have cost more than $40,000 million. Life on the Russian *Mir* space station continued with less drama than the previous year and included the delivery by space shuttle in January of Andy Thomas, the last of seven US astronauts scheduled to spend time on *Mir*. Meanwhile, it was suggested that *Mir* would be slowly lowered from orbit so as to re-enter the atmosphere and burn up safely towards the end of 1999, though it seemed that this announcement may have resulted from US pressure on the Russians not to divert their scarce resources from the ISS.

The 77-year-old US astronaut and senator, John Glenn, made history for the second time by becoming the oldest person to have visited space. His shuttle flight in October came 36 years after he had become the first American to orbit the Earth. The NASA craft *Deep Space One* was launched, testing a new Ion drive to set it in progress towards a rendezvous with an asteroid. But one of the NEAR spacecraft failed to fire its conventional rockets to steer it to a rendezvous with the asteroid Eros. Scientists still hoped that it could complete its mission at a later date. There was a second successful launch of an *Ariane V* rocket during the year, and a Russian nuclear submarine successfully placed two small German research satellites into orbit.

At the beginning of the year the first civilian US Moon mission for 25 years, *Lunar Prospector*, was launched. Along with its scientific instruments, it carried the ashes of lunar geologist Eugene Shoemaker, who had died the previous year, fulfilling his ambition to visit the Moon. A few weeks later mission scientists were able to announce that they had detected frozen water on the Moon, possibly in sufficient quantities to supply a lunar base. Meanwhile, the US *Mars Global Surveyor* craft detected more evidence that Mars had had rivers, floods and possibly even oceans billions of years ago. The European Infra-red Space Observatory finally ran out of liquid helium to cool its heat sensors in April, but not until after it had completed all the mission objectives, including detecting water molecules in vast clouds in interstellar space. The space probe *Ulysses* completed its first full orbit over the Sun's poles and a US craft called *TRACE* was launched to look at X-rays from the Sun. There was excitement and tension for scientists running Europe's solar observatory spacecraft, *SOHO*, after they lost contact with it, following an incorrect sequence of instructions. By the time they found it again, its fuel had frozen solid and there were fears that its instruments would have been damaged. However, slowly and carefully *SOHO* was brought back to life in full working order.

The journal *Science* awarded 'breakthrough of the year' status to the implications of a series of observations of the brightness of distant exploding stars or supernovae. Certain supernovae were of a precisely-known absolute brightness so, by observing their actual brightness in distant galaxies, the astronomers, under Dr Saul Perlmutter, were able to estimate how far away the galaxies were. By comparing the distances of more than 40 supernovae up to nine billion light years away with the red shifts of the galaxies they were in, they concluded that the expansion of the Universe seemed to be accelerating. The reason was not fully understood, but implied that the Universe would go on expanding forever. Observations of differences in the absorption lines of magnesium and iron atoms in distant quasars led researchers to suggest that one of the most fundamental constants of the Universe, the fine structure constant, may have been different in the past. Measurements from the Super Kamiokande neutrino detector in Japan suggested that the neutrino might have a small but real mass, sufficient for neutrinos to make up the bulk of the mass of the Universe.

Observations from the *COBE* satellite of the infra-red glow in the Universe suggested that there were once far more stars than we can see today, perhaps a lost generation of short-lived stars. The record for the most distant galaxy detected was broken several times during the year by British and US astronomers, who detected galaxies that must have existed when the Universe was less than 800 million years old. Among the distant objects seen was an active galaxy or quasar ten times brighter than anything previously detected. Several big new telescopes were under construction around the world, suggesting that such records would not stand for long. Among the instruments was the Very Large Telescope of the European Southern Observatory in Chile. The first of four giant telescopes there began operations and it was expected that the completed instrument would be as powerful as a single telescope 16 metres in diameter.

There was evidence of several more solar systems around nearby stars, including possible planets the size of the Earth, and radio telescopes detected dust disks out of which planets might form. The Hubble Space Telescope produced what might be the first image of a planet outside our solar system around a nearby star. Astronomers continued to search for asteroids that might pose a threat to the Earth and, at one stage, thought they had found one that could collide in 2028, though later calculations concluded that it would miss. More geological evidence for past collisions was found. Meanwhile, observers prepared for a harmless but potentially spectacular meteor storm in November during the annual Leonid meteor shower. There were many fine shooting stars observed, but they did not amount to a storm.

The technology of landmine detection received added impetus from the death of Diana, Princess of Wales, the preceding year (see AR 1997, pp. 4, 165, 442-3, 566-8). Hand-held metal detectors had proved too slow, dangerous and unable to detect plastic mines; blast-proof mine clearance vehicles were too expensive and unable to operate in rough terrain. Advances were made in vehicle-based ground-penetrating radar systems to clear mines quickly from roads. Infra-red sensors were showing promise for detecting whole minefields and various techniques for detecting the explosives within a mine were under development, including one called 'nuclear quadrupole resonance' for remotely sensing explosives and sensitive chemical sensors for sniffing out faint traces of molecules of explosive in the air.

In the year in which the 50th anniversary of the world's first programmable computer was celebrated in Manchester, there were several fundamental advances that were expected to lead to faster, smaller computers in the future. Dutch scientists created a micro-electronic component, a transistor, from a single molecule, a buckytube or cylinder of the form of carbon called a fullerene. Researchers at Harvard University used a buckytube as a probe a million times smaller than the tip of a needle. They believed it could be adapted into a sort of nano-scalpel to repair individual genetic defects.

Israeli scientists used the ability of the genetic material DNA to self-assemble to grow an ultra-miniaturized connection between two electrodes; and a team from the Cavendish Laboratory in Cambridge made the world's first integrated circuit based not on silicon but on plastic. Researchers in Arizona built a molecular machine that mimicked photosynthesis. They hoped that its ability to trap solar energy and store it as chemical fuel would help it to power micro-machines of the future. Solar-powered machines on a different scale were announced by the US space agency NASA: a fleet of solar planes designed to patrol the upper atmosphere powered by nothing but sunlight. They unveiled a prototype with a wingspan of more than 60 metres in the Californian desert.

A company in the USA developed a way of converting methane or natural gas into methyl alcohol, a liquid that could be stored and transported as a fuel more easily. They hoped that, using their technique, natural gas might become a replacement for petrol. To harness a simpler form of energy, the South African President, Nelson Mandela, opened a new factory for clockwork torches. The invention came from Trevor Bayliss, whose design of a clockwork radio was already proving very successful. Researchers at the MIT developed a sort of electronic ink that changed colour when an electric field was applied and stayed that way until it received a new field. They anticipated its use in displays and as a sort of instant electronic book that could be printed in an instant and re-used after having been read.

The British computer scientist, Professor Kevin Warwick, became the first person to be implanted with a silicon chip to track his movements. He underwent the implant to illustrate how technology could affect personal freedom. Researchers at the Los Alamos laboratory in the US believed they had developed an uncrackable code using a technique called quantum cryptography which they demonstrated over a satellite link. The prospect of a satellite phone that would work anywhere in the world became a reality with the launch of the last of 66 satellites to complete the Iridium network.

BIOLOGICAL AND MEDICAL SCIENCES. In its 1998 *World Health Report*, the World Health Organization (WHO) predicted that life in the 21st century would be healthier and longer for more people than ever before. It predicted that average global life expectancy at birth would rise from 66 years in 1998 to 73 years by 2025. But the report warned that those extra years would be unequally shared among people in rich and poor nations, with life expectancy in Japan and Sweden reaching 82 while that in Sierra Leone would still be just 51. It was predicted that the number of people aged 65 and over in the world would grow by almost a million every month, and with that increase would come a rise in degenerative diseases and an increased burden on health services.

In another report, an international group of eminent doctors predicted that it would become impossible to deal with health problems without also tackling poverty, so the health of the world would depend not only on doctors and nurses but on those providing clean water and sanitation, adequate food and economic stability. World Health Day in 1998 also focused on deaths that had been linked with poverty: those of women dying from the complications of pregnancy or childbirth. During 1998 one woman was dying from such causes every minute—deaths which the WHO believed could be prevented. There were research results to suggest that life expectancy might become even longer in the more distant future. Genetic studies in fruit flies revealed a gene without which the insects could live 40 per cent longer. Research showed that cells aged and died when the ends of the chromosomes that contained their genetic material became damaged. These ends were normally capped by structures called telomeres and research in the US showed that the healthy lives of living human cells could be extended using an enzyme called telomerase, which rebuilt the protective telomeres.

Doctors continued to express concerns that emerging diseases would be a major problem in the future, particularly as a consequence of global warming. It was revealed that an epidemic in Romania in 1996 had been caused by West Nile fever, spread by mosquitoes usually only seen in warmer climates. There was an outbreak of dengue fever in south-east Asia and of sleeping sickness in Angola, and an epidemic of typhus in Burundi. Malaria continued to be a serious problem and WHO announced a major new initiative to hold back the disease. Another serious concern was the spread of antibiotic resistance among disease-causing organisms. It was estimated to that there were a million new cases of bacterial infection occurring within the world's hospitals every day, many of them resistant to antibiotics. Britain's Public Health Laboratory Service discovered a strain of bacteria resistant to all known antibiotics, fuelling fears that such super-bugs would soon spread out of control. The blame was placed on the widespread use of antibiotics in farm animals and their excessive use to treat human diseases, often including viral infections for which they were ineffective. However, a new breath test was developed to diagnose such infections correctly and it was discovered that both bacteria and cancer cells used the same mechanism to pump out drugs to which they were resistant, leading to hopes that the mechanism might be blocked by new treatments.

One of the infections in which drug resistance was still a major problem was tuberculosis (TB). In a report, WHO said that, although some countries were tackling TB successfully, others were not and just 22 countries accounted for 80 per cent of all cases. TB was thought to be the biggest killer of young women in the world and it was estimated that the diseases would kill 70 million people before the year 2020. However, there were some advances in treating the disease: the entire genome of the bacterium responsible was sequenced and researchers discovered a gene essential for the bacteria to multiply in human cells to cause the disease. They hoped to target treatments against it.

Multiple drug resistance was also seen for the first time in the AIDS virus HIV, although the first significant fall in the number of deaths due to AIDS in the USA and Europe was reported. This was believed to have been due to a greater awareness in those regions of the need for safe sex plus the widespread use of what was known as 'triple therapy', a combination of three different drugs. However, it was not clear whether the treatment cured the disease or merely delayed it. By contrast, 95 per cent of AIDS cases were in the developing world, where the drugs could seldom be afforded, in spite of price cuts of up to 75 per cent during the year. In Zambia, for example, a quarter of the population was believed to be infected with HIV and two million Zambians were expected to die of AIDS by 2010. Meanwhile, the first-ever recorded case of AIDS was discovered. The virus was found in a frozen blood sample taken from an African man who had died in 1959.

The implications of the previous year's cloning of Dolly the sheep (see AR 1997, p. 457) continued to reverberate around the bio-medical world. At the start off the year, a former US physicist, Dr Richard Seed, claimed to be ready to begin experiments that would lead to the cloning of humans.

Later, South Korean researchers claimed to have produced a cloned human, but did not allow it to grow beyond a four-cell embryo. The US subsidiary of the company that produced Dolly announced the birth of Mr Jefferson, a cloned calf, but he was produced from a foetal cell rather than that of an adult. A Japanese team claimed a high success rate for cloning an adult animal, producing eight cloned calves. It was hoped that cloned cattle might produce uniformly high-quality beef as well as herds of animals resistance to BSE or 'mad cow disease' and perhaps able to produce useful pharmaceutical products in their milk. Genetic tests proved that Dolly herself was a true clone of an adult cell, and she went on to give birth to a lamb named Bonnie, confirming that cloning did not result in infertility or premature ageing.

Scientists in Wisconsin developed a technique for growing laboratory cultures of stem cells taken from human embryos. It was speculated that such cells might be grown into transplant material to treat a range of diseases such as Parkinson's and Alzheimer's diseases. An advisory panel in Britain gave limited approval to the use of cloned human tissue in this way. There were also significant advances in tissue engineering. By allowing cloned cells or a patient's own cells to grow up onto some sort of artificial scaffolding, it was hoped that whole organs might be grown for transplantation. This would avoid the need for human donors and the ethical dilemmas and risks of viral infection that had plagued suggestions of transplanting organs from animals. To demonstrate the possibilities, Dr Charles Vacanti of MIT, who had previously grown a human ear on the back of a mouse, went on to produce blood vessels, heart valves and nipples from animal tissue. In October he reconstructed a metal worker's crushed thumb, using a piece of coral into which the patient's own bone cells grew and then covering it with soft tissue grown from the remains of the original thumb. There were also research results to indicate that cells of the central nervous system might be stimulated into growth again, leading to possible repair of degenerative brain diseases and severed spinal cords.

The culmination of 35 years of work was announced by scientists in Cambridge who had succeeded in sequencing the entire genome off a multicellular organism, albeit a tiny worm called *Cenorhabditis elegans*. The worm shared 40 per cent of its genes with humans and the research was already helping the understanding of human genetic make-up. Cloning and genetic engineering came together with a technique for producing cloned mice with a single gene deleted. Mass production of such animals was expected to make discovering the function of each gene much easier. Among the many other genes identified during the year were genes predisposing to drug addiction and alcoholism, genes involved in our internal body clocks, a gene involved in speech and language, a gene for baldness, a gene involved in sporting ability, the gene that laid down the symmetry of the body and the gene that gave modern humans their comparatively flat faces.

Several new pieces were put in place in the evolutionary jigsaw of life during 1998. German researchers found that some of the protein precursors of life could form on iron sulphide minerals around undersea volcanic vents and a Japanese team found that comparatively short fragments of RNA could make proteins begin to form in the same way. The oldest fossils of multi-cellular life-forms were found in Chinese deposits 600 million years old. They included tiny sponges a millimetre across and what appeared to be the embryos of primitive worms. The 340-million-year-old fossil remains of a land animal were found near Edinburgh, displaying intermediate characteristics between amphibians and reptiles. The creature was named *Eucritter melanolimnetes*, literally 'beautiful creature from the black lagoon'. Modern specimens of a coelacanth were recovered off Indonesia, more than 10,000 kilometres from the only place where such living fossils had been found before.

The remains of the world's oldest flowering plant were discovered in volcanic ash 140 million years old in China and there was a major reclassification of the plant kingdom, based on DNA analysis. A vast nesting-site of dinosaurs was discovered in Argentina, with eggs containing dinosaur embryos, and a fossil dinosaur was found in Italy with traces of its internal organs preserved. Fossils showed that ants dated back to the time of the dinosaurs. Two small fossil dinosaurs about the size of turkeys were discovered in China. They could not fly but were covered with downy feathers, suggesting that birds must have evolved from dinosaurs. The fossilized jawbone of what could have been a Jurassic parrot was unearthed in Wyoming. The oldest intact skull and skeleton of a possible human ancestor was discovered at Sterkfontein near Johannesburg. At 1.2 metres tall and 3.5 million years old, though ape-like, it walked erect, suggesting possible human ancestry.

NOBEL PRIZES. The 1998 Nobel Prize for Medicine or Physiology was awarded to US scientists Robert Furchgott, Louis Ignarro and Ferid Murad for their discovery of the role of nitric oxide as a chemical messenger in our bodies. It was a discovery that eventually led to the impotence drug Viagra becoming a best-seller in 1998. For the third year running, the Physics Prize went for the study of phenomena at extremely low temperatures: in this case to Horst Störner (Germany), Daniel Tsui and Robert Laughlin (USA) for their work on how metals conduct electricity at almost absolute zero. The Chemistry Prize was awarded to two theoreticians, John Pople (UK) and Walter Krohn (USA), for developing ways of making quantum calculations feasible.

2. INFORMATION TECHNOLOGY

DEMOCRACY and popular prurience were the gainers as traditional media ran a poor second to Internet communication on Friday 18 September, the day when Kenneth Starr's report on US President Bill Clinton's relationship with Monica Lewinsky was released for publication (see IV.1; XVII.4). Members of the public were able to access the report directly on the worldwide web, to search the full text for the parts of greatest interest and to download all 450 pages, or merely extracts selected by themselves, without having to wait for the printing process to be completed or to order a copy from a bookshop.

Unprecedented volume of traffic manifested itself, with, for example, America Online (AOL) recording 10 million hours' usage in a single day for the first time ever. Yet there were no reports of major system failures such as had happened on previous occasions when usage had peaked (see AR 1997, p. 462), although users were not necessarily able to connect to their chosen web site at first attempt. On this occasion, a surge in usage had been expected and congressional technical staff had had the foresight to distribute copies of the report on CD-ROM in HTML (hypertext mark-up language) format to key third-party distributors, such as Yahoo! and AOL. Newspapers could not react so quickly, and even television reports showed pictures of computer screens displaying the text online.

A 'digital declaration of independence' was the ambitious designation given by US Vice-President Al Gore to five challenges which he enunciated shortly after the surge of Internet usage witnessed on 18 September. Mr Gore had already gained a reputation as an enthusiastic advocate of the information society when, in 1993, he launched the US National Information Infrastructure (see AR 1993, pp. 459–60). On this more recent occasion, he was inaugurating the plenipotentiary conference of the International Telecommunication Union (ITU), the UN specialized agency with responsibility for standards in that field, which was held in Minneapolis from 18 October. In summary, his challenges were: (i) to improve access so that everyone in the world would be in walking distance of voice and data communications services within the coming decade; (ii) to overcome language barriers with 'real-time' (i.e. almost instantaneous) digital translation; (iii) to create a global network of people working to improve the delivery of education, health care, agricultural resources and sustainable development; (iv) to use communications to ensure the free flow of ideas and support democracy and free speech; and (v) to use communication technology to expand economic opportunity to all communities around the world.

INTERNET DEVELOPMENTS. Important changes relating to the management structure of the Internet were agreed during 1998. Originally, the Internet had been established as a public sector, military and academic network (see AR 1993, p. 461) and had been managed and funded as such. Prior to 1998, key decisions concerning the protocols and standards which enabled the Internet to function were channelled through the Internet Assigned Numbers Authority (IANA), which was also responsible for the coordination of the domain name system (DNS). Subject to the coordinating role of IANA, however, the issue of names to users was devolved to a variety of organizations in different parts of the world, including Network Solutions Inc (NSI) in the USA, acting as contractor to the National Science Foundation (NSF), a US government agency. As the Internet became increasingly used by commercial as well as public sector entities and took on international dimensions, it was gradually recognized, albeit not quickly and not without controversy, that management of the Internet should no longer reside effectively under the control of the US government.

After wide consultation, by the end of 1998 proposals had been drawn up and accepted by the US government for the formation of a non-profit-making company based in California, but with wide international representation on the board, to take over the central coordinating functions of the Internet. Amongst the first priorities of the newly-formed Internet Corporation for Assigned Names and Numbers (ICANN) were to introduce competition into the registration of domain names around the world and to resolve the vexed question of the creation of new top-level domains (such as .com, .net and .org), a subject which had attracted much debate over the previous 12 months or more.

One of the architects of ICANN had been Dr Jon Postel, head of the Computer Networks Division of the Information Sciences Institute at the University of Southern California in Los Angeles. Dr Postel had been involved in the coordination of the Internet and its forerunner networks for over a quarter of a century. Shortly after delivering his final recommendations to the US Department of Commerce, however, he died on 16 October as a result of complications during heart surgery (see Pt XVIII: Obituary). Earlier in the year he had demonstrated the extent of his influence over the Internet when he arranged for key network traffic to be diverted via his computer. Although he described his actions as an 'experiment', some commentators believed that his intention had been to give added weight to his opinions.

CONSUMER ELECTRONICS. In the UK, British Sky Broadcasting (BSkyB) began digital television broadcasting by satellite and was followed swiftly by cable and terrestrial broadcasters with their own digital offerings (see also XV.1.vi). The advent of these services posed a difficult problem for government, namely when to 'turn off' analogue television broadcasting. In the event, unlike the US government, which had set 2006 as a firm date for the end of analogue television broadcasting, the UK government decided not to fix a date, thereby ruling out, above all, a proposed five-year target. Government concerns focused upon the cost to consumers, especially the poor and elderly, who would need to replace television sets or acquire conversion devices in order to be able to receive digital signals.

In the realm of consumer video, DVD (digital versatile disc) showed tangible signs of taking off and, therefore, in the longer run of replacing the analogue VHS cassette as the medium of preference for video distribution. By Christmas approximately 2,000 DVD titles were on sale in the USA and 500 in Europe, and it was being reported that sales of players had exceeded one million during the year. At the same time, however, agreement had still not been reached on a standard format for DVD audio and a smooth transition from CD to DVD for the distribution of music was endangered by the development of opposing camps in the audio industry.

Meanwhile, the music industry also perceived itself as under threat from the appearance in the marketplace of modestly-priced (under US$200) portable devices which could store and replay approximately one hour of recorded music downloaded from the Internet using MP3 technology, a software capable of compressing sound and reproducing it with little loss of quality. Late in the year the Recording Industry Association of America (RIIA) failed in legal action aimed at preventing Diamond Multimedia Systems from manufacturing and marketing such a device, known as the Rio digital music player. The court decision left the RIIA reassessing its strategies to combat piracy, with the focus necessarily being redirected at technological rather than legal solutions.

COMPUTER TECHNOLOGY. Intel Corporation, the world's largest chip manufacturer, announced that it was on course to introduce the first of its new 'IA-64' generation of 64-bit microprocessors in 2000 (the well-established Pentium family being 32-bit processors). The IA-64 series was designed to work with special software which would facilitate parallel processing. Intel dubbed its approach, which was not without competitors, EPIC (explicit parallel instruction computing) and expected the IA-64 series to perform better than the fastest processors previously produced. In view of the absence of 64-bit operating systems and applications software, however, Intel was also proceeding with a new range of 32-bit processors.

In a different area of technology, 1998 could be recorded as the beginning of the end for the 'network computer', a machine with limited local intelligence, designed to access resources through the network to which it was connected. At least, that was the claim of Bill Gates, chief executive of the world's largest software company, Microsoft Corporation, speaking at a conference in Paris in September. Indeed, in an independent survey carried out for Compaq Computer earlier in the year, three-quarters of IT professionals interviewed had seen no role for the network computer. Originally the network computer had been championed by Larry Ellison of Oracle Corporation (see AR 1995, p. 453) as a technology which might ultimately weaken the position of Microsoft through the elimination of the need for operating systems and applications software other than at the 'centre' of a network.

MARKET FORCES *V.* REGULATION. Legal actions in the USA against Microsoft continued through the year. Action started in 1997 (see AR 1997, p. 462), seeking to force Microsoft to stop integrating its Internet browser software with its 'Windows' operating systems software failed in relation to both Windows 95 and Windows 98. In May, however, the federal Justice Department and the attorneys-general of 20 US states jointly launched a major new anti-trust suit against Microsoft, focusing on a number of specific anti-competitive business practices alleged to be employed by the corporation. Nevertheless, underlying the case was the more fundamental issue of whether consumers' interests were best served by market forces alone, especially in the fast-developing technology sector, or whether regulatory intervention was necessary. The case went to trial in September and was still proceeding at the end of the year.

More or less contemporaneously, the US Federal Trade Commission filed an action against Intel, on the grounds that it was using its power in the marketplace to reduce competition by refusing to provide companies deemed to be possible competitors with technical information necessary for them to develop products built around Intel chips. The hearing was scheduled to commence in January 1999.

GOVERNMENT INITIATIVES. With the coming-into-force in October 1998 of the European Union (EU) directive on data protection, a policy issue over which the EU and the USA had little common ground (see AR 1997, p. 464) became the focus of potential dispute. The new directive prohibited the export of personal data to countries deemed not to have adequate data protection laws. Because of a fundamental difference in philosophy, the USA fell into this latter category, the US administration consistently maintaining the view that industry self-regulation was preferable to legislative intervention. Bilateral talks failed to resolve the issue and there was a possibility the USA might refer the matter to the World Trade Organization (WTO).

THE MILLENNIUM. The issue commonly referred to as the 'millennium bug' or the 'Y2K problem' was not at all new (see AR 1996, p. 449), but, as the year 2000 approached, awareness of the possible problems increased. At the root of the problem was earlier practice, on the part of computer programmers, of using two digits rather than four to register year dates. At the turn of the century, computers programmed in this way would be likely either to reject or to fail to assign any significance to an '00' date, with the possible consequence that systems would stop completely. Alternatively, an '00' date might be interpreted as '1900', with a variety of other possible results. For example, in a retail application, a system might classify all stock as beyond its sell-by date and, therefore, automatically stop sales and/or order the destruction of the stock. Potential risks were considered most serious for critical systems, such as security or defence installations, or for applications in the civil aviation or emergency services fields. A major concern was that since date registering could be thought trivial, and in some applications would appear not to be a material consideration, the problem might be overlooked in smaller organizations.

As a response to the problem, many governments, including those of the USA and the UK, launched initiatives to raise awareness and to promote actions, including contingency plans in the event of failures, to ensure that there would be no interruption of operations of whatever sort. In the important field of communications, the ITU set up a dedicated task-force which embarked upon a series of actions to advise telecommunications operators, especially in developing countries, on millennium compliance.

3. THE ENVIRONMENT

THE quality of the food in our mouths, and the rights of people consuming and producing that food, were the environmental issues debated most warmly during 1998 on several continents. Whether foods containing genetically-engineered ingredients should be labelled, whether companies had the right to patent existing names of crop strains, and the meaning of the word 'organic' were all ingredients of that debate. The year also saw several major climate-related disasters such as Hurricane Mitch, the first inclusion of a Green political party in a major government, and a row over whether ordinary Americans would be allowed merely to discuss climate change.

'Frankenstein food' which exposed its consumers to a potential welter of unknown frightening medical consequences? Or a safe and efficient technology that the human race needed in order to continue feeding itself? As 1998 began, the two sides of the genetic engineering debate girded their loins for battle. In Europe, foods containing genetically-modified organisms (GMOs), notably soya, were already on supermarket shelves—in the main without being labelled as such. This was the result of a 1997 European Union (EU) ruling that labelling was unnecessary. Early in 1998 some activists started campaigns of direct action. In the UK, fields of experimental genetically-modified (GM) crops were destroyed. In Germany, campaigners staged sit-ins in fields which were about to be planted with such crops. Although the people of Switzerland voted in a referendum against a general ban on genetic research [see II.3.vii], commentators suggested that the vote would have gone the other way had the question been about GMOs in food only. The Prince of Wales spoke publicly against genetic modification of food, and the British retail chain Iceland said that it would not stock food which might contain GM ingredients. The UK parliament showed exquisite leadership by proclaiming the technology safe, whilst banning GM food from its own restaurants.

In India, too, GMOs in food became a major issue. An American biotechnology company, Ricetech, had patented a genetically-modified strain of basmati rice, a speciality variety which had been grown in India for generations. Ricetech claimed that the patent gave them rights to the term 'basmati' as well as to their own strain and had taken legal action against Indians using the name to refer to unmodified basmati. Following protests from Indian farmers, which included mass demonstrations outside the US embassy in Delhi, the government filed a protest with the World Trade Organization (WTO), which subsequently ruled in favour of Ricetech.

In the USA itself, the Department of Agriculture (USDA) found itself swamped during the first quarter of the year by protest letters about its proposed definition of the term 'organic'. In 1997 the USDA had decided that the word should be strictly defined so that consumers would know precisely what was meant by labelling a food organic. Its draft definition said that the term should be able to encompass crops grown on sewage and GMOs. The USDA asked for feedback, and 200,000 letters arrived, overwhelmingly critical. By April it was working on a new draft definition excluding sewage-grown crops and GMOs. In September scientists in Chicago discovered that GM plants were more likely to cross-breed with related plants nearby than non-GM varieties, so increasing the chances of genes for herbicide resistance, for example, spreading into weeds, which would then become very difficult to control.

All these issues were, however, overshadowed in the second half of the year by the so-called 'terminator' gene, nick-named after the popular films starring Arnold Schwartzenegger, and developed jointly by the USDA and the company Delta Pine and Land. When inserted into a plant's genetic material, the gene made the seeds of that plant sterile. Thus it would prevent a farmer saving and using those seeds, forcing him to buy new stock each year. The world's largest biotech company, Monsanto, acquired Delta Pine and Land early in the year, and thus at least part of the 'terminator' patent. Farmers in several developing countries, notably India, protested vigorously. Discussions on the precise assignation of rights between Monsanto and the USDA were continuing as 1998 ended.

Whatever the science behind GMOs, there was no doubt that the 'terminator' affair was a public relations disaster for the biotechnology industry. Another was a bungled attempt, led by Monsanto, to persuade several prominent African leaders to endorse genetic engineering as necessary to avert starvation amongst an increasing population. Instead, several of the targeted leaders spoke out against the technology. As the year ended, opinion polls in Europe were showing a marked distrust of GMOs, and plans were being laid for mandatory labelling of foods containing them. A senior executive of one biotech giant acknowledged that 'we now have a PR mountain to climb'.

Several scientific papers emerging during the year mapped out a different, more nature-based, potential path towards increasing crop yields. A 15-year study by American researchers, published in November, showed that organic fertilizers could boost plant growth as effectively as conventional high-intensity inorganic ones, and bring additional environmental benefits such as reduced nitrate run-off and lower emissions of greenhouse gases. German scientists showed that ploughing at night-time reduced the amount of herbicide needed. International conferences in February and June heard delegates warning of increasing stress on water supplies. United Nations experts said that one in five people lived without access to safe drinking water, and that this number would rise to one in three by 2025.

Away from agriculture, the image of genetic research suffered another blow when news emerged from South Africa's Truth and Reconciliation Commission (see VII.3) that the former apartheid regime had been researching the idea of making biological weapons which would target specific racial groups, using genetic differences between races to discriminate. The British government said that it would press for tighter international controls on biological weapons research as a result.

More evidence that the planet Earth was warming up, and that human activities were responsible, emerged during 1998. In April American researchers published a statistical analysis of existing data from many sources demonstrating that the pace of warming—around one degree Celsius over the last 100 years—was very fast in historical terms and that the man-made 'greenhouse effect' was the reason why. Attention was also focused on climate because the latest El Niño effect, which had started in 1997 (see AR 1997, pp. 468-9), continued for the first few months of the year before gradually abating. It was succeeded by La Niña—loosely defined as El Niño in reverse but not as severe—which lasted into 1999.

The combination of global warming and El Niño made the first three months of 1998 the warmest on record. Many health-related events were ascribed to climatic change. These included outbreaks of dengue fever in South-East Asia early in the year; what the World Health Organization called 'quantitative leaps' of malaria transmission in several regions previously thought too high and so too cold for the parasite-bearing Anopheles mosquitoes to survive, including parts of southern Africa and of Indonesia; an outbreak of Rift Valley fever in Kenya and Somalia; increases in the incidence of cholera in Latin America and Africa; and of hantavirus and E-coli infection in North America. In November researchers discovered that Arctic ice was 20 to 30 per cent thinner than 20 years ago, a finding which was also laid at the door of global warming, as was the breaking-up in February of a large part of the Larsen ice shelf in Antarctica.

In December the ozone hole over the Antarctic set a new record by lasting more than 100 days. Activists uncovered new evidence of a major black market in chlorofluorocarbons (CFCs), the substances primarily responsible for ozone depletion. Campaigners from the Environmental Investigation Agency (EIA) pressure group posed as buyers of CFCs on the Internet and received a vast number of offers, one potential deal being worth $52 million.

The latest computer model of global climate change from the Hadley Centre, part of the British Meteorological Office, suggested that current projections of temperature rise were too conservative; rather than increasing by between one and four degrees Celsius by the year 2010, as the UN's intergovernmental panel on climate change had concluded, a rise of six degrees was likely. This model projected that over the next century the Amazon rain-forest would largely turn to desert. American researchers demonstrated that hurricanes and tropical storms would spin faster in a warmer climate, increasing their destructive potential.

The Hadley Centre data were unveiled at November's UN Climate Change Treaty meeting in Buenos Aires, known as the fourth Conference of the Parties or COP-4. The meeting was supposed to fill in much of the detail left out by the agreement signed in Kyoto in December 1997 (see AR 1997, pp. 466–7; 568–72). Significant issues were the setting-up of a trading mechanism for so-called emissions credits, agreed in principle at Kyoto, and the path to be taken by nations outside the Annex One group (OECD and former Soviet bloc countries, broadly-speaking) already bound to reductions targets. (In the run-up to Buenos Aires the United States had repeatedly called for some kind of target to be set for developing nations.) A major dispute on the latter issue was partially averted when the host nation, Argentina, set voluntary targets on emissions cuts. However, the mechanism for emissions trading was not decided; and several independent bodies, such as the London-based International Petroleum Exchange, announced their own plans to set up privately-operated trading schemes by the end of 1999.

The absence of a concrete emissions trading plan from Buenos Aires did not seem of itself to be a major worry for climate campaigners. More serious by far was the fact that, as 1998 ended, the United States had not ratified the Kyoto treaty and, if leaders of the Senate were to be believed, did not intend to ratify it. Indeed, in the first half of the year it seemed likely that the House of Representatives would prevent President Clinton's administration from spending money on even discussing climate change by refusing to allocate funds for it in the annual budget; in the end the President did get his money. By the end of 1998, just under a third of the 160 signatories to Kyoto had ratified the treaty. In September, however, official reports in France and in the Netherlands indicated that neither nation was on track to meet the emissions reductions targets it had signed up to in Kyoto.

The changes in disease patterns mentioned above were only one of the consequences of the 1997–98 El Niño, one of the strongest such events on record. In May Ecuador announced that it would have to spend $2,000 million repairing damage to roads and other infrastructure, recovering agricultural land and resettling homeless people. Brazil and Mexico were badly affected by forest fires, made worse by drought—another El Niño consequence. The more widely-reported fires in South-East Asia, again exacerbated by drought, cost the region $4,000 million, according to a report by the Worldwide Fund for Nature (WWF) and the Singapore-based Economy and Environment Programme for South-East Asia. August saw severe floods in much of Asia. In Bangladesh, rising waters affected 20 million people and over half of the country's land (see VIII.2.iii), while an estimated four million people died in China (see IX.2.i). Although the Chinese floods were widely blamed on El Niño, the underlying reasons seemed a little more complex. Intense monsoon rain fell on ground which had been much dryer than usual because of the previous year's weak rains, and so did not penetrate into the soil so deeply. The clearing of forests around the affected areas had also played a part, making it far easier for excess water to reach rivers. Indeed, in the aftermath of the 1998 floods, the Chinese government mobilized police to crack down on illegal logging in the Yangtse valley, where the worst floods occurred; one estimate put the number of people making a living from illegal logging there at over a million. The authorities intended to put the perpetrators to work planting new trees.

The worst disaster of the year was Hurricane Mitch, the most destructive Atlantic storm for 200 years, which hit central America in November (see IV.3.xiii). Honduras and Nicaragua bore the brunt of its assault, though neigbouring countries and some Caribbean islands were also touched. Well over 20,000 people died—as the year ended no exact figure was available. Much of the region was left without power, food, medicines, housing or drinking water. Honduras declared a national state of alert because of epidemics of several diseases—diarrhoea, cholera, and leptospirosis (also known as Weil's disease) among them.

The Indonesian forest fires took a devastating toll on wildlife as well as people. Among the animals to suffer were orang-utans. The fires destroyed their food and drove them into villages, where frequently they were killed by poachers. Orang-utan numbers had in any case been declining in previous years, primarily through habitat loss. In July a survey by the EIA found that only 15–20,000 remained.

The year saw the discovery of a previously-unknown fungus which attacked frogs and toads. It had been known for ten years previously that amphibian numbers were declining worldwide, but the reason had been a mystery until the fungus was identified. However, scientists believed it likely that the fungus was able to kill only because the amphibians' immune systems had already been weakened by pollution. In Australia, large numbers of fruit-bats were born with defects such as extra fingers, enlarged heads and cleft palates. It was thought that, because of habitat loss, the bats had been forced to eat fruit sprayed with pesticides.

In June the Cambridge-based World Conservation Monitoring Centre launched a report saying that over half the world's coral reefs were under threat from, amongst other things, pollution, excess sedimentation and over-fishing. Sea turtles became the subject of a WTO dispute between the USA on the one hand and India, Pakistan, Thailand and Malaysia on the other. The USA had unilaterally banned the import of shrimps caught using nets which could also snare turtles. The WTO ruled the ban illegal in October, leading campaigners such as the WWF to call for a revision of WTO regulations to allow for environmental concerns. Also in October, 70 nations, including Japan and South Korea, signed an agreement banning the practice of 'finning' sharks—slicing off the dorsal fin (to make delicacy foods) and then throwing the fish back in the water. The UN Food and Agriculture Organization (FAO), which set up the deal, hoped that fewer sharks would be caught as a consequence of boats having to bring the entire carcass to shore.

Two accords signed at Interpol, again in October, promised harsher penalties for anyone found engaging in trade in endangered species. The following month Indian scientists announced that they had developed a DNA test able to identify the source of powdered rhinoceros horn. From Uganda came a suggestion that ivory poaching had exerted an extreme kind of evolutionary force on elephants. Over 10 per cent of elephants born in the Queen Elizabeth National Park had no tusks, an extraordinarily high number (in 1930 the figure was less than one per cent). In the wild, individual animals with this genetic mutation were at a severe disadvantage, being unable to dig for food and water or to defend themselves. The explanation was that elephants with this mutation had been surviving the attentions of poachers, who could get no ivory from them.

For the first time, the threat to the plant kingdom from human activities was quantified. In April the International Union for the Conservation of Nature published what it called a 'Red List', naming 34,000 plant species—one in every nine—at risk from habitat loss.

In October the German Green Party became a junior member of the ruling coalition following the previous month's general election, which had seen the Social Democrats emerge as the largest single party (see II.2.i). Among the declared policies of the German Greens were pledges to triple the price of petrol within ten years and to close the country's nuclear power stations. There had been widespread protests against the transportation of nuclear waste across Germany earlier in the year. An end to nuclear power became government policy. However, following representations from the nuclear industry—which pointed out, among other things, the likely costs of severing waste-reprocessing contracts with Britain's Sellafield plant—the decision was put on hold. As the year ended, the final picture on this issue remained unclear.

The year saw oil and chemical spills in several parts of the world. In January a barge ran aground on the coast of the United Arab Emirates, disgorging thousand of tonnes of oil which affected over 80 kilometres of coastline. A 40-kilometre stretch of the Grand Canal in eastern China was contaminated during the same period by industrial waste, principally from paper mills. In Cambodia fears were expressed that the country's beaches could become a target for the dumping of toxic waste from other countries, after nearly 3,000 tonnes of waste containing radioactive materials were found on the south coast.

In Europe Shell Oil began to dismantle the former North Sea oil platform, the *Brent Spar,* in November. (The company had planned to dump it in the Atlantic Ocean in 1995 but had been forced to change its plans by force of public protest.) The *Brent Spar* was to be taken apart in the Norwegian fjord which had been its home since 1995 and parts of it used to make a car ferry quay. From Alaska came news that the ecology of Prince William Sound, devastated by the Exxon Valdez oil spill in 1989, which had released 50 million litres of oil, was beginning to recover (see AR 1989, pp. 444–5). Local scientists said in January that bird and fish populations were climbing. To try and make such spillages less likely in European waters, the 15 members of the OSPAR convention (EU member states, broadly-speaking) signed a new deal in July. Oil rigs would now have to be disposed of on land rather than at sea, and member states would reduce levels of radioactive discharge to 'close to zero' by 2020.

In September more than 100 nations agreed a new treaty aimed at regulating the trade in potentially hazardous chemicals. The FAO, which negotiated the agreement, estimated that thousands of tonnes of unwanted, unlabelled and therefore dangerous pesticides lay abandoned in rusting barrels on developing-world farms. Industrial chemicals such as carcinogenic PCBs were also included in the treaty. Called PICS (short for Prior Informed Consent), the agreement would force exporters to provide proper documentation on the health hazards of chemicals and to give potential recipient nations the right to refuse consignments of regulated substances.

New evidence for the health effects of pollution emerged. In January Swedish scientists found that men who worked with PVC had a six-fold increase in their risk of testicular cancer. In August a team of British researchers published data showing that women living near hazardous waste landfill sites in West European countries had a higher chance of giving birth to children with defects.

Two reports published during 1998 showed that air quality in Western Europe had improved over the last 30 years. Linked to this was a reduction of 30 per cent in levels of acid rain across the continent. Further measures to clean up air pollutants were announced in October by the EU; these set lower permitted levels of substances hazardous to health such as dioxins and cadmium.

In August scientists in Arizona demonstrated that air pollution disrupted weather on a weekly basis. They showed that in industrialized nations, weekends were significantly wetter than weekdays. Higher emissions of pollutants during the working week were believed to suppress rainfall by an as yet undetermined mechanism. Canadian scientists, meanwhile, discovered pollutants even in the most remote parts of this vast country. They found organochlorides (used in industry and agriculture) on snow-crested peaks and in mountain streams; presumably they had been carried by winds. The scientists concluded that there was probably no place on Earth free from pollution.

One eco-friendly branch of science which progressed well during 1998 was bio-remediation—the use of natural organisms to clean up waste. In March a British team identified a lichen able to absorb uranium. In India researchers discovered that banana pith could remove dyes from streams. And researchers within the Russian space programme examined the use of bacteria to dissolve paper underwear discarded by long-term residents of space stations.

A modern-day successor to the famous photograph of the Earth taken by *Apollo* astronauts was unveiled by the European Joint Research Centre in November. Rather than the sparkling blue oceans and white clouds of 30 years earlier, it showed vast plumes of smoke coming from forest fires in South-East Asia, Brazil, West Africa, China and Russia. If the *Apollo* pictures summed up the promise of the new, gleaming technological era and the fresh perspectives it could give, those of 1998 suggested a planet submerged under the weight of modern humanity and fighting desperately for air.

XIV THE LAW

1. INTERNATIONAL LAW—EC LAW

i. INTERNATIONAL LAW

THE International Court of Justice did not give judgment on the merits in any of the ten cases before it. Inadequate resources and lengthy procedures meant that cases typically took four years to complete; the Court accordingly began the revision of its working methods. Three new cases came to the Court. On 3 April Paraguay brought an action against the USA; it alleged violations of the Vienna Convention on Consular Relations with regard to Angel Francisco Breard, a Paraguayan national convicted of murder in the USA, due to be executed on 14 April. Paraguay sought a declaration that because the USA had not notified Paraguay of the detention of Breard it had violated its obligations and should re-establish the situation that existed before the violation. Paraguay also made an urgent request that the Court indicate provisional measures. The Court unanimously indicated that the USA should take all measures at its disposal to ensure that Breard was not executed pending the final decision of the Court. However, the USA went ahead with the execution. The case raised important questions of the binding nature of provisional measures and of the implementation of international law in federal states. On 11 November Paraguay withdrew its case.

On 2 November Indonesia and Malaysia jointly brought to the Court a case concerning sovereignty over two islands in the Celebes sea; and on 30 December Guinea brought a case against the Democratic Republic of the Congo for grave breaches of international law against a Guinean national.

There was also a new request for an advisory opinion by the UN Economic and Social Council (ECOSOC). A difference had arisen between the UN and Malaysia on the interpretation and application of the 1946 Convention on Privileges and Immunities of the UN. This protected persons in the service of the UN from interference by national authorities. A Malaysian lawyer was appointed by the UN Commission on Human Rights, an organ of ECOSOC, as a special rapporteur on the independence of judges and lawyers. He was sued in the Malaysian courts for his comments on the Malaysian justice system. UN legal counsel claimed that he had spoken in an official capacity and was immune from the legal process but the Malaysian courts ignored this. ECOSOC accordingly sought an advisory opinion on the legal question of the applicability of the Convention of Privileges and Immunities.

The Court decided three cases on jurisdiction and admissibility. The USA and UK contested the Court's jurisdiction to hear the *Lockerbie* cases.

These arose out of the destruction of Pan Am flight 103 over Lockerbie in 1988; the USA and UK sought the surrender of two Libyans for trial but Libya argued on the basis of the Montreal Convention for the Suppression of Unlawful Acts against the Safety of Civil Aviation that it was not bound to extradite its own nationals. Libya took the cases to the Court. The main argument of the respondents was that this was not a matter for the Court because the UN Security Council had dealt with it in resolutions 731, 748 and 833, which required Libya to surrender the two accused and to demonstrate its renunciation of support for terrorism. Libya argued that the resolutions did not in fact require surrender of the accused, but that, if they did, they were outside the power of the Security Council. The Court gave a brief and technical judgment, avoiding the fundamental issue of its power to allow judicial review of Security Council decisions. Because the resolutions were passed after the Libyan application to the Court they did not make the case inadmissible. The argument that the Security Council resolutions determined the rights of the parties was interwoven with the merits and could not be decided at this preliminary stage. The Court had jurisdiction and the case was admissible.

In *Cameroon/Nigeria*, a land and maritime boundary case, Nigeria made eight preliminary objections on jurisdiction and admissibility. Cameroon based the Court's jurisdiction on acceptance by both states of the Court's compulsory jurisdiction under Article 36(2) of the statute of the Court. Nigeria's most controversial argument was that Cameroon could not invoke its declaration under Article 36(2) because it had not notified Nigeria that it had made such a declaration. Therefore Cameroon had acted prematurely and in abuse of the system. This argument challenged a clear line of previous decisions by the Court and was rejected. Any state party to the statute, in making a declaration under Article 36(2), made a standing offer to other states parties to the statute which had not yet deposited a declaration of acceptance. There was no duty on Cameroon to inform Nigeria that it intended to accept the Court's jurisdiction and to bring proceedings. Nigeria's other objections were that the case involved third parties, that Cameroon was obliged to exhaust other means of settlement and that it had not given enough detail of its claims; the Court rejected all these arguments. Following this decision, Nigeria filed a request for interpretation of the judgment. This was the first time that the Court had been seized of a request for the interpretation of a judgment on preliminary objections while proceedings on the merits were still pending, and technically it gave rise to a new case.

The third case on jurisdiction and admissibility was *Fisheries Jurisdiction* (*Spain* v. *Canada*). Spain claimed that the boarding on the high seas of a Spanish fishing boat, the *Estai*, by a Canadian patrol boat had violated international law on freedom of navigation and fishing on the high seas. Spain based the Court's jurisdiction on Article 36(2) of the Statute of the Court. However, Canada had made a reservation excluding from the Court's jurisdiction disputes arising out of conservation and management measures taken by Canada and the enforcement of such measures. The case turned on the interpretation of this reservation. Spain argued that it should be narrowly interpreted so as to make it consistent with international law. Canada emphasized the unilateral nature of reservations and said that they were to be interpreted in a natural way and with particular regard for the intentions of the reserving state. The Court by 12–5 accepted the Canadian argument; reservations operated to define the limits of the Court's acceptance of the compulsory jurisdiction of the Court and there was thus no reason to interpret them restrictively. Therefore, the Canadian reservation covered the case and the Court had no jurisdiction.

There was also a major arbitration award in a territorial dispute between Eritrea and Yemen concerning certain Red Sea islands—small, waterless and barely habitable, but straddling one of the most important and busiest seaways in the world (see V.3.ii; VI.1.i). Eritrea based its claim on a chain of title through Ethiopia and Italy. Yemen based its claim on historic Yemeni title going back to the sixth century. The tribunal held that neither party had persuaded it of the existence of historic title as a source of territorial sovereignty. It was the recent history of use and possession that ultimately proved to be the main base of the tribunal's decision. The geographical situation of the islands was also important; the tribunal applied a presumption that islands off a particular coast belonged by appurtenance to that coast. The tribunal divided the islands into groups and then assigned some to each party.

The International Criminal Tribunal for Rwanda started the year still handicapped by lack of resources and without a clear schedule (see also VII.1.ii). But important progress was made when the first sentence and judgment were given and a third trial chamber was established, following which new judges were elected on 3 November. The first sentence was passed in the case of *Jean Kambanda*, the Prime Minister in the extremist Hutu government in 1994 when at least 500,000 Tutsis and moderate Hutus were massacred in 100 days (see AR 1994, pp. 292–4). On 1 May Kambanda pleaded guilty to six counts of genocide and crimes against humanity. In passing sentence on 4 September, the tribunal ranked the crimes: violations of the Geneva Conventions were lesser crimes than crimes against humanity or genocide. Genocide was unique—the crime of crimes—and this must be taken into account in deciding the sentence. Kambanda had personally participated in genocide; he had also failed to take reasonable measures to prevent subordinates from committing crimes against the people. In mitigation it was argued that he had pleaded guilty and had cooperated with the prosecutor. The tribunal was not convinced that he had genuinely shown any remorse. Therefore, he was sentenced to life imprisonment.

The first judgment was given on 2 September when *Jean-Paul Akayesu* was found guilty of genocide, incitement to commit genocide and seven other charges of crimes against humanity, including rape. Akayesu was acquitted on six other counts; both he and the prosecutor appealed against the judgment. Akayesu was the mayor of Taba in 1994 when at least 2,000 Tutsis were killed there. He failed to take measures to prevent the massacres and himself ordered murders and called for the annihilation of Tutsis. This was the first international decision on genocide and the tribunal elaborated on the definition; it involved acts aimed at the annihilation of a specially targeted group, with an intent to destroy in whole or in part a national, ethnic, racial or religious group. On 2 October Akayesu was sentenced to life imprisonment for genocide.

The International Criminal Tribunal for the former Yugoslavia also made progress. A third trial chamber was established to speed up the work of the tribunal and three new judges took office on 16 November. However, there were problems in securing the cooperation of the Federal Republic of Yugoslavia (FRY). The president of the tribunal and the prosecutor communicated to the UN Security Council the urgent need to impress upon the FRY the need to honour its obligations under the Dayton Agreement and under Security Council resolutions. The FRY had failed to execute arrest warrants and was a haven for fugitives from international law. In response to events in Kosovo (see III.2.vi) the prosecutor announced that the statute empowered the tribunal to prosecute persons responsible for serious violations of international humanitarian law committed in the territory of the former Yugoslavia since 1991; this jurisdiction was ongoing and covered the recent violence in Kosovo.

Judgment was given in two cases. In the *Celebici* case on 16 November Zdravko Mucic, a Bosnian Croat prison camp commander, and two Bosnian Muslims, Hazim Delic and Esad Landzo, were convicted for their treatment of Serb detainees in the Celebici camp in 1992. Zejnil Delalic was acquitted because it had not been proved that he had command and control of the camp such as to entail criminal responsibility. The 500-page judgment addressed complex issues of law and fact. It gave an overview of the disintegration of the former Yugoslavia and discussed the nature of the conflict. It also examined at length the definitions of the crimes charged in the indictment. It elucidated the concept of command responsibility for the first time since the Nuremberg and Tokyo trials after World War II. Mucic, as commander of the camp, was found guilty on 11 counts of grave breaches of the Geneva Conventions and violation of the laws and customs of war. He had allowed those under his authority to commit the most heinous offences. Because he had acted out of frailty rather than malice his sentence was seven years imprisonment. Delic, deputy commander of the camp, was guilty of 13 counts of murder, torture, rape and causing great suffering and inhumane acts; he was sentenced to 20 years for his singular brutality and calculated cruelty. Landzo was guilty on 17 counts and was sentenced to 15 years; despite his youth he had not been a mere instrument of his superiors.

The second judgment was given on 10 December when *Anto Furundzija*, a Bosnian Croat military commander, was convicted of serious violations of the laws and customs of war. This was the first case to focus exclusively on an act of rape. It followed the definition of rape first adopted by the Rwanda tribunal in the *Akayesu* case and then applied in the *Celebici* case. It also upheld the *Celebici* ruling that rape could amount to torture. Furundzija was found guilty of two counts of torture in violation of the laws and customs of war and also of aiding and abetting outrages on personal dignity; he was sentenced to ten years' imprisonment.

Partly as a result of the creation of the Rwanda and Yugoslavia tribunals, states overwhelmingly agreed on the adoption of the statute for a permanent international criminal court at the Rome conference on 17 July (see XVII.2). The court was to be established at The Hague, to have jurisdiction over persons for the most serious crimes, and to be complementary to national criminal jurisdictions. The crimes within the jurisdiction of the court were genocide, crimes against humanity, war crimes and (in the future) the crime of aggression.

The year marked a fundamental reform of the Council of Europe system for the implementation of the European Convention on Human Rights; in order to cope with the vast increase in the number of cases and the accession of new states parties the original two-tier system of commission and court was replaced by a single full-time court which came into operation on 1 November (see also XI.5.i). It consisted of one judge for each contracting party to the convention; it was to sit in committees of three judges, chambers of seven judges and in a grand chamber of 17 judges. The right of individual petition became automatic.

The Court decided over 100 cases in 1998. As usual the largest single group concerned the right to a fair trial under Article 6; the largest number of these were against France and the most significant cases were *Rheinhardt*, *Omar* and *Guerin*, which found that the French criminal justice system was fundamentally defective. There were also many important cases against Turkey. Several cases were decided under Article 2, the right to life. The Turkish security forces were not held directly responsible for causing deaths, but the failure of Turkey adequately to investigate the deaths was held to amount to a violation of Article 2. Many cases arose out of Turkey's treatment of the Kurds (see II.4.vii). It was found to have interfered with their rights of free speech and of property and to have unduly prolonged detention of terrorist suspects in police custody. The dissolution of communist and socialist parties sympathetic to the Kurds was held to violate the right of freedom of association.

Another development in human rights was the entry into force of the *Framework Convention for the Protection of National Minorities* on 1 February. This was the first ever legally-binding multilateral instrument devoted to the protection of national minorities. It provided for non-discrimination and the promotion of effective equality. Monitoring was to be carried out by a committee of ministers, assisted by an advisory committee.

The 1991 *Madrid Protocol to the Antarctic Treaty* entered into force on 14 January after ratification by Japan, the last of the 26 consultative parties to the Antarctic Treaty to ratify. The protocol was intended to protect Antarctica from oil exploration and mining for 50 years. The UN General Assembly opened the *International Convention for the Suppression of Terrorist Bombings* for signature on 12 January. The proposal for this treaty had been made by the USA in response to the terrorist bombing of a US air base in Saudi Arabia in 1996 (see AR 1996, pp. 216-7). The convention required parties to criminalize attacks by terrorists in public places, and also to prosecute or extradite persons in their territory and to cooperate in investigation and prosecution of offences.

ii. EUROPEAN COMMUNITY LAW

THE hectic pace of constitutional change in recent years dwindled to a lull during 1998, as ratification of the Treaty of Amsterdam (ToA) by the European Union (EU) member states slowly wound its way through the year, only four ratifications being outstanding at the year's end. But it was a lull before the storm: when the ToA came into force, sometime in 1999, there would be massive adjustments for lawyers to make. Already they were beginning to come to terms with the renumbering of the articles of the European Community (EC) and EU Treaties; textbooks began to appear using the new numbers; and the European Court of Justice (ECJ) issued a complicated notice explaining how it would distinguish between old numbers (in cases based on the old law) and new numbers (in more recent cases).

To some extent, the lull could be attributed to the diversion of the attention of the EU institutions to the introduction of the single currency (the 'euro') at the end of the year (see XI.4). Otherwise, however, energies seemed to be devoted to the starting of significant initiatives, such as the official opening in March of the Inter-governmental Conference on the fifth enlargement of the Union and the detailed discussions thereafter with the six applicant countries (Poland, Hungary, Czech Republic, Estonia, Slovenia and Cyprus).

Such initiatives also touched the core area of the Community legal system itself. The ECJ made a formal proposal to the Council of Ministers in February that the Court of First Instance (CFI) should be entitled in certain circumstances to sit with a single judge—a revolutionary innovation in the eyes of continental lawyers, which the CFI had itself proposed the previous year. It also asked the Council to transfer to the CFI jurisdiction over a further series of case types: state aid cases brought by member states, Article 90 competition cases relating to public enterprises, cases about clearance of FEOGA accounts under the common agricultural policy and contractual disputes between the Commission and its suppliers under Article 215(1). On the other hand, the ECJ severely criticized the CFI for excessive delay in *Baustahlgewebe* v. *EC Commission,* a very complex competition case which had taken 5½ years to reach judgment, and reduced the 3 million ecu fine by 50,000 ecu as compensation for the delay. This was a long-standing problem and also affected the ECJ (which had itself taken 3½ years on the appeal in *Baustahlgewebe*), despite strenuous efforts by successive presidents of the Court to solve it. During 1998 the European Commission announced its intention to set up a high-level 'committee of wise men' (mostly former members of the ECJ and CFI) to examine fundamental reform of the Court and the 'very architecture' of the Community judicial system. During the year the Court hosted a series of visits by senior judges and politicians during which discussions touched on the role and functioning of the two courts (ECJ and CFI) and the future of the Community judicial system. Clearly some fundamental rethinking was being prepared.

Something of the same applied to the substantive law of the Community. Hitherto, most Community legislation had, for obvious reasons, been in the field of commerce and industry, filling out the principles laid down in the EC Treaty. Even there, most of it had a public, regulatory character. Only occasionally was it aimed at private law governing ordinary relations between ordinary people; but there too a strong commercial bias was apparent, as with the directives on unfair terms in contracts and on a manufacturer's liability for defective products. General legal areas such as contract law, the law of negligence, family law and criminal law had for the most part been excluded from Community action. More particularly, the procedural aspects of law—the procedures of the national courts, the police and other enforcement agencies—had as a matter of principle been left to the member states as part of the partnership between them and the Community. That was now all changing.

The trail-blazer for this move into 'ordinary' law was the field of private international law—the rules applying to situations involving two or more different legal systems, such as a contract between a German in Germany and an Italian in Italy, or a motor-car accident in France between a British and a Belgian car. These had nothing specific to do with commerce, but of course were relevant to free movement of people, goods and services. Consequently, there had long been rules on which national courts were entitled to hear cases of this sort and on the enforcement of their judgments throughout the Community. The 30-year old Brussels Convention on jurisdiction and the execution of judgments in civil and commercial matters, which was extended to the EFTA states by a parallel Lugano

Convention, revealed a number of difficulties, which led to an extensive re-examination of both conventions on the basis of a Commission draft published in January 1998. Shortly afterwards, in May, the member states adopted a follow-up convention, 'Brussels II', which dealt in the same way with matrimonial cases. At the same time, preliminary work was being devoted to a follow-up to the Rome Convention on the choice of law in contract disputes, 'Rome II', which would lay down similar rules in cases involving civil wrongs.

Criminal law as such had in the past been regarded as outside the scope of Community law (except where criminal penalties were used to enforce other EC rules). The influence of the third pillar of the EU Treaty, on justice and home affairs, had been crucial in bringing 'pure' criminal law into the Community legal system. The fight against organized crime (the money-laundering directive) and policing of aliens prepared the way for conventions on uniform procedures to combat fraud against the EU and that in turn led to proposals, under close discussion during the year, for a *'corpus juris'* and for a Union-wide prosecution function, possibly involving an EU public prosecutor. This was initially being postulated in connection with fraud against the Community, but pressures to extend it more widely had already emerged.

Even more revolutionary were the proposals, at various stages of discussion, for a uniform law of contract throughout the EU and, separately, for a European uniform code of civil procedure. These latter formed part of a small but growing movement towards what was called a 'European legal space'.

Concern with the reform of legal structures extended also to internal Community procedures, particularly to the wholesale re-examination and reform of the competition enforcement by the Commission's fourth directorate-general (DG-IV). This had led to proposals to reform the formal hearings procedure by which companies accused of anti-competitive conduct under Articles 85 or 86 presented their defence arguments: draft general regulations on the hearing officer were published during the year. New regulations on the procedure in state aid cases were adopted in November. A very far-reaching proposal to repeal all the block exemption regulations (enabling companies to avoid Article 85 proceedings in certain cases) and replace them with a single all-embracing regulation was under intense discussion.

The background to all these reforms was that DG-IV faced the same problem as that experienced by the ECJ: inability to cope with a large and increasing case-load. There was a growing sense of desperation visible in the Community that its law enforcement machinery would not be able to cope with the increasing demands upon it, as Community law itself expanded and as new states, and therefore new 'customers' for law enforcement, joined the Union. Both from DG-IV and from the ECJ suggestions were being made that the national courts and national agencies should take on more of this burden even than they already did, in spite of the danger of fragmentation which would follow from such a decentralization of Community effort.

This internal rethinking about the Community legal system took place against an increasingly importunate global background, as the World Trade Organization (WTO) began to develop its own legal role in world trade (see XI.2.ii). Its new dispute settlement mechanism, adding an effective appellate body to the earlier dispute panels, had achieved remarkable success and underlay a series of serious trade disputes between the EU and the United States. Two of these, in particular, led during the year to serious threats of retaliatory US trade sanctions relating to the EU bananas regime, which discriminated in favour of associated Lomé Convention countries, and to Community legislation banning the use of certain growth hormones in cattle—in both cases to the disadvantage of US exporters. Apart from these specific disputes, both the EU and the US submitted proposals to the WTO for reforms to its disputes procedure.

2. LAW IN THE UNITED KINGDOM

THE year saw two fundamental constitutional changes. The *Scotland Act* and the *Government of Wales Act* provided for considerable devolution of powers from Westminster to Scotland and Wales respectively (see II.1.ii; II.1.iii; XVII.3); and the *Human Rights Act* incorporated the European Convention on Human Rights into English law. The latter statute introduced a requirement that the courts interpret legislation consistently with the Convention, and provided mechanisms to remove incompatibilities between the Convention and domestic law.

The House of Lords overturned a judgment of the Queen's Bench Divisional Court, ruling that the former head of state of Chile might be extradited to Spain to face charges of genocide and torture;[1] the defence of sovereign immunity was held not to be available in such circumstances (see II.1.i; IV.3.iv). Almost unprecedentedly, a differently-constituted House of Lords subsequently vacated this judgment on the grounds that one of the members of the first court might have given the impression of bias against the applicant.[2] In another important case on the law of extradition, the House of Lords held that extradition might be appropriate when a warrant had been issued in respect of pre-trial proceedings; the variations in the criminal procedures of different states meant that it would be unwise to insist on a rigorous interpretation of the statutory requirement that the individual be 'accused' of a offence.[3] The Divisional Court held that it might be lawful to make an order for extradition even though the defendant was not present at the extradition hearing,[4] though there was a general right of the accused person to give evidence in extradition proceedings.[5] There was some confusion over the rules of extradition to the United States. It was first held that there was no jurisdiction to extradite a person to America on charges of conspiracy to defraud or to commit theft,[6] but a later case declined to follow this and held that the conspiracy to commit an extraditable offence was itself extraditable.[7]

Other statutes gave effect to the international obligations of the United Kingdom: the *Nuclear Explosions (Prohibition and Inspections) Act* following the Comprehensive Nuclear Test-Ban Treaty of 1996 (see AR 1996, pp. 542–3), and the *Landmines Act* following the Ottawa Convention of 1997 (see AR 1997, pp. 566–8). The *Competition Act* brought English competition law in line with European law, while the *Data Protection Act* reformed and consolidated the law relating to personal data in the light of a European directive.

The courts continued to exercise control over local authorities. The duty to provide suitable education imposed on them by the *Education Act 1993* was to be strictly enforced, based on the educational needs of the child; financial resources were not to be taken into account;[8] similarly, financial resources were held to be an irrelevant factor in making a disabled facilities grant.[9] The House of Lords held that it was open to the defendant charged under a by-law to allege that it had been improperly made and was therefore *ultra vires*; though on the facts of the case the defendant did not succeed.[10] A trishaw was held not to be a stage-coach, with the result that a local authority had the power to impose terms on a licence for its use.[11]

A cluster of cases clarified aspects of the law relating to the operation of the criminal justice system. It was held that the Home Secretary had power to refuse to allow the release of a person serving a mandatory life sentence if there was thought to be a risk of his committing serious non-violent offences after his release;[12] and that he had been within his powers to impose a whole life tariff on a convicted child killer.[13] A person kept in prison for a longer period than was justified was held entitled to damages for false imprisonment, notwithstanding that the governor of the prison had been following guidelines set down by the courts in cases which had only subsequently been overruled.[14] A wide discretion was allowed to the police in the interests of keeping public order: the House of Lords refused to quash the decision of a chief constable to restrict the sailings of boats carrying animals on the grounds that the costs of policing demonstrations by those opposed to the sailings was unacceptably high.[15] The appropriateness of disclosure by the police of the identity of convicted paedophiles who had served their sentences was considered by the Court of Appeal: it was held that in the instant case the police had been right to release the information, but that such a step should be taken only when there was a pressing need to do so.[16] On the other hand, a local authority was held to have no general duty or power to disclose to others findings of sexual abuse in civil proceedings.[17] The procedural rules relating to the taking of blood samples from a driver suspected of driving with excess alcohol in the blood were clarified by the House of Lords.[18] Principles for the sentencing of young offenders,[19] for the offence of arson,[20] and for offences committed on aeroplanes[21] were laid down by the Court of Appeal, which also specified important guidelines to deal with the conflict between an individual's right to information needed to obtain redress in the courts and the public interest that certain information should be kept confidential in so far as it related to ongoing criminal investigations.[22] Many changes were introduced by the *Crime and Disorder Act*, including the creation of a Sentencing Advisory Council to assist the Court of Appeal and the stiffening of penalties for crimes aggravated by a racial motive. The *Magistrates' Courts (Procedure) Act*, described by the Lord Chancellor as 'modest but important', streamlined the procedure for the prosecution of minor motoring offences.

A crown court was held to have acted correctly in refusing to hear expert evidence of the competence of young children to testify: it was a matter for the court itself to decide whether the children were capable of giving intelligible evidence;[23] similarly, it was for the court to decide, without expert evidence, whether or not unidentified individuals in indecent photographs were children.[24] The conviction of Derek Bentley, hanged for murder in 1953, was quashed on the grounds that the judge's direction to the jury had been inadequate;[25] and the Court of Appeal overturned the conviction of a man prosecuted for offences alleged to have occurred over 30 years earlier, stressing that in such a case the judge must make very clear to the jury the difficulties of responding to charges after such a long delay.[26] The meaning of 'intention' in the crime of murder was further clarified by the House of Lords.[27] A person demolishing a wall in the belief that it was blocking a right of way was held to have a lawful excuse, and so not to be guilty of causing criminal damage.[28] A dentist who continued to work after having been suspended from practice was held not to have committed assault on her patients.[29] The House of Lords gave consideration to the meaning of the word 'road' in the context of statutory rules relating to compulsory insurance policies, and held that it did not include a carpark.[30]

In *Mansfield* v. *Weetabix*[31] the Court of Appeal stressed that liability in negligence was based on the defendant's culpable failure to take reasonable care, so that a driver who caused injury while in a hypoglycaemic state was not required to compensate the victim; but liability was established where a professional footballer had injured another player in a tackle which any reasonable professional footballer would have recognized as carrying the risk of serious injury.[32] A student trespasser injured after climbing into a college swimming pool at night was held to have taken the risk of injury on himself.[33] The vexing question of the extent of liability in tort for the negligent causation of purely economic loss was yet again considered by the House of Lords; their lordships further consolidated the principle that liability should depend on whether the defendant had made an assumption of responsibility to the plaintiff,[34] so that an accountant was not held liable when he assisted a client to make representations to a third party;[35] but a person claiming to have been deprived of a legacy under a will as a result of a solicitor's negligence was required to make use of proceedings to rectify the will rather than simply suing the solicitor.[36] The equally vexing question of the Common Law liability of public authorities was further considered by the Court of Appeal, holding that no liability in negligence attached to a local authority making arrangements to foster out children in their care, but that an action might lie against the ambulance service after an emergency call had been accepted.[37] In continuing litigation arising out of the Hillsborough football stadium disaster in 1989, the House of Lords held that claims of police officers present at the scene to recover in respect of psychiatric injury should be judged on the same basis as claims by relatives of those who had been injured;[38] a workmate was held able to recover damages for psychiatric injury stemming from the death of a fellow-worker through the defendants' negligence only if he actually witnessed the death;[39] changes in the law, mostly of a minor nature, were recommended by the Law Commission.[40] Limits were put on the immunity of barristers from a suit in negligence based on their negligent conduct of legal proceedings,[41] and the boundaries of the immunity of solicitors were explored.[42] In *Wells* v. *Wells* the House of Lords reformed the rules relating to the assessment of damages for personal injuries to take account of changes in the forms of available investments for damages. The Court of Appeal stressed the importance of free speech in a modern plural democracy, allowing a widening of the defence of qualified privilege to newspapers in actions for defamation.[43] The right of an adult of sound mind to refuse medical treatment deemed necessary by doctors was trenchantly reasserted,[44] though it was held that the Common Law doctrine of necessity justified the treatment of a mentally-disabled patient who was incapable of giving consent for himself.[45]

A difficulty of interpretation of the *Limitation Act 1980* was cleared up by the House of Lords, holding that a judgment might be enforced more than six years after it had been given, but that the ordinary six-year limitation period applied to claims to recover arrears of interest.[46] A contingent fee arrangement by a solicitor in a criminal case was held to be lawful, provided that the solicitor's charges should the case be won were no more than the ordinary charges,[47] though the decision was subsequently heavily criticized as having been made without reference to a relevant decision of the House of Lords;[48] and a contingent fee agreement in arbitration proceedings was similarly held to be lawful.[49] In an important case on the interpretation of the Brussels Convention, the House of Lords took a rigorous approach to the rule that an insurer could only bring proceedings in the state where the defendant was domiciled,[50] and a careful stance was taken towards the issue of anti-suit injunctions, the courts refusing to prevent the hearing of a case in Texas when it was admittedly more appropriate for the issue to be tried in India.[51] The House of Lords applied to accountants the same rules normally applied to solicitors, and granted an injunction to a former client on terms which would prevent the disclosure of confidential information to other clients;[52] a firm of solicitors was held not to have been in breach of its duty to a client when it failed to pass on information which the client had not requested.[53]

A group of long-standing problems in commercial law were resolved. In *Kleinwort Benson* v. *Lincoln City Council*, the centuries-old rule prohibiting a restitutionary claim arising out of a mistake of law was grubbed out, even where the payment had been made under a settled belief as to the state of the law which had subsequently been changed by judicial decision. In a case on appeal from Northern Ireland, the House of Lords removed a difficulty associated with standard-form building contracts, allowing that the courts had inherent jurisdiction to revise architects' interim certificates;[54] and a difficulty over the Common Law rules relating to the carriage of dangerous goods was resolved in *Effort Shipping Company Ltd* v. *Linden Management SA*. The *Late Payment of Commercial Debts (Interest) Act* reversed the common law rule that interest could be charged on unpaid debts only if there was a specific provision permitting this in the parties' contract. A rather newer problem was nipped in the bud when injunctions were granted against a company registering distinctive Internet domain names where the use of such a domain name would lead to confusion with a well-known company, or where the name constituted a trademark.[55]

The law relating to employment relationships was remoulded. The *National Minimum Wage Act* reduced the freedom of employers to offer low wages; the *Public Interest Disclosure Act* laid down a framework within which employees might report on illegal or improper practices by their employers without the risk of victimization; and the *Employment Rights (Dispute Resolution) Act* reformed the law relating to industrial tribunals.

The House of Lords held that the normal power of the County Court to adjourn proceedings was not altered by the provisions of the *Housing Act* 1985, and that it was appropriate to do so when a relevant issue lay to be determined in collateral proceedings;[56] but a husband attempting to obtain a property adjustment order after his wife had already terminated a tenancy was held to have acted too late.[57] The *Housing Act* 1985 was construed strictly so as to require a local authority to investigate afresh whether an applicant for housing was intentionally homeless, notwithstanding that a determination to this effect had been made on a previous application.[58] A homosexual partner was not recognized as equivalent to a wife or husband within the terms of the Rent Acts, so that there was no right of succession to a tenancy after the death of the original tenant;[59] nor was a person in exclusive occupation of a flat in an almshouse entitled to a protected tenancy.[60] The usual covenant for quiet enjoyment in a domestic tenancy agreement was construed to cover disturbance caused by noise which it was within the power of the landlord to control, but that it did not impose an obligation to alter or improve premises;[61] and it was similarly held that the landlord would not be liable in nuisance.[62]

1. *R v. Bow Street Metropolitan Stipendiary Magistrate*, ex parte Pinochet Ugarte 3 WLR 1456
2. re *Pinochet, The Times*, 18 December
3. re *Ismail* 3 WLR 495
4. *R v. Bow Street Magistrates' Court, ex parte Government of Germany* 2 WLR 498
5. *R v. Governor of Brixton Prison, ex parte Gross* 3 WLR 1420
6. *R v. Secretary of State for the Home Department, ex parte Gilmore* 2 WLR 618
7. *R v. Bow Street Metropolitan Stipendiary Magistrate, ex parte Government of the United States of America* 3 WLR 1156
8. re *T (a minor)* 2 WLR 884
9. *R v. Birmingham City Council, ex parte Mohammed* 3 All ER 788
10. *Boddington v. British Transport Police* 2 WLR 639
11. *R v. Cambridge City Council, ex parte Lane, The Times*, 13 October
12. *R v. Secretary of State for the Home Department, ex parte Stafford* 3 WLR 372
13. *R v. Secretary of State for the Home Department, ex parte Hindley, The Times*, 6 November
14. *R v. Governor of Brockhill Prison, ex parte Evans*, (1998) 148 New Law Journal 977
15. *R v. Chief Constable of Sussex, ex parte International Trader's Ferry Ltd, The Times*, 16 November
16. *R v. Chief Constable of the North Wales Police, ex parte A.B.* 3 WLR 57
17. In re *V (Minors) (Sexual Abuse: Disclosure), The Times*, 9 October
18. *Director of Public Prosecutions v. Jackson* 3 WLR 514; cf *R v. Warren* AC 319
19. *R v. A.M.* 1 WLR 363
20. *R v. Mitchell, The Times*, 4 September
21. *R v. Oliver, The Times*, 13 October
22. *C v. S, The Times*, 5 November
23. *G v. Director of Public Prosecutions* 2 WLR 609
24. *R v. Land* 3 WLR 322
25. *R v. Bentley, The Times*, 31 July
26. *R v. Percival, The Times*, 20 July
27. *R v. Woollin* 3 WLR 382
28. *Chamberlain v. Lindon* 1 WLR 1252
29. *R v. Richardson* 3 WLR 1292
30. *Clark v. Kato, Smith and General Accident Fire & Life Assurance Corporation plc, The Times*, 23 October
31. 1 WLR 1263
32. *Watson v. Gray, The Times*, 26 November
33. *Ratcliff v. McConnell, The Times*, 3 December
34. *Williams v. Natural Life Health Foods Ltd* 1 WLR 830
35. *Abbot v. Strong, The Times*, 9 July
36. *Walker v. Geo H. Medlicott* (a firm), *The Times*, 25 November; cp *Carr-Glyn v. Frearsons* 4 All ER 225
37. *W v. Essex County Council* 3 WLR 534; *Kent v. Griffiths, The Times*, 23 December
38. *Frost v. Chief Constable of South Yorkshire Police* 3 WLR 1509
39. *Hunter v. British Coal Corporation* 3 WLR 685

40. *Law Commission Report 249, Liability for Psychiatric Illness*
41. *Atwell v. Perry & Co* 4 All ER 65
42. *Arthur J.S. Hall & Co* (a firm) v. *Simons, The Times*, 18 December
43. *Reynolds v. Times Newspapers Ltd* 3 WLR 862
44. *St George's Healthcare NHS Trust v. S* 3 WLR 936
45. *Re L* 3 WLR 107
46. *Lowsley v. Forbes* 3 WLR 501
47. *Thai Trading Co v. Taylor* 2 WLR 893
48. *Hughes v. Kingston upon Hull City Council, The Times*, 9 December
49. *Bevan Ashford* (a firm) v. *Geoff Yeandle (Contractors) Ltd* 3 WLR 172
50. *Baltic Insurance Group v. Jordan Grand Prix Ltd, The Times*, 17 December
51. *Airbus Industrie GIE v. Patel* 2 WLR 686
52. *Prince Jefri Bolkiah v. KPMG* (a firm) (House of Lords, 18 December)
53. *National Home Loans Corporation v. Giffen* 1 WLR 207
54. *Beaufort Development (NI) Ltd v. Gilbert-Ash (NI) Ltd* 2 WLR 860
55. *British Telecommunications plc v. One in a Million Ltd* (1998) 148 New Law Journal 1179
56. *Bristol City Council v. Lovell* 1 WLR 446
57. *Newlon Housing Trust v. Al-Sulaimen* 3 WLR 451
58. *R v. Harrow London Borough Council, ex parte Fahia* 1 WLR 1396
59. *Fitzpatrick v. Sterling Housing Association Ltd* 2 WLR 225
60. *Gray v. Taylor* 1 WLR 1093
61. *Southwark London Borough Council v. Mills* 3 WLR 49
62. *Baxter v. Camden London Borough Council (No. 2), The Times*, 11 November

3. UNITED STATES LAW

THE Supreme Court under Chief Justice William Rehnquist continued its moderately conservative interpretation of the US constitution in 1998, and the federal courts of appeal followed its path. The Court held that the line-item veto the right of the President created by legislation to veto specific clauses in bills submitted for presidential signature violated the constitutional separation of powers between Congress and the President. A federal appeals court held, in *Condon v. Reno*, that the federal Driver's Privacy Act, which prohibited the disclosure, by state agencies which licensed drivers, of information about drivers, violated the 10th Amendment, which reserved to the states powers not specifically granted to the federal government.

However, in two cases the Court reached a pragmatic consensus on sexual harassment in the workplace, with seven justices supporting the decisions, in contrast to the deep ideological divisions in such cases previously. In *Onacle v. Sundower Offshore Services*, the Court recognized that sexual harassment of a man by a male superior—in this case the man claimed he had been grabbed, taunted and threatened with rape in a shower— constituted discrimination and violated Title VII of the Civil Rights Act. The Court remanded another case, *City of Belleville v. Doe*, where two boys, who were called 'fag' and 'queer' by co-workers and claimed that they had been sexually harassed, for reconsideration in light of its decision in *Onacle*.

The tension between aggressive exercises of freedom of speech and press, on the one hand, and others' rights, on the other, posed difficult questions for the courts. The Washington Supreme Court, in *State Public Disclosure Commission* v. *119 Vote No! Committee*, held that a state statute, which imposed fines of up to $10,000 for publishing false statements of material facts with actual malice in political campaigns, violated the 1st Amendment. Defamation laws permissibly protected private reputations, but a law which restricted falsehoods about political issues was unjustified. The Illinois Supreme Court, in *People* v. *Sanders*, held unconstitutional a statute that made it illegal to disturb a hunter with intent to dissuade him from killing an animal. The Texas Supreme Court, in *Orozco* v. *Dallas Morning News, Inc.*, held that a newspaper was not obliged to refrain from publishing the street name and address of a criminal suspect even though there was a foreseeable risk of a retaliatory shooting of the suspect or his family, which occurred in this case. The reporting of crimes and arrests was an important task of newspapers, and the public had a right to know about criminal activity, including the names and addresses of suspects arrested for crimes.

The dilemma between holding individuals responsible for their mistakes and manufacturers responsible for their defective products continued to be the focal point for the development of tort law. The federal court of appeals in Florida reversed the only recent judgment (for $750,000 in 1996) against a tobacco manufacturer because the plaintiff's claim that he had not been warned about the dangers of smoking could not be sustained in the wake of legislation, adopted in 1969, which required warnings on cigarette packages. In two separate cases, the Texas Supreme Court and the US Court of Appeals for the District of Columbia Circuit, however, adopted the new *Restatement (Third) of Torts: Products Liability* rule that warnings on a product were only one factor in deciding whether a product was defective. In *Uniroyal Goodrich Tyre Co.* v. *Martinez*, the Texas Supreme Court upheld a judgment of $10.3 million for injuries which the plaintiff sustained when he mounted a tyre on a rim designed for a larger tyre. He ignored the warning, which illustrated, with yellow and red highlights, a worker being thrown into the air by an exploding tyre when the worker mounted a tyre on such a rim. The court repeated the *Restatement* to the effect that a warning could not insulate a manufacturer from its defective products.

Litigation against the tobacco manufacturers for the diseases caused by smoking resulted in the largest settlements ever. In 1997 the states, which had sued tobacco companies for costs borne by them in providing medical care to smokers, and the tobacco manufacturers had tentatively agreed to settle (see AR 1997, p. 485); however, their settlement required that Congress enact legislation granting immunity to the tobacco manufacturers. In January the state of Texas settled its claims for $15,300 million (Mississippi and Florida having settled in 1997 for $3,600 million and $11,000 million, respectively). Congress then abandoned its effort to adopt legislation implementing the 1997 proposed settlement, and the tobacco manufacturers withdrew their support for that proposal. Later in the year 46 states and five US territories agreed to settle their claims for $206,000 million. The payments by the tobacco manufacturers would be paid over 25 years.

Dow Corning, once the largest manufacturer of silicon breast implants, had filed for a chapter 11 bankruptcy proceeding in response to a class action suit brought by 170,000 women for injuries allegedly caused by such implants. In 1998 the corporation settled with the women for $3,200 million.

The procedural fairness of the settlement of mass tort claims continued to be questioned, following the Supreme Court's decision in *Amchem Products* v. *Windsor* (see AR 1997, pp. 484-5)). In 1997, in *Ortiz* v. *Fibreboard*, the Court reversed a proposed $1,500 million settlement of asbestos claims. In 1998, in *Flanagan* v. *Ahearn*, the Fifth Circuit Court of Appeals, however, reaffirmed its ruling in a brief opinion. The petitioners, again, appealed to the Supreme Court, which agreed to hear the case, and a decision was expected in 1999.

The difficult balance between individual rights and society's interest in effective enforcement of criminal law remained the theme in the most important decisions in criminal procedure. The Supreme Court, in *Knowles* v. *Iowa*, held that the police might not order a 'full field-type search' of a driver and his passengers after stopping the driver for a traffic offence, such as speeding. An officer who suspected that a driver or passenger, in such a case, had a weapon might only perform a 'pat-down'. Two federal appeals courts held that police officers must have a warrant to use thermal imagers used to sense heat from high-intensity lights often used to grow marijuana indoors on private property.

XV THE ARTS

1. OPERA—MUSIC—BALLET & DANCE—THEATRE—CINEMA—
TELEVISION & RADIO

i. OPERA

THE Royal Opera's season at London's Shaftesbury Theatre, which had begun so disastrously at the end of 1997, ended more happily at the beginning of the new year with a production of Mozart's enchanting *Le Nozze di Figaro*, sensibly entrusted to Patrick Young, one of the company's staff directors, and conducted by the Israeli-American Steven Sloane, who was making his Royal Opera debut. Between them Young and Sloane did full justice to the musical and dramatic elements of the opera, the director emphasizing the underlying seriousness of the play by Beaumarchais on which the work was based, and the conductor bringing an elegant stylishness and warmth to the performance of Mozart's glorious score.

The future of the Royal Opera continued to remain uncertain. A new executive director, the American Michael Kaiser, was appointed, but the ongoing hostility of both the Arts Council and the Department of Culture to the company and, indeed, to the serious arts in general, was apparent throughout the year. Meanwhile, the rebuilding of the Royal Opera House itself, which was expected to reopen at the end of 1999, proceeded apace.

It fell to English National Opera to provide London with its major operatic experiences throughout the year. The Minister for Culture had made the suggestion, unacceptable to all concerned, that the Royal Opera and English National Opera should merge. But if any justification were needed for the continued existence of ENO as a completely separate entity from the Royal Opera, it was triumphantly provided by ENO's revival of Nicholas Hytner's elegant 1985 staging of Handel's *Xerxes*. The entire cast, led by Sarah Connolly and Jean Rigby, was superb, and Hytner's literate and singable translation was clearly articulated by all.

Of ENO's new productions, the most successful was Graham Vick's staging of Offenbach's problematic *Tales of Hoffman*. Left unfinished by the composer, the work had no really definitive performing score, but ENO opted for a recent scholarly edition by Michael Kaye, and Tobias Hoheisel's single, adaptable set brought a welcome touch of glamour to the Coliseum stage. Julian Gavin was an impressive Hoffman, and the Wagnerian bass John Tomlinson enjoyed himself hugely as all four villains. The dynamic conductor was the company's music director, Paul Daniel.

Other new productions by ENO included Puccini's *Trittico*, refreshingly traditional, well-paced and dramatically vivid, and Massenet's *Manon*, drably designed and messily directed. On the opening night of *Manon*, the conductor Paul Daniel was applauded while the production team was roundly booed. Daniel drew stylish and vigorous playing from the orchestra also in Verdi's *Otello*, which opened the company's 1998–99 season in September. The director, David Freeman, set the action in present-day Cyprus, in a cage-like military fort designed by Tom Phillips RA, its wire-mesh detail impressive and its usefulness to the advancement of the plot immense. Undertaking the role of Otello for the first time, David Rendall was exciting in his outbursts of jealous rage, and finally extremely moving.

The regional opera companies all offered lively new productions. Opera North staged Stephen Sondheim's *Sweeney Todd*, a brilliant piece of 20th-century music theatre. Steven Page sang the title-role extremely well, and his naturally imposing stage persona saw him safely through the basics of the action. The company's repertoire also included Tchaikovsky's popular *Eugene Onegin* and a welcome staging of Verdi's rarely-heard but fascinating early work, *Giovanna d'Arco*.

Welsh National Opera's production (in partnership with Australian Opera) of Benjamin Britten's *Billy Budd* was one of the most exciting new stagings of an opera by Britten to have emerged for many years. The action takes place on board a British naval vessel during the war with France in 1797, but Brian Thomson, Australia's leading stage designer, opted for a huge platform which tilted in every possible direction. It poetically simulated the motion and also the atmosphere of the ship on which the handsome young Billy meets his death. The production by Neil Armfield, another Australian, was both intelligent and imaginative, and virtually every role was finely sung, especially Phillip Ens's youngish villain, Claggart, and Christopher Maltman's charismatic Billy. The chorus and orchestra under Andrew Litton performed thrillingly.

Scottish Opera offered a light-hearted production by Stewart Laing of Mozart's *Cosi fan tutte* set in the present day, with Guglielmo wearing football gear and Ferrando dressed as the school swot in grey sweater and spectacles. Comedy took precedence over music throughout, in the singing as well as in the staging.

Glyndebourne Festival Opera, too, played tricks on *Cosi fan tutte*. Graham Vick placed the action in a bare rehearsal room, with the singers in jeans and casual wear. After that initial joke, there was nowhere to go, but musically things were better. Barbara Frittoli was an enchanting Fiordiligi, Roberto Sacca an engaging Ferrando, and Alan Opie an ideal Alfonso. Also at Glyndebourne, Sir Peter Hall's new staging of *Simon Boccanegra* was a clear, intelligent presentation of the work as Verdi conceived it, with a masterly handling of the crowd scenes, and sensitive, imaginative direction of the intimate encounters between individual characters. Without being representational, John Gunter's superb sets magically conjured up 14th-century Genoa, and Elena Prokina brought a beautiful voice and presence to the role of Amelia. Glyndebourne's revival of John Cox's elegant 25-year-old production of Strauss's final opera, *Capriccio*, looked as good as new.

Sir Michael Tippett, the doyen of British opera composers, died in January at the age of 93 (see XVIII: Obituary). Among singers who died during the year were Richard Cassilly, the American tenor who was a favourite at Covent Garden in the 1960s and '70s; Todd Duncan, the American baritone who created the role of Porgy in Gershwin's *Porgy and Bess*; Oreste Kirkop, the Maltese tenor who sang with Sadler's Wells Opera for many years; Michel Roux, the French bass-baritone who appeared at Glyndebourne in the '50s; Anne Wood, the British contralto and opera administrator; Hermann Prey, the famous German baritone; and Ilva Ligabue, the Italian soprano who was active in Italian and British opera houses in the '60s.

ii. MUSIC

THE year 1998 saw a continuation from previous years of the trends and divisions in classical music: much diverse activity, little aesthetic unanimity. The reaction against modernism grew apace; the middle ground, which made up far the greater part of the concert and opera season, continued to provide the livelihood for most musicians; in the popularity stakes there was perhaps a slight challenge to Mahler from Prokofiev, Janacek and Shostakovich; the trend towards early music, and performance on 'period' instruments, showed little sign of abating, though it was stronger in Europe than in America; contemporary composers continued to be a minority taste, with the lowest proportion of time—about 4 per cent of the total musical output—being allotted to living British composers in Britain.

There was some philosophical questioning on the part of critics and writers into the failure of modernism, the mindless decadence of pop culture, and the state of classical music generally. One German composer, Helmut Lachenman, clearly more musican than philosopher, dismissed comprehensively 'the cheap pretensions of *avant-garde* hedonists, sonority chefs, exotic meditationists and nostalgia-merchants'; one English writer, Roger Scruton, more philosopher than musician, took an inclusive swipe at both pop music and modernism: 'Young people are exposed on all sides to soul-destroying rubbish.' The death in 1998 of Sir Michael Tippett (see XVIII: Obituary) led to speculation by writers of every persuasion about his place as a composer. There was no unanimity. How could there be? In a culture which boasted of its 'plurality', was there such a thing as a contemporary master? The musical language itself was evolving; how could there be universality?

This was sharply illustrated by two contrasted premieres in 1998 by the Tweedledum and Tweedledee of British music, Sir Peter Maxwell Davies and Sir Harrison Birtwistle. Each piece was commissioned and first performed in America before being heard in England; each composer reacted differently to the post-serial situation of the 1990s. Davies's *A Reel of Seven Fishermen* was premiered by the San Francisco Symphony, conducted by the composer. His style had gradually evolved outwards, becoming more accessible to the listener, consistent with his greater experience as conductor. Structure, tonality and melodic line were simplified; the material was a pastiche of Scottish dance, folk song and plainchant.

Birtwistle's *Exody* was premiered by the Chicago Symphony Orchestra, conducted by Daniel Barenboim. Birtwistle's style had evolved inwards into itself, becoming less accessible to the listener. The texture became progressively denser and more static, the structure and tonality more anarchic. The material was 'endless exposition', with self-multiplying complexity and unrelated layers of sound, which far from being a source of richness and colour were aesthetically nihilistic.

At the other end of the stylistic spectrum, the minimalist John Adams also had an active year, on both sides of the Atlantic. The workings of the global market in music, which was becoming more integrated through a network of promotions and festivals, meant that activity led to further activity. The more performances a composer achieved, particularly of works in the larger categories of opera or symphony, the more he obtained. He became known for being known. Following the favourable reception of his Piano Concerto *Century Rolls* in 1997, his very popular, if lightweight, opera *Nixon in China* (see AR 1988, p. 477) was given a concert performance in London at the Barbican in February; thereafter a concert suite was made from it, and this was heard at Aspen, Colorado, in July. A further Adams' piece, *Hallelujah Junction* for piano duet, was heard in Los Angeles in April, the first of many performances.

Judging by performances, the most popular American composer of the year was probably Leonard Bernstein. His music crossed boundaries and categories; it could therefore be heard in differing contexts. It featured prominently in a series of concerts at the Barbican between October and December, under the title 'Inventing America'. Then again, extracts from various well-known scores were stitched together by the choreographer John Neumeier to make a new ballet *Bernstein Dances*. After the premiere in Hamburg in June, the work was repeated at a 'Bernstein Celebration' in the Lincoln Center in July.

Following Bernstein—an American musician for whom composition was an extension of his piano playing and conducting, both being a reflection of a close affinity with the roots of American culture—André Previn achieved a distinct success and popular acclaim when his folk-opera, based on Tennessee Williams's classic *A Streetcar Named Desire,* was first heard in San Francisco in September. It had taken a decade and more to reach fruition, and only came about after Bernstein himself and Stephen Sondheim had turned down the idea—the latter on the grounds that it was already 'such a good play, it doesn't need music'. The same could be said of *Romeo and Juliet*; but success as a folk-opera came with the extra dimension of music, which was integral to the material of the story itself, whether in *West Side Story* or *A Streetcar Named Desire*.

A runner-up to Bernstein, if appealing to a more limited public, was his fellow American Elliott Carter, whose ninetieth birthday was duly marked, hyped and celebrated in 1998. The chief event of his year was the first complete performance, lasting 45 minutes, of the orchestral triptych *Symphonia: Sum Fluxae Pretium Spei*, whose composition had dominated Carter's output in the 1990s. The three constituent parts, which could also be performed separately, were *Partita* (see AR 1994, p. 506–7), *Adagio Tenebroso* (see AR 1995, p. 477) and *Allegro Scorrevole*. The first performance of all three took place in Manchester in April, as part of the ISCM Festival. Numerous other performances of his works during the year included two other premieres, *Luimen* for chamber ensemble, first heard in Amsterdam in March, and the *Piano Quintet*, first heard at the Library of Congress in Washington in November.

If birthdays divisible by five could be used to draw attention to a particular musician, another one occurred in 1998, not perhaps as internationally well-known as Elliott Carter's, but no less distinctive. The American Ned Rorem was 75, and the chief event of his year was the premiere in New York in January of *Evidence of Things Not Seen*, a suite of 36 songs for four solo singers and piano. Solo songs alternated with accompanied duets, trios and quartets. Rorem was best known as a songwriter, and this was his most substantial project to date, with poems by many writers, organized into three collections—*Beginnings, Middles, Ends*—descriptive of the different perspectives in the life of a man. Another commission for 1998 was for the *Double Concerto* for violin, violoncello and orchestra, which was heard first in Indianapolis in October, later in Edinburgh.

In London the most publicized premiere of the year heralded the completion by Anthony Payne of Elgar's *Third Symphony*. This was left unfinished on the composer's death in 1934; Payne, a writer on music specializing in British composers and also a neo-Webernian composer himself, described his additions as an 'elaboration'. The work was instantly successful with the public, and numerous further performances were scheduled; indeed it almost reached cult status. It was also a fake, being neither genuine Elgar nor genuine Payne. It was published by a firm other than Elgar's chief publisher. In completing Elgar's symphony, moreover, Payne had contravened the composer's express wish, made at the close of his life to his friend W.H. Reed, that 'no-one must tinker with it'. Such treatment could at best amount only to pastiche, or an academic parlour game of the sort already witnessed in the case of some other well-known incomplete works, such as Schubert's *Unfinished Symphony*, or Mahler's tenth.

The latest developments in modernism, or post-modernism, were to be found in Germany, where a strong influence could be seen from oriental musicians. At the sixth Münchener Biennale the new artistic director, Peter Ruzicka presented Helmut Lachenman's *Das Mädchen mit den Schwefelholzern*, greatly influenced by the oriental *Sho*, as well as music-theatre from Indian and Japanese composers, including Toshio Hosokawa (*Vision of Lear*) and Sanleep Bhagwati (*Ramanujan*). Other theatre works included *Komëdie ohne Titel* (from Lorca), by a Henze pupil Jan Müller-Wieland, and the festival ended with Weltmusik-Nacht, including Isang Yun's *First Chamber Symphony* and Hans Zender's *5 Haiku*.

The Wittener Tage für Neue Kammermusik included among its *avant-garde* pieces some work by the Japanese composer, Misulo Mochiuuki, who had studied at IRCAM in Paris, where his *Si Bleu, Si Calme* was made. Featured composers were the Italian Salvatore Sciarrino and the British composer Brian Ferneyhough, as well as the German composers York Höller and Walter Zimmerman and several others.

Among those who died in 1998 were the composers Sir Michael Tippett, Alfred Schnittke and Geoffrey Bush; the conductors Klaus Tennstedt and Lamberto Gardelli; and the Italian organist Fernando Gemani (For Tippett, Schnittke, Tennstedt and Germani, see XVIII: Obituary).

BOOKS OF THE YEAR. *Gershwin, Rhapsody in Blue*, by David Schiff; *Michael Tippett*, by Meirion Bowen; *The Cambridge Companion to Berg*, ed. Anthony Pople; *The Aesthetics of Music*, by Roger Scruton; *Bela Bartok and Turn-of-the-Century Budapest*, by Judit Frigyesi; *Ludwig van Beethoven: Briefwechsel: Gesamtausgabe Vol.1–7*, ed. Sieghard Brandenburg; *The Frontiers of Meaning; Three Informal Lectures on Music*, by Charles Rosen; *Virgil Thomson: Composer on the Aisle*, by Anthony Tommasini; *Bohemian Fifths: an Autobiography*, by Hans Werner Henze; *Leonard Bernstein*, by Paul Myers; *The Music of Elliott Carter*, by David Schiff (updated edition; first published 1983).

iii. BALLET & DANCE

ALTHOUGH marred by the deaths of several leading personalities including the great Soviet ballerina Galina Ulanova and American choreographer Jerome Robbins (see XVIII: Obituary), 1998 will be remembered as a year of celebrations. These marked the 225th anniversary of the Royal Swedish Ballet, the 100th birthday of Dame Ninette de Valois, founder of the Royal Ballet in Britain, and the 50th birthdays of dancer Wayne Sleep and choreographer Richard Alston. It was again a year in which memorable performances by individual dancers made a greater impression than the productions in which they danced.

The Royal Swedish Ballet, under the direction of Frank Andersen, chose to celebrate by presenting a showcase of its current repertory and rich history in a nine-day festival in June with a programme of performances, seminars, exhibitions and a final gala. The festival opened with a revelatory programme of four works created for the Ballets Suédois (a 1920s breakaway company that rivalled Serge Diaghilev's Ballets Russes and was noted for commissioning of scores from eminent composers and designs from innovative artists). It continued with particularly memorable recreations of eighteenth- and early nineteenth-century ballets (*Pygmalion*; an extract *from Opportunity Makes the Thief*; *The Return of Springtime, Harlequin, Magician of Love*; *The Highwayman, or, The Magnanimous Soldier*) performed in the charming court theatres at Ulriksdal and Drottingholm.

The most successful presentations in the Royal Opera House were Kenneth MacMillan's *Mayerling* (in which Jan-Erik Wikström was a dramatic Rudolf while all the company impressed with their attention to detail) and *The Nutcracker*. This had been adapted by Pär Isberg and Erik Näslund to incorporate characters from the children's stories by Elsa Beskow so that the housemaid and the charcoal burner, Marie Lindquist and Hans Nilsson, became the Sugar Plum Fairy and her Prince. As Beskow's stories featured the black dog Prick, Happy also had a featured role and, naturally, stole the show. His role was 'choreographed' with the aid of 'rewards' of cheese.

The Royal Ballets in Denmark and Britain experienced a year of chaos. In Copenhagen the dancers were frustrated by the repertory they danced and seemed unhappy with the leadership of their artistic director, Maina Gielgud, while in London the company was a victim of the managerial chaos of the whole Royal Opera House. Although it lost many of its male dancers to a new company headed by Japanese star, Tetsuya Kumakawa, its immediate problems over contracts and working conditions seemed resolved by the end of the year. With Michael Kaiser appointed as executive director the whole organization began to plan for the future on a more positive note. It was, nevertheless, a difficult year for the company made homeless during the rebuilding of the Opera House but none of its performances were of the standard the company achieved in past years. Life on the road during its first year as an itinerant company was recorded in Deborah Bull's diary, *Dancing Away*.

It was therefore left to the lively and creative Birmingham Royal Ballet to celebrate Ninette de Valois' centenary in the style it deserved. This took the form of David Bintley choreographing a new ballet, *The Protecting Veil*, in homage to de Valois and an impeccable revival of her own *The Prospect Before Us*. Last performed 46 years ago, *The Prospect Before Us* was a comic ballet about rival late eighteenth-century theatre managers; its witty, period-pastiche choreography was revived by Jean Bedells and Roger Furse's set and costume designs were restored by David Dean.

Wayne Sleep was probably the best-known dancer in Britain. He interrupted a nationwide tour to present a birthday gala in London in which he recreated many of his most successful roles and proved he could still whiz round the stage. Richard Alston celebrated on a more modest scale at the Queen Elizabeth Hall, London, presenting a satisfying programme that combined the old and the new. Brief sections of past successes were danced by his present company under the title *Sophisticated Curiosities (1970–1990)*. Eva Karczag, Siobhan Davies, Darshan Singh Buller and Alston himself returned to the stage in new choreography and Alston also created a major new work, *Waltzes in Disorder* (to Brahms' *Liebeslieder Wältzer*), superbly performed by dancers (including Martin Lawrence and Christopher Tudor) and musicians. For many British dance-goers this evening was the highlight of the contemporary dance calendar. Other important events were the visit of Merce Cunningham's company with a repertory of Events and new dances and Siobhan Davies' company celebrating its tenth anniversary with a new staging of *Winnsboro' Cotton Mill Blues* and the creation of *Eighty-eight*.

June and July saw stunning performances by Tamara Rojo and Nicolas Le Riche as the protagonists in *Romeo and Juliet*. Unfortunately this couple was divided not by feuding families but by the English Channel. Rojo was appearing in Derek Deane's production in the round (complete with rotating balcony) at the Royal Albert Hall, London, while Le Riche was the dramatic hero in Rudolf Nureyev's version at the Paris Bastille. For both English National Ballet (ENB) and the Paris Opéra it was a year in which they concentrated on full-evening presentations. Nevertheless, this allowed certain dancers to stand out. For ENB Agnes Oaks was a brilliant Aurora, secure in her balances, sincere in her acting. For Paris Opéra Elisabeth Platel shone as Giselle and Gamzatti; Laurent Hilaire brought authority and superb technique to Solor and de Grieux (the latter in stunning partnership with Sylvie Guillem as Manon); and Charles Jude said farewell to the Opéra as the romantic Albrect, having played a dangerous Tybalt in *Romeo and Juliet* the previous night.

Similarly, American Ballet Theatre (ABT) revealed that they had become once again a strong company. In June their first performances of *Le Corsaire* fielded as powerful collection of male dancers as could be hoped for. In four leading roles José Manuel Carrero, Angel Corella, Vladimir Malakov, Keith Roberts, Ethan Stiefel and Giuseppe Picone alternated to thunderous applause. Stiefel also triumphed in the challenging lead role in Frederick Ashton's *Les Patineurs*. ABT's other major acquisition was Ben Stevenson's *The Snow Maiden*, co-produced with Houston Ballet and charmingly designed by Desmond Heeley (his farewell to the stage). Nina Ananiashvili created the title role of the girl who melts in the sun's rays for both companies. The talented Cuban dancer, Carlos Acosta (now also revitalizing the Royal Ballet) was her original Misgir in Houston. This role was impressively danced by Corella at ABT where it was also a treat to see Irina Kolpakova in the cameo role of the Czarina.

The 1998 Edinburgh Festival included two major dance events. Firstly there was Pacific North West's first visit to Britain presenting their striking staging of George Balanchine's full-evening *A Midsummer Night's Dream*. Secondly there was a tribute to Hans van Manen celebrating his 40 years as a choreographer with performances by both Dutch National Ballet and two parts of Netherlands Dance Theatre (NDT2—the apprentice company, and NDT3—the seniors). Van Manen was worthy of such an honour as his choreography had always crossed boundaries of dance styles and pioneered the incorporation of new technology. His 1979 production, *Live*, for dancer and video camera continued to be highly praised. Between the companies programmes included long-recognized masterworks such as *Grosse Fuge* and *5 Tangos* as well as a new work to Astor Piazolla's tangos, *Zero Hour*. The most satisfying of van Manen's recent works was the brief dance, *The Old Man and Me*, for Sabine Kupferber and Gérard Lemaitre. This was free of the misogynistic elements that had marred some of his choreography.

In October the new Sadler's Wells (the sixth theatre on the site in Islington) was opened by Rambert Dance Company revealing a magnificent new stage for dance in London. This allowed major companies from abroad to be seen, the most significant to date being William Forsythe's Frankfurt Ballet. Forsythe's choreography, extreme and exciting, was much admired and British audiences at last saw his own dancers performing the revolutionary works they had created.

Trisha Brown became the latest choreographer to tackle *L'Orfeo*, this time using Claudio Monteverdi's version, for a cool production that effectively intermingled singers and dancers. Another interesting production was the Royal New Zealand Ballet's *The Sleeping Beauty*. For this they invited Kim Brandstrup to mount the ballet, in which he retained Marius Petipa's choreography for soloist whilst avoiding production clichés and provided new choreography for the corps de ballet. The most exciting completely new classical ballet was Christopher Hampson's *Country Garden* for English National Ballet and London had the opportunity to see some of New York City Ballet's newer creations during a short visit by a group of dancers led by Peter Boal, Albert Evans and Wendy Whelan. In November New York City Ballet embarked on a year-long celebration of their 50th anniversary. Meanwhile, to mark the centenary of the birth of Federico Garcia Lorca, Rambert Dance Company revived their dramatic *Cruel Garden*, created 21 years ago by Lindsay Kemp and Christopher Bruce.

Among others from the world of ballet who died in 1998 were Svetlana Beriosova (see XVIII: Obituary), Alexander Bogatiriev, Christopher Gable and Alla Shelest.

iv. THEATRE

THE familiar difficulties of funding continued to plague theatres, large and small, both in London and in the regions, but signs appeared that the rigid restrictions imposed upon the use of money derived from the National Lottery were to be eased. Companies and individual productions would start to benefit directly, replacing the short-sighted practice in operation hitherto whereby the money could be spent only upon the physical structures, the 'bricks and mortar', or upon secondary concerns such as educational tie-ins–which, though unquestionably of great value, would be unable to function at all if the local theatre lacked the wherewithal to stay open.

Chris Smith, the Culture Minister, succeeded in wringing from the Treasury a 15 per cent increase in Arts Council funding but uncertainty grew about the future of the Council itself, accused on all sides of bad decision-making, lack of forward thinking and cronyism. Nothing in its dealings with the theatre brought the Council the abuse that came its way over the sequence of errors to do with the Royal Opera House, but in the autumn the entire drama panel resigned when internal reconstruction, described as 'streamlining', reduced its advisory functions to a minimum.

Other resignations were threatened when the Royal Court Theatre, still in voluntary exile to two West End theatres while rebuilding continued at its Chelsea home, announced that it was to accept £3 million from the Jerwood Foundation and would accordingly add Jerwood to its name. Some writers protested at what they called a submission to mammon, arguing that under its familiar name the theatre had been the standard-bearer for new British writing since 1956. The theatre management pointed out that the alternative was bankruptcy and closure. The Jerwood Foundation, established by the pearl trader John Jerwood to support young and emerging artists, had been particularly generous to the Royal Court in previous years, and after further discussion it was decided that the theatre's name should remain unchanged but that its two auditoria, scheduled to reopen in 1999, would be known as the Jerwood Theatre Upstairs and the Jerwood Theatre Downstairs.

A striking feature of the year's London productions was the number of movie stars who appeared in them. Hollywood stars had trod the London boards before: Dustin Hoffman played Shylock in a production by Sir Peter Hall, who subsequently directed Jessica Lange as Blanche DuBois; Lauren Bacall, Leslie Caron and Julie Christie had appeared, though not with great success, at various Chichester Festival seasons; but in 1998 the trickle became a torrent.

In a revival of Luigi Pirandello's 1921 play *Naked* at the Almeida the French actress Juliette Binoche, with memories of her performance in the film *The English Patient* still fresh in the public mind, played the young nanny in whose care a child died in mysterious circumstances. The attempts by various men to discover the truth of the matter, and her own struggle first to please them and then to establish the truth for herself, became intensely moving as Juliette Binoche, an electrifying presence, moved between grief and hysteria to her eventual despair.

The Almeida's artistic co-directors, Ian McDiarmid and Jonathan Kent, had lured Ralph Fiennes and Liam Neeson to their theatre the previous year, and Neeson returned to play Oscar Wilde in David Hare's *The Judas Kiss*, where he gave a strong, muscular performance, notably freed from affectation and considerably better than the play Hare had written.

Infinitely more successful was Howard Davies's eloquent direction of Eugene O'Neill's *The Iceman Cometh*, again at the Almeida, from where it transferred to the Old Vic and subsequently to Broadway. Here the movie star was Kevin Spacey, an actor with a wealth of stage experience behind him, and in this marathon of a play, one of the 20th century's towering masterpieces, he played Hickey, the messianic salesman with a frightening secret. Spacey's mesmerising performance, combining holiness with hollowness, and laced with panic, showed that his presence was far from being a piece of opportunistic casting, and the ease with which his playing blended with the otherwise all-British cast (including Tim Pigott-Smith and Rupert Graves) helped earn the play its fistfull of awards.

The Australian-born actress Nicole Kidman also trained in the theatre before going on to achieve success in Hollywood, a preparation that enabled her to give variety to the five roles provided for her, in various states of undress, in David Hare's version of *Der Reigen* at the Donmar. Better known as *La Ronde*, Hare renamed Arthur Schnitzler's circular chain of love-stories *The Blue Room*, and in updating it he surprisingly jettisoned the original's social concerns. However, the comedy was not lost and the presence of the very beautiful Nicole Kidman guaranteed full houses at the Donmar throughout its relatively short run. Towards the end ticket touts were rumoured to be asking £500 for a ticket. The dashing and subtle performances given by her stage partner Iain Glen should not be forgotten.

David Hare, astonishingly prolific, also provided one of the year's least-anticipated successes with *Via Dolorosa* (Royal Court), an account of a visit to Israel and Palestine. He both wrote and performed this one-man work, and what initially looked set to be a journalistic report developed into a humane and moving meditation on the area's seemingly intractable problems, where both Jews and Arabs were as bitterly divided among themselves as with each other. 'What matters', he asked at the end, 'stones or ideas?', leaving to us or to the future the task of supplying an answer.

Inevitably, some productions were insults to the intelligence of any audience, but the year brought two new plays that merited the status of modern classics. Michael Frayn's *Copenhagen* (National Theatre) took as its starting-point the controversial, and never convincingly explained, visit paid in 1941 by the German physicist Werner Heisenberg to his old teacher, the half-Jewish Niels Bohr, in Nazi-occupied Denmark. Famous for introducing the so-called 'uncertainty principle' into quantum mechanics, Heisenberg was at that time at work on research that could have provided Hitler with the atomic bomb and so altered the course of history. Acted on a stark lecture-hall set by only three actors, David Burke and Matthew Marsh as the two scientists and Sara Kestelman as Bohr's wife (all three superb), the play seemed at first to be redefining drama as argument, yet so gripping was this argument, and so cunningly had Frayn woven other notions of uncertainty into the structure, that it was soon apparent that we were present at one of the finest and most intelligently passionate plays of the Nineties. Certainly it was the most important work of Frayn's theatrical career, his earlier plays having frequently revealed an attentive and humane concern with moral questions but never before demonstrating these with such dramatic power.

The second of these ambitious and moving plays enjoyed only its scheduled month's run at Birmingham's Repertory Theatre, a company whose reputation continued to grow under the artistic direction of Bill Alexander. *Frozen*, by Bryony Lavery, trod the emotional minefield of child murder, again using only three actors and employing the form, until the closing scenes, of three interwoven monologues. Ruari Murchison's starkly monochrome setting, against a rear wall made up of a grid of light beams, emphasized the terrible isolation of the distraught mother, the numbed murderer and, to a lesser degree, the American psychiatrist visiting from another Birmingham (Alabama). Lavery suggested that both the mother (Anita Dobson, never better) and her child's killer (Tom Georgeson) had become locked in an icy, lifeless rigidity, the one through shock and the other resulting from parental abuse in childhood. The hauntingly tender restraint of Lavery's writing, and the power thus concentrated on some of the distressing details, were major creative achievements.

No restraint was evident in *You'll Have Had Your Hole*, a first play by Irvine Welsh, the author of *Trainspotting*, which premiered in Leeds and added torture and anal rape to his familiar landscape of drugs and verbal abuse. The writing was banal and the construction inept. Sarah Kane's no less horror-soaked *Cleansed* (Royal Court) also dealt in punishment, dismemberment and cruel death but a moral purpose, investigating notions of love, could be discerned within the murk. This purpose came to the fore in her short play *Crave* (a Paines Plough production at the Royal Court) where four figures seated on chairs, spoke reproachfully and longingly of love, sometimes to one another but often just to themselves. The plays of Kane, author of the notorious *Blasted*, had often enraged conservatively disposed audiences but their structural competence and the shafts of poetic language consistently held the stage.

Conventional wisdom had always held that the classical tragedies of Jean Racine never worked in the English theatre. The Almeida company defied this wisdom by presenting two, *Phèdre* and *Britannicus*, and not in their Islington home but in a West End theatre (Albery). Jonathan Kent's direction, sober yet tense with ritual, discovered unfamiliar psychological depths in both these studies of sexual obsession, which had the great advantage of starring Diana Rigg in each, as the thwarted stepmother in the first and as Nero's relentless mother, Agrippina, in the second.

A discovery of a different order occurred earlier in the year when *Not About Nightingales* opened at the National Theatre. Written by Tennessee Williams at the very start of his career, when still uncertain if his future lay as a dramatist or a shoe salesman, the manuscript had lain forgotten in a university archive for sixty years until noticed by Vanessa Redgrave. She brought it to the attention of the Alley Theatre, Houston, and to Trevor Nunn at the National, who gave a magnificent production of this raw account of a battle of wills in a hellish prison in Philadelphia. Williams based this prentice work on a true incident, where four prisoners were literally cooked to death in a punishment cell when the radiators were turned up to full, and although the play was by no means faultless it offered fascinating insights into the early creative processes of a dramatist, notoriously uneven but when at his best standing in the very highest rank. Corin Redgrave played the sadistic prison governor, and the inhumanity of his 'ideal prison' found visible expression in Richard Hoover's award-winning set, entirely grey, even down to the Stars and Stripes hanging on the wall.

The European premiere of Neil Simon's attractively elegiac *Proposals*, set in a country cottage in the Pocono Mountains of Pennsylvania, opened in Leeds, and Terrence McNally's poignant *Love! Valour! Compassion!* was given an exemplary staging by Roger Haines at his relatively low-profile Library Theatre in Manchester. Regrettably, neither of these productions made the further journey to London, and though McNally's play did make an appearance there, in an award-winning production from the Edinburgh Festival, it played at the small 100-seater Tristan Bates Theatre. Sometimes the decisions made by theatre managements, commercial and subsidized, seemed both illogical and crass.

Other American plays fared a little better. David Mamet's buoyant *Lakeboat*, written during his college days and set on a freighter steaming across Lake Michigan, received its belated British premiere at the Lyric, Hammersmith; Edward Albee's *The Play About the Baby* (Almeida), though superbly acted, baffled its audience; Paula Vogel successfully introduced a chorus into her *How I Learned to Drive* (Donmar), the subject being child abuse, or the threat of it, the 'concern of the year'.

American musicals fared best of all. A revival of *Sweet Charity* came and went but *Rent*, a kind of New York *La Bohème*, triumphed. The revival of Stephen Sondheim's *Into the Woods* enjoyed a long run at the Donmar, as did Charles Strouse's *Annie* at the Victoria Palace. A vigorous production of *Oklahoma!* earned some much-needed cash for the National Theatre, first at the South Bank and then in its West End transfer. Revivals of popular musicals were not the sort of work envisaged by those who campaigned for a national theatre in the days before Laurence Olivier established it in 1963, at that time in the Old Vic. But even national theatres had to swim with the financial tide or sink.

The Royal Shakespeare Company (RSC), the country's other major national organization, again enjoyed a season of mixed successes where nothing was ever seriously bad but few offerings greatly thrilled the imagination. David Calder gave a commanding and intelligent portrayal of Prospero in Adrian Noble's production of *The Tempest*, and Robert Glenister played a frantic and stuttering Duke in a *Measure for Measure* most impressively directed by Michael Boyd, with Stephen Boxer, one of the best verse-speakers of his generation, as the devilish Angelo. C.S. Lewis's ever-popular children's tale *The Lion, the Witch and the Wardrobe* became the first family Christmas show to be produced on Stratford's main stage for thirty years. The book's militant Christianity never appealed to all tastes, and Noble's production only occasionally caught its undeniable magic, but in Patrice Naiambana, majestically golden and husky-voiced, the show found an eloquent Aslan, the Christ-like lion who triumphs over the wicked witch.

Irish drama continued to flourish, north and south of the border, ranging in subject from the existence and implications of the border to the sometimes harsh conditions of modern urban life. The RSC recalled an earlier Ireland in *Shadows*, grouping together two short haunted plays by J. M. Synge and one by W. B. Yeats. A rural Ireland of the 1930s was conjured up in *Tarry Flynn*, adapted by Conall Morrison from Patrick Kavanagh's autobiography of that name. Morrison's strikingly unnaturalistic production for the Abbey Theatre, Dublin, played a short season in London at the National Theatre where the impresario Cameron Mackintosh was sufficiently impressed to choose Morrison to direct yet another attempt to make the musical *Martin Guerre* a success. Rewritten, refocused and greatly improved, this production opened in Leeds but whether plans existed for a further life in London remained uncertain.

London's Gate Theatre at Notting Hill, long recognized as London's foremost house for staging foreign work, recovered from a dip in its fortunes with the appointment of 28-year-old Mick Gordon as its new artistic director. Himself born in Ulster, he unearthed *Volunteers*, a multi-layered Brian Friel play set on an archaeological dig, that had displeased the Irish critics in 1975 and not been seen since. Resonant, sardonic and passionately acted, unforgettably so by Patrick O'Kane as a mordantly Hamlet-like Republican prisoner, the play asked uncomfortable questions about the past and the distortions imposed upon it by a present forever hunting for victims.

Mick Gordon had preceded this production with *Une Tempête*, a reinvention of Shakespeare's play by Aimé Césaire, the Martiniquan writer who coined the word 'negritude'. This absorbing study of colonialism, in which Ariel and Caliban, both black, argued over the route to freedom, was also astonishingly funny and began Gordon's tenure on a high note which it sustained to the end of the year. Surviving on modest funding and individual sponsorship the continuing ability of theatres such as the Gate to create great theatre was a marvel to cherish.

v. CINEMA

ANYONE in the film business who feared that the cinema might be in for a bad time with the advent of multi-channel television must have been considerably cheered by Hollywood's success in 1998. In America, the year's gross box-office takings rose 10 per cent over 1997, reaching an estimated $6,860 million. The sale of 1,380 million individual tickets was the best showing of the 1990s, and you had to go back to 1966 to find a better one. A record of 15 movies grossed more than $100 million on the home market, and internationally too Hollywood did exceptionally well, with 17 films passing the same mark. It could still truly be said that America's best exports were films and aeroplanes.

The phenomenon of the year, though it came out in 1997, was undoubtedly James Cameron's multi-Oscared *Titanic* which, by the end of 1998, had grossed the fantastic sum of $1,697 million—$488 million in America and $1,209 million internationally. No wonder Cameron proclaimed himself 'king of the world' at the Oscar ceremonies. One of the reasons for this enormous success was that Hollywood's best-publicized and hyped titles were now seen everywhere. And while that did not mean instant success, there was no doubt that if the public liked the idea of them, the box-office ball started rolling as never before. *Titanic* managed to double the performance of Steven Spielberg's *Jurassic Park*, the previous box-office champion. It ruled the waves and waived the rules. It would be nice to be able to give a good reason why. But perhaps it was because this once-derided film, almost stopped in the middle of its making when the budget got too big, was a clever combination of history and fiction which satisfied those who wanted both the spectacular and the romantic. The simplistic love story between Kate Winslet and Leonardo DiCaprio was liked by as many people as were thrilled by the special-effects-dominated final sinking of the liner itself. If the film was made with great sophistication technically, it was its lack of sophistication emotionally which helped to draw the crowds.

Of the other successful Hollywood films, it was hard to find one which would last in the memory, except perhaps Steven Spielberg's *Saving Private Ryan*, a war epic which contained some extraordinary battle sequences and an equal measure of banalities. In that respect it resembled *Titanic*. But its best moments, such as the long opening sequence of the storming of the Normandy beaches, filmed with a hand-held camera and a real appreciation of the sound as well as the sights of battle, were surely more memorable than anything *Titanic* achieved. The film made $464 million worldwide and between it and *Titanic* came the science fiction *Armageddon* with $410 million. *Godzilla* and *Deep Impact*, also science fiction fantasies, were close behind those three. It was hardly a year to celebrate artistically; no doubt if it had been, the box-office returns would have been less. In a world sliding into recession, it seemed that the still predominantly young audience wanted escapist spectacle above all else.

Despite all this, European film-making remained reasonably buoyant. Its leader was still Britain, as much because of the language problem for non-English-speaking films as because of its quality. But it was a little depressing to note that most of the successful British films were made with American money. It looked as if 1998 would be a bad year. National Lottery financing did not come up with any hits, general production was down from 1997 and the Blair government's schemes to help could not be said to have come to fruition. But suddenly things changed in the last three months of the year, when America took note of a whole posse of British films, notably John Madden's entertaining romantic fantasy *Shakespeare in Love*, which added to the success of his *Mrs Brown*, Anand Tucker's *Hilary and Jackie*, the controversial story of the cellist Jacqueline Du Pré, Mark Harmon's *Little Voice*, which gave Jane Horrocks and Michael Caine parts to remember, and the laddish East End thriller *Lock, Stock And Two Smoking Barrels*.

Previously, only the romantic *Sliding Doors* had hit the mark in Britain and America, while Ken Loach's, *My Name is Joe*, prize-winner at the Cannes Festival, had not had very rewarding returns in its home country. There was, however, no *Full Monty* or *Bean*. Had Britain financed the majority of these films, there would have been no argument at all about the success or failure of the British film industry. The American money which enabled most of them to be made meant that Americans got the profits and the British the kudos.

Fortunately for non-English-speaking European cinema, there was a film which broke down national barriers in several countries. Roberto Benigni's *Life is Beautiful* broke all box-office records in Italy and then went on to win prizes almost everywhere, including the European Academy's 'Best film of 1998'. Considering it was a tragi-comedy, a large part of which was set in a Nazi concentration camp, this was a considerable surprise. Benigni had previously appeared as an actor in two American films but had not reached international prominence with his own work as writer, actor and director. *Life is Beautiful* altered that. Its combination of eccentric comedy, Italian sentimentality and serious comment about hope amidst horror hit audiences in the gut all over the world. Even the best of Fellini or Visconti could not measure up to its success, and the Italian cinema, which had been through at least a decade of lean years, now seemed more confident about itself.

In France, where attendances for Hollywood films increased but for French films reached an all-time low of some 30 per cent of the total, there were still some successes. But most were purely on a national level, except Erick Zonka's splendid debut *The Dreamlife of Angels*, which became an international *succès d'estime* and more than paid back its small budget. About two young women making their way through a host of difficulties in the French provinces, *Dreamlife* boasted superb performances from Elaine Bouchez and Natalie Regnier and eschewed nearly all the clichés of youth movies.

It should be remembered that the films that did well in profit percentage terms were either the big budget spectaculars or the small budget art movies. It was those in the middle of the range that most frequently failed. This at least gave most European films a bit of hope, provided they could find room in the cinemas beside the American blockbusters—not often an easy task. In Germany, however, some 25 per cent of the cinema-going audience was for home-grown films, which would not seem good for France but was excellent for Germany, where the film industry had been in decline, as in Italy, for some time. The chief recipient of this rare accolade was *Run Lola Run*, in which a girl had 40 minutes to save her boyfriend, and did so in the last reel. The film made more money than any other German film of the 1990s, and sold well internationally too.

In Scandinavia, the big success came from Denmark, where a group of film-makers, including Lars Von Trier and Thomas Vinterberg, had fashioned *Dogme 95*—ten rules that should not be broken when making films, including the use of nothing but hand-held cameras, no credits for the director and a vow of chastity while shooting. This amused many but was really a reaction against the stodgy literary adaptations of the Danish cinema. It produced Von Trier's *The Idiots*, the swingeing portrayal of a madhouse, which included some pornographic passages, and Vinterberg's *The Celebration*. The latter was a big success, tracing the terrible moment when, at a family gathering to celebrate the 70th birthday of the paterfamilias, the old man was accused of sexually abusing two young members of the brood, one of whom had committed suicide.

The Russian cinema was not so lucky, since a chronic shortage of finance and cinemas predicated to showing only the latest from Hollywood meant that production levels were down again from the low level of 1997. Only a handful of films either from Russia or what used to be the Soviet Union reached the West at all, the best being Dinara Drukarova's eccentric but notable *Of Freaks and Men*. Nor was the cinema of Eastern Europe much better served. But Greece produced the Cannes Palme d'Or in Theo Angelopoulos' *Eternity and a Day*, the intricate story of a dying writer raging against his fate but finally coming to terms with it. And the former Yugoslavia, produced two films which were noted at the film festivals of the world: Emir Kusturica's comedy *Black Cat White Cat* and Goran Paskaljevic's *The Powder Keg*. Both films were from Serbia, the former being the Grand Jury prize at Venice and the latter, a highly critical film about the Serbian mentality, the European Critics' Prize for the year.

The Iranian cinema continued to attract international attention, notably with Samirah Makhmalbaf's *The Apple*, the story of an old man who locked his two daughters in the house to save them from the world and then got reported to the authorities for doing so. The daughter of the distinguished director Mohsen Makhmalbaf, Samirah was only 17 when she made the film, which won prizes at Cannes and was sold all over the world.

In Asia, film production became ever-more difficult as a result of economic recession. India produced its fair share of hits from Bombay ('Bollywood') and Madras ('Mollywood'), but the huge Indian audience seemed to be becoming more fussy by the day, rendering some of the more traditional song-and-dance spectaculars profitless. The influx of American films continued apace and some were successful, notably *Titanic*. The West, it seemed, exerted an increasing influence on popular Indian films, many of which shamelessly borrowed the plots of the most successful Hollywood examples. About 700 films were still churned out each year, technically better than before but artistically of rather less value than such old-time hits as *Mother India*.

The year saw the death of Akira Kurosawa (see XVIII: Obituary), the great Japanese director of *Rashomon*, *The Seven Samurai* and *Living*, and also (in a car crash) of Alan Pakula the American director of *Klute* and *All the President's Men*. It would not be easy to find similar talents, either in Japan or America, to replace them.

vi. TELEVISION & RADIO

PESSIMISTS looking for evidence that increased commercialism and ratings pressure was starting to undermine the British tradition of public service broadcasting had no difficulty finding it in 1998. What for many was a defining moment came on 11 November when Sir Robin Biggam, chairman of the Independent Television Commission (ITC), announced that the regulatory body, by a seven to three majority, had decided to give permission for the moving of *News at Ten* from its prime-time slot after 31 years. 'In a multi-channel age, direct intervention by a regulator to dictate the precise scheduling of a programme, even an institution such as *News at Ten*, looks increasingly inappropriate', Sir Robin told a press conference. From March 1999 the main ITV news would be at 6.30pm, with only headlines at 10pm, followed by a new 20-minute programme from Independent Television News (ITN) at 11pm.

Although the ITC insisted that the permission was being given on condition that there would be no reduction in the funding, range and quality of news on ITV, commission chief executive Peter Rogers admitted that 'the genie could not be put back in the bottle'. There would be no return for *News at Ten*. The decision was denounced as 'a grave mistake' by former Prime Minister John Major, whose successor, Tony Blair, made it clear that he would have preferred *News at Ten* to have stayed where it was. Critics argued that the still profitable ITV companies should not, so easily, have been allowed to escape their obligations to provide news at the heart of the evening schedule.

Ironically, a week later the ITC itself made 11 of the ITV companies even richer when it agreed, as part of a re-licensing process, to cut the amount they paid to government by around £75 million a year. The ITV companies argued successfully, however, that unless *News at Ten* was moved they could not modernize their schedule between 9pm and 11pm and show uninterrupted films and more adult drama in the face of ever-increasing competition. They had been suffering a serious loss of audience, particularly among young viewers, and in January the new ITV chief executive, Richard Eyre, had promised a counter-attack. He even took the risk of setting public targets—that ITV would get back to a 38 per cent audience share in 1999 and to 40 per cent in the year 2000. As 1998 ended, the first target looked like being narrowly achieved; but the 2000 target was a much taller order.

Pressure to increase audiences was also blamed for radical changes to the BBC Radio 4 schedule introduced on 1 April by new controller James Boyle. Established programmes such as *On Your Farm*, *Medium Wave* and *Break Away* were ended, and many others were moved. The morning farming programme was switched to 5.30am and the *Today* news and current affairs programme extended so that it began at 6am. More controversially, the *Today in Parliament* segment of *Today* was moved to long wave (and given a longer slot), at the inevitable cost of lower audiences. Betty Boothroyd, the Speaker of the House of Commons, was among those who expressed disquiet, although the BBC said that the change would be reviewed in 12 months. Overall, the modernization of the Radio 4 schedule sparked a large number of complaints from its notoriously conservative audience, and an initial loss of listening. By year-end, however, the figures had recovered, and just under 8 million people were listening to the channel for more than 11 hours a week.

Concerns were also expressed that a worldwide alliance signed in March by the BBC with Discovery Communications of the US, a commercial broadcaster which specialized in factual programming, would over time change the nature of the BBC. As part of the deal the BBC got, at no investment cost, a 50 per cent stake in all new Discovery channels outside the USA, including Animal Planet, and a 20 per cent stake in Animal Planet in the USA. Sir John Birt, the BBC director-general, who announced during the year that he planned to step down at the end of his current contract in April 2000, insisted that the BBC's programme commissioning policy would not be influenced by the demands of Discovery.

The biggest concern of all was about the quality of documentaries—quite apart from surge of 'docu-soaps'—and whether viewers could believe what they saw on their screens any more. The most notorious example concerned *The Connection*, a hard-hitting documentary made for Carlton Television which purported to tell the story of a Colombian cartel planning to open up a new drug route into the UK. An investigation by *The Guardian* newspaper, later confirmed by Carlton itself, claimed that many sequences in the programme were not true and that viewers had been misled. In December the ITC fined Carlton an unprecedented £2 million and warned that the company's broadcasting licence would be shortened if anything like it ever happened again.

If it had been only one rogue programme, then *The Connection* affair, however dramatic, would have quickly been forgotten. Unfortunately, however, there was growing evidence that a number of producers were at best naive and sometimes downright misleading in the battle to get the dramatic pictures they wanted. The BBC admitted that some scenes in *Driving School* (see AR 1997, p. 504) were not what they had seemed to be. In September a Channel 4 documentary about a 'father' and daughter called *Daddy's Girl* was withdrawn from the schedules at the last minute when the man was found to be the woman's boyfriend. In November a researcher on *Much Too Young: Chickens*, a Channel 4 documentary about Glasgow rent boys, said that 'clients' of the boys negotiating for sex were actually researchers on the programme or their friends.

On more orthodox ground, the biggest television event of the year was the World Cup football finals in France (see Pt XVI). Although the total audience did not reach the 31 million who watched the funeral of Princess Diana in 1997, the final was watched by 15.6 million people on BBC1 and 6.6 million on ITV. The whole issue of sports coverage became progressively difficult for the BBC during the year. Not only was 1998 the last year in which the corporation covered the FA Cup Final (having been outbid by ITV), but the BBC also surprisingly lost Test Match cricket to Channel 4.

The Secretary for Culture, Media and Sport, Chris Smith, did make efforts to ensure that the main sporting events that helped to unite the nation would remain on terrestrial television. First he set up a task force under the chairmanship of Lord Gordon, the Scottish commercial broadcaster, and then went further than its recommendations in strengthening the 'listed' events preserved for terrestrial television. Not only did he protect all the finals of the World Cup, but he also included the qualifying matches of the home nations, although some Test cricket was released for subscription television.

Increasingly, television sports rights were a major commercial and legal battle-ground. By December football's Premier League and the Office of

Fair Trading were limbering up for a four-month case before the Restrictive Practices Court on whether the League's collective rights deal with British Sky Broadcasting (BSkyB) was an illegal cartel or not. If the court overturned the agreement and decided that each club should negotiate its television rights separately, not only would BSkyB lose its all-important exclusive Premier League coverage, but the BBC's *Match of the Day* (taking match highlights from BSkyB) would be impossible to produce. It was because of such threats that Rupert Murdoch authorized BSkyB to make a £623 million bid for Manchester United—a deal that was sent for investigation to the Monopolies and Mergers Commission.

Against such a wide range of uncertainties, at least Mr Smith was able to provide some certainties for the BBC. At a Royal Television Society conference in October he endorsed the BBC's role as a public service broadcaster and said that the principle of the licence fee was not in question until at least 2006, when the corporation's present Royal Charter expired. 'Though an imperfect funding mechanism, the licence remains, for the foreseeable future the best means to provide the BBC with sufficient security to continue to meet its obligations to all its audiences', Mr Smith said. He promised to set up a committee to see how the BBC could earn more private funds without endangering its main role and to look at reforming the system of concessionary licences for the elderly.

In July Mr Smith also produced, in conjunction with the Department of Trade and Industry, a Green Paper, *Regulating Communications— Approaching Convergence in the Communications Age*. The document took a pragmatic approach and ruled out any sudden move to a single regulatory body covering all communications media. It was equally cautious about setting a switch-off date for existing analogue broadcasting. The prize was to move the entire population on to digital television and then auction off the old analogue frequencies for the billions that mobile communications operators would pay. Manufacturers of digital equipment wanted the government set a cut-off date in ten years but Mr Smith refused to set a date until he could see how quickly the country took to digital television, and in particular digital terrestrial television, which would be at the heart of such a transition. The ITC believed that it might be 20 years before everyone had made the move to digital.

However, after all the hype and delays, digital television did finally arrive in the UK. BSkyB came first with the launch of SkyDigital on 1 October. It was not exactly the 'up to 200 channels' promised, but it did offer unprecedented choice. There were no fewer than ten news and documentary channels, including Discovery and Animal Planet, whose slogan was 'all of the animals all of the time'. The total number of channels was actually 140 and that included 40 channels of digital music plus 48 channels devoted to the latest movies on a pay-per-view basis.

OnDigital, the commercial digital terrestrial service which was broadcast from ordinary transmitters and required neither satellite dish nor cable connection, launched its 16-channel service with a ceremony at London's Crystal Palace on 15 November. The line-up included ITV 2, a new service only available on terrestrial and cable. Meanwhile, the BBC launched BBC Choice, a new channel which offered another chance to see some of the week's best programmes as well as taking viewers behind the scenes of major programmes. BBC Choice and BBC News 24, also launched in digital, were both paid for by the licence fee, as were BBC Online (the corporation's Internet service) and the Learning Channel, planned for spring 1999. By the turn of the year it was too early to tell how successful the new services were proving to be in attracting viewers, but BSkyB said that it had easily reached its end-of-year target of more than 200,000 digital satellite subscribers.

After a further series of mergers there were really only three large surviving cable companies, Telewest, NTL and Cable & Wireless Communications. They said that they would introduce their digital services in 1999, including interactive services such as home shopping and home banking as well as fast Internet access. After years in the doldrums, the cable companies started to market their wares better, helped by an ITC decision that customers should not be forced to pay for packages of basic channels they did not want in order to be able to buy premium channels such as sport and movies. Telewest, for instance, had growing success with its 'millennium package'—14 channels and a telephone line, all for £12.99 a month.

Notwithstanding the controversy over Radio 4, BBC Radio had a good year, narrowing the gap with the commercial sector despite the launch of new commercial stations. Radio 5 Live continued to attract new listeners, and in the battle with Chris Evans, in his first year in charge of Virgin Radio, Zoe Ball emerged victorious. In the final quarter of the year, her first in sole charge of the Radio 1 *Breakfast Show*, Ms Ball added 500,000 new listeners, to take the total audience to 5.5 million.

Kelvin MacKenzie, equally colourful as managing director of Mirror Television in charge of Live TV as he had been as editor of *The Sun* newspaper, decided to take his talents to radio. He led a consortium which took control of Talk Radio, the national commercial speech station. The usual sackings associated with Mr MacKenzie ensued. Financially, commercial radio continued to forge ahead, and in 1998, excluding local classified advertisements, had advertisement revenue of £426 million, an increase of 18.6 per cent on the previous year.

The final irony for a year that once promised 200 channels or more was the fact that some channels did not manage to survive. Channel One, which was backed by the financial muscle of Associated Newspapers (publishers of the *Daily Mail*) and had promised to be the London equivalent of Channel One in Manhattan, was virtually closed down, leaving only a rudimentary service. And Britain, a country allegedly obsessed like no other with the weather, could not support the Weather Channel, which collapsed during the summer.

2. VISUAL ARTS—ARCHITECTURE

i. VISUAL ARTS

It was a year for major artistic commissions in Britain, a country not accustomed since Victorian times to official monuments save those of a martial nature. The long-delayed opening of the new British Library building at St Pancras brought with it several important works of public art. Visually dominating the vast lobby of Sir Colin St John Wilson's building was a tapestry based on a 1970s painting by R.B. Kitaj, *If Not Not*, a jumbled and ethereal dreamscape inspired both by T.S. Eliot's poem, *The Wasteland*, and by the Holocaust, a conflation typical of the imagination of this artist of suitably bookish reputation. His wall-hanging was the largest single loom tapestry to have been woven in the twentieth century, and reportedly required 7,000 hours of work. It was made in Edinburgh, where the original painting was in the collection of the Scottish National Gallery of Modern Art. Other important works at the library complex were Sir Eduardo Paolozzi's sculptural transcription of William Blake's portrait of Sir Isaac Newton which presided over the impressive forecourt, and artist Tom Phillips's text-based open-latticed gates.

The plans for the controversial Millennium Dome for the year 2000, at Greenwich in London, were unveiled in 1998 and included a proposed androgynous figure, larger than New York's Statue of Liberty, which would dominate the 'Body Zone', one of 12 mammoth pavilions housed within the Dome. The statue would feature an observation platform within its head and was to be covered, head to foot, by one million photographs of children. It was not to be designed by an artist, and thus promised to be a curiosity rather than a work of art. However, by coincidence, just as these plans were being discussed, a sculpture by Anthony Gormley, his *Angel of the North*, was erected at a motorway site at Gateshead in the north of England. This commission succeeded in gaining world attention as much for its impressive structural and financial statistics as for its aesthetic merit: at 65 ft in height, 200 tons in weight, and with a wingspan about that of a Jumbo jet (175 ft), *Angel* was one of the world's largest public works of art, and cost £800,000. Its instigators reckoned that 33 million people a year would see it, most of them motorists able to afford the piece a momentary glance.

By another neat coincidence, as if gently mocking these various schemes, the Russian artists Ilya and Emilia Kabakov staged an exhibition in London entitled 'Palace of Projects', conceived as a satire of utopianism. Their installation—brought about by the aptly named Artangel, the agency which had been responsible for Rachel Whiteread's 1993 *House*—actually took place in a dome: the Round House in Chalk Farm, north London. The work consisted of a mass of invented projects of Gogol-like absurdity, each assigned to a fictional Russian character, presented as clumsy models with pompous accompanying texts in a spiral structure resembling Breughel's *Tower of Babel* (or Tatlin's *Monument to the Third International*).

Following the successes and controversies of the previous year's 'Sensation' exhibition at the Royal Academy of Arts (see AR 1997, pp. 510–1), which transformed that institution's previous deficit into a surplus, London continued to bask in an internationally-perceived artistic buoyancy. The most emphasis was on the young neo-conceptual artists featured in the 'Sensation' exhibition, which had been drawn from the Saatchi Collection. Charles Saatchi held a sale of 800 works by young British artists for the benefit of student bursaries at four of the capital's art schools. The sale, managed by Christies, established significant prices for many of the artists represented in his collection. Among them was Damien Hirst, whose celebrity continued to grow in 1998 as he opened what became a highly fashionable restaurant in west London. This venue was called 'Pharmacy' and featured, among its decorations, medicine cabinets filled with pharmaceutical products and pill-motif wall-papers. After being sued by the Royal Pharmaceutical Society on the basis that the establishment would deceive the public, the management reluctantly changed the name to 'Achy Ramp', an anagram of pharmacy.

A significant new gallery opened in north London to show the Estorick Collection of Italian modern art, which had particularly rich holdings in the Futurist movement. The Tate Gallery received a gift of 56 British and American works, mostly of the 1980s and 1990s, from the collector Janet de Botton, reckoned to be worth over £2 million, and destined for the Tate Gallery of Modern Art at Bankside, which was to open in 2000. While building works continued apace inside the former power station which was to house that museum, a series of avant-garde films were projected onto one of its outer walls in giant size. In a similar spirit, the National Gallery celebrated its acquisition of Stubbs's horse-portrait, *Whistlejacket*, which had been on loan to them for some while, by projecting the image onto the side of its Sainsbury wing overlooking Trafalgar Square. The painting itself was sent on a national tour. While these schemes brought work into visibility for people who might not otherwise have a chance to see them, an important series of mural paintings by Goya became visible, in Spain, to a constituency previously denied sight of them. Since they were housed in a monastery in northern Spain, the frescoes had not previously been seen by a woman.

One of the principal exhibitions for 1998 was the Bonnard retrospective at the Tate Gallery, which also visited the Museum of Modern Art in New York and offered a fresh perspective on this artist by focusing on his twentieth-century achievements. At the end of the year a major Jackson Pollock exhibition was similarly shared between the two institutions, this time starting at the Modern. Also at the Tate were the Patrick Heron retrospective and a display of new works by Lucian Freud. Heron received his due recognition as an abstract painter of subtlety and distinction with this show. A Freud group portrait of the 1980s, meanwhile, achieved a staggering price at auction in New York, fetching the equivalent of over £5.8 million. The highest price paid for a work at auction in 1998—a generally buoyant year in all markets—was the US$70.1 million paid for a Van Gogh self-portrait.

Anthony Caro's sculptural transcriptions of old master paintings were the subject of an exhibition at the National Gallery. His was the first exhibition by a sculptor at the National, a gallery traditionally committed to painting. Since all of the works which Caro had previously translated into three-dimensional form belonged to other collections, he made three pieces after a Van Gogh chair belonging to the National. The year marked the centenary of Caro's one-time mentor, Henry Moore, a travelling retrospective of whose work drew record attendances in South America. Other major shows abroad included a reconsideration of the late work of Delacroix, staged in Paris and Philadelphia.

An extraordinary new museum, dubbed 'the Louvre of Las Vegas', opened in the Nevada gambling town, featuring $300 million worth of masterpieces, all assembled within the last few years, and set within the world's most lavish casino, the Bellagio. The impresario behind this collection, Stephen Wynn, had acquired works at twice the rate of the notoriously fast-spending Getty Museum. Meanwhile, outside the real Louvre, in Paris, modern and contemporary sculptures were sited in the Tuilleries gardens, a move instigated by the New York-based French sculptor Alain Kirili.

In Amsterdam a painting by the abstract expressionist Barnett Newman, *Cathedral*, was slashed at the Stedelijk Museum by the same vandal who, 11 years previously, had attacked *Who's Afraid of Red, Yellow and Blue* by the same artist, a crime for which he had served just five months in prison. He told police after the 1998 incident that he had been attempting to 'restore' his handiwork to the restored earlier picture, but had found that it was not on view.

The art world continued to be haunted by the shameful looting and robbery carried out during World War II. The movement to repatriate works taken by Stalin's armies from German museums at the end of the war received a blow when the Russian Duma obliged President Yeltsin to sign legislation making restitution virtually impossible. There were several high-profile instances around the world of heirs of Holocaust victims claiming pillaged artworks. During the exhibition of Egon Schiele at the Museum of Modern Art, New York, two separate claims were issued on pieces from the Rudolf Leopold Collection, Vienna, which were allegedly stolen from Austrian Jewish collectors during the Nazi period. Families had requested of MoMA director Glenn Lowry that the pictures be held once the show concluded, but they were told that the museum was under contractual obligation to send the works to the next exhibition venue. A subpoena was then served by the Manhattan district attorney, and the works were seized during the run of the exhibition. This had the predicted side-effect, from the museum's point of view, of frightening future lenders to exhibitions who were worried by the shaky provenance of their holdings: three works promised to the MoMA for the Bonnard retrospective were withheld by European private collectors. A task-force of American museums looking into the issue of claims from victims and their heirs was established under the leadership of Phillipe de Montebello, director of the Metropolitan Museum of Art, and expressed its commitment to treating all claims fairly and honorably. Other claims were made concerning Braque paintings in the collection of the Pompidou Centre in Paris and a Matisse in the Seattle Art Museum.

Unrelated to the moral issues of war, but equally worrying to curators, was an incident in Fort Worth, Texas, where important works by the living artist Robert Rauschenberg were seized from a museum retrospective by sheriffs pursuing a claim from an aggrieved business associate of the artist. The matter was later settled between the parties.

Rauschenberg, meanwhile, was among the winners of the 1998 Praemium Imperiale awarded by the Japanese government; the sculptor Dan Karavan and the architect Alvaro Siza were also recipients. The Kyoto Prize, worth $350,000, went to pioneer video sculptor Nam June Paik, while the second Hugo Boss Prize, awarded through the Guggenheim Museum, went to British artist Douglas Gordon, who also worked with film. Gordon had won the Turner Prize in 1996 (see AR 1996, p. 488). The 1998 Turner Prize was awarded to Chris Ofili, whose primitive-charged, multi-coloured paintings exploring issues of black cultural identity incorporated elephant dung. The artists short-listed for the Turner, Tacita Dean, Cathy de Monchaux and Sam Taylor-Wood, featured in an exhibition at the Tate Gallery, which administered the prize. Ofili was also short-listed for the Jerwood Prize for Painting, which was awarded to Madalena Strindberg.

Among those who died in 1998 were Victor Pasmore, British painter; César, French sculptor; Beatrice Wood, American ceramist; Ilse Bing, photographer; Wolf Vostell, of the German conceptual art movement 'fluxus'; Milton Brown, art historian; David Bourdon, art critic; Jean-François Lyotard, aesthetician; Eric Orr, sculptor; Jean Lipman, curator and collector; Dieter Roth, conceptual artist; Mario Schifano, Italian painter; and Federico Zeri, Italian art critic. (For Pasmore, Wood and Zeri, see Pt XVIII: Obituary.) Three influential art dealers, Richard Bellany, Harry Lunn and Frank Lloyd, also died.

ii. ARCHITECTURE

THE year in architecture was marked by the drive for new parliament buildings—representing new national identities—in Scotland and Wales, as the 'New Labour' government aimed to realise its promises of political devolution (see II.1.ii; II.1.iii).

In Scotland, initially it was a case of deciding which city should hold the seat of power and then, when Edinburgh had been picked, where in the city it should be sited and how the design should be procured. The end-result was Holyrood, and an architectural competition for the site followed. This was won by the Catalan architect Enric Miralles (with the Scottish office of RMJM), who proposed a £50 million scheme reminiscent of a series of 'upturned boats' in the richly historic environment. In Wales the Richard Rogers Partnership emerged triumphant, after more inter-city squabbling over who should get the building. Rogers' £10 million scheme, themed around transparency and openness, was to be built in the Cardiff Bay area, alongside a 'Wales Millennium Centre' proposed by the Percy Thomas Partnership. This was the site of the abortive Cardiff Bay Opera House designed by Zaha Hadid but rejected by the Millennium Commission in 1995 (see AR 1995, p. 499; 1996, p. 492). The Percy Thomas designs, by Jonathan Adams, featured a gently undulating roof pierced by conical cooling towers for the assembly chamber below.

In London, the open competition route was controversially eschewed as a method of procurement for creating a headquarters for the capital's planned new mayor and elected assembly (see II.1.i). Instead, the government invited developers and architects to make proposals for different sites and buildings. A shortlist was whittled down to two—a site next to Tower Bridge called London Bridge City, with 'new-build' designs by Foster and Partners, and Victoria House in Bloomsbury, a bold Will Alsop-designed amendment to a neo-classical pile. Foster emerged triumphant.

The minister responsible for London, Nick Raynsford, made it clear that the process by which he had decided in favour of the Tower Bridge site was in line with the 'Rethinking Construction' Egan report, published during the year. Sir John Egan, chief executive of the British Airports Authority, chaired the committee which produced the report, outlining strategies for efficiency and cost-savings through standardization of components and repeat delivery. Architects felt marginalized by the report, which was seen in some quarters to give more power to the elbow of the contractor at the expense of design.

Faced with the problems of meeting requirements for 4.4 million new homes by 2016, the government turned to Lord (Richard) Rogers of Riverside. He was chosen to head a new Urban Task Force, which set itself the agenda of trying to repopularize the notion of living in the city, to increase housing densities and to encourage development on so-called 'brownfield sites' (i.e. previously-developed land). Meanwhile, Deputy Prime Minister John Prescott threw his weight behind a push for an 'integrated transport strategy'.

Elsewhere in government, a reshuffle ended Arts Minister Mark Fisher's term in office, with little to show for his work on architectural issues. Hopes were voiced that his replacement, former Conservative MP Alan Howarth, would fare better in the role. Mr Howarth, a minister in the Department of Culture, Media and Sport, proposed the abolition of the Royal Fine Art Commission and its replacement by a new Architecture Commission headed by a 'champion' of architecture. Plans for the new commission suggested that it would come into existence by the end of 1999.

Much of the year's media interest continued to focus on the Millennium Dome at Greenwich, designed by the Richard Rogers Partnership. With the millennium approaching, the New Millennium Experience Company finally unveiled some of the contents, with separate zones designed by different architects and sponsored by companies including BT, Boots and GEC. Architects inside included Zaha Hadid (the Mind Zone) and Eva Jiricna and Jasper Jacobs' Spirit Zone, which struggled to find both a sponsor and agreement about content among religious leaders. Branson Coates designed the exhibit with perhaps the most column-inches ascribed to it, the Body Zone—a huge two-headed figure which had metamorphosed from a single millennium figure to boast the curvature of both genders.

Branson Coates was in demand elsewhere as architects representative of popular culture. The government commissioned the practice to create 'Powerhouse UK'—a series of four exhibition 'pods' showing off the products of 'Cool Britannia', sited on Horse Guards' Parade. In May G-8 summit leaders were shown around the celebration of British ingenuity and design, a mini-Dome all by itself. Branson Coates was on similar ground in Sheffield, where it completed its Lottery-backed Centre for Popular Music. Again it was an exhibition space in four huge metallic 'pods' like drums, but conceived of before its London relation.

Adventurous design in the shape of a bold deconstructivist proposal for the Victoria and Albert Museum by Daniel Libeskind was unexpectedly approved by Kensington & Chelsea's planning committee, even though planning officials had recommended refusal. The architectural community rejoiced at the decision, talked excitedly about London's version of Frank Gehry's Guggenheim Museum in Bilbao and hoped that funding would materialize. Further details of the Libeskind 'spiral' scheme were awaited with eagerness.

Ian Ritchie's scheme for a great glass multiplex complex on the site of the former Crystal Palace in south London received planning consent, despite great local controversy which resulted in campaigners taking the decision all the way to the High Court over issues of 'style'—but they lost. Other busy practices included Nicholas Grimshaw & Partners, which unveiled its Millennium Point project in Birmingham and finalized its designs for the huge Millennium-funded environmental 'biome Eden' project in Cornwall.

Sir Norman Foster's conquest of major projects in the UK continued apace, with his 'World Squares for All' project getting approval from Westminster council. The plan envisaged the pedestrianization of the south side of Parliament Square and the north side of Trafalgar Square, creating public squares and new routes, symbolizing the increased attention being given to pedestrians in the capital. The Foster practice was also a major prize winner, scooping the RIBA's Stirling Prize for its Duxford Air Museum. The same building shared joint top prize with Sidell Gibson and Donald Insall's Windsor Castle restoration, in the Royal Fine Art Commission's 'building of the year' award. Foster also opened the doors, and runways, on another air-related project, the mammoth £12,000 million Chek Lap Kok airport in Hong Kong, the world's biggest building project for many years (see also IX.2.ii). Closer to home, Niels Torp's spacious and civilized headquarters for British Airways opened to acclaim at Heathrow, and there were similar plaudits for Benson and Forsyth's Museum of Scotland and Colin St John Wilson's British Library. Wilson was duly made a knight after the epic struggle to complete a project which took three decades.

Pimlico School, completed in the 1970s, became the subject of furious controversy following a proposal by Westminster council to demolish it and replace it with a new school and a private housing development. A competition was held under the aegis of Home Secretary Jack Straw, chairman of the governors. He was keen to make the project work as an example of how private finance could be used to underwrite education projects around the country and thus reduce the cost to the Treasury. Protests continued.

The redevelopment proposal for Paternoster Square, next to St Paul's Cathedral, to a master-plan by Whitfield Partners, was finally given planning approval, marking an end to a long saga. Elsewhere in London, the South Bank arts complex found a new chairman in property tycoon Elliott Bernard, brought in to oversee Richard Rogers' scheme for a glass-wave roof over much of the site; but he ended up scrapping it because of a shortage of Lottery funds to finance the project. English Heritage moved to settle another long-running controversy by proposing a new plan for Stonehenge, including a new visitor centre and approach to the stones.

The London-based Architecture Foundation embarked on a series of road-shows in London boroughs with the aim of introducing architects to problem sites and the public in a bid to improve local environments. The RIBA started to feel the effects of the newly-formed Architects' Registration Board, with which it battled over a new code of conduct and the board's control of architectural education.

Losses to the profession in 1998 included Peter Moro, co-designer of the Royal Festival Hall; the concrete engineer Felix Candela; Ove Arup research head Steven Groak; David Green of Taylor & Green, exponent of rural housing; Modernist conservation champion Christopher Dean; and 45-year-old Benoît Cornette of the French practice Decq and Cornette, killed in a car crash.

The Royal Gold Medal was awarded to the nonagenarian Brazilian Oscar Niemeyer, creator of Brasilia. The Pritzker Prize went to the Italian Renzo Piano, and the landscape architect Kathryn Gustafson was the inaugural winner of the Jane Drew Prize. The largest architectural prize in monetary terms, the £130,000 Carlsberg award, went to the Swiss architect Peter Zumthor.

3. LITERATURE

ONE name dominated the British and to some extent the world literary scene in 1998: that of Ted Hughes (see XVIII: Obituary). Poet Laureate since the death of John Betjeman in 1984, Hughes himself died in the course of an extraordinary couple of years during which he won virtually every literary prize in his own country for which he was eligible and was honoured with the Order of Merit. Some of these awards were posthumous, such as the Forward and T.S. Eliot Prizes; another spanned the periods both before and after his death, because he became the first writer to win the overall Whitbread Prize twice running. He was regarded as once more writing at the peak of his powers, being honoured with these prizes both for *Birthday Letters* and for *Tales from Ovid*. The first of these was an extraordinarily vivid and ultimately anguished sequence of poems, written over 25 years, in which Hughes assessed his first marriage, which was to the American poet Sylvia Plath, who had committed suicide in 1963. Its publication astonished the normally knowing literary public and the book was well on course by the end of the year to becoming in Britain the best-selling volume of poetry published in the twentieth century. Hughes's death left a gaping hole in the literary life of the country. He was regarded as an outstandingly successful Laureate, who had helped to redefine its role in relation to the state. No obvious heir was waiting in the wings, though one or two poets conspicuously positioned themselves within reach of the limelight in the evident hope that they would be called to the centre of the stage.

In world terms there were the deaths of other poets of equal prominence, notably Zbigniew Herbert from Poland, Miroslav Holub from the Czech Republic, Nizar Kabbani from Syria and the Nobel Prize winner Octavio Paz from Mexico. Scottish writing, so denuded in recent years of its doyens, unexpectedly lost Iain Crichton Smith, who wrote in Gaelic as well as in English. The great Danish writer Henrik Stangerup died, as did two notable examiners of sexuality, both from France: Dominique Aury, creator of the erotic classic *The Story of O*, and Julien Green. Among other authors who died in 1998 were Attia Hosain from India and the American journalist and critic Martha Gellhorn. Some of the most commercially successful writers in the world also departed, including Dame Catherine Cookson, who for years had been by far the most bought and borrowed novelist in the United Kingdom, Francis Durbridge, Hammond Innes and Wolf Mankowitz. (For Cookson, Gellhorn, Hughes and Paz, see XVIII: Obituary.)

XV.3. LITERATURE

The end of a century was a time for taking stock, but so intent were readers on peering into the next millennium that some notable centenaries were almost overlooked. Very little fuss was made of Brecht's and Lorca's, for example. It was, however, the year in which a particular day, 23 April (Shakespeare's birthday), was designated World Book Day. In Britain every child was given a one-pound book token on this day, in order to encourage the habit of book-buying, and from October there was a Year of Reading in full swing.

The Nobel Prize for Literature went to the Portuguese novelist José Saramago. This was a virtuous and overdue choice, though sadly in all the coverage of the event it seemed that no-one remembered the work of the late Giovanni Pontiero in so assiduously translating Saramago's books into English so that readers could, without delay, assess for themselves the merits of this distinguished writer.

In Britain there was little excitement attached to those prizes which were not awarded to Ted Hughes. The Booker Prize for fiction had a sentimental favourite, Beryl Bainbridge, who was shortlisted for the fifth time, but it went instead to the also frequently-tipped Ian McEwan, for his brief novel *Amsterdam*. This was the 30th anniversary of the Booker Prize and there were public readings at the new British Library by way of celebration. The Stakis Prize for Scottish Writer of the Year was shared between James Kelman and Edwin Morgan, two brilliant writers both at the peak of their powers. The Orange Prize, which was reserved for female writers, went to the Canadian novelist Carol Shields.

The International IMPAC Dublin Literary Award—the Nobel Prize apart, monetarily the largest literary prize of all—went to the Romanian author Herta Muller, for *The Land of Green Plums*, written in German and translated into English by Michael Hofmann. The Commonwealth Writers' Prize was awarded to Peter Carey for *Jack Maggs*, a book inspired by Dickens's *Great Expectations*.

There were the usual storms in literary tea-cups of a kind which filled the headlines for a day or two before being largely forgotten. Media magnate Rupert Murdoch's refusal to publish Chris Patten's account of his period as the last governor of Hong Kong was one such, motivated, it was assumed, by Murdoch's desire to expand his news empire into mainland China and therefore not to give offence to that vast nation. Another *petite scandale* was a much-publicized family row surrounding Hanif Kureishi's unsympathetic depiction of his father in his novel, *Intimacy*. A third was Paul Theroux's deconstruction in *Sir Vidia's Shadow* of his personal and professional relationship with V.S. Naipaul, which was regarded as entering new realms of poor taste.

Overshadowing all these matters was the publication in the United States, in printed form but significantly too on the Internet, of the Starr Report—the document which led to the impeachment of President Clinton (see IV.1; XIII.2; XVII.4). Though hardly a work of literature, it was undoubtedly the most talked-about publication of the year and potentially the most historic. It was thought that its influence would extend beyond the political domain because it put into common currency sexual language which had previously belonged mainly to the realm of pornography and which now became the stuff of daily comment on television screens and newspaper front pages all round the world.

Threshholds were crossed—or proprieties transgressed if one took a morally condemning view of them—by several publications during the year. Paul Theroux's book on V.S. Naipaul was one example, but of greater consequence was Gitta Sereny's *Cries Unheard*, her account of the life of Mary Bell, who as a child had murdered younger children. Ms Sereny was considered by many to have betrayed the trust which Mary Bell had placed in her by exposing this now adult woman to insatiable public curiosity. Fundamental ethical and moral attitudes were debated as a consequence of the book. Marina Warner, in a far more scrupulous work, enticingly called *No Go the Bogeyman: Scaring, Lulling and Making Mock*, explored some of the same subliminal territory (or 'terrortry', as one critic termed it) as Ms Sereny, but her examples were manifold and her authorial position was sounder.

The other big discussion sparked by the world of books concerned the nature of Englishness. Devolved political authority was planned for Northern Ireland, Scotland and Wales, resulting partly from the cultural regeneration evident in those places over at least the past ten years (see II.1.ii; II.1.iii; II.1.iv). At last there was a sense of England catching up, with a number of well-received books exploring the nature of the English personality. Julian Barnes and Jeremy Paxman were leading contributors to this debate, with *The Oxford Book of English Short Stories*, edited by A.S. Byatt, ushering it in with her pointedly rigorous limiting of her selection to tales told by writers from England, as opposed to others from different parts of the United Kingdom.

With 100,000 books published in Britain alone, and with growing publishing industries in the United States and India, there seemed to be little serious challenge to traditional modes of publishing coming forth from the worldwide web or from digitalized technology. There were signs of change in other parts of the book industry, however. This was the first year in which book-purchasing through the Internet outstripped buying by mail order or across the counter. Publications on the Internet were for the first time allowed to be considered as proper entrants to major literary prizes. Discussion groups on the web became more common than ever before, allowing, for example, reading circles with memberships around the world to share views about books. Self-publication was rapidly becoming legitimized, with a novel by David Caute, *Fatima's Scarf*, which had been turned down by conventional publishers, becoming one of the most admired works of fiction in the year.

It was an impressive year for fiction as a whole. Several of the great international names produced good new work, among them J.P. Donleavy, Nadine Gordimer, Milan Kundera, Toni Morrison, Philip Roth, John Updike and Alice Walker. In Britain Beryl Bainbridge's *Master Georgie*, set at the time of the Crimean War, continued her greatly-admired series of historical reconstructions. There was a small revival of the short story, with A.S. Byatt's *Elementals* considered to be among her best work. George Mackay Brown was the author of a notable collection published posthumously, and Alice Munro once again showed herself to be the consummate artist of this most difficult genre. Among new novelists Giles Foden made a slightly controversial stir with *The Last King of Scotland*, in which the demonized former Ugandan dictator Idi Amin was almost sympathetically realized. Kiran Desai and Jackie Kay were first-time novelists whose work was very warmly greeted.

Ted Hughes so dominated the world of poetry that it was hard for anyone else to be noticed in what was nevertheless a busy year. Two great veteran poets, Allen Curnow and D.J. Enright, had new *Collected Poems* published, both spanning work of 50 years or more. Séamus Heaney published his first book since winning the Nobel Prize in 1995. Towards the end of the year the poetry world in Britain found itself up-in-arms over the unanticipated withdrawal of the Oxford University Press from the publication of contemporary poetry, the most significant publisher's withdrawal of support for poetry of the several which had happened in recent years.

Among the rest of the year's publications there were some long-awaited autobiographies. Edward Heath's *The Course of My Life* was well-written, which in itself surprised a lot of reviewers sceptical of the literary skills of politicians. There were outstanding biographies of Isaiah Berlin (by Michael Ignatieff), Samuel Taylor Coleridge (by Richard Holmes), Thomas More (by Peter Ackroyd) and Henri Matisse (by Hilary Spurling), as well as moving personal memoirs from the actors Keith Baxter and Felicity Kendal and the poet-editor Alan Ross. The memoir that earned the most publicity, mixing plaudits with some opprobrium, was John Bayley's *Iris*, in which he depicted the failing mental condition of his famous wife, the novelist Dame Iris Murdoch.

Curiously, the year also saw the 'completion' of a 'new' detective novel by Dorothy L. Sayers (who died in 1957), *Thrones, Dominations*, in which Jill Paton Walsh brought to fruition an abandoned manuscript. Charles Osborne wrote a 'new' Agatha Christie thriller by converting into novel form her play *Black Coffee*. Perhaps the grandest literary achievement of the year was the publication in 20 volumes of the complete works of George Orwell, edited by Peter Davison.

Several books were published for the first time which had been written a long time ago. Most important of these was Mary Shelley's *Maurice, or The Fisher's Cot*, a lost story now edited by Claire Tomalin. The title was reminiscent of E.M. Forster's posthumously-published novel *Maurice* (1971); and Forster made another belated appearance with *The Prince's*

Tale and Other Uncollected Writing. Two plays by Joe Orton were discovered, *Fred and Madge* and *The Visitors*, as well as a novella by him called *Between Us Girls*. There was also, in the year of the blockbuster film *Titanic* (see XV.1.v), the intriguing memoir of Violet Jessop, a survivor of the famous sinking, whose memories of the event had remained unseen since they were written in 1934.

Great attention was paid to the apparent lifting of the restrictions on Salman Rushdie, imposed as a consequence of the Iranian *fatweh* in 1989 (see AR 1989, pp. 428-9, 493-4). Sadly the jubilation proved short-lived, and by the end of the year Rushdie was as closely-protected as ever. While millennial momentum built up throughout much of the world, many writers, among whom Rushdie was only one, continued to be hounded by governments in ways which seemed positively medieval. Though the Nobel Prize laureate of 1986, Wole Soyinka, was able to return to Nigeria (see VI.2.ii), where there were some tentative improvements in the political conditions, it was evident that the lives of writers in many nations, notably in Myanmar (Burma), China and Kenya, were as circumscribed as ever.

Among the leading titles published in 1998 were the following:

FICTION. Antoni, Robert, *Blessed is the Fruit* (Faber); Ashworth, Andrea, *Once in a House on Fire* (Picador); Bainbridge, Beryl, *Master Georgie* (Duckworth); Baker, Nicholson, *The Everlasting Story of Nory* (Chatto); Barker, Nicola, *Wide Open* (Faber); Barker, Pat, *Another World* (Viking); Barnes, Julian, *England, England* (Cape); Barry, Sebastian, *The Whereabouts of Eneas McNulty* (Picador); Beaven, Derek, *Acts of Mutiny* (Fourth Estate); Booth, Martin, *The Industry of Souls* (Dewi Lewis); Boyd, William, *Armadillo* (Hamish Hamilton); Boyd, William, *Nat Tate: An American Artist 1928-1960* (21 Publishing); Boyle, T. Coraghesan, *Riven Rock* (Bloomsbury); Brookner, Anita, *Falling Slowly* (Viking); Brown, George Mackay, *The Island of the Woman and Other Stories* (John Murray); Byatt, A.S., *Elementals* (Chatto & Windus); Carr, Rocky, *Brixton Bwoy* (Fourth Estate); Cartwright, Justin, *Leading the Cheers* (Sceptre); Caute, David, *Fatima's Scarf* (Totterdown); Chandra, Vikram, *Love and Longing in Bombay* (Faber); Chaudhuri, Amit, *Freedom Song* (Picador); Coupland, Douglas, *Girlfriend in a Coma* (Flamingo); Darling, Julia, *Crocodile Soup* (Anchor); Dennis, Ferdinand, *Duppy Conqueror* (Flamingo); Desai, Kiran, *Hullabaloo in the Guava Orchard* (Faber); Donleavy, J.P., *Wrong Information is Being Given Out at Princeton* (Little, Brown); Doughty, Louise, *Honey-Dew* (Touchstone); Duffy, Maureen, *Restitution* (Fourth Estate); Dunmore, Helen, *Your Blue-Eyed Boy* (Viking); Dyer, Geoff, *Paris Trance* (Abacus); Echenoz, Jean (translated Waldman, Guido), *Lake* (Harvill); Ellmann, Lucy, *Man or Mango?* (Hodder Headline); Faulks, Sebastian, *Charlotte Gray* (Hutchinson); Fine, Anne, *Telling Liddy* (Bantam); Flanagan, Richard, *The Sound of One Hand Clapping* (Picador); Foden, Giles, *The Last King of Scotland* (Faber); Garland, Alex,*The Tesseract* (Viking); Gee, Maggie, *The Ice People* (Richard Cohen); Gordimer, Nadine, *The House Gun* (Bloomsbury); Gunesekera, Romesh, *The Sandglass* (Granta); Hensher, Philip, *Pleasured* (Chatto); Higgins, Aidan, *Dog Days* (Secker & Warburg); Hill, Susan, *The Service of Clouds* (Chatto & Windus); Hoban, Russell, *Mr Rinyo-Clacton's Offer* (Cape); Hollinghurst, Alan, *The Spell* (Chatto & Windus) Hornby, Nick, *About a Boy* (Gollancz); Hudson, Mark, *The Music in My Head* (Cape); Hurd, Douglas, *The Shape of Ice* (Little, Brown); Huth, Angela, *Wives of the Fishermen* (Little, Brown); Irving, John, *A Widow for One Year* (Bloomsbury); Jhabvala, Ruth Prawer, *East into Upper East: Plain Tales from New York and New Delhi* (Murray); Kay, Jackie, *Trumpet* (Picador); Kelman, James, *The Good Times* (Secker & Warburg); Kempadoo, Oonya, *Buxton Spice*

(Phoenix House); Kundera, Milan (translated by Asher, Linda), *Identity* (Faber); Kureishi, Hanif, *Intimacy* (Faber); Langley, Lee, *False Pretences* (Chatto); Lively, Penelope, *Spiderweb* (Viking); Lurie, Alison, *The Last Resort* (Chatto); Mackay, Shena, *The Artist's Widow* (Cape); McCabe, Patrick, *Breakfast on Pluto* (Picador); McEwan, Ian, *Amsterdam* (Cape); McInerney, Jay, *Model Behaviour* (Bloomsbury); Mamet, David, *The Old Religion* (Faber); Mantel, Hilary, *The Giant, O'Brien* (Fourth Estate); Melville, Pauline, *The Migration of Ghosts* (Bloomsbury); Miller, Andrew, *Casanova* (Sceptre); Mootoo, Shani, *Cereus Blooms at Night* (Granta); Morrison, Toni, *Paradise* (Chatto & Windus); Munro, Alice, *The Love of a Good Woman: Stories* (Chatto & Windus); Nye, Robert, *The Late Mr Shakespeare* (Chatto & Windus); Okri, Ben, *Infinite Riches* (Phoenix House); Owens, Agnes, *For the Love of Willie* (Bloomsbury); Perkins, Emily, *Leave Before You Go* (Picador); Raphael, Frederic, *Coast to Coast* (Orion); Rathbone, Julian, *Trajectories* (Gollancz); Roth, Philip, *I Married a Communist* (Richard Cohen); Rose, Dilys, *War Dolls* (Review); St Aubyn, Edward, *On the Edge* (Chatto & Windus); Sayers, Dorothy L. and Walsh, Jill Paton, *Thrones, Dominations* (Hodder & Stoughton); Sealy, I. Allan, *The Everest Hotel* (Doubleday); Sebald, W.G. (translated by Hulse, Michael), *The Rings of Saturn* (Harvill); Self, Will, *Tough, Tough Toys for Tough, Tough Boys* (Bloomsbury); Shelley, Mary (ed. Tomalin, Claire), *Maurice, or The Fisher's Cot* (Viking); Sillitoe, Alan, *The Broken Chariot* (Flamingo); Storey, David, *A Serious Man* (Cape); Taylor, D.J., *Trespass* (Duckworth); Theroux, Marcel, *A Stranger in the Earth* (Phoenix House); Thorpe, Adam, *Pieces of Light* (Cape); Trapido, Barbara, *The Travelling Hornplayer* (Hamish Hamilton); Updike, John, *Toward the End of Time* (Hamish Hamilton); Vine, Barbara, *The Chimney Sweeper's Boy* (Viking); Walker, Alice, *By the Light of My Father's Smile* (Women's Press); Warner, Alan, *The Sopranos* (Cape); Weldon, Fay, *Big Women* (Flamingo); Weldon, Fay, *A Hard Time to be a Father* (Flamingo); Welsh, Irvine, *Filth* (Cape); Wicks, Susan, *Little Things* (Faber); Wilson, A.N., *Dream Children* (John Murray); Winterson, Jeanette, *The World and Other Places* (Cape); Wolf, Christa (translated by Cullen, John), *Medea* (Virago); Wolfe, Tom, *A Man in Full* (Cape).

POETRY. Abse, Dannie, *Welsh Retrospective* (Seren); Armstrong, Peter, *The Red-Funnelled Boat* (Picador); Ashbery, John, *Wakefulness* (Carcanet); Beer, Patricia, *Autumn* (Carcanet); Carson, Anne, *Glass and God* (Cape); Constantine, David, *The Pelt of Wasps* (Bloodaxe); Curnow, Allen, *Early Days Yet: New and Collected Poems, 1941–1997* (Carcanet); D'Aguiar, Fred, *Bill of Rights* (Chatto); Dawes, Kwame, *Shook Foil* (Peepal Tree); Dharker, Imtiaz, *Postcards from God* (Bloodaxe); Duhig, Ian, *Nominies* (Bloodaxe); Enright, D.J., *Collected Poems 1948–1998* (OUP); Fainlight, Ruth, *Sugar-Paper Blue* (Bloodaxe); Falck, Colin, *Post-Modern Love* (Stride); Gross, Philip, *The Wasting Game* (Bloodaxe); Harsent, David, *A Bird's Idea of Flight* (Faber); Heaney, Seamus, *Opened Ground: Poems 1966–1996* (Faber); Heath-Stubbs, John, *Galileo's Salad* (Carcanet); Heath-Stubbs, John, *The Torriano Sequences* (Hearing Eye); Hooker, Jeremy, *Our Lady of Europe* (Enitharmon); Hughes, Ted, *Birthday Letters* (Faber); Jennings, Elizabeth, *In the Meantime* (Carcanet); Khalvati, Mimi, *Entries on Light* (Carcanet); Kinsella, John, *Collected Poems 1980–1994* (Bloodaxe); Levi, Peter, *Reed Music* (Anvil); Lewis, Gwyneth, *Zero Gravity* (Bloodaxe); Maxwell, Glyn, *The Breakage* (Faber); Morgan, Edwin, *Virtual and Other Realities* (Carcanet); Muldoon, Paul, *Hay*, (Faber); Murray, Les, *Collected Poems* (Carcanet); Padel, Ruth, *Rembrandt Would Have Loved You* (Chatto & Windus); Satyamurti, Carol, *Selected Poems* (OUP); Sewell, John, *Bursting the Clouds* (Cape); Stead, C.K., *Straw into Gold: Poems New and Selected* (Arc); Szirtes, George, *Portrait of My Father in an English Landscape* (OUP); Tate, James, *Selected Poems* (Carcanet); Thwaite, Anthony, *Selected Poems, 1956–1996* (Enitharmon); Tomlinson, Charles, *Selected Poems 1955–1997* (OUP); Wallace-Crabbe, Chris, *Whirling* (OUP); Williams, C.K., *The Vigil* (Bloodaxe).

AUTOBIOGRAPHY AND BIOGRAPHY. Ackroyd, Peter, *The Life of Thomas More* (Chatto & Windus); Angelou, Maya, *Even the Stars Look Lonesome* (Virago); Bailey, John, *Iris* (Duckworth); Baxter, Keith, *My Sentiments Exactly* (Oberon); Brook, Peter, *Threads of Time:*

XV THE ARTS

A Memoir (Methuen); Callow , Phillip, *Chekhov: The Hidden Ground* (Constable); Carpenter, Humphrey, *Dennis Potter: The Authorised Biography* (Faber); Chisholm, Anne, *Rumer Godden: a Storyteller's Life* (Macmillan); Chisholm, Kate, *Fanny Burney: Her Life* (Chatto); Dankworth, John, *Jazz in Revolution* (Constable); Davis, Gregson, *Aime Cesaire* (CUP); Doran, Jamie and Bizony, Piers, *Starman: the Truth behind the Legend of Yuri Gagarin* (Bloomsbury); Gandhi, Arun, *Daughter of Midnight: The Child Bride of Gandhi* (Blake); Glendinning, Victoria, *Jonathan Swift* (Hutchinson); Hadda, Janet, *Isaac Bashevis Singer: A Life* (OUP); Hale, Keith (ed.), *Friends and Apostles: The Correspondence of Rupert Brooke and James Strachey, 1905–1914* (Yale); Hamilton, Ian, *A Gift Imprisoned: The Poetic Life of Matthew Arnold* (Bloomsbury); Heath, Edward, *The Course of My Life: My Autobiography* (Hodder); Hibbert, Christopher, *George III: A Personal History* (Viking); Hoban, Phoebe, *Basquiat: A Quick Killing in Art* (Quartet); Holmes, Richard, *Coleridge: Darker Reflections* (HarperCollins); Honan, Park, *Shakespeare: A Life* (OUP); Huntford, Roland, *Nansen: The Explorer as Hero* (Duckworth); Ignatieff, Michael, *Isaiah Berlin* (Chatto & Windus); Jacobson, Dan, *Heshel's Kingdom* (Hamish Hamilton); Jardine, Lisa and Stewart, Alan, *Hostage to Fortune: the Troubled Life of Francis Bacon* (Gollancz); Jessop, Violet, *Titanic Survivor: The Memoirs of Violet Jessop, Stewardess* (Sutton); Kendal, Felicity, *White Cargo* (Michael Joseph); Kincaid, Jamaica, *My Brother* (Vintage); McBrien, William, *Cole Porter: the Definitive Biography* (HarperCollins); McCabe, John, *Cagney* (Aurum); McLynn, Frank, *Napoleon* (Cape); MacNiven, Ian, *Lawrence Durrell* (Faber); Miller, Karl, *Dark Horses* (Picador); Naipaul, V.S., *Beyond Belief* (Little, Brown); O'Brien, Conor Cruise, *Memoir: My Life and Themes* (Profile); Callaghan, Sean, *The Informer* (Bantam); Patten, Chris, *East and West* (Macmillan); Phillips, Brian, *Primo Levi: Tragedy of an Optimist* (Aurum); Plimpton, George, *Truman Capote* (Picador); Rae, Simon, *W.G.Grace: A Life* (Faber); Ricketts, Harry *The Unforgiving Minute: A Life of Rudyard Kipling* (Chatto & Windus); Rooksby, Rikky, *A.C.Swinburne: A Poet's Life* (Scolar); Ross, Alan, *Winter Sea* (Harvill); Routledge, Paul, *Gordon Brown: The Biography* (Simon & Schuster); Schmidt, Michael, *Lives of the Poets* (Weidenfeld); Sinclair, Andrew, *Death By Fame: A Life of Elisabeth, Empress of Austria* (Constable); Soames, Mary (ed.), *Winston and Clementine Churchill Speaking for Themselves: The Personal Letters of Winston and Clementine Churchill* (Doubleday); Spurling, Hilary, *The Unknown Matisse: A Life of Henri Matisse, Vol.1, 1869–1908* (Hamish Hamilton); Stanford, Peter, *The She-Pope: A Quest for the Truth Behind the Mystery of Pope Joan* (Heinemann); Theroux, Paul, *Sir Vidia's Shadow: a Friendship across Five Continents* (Hamish Hamilton); Thomas, D.M., *Alexander Solzhenitsyn: a Century in His Life* (Little, Brown); Wilson, Elizabeth, *Jacqueline Du Pre* (Weidenfeld); Wilson, Jean Moorcroft, *Siegfried Sassoon: the Making of a War Poet* (Duckworth); Zeepvat, Charlotte, *Prince Leopold: the Untold Story of Queen Victoria's Youngest Son* (Sutton); Ziegler, Philip, *Osbert Sitwell* (Chatto & Windus).

OTHER BOOKS. Beevor, Anthony, *Stalingrad* (Viking); Cannadine, David, *History in Our Time* (Yale University Press); Conrad, Peter, *Modern Times: Modern Places* (Thames and Hudson); Dawkins, Richard, *Unweaving the Rainbow* (Allen Lane); Forster, E.M., *The Prince's Tale and Other Uncollected Writing* (Andre Deutsch); Fowles, John, *Wormholes: Essays and Occasional Writings* (Cape); Fuentes, Carlos (translated Castaneda, Marina Gutman), *A New Time for Mexico* (Bloomsbury); Gilbert, Martin, *Israel: a History* (Doubleday); Goldsworthy, Verna, *Inventing Ruritania: The Impersonation of the Imagination* (Yale University Press); Hoffman, Eva, *Shtetl: The history of a small town and an extinguished world* (Secker & Warburg); Ignatieff, Michael, *The Warrior's Honour: Ethnic War and the Modern Conscience* (Chatto & Windus); Keillor, Garrison, *Wobegon Boy* (Faber); Lively, Adam, *Masks: Blackness, Race and the Imagination* (Chatto); Lummis, Trevor, *Pitcairn Island: Life and Death in Eden* (Ashgate); Malcolm, Noel, *Kosovo: A Short History* (Macmillan); Marwick, Arthur, *The Sixties: Cultural Revolution in Britain, France, Italy and the United States 1958–1974* (OUP); Morrison, Blake, *Too True* (Granta); Naipaul, V.S., *Beyond Belief* (Little, Brown); Parsons, Neil, *King Khama, Emperor Joe and the Great White Queen: Victorian Britain through African Eyes* (University of Chicago Press); Phillips, Mike and Trevor, *Windrush: The*

Irresistible Rise of Multi-Racial Britain (HarperCollins); Pinker, Steven, *How the Mind Works* (Allen Lane/Penguin Press); Pinter, Harold, *Various Voices: Prose, Poetry, Politics 1948–1998* (Faber); Rose, Steven, *Lifelines: Biology, freedom, determinism* (Allen Lane/The Penguin Press); Sereny, Gitta, *Cries Unheard: the Story of Mary Bell* (Macmillan); Smith, Chris, *Creative Britain* (Faber); Warner, Marina, *No Go the Bogeyman: Scaring, Lulling and Making Mock* (Chatto & Windus); Watkins, Alan, *The Road to Number 10: from Bonar Law to Tony Blair* (Duckworth); Witts, Richard, *Artist Unknown: an Alternative History of the Arts Council* (Little, Brown).

XVI SPORT

PROBLEMS AND POLITICS. Drugs were again a problem. The exceptional progress of some Chinese athletes and swimmers had long caused suspicion, and disbelief of the explanation that turtle's blood was the secret of success. A Sydney customs' officer discovered the real reason when swimmer Yuan Yuan was found to have enough growth hormone in her suitcase to improve the whole team's performance. An Irish swimmer, Michelle de Bruin, was the next to suffer suspension. There had been long-running suspicion about her amazing improvement, as Michelle Smith, to win three golds and a bronze in the 1996 Olympics (see AR 1996, p. 502), Ireland's total medal tally. Now a high percentage of whiskey was found in a sample from this much-tested performer.

Inevitably, de Bruin appealed against her suspension, claiming that there had been tampering with the sample, but her brilliant career was now inevitably shadowed. Such an appeal was, however, won by England's best 800-metres runner. Diane Modahl had had to sacrifice house and family savings before it was conclusively proved that her positive test result in 1994 (see AR 1994, p. 540) had been farcical rubbish. After four wasted years there was a happy ending when, with her reputation restored, she won a bronze in the Commonwealth Games. For the authorities the sequel was likely to be less pleasant. The bankrupt Amateur Athletic Association (AAA) and the international body both faced massive claims for damages for the loss and suffering unfairly inflicted on Modahl.

The biggest scandal of the year left the prestigious Tour de France cycle race in a shambles. The Festina team was withdrawn after admissions of long-term use of eythropoietin. The TVM Dutch squad was targeted next, and as police searches widened several more teams withdrew. The remaining cyclists stopped for a time in protest. Tennis then had a problem as Australian Open winner Petr Korda tested positive for steroids, and lost the relevant prize money and ranking points.

Cricket had different problems. It came to light that Australia's Mark Waugh and Shane Warne had accepted thousands of pounds from bookmakers some years earlier. The Australian Cricket Board had fined them, but kept the matter secret. These two had also volunteered themselves as witnesses accusing leading Pakistani cricketers of trying to fix matches. That inquiry was continuing, but the Pakistan authorities called for Waugh and Warne to be banned in light of the latest disclosures.

Football hooliganism in England was on the wane, but the hard core disgraced the country again with riotous behaviour in Marseilles at the start of the World Cup. This was soon under control, but the English miscreants were not alone. Tunisians reacted similarly, and the worst incident involved the Germans, a French gendarme being crippled by a blow on the head with an iron bar.

Administrators also had cause to blush. Marc Holder, an International Olympic Committee (IOC) official, publicly denounced some fellow committee members for soliciting bribes from cities bidding for the Olympics. The secretary of the English Football Association (FA), Graham Kelly, resigned in December when he and FA chairman Keith Wiseman were accused of giving a large loan to the Welsh FA without proper authorization in the hopes of voting support internationally for Mr Wiseman and for England's bid to host the 2006 World Cup.

WINTER OLYMPICS. The impressive opening ceremony for the 18th Winter Olympics set the tone for a splendidly-organized games in Nagano, Japan (see also IX.2.iv). The initial day brought the first of several postponements through fog, or rain, of the most prestigious event, the men's downhill ski race. Elsewhere the competition went ahead, with Russia claiming the first gold medal as Olga Danilova overtook compatriot Larissa Lazutina in a women's cross-country skiing event. Canada won the first gold in the new snow-boarding event. Its inclusion had caused controversy, and more followed as Canadian Ross Rebegliati tested positive for marijuana. Rebegliati was first disqualified, but then reinstated on appeal. There were many world records in speed-skating as the new longer skates improved performance. Several of these were set by Dutch skaters, who won ten medals overall. Most notable was Marianne Timmer's two records. Japan also had a speed-skating gold medal, as Hiroyasu Shimizou won the men's 500 metres.

Germany soon established itself as the most prolific medal winner of these Games because of its all-round strength. In the speed-skating Claudia Pechstein and Gunter Niemann-Stirnemann were outstanding. Germans also excelled in snow-boarding and made a clean sweep of the three luge events. In the pairs Americans won silver and bronze, their country's first medals in luge. When the alpine events were finally raced, after much rescheduling, America's Picabo Street was surprise winner of the women's downhill. In the men's the favourite, Austria's Hermann Maier, crashed spectacularly, cart-wheeling over two lines of safety-netting. That let in France's Jean Luc Cretier to take gold. Bruised but undaunted, Maier still won gold in both super-giant and giant slaloms. In these two women's events, Katja Seizinger of Germany took golds, and also a bronze in the slalom, which was dominated by Italy's Deborah Compagnoni.

Norway's Bjoern Daehlie was the man of the games with three golds in cross-country skiing to bring his Olympic total to a record eight. One of these was the team relay event which Norway won by inches in a hectic finish. Japan, as usual, excelled in its national winter sport of ski-jumping. Only on the normal hill did the gold elude them as Finland's Jani Soininen out-jumped the rest. But the silver went to Kazuyardi Funaki, who also won gold on the big hill. In the team event Japan's favourite jumper, Masahiko Harada, managed a record 137 metres after a poor first jump.

Russia dominated the ice-dancing and also the figure-skating, except for the women's event. That provided two notable performances by young Americans. Going into the final session 17-year-old Michelle Kwan was leading. But an inspired and joyous performance by 15-year-old world champion Tara Lipinski gave her the gold.

The final event of the Olympics ended with one of the major upsets. In the men's ice hockey final the Czech Republic beat Russia 1–0. Petr Svoboda's third-period goal confirmed the unfancied Czechs as the team of the tournament. On the way to the final they beat the USA 4–1 and then knocked out world champions Canada in a penalty shoot-out. Their outstanding player, goal-tender Dominik Hasek, was crucial to their victories. The Americans had the consolation that, in the first Olympics event for women's ice hockey teams, they defeated world champions Canada in the final. To offset that success, their men's team disgraced themselves by taking their frustrations out on their hotel furniture and causing considerable damage. For Canada there was no consolation whatever. Even with the legendary Wayne Gretzky in their team, they lost the third-place match 2–3 to Finland.

Overall winners Germany won 29 medals, 12 of them gold; Norway came second with 25, 10 of them gold. The Russian Federation was third, Canada fourth, the USA fifth and the Netherlands sixth.

COMMONWEALTH GAMES. Malaysia staged the 16th Commonwealth Games in September. The colourful opening ceremony in Kuala Lumpur set the tone of an event more noted for friendliness than top-line competition. Sadly, the background was not so friendly, in that internal political problems led to riots even during Queen Elizabeth II's visit (see IX.1.iii).

With the event involving a variety of sports ranging from athletics to cricket and rugby, Australia proved to have the greatest strength in depth. Their tally was 59 golds and 135 medals in all. England came second with 21 golds and 75 medals overall. Canada was third with 16 golds and a total tally of 65. Australia was most dominant in swimming, while England had ten golds in athletics.

Diane Modahl's bronze in the women's 800 metres, with the drug charge against her totally disproven (see above), was the most emotional of several such moments. Shot-putter Judy Oakes won her sixth medal in these competitions, and for the first time it was gold. In the hurdles Tony Jarrett won his 14th major medal, and again it was a first gold. The most courageous performance was by Wales's Iwan Thomas, who arrived only just in time to take gold again in the 400 metres at the end of a tiring season.

ASSOCIATION FOOTBALL. The World Cup championship was a triumph for France on and off the field. The organization was outstanding, and the host nation was a deserved winner on the field. Despite merited complaints about the standard of refereeing, and the disruption caused by the shoals of red and yellow cards in response to FIFA's instructions that referees should be severer than usual, the climax was as forecast. What was not expected was that the host nation should overwhelm holders Brazil in the final, despite having Marcel Desailly sent off.

For the Brazilians it was a sad and confusing day. Their great star, Dadado Ronaldo, suffered a panic attack in the night and was taken to hospital. He was first left out of the team, then reinstated when the doctor passed him fit. But fit for football at this level he was not. With Ronaldo making no contribution, his dispirited team was overwhelmed 3–0, even though France started without captain and key defender Laurent Blanc and then lost Desailly.

Blanc had been sent off in France's 2–1 semi-final win against the brave and talented Croatian team. Croatia had led with a goal from Davor Suker, whose six in the competition won him the 'golden boot' as top scorer. Right-back Lilian Thuram then scored twice to lift France to the final. The one weakness of the French team was the lack of goal-scoring forwards. Defenders like Thuram and Blanc had done the job instead, and in the final mid-fielders scored the three French goals. The player of the match, Zedinine Zidane, headed two, while Emmanuel Petit completed the rout of Brazil with a fine individual strike.

Brazil's outstanding performance was in beating the Netherlands in the semi-final, with Ronaldo outshining Dennis Bergkamp, whose brilliant late goal had defeated Argentina in the previous match. Argentina had just defeated England in a penalty shoot-out at the end of a fascinating quarter-final. Liverpool's 18-year-old Michael Owen made himself a star when he put England ahead with a remarkable individual goal. But with the score 2–2 David Beckham was sent off for a petty retaliation. Down to ten men, England still had the edge: a goal by Sol Campbell was disallowed and an obvious penalty not given them. Two penalty misses then eliminated the English team, which had gone out in the same heart-breaking way in the 1996 European Nations finals (see AR 1996, p. 503).

The expected advance of African and Asian teams did not materialize. Of the eight quarter-finalists, six teams were European, and two South America; so the old order was unchanged. Only the fancied Olympic champions, Nigeria, even made the last 16. England also got to that stage, showing much promise in defeating Columbia and Tunisia, each by 2–0. Scotland, however, failed to qualify for the play-off stages.

In domestic competition, north London side Arsenal, managed by Frenchman Arsène Wenger, were at one stage 13 points behind Manchester United. In a spirited finish, however, a surge of victories took them to the Premier League championship. They completed the double by defeating Newcastle United in the Cup Final. In Scotland, there was a rare Premier

Division triumph for Celtic, who ended Rangers' run of nine successive championships.

In Europe, Manchester United again reached the semi-finals of the prestigious Champions League, only to lose to Monaco on the 'away goal rule'. The final was between two of the great names of the competition, Real Madrid beating Juventus by the only goal. Chelsea not only won the English League Cup, but also defeated Stuttgart in the final of the European Cup Winners' Cup.

ATHLETICS. Great Britain and Northern Ireland shrugged off a poor 1997 season by winning the European Cup, then topping the rank order in the European championship in Budapest. Their nine golds equalled their best previous performance, with Germany close behind on eight, then Russia on six. The ranking was based on golds, but with eight silvers as well Germany was strongest in depth. Outstanding winners for Britain were Steve Backley in the javelin and Jonathan Edwards in the triple jump. Both left the other competitors far behind from their first throw or jump. In the javelin Mick Hill came second, his first medal in major competition after many years of trying.

In middle-distance running the Germans excelled, while Britain was outclassed in events that it once dominated. Instead, it was in the sprints that Britain was superior. Darren Campbell won the 100 metres, and a clean sweep in the 200 metres followed when Doug Walker's late surge for gold took him ahead of Doug Turner and Julian Golding. Golding's dip to the line brought him bronze fractionally ahead of Dutchman Troy Douglas, who was disqualified for swearing at an official when the result was announced.

Welshman Iwan Thomas comfortably won the 400 metres ahead of the fancied Mark Richardson, who was beaten into third place by the Pole, Robert Mackowiak. Not surprisingly, Britain also took both the 4 x 100-metre men's relay and the 4 × 400, in which Poland pressed them hard. Another outstanding effort was Colin Jackson's win in the 110-metre hurdles, proving that he was back to his best. Diane Lewis at last won gold in the heptathlon to underline her steady improvement. But the best performance of the championship was from Ireland's Sandra O'Sullivan, who won by a distance in both the 5,000 metres and 10,000 metres. O'Sullivan also won two world cross-country championships over different distances on successive days as well as the prestigious Great North Run.

CRICKET. England's cricketers had mixed fortunes. Returning from heavy defeat in the West Indies, they won their first major series at home for 11 years. Victory over the formidable South Africans was a fine start for Alec Stewart, who took over as captain from Michael Atherton. South Africa dominated the first three Tests and would have gone two up in the third had not a century by Stewart and dogged resistance by tail-ender Robert Croft forced a second draw. England then won at Trent Bridge by eight wickets, and by the narrowest of margins in the final Test, thanks to fine bowling by Darren Gough and Angus Fraser.

Joy was short-lived as Sri Lanka, the world one-day champions, defeated England by ten wickets in a one-off Test. Off-spinner Muttiah Muralitharan took 16 wickets, the fifth highest haul in Test cricket. The winter tour of Australia started badly, only rain saving England in the first Test and the next two being lost, to ensure that Australia kept the Ashes. There was then some Christmas cheer as superb bowling by Dean Headley and Gough snatched victory against the odds in the fourth Test, leaving England a chance to square the series in the new year. Highlights of the many other Tests included Zimbabwe's first away-series win, in India, and South Africa's three successive wins over the West Indies, whose troubled team had refused to fly on from London without negotiations over pay and the captaincy.

Individual records included a ninth-wicket partnership of 195 by Pat Symcox and Mark Boucher for South Africa against Pakistan, and Mark Taylor's 334 to equal Don Bradman's Australian record. Taylor might have gone on to beat the world record had he not declared to aid a win against Pakistan. Australian wicket-keeper Ian Healey's 356th dismissal took him past Rodney Marsh's Test record. The highest run-scorer in Tests in 1998 was Alec Stewart with 1,222.

In England, Leicestershire won the County Championship, Lancashire the NatWest trophy and the Axa Sunday League. In the last-ever Benson & Hedges final, Essex demolished Derbyshire.

GOLF. Tiger Woods retained his number one ranking throughout the year, but it was his close friend and fellow American, Mark O'Meara, who was man of the year. Always consistent, and often devastating over the final nine holes of the 72, O'Meara finished strongly to win the US Masters. He did it again to win the British Open, then came from behind to beat Woods in the final of the World Match Play championship at Wentworth.

In Europe, Scotland's Colin Montgomerie was leading money-taker for the sixth successive year, narrowly beating Ireland's Darren Clarke and Lee Westwood. Westwood, however, was voted European player of the season for his seven wins in six different countries and three different continents.

In the US PGA tour money list, O'Meara came seventh with $1,837,246. The leader with $2,591,031 was David Duval. He won the Vardon trophy as well with an overall average of 69.13 strokes per round, edging out Woods by 0.08 of a stroke. O'Meara was fifth with 69.63. Second in the money list was Fiji's Vijay Singh, followed by Jim Furyk, Woods, Hal Sutton, Phil Mickelson, O'Meara, Justin Leonard, Fred Couples and John Huston as the top ten. The other two winners of majors were Vijay Singh in the US PGA at Sahalee and Lee Janzen in the US Open. All the victors were quoted at heavy odds against in the pre-tournament betting, before triumphing against expectation. For 41-year-old O'Meara and Singh, theirs were first-ever major victories.

In becoming number one again on the European tour, Colin Montgomerie needed a late surge with wins in the British and the German Masters to add to previous success in the Volvo PGA championship. In number of wins, Lee Westwood went one better. In addition, he won the Freeport-McDermott Classic on the US tour and had back-to-back wins in Japan. Darren Clarke had only two wins, but topped the all-round *Guardian* performance data rankings. By contrast, Nick Faldo was on the slide, in 82nd place. Yet it was his brilliant performance, ably backed by David Carter, which won England the World Cup for the first time. The Alfred Dunhill Nations' Cup at St Andrews was won by South Africa.

In women's golf, the Americans were comfortable victors in both the professional Solheim Cup and the amateur Curtis Cup. In both competitions, the Americans surged ahead in the early matches and held on to win the Solheim 16–12 and the Curtis 10–8. Player of the year was Korea's Se Ri Pak. Aged only 20, she became the youngest-ever US Women's Open champion, and took another major, the LPGA championship, among her four tour victories. In the money list, she finished second with $862,170, behind Gunika Sorenstam, who pocketed more than a million dollars. With her sponsors Samsung reportedly doubling her winnings, Se Ri Pak was expected to become the world's best-paid sportswoman. But with such expectations, the pressure became intense too. On returning to Korea she was admitted to hospital suffering from stress.

MOTOR SPORT. Grand Prix racing this season turned into a battle between two cars and two drivers. In the end all the honours went not to Michael Schumacher and Ferrari, but to Mikka Hakkinen and McLaren-Mercedes. Hakkinen's was a remarkable performance after a terrible crash in the 1996 Australian Grand Prix had left him close to death. The drivers' championship was only decided in a remarkable final race on Japan's Suzuka track. Early on McLaren was totally dominant. In Australia Hakkinen won with David Coulthard second. That caused controversy as Coulthard deliberately slowed at the end to let his team-mate through, according to a pre-race agreement. Thereafter, Hakkinen truly proved himself the better driver, recording eight wins to Coulthard's one. Schumacher began to eat into Hakkinen's lead as the season progressed, his win at Monza leaving both drivers on 80 points. The crucial event in the tense final four races came earlier on Luxembourg's Nurburgring track, where Schumacher was set to win until he drove into the lapped Coulthard, irreparably damaging both cars. A furious Schumacher claimed that Coulthard had deliberately risked killing him, but clearly it was an accident caused by atrocious weather. So bad were the conditions that none of the top drivers finished, with Damon Hill winning and his Jordan-Mugen team mate Ralf Schumacher coming second.

Hakkinen drove superbly to win the penultimate race, which gave him a four-point lead before the final challenge of Suzuka. Schumacher was in pole position, but after a re-start stalled his engine on the grid and had to start from the back. That allowed Hakkinen to win comfortably, as Schumacher blew a tyre in his desperate attempts to carve his way through the field. The constructors' championship was also settled at Suzuka, with McLaren clear winners over Ferrari. Williams came third and Jordan, in fourth place, achieved their highest-ever placing.

RUGBY UNION. World champions South Africa confirmed their status with a record-equalling run of 17 successive wins, until being narrowly defeated by England when going for the 18th. Their run included victories over Australia and New Zealand in the Tri-Nations Cup and a 96-13 hammering of a below-strength England touring team. Finally, South Africa seemed to be heading for a clean sweep in a tour of Britain. Wales gave them a shock, leading 20-17 before a final Springbok surge took them home. Scotland and Ireland were brushed aside but, at Twickenham, England came from behind, stimulated by a Jeremy Guscott try, to end their remarkable run.

In the Five Nations' championship, France won the grand slam, England the triple crown and the Calcutta Cup as in the previous year. The crucial match was the first, as France stormed ahead of England in the first 20 minutes in Paris and were never caught. Later the French scored 50 points or more against both Scotland and Wales, the latter's 51-0 thrashing setting a record for this competition. Ireland, however, came very close to achieving an upset in Paris, only a late try giving France an 18-16 win. England had comfortable wins against the other three, with Paul Grayson's 19 points overwhelming Scotland in the first Five Nations match played on a Sunday.

Bath won the European club championship, all their points in the final coming from full-back Jonathan Callard. Newcastle, led by Rob Andrew, won the Premiership title, and Saracens the Tetley Bitter Cup. In Wales, Swansea won the League, Llanelli the Cup. Watsonians won the Scottish League and Glasgow Hawks the Cup, while Shannon were Irish champions for the fourth successive season.

RUGBY LEAGUE. In league rugby visiting New Zealand overwhelmed Great Britain in the first two Tests, and were a point ahead with seconds to go in the third, when a dropped goal levelled the scores. Wigan were back to top form, ending head of the Super-League table and beating Leeds in the grand final. At Wembley the Challenge Cup final produced the greatest upset in the competition's history. Unfancied Sheffield Eagles overwhelmed 'mighty' Wigan against all the odds.

TENNIS. For only the second time the four men's and women's grand slam events were won by different players. The year started with America's Pete Sampras and Switzerland's Martina Hingis undisputed number ones, a ranking both had a struggle to sustain. Sampras eventually retained his ranking for a record sixth successive year, but was put under immediate pressure when Petr Korda won the Australian Open. Sampras was then eliminated early in the French Open, where the clay courts did not suit his power game. On Wimbledon's grass, however, he was still the master, beating Croatia's Goran Ivanisevic in five hard-fought sets in the final. In the US Open Sampras was leading 2–1 in the semi-final against Australia's Patrick Rafter, when an injured ankle let him down. Rafter went on to win the final and became Sampras's closest challenger for the top ranking.

Two Britons, Tim Henman (fifth) and Greg Rusedski (tenth) continued to be highly-ranked, both being involved in the big money-spinning ATP tour championship at the end of the season. The Davis Cup had lost so much of its past prestige that none of the three top Americans turned out for the semi-final, which was won by Italy. In the final in Milan, Sweden raced to a winning 3–0 lead over the Italians.

In women's tennis, Martina Hingis began with victory in the Australian Open, but was soon pressed hard by several other players. At Wimbledon it was third-time-lucky for Jana Novotna, who at last controlled her nerves to win the final against France's Nathalie Tauziat. American Lindsay Davenport was the appropriate winner of the US Open, beating Hingis in the final. As consolation, Hingis completed a clean sweep of all four grand slam doubles, though with different partners.

THE TURF. This year the Grand National went off slickly enough, but not without controversy. The heavy going added an extra burden to this exceptionally testing event. Only six of the 37 runners finished and there were three fatalities. Leading trainer Jenny Pitman criticized the inclusion of so many horses without the pedigree for such a challenge. The top-weight Suny Bay showed that the fittest could do it by finishing a gallant second. The winner was Earth Summit, ridden by Carl Llewellyn, for his second National victory.

There was triumph and tragedy for one of the most popular horses. The grey, One Man, was cheered to victory in the Queen Mother Champion Chase, then had a fatal fall at Anfield shortly before the National. Irish horse Istabraq comfortably won the Champion Hurdle, while Cool Dawn took the Gold Cup. Tony McCoy was again champion jumps jockey, this time by a record margin. Before the end of March he had already passed Peter Scudamore's 221 wins in a season.

On the flat, the outstanding European jockey was Olivier Peslier, rivalling Frankie Dettori on performance and personality. Peslier had a third successive Arc de Triomphe win on Sagomix, who gave trainer André Fabré his fifth success in this prestigious race. Peslier also won the Derby on

High Rise, as well as riding Europe's champion miler, Desert Prince. Dettori had his successes as well, recording seven wins during Royal Ascot. In the King George he had a masterly ride on Swain to beat High Rise and the rest. The champion jockey, however, was Kieran Fallon with over 200 winners. The champion trainer was Godolphin's Said Bin Saroor.

Australia's Caulfield Cup was 135 years old and there was a rare British success for 66-1 outsider Taufan's Melody, trained by Lady Herries. The Melbourne Cup was won by Jezabeel. In the most prestigious of the Breeder's Cup races in America, Frankie Dettori was heavily criticized for allowing Swain to drift, thereby losing to Awesome Again.

AMERICAN ASPECTS. American football's Super Bowl XXXII in San Diego's Qualcomm Stadium became very special as Denver Broncos finally ended the NFC's 13-year dominance of the event. Denver were only a wild-card entry from the AFC, but deserved their 31-24 win over holders Green Bay Packers. Denver had reached this NFL final three times before only to lose by ever-larger margins. Their quarter-back, John Elway, had been outscored 136-40 in those previous encounters, so victory at last was especially sweet for him. His opposite number, Brett Favre, had been outstandingly successful all season and gave Packers the ideal start with a long touchdown pass to Antonio Freeman. But Elway began even more forcefully, sweeping the Broncos to a 17-7 lead with much assistance from running-back Terrell Davis. Packers fought back to 17-17, and again to 24-24, but the decisive thrust came from Davis, who scored his third touchdown to earn the 'most valuable player' award. For the third touchdown he had only one yard to go, but overall he rushed 157 yards, a tribute to his skill, but also an indication of how the power of the Broncos wore down the Packers.

For baseball fans this was an enthralling year in which two players shattered its most hallowed record. When the legendary Babe Ruth's record of 60 home runs was beaten some years ago there had been widespread annoyance that a national hero had finally been bettered. This time the country was absorbed as Mark McGwire of St Louis Cardinals and Sammy Sosa of Chicago Cubs raced each other. McGwire was the first to push the record to 62; then Sosa caught up at 65 each; thereafter, McGwire eased away to a remarkable 70.

Detroit Redwings won the Stanley Cup, ice hockey's most prestigious trophy, for the second successive year. Redwings had previously gone 43 years without winning a trophy; but they confirmed their present quality with a 4-1 drubbing of Washington Capitals.

XVII DOCUMENTS AND REFERENCE

1. NORTHERN IRELAND: GOOD FRIDAY AGREEMENT

Printed below are extracts from the agreement reached in multi-party negotiations in Northern Ireland on 10 April 1998, commonly known as the Good Friday Agreement and also referred to officially as the Belfast Agreement. (Text supplied by Northern Ireland Office.)

I DECLARATION OF SUPPORT

1. We, the participants in the multi-party negotiations, believe that the agreement we have negotiated offers a truly historic opportunity for a new beginning.

2. The tragedies of the past have left a deep and profoundly regrettable legacy of suffering. We must never forget those who have died or been injured, and their families. But we can best honour them through a fresh start, in which we firmly dedicate ourselves to the achievement of reconciliation, tolerance, and mutual trust, and to the protection and vindication of the human rights of all.

3. We are committed to partnership, equality and mutual respect as the basis of relationships within Northern Ireland, between North and South, and between these islands.

4. We reaffirm our total and absolute commitment to exclusively democratic and peaceful means of resolving differences on political issues, and our opposition to any use or threat of force by others for any political purpose, whether in regard to this agreement or otherwise.

5. We acknowledge the substantial differences between our continuing, and equally legitimate, political aspirations. However, we will endeavour to strive in every practical way towards reconciliation and rapprochement within the framework of democratic and agreed arrangements. We pledge that we will, in good faith, work to ensure the success of each and every one of the arrangements to be established under this agreement. It is accepted that all of the institutional and constitutional arrangements—an Assembly in Northern Ireland, a North/South Ministerial Council, implementation bodies, a British-Irish Council and a British-Irish Intergovernmental Conference and any amendments to British acts of parliament and the constitution of Ireland—are interlocking and interdependent and that in particular the functioning of the Assembly and the North/South Council are so closely inter-related that the success of each depends on that of the other.

6. Accordingly, in a spirit of concord, we strongly commend this agreement to the people, North and South, for their approval.

II CONSTITUTIONAL ISSUES

1. The participants endorse the commitment made by the British and Irish governments that, in a new British-Irish Agreement replacing the Anglo-Irish Agreement, they will:

(i) recognize the legitimacy of whatever choice is freely exercised by a majority of the people of Northern Ireland with regard to its status, whether they prefer to continue to support the Union with Great Britain or a sovereign united Ireland;

(ii) recognize that it is for the people of the island of Ireland alone, by agreement between the two parts respectively and without external impediment, to exercise their right of self-determination on the basis of consent, freely and concurrently given, North and South, to bring about a united Ireland, if that is their wish, accepting that this right must be achieved and exercised with and subject to the agreement and consent of a majority of the people of Northern Ireland;

(iii) acknowledge that while a substantial section of the people in Northern Ireland share the legitimate wish of a majority of the people of the island of Ireland for a united Ireland, the present wish of a majority of the people of Northern Ireland, freely exercised and legitimate, is to maintain the Union and, accordingly, that Northern Ireland's status as part of the United Kingdom reflects and relies upon that wish; and that it would be wrong to make any change in the status of Northern Ireland save with the consent of a majority of its people;

(iv) affirm that if, in the future, the people of the island of Ireland exercise their right of self-determination on the basis set out in sections (i) and (ii) above to bring about a united Ireland, it will be a binding obligation on both Governments to introduce and support in their respective Parliaments legislation to give effect to that wish;

XVII.1. NORTHERN IRELAND: GOOD FRIDAY AGREEMENT

(v) affirm that whatever choice is freely exercised by a majority of the people of Northern Ireland, the power of the sovereign government with jurisdiction there shall be exercised with rigorous impartiality on behalf of all the people in the diversity of their identities and traditions and shall be founded on the principles of full respect for, and equality of, civil, political, social and cultural rights, of freedom from discrimination for all citizens, and of parity of esteem and of just and equal treatment for the identity, ethos, and aspirations of both communities;

(vi) recognize the birthright of all the people of Northern Ireland to identify themselves and be accepted as Irish or British, or both, as they may so choose, and accordingly confirm that their right to hold both British and Irish citizenship is accepted by both Governments and would not be affected by any future change in the status of Northern Ireland.

2. The participants also note that the two Governments have accordingly undertaken in the context of this comprehensive political agreement, to propose and support changes in, respectively, the Constitution of Ireland and in British legislation relating to the constitutional status of Northern Ireland.

Annex A: Draft clauses/schedules for incorporation in British legislation

1(i). It is hereby declared that Northern Ireland in its entirety remains part of the United Kingdom and shall not cease to be so without the consent of a majority of the people of Northern Ireland voting in a poll held for the purposes of this section in accordance with Schedule 1. (ii) But if the wish expressed by a majority in such a poll is that Northern Ireland should cease to be part of the United Kingdom and form part of a united Ireland, the Secretary of State shall lay before Parliament such proposals to give effect to that wish as may be agreed between Her Majesty's Government in the United Kingdom and the Government of Ireland.

2. The Government of Ireland Act 1920 is repealed; and this Act shall have effect notwithstanding any other previous enactment.

Schedule 1: Polls for the purpose of Section 1

1. The Secretary of State may by order direct the holding of a poll for the purposes of section 1 on a date specified in the order.

2. Subject to paragraph 3, the Secretary of State shall exercise the power under paragraph 1 if at any time it appears likely to him that a majority of those voting would express a wish that Northern Ireland should cease to be part of the United Kingdom and form part of a united Ireland.

3. The Secretary of State shall not make an order under paragraph 1 earlier than seven years after the holding of a previous poll under this Schedule.

4. (Remaining paragraphs along the lines of paragraphs 2 and 3 of existing Schedule 1 to 1973 Act.)

Annex B: Irish government draft legislation to amend the constitution

Add to Article 29 the following sections:

7. The state may consent to be bound by the British-Irish Agreement done at Belfast on the day of 1998, hereinafter called the Agreement. Any institution established by or under the Agreement may exercise the powers and functions thereby conferred on it in respect of all or any part of the island of Ireland notwithstanding any other provision of this constitution conferring a like power or function on any person or any organ of state appointed under or created or established by or under this constitution. Any power or function conferred on such an institution in relation to the settlement or resolution of disputes or controversies may be in addition to or in substitution for any like power or function conferred by this constitution on any such person or organ of state as aforesaid. If the government declare that the state has become obliged, pursuant to the Agreement, to give effect to the amendment of this constitution referred to therein, then, notwithstanding Article 46 hereof, this constitution shall be amended as follows:. . .

ii. The following Articles shall be substituted for Articles 2 and 3 of the English text:

'*Article 2*: It is the entitlement and birthright of every person born in the island of Ireland, which includes its islands and seas, to be part of the Irish nation. That is also the entitlement of all persons otherwise qualified in accordance with law to be citizens of Ireland. Furthermore, the Irish nation cherishes its special affinity with people of Irish ancestry living abroad who share its cultural identity and heritage.

'*Article 3*: 1. It is the firm will of the Irish nation, in harmony and friendship, to unite all the people who share the territory of the island of Ireland, in all the diversity of their identities and traditions, recognizing that a united Ireland shall be brought about only by peaceful means with the consent of a majority of the people, democratically expressed, in both jurisdictions in the island. Until then, the laws enacted by the parliament established by this constitution shall have the like area and extent of application as the laws enacted by the parliament that existed immediately before the coming into operation of this constitution. 2. Institutions with executive powers and functions that are shared between those jurisdictions may be established by their respective responsible authorities for stated purposes and may exercise powers and functions in respect of all or any part of the island.. . .

III STRAND ONE: DEMOCRATIC INSTITUTIONS IN NORTHERN IRELAND

1. This agreement provides for a democratically elected Assembly in Northern Ireland which is inclusive in its membership, capable of exercising executive and legislative authority, and subject to safeguards to protect the rights and interests of all sides of the community.

The Assembly. 2. A 108-member Assembly will be elected by PR(STV) [proportional representation (single transferable vote)] from existing Westminster constituencies.

3. The Assembly will exercise full legislative and executive authority in respect of those matters currently within the responsibility of the six Northern Ireland government departments, with the possibility of taking on responsibility for other matters as detailed elsewhere in this agreement.

4. The Assembly—operating where appropriate on a cross-community basis—will be the prime source of authority in respect of all devolved responsibilities.

Safeguards. 5. There will be safeguards to ensure that all sections of the community can participate and work together successfully in the operation of these institutions and that all sections of the community are protected, including: (*a*) allocations of committee chairs, ministers and committee membership in proportion to party strengths; (*b*) the European Convention on Human Rights (ECHR) and any Bill of Rights for Northern Ireland supplementing it, which neither the Assembly nor public bodies can infringe, together with a Human Rights Commission; (*c*) arrangements to provide that key decisions and legislation are proofed to ensure that they do not infringe the ECHR and any Bill of Rights for Northern Ireland; (*d*) arrangements to ensure key decisions are taken on a cross-community basis; (i) either parallel consent, i.e. a majority of those members present and voting, including a majority of the unionist and nationalist designations present and voting; (ii) or a weighted majority (60 per cent) of members present and voting, including at least 40 per cent of each of the nationalist and unionist designations present and voting. Key decisions requiring cross-community support will be designated in advance, including election of the Chair of the Assembly, the First Minister and Deputy First Minister, standing orders and budget allocations. In other cases such decisions could be triggered by a petition of concern brought by a significant minority of Assembly members (30/108). (*e*) an Equality Commission to monitor a statutory obligation to promote equality of opportunity in specified areas and parity of esteem between the two main communities, and to investigate individual complaints against public bodies.

Operation of the Assembly. 6. At their first meeting, members of the Assembly will register a designation of identity—nationalist, unionist or other—for the purposes of measuring cross-community support in Assembly votes under the relevant provisions above.

7. The Chair and Deputy Chair of the Assembly will be elected on a cross-community basis, as set out in paragraph 5(*d*) above.

8. There will be a committee for each of the main executive functions of the Northern Ireland administration. The chairs and deputy chairs of the Assembly committees will be allocated proportionally, using the d'Hondt system. Membership of the committees will be in broad proportion to party strengths in the Assembly to ensure that the opportunity of committee places is available to all members.

9. The committees will have a scrutiny, policy development and consultation role with respect to the department with which each is associated, and will have a role in initiation of legislation. They will have the power to: consider and advise on departmental budgets and annual plans in the context of the overall budget allocation; approve relevant secondary legislation and take the committee stage of relevant primary legislation; call for persons and papers; initiate enquiries and make reports; consider and advise on matters brought to the committee by its minister.

10. Standing committees other than departmental committees may be established as may be required from time to time.

11. The Assembly may appoint a special committee to examine and report on whether a measure or proposal for legislation is in conformity with equality requirements, including the ECHR/Bill of Rights. The committee shall have the power to call people and papers to assist in its consideration of the matter. The Assembly shall then consider the report of the committee and can determine the matter in accordance with the cross-community consent procedure.

12. The above special procedure shall be followed when requested by the executive committee, or by the relevant departmental committee, voting on a cross-community basis.

13. When there is a petition of concern, as in 5(*d*) above, the Assembly shall vote to determine whether the measure may proceed without reference to this special procedure. If this fails to achieve support on a cross-community basis, as in 5(*d*)(i) above, the special procedure shall be followed.

Executive authority. 14. Executive authority to be discharged on behalf of the Assembly by a First Minister and Deputy First Minister and up to ten ministers with departmental responsibilities.

15. The First Minister and Deputy First Minister shall be jointly elected into office by the Assembly voting on a cross-community basis, according to 5(*d*)(i) above.

16. Following the election of the First Minister and Deputy First Minister, the posts of ministers will be allocated to parties on the basis of the d'Hondt system by reference to the number of seats each party has in the Assembly.

17. The Ministers will constitute an Executive Committee, which will be convened, and presided over, by the First Minister and Deputy First Minister.

18. The duties of the First Minister and Deputy First Minister will include, *inter alia*, dealing with and co-ordinating the work of the Executive Committee and the response of the Northern Ireland administration to external relationships.

19. The executive committee will provide a forum for the discussion of, and agreement on, issues which cut across the responsibilities of two or more ministers, for prioritizing executive and legislative proposals and for recommending a common position where necessary (e.g. in dealing with external relationships).

20. The executive committee will seek to agree each year, and review as necessary, a programme incorporating an agreed budget linked to policies and programmes, subject to approval by the Assembly, after scrutiny in Assembly committees, on a cross-community basis.

21. A party may decline the opportunity to nominate a person to serve as a minister or may subsequently change its nominee.

22. All the Northern Ireland departments will be headed by a minister. All ministers will liaise regularly with their respective committee.

23. As a condition of appointment, ministers, including the First Minister and Deputy First Minister, will affirm the terms of a pledge of office (Annex A) undertaking to discharge effectively and in good faith all the responsibilities attaching to their office.

24. Ministers will have full executive authority in their respective areas of responsibility, within any broad programme agreed by the executive committee and endorsed by the Assembly as a whole.

25. An individual may be removed from office following a decision of the Assembly taken on a cross-community basis, if (s)he loses the confidence of the Assembly, voting on a cross-community basis, for failure to meet his or her responsibilities including, *inter alia*, those set out in the pledge of office. Those who hold office should use only democratic, non-violent means, and those who do not should be excluded or removed from office under these provisions.

Legislation. 26. The Assembly will have authority to pass primary legislation for Northern Ireland in devolved areas, subject to: (*a*) the ECHR and any Bill of Rights for Northern Ireland supplementing it which, if the courts found to be breached, would render the relevant legislation null and void; (*b*) decisions by simple majority of members voting, except when decision on a cross-community basis is required; (*c*) detailed scrutiny and approval in the relevant departmental committee; (*d*) mechanisms, based on arrangements proposed for the Scottish parliament, to ensure suitable coordination, and avoid disputes, between the Assembly and the Westminster parliament; (*e*) option of the Assembly seeking to include Northern Ireland provisions in United Kingdom-wide legislation in the Westminster parliament, especially on devolved issues where parity is normally maintained (e.g. social security, company law).

27. The Assembly will have authority to legislate in reserved areas with the approval of the Secretary of State and subject to parliamentary control.

28. Disputes over legislative competence will be decided by the courts.

29. Legislation could be initiated by an individual, a committee or a minister.

Relations with other institutions. 30. Arrangements to represent the Assembly as a whole, at summit level and in dealings with other institutions, will be in accordance with paragraph 18, and will be such as to ensure cross-community involvement.

31. Terms will be agreed between appropriate Assembly representatives and the government of the United Kingdom to ensure effective coordination and input by ministers to national policy-making, including on EU issues.

Role of Secretary of State: 32. (*a*) to remain responsible for Northern Ireland Office matters not devolved to the Assembly, subject to regular consultation with the Assembly and ministers; (*b*) to approve and lay before the Westminster parliament any Assembly legislation on reserved matters; (c) to represent Northern Ireland interests in the United Kingdom cabinet; (d) to have the right to attend the Assembly at their invitation.

33. The Westminster parliament (whose power to make legislation for Northern Ireland would remain unaffected) will: (a) legislate for non-devolved issues, other than where the Assembly legislates with the approval of the Secretary of State and subject to the control of parliament; (b) to legislate as necessary to ensure that the United Kingdom's international obligations are met in respect of Northern Ireland; (c) scrutinize, including through the Northern Ireland Grand and Select Committees, the responsibilities of the Secretary of State.

34. A consultative Civic Forum will be established. It will comprise representatives of the business, trade union and voluntary sectors, and such other sectors as agreed by the First Minister and the Deputy First Minister. It will act as a consultative mechanism on social, economic and cultural issues. The First Minister and the Deputy First Minister will by agreement provide administrative support for the Civic Forum and establish guidelines for the selection of representatives to the Civic Forum.

Transitional arrangements. 35. The Assembly will meet first for the purpose of organization, without legislative or executive powers, to resolve its standing orders and working practices and make preparations for the effective functioning of the Assembly, the British-Irish Council and the North/South Ministerial Council and associated implementation bodies. In this transitional period, those members of the Assembly serving as shadow ministers shall affirm their commitment to non-violence and exclusively peaceful and democratic means and their opposition to any use or threat of force by others for any political purpose; to work in good faith to bring the new arrangements into being; and to observe the spirit of the pledge of office applying to appointed ministers.

Review. 36. After a specified period there will be a review of these arrangements, including the details of electoral arrangements and of the Assembly's procedures, with a view to agreeing any adjustments necessary in the interests of efficiency and fairness.. . .

IV STRAND TWO: NORTH/SOUTH MINISTERIAL COUNCIL

1. Under a new British/Irish Agreement dealing with the totality of relationships, and related legislation at Westminster and in the Oireachtas, a North/South Ministerial Council to be established to bring together those with executive responsibilities in Northern Ireland and the Irish government, to develop consultation, cooperation and action within the island of Ireland—including through implementation on an all-island and cross-border basis—on matters of mutual interest within the competence of the Administrations, North and South.

2. All Council decisions to be by agreement between the two sides. Northern Ireland to be represented by the First Minister, Deputy First Minister and any relevant ministers, the Irish government by the Taoiseach and relevant ministers, all operating in accordance with the rules for democratic authority and accountability in force in the Northern Ireland Assembly and the Oireachtas respectively. Participation in the Council to be one of the essential responsibilities attaching to relevant posts in the two administrations. If a holder of a relevant post will not participate normally in the Council, the Taoiseach in the case of the Irish government and the First and Deputy First Minister in the case of the Northern Ireland administration to be able to make alternative arrangements.

3. The Council to meet in different formats: (i) in plenary format twice a year, with Northern Ireland representation led by the First Minister and Deputy First Minister and the Irish government led by the Taoiseach; (ii) in specific sectoral formats on a regular and frequent basis with each side represented by the appropriate minister; (iii) in an appropriate format to consider institutional or cross-sectoral matters (including in relation to the EU) and to resolve disagreement.

4. Agendas for all meetings to be settled by prior agreement between the two sides, but it will be open to either to propose any matter for consideration or action.

5. The Council: (i) to exchange information, discuss and consult with a view to co-operating on matters of mutual interest within the competence of both Administrations, North and South; (ii) to use best endeavours to reach agreement on the adoption of common policies, in areas where there is a mutual cross-border and all-island benefit, and which are within the competence of both Administrations, North and South, making determined efforts to overcome any disagreements; (iii) to take decisions by agreement on policies for implementation separately in each jurisdiction, in relevant meaningful areas within the competence of both Administrations, North and South; (iv) to take decisions by agreement on policies and action at an all-island and cross-border level to be implemented by the bodies to be established as set out in paragraphs 8 and 9 below.

6. Each side to be in a position to take decisions in the Council within the defined authority of those attending, through the arrangements in place for coordination of executive functions within

each jurisdiction. Each side to remain accountable to the Assembly and Oireachtas respectively, whose approval, through the arrangements in place on either side, would be required for decisions beyond the defined authority of those attending.

7. As soon as practically possible after elections to the Northern Ireland Assembly, inaugural meetings will take place of the Assembly, the British/Irish Council and the North/South Ministerial Council in their transitional forms. All three institutions will meet regularly and frequently on this basis during the period between the elections to the Assembly, and the transfer of powers to the Assembly, in order to establish their *modus operandi*.

8. During the transitional period between the elections to the Northern Ireland Assembly and the transfer of power to it, representatives of the Northern Ireland transitional administration and the Irish government operating in the North/South Ministerial Council will undertake a work programme, in consultation with the British government, covering at least 12 subject areas, with a view to identifying and agreeing by 31 October 1998 areas where cooperation and implementation for mutual benefit will take place. Such areas may include matters in the list set out in the Annex. 9. As part of the work programme, the Council will identify and agree at least six matters for cooperation and implementation in each of the following categories: (i) matters where existing bodies will be the appropriate mechanisms for cooperation in each separate jurisdiction; (ii) matters where the cooperation will take place through agreed implementation bodies on a cross-border or all-island level.

10. The two governments will make necessary legislative and other enabling preparations to ensure, as an absolute commitment, that these bodies, which have been agreed as a result of the work programme, function at the time of the inception of the British-Irish Agreement and the transfer of powers, with legislative authority for these bodies transferred to the Assembly as soon as possible thereafter. Other arrangements for the agreed co-operation will also commence contemporaneously with the transfer of powers to the Assembly.

11. The implementation bodies will have a clear operational remit. They will implement on an all-island and cross-border basis policies agreed in the Council.

12. Any further development of these arrangements to be by agreement in the Council and with the specific endorsement of the Northern Ireland Assembly and Oireachtas, subject to the extent of the competences and responsibility of the two Administrations.

13. It is understood that the North/South Ministerial Council and the Northern Ireland Assembly are mutually inter-dependent, and that one cannot successfully function without the other.

14. Disagreements within the Council to be addressed in the format described at paragraph 3(iii) above or in the plenary format. By agreement between the two sides, experts could be appointed to consider a particular matter and report.

15. Funding to be provided by the two administrations on the basis that the Council and the implementation bodies constitute a necessary public function.

16. The Council to be supported by a standing joint secretariat, staffed by members of the Northern Ireland Civil Service and the Irish Civil Service.

17. The Council to consider the European Union dimension of relevant matters, including the implementation of EU policies and programmes and proposals under consideration in the EU framework. Arrangements to be made to ensure that the views of the Council are taken into account and represented appropriately at relevant EU meetings.

18. The Northern Ireland Assembly and the Oireachtas to consider developing a joint parliamentary forum, bringing together equal numbers from both institutions for discussion of matters of mutual interest and concern.

19. Consideration to be given to the establishment of an independent consultative forum appointed by the two administrations, representative of civil society, comprising the social partners and other members with expertise in social, cultural, economic and other issues.. . .

V STRAND THREE

British-Irish Council

1. A British-Irish Council (BIC) will be established under a new British-Irish Agreement to promote the harmonious and mutually-beneficial development of the totality of relationships among the peoples of these islands.

2. Membership of the BIC will comprise representatives of the British and Irish Governments, devolved institutions in Northern Ireland, Scotland and Wales, when established, and, if appropriate, elsewhere in the United Kingdom, together with representatives of the Isle of Man and the Channel Islands.

3. The BIC will meet in different formats: at summit level, twice per year; in specific sectoral formats on a regular basis, with each side represented by the appropriate minister; in an appropriate format to consider cross-sectoral matters.

4. Representatives of members will operate in accordance with whatever procedures for democratic authority and accountability are in force in their respective elected institutions.

5. The BIC will exchange information, discuss, consult and use best endeavours to reach agreement on cooperation on matters of mutual interest within the competence of the relevant administrations. Suitable issues for early discussion in the BIC could include transport links, agricultural issues, environmental issues, cultural issues, health issues, education issues and approaches to EU issues. Suitable arrangements to be made for practical co-operation on agreed policies.

6. It will be open to the BIC to agree common policies or common actions. Individual members may opt not to participate in such common policies and common action.

7. The BIC normally will operate by consensus. In relation to decisions on common policies or common actions, including their means of implementation, it will operate by agreement of all members participating in such policies or actions.

8. The members of the BIC, on a basis to be agreed between them, will provide such financial support as it may require.

9. A secretariat for the BIC will be provided by the British and Irish governments in coordination with officials of each of the other members.

10. In addition to the structures provided for under this agreement, it will be open to two or more members to develop bilateral or multilateral arrangements between them. Such arrangements could include, subject to the agreement of the members concerned, mechanisms to enable consultation, cooperation and joint decision-making on matters of mutual interest; and mechanisms to implement any joint decisions they may reach. These arrangements will not require the prior approval of the BIC as a whole and will operate independently of it.

11. The elected institutions of the members will be encouraged to develop inter-parliamentary links, perhaps building on the British-Irish Inter-Parliamentary Body.

12. The full membership of the BIC will keep under review the workings of the Council, including a formal published review at an appropriate time after the Agreement comes into effect, and will contribute as appropriate to any review of the overall political agreement arising from the multi-party negotiations.

British-Irish Intergovernmental Conference

1. There will be a new British-Irish Agreement dealing with the totality of relationships. It will establish a standing British-Irish Intergovernmental Conference, which will subsume both the Anglo-Irish Intergovernmental Council and the Intergovernmental Conference established under the 1985 Agreement.

2. The Conference will bring together the British and Irish governments to promote bilateral cooperation at all levels on all matters of mutual interest within the competence of both governments.

3. The Conference will meet as required at summit level (Prime Minister and Taoiseach). Otherwise, governments will be represented by appropriate ministers. Advisers, including police and security advisers, will attend as appropriate.

4. All decisions will be by agreement between both governments. The governments will make determined efforts to resolve disagreements between them. There will be no derogation from the sovereignty of either government.

5. In recognition of the Irish government's special interest in Northern Ireland and of the extent to which issues of mutual concern arise in relation to Northern Ireland, there will be regular and frequent meetings of the Conference concerned with non-devolved Northern Ireland matters, on which the Irish government may put forward views and proposals. These meetings, to be co-chaired by the Minister for Foreign Affairs and the Secretary of State for Northern Ireland, would also deal with all-island and cross-border cooperation on non-devolved issues.

6. Cooperation within the framework of the Conference will include facilitation of cooperation in security matters. The Conference also will address, in particular, the areas of rights, justice, prisons and policing in Northern Ireland (unless and until responsibility is devolved to a Northern Ireland administration) and will intensify cooperation between the two governments on the all-island or cross-border aspects of these matters.

7. Relevant executive members of the Northern Ireland administration will be involved in meetings of the Conference, and in the reviews referred to in paragraph 9 below to discuss non-devolved Northern Ireland matters.

XVII.1. NORTHERN IRELAND: GOOD FRIDAY AGREEMENT

8. The Conference will be supported by officials of the British and Irish governments, including by a standing joint secretariat of officials dealing with non-devolved Northern Ireland matters.

9. The Conference will keep under review the workings of the new British-Irish Agreement and the machinery and institutions established under it, including a formal published review three years after the Agreement comes into effect. Representatives of the Northern Ireland administration will be invited to express views to the Conference in this context. The Conference will contribute as appropriate to any review of the overall political agreement arising from the multi-party negotiations but will have no power to override the democratic arrangements set up by this Agreement.. . .

VII DECOMMISSIONING

1. Participants recall their agreement in the Procedural Motion adopted on 24 September 1997 'that the resolution of the decommissioning issue is an indispensable part of the process of negotiation', and also recall the provisions of paragraph 25 of Strand One above.

2. They note the progress made by the Independent International Commission on Decommissioning and the governments in developing schemes which can represent a workable basis for achieving the decommissioning of illegally-held arms in the possession of paramilitary groups.

3. All participants accordingly reaffirm their commitment to the total disarmament of all paramilitary organizations. They also confirm their intention to continue to work constructively and in good faith with the Independent Commission, and to use any influence they may have, to achieve the decommissioning of all paramilitary arms within two years following endorsement in referendums North and South of the agreement and in the context of the implementation of the overall settlement.

4. The Independent Commission will monitor, review and verify progress on decommissioning of illegal arms, and will report to both Governments at regular intervals.

5. Both governments will take all necessary steps to facilitate the decommissioning process to include bringing the relevant schemes into force by the end of June.

VIII SECURITY

1. The participants note that the development of a peaceful environment on the basis of this agreement can and should mean a normalisation of security arrangements and practices.

2. The British government will make progress towards the objective of as early a return as possible to normal security arrangements in Northern Ireland, consistent with the level of threat and with a published overall strategy, dealing with: (i) the reduction of the numbers and role of the Armed Forces deployed in Northern Ireland to levels compatible with a normal peaceful society; (ii) the removal of security installations; (iii) the removal of emergency powers in Northern Ireland; and (iv) other measures appropriate to and compatible with a normal peaceful society.

3. The Secretary of State will consult regularly on progress, and the response to any continuing paramilitary activity, with the Irish government and the political parties, as appropriate.

4. The British government will continue its consultation on firearms regulation and control on the basis of the document published on 2 April 1998.

5. The Irish government will initiate a wide-ranging review of the Offences Against the State Acts 1939–85 with a view to both reform and dispensing with those elements no longer required as circumstances permit.

IX POLICING AND JUSTICE

1. The participants recognize that policing is a central issue in any society. They equally recognize that Northern Ireland's history of deep divisions has made it highly emotive, with great hurt suffered and sacrifices made by many individuals and their families, including those in the Royal Ulster Constabulary (RUC) and other public servants. They believe that the agreement provides the opportunity for a new beginning to policing in Northern Ireland with a police service capable of attracting and sustaining support from the community as a whole. They also believe that this agreement offers a unique opportunity to bring about a new political dispensation which will recognize the full and equal legitimacy and worth of the identities, senses of allegiance and ethos of all sections of the community in Northern Ireland. They consider that this opportunity should inform and underpin the development of a police service representative in terms of the make-up of the community as a whole and which, in a peaceful environment, should be routinely unarmed.

2. The participants believe it essential that policing structures and arrangements are such that the

police service is professional, effective and efficient, fair and impartial, free from partisan political control; accountable, both under the law for its actions and to the community it serves; representative of the society it polices, and operates within a coherent and cooperative criminal justice system, which conforms with human rights norms. The participants also believe that those structures and arrangements must be capable of maintaining law and order including responding effectively to crime and to any terrorist threat and to public order problems. A police service which cannot do so will fail to win public confidence and acceptance. They believe that any such structures and arrangements should be capable of delivering a policing service, in constructive and inclusive partnerships with the community at all levels, and with the maximum delegation of authority and responsibility, consistent with the foregoing principles. These arrangements should be based on principles of protection of human rights and professional integrity and should be unambiguously accepted and actively supported by the entire community.

3. An independent commission will be established to make recommendations for future policing arrangements in Northern Ireland including means of encouraging widespread community support for these arrangements within the agreed framework of principles reflected in the paragraphs above and in accordance with the terms of reference at Annex A. The commission will be broadly representative with expert and international representation among its membership and will be asked to consult widely and to report no later than summer 1999.

4. The participants believe that the aims of the criminal justice system are to: deliver a fair and impartial system of justice to the community; be responsive to the community's concerns, and encouraging community involvement where appropriate; have the confidence of all parts of the community; and deliver justice efficiently and effectively.

5. There will be a parallel wide-ranging review of criminal justice (other than policing and those aspects of the system relating to the emergency legislation) to be carried out by the British government through a mechanism with an independent element, in consultation with the political parties and others. The review will commence as soon as possible, will include wide consultation, and a report will be made to the Secretary of State no later than autumn 1999. Terms of reference are attached at Annex B.

6. Implementation of the recommendations arising from both reviews will be discussed with the political parties and with the Irish government.

7. The participants also note that the British government remains ready in principle, with the broad support of the political parties, and after consultation, as appropriate, with the Irish government, in the context of ongoing implementation of the relevant recommendations, to devolve responsibility for policing and justice issues.. . .

X PRISONERS

1. Both governments will put in place mechanisms to provide for an accelerated programme for the release of prisoners, including transferred prisoners, convicted of scheduled offences in Northern Ireland or, in the case of those sentenced outside Northern Ireland, similar offences (referred to hereafter as qualifying prisoners). Any such arrangements will protect the rights of individual prisoners under national and international law.

2. Prisoners affiliated to organizations which have not established or are not maintaining a complete and unequivocal ceasefire will not benefit from the arrangements. The situation in this regard will be kept under review.

3. Both governments will complete a review process within a fixed time frame and set prospective release dates for all qualifying prisoners. The review process would provide for the advance of the release dates of qualifying prisoners while allowing account to be taken of the seriousness of the offences for which the person was convicted and the need to protect the community. In addition, the intention would be that should the circumstances allow it, any qualifying prisoners who remained in custody two years after the commencement of the scheme would be released at that point.

4. The governments will seek to enact the appropriate legislation to give effect to these arrangements by the end of June 1998.

5. The governments continue to recognize the importance of measures to facilitate the reintegration of prisoners into the community by providing support both prior to and after release, including assistance directed towards availing of employment opportunities, re-training and/or re-skilling, and further education.

XI VALIDATION, IMPLEMENTATION AND REVIEW

Validation and implementation. 1. The two governments will as soon as possible sign a new British-Irish Agreement replacing the 1985 Anglo-Irish Agreement, embodying understandings on constitutional issues and affirming their solemn commitment to support and, where appropriate, implement the agreement reached by the participants in the negotiations which shall be annexed to the British-Irish Agreement.

2. Each government will organize a referendum on 22 May 1998. Subject to parliamentary approval, a consultative referendum in Northern Ireland, organized under the terms of the Northern Ireland (Entry to Negotiations, etc.) Act 1996, will address the question: 'Do you support the Agreement reached in the multi-party talks on Northern Ireland and set out in Command Paper 3883?' The Irish government will introduce and support in the Oireachtas a bill to amend the constitution as described in paragraph 2 of the section 'Constitutional Issues' and in Annex B, as follows: (a) to amend Articles 2 and 3 as described in paragraph 8.1 in Annex B above and (b) to amend Article 29 to permit the government to ratify the new British-Irish Agreement. On passage by the Oireachtas, the bill will be put to referendum.

3. If majorities of those voting in each of the referendums support this agreement, the governments will then introduce and support, in their respective parliaments, such legislation as may be necessary to give effect to all aspects of this agreement, and will take whatever ancillary steps as may be required including the holding of elections on 25 June, subject to parliamentary approval, to the Assembly, which would meet initially in a 'shadow' mode. The establishment of the North-South Ministerial Council, implementation bodies, the British-Irish Council and the British-Irish Intergovernmental Conference and the assumption by the Assembly of its legislative and executive powers will take place at the same time on the entry into force of the British-Irish Agreement.

4. In the interim, aspects of the implementation of the multi-party agreement will be reviewed at meetings of those parties relevant in the particular case (taking into account, once Assembly elections have been held, the results of those elections), under the chairmanship of the British government or the two governments, as may be appropriate; and representatives of the two governments and all relevant parties may meet under independent chairmanship to review implementation of the agreement as a whole.

Review procedures following implementation. 5. Each institution may, at any time, review any problems that may arise in its operation and, where no other institution is affected, take remedial action in consultation as necessary with the relevant government or governments. It will be for each institution to determine its own procedures for review.

6. If there are difficulties in the operation of a particular institution, which have implications for another institution, they may review their operations separately and jointly and agree on remedial action to be taken under their respective authorities.

7. If difficulties arise which require remedial action across the range of institutions, or otherwise require amendment of the British-Irish Agreement or relevant legislation, the process of review will fall to the two governments in consultation with the parties in the Assembly. Each government will be responsible for action in its own jurisdiction.

8. Notwithstanding the above, each institution will publish an annual report on its operations. In addition, the two governments and the parties in the Assembly will convene a conference four years after the agreement comes into effect, to review and report on its operation.

ANNEX: AGREEMENT BETWEEN THE GOVERNMENT OF THE UNITED KINGDOM OF GREAT BRITAIN AND NORTHERN IRELAND AND THE GOVERNMENT OF IRELAND

The British and Irish governments:

Welcoming the strong commitment to the Agreement reached on 10 April 1998 by themselves and other participants in the multi-party talks and set out in Annex 1 to this Agreement (hereinafter 'the Multi-Party Agreement');

Considering that the Multi-Party Agreement offers an opportunity for a new beginning in relationships within Northern Ireland, within the island of Ireland and between the peoples of these islands;

Wishing to develop still further the unique relationship between their peoples and the close cooperation between their countries as friendly neighbours and as partners in the European Union;

Reaffirming their total commitment to the principles of democracy and non-violence which have been fundamental to the multi-party talks;

Reaffirming their commitment to the principles of partnership, equality and mutual respect and to the protection of civil, political, social, economic and cultural rights in their respective jurisdictions;

Have agreed as follows:

Article 1

The two governments:
(i) recognize the legitimacy of whatever choice is freely exercised by a majority of the people of Northern Ireland with regard to its status, whether they prefer to continue to support the Union with Great Britain or a sovereign united Ireland;
(ii) recognize that it is for the people of the island of Ireland alone, by agreement between the two parts respectively and without external impediment, to exercise their right of self-determination on the basis of consent, freely and concurrently given, North and South, to bring about a united Ireland, if that is their wish, accepting that this right must be achieved and exercised with and subject to the agreement and consent of a majority of the people of Northern Ireland;
(iii) acknowledge that while a substantial section of the people in Northern Ireland share the legitimate wish of a majority of the people of the island of Ireland for a united Ireland, the present wish of a majority of the people of Northern Ireland, freely exercised and legitimate, is to maintain the Union and accordingly, that Northern Ireland's status as part of the United Kingdom reflects and relies upon that wish; and that it would be wrong to make any change in the status of Northern Ireland save with the consent of a majority of its people;
(iv) affirm that, if in the future, the people of the island of Ireland exercise their right of self-determination on the basis set out in sections (i) and (ii) above to bring about a united Ireland, it will be a binding obligation on both Governments to introduce and support in their respective Parliaments legislation to give effect to that wish;
(v) affirm that whatever choice is freely exercised by a majority of the people of Northern Ireland, the power of the sovereign government with jurisdiction there shall be exercised with rigorous impartiality on behalf of all the people in the diversity of their identities and traditions and shall be founded on the principles of full respect for, and equality of, civil, political, social and cultural rights, of freedom from discrimination for all citizens, and of parity of esteem and of just and equal treatment for the identity, ethos and aspirations of both communities;
(vi) recognize the birthright of all the people of Northern Ireland to identify themselves and be accepted as Irish or British, or both, as they may so choose, and accordingly confirm that their right to hold both British and Irish citizenship is accepted by both Governments and would not be affected by any future change in the status of Northern Ireland.

Article 2

The two governments affirm their solemn commitment to support, and where appropriate implement, the provisions of the Multi-Party Agreement. In particular there shall be established in accordance with the provisions of the Multi-Party Agreement immediately on the entry into force of this Agreement, the following institutions:
(i) a North/South Ministerial Council;
(ii) the implementation bodies referred to in paragraph 9 (ii) of the section entitled 'Strand Two' of the Multi-Party Agreement;
(iii) a British-Irish Council;
(iv) a British-Irish Intergovernmental Conference.

Article 3

(1) This Agreement shall replace the Agreement between the British and Irish Governments done at Hillsborough on 15h November 1985 which shall cease to have effect on entry into force of this Agreement.
(2) The Intergovernmental Conference established by Article 2 of the aforementioned Agreement done on 15 November 1985 shall cease to exist on entry into force of this Agreement.

Article 4

(1) It shall be a requirement for entry into force of this Agreement that: (*a*) British legislation shall have been enacted for the purpose of implementing the provisions of Annex A to the section entitled 'Constitutional Issues' of the Multi-Party Agreement; (*b*) the amendments to the Constitution of Ireland set out in Annex B to the section entitled 'Constitutional Issues' of the Multi-Party Agreement shall have been approved by Referendum; (*c*) such legislation shall have

been enacted as may be required to establish the institutions referred to in Article 2 of this Agreement.

(2) Each government shall notify the other in writing of the completion, so far as it is concerned, of the requirements for entry into force of this Agreement. This Agreement shall enter into force on the date of the receipt of the later of the two notifications.

(3) Immediately on entry into force of this Agreement, the Irish government shall ensure that the amendments to the constitution of Ireland set out in Annex B to the section entitled 'Constitutional Issues' of the Multi-Party Agreement take effect. In witness thereof the undersigned, being duly authorized thereto by the respective governments, have signed this Agreement.. . .

Annex 1. The Agreement Reached in the Multi-Party Talks [above].

Annex 2. Declaration on the Provisions of Paragraph (vi) of Article 1 in relation to Citizenship: The British and Irish governments declare that it is their joint understanding that the term 'the people of Northern Ireland' in paragraph (vi) of Article 1 of this Agreement means, for the purposes of giving effect to this provision, all persons born in Northern Ireland and having, at the time of their birth, at least one parent who is a British citizen, an Irish citizen or is otherwise entitled to reside in Northern Ireland without any restriction on their period of residence.

2. STATUTE OF INTERNATIONAL CRIMINAL COURT

Printed below are extracts from the Statute of the International Criminal Court adopted by a UN conference in Rome on 17 July 1998, with 120 states voting in favour, seven against and 21 abstaining. (Text supplied by United Nations, New York.)

PART 1: ESTABLISHMENT OF THE COURT

Art. 1: The Court. An International Criminal Court ('the Court') is hereby established. It shall be a permanent institution and shall have the power to exercise its jurisdiction over persons for the most serious crimes of international concern, as referred to in this Statute, and shall be complementary to national criminal jurisdictions. The jurisdiction and functioning of the Court shall be governed by the provisions of this Statute.

Art. 2: Relationship of the Court with the United Nations. The Court shall be brought into relationship with the United Nations through an agreement to be approved by the Assembly of States Parties to this Statute and thereafter concluded by the President of the Court on its behalf.

Art. 3: Seat of the Court. 1. The seat of the Court shall be established at The Hague in the Netherlands ('the host state').

2. The Court shall enter into a headquarters agreement with the host state, to be approved by the Assembly of States Parties and thereafter concluded by the President of the Court on its behalf.

3. The Court may sit elsewhere, whenever it considers it desirable, as provided in this Statute.

Art. 4: Legal status and powers of the Court. 1. The Court shall have international legal personality. It shall also have such legal capacity as may be necessary for the exercise of its functions and the fulfilment of its purposes.

2. The Court may exercise its functions and powers, as provided in this Statute, on the territory of any state party and, by special agreement, on the territory of any other state.

PART 2: JURISDICTION, ADMISSIBILITY AND APPLICABLE LAW

Art. 5: Crimes within the jurisdiction of the Court. 1. The jurisdiction of the Court shall be limited to the most serious crimes of concern to the international community as a whole. The Court has jurisdiction in accordance with this Statute with respect to the following crimes: (*a*) the crime of genocide; (*b*) crimes against humanity; (*c*) war crimes; (*d*) the crime of aggression.

2. The Court shall exercise jurisdiction over the crime of aggression once a provision is adopted in accordance with Articles 121 and 123 defining the crime and setting out the conditions under which the Court shall exercise jurisdiction with respect to this crime. Such a provision shall be consistent with the relevant provisions of the Charter of the United Nations.

Art. 6: Genocide. For the purpose of this Statute, 'genocide' means any of the following acts committed with intent to destroy, in whole or in part, a national, ethnical, racial or religious group, as such: (*a*) killing members of the group; (*b*) causing serious bodily or mental harm to members of the group; (*c*) deliberately inflicting on the group conditions of life calculated to bring about its physical destruction in whole or in part; (*d*) imposing measures intended to prevent births within the group; (*e*) forcibly transferring children of the group to another group.

Art. 7: Crimes against humanity. 1. For the purpose of this Statute, 'crime against humanity' means any of the following acts when committed as part of a widespread or systematic attack directed against any civilian population, with knowledge of the attack: (*a*) murder; (*b*) extermination; (*c*) enslavement; (*d*) deportation or forcible transfer of population; (*e*) imprisonment or other severe deprivation of physical liberty in violation of fundamental rules of international law; (*f*) torture; (*g*) rape, sexual slavery, enforced prostitution, forced pregnancy, enforced sterilization, or any other form of sexual violence of comparable gravity; (*h*) persecution against any identifiable group or collectivity on political, racial, national, ethnic, cultural, religious, gender as defined in paragraph 3, or other grounds that are universally recognized as impermissible under international law, in connection with any act referred to in this paragraph or any crime within the jurisdiction of the Court; (*i*) enforced disappearance of persons; (*j*) the crime of apartheid; (*k*) other inhumane acts of a similar character intentionally causing great suffering, or serious injury to body or to mental or physical health.

2. For the purpose of paragraph 1: (*a*) 'attack directed against any civilian population' means a course of conduct involving the multiple commission of acts referred to in paragraph 1 against any civilian population, pursuant to or in furtherance of a State or organizational policy to commit such attack; (*b*) 'extermination' includes the intentional infliction of conditions of life, *inter alia* the deprivation of access to food and medicine, calculated to bring about the destruction of part of a population; (*c*) 'enslavement' means the exercise of any or all of the powers attaching to the right of ownership over a person and includes the exercise of such power in the course of trafficking in persons, in particular women and children; (*d*) 'deportation or forcible transfer of population' means forced displacement of the persons concerned by expulsion or other coercive acts from the area in which they are lawfully present, without grounds permitted under international law; (*e*) 'torture' means the intentional infliction of severe pain or suffering, whether physical or mental, upon a person in the custody or under the control of the accused; except that torture shall not include pain or suffering arising only from, inherent in or incidental to, lawful sanctions; (*f*) 'forced pregnancy' means the unlawful confinement, of a woman forcibly made pregnant, with the intent of affecting the ethnic composition of any population or carrying out other grave violations of international law. This definition shall not in any way be interpreted as affecting national laws relating to pregnancy; (*g*) 'persecution' means the intentional and severe deprivation of fundamental rights contrary to international law by reason of the identity of the group or collectivity; (*h*) 'the crime of apartheid' means inhumane acts of a character similar to those referred to in paragraph 1, committed in the context of an institutionalized regime of systematic oppression and domination by one racial group over any other racial group or groups and committed with the intention of maintaining that regime; (*i*) 'enforced disappearance of persons' means the arrest, detention or abduction of persons by, or with the authorization, support or acquiescence of, a state or a political organization, followed by a refusal to acknowledge that deprivation of freedom or to give information on the fate or whereabouts of those persons, with the intention of removing them from the protection of the law for a prolonged period of time.

3. For the purpose of this Statute, it is understood that the term 'gender' refers to the two sexes, male and female, within the context of society. The term 'gender' does not indicate any meaning different from the above.

Art. 8: War crimes. 1. The Court shall have jurisdiction in respect of war crimes in particular when committed as a part of a plan or policy or as part of a large scale commission of such crimes.

2. For the purpose of this Statute, 'war crimes' means:

(*a*) grave breaches of the Geneva Conventions of 12 August 1949, namely, any of the following acts against persons or property protected under the provisions of the relevant Geneva Convention: (i) wilful killing; (ii) torture or inhuman treatment, including biological experiments; (iii) wilfully causing great suffering, or serious injury to body or health; (iv) extensive destruction and appropriation of property, not justified by military necessity and carried out unlawfully and wantonly; (v) compelling a prisoner-of-war or other protected person to serve in the forces of a hostile power; (vi) wilfully depriving a prisoner of war or other protected person of the rights of fair and regular trial; (vii) unlawful deportation or transfer or unlawful confinement; (viii) taking of hostages;

(*b*) other serious violations of the laws and customs applicable in international armed conflict, within the established framework of international law, namely, any of the following acts: (i) intentionally directing attacks against the civilian population as such or against individual civilians not taking direct part in hostilities; (ii) intentionally directing attacks against civilian objects, that is, objects which are not military objectives; (iii) intentionally directing attacks against personnel, installations, material, units or vehicles involved in a humanitarian assistance or peace-keeping mission in accordance with the Charter of the United Nations, as long as they are entitled to the protection given to civilians or civilian objects under the international law of armed conflict; (iv) intentionally launching an attack in the knowledge that such attack will cause incidental loss of life or injury to civilians or damage to civilian objects or widespread, long_term and severe damage to the natural environment which would be clearly excessive in relation to the concrete and direct overall military advantage anticipated; (v) attacking or bombarding, by whatever means, towns, villages, dwellings or buildings which are undefended and which are not military objectives; (vi) killing or wounding a combatant who, having laid down his arms or having no longer means of defence, has surrendered at discretion; (vii) making improper use of a flag of truce, of the flag or of the military insignia and uniform of the enemy or of the United Nations, as well as of the distinctive emblems of the Geneva Conventions, resulting in death or serious personal injury; (viii) the transfer, directly or indirectly, by the occupying power of parts of its own civilian population into the territory it occupies, or the deportation or transfer of all or parts of the population of the occupied territory within or outside this territory; (ix) intentionally directing attacks against buildings dedicated to religion, education, art, science or charitable purposes, historic monuments, hospitals and places where the sick and wounded are collected, provided they are not military objectives; (x) subjecting persons who are in the power of an adverse party to physical mutilation or to medical or scientific experiments of any kind which are neither justified by the medical, dental or hospital treatment of the person concerned nor carried out in his or her interest, and which cause death to or seriously endanger the health of such person or persons; (xi) killing or wounding treacherously individuals belonging to the hostile nation or army; (xii) declaring that no quarter will be given; (xiii) destroying or seizing the enemy's property unless such destruction or seizure be imperatively demanded by the necessities of war; (xiv) declaring abolished, suspended or inadmissible in a court of law the rights and actions of the nationals of the hostile party; (xv) compelling the nationals of the hostile party to take part in the operations of war directed against their own country, even if they were in the belligerent's service before the commencement of the war; (xvi) pillaging a town or place, even when taken by assault; (xvii) employing poison or poisoned weapons; (xviii) employing asphyxiating, poisonous or other gases, and all analogous liquids, materials or devices; (xix) employing bullets which expand or flatten easily in the human body, such as bullets with a hard envelope which does not entirely cover the core or is pierced with incisions; (xx) employing weapons, projectiles and material and methods of warfare which are of a nature to cause superfluous injury or unnecessary suffering or which are inherently indiscriminate in violation of the international law of armed conflict, provided that such weapons, projectiles and material and methods of warfare are the subject of a comprehensive prohibition and are included in an annex to this Statute, by an amendment in accordance with the relevant provisions set forth in articles 121 and 123; (xxi) committing outrages upon personal dignity, in particular humiliating and degrading treatment; (xxii) committing rape, sexual slavery, enforced prostitution, forced pregnancy, as defined in article 7, paragraph 2(*f*), enforced sterilization, or any other form of sexual violence also constituting a grave breach of the Geneva Conventions; (xxiii) utilizing the presence of a civilian or other protected person to render certain points, areas or military forces immune from military operations; (xxiv) intentionally directing attacks against buildings, material, medical units and transport, and personnel using the distinctive emblems of the Geneva Conventions in conformity with international law; (xxv) intentionally using starvation of civilians as a method of warfare by depriving them of objects indispensable to their survival, including wilfully impeding relief supplies as provided for under the Geneva Conventions; (xxvi) conscripting or enlisting children under the age of fifteen years into the national armed forces or using them to participate actively in hostilities.

(*c*) In the case of an armed conflict not of an international character, serious violations of article 3 common to the four Geneva Conventions of 12 August 1949, namely, any of the following acts committed against persons taking no active part in the hostilities, including members of armed forces who have laid down their arms and those placed hors de combat by sickness, wounds, detention or any other cause: (i) violence to life and person, in particular murder of all kinds, mutilation, cruel treatment and torture; (ii) committing outrages upon personal dignity, in particular humiliating and degrading treatment; (iii) taking of hostages; (iv) the passing of sentences and the carrying out of executions without previous judgement pronounced by a regularly constituted court, affording all judicial guarantees which are generally recognized as indispensable.

(*d*) Paragraph 2 (*c*) applies to armed conflicts not of an international character and thus does not apply to situations of internal disturbances and tensions, such as riots, isolated and sporadic acts of violence or other acts of a similar nature.

(*e*) Other serious violations of the laws and customs applicable in armed conflicts not of an international character, within the established framework of international law, namely, any of the following acts: (i) intentionally directing attacks against the civilian population as such or against individual civilians not taking direct part in hostilities; (ii) intentionally directing attacks against buildings, material, medical units and transport, and personnel using the distinctive emblems of the Geneva Conventions in conformity with international law; (iii) intentionally directing attacks against personnel, installations, material, units or vehicles involved in a humanitarian assistance or peace-keeping mission in accordance with the Charter of the United Nations, as long as they are entitled to the protection given to civilians or civilian objects under the law of armed conflict; (iv) intentionally directing attacks against buildings dedicated to religion, education, art, science or charitable purposes, historic monuments, hospitals and places where the sick and wounded are collected, provided they are not military objectives; (v) pillaging a town or place, even when taken by assault; (vi) committing rape, sexual slavery, enforced prostitution, forced pregnancy, as defined in article 7, paragraph 2(f), enforced sterilization, and any other form of sexual violence also constituting a serious violation of article 3 common to the four Geneva Conventions; (vii) conscripting or enlisting children under the age of 15 years into armed forces or groups or using them to participate actively in hostilities; (viii) ordering the displacement of the civilian population for reasons related to the conflict, unless the security of the civilians involved or imperative military reasons so demand; (ix) killing or wounding treacherously a combatant adversary; (x) declaring that no quarter will be given; (xi) subjecting persons who are in the power of another party to the conflict to physical mutilation or to medical or scientific experiments of any kind which are neither justified by the medical, dental or hospital treatment of the person concerned nor carried out in his or her interest, and which cause death to or seriously endanger the health of such person or persons; (xii) destroying or seizing the property of an adversary unless such destruction or seizure be imperatively demanded by the necessities of the conflict;

(f) Paragraph 2(e) applies to armed conflicts not of an international character and thus does not apply to situations of internal disturbances and tensions, such as riots, isolated and sporadic acts of violence or other acts of a similar nature. It applies to armed conflicts that take place in the territory of a state when there is protracted armed conflict between governmental authorities and organized armed groups or between such groups.

3. Nothing in paragraphs 2(c) and 2(d) shall affect the responsibility of a government to maintain or re_establish law and order in the state or to defend the unity and territorial integrity of the state, by all legitimate means.. . .

PART 4: COMPOSITION AND ADMINISTRATION OF THE COURT

Art. 34: Organs of the Court. The Court shall be composed of the following organs: (a) the Presidency; (b) an Appeals Division, a Trial Division and a Pre-Trial Division; (c) the Office of the Prosecutor; (d) the Registry.

Art: 35 *Service of judges.* 1. All judges shall be elected as full-time members of the Court and shall be available to serve on that basis from the commencement of their terms of office.. . .

PART 7: PENALTIES

Art. 77: Applicable penalties. 1. Subject to article 110, the Court may impose one of the following penalties on a person convicted of a crime under article 5 of this Statute: (a) imprisonment for a specified number of years, which may not exceed a maximum of 30 years; or (b) a term of life imprisonment when justified by the extreme gravity of the crime and the individual circumstances of the convicted person.

2. In addition to imprisonment, the Court may order: (a) a fine under the criteria provided for in the Rules of Procedure and

Evidence; (b) a forfeiture of proceeds, property and assets derived directly or indirectly from that crime, without prejudice to the rights of bona fide third parties.. . .

Art. 79: Trust Fund. A Trust Fund shall be established by decision of the Assembly of States Parties for the benefit of victims of crimes within the jurisdiction of the Court, and of the families of such victims.

2. The Court may order money and other property collected through fines or forfeiture to be transferred, by order of the Court, to the Trust Fund.

3. The Trust Fund shall be managed according to criteria to be determined by the Assembly of States Parties.. . .

3. SCOTLAND AND WALES: DEVOLUTION ACTS

Printed below are extracts from the Scotland Act enacted by the UK parliament on 19 November 1998 and the Government of Wales Act enacted on 31 July 1998. (Text from Her Majesty's Stationery Office, London.)

SCOTLAND ACT

PART I: THE SCOTTISH PARLIAMENT

1. The Scottish parliament

(1) There shall be a Scottish parliament.

(2) One member of the parliament shall be returned for each constituency (under the simple majority system) at an election held in the constituency.

(3) Members of the parliament for each region shall be returned at a general election under the additional member system of proportional representation provided for in this part and vacancies among such members shall be filled in accordance with this part.

(4) The validity of any proceedings of the parliament is not affected by any vacancy in its membership.. . .

5. Candidates

(1) At a general election, the candidates may stand for return as constituency members or regional members.

(2) A person may not be a candidate to be a constituency member for more than one constituency.

(3) The candidates to be regional members shall be those included in a list submitted under sub-section (4) or individual candidates. ·

(4) Any registered political party may submit to the regional returning officer a list of candidates to be regional members for a particular region (referred to in this Act, in relation to the region, as the party's 'regional list').

(5) A registered political party's regional list has effect in relation to the general election and any vacancy occurring among the regional members after that election and before the next general election.

(6) Not more than 12 persons may be included in the list (but the list may include only one person).

(7) A registered political party's regional list must not include a person (*a*) who is included in any other list submitted under sub-section (4) for the region or any list submitted under that sub-section for another region, (*b*) who is an individual candidate to be a regional member for the region or another region, (*c*) who is a candidate to be a constituency member for a constituency not included in the region, or (*d*) who is a candidate to be a constituency member for a constituency included in the region but is not a candidate of that party.

(8) A person may not be an individual candidate to be a regional member for a particular region if he is (*a*) included in a list submitted under sub-section (4) for the region or another region, (*b*) an individual candidate to be a regional member for another region, (*c*) a candidate to be a constituency member for a constituency not included in the region, or (*d*) a candidate of any registered political party to be a constituency member for a constituency included in the region.

(9) In this Act, 'registered political party' means a party registered under the Registration of Political Parties Act 1998.

6. Poll for regional members

(1) This section and sections 7 and 8 are about the return of regional members at a general election.

(2) In each of the constituencies for the parliament, a poll shall be held at which each person entitled to vote as elector may give a vote (referred to in this Act as a 'regional vote') for (*a*) a registered political party which has submitted a regional list, or (*b*) an individual candidate to be a regional member for the region.

(3) The right conferred on a person by sub-section (2) is in addition to any right the person may have to vote in any poll for the return of a constituency member.

7. Calculation of regional figures

(1) The persons who are to be returned as constituency members for constituencies included in the region must be determined before the persons who are to be returned as the regional members for the region.

(2) For each registered political party which has submitted a regional list, the regional figure for the purposes of section 8 is (*a*) the total number of regional votes given for the party in all the constituencies included in the region, divided by (*b*) the aggregate of one plus the number of candidates of the party returned as constituency members for any of those constituencies.

(3) Each time a seat is allocated to the party under section 8, that figure shall be recalculated by increasing (or further increasing) the aggregate in sub-section (2)(*b*) by one.

(4) For each individual candidate to be a regional member for the region, the regional figure for the purposes of section 8 is the total number of regional votes given for him in all the constituencies included in the region.

8. Allocation of seats to regional members

(1) The first regional member seat shall be allocated to the registered political party or individual candidate with the highest regional figure.

(2) The second and subsequent regional member seats shall be allocated to the registered political party or individual candidate with the highest regional figure, after any recalculation required by section 7(3) has been carried out.

(3) An individual candidate already returned as a constituency or regional member shall be disregarded.

(4) Seats for the region which are allocated to a registered political party shall be filled by the persons in the party's regional list in the order in which they appear in the list.

(5) For the purposes of this section and section 10, a person in a registered political party's regional list who is returned as a member of the Parliament shall be treated as ceasing to be in the list (even if his return is void).

(6) Once a party's regional list has been exhausted (by the return of persons included in it as constituency members or by the previous application of sub-section (1) or (2)) the party shall be disregarded.

(7) If (on the application of sub-section (1) or any application of sub-section (2)) the highest regional figure is the regional figure of two or more parties or individual candidates, the sub-section shall apply to each of them.. . .

Franchise and conduct of elections

11. Electors

(1) The persons entitled to vote as electors at an election for membership of the parliament held in any constituency are those who on the day of the poll (*a*) would be entitled to vote as electors at a local government election in an electoral area falling wholly or partly within the constituency, and (*b*) are registered in the register of local government electors at an address within the constituency.

(2) A person is not entitled to vote as elector in any constituency (*a*) more than once at a poll for the return of a constituency member, or (*b*) more than once at a poll for the return of regional members, or to vote as elector in more than one constituency at a general election.. . .

PART II: THE SCOTTISH ADMINISTRATION

Ministers and their staff

44. The Scottish executive

(1) There shall be a Scottish executive, whose members shall be (*a*) the First Minister, (*b*) such ministers as the First Minister may appoint under section 47, and (*c*) the Lord Advocate and the Solicitor General for Scotland.

(2) The members of the Scottish executive are referred to collectively as the Scottish ministers.

(3) A person who holds a ministerial office may not be appointed a member of the Scottish executive; and if a member of the Scottish executive is appointed to a ministerial office he shall cease to hold office as a member of the Scottish executive.

(4) In sub-section (3), references to a member of the Scottish executive include a junior Scottish minister and 'ministerial office' has the same meaning as in section 2 of the House of Commons Disqualification Act 1975.

45. The First Minister.

(1) The First Minister shall be appointed by Her Majesty from among the members of the parliament and shall hold office at Her Majesty's pleasure.

(2) The First Minister may at any time tender his resignation to Her Majesty and shall do so if the parliament resolves that the Scottish executive no longer enjoys the confidence of the parliament.

(3) The First Minister shall cease to hold office if a person is appointed in his place.

(4) If the office of First Minister is vacant or he is for any reason unable to act, the functions exercisable by him shall be exercisable by a person designated by the Presiding Officer.

(5) A person shall be so designated only if (a) he is a member of the parliament, or (b) if the parliament has been dissolved, he is a person who ceased to be a member by virtue of the dissolution.

(6) Functions exercisable by a person by virtue of sub-section (5)(a) shall continue to be exercisable by him even if the parliament is dissolved.

(7) The First Minister shall be the Keeper of the Scottish Seal.

46. Choice of the First Minister

(1) If one of the following events occurs, the parliament shall within the period allowed nominate one of its members for appointment as First Minister.

(2) The events are (a) the holding of a poll at a general election; (b) the First Minister tendering his resignation to Her Majesty; (c) the office of First Minister becoming vacant (otherwise than in consequence of his so tendering his resignation); (d) the First Minister ceasing to be a member of the parliament otherwise than by virtue of a dissolution.

(3) The period allowed is the period of 28 days which begin with the day on which the event in question occurs; but (a) if another of those events occurs within the period allowed, that period shall be extended (subject to paragraph (b)) so that it ends with the period of 28 days beginning with the day on which that other event occurred, and (b) the period shall end if the parliament passes a resolution under section 3(1)(a) or when Her Majesty appoints a person as First Minister.

(4) The Presiding Officer shall recommend to Her Majesty the appointment of any member of the parliament who is nominated by the parliament under this section.

47. Ministers

(1) The First Minister may, with the approval of Her Majesty, appoint ministers from among the members of the parliament.

(2) The First Minister shall not seek Her Majesty's approval for any appointment under this section without the agreement of the parliament.

(3) A minister appointed under this section (a) shall hold office at Her Majesty's pleasure, (b) may be removed from office by the First Minister, (c) may at any time resign and shall do so if the parliament resolves that the Scottish executive no longer enjoys the confidence of the parliament, (d) if he resigns, shall cease to hold office immediately, and (e) shall cease to hold office if he ceases to be a member of the parliament otherwise than by virtue of a dissolution.. . .

PART IV: THE TAX-VARYING POWER

73. Power to fix basic rate for Scottish taxpayers

(1) Subject to section 74, this section applies for any year of assessment for which income tax is charged if (a) the parliament has passed a resolution providing for the percentage determined to be the basic rate for that year to be increased or reduced for Scottish taxpayers in accordance with the resolution, (b) the increase or reduction provided for is confined to an increase or reduction by a

number not exceeding three which is specified in the resolution and is either a whole number or half of a whole number, and (c) the resolution has not been cancelled by a subsequent resolution of the parliament.

(2) Where this section applies for any year of assessment the Income Tax Acts (excluding this Part) shall have effect in relation to the income of Scottish taxpayers as if any rate determined by the parliament of the United Kingdom to be the basic rate for that year were increased or reduced in accordance with the resolution of the Scottish parliament.. . .

SCHEDULE 1: CONSTITUENCIES, REGIONS AND REGIONAL MEMBERS

General

1. The constituencies for the purposes of this Act are (a) the Orkney Islands, (b) the Shetland Islands, and (c) the parliamentary constituencies in Scotland, except a parliamentary constituency including either of those islands.

2.(1) There shall be eight regions for the purposes of this Act.(2) Those regions shall be the eight European Parliamentary constituencies which were provided for by the European Parliamentary Constituencies (Scotland) Order 1996.(3) Seven regional members shall be returned for each region. (4) Sub-paragraphs (2) and (3) are subject to any Order in Council under the Parliamentary Constituencies Act 1986 (referred to in this Schedule as the 1986 Act), as that Act is extended by this Schedule.. . .

GOVERNMENT OF WALES ACT

PART I: THE NATIONAL ASSEMBLY FOR WALES

1. The Assembly

(1) There shall be an assembly for Wales to be known as the National Assembly for Wales or Cynulliad Cenedlaethol Cymru (but referred to in this Act as the Assembly).(2) The Assembly shall be a body corporate.

(3) The exercise by the Assembly of its functions is to be regarded as done on behalf of the Crown.

2. Membership

(1) The Assembly shall consist of (a) one member for each Assembly constituency, and (b) members for each Assembly electoral region.

(2) The Assembly constituencies and Assembly electoral regions, and the number of Assembly seats for each Assembly electoral region, shall be as provided for by or in accordance with Schedule 1.

(3) Members of the Assembly (referred to in this Act as Assembly members) shall be returned in accordance with the provision made by and under this Act for (a) the holding of ordinary elections of Assembly members, and (b) the filling of vacancies in Assembly seats.

(4) An ordinary election involves the holding of elections for the return of the entire Assembly.

(5) The term of office of an Assembly member (a) begins when he is declared to be returned as an Assembly member, and (b) continues until the end of the day before the day of the poll at the next ordinary election.

(6) But an Assembly member may at any time resign his seat by giving notice to (a) the presiding officer, or (b) any person authorized by the standing orders of the Assembly to receive the notice.

(7) The validity of anything done by the Assembly is not affected by any vacancy in its membership.

3. Time of ordinary elections

(1) The poll at the first ordinary election shall be held on a day appointed by order made by the Secretary of State.

(2) The poll at each subsequent ordinary election shall be held on the first Thursday in May in the fourth calendar year following that in which the previous ordinary election was held.

(3) But the Secretary of State may by order require the poll at such an ordinary election to be held on a day which is neither (*a*) more than one month earlier, nor (*b*) more than one month later, than the first Thursday in May.

(4) Where the poll at an ordinary election would be held on the same day as polls at ordinary elections of community councillors, the Secretary of State may by order provide for the polls at ordinary elections of community councillors to be postponed, for not more than three months, to a day specified in the order.

(5) An order under sub-section (4) may make provision for (*a*) any provision of, or made under, the Representation of the People Acts, or (*b*) any other enactment relating to elections of community councillors, to have effect with such modifications or exceptions as the Secretary of State considers appropriate in connection with the postponement of polls for which it provides.

(6) No order shall be made under sub-section (3), and no order in connection with an ordinary election subsequent to the first shall be made under sub-section (4), unless the Secretary of State has consulted the Assembly.

4. Voting at ordinary elections

(1) Each person entitled to vote at an ordinary election in an Assembly constituency shall have two votes.

(2) One (referred to in this Act as a constituency vote) is to be given for a candidate to be the Assembly member for the Assembly constituency.

(3) The other (referred to in this Act as an electoral region vote) is to be given for (*a*) a registered political party which has submitted a list of candidates to be Assembly members for the Assembly electoral region in which the Assembly constituency is included, or (*b*) an individual who is a candidate to be an Assembly member for that Assembly electoral region.

(4) The Assembly member for the Assembly constituency shall be returned under the simple majority system.

(5) The Assembly members for the Assembly electoral region shall be returned under the additional member system of proportional representation in accordance with sections 5 to 7.

(6) The person who is to be returned as the Assembly member for each Assembly constituency in the Assembly electoral region must be determined before it is determined who are to be returned as the Assembly members for that Assembly electoral region.

(7) At an ordinary election a person may not be a candidate to be the Assembly member for more than one Assembly constituency.

(8) In this Act 'registered political party' means a party registered under any enactment providing for the registration of political parties.

5. Party lists and individual candidates

(1) Any registered political party may submit a list of candidates to be Assembly members for the Assembly electoral region.(2) The list is to be submitted to the regional returning officer.

(3) The list has effect in relation to (*a*) the ordinary election, and (*b*) any vacancies in seats of Assembly members returned for Assembly electoral regions which occur after that election and before the next ordinary election.

(4) The list must not include more than 12 persons (but may include only one).(5) The list must not include a person (*a*) who is included on any other list submitted for the Assembly electoral region or any list submitted for another Assembly electoral region, (*b*) who is an individual candidate to be an Assembly member for the Assembly electoral region or another Assembly electoral region, (*c*) who is a candidate to be the Assembly member for an Assembly constituency which is not included in the Assembly electoral region, or (*d*) who is a candidate to be the Assembly member for an Assembly constituency included in the Assembly electoral region but is not a candidate of the party.

(6) A person may not be an individual candidate to be an Assembly member for the Assembly electoral region if he is (*a*) included on a list submitted by a registered political party for the Assembly electoral region or another Assembly electoral region, (*b*) an individual candidate to be an Assembly member for another Assembly electoral region, (*c*) a candidate to be the Assembly member for an Assembly constituency which is not included in the Assembly electoral region, or (*d*) a candidate of any registered political party to be the Assembly member for an Assembly constituency included in the Assembly electoral region.

6. Calculation of electoral region figures

(1) For each registered political party by which a list of candidates has been submitted for the Assembly electoral region (*a*) there shall be added together the number of electoral region votes given for the party in the Assembly constituencies included in the Assembly electoral region, and (*b*) the number arrived at under paragraph (*a*) shall then be divided by the aggregate of one and the number of candidates of the party returned as Assembly members for any of those Assembly constituencies.

(2) For each individual candidate to be an Assembly member for the Assembly electoral region there shall be added together the number of electoral region votes given for him in the Assembly constituencies included in the Assembly electoral region.

(3) The number arrived at (*a*) in the case of a registered political party, under sub-section (1)(*b*), or (*b*) in the case of an individual candidate, under sub-section (2), is referred to in this Act as the electoral region figure for that party or individual candidate.

7. Return of electoral region members

(1) The first seat for the Assembly electoral region shall be allocated to the party or individual candidate with the highest electoral region figure.

(2) The second and subsequent seats for the Assembly electoral region shall be allocated to the party or individual candidate with the highest electoral region figure. . ...

(4) An individual candidate already returned as an Assembly member shall be disregarded.

(5) Seats for the Assembly electoral region which are allocated to a party shall be filled by the persons on the party's list in the order in which they appear on the list.. . .

PART II: ASSEMBLY FUNCTIONS

21. Introductory

The Assembly shall have the functions which are (*a*) transferred to, or made exercisable by, the Assembly by virtue of this Act, or (*b*) conferred or imposed on the Assembly by or under this Act or any other Act.

22. Transfer of Ministerial functions to Assembly

(1) Her Majesty may by Order in Council (*a*) provide for the transfer to the Assembly of any function so far as exercisable by a minister of the Crown in relation to Wales, (*b*) direct that any function so far as so exercisable shall be exercisable by the Assembly concurrently with the minister of the Crown, or (*c*) direct that any function so far as exercisable by a minister of the Crown in relation to Wales shall be exercisable by the minister only with the agreement of, or after consultation with, the Assembly.

(2) The Secretary of State shall, before the first ordinary election, lay before each House of Parliament the draft of an Order in Council under this section making provision for the transfer of such functions in each of the fields specified in Schedule 2 as the Secretary of State considers appropriate.

(3) An Order in Council under this section may contain any appropriate consequential, incidental, supplementary or transitional provisions or savings (including provisions in the form of amendments or repeals of enactments).

(4) No recommendation shall be made to Her Majesty in Council to make an Order in Council under this section (*a*) unless a draft of the statutory instrument containing the Order in Council has been laid before, and approved by a resolution of, each House of Parliament, and (*b*) in the case of an Order in Council varying or revoking a previous Order in Council, unless such a draft has also been laid before, and approved by a resolution of, the Assembly.. . .

SCHEDULE 1: ASSEMBLY CONSTITUENCIES AND ASSEMBLY ELECTORAL REGIONS

General

1. The Assembly constituencies shall be the parliamentary constituencies in Wales.
2.(1) There shall be five Assembly electoral regions. (2) The Assembly electoral regions shall be

the five European parliamentary constituencies in Wales provided for by the European Parliamentary Constituencies (Wales) Order 1994. (3) There shall be four Assembly seats for each Assembly electoral region.. . . .

4. THE STARR REPORT

Printed below is the executive summary of the 445-page report ('referral') submitted to the US Congress on 9 September 1998 by Independent Counsel (Special Prosecutor) Kenneth W. Starr, who had been authorized in January 1998 to extend his investigation of the Whitewater affair to encompass President Clinton's conduct in respect of his alleged relationship with a former White House intern, Monica Lewinsky. (Text from US Congress, Washington.)

Introduction

As required by Section 595(c) of Title 28 of the United States Code, the Office of the Independent Counsel ('OIC' or 'Office') hereby submits substantial and credible information that President William Jefferson Clinton committed acts that may constitute grounds for an impeachment.

The information reveals that President Clinton:
—lied under oath at a civil deposition while he was a defendant in a sexual harassment lawsuit; lied under oath to a grand jury;
—attempted to influence the testimony of a potential witness who had direct knowledge of facts that would reveal the falsity of his deposition testimony;
—attempted to obstruct justice by facilitating a witness's plan to refuse to comply with a subpoena;
—attempted to obstruct justice by encouraging a witness to file an affidavit that the President knew would be false, and then by making use of that false affidavit at his own deposition;
—lied to potential grand jury witnesses, knowing that they would repeat those lies before the grand jury; and
—engaged in a pattern of conduct that was inconsistent with his constitutional duty to faithfully execute the laws.

The evidence shows that these acts, and others, were part of a pattern that began as an effort to prevent the disclosure of information about the President's relationship with a former White House intern and employee, Monica Lewinsky, and continued as an effort to prevent the information from being disclosed in an ongoing criminal investigation.

Factual Background

In May 1994, Paula Corbin Jones filed a lawsuit against William Jefferson Clinton in the United States District Court for the Eastern District of Arkansas. Ms Jones alleged that while he was the Governor of Arkansas President Clinton sexually harassed her during an incident in a Little Rock hotel room.

President Clinton denied the allegations. He also challenged the ability of a private litigant to pursue a lawsuit against a sitting President. In May 1997, the Supreme Court unanimously rejected the President's legal argument. The Court concluded that Ms Jones, '[l]ike every other citizen who properly invokes [the District Court's] jurisdiction. . ., has a right to an orderly disposition of her claims', and that therefore Ms Jones was entitled to pursue her claims while the President was in office. A few months later, the pre-trial discovery process began.

One sharply disputed issue in the *Jones* litigation was the extent to which the President would be required to disclose information about sexual relationships he may have had with 'other women'. Ms Jones's attorneys sought disclosure of this information, arguing that it was relevant to proving that the President had propositioned Ms Jones. The President resisted the discovery requests, arguing that evidence of relationships with other women (if any) was irrelevant.

In late 1997, the issue was presented to United States District Judge Susan Webber Wright for resolution. Judge Wright's decision was unambiguous. For purposes of pre-trial discovery, President Clinton was required to provide certain information about his alleged relationships with other women. In an order dated 11 December 1997, for example, Judge Wright said: 'The Court finds, therefore, that the plaintiff is entitled to information regarding any individuals with whom the President had sexual relations or proposed or sought to have sexual relations and who were during the relevant time frame state or federal employees.' Judge Wright left for another day the issue whether any information of this type would be admissible were the case to go to trial. But for purposes of answering the written questions served on the President, and for purposes of answering questions at a deposition, the District Court ruled that the President must respond.

In mid-December 1997, the President answered one of the written discovery questions posed by Ms Jones on this issue. When asked to identify all women who were state or federal employees and with whom he had had 'sexual relations' since 1986, the President answered under oath: 'None.' For purposes of this interrogatory, the term 'sexual relations' was not defined.

On 17 January 1998, President Clinton was questioned under oath about his relationships with other women in the workplace, this time at a deposition. Judge Wright presided over the deposition. The President was asked numerous questions about his relationship with Monica Lewinsky, by then a 24-year-old former White House intern, White House employee and Pentagon employee. Under oath and in the presence of Judge Wright, the President denied that he had engaged in a 'sexual affair', a 'sexual relationship', or 'sexual relations' with Ms Lewinsky. The President also stated that he had no specific memory of having been alone with Ms Lewinsky, that he remembered few details of any gifts they might have exchanged, and indicated that no one except his attorneys had kept him informed of Ms Lewinsky's status as a potential witness in the *Jones* case.

The Investigation

On 12 January 1998, this Office received information that Monica Lewinsky was attempting to influence the testimony of one of the witnesses in the *Jones* litigation, and that Ms Lewinsky herself was prepared to provide false information under oath in that lawsuit. The OIC was also informed that Ms Lewinsky had spoken to the President and the President's close friend Vernon Jordan about being subpoenaed to testify in the *Jones* suit, and that Vernon Jordan and others were helping her find a job. The allegations with respect to Mr Jordan and the job search were similar to ones already under review in the ongoing Whitewater investigation.

After gathering preliminary evidence to test the information's reliability, the OIC presented the evidence to Attorney-General Janet Reno. Based on her review of the information, the Attorney-General determined that a further investigation by the Independent Counsel was required.

On the following day, Attorney-General Reno petitioned the Special Division of the United States Court of Appeals for the District of Columbia Circuit, on an expedited basis, to expand the jurisdiction of Independent Counsel Kenneth W. Starr. On 16 January 1998, in response to the Attorney-General's request, the Special Division issued an order that provides in pertinent part: [that] The Independent Counsel shall have jurisdiction and authority to investigate to the maximum extent authorized by the Independent Counsel Reauthorization Act of 1994 whether Monica Lewinsky or others suborned perjury, obstructed justice, intimidated witnesses, or otherwise violated federal law other than a Class B or C misdemeanor or infraction in dealing with witnesses, potential witnesses, attorneys, or others concerning the civil case *Jones* v. *Clinton*.

On 28 January 1998, after the allegations about the President's relationship with Ms Lewinsky became public, the OIC filed a Motion for Limited Intervention and a Stay of Discovery in *Jones* v. *Clinton*. The OIC argued that the civil discovery process should be halted because it was having a negative effect on the criminal investigation. The OIC represented to the Court that numerous individuals then under subpoena in *Jones*, including Monica Lewinsky, were integral to the OIC's investigation, and that courts routinely stayed discovery in such circumstances.

The next day Judge Wright responded to the OIC's motion. The court ruled that discovery would be permitted to continue, except to the extent that it sought information about Monica Lewinsky. The court acknowledged that 'evidence concerning Monica Lewinsky might be relevant to the issues in [the *Jones*] case'. It concluded, however, that this evidence was not 'essential to the core issues in this case', and that some of that evidence 'might even be inadmissible'. The court found that the potential value of this evidence was outweighed by the potential delay to the Jones case in continuing to seek discovery about Ms Lewinsky. The court also was concerned that the OIC's investigation 'could be impaired and prejudiced were the court to permit inquiry into the Lewinsky matter by the parties in this civil case'.

On 9 March 1998, Judge Wright denied Ms Jones's motion for reconsideration of the decision regarding Monica Lewinsky. The order states: 'The court readily acknowledges that evidence of the Lewinsky matter might have been relevant to plaintiff's case and, as she argues, that such evidence might possibly have helped her establish, among other things, intent, absence of mistake, motive, and habit on the part of the President. Nevertheless, whatever relevance such evidence may otherwise have. . .it simply is not essential to the core issues in this case. . ..'

On 1 April 1998, Judge Wright granted President Clinton's motion for summary judgment, concluding that even if the facts alleged by Paula Jones were true, her claims failed as a matter of law. Ms Jones has filed an appeal, and as of the date of this Referral, the matter remains under consideration by the United States Court of Appeals for the Eighth Circuit.

After the dismissal of Ms Jones's lawsuit, the criminal investigation continued. It was (and is) the view of this Office that any attempt to obstruct the proper functioning of the judicial system, regardless of the perceived merits of the underlying case, is a serious matter that warrants further inquiry. After careful consideration of all the evidence, the OIC has concluded that the evidence of wrongdoing is substantial and credible, and that the wrongdoing is of sufficient gravity that it warrants referral to Congress.

The Significance of the Evidence of Wrongdoing

It is not the role of this Office to determine whether the President's actions warrant impeachment by the House and removal by the Senate; those judgments are, of course, constitutionally entrusted to the legislative branch. This Office is authorized, rather, to conduct criminal investigations and to seek criminal prosecutions for matters within its jurisdiction. In carrying out its investigation, however, this Office also has a statutory duty to disclose to Congress information that 'may constitute grounds for an impeachment', a task that inevitably requires judgment about the seriousness of the acts revealed by the evidence.

From the beginning, this phase of the OIC's investigation has been criticized as an improper inquiry into the President's personal behaviour; indeed, the President himself suggested that specific inquiries into his conduct were part of an effort to 'criminalize my private life'. The regrettable fact that the investigation has often required witnesses to discuss sensitive personal matters has fueled this perception.

All Americans, including the President, are entitled to enjoy a private family life, free from public or governmental scrutiny. But the privacy concerns raised in this case are subject to limits, three of which we briefly set forth here.

First. The first limit was imposed when the President was sued in federal court for alleged sexual harassment. The evidence in such litigation is often personal. At times, that evidence is highly embarrassing for both plaintiff and defendant. As Judge Wright noted at the President's January 1998 deposition, 'I have never had a sexual harassment case where there was not some embarrassment.' Nevertheless, Congress and the Supreme Court have concluded that embarrassment-related concerns must give way to the greater interest in allowing aggrieved parties to pursue their claims. Courts have long recognized the difficulties of proving sexual harassment in the workplace, inasmuch as improper or unlawful behaviour often takes place in private. To excuse a party who lied or concealed evidence on the ground that the evidence covered only 'personal' or 'private' behaviour would frustrate the goals that Congress and the courts have sought to achieve in enacting and interpreting the Nation's sexual harassment laws. That is particularly true when the conduct that is being concealed—sexual relations in the workplace between a high official and a young subordinate employee—itself conflicts with those goals.

Second. The second limit was imposed when Judge Wright required disclosure of the precise information that is in part the subject of this Referral. A federal judge specifically ordered the President, on more than one occasion, to provide the requested information about relationships with other women, including Monica Lewinsky. The fact that Judge Wright later determined that the evidence would not be admissible at trial, and still later granted judgment in the President's favor, does not change the President's legal duty at the time he testified. Like every litigant, the President was entitled to object to the discovery questions, and to seek guidance from the court if he thought those questions were improper. But having failed to convince the court that his objections were well founded, the President was duty bound to testify truthfully and fully. Perjury and attempts to obstruct the gathering of evidence can never be an acceptable response to a court order, regardless of the eventual course or outcome of the litigation.

The Supreme Court has spoken forcefully about perjury and other forms of obstruction of justice:
In this constitutional process of securing a witness' testimony, perjury simply has no place whatever. Perjured testimony is an obvious and flagrant affront to the basic concepts of judicial proceedings. Effective restraints against this type of egregious offense are therefore imperative.

The insidious effects of perjury occur whether the case is civil or criminal. Only a few years ago, the Supreme Court considered a false statement made in a civil administrative proceeding: 'False testimony in a formal proceeding is intolerable. We must neither reward nor condone such a "flagrant affront" to the truth-seeking function of adversary proceedings. . . . Perjury should be severely sanctioned in appropriate cases.' Stated more simply, '[p]erjury is an obstruction of justice'.

Third. The third limit is unique to the President. 'The Presidency is more than an executive responsibility. It is the inspiring symbol of all that is highest in American purpose and ideals.' When he took the Oath of Office in 1993 and again in 1997, President Clinton swore that he would 'faithfully execute the Office of President'. As the head of the Executive Branch, the President has the constitutional duty to 'take care that the laws be faithfully executed'. The President gave his testimony in the *Jones* case under oath and in the presence of a federal judge, a member of a co-equal branch of government; he then testified before a federal grand jury, a body of citizens who had themselves taken an oath to seek the truth. In view of the enormous trust and responsibility attendant to his high office, the President has a manifest duty to ensure that his conduct at all times complies with the law of the land.

In sum, perjury and acts that obstruct justice by any citizen—whether in a criminal case, a grand jury investigation, a congressional hearing, a civil trial, or civil discovery—are profoundly serious matters. When such acts are committed by the President of the United States, we believe those acts 'may constitute grounds for an impeachment'.

The Scope of the Referral

1. *Background of the Investigation*. The link between the OIC's jurisdiction—as it existed at the end of 1997—and the matters set forth in this Referral is complex but direct. In January 1998, Linda Tripp, a witness in three ongoing OIC investigations, came forward with allegations that: (i) Monica Lewinsky was planning to commit perjury in *Jones* v. *Clinton*, and (ii) she had asked Ms Tripp to do the same. Ms Tripp also stated that: (i) Vernon Jordan had counseled Ms Lewinsky and helped her obtain legal representation in the *Jones* case, and (ii) at the same time, Mr Jordan was helping Ms Lewinsky obtain employment in the private sector.

OIC investigators and prosecutors recognized parallels between Mr Jordan's relationship with Ms Lewinsky and his earlier relationship with a pivotal Whitewater-Madison figure, Webster L. Hubbell. Prior to January 1998, the OIC possessed evidence that Vernon Jordan—along with other high-level associates of the President and First Lady—helped Mr Hubbell obtain lucrative consulting contracts while he was a potential witness and/or subject in the OIC's ongoing investigation. This assistance took place, moreover, while Mr Hubbell was a target of a separate criminal investigation into his own conduct. The OIC also possessed evidence that the President and the First Lady knew and approved of the Hubbell-focused assistance.

Specifically, in the wake of his April 1994 resignation from the Justice Department, Mr Hubbell launched a private consulting practice in Washington, DC. In the startup process, Mr Hubbell received substantial aid from important public and private figures. On the day prior to Mr Hubbell announcing his resignation, White House Chief of Staff Thomas 'Mack' McLarty attended a meeting at the White House with the President, First Lady, and others, where Mr Hubbell's resignation was a topic of discussion.

At some point after the White House meeting, Mr McLarty spoke with Vernon Jordan about Mr Jordan's assistance to Mr Hubbell. Mr Jordan introduced Mr Hubbell to senior executives at New York-based MacAndrews & Forbes Holding Co. Mr Jordan is a director of Revlon Inc., a company controlled by MacAndrews & Forbes. The introduction was successful; MacAndrews & Forbes retained Mr Hubbell at a rate of $25,000 per quarter. Vernon Jordan informed President Clinton that he was helping Mr Hubbell.

By late 1997, this Office was investigating whether a relationship existed between consulting payments to Mr Hubbell and his lack of cooperation (specifically, his incomplete testimony) with the OIC's investigation. In particular, the OIC was investigating whether Mr Hubbell concealed information about certain core Arkansas matters, namely, the much-publicized Castle Grande real estate project and related legal work by the Rose Law Firm, including the First Lady.

Against this background, the OIC considered the January 1998 allegations that: (i) Ms Lewinsky was prepared to lie in order to benefit the President, and (ii) Vernon Jordan was assisting Ms Lewinsky in the *Jones* litigation, while simultaneously helping her apply for a private-sector job with, among others, Revlon Inc.

Based in part on these similarities, the OIC undertook a preliminary investigation. On 15 January 1998, this Office informed the Justice Department of the results of our inquiry. The Attorney-General immediately applied to the Special Division of the Court of Appeals for the District of Columbia Circuit for an expansion of the OIC's jurisdiction. The Special Division granted this request and authorized the OIC to determine whether Monica Lewinsky or others had violated federal law in connection with the *Jones* v. *Clinton* case.

2. *Current Status of the Investigation*. When the OIC's jurisdiction was expanded to cover the Lewinsky matter in January 1998, several matters remained under active investigation by this Office. Evidence was being gathered and evaluated on, among other things, events related to the Rose Law Firm's representation of Madison Guaranty Savings & Loan Association; events related to the firings in the White House Travel Office; and events related to the use of FBI files. Since the current phase of the investigation began, additional events arising from the Lewinsky matter have also

come under scrutiny, including possible perjury and obstruction of justice related to former White House volunteer Kathleen Willey, and the possible misuse of the personnel records of Pentagon employee Linda Tripp.

From the outset, it was our strong desire to complete all phases of the investigation before deciding whether to submit to Congress information—if any—that may constitute grounds for an impeachment. But events and the statutory command of Section 595(c) have dictated otherwise. As the investigation into the President's actions with respect to Ms Lewinsky and the Jones litigation progressed, it became apparent that there was a significant body of substantial and credible information that met the Section 595(c) threshold. As that phase of the investigation neared completion, it also became apparent that a delay of this Referral until the evidence from all phases of the investigation had been evaluated would be unwise. Although Section 595(c) does not specify when information must be submitted, its text strongly suggests that information of this type belongs in the hands of Congress as soon as the Independent Counsel determines that the information is reliable and substantially complete.

All phases of the investigation are now nearing completion. This Office will soon make final decisions about what steps to take, if any, with respect to the other information it has gathered. Those decisions will be made at the earliest practical time, consistent with our statutory and ethical obligations.

The Contents of the Referral

The Referral consists of several parts. Part One is a Narrative. It begins with an overview of the information relevant to this investigation, then sets forth that information in chronological sequence. A large part of the Narrative is devoted to a description of the President's relationship with Monica Lewinsky. The nature of the relationship was the subject of many of the President's false statements, and his desire to keep the relationship secret provides a motive for many of his actions that apparently were designed to obstruct justice.

The Narrative is lengthy and detailed. It is the view of this Office that the details are crucial to an informed evaluation of the testimony, the credibility of witnesses, and the reliability of other evidence. Many of the details reveal highly personal information; many are sexually explicit. This is unfortunate, but it is essential. The President's defence to many of the allegations is based on a close parsing of the definitions that were used to describe his conduct. We have, after careful review, identified no manner of providing the information that reveals the falsity of the President's statements other than to describe his conduct with precision.

Part Two of the Referral is entitled 'Information that May Constitute Grounds for An Impeachment'. This 'Grounds' portion of the Referral summarizes the specific evidence that the President lied under oath and attempted to obstruct justice. This Part is designed to be understandable if read without the Narrative, although the full context in which the potential grounds for impeachment arise can best be understood if considered against the backdrop of information set forth in Part One.

Several volumes accompany the Referral. The Appendix contains relevant court orders, tables, a discussion of legal and evidentiary issues, background information on the Jones litigation. . .and other reference material. . . .

In the course of its investigation, the OIC gathered information from a variety of sources, including the testimony of witnesses before the grand jury. Normally a federal prosecutor is prohibited by Rule 6(e) of the Federal Rules of Criminal Procedure from disclosing grand jury material, unless it obtains permission from a court or is otherwise authorized by law to do so. This Office concluded that the statutory obligation of disclosure imposed on an Independent Counsel. . .grants such authority. Nevertheless, out of an abundance of caution, the OIC obtained permission from the Special Division to disclose grand jury material as appropriate in carrying out its statutory duty. . .. We also advised Chief Judge Norma Holloway Johnson, who supervises the principal grand jury in this matter, of our determination on that issue.

5. UNITED KINGDOM LABOUR CABINET
(as at 31 December 1998)

Prime Minister, First Lord of the Treasury and Minister for the Civil Service	Rt. Hon. Tony Blair, MP
Deputy Prime Minister and Secretary of State for the Environment, Transport and the Regions	Rt. Hon. John Prescott, MP
Lord Chancellor	Rt. Hon. The Lord Irvine of Lairg
Chancellor of the Exchequer	Rt. Hon. Gordon Brown, MP
Secretary of State for the Home Department	Rt. Hon. Jack Straw, MP
Secretary of State for Foreign and Commonwealth Affairs	Rt. Hon. Robin Cook, MP
Secretary of State for Trade and Industry	Rt. Hon. Stephen Byers, MP
President of the Council and Leader of the House of Commons	Rt. Hon. Margaret Beckett, MP
Secretary of State for Social Security	Rt. Hon. Alistair Darling, MP
Chief Secretary to the Treasury	Rt. Hon. Alan Milburn, MP
Secretary of State for Northern Ireland	Rt. Hon. Marjorie (Mo) Mowlam, MP
Secretary of State for Culture, Media and Sport	Rt. Hon. Chris Smith, MP
Secretary of State for Education and Employment	Rt. Hon. David Blunkett, MP
Secretary of State for Defence	Rt. Hon. George Robertson, MP
Secretary of State for Health	Rt. Hon. Frank Dobson, MP
Lord Privy Seal, Leader of the House of Lords and Minister for Women	Rt. Hon. Baroness Jay of Paddington
Minister of Agriculture, Fisheries and Food	Rt. Hon Nick Brown, MP
Secretary of State for Scotland	Rt. Hon. Donald Dewar, MP
Chancellor of the Duchy of Lancaster and Minister for the Cabinet Office	Rt. Hon. Jack Cunningham, MP
Secretary of State for Wales	Rt. Hon. Alun Michael, MP
Secretary of State for International Development	Rt. Hon. Clare Short, MP
Chief Whip	Rt. Hon. Ann Taylor, MP

6. UNITED STATES DEMOCRATIC ADMINISTRATION
(as at 31 December 1998)

Members of the Cabinet:

President	Bill Clinton
Vice-President	Al Gore
Secretary of State	Madeleine K. Albright
Secretary of the Treasury	Robert E. Rubin
Secretary of Defence	William S. Cohen
Secretary of the Interior	Bruce Babbitt
Secretary of Agriculture	Dan Glickman
Secretary of Commerce	William M. Daley
Secretary of Housing & Urban Development	Andrew M. Cuomo
Secretary of Transportation	Rodney E. Slater
Secretary of Health & Human Services	Donna E. Shalala
Attorney-General	Janet Reno
Secretary of Labour	Alexis M. Herman
Secretary of Energy	Bill Richardson
Secretary of Education	Richard W. Riley
Secretary of Veterans' Affairs	Jesse Brown

Other Leading Executive Branch Officials:

White House Chief of Staff	Erskine Bowles
Director of Office of Management & Budget	Franklin D. Raines
Chairman of Council of Economic Advisers	Janet L. Yellin
National Security Adviser	Samuel D. Berger
Head of Environmental Protection Agency	Carol Browner
Director of Central Intelligence Agency	George Tenet
Representative for Trade Negotiations	Charlene Barshefsky
Ambassador to United Nations	(vacant)
Director of National Economic Council	Gene Sperling
Director of Small Business Administration	Aida Alvarez
Director of US Information Agency	Joseph Duffey

7. INTERNATIONAL COMPARISONS: POPULATION AND GDP

The following table gives population and gross domestic product (GDP) data for the member states of the Organization for Economic Cooperation and Development plus selected other countries. (Sources: OECD, Paris; UN Population Fund, New York; World Bank, Washington.)

	Population 1998 (million)	Population growth %	GDP ('000 million)* 1997	GDP ('000 million)* 1998
Argentina	36.27	1.3	348.2	n/a
Australia	18.61	0.9	392.9	349.9
Austria	8.20	0.4	206.2	211.9
Belgium	10.17	0.1	242.5	249.3
Canada	30.68	1.1	607.7	584.2
China (incl. Hong Kong)	1,236.92	0.8	1,000.0	n/a
Czech Republic	10.29	0.0	52.0	55.3
Denmark	5.33	0.5	170.0	174.8
Finland	5.15	0.2	119.8	126.2
France	58.81	0.3	1,394.1	1,435.5
Germany	82.08	0.02	2,089.9	2,142.1
Greece	10.66	0.4	119.9	119.3
Hungary	10.21	0.0	45.3	47.5
Iceland	0.27	0.5	7.4	8.1
India	984.00	1.7	360.0	n/a
Irish Republic	3.62	0.4	77.2	82.3
Israel	5.64	1.9	96.7	n/a
Italy	57.00	0.7	1,145.4	1,171.8
Japan	125.93	0.2	4,190.2	3,797.2
South Korea	46.41	1.0	442.5	295.3
Luxembourg	0.43	1.0	15.8	16.5
Mexico	98.55	1.8	402.1	417.3
Netherlands	15.73	0.5	363.3	378.3
New Zealand	3.62	1.0	65.0	52.7
Norway	4.42	0.4	153.4	145.5
Poland	38.61	0.0	135.6	150.6
Portugal	9.93	0.0	101.3	105.4
Saudi Arabia	20.79	3.4	206.5	n/a
South Africa	42.84	1.4	270.0	n/a
Spain	39.13	0.1	532.0	556.3
Sweden	8.89	0.3	227.8	228.8
Switzerland	7.26	0.2	255.3	262.4
Turkey	64.57	1.6	189.9	206.5
UK	58.97	0.3	1,282.9	1,362.3
USA	270.31	0.9	7,824.0	8,178.8

*At current prices and exchange rates.

8. MAASTRICHT CONVERGENCE CRITERIA PERFORMANCE

The following table shows the performance of the European Union (EU) member states in respect of the main convergence criteria established by the 1991 Maastricht Treaty for participation in economic and monetary union (EMU) and the single European currency. (Source: Eurostat, Luxembourg.)

	Budget deficit(1) % of GDP (2.7% ceiling)					Government debt % of GDP (60% ceiling)				
	1994	*1995*	*1996*	*1997*	*1998*	*1994*	*1995*	*1996*	*1997*	*1998*
Belgium	5.1	4.1	3.3	2.1	1.3	135.0	133.7	130.6	122.2	117.3
Germany	2.4	3.5	4.0	2.7	2.1	50.4	58.1	60.8	61.3	61.0
Greece	12.1	9.1	7.9	4.0	2.4	110.4	111.8	110.6	108.7	106.5
Spain	6.3	6.6	4.4	2.6	1.8	63.1	65.7	67.8	68.8	65.6
France	5.6	4.8	4.0	3.0	2.9	48.4	52.8	56.4	58.0	58.5
Ireland	1.7	2.0	1.4	−0.9	−2.3	87.9	81.6	74.7	66.3	52.1
Italy	9.0	7.1	6.6	2.7	2.7	125.5	124.9	123.4	121.6	118.7
Luxembourg	−2.6	−1.5	−0.9	−1.7	−2.1	5.7	6.0	7.8	6.7	6.7
Netherlands	3.4	4.0	2.6	1.4	0.9	77.4	79.7	78.7	72.1	67.7
Austria	4.4	5.9	4.3	2.5	2.1	65.1	69.0	71.7	66.1	63.1
Portugal	5.8	5.1	4.0	2.5	2.3	69.6	71.7	71.1	62.0	57.8
Finland	6.2	5.2	3.3	0.9	−1.0	59.5	59.2	61.3	55.8	49.6
Sweden	10.8	8.1	3.9	0.8	−2.0	79.3	78.7	78.1	76.6	75.1
Denmark	3.5	1.6	1.4	−0.7	−0.8	76.0	71.9	70.2	65.1	58.1
UK	6.8	5.8	4.6	1.9	−0.6	50.4	54.1	56.3	53.4	49.4

(1) Minus sign indicates budget surplus.

XVIII OBITUARY

Abacha, General Sani (b. 1943), President of Nigeria since 1993, succeeded two previous military dictators who had ruled the country over the past ten years. His regime was as cruel and murderous as any in Africa. One victim, slain in 1995 with eight others on trumped-up charges after undergoing vile indignities, was the distinguished environmentalist and playwright Ken Saro-Wiwa. Abacha was commissioned in the army in 1963 after attending the Mons officer cadet training college in England, and rose rapidly in rank during 20 years thereafter. He made himself defence minister under the dictator General Babangida, whom he soon ousted. Died 8 June

Abiola, Chief Moshood (M.K.O.) (b. 1937), Nigerian businessman and politician, became a symbol of democracy in Nigeria through five years of detention after disputed presidential elections in 1993 in which he claimed a majority: it was immediately followed by a seizure of power by his autocratic rival Sani Abacha (*q.v.*) and subsequent military rule. Abiola, educated first at a Baptist high school, studied accountancy at Glasgow University. Back in Nigeria, he rose in his profession to become chairman of the American-owned firm ITT Nigeria, founding, in 1978, a powerful publishing business which reinforced his close connection with successive military regimes. He had grown rich, and gave generously to charities, for education in particular. A 'prisoner of conscience', on the eve of his expected release he suffered a heart attack and died 7 July

Ambler, Eric (b. 1909), British novelist and screenwriter, became the master of the spy story, starting with six books, written before World War II, from *The Dark Frontier* (1936) to *Journey into Fear* (1940). Expelled from school, he contrived to get a degree in engineering from London University, and then took up copywriting for advertisements, meanwhile writing his first spy story, which proved a huge success. In World War II he was drafted into the Army Film Unit, where he joined up with the actor Peter Ustinov and which he left as a lieutenant-colonel with a US Bronze Star. While a scriptwriter and producer for J. Arthur Rank, he returned to writing spy thrillers, with renewed success, as in *Passage of Arms* (1959). A spell in Hollywood was less successful, but he lived with his second wife in California for some years. Retiring to Switzerland, he wrote the autobiographical *Here Lies Eric Ambler* (1985), and then he moved for health reasons to London. Died 22 October

Barton, Professor Sir Derek, FRS (b. 1918), shared with Odd Hassel the 1969 Nobel Prize for Chemistry for their fundamental discoveries in conformational analysis, concerning the behaviour of organic molecules. Educated at Tonbridge School and Imperial College, London, where he graduated in 1940 and took a doctorate in 1942, after specialist service in World War II he returned to Imperial College as a lecturer. He then took a readership at Birkbeck College (after a year as visiting professor at Harvard), which gave him ample time for research. In 1955 he became Regius Professor of Chemistry at Glasgow, and in 1957 Hoffman Professor of Chemistry at Imperial College, all the time researching fruitfully in organic chemistry. Retiring at the age of 60, he became director of the Institut de Chemie des Substances Naturelles in France, then in 1986 moved to Texas A&M University as distinguished professor and later Dow Professor of Chemical Invention. His academic honours were many, and besides his knighthood (1972) he was awarded the

Légion d'Honneur from France and the Order of the Rising Sun from Japan. Died 16 March

Bassey, Hogan (b. in Nigeria, 1932), was world featherweight boxing champion 1956–59. Moving to England in 1952, he won the British Empire title in 1955 and defended it against various challengers. In the following year he beat the (French) Algerian Cherif Hamia, the reigning European champion, in a match for the vacant world title, which he defended successfully twice, before losing it to Davey Moore (USA) in March 1959. Bassey then retired, returning to Nigeria and coaching amateur boxers for the Olympic Games. Died 26 January

Beriosova, Svetlana (b. in Lithuania, 1932), British ballerina, took her first lessons from her father, the dance and ballet-master Nicholas Beriozoff, before studying in the USA. She made her professional debut with the Ottawa Ballet in 1947 and was subsequently engaged by a small English company, Metropolitan Ballet, where her roles included *Giselle* and Odette in *Swan Lake*. Invited by Ninette de Valois to join Sadler's Wells Theatre Ballet in 1949, she transferred in 1952 to Covent Garden where she was renowned for her interpretation of the most famous classical roles for over 20 years. She also had notable success in leading parts created for her by the choreographers John Cranko, Kenneth Macmillan and Frederick Ashton. Died 10 November

Brisby, Liliana Daneva (b. in Bulgaria, 1923), author and broadcaster, born into the Bulgarian political/cultural elite, met her British husband while studying in Switzerland during World War II, after which she lived in England, later working at the Foreign Office and Chatham House. A fierce opponent of the post-war communist regime in her homeland, she broadcast and wrote prolifically on East European affairs and was for many years *The Annual Register*'s contributor on Bulgaria. Died 30 October

Carmichael, Stokely (b. in Trinidad, 1941), American civil rights campaigner and Black Power activist who became an icon of the worldwide student protest movements of the 1960s. His role in fomenting riots by US urban blacks alarmed less radical black leaders, such divisions prompting his decision in 1969 to settle in black Africa (Guinea) and to adopt the name Kwame Ture. Died 15 November

Casaroli, HE Cardinal Agostino (b. 1914), as Vatican Secretary of State 1979–90 led the Roman Church into a policy of dialogue with Soviet communism in protection of its own faithful and the survival of Christianity in Soviet-dominated countries in Europe. Born to a family closely related to the Church, he studied canon law at the Lateran University and then diplomacy at the Pontifical Ecclesiastical Academy. He was ordained priest in 1937, and in 1940 joined the Vatican's Secretariat of State. As Under-Secretary for Extraordinary Affairs he led the Vatican delegation to the UN conference on diplomatic relations. Master of half-a-dozen languages, he opened relations with the satellite countries of Eastern Europe, and in 1971 talked with Soviet officials in Moscow. In 1975 he signed the Helsinki Final Act on behalf of the Holy See. In 1979 he became Pro-Secretary of State and a cardinal. His diplomacy followed the dictum of Pope John XXIII: 'There are many enemies of the Church, but the Church is enemy to no-one'. Gorbachev's *perestroika* was Casaroli's triumphant opportunity. He retired in 1990 and died 8 June

Clifford, Clark (b. 1906), American lawyer and politician, was Special Counsel to US President Truman 1946–50 and Defence Secretary in President Lyndon Johnson's administration 1968–69. The thrust of his advice in the 1940s was to define and conduct the Cold War between the USA and the Soviet Union. But his prime interest remained the law. After taking a law degree at Washington University,

St Louis, Missouri, he quickly built up a lucrative practice. In World War II he was commissioned in the US Naval Reserve and posted to Washington, where the patronage of James Vardaman led to his intimacy with President Truman, for whom, *inter alia*, he drafted the National Security Act of 1947. The law practice in Washington, of which he was senior partner, flourished exceedingly, but his involvement with the crooked Bank of Credit and Commerce International (BCCI) shattered his reputation for probity. Died 10 October

Commager, Henry Steele (b. 1902), American historian, was one of the most distinguished writers on the US constitution in the twentieth century. His first book, *The Growth of the American Republic*, with Samuel Eliot Morrison as co-author, was published in 1930, and was followed by a stream of books, including *The Commonwealth of Learning* (1968) and the multi-volume *The Rise of the American Nation*. He was educated at Chicago and Copenhagen universities, and held professorships at New York University 1925–39 and Columbia University 1939–56. From that base he was given short-term professorships at Cambridge, Oxford and Uppsala, and at other US academies. Politically, he was profoundly opposed to Senator McCarthy's inquisitorial campaign, and he scorned US involvement in Vietnam. Unrivalled as polemicist and as historian of the nation, he was highly popular on campus. Died 2 March

Cookson, Dame Catherine, DBE (b. 1906), British novelist, sold over 100 million copies of more than 70 novels. Year after year they topped the list of titles borrowed from British public libraries. These books were not romantic potboilers, but strong stories of life in England's industrial northeast, where she was born illegitimate and brought up in poverty. She went to work at 13 in a laundry, became head laundress of a workhouse in Hastings, Sussex, and married Thomas Cookson, a schoolmaster, in 1940. She contracted a blood disease and had four miscarriages. Her first novel, *Kate Hannigan*, was published in 1950, and thereafter her output flowed unceasingly. Her autobiography, *Our Kate*, was published in 1969. She lost her sight in old age, but continued to dictate. Her books had made her rich, and she gave munificently to charitable causes, including £100,000 to St Hilda's College, Oxford, and the launch of a foundation for research in molecular haematology. Died 11 June

Davis, Fred, (b. 1913), British greenbaize professional, won the world snooker championships in every year bar one (1950) from 1948 to 1956, and the world billiards championship in 1980. He was 12 years younger than his even more famous brother Joe Davis, repeatedly world billiards champion, who thought little of his brother's talent until, at the age of 16, he won the junior professional billiards championship for the first of three successive years. Snooker, however, was his forte, and he began his world successes soon after the interruption of military service in World War II. He retired from the professional game in 1993. Died 15 April

Gellhorn, Martha (b. 1908), American war correspondent and novelist, was married three times, to Bertrand de Jouvenel, Ernest Hemingway and T.S. Matthews, but marriage was incidental to her own pursuit of news and information in troubled and violent times and places. These included the Spanish Civil War, the German rape of Czechoslovakia in 1939, the Russo-Finnish war of 1939–40, the D-Day landings in 1945, Vietnam, Lebanon and El Salvador. After education at Bryn Mawr, she started her journalistic career in Paris, but returned to America and made her name with reports for the Emergency Relief Administration on communities stricken by the great depression beginning in 1929. They were the material of her book, *The Trouble I've Seen*, whose title summed up most of her subsequent experience as a roving journalist. The last years of her life were spent in Wales and London. Died 15 February

Germani, Fernando (b. 1906), Italian organist, was titular organist of St Peter's in the Vatican 1948–59. A musical child prodigy, at the age of eight he joined the Royal Conservatory in Rome, and at 15 was appointed organist of Rome's Augusteo Symphony Orchestra. In 1927 he drew huge audiences for recitals in the USA, and in 1932 made his first tour in England. From 1932 until 1971 he taught the organ to pupils from all over the world at the Accademia Musicale Chigiani in Siena; from 1934 until 1976 he was professor of organ at the Conservatorio Regio in Rome. In 1945 he performed the complete organ works of J.S. Bach, a feat he repeated seven times elsewhere in the world. Other favoured composers were Frescobaldi, Franck and Reger. Germani himself composed works for organ and for violin and piano, and published *Method for Organ* in four volumes (the first in 1939) which revolutionized pedal technique. Though he retired before the era of compact discs, many recordings of his finest performances survive. Died 10 June

Goldwater, Barry (b. 1909), was US senator for Arizona 1953–64 and 1967–69: in 1964 he was Republican candidate for the presidency, but was beaten by Lyndon Johnson in a landslide. He was an extreme libertarian: in his book *The Conscience of a Conservative* (1960) he wrote 'I do not undertake to promote welfare, for I propose to extend freedom'. Of Jewish descent, he married an Episcopalian, whose religion was passed to their four children. After an erratic education he joined his father's department store and became its president in 1937. In World War II he served as a pilot of planes bringing American goods to Europe; in 1949 he entered politics, and was first elected senator in 1953. He opposed increases in federal spending, and was one of the few senators to back the infamous Joe McCarthy. His epitaph could be his own words: 'Extremism in defence of liberty is no vice.' Died 29 May

Gordon, Margot (b. Lamb, 1912), British tennis and squash player, won the US tennis championship at Forest Hills in 1938. She had already won both the US and British squash titles in 1936, and was British champion six times in succession. She married Bill Gordon in 1944, and with him spent 20 years in Central Africa, taking part in political life in Uganda and Nigeria. Active through a long retirement in England and France, she died 3 January

Gowing, Professor Margaret, CBE, FRS, FBA (b. Elliott, 1921), British historian and archivist, took a first-class degree in economics at the London School of Economics and served at the Board of Trade during World War II. From 1944–59 she served in the historical section of the Cabinet Office where she worked on the war histories project with Sir Kenneth Hancock with whom she co-authored *British War Economy* (1949). She was a member of the Grigg Committee which led to the Public Records Act in 1958. In 1959 she was appointed archivist/historian to the UK Atomic Energy Authority where, despite her initial ignorance of science, she soon found a ripe subject for research, culminating in the publication of her highly successful *Britain and Atomic Energy 1939–45* (1964). After a spell at the University of Kent she was appointed Oxford University's first Professor of the History of Science 1972–86. A member of many public bodies, she also lectured widely in Britain and abroad and was instrumental in setting up the Contemporary Scientific Archives Centre (now at Bath). Her two-volume *Independence and Deterrence* (with Lorna Arnold, 1974), on British nuclear policy 1945–52, was widely acclaimed and became a classic in its field. Died 7 November

Grade, Lord (Lew) (b. in Ukraine, 1906), British film and television producer, was one of the most influential and flamboyant personalities in post-war British show business. Arriving in England in 1912, he left school at 14 and started work in the rag trade in London's East End. He spent ten years as a professional dancer before forming a theatrical agency with his brother in 1943. In 1955 the arrival of commercial television led him to invest in the Birmingham-based company Associated Television (ATV), of which he became chief executive in 1962. Among the many popular programmes he brought to the small screen were the long-running soap opera *Coronation Street*, *The Saint* series based (loosely) on the Charteris character and spectacular variety shows such as *Saturday Night at the London Palladium*, earning the company more than £100 million in the US and other foreign markets. In the 1970s he turned, rather less successfully, to international film production, his few triumphs including *The Return of the Pink Panther* and *On Golden Pond*, whose veteran stars, Katherine Hepburn and Henry Fonda, received Academy awards. His entertainment empire included, at various times, London's Classic cinema chain, Stoll Moss Theatres, Elstree film studios, Pye Records and, latterly, The Grade Company, which he set up in 1985. He was created a life peer in Harold Wilson's resignation honours list. Died 13 December

Hodgkin, Professor Sir Alan Lloyd, OM, KBE, FRS (b. 1914), British scientist, was jointly awarded the Nobel Prize for Physiology or Medicine in 1963 for his experiments in electrophysiology which transformed knowledge of the mechanism of conduction of the nervous impulse. Educated at Gresham's School, Holt, and Trinity College, Cambridge (Fellow 1936), he spent a year at the Rockefeller Institute in 1938. During World War II, he was engaged on development of airborne radar for the RAF. Returning to the Physiological Laboratory in Cambridge 1945–52, he became Fullerton Research Professor of the Royal Society 1952–69. In 1969 he was appointed John Henry Plummer Professor of Biophysics in the University of Cambridge and served as Master of Trinity College 1978–84. He was President of the Royal Society 1970–85, having been awarded its Royal Medal in 1958 and the Copley Medal in 1965. His many academic honours and awards included the chancellorship of Leicester University (1971–84), presidency of the Marine Biological Association (1966–76), membership of several foreign scientific academies and numerous honorary degrees. Among his publications were a series of papers on new approaches to cellular neurophysiology in the *Journal of Neurophysiology* and an autobiography, *Chance and Design* (1992). He was appointed to the Order of Merit in 1973. Died 20 December

Huddleston, Rt Rev Trevor, KCMG (b. 1913), was for many years the mouthpiece of the non-white victims of apartheid in South Africa. Educated in the High Anglican tradition at Lancing College, Christ Church (Oxford) and Wells Theological College, he was ordained priest in 1937 and two years later joined the monastic Order of the Community of the Resurrection. In 1943 he was sent to South Africa to take charge of the Community's mission in Sophietown, a black area of Johannesburg, and in 1947 became its Provincial in South Africa. His book, *Naught for Your Comfort*, published in 1956, describing his experiences, became a worldwide best-seller and caused his withdrawal from South Africa by the Community. Five years in England, spent promoting the cause of the South African black majority, were followed by his election as Bishop of Masasi in Tanzania, and in 1968 by his appointment as Bishop of Stepney, in London's poor East End with a large population of non-white immigrants. In 1978 he became Bishop of Mauritius, and later Archbishop of the Anglican province of the Indian Ocean. Retiring in 1983, he became president of the Anti-Apartheid Movement and Provost of an Anglican-Nonconformist theological college. Invited by Nelson Mandela, he paid a last brief visit to South Africa in 1991. His knighthood was gazetted in the first full honours list issued by the new Labour government in 1997. Died 20 April

Hughes, Ted (Edward James) OM (b.1930), British poet, became Poet Laureate in 1984. Born in the Yorkshire Pennines, he was educated at Mexborough Grammar School and (after two years' national service) at Pembroke College, Cambridge, where he began to write poems. His first collection was published as *The Hawk in the Rain* (1957), followed by *Lupercal* (1958), which won the Hawthornden Prize. In 1956 he had married the American poet Sylvia Plath, and they spent two years in academic posts in the USA. After frictions in the marriage, which had given them a son and a daughter, Sylvia Plath took her own life in 1963. Hughes thereupon stopped writing poetry for three years. In 1970 he married Carol Orchard, and they remained happily together until his death. Two books of poetry—*Wodwo* (1967) and *Crow* (1970)—mirrored his personal emotions. Another collection, *Moortown* (1979), a verse journal of farming life in Devon, proved his lyrical power was as great as ever. In the same year there appeared *The Remains of Elmet*, poems honouring his native Yorkshire. He also wrote books and poetry for children, notably *The Iron Man* (1968). Finally, in 1998 he published *Birthday Letters*, relating his side of the Sylvia Plath story, also the prize-winning *Tales from Ovid*. In August of that year he was appointed to the Order of Merit. Died 28 October

Hunt, Lord (Sir John), KG, DSO (b. in India 1910), British soldier and mountaineer, was the leader of the British expedition which conquered Everest in 1953, the final ascent to the summit being achieved by Sir Edmund Hillary and Sherpa Tenzing. He subsequently led a distinguished life in public affairs. Henry C.J. Hunt was educated at Marlborough College and Sandhurst, from which he passed out first with the King's Gold Medal. He served with the King's Royal Rifle Regiment in India and Burma 1931–40, and returned to become chief instructor in the Commando Mountain and Snow Warfare School. Rejoining his regiment in 1944, he won the DSO and commanded the 11th Indian Infantry Brigade. After the war and staff college training he served in the Middle East and West Germany before getting special leave to lead the Mount Everest expedition. A keen mountaineer from his youth, he had taken part in several Himalayan climbs while serving in India. Three years after the Everest triumph in 1953, for which he was knighted, he retired from the Army, to become secretary to the Duke of Edinburgh's Award Scheme for young people. As president of the Alpine Club (1956–58), he chaired the club's centenary meeting at Zermatt in 1957. He became chairman of the Parole Board for England and Wales and president of the Council for Volunteers Overseas 1968–69. Created a life peer in 1966, he was appointed a Knight of the Garter in 1979. Died 8 November

Iryani, Sheikh Abdul Rahman al- (b. 1911), was President of North Yemen 1967–74. In the turbulent politics of his country, he spent nearly 15 years in prison, narrowly escaping execution, but in 1962 he became Minister of Religious Endowments, then, after a coup, Vice-President and Prime Minister, resigning in 1966. Egypt's defeat in the Arab-Israeli war brought a new situation in which Iryani headed a three-man presidential committee, but he was forced to resign after seven years during which he had striven to create a democratic state pinioned between extremes of marxism and Islamism. Died 14 March

Jünger, Ernst (b. 1895), German writer, based much of his published work on his diaries. Intensely nationalist and right-wing, he nevertheless distanced himself from the Nazis, and was fortunate to escape execution after the 1944 plot against Hitler's life. His first and most durable book, *Storm of Steel* (1920), was based on his heroic experiences as a soldier in World War I. Rejoining the army in 1939, he spent most of World War II in occupied Paris. Meanwhile, he had published a great number of books reflecting, in one way or another, his political philosophy, which idealized a permanent authoritarian economy whose citizens behaved like soldiers under command. He scorned the Weimar Republic and sometimes saw Germany as a partner with Soviet Russia against the effete liberal democracy of the West, but in his last reclusive years he turned his interest to defence of the natural environment. Died 17 February

Karamanlis, Konstantinos (b. 1907), President of Greece 1980–85 and 1990–95, had been Prime Minister 1955–63 and 1974–80. Graduating from the Law School of Athens University, he started in practice but was soon drawn into regional politics, until the Metaxas dictatorship banned all political activity. In 1935 he was elected to parliament on the ticket of the Populist Party, which swept the polls in the 1946 elections, after Greece had been occupied in World War II. He held several cabinet posts, before joining the new right-wing Greek Rally, which took power under Alexander Papagos. When Papagos died in 1955, King Paul chose Karamanlis to form a government. He dissolved the Greek Rally and formed the National Radical Union, which won the 1956 elections. The chief coup of his eight years in office was the pact with Britain and Turkey establishing Cyprus as an independent republic in 1960. Resigning after losing to George Papadopoulos in the 1963 elections, he exiled himself to Paris for the next 11 years. The rule of 'the Colonels' from 1967 to 1974 was ended with his return to Greece at the head of a government of national unity. He set up a new party, New Democracy, and after he had won a triumphant electoral victory he launched a referendum which gave a large majority for making Greece a republic. A new constitution was approved in 1975, giving the President increased power. Faced with rising opposition from Andreas Papandreou's PASOK, Karamanlis resigned the party leadership and was voted President by parliament in 1980. As President, Karamanlis did not intervene in domestic politics, but his moderating influence was evident in Papandreou's foreign policy, which became more pro-European. He resigned the presidency in 1985 and went into retirement, but in 1990 was persuaded to stand for another term, finally resigning in 1995. Died 23 April

Kurosawa, Akira (b. 1910), Japanese film director, was popularly known in the West for his film *The Seven Samurai* (1954), remade by Hollywood as *The Magnificent Seven* (1960); but at the Venice Festival in 1951 his film *Rashomon* had been enthusiastically received, gaining the top award of the Golden Lion, followed by an Oscar in Hollywood for best foreign film. A second Oscar awaited his film *Dersu Uzala* (1975), a story of Siberia which was shot in Soviet Russia. His last film, *Ran* (1984), invested Shakespeare's *King Lear* with sons instead of daughters. Much earlier (1957) he had made *Throne of Blood*, borrowing from Shakespeare a Macbeth-like story, starring Toshiro Mifune, who appeared in other Kurosawa films between 1948 and 1965. Died 6 September

Laxness, Halldor (b. 1902), Icelandic writer, won the Nobel Prize for Literature in 1955. His life followed a pattern of changes and reversals. Born of well-to-do parents, he left school early and travelled widely in Europe. Embracing Catholicism, he spent a year in a monastery, where he wrote his first novel, *At the Holy Mountain* (1920). In 1927, having renounced his Catholic faith, he published the novel *The Great Weaver from Kashmir*, sceptical of Christianity. Two years in America turned him into a socialist, a transition recorded in his autobiography, *Poet's Time* (1963). He now settled into writing novels with an historical and nationalistic flavour. A vast tetrology, *Hiernsijos* (1937–40, published in English in 1969 as *World Light*), confirmed his left-wing philosophy. There followed a sequence of other novels and political tracts, less polemical and more philosophical than his previous work. Died 8 February

Limann, Hilla (b. 1934), was President of Ghana 1974–81. Though democratically elected as candidate of the People's National Party, he was overshadowed and eventually overthrown by Jerry Rawlings. After a short spell in prison, he continued in politics but could win only about 7 per cent of the vote for the presidency in 1992. Educated at schools in Ghana, at the London School of Economics and the University of Paris, he had started a diplomatic career before turning to politics. Died 23 January

Lloyd, George (b. 1913), British musical composer, enjoyed two highly creative periods, separated by a sequence of traumatic experience in World War II, ill-health and retreat to his native West Country for 20 years as a market gardener. He disliked the tuneless dissonance of most serious modern music, and composed in a more conventional style with an idiom of his own. Supported by a well-to-do musical family, as a youth he studied violin and composition under eminent teachers, and composed his *First Symphony* at the age of 19. His first three symphonies were performed (1933–36) by distinguished orchestras, and two operas, *Iernin* and *The Serf*, came to London, the latter to Covent Garden. Before, during and after that long retreat, which was followed by difficulty in regaining recognition, he composed three operas, four piano concertos, 12 symphonies and two massive choral works, a symphonic Mass and finally a Requiem. A deal forged with the Albany N.Y. Symphony Orchestra brought worldwide recognition and wealth from recordings of old and new works. Died 3 July

Martin, William McChesney (b. 1906), was chairman of the US Federal Reserve Board 1951–70, responsible for central bank control of the money supply for close on 20 years. His steadfast policy of prudence often brought conflict with political pressures, but was rewarded by a long period of stable values and economic growth. The son of a leading banker in St Louis, in 1931 he was sent to Wall Street, where in 1938 he became chairman of the New York stock exchange. After military service in World War II he was president of the Export-Import Bank before becoming assistant secretary to the Treasury in Washington 1949–51. His appointment as chairman of the Federal Reserve Board by President Truman was confirmed by successive US Presidents until President Nixon replaced him, after which he continued his public service in unofficial ways. Died 27 July

Moody, Helen Wills (b. 1905), American tennis player, won the Wimbledon singles title eight times between 1926 and 1936, and was US champion seven times and French champion four times. The daughter of a successful Californian doctor, Helen Wills became Mrs Moody in 1929. In 1926 she had been matched against Suzanne Lenglen, who won despite Wills's harder hitting. After Lenglen turned professional, Wills was acknowledged to be the best amateur in the world: in 1928 she won both the Wimbledon and the French championships. Divorced from Moody, she married Aidan Roark, a polo international. Died 1 January

Moore, Archie, (b. 1913), American boxer, was world light-heavyweight champion in the 1950s, coming to the title at the advanced age of 39. Vastly esteemed for his ring-craft, hard punch and durability, he dominated his natural weight division for a decade, only coming unstuck when he went in with real heavyweights such as Rocky Marciano (1955) and Floyd Patterson (1956). Died 9 December

Nanda, Gulzari Lal (b. 1898), was twice Prime Minister of India, but in each case only for a very short time. In 1964 he was Home Minister when Jawaharlal Nehru died in office, and was called upon by the President to fill the gap until the Congress Party elected a new leader (Lal Bahadur Sastri). The same sequence followed when Sastri himself died in 1965. As soon as Congress chose Indira Gandhi, Nanda gave way. Again Home Minister, he was obliged to resign at the end of 1966 when in Delhi a mass demonstration of orthodox Hindus against the slaughter of cows ended in violence, police gunfire and a number of deaths. Nanda remained on the back benches for another decade. Died 15 January

Nguyen Van Linh (b. 1915), was general secretary of the Communist Party of Vietnam (CPV) 1986–91. His political career had begun with imprisonment 1930–36 for distributing leaflets. On his release he joined the party and served a second term in prison 1941–45. An underground activist in South Vietnam for 30 years, he was eventually promoted to full membership of the party politburo in 1976. In 1982 he lost his place in the CPV politburo and the central secretariat, but recovered it three years later in a climate of reform, and in 1986 became the party's general secretary. In 1991 he retired, but remained influential as a modest critic of inefficiency and corruption. Died 27 April

Pasmore, Victor, CH, CBE (b. 1908), British artist, had two distinct phases of painting, objective and abstract. The son of a distinguished surgeon, and educated at Harrow school, he was obliged by his father's death to take work as a clerk while painting and studying art in his spare time until 1938. He had already had a one-man show and joined with other artists in what became known as the Euston Road School. A conscientious objector in World War II, he was briefly imprisoned before returning to paint views which became less and less naturalistic, until by 1948 his work had become completely abstract. A visiting teacher at two London art schools 1943–55, he was appointed Master of Painting at King's College, Durham 1954–65. While he became a consultant on urban design, his painting continued and developed, turning bright and colourful after he bought a house in Malta. He was elected Senior Academician of the Royal Academy in 1984. Died 23 January

Paz, Octavio (b. 1914), Mexican poet and essayist, won the Nobel Prize for Literature in 1990. Born to a politically-involved family, he published his first collection, *Luna Silvestre*, in 1933 and his second, *Raiz del Hombre*, in 1937. He was enticed by the Spanish Civil War, but returned disillusioned with communism. After World War II he entered the diplomatic service, and after postings to Paris, Delhi and Tokyo became Mexico's ambassador to India 1962–68. Meanwhile, he had published a prose work, *El Laberinto de la Soledad* (1950) about the forces that had made modern Mexico, a series of prose poems, *Augila o Sol* (1951), and the poetic *Piedra de Sol* (1957). His poems were collected in the bilingual *Configurations* (1971). He also wrote essays of literary criticism, and in 1976 he founded an influential literary magazine, *Vuelta*. Died 19 April

Pol Pot, (b. Saloth Sar, 1925), erstwhile Prime Minister of Cambodia (Kampuchea), was one of the most ruthless political dictators of the twentieth century: in power he ordered the killing of a large part of the country's small population, in the interest of entrenching communism. In his youth he had joined the Democratic Party, which sent him to Paris where his nationalism caught a marxist infection. In 1953 he returned to Cambodia, and soon took command of a revolutionary movement known as the Khmers Rouges. There followed a long struggle with the country's monarch, Norodom Sihanouk, who was overthrown by a military coup in 1970. By 1975 Pol Pot's communist forces were able to take over control of the country, and his murderous rule began. First he ordered all civil servants and military officers from the previous regime to be killed, then communist intellectuals, then bourgeois party members and party peasant leaders, and finally most veterans of the party. In 1977 he renamed the country Democratic Kampuchea, with himself as Prime Minister. In 1979 Vietnam invaded and drove Pol Pot into the jungle, where he lurked for a decade, vainly trying to regain power by guerrilla warfare. Died 15 April

Postel, Jonathan (b. 1943), American computer expert, founded the World Wide Web and pioneered network pathways and domain names for the Internet. He had won an MSc in engineering and a PhD in computer science from the University of California at Los Angeles, both in 1968. Working on problems of Internet communication, he created the Internet Assigned Numbers Authority (IANA) and led the development of a standard protocol for e-mail. He was a founding member of the Internet Architecture Board and a trustee of the Internet Society. In 1998 he gained the silver medal of the International Telecommunications Union for his work on IANA. Died 16 October

Powell, Rt Hon Enoch (b. 1912), British politician who exerted a powerful influence on British political life by the sheer force of his personality and his logically-advanced right-wing views. Classical scholar, poet, soldier (rising from the ranks to brigadier in World War II), he was essentially a lone thinker and orator. Educated at King Edward's School, Birmingham, and Trinity College, Cambridge, he started an academic career as professor of Greek at Sydney University 1938–39. After the war he became Conservative MP for Wolverhampton South-West 1950–74, rising into the Tory hierarchy (and serving in government 1960–63) but being dismissed from the opposition front bench by Edward Heath in 1968 over his 'rivers of blood' speech questioning the wisdom of large-scale non-white immigration into Britain. Also vehemently opposed to surrender of British sovereignty to Europe, in 1974 he recommended Conservatives to vote for the then anti-European Labour Party, but lost his seat. Eight months later he returned to parliament, having found a congenial base as an Ulster Unionist, on the strength of his view that Northern Ireland should remain part of the UK. Died 8 February

Robbins, Jerome (b. Rabinowitz, 1918), American choreographer and impresario, was famed far beyond ballet circles for his direction and choreography of the Broadway musical *West Side Story* (1957), followed by *Fiddler on the Roof* (1964); but he was also a master of 'pure' ballet, starting with *Fancy Free*, which he made for Ballet Theatre in 1944, and which also became the fabric of a Broadway musical, *On the Town*. He had begun his theatrical career at 18 as an actor. In 1949 he joined George Balanchine's New York City Ballet as associate (later joint) ballet master, creating a succession of ballets before and after Balanchine's death in 1983. His contribution to the history of dance through its integration with splendiferous musicals was unique. Died 29 July

Roberts, Sir Frank, GCMG, GCVO (b. 1907), British diplomat, was ambassador to Yugoslavia 1954–57, to NATO 1957–60, to the Soviet Union 1960–63 and to West Germany 1963–68, and crowned his official career with outstanding service to Anglo-German relations. Short in stature, quick in movement and mind, he was a brilliant exponent of foreign affairs. From Trinity College, Cambridge, he joined the Foreign Office in 1930, rising to deputy under-secretary of state, with a break as high commissioner in India, before his first embassy in Belgrade. After his retirement, he became a director of three German business firms, president of the Anglo-German Association, chairman of the German Chamber of Commerce in the UK, and president of the Great Britain-USSR Association. Died 7 January

Rogers, Roy (b. 1911), American singer and actor, was in his time the most celebrated cowboy actor in Hollywood. Of part Indian descent, he began his career as a radio singer in the 1930s, but turned to films and learned to ride and shoot. In Hollywood he became top star of the Western film industry from 1941, with his famous palomino horse Trigger, who died in 1965. Television ousted that sort of film, but Rogers found ways of exploiting it, and returned successfully to singing, releasing an album of songs in 1991, and to business promotion helped by his earlier cowboy fame. Died 6 July

Rothermere, (Vere Harmsworth) third Viscount (b. 1925), British newspaper proprietor, inherited from his father and grandfather a press empire centred on the London *Daily Mail*, which he successfully defended against rivals and predators. He found a valuable ally in the journalist David English (knighted in 1992), who eventually became editor of the *Mail* and editor-in-chief of the *Mail on Sunday*, launched in 1982. The *Mail* had changed from broadsheet to tabloid in 1971, a move which cost circulation and jobs but eventually succeeded. Rothermere was able to replace the failing *Evening News* by the *Standard*, which he bought in 1980, but he lost the competition for control of *The Times* to Rupert Murdoch in the same year. Born to wealth and privilege, he had been evacuated in World War II and educated, after a year at Eton, at Kent School in Connecticut. His business career had begun, after national service, at Anglo-Canadian Paper Mills in Quebec at the age of 23, but his father brought him to his newspaper inheritance three years later. Died 1 September

Rowland, R. W. ('Tiny') (b. 1917), British business entrepreneur, made his first fortune in the turbulent financial ambiance after the end of World War II, but in 1948 he emigrated to Rhodesia, where he operated through a conglomerate called Lonrho. Regarded by the City of London as an outsider, he amassed great wealth by personal contacts with political leaders of newly-independent African countries. Often in conflict with the British authorities and other companies, in 1985 he fought his most notorious battle for control of Harrods, the famous London department store, which he lost to Mohamed al-Fayed. At that time he was proprietor of *The Observer* Sunday newspaper. Born in Hamburg, Germany, he was sent to England in 1934, and after school education was directed to civilian work in the war, as the son of an enemy alien. Worth, it was reckoned, £650 million, he died 24 July

Schnittke, Alfred (b. 1934), Russian composer, had a German as well as a Jewish strain in his blood and his music, which combined 12-tone serialism with traditional tonality and occasional echoes of less modernist composers. Born in the Soviet Union, he began his musical education in Vienna at the age of 12, but returned with his parents to Russia and entered the Moscow Conservatoire. There he remained, studying and teaching, until 1972. His First Symphony, banned in Moscow, was premiered in Gorki under the patronage of the conductor Gennadi Rozhdestvensky. He visited the West in 1977 posing as an orchestral pianist and participating in the first performance of his Concerto Grosso No 1; but his full international recognition awaited the performance of more than 30 of his works in 1989 in a Stockholm festival. In that year he became professor of composition at the Hochschule für Musik in Hamburg. Though handicapped by a succession of strokes he continued composing, winning an ever wider circle of admirers. Died 3 August

Schumann, Maurice (b. 1913), Foreign Minister of France 1969–73, was one of the ideologists of the EEC, which eventually became the European Union, and the catalyst for British entry under Edward Heath in 1972. Jewish by birth, he embraced Catholicism and Christian Democratic politics. Educated at the Lycée Henri IV and the Sorbonne, he became a journalist and broadcaster. In World War II, he joined General de Gaulle in London and fought in the liberation of France. Thereafter he pursued a political career and rose through junior office and ministerial posts to the Foreign Ministry. Defeated in his constituency in 1973, he took to authorship, publishing novels and other books on a wide variety of subjects. Died 10 February

Serapheim, Archbishop, (b. Vissarion Tikos, 1913), was Primate of the Greek Orthodox Church from 1974. Of peasant birth, he entered a seminary at the age of 18 and in due course was ordained priest. He soon showed his militant toughness in fighting with the Greek resistance against the German occupation in World War II; then as Metropolitan of Ioannina he bought arms for the EOKA rebels against British rule in Cyprus. He was elected Archbishop of Greece under the regime of 'the Colonels' and retained his ultra-conservative opinions for the next quarter-century, rejecting all ecumenical overtures from other churches. Died 10 April

Sharif-Emami, Jafar (b. 1910), was Prime Minister of Iran for two short terms under the Pahlevi regime. An engineer by profession, he rose to be Minister of Industry and Mines before being appointed Prime Minister 1960–62, then becoming president of a royal ecclesiastical foundation. In 1978 the Shah again made him Prime Minister. A series of political and social reforms did not placate the fundamentalist opposition, and after a period of civil strife Sharif-Emami resigned, fleeing to the USA in 1979. There he lived a quiet studious life, and died 11 June

Sinatra, Frank (b. 1915), American popular singer and actor, was for two generations the supreme idol in the temple of popular music. Born in Hoboken, N.J., he dropped out of high school, took odd jobs and sang in his spare time, with Bing Crosby as his hero. His first record with the Harry James' band was issued in 1939. Very soon he was recruited by the trombonist Tommy Dorsey, from whom he learned, with strict self-discipline, the breath control that enabled him to sing a long-drawn-out melodic line. Setting out on a solo career in 1942, he made records for Columbia, such as *Someone to Watch Over Me*, before moving to Hollywood and teaming with Gene Kelly in films, including *On the Town* (1949). After a low period he made a brilliant come-back in the role of GI Maggio in *From Here to Eternity* (1953), which won him an Oscar as best supporting actor. His career restarted in such renowned musicals as *Guys and Dolls* and *Pal Joey*. A single record, *I've Got the World on a String*, revived his public acclaim. He next went in for albums of songs on disc: *Songs for Swinging Lovers* (1956) included *I've Got You Under My Skin* and *Anything Goes*.

In 1961 he parted from Capital Records, with which he had signed in 1955, to form his own company, Reprise, later swallowed by Warner Brothers. In 1966 the disc of *Strangers in the Night* was his biggest single success. During this period he first sang *My Way*, which became his signature tune for the rest of his life. In 1971 he announced his retirement, but it was not to be for long: two years later he was on television in the show *Blue Eyes is Back*. His albums of the 1980s included the song *New York, New York*. A retrospective disc, *Live in Concert*, was released for his 80th birthday. By then he had been married three times, most famously to screen goddess Ava Gardner. Politically, once a Democrat and a close supporter of President Kennedy, he became a committed Reaganite Republican. In 1985 he was awarded the President's Medal of Freedom. Died 14 May

Soper, Rev Lord (Donald) (b. 1903), was one of the most outstanding and controversial churchmen of the century. An evangelist in the tradition of John Wesley, for 60 years he preached twice weekly and in all weather at London's Tower Hill and Speakers' Corner, where his wit, charm and gift for repartee made him no soft target for hecklers. A committed socialist, fervent champion of the homeless and vociferous pacifist (he supported nuclear disarmament), lifelong teetotaller and opponent of gambling, he wrote a regular column for the left-wing weekly *Tribune* for 20 years. After leaving Cambridge, and following his ordination, he was successively minister at the South London Mission (1926–29), the Central London Mission (1929–36) and Superintendent of the West London Mission, Kingsway Hall 1936–78. He was president of the Methodist Conference in 1953 and served as an alderman on the London County Council in the early 1960s. Created a life peer by Harold Wilson in 1965, he was the first Methodist minister to sit in the House of Lords. He was awarded an honorary DD by the University of Cambridge in 1988. Died 22 December

Spock, Dr Benjamin (b. 1903), American paediatrician, became a household name among parents everywhere with the publication of his book *Baby and Child Care* in 1946. His theme, 'to respect children because they are human beings and they deserve respect', was castigated by some as a cult of permissiveness, but others welcomed its challenges to stern parental discipline. The book sold 50 million copies of successive editions. Spock was educated at a private academy and Yale University, where he stroked the American gold-winning rowing eight in the 1924 Olympics in Paris, and then at Columbia University College of Physicians, specializing in paediatrics and child psychology. After the success of his book he gave up his private practice to join the staff of the Mayo Clinic and then held professional posts in the universities of Minnesota, Pittsburgh and Cleveland. He took left-wing stances on the Vietnam War and nuclear armament. In later life his views on child-rearing approached the conventional idea of parental responsibility, and in *Bringing Up Children in Difficult Times* (1974) he came close to recanting his original permissive theme. He became a popular lecture-tourist, using his fame as a paediatrician to promote his opinions on war and peace. Died 15 March

Suzuki, Shinichi (b. 1898), Japanese violinist, became famous for his philosophy of teaching very young children to play the violin: it was based on the assertion that if children could learn to speak a complete native language by the age of three or four they could do likewise with a musical instrument if encouraged by their parents. In the 1920s he spent eight years in Germany, where he became close to Albert Einstein and was friendly with leading musicians like Karl Klinger, Fritz Kreisler and Bruno Walter. In 1928 he married the soprano Waltraud Prange. Back in Japan he became the country's first professional concert violinist and began the work of teaching young children. In the 1950s he hosted mammoth concerts of young violinists, of whom he took a group to the USA in 1964. In the late 1970s the European Suzuki Association was formed, followed in 1983 by the International Suzuki Association. He was honoured by the Emperor and by universities and lay bodies all over the world. Died, aged 99, 26 January

Tabarly, Eric (b. 1931), French yachtsman, won *The Observer* Single-handed Trans-Atlantic Race in 1964, for which he was honoured as an Officier de la Légion d'Honneur, and again in 1976. In 1969 he won a similar race across the Pacific from California to Japan. Other victories in his yachts, always called *Pen Duick*, included two Sydney-Hobart races and the Cowes Channel race, and in 1988 he broke the longstanding record for the Atlantic crossing from New York to the Lizard in his trimaran *Paul Ricard.* He had originally joined the French navy, from which he retired in 1966 to work in the Ministry of Youth and Sport, and from 1971 at the inter-service sports school. Sailing with a novice crew, he fell off his yacht off the Welsh coast and was drowned 13 June

Taylor, Telford (b. 1908), American lawyer and democratic rights activist, first came to international prominence at the Nuremberg trials of alleged German war criminals after World War II: though the German general staff, against whom he led the prosecution, was ultimately acquitted, his conduct of the case had been impressive, and he succeeded in his prosecution of numerous individuals on similar charges. Educated at Williams College and the Harvard Law School, he served the Roosevelt administration from 1933 as a departmental lawyer and strategist of the New Deal, drafting the Securities Exchange Act and becoming branded as a leftist. When the USA entered the war in 1941, Taylor was posted to the British code-breaking unit at Bletchley Park. After the war and the Nuremberg trials, from which he emerged a public hero, he led a Washington practice which became linked with defence of communists and others hounded by Senator McCarthy. In 1970 he published a book condemning the Vietnam War as a crime and a blunder. His later books included *Courts of Terror* (1975), *Munich: The Price of Peace* (1979) and an account of the first Nuremberg trial (1992), all inspired by his principled liberalism. Died 23 May

Tazieff, Haroun (b. 1914 in Poland), French volcanologist, became world-famous for his film *Les Rendezvous du Diable* in 1959. After his widowed mother had taken him to Brussels, where he took part in the World War II resistance, from a budding academic career he saw his first active volcano in Africa in 1948, and in the 1950s visited volcanoes around the world, daring to the point of danger but safety-conscious and well-living. Moving to France, he became director of the National Council of Scientific Research and entered politics as a socialist and rose to become a secretary of state under President Mitterrand. Died 2 February

Tennstedt, Klaus (b. in Germany 1926), orchestral conductor, became principal conductor of the London Philharmonic Orchestra (LPO) 1983-87. He first followed his father as a violinist, but soon turned to the piano and to conducting. He defected from East Germany to Sweden 1971-76. An invitation to conduct Bruckner's Eighth Symphony in Boston in 1974 proved a triumph, and Tennstedt went on to conduct several other leading American orchestras. From 1976 he added engagements in London, Paris and elsewhere in Europe. In 1983 he was appointed principal conductor of the LPO, but resigned in 1987, suffering from heart trouble and lung cancer, whereupon the LPO named him conductor laureate. Died 11 January

Tippett, Sir Michael, OM, CH (b. 1905), British musician, was in the forefront of musical composition in traditional forms in the latter part of the twentieth century. The aptly-named *A Child of Our Time* (1944) was a key work, reflecting both his debt to earlier British composers like Purcell and his own pacifism and humanitarianism. The son of a lawyer, Tippett had a normal school education before entering the Royal College of Music in 1923, where he returned after a spell conducting musical groups. In 1932 he succeeded Gustav Holst as conductor of the Morley College orchestra for out-of-work musicians. His ardent pacifism won him three months in prison, which he took in his stride. Before and after *A Child of Our Time*, he composed a catalogue of works, including five operas (*The Midsummer Marriage* of 1955, *King Priam* of 1962, *The Knot Garden* of 1970, *The Ice Break* of 1977 and *New Year* of 1989), five string quartets, four piano sonatas, four symphonies and the dramatic work *The Mask of Time* (1984). He was knighted in 1960, made a Companion of Honour in 1970 and given the Order of Merit in 1983. He never married, but had a long homosexual relationship with the musicologist Meirion (Bill) Bowen. Died 8 January

Ulanova, Galina (b. 1910), Russian dancer, was among the greatest ballerinas of the century. At the age of nine she entered the school linked to the Mariinsky Theatre, where she was taught by her mother, Maria Romanova, and by Agrippina Vaganova. Her graduation performance in 1928 revealed her unique talent, which reached a peak in Leonid Lavrosky's 1940 presentation of *Romeo and Juliet* at the Kirov Theatre. *Giselle* was perhaps her finest role. In 1944 she joined the Bolshoi Ballet, which brought her to London in 1956 as a ballerina of superb genius. She retired from dancing in 1962, but film recordings were made of some of her greatest performances. Died 21 March

Wallace, George (b. 1919), American politician, was three times a candidate for the presidency 1964–72, and four times governor of Alabama between 1963 and 1987. It was during the presidential election primary in 1972 that he was shot by a white gunman and suffered injuries which paralysed him from the waist down so that he spent the rest of his active life in a wheelchair. His attitude was unashamedly racist and segregationist: 'segregation for ever' he trumpeted in the 1972 presidential campaign, in which he carried five states and won nearly ten million votes. When, in 1968, the Democratic Party set about ridding itself of segregationism, his presidential candidature carried the banner of the American Independence Party. As a young man, Wallace had worked his way through university and was called to the bar in 1942. In 1953 he became a district judge, but within a decade he had launched his political career. Died 13 September

Wills, Helen, *see* Moody, Helen Wills

Wood, Beatrice (b. 1893), American artist, came from a rich Californian family, but lost her fortune to debts incurred by a pseudo-husband who was found to have another legal wife. In her early life she had studied painting, stage design and acting in Paris, falling in with the French Dadaiste Marcel Duchamp, with whom she collaborated in producing a magazine, *The Blindman*. In 1928 she returned to California, where she became fascinated by ceramics, setting up her own studio in Los Angeles in 1937. Her ceramic work was of two kinds: some beautifully traditional, some inspired by her earlier *avant-garde* experiences, and she also made prints and drawings until well after he 100th birthday. Died 12 March

Zeri, Federico (b. 1921), Italian art critic, was known to the wider world for his trenchant attacks on state bureaucracy and myopia in the field of art, and for his championship of Renaissance artists whose work had been under-rated. He held visiting professorships at Harvard and Columbia universities and was a founding member of the board of the Getty Museum in Malibu. Born into a wealthy and cultivated Roman family, he graduated in fine arts at Rome University in 1944 and spent the next ten years working for the state museum administration. His catalogues of the Spada and Pallavicini collections (1954 and 1959) fortified his reputation as an authority on medieval and Renaissance art. Called to catalogue the Italian paintings in the Metropolitan Museum in New York, he published three monographs on the Florentine, Venetian and Sienese schools. His acute judgment and sharp tongue brought him, back in Italy, a regular newspaper column and frequent television appearances. Died 5 October

Zhivkov, Todor (b. 1911), Bulgarian communist leader, became First Party Secretary and Prime Minister in 1962, and President of the Council of State from 1971, holding office until 1989, when he was expelled under charges of embezzlement of state funds. Born of a peasant family, he joined the Communist Party in 1932 and was active in the partisan movement against German control in World War II. Rising in the Sofia party organization, he became a secretary to the central committee and a candidate member of the politburo, taking supreme office in 1962. In policy he slavishly followed Moscow's example, integrating Bulgaria into Comecon. After his dismissal by a reformist upsurge in 1989, he was charged with misappropriation of state funds, found guilty and sentenced to imprisonment, but was released on appeal. Died 5 August

CHRONICLE OF PRINCIPAL EVENTS IN 1998

JANUARY

4   In Lithuania, Valdas Adamkus defeated Arturas Palauskas in presidential election; he was inaugurated on 26 Feb.
5   Amnesty International estimated that more than 80,000 had died in violence in Algeria since 1992; further massacres by Islamic insurgents were reported on 7 Jan.
9   British PM Tony Blair on official visit to Japan.
    President Clinton launched emergency initiative with IMF to rescue Indonesia from threatened economic collapse.
    Britain's N. Ireland Secretary, Mo Mowlam, made unprecedented visit to convicted loyalist terrorists in Belfast's Maze prison to appeal for support in peace talks.
12 Hong Kong's share index down 9 per cent: it had lost 27 per cent since 1 Jan. amid growing economic crisis in Far East.
17 Iraqi leader Saddam Husain issued ultimatum to UN to lift trade sanctions by 20 May or he would end arms inspections.
20 Václav Havel re-elected President of Czech Republic for second five-year term; he was sworn in on 2 Feb.
21 Pope John Paul on historic five-day visit to Cuba, including talks with President Castro.
    In USA, special prosecutor Kenneth Starr launched investigation into allegations that President Clinton had committed perjury over his alleged affair with Monica Lewinsky; in response to mounting scandal, Mr Clinton denied affair on 26 Jan. (see 18 Aug., 9 Sept., 19 Dec.).
25 Eleven died in suicide lorry bomb attack by Tamil Tigers on Sri Lanka's holiest shrine, the Temple of the Tooth in Kandy.
28 In India, 26 people sentenced to death for their part in assassination of Rajiv Gandhi in 1991.

FEBRUARY

2   In USA, President Clinton presented to Congress $1,700,000 million budget for fiscal 1999, first balanced budget since 1969; it included major childcare initiative and other increases in social expenditure.
3   In Italy, 20 died when low-flying US military aircraft cut wire supporting cable car in Dolomites ski resort.
    Prince of Wales on three-day visit to Sri Lanka, celebrating 50th anniversary of independence; he later visited Bhutan and Nepal.
4   At elections in Costa Rica, opposition leader Miguel Angel Rodríguez Echeverria narrowly defeated ruling PLN candidate; he was sworn in as President on 8 May.
    4,000 died in earthquake in remote northern region of Afghanistan.
5   British PM Tony Blair in Washington for talks with President Clinton; escalation of crisis over UN weapons inspection in Iraq was major item on agenda.
10 President Yeltsin of Russia on state visit to Italy for talks with PM Romano Prodi and audience with Pope John Paul II.
13 In Sierra Leone, senior junta officials fled following overthrow of regime of Lt.-Col. Johnny Koroma by Nigerian-led ECOMOG forces seeking reinstatement of government of Ahmed Tejan Kabbah, ousted in May 1997 (see 10 March, 8 May).
    Australia's Constitutional Convention voted overwhelmingly to hold referendum on ending links with Britain and declaration of republic.

15 In Cyprus, incumbent President Glafkos Clerides narrowly defeated George Iakovou in second round of presidential election.
16 206 died when Taiwanese A-300 Airbus crashed on approach to Taipei.
Two weeks of voting commenced in India's general election (see 3 March).
23 Following talks in Baghdad between UN Secretary-General Kofi Annan and Iraqi leaders, a deal was signed to allow UN weapons inspectors unrestricted access to all sites (see 14 Nov., 16 Dec.).
Laos National Assembly approved appointment of Khamtay Siphandon as President; he was replaced as PM by Sisavath Keobounphanh.
25 Kim Dae Jung, former pro-democracy campaigner, inaugurated as President of South Korea following Dec. 1997 election.

MARCH

1 In UK, 250,000 took part in 'Countryside Alliance' march in London to highlight perceived government threat to traditional rural way of life.
A two-week sale of artefacts of late Duke and Duchess of Windsor opened at Sotheby's, New York; it raised $23.35 million for charity.
2 In Pristina, capital of Kosovo, Serb riot police attacked demonstration by 50,000 ethnic Albanians seeking autonomy.
3 Final results of Indian general election gave no party overall majority; on 19 March a coalition headed by Hindu-nationalist Bharatiya Janata Party was sworn in, led by Atal Behari Vajpayee.
4 Ezer Weizman re-elected President of Israel for second term by Knesset.
5 NASA scientists reported that satellite *Lunar Prospector* had discovered pockets of water around north and south poles of Moon.
10 Ahmed Tejan Kabbah, overthrown in 1997, reinstated as President of Sierra Leone, following intervention of ECOMOG forces.
In Indonesia, Gen. Suharto re-elected President for seventh successive term by People's Consultative Assembly (see 21 May).
11 At general election in Denmark, ruling Social Democratic coalition returned with majority of one; PM Poul Nyrup Rasmussen named reshuffled government on 23 March.
Angolan government offered final peace deal to rebel leader Jonas Savimbi, legalizing Unita as political party.
12 European Union held 26-nation summit in London to mark launch of its planned expansion into Eastern Europe and Cyprus; negotiations opened in Brussels on 31 March with six 'fast-track' applicants.
14 In India, Sonia Gandhi, widow of murdered PM Rajiv Gandhi, appointed president of Congress Party.
17 In UK, budget day: Chancellor offered new incentives for low-paid working families and pledged more cash for NHS and education.
In China, National People's Congress endorsed economic reformer Zhu Rongji as PM in succession to Li Peng, who was named party chairman.
21 Pope John Paul on three-day visit to Nigeria.
22 In general elections in Moldova, Communists emerged as largest single party but were excluded from coalition government formed by PM Ion Ciubiu on 21 May.
23 President Clinton began 11-day tour of Africa, visiting Ghana, Senegal, Uganda, Rwanda, Botswana and S. Africa.
In Russia, President Yeltsin dismissed government of Viktor Chernomyrdin, calling for more dynamic approach to economic reform; Sergei Kiriyenko named PM (see 23 Aug.).
25 Tony Blair became first British PM to address French National Assembly.
In USA, two boys aged 11 and 13 detained following shooting incident at school in Jonesborough, Arkansas, in which five died.

25 European Commission declared that 11 states would join monetary union and launch of 'euro' single currency in Jan. 1999.
   In UK, government White Paper outlined proposals for a new elected mayor and 25-member assembly for London.
26 Presidents Yeltsin of Russia and Chirac of France plus Chancellor Kohl of Germany held first annual 'troika' summit near Moscow: agenda included Iraq and mounting ethnic violence in Kosovo.
27 UN Security Council approved dispatch of 1,350 peacekeeping troops to Central African Republic.
28 In UK, Cambridge beat Oxford by 2½ lengths in University Boat Race.
29 Ukraine held parliamentary elections: Communists emerged as largest single party but without overall majority.
30 In Armenia's presidential election, former PM Robert Kocharyan gained landslide victory, following resignation of Levon Ter-Petrosyan on 3 Feb.
31 China's new PM Zhu Rongji began official visit to UK, including talks with Tony Blair on 2 April.

APRIL

1 In USA, federal judge in Arkansas dismissed charges of sexual harassment brought by Paula Jones against President Clinton.
   Israel's security cabinet voted to adopt UN resolution 425 (March 1978) calling for withdrawal of troops from southern Lebanon.
   Festus Mogae sworn in as President of Botswana following retirement of Sir Ketumile Masire.
2 Second Asia-Europe Meeting (ASEM) opened in London: Asian financial crisis was main topic on agenda.
   Radu Vasile appointed PM of Romania following resignation of Victor Ciorbea.
   Former French cabinet minister Maurice Papon (87) gaoled for ten years by Bordeaux court for his role in deportation of Jews to Nazi death camps in World War II.
4 In UK, Grand National won by Earth Summit at 7–1.
9 In Saudi Arabia, at least 118 Muslim pilgrims died in stampede near Mecca during annual *haj*.
10 British and Irish governments and eight N. Ireland political parties (including Ulster Unionists and Sinn Féin) signed peace settlement for Province (the so-called Good Friday Agreement—see XVII.1) following talks brokered by former US Senator George Mitchell (see 22 May).
   In UK, five died in worst flooding to affect Midlands and East Anglia for 50 years.
15 Cambodia's Khmer Rouge dictator Pol Pot, responsible for deaths of an estimated 1.7 million people in 1970s, died (see XVIII: Obituary).
   Girija Prasad Koirala sworn in as PM of Nepal, following resignation of government of Surya Bahadur Thapa.
17 British PM Tony Blair began five-day tour of Egypt, Saudi Arabia, Jordan and Israel in effort to bolster Middle East peace process.
18 President Yeltsin of Russia on two-day visit to Japan for talks with PM Ryutaro Hashimoto.
   Thomas Klestil re-elected President of Austria for second six-year term.
24 In Rwanda, thousands watched public execution of 22 men and women for their part in 1994 massacres.
26 In UK, London Marathon won by Abel Anton (Spain) in 2 hr 7 min 57 sec.
27 Kosovo on verge of war as Serb police and Yugoslav army poured into province to suppress separatist Kosovo Liberation Army rebels.
30 Israel held celebrations to mark 50th anniversary of foundation of nation state.

31 UN Security Council adopted resolution 1160, imposing arms embargo on Federal Republic of Yugoslavia and urging dialogue between Belgrade and ethnic Albanian community in Kosovo.

MAY

1 European Union began special summit in Brussels: it formally decided to launch single currency in Jan. 1999 with 11 of its 15 members participating.
3 US, Israeli and Palestinian officials held two days of talks in London on stalled Middle East peace process but failed to achieve a breakthrough.
4 At the Vatican, newly-appointed commander of Swiss Guard Col. Alois Estermann and his wife found murdered; assumed murderer also found dead.
6 In the Netherlands, ruling Labour Party, led by Wim Kok, gained increased share of vote in general election; a new Labour-led coalition took office on 3 Aug.
  In southern Italy, 135 died in series of mudslides set off by heavy rain in Campania region.
8 UK company, Sandline International, named five senior British diplomats who allegedly approved shipment of weapons to Sierra Leone, in breach of UN sanctions.
10 At Dublin conference, Sinn Féin voted to support Ulster peace agreement and pursue a united Ireland by peaceful means.
  Paraguay held presidential and parliamentary elections; Raúl Cubas Grau of ruling Colorado Party won presidential contest; he was sworn in on 15 Aug.
11 In the Philippines, Joseph Estrada gained landslide victory in presidential elections; he was sworn in on 30 June.
  India carried out three underground nuclear weapons tests in Rajasthan desert, despite Western warnings of international sanctions.
14 In Indonesia, more than 200 died in rioting in Jakarta amid rising tide of protests calling for resignation of President Suharto (see 21 May).
  Israeli forces shot dead eight Palestinians during rioting in Gaza Strip where Palestinian demonstrators sought to attack isolated Jewish settlements.
15 G-8 summit opened in Birmingham, UK, ending 17 May; debt relief measures for some of world's poorest countries was high on agenda but no new measures were agreed.
18 President Clinton and PM Blair held talks at Chequers prior to EU/US summit held in London at which agreement was reached over threatened US sanctions on European companies trading with Cuba, Libya and Iran.
21 Gen. Suharto resigned as President of Indonesia after 32 years, following nationwide protests; his deputy B.J. Habibie sworn in as new President.
22 In referendums in N. Ireland and Republic of Ireland, voters overwhelmingly approved multi-party peace accord signed on 10 April, so-called Good Friday Agreement.
24 At first post-colonial elections in Hong Kong, pro-democracy candidates won 14 of 20 directly-elected seats in legislative assembly.
26 Emperor Akihito of Japan on four-day state visit to UK: there were protests in London by former prisoners-of-war.
27 In Russia, interest rates raised to 150 per cent in response to stock market panic over mounting economic crisis (see 17 Aug.).
  In UK, Low Pay Commission recommended minimum wage of £3.60 per hour.
28 In a referendum, Danish voters approved Amsterdam Treaty providing for changes in European Union.
  Pakistan carried out five underground nuclear tests; a state of emergency was declared as President Clinton announced imposition of sanctions.
30 3,000 died in second earthquake to strike remote region of northern Afghanistan this year.
31 At parliamentary elections in Yugoslav republic of Montenegro, reformist coalition led by President Djukanovic defeated Slobodan Milošević's loyalists.

JUNE

3 More than 100 died when a high-speed train was derailed near Eschede: it was Germany's worst rail accident since World War II.
 Heavy fighting erupted between Ethiopian and Eritrean troops on disputed border.
4 UN Security Council held emergency meeting in Geneva to consider growing arms race between India and Pakistan.
8 Nigeria's military dictator Gen. Sani Abacha died suddenly (see XVIII: Obituary); Gen. Abdulsalam Abubakar sworn in as head of state on 9 June.
 UN imposed economic sanctions against Yugoslavia in response to Serb attacks on ethnic Albanians in Kosovo.
9 World Cup football competition opened in France; France beat Brazil 3–0 in final on 12 July.
10 EU Commission declared that meat from younger cattle in Britain was safe from BSE and recommended lifting of ban on export of British beef (see 23 Nov.).
12 World stock markets slumped in response to news that Japan was officially in recession.
 Queen Margrethe of Denmark opened four-mile Storebaelt Bridge linking eastern and western Denmark: it was world's second-longest suspension bridge.
15 EU leaders attended two-day Council meeting in Cardiff; Germany demanded large reduction in its £7,000 million contribution to EU's running costs.
 NATO aircraft staged six-hour Operation Falcon through Albania and Macedonia as warning to Serbia to cease repression in Kosovo.
 Hundreds reported dead in fighting in Guinea-Bissau in aftermath of attempted coup on 7 June.
16 President Miloševic of Yugoslavia agreed to begin talks on autonomy for Kosovo; 300 had died and more than 100,000 ethnic Albanians had fled province since fighting began in March.
 World Bank warned that Asia was on brink of deep recession which could trigger world recession if Japan took no action over its ailing economy.
 1,300 reported dead, 10,000 missing in cyclone in northern India.
17 President Clinton announced $2,000 million package in support of Japanese yen, which had fallen to eight-year low against dollar.
19 Czech Republic held elections; Social Democrats, led by Milos Zeman, formed minority government on 9 July.
21 In Colombia's presidential election, Andrés Pastrana Arango (Conservative) gained narrow victory over Horacio Serpa (ruling Liberals): he was sworn in on 8 Aug.
23 In response to call from President Yeltsin, Russia's PM Sergei Kiriyenko outlined programme of economic measures intended to combat country's economic crisis.
25 President Clinton began nine-day state visit to China and Hong Kong, holding talks with President Jiang Zemin.
 In N. Ireland, voters went to polls to elect members to new Belfast Assembly: Ulster Unionists emerged as largest party.
27 More than 120 died in earthquake which devastated Turkish city of Adana.

JULY

1 David Trimble, leader of Ulster Unionist Party, elected First Minister at first meeting of new N. Ireland Assembly.
2 President Jiang Zemin of China formally opened Hong Kong's new $12,000 million Chek Lap Kok airport: it had the world's largest terminal.
6 Britain's National Health Service celebrated 50th anniversary of its foundation.
7 Chief Moshood Abiola, Nigeria's detained opposition leader and presumed 1993 election winner, died suddenly; his release from custody was believed to have been imminent (see XVIII: Obituary).

10 In China, 600 people reported dead in severe flooding in south-western province of Sichuan.
12 In N. Ireland, three young brothers died in arson attack on their home in loyalist area of Ballymoney, Co. Antrim, following week of violence by loyalist Orangemen demanding right to march in Drumcree.
Jamil Mahuad Witt elected President of Ecuador.
13 Japanese PM Ryutaro Hashimoto resigned in aftermath of sharp reverse for ruling Liberal Democrats (LDP) in Upper House elections; he was succeeded by Keizo Obuchi, newly-appointed president of LDP, on 30 July.
14 In UK, Chancellor announced £40,000 million package for investment in health and education over next three years.
17 Some 3,000 died when tidal wave struck north-western coast of Papua New Guinea.
In Russia, a state funeral was held in St Petersburg for the interment of the remains of Tsar Nicholas II, his family and servants, who were shot by the Bolsheviks at Yekaterinburg in 1918.
In Rome, UN conference adopted statute of new International Criminal Court (see XVII.2).
20 Nigeria's new military ruler announced intended return to civilian rule following May 1999 election.
In UK, government published White Paper on transport: it foreshadowed new charges and taxes to discourage private motoring.
24 In USA, two policemen shot dead when lone gunman opened fire in Washington's Capitol building.
26 Cambodian People's Party, led by Hun Sen, gained most of 122 seats in elections for National Assembly.
27 In UK, PM Tony Blair announced government reshuffle, sacking four cabinet ministers: Peter Mandelson appointed Trade and Industry Secretary (see 22 Dec.).
Pakistan's former PM Benazir Bhutto appeared in court in Lahore, charged with corruption.

AUGUST

3 Serbian security forces carried out scorched-earth policy against ethnic Albanian towns in Kosovo: more than 180,000 had been displaced since start of conflict in March.
4 In China, 2,500 reported dead in severe flooding on Yangtse river in Hunan, Hubei and Jiangxi provinces since June.
5 Iraqi parliament called for immediate freeze on work of UN weapons inspectors and end to eight-year oil embargo.
7 In Kenya, at least 240 died, 5,000 injured in terrorist suicide car bomb attack on US embassy in Nairobi; 10 died in another attack on US embassy in Dar es Salaam, Tanzania (see 20 Aug.).
10 In Democratic Republic of Congo, Tutsi-led rebel forces advanced on Kinshasa, threatening government of Laurent Kabila.
11 British Petroleum announced agreed £53,000 million takeover of US oil company Amoco in history's biggest industrial merger.
12 Tajikistan appealed for international intervention as fundamentalist Islamic Taleban troops were reported to be within five miles of Afghanistan's border with central Asian states.
King Husain of Jordan, in hospital in USA for prolonged cancer treatment, delegated domestic powers to his brother, Crown Prince Hasan; a new cabinet, led by Fayez Tarawneh, was sworn in on 20 Aug.
13 Swiss banks agreed to pay £767 million into a fund for victims of the Jewish Holocaust whose assets were lost or plundered.
15 In Northern Ireland, 28 died, 200 injured in massive car bomb explosion in Omagh, Co. Tyrone; the 'Real IRA' claimed responsibility.

17 Russia announced 50 per cent devaluation of the rouble.
18 In USA, President Clinton admitted an improper relationship with Monica Lewinsky which he had previously denied under oath (see 9 Sept., 19 Dec.).
19 Irish PM Bertie Ahern announced tough package of anti-terrorist measures in wake of Omagh bombing.
20 US launched cruise missile attacks on suspected terrorist bases in Afghanistan and chemical weapons facility in Sudan, claiming it had evidence that Islamic fundamentalist groups had been involved in US embassy bombings in East Africa on 7 Aug.
23 In Russia, President Yeltsin dismissed government following devaluation of rouble (see 10 Sept.)
24 Angolan troops advanced into south-western area of Democratic Republic of Congo in attempt to halt advance of Tutsi rebels.
  Britain and US offered to hold trial in Netherlands of two Libyans suspected of 1988 bombing of Pan Am airliner over Lockerbie, Scotland, but according to Scottish law.
25 In S. Africa, terrorist bomb attack on Cape Town restaurant killed one and injured 24; Islamic militants claimed it was retaliation for US attacks in Afghanistan and Sudan.
26 Stock markets fell sharply in response to heavy losses by Russian rouble on world currency markets and fears that Russian crisis might trigger global collapse.
29 In Ecuador, 78 died when Cuban airliner crashed on take-off from Quito.

SEPTEMBER

1 President Clinton in Moscow for two days of talks with President Yeltsin; he called on Russia to persist with economic reform.
  In Belgium, trial of former NATO secretary-general Willy Claes and nine others, on charges of corruption, opened in Brussels.
2 In UK, parliament recalled to pass emergency bill to combat terrorism in wake of Omagh bombing on 15 Aug.
  Malaysia's PM, Mahathir Mohamad, dismissed his deputy, Anwar Ibrahim (see 21 Sept., 2 Nov.).
3 President Clinton on three-day visit to N. Ireland and Irish Republic.
  229 died when Swissair McDonnell Douglas MD11 crashed off Nova Scotia, Canada.
4 Former Rwandan PM Jean Kambanda gaoled for life by UN International Criminal Tribunal for Rwanda (sitting in Arusha, Tanzania) for genocide in Rwanda in 1994.
5 Elections in Malta were won by Nationalist Party; its leader, Eddie Fenech-Adami sworn in as PM on 6 Sept.
8 Rupert Murdoch's BSkyB offered £623 million for Manchester United Football Club in what would be world's biggest sports takeover if approved.
  A peace summit of rival factions in Congo-Kinshasa's civil war at Victoria Falls failed to agree date for implementation of ceasefire.
9 In USA, 445-page report of Kenneth Starr's investigation of President Clinton's affair with Monica Lewinsky delivered to Congress for scrutiny by House judicial committee considering possible impeachment (see XVII.4); on 11 Sept. Mr Clinton's lawyers issued 73-page rebuttal (see 19 Dec.).
  Two months of incessant rain had left two-thirds of Bangladesh under water and threatened flooding to Dhaka.
10 President Yeltsin named Yevgenii Primakov as PM: his previous candidate, former PM Viktor Chernomyrdin, had been rejected twice by Duma; nomination approved by Duma on 11 Sept.
12 Bosnia held its second elections since 1995 Dayton Peace Accord; ethnic hardliners returned to most senior positions in Republika Srpska and Muslim-Croat Federation.
13 In Albania, crowds protesting over assassination of an opposition politician stormed government offices, forcing PM Fatos Nano and ministers to flee (see 29 Sept.).

CHRONICLE OF PRINCIPAL EVENTS IN 1998 609

14 New Northern Ireland Assembly met for first time at Stormont.
 More than 50,000 ethnic Albanians reported to have fled from Kosovo in past week; nearly a quarter of province's population had now been displaced since start of ethnic troubles in March.
17 HM Queen Elizabeth II began week-long state visit to Brunei and Malaysia, where she closed Commonwealth Games on 21 Sept.
21 In Malaysia, demonstrators took to streets of Kuala Lumpur, protesting over arrest of former Deputy PM Anwar Ibrahim and demanding resignation of PM Mahathir Mohamad (see 2 Nov.).
 British PM Tony Blair in New York to address UN General Assembly and New York Stock Exchange, where he called for major reform of international financial system.
22 More than 300 died when Hurricane Georges struck Dominican Republic and other areas of northern Caribbean.
 Several died in skirmishes in Maseru where S. African troops had been invited by Lesotho's PM to restore order among anti-government protesters.
24 Britain's Foreign Secretary announced agreement with Iranian government over safety of author Salman Rushdie, under threat of death since declaration of *fatweh* in 1989 (see AR 1989, p. 493–4).
26 At general elections in Sovakia, leading opposition parties overwhelmingly defeated six-year-old government of PM Vladimir Meciar; a new government, led by Mikulas Dzurinda took office on 30 Oct.
27 A general election in Germany ended 16-year rule of Chancellor Kohl and Christian Democratic Union; Social Democrats, led by Gerhard Schröder, gained largest share of vote; Schröder formed coalition with Greens and took office on 27 Oct.
29 Sixteen Albanian civilians found massacred in remote Kosovo village; a further 14 murdered men found on 30 Sept., as calls for NATO air strikes against Serb targets in Kosovo intensified.
 In Albania, ruling Socialist Party named Pandeli Majko PM following resignation of Fatos Nano.
 President Mandela held talks in Cape Town with King Letsie III over S. African intervention in Lesotho, where more than 100 had died in recent troubles.

OCTOBER

3 At general election in Australia, Liberal-National coalition led by PM John Howard returned to office with reduced majority.
 G-7 Finance Ministers held talks in Washington, DC, to discuss response to deepening global economic crisis, following a week in which world stock market prices had plummeted.
4 At elections in Brazil, Fernando Henrique Cardoso re-elected President for unprecedented second term.
6 British PM Tony Blair on five-day official visit to China and Hong Kong.
12 Following talks with US negotiator Richard Holbrooke, President Miloševic of Yugoslavia, under threat of NATO air strikes, agreed deal for deployment of 2,000-strong OSCE observer force in Kosovo to ensure no further harassment of ethnic Albanians by Serb forces.
15 Lebanese parliament elected Gen. Émile Lahoud as President; he was sworn in on 24 Nov.
 Nobel Peace Prize awarded jointly to Ulster Unionist leader David Trimble and SDLP leader John Hume for their efforts towards peace in N. Ireland
18 Former Chilean head of state Gen. Augusto Pinochet (82) arrested at a London hospital on extradition request by Spanish judge investigating murder of Spanish citizens in Chile during his time in office (1973–90) (see 25 Nov., 9 Dec.).
19 President Václav Havel of Czech Republic on official visit to UK.

In Italy, PDS leader Massimo D'Alema named PM following resignation of government of Romano Prodi on 9 Oct.
23 Following nine days of talks at Wye Plantation, near Washington, between Israeli PM Binyamin Netanyahu and PLO leader Yassir Arafat and hosted by President Clinton, a new agreement on Middle East peace was signed, ending 19-month deadlock: the Wye River Memorandum pledged further Israeli withdrawal from West Bank and Palestinian curb on anti-Israeli terrorism.
25 EU leaders concluded two-day informal summit in Pörtschach, Austria.
26 Presidents of Peru and Ecuador signed historic treaty ending century-old border dispute.
27 President Carlos Menem, on six-day official visit to UK, first by an Argentine leader since Falklands war in 1982.

In UK, Welsh Secretary Ron Davies resigned over 'serious lapse of judgment' on Clapham Common, south London; replaced by Alun Michael.
29 John Glenn (77), America's first man to orbit Earth in 1962, returned to space in nine-day mission aboard *Discovery* shuttle.

In S. Africa, final report of Truth and Reconciliation Commission published: it contained indictments of leading politicians and their parties (including ruling ANC) during apartheid era.
30 Some 10,000 people died in Honduras and Nicaragua when Hurricane Mitch caused flash flooding and mudslides in large areas of Central America.

NOVEMBER

1 Russian government approved economic reform package aimed at ending country's economic crisis, but plan was rejected by IMF.
2 New German Chancellor Gerhard Schröder in London for first official talks with PM Tony Blair: they agreed to set up Anglo-German think tank.

In Malaysia, trial opened in Kuala Lumpur of former deputy PM Anwar Ibrahim, charged with corruption and sexual offences.
3 In US mid-term elections Republicans retained control of Senate and House of Representatives; Democrats gained five House seats and governorship of California; there was no change in Senate split (Republicans 55, Democrats 45).
8 In Bangladesh, court sentenced to death 15 army officers and politicians for their role in assassination of country's first President, Sheikh Mujibur Rahman (see AR 1975, p. 262).
9 At general election in Bermuda, Progressive Labour Party won 26 of 40 seats in parliament, defeating ruling United Bermuda Party after 35 years; its leader, Jennifer Smith, was sworn in as PM on 10 Nov.
13 In Indonesia, several died in riots in Jakarta where students were demanding political reform.
15 President Clinton called off threatened cruise missile attacks against Iraq at last minute following President Saddam Husain's agreement to cooperate with UN weapons inspectors in Iraq (see 16 Dec.).
20 President Clinton on two-day official visit to S. Korea.

Galina Starovoitova, a reformist member of Russian parliament and presidential contender, assassinated in St Petersburg.
23 EU Agriculture Ministers lifted three-year ban on export of British beef because of BSE fears; 4.4 million cattle had been slaughtered at a cost of £4,000 million.

President Yeltsin, in hospital in Moscow, held talks with Chinese President Jiang Zemin.
24 The opening of Yassir Arafat International Airport in Gaza Strip gave one million Palestinians their first direct link with the outside world.

In UK, state opening of parliament: Queen's Speech foreshadowed 22 bills including one to end voting rights of hereditary peers and another to overhaul social security system.

25 In UK, House of Lords' panel delivered 3–2 ruling that former Chilean dictator Gen. Pinochet did not have immunity against extradition to Spain (see 9 Dec.).
President Jiang Zemin on historic state visit to Japan: he was first Chinese leader to visit Japan since World War II.
26 Tony Blair addressed Irish parliament in Dublin: he was first British PM to do so since partition in 1922.
In Japan, a Tokyo court rejected claim by former British prisoners-of-war for compensation for mistreatment by Japan during World War II.
In Latvia, a new coalition government was formed by Vilis Kristopans, whose Latvia's Way party gained largest number of parliamentary seats in 3 Oct. election.
28 Israel carried out heavy shelling of Hizbullah positions in occupied southern Lebanon, following deaths of seven Israeli soldiers in ambush.
President Chirac hosted Franco-African summit in Paris: he announced that governments of Uganda, Rwanda and Congo had agreed ceasefire in four-month conflict in Congo-Kinshasa, on basis of deal negotiated by UN Secretary-General; Congolese rebels were not present at talks.
30 In provincial elections in Quebec, separatist Parti Québécois government of Lucien Bouchard won majority of seats, but insufficient for early further referendum on independence.

DECEMBER

1 President Roman Herzog of Germany on state visit to UK.
US oil giant Exxon announced takeover of Mobil in $82,000 million deal, the biggest in history of world stock markets.
2 In UK, government published White Paper, *Modernizing Justice*, including proposals to reform legal aid and lawyers' monopolies.
Salim al Hoss succeeded Rafiq Hariri as PM of Lebanon.
Bülent Ecevit designated PM of Turkey to succeed Mesut Yilmaz.
3 Two-day Anglo-French summit opened in St Malo: joint initiatives on defence, transport and the 'millennium computer bug' were main items under discussion.
6 In presidential elections in Venezuela, Col. Hugo Chávez, previously gaoled for role in 1992 coup attempt, gained landslide victory.
7 Four Western hostages, including three Britons, kidnapped in Chechenya in October, found murdered by their abductors after a botched rescue mission by Chechen security forces.
9 UK Home Secretary Jack Straw approved opening of proceedings against Gen. Pinochet for his extradition to Spain; however, on 17 Dec. law lords quashed 25 Nov. ruling enabling extradition, because of one judge's undeclared links with Amnesty International.
Parliamentary deputies elected Ruth Dreifuss as Switzerland's first woman President (for 1999).
11 EU leaders began two-day summit in Vienna.
12 President Clinton arrived in Jerusalem to begin historic three-day visit to Israel and Palestinian-controlled Gaza Strip.
16 US and UK launched Operation Desert Fox, four nights of massive bombing raids against Iraq, in response to Saddam Husain's continued refusal to cooperate with UN weapons inspectors.
19 US House of Representatives voted for impeachment of President Clinton for 'high crimes and misdemeanours', charges arising from his affair with Monica Lewinsky.
22 In UK, Trade and Industry Secretary Peter Mandelson and Paymaster-General Geoffrey Robinson resigned from government over a financial loan scandal.
28 Six died when severe weather hit boats competing in Sydney-Hobart yacht race, event's worst disaster in its 54-year history.
29 Three Britons and an Australian died in shoot-out when Yemeni security forces raided mountain hideout where kidnappers were holding 16 Western hostages.

INDEX

Page references in bold indicate location of main coverage.

Abacha, Gen. Sani, 90, 269, 270, 271, 421, 454, 456, 468, 586 (obit.), 606
Abayomi, Alhaji, 270
Abdullah ibn Abdul Aziz, Crown Prince, 235, 237, 238, 450
Abessole, Father Paul Mba, 285
Abiola, Chief Moshood (M.K.O.), 269, 270, 421, 586 (obit.), 606
Abkhazia, 157, 443
Abse, Dannie, 543
Abu Dhabi, 242, 451
Abu Musa & Tunbs Islands, 244, 314, 451
Abubakar, Gen. Abdulsalam, 269, 270, 271, 421, 456, 606
Ackroyd, Peter, 541, 543
Acosta, Capt. Jorge, 183
Acosta, Carlos, 516
Adami, Mohamed, 253
Adams, Gerry, 49, 50
Adams, John, 512
Adams, Jonathan, 535
Addo, Nana Akufo, 267
Advani, L.K., 327
Afewerki, Issaias, 257, 258, 259
Afghanistan, 2, 3, 4, 65, 176, 262, 314–5, **316–9**, 323, 324, 334, 400, 407, 412, 427, 602, 608
African Development Bank (AfDB), 456–7
African Organizations & Conferences, 304, **453–7**
Agayev, Avez, 321
Agyeman, Nana Konadu, 267
Ahern, Bertie, 45, 50, 70, 608
Aho, Esko, 80
Ahtisaari, Martti, 80, 81
Ahwoi, Kwamena, 267
AIDS/HIV, 6, 58, 305, 310, 477
Akayesu, Jean-Paul, 293, 494, 495
Akayev, Askar, 319, 321, 322, 326
Akihito, Emperor Tsugu no Miya, 37, 43, 376, 377, 381, 605
Alanis of Urgel, Bishop Joan Martí, 87
Alarcón Rivera, Fabián, 190

Albania, 13, 64, **130–3**, 146, 439, 440, 442, 449, 606, 608
Albee, Edward, 521
Albert II, King, 65
Albright, Madeleine K., 116, 176, 441, 583
Alderdice, Lord, 47
Alemán Lacayo, Arnaldo, 198, 200
Alexander, Bill, 520
Alexis, Jacques Edouard, 197
Alexis, Patriarch, 470
Algeria, 4, 60, 66, **251–3**, 255
Aliyev, Geidar, 156, 157
Almunia, Joaquín, 94
Alston, Richard, 516
Alvarez, Aida, 583
Amamou, Mohammed, 450
Amangwe, Dr Amukowa, 262
Amarjargal, Rinchinnyamyn, 386
Amato, Giuliano, 64
Ambler, Eric, 586 (obit.)
American & Carribbean Organizations, **462–5**
Amin, Idi, 541
Ammush, Bassam al, 227
Amnesty International, 37, 259, 263, 294, 348, 350, 472, 602
Amour, Dr Salmin, 265
Anafu, Dr Moses, 422
Ananiashvili, Nina, 516
Andean Community (CA/Ancom), **463**, **465**
Andersen, Frank, 514
Andorra, **87**, **88**
Andrikiene, Laima, 115
Angelou, Maya, 543
Angeloz, Eduardo César, 184
Angola, 286, 288, 290, **297–9**, 302, 306, 312, 400, 410, 412, 425, 426, 428, 455, 477, 603, 608
Anguilla, 212 465
Anguita, Julio, 94
Ani, Chief Anthony, 269

INDEX

Annan, Kofi, 106, 187, 244, 248, 255, 293, 353, 400, 405, 425, 451, 603
Anomeritis, Georgios, 102
Antarctica, 486–7, 497
Anthony, Kenny D., 210, 211
Antigua & Barbuda, 209, 210
Anton, Abel, 604
Antoni, Robert, 542
Antrobus, Charles James, 210
Anwar Ibrahim, 352, 353, 461, 608, 609, 610
Anyaoku, Chief Emeka Chukwuemeka, 421, 422
Arab League, 3, 233, 314, **450, 452**
Arab Maghreb Union (AMU), 450
Arab Organizations, 450–2
Arab States of the Gulf, 240–4, 450–2
Arafat, Yassir, 218, 221, 222, 223, 224
Aragona, Giancarlo, 440
Araujo, Francisco de Assis, 186
Archer, Lord (Jeffrey), 18
Architecture, 40, 322, **534–8**
Arctic Council, 445, 446
Arctic Ocean, 486
Ardanza, José Antonio, 91
Argaña, Luis María, 192
Argentina, 37, 92, **183–4**, 247, 400, 418, 464, 610
Armenia, 13, **156–7**, 426, 443, 604
Armey, Dick, 168
Armfield, Neil, 510
Arms Control, see Defence, Disarmament & Security
Armstrong, Peter, 543
Arnold, Lorna, 589
Art, see Visual Arts
Arthur, Owen, 206, 423
Aruba, 215
Arzú Irigoyen, Alvaro, 198, 200
Asad, Hafiz al-, 228, 229
Åsbrink, Erik, 79
Ashbery, John, 543
Ashdown, Paddy, 24
Asher, Linda, 543
Ashimolowo, Matthew, 469
Ashrawi, Hannan, 223
Ashton, Frederick, 516, 587
Ashworth, Andrea, 542
Asia-Europe Meeting (ASEM), 369, **458**
Asian Development Bank (ADB), 461, 462

Asian Economic Crisis, 7, **8–10**, 14, 31, 71, 77, 94, 97, 110, 160–1, 181–2, 236, 242, 284, 343, 351, 354, 356–7, 360, 363, 366, 376–7, 379, 380–1, 387, 392, 394, 420, 422, 437, 455, 458, 459, 461–2, 606
Asia-Pacific Economic Cooperation (APEC), 353, 369, 379, 395, **457, 460–2**
Asia-Pacific Organizations, 457–62
Asrat Woldeyes, Prof., 259
Association of Caribbean States (ACS), 463
Association of South-East Asian Nations (ASEAN), 9, 352, 362 369, 379, **457, 458–60**
Astiz, Capt. Alfredo Ignacio, 183
Atef, Mohammed, 174
Atherton, Michael, 550
Atta-Mills, John, 267
Aubry, Martine, 56
Aury, Dominique, 538
Australia, 328, 354, **387–91**, 392, 395, 398, 402, 420, 458, 461, 462, 467, 470, 488, 546, 602, 611
Austria, 35, **81–3**, 90, 119, 121, 151, 250, 431, 433, 450, 604
Avebury, Lord, 36
Avramopoulos, Dimitris, 103
Axworthy, Lloyd, 182
Ayala Lasso, José, 190
Ayales, Farid, 201
Azerbaijan, 13, **156, 157**, 326, 439, 443
Aziz, Rafidah, 461
Azizah Ismail, 353
Aznar López, José María, 91, 185

Ba, Mamadou, 279
Babangida, Gen. Ibrahim, 270, 586
Babbitt, Bruce, 216, 583
Babiniotis, Prof. George, 104
Bacall, Lauren, 518
Bach, J.S., 589
Bacon, Jim, 390
Bagabandi, Natsagiyn, 326, 384, 385, 386
Bahamas, The, 208–9, 422
Bahrain, 241, 242, 243, 244, 400
Bailey, John, 543
Bainbridge, Beryl, 539, 541, 542
Baker, Nicholson, 542
Balaguer, Joaquín, 197
Balanchine, George, 517, 595

Balasuriya, Fr Tissa, 466
Balcerowicz, Leszek, 112
Balfour, Arthur, xvi
Balgimbayev, Nurlan, 319
Balladur, Edouard, 58, 60
Ballet & Dance, 514–7
Baltic Council/Assembly, 445, 447
Banda, Hastings, 300
Bangladesh, 13, **334–7**, 428, 488, 608, 610
Banzer Suárez, Hugo, 185
Baranyi, Francisc (Ferenc), 125
Barbados, 206–7, 210, 423
Bardé, Laokein 'Frisson', 284
Barenboim, Daniel, 512
Barents Euro-Arctic Region (BEAR), 446
Barents Sea, 447
Barker, Nicola, 542
Barker, Pat,, 542
Barnes, Julian, 540, 542
Barr, Glenn, 71
Barrionuevo, José, 92
Barrow, Dean Oliver, 207
Barry, Sebastian, 542
Barshefsky, Charlene, 583
Bartholomew, Patriarch, 470
Barton, Prof. Sir Derek, 586 (obit.)
Baruch, Leonel, 201
Barzani, Mesud, 109
Barzani, Mustafa, 235
Bashir, Omar Hasan Ahmed al-, 245
Basque Question, 91–2
Basri, Driss, 254
Bassey, Hogan, 587 (obit.)
Bassolino, Antonio, 64
Bastien, Kely, 197
Batalla, Hugo, 194
Batbayar, Bat-Erdeniyn, 386
Baxter, Keith, 541, 543
Baykal, Deniz, 108
Bayley, John, 541
Beatrix, Queen, 67
Beattie, Peter, 388
Beaumarchais, Pierre, 509
Beaven, Derek, 542
Beazley, Kim, 389
Beckett, Margaret, 22, 32, 582
Beckham, David, 549
Bedells, Jean, 515
Beer, Patricia, 543
Beevor, Anthony, 544
Begin, Benny, 217
Béjar Molina, Gen. Carlos, 185

Belarus, 13, 112, **153–4**, 415, 426, 440, 443
Belgium, **65–7**, 71, 290, 431, 433, 466, 608
Belize, 207
Bell, Mary, 540
Ben Ali, Gen. Zayn al-Abdin, 249, 250, 251
Ben Yahia, Habib, 251
Benesova, Libuse, 119
Benin, 282
Bentley, Derek, 502
Berceanu, Radu, 125
Berenson, Lori, 193
Bergkamp, Dennis, 549
Beriosova, Svetlana, 587 (obit.)
Beriozoff, Nicholas, 587
Berisha, Sali, 130, 131, 132
Berlin, Isaiah, 541
Bermuda, 212–3 610
Bernard, Elliott, 537
Bernstein, Leonard, 512, 513
Berrios Sagredo, Eugenio, 194
Berti, Pietro, 88
Bertinotti, Fausto, 63
Beskow, Elsa, 515
Betchine, Gen. Mohamed, 253
Betjeman, John, 538
Beye, Alioune Blondin, 298
Bhumibol Adulyadej (Rama IX), King, 351
Bhutan, 338, **339–41**, 602
Bhutto, Benazir, 332, 607
Bicakćić, Edhem, 134
Bildt, Carl, 79
Billah Bolkiah, Prince Al-Muhtadee, 354
Bin Laden, Osama, 133, 174, 176, 245, 262, 318, 319, 334
Bing, Ilse, 534
Binoche, Juliette, 518, 519
Bintley, David, 515
Bird, Lester, 209
Birendra Bir Bikram Shah Deva, King, 338, 339
Birtwistle, Sir Harrison, 512
Biwott, Nicholas, 262
Biya, Paul, 283
Bizimungu, Pasteur, 291
Bizony, Piers, 544
Black Sea Economic Cooperation (BSEC), 447, 450
Black Sea, 325

Blair, Tony, 18, 21, 23, 28, 30, 34, 35, 36, 38, 49, 50, 56, 223, 437, 605
Blanc, Laurent, 549
Blas Salazar, Col. Juan, 199
Bleiler, Andy, 160
Blunkett, David, 582
Boal, Peter, 517
Bogatiriev, Alexander, 517
Bohr, Niels, 520
Bol, Kerubino Kuanyin, 246
Bolger, Jim, 393
Bolivia, 185
Bollini, Paolo, 88
Bondevik, Kjell Magne, 76
Bongo, Omar, 283, 285, 425
Bonhöffer, Dietrich, 469
Bonnard, Pierre, 532, 534
Booker Prize, 539
Booth, Martin, 542
Boothroyd, Betty, 22, 527
Borday-Tornay, Muguette, 89
Borrell, José, 94
Bosić, Boro, 134
Bosnia & Hercegovina, 79, **134–7,** 161, 405, 409, 430, 440, 441, 449, 495, 496, 608
Bostwick, Janet, 209
Botha, P.W., 309
Botrero Zea, Fernando, 188
Botswana, 302, **303, 304–5,** 306, 307, 422, 603, 604
Bouchard, Lucien, 178, 179, 180, 611
Boucher, Mark, 551
Bouchez, Elaine, 525
Bougainville, 391–2, 395, 397
Bourdon, David, 534
Boutros-Ghali, Boutros, 423, 424
Bowen, Meirion (Bill), 514, 600
Bowles, Erskine, 583
Boyd, Michael, 522
Boyd, William, 542
Boyle, James, 527
Boyle, T. Coraghesan, 542
Bradman, Don, 551
Brahimi, Lakhdar, 318
Brandstrup, Kim, 517
Brandt, David, 212, 213
Braque, Georges, 534
Brazil, 10, 96, 183, **186–7,** 195, 326, 400, 403, 418, 426, 464, 488, 491, 609
Breard, Angel Francisco, 492
Brecht, Bertolt, 539

Briceño, John, 207
Brisby, Liliana Daneva, 587 (obit.)
British Virgin Islands, 212, 213
Britten, Benjamin, 510
Broadcasting, see Television & Radio
Brook, Peter, 543
Brookner, Anita, 542
Brown, George Mackay, 542
Brown, Gordon, 19, 30, 31, 33, 46, 582
Brown, Jesse, 583
Brown, Milton, 534
Brown, Nick, 22, 27, 582
Browner, Carol, 583
Bruce, Christopher, 517
Brunei, 354, 429, 458, 609
BSE (bovine spongiform encephalopathy), 35–6, 98–9
Bucaram Ortiz, Abdalá, 190
Buckley, Fr Pat, 467
Bulatović, Momir, 142, 147
Bulgaria, 13, **127–30**, 402, 434, 439, 450, 587, 601
Bull, Deborah, 515
Buller, Darshan Singh, 516
Burke, David, 520
Burkina Faso, 276, 280–1, 286, 430, 454, 455
Burma, see Myanmar
Burundi, 291–3, 477
Bush, Geoffrey, 514
Bush, George W., 167, 173
Bush, Jeb, 167
Buthelezi, Chief Mangosuthu, 309
Butler, Richard, 233, 234
Buyoya, Col. Pierre, 291, 292, 293
Buzek, Jerzy, 111, 449
Byatt, A.S., 540, 541, 542
Byrd, James, 174

Cabezas, José Luis, 184
Caine, Michael, 524
Calder, David, 522
Calderón Sol, Armando, 198, 199
Caldera Rodríguez, Rafael, 194, 195
Callard, Jonathan, 553
Callow, Phillip, 544
Cambodia, 1, 101, **360–2**, 405, 459, 490, 594–5, 604, 607
Camdessus, Michel, 417, 455
Cameron, James, 523
Cameroon, 283, 284–5, 422, 493
Campbell, Alastair, 23

Campbell, Darren, 550
Campbell, Graeme, 389
Canada, 76, **178–83**, 196, 286, 305, 328, 400, 402, 422, 448, 469, 491, 493–4
Candela, Felix, 537
Cannadine, David, 544
Canterbury, Archbishop of, 469
Cape Verde, **294, 295**, 298, 425
Caprivi Strip, 307
Cardoso, Fernando Henrique, 186, 187, 326, 609
Carey, Peter, 539
Caribbean Community (Caricom), 204, 205, 206, 211, **463, 464–5**
Carl XVI Gustav, King, 78
Carmichael, Stokely, 587 (obit.)
Caro, Anthony, 533
Caroline, Princess, 88
Caron, Leslie, 518
Carpenter, Humphrey, 544
Carr, Rocky, 542
Carrera Fuentes, Adrián, 202
Carrero, José Manuel, 516
Carrington, Edward, 463
Carson, Anne, 543
Carter, David, 552
Carter, Elliott, 513
Carter, Jimmy, 171, 312
Cartwright, Justin, 542
Caruana, Peter, 94, 95
Casaroli, Cardinal Agostino, 587 (obit.)
Caspian Sea, 157, 324, 325, 326
Cassar, Michael, 101
Castro Ruz, Dr Fidel, 99, 195, 196, 204, 208, 465, 468, 602
Caute, David, 540, 542
Cavallo, Domingo, 184
Cayman Islands, **212, 213**
Cem, Ismail, 109
Central African Republic, **283, 286**, 288, 290, 375, 411, 604
Central Asian Economic Community (CAEC), 323
Central Asian Republics, 319–26
Central European Free Trade Association (CEFTA), 129, **447, 448–9**
Central European Initiative (CEI), 447, 449–50
Césaire, Aimé, 522
Chad, **283, 284**, 286, 290
Chaiyawat Wibulswasdi, 351

Chalerm Yubamrung, 352
Chan, Anson, 371
Chandra, Vikram, 542
Channel Islands, 46, 106
Chaovalit Yongchaiyut, 352
Charest, Jean, 178, 179, 180, 181
Charikane, Ahmed, 346
Charles, Dame Eugenia, 210
Chatham Islands, 398
Chatichai Choonhavan, 352
Chaudhuri, Amit, 542
Chávez Frias, Col. Hugo, 194, 195, 611
Chea Sim, 362
Chechenya, 39, 443, 611
Chernomyrdin, Viktor, 148, 150
Chi Haotian, 370
Chia Thye Poh, 355
Chile, 8, 37, 92–3, 99, **187–8**, 303, 464, 609
Chiluba, Frederick, 299, 300
China, 5, 6, 8, 10, 12, 38, 99, 152, 163, 164, 247, 258, 261, 300, 317, 322, 326, 328, 339, 360, **364–71**, 372, 373, 374–5, 379, 381, 382, 384, 398, 405, 407, 426, 428, 458, 469, 479, 488, 490, 491, 542, 603, 604, 606, 607, 611
Chinyata, Kasasa Mutati, 453
Chirac, Jacques, 56, 57, 58, 60, 87, 112, 431, 604, 611
Chisholm, Anne, 544
Chisholm, Kate, 544
Chissano, Joaquim Alberto, 296, 297
Chrétien, Jean, 178, 181, 196
Christie, Agatha, 541
Christie, Julie, 518
Chronicle of 1998, 602–11
Chuan Leekpai, 351
Chuayffet Chemor, Emilio, 201
Chubais, Anatolii, 150
Chung Ju Yung, 382
Chung, Johnny, 162, 163
Cinema, 523–6
Ciorbea, Victor, 124, 125
Ciubiu, Ion, 153, 603
Clark, David, 21
Clark, Helen, 394
Clark, Joe, 181
Clarke, Darren, 551, 552
Clarke, Kenneth, 24
Clerides, Glafkos, 103, 105, 107, 603
Clifford, Clark, 587–8 (obit.)

Clinton, Bill (US President), 5, 6, 8, 174, 468, 583, 602, 603, 604, 605, 606, 608, 610, 611; Africa, 176, 268, 312, 454; Americas, 196; Asia/Pacific, 176, 328, 360, 365, 369, 373, 379, 382, 384, 461; Central/E. Europe, 152, 176, 414; economy, 175; elections, 166, 167; gun control, 174; impeachment, 168, 170–1; Lewinsky affair/scandals, 2, 158, 159–60, 161–2, 164–6, 168, 234, 480, 539, 577–9; Middle East, 38, 170, 176–7, 218, 219, 221, 222, 227; State of the Union, 160–1; W. Europe, 46, 102, 103, 176–7, 436
Clinton, Hillary Rodham, 160, 163, 170
Clodumar, Kinza, 399
Collins, Fr Paul, 467
Collor de Mello, Fernando, 186
Colombia, 94, **188–90**, 426, 606
Commager, Henry Steele, 588 (obit.)
Common Market for Eastern & Southern Africa (COMESA), 453
Commonwealth of Independent States (CIS), 155, 322, 323, 324
Commonwealth, The, 36, 269, 328, 395, 399, **421–3**, 546, 548
Community of Portuguese-Speaking Countries (CPLP), 99, 295, **424, 425–6**, 454
Community of Sahel & Saharan States (Comessa), 249
Comoros, 345, 346–7
Compagnoni, Deborah, 547
Compaoré, Capt. Blaise, 276, 280, 281, 455, 455
Condé, Alpha, 279
Conedera, Bishop Juan, 468
Congo, Democratic Republic of the, 60, 246, 266, 271, 280, 286, **288–91**, 293, 294, 298, 300, 302, 303, 306, 312, 405, 425, 428, 454, 455, 492, 607, 608, 611
Congo, Republic of, 283, 285–6, 288, 290
Connor, Joseph, 402, 403, 404
Conrad, Peter, 544
Constantine, David, 543
Constantine, King, 103
Constantinescu, Emil, 124, 125
Conté, Gen. Lansana, 275, 279
Cook Islands, 399
Cook, Robin, 20, 36, 142, 582
Cookson, Dame Catherine, 538, 588 (obit.)

Córdovez, Diego, 106
Corea, Gamani, 428
Corella, Angel, 516
Cornette, Benoît, 537
Corrales, José Miguel, 201
Corsica, 57
Cosma, Miron, 126
Cossiga, Francesco, 62
Costa Rica, 198, 200, **201**, 464, 602
Côte d'Ivoire, 276, 280, 286
Cotti, Flavio, 84
Couchpin, Pascal, 87
Coulthard, David, 552
Council of Europe, 438–40, 443, 496
Council of the Baltic Sea States (CBSS), 445–6
Coupland, Douglas, 542
Couples, Fred, 551
Cox, Baroness, 472
Cox, Eugene, 213
Cox, John, 511
Cox, Paula, 213
Craig, Greg, 170
Cranko, John, 587
Cretier, Jean Luc, 547
Crichton Smith, Iain, 538
Croatia, 13, 89, **137–9**, 141, 426, 439, 440, 442, 449
Cros, Marcel, 279
Crosby, Bing, 597
Cruickshank, Allan, 211
Csurka, Istvan, 122
Cuba, 1, 90, 93, 99, **195–6**, 204, 208, 209, 404, 428, 436, 464, 465, 468, 605
Cubas Grau, Raúl, 191, 605
Cullen, John, 543
Cuneo, M.W., 472
Cunningham, Jack, 22, 582
Cunningham, Merce, 516
Cuomo, Andrew M., 583
Curnow, Allen, 541, 543
Currie, Betty, 161
Cutileiro, José, 414
Cyprus, 7, 103, **105–8**, 408, 434, 448, 497, 603
Czech Republic, 75, 93, 107, **118–9**, 121, 414, 415, 434, 449, 497, 538, 602, 606, 609

da Costa, Guiherme Posser, 295, 296
da Costa, Manuel Pinto, 295
da Silva, Luiz Inácio ('Lula'), 186

D'Aguiar, Fred, 543
D'Alema, Massimo, 61, 435, 610
D'Amato, Alfonse, 167
Daehlie, Bjoern, 547
Daianu, Daniel, 125
Daim Zanuddin, 352
Dalai Lama, 176, 369
Dalbins, Col. Juris, 117
Daleus, Lennart, 79
Damascus Declaration Group, 452
Damitov, Kadyrjan, 320
Daniel, Paul, 509, 510
Danilova, Olga, 547
Dankworth, John, 544
Dao Trong Lich, Gen., 360
Darbinyan, Armen, 156
Darling, Alistair, 22, 582
Darling, Julia, 542
Davenport, Lindsay, 554
Davies, D.J., 472
Davies, Howard, 519
Davies, Omar, 204
Davies, Ron, 26, 42, 43, 610
Davies, Sir Peter Maxwell, 512
Davis, Fred, 588 (obit.)
Davis, Gray, 167
Davis, Gregson, 544
Davis, Joe, 588
Davis, Terrell, 555
Davison, Peter, 541
Dawes, Kwame, 543
Dawkins, Richard, 544
de Botton, Janet, 532
de Bruin, Michelle, 546
de Cerqueira Antúnes, Antônio, 463
de Gaulle, Gen. Charles, 597
de Jouvenel, Bertrand, 588
de la Rua, Fernando, 184
de Mello, Fr Anthony, 466
de Monchaux, Cathy, 534
de Montebello, Phillipe, 534
de Soto, Alvaro, 349
de Trazegnies, Fernando, 193
de Valois, Dame Ninette, 514, 515, 587
de Venecia, Jose, 357
Dean, Christopher, 537
Dean, David, 515
Deane, Derek, 516
Déby, (Col.) Idriss, 283, 284
Defence, Disarmament & Security,
defence organizations, **413–7**;
Indian/Pakistan nuclear tests, 1, 5,
327–8, 333–4, 371, 397, 412, 427, 460;
landmines treaty, 182, 427; NPT, 187,
451; Pacific nuclear tests, 462;
START-II, 117, 152; test-ban treaty,
5, 161, 187, 334, 427
Dehaene, Jean-Luc, 65, 66
Delacroix, Eugène, 533
Delamuraz, Jean-Pascal, 86
Delic, Hazim, 495
Delors, Jacques, 114
Demirchyan, Karen, 156
Demirel, Süleyman, 108, 110, 322, 326
Deng Xiaoping, 364
Denis, Hervé, 197
Denktash, Rauf, 105, 106
Denmark, 73–5, 133, 175, 377, 431, 433,
441, 445, 446, 515, 525, 603, 605, 606
Dennis, Ferdinand, 542
Desai, Kiran, 541, 542
Desailly, Marcel, 549
Dettori, Frankie, 554, 555
Dewar, Donald, 39, 41, 582
Dharker, Imtiaz, 543
Di Pietro, Antonio, 62
Diallo, Issa, 298
Diana, Princess of Wales, 475, 528
DiCaprio, Leonardo, 523
Dickens, Charles, 539
Dill, Jerome, 212
Ding Guangen, 364
Dini, Lamberto, 251
Diouf, Abdou, 275, 277, 278
Disasters & Accidents (see also
Environmental Questions), Australia,
391; Bolivia, 185; Brazil, 488;
Canada, 182; China, 367, 488; Cuba,
196; Ecuador, 488; Fiji, 398; Greece,
104; Hong Kong, 372; Hurricane
Georges, 197, 210; Hurricane Mitch,
94, 198–9, 484, 488; Indonesia, 488;
Mexico, 488; Montserrat, 213–4;
Nigeria, 271; Papua New Guinea,
392; Peru, 192; Slovakia, 121; Spain,
94; Sudan, 247; Thailand, 352; USA,
158–9
Diya, Lt.-Gen. Oladipo, 269
Djibouti, 257, 261
Djordjević, Nenad, 146
Djoussouf, Abbas, 345, 347
Djukanović, Milo, 142, 146, 147, 605
Djunić, Danko, 146
Dobelis, Juris, 116

Dobson, Anita, 520
Dobson, Frank, 582
Documents & Reference, 556–85
Dodik, Milorad, 134
Dominica, 209, 210
Dominican Republic, 196, **197,** 464, 609
Dondo, Margaret, 301
Donleavy, J.P., 541, 542
Doran, Jamie, 544
Dorligjav, Dambyn, 385
dos Santos, José Eduardo, 297, 298, 312
Dostam, Gen. Abdul Rashid, 316
Doughty, Louise, 542
Douglas, Denzil, 209, 211
Dowiyogo, Bernard, 396
Draper, Derek, 21
Drnovšek, Janez, 141
Drukarova, Dinara, 525
Du Pré, Jacqueline, 524
Dubai, 190
Duchamp, Marcel, 600
Duffey, Joseph, 583
Duffy, Judge Kevin, 172
Duffy, Maureen, 542
Dugan, Angel Serafin Seriche, 284
Duhalde, Eduardo, 184
Duhig, Ian, 543
Duisenberg, Wim, 34, 68, 432
Dumont, Mario, 180
Dun, Bob, 457
Duncan, Daniel Kablan, 276
Dunmore, Helen, 542
Dunn, Jennifer, 168
Dupuis, Fr Jacques, 466, 467
Durbridge, Francis, 538
Dutroux, Marc, 65
Duval, David, 551
Duve, Freimut, 443
Dyer, Geoff, 542
Dzurinda, Mikulas, 120, 121, 609

East African Commission (EAC), 453, 456
East Timor, 99, 357, 425, 472
Ecevit, Bülent, 129, 611
Echenoz, Jean, 542
Economic Community of Central African States (CEEAC), 453
Economic Community of West African States (ECOWAS), 272, 282, 295, 405, **453**, 454, **456**
Economic Organizations, 417–21

Ecuador, 190–1, 193, 437, 465, 488, 607, 610
Edinburgh, Duke of, 591
Edwards, Jonathan, 550
Egal, Mohammed Ibrahim, 260
Egypt, 13, 110, 133, **224–6**, 229, 234, 244, 245–6, 260, 425, 448, 452, 604
Einstein, Albert, 598
El Salvador, 198, 199, **200**, 468, 469
Elbegdorj, Tsahiagiyn, 385
Elgar, Edward, 513
Elgin Marbles, 103
Elizabeth II, Queen, 16, 37, 50, 71, 94, 178, 203, 206, 207, 208, 209, 210, 353, 387, 391, 393, 396, 397, 469, 548, 609
Elizabeth, Grand Duchess, 469
Ellison, Larry, 482
Ellmann, Lucy, 542
Elway, John, 555
Eman, Jan Hendrick (Henny), 215
English, Sir David, 596
Enhbayar, Nyambaryn, 384, 385
Enright, D.J., 541, 543
Ens, Phillip, 510
Environmental Questions, 484–91
Equatorial Guinea, 283, 286–7
Erbakan, Necmettin, 109
Erdogan, Recep Tayyip, 109
Erignac, Claude, 57
Eritrea, 240, 245, 246, **257**, 258, *map* 259, **260**, 261, 280, 454, 455, 494, 606
Ermán González, Antonio, 184
Ernst August of Hanover, Prince, 88
Eroglu, Dervis, 105
Ershad, Gen. Mohammed Hossain, 336
Esack, Farid, 472
Espy, Mike, 170
Esquivel, Manuel, 207
Estermann, Col. Alois, 88, 605
Estonia, 13, 107, **114–7,** 434, 447, 497
Estrada, Joseph Ejercito, 353, 357, 358, 359, 605
Ethiopia, 226, 240, 246, **257–9** (*map* 259), 260, 261, 280, 454, 455, 606
European Bank for Reconstruction & Development (EBRD), 140, 155, **444–5**
European Community Law, 497–500
European Court of Human Rights (ECHR), 439
European Court of Justice (ECJ), 497–8
European Economic Area (EEA), 448

European Free Trade Association (EFTA), 76, **447–8**, 498
European Union (see also European Community Law), **430–8**; Africa, 250, 251–2, 255, 281, 292, 295, 304, 312, 424, 456; Agenda 2000, 35, 82, 93, 435–6; Asia, 6, 369, 370, 458, 460; Central/E. Europe, 133, 134, 138, 142–3, 151, 155, 444; Commission problems, 438; data protection, 483; EMU/single currency, 7, 10, 14, 15, 16, 24, 31, 34–5, 55–6, 58, 59–60, 61, 64, 67, 68, 69, 70, 72–3, 74–5, 80, 82, 93, 99, 101, 431–3, 585; enlargement, 100, 106–7, 109, 111, 116, 119, 121, 123–4, 127, 128, 129, 141–2, 434–5, 447, 449; environmental questions, 484, 490; European organizations, 439, 443, 448, 449–50; foreign & security policy, 417, 437; Latin America, 464; Mid East, 222, 224, 314; Nordic/EFTA/EEA states, 84–5, 446, 447, 448; Schengen accord, 76, 77, 124; taxation policy, 433–4; USA/bananas, 175–6, 210, 419, 436–7
Eustace, Arnhim, 211
Evans, Albert, 517
Evans, Chris, 530
Evans, Gareth, 389
Extracts from Past Volumes, xvi
Eyadéma, Gen. Gnassingbé, 276, 281, 282, 424

Fabius, Laurent, 58
Fabré, André, 554
Fadul, Francisco, 294
Fahd ibn Abdul Aziz, King, 235, 236, 237, 238
Fainlight, Ruth, 543
Falck, Colin, 543
Faldo, Nick, 552
Falkland Islands/Malvinas, 37, 184
Fallon, Kieran, 555
Faroe Islands, 74, 76
Farrakhan, Louis, 247
Fatchett, Derek, 246
Faulks, Sebastian, 542
Favre, Brett, 555
Fayed, Mohamed al-, 596
Fellini, Federico, 524
Fenech Adami, Dr Eddie, 99, 100, 101, 608

Fernandes, George, 327, 328
Fernández de Soto, Guillermo, 189
Fernández Faingold, Hugo, 194
Fernández, Leonel, 197
Ferneyhough, Brian, 514
Ferreira, Mega, 96
Ferrero Costa, Eduardo, 193
Field, Frank, 22
Fiennes, Ralph, 519
Fiji, 396, 398
Filali, Abdellatif, 254
Fine, Anne, 542
Finland, 78, **80–1**, 431, 432, 433, 446
Fischer, Joschka, 55
Fisher, Mark, 535
Fitzgerald, Peter, 166
Five-Power Defence Arrangements, 354
Flanagan, Richard, 542
Fletcher, Dr Raphael, 208
Flores Facussé, Carlos Roberto, 198
Flowers, Gennifer, 159
Foden, Giles, 541, 542
Fonda, Henry, 590
Food & Agriculture Organization (FAO), 489, 490
Ford, Gerald, 166, 171
Forné Molne, Marc, 87, 88
Forster, E.M., 541, 544
Forsythe, William, 517
Fortier, Michael, 172
Foruhar, Dariush, 313
Fowles, John, 544
France, 14, 35, 38, **56–60**, 61, 93, 112, 144, 152, 154, 228, 229, 231, 233, 243, 249, 251, 255, 261, 277, 281, 285, 286, 290, 314, 346, 347, 376, 420, 430, 431, 432, 433, 436, 442, 445, 456, 462, 487, 496, 525, 538, 546, 548–9, 553, 597, 598–9, 604, 606
Franco-African Summit, 285, 286, 290, 424–5
Francophone Agency, 424
Francophone Community, 422, **423–5**
Fraser, Angus, 551
Frayn, Michael, 519, 520
Fréchette, Louise, 402
Freeman, Antonio, 555
Freeman, David, 510
Frei Ruiz-Tagle, Eduardo, 184, 187, 188
French Polynesia, 397
Freud, Lucian, 532
Frick, Mario, 87, 88

INDEX 621

Friel, Brian, 522
Frigyesi, Judit, 514
Frittoli, Barbara, 510
Frutos, Francisco, 94
Fuentes, Carlos, 544
Fujimori, Alberto Keinya, 191, 192, 193
Funaki, Kazuyardi, 547
Furundzija, Anto, 496
Furyk, Jim, 551

Gable, Christopher, 517
Gabon, 283, 285, 286, 290, 400, 425
Gambia, The, 273, 400
Gamboa ('El Caracol'), Alberto Orlandes, 189
Ganbold, Davaadorjiyn, 385, 386
Ganbold, Dogsomyn, 386
Gandhi, Arun, 544
Gandhi, Indira, 327, 594
Gandhi, Rajiv, 327, 602, 603
Ganić, Ejup, 134
Ganzuri, Kamal Ahmad, 224
Garang, Col. John, 246
Garayev, Bayramberdi, 321
García Belaunde, José Antonio, 463
García, Antonio, 189
Gardelli, Lamberto, 514
Gardner, Ava, 598
Garland, Alex, 542
Garzón, Baltasar, 92
Gasana, Anastace, 293
Gates, Bill, 404, 482
Gavin, Julian, 509
Gaviria Trujillo, César, 462
Gayoom, Abdul, 345, 347
Gbagbo, Laurent, 280
Gbedemah, K.A., 268
Gbezera-Bria, Michel, 283
Gee, Maggie, 542
Geingob, Hage, 304, 307
Geitonas, Costas, 102
Gelbard, Robert, 142
Gellhorn, Martha, 538, 588–9 (obit.)
Gemani, Fernando, 514
George, Eddie, 32
Georgia, 156, 157, 408, 440, 443
Georgievski, Ljubčo, 139, 140
Gerardi Conadera, Mgr Juan José, 200
Geremek, Bronislaw, 441, 442
Germani, Fernando 514, 589 (obit.)

Germany, 7, 14, 15, **51–6**, 60, 79, 85, 93, 112, 116, 119, 140, 144, 152, 154, 228, 230, 239, 247, 281, 326, 399, 401, 430, 431, 432, 433, 434, 436, 443, 444, 446, 467, 469, 473, 479, 484, 486, 489, 514, 525, 591–2, 604, 606, 609, 610, 611
Gershwin, George, 511
Ghana, 265, **267–8**, 281, 286, 424, 593, 603
Ghanem, Faraj Said bin, 239
Ghannouchi, Mohamed, 251
Gibraltar, 94–5
Gidada, Negaso, 257
Giddens, Prof. Anthony, 23
Gielgud, Maina, 515
Gilbert, Martin, 544
Gilchrist, Olympio, 424
Gingrich, Newt, 165, 168
Gladstone, William, xvi
Glemp, Cardinal Joseph, 471
Glen, Iain, 519
Glendinning, Victoria, 544
Glenn, John, 473, 610
Glickman, Dan, 583
Gligorov, Kiro, 139
Goh Chok Tong, 355, 459
Golding, Julian, 550
Goldsworthy, Verna, 544
Goldwater, Barry, 589 (obit.)
Göncz, Árpád, 122
Gorbachev, Mikhail, 587
Gordimer, Nadine, 541, 542
Gordon, Bill, 589
Gordon, Douglas, 534
Gordon, Lord, 528
Gordon, Margot, 589 (obit.)
Gordon, Mick, 522, 523
Gordon, Pamela F., 212
Gore, Al, 170, 353, 395, 461, 480, 583
Gormley, Anthony, 531
Gough, Darren, 551
Gouled Aptidon, Hassan, 257, 261
Gourad Hamadou, Barkat, 257
Gowing, Prof. Margaret, 589 (obit.)
Grade, Lord (Lew), 590 (obit.)
Grandcourt, Alvina, 346
Grayson, Paul, 553
Greece, 101–4, 107–8, 129, 141, 431, 466, 592, 597
Green, David, 537
Green, Julien, 538
Greenland, 76

Grenada, 208
Grimshaw, Nicholas, 536
Grímsson Ólafur Ragnar, 75, 76
Groer, Cardinal Hans Hermann, 90
Gross, Philip, 543
Group of 77, 426, 428
Group of Eight (G-8), 15, 16, 31, 46, 328, 329
Gryn, Rabbi Hugo, 470
Guardado, Facundo, 200
Guatemala, 198, 200–1, 207, 400, 468
Guelendouksia, Nassour Owaido, 283
Guellah, Ismail Omar, 261
Guig, Mohammed Lemine Ould, 278
Guinea, 272, 274, **275, 279**, 295, 454, 492
Guinea-Bissau, 277, **294–5**, 375, 425, 454, 456, 606
Guirma, Frederic, 280
Gujadhur, Anil, 344
Gujadhur, Bud, 344
Gujral, I.K., 336
Gulf Cooperation Council (GCC), 448, **450–2**
Gunesekera, Romesh, 542
Gunter, John, 510
Gurría Treviño, José Angel, 202
Guscott, Jeremy, 553
Gustafson, Kathryn, 537
Guterres, António, 96
Guyana, 195, **205**, 214, 464
Guzmán Morales, Gen. Jaime, 200
Gwarzo, Ishmael, 271

Habibie, Bacharuddin J., 353, 355, 356, 357, 425, 605
Hadda, Janet, 544
Hague, William, 18, 21, 23, 28
Haider, Jörg, 82, 83
Haiti, 197, 410
Haiveta, Chris, 391, 392
Hajdari, Azem, 131, 132
Hakkinen, Mikka, 552, 553
Hale, Keith, 544
Halliday, Dennis, 407
Hama, Amadou, 282
Hamdani, Ismael, 251, 253
Hamia, Cherif, 587
Hamid Albar, 354
Hamilton, Ian, 544
Hampson, Christopher, 517
Hanish Islands, 240, 260
Hans Adam II, Prince, 87

Hanson, Pauline, 389
Harada, Masahiko, 548
Harald V, King, 76, 78
Hare, David, 519
Hariri, Rafiq, 230, 231, 232, 611
Harman, Harriet, 21, 22
Harmon, Mark, 524
Harris, Larry Wayne, 173
Harsent, David, 543
Harte, Paddy, 71
Hasan bin Talal, Crown Prince, 226, 472, 607
Hasan, Nacem ul-, 457
Hasek, Dominik, 548
Hashimoto, Ryutaro, 377, 378
Hassan II, King, 253
Hassel, Odd, 586
Headley, Dean, 551
Healey, Ian, 551
Heaney, Seamus, 543
Heath, Sir Edward, 541, 544, 595, 597
Heath-Stubbs, John, 543
Heeley, Desmond, 516
Heisenberg, Werner, 520
Helms, Jesse, 196
Hemingway, Ernest, 588
Henderson, Ian, 243
Henri, Prince, 70
Hensher, Philip, 542
Henze, Hans Werner, 514
Hepburn, Katherine, 590
Herbert, Zbigniew, 538
Hercus, Dame Ann, 106
Hermoza Ríos, Gen. Nicolás, 193
Heron, Patrick, 532
Herries, Lady, 555
Herzog, Roman, 51, 326, 611
Heseltine, Michael, 24
Hibbert, Christopher, 544
Hierro López, Luís, 194
Higgins, Aidan, 542
Hilaire, Laurent, 516
Hill, Christopher, 144, 145, 146
Hill, Damon, 553
Hill, Heather, 389
Hill, Mick, 550
Hill, Susan, 542
Hingis, Martina, 554
Hirschfeld, Abe, 168
Hirst, Damien, 532
Hitler, Adolf, 520

Hoban, Phoebe, 544
Hoban, Russell, 542
Hochschild Pflaud, Luis, 193
Hodgkin, Prof. Sir Alan Lloyd, 590 (obit.)
Hodson, H.V. (Harry), xv
Hoffman, Dustin, 518
Hoffman, Eva, 544
Hoffmann, Lord, 37
Hofmann, Michael, 539
Holbrooke, Richard, 144, 145, 146
Holder, Marc, 547
Hollinghurst, Alan, 542
Holmes, Richard, 544
Holness, Andrew, 203
'Holocaust Gold' issue, 79, 83, 84, 533–4, 607
Holst, Gustav, 599
Holub, Miroslav, 538
Holy See, see Vatican
Honan, Park, 544
Honduras, 198, 199, 488, 610
Hong Kong, 12, 365, 370, **371–3**, 602, 605, 606
Hong Song Nam, 382, 383
Hong Soon Yung, 380
Hooker, Jeremy, 543
Hornby, Nick, 542
Horne, John, 211
Horrocks, Jane, 524
Hosain, Attia, 538
Houngbedji, Adrien, 282
Howard, John, 387, 388, 389, 462, 609
Howarth, Alan, 535
Hoyte, Desmond, 205, 464
Hrawi, Elias, 230, 231
Hu Jintao, 364, 368
Hubbell, Webster, 163, 168, 580
Huddleston, Rt Rev Trevor, 590–1 (obit.)
Hudghton, Ian, 41
Hudson, Mark, 542
Hughes, Hubert, 212
Hughes, Ted, 538, 543, 591 (obit.)
Hujilan, Jameel al-, 450, 452
Hulse, Michael, 543
Hume, Cardinal, 469
Hume, John, 44, 46, 609
Hun Sen, 360, 361, 362, 607
Hung Pacheco, Gen. Mario Raúl, 199
Hungary, 13, 75, 107, 121, **122–4**, 127, 326, 414, 415, 417, 434, 449, 497
Hunt, Lord (Sir John), 591 (obit.)

Huntford, Roland, 544
Hurd, Douglas, 542
Hurtado Larrea, Osvaldo, 190
Husain ibn Talal, King, 218, 226, 227, 229, 607
Huston, John, 551
Huth, Angela, 542
Hyde, Henry, 168
Hytner, Nicholas, 509

Iakovou, George, 105
Ibero-American Summit, 93, 99, **463–4**
Ibrahim, Abdallah, 347
Ibrahim, Ilyas, 347
Ibrahimov, Jumabek, 319, 321
Iceland, 75–6, 77, 448, 592–3
Ignarro, Louis, 479
Ignatieff, Michael, 541, 544
Iliescu, Ion, 126
Inamine, Keiichi, 379
India, 1, 5, 13, 151, 300, **326–31**, 333, 334, 336, 337, 338, 339, 343, 371, 397, 412, 418, 419, 427, 429, 458, 460, 466, 485, 489, 526, 538, 594, 602, 603, 605, 606
Indian Ocean Rim Association for Regional Cooperation (IORARC), 458
Indonesia, 7, 9, 12, 15, 99, 352, 353, **355–7**, 367, 371, 380, 387, 418, 425, 429, 458, 459, 460, 472, 488, 492, 603, 605, 610
Information Technology, 8, 36, 39–40, **479–84**
Ingraham, Hubert, 208
Innes, Hammond, 538
Insall, Donald, 537
Insulza, José Miguel, 93, 188
Inter-American Development Bank (IADB), 194, 464
Inter-Governmental Authority on Development (IGAD), 246
International Atomic Energy Agency (IAEA), 397, 406
International Court of Justice (ICJ), 199, 240, 244, 248, 285, 314, 492–4
International Development Association (IDA), 419
International Finance Corporation (IFC), 445
International Labour Organization (ILO), 9

International Monetary Fund (IMF), 8–10, 13, 110, 116, 126, 128, 133, 149, 151, 154, 161, 175, 186, 197, 199, 200, 205, 206, 210, 224, 226, 239, 247, 259, 261, 263, 264, 265, 269, 280, 296, 302, 305, 332, 333, 351, 356, 357, 392, **417, 418**, 419, 428, 455, 458
International Telecommunication Union (ITU), 480, 484
Interpol, 311, 489
Iran, 3, 5, 13, 155, 184, 229, 234, 236, 237, 244, **314–5**, 317, 318, 325, 334, 383, 400, 436, 451, 526, 542, 597, 605, 609
Iraq, 3, 5, 6, 17, 38–9, 60, 65, 94, 152, 170, 224, 226, 227, 228, 229, **232–5**, 237, 244, 245, 251, 313, 315, 371, 383, 400, 406–7, 408, 430, 437, 451, 452, 461, 602, 607, 610, 611
Ireland, Northern, see Northern Ireland
Ireland, Republic of, 10, 15, 46, 47, 50, **70–3**, 431, 433, 522
Irian Jaya, 357
Irvine of Lairg, Lord, 20, 582
Irving, John, 542
Iryani, Abdulkarim al-, 238, 239
Iryani, Sheikh Abdul Rahman al-, 591 (obit.)
Isaac, Mark, 208
Isberg, Pär, 515
Islamic Conference Organization, see Organization of the Islamic Conference
Islamic factor, 5, 39, 109, 133, 174–5, 176, 224–5, 245, 247, 252, 262, 318, 348
Isle of Man, 46
Ismoil, Eyad, 172
Israel, 3, 4, 94, 113, 176, 177, 184, **217–21**, 222–3, 224, 226, 227, 228, 231, 234, 251, 326, 401, 402, 428, 451, 452, 466, 471, 475, 603, 604, 611
Issing, Otmar, 432
Italy, 14, **61–4**, 67, 110, 133, 141–2, 152, 249, 251, 255, 261, 430, 431, 432, 433, 435, 445, 589, 600–1, 602, 605, 610
Ivanisevic, Goran, 554
Ivanov, Igor, 117
Ivcher, Baruch, 193
Izetbegović, Alija, 135
Izurieta, Gen. Ricardo, 93, 187, 188

Jackson, Colin, 550
Jacobs, Jasper, 536
Jacobson, Dan, 544
Jacolin, Henry, 442
Jagan, Janet, 205, 214, 464
Jakarta, Archbishop of, 472
Jamaica, 203–5, 437
Jameel, Fathulla, 347
James, Edison, 209, 210
James, Harry, 597
Jammeh, Col. Yahya, 273
Janacek, Leos, 511
Janos, James George, 167
Janzen, Lee, 552
Japan, 6, 9, 10, 12, 15, 37, 43, 44, 119, 177, 261, 322, 325, 328, 329, 365, 368, 369, 370–1, **376–80**, 381, 382, 383, 401, 426, 458, 461, 462, 476, 478, 489, 547, 592, 598, 605, 606, 607, 611
Jardine, Lisa, 544
Jay of Paddington, Baroness, 22, 28, 582
Jean, Grand Duke, 69, 70
Jefri, Prince, 354
Jelavić, Ante, 135
Jenkins of Hillhead, Lord, 25
Jennings, Elizabeth, 543
Jerwood, John, 518
Jessop, Violet, 544
Jeyaratnam, J.B., 355
Jhabvala, Ruth Prawer, 542
Jiang Zemin, 5, 176, 364, 365, 368, 369, 370, 372, 373, 375, 379, 382, 606, 610, 611
Jigme Singye Wangchuk, Dragon King, 339, 340
Jiricna, Eva, 536
Jóhannsson, Kjartan, 447
Johansson, Olof, 79
John Paul II, Pope, 87, 89, 466, 468, 471, 472, 602, 603
John XXIII, Pope, 587
John, Esther, 469
Johnson, Andrew, 158, 171
Johnson, Daniel, 178, 180
Johnson, Lyndon, 587, 589
Johnson, Norma Holloway, 581
Johnston, Donald, 417
Jones, Paula Corbin, 158, 159, 161, 162, 168, 170, 577, 578, 604
Jorabekov, Ismoil, 321
Jordan, 13, 218, 223, **226–8**, 229, 234, 448, 604, 607

Joseph, Bishop John, 471
Jospin, Lionel, 56, 59
Juan Carlos, King, 91, 93, 103, 326
Jude, Charles, 516
Jumagulov, Apas, 320
Jumaliyev, Kuvachbek, 320
Jumeau, Esme, 345
Juncker, Jean-Claude, 69
Jünger, Ernst, 591–2 (obit.)
Juppé, Alain, 60

Kâ, Djibo, 277
Kabakov, Ilya and Emilia, 531
Kabbah, Alhaji Ahmed Tejan, 36, 272, 421, 456, 602, 603
Kabbani, Nizar, 538
Kabila, Laurent, 246, 266, 288, 289, 290, 293, 298, 302, 306, 312, 455, 607
Kabua, Imata, 397, 399
Kaiser, Michael, 509, 515
Kalpokas, Donald, 397, 399
Kambanda, Jean, 494, 608
Kamougué, Abdelkader, 284
Kane, Sarah, 520
Karadžić, Radovan, 134, 136, 137
Karamanlis, Konstantinos, 104, 592 (obit.)
Karamanlis, Kostas, 104
Karamanski, Ivo, 130
Karamat, Gen. Jehangir, 332
Karavan, Dan, 534
Karbaschi, Gholamhossein, 313
Karczag, Eva, 516
Karimov, Islam, 320, 321, 326
Kartman, Charles, 383
Kashmir, 427, 429
Kaunda, Kenneth, 299, 300
Kaura, Katuutire, 307
Kavanagh, Patrick, 522
Kay, Jackie, 541, 542
Kaye, Michael, 509
Kazakhstan, 151, **319–26**, 370, 426, 473
Kazhegeldin, Akezhan, 321
Kedikilwe, Ponatshego, 305
Keillor, Garrison, 544
Keita, Ibrahim Boubakar, 275
Kelly, Gene, 597
Kelly, Graham, 547
Kelly, John, 212
Kelman, James, 539, 542
Kemp, Lindsay, 517
Kempadoo, Oonya, 542

Kendal, Felicity, 541, 544
Kent, Jonathan, 519, 521
Kérékou, Mathieu, 276, 282
Kenya, 174, 245, **261–3**, 264, 293, 400, 422, 456, 486, 542, 607
Kernot, Cheryl, 389
Khalvati, Mimi, 543
Khama, Lt.-Gen. Ian, 305
Khamenei, Ayatollah Seyed Ali, 313, 314
Khamphoui Keoboualapha, 363
Khamtay Siphandon, 363, 603
Kharrazi, Kamal, 244, 314
Khashoggi, Hussein, 398
Khatami, Mohammed, 313, 314, 315
Khieu Samphan, 362
Khin Nyunt, Lt.-Gen., 349, 350
Khouna, Cheikh El-Avia Ould Mohammed, 275, 278
Kibaki, Mwai, 262
Kidman, Nicole, 519
Kim Dae Jung, 379, 380, 381, 603
Kim Il Chol, 383
Kim Il Song, 382
Kim Jong Il, 382, 383, 384
Kim Jong Pil, 380
Kim Yong Nam, 381, 382, 383
Kincaid, Jamaica, 544
King, Martin Luther, 469
Kinkel, Kipland, 174
Kinnock, Neil, 85
Kinsella, John, 543
Kiribati, **396**, **397**, 398
Kirienko, Sergei, 148, 150
Kirili, Alain, 533
Kirkop, Oreste, 511
Kirton, Neil, 393
Kitaj, R.B., 531
Ki-Zerbo, Joseph, 280
Klaus, Vaclav, 118
Klima, Viktor, 81, 82
Klinger, Karl, 598
Klutse, Kouassi, 276, 282
Knights of Malta, 101
Kobena, Djény, 280
Kocharyan, Robert, 156
Kohl, Helmut, 52, 53, 54, 55, 112, 152, 431, 432, 434, 435, 604, 609
Köhler, Horst, 444
Koirala, Girija Prasad, 338, 339, 604
Kok, Wim, 67, 68
Kolélas, Bernard, 285
Kolbe, Fr Maximilian, 469

INDEX

Kolpakova, Irina, 516
Konan Bédié, Henri, 276
Konaré, Alpha Oumar, 275, 278
Kontić, Radoje, 147
Koo Chen-fu, 371, 374, 375
Koolman, Olindo, 215
Korda, Petr, 546, 554
Korea, Democratic People's Republic of (North Korea), 5, 334, 378–9, 381, **382–4**
Korea, Republic of (South Korea), 12, 44, 363, 367, 368, 379, **380–2**, 383, 384, 418, 458, 478, 489, 603, 610
Koroma, Alhaji G.V., 274
Koroma, Lt.-Col. Johnny Paul, 272, 602
Kosovo crisis, 6–7, 127, 129, 132–3, 139–40, **142–6** (*map* 143), 147, 192, 371, 405, 407, 430, 437, 442, 449, 495, 603, 604, 605, 606, 607, 609
Kostov, Ivan, 127, 128
Kouyate, Lamine, 453
Kovác, Michal, 121
Krasts, Guntars, 115
Kreisler, Fritz, 598
Kristopans, Vilis, 114, 115
Ksila, Khemais, 250
Kučan, Milan, 141
Kuchma, Leonid, 153, 155, 450
Kufuor, John Agyekum, 267
Kulov, Feliks, 320
Kumaratunga, Chandrika Bandaranaike, 341, 342, 343
Kundera, Milan, 541, 543
Kurdish question, 65–5, 108, 109–10, 228, 229, 235, 496
Kureishi, Hanif, 539, 543
Kurokawa, Kise, 322
Kurosawa, Akira, 526, 592 (obit.)
Kusturica, Emir, 525
Kutan, Recai, 109
Kuwait, 232, 234, **240**, 241, 242, 243, 244, 408
Kwan, Michelle, 548
Kwasniewski, Aleksander, 111, 112, 113
Kwitny, Jonathan, 472
Kyrgyzstan, 319–26, 426

La Fontaine, J.S., 472
Labastida Ochoa, Francisco, 202
Lachenman, Helmut, 511, 514
Lafontaine, Oskar, 35, 53, 55, 432, 433
Lahad, Gen. Antoine, 231

Lahnstein, Anne Enger, 77
Lahoud, Émile, 230, 231, 609
Lahure, Johnny, 69
Laino, Domingo, 191
Lajevardi, Assadollah, 313
Lake, Anthony, 258
Lally, Pat, 41
Lamari, Lt.-Gen. Mohammed, 253
Landazábal Reyes, Gen. (retd) Fernándo, 189
Landell-Mills, Pierre, 335
Landsbergis, Vytautas, 115, 116
Landzo, Esad, 495
Langa, Judge Pius, 306
Lange, Jessica, 518
Langenberger, Christiane, 87
Langley, Lee, 543
Laos, 360, **363**, 459, 603
Laraki, Azeddine, 429
Lari, Moussavi, 313
Larsen, Berit Brørby, 446
Lasaro, Iairo, 392
Latin American Economic System (SELA), 463, 465
Latin American Integration Association (ALADI), 463, 465
Latvia, 13, **114–7**, 434, 439, 443, 445, 446, 447, 611
Lavaka-Ata-'Ulukalala, Prince, 398
Lavery, Bryony, 520
Lavrosky, Leonid, 600
Law & Legal Affairs (see also European Court of Human Rights, International Court of Justice, War Crimes Tribunals), **492–508**; European Community Law, **497–500**; international law, **492–7**; UK law, 500–6; US law, 171–4, **506–8**
Lawrence, Martin, 516
Laxness, Halldor, 592–3 (obit.)
Lazutina, Larissa, 547
Le Kha Phieu, Gen., 359
Le Pen, Jean-Marie, 58
Le Riche, Nicolas, 516
Lebanon, 220, 223, 228, 229, **230–2**, 408, 452, 609, 611
Lebed, Alexander, 148, 152
Lee Hoi Chang, 380
Lee Kuan Yew, 354, 355
Lee Teng-hui, 374, 375
Leifland, Leif, 79
Lemaitre, Gérard, 517

INDEX

Leonard, Justin, 551
Leopold of the Belgians, King, 288
Léotard, François, 58
Lesotho, 303, 304, 305, **306**, 312, 609
Letsie III, King, 303, 306, 609
Leuenberger, Moritz, 85
Lévêque, Michel, 88
Levi, Noel, 457
Levi, Peter, 543
Levy, David, 217
Lewinsky, Monica, 2, 158, 159, 160, 161, 162, 164, 165, 166, 218, 480, 577, 578, 580, 581, 602, 608, 611
Lewis, C.S., 522
Lewis, Diane, 550
Lewis, Gwyneth, 543
Leye Lenelgau, Jean-Marie, 397
Li Lanqing, 364
Li Peng, 364, 368, 369, 603
Li Ruihuan, 364
Liberia, 273, **274,** 428
Libeskind, Daniel, 536
Libya, 3, 5, 41–2, 246, **247–9**, 251, 260, 430, 436, 452, 493, 605
Lieberman, Joseph, 165
Liechtenstein, 87, 88, 448
Lien Chan, 375
Ligabue, Ilva, 511
Limani, Beqir, 140
Limann, Hilla, 268, 593 (obit.)
Lindquist, Marie, 515
Lindsey, Bruce, 162
Lipkin-Shahak, Gen. Amnon, 221
Lipman, Jean, 534
Lipponen, Paavo, 80, 81
Lissouba, Pascal, 285
Literature, 538–45
Lithuania, 13, **114–7**, 434, 445, 447, 587, 602
Littlechild, Prof. Stephen, 34
Litton, Andrew, 510
Lively, Adam, 544
Lively, Penelope, 543
Livingston, Bob, 168, 171
Livingstone, Ken, 18
Llewellyn, Carl, 554
Lloyd, Frank, 534
Lloyd, George, 593 (obit.)
Loach, Ken, 524
Lockerbie bombing, 41–2, 248, 406, 412, 452, 492–3
Lorca, Federico Garcia, 514, 517, 539

Louima, Abner, 173
Louisy, Perlette, 210
Loum, Mamadou Lamine, 275, 277
Lowry, Glenn, 533
Lucinschi, Petru, 153
Lukashenka, Alyaksandr, 153, 154
Lummis, Trevor, 544
Lungren, Dan, 167
Lunn, Harry, 534
Luo Gan, 364
Lurie, Alison, 543
Luwum, Archbishop Janani, 469
Lux, Josef, 118
Luxembourg, 69–70, 431, 433, 434
Lyotard, Jean-François, 534

Mabuku, Johnnie, 307
Macao, 99
McAleese, Mary, 50, 70, 71
McBrien, William, 544
McCabe, John, 544
McCabe, Patrick, 543
Macapagal-Arroyo, Diosdado, 358
Macapagal-Arroyo, Gloria, 358
McCarthy, Callum, 34
McCarthy, Joe, 589
Macartney, Allan, 41
McCreevey, Charlie, 72
McDiarmid, Ian, 519
McDougal, James (Jim), 163
McEwan, Ian, 539, 543
McGuigan, Harry, 41
McGuinness, Martin, 49
McGwire, Mark, 158, 555
McInerney, Jay, 543
Mackay Brown, George, 541
Mackay, Shena, 543
MacKenzie, Kelvin, 530
MacKilligin, David, 212
McKinnon, Don, 395
Mackintosh, Cameron, 522
McLachlan, John, xv
McLauchlan, Lucille, 238
McLetchie, David, 41
McLynn, Frank, 544
MacMillan, Kenneth, 515, 587
McNally, Terrence, 521
MacNiven, Ian, 544
Macedonia, 13, 129, **139–41**, 146, 409, 439, 442, 606
'Mad cow disease', see BSE
Madagascar, 348, 375

Madden, John, 524
Madi, Mohammed Abou, 346
Mahathir Mohamad, Dr, 352, 353, 355, 395, 459, 461, 608, 609
Mahler, Gustav, 511, 513
Mahuad Witt, Jamil, 190, 607
Maier, Hermann, 547
Mainassara, Brig.-Gen. Ibrahim Barre, 276
Maiyaki, Ibrahim Assane, 276
Majali, Abdul Salam, 226
Majko, Pandeli, 130, 131, 132, 609
Major, John, 46, 527
Makhmalbaf, Mohsen, 526
Maksim, Patriarch, 128
Malawi, 300
Malaysia, 4, 7, 9, 12, 261, **352–4**, 355, 380, 395, 400, 419, 422, 458, 459, 461, 489, 492, 608, 609, 610
Malcolm, Noel, 544
Maldives, 345, 347–8
Mali, 275, 278
Mallon, Seamus, 47, 50
Malta, 99–101, 434, 608
Maltman, Christopher, 510
Mamboundou, Pierre, 285
Mamet, David, 521, 543
Mandela, Nelson, 43, 302, 308, 309, 342, 426, 427, 454, 475, 591, 609
Mandelson, Peter, 16, 21, 26, 29, 30, 34, 607, 611
Mane, Gen. Ansumane, 294, 295
Manning, Patrick, 206
Manqoush, Mohammed Ahmed al-, 247
Mantel, Hilary, 543
Mara, Ratu Sir Kamisese, 396
Maraye, Dan, 344
Marcos, Bong Bong, 358
Marcos, Ferdinand, 358
Marcos, Imee, 358
Marcos, Imelda, 358
Margrethe II, Queen, 73, 606
Marin, Florencio, 207
Marjanović, Mirko, 142, 144, 145, 146
Marsh, Matthew, 520
Marshall Islands, 375, **397, 399**, 402
Marshall Plan (1948), xvi
Martin, Paul, 182
Martin, William McChesney, 593 (obit.)
Marulanda Vélez ('Tirofijo'), Manuel, 189
Marullo, Count Carlo, 101

Marwick, Arthur, 544
Masemola, Manche, 469
Masih, Ayub, 471
Masiyiwa, Strive, 301
Massera, Adm. Eduardo Emilio, 184
Masud, Gen. Ahmed Shah, 317, 318
Matisse, Henri, 534, 541
Matoub, Lounes, 253
Matsch, Judge Richard, 172
Matutes, Abel, 93, 95
Mauritania, 275, 278
Mauritius, 343–4, 422, 455
Maxwell, Glyn, 543
Mbeki, Thabo, 310
Mbuende, Kaire, 453
Meciar, Vladimir, 120
Medical Research, see Scientific, Medical & Industrial Research
Mégret, Bruno, 58
Meguid, Ahmad Esmat Abdel, 450, 452
Meigh, Frances, 467
Meles Zenawi, 258
Melville, Pauline, 543
Memené, Gen. Seyi, 281
Menem, Carlos Saúl, 37, 183, 184, 610
Mensah, J.H., 268
Mercosur, see Southern Common Market
Meri, Lennart, 114, 116
Meridor, Dan, 217
Mexico, 188, **201–3**, 236, 465, 488, 538, 594
Michael, Alun, 26, 43, 582, 610
Michiko, Empress, 377
Mickelson, Phil, 551
Micronesia, Federated States of, 395, **397**, 402, 462
Migas, Jozef, 120
Mihaylova, Nadezhda, 128, 129
Mihov, Col.-Gen. Miho, 129
Milburn, Alan, 30, 582
Miller, Andrew, 543
Miller, Karl, 544
Millon, Charles, 58
Milne, Christine, 390
Milošević, Slobodan, 142, 144, 145, 146, 147, 606, 609
Milutinović, Milan, 142
Mindanao, 359
Mintoff, Dom, 100
Miralles, Enric, 40, 535

Mishra, Brijesh, 328
Mitchell, George, 45, 604
Mitchell, Keith, 208
Miyazawa, Kiichi, 378
Mkapa, Benjamin, 264, 265
Mladić, Ratko, 136
Mobutu, ex-President, 288, 289
Mochiuuki, Misulo, 514
Moco, Marcolino, 424, 426
Mocumbi, Pascoal, 296
Modahl, Diane, 546, 548
Mofaz, Gen. Shaul, 221
Mogae, Festus, 303, 304, 305, 604
Mohammed, Abdou, 347
Moi, Daniel Arap, 261, 262, 263
Mokhehle, Ntsu, 306
Moldova, 153, 154, 439, 443, 603
Momoh, Joseph, 272
Monaco, 88
Mondrian, Piet, 68
Moneta, Carlos, 463
Mongolia, 326, **384–6**, 460
Monteiro, Antonio Mascarenhas, 294
Monteiro, Manuel, 98
Montenegro, Yugoslav Republic of, 146–7
Montesinos, Capt. Vladimiro, 192
Monteverdi, Claudio, 517
Montgomerie, Colin, 551, 552
Monti, Mario, 433
Montserrat, 212, 213–4
Moody, Helen Wills, 593 (obit.)
Moore, Archie, 593–4 (obit.)
Moore, Davey, 587
Moore, Henry, 533
Moore, Mike, 395
Mootoo, Shani, 543
Morawski, Eugeniusz, 111
Morgan, Edwin, 539, 543
Morgan, Rhodri, 42, 43
Moro, Peter, 537
Morocco, 96, **253–5**, 256, 285
Morrison, Blake, 544
Morrison, Conall, 522
Morrison, Toni, 543
Morwood, Fr Michael, 467
Moseley-Braun, Carol, 166
Mosisili, Bethuel Pakalitha, 303, 306
Mowlam, Marjorie (Mo), 45, 48, 582, 602
Moynihan, Daniel Patrick, 165
Mozambique, 96, **296–7**, 306, 426

Mozart, 509, 510
Mswati III, King, 304
Mubarak, Mohammed Husni, 110, 224, 225, 245
Mudavadi, Musalia, 262
Mudenge, Stan, 421
Mugabe, Robert, 301, 302, 303, 455
Mukasi, Charles, 292
Muldoon, Paul, 543
Muller Costas, Herbert, 185
Muller, Herta, 539
Müller-Wieland, Jan, 514
Mulroney, Brian, 178
Muluzi, Bakili, 300
Munro, Alice, 541
Murad, Ferid, 479
Muralitharan, Muttiah, 551
Murdoch, Dame Iris, 541
Murray, Les, 543
Museveni, Yoweri, 265, 266
Musharaf, Gen. Parvez, 332
Music, 511–4
Musoke, Kintu, 265
Musonge, Peter Mafany, 283
Mutharika, Bingo wa, 453
Muyongo, Meshake, 307
Myanmar (Burma), **349–50**, 459, 460, 542
Myers, Paul, 514

Nagorno-Karabakh, 156, 443
Naiambana, Patrice, 522
Naimi, Ali al-, 235
Naipaul, V.S., 544
Najjar, Bashir, 229
Nali, Michael, 391
Namibia, 290, 291, 302, **304**, 305, **306–7**, 400, 425, 455
Nanda, Gulzari Lal, 594 (obit.)
Nano, Fatos, 130, 131, 608, 609
Narantsatsralt, Janlavyn, 384, 386
Narayanan, Kocheril Raman, 326, 331
Näslund, Erik, 515
Nauru, 396, 399
Nayef, Prince, 237
Nazarbayev, Nursultan, 319, 321, 324, 370
Neeson, Liam, 519
Nehru, Jawaharlal, 594
Neill of Bladen, Lord, 25
Nelson, Adm. Horatio, xvi
Nemtsov, Boris, 150

Nena, Jacob, 395
Nepal, 338–9, 340, 602, 604
Neruda, Pablo, 454
Netanyahu, Binyamin, 4, 94, 176, 217, 218, 219, 220, 221, 222, 223, 224, 227, 231, 610
Netherlands Antilles, 214, 215
Netherlands, The, 42, **67–9**, 140, 176, 182, 248, 359, 400, 406, 413, 431, 432, 433, 444, 445, 471, 487, 605
Neto, Raul Bragança, 296
Neumeier, John, 512
New Caledonia, 399
New Zealand, 106, 328, 354, 392, **393–5,** 399, 458, 461, 462, 469
Newman, Barnett, 533
Nguyen Co Thach, 360
Nguyen Van Linh, 360, 594 (obit.)
Niasse, Moustapha, 277
Nicaragua, 198, 199–200, 488, 610
Nicholas II, Tsar, 151, 470
Niemann-Stirnemann, Gunter, 547
Niemeyer, Oscar, 537
Niger, 276, 282
Nigeria, 90, **269–72,** 274, 282, 287, 295, 421, 425, 426, 454, 456, 468, 469, 493, 542, 586, 587, 603, 606, 607
Nilsson, Hans, 515
Nimrod, Elvin, 208
Nixon, Richard M., 593
Niyazbiyev, Orazmurad, 321
Niyazov, Gen. Saparmurad, 320, 326
Nkrumah, Kwame, 268
Nobel Prizes, chemistry, 479; economics, 331, 423; literature, 539; medicine, 479; peace, 44, 50; physics, 479
Noble, Adrian, 522
Noboa Pontón, Alvaro, 190
Non-Aligned Movement (NAM), 312, 336, **426–8**
Nong Duc Manh, 359
Nordic Council, 76, **445, 446–7**
North American Free Trade Agreement (NAFTA), 465
North Atlantic Treaty Organization (NATO), 55, 65, 75, 94, 112, 116–7, 125, 127, 128, 129, 133, 136, 140, 144, 152, 161, 405, **414–7,** 426, 438, 442, 447, 449
Northern Ireland, 7, 16, **44–51,** 70–1, 467, **556–67**
Norway, 76–8, 247, 446, 448, 490

Nouhak Phoumsavan, 363
Nouri, Abdollah, 237, 313
Novotna, Jana, 554
Noyer, Christian, 432
Nujoma, Sam, 304, 307
Nuon Chea, 362
Nyachae, Simeon, 262, 263
Nye, Robert, 543
Nzimande, Blade, 310

O'Brien, Conor Cruise, 544
O'Kane, Patrick, 522
O'Meara, Mark, 551, 552
O'Neal, Ralph, 212
O'Neill, Eugene, 519
O'Sullivan, Sonia, 550
Oakes, Judy, 548
Oaks, Agnes, 516
Obame-Nguema, Paulin, 283
Obasanjo, Gen. Olusegun, 270, 271
Obiang Nguema Mbasogo, Brig.-Gen. Teodoro, 284, 286, 287
Obituaries, 586–601
Obuchi, Keizo, 365, 371, 376, 377, 378, 379, 381, 607
Öcalan, Abdullah, 64, 110, 229
Oddsson, Davíd, 75
Odeh, Mohammed Saddiq, 174
Odinga, Raila, 262
Odlum, George, 211
Offenbach, 509
Ofili, Chris, 534
Okri, Ben, 543
Olarreaga, Manuel, 463
Olisemeka, Ignatius, 270, 421
Olivier, Laurence, 522
Olmert, Ehud, 220
Olympio, Gilchrist, 281, 424
Oman, 241, 242, 326
Omar, Chamassi Said, 347
Omar, Mullah Mohammad, 316, 318
Ona, Francis, 392
Opera, 509–11
Opertti, Didier, 194, 400
Opie, Alan, 510
Orchard, Carol, 591
Organization for Economic Cooperation & Development (OECD), 9, 10, 12, 14, 98, **417, 420,** 465, 487
Organization for Security & Cooperation in Europe (OSCE), 145, 417, 439, **440–3**

Organization of African Unity (OAU), 248, 258, 271, 280, 290, 346, 425, 452, **453–5**
Organization of American States (OAS), **462**, 464
Organization of Eastern Caribbean States (OECS), 210, **463**
Organization of the Islamic Conference (OIC), **429–30**
Organization of the Petroleum Exporting Countries (OPEC), 235–6, **418, 420**, 451
Orr, Eric, 534
Ortega Saavedra, Daniel, 199
Ortega, Ramón 'Palito', 184
Ortiz Martínez, Guillermo, 203
Orton, Joe, 542
Orwell, George, 541
Osborne, Charles, 541
Oscar awards, 523
Ota, Masahide, 379
Otgonbileg, Shagdaryn, 385
Otunnu, Olara, 341
Ouattara, Alassane, 280
Oudom Khattigna, 363
Ouedraogo, Herman, 280
Ouedraogo, Kadre Desiré, 276
Ouedraogo, Ram, 280
Ouyahia, Ahmed, 253
Overviews of the year, 1–15
Oviedo Silva, Gen. (retd) Lino César, 191, 192
Owen, John, 212
Owen, Michael, 549
Owens, Agnes, 543
Owhali, Mohammed Rashed Daoud, 174
Ozawa, Ichiro, 378

Pacific Community, Secretariat of (SPC), 457, 462
Pacific Island States, 395–9
Padel, Ruth, 543
Paek Nam Sun, 383
Paeniu, Bikenibeu, 396, 397
Paik, Nam June, 534
Pakistan, 1, 3, 5, 13, 315, 316, 317, 318, 319, 324, 327, 328, 329, **331–4**, 336, 343, 371, 383, 397, 408, 412, 419, 427, 458, 460, 469, 471, 489, 546, 605, 606, 607
Pakula, Alan, 526
Palauskas, Arturas, 602

Palestinian Entity, 4, 176–7, 218–20, **221–4**, 226–7, 228, 234, 427–8, 448
Panama, 198, 200, **201**, 464, 465
Panday, Basdeo, 206
Pandolfi Arbulu, Alberto, 192, 193
Papadopoulos, George, 592
Papagos, Alexander, 592
Papandreou, Andreas, 104, 592
Papon, Maurice, 604
Papua New Guinea, 391–2, 395, 397, 462, 469, 607
Paracel Islands, 360
Paraguay, 191–2, 492, 605
Paris Club, 136, 199, 200
Parizeau, Jacques, 179
Park Chung Soo, 380
Parris, Matthew, 26
Parsons, Neil, 544
Partnership for Peace, 414, 417
Paskaljevic, Goran, 525
Pasmore, Victor, 534, 594 (obit.)
Pastora Gómez, Edén, 200
Pastrana Arango, Andrés, 188, 189, 427, 606
Pastrana Borrero, Misael, 189
Patassé, Ange-Félix, 283, 286
Patten, Chris, 539, 544
Patterson, Floyd, 594
Patterson, Percival J., 203
Paul VI, Pope, 466
Paxman, Jeremy, 540
Payne, Anthony, 513
Paz, Octavio, 538 (obit.)
Pechstein, Claudia, 547
Peña Gómez, José Francisco, 197
Penfold, Peter, 36
Perez, Carlos Andrés, 194
Pérez Balladares, Ernesto, 198, 201
Pérez Martínez, Gregorio Manuel, 189
Pérez Yoma, Eduardo, 187
Perišić, Gen. Momčilo, 146
Perkins, Emily, 543
Perlmutter, Dr Saul, 474
Persson, Göran, 78, 79
Peru, 94, 188, 191, **192–3**, 460, 610
Peslier, Olivier, 554
Peters, Winston, 393, 394
Petipa, Marius, 517
Petit, Emmanuel, 549
Petsalnikos, Phillipos, 102
Pettersson, Christer, 79
Pham The Duyet, 359

Phan Van Khai, 359, 459
Philippines, 9, 353, **357–9**, 418, 458, 459, 460, 466, 605
Philips, Peter, 203
Phillips, Brian, 544
Phillips, Mike, 544
Phillips, Trevor, 544
Piazolla, Astor, 517
Picone, Giuseppe, 516
Pilolevu Tuita, Princess, 398
Pineiro Losada ('Barba Roja'), Manuel, 196
Pinheiro, João de Deus, 281
Pinker, Steven, 545
Pinochet Ugarte, Gen. (retd) Augusto, 37, 38, 92, 93, 99, 187, 303, 609, 611
Pinter, Harold, 545
Pirandello, Luigi, 518
Pitman, Jenny, 554
Pius XII, Pope, 89, 470, 471
Platel, Elisabeth, 516
Plath, Sylvia, 538
Plavšić, Biljana, 134, 135
Plimpton, George, 544
Pohiva, 'Akilisi, 398
Pol Pot, 360, 361, 594–5 (obit.), 604
Poland, 13, 75, 93, 96, 107, **112–4**, 399, 414, 415, 417, 434, 441, 448, 449, 469, 471, 497, 538
Pollard, Jonathan, 177, 219
Pollock, Jackson, 532
Pontiero, Giovanni, 539
Poole, Alan, 212
Poplašen, Nikola, 134, 135
Pople, Anthony, 514
Pople, John, 479
Portas, Paulo, 98
Portugal, 96–9, 252, 255, 296, 298, 312, 377, 431, 433, 463
Posada Carriles, Luis, 196
Postel, Jonathan (Jon), 481, 595 (obit.)
Powell, Enoch, 595 (obit.)
Prabowo Subianto, Gen., 356, 357
Prescott, John, 19, 582
Preudhomme, Herbert, 208
Previn, André, 512
Prey, Hermann, 511
Primakov, Yevgenii, 147, 150, 151, 152
Primarolo, Dawn, 30
Prior, Michael, 472
Prodi, Prof. Romano, 61, 62, 63
Prokina, Elena, 510

Prokofiev, 511
Puccini, 509
Puerto Rico, 106, **216–7**
Qabbani, Nizar, 230
Qadafi, Col. Muammar, 247, 248, 249
Qalamuddin, Mohammed, 318
Qarwi, Hamid, 249
Qatar, 227, 229, **241**, 242, 243, 244, 246, 429
Quebec, 178–81, 611
Quinteros Ayllón, Pedro Domingo, 193
Rabbani, Mullah Mohammed, 316
Rabuka, Maj.-Gen. Sitiveni, 396
Racine, Jean, 520
Radhakishum, Pretaapnarain, 214
Radišić, Živko, 134, 135
Rae, Simon, 544
Rafiqdust, Mohsen, 313
Rafsanjani, Ali Akbar, 237, 244, 314, 451
Rafter, Patrick, 554
Raines, Franklin D., 583
Rainier III, Prince, 88
Rais, Amien, 356
Rakhmanov, Imamali, 320, 323
Rakkiat Sukthana, 351
Ramírez Durand ('Feliciano'), Oscar, 193
Ramgoolam, Navin, 343, 344
Ramos, Alvaro, 194
Ramos, Fidel, 357
Ranariddh, Prince Norodom, 361, 362
Raphael, Frederic, 543
Rasizade, Artur, 156, 157
Rasmussen, Anders Fogh, 74
Rasmussen, Poul Nyrup, 73, 74, 603
Rathbone, Julian, 543
Ratsirahonana, Norbert, 348
Ratsiraka, Didier, 348
Rawlings, Jerry, President, 267, 268, 593
Raynsford, Nick, 535
Rebegliati, Ross, 547
Rebelo de Sousa, Marcelo, 98
Redgrave, Corin, 521
Regnier, Natalie, 525
Rehn, Elizabeth, 81
Reina Idiaquez, Carlos Roberto, 199
Reith, Peter, 390
Religion, 1, 66, 89–90, 97, 104, 196, **466–72**
René, France-Albert, 345, 424
Rendall, David, 510
Reno, Janet, 170, 578, 583

Revoredo Marsana, Delia, 192
Richard, Alain, 243
Richard, Lord, 21
Richardson, Bill, 316, 583
Richardson, Mark, 550
Ricketts, Harry, 544
Rigby, Jean, 509
Rigg, Diana, 521
Rio Group, 462, 464
Ritchie, Ian, 536
Roark, Aidan, 593
Robbins, Jerome, 514, 595 (obit.)
Roberts, Sir Frank, 595–6 (obit.)
Roberts, Keith, 516
Robertson, George, 39, 582
Robertson, Paul, 203
Robinson, Arthur N.R., 206
Robinson, Geoffrey, 20, 29, 30, 611
Robinson, Mary, 362
Rodinson, Maxime, 225
Rodríguez Bautista, José Nicolás, 189
Rodríguez Echeverría, Miguel Angel, 198, 201, 602
Rogers, Peter, 527
Rogers, Roy, 596 (obit.)
Roi, Rameshwurlall Basant, 344
Rojas Parr, Freddy, 194
Rojo, Tamara, 516
Roma (Gypsies), 121
Romaios, Georgios, 102
Romania, 123, **124–7**, 326, 402, 448, 449, 470, 476, 604
Romanova, Maria, 600
Romero, Archbishop Oscar, 468, 469
Romiti, Cesare, 61
Ronaldo, Dadado, 549
Rooksby, Rikky, 544
Rorem, Ned, 513
Rose, Dilys, 543
Rose, Steven, 545
Rosen, Charles, 514
Rosenstingl, Peter, 82
Ross, Alan, 541, 544
Rosselló, Pedro, 215
Roth, Dieter, 534
Roth, Philip, 541, 543
Rothermere (Vere Harmsworth), Viscount, 596 (obit.)
Roudhan, Abdullah al-, 243
Routledge, Paul, 544
Roux, Michel, 511
Rowland, R. W. ('Tiny'), 596 (obit.)

Rozhdestvensky, Gennadi, 596
Rudolph, Eric Robert, 172
Rugova, Ibrahim, 144, 146
Ruiz Ferro, Julio César, 202
Ruiz Massieu, José Francisco, 203
Ruiz, Bishop Samuel, 202
Rusedski, Greg, 554
Rushdie, Salman, 542
Russian Federation, 6, 7, 10, 12, 13, 31, 38, 77, 78, 81, 110, 112, 115, 116, 117, 124, 128, **147–52**, 153, 154, 155, 176, 230, 233, 298, 317, 322, 324, 325, 326, 328, 343, 365, 369, 370, 377, 379, 382, 383, 385, 403, 407, 414, 415, 418, 426, 429, 439, 443, 444, 446, 447, 460, 469, 470, 473, 491, 525–6, 596, 600, 602, 603, 604, 607, 608, 610
Ruth, Babe, 555
Ruzicka, Peter, 514
Rwanda, 60, 258, 288, 289, **291, 293–4**, 302, 500, 405, 413, 425, 494, 496, 603, 604, 608, 611
Rwigyema, Pierre-Célestin, 291

São Tomé & Príncipe, 295–6
Saad al-Abdullah as-Salim as-Sabah, Crown Prince Shaikh, 240
Saadi, Jaime Nebot, 190
Saatchi, Charles, 532
Sabumei, Benias, 392
Sacks, Chief Rabbi Jonathan, 470
Sadat, Anwar al-, 226
Saddam Husain, 3, 38, 150, 177, 222, 232, 234, 602, 610, 611
Sáez, Irene, 195
Saitoti, George, 262, 263
Sakić, Dinko, 139
Salas Römer, Henrique, 195
Salazar Monroe, Gen. Julio, 193
Saleh, Ali Abdullah, 238, 239
Saleh, Jaime M., 214
Saleh, Maj.-Gen. Al-Zubair Muhammed, 247
Saleh, Maj.-Gen. Salim, 266
Salinas de Gortari, Carlos, 202
Salinas de Gortari, Raúl, 202
Salisbury, 6th Marquess of, 29
Sam Rangsi, 361, 362
Samoa, 396, 397–8
Sampaio, Jorge, 96
Samper Pizano, Ernesto, 188
Sampras, Pete, 554

San Marino, 88
San San, Daw, 350
Sanguinetti, Julio María, 194
Sankoh, Foday, 272
Sant, Dr Alfred, 99, 100
Santamaria, Bob, 391
Santer, Jacques, 69, 370, 430, 438
Santiestevan de Noriega, Jorge, 192
Saramago, José, 96, 539
Šarinić, Hrvoje, 138
Saro-Wiwa, Ken, 586
Sarwar, Mohammed, 41
Sassou-Nguesso, Denis, 283, 285, 286
Sastri, Lal Bahadur, 594
Sato, Mitsuo, 462
Satyamurti, Carol, 543
Saucedo Sánchez, Gen. César, 193
Saudi Arabia, 13, 174–5, 229, 232, 234, **235–8**, 239, 240, 244, 262, 314, 319, 398, 450, 451, 452, 497, 604
Savage, Frank J., 212
Savimbi, Jonas, 297, 298, 299, 405, 428, 603
Sayers, Dorothy L., 541, 543
Scalfaro, Oscar Luigi, 61
Schäuble, Wolfgang, 54
Schiele, Egon, 533
Schifano, Mario, 534
Schiff, David, 514
Schmidt, Michael, 544
Schnittke, Alfred, 514, 596 (obit.)
Schnitzler, Arthur, 519
Schröder, Gerhard, 35, 51, 52, 53, 56, 60, 65, 433, 435, 609, 610
Schubert, 513
Schumacher, Michael, 552
Schumacher, Ralf, 553
Schumann, Maurice, 597 (obit.)
Schumer, Charles, 167
Schwartzenegger, Arnold, 485
Schyman, Gudrun, 79
Scientific, Medical & Industrial Research, 473–9
Scotland, 7, 16, 17, **40–2**, 46, 238, 248, 406, 452, 534–5, **571–4**
Scudamore, Peter, 554
Se Ri Pak, 552
Sealy, I. Allan, 543
Sebald, W.G., 543
Seed, Dr Richard, 477
Segmüller, Col. Pius, 89
Seizinger, Katja, 547
Selebi, Jacob, 404
Seleznev, Gennadii, 148
Self, Will, 543
Sen, Prof. Amartya Kumar, 331, 423
Sendawula, Gerald, 265
Senegal, 273, **275, 276–8**, 286, 294, 295, 454, 603
Serapheim, Archbishop, 597 (obit.)
Serbia, see Yugoslavia, Federal Republic of
Sereny, Gitta, 540, 545
Serfaty, Abraham, 255
Serpa Uribe, Horacio, 189, 606
Serrano Elias, Jorge, 200
Šešelj, Vojislav, 135
Sewell, John, 543
Seychelles, 345–6, 422, 424
Shalala, Donna E., 583
Sharif, Mohammed Nawaz, 331, 332, 333, 336
Sharif-Emami, Jafar, 597 (obit.)
Sharjah, 451
Sharon, Ariel, 218, 227
Shattock, David, 344
Shelest, Alla, 517
Shelley, Mary, 541, 543
Shephard, Matthew, 174
Shevardnadze, Eduard, 156, 157
Shields, Carol, 539
Shihabi, Gen. Hikmat, 229
Shimizou, Hiroyasu, 547
Shipley, Jenny, 393, 394, 395, 462
Shoemaker, Eugene, 473
Short, Clare, 582
Shostakovich, 511
Shubailat, Leith, 227
Sierra Leone, 36, **272–3**, 274, 405, 406, 411, 412, 421, 428, 456, 476, 602, 605
Siew, Vincent, 374, 375, 376
Sihanouk, King Norodom, 360, 361, 362, 595
Siimann, Mart, 114, 117, 447
Silajdzic, Haris, 134
Silayev, Boris, 320
Sillitoe, Alan, 543
Simeon, ex-King, 130
Simitis, Kostas, 101, 102, 103
Simmons, David, 207
Simon, Neil, 521
Sinatra, Frank, 597–8 (obit.)
Sinclair, Andrew, 544
Singapore, 354–5, 458, 459

Singh, Jaswant, 328
Singh, Vijay, 552
Singherok, Brig.-Gen. Jerry, 392
Sisavath Keobounphanh, 363, 603
Sithole, Jan, 308
Sivapalan, Ponnuthurai, 342
Siza, Alvaro, 534
Sizimbo, Francis, 307
Skate, Bill, 391, 392, 462
Skele, Andris, 115
Skinner, Dennis, 23
Slepian, Barnett, 173
Sloane, Steven, 509
Slovakia, 83, 119, **120–1**, 123, 439, 449, 609
Slovenia, 107, 140, **141–2**, 400, 434, 449, 497
Smith, Andrew, 20
Smith, Chris, 518, 528, 529, 545, 582
Smith, Jennifer, 212, 213, 610
Smith, Michelle, 546
Soames, Mary, 544
Soares, Mario, 252
Sock, Mademba, 277
Sodano, Cardinal Angelo, 87
Sofia, Queen, 93, 103
Soininen, Jani, 547
Solana, Javier, 117, 129, 413
Solans, Eugenio Domingo, 432
Solomon Islands, **397**, 399
Somalia, 174, **257, 260–1**, 404, 428, 486
Somaliland, 260–1
Sonja, Queen, 78
Soper, Rev Lord (Donald), 598 (obit.)
Sorenstam, Gunika, 552
Sorhaindo, Crispin, 210
Soros, George, 149
Sosa, Sammy, 158, 555
Sousa Franco, António, 98
South Africa, 6, 43, 176, 269, 296, 300, 302, 304, 306, 307, **308–12**, 336, 343, 404, 422, 425, 426, 427, 454, 455, 467, 468, 469, 475, 486, 603, 608, 610
South Asian Association for Regional Cooperation (SAARC), 336, 339, 343, **457**
South Ossetia, 443
South Pacific Forum (SPF), 397, **457, 462**
Southern African Customs Union (SACU), 304

Southern African Development Community (SADC), 290, 298, 302, 304, 306, 312, **453, 455**, 456
Southern Common Market (Mercosur), **463, 464**, 465
Space Research, see Scientific, Medical & Industrial Research
Spacey, Kevin, 519
Spain, 8, 37, 38, **91–4**, 95, 96, 99, 103, 188, 189, 196, 255, 287, 312, 326, 431, 432, 433, 445, 463, 493–4, 611
Sperling, Gene, 583
Spicer, Lt.-Col. (retd) Tim, 36
Spock, Dr Benjamin, 598 (obit.)
Sport, 59, 158, 314, 377, 399, 422, **546–55**
Spottiswoode, Clare, 34
Spurling, Hilary, 541, 544
Spychalska, Ewa, 112
Sri Lanka, 340, **341–3**, 466, 602
St Aubyn, Edward, 543
St Kitts & Nevis, 209, 210–1
St Lucia, 205, **210, 211**, 422, 464
St Vincent & the Grenadines, 210, 211
Stalin, Joseph, 113
Stamatopoulos, Haris, 102
Stanford, Peter, 544
Stangerup, Henrik, 538
Stanišić, Ljubiša, 146
Starovoitova, Galina, 152, 610
Starr, Kenneth W., 158, 159, 160, 161, 163, 164, 165, 168, 168, 480, 577, 578, 602, 608
Stead, C.K., 543
Stein, Edith, 471
Stephanopoulos, Kostas, 101
Stephen, Marcus, 399
Stepinac, Cardinal Aloysius, 89
Stevenson, Ben, 516
Stewart, Alan, 544, 551
Stewart, Alec, 550, 551
Stiefel, Ethan, 516
Stiglitz, Joseph, 9
Stoiber, Edmund, 54, 55
Storey, David, 543
Störner, Horst, 479
Stoyanov, Petar, 127, 128, 130
Strang, Gavin, 21
Strathclyde, Lord, 29
Strauss-Kahn, Dominique, 59
Straw, Jack, 20, 27, 37, 188, 537, 582, 611
Street, Picabo, 547
Strindberg, Madalena, 534

Strouse, Charles, 521
Sušak, Gojko, 138
Sudan, 3, 4, 65, 176, **245–7**, 258, 260, 262, 290, 400, 472
Suharto, Gen., 352, 355, 356, 357, 425, 603, 605
Sukarno, Gen., 356
Sukarnoputri, Megawati, 356
Suker, Davor, 549
Sultonov, Otkir, 320
Sumatra, 357
Sumaye, Frederick, 264
Summit of the Americas, 464
Surayud Chulanot, Gen., 352
Surin Pitsuwan, 352
Suriname, 214
Sutherland, Dame Veronica, 423
Sutton, Hal, 551
Suu Kyi, Aung San, 349, 350
Suzuki, Shinichi, 598 (obit.)
Svoboda, Petr, 548
Swaziland, **304, 308**, 402
Sweden, **78–80**, 431, 446, 476, 490
Switzerland, **84–7**, 184, 448, 484, 607, 611
Symcox, Pat, 551
Synge, J. M., 522
Syria, 5, 110, 223, 226, **228–30**, 231, 234, 383, 452, 538
Szirtes, George, 543

Ta Mok, 361
Tabarly, Eric, 598–9 (obit.)
Taha, Ali Uthman Muhammed, 247
Taiwan, 6, 12, 176, 365, 369, 371, **374–6**, 379, 398, 603
Tajikistan, 317, **320–6**, 400, 409, 607
Taki, Mohammed, 346, 347
Talabani, Jalal, 110
Talić, Gen. Momir, 134
Tang Liang Hong, 355
Tanoh, Augustus, 267
Tansi, Fr Cyprian, 468
Tanzania, 174, 245, **264–5**, 292, 400, 422, 456, 607
Tapiedi, Lucian, 469
Tarar, Mohammed Rafiq, 331
Tarawneh, Fayez, 226, 228, 607
Tarschys, Daniel, 438
Tate, James, 543
Taufa'ahua Tupou IV, King, 396
Tauziat, Nathalie, 554

Taya, Col. Maaouyia Ould Sidi Mohammed, 275
Taylor, Ann, 22, 582
Taylor, Charles, 274
Taylor, D.J., 543
Taylor, Derek H., 212, 214
Taylor, Mark, 551
Taylor, Telford, 599 (obit.)
Tazieff, Haroun, 599 (obit.)
Tchaikovsky, 510
Television & Radio, 526–30
Tenet, George, 583
Tennstedt, Klaus, 514, 599 (obit.)
Ter-Petrosyan, Levon, 156, 604
Thailand, 9, 12, **351–2**, 363, 367, 380, 418, 419, 458, 459, 460, 489
Than Shwe, Gen., 349
Thapa, Surya Bahadur, 338
Thatcher, Baroness, 35, 37, 56
Theatre, 518–23
Theroux, Marcel, 543
Theroux, Paul, 539, 540, 544
Thiam, Habib, 277
Thomas, Andy, 473
Thomas, D.M., 544
Thomas, Iwan, 548, 550
Thomas, Percy, 535
Thomson, Brian, 510
Thorpe, Adam, 543
Thuram, Lilian, 549
Thwaite, Anthony, 543
Tiberi, Jean, 58
Tibet, 176, 369
Timmer, Marianne, 547
Tippett, Sir Michael, 514, 599–600 (obit.)
Tkachenko, Oleksandr, 154
Togo, 276, 281–2, 285, 286, 295, 424
Tokayev, Kasymzhomart, 326
Tomalin, Claire, 541, 543
Tomlinson, Charles, 543
Tomlinson, John, 509
Tommasini, Anthony, 514
Tonga, 375, 396, 398
Tornay, Cedric, 89
Torp, Niels, 537
Torrijos Espino, Martin, 201
Torrijos Herrera, Omar, 201
Tosovsky, Josef, 118
Totobi-Quakyi, Kofi, 267
Tran Duc Luong, 359
Transdnestria, 443
Traoré, Moussa, 278

Trapido, Barbara, 543
Treviño, Gurría, 203
Trichet, Jean-Claude, 431, 432
Trimble, David, 44, 46, 47, 50, 71, 606, 609
Trinidad & Tobago, 206, 211
Tripp, Linda, 159, 161, 580, 581
Trovoada, Miguel, 295
Truman, Harry S., 587, 593
Tsang, Donald, 372
Tshering, Lyonpo Dawa, 341
Tshisekedi, Etienne, 288
Tsokhatzopoulos, Akis, 103
Tsui, Daniel, 479
Tucker, Anand, 524
Tucker, Karla Faye, 173
Tudjman, Franjo, 137, 138
Tudjman, Miroslav, 138
Tudor, Christopher, 516
Tudor, Corneliu Vadim, 126
Tung Chee-hwa, 371, 372
Tung, Brian Kwei, 206
Tunisia, 64, 66, **249–51**, 448, 452
Tupuoto'a, Crown Prince, 398
Turajonzoda, Haji Akbar, 322
Turaljić, Hakija, 136
Ture, Kwame, 587
Turkey, 64–5, 102–3, 105, 106, 107, **108–10**, 228, 229, 322, 326, 434, 439, 496
Turkish Republic of Northern Cyprus (TRNC), 105–6, 109
Turkmenistan, 317, **320–6**, 426, 428
Turks & Caicos Islands, 212, 214
Turner, Doug, 550
Tutu, Archbishop Desmond, 308
Tuvalu, 396, 397

Uganda, 176, 246, **265–6**, 288, 289, 290, 291, 302, 425, 456, 469, 489, 603, 611
Ukraine, 13, 124, **153, 154–5**, 273, 403, 415, 418, 426, 439, 443, 450, 604
Ulanova, Galina, 514, 600 (obit.)
Ulenga, Ben, 307
Ulmanis, Guntis, President, 114, 115
Ulufa'alu, Bartholomew, 397, 399
United Arab Emirates (UAE), 232, **240, 241–2**, 243, 244, 314, 319, 451, 490
United Kingdom (see also Northern Ireland, Scotland, Wales), **16–51**; 'arms to Africa' affair, 36–7; arts, 509–45; BSE, 35–6; cabinet changes, 21–2, 26, 30, 43, 582; 'cash for access' affair, 20–1; defence & security, 5, 39–40; Davies affair, 25–6, 43; devolution, 7, 16, 17, 40, 42–3, 45–6, **571–7**; economy, 14–5, **31–4**; environment, 484, 489; EU/single currency, 7, 15, 16–7, 18, 24, 28, 29, 31, 34–5, 56, 72, 431, 432, 434, 437; external relations, **34–40**, 66–7, 94–5, 101, 103, 157, 218, 223, 224, 238, 239, 245, 246, 269, 307, 328, 354, 370, 373, 377–8, 379, 401, 426, 445, 458, 462; Falklands, 37, 184; House of Lords, 17–8, 28–9; local government, 18–9; Iraq crisis, 38–9, 60, 65, 94, 232, 233, 234, 237, 244, 315, 407, 451, 452; law, **500–6**; Libya/Lockerbie, 248, 452, 492–3; London authority, 18; Mandelson affair, 29–30; millennium bug, 39–40, 484; Pinochet arrest, 8, 37–8, 92–3, 99, 187–8; obituaries, 586ff; political affairs, 22–3, 23–4, 24–5; 27; political asylum, 27; religion, 467, 469, 470–1; scandals, 20–1, 25–6, 29–30, 36–7, 43; science, 479; sport, 546–55; welfare reform, 19–20, 22
United Nations, 400–13; Afghanistan, 316, 317, 318, 407, 412; Africa, 36, 245, 246, 258, 261, 272, 286, 289, 292, 293, 294, 405, 406, 425; Americas, 187, 195; Angola, 298, 299, 405, 412; Asia, 323, 325, 336, 341, 343, 349, 353, 362, 370, 384; Cyprus, 105–6, 108; East Timor, 425; environment, 486, 487; finance, 175, 402–4; human rights, 6, 8, 83, 196, 200, 209, 252, 362, 370, 404–5, 492, 496–7; Iraq, 3, 6, 38–9, 60, 65, 152, 177, 233–4, 244, 315, 406–7, 412, 430, 451, 452; Kosovo & former Yugoslavia, 137, 138, 139, 142, 144, 145, 405, 407, 442, 495; Libya/Lockerbie, 247–8, 406, 430; Mid East, 222, 229, 231, 401–2, 428; NAM, 428; OSCE, 443; peacekeeping forces, 406, 408–11; reform, 182, 401, 402; special debates, 412; transparency, 412–3; war crimes tribunals, 145, 182–3, 400, 413, 494–6, 567–70; Western Sahara, 255–6
United States of America, 158–77; administration list, 583; African embassy bombings, 2–3, 65, 133, 174,

176, 245, 262–2, 265, 318, 319, 427; Africa, 176, 251, 258, 290, 294, 312, 454; Americas, 99, 196, 204, 211, 464, 465, 492; arts, 512–3, 516, 521, 523–4, 533–4; Asia/Pacific, 314, 316, 317, 326, 327, 328, 329, 333, 334, 353, 355, 360, 365, 369–70, 373, 376, 377, 381, 383–4, 393, 395, 460, 461, 462; China, 5, 176, 365, 369–70, 373; economy, 10–11, 12, 14, 160, 175–6; environmental issues, 419, 485, 486, 487, 489, 491; EU/bananas, 175–6, 210, 419, 436–7; information technology, 480–1, 482–3, 484; Iraq crisis, 3–4, 17, 38, 60, 65, 94, 170, 177, 232, 233–4, 237, 244, 315, 407, 451, 452, 461; Israel-Palestine, 176–7, 217–20, 222–3, 231, 402, 429; Kosovo crisis, 142, 144, 145–6; Lewinsky scandal, 2, 8, 158, 159–60, 161–2, 163, 164–6, 167–8, 170, 171, 176, 177, 218, 480, **577–81**; Libya/Lockerbie, 248–9, 430, 452, 492–3; Mid East, 224, 228, 229, 243, 314; mid-term elections, 166–70 (*map* 169); NATO, 414, 416; obituaries, 587ff; OSCE, 440; political affairs, 160–1, 162, 170, 171; religion, 469; Russia, 150, 152; science & space research, 473–6, 477–8; social & legal affairs, 171–5, 506–8; sport, 158, 548, 551–2, 555; storms & tornadoes, 158–9; UN, 403; Europe, 49, 84, 102–3, 113, 116–7, 125, 128, 135, 150, 152, 154; Whitewater affair, 162–3, 164
Updike, John, 541, 543
Urrego Cárdenas, José Nelson, 188
Uruguay, 194, 400, 464
US Virgin Islands, 215, 216
Usman, Ismaila, 270
Ustinov, Peter, 586
Uteem, Cassam, 343
Uzbekistan, 151, 316, 317, **320–6**, 426, 443

Vacanti, Charles, 478
Vaea, Baron, 396
Vaganova, Agrippina, 600
Vagnorius, Gediminas, 114, 115
Vajpayee, Atal Bihari, 326, 327, 603
Valentim, Jorge, 299
Vallarino, Alberto, 201

Valle Riestra, Javier, 193
van den Broek, Hans, 129
van Dunem, Fernando José da França Dias, 297
Van Manen, Hans, 517
Vanhala, Matti, 80
Vanuatu, 397, 399
Vardaman, James, 588
Vasić, Goran, 136
Vasile, Radu, 124, 125, 604
Vassiliou, George, 105
Vassilopoulos, Lt.-Gen. Athanasios, 102
Vatican, 1, 87, 88–90, 152, 196, 466, 467, 468, 470–1, 587, 602, 605
Veiga, Carlos, 294
Venezuela, 194–5, 236, 611
Venizelos, Evangelos, 103
Ventura, Jess 'the body', 167
Vera, Rafael, 92
Verdi, 510
Vick, Graham, 509, 510
Victoria, Queen, 388
Videla, Jorge Rafael, 183
Vieira, João Bernardo, 273, 277, 294, 295, 454
Vietnam, 359–60, 373, 458, 460, 494
Viljoen, Gen. Constand, 309
Villiger, Kaspar, 86
Vine, Barbara, 543
Vinterberg, Thomas, 525
Virat Rattanaset, 351
Visconti, Luchino, 524
Visegrad Group, 129, 449
Visual Arts, 531–4
Vogel, Paula, 521
Vollebæk, Knut, 77
Von Trier, Lars, 525
Voynet, Dominique, 59
Vu Van Mau, 360
Vujanović, Filip, 142

Wade, Maître Abdoulaye, 276, 277
Waigel, Theo, 54, 55
Waldman, Guido, 542
Wales, 7, 16, 17, 26, **42–4**, 46, 534–5, **574–7**
Wales, Charles, Prince of, 103, 340, 342, 484, 602
Walesa, Lech, 111, 114
Walker, Alice, 541, 543
Walker, Danville, 204
Walker, Doug, 550

Wallace, George, 600 (obit.)
Wallace-Crabbe, Chris, 543
Walsh, Jill Paton, 541, 543
Walter, Bruno, 598
Wamba, Ernest Wamba dia, 289
Wang Daohan, 374, 375
Wang Zhiming, Pastor, 469
War Crimes Tribunals, 145, 182–3, 400, 413, 494–6, **567–70**
Warne, Shane, 546
Warner, Alan, 543
Warner, Marina, 540, 545
Warwick, Prof. Kevin, 476
Wasmosy, Juan, 192
Watkins, Alan, 545
Waugh, Mark, 546
Wei Jianxing, 364
Weimar Triangle, 112
Weizman, Ezer, 217, 221, 603
Weldon, Fay, 543
Wellink, Nout, 68
Welsh, Irvine, 520, 543
Wen Jiabao, 364
Wenger, Arsène, 549
Wenström, Anders, 445
Werner, Pierre, 69
West African Economic & Monetary Union (UEMOA), **453, 456**
Westendorp, Carlos, 135
Western European Union (WEU), **414, 417**, 438
Western Sahara, **255–6**, 408
Westwood, Lee, 551, 552
Whelan, Charlie, 30
Whiteread, Rachel, 531
Whittleton, Jack A., 457
Wicks, Susan, 543
Widdecombe, Ann, 24
Wijdenbosch, Jules, 214
Wijffels, H.H.F., 68
Wijngaards, Fr John, 467
Wilde, Oscar, 519
Wilkstrom, Jan-Erik, 515
Willey, Kathleen, 161, 162, 168, 581
Williams, C.K., 543
Williams, Tennessee, 521
Wills, Helen, see Moody, Helen Wills
Wilson, A.N., 543
Wilson, Colin St John, 537
Wilson, David, 210
Wilson, Elizabeth, 544
Wilson, Harold, 590, 598

Wilson, Jean Moorcroft, 544
Win Ayung, 349
Windsor, Duke and Duchess of, 603
Windward & Leeward Islands, 209–11
Winslet, Kate, 523
Winterson, Jeanette, 543
Wiranto, Gen., 356
Wiseman, Keith, 547
Witts, Richard, 545
Wolf, Christa, 543
Wolfahrt, Georges, 69
Wolfe, Tom, 543
Wolfensohn, James D., 417, 419
Wood, Anne, 511
Wood, Beatrice, 534, 600 (obit.)
Woods, Tiger, 551
Woodward, Louise, 174
World Bank, 9, 126, 140, 205, 210, 223, 228, 230, 264, 280, 284, 328, 330, 334, 335, 336, 360, 392, **417, 419**, 428, 445, 461, 464
World Health Organization (WHO), 404, 476
World Trade Organization (WTO), 204, 242, 395, **417, 419**, 428, 436, 437, 449, 451, 461, 483, 485, 489, 500
Wright, Billy, 45
Wright, Judge Susan Webber, 160, 162, 577, 578
Wye River Accords, 176–7, 217–20, 221, 222–3
Wyllie, Bernard, 211

Yabrán, Alfredo, 184
Yadav, Lalu Prasad, 331
Yang Shangkun, 365
Yellin, Janet L., 583
Yeltsin, Boris, 117, 147, 148, 149, 150, 151, 152, 153, 155, 176, 328, 365, 370, 377, 379, 385, 470, 533, 602, 603, 604, 604, 606, 608, 610
Yemen, 39, 175, **238–40**, 260, 452, 494, 591, 611
Yi Hoe Chang, 380
Yilmaz, Mesut, 108, 611
Yogi, Maharishi Mahesh, 330
Yona, Daniel, 264
Young, Patrick, 509
Yousef, Ramzi Ahmed, 172
Youssoufi, Abderrahmane, 253, 254, 255
Yuan Yuan, 546

Yugoslavia, Federal Republic of, (see also Kosovo crisis) 6–7, 55, 89, 124, 129, 137, 138–9, **142–7**, 371, 404, 405, 407, 413, 417, 426, 430, 441, 449, 495, 496, 605, 606
Yun, Isang, 514

Zaïre, see Congo, Democratic Republic of the
Zabala Ossio, Adm. Jorge, 185
Zadornov, Mikhail, 151
Zafy, Albert, 348
Zahid Hamid, 352
Zalm, Gerrit, 68
Zamarreño, Manuel, 91
Zambia, 290, 293, **299–300**, 306, 422, 455
Zanzibar & Pemba, 264–5, 422
Zedillo Ponce de León, Ernesto, 201
Zeepvat, Charlotte, 544
Zeman, Milos, 118, 119, 449, 606
Zender, Hans, 514
Zeng Qinghong, 364
Zeri, Federico, 534, 600–1 (obit.)
Zerić, Dr Mustafa, 136
Zéroual, Brig.-Gen. Liamine, 251, 253
Zhelev, Dr Zhelyu, 128
Zhivkov, Todor, 601 (obit.)
Zhu Rongji, 364, 367, 368, 370, 603, 604
Zia, Begum Khaleda, 334, 335, 336, 337
Ziegler, Philip, 544
Zimbabwe, 290, **301–3**, 306, 312, 422, 425, 455
Zobel, Judge Hiller, 174
Zolić, Maj.-Gen. Pero, 134
Zongo, Norbert, 281
Zonka, Erick, 525
Zorig, Sanjaasürengiyn, 386
Zuabi, Mahmud, 228
Zubak, Krešimir, 134
Zumthor, Peter, 538
Zyuganov, Gennadii, 150, 152

REF D 2.A7 1998